HISTORY OF
ENGLAND

HARPER'S HISTORICAL SERIES

Under the Editorship of
GUY STANTON FORD

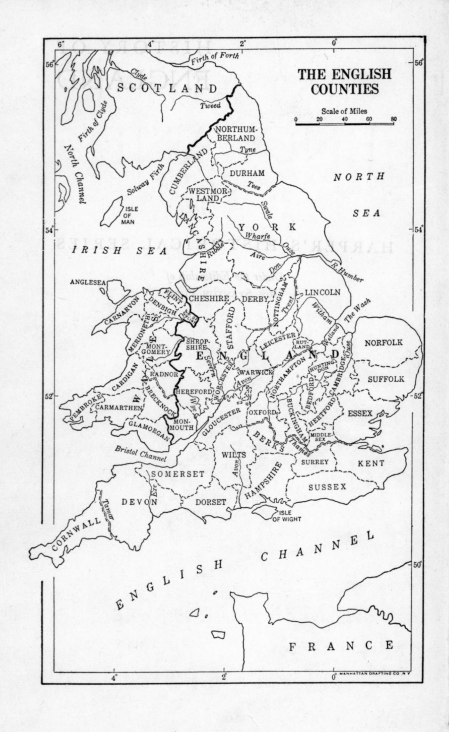

THE ENGLISH
COUNTIES

Scale of Miles
0   20   40   60   80

SCOTLAND

Firth of Forth

Clyde

Tweed

Firth of Clyde

North Channel

NORTHUM-
BERLAND

Tyne

Solway Firth

CUMBERLAND

DURHAM

Tees

WESTMOR-
LAND

ISLE
OF
MAN

YORK

Wharfe

LANCASHIRE

Ribble

Aire

Don

Ouse

R. Humber

IRISH SEA

NORTH

SEA

ANGLESEA

FLINT

DENBIGH

CHESHIRE

DERBY

LINCOLN

The Wash

CARNARVON

Dee

STAFFORD

NOTTINGHAM

Trent

Witham

MERIONETH

MONT-
GOMERY

SHROP-
SHIRE

LEICESTER

RUT-
LAND

Welland

NORFOLK

CARDIGAN

RADNOR

WARWICK

NORTHAMPTON

HUNTING-
DON

CAMBRIDGE

Ouse

SUFFOLK

WALES

BRECKNOCK

HEREFORD

WORCESTER

Avon

BEDFORD

PEMBROKE

CARMARTHEN

Wye

Severn

OXFORD

BUCKINGHAM

HERTFORD

MIDDLE-
SEX

ESSEX

ENGLAND

GLAMORGAN

MON-
MOUTH

GLOUCESTER

BERKS

Thames

SURREY

KENT

Bristol Channel

WILTS

HAMPSHIRE

SUSSEX

SOMERSET

Avon

Exe

DEVON

DORSET

ISLE
OF WIGHT

CORNWALL

Tamar

ENGLISH   CHANNEL

FRANCE

MANHATTAN DRAFTING CO. N.Y.

HISTORY OF ENGLAND

Third Edition

By

W. E. LUNT

Professor of History in
Haverford College

HARPER & BROTHERS

New York   London

To My Wife

ELIZABETH ATKINSON LUNT

CONTENTS

vii

Contents

MAPS

MAPS

GENEALOGICAL TABLES

EDITORIAL FOREWORD

THE passing years in no sense diminish, they rather increase the appreciation of the importance of English history. Nowhere is that more evident than in the United States. We long since ceased to be a part of Great Britain's empire overseas, but so long as our institutions, language and culture remain in any degree what they are today, we shall seek their origins in England and in doing it, pay tribute to a British Empire more enduring than the visible evidences of its power and dominion.

One evidence of this growing appreciation of the importance of English history and civilization in which our own takes root is the several books on English history, each with its own excellencies, which have appeared recently. When author, editor and publisher combine to add another to the list, they may properly be asked to offer a word of explanation of just what has been done and why.

Frankly this book does not seek to be all things to all students from the junior high school to the graduate student. It is primarily a college textbook for the general course in English history. It is therefore free to give a treatment suitable to the importance of the topics included. Even more important is the maintenance of a sense of selection and proportion by which alone a history of England can be kept from an unmanageable overload of names and political details. England has played an important rôle in many ways and through a long period. The eagerness to know our own day through contemporary history is more likely in English history than in any field to obscure the fact that to know today we must know the yesterdays. But that less familiar past in which the present of both England and America finds its roots requires its just attribution of emphasis and proper space for its interpretation. It seems to me that in this matter, Professor Lunt has most sturdily and successfully maintained or perhaps restored a balance in the treatment of past and present, medieval and modern.

England's political history treated usually in chronological sequence has furnished in this volume the thread so necessary for the guidance of the student. It enables him to follow in orderly fashion the author's treatment of English social, economic, constitutional, religious and intellectual developments. It was not Professor Lunt's purpose to write a history of the British Empire, but imperial policies and interests are dealt with where they have notably affected the history of England.

The whole organization and treatment is easily followed and can be reviewed by the use of topic side headings which do not interrupt the thread of the narrative.

The scholarship and teaching experience of the author are represented in the text. The bibliographies have been added not as evidences of erudition but as aids to the student and teacher who would pursue further for himself any of the many topics that arouse his particular interest.

After reviewing this volume in both manuscript and printed form, I can say that so far as editorial complicity in producing another English history is concerned, I feel quite cheerful and conscience free, and quite ready to see the appraisal I have expressed in this foreword put to the test which comes by use.

GUY STANTON FORD

March, 1928

ACKNOWLEDGMENTS

I REGRET that the detailed notation of the sources of my information would so increase the length and complexity of the book as to defeat one of its principal purposes. For quotations and conscious paraphrases of the words of another I have attempted to give references. Since my reading on the subject has extended over a period of many years, I may have failed through inadvertence to acknowledge some such direct borrowings. If that proves to be the case, I ask indulgence. To the host of other authors from whose researches my knowledge has been largely derived I take this opportunity to express my thanks and my appreciation of their scholarly guidance. In establishing the proportion and perspective, which are of such fundamental importance in the present type of treatment, I have been aided by a factor of such a character that it admits of no precise definition. Lectures delivered by Professor Alfred L. P. Dennis, Professor Roger B. Merriman, President A. Lawrence Lowell, Professor Edwin F. Gay, Professor Charles H. Haskins, and the late Professor Charles Gross, to which I listened with enjoyment as a student, have influenced profoundly the development of my views with regard to the significance of many aspects of English history. Though I have not intentionally adopted their views or borrowed their ideas directly, it is possible that even the turn of a phrase has lingered unconsciously in my thought to find expression in the following pages. If any of the interest with which they endowed the subject has found its way into my narrative, my indebtedness to them is indeed great.

To those who assisted in the preparation of the book I am deeply grateful. Portions of the manuscript which fall within the respective fields of their expert knowledge were read by Dr. Isaiah Bowman, Director of the American Geographical Society, Dr. G. M. Wrigley, editor of the American Geographical Review, Professor Roland B. Dixon of Harvard, Professor E. A. Hooton of Harvard, Professor William A. Morris of the University of California, Professor Albert B. White of the University of Minnesota, Professor Howard L. Gray of Bryn Mawr, Professor Roger B. Merriman of Harvard, Professor Wallace Notestein of Cornell University, Professor Avery O. Craven of the University of Illinois, Professor Bernadotte Schmitt of the University of Chicago, and Professor Herbert C. Bell of Wesleyan University. The editor of the series, Dean Guy Stanton Ford, gave to the whole manuscript the benefit of his ripe scholarship. The constructive and stimulating criticisms of these generous scholars helped me to discover errors of fact and judgment and to improve the narrative in many other ways. In the final stages of preparation the publishers have rendered valued assistance. To my wife I am happily indebted for much criticism and aid. For the errors and shortcomings which remain, the responsibility is mine.

W. E. L.

Haverford, Pennsylvania
March 6, 1928

FURTHER ACKNOWLEDGMENTS

THE changes incorporated in the second edition rest largely upon the suggestions made by teachers and students who have used the book in its earlier form. It is a pleasure to extend to these friendly and constructive critics my sincere thanks for their generous assistance. I wish also to acknowledge my indebtedness to several of my colleagues at Haverford for advice on certain problems which fell within their respective fields of knowledge.

W. E. L.

Chebeague, Maine
June 29, 1937

NOTE

THE principal purpose of the third edition is to bring the period after 1918 up to date, but I have taken the opportunity to make some changes elsewhere in the text and in the Suggestions for Further Reading.

Haverford, Pennsylvania
January 9, 1945

W. E. L.

HISTORY OF
ENGLAND

CHAPTER I

THE LAND AND ITS EARLY INHABITANTS

THE development of civilization by the inhabitants of England has been affected profoundly by the location of the British Isles on the globe. Physically and culturally they form part of the continent of Europe. Centuries before written history begins they were attached to the continent by land. The earliest men who lived in Britain may have walked from the site of Calais to that of Dover dry-shod. The creation of the seas around the British Isles in prehistoric times rendered communication more difficult, but left it comparatively easy. The strait of Dover is only twenty-one miles wide at its narrowest part. For many centuries peoples migrated from the continent to the islands, bringing with them new civilizations. Each new group kept more or less in touch with the people of the mainland. Every great intellectual, religious, economic, or social development which occurred in western Europe affected England sooner or later. English civilization consequently has been a European civilization, and England from the earliest times has taken a part in European affairs.

Location
of the
British
Isles

The separation of the water has been enough, nevertheless, to produce in Britain a certain independence in the development of her civilization. Before the days of steam navigation communication across Britain's water frontier was not as easy as communication across most of the land frontiers surrounding the peoples of the continent. The fundamental ideas—moral, political, social, commercial, or what not—which from time to time have been carried from one portion of Europe to another to influence deeply the modes of life followed by the peoples of western Europe, have generally come to Britain late. They have also come more slowly, giving more time for assimilation and more opportunity for independent development. The Reformation, for example, took a course in England different from that taken anywhere on the continent. The Teutonic dialects carried to England by the Anglo-Saxons grew into English, which differs from modern German. The Christianity established in Britain by the Romans developed an ecclesiastical organization unlike that established generally in western Europe. To say that the isolation of Britain was the sole cause of any of these developments used as illustrations, or of the multitude that might be cited, would be an exaggeration; but the isolation was without doubt an important contributory cause. The independent views of the average Englishman, his conservatism, his love of precedent—what in short is often termed his insularity of mind—may be attributed in large degree to his insular environment. A contemporary may well question whether the rapidity of communication which has developed within the past century is not breaking down before his eyes the isolation productive of this independence of thought; but there can be no question of its existence under the conditions which surrounded human life in the past.

The water barrier has also protected the islands from attack. It has not been a complete protection. In the early period of England's history several peoples crossed the water and obtained a foothold for the successful conquest of the land. Yet it has made invasion difficult. Since the eleventh century Britain has never suffered any significant armed invasion from an external foe coming across the water, except two occasions when large groups of Englishmen assisted the invaders. The necessity of transport by water, moreover, has forced the invaders who have conquered the islands to advance their occupation slowly, resulting generally in the assimilation of the invaders by the invaded, or in an adjustment between the two. The security provided by the "salt-water girdle" has helped to give to English history a continuity of development unrivaled by that of any area of equal size on the continent. Since the fifth century there have been no sharp breaks in English history.

The location of Britain in relation to the world as a whole was once very different from what it is now. Before the discoveries of Columbus and Vasco da Gama, Britain was at the outside edge of the known world. Europe, northern Africa, and Asia constituted the realm of the known, and the knowledge of the far parts of these areas was slight. In ancient and medieval times the Mediterranean was the center of civilization and of commerce. Oriental products were brought by caravan to the shores of that sea, whence the Mediterranean peoples distributed them throughout Europe. England was in touch with this current of world trade from prehistoric times, but it was too remote from the center of exchange to have an influential part. Its position was similar with regard to civilization, which went hand in hand with commerce. Civilization radiated from the shores of the Mediterranean. The farther from this center a people was located, the more backward was its culture. Until modern times, England in the "utmost corner of the west" was slow in the development of its civilization.

With the vast expansion of the known world which took place in

the fifteenth and sixteenth centuries Britain's situation was reversed. The ocean on its western flank ceased to be a barrier. Gradually, as exploration, exploitation, and colonization of the newly discovered lands progressed, the ocean became the principal pathway of communication. The Atlantic superseded the Mediterranean as the center of commercial activity. England ceased to be at the end of the world and almost literally became the center. It was thus favorably located to become the transit point of a large share of the new commerce which rapidly came into being. The English took full advantage of the opportunity. Ocean exploration, colonization, and development of a sea-borne trade supplemented one another, until today a political map of the globe displays England as the heart of the greatest empire in the world, while the red lines of a commercial map converge upon England in a way that demonstrates conclusively her dominant position as an *entrepôt*. The exchange of a marginal for a central position has been of vital moment in England's history.

The salient characteristics of the surface of Great Britain become apparent, if a line, slightly convex toward the east, is drawn from the mouth of the Exe in Devonshire to the mouth of the Tees in Yorkshire. To the north and west of this Exe-Tees line are the highlands, and to the south and east the lowlands. The mountains and hills of the north and west are not generally very high, few peaks exceeding a height of 3,000 feet, but they cover most of the surface in this region. They are so distributed as to break the island into several well-defined physical sections. The highest mountains are the highlands of Scotland. South of them, where the firths of Forth and Clyde carry the coast line far inland, is a narrow plain, where dwells the largest part of the population of Scotland. Between this plain and England is a broad mountainous band which runs approximately east and west from coast to coast. A narrow belt of coastal lowland around the eastern end and river valleys on the west provide natural routes of communication. They have not been sufficient to counteract entirely the tendency of the mountain barrier to separate the two portions of the island. To this day Scotland retains an individuality of its own; and throughout most of the historic period Scotland and England have been inhabited by peoples more or less alien to each other. From the Cheviots the Pennine chain extends south into the center of the plain. In the lake district the Cumbrian mountains carry the highlands out to the western coast, but for most of their course the Pennines divide the lowlands of the east from the lowlands of the west. They are cut by the two narrow gaps of the Tyne and the Aire, which facilitate com-

Surface

munication between east and west. To the west the Cambrian mountains cover Wales except for a narrow strip of coastal lowland. They
are deeply scored by valleys, and the broken character of the surface
impedes internal communication. The water-parting, however, is far
to the west. Short streams flow down to the western coast, while the
longer rivers follow the eastern slope. The character of the surface
tends to segregate the inhabitants of the district. For many centuries
they were practically independent of the peoples who controlled the
plain. The difficulty of internal communication, however, made national unity difficult to attain, and eastward-flowing streams enabled
the invaders to penetrate far into the interior. The several centuries
by which the union of Wales with England preceded that of Scotland
find a partial explanation in topography. South of the Cambrian mountains are the heights of Cornwall and Devon in the extreme southwest
of England. The continuity of the uplands in the western part of the
island is broken by the Chester gap, a broad belt of lowland which
penetrates to the western coast between the Pennines and northern
Wales, and by the Severn gap between southern Wales and the heights
to the south. When the peoples of the hills and the plain have been
hostile, as has often been the case, these gaps have been of advantage
to the latter. They have also served to give the people of the plain
direct access to the ocean, which has been of great value for purposes
of communication, especially in modern times.

The plain to the south and east of the Exe-Tees line occupies the
major portion of England. It is crossed by several ridges or uplands,
running from the southwest toward the northeast or east. They include
the Cotswolds, the Chilterns, and the North and South Downs. The
tops of these rarely rise to 1,000 feet above the level of the sea, and most
of the surface is below the contour line of 500 feet. The ridges give to
most of the plain the character of rolling country. The plain is the
most fertile and most habitable portion of the islands. Its location in
the southeast places it in the path of invaders from the continent. It is
the easiest for invaders to approach and the most desirable to hold.
Consequently newcomers from across the seas more than once have
driven the natives of the plain to seek protection in the more inaccessible highlands of the west and north. Wales and Scotland were long
inhabited by peoples of speech different from that of those who lived
on the plain. The antipathy thus begun was fostered by the terrain,
and it survived to color many centuries of British history.

The Exe-Tees line also divides the country geologically. North and
west are the harder rocks of the older formations; south and east are

the softer rocks of more recent formations. In the region of the harder rocks the soil is generally scanty and infertile. Such soil as can be used is given mainly to pasture. Large portions of the highlands of Scotland and parts of the interior of Wales are barren moorlands, which are waste, or at best poor pasture. Cultivated land in this section is confined mainly to the valleys and to the small areas of plain. In Scotland twelve per cent of the land is now under cultivation and eight per cent is in permanent pasture; in Wales the corresponding figures are fifteen and forty-three per cent; but in England, where the land is mostly plain of the more recent geological formations, thirty-two per cent of the land is arable and forty-two per cent is in permanent pasture. During the many centuries when the pursuits of the people of Britain were predominantly rural, the north and west were more sparsely inhabited than the south and east.[1] For large parts of the two areas this proportion still holds good, but the growth of industry since the industrial revolution began in the eighteenth century has concentrated population near the fields of coal and iron, which lie north of the Exe-Tees line. Outside of the metropolitan area of London the most densely populated districts today are found in the south of Wales, in the lowlands east and west of the Pennines, and in the lowlands of Scotland.

One aspect of the surface which had great influence upon the early history of Britain no longer exists. Today only five per cent of the land is wooded. In later prehistoric times primeval forests were so nearly universal that the chalk downs and the moorlands, because they were free from the thick growth, became the principal centers of human habitation and the main trackways of communication. Even in the time of Celt and Saxon, Dane and Norman parts of the land were so heavily wooded as to impede communication, break up portions of the plain into isolated sections, and hinder the progress of national unity. Marsh and fen, which have now disappeared before the hand of man, also helped to divide the country into separate units and to retard the progress of civilization. In the south, for example, the dense forest of the Weald obstructed communication between the coast and the interior. The South Saxons, who conquered Sussex at the time of the Anglo-Saxon conquest, were so isolated from the rest of Britain by the forest and by Romney marsh on the east, that they were the last of the Anglo-Saxon peoples to receive Christianity, although the religion was first introduced into the neighboring kingdom of Kent. In the east a great marsh called the Fens occupied a large part of the county

---

[1] The historical changes in the density of population are well illustrated by maps in A. P. Usher's *Introduction to the Industrial History of England*, pp. 95–99.

of Cambridge and adjoining districts, made that now fertile land a waste, and gave to East Anglia a seclusion which more than once becomes apparent in the history of the locality. Many other forests and marshes effected similar results in a lesser degree.[2]

The coast line of the British Isles is exceptionally broken. The continent of Europe, which is well endowed with coast, has one mile of it for about every two hundred square miles of surface; Great Britain has one mile of coast for every twenty square miles of surface. The many indentations in the coast provide harbors which facilitate communication with the outside world. The harbors, moreover, are readily accessible to the people of the interior, for numerous rivers flow down to the sea, and no place in Great Britain is more than seventy miles from the coast. In the era of small boats almost any depression in the coast was a possible landing place, although the mouths of streams were generally favored, since their valleys offered routes into the interior. The larger ships of modern times need deeper water in harbors protected from storms. These are provided plentifully by the many rivers which receive tidal waters. Though the western coast of Great Britain has a more indented outline than the eastern, it has fewer important ports, because the mountains offer a barrier to communication with the interior, and the streams flowing into the sea on that side of the island are generally short and steep.

The most significant aspect of the English river system is the location of the main water-parting. Since this is in the west, the rivers flow comparatively long distances through the plain to the east. The gradients are easy, the waters flow gently, and hence they are navigable for small boats for long distances. During the many centuries of poor roads, when goods had to be carried overland mainly on pack animals, the existence of these numerous waterways was of the highest importance for the facilitation of transportation. Even in these days of good roads and railways, carriage by water has the advantage of cheapness. In the early dawn of English history the rivers supplied the only available routes of transportation to many places in England, and the easiest ways of communication. The rivers, moreover, offered early invaders available routes into the interior, and often the most desirable places for settlement. The rivers provide water, a vital necessity, and the alluvial soil of their valleys is fertile and well watered. A glance at the map of the Anglo-Saxon kingdoms demonstrates that in more than one instance river basins determined the course and settled the limits

---

[2] Green. *Making of England,* pp. 7-12, and the maps *passim.*

of the political expansion of a group of the Teutonic invaders.[3] The rivers of Britain have been important agents in the development of British civilization.

In their climate the British Isles are particularly fortunate. They are located between 50° and 60° north of the equator, where they receive from the sun the same amount of heat as Labrador or central Russia. Their climate, however, is much milder than that common in this latitude. They never suffer such snow and cold as defeated Napoleon's campaign to Moscow, nor are their ports ever icebound as are those of Labrador. Their climate is profoundly modified by their location in the ocean and in relation to prevailing winds and currents. The ocean in the winter is warmer than the land and in summer it is cooler, because the land radiates heat more rapidly than water. The prevailing winds over the British archipelago are from the west or southwest, and in the winter they come from warmer latitudes as well as over the warmer ocean. They also cause a northeasterly drift of the surface of the North Atlantic, which brings warmer water to the shores of Great Britain. These factors so modify the temperature due to the direct rays of the sun, that Great Britain is warmer in winter and cooler in summer than inland districts located in the same latitude. Around London, where the greatest variation between the temperatures of winter and summer occurs, the average temperature during January is 39° Fahrenheit and during July 63°; in Moscow the averages are 13° and 67°. In the British Isles snow seldom lies on the ground for more than a few days. In the summer extreme heat such as occurs even in the northern part of the United States is almost unknown. Refrigerators are not commonly found among the household effects of English families. The British Isles enjoy a remarkably equable climate. Because of the location of the highlands in relation to the moist winds from the ocean the rainfall is abundant. It is well distributed throughout the year and hence is of the greater value for the production of vegetation.

With natural resources the British Isles are well supplied. The soil and the climate are favorable for the production of "victuals and drink," the most fundamental of man's material needs. Some plants grown in the northern part of the United States cannot be raised in England, but of the common cereals and grasses which constitute the basis of human sustenance corn (i.e., maize) is the only one of importance which will not mature in England. Pasture-grass is the most

Climate

Natural resources

---

[3] A map which illustrates this particularly well is given by Leeds in his *Archæology of the Anglo-Saxon Settlements*, p. 19.

common crop of Great Britain. The plentiful moisture makes it of exceptionally good quality, and the equable climate renders its growth possible all the year round in the western part of the islands. Since it grows best in the wetter regions, the west and north are pastoral. Oats may be grown in nearly all parts of the island where the soil is suitable. Wheat can be ripened regularly only in the warmer and drier eastern counties. The east and the southeast of England, where the soil as well as the climate is most fit, are the agricultural sections of chief importance. Early peoples whose principal pursuits were pastoral or agricultural found the islands well adapted to their needs. Their crops, their cattle, and their swine constituted their principal wealth. In the Middle Ages sheep-growing also became a leading industry. Fishing has been pursued from the earliest times, and the rich supply of fish located in the shoals of the North Sea has made it a staple industry. In the Early and Middle Ages these were the natural resources of chief value to the inhabitants, and they are still of fundamental importance in the economic life of the islands.

The mineral wealth of the islands was utilized only in small part before 1800. Our first written evidence concerning Britain relates to the tin mines of Cornwall, and until the nineteenth century they remained the chief source of the world's supply. Copper, lead, and iron have been mined since before Roman times. The deposits of lead and iron are still extensive, although the copper has been nearly exhausted. Only traces of the precious metals have been found. Coal, the most important of England's mineral resources today, was but little used before the seventeenth century. Charcoal, produced from wood, was employed for smelting, and wood and peat were employed for fuel. Granite, sandstone, limestone, and slate, which are used in place of wood for building purposes, abound in many parts of the islands. In the southeast of England bricks are the common building material. Elsewhere there are deposits of clay suitable for potteries.

In the natural resources the different parts of the islands do not share equally. England has the largest amount of good agricultural land and the richest supplies of iron and coal. The highlands of Scotland are in large part too barren even for pasture, and they are exceptionally poor in mineral deposits. Ireland lacks sufficient coal to promote its industrial development. This disproportion in the distribution of natural resources holds good with regard to many other geographic factors. England has the largest share of the plain, of the rivers, and of the good harbors; it is located in the most advantageous place for intercourse with the continent; and its surface is sufficiently diversified to

England's pre-eminence

supply a greater variety of human wants than that of any of the other divisions, but not so broken by mountains as to oppose the obstacles to political and social unity found in Scotland and in Wales. Thus England, the largest of the natural divisions of the islands, is designated geographically for the position of leadership it has always held historically.

Our knowledge of the men who were the earliest inhabitants of Britain is derived from material remains, which have to be interpreted for us by the archaeologist, the anthropologist, and the geologist. Written evidence is so preeminently the material from which the historian works, that the period of a people's history antecedent to the appearance of written records is commonly called prehistoric. In Britain written evidence becomes common only with the coming of the Romans. The story of human activities in Britain before 55 B.C. rests upon inferences drawn from the implements, dwellings, fortifications, burial mounds, and bones which have survived the intervening centuries.[4]

Evidence of prehistoric period

Since this evidence supplies no dates, the successive developments of civilization in the prehistoric period are classified by types of culture. The peoples of Britain, along with those of western Europe, generally passed successively through three principal stages, distinguished by the character of the tools and weapons which they used. In order of succession they were the stages of stone, bronze, and early iron. The stage of stone lasted so much longer than the other two that subdivisions have been found convenient. In Britain these are the eolithic (dawn of stone), the paleolithic (old stone), mesolithic (transitional) and neolithic (new stone) stages. The temporal length of these stages can be estimated only by the roughest of approximations. When an archaeologist discovers in the earth stone tools which were made by man, he can assign them to one of these stages by their types. If they are found in a recognizable stratum of the earth's surface, the geologist can give them an approximate date. Geologists have determined the order in which the strata of the earth's surface were formed and the approximate length of time which the deposit of each layer consumed. The evidence which is used to estimate the time is far from exact, and as a consequence scholars differ with regard to the probable length of the several periods.[5] Implements of the eolithic stage have been found

Stages of prehistoric culture

---

[4] Britain is mentioned briefly by a few Greek writers before 55 B.C.

[5] Compare, for example, the timetables given by Osborn, *Men of the Old Stone Age*, pp. 18–23, 280; Osborn, *Man Rises to Parnassus*, pp. 24, 25; Vulliamy, *Our Prehistoric Forerunners*, p. 15; Burkitt, *The Old Stone Age*, p. 138.

in a stratum which belongs to the period classified by geologists as the pleiocene epoch of the tertiary era, and a reasonably conservative estimate gives to these objects an age of 500,000 years. The paleolithic stage began during the pleistocene epoch of the quaternary era, which is known also as the age of ice. During this epoch the glacial ice advanced and retreated in northern Europe several times, causing changes of climate from warm to cold and leaving new deposits of soil after each advance. Paleolithic tools are often found associated with the remains of fauna and flora which indicate that the climate was warm or cold and make it possible to determine that the users of the tools lived in a glacial or an interglacial period. Since it is generally assumed that there were four glaciations, it is not always possible to assign a culture with precision to a given glacial or interglacial period, and differences of opinion among scholars with regard to such ascriptions have resulted in chronological estimates of the beginning of the paleolithic stage which vary by tens of thousands and even by hundreds of thousands of years. It seems to be the present tendency to associate the earliest paleolithic culture with the second interglacial period, which is often estimated to have been taking place 200,000 years ago. The date has won nothing like universal acceptance, but it is no longer as important as it was when it was thought to mark the time of the earliest implements formed by the hand of man. Recent discoveries seem to indicate that human civilization was developing with more or less continuity from the eolithic to the paleolithic stage. The paleolithic culture was superseded by the mesolithic after the close of the pleistocene epoch at a date which may perhaps be placed between 12,000 and 8,000 years ago. The advance to neolithic culture was made in Britain in the neighborhood of 3000 B.C., to bronze somewhere between 2000 and 1800 B.C., and to iron probably between 600 and 400 B.C.

Eolithic

The existence of man in England in the pleiocene epoch is attested by the discovery of tools made by the rough chipping of flints. The flints are so crudely fashioned that for a long time many archaeologists believed them to have been shaped by processes of nature, but several of those found in recent years are now acknowledged by eminent and conservative prehistorians to have been the handiwork of man. The men who produced this eolithic culture were hunters who derived their food from the chase. In this they did not differ from their successors until the end of the mesolithic stage, but the nature of their implements indicates that their civilization was on a lower plane. They were not only intelligent enough to manufacture tools which increased the efficiency of their labor, but they apparently knew also how to

PREHISTORIC BRITAIN

Scale of Miles

0   20   40   60   80

○ Paleolithic finds
● Mesolithic discoveries
▨ Areas inhabited in Neolithic and Bronze Stages
▲ Tin Deposits
■ Copper Deposits
+ Flint Quarries
-- Pathways
Wood and Swamps
Land over 500 feet above Sea Level

Firth of Forth

Firth of Clyde

Tweed

SOUTHERN UPLANDS

CHEVIOT HILLS

Tyne

Solway Firth

CUMBRIAN MTS.

ISLE OF MAN

P E N N I N E   C H A I N

YORK MOORS

I R I S H

S E A

Humber

ANGLESEA

The Wash

C A M B R I A N   M T S.

Bristol Channel

Thames

CHILTERN HILLS

NORTH DOWNS

EXMOOR

SOUTH DOWNS

DARTMOOR

Ouse

Solent

Strait of Dover

E N G L I S H   C H A N N E L

F R A N C E

MANHATTAN DRAFTING CO., N.Y.

build a fire and thus to make their lives more comfortable. Concerning the type of men who wrought these beginnings nothing is known, because no human skeletons have been found in authentic association with them. The meagerness of this information about man and his earliest works is disappointing, but it is of no small importance to have established as highly probable that man had already begun "that conquest of material which is the essential and distinguishing characteristic of his species."[6]

In the early pleistocene epoch man gradually improved the quality of his tools and increased their variety until he reached the stage designated as lower paleolithic.[7] The men of this stage enjoyed a mild and genial climate which enabled them to live in the open. Their remains are now found principally in alluvial deposits, whence they are sometimes known as men of the river drift. Their tools were better than those of their predecessors. More expert chipping and fuller trimming of the flints gave them sharper edges. The methods of manufacture improved, moreover, during the thousands of years through which this culture endured. Two skulls excavated in deposits of soil made by a river give some idea of the manner of men who developed this industry. One found at Piltdown in Sussex has a jaw similar in some aspects to that of an ape, but a forehead which is straight like that of a man.[8] The other, which was discovered at Swanscombe in Kent, is said to be of the same general type as the Piltdown specimen, but it is more primitive in its development, and consequently earlier. It was definitely associated with one of the later phases of the lower paleolithic culture. *(margin: Lower paleolithic)*

Toward the close of the interglacial epoch the colder climate forced men to seek protection in rock shelters and in caves. There they lived during the next glaciation, developing the higher type of culture of the middle paleolithic. The cavemen certainly had fire; they had clothes made of skins; their tools and weapons display an improved *(margin: Middle paleolithic)*

---

[6] Vulliamy, *Our Prehistoric Forerunners*, p. 43.

[7] The paleolithic culture, which endured for such an unimaginable length of time, underwent slow but steady development. Archaeologists distinguish six phases of this progress, which are named after the places where good archaeological examples of each type have been found. They are, in order from earliest to latest: Chellean, Acheulean (grouped above as lower paleolithic), Mousterian (middle paleolithic), Aurignacian, Solutrean, Magdalenian (upper paleolithic).

[8] The date of the skull is disputed. It was found with tools too rough to be assigned certainly to any culture, with bones of pleiocene fauna which had been rolled by the action of water, and with unrolled bones of pleistocene fauna. Since the human bones had been little rolled, they seem more likely to belong to the pleistocene epoch: Burkitt, *Old Stone Age*, p. 124.

technique and a greater variety. The apparently formal burials of some of the human remains contemporary with this culture are the basis of an inference that the middle paleolithic men had a religion. They were still hunters, though reindeer and other animals of a subarctic climate were now the objects of their pursuit. Racially these men were of the Neanderthal type, having a long head,[9] a low and retreating forehead, heavy eye ridges, an undeveloped chin, and a massive body about five feet in height.

Eventually a superior type of culture, which may be called upper paleolithic, appeared. Men still lived principally in caves and obtained their food from the chase. They developed a much larger variety of tools and weapons, using bone as well as stone for their manufacture, and they gave their flints a beauty of form and a fineness of finish hitherto unapproached. Most remarkable of all, however, was their development of a graphic art. On horn and bone and on the walls of caves they drew, carved, or painted realistically the animals which they saw about them. Few of these drawings have yet been found in Britain, but the evidence of the existence of the upper paleolithic culture there is ample. The transition to the upper paleolithic culture coincided with the appearance of man of a higher type. He was longheaded, with a high forehead, a broad face, a well-formed chin, and a stature generally tall. Man of this type, which is called Cro-Magnon, resembled modern man much more closely than did his Neanderthal predecessor.[10] Though this race predominated in Britain during the upper paleolithic stage, some of the men who lived there belonged to a round-headed race.[11]

As the climate gradually became temperate in the post-glacial epoch, the upper paleolithic was superseded by the transitional stage of the mesolithic. This culture was marked by a deterioration in some of its aspects. The day of bountiful big game had departed. The nature of the implements and the heaps of shells indicate that man eked out a barer existence on small game and fish. The men of this period spread over a wider area than their paleolithic predecessors, who seem to have been confined to England and Wales. They lived both in caves and in

Marginal notes:
Upper paleolithic
Mesolithic

---

[9] The skull, which is one of the principal distinguishing marks of race, is measured by an instrument called the cephalometer. It determines the ratio between the length from forehead to back and the breadth from ear to ear. A comparatively long head is called dolichocephalic (long-headed) and a comparatively broad head brachycephalic (round-headed).

[10] On the continent another long-headed race known as the Combe Capelle was associated with this culture, and traces of a negroid race have been found.

[11] Burkitt, *Our Early Ancestors,* p. 100; Clark, *Mesolithic Age,* pp. 11, 107.

the open. One type of home occupied by those who did not live in caves was the pit-dwelling, which was built by digging a circular hole in the earth, throwing up the excavated earth around the hole, and covering the top with poles and branches or skins. In one instance mesolithic pit-dwellings have been found in a group, but the discovery hardly warrants the assumption that communal life was common. This culture was developed partly by the descendants of the people who inhabited England in upper paleolithic times, and partly by two separate streams of immigrants who came from the east and south. The racial history of Britain in this period cannot be told definitely for lack of skeletal remains,[12] but the newcomers, like the natives, appear to have been mainly of Cro-Magnon stock.[13]

The neolithic culture seems to have been brought to Britain principally by a people who came along the Atlantic seaboard from the Iberian peninsula.[14] They had long heads, but their narrow faces contrasted strongly with the broad faces of the Cro-Magnons. They probably belonged to the Mediterranean race which appears to have preceded the Alpine and the Nordic races everywhere in western Europe.[15] The immigrants settled among the people who already inhabited Britain, and the intermixture of the two races had the result that the blood of paleolithic man runs in the veins of modern Englishmen. When the new culture was established in Britain, it marked a tremendous stride in the advancement of civilization. It was distinguished by four principal characteristics. (1) Implements of polished stone were common. Many implements of chipped flint continued in use, but neolithic men could make far more finely finished tools than their predecessors, and they had more varieties. (2) Pottery was manufactured. (3) Animals, including horses, cattle, sheep, hogs, and goats, were domesticated. Neolithic men still relied upon the chase for a considerable part of their food, but they were no longer entirely dependent upon it. (4) Agriculture was invented. Though it was of

> Neolithic stage

---

[12] Clark, *Mesolithic Age*, p. 107.

[13] Burkitt, *Our Early Ancestors*, pp. 20, 21, 38, 39.

[14] One element of neolithic culture seems, however, to have come to eastern England from the Baltic.

[15] The principal distinguishing marks of these three races are as follows:

Race	Head	Stature	Eyes	Hair
Mediterranean	long	medium	dark	dark
Alpine or Celtic	round	medium	dark	dark
Nordic or Teutonic	long	tall	blue	light

A variant of the Alpine type, which is tall, dark, and has a round head of a peculiar shape, is called Dinaric or Armenoid. It is classified by some as a fourth race.

the most primitive sort, it was the greatest contribution to European civilization made by neolithic men.

Neolithic men not only appeared in all parts of the British Isles, but they also inhabited the country more thickly than their predecessors. They generally lived on the low ridges of chalk and limestone, which supplied water, were bare of the overgrown forest which choked the lowlands, and supplied good grazing grounds. They usually occupied huts of the pit-dwelling type, and they often grouped their huts in hamlets or small villages. Neolithic men constructed a few of the numerous prehistoric fortifications of earth found in Britain. They also built several types of sepulchral chambers, the most distinctive of which are called long barrows because of their shape.

These material indications of organization in groups necessitate the assumption of a complete transformation of economic and social life since paleolithic times. A hunting population must necessarily inhabit a country sparsely and live singly or in small isolated groups in order not to destroy its source of food. With neolithic man we arrive at the stage of community life. Since such works as the long barrows imply communal action, there must have been some political organization, however crude, and some customs to regulate the rights and duties of members of the community in relation to other members. In all probability, too, there was some trade. Implements have been discovered made of a kind of stone which is not to be found in the immediate locality. The men of this age also worked flint mines on a scale which implies commercial exchange of the product. One of them has a shaft fifty feet deep and lateral galleries. The trade routes were the rivers and the pathways along the unwooded ridges, such as the downs of southern England. Probably coastal navigation had also begun.

Stage of bronze

The stage of bronze, which began around 2000 B.C., was probably coincident with the appearance of new immigrants in England. The long barrows typical of the neolithic culture were superseded by round barrows. In these the majority of the skeletons belong to a new race of men whose heads were round and whose height was generally above that of the resident population of long-heads. The men of the new race who came from the vicinity of the Rhine to the eastern and southeastern shores of England, appear to have introduced the round barrows, a new style of pot called a beaker, and metal implements. Because the new pottery is the most distinguishing mark of their culture found among their material remains, they are often designated as the Beaker folk, but their chief contribution to the advancement of

British civilization was their knowledge of the use of metal in the place of stone.[16] They settled most thickly in the regions which had been favored by their predecessors. Some of the native long-heads probably retired to the north and west before the newcomers, but the two peoples appear commonly to have intermingled.

The progress of civilization in the stage of bronze was comparatively rapid, because the new tools could take a sharper edge and were much more efficient than the old. Progress was made chiefly along the lines already laid down in the preceding stage. The habitations remained much the same in character. Some stone huts may be assigned to this stage, and the hamlets were sometimes surrounded by defensive earthworks. The peoples of this stage also erected the great circles of huge upright stones, connected with religious observance, of which the best known is Stonehenge on Salisbury plain. The new implements of bronze were at first patterned upon the neolithic models. Eventually new shapes were produced, which made the implements better adapted to their respective purposes, and new tools, such as wheeled vehicles, were devised. The use of bronze, which is copper mixed with ten per cent of tin, resulted in the utilization of the tin located in Cornwall and of the copper in that locality and in south Wales, and in the establishment of mines and foundries. Before the end of the stage of bronze Britain had begun to export tin to the continent. The presence of ornaments made of glass, gold, and amber, which came respectively from Mediterranean lands, Ireland, and the Baltic, testifies to an import trade. Pastoral pursuits were becoming more common, since the people of this day lived less upon the products of the chase and more upon the flesh of domesticated animals. Agriculture still remained primitive in the early part of the period. The inhabitants of a hamlet cultivated a plot of land for a few years until it was exhausted, when they moved to new lands. Before the close of the period agricultural pursuits were followed not only more extensively but also more intensively. In some portions of Britain the technique of cultivation improved so greatly that the settlements became more permanent. The people of the bronze stage also knew how to weave cloth, which they used for clothing. The accumulation of wealth, which might be expected to accompany these developments, is witnessed by the many

---

[16] The invention of bronze does not appear to have been made indigenously in Britain. The earliest tools of bronze give evidence of derivation from across the Channel, where bronze was used long before its appearance in Britain. Some of the early bronze implements found in southwestern England may have come from the Iberian peninsula as the result of commercial intercourse.

discoveries of personal adornments. The most striking testimony of the amelioration of the conditions of human existence, however, is the longer average of age which had been attained by the people buried in the round barrows, as compared with those buried in the long barrows. Hand in hand with this economic advancement must have gone development of religious belief and improvement of political organization, but the evidence admits of nothing beyond pure speculation as to the actual course of these changes.

The coming of the Celts

The people whom the Romans found in possession of Britain were in the stage of early iron. Because they spoke the Celtic language they are known as Celts. By whom and when the Celtic tongue was brought to Britain is an unsolved problem, because it has not yet become possible to correlate the philological and the archaeological evidence. A theory that the Beaker folk who initiated the bronze stage spoke Celtic is difficult to reconcile with the distribution of the archaeological remains. Another theory that slashing swords and socketed axes, which appeared in England in the neighborhood of 1000 B.C., were brought by Celtic invaders meets no serious obstacle in the archaeological evidence. For that reason it receives wider acceptance from scholars, but it does not yet appear to rest upon a very firm evidential foundation. Later in the bronze age at least two invasions from the continent took place; and the second group of invaders, who probably came from the Rhine basin and central Europe to southeastern England in the course of the sixth and fifth centuries B.C., introduced iron tools and almost certainly spoke Celtic. During the stage of iron still other peoples whose language was Celtic migrated to Britain. One group came from western Gaul to southwestern Britain around 200 B.C., and the Belgae, who were the last to arrive, began to cross from north-eastern Gaul to the opposite shore only a few years before Caesar visited the island. However doubtful may be the origin of Celtic speech in Britain, it was the dominant language by the time of Caesar, if it was not the only one. The iron culture introduced by the Celts also prevailed except in remote parts of the west and north. Yet the invaders did not supplant the older population. On the contrary, they mingled with the natives and added a long-headed Nordic strain to the racial intermixture which already existed.[17]

---

[17] Based upon the evidence of skeletal remains, which are still so few as to leave the situation somewhat obscure. The skeletons discovered in association with the early iron culture before Roman times are nearly all dolichocephalic, though some approach so near to brachycephalism that they give rise to a theory of racial intermixture among some of the invading Celtic peoples before they left the continent. At least one round skull

The new economic organization is called the stage of early iron to distinguish it from the Roman and later civilizations, for we still live in the stage of iron. The effect of the introduction of iron was to increase the efficiency of human labor. New types of tools appeared, and old tools, such as those used for agricultural purposes, were improved to so great an extent, that man, with the same expenditure of energy, could make the soil yield larger crops. The same area could and did support a much larger population; commerce increased; wealth accumulated; living conditions became more comfortable; in short, a higher type of civilization was developed.

Economic organization

Agriculture and grazing continued to be the chief industries. Both were conducted on a much larger scale than formerly. Apparently some of the valleys began to be cleared and settled in this epoch with the aid of the new iron tools. Survivals, as well as allusions by classical authors, indicate that pastoral pursuits predominated over agricultural. Iron and lead began to be mined and worked, the potter's wheel began to be employed for the production of more and improved pottery, the weaving of woolen and linen cloths became common, and carpenters, coopers, leather-workers, boatbuilders, and other artisans acquired a considerable degree of skill in their respective occupations. The natural result was a notable increase of internal and external commerce. Tin, which was sent across the Channel and to the Mediterranean, probably remained the staple export. A Roman, writing a few years before the Roman conquest, enumerated grain, cattle, skins, gold, silver, iron, slaves, and hunting dogs among the commodities brought to Italy from Britain. Their exports were thus raw materials. Their imports were principally luxuries, such as necklaces, bracelets, amber, and glassware. The most striking evidence of the economic development, however, was the introduction of money to facilitate the exchange of commodities, which previously appears to have been accomplished by the direct barter of one commodity for another. The earliest money was in the form of bars of iron made in certain standard weights to represent different values. This currency was followed well before Roman times by stamped coins of gold and other metals patterned upon Greek coins.

The increase in economic prosperity had a variety of results which can still be traced. Habitations remained much the same in their

---

typically different from the skulls of the earlier Beaker folk has been found in England in connection with the remains of early iron age culture. The remains, on the other hand, leave no doubt that a large element of the long-heads originally associated with the neolithic culture survived the Celtic inroads.

general types, although a few of the rich probably had houses containing several rooms. Household conveniences, such as ovens, wooden doors, and floors became common, and household utensils increased in number and in variety in the ordinary dwellings. Personal adornment occupied considerable attention. For clothing bright-colored tartans were favored. Jewelry, as the list of imports indicates, was more popular than ever. The gentlemen of the period have left behind large numbers of the razors with which they shaved, and the ladies failed to remove all traces of the cosmetics which we are wont to associate with the toilets of the old ladies of the nineteenth century and of the young ladies of the twentieth. With such ultra refinements of civilization as these went, as we should expect, association in larger communities. One complete village, lately unearthed, contained eighty dwellings, which for those days must have been a considerable town. Some of the communities, in fact, deserve the title of towns, since they were the commercial and political centers of considerable districts. The most notable concomitant of the greater prosperity was the development of a native art. This was not entirely indigenous. The Britons borrowed certain motives from across the Channel, but they developed them into a decorative art so distinctive that it is known as late Celtic or as early British.

Political organization

The largest unit of political organization was the tribe. It was ruled by a king or chieftain, who appears, in some instances at least, to have held his office by hereditary right. There was much intertribal warfare. Occasionally a strong king was able to subdue neighboring tribes and thus to extend his dominions, but this process of unification was always on a small scale. When the Roman conquest began, the land was still divided among a large number of turbulent tribes. Their rivalries and their inability to combine for a common purpose aided the progress of Roman arms. The tribes were divided into smaller units called clans. The clan was a patriarchal group of relatives descended from a common ancestor. It was ruled presumably by the oldest competent male member. The basis of the political organization was thus a personal group, as usually is the case in a primitive society. The territorial unit generally develops only with a more highly organized type of government.

Social organization

Celtic society presents the great inequalities in social ranks often found in primitive societies. Besides the ordinary freemen there were nobles and slaves. The class of slaves was doubtless drawn from the conquered population. About its rights or lack of rights we have no certain information. Judging by later survivals, it seems probable that the slaves often lived in separate communities and paid tribute to the heads of free clans, instead of working directly for the freemen. The aristocracy, if it was comparable to that of Gaul, was influential in the government of the tribe. About the social status and the political influence of the ordinary freemen we know nothing.

The Celts, like the Romans, had a number of gods. They were local, excepting a few more or less common to several tribes. Often they represented the personification of natural things, such as a wood, a stream, or a spring. The Celts worshiped in the natural temples provided by groves, and they made no images of their gods. They believed in a future life. The most characteristic aspect of their religious organization was their priesthood of druids. Of the British druids Caesar gives no description, but he records a tradition that the institution originated in Britain, and he states that the druids of Gaul often went to Britain to receive instruction in the higher branches of their cult. What Caesar says about the position of the druids of Gaul may consequently be applied to the druids of Britain without fear of great error. They presided at religious ceremonies, which consisted mainly of divinations and sacrifices. Their practices, which sometimes extended to the immolation of human beings, appear to have impressed the Romans with their grimness and horror. They also preserved the religious doctrine, the traditions, and the lore of the tribe. In order to become a druid a long period of training was necessary. A principal part of the education was to commit to memory enormous quantities of sacred verse, which was preserved only in oral form. The druids, who were the learned men of the day, gave such instruction as was available to the youths who sought an education. They also acted in a judicial capacity in such few cases as may be supposed to have come before public tribunals for decision. They appear to have been a queer combination of priests, magicians, medicine men, teachers, and magistrates. They constituted a highly respected class with great influence in the community. When the Romans were conquering Britain, they found that the druids were providing much of the inspiration behind the strong resistance of the natives.

Thus the natives of Britain whom Caesar attacked were in a far more primitive stage of civilization than the Romans, but, despite the assurance of Caesar that they painted their bodies for battle, they were far above the stage of civilization we are wont to associate with savages. Yet this civilization was most unevenly distributed. In the remote parts of the west and the north the civilization was still of the stages of bronze and stone. Iron implements, the basis of the economic pros-

Religion

Distribution of culture

perity on which rested the higher civilization of the south and east had hardly penetrated to these parts in Caesar's day. Even in the portion south of the Exe-Tees line the culture was by no means uniform. Within this district caves still supplied permanent homes occasionally, and the pit-dwellings and thatched huts of wattle and dried mud were the most common abodes. The large number of fortifications maintained in this period demonstrates that warfare, the negation of all civilization, was still the order of the day; and the ladies and gentlemen of Glastonbury, who had wooden floors and doors, mirrors and rouge, finally lost their heads when their well-fortified village was attacked by their foes.

CHAPTER II

ROMAN BRITAIN AND THE ANGLO-SAXON CONQUEST

FROM 55 B.C. to the early part of the fifth century Britain was in contact with the Roman world. During that period a few Roman historians and geographers devoted brief passages to affairs in Britain. They may be supplemented by archaeological evidence, which becomes more abundant and supplies the greater and more trustworthy part of our information.

Sources of information

In the development of the civilization described in the preceding chapter Britain occupied the backward position dictated by her remote geographical position in relation to the rest of Europe. Long before the neolithic stage ended in Britain, the peoples of the Mediterranean lands used bronze, built palaces, temples, and monuments, lived in cities, and committed their thoughts to writing. While Britain was in the stage of bronze, Egyptian and Aegean, Phoenician and Greek civilizations waxed and waned. During Britain's stage of iron "the glory that was Greece" gave place to "the grandeur that was Rome." Beginning as a small hill-town, Rome piled conquest upon conquest, until, by the beginning of the Christian era, the Mediterranean was a Roman lake, and all of Europe south of the Danube and west of the Rhine acknowledged her sway. Wherever the Roman legions went, Roman commerce and Roman civilization followed. Whenever a new territory was added to the Roman dominions, armed forces were stationed permanently upon its borders to repel hostile invaders and at points of vantage in the interior to prevent internal insurrection. By this means Rome gave to the lands under her sway a deep and lasting peace, which brought prosperity to many a people never before long free from the turmoil of war. When the soldiers had been placed on guard, building began. Cities were reared and filled with Roman and Italian colonists, who spread the Roman civilization among the natives. The cities were connected by well-constructed roads, which became avenues of commerce and communication over the length and breadth of the empire. By this slow but certain process the Roman civilization was allowed to permeate among the conquered provincials. Never did Rome attempt to force the adoption of her civilization by the natives. The results varied from one part of the empire to another.

Britain and the Roman Empire

In the east, where the Roman civilization met the Greek of kindred type, the Roman did not prevail; in central and western Europe, where the native civilizations were of lower standards, the Romanization became complete. Within this vast area was one language, one set of institutions, one culture. Civilized Europe was included within the frontiers watched by the Roman legions; outside was barbarism. The conquest which added Britain to this vast empire brought her also within the pale of the highest civilization of the age.

Caesar in Britain

The first direct political contact between Rome and Britain was brought about by Julius Caesar. The great general was engaged between 58 and 50 B.C. in the conquest of Gaul, that is, what is now approximately France and Belgium. In the course of his campaigns he found that the Celts of Gaul were receiving aid from the Celts of Britain. In order to persuade the British Celts to mind their own business, he made armed demonstrations against them in 55 and 54 B.C. On the first expedition he engaged the local tribesmen of Kent without notable success, and retired without having penetrated the country more than a few miles beyond his landing place. On the second he marched through Kent and advanced a few miles across the Thames. He defeated a confederacy of the Celtic tribes which opposed him, received hostages, exacted a futile promise of the payment of annual tribute, and withdrew his legions across the Channel never to return.

A century of intercourse

Caesar's expeditions brought Britain to the attention of the Roman world. Thereafter visions of British conquest haunted Roman statesmen, but civil wars and the more pressing necessities for campaigns in other directions prevented the fulfillment of the dream for nearly a century. Meanwhile the Celts of Britain were coming under the influence of the Roman civilization. After Caesar's conquest of Gaul, a Roman province was organized across the Channel from Britain. The continuation by the Celts of Britain of their intercourse with the Celts of Gaul brought them into contact with things Roman, while the foreign commerce of Britain, which seems now to have quickened, brought to the island Roman merchants, the forerunners of empire. In this interval British coins began to be patterned on those of Rome; British princes began to pay their respects to the emperors at Rome; and more than one prince, who had suffered reverses in the civil wars of his native land, besought Roman intervention in British affairs. The Romans on their side acquired greater familiarity with the geography, the politics, and the resources of the island. Thus the way was prepared for the conquest which was undertaken by the emperor Claudius in 43 A.D.

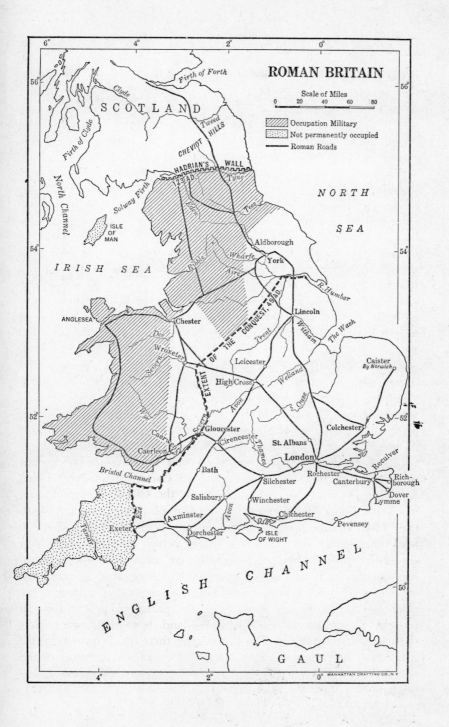

ROMAN BRITAIN

Scale of Miles

0   20   40   60   80

Occupation Military
Not permanently occupied
Roman Roads

SCOTLAND

Firth of Forth

Clyde

Firth of Clyde

North Channel

Solway Firth

Tweed

CHEVIOT HILLS

HADRIAN'S WALL
23 AD

Tyne

NORTH SEA

ISLE OF MAN

IRISH SEA

Eden

Tees

Aldborough

Ribble

Wharfe

York

Aire

EXTENT OF THE CONQUEST, 49 AD

R. Humber

ANGLESEA

Chester

Dee

Lincoln

Witham

The Wash

Wroxeter

Severn

Trent

Leicester

Welland

Caister By Norwich

High Cross

Wye

Avon

Ouse

Caerws

Severn

Gloucester

Cirencester

St. Albans

Colchester

Caerleon

Thames

London

Reculver

Bristol Channel

Bath

Rochester

Canterbury

Richborough

Salisbury

Silchester

Dover

Exe

Winchester

Chichester

Lymme

Axminster

Avon

Pevensey

Roman

Exeter

Dorchester

ISLE OF WIGHT

ENGLISH CHANNEL

GAUL

MANHATTAN DRAFTING CO., N Y

The Roman army landed in the southeastern corner of Britain. The first advance resulted in the conquest of the strong confederacy of Belgic tribes holding that section of the island. Thence the legions advanced on the radii of a circle to the southwest, northwest, and north, where they met with slight resistance from tribes which had previously been the foes of the Belgae. Within five years the Romans had control of the plain. The Roman authority in this district, however, was not yet firmly established. Petty rebellions and disorders occurred, which culminated in 61 with an outbreak that nearly overwhelmed the Roman power. The natives of the east, angered by the injustice and extortion of Roman officials, were led by Queen Boudicca[1] against the principal Roman settlements. They massacred the inhabitants and defeated the only section of the Roman army stationed in the neighborhood. The tide turned with the arrival of the Roman governor, who had been conducting a campaign in Wales. Hurrying east with a small army, he risked successfully a critical battle which scattered the forces of Boudicca. A reorganization of the government, which laid the foundation of orderly provincial administration, followed during the next decade. By about 70 the Roman control of the plain south of Humber and Mersey was thoroughly established.

Conquest of the plain

Meanwhile the conquest of the hill-tribes had been begun. This was a more difficult task, requiring a longer time for its accomplishment. Campaigns begun in Wales in 48 were not completed until 79. The last campaign was conducted by Agricola, governor of Britain from 78 to 85, who turned next to the task of extending the Roman power toward the north, where the conquest had begun a few years earlier. In successive campaigns he led his armies up to the lowlands of Scotland, established garrisons on the short line between Clyde and Forth, and was fighting in the highlands when he was recalled to Rome. The attempt to make the ocean the boundary of the empire on the north was not again renewed. Shortly after Agricola's time the outposts in the lowlands of Scotland had to be withdrawn because the ambitious governor had left too many natives unsubdued in his rear. The Pennines, indeed, were so insecurely held that the warfare with the inhabitants of these mountains lasted intermittently until 120, when the emperor Hadrian came in person to complete the conquest. Even after his thorough work a formidable revolt had to be quelled thirty-five years later, before permanent peace was firmly established behind the northern boundary of the province of Britain. This frontier

Conquest of the uplands

---

[1] Long known as Boadicea through the misreading of a medieval manuscript.

was fixed by Hadrian, who had a wall built across the island from Tyne to Solway. North of the wall warfare did not cease until the early years of the third century.

Era of peace

The second century, which witnessed prolonged warfare in the north of Britain, was for the empire as a whole a period of prosperity. The historian, Gibbon, characterized it as "the period in the history of the world during which the condition of the human race was most happy and prosperous."[2] The third century, on the other hand, was a time of disaster, when civil wars and invasions seemed to threaten the disruption of the empire. In contrast with all this Britain entered upon a period of peace. Her frontiers were free from serious attack, and her legions took little part in the civil wars. This peaceful epoch was the time when many new residences were built in the country, but for the towns it was not a period of prosperity. In Britain, as elsewhere in the empire, the towns began to decay in the middle of the century, borne down by a burden of imperial taxation which was too heavy and by an inflation of the currency.

End of the Roman régime

About 350 began a series of events which ended in the downfall of Roman rule in Britain. The independent Celts in the north renewed their attacks on the wall. The Celts of Ireland, who were known as Scots, settled in the west of Scotland, gave the land their name, assisted in the attacks upon the wall, and raided the coast of Wales. The Franks and Saxons, German peoples living at the mouth of the Rhine and beyond, had begun to make piratical descents upon the coasts of Britain toward the end of the third century. Already a fleet and a system of fortification on the eastern coast had been organized for defense and placed under the command of a Roman officer known as the count of the Saxon Shore. Coincidently with the attacks of the Celts, the piratical raids of the Germans appear to have increased in scope and frequency. The invaders broke the defenses to such an extent that country houses began to be abandoned because residence in the open country was no longer safe. Though the wave of invasion was temporarily turned back, it could not be held in check permanently. The empire itself was beginning to crumble. In 378 the battle of Adrianople broke for all time the Rhine-Danube frontier and marked the beginning of those barbarian invasions before which the might of Rome was destined to fall. In the face of these attacks the imperial government found it necessary to concentrate on the defense of the heart of the empire, and to leave the provinces on the outskirts to their own

---

[2] Edition by Bury, i, 78.

resources. In Britain the situation was further complicated by the attempt of an officer stationed in Britain to usurp the purple. In 383 he crossed to Gaul, carrying most of the British garrisons with him. After he was defeated and slain the legions probably were never restored to their full complement. Soon troops began to be withdrawn from Britain for the defense of Italy. In 407 another prospective usurper took more of the soldiers across the Channel, never to return. Thereafter Rome may have sent governors and troops to the island for a few years, but the Romano-Celtic inhabitants were soon left to shift for themselves against the attacks of Celtic and German barbarians.

The provincial organization of Britain was begun immediately after the initial stages of the conquest. The frontier provinces, such as Britain was destined to be, were ruled by a governor who had command of the army as well as headship of the civil government. His powers were nearly absolute except for his responsibility to the emperor. The natives, however, were given some autonomy in local affairs, as soon as they were regarded as sufficiently assimilated to be intrusted with political power. The form taken by the local government was municipal. Rome, itself a city, naturally modeled the governments of conquered lands upon its own organization. The first governors of Britain had not only to plan and execute campaigns, but also to provide for the defense of the conquered portions and to establish there the civil institutions which alone could be counted upon to influence the natives to adopt Roman ways of life. Of the early governors, Agricola (78-85) was the most successful in the work of civil administration. He encouraged the natives to undertake the construction of public buildings, to adopt the dress and other fashions of the Romans, and to use Latin. He made provision too for the education of the sons of influential Britons. By the close of his term of office, the provincial organization, which was successfully Romanizing the natives of other provinces, was firmly established in Britain.

Provincial organization of Britain

Among the Roman institutions in Britain, the army occupied an exceptionally prominent place throughout the whole period of the occupation. The troops were stationed principally at three centers near the highlands,[3] and in the hills small fortified garrisons were kept thickly placed. In Wales and in all of the uplands north of Trent the Roman occupation remained primarily military. In these regions Roman culture had little opportunity to influence the natives. Military institutions, as contrasted with civil, are poor agents for the propagation

The army

---

[3] At Caerleon, Chester, and York.

of civilization. The Roman armies in Britain did little themselves to Romanize the natives, though by holding the barbarians on the north at bay and by keeping the hillsmen quiet, they gave to the plain behind the long period of peace which enabled the civil institutions to do their slow, quiet work of penetration.

Cities   In the plains the Romans established to some extent the agencies which had been used to Romanize other provinces. The most important of these was the urban center. In newly conquered territories, such as northern France or Britain, the Romans, after founding municipalities in natural geographical centers and filling them with colonists who spoke Latin, could rely upon the intercommunication between town and country to radiate Roman culture from one center through a large district. In Britain only four urban units of this sort are known to have been established,[4] though three others became important centers of Romanized life.[5] Besides these cities there were some ten to twenty smaller towns,[6] which were built on the Roman model, with squares, market places, temples, and public baths. Silchester, a typical town of this class, probably had a population of less than 2,000. Judging by a single inscription found in one of these towns, they were of the type prevalent in northern France. They were tribal towns, where the government was managed, not by Roman citizens, but by leaders of the tribe. The population of such a town would be mainly native, though it might contain a small element of Roman merchants and settlers. These municipalities were not as potent agents for the spread of Roman civilization as were the larger towns, though their organization on the Roman model implies the absorption by their inhabitants of some part of the Roman culture. The inhabitants were free, on the other hand, to retain the Celtic language and customs, and possibly did so to some extent. The towns of these two types account for the government of the larger part of the plain, though there must have been some parts remote from the urban influence which disseminated the Roman culture.

Villas and villages   The greater part of the population still lived in the country, either in scattered country residences called villas, or in villages. The villas varied all the way from comparatively simple farmhouses of moderate size to large and sumptuous country houses supplied with furnaces and bathrooms and decorated with frescoes and mosaics. They were uniformly of Roman provincial types of architecture, which were

---

[4] Colchester, Lincoln, Gloucester, and York.

[5] London, St. Albans, and Bath.

[6] In England "town" is a generic term for urban units, and it is so used in this book

distinctively different from the round stone huts of the Celts; and those which have been excavated contain many material remains indicating that the people who lived in them were mainly Romanized natives. Some of the villas were located upon large estates which were cultivated by means of native laborers, who probably were for the most part slaves or serfs. The villas were small centers from which the influence of the Roman culture radiated in rural districts to some extent. On the other hand, many of the inhabitants still lived in small villages. In a few regions the villages and the villas were neighbors; but villages were rarely located upon the estates of villas, and in many districts only villages or only villas have been found. The homes of the villagers were huts of the Celtic type, and the plan and organization of the villages remained the same as those of the villages which had existed before the Roman occupation. In a few villages some of the inhabitants used Roman pottery and coins, but the traces of Roman influence are small. The villages represent a large section of the community which retained the native methods of life and was affected only slightly by Roman culture.

"Of all inventions," says Macaulay,[7] "the alphabet and the printing press alone excepted, those inventions which abridge distance have done most for the civilization of our species." The Roman roads were such an invention. The roads existing before the Roman conquest were probably little better than rough paths and trails, following the sinuous courses of the cleared ridges of chalk and limestone. The Roman roads were so carefully and solidly constructed that their remains can be traced in many parts of England to this day. They were laid down generally on a straight line between points, unless some insuperable physical obstacle intervened, because their principal purposes were to increase the speed with which troops could be moved from one place to another and to keep the central government at Rome in touch with all parts of the empire. The Roman engineers had an eye for natural routes of communication. The trunk roads of the Romans with one exception radiated from London. They followed closely the routes taken today by three of the principal English railways. Along these roads went commerce, and hard on the heels of commerce follows civilization. **Roads**

The commerce and industry of the Roman period seem to have been largely of the same kind as in the preceding epoch, but much greater in amount. Metals constituted an important part of the exports **Commerce and industry**

---

[7] *History of England* (Boston, 1855), i, 290.

from Britain, and the demands of a higher civilization increased their use greatly in Britain itself. Tin, lead, copper, and iron were the principal metals produced. Manufactures of implements and appliances of bronze and iron developed many improvements of technique and turned out a far greater quantity and variety of articles. Agriculture must have been practiced more extensively than formerly, since in the fourth century Britain was one of the regular sources of grain supply for some of the provinces across the Channel. Agriculture, indeed, seems for the time to have been the leading industry. Cattle, hides, and slaves were still exported. Cloth was woven on a sufficient scale to provide a surplus for export. The taste of the Romans for luxuries of the table brought Kentish oysters to Rome, and, lest we should forget the wild character still preserved by most of Britain's surface, we are reminded that Britain supplied wild beasts for the shows at Rome. Wine, oil, ivory, amber, pottery, and glassware were among the imports, but they probably constitute only a partial list. Despite the importation of pottery, a large industry in that ware was developed in England, and an industry in glassware as well. The building trades flourished. Slates and other stones were quarried, and bricks were made in large quantities. In the fourth century, when a Gallic city had to be rebuilt, masons and other workmen were obtained from Britain. The hoards of coins which are frequently dug up give the most impressive testimony to the commercial and industrial prosperity of the island during the Roman era. Without much doubt the volume of business was larger than it had ever been before, or than it was to be again for many centuries after Roman rule ended.

Religion   With regard to religion, the Romans followed the same policy as with regard to other native institutions; they made no attempt to uproot the native cult; they merely established their own, allowing the Celts to worship what gods they chose. The Romans were becoming sufficiently sceptical about their own religion to tolerate others, as long as they did not conflict with the state. But the Romans who lived in Britain came from many parts of the empire, and they brought with them many gods. Beside the altars of Jupiter and Mars are found the shrines of the eastern Mithra and Isis. Among these eastern religions came Christianity. By the beginning of the third century individual Christians were present in Britain, and at the beginning of the fourth there was a fully developed Christian church. During the fourth century, under first the toleration and then the encouragement of the imperial government, Christianity became more widespread in Britain. Paganism probably survived to the end of the Roman régime; whether Christianity was then the religion of the majority or of the minority in Britain is unknown; but Christianity is one of the few Roman institutions, if not the only one, which survived the destructive conquest of the Anglo-Saxons in the fifth century.

One of the best tests of community of civilization is community of language. So long as two peoples speak different languages they must remain more or less alien to each other's thought. In Britain the government began early to encourage the use of Latin by the natives. Literary allusions give some ground for the assumption that the aristocratic and professional classes spoke Latin. More valuable are the inscriptions scratched on tiles and pots by workmen and servants. Enough inscriptions of this sort have been found to establish a probability that in the third and fourth centuries Latin was a familiar tongue to such urban classes as artisans and servants, who were recruited mainly from the native population. They indicate a possibility, indeed, that Latin was used by similar classes on some of the rural estates. The evidence is not sufficient, on the other hand, to preclude the possibility that Celtic remained the language of common usage among the peasants and even among the artisans of some of the towns. The evidence throws but a flickering light on the linguistic situation in Roman Britain.

Latin language

These are the salient characteristics of the civilization which the Romans established in Britain. It did not extend to all parts of the island. North of the wall the Roman legions never secured a permanent foothold. In the uplands south of the wall and north of the Mersey and the Humber, and in Wales, the failure of civil institutions to penetrate gave the process of Romanization no opportunity to work. Cornwall, too, saw little of the Roman culture. In all these districts the Celtic culture survived. The Roman sphere of cultural influence was confined to the plain. Within that area Roman civilization was adopted to some extent by the natives. Latin appears to have been used by a much wider group of the natives than that composed of the officials and the nobles. The cities, the villas, the roads, and the commerce must have brought about some Romanization of the natives. The survival of Christianity suggests that the process went deep. Yet in some Celtic villages which have been excavated the traces of Roman influence are slight. These are vague and not entirely harmonious conclusions; but, on the whole, the most probable interpretation of the evidence seems

Extent of the Romanization

to be that there was an amalgamation of the two civilizations. In this mixture the Roman civilization predominated except in isolated rural districts. It was, however, the crude civilization of a frontier province, not the polished culture that flourished in much of Gaul.

Effect on later history

After Britain was cast adrift from the empire, a curtain of historical darkness descended upon the island. When it was lifted two centuries later, Anglo-Saxon German-speaking peoples occupied the plain and Celtic-speaking peoples held the hills. The Romanized provincials of the plain had been driven to seek refuge among the hillsmen whose culture was still Celtic. There the plainsmen were forced to revert to the simpler and cruder modes of life practiced by the hillsmen. Their Roman culture was too superficial in character long to survive the reversion. Latin and along with it nearly the whole fabric of Roman civilization disappeared. Christianity survived, and possibly in the southeastern counties, where Roman influence began earliest and was always strongest, the agrarian system (that is, the method of parceling out land for agricultural purposes) may have modified the agricultural methods of the Anglo-Saxon invaders. Aside from these, no institutions have been found in Britain the beginnings of which can be assigned with any high degree of probability to the Roman period. The Romans during their occupation of England contributed little to the stock of institutions which constitute the heritage of Englishmen.

Evidence about the Anglo-Saxon conquest

Although the Anglo-Saxon conquest exerted a profound influence upon the course of English history, it left scant trace upon written records. Of its general character and its results we may judge somewhat from the survivals of a later time, but its course remains unchronicled. Though a native monk named Gildas wrote a work on the destruction of Britain while the conquest was still in progress, he wrote a century or more after its beginning, and he recorded astonishingly few facts. Two later chronicles, which have been followed by many modern historians, are Bede's *Ecclesiastical History*, which was finished in 731, and the *Anglo-Saxon Chronicle*, which was not begun until the ninth century. They are excellent authorities for the periods with which they are contemporary, and they preserve some earlier contemporary records of the period after 597; but for the fifth and sixth centuries, when the Anglo-Saxon conquest was taking place, they have little worth.[8] Archaeology adds much less to our knowledge of

---

[8] The *Historia Brittonum*, though redacted in the ninth century, contains a core of narrative written near the end of the seventh century. It is difficult to disentangle and has as yet slight historical value.

this period than of the Roman. The Anglo-Saxons of the period of
the conquest made their buildings of wood and left behind them few
enduring material remains except in their cemeteries.

The Anglo-Saxon conquest of Britain was part and parcel of the
barbarian invasions of the empire in the fifth century. After centuries
of pressure against the Rhine-Danube frontier, the Germans burst
the bounds, overran the western part of the empire, and broke it up
into independent German kingdoms. While Goth and Vandal, Burgundian and Frank were crossing the land frontier, the German peoples
who lived on the north shore east of the Rhine and in the peninsula
of Jutland began to cross the water frontier to Britain. These peoples
were the Jutes, the Angles, and the Saxons,[9] but the three intermixed
to some extent both before they left the continent and during the
course of the conquest. They came in long narrow boats, propelled
by oars rather than by sail. The keels, as they were called, were so
low amidships that they must have been a hazardous means of
transport across the open sea, but their rowers knew no fear. "The
dangers of the deep," said a contemporary, "are to them, not casual
acquaintances, but intimate friends, for since a tempest throws the
invaded off their guard, and prevents the invaders from being descried
from afar, they hail with joy the crash of waves on the rocks which
gives them their best chance of escaping from other enemies than the
elements."[10] These bold navigators conducted plundering raids against
Britain intermittently for more than a century before they began to
conquer the land for the purpose of settlement. The attacks changed
their character probably around the middle of the fifth century. Though
some of the early invaders who came for settlement appear to have
swept far inland and caused the destruction or final abandonment of
many towns, they were unable to hold so much territory, and the
earliest settlements were made in the southeast, the east, and the valley
of the Thames. The conquerors probably did not come in large armies,
but rather in successive small groups, each group winning a separate
district in which to make its home. The many small wars which resulted from this method of penetration followed one another more
or less continuously until the early years of the sixth century, when
a period of comparative peace intervened. During the interval the

The course of the conquest

---

[9] This, at least, is the tradition preserved by Bede, which receives some confirmation
from archaeological evidence, although philology indicates a possibility that Angle and
Saxon may have been two names for one people. For the latter view see Chadwick,
Origin of the English Nation, ch. iv. Compare Hodgkin, *A History of the Anglo-Saxons*,
i, 157–161.

[10] Sidonius, quoted by Hodgkin, *A History of the Anglo-Saxons*, i, 19.

invaders were probably consolidating their holdings and forming coalitions among themselves. In the second half of the sixth century, when they renewed their aggressions, they fought in larger groups. This second series of wars may be said to have ended with two Anglo-Saxon victories in the west which were won during the closing years of the sixth century and the opening years of the seventh. The conclusion of the conquest, which had been going forward intermittently for 150 years or more, left the Anglo-Saxons in possession of nearly all of the land which is now included in England, except the Cornish peninsula in the southwest and the region of the Cumbrian mountains in the northwest. These upland districts, together with Wales and Scotland, were still in the hands of the unconquered natives.

Character of the conquest

The Anglo-Saxon conquest was utterly different in character from the Roman. The Anglo-Saxons migrated as a people; the warriors brought with them their wives and children, and set up their household gods on the newly conquered soil. A German civilization was thus brought to England. The new civilization did not amalgamate extensively with the old, for the Anglo-Saxons appear to have waged a war of extermination. They did not kill all the Celts in the territories which they occupied, but, except in the west, the north, and possibly the southeast, they appear either to have killed or to have driven out the larger portion of them. In some regions they may have retained some of the Celts as slaves, and there may have been some intermarriage with Celtic women, but the contact between the two peoples was not enough to effect any significant modification in the institutions of the conquerors. Such, at least, is the only hypothesis which seems adequately to explain the divergence between the results of the Anglo-Saxon conquest and those of the conquests made by other German peoples in other parts of the empire. In Gaul, for example, the Franks, after a period of warfare, were accepted as rulers by the native provincials. The two peoples settled down peacefully side by side and intermingled freely. The German conquerors soon adopted the Latin of the conquered in place of their mother tongue and abandoned their paganism in favor of the Christianity of the subject population. In Britain the conquest extended over a much longer period, the natives contested the progress of the invaders more stubbornly, and the opportunity for peaceful intercourse between the conquerors and the conquered was less. In Britain the language of the conquerors remained almost purely Germanic. Nor did the Anglo-Saxons accept Christianity from the conquered. Christianity survived among the Celts of Britain, but the Anglo-Saxons were first converted by missionaries sent from Rome, when the conquest had been nearly completed.[11] A contact between the Anglo-Saxons and the Celts which was not sufficiently close to cause any significant change in either the language or the religion of the conquerors could hardly have wrought any vital change in other Anglo-Saxon institutions. Even the material aspects of the civilization of the Roman period disappeared. In all probability the Anglo-Saxon conquest resulted in the substitution of the Anglo-Saxon civilization for that of the native Celts in the largest part of what is now England. The origin of most English institutions must be traced back to Germany.[12]

Any attempt to portray the civilization of the Anglo-Saxons, as it existed before its transplantation to England, must be handicapped by lack of sufficient knowledge. Specific information about the institutions of the Angles, Saxons, and Jutes, except such uncertain knowledge as can be gleaned from survivals in their laws and literature written long after their arrival in England, is almost entirely absent. Two descriptions of the Germans as a whole are extant. Since the Anglo-Saxon culture was, with possible variations in detail, that common to the Teutonic people, these descriptions may probably be accepted as applicable in broad outline to the institutions of the Anglo-Saxons. Unfortunately they were written some centuries before the time of the Anglo-Saxon invasion of Britain. The first was by Caesar, who devoted six brief chapters of his *Gallic Wars* to a characterization of the Germans as he saw them. In 98 A.D., Tacitus wrote the *Germania*, which is a more circumstantial account. Between that time and the Anglo-Saxon conquest some changes in German institutions indubitably took place, but contemporary evidence of what happened in this interval is almost non-existent. The later institutions of the Anglo-Saxons, however, when compared with those described by Caesar and Tacitus, present a remarkable family likeness. It appears to be a reasonably safe assumption that these two Roman historians describe the roots from which grew many parts of the English constitution.

The largest political unit among the Germans was the tribe. In many tribes the only organ of central government was the council

Our knowledge of the early Germans

---

[11] In the course of the seventh century Celtic missionaries began to win converts among the Anglo-Saxons in the north, and on the west also there was some reactionary influence of Celtic upon German institutions, but Anglo-Saxon institutions by then had had time to take firm root in English soil undisturbed by outside influence.

[12] This hypothesis, which is based mainly upon the evidence of survivals, has the general acceptance of historians, although it is still denied by some. A convenient, brief exposition of the two points of view is given by A. M. Chambers in her *Constitutional History of England* (London, 1911), pp. 7–16.

composed of all the freemen of the tribe. They deliberated upon
questions of interest to the whole group, such as war and peace, and
settled all affairs of importance. There was no voting in the modern
sense of the term, but the approval of the council of freemen was
essential to secure common action. The nature of the institution implies an undisciplined, rough and ready freedom. In the time of
Tacitus some tribes had kings, who appear to have been permanent
leaders of their peoples rather than the authoritative heads of states.
In these tribes the tribal councils were still maintained. Some of the
Anglo-Saxon tribes had kings before they began the conquest of
Britain; others probably developed their kings from temporary military leaders during the turmoil of the conquest. When the conquest
ceased, every independent group of the Anglo-Saxons had its king.
On the other hand, there is no evidence that the democratic tribal
assembly ever existed in England. The tradition preserved in later
literature places power in the hands of the king and of his court,
which was filled with royal officials and military retainers. Whether
this democratic element disappeared before, during, or after the Anglo-
Saxon conquest, it is impossible to say.

The tribal unit was subdivided into smaller units, which Caesar
and Tacitus call *pagi*. They were probably the divisions called hundreds by the Germans. The chieftains selected in the tribal council
administered the affairs of the hundreds and presided over the local
courts, which probably transacted most of the judicial business of the
tribesmen. The chieftains were not absolute in their power, since
many freemen were associated with them in their work. In Anglo-
Saxon laws the hundred is not mentioned until the tenth century,
but the institution may have existed earlier. In the early Anglo-Saxon
laws, on the other hand, the local officials seem to have been appointed
by the king. In each hundred were several villages. They appear to
have had few independent political functions.

In the time of Caesar and Tacitus the clan was an important agent
of government, and among the early Anglo-Saxons the kindred bond
was still strong. The personal basis of the political organization appears clearly in the mode of administering justice. The law of private
vengeance, the "eye for eye, tooth for tooth" principle of the laws
of Moses, which regarded a crime primarily as an offense against
the individual rather than against society as a whole, was the law
of the early Germans. The person who suffered injury from another
could seek his own redress, or, if he were slain or disabled, it was
the duty of his clan to exact atonement from the transgressor. In the

Political organization

Justice

time of Tacitus the courts could be used in place of self-help, though the alternative right of private vengeance was still retained. In the case of homicide a fine called the wergeld (man-money) was paid to the clansmen of the deceased. Lesser injuries could be expiated by fines paid in part to the injured party and in part to the state. These fundamental principles of criminal law still prevailed among the Anglo-Saxons at the time of the conquest. Their earliest written laws are taken up largely with the tariff of fines assessed against all conceivable kinds of bodily injury.

One of the principal purposes for which the German tribal state existed was for waging war. "The German people revel in war," says **Warfare** Tacitus, and his assertion is amply verified in the pages of his own histories. The military organization of the Germans, like their political organization, was a rough and ready one. Every freeman was a warrior; the army was the tribe in arms. The emphasis placed upon military affairs remained prominent among the Anglo-Saxons long after their conquest of Britain. An institution connected with the military organization, which had a deep influence upon German life, was the *comitatus*. This was a body of personal companions and followers whom a chieftain or some other influential man gathered around him for the purpose of warfare. The members were dependent on the leader, though the position was one of honor. The *comitatus* was a permanent part of the leader's household. He supplied the members with weapons and horses, shared with them the spoils of war, and provided for their maintenance. The members were bound to him by a special oath of fidelity. Their principal duty was military service, but it was service of an exceptional sort, for so close was the bond that it was a dishonor to survive the leader unavenged, if he fell in battle. This institution, which must have done much to foster high ideals of loyalty and honor, as well as war, appears in England in the early days of the Anglo-Saxon kingdoms.

Among the Germans Tacitus distinguishes four social classes. The foundation of German society was the freeman.[13] The council com- **Ranks and** posed of freemen transacted the business of the community, and the **classes** host of freemen went forth in battle array. Above the freemen in the social scale were the nobles. Nobility carried with it honor and esteem; doubtless it gave its possessors greater influence in the con-

---

[13] There is a school of writers who would have us believe that German society was composed of a small ruling caste of free landowners, upon whom the remaining people were economically and politically dependent; but this does not accord with the picture of Tacitus, who emphasizes the freedom of the rank and file of the Germans.

duct of public affairs than that possessed by the ordinary freeman; but the nobles did not form a ruling caste. Below the freemen were the slaves, who had no political rights and no wergeld. They were the chattels of their masters, who had the same rights over them as over an ox or a horse. In practice their lot was not so bad as that of the Roman slaves. The German slave generally had a dwelling of his own, and the main element of his servitude consisted of a tribute paid in produce to his owner. Above the slave and below the freemen in social rank were the freedmen, who originally were emancipated slaves. They were distinguished from the slaves in that they were not mere chattels; they could not be bought and sold; they had a wergeld; they could not be slain with impunity. Beyond these, however, they had no political rights. Their position was distinctly inferior to that of the freemen. In the Anglo-Saxon laws, written in England in the seventh century, all of these classes are mentioned. The nobles are known as eorls, the ordinary freemen as ceorls, and those in the class intermediate between the free and the slave as laets.

Economic development

The Anglo-Saxons who conquered England made agriculture the mainstay of their existence. They were preeminently a rural people, who preferred to live in the open spaces and disliked the confinement of the walls of a town. After their advent, most of the Roman towns, whence the native inhabitants had departed, were left to fall into ruin and decay. A few continued to be occupied after the conquest, but their populations dwindled and all traces of urban life disappeared. The villa system of the Romans was likewise abandoned. Even the Roman roads were not kept in repair, although the main highways continued to be used to such an extent that they received Anglo-Saxon names. The invaders did not settle along the roads, however. They came by boat, penetrated the interior, mainly by means of the rivers, and settled in the valleys. The thriving commerce of the Roman period came to an end. With the Franks across the Channel the Anglo-Saxons maintained a commercial intercourse, in which the chief article of export was slaves, but the volume of trade was insignificant compared with that of Roman days. Many of the industries of the Roman period ceased to exist, while others deteriorated. The use of the potter's wheel, for example, appears to have been unknown, except to the Jutes. The Anglo-Saxon decorative art was barbaric and weak in its design, although it displays a highly developed technique of execution. Cultured municipal life with its commercial and industrial concomitants vanished with the coming of the Anglo-Saxons, and English life became rural, rude, and predominantly agricultural.

In religion the Anglo-Saxons were still as pagan as their ancestors had been in the first century. Like the Celts and the Romans of an earlier time, they worshiped many gods. Among them Woden, the god of war, and Thunor, the god of the weather, were prominent, and worship of the personified aspects of nature which affected the crops was also popular.

Religion

The Anglo-Saxons spoke dialects of a language which belonged to the low-German linguistic family. At the time of the conquest the language was not a written one. The Anglo-Saxons had a rude alphabet of characters known as runes, which they used only in brief inscriptions. In the seventh century knowledge of the Roman alphabet brought by the Christian missionaries caused Anglo-Saxon to become a written language. It was first employed early in the seventh century to reduce to written form a set of Anglo-Saxon laws in the native tongue. Though no written literature existed before that time, the recitation of poems and songs was a favorite form of amusement at courts of kings and in halls of nobles. Many poems which were not written down until later either took their form in the centuries when the Anglo-Saxon conquest was taking place, or preserved legends developed in that heroic epoch. *Beowulf* is the obvious example known to every student of English literature. This literature preserves the thoughts, ideals, and traditions of the Germans of the time of the Anglo-Saxon conquest and gives us a glimpse of the intellectual outlook of the conquerors of Britain, who gave to the portion of the island which they won the name of England.

Language and literature

CHAPTER III

THE DEVELOPMENT OF ANGLO-SAXON ENGLAND

The
heptarchy

WHEN the historical darkness surrounding the period of the conquest gives way to the half-light provided by the flickering flames of such candles as Bede, the *Anglo-Saxon Chronicle,* and the Anglo-Saxon laws, England was not yet a political entity. The conquered land had been settled by several separate groups, which formed independent kingdoms. At the beginning of the seventh century some of these had already disappeared, swallowed up by their larger and stronger neighbors, and others were shortly to be absorbed. The seven kingdoms which played important parts in the seventh century are known as the heptarchy. The kingdom of Kent in the southeast was settled by the Jutes. The Saxons settled all around the Jutes, forming the three kingdoms of Essex, Sussex, and Wessex. North of the Saxons were the Angles, who organized the three kingdoms of East Anglia, Mercia, and Northumbria.

Unifying
forces

The making of England is the story of the deeds by which the peoples of these independent kingdoms were united under the rule of one king. Three forces helped in varying degrees to bring about this result. (1) The warfare among the different groups of the conquerors, begun before the conquest was finished, continued in the seventh and eighth centuries. The stronger and more ambitious kings secured superiority over neighboring kingdoms. (2) The church was the second force which contributed to the production of a united England. Within a century of its introduction Christianity spread to all the kingdoms. When an ecclesiastical organization common to all of Anglo-Saxon Britain had once been established, it became by example an influence in the direction of political unity. (3) These two forces, however, failed to accomplish unity, until the third, the pressure of a common enemy, was applied. Toward the close of the eighth century the Danes began to invade the country from the sea. When they had nearly overrun the land, the kings of Wessex, by conquering the Danes, became the kings of a united England. Internal strife, Christianity, and foreign invasion were the principal forces at work to produce unity.

Supremacy
of Kent

The story of their working begins with the supremacy established by King Ethelbert of Kent, who ruled from 560 to 616. Before the end of the sixth century he had won acknowledgment of his leadership from the kingdoms south of the Humber. He had also cemented an alliance with the powerful king of the Franks by the marriage of his daughter. This marriage prepared the way for the most important event of his reign, the coming of Christianity. The Franks had long since been converted to Christianity, and Ethelbert's queen was allowed to bring priests to Kent and to practice her own worship. Ethelbert had thus acquired familiarity with the new faith, when the Christian mission which brought the religion to the Anglo-Saxons landed on the shore of Kent in 597.

The mission, which was headed by Augustine, had been despatched from Rome by Pope Gregory the Great. The conversion of the Anglo-Saxons was part of a task which the Christians of the west had undertaken with the coming of the barbarians into the empire. When the empire fell, Christianity rose triumphant above the political ruins and began the conquest of the conquerors. The guidance of the movement was taken by the bishops of Rome, who received the title of popes and were acknowledged by the Christian communities of the west as the leaders of the church. When Gregory the Great became pope, the Anglo-Saxons constituted the last large group of the conquerors who were still heathen. Augustine and his companions were hospitably received by Ethelbert. Within a few months the king and a large number of his subjects had been baptized. Within a few years the new religion had spread to neighboring kingdoms where Ethelbert was influential. When he died in 616, the supremacy of Kent ended, and no further progress in the expansion of Christianity was made from that kingdom.

Introduction of Christianity

A new impetus was given to the movement, however, by the conversion of Edwin, king of Northumbria, who acquired the leadership of the heptarchy soon after the death of Ethelbert. The event which brought Christianity to his realm was his marriage to the sister of the king of Kent. She stipulated that she should be allowed to worship in her own faith. The bishop whom she brought with her thus became the apostle of the faith among the Northumbrians. His eloquence soon converted Edwin and many of his subjects. Before the new religion was firmly rooted, the supremacy of Northumbria was overthrown. The heathen king of Mercia, chafing under his dependence upon Edwin, defeated the Northumbrians in 633 in a battle which cost Edwin his life and resulted in the spread of pillage and destruction throughout the kingdom. The bishop fled before the storm, leaving Christianity to be overwhelmed.

Supremacy of Northumbria

The reversal of the fortunes of Northumbria and Christianity was only temporary. Oswald, a prince of a rival royal house, who had been in exile during Edwin's reign, assumed the leadership and freed Northumbria of her foes. He brought with him a Christian influence from a new quarter. During his exile he had been converted to the faith by the Scots, whose church was descended from that established in Britain during the Roman régime. During the period of the Anglo-Saxon conquest the Celtic Christians had been out of touch with the Christians of the continent. Consequently some of their practices and observances differed from those followed by the rest of the church and by the missionaries from Rome, who so far had done all the work of spreading Christianity among the Anglo-Saxons. Oswald brought back with him as a missionary the Scot, Aidan, whose efforts re-established Christianity in Northumbria. Oswald also began the attempt to recover supremacy over the other kingdoms, but the conclusion of this task was left to his brother Oswy, who succeeded him (642-670).

A few years after Oswy's death the three great kingdoms of Northumbria, Mercia, and Wessex established a temporary balance of power, which gave to England an interval of comparative freedom from internal wars during the closing years of the seventh century. During this period, however, Wessex secured control of Sussex and Kent by force of arms.

In this interval the Christian communities established among the Anglo-Saxons received the organization which made the church a potent influence in Anglo-Saxon life and provided a persuasive argument in favor of political unity. The first step was taken under Oswy's guidance at a council held at Whitby in 664. Here the representatives of the Celtic form of worship brought to Northumbria by Aidan and those of the form brought to Kent by Augustine met and debated in the presence of the king the merits of their respective observances. The debate centered around differences of forms and ceremonies, such as the date at which Easter should be celebrated. The fundamental point at issue had small place in the discussion, as Bede reports it. If the Northumbrians, Mercians, and East Saxons abided by the Celtic ceremonies, England would be split between two rival ecclesiastical organizations; part of the Anglo-Saxons would have a community of interests with the Celts, and part with the neighboring peoples of the continent. The issue was between ecclesiastical disunity and isolation on the one side, and ecclesiastical unity and community of interest with the rest of Europe on the other. That issue probably swayed

Organization of the church

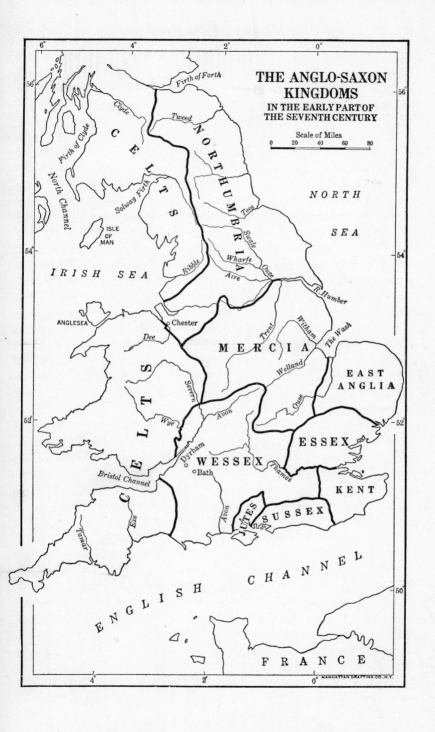

THE ANGLO-SAXON
KINGDOMS
IN THE EARLY PART OF
THE SEVENTH CENTURY

Scale of Miles
0   20   40   60   80

6°   4°   2°   0°

56   56

Firth of Forth

Clyde

Tweed

Firth of Clyde

C E L T S

N O R T H U M B R I A

North Channel

Solway Firth

N O R T H

S E A

54   54

Tees

ISLE
OF
MAN

Swale

Ribble

Wharfe

I R I S H   S E A

Aire

Ouse

ANGLESEA

R. Humber

Chester

Dee

Trent

Witham

The Wash

M E R C I A

C E L T S

Severn

Welland

E A S T
A N G L I A

52   52

Wye

Avon

Ouse

Dyrham

E S S E X

Bristol Channel

W E S S E X

Bath

Thames

K E N T

Exe

Avon

J U T E S

S U S S E X

Tamar

E N G L I S H   C H A N N E L

50

F R A N C E

4°   2°   0°   MANHATTAN DRAFTING CO., N.Y.

Oswy's decision, though the better case presented by the exponents of the Roman communion for the control of the keys by their priesthood was the reason which he assigned. At any rate, he declared in favor of the usage followed by Augustine and his successors. His decision was accepted by the Northumbrians and other Anglo-Saxons of like belief. Thus there was an English church before there was an English nation.

The council of Whitby made possible the unified and efficient organization of the Anglo-Saxon church. This was the work mainly of Theodore of Tarsus. He was a Greek, prominent in the church at Rome, who was appointed archbishop of Canterbury by the pope. When he reached England in 669, he found the existing ecclesiastical organization loose and weak. A bishopric had been established in each Christian kingdom. In the larger kingdoms this made the diocese, the district in which the bishop had supervision of the clergy, too large. The church also lacked a well-ordered parochial system. The priests were mainly of the itinerant missionary type, and the dioceses were not yet divided into territorial parishes with a priest in each parish. Theodore increased the number of dioceses, defined the duties of the bishops, and secured from them acknowledgment of the supremacy of the archbishop. By a requirement that priests should be attached to a definite diocese he laid the foundation on which a settled system of parishes was built at a later day. He also held the first ecclesiastical council, or synod, in which the bishops and leading priests made laws for the rule of the whole church. These were the first laws enacted for all the Anglo-Saxons, and Theodore was the first archbishop whom all the Anglo-Saxon clergy acknowledged as their head. The subsequent creation in 735 of an archbishopric of York, with jurisdiction north of the Humber, impaired the ideal of ecclesiastical unity, but the province of York was much smaller than the older southern province, and the archbishop of Canterbury was more influential in ecclesiastical and political affairs than his northern colleague.

The dominating factor in the political development of the eighth century was the supremacy of Mercia. In 733 the king of Mercia conquered Wessex and established supremacy over all of England south of the Humber. Of the two kings who ruled Mercia during most of this century, Offa II (757-796) was the more famous. He was the ablest and most powerful of the Anglo-Saxon kings who had yet ruled. His hegemony never included Northumbria, which went its way of isolation. Acknowledgment of his greatness was not confined

Supremacy of Mercia

to England, for Charles the Great, the mightiest European monarch of his day, considered it worth while to maintain with him a generally friendly correspondence, and the papacy showed him favor, addressing him on one occasion as "king of the English." Yet he did not build the supremacy of Mercia upon a firm foundation, for soon after his death the leadership passed to Wessex.

Supremacy of Wessex

The king who brought Wessex to the fore was Egbert, who ruled from 802 to 839. By the conquest of Mercia he reversed completely the positions of the two kingdoms. So strong did he become that even the king of Northumbria gave him a nominal allegiance. Egbert was followed by his son Ethelwulf, who was a weaker king, although he appears to have maintained the West Saxon supremacy undiminished territorially during his reign of nearly twenty years. In his time it became apparent that Egbert had brought Wessex to the headship of Anglo-Saxon affairs just in time to throw upon her the brunt of the struggle against the Danes, who were now beginning to harry the land.

The Danes

The people whom the Anglo-Saxons called the Danes lived in what is now Denmark, Norway, and Sweden. They were of the same Nordic race as the Anglo-Saxons themselves. They spoke German dialects, which have since become the Scandinavian languages. Their civilization was much like the Anglo-Saxon before it had become subject to the influences of Christianity and of settled life in Britain. They displayed in the ninth century the same wild love of the ·sea and the same lust for plunder that had been characteristic of the Anglo-Saxons in the fifth. Their boats were long and open, worked both by rowers and by sail, well adapted for navigation in bays and rivers, but perilous conveyances for the passage of the open sea. Toward the close of the eighth century, nevertheless, they began to fare forth across the blue water, seeking adventure and wealth. During the two following centuries they wrought havoc in many parts of Europe. To the land of the Franks and to Ireland, as well as to Britain, they came, receiving from the first the name of the Northmen. Wherever they went they left destruction and terror in their wake. They penetrated the rivers far inland, made surprise attacks, and escaped with the booty to their ships. For many years the attacked peoples were unable to organize any adequate defense; if the pirates found a strong opposing force at one place, they merely took to their boats and attacked elsewhere. The harassed peoples came to live in constant dread of these incursions. Eventually the vikings, as these sea kings were often called, established settlements in all of these lands; but their rovings did not stop there. They appeared in Spain and even in the Mediterranean. They also sailed west into the unknown, where they settled Iceland and Greenland and landed in America many centuries before the time of Columbus. Others went overland through Russia, where they established trade and became for a time the ruling caste among the native Slavs of a large area. Some of them even reached Constantinople, where they constituted a famous bodyguard of the eastern emperor. The ninth and tenth centuries constituted a period when the vikings worked out their destinies in wide fields.

The Danes first came to England a few years before the end of the eighth century. During the early years of the ninth century they were diverted to Ireland, which they completely overran, remaining in occupation of the northern part of it. In 834 they extended their operations to England and to the continent. Thereafter their raids in these directions increased steadily in frequency. Whenever an attack failed on one side of the Channel, they were likely to repair to the other. Their invasions of England followed much the same course as the Anglo-Saxon invasions appear to have taken three centuries earlier. At first they came in small bands, landed in an unexpected place, ravaged the district, and departed with their booty before adequate defense could be organized. About the middle of the century their attacks entered upon a new and more serious phase, when a large fleet of ships brought a whole army of invasion, which remained in England over the winter. In 865 they came in a great host, bent upon conquest and settlement. Within five years they had subdued Northumbria and East Anglia and ravaged the eastern half of Mercia. At the end of 870 they turned their attention to Wessex, which was now practically all that stood between them and the complete subjugation of England. The leader who prevented the consummation of their design and saved England to the Anglo-Saxons was King Alfred.

The coming of the Danes to England

Alfred, the greatest figure in Anglo-Saxon history, was the fourth son of Ethelwulf. He was brought to the throne in 871 by the death of his last surviving brother,[1] when the Danes had already begun the invasion of Wessex. Coming from East Anglia, they built a camp at Reading on the Thames. From this base they sallied forth into the region of Wessex roundabout to give Alfred his famous "year of battles." Eight times within the year the army of Wessex joined issue with the Danes, success going sometimes to one side and sometimes to the other. In the midst of the campaign Alfred's brother died, leaving

Alfred's campaigns against the Danes

---

[1] His brothers, who ruled in turn, were Ethelbald, 858–860; Ethelbert, 860–866; Ethelred, 866–871.

Alfred alone to finish the war. The end of this series of battles seems to have been a draw. In 872 Alfred bought peace from the Danes; but they had not been able to penetrate Wessex. For nearly four years the Danes kept their treaty, using the interval to conquer Mercia, to consolidate their conquests elsewhere, and to continue the process of settlement. In 876 they attacked Wessex again, this time in the west. They marched straight to the coast, where they fortified themselves at Wareham. Alfred, who had reorganized his army, besieged them so successfully that they could accomplish nothing, and eventually they agreed to leave Wessex. In 878, however, the Danes, who had retired to Mercia, broke their agreement, invaded Wessex in midwinter, and seized the royal vill of Chippenham. The attack was a complete surprise. The soldiers of Wessex were dispersed to their homes for the winter, and Alfred was forced to seek refuge with a handful of companions in the isle of Athelney located in a swamp. Alfred's fortunes appeared to be at their lowest ebb. It is to this period that the legend of the burnt cakes belongs. Despite the personal hardships which he was forced to undergo, he was really in a better position than he had been in 872, for he now had a well-trained and well-seasoned army, when he could assemble it. In the spring he accomplished the task and met the Danes at Edington. Alfred won a complete victory, which was the turning point of the war. The Danish leader, Guthrum, agreed to accept Christianity, to withdraw his forces from Wessex, and to keep the peace henceforth. Though he did not keep the letter of his oath, Wessex never again had its independence seriously threatened by the Danes.

Subsequently Alfred had to undertake two sets of campaigns. In 884 a group of Danes who had been operating across the Channel landed in Kent, where they received some aid from the Danes settled in East Anglia, for whom Guthrum was responsible. Alfred drove out the invaders, and in the next year chastised the East Anglian Danes, capturing London in the process. On this occasion he forced Guthrum to sign a treaty which added considerably to the territory under Alfred's control. The boundary ran from east of London to Bedford, and thence approximately along Watling Street, the old Roman road to Chester. The district to the northeast of that line, known as the Danelaw, was left to the Danes. The southwestern half of England was now united under Alfred as one corporate whole. The pressure of the Danes had wrought unity in that part of England still left in Anglo-Saxon hands, and a solid foundation had been laid for the unity of all England.

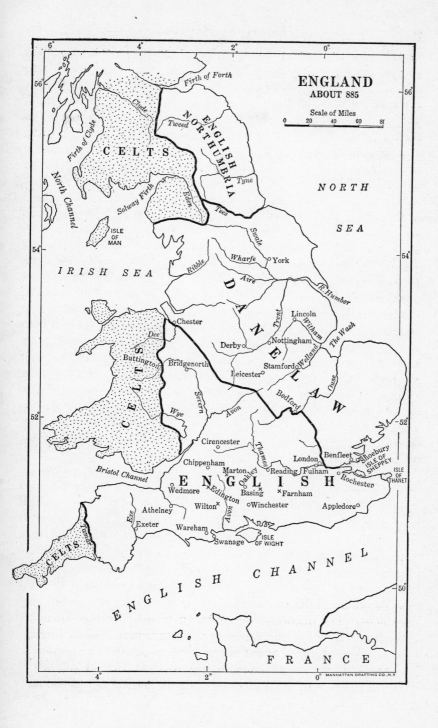

ENGLAND
ABOUT 885

Scale of Miles
0   20   40   60   80

NORTH
SEA

IRISH SEA

Firth of Forth

Tweed

ENGLISH
NORTHUMBRIA

CELTS

Firth of Clyde

Clyde

North Channel

Solway Firth

Eden

Tyne

Tees

ISLE
OF
MAN

Ribble

Wharfe

Swale

York

Aire

DANELAW

Chester

Dee

Buttington

Bridgenorth

Derby

Trent

Lincoln

Nottingham

Witham

The Wash

R. Humber

CELTS

Wye

Severn

Avon

Leicester

Stamford

Welland

Ouse

Bedford

Bristol Channel

Cirencester

Chippenham

Marton

Oakley

Thames

Reading

London

Fulham

Benfleet

Shoebury

ISLE OF
SHEPPEY

Rochester

ISLE
OF
THANET

ENGLISH

Wedmore

Edington

Basing

Farnham

Winchester

Appledore

Athelney

Wilton

Avon

Exe

Exeter

Wareham

Swanage

ISLE
OF WIGHT

CELTS

Tamar

ENGLISH CHANNEL

FRANCE

MANHATTAN DRAFTING CO., N.Y.

The last incursion of the Danes began in 892. Again a group which had been worsted across the Channel landed in the southeast. It was a formidable force, which intended to win new homes in England. The invaders found the situation changed since 865. Alfred kept them constantly on the defensive, defeating them whenever he could force an engagement. In 896 they finally gave up the attempt and sailed away. Alfred, who died in 899, had no more serious trouble from the Danes. Subsequently there was fighting between the English and the Danes settled in England, but this was the last systematic attempt at invasion by the Danes for a century.

Alfred was not only a great leader in the field; he was also a good strategist. His success was due to his ability to see the fundamental characteristics of the Danish offense as a whole and to devise new modes of defense to meet their tactics. In the defenses of England he instituted three principal changes. (1) He reorganized the principal fighting force, called the fyrd. This was a militia, still composed, as it had been in the time of Tacitus, of the ordinary freemen. It could be held together only for the briefest campaigns because long absence of the soldiers from their farms would bring their families to the verge of starvation. Alfred met the difficulty by dividing the fyrd into two halves, which relieved each other at fixed periods. (2) He fortified places strategically situated, and either he or his son arranged a system to provide for their garrisons. To each fortified place a district was attached, in which certain of the resident nobles were required to have a house within the walled area where they resided or kept in residence a military retainer. Thus there would always be a permanent garrison, and, when the Danes approached, all the people of the countryside would have a refuge. (3) Alfred began the construction of a navy, although it appears to have played only a minor part in his principal campaigns.

Alfred's military reforms

Alfred was even more interested in the arts of peace than in those of war, and he cultivated them with equal assiduity and success. Here his work was that of restoration rather than of innovation. In the civil administration Alfred attempted to restore the régime of law and order which had necessarily been badly disrupted during the long period of the invasions. He issued a set of laws, which consists largely of a repetition of selections from the Mosaic laws and the laws of his predecessors. He insisted upon the impartial administration of justice, and he was active personally in the supervision of this branch of the governmental service. He ruled with an authority such as no Anglo-Saxon king had exercised before him, although the centraliza-

Alfred's government

tion was still far from that to which we are accustomed in the governments of our own day.

With the revival of intellectual pursuits Alfred was especially concerned. Here the destruction caused by the Danes had been exceptionally complete. The monasteries, which were the principal centers of learning, had been singled out for attack by the Danes because of their wealth. So nearly extinct had a knowledge of letters become that Alfred himself wrote: "But so clean fallen away was learning now in the Angle race, that there were very few on this side Humber who would know how to render their service-book into English, or to read off an epistle out of Latin into English, and I ween there would not be many on the other side of Humber. So few of them were there that I cannot think of so much as a single one South of Thames when I took to the realm."[2] Since Latin was then the all but universal vehicle of literary expression and the language of the church and of diplomacy, as well as to some extent of civil service, law, and business, the revival of its study was imperative for the training of leaders in church and state, as well as for the national welfare. To meet this crisis Alfred gathered around him the only four learned Englishmen whom he could find, and several foreign scholars, among whom was his biographer Asser, a Welshman. With their aid he founded a court-school, which the sons of the nobility were urged to attend. From this nucleus Alfred developed a group of trained clergymen, who could disseminate knowledge more widely, and a group of educated laymen, whence could come competent administrators. Alfred himself took delight in his intercourse with these scholars. With their help he translated from Latin several books on moral and historical subjects, which, in his estimation, it was "most needful for every man to know." It was at his inspiration that the *Anglo-Saxon Chronicle* was begun. Alfred's endeavors in this field met with a deserved success, and his intellectual impulse long survived him. Seventy-five years later, at a time when few European noblemen could read Latin, much less write it, his kinsman wrote a chronicle in Latin, while the stream of Anglo-Saxon prose, which had its source in Alfred's translations, still flowed.

Although these cares would seem enough to occupy fully the time of an ordinary king, Alfred found the energy for many other activities. His deep religious faith led him to aid in the revival of monastic life, which was the ideal form of religious expression in that age, though

---

[2] As translated by Oman, *England Before the Norman Conquest*, p. 476.

his efforts in this field were not notably successful. Along with his intellectual interests went a lively concern for the restoration of the industrial arts, which made him the liberal patron of skilled artificers of all kinds. He maintained intercourse with many foreign rulers and prelates, and his envoys, bearing alms, went often to Rome, which he had visited twice during his childhood. The pleasure which he derived from the conversations about other lands with foreigners whom he welcomed at his court is but one indication of the many-sidedness of his interests. Alfred's deeds won him fame both at home and abroad in his own day, and his truly noble character won him the love of his people. Time has not reversed the contemporary judgment. Today Alfred is deservedly the one royal name of the Anglo-Saxon period with which every English-speaking schoolboy is familiar through story and legend, if not through history.

Alfred's son Edward[3] (899-924) and Edward's three sons[4] each in turn waged war against the Danes settled in England, until they restored the Danelaw to English control. Edward began the systematic conquest of the Danelaw. He advanced slowly, stopping to build forti-fied places in each new district that he invaded. In the course of eight years he completely subdued the Danes south of the Humber, and the Northumbrian Danes gave in their submission. South of the Humber the reconquered land was divided into shires and placed under the control of English officials, but north of that estuary the Danes were allowed to govern themselves locally. Early in the reign of Edward's oldest son, Ethelstan, when the Danish king of Northumbria died, the kingship was suppressed and the kingdom was annexed to the English crown. The act was premature, for this district had not been subdued by conquest and occupied by fortified garrisons. Ethelstan's brothers had to crush many rebellions before the English hold on Northumbria was secure. Only when the last rebellion had been quelled in 954 was the reconquest of the Danelaw finished. There was now in reality a king of all England. National consciousness on the part of the Danes was still quiescent, the machinery of the central government was still weak, but the nominal unity of England had been accomplished.

Though the Danes thus affected the course of English history pro-foundly, they did not add many new elements to English civilization. In southern Northumbria and in eastern Mercia they settled in large numbers. The process of assimilation began at once. The Danes located

Recon-quest of the Danelaw

Effects of the Danish invasions

---

[3] Known as Edward the Elder to distinguish him from Edward the Martyr who ruled from 975 to 978.

[4] Ethelstan (924–939), Edmund (939–946), and Edred (946–955).

beside the conquered Anglo-Saxons, and free intercourse between the two peoples developed at an early time. The Danes, for example, generally accepted Christianity soon after their colonization. So large was the alien element, however, that the Danish region retained an individual character for over two centuries. Despite the political unity established in the middle of the tenth century, the consciousness of national difference was still strong enough in Danish England half a century later to aid greatly the Danish kings Swegen[5] and Canute[6] in their conquest of England. Fully two centuries after the Danish conquest of Northumbria the social organization in Danish England differed in many respects from that in Anglo-Saxon England. In this long period of amalgamation the Danes gave as well as received. Although they seemed to contemporaries to bring only destruction, yet they displayed wherever else they settled in Europe a constructive ability for political organization. Presumably this genius was not lacking among those who made their homes in Britain, but few indeed are the elements of law or government in the later constitution of England which can be traced definitely to a Danish origin. The reason is obvious. The political institutions of the Danes differed from those of the Anglo-Saxon only in degree; in kind they were alike. Racially the two peoples were the same. Linguistically, too, Dane and Angle were closely akin, though philologists have traced to a Danish source a small group of words current in the English language. Perhaps the principal contribution of the Danes, which can still be recognized, was the stimulus given to trade. The Danes were as good traders as they were pirates. When settled life ended piracy, commerce was left. They shared with their kinsmen the monopoly of the trade of the Baltic, and far-flung Norse outposts across Russia brought the merchants of the Baltic into touch with the Byzantines and with the Mohammedans, who between them nearly monopolized the trade of the Mediterranean and the east. York under the Danes became a thronged mart "filled," says a contemporary observer, "with the riches of merchants who come from everywhere, especially from the Danish nation,"[7] and many a lesser settlement became the center of an active trade. The increase of commercial intercourse must have quickened the development of English civilization, but this is a result too elusive to be submitted to any exact measurement. So it was with practically the whole of their contribution. They reinvigorated the civilization existing

[5] Otherwise *Sweyn, Svend,* or *Svein*. See below, p. 52.
[6] Otherwise *Cnut*.
[7] Quoted from Larson, *Canute,* p. 21

among the Anglo-Saxons, but their tangible additions to that civilization were few.

The death of the last of Edward's sons was followed by a short reign[8] filled with the quarrels of factions striving for political power. They ended in 959 with the accession of Edgar. His reign of sixteen years (959-975) is nearly the only one of which the *Anglo-Saxon Chronicle* finds no wars to record. "Edgar the Peaceful" men called him. Of his reign the *Chronicle* says: "In his days it prosper'd well, and God him granted that he dwelt in peace."[9] So quiet was his reign, in fact, that it is nearly without annals. He ruled all England with an undisputed sway; he enacted wise legislation; he appears to have been an able ruler; but of his policies in secular affairs little is known.

Edgar the Peaceful

Among Edgar's advisers was Dunstan, who stands out as the first of a long line of ecclesiastical statesmen. As a boy Dunstan attended the palace-school. There he displayed such intellectual ability and religious zeal that he became one of the royal counselors and abbot of Glastonbury. At the monastery he maintained a school, where he roused in his pupils a love of letters, inspiring some of them with a desire for the reform of the church. Edgar made him archbishop of Canterbury. Under the influence of Dunstan and his disciples and friends Edgar lent the weight of the royal authority to the cause of monastic reform.

Dunstan

Monasticism had been established in England by the early missionaries. The object of the monastic life was to develop more perfectly the spiritual side of man's nature by the suppression of the material and baser part. The seclusion of the monastic walls protected the inmates from the contamination of the world, and the organization of the life within the walls was designed to remove worldly temptations, to eradicate material ambitions and carnal desires, and to promote the spiritual instinct by asceticism and by prayer. It was of the essence of the institution that the monks should live regular lives according to rule. So prominent was this aspect of the life, indeed, that the monks were known as the regulars,[10] as distinguished from the secular clergy, who lived in the world,[11] attempting to save the souls of other men.

Monastic life

The rule which prevailed in England was that established in Italy by St. Benedict in the sixth century. It provided for the entrance of men from all classes of society, after they had passed a satisfactory

[8] Edwig, 955–959.
[9] *Anglo-Saxon Chronicle,* ed. by Thorpe, ii, 92.
[10] From the Latin *regula,* meaning rule.
[11] In Latin *saeculum.*

novitiate. On entrance the new member took a vow of obedience and chastity and renounced all connection with the world outside. He was allowed to own no property. Upon him was urged above all things the cultivation of the spirit of humility and obedience. The daily life was apportioned among devotional exercises, manual labor, and study. Attendance daily at seven divine services, one of which came in the middle of the night, was the chief duty, but work in the fields or at an artisan's craft, copying of manuscripts, teaching, and study were no less regular parts of the daily routine. The life of the monastic community was lived in common. The monks partook of common meals, slept in common dormitories, attended services together, and carried on their occupations within sight and hearing of one another. The constitution of the monastery was monarchical. The head of each monastery was an abbot, who held office for life. Normally he was elected by the monks, but in the Anglo-Saxon period kings often designated the holders of important abbacies and nobles influenced the appointments to those of lesser importance. Once appointed, however, the rule of the abbot within the monastery was absolute, except so far as it was supervised by the bishop.

When the monasteries were first established in England they made a tremendous appeal to the spirit of the age. The example of men and women, renouncing all worldly pleasures and ambitions, living humble lives of hardship, and devoting themselves solely to the glorification of God, became a spiritual inspiration in the lives of many who did not themselves become monks or nuns. The monasteries soon had the patronage of kings and nobles, whose liberality provided them with great wealth in lands. The manual labor of the monks helped to develop the agiculture of the country and to foster and improve the industrial arts. Their intellectual pursuits made the monasteries centers of learning. The brilliance of the contribution made by the monasteries to intellectual life is typified in the career of Bede, whose reputation as a scholar brought fame to his monastery throughout western Europe. Before Bede's death in 735, however, the first ardor which had carried English monasticism to this high eminence was beginning to wane. Bede complains of monasteries which were such only in name. Their rich revenues were in the hands of laymen, and their inmates did not pretend to follow the rule. The ninth century saw monastic life nearly blotted out as a result of the Danish invasions. Alfred's attempts to restore it were unsuccessful. In Edgar's reign the ideal of St. Benedict was upheld in few English monasteries.

The reforms undertaken by Dunstan and his colleagues had their inspiration in the monastic life of the continent.[12] Across the Channel monastic life had suffered a similar deterioration, but early in the tenth century a reform had been begun which was destined to restore the institution to its pristine vigor. Some of the group around Dunstan became inmates of a French monastery, where the discipline had been restored, in order to become familiar with the practices of the strict rule. Subsequently, with the support of Edgar and Dunstan, they evicted the seculars, who occupied several monastic foundations without practice of the common life, and put monks in their places. They also founded many new houses. The royal council (witan) prescribed a version of the Benedictine rule to be observed in all monasteries. In the south of England the revival accomplished excellent results. The secular clergy, which had ceased to observe the rule of celibacy and was lax in many other respects, began to respond to the urgings of Dunstan and others and to the example of the reformed monastic discipline, lay morals displayed a better tone, and the intellectual impulse given by Alfred was caught up and carried to fruition. The results of the revival, however, were only temporary. During the course of the eleventh century both spirituality and learning fell into a state of decay, whence they were rescued only by the Norman conquest.

Dunstan's reforms

The death of Edgar in 975 saw a renewal of the strife of factions. The nobles were becoming so wealthy and so influential that they were without regard for the national welfare, the royal authority, or the maintenance of law and order. Edgar was strong enough to hold them temporarily in check, but after his death they began again to pursue their own selfish interests and to fight their personal quarrels. When Ethelred became king in 978, he was only ten years old. His minority was a period of dissension among the magnates responsible for the government. When he took the government into his own hands, the situation did not improve. He displayed such an infinite capacity for doing the wrong thing that he was soon known as the king "devoid of counsel" (redeless). Seldom, if ever, has a more incompetent king sat upon the English throne. Under his weak leadership the nobles continued their quarrels with unabated vigor.

Ethelred the Redeless

During Ethelred's reign, while the English suffered from weak and divided leadership, they were called upon to meet the invasion of a foreign foe. During the tenth century the viking spirit had been dormant, but about 980 the pirates began again to sail their dragon

Renewed Danish invasions

---

[12] This is the commonly accepted view. Robinson maintains that the movement was native at the outset, coming under foreign influence only when it was well established: *Times of St. Dunstan*, p. 127.

ships. Their attacks, which were directed against England, developed through three phases. For a few years they were isolated raids upon the coasts. Later the invasions were made by large armies which penetrated far inland. The armies were sometimes led by Swegen, king of Denmark, who in this period seems to have been bent only upon plunder. In 1013, however, he began a deliberate attempt to win the English crown, which his son Canute carried to a successful termination in 1017.

The English defense was inadequate for lack of leadership. If the invaders landed in the east, Ethelred would have the English army in the west; if an exceptionally large army of defense was collected, it would be disbanded before the vikings attacked, or it would be rendered useless by the quarrels and divided counsels of the commanders. "Ever as it should be forwarder, so was it later," says the chronicler.[13] In 991, Ethelred bought peace from the invaders by the payment of a large sum, which was called the Danegeld. Thereafter this humiliating expedient became of frequent occurrence, and the Danegeld became a tax levied on land. As the people became more disgusted with the lack of central guidance, local particularism began to thrive. The record of the chronicler for 1010 reads: "Then were all the witan [members of the royal council] summoned to the king, and they would then advise how this country could be defended. But though something was then resolved, it stood not even for a month: at last there was not a chief man who would gather a force, but each fled as he best might; nor even at last would any shire assist another."[14]

The unity of the kingdom so recently wrought could not endure the strain of continual disaster. When Swegen came in 1013 to strike for the crown, the people of the old Danelaw offered to accept him as king. When he advanced across Watling Street the people of the south yielded after comparatively slight resistance. Ethelred, deserted by his people, fled to the court of his brother-in-law, the duke of Normandy. Swegen had hardly won the crown when death overtook him. The death of Ethelred in 1016 gave the English a leader in Edmund Ironside, Ethelred's son. He waged war against Canute, Swegen's son, so successfully that he forced the Dane to agree to a partition of England something like that of Alfred's time. Edmund's career was cut short, however, by his death near the end of 1016, no new

The English defense

The conquest of the kingdom

---

[13] Edition by Thorpe, ii, 109.
[14] *Ibid*, ii, 116.

leader appeared, and early in 1017 the witan acknowledged Canute as king of all England.

Canute ruled England well. From the first he tried to act as king of England and not as a conqueror. He sent his troops home, except three or four thousand which he kept as a personal bodyguard and household troop. They were known as the housecarles. Their position was a favored one, something like that of the companions in the *comitatus*. Practically they formed an efficient mercenary force, sufficient to meet any incipient rebellion, but not large enough to appear oppressive to Canute's English subjects. His chief advisers, his earls, and probably the members of his household were in large majority Scandinavians in the early years of his reign, though the number of Englishmen in these positions increased later. He early made known his intention to maintain the English law, and he introduced few new customs. He was a liberal patron of the church. To the clergy he gave an ostentatious support which they requited in kind. But that which did most to win the loyalty of his new subjects was the peace and order which he maintained. Canute was an executive of ability. Under his government England recovered from the disasters of Ethelred's reign and enjoyed a period of peace and prosperity which contemporaries could compare only with the happy days of Edgar the Peaceful.

Canute's government, 1017–1035

Under Canute's rule England became part of a great northern empire, which temporarily rivaled the Holy Roman Empire in fact, if not in name. Canute inherited the crown of Denmark, and won the Norwegian kingship by conquest. Although these territories were never called an empire, they gave to Canute a power imperial in its magnitude. He figured more largely in the international affairs of Europe than any king of the Anglo-Saxons before his day. His alliance was sought by the emperor, he was received favorably by the pope, and he was able to make advantageous treaties with them and with other rulers concerning the privileges of English merchants and travelers in foreign lands. The union was, indeed, of commercial benefit to the English, since it gave their king virtual control of the trade of the Baltic and North Seas. This empire was bound together, however, only by the personality of Canute. When he died, Norway fell away from the control of the family, his son Harthacanute secured Denmark, and his son Harold became king of England. Upon the death of the latter in 1040, Harthacanute added the crown of England to that of Denmark, but he lived only two years more. After his death no near heirs of Canute were left; the English turned

Canute's empire

back to a representative of the line of Alfred; and the connection between England and Denmark, upon which Canute's empire had been based, was broken for all time.

Edward the Confessor

Edward, later called the Confessor because of his reputed piety, was the descendant of Alfred whom the English chose as their king. He was the last surviving son of Ethelred. Since early childhood he had lived at the court of his uncle, the duke of Normandy. His language and culture were French, and his friends and intimates were Normans. As he was too old to adapt himself readily to English modes of life and thought, he attempted to introduce Norman fashions into the English court and to surround himself with Norman retainers, upon whom he bestowed lands and offices with a liberal hand. His reign resulted in the establishment of a Norman influence in England, which helped to prepare the way for the Norman conquest.

The Normans

The Normans, who then became so closely associated with English history, occupied Normandy, a French duchy across the Channel from England. Their language and civilization were French, but their dominant racial strain was Nordic. The duchy of Normandy, like the Danelaw in England, was the product of the raids of the vikings. In 911 the king of France had ceded the territory to the leader of the invading Northmen in order to bring an end to the ravaging of France. Within a short time the northern pirates had settled the land and within a century they had exchanged their own culture for that of their French subjects and neighbors. The dukes of Normandy, one after another, were masterful men whose skill in political organization and daring in aggressive warfare made Normandy the most powerful and best-governed principality in France. By the eleventh century Normandy had become practically an independent state, ruled by dukes ambitious for power and eager for conquest, whose well-ordered administration gave them command of the resources of a prosperous people. Their subjects, moreover, still displayed the same love of adventure and the same energy of enterprise which had originally brought the Northmen to Normandy. They went restlessly forth to seek their fortunes in many lands. One group of Normans had already begun the formation of a Norman state in southern Italy, when Edward's accession brought another group to place and power in England.

Edward the Confessor was not able to confer offices upon his Norman friends and followers without opposition from the English nobles, who regarded royal place and favor as the birthright of themselves and their henchmen. When Canute chose to appoint Danes to high places, the English earls could not gainsay the army at his back; but Edward, who had no mercenaries, was dependent upon the support of the native nobility. The nobles were led by a few wealthy and powerful earls. Originally there appears to have been an earl to each shire, but in the course of the tenth century the number decreased, each earl ruling several shires. During Canute's reign the four earldoms of Wessex, East Anglia, Mercia, and Northumbria stood out as far larger and more important than the other seven mentioned in his charters. So influential had the holders of these earldoms become, that it required a strong king like Canute or Edgar to control them. Under a weak king the earls went their own way. The quarrels of factions which disturbed the reigns of some of the kings of the tenth century and did much to render Ethelred impotent against the Danes were the landmarks of the road they traveled. Edward was not an excessively weak king, but his ability was only that of respectable mediocrity. He was most devout, though he was more interested in his own devotions and almsgiving than in ecclesiastical affairs generally. In other business he was generally easy-going, although he held to his attempt to import Norman men and customs with considerable tenacity. Edward could not dominate the earls, but to some extent he was able to play upon their rivalries and set them one against another to his own advantage. The result was a struggle during most of his reign among those who sought to control the grants of royal favors. Occasionally the English earls united against the Norman favorites. More frequently their jealousies of one another outweighed their dislike of the foreigners. So Edward's effort to place Normans in civil and ecclesiastical offices and to endow them with lands was partially successful, and a new element of dissension was added to the many which would soon make England the prey of William the Conqueror.

English opposition to the Normans

The earl who stood forth as most influential at Edward's accession was Godwin of Wessex. He had been chiefly responsible for Edward's election, and he held first place in the king's counsels in the early years of his reign. In 1045 Edward married Godwin's daughter, and shortly after he gave earldoms to two of Godwin's sons and to one of his nephews. These favors may well have prepared the way for a reversal of Godwin's fortunes by arousing the envy of his rivals. Eventually Godwin wrought his downfall by championship of the cause of the English citizens of Dover against a French nobleman who was the friend of the king. The earls of Northumbria and Mercia

Edward and Godwin

supported Edward in his attempt to force Godwin to punish the citizens of Dover for an alleged attack upon the followers of the French nobleman, and Godwin and his sons found it necessary to seek safety in flight. After the fall of Godwin's house the English earls soon discovered that the foreign favorites were the chief gainers thereby. Public sentiment veered rapidly in Godwin's favor. In 1052, after a year of exile, he was able to return practically without opposition. The northern earls would no longer help the king, and many of his foreign protégés fled to the continent. The king was constrained to restore to Godwin and his sons their offices and lands, and again to accept Godwin's domination.

One result of Godwin's restoration was fraught with dire consequences for the future of his house. The assembly of the witan, which formally revoked the sentence of outlawry against Godwin and his sons, also decreed the outlawry of several of the foreigners who had fled. Among them was the Norman archbishop of Canterbury. Thus the highest office in the English church was left actually vacant. The office was given to an Englishman, Stigand, who had been one of Godwin's supporters. Legally, however, the position was not vacant, since, according to the law of the church, only the pope or death could depose an archbishop. Stigand consequently could not obtain the pallium. This was a scarf conferred by the pope as an indication of papal approval of the appointment of an archbishop. Without this insignia an archbishop could not legally fulfill some of the duties of his office. When Stigand was named archbishop, the pope who had given the pallium to his Norman predecessor was still in office. He naturally regarded the Norman as the rightful archbishop. At the time, the papacy, after many years of corruption and inefficiency, was undergoing a moral regeneration, which was causing a vigorous assertion of the papal authority over the episcopate. Since the power to award the pallium was the keystone of the arch upon which rested the papal control of the local clergy, the papacy regarded Stigand's exercise of the archiepiscopal functions without it as a flagrant usurpation. When he later obtained the scarf from an antipope, he merely heightened his offense in the eyes of the legitimate popes. The papacy, however, could not secure the removal of the offender so long as he was tacitly supported by the house of Godwin; and so long as the papal superiority over the archbishop was thus defied, its control over the greater part of the English clergy, which was subordinate to the archbishop of Canterbury, was defective. The papacy was thus thrown into political opposition to the house of Godwin at a time when the

(margin) Stigand

Holy See was beginning to exercise greater moral influence in the affairs of Europe than it had possessed for centuries. When William, the duke of Normandy, decided to attack England, the approval of the papacy was consequently given to the invader, and this moral support contributed in no small degree to William's success and to the overthrow of Godwin's house.

After Godwin's restoration his house practically controlled the government of England for the remainder of the Anglo-Saxon period. Godwin himself died soon after his return, but his oldest surviving son, Harold, stepped into his place as earl of Wessex and chief adviser of the king. Though Harold was no less ambitious than his father for the power and influence of his family, he was more moderate and politic. When the earls of Northumbria and Mercia died, he secured the former earldom for his brother Tostig and part of the latter for another brother. He did not support Tostig, however, when the Northumbrians revolted in 1065. Instead, he allowed his brother to be exiled, and let the north and center of England, a portion as large as that left in the hands of his kin, come under the control of the descendants of the former earls, who were the hereditary rivals of his house. Such was the situation when Harold himself became king. Edward the Confessor died at the beginning of 1066. He had no children, and the only direct descendant of Alfred's line had lived in exile, was little known in England, and was too young to rule. He was no candidate to place upon the throne in the face of the known ambitions of William the Norman. Harold, though he lacked royal blood, was the most influential man in England politically, and he had long borne the actual responsibility for the government of the kingdom. The dying king recognized the situation by giving his sanction to Harold's candidacy. On the day after Edward died the witan chose Harold king. Since no opposition is recorded, presumably Harold's conciliatory policy had won the acquiescence of the northern earls, though later events were to show that jealousy of the rival house of Godwin still remained with them a stronger motive than dislike of the rule of a foreigner. Nationality was as yet a flame which gave but fitful gleams.

"And in this year also," says the *Chronicle*, "earl Harold was hallowed king; and he experienced little quiet therein, the while that he ruled the realm."[15] Duke William received the news of Harold's coronation with a great display of wrath, and forthwith began prepara-

Harold, Godwin's son

Tostig and Hardrada

---

[15] Translation by Thorpe, p 164.

tions to support his own claims to the English crown by armed invasion. His record of victories over Norman vassals and neighboring feudal magnates gave presage óf a formidable foe. Harold, who soon learned of his intentions, did not underestimate the strength of his rival. He began elaborate preparations for defense. The attack was begun by Tostig, who bitterly resented his brother's desertion of his cause. After negotiating with William, he attempted to invade England with his own followers without success. An alliance with Harold Hardrada, the king of Norway, who sought to renew the bond between Scandinavia and England, rendered him a serious menace. The united forces of Harold Hardrada and Tostig landed in Northumbria in September. They defeated the opposing army of the northern earls, but five days later had to face the army of Harold, Godwin's son, at Stamford Bridge. The English king had kept a large army and a fleet on the southern coast all summer, waiting the expected arrival of William. Early in September a large part of the force, which consisted mainly of local militia, had to be disbanded in order that the crops might be gathered. With the remainder and with his thegns and household troops Harold hastened north leaving the southern coast unguarded. The battle, which was the greatest yet fought between Scandinavians and Englishmen, was a complete victory for Harold, Godwin's son. Harold Hardrada and Tostig were both left dead upon the field. Only a remnant of the invaders escaped to their boats.

William's preparations

Three days after the battle of Stamford Bridge, on September 28, William landed in the south, a few miles from Hastings. His careful preparations had provided him with a well-equipped army probably numbering between 10,000 and 15,000 men. Immediately on receipt of the news of Harold's accession, William had begun to circulate the statement of his claims at the courts of Europe. William, though he had none of Alfred's blood in his veins, was the first cousin, once removed, of Edward the Confessor. In current thought on such topics any relationship was likely to be held better than none. William asserted, moreover, that Edward had acknowledged him as his heir and that Harold had taken an oath to support his candidacy. These stories, circulated far and wide, probably helped to create a public opinion favorable to his enterprise. His most valuable moral backing came from the papacy. Since Stigand still continued to act as archbishop in defiance of the papal will, the pope was easily persuaded to send to William a consecrated banner as a sign of the papal approval. This gave to the expedition the highest moral sanction it could have. William also made it attractive by the offer of spoils to those who participated. The combination of pseudo-sanctity and loot made so strong an appeal to the warriors of that age that he had no difficulty in obtaining followers. Though his barons refused to serve in his army as a part of their required military service, many of them came as volunteers. Lords who owed him no allegiance came from many parts of France and even from Italy and Spain. With this host William disembarked and awaited the coming of King Harold.

When the news reached Harold, he marched rapidly to London with his victorious army. Here he waited a few days to gather local militia. The northern earls followed with their levies, but, despite the haste with which Harold had just come to their aid, they failed to arrive in time to participate in the battle against William. With an army probably about the size of William's Harold marched south and took up his position on a hill near Hastings between the Normans and the interior. William advanced to the attack on October 14. The English fought with the professional troops in front, protected by a wall of shields, and with the poorly armed, badly disciplined militia on the rear and flanks. When the Norman archers and heavy-armed infantry failed to open gaps in the English line, the cavalry charged, only to be driven back in confusion. William rallied them, however, and turned the incident to his advantage. The retreat had induced some of the English to follow their enemies down the hill. When the Normans turned, they were able to cut their pursuers to pieces. Still the wall of shields held, but in the course of the day feigned retreats and the expedient of shooting arrows into the air to fall perpendicularly upon the English wore away their power of resistance. William's cavalry finally drove home a charge, Harold fell mortally wounded, and the remainder of the English fled.

William's victory

The road to the interior now lay open to William. He advanced slowly to Dover and thence toward London, taking possession of the towns and fortified places on the way. He crossed the Thames above London, and approached the city from the north. Meanwhile there had been divided counsels in London. The spirit of resistance was strong, but no leader appeared. Eventually the witan elected Edgar, the grandson of Edmund Ironside and the only surviving representative of the royal house of Wessex. He was too young to organize the defense, and the northern earls, whose position and rank should have made them the chief advisers of the king, appear to have sulked. When William finally came within sight of London, nothing had been done. Since the position was hopeless, the chief men of state and church came out to meet William with an offer of the crown which Edgar resigned. Substantially this was a tender of the crown by the English witan. William sought the advice of his Norman barons, and, assured of their adherence to him as king, he accepted. On Christmas Day of 1066 he was crowned, and the reign of the first Norman king was begun.

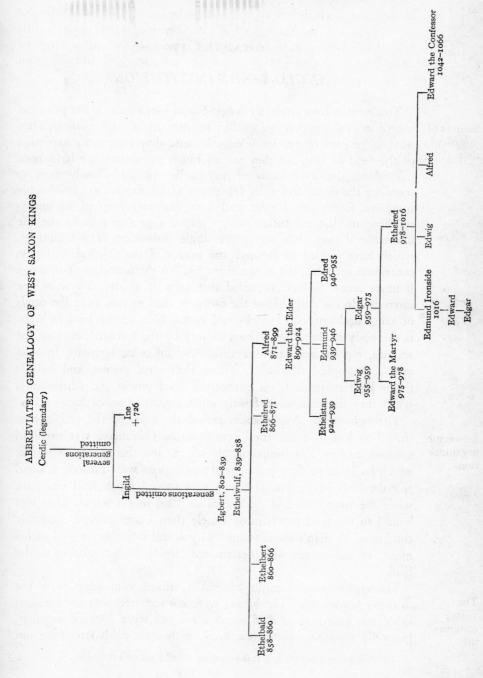

ABBREVIATED GENEALOGY OF WEST SAXON KINGS

Cerdic (legendary)

Ingild

several generations omitted

Ine
+ 726

Egbert, 802–839

Ethelwulf, 839–858

generations omitted

Ethelbald
858–860

Ethelbert
860–866

Ethelred
866–871

Alfred
871–899

Edward the Elder
899–924

Ethelstan
924–939

Edmund
939–946

Edred
946–955

Edwig
955–959

Edgar
959–975

Edward the Martyr
975–978

Ethelred
978–1016

Edmund Ironside
1016

Edward

Edgar

Edwig

Alfred

Edward the Confessor
1042–1066

CHAPTER IV

ANGLO-SAXON INSTITUTIONS

THE written laws issued by Anglo-Saxon kings provide the principal source of information about the institutions of this period. They leave large gaps in our knowledge because they cover only a portion of the field of law, but they tell us much more than we have been told about the institutions of any earlier period. Closely akin to them are the deeds and wills (charters) which survive in considerable numbers. Ecclesiastical rules and laws (canons) help to an understanding of that institution which played a greater part in the life of medieval man than any other single institution. The chronicles, which have guided us through the mazes of the political narrative, contribute their bit, but it is a sorry bit. To the historian of that age it never seems to have occurred that men of a later day would be interested in the daily life of the ordinary man as well as in the deeds of kings and armies, of clerks and saints. Next to the laws in value is the body of literature written mainly by the learned clergy of the seventh, eighth, and tenth centuries. Schoolbooks, sermons, lives of saints, theological discourses, letters, devotional poems, and ballads throw light particularly on intellectual development and Christianity, while they illumine more faintly some aspects of social life.

Throughout the Anglo-Saxon period the mass of the people continued to live in small rural communities. Commerce was small in amount, money was comparatively scarce, and the systems of credit which facilitate modern commercial transactions were unknown. Land was the basis of wealth. The man who owned much land was rich, while the man who had the use of no land might starve. Man was bound to the land much more closely than under present economic conditions. A man's social status and political influence as well as his means of subsistence were determined largely by his relation to the land.

The typical rural community was a village, containing from ten to thirty households.[1] The homes were not scattered over the countryside, each guarding its own broad acres, but were grouped together, generally straggling along one street, with open fields stretching out

---

[1] The Anglo-Saxon term is tun. It is sometimes called a vill or a township.

spaciously from the cluster of houses. This form of settlement has been expressively termed the nucleated village. Contrasted with it is the settlement of scattered hamlets, consisting of two, three, or four households. Hamlets prevailed in western England and they were not uncommon in some other parts of England; but the nucleated village was the usual form of settlement in the greater part of Anglo-Saxon England.

In such a community the homes of the ordinary villagers were thatched huts, generally of one room, built of wood, clay, wattles, or a combination of these materials. They were without chimneys, the smoke being allowed to escape through a hole in the roof; they were barely furnished; and sometimes the villager's cattle and pigs shared the hovel with his family in the winter. In many villages, by the tenth century, there was one landholder who was much wealthier than the rest. He was the lord of the village. His more elaborate house was located somewhat apart from the rest. It was generally a timbered house, built frequently of split logs. Often it contained only one large room, though it might have a kitchen ,and sleeping-rooms separate from the hall or living room. The best of the houses might contain rich decorations of tapestry and ornamental vessels of gold, silver, or bronze; but, from the point of view of comfort, the furnishings were more crude than in Roman times, and extremely bare compared with our modern conveniences.

Economically the village was nearly self-sufficient. The food consumed by the community was produced in the fields, pastures, and woods surrounding the village, where grains and a few vegetables and fruits were grown, and cattle, sheep, and swine were reared. Fuel was supplied by the woods or by the peat in the locality. Clothing was manufactured in the homes. Local carpenters, smiths, and potters made most of the buildings, house furnishings, and implements required. Some raw materials, such as salt and iron, personal adornments brought probably by itinerant peddlers, and household utensils and ornaments used by the rich were bought outside the village; but throughout the Anglo-Saxon period the commercial intercourse of the average village with the outside world was small. If we apply the measure of our modern standards, the rural economic organization was crude and rural life was hard.

The prevailing method of agriculture was that known as the open-field system.[2] The land of each villager, instead of being in one com-

---

[2] In the southeastern counties the holdings of the villagers were more compact than in the open-field system. This was probably a survival from Roman times. In the south-

pact block, was intermingled with that of his neighbors. The unenclosed arable land was divided into strips, usually an acre in extent. If a villager had thirty acres, they would lie scattered over the whole area devoted to tillage, and between one of his strips and the next would lie several of his neighbors' strips. Since fertilization of the soil was not practiced on a sufficient scale to make it possible to raise successive crops of grain on the same land year after year, it was necessary to allow the land to lie fallow frequently, in order that it might recuperate its growing power. Provision for this was made by dividing the arable lands of the village into two fields, one of which lay fallow each year, while the other was cultivated.[3] The land of each villager was apportioned approximately equally between the two fields. Each village had a stretch of land used for pasture, and probably some woodland, which the inhabitants shared in common. Each village, too, was likely to have its natural meadow, where each villager had an allotment from which he cut the hay. The system as a whole was wasteful, resulting in meager returns from the soil. It was so difficult for the small proprietor to store up any surplus against a time of need that local famines were not uncommon.

In this system of agriculture the communal element was prominent. The ownership of the lands appears to have been individual. From the point of view of ownership the villages were of two kinds. In free or lordless villages the inhabitants were free and owned the land they tilled.[4] In others the men were unfree, being dependent upon a lord who owned all the land of the village. The villagers cultivated for their own use portions of the arable fields not used by the lord, pastured their cattle in the common pasture, and in general lived like the men in the free villages; but they were bound to the soil, and they owed the lord rents and agricultural services. In both kinds of villages the use of the lands in accordance with such a com-

---

western and northwestern counties the Celtic runrig system prevailed. In this the holdings were intermingled strips, but the rotation was different, and there was no division into two or three great fields. Elsewhere in England is found the open-field system, which appears to be distinctively Teutonic. See map in H. L. Gray's *English Field Systems*, which is an authoritative work on this subject.

[3] Later a three-field rotation, in which the land lay fallow only once in three years, became common. Contemporary evidence that either a two- or three-field rotation existed in the Anglo-Saxon period is lacking, and the above assumption that the two-field rotation prevailed is based on inference from survivals.

[4] The question of the ownership of the lands in the villages of free men has been hotly debated by modern historians. The earliest documents which throw light on the subject display individual ownership of the arable, and there are no survivals pointing to earlier communal ownership.

plicated agricultural system seems necessarily to have involved some communal regulation. Each village probably had a headman, called the reeve, and the villagers probably assembled in meetings to establish rules governing the rights of common pasture, the course of rotation in the arable fields, and kindred affairs.[5]

Commerce occupied an unimportant place among the early Anglo-Saxons. The first apparent stimulus to trade came from the early Christian missionaries, who brought so many other things to Britain besides Christianity. They developed among the Anglo-Saxons a religious zeal which found frequent expression in pilgrimages to the holy places at Rome. The pilgrims sometimes paid their way by trading. They brought back new tastes and fashions, which, as they spread, caused importation. The missionaries themselves created new needs and desires, which could be satisfied only by intercourse with the continent. The Danes, however, gave to Anglo-Saxon commerce the greatest impetus which it received. The character of the trade is nowhere clearly described. The imports were largely products not native to England, such as silk, gems, wine, oil, and ivory from the south and east, although furs, skins, weapons, and ironwork were brought from the Scandinavian north. At the end of the tenth century merchants from Germany, Flanders, Normandy, and Aquitaine were bringing goods to the port of London. The export of slaves continued despite the efforts of the church to stop it, tin was still a staple product, and wool was also an active article of commerce. The exports appear to have been chiefly raw materials.

Industry, too, developed during the Anglo-Saxon period. The skill which the Anglo-Saxons of the era of the conquest displayed in the decorative working of metals was inherited by their descendants, and the art was patronized by Alfred and fostered by Dunstan. The early missionaries brought some new industrial arts, such as that of illuminating manuscripts, in which the Anglo-Saxons attained proficiency. The importation of artisans to build and decorate churches must also have led to the introduction of some new industries. Agriculture, however, remained throughout the period the industry of fundamental importance. Those who earned a living other than from the soil were few. The rise of towns after the Danish conquest may have enabled a few artisans to live primarily by their respective trades, but the crafts were practiced mainly in the households of the peasants whose

Commerce

Industry

---

[5] That such communal management existed is deduced from the nature of the agricultural arrangement and from survivals. There is no certain contemporary proof of the existence of a reeve or of village-moots. See below, p. 72.

chief concern was tillage. At the close of the Anglo-Saxon period England was still less advanced both industrially and commercially than it had been in the time of the Romans.

Towns

One result of the increased commercial activity of the tenth and eleventh centuries was the rise of a few towns. From the time of the Anglo-Saxon conquest to the coming of the Danes urban life seems to have been extinct. The shell within which a new urban life developed was provided by the walled enclosures built for purposes of defense during the Danish wars. These fortified centers, which were called boroughs, were erected by both the Anglo-Saxons and the Danes. After the wars many of them were left vacant, but others, which had received permanent garrisons, continued to be inhabited. The residents were at first engaged in agricultural pursuits like the dwellers in the surrounding open villages. As commerce increased during the tenth and eleventh centuries, some members of the community began to make a living primarily by buying and selling. They tended to settle in the boroughs which enjoyed favorable geographical locations for the transaction of commerce and provided the protection of walls against the violence which traders of that age often encountered. In this manner settlements of traders were established in several boroughs, and these boroughs may be regarded as towns. The settlements marked only the beginning of a renewal of urban life. At the close of the Anglo-Saxon period some of the boroughs still lacked mercantile settlements, and even the boroughs which had them remained partly rural in their economic organization. Some of their inhabitants still followed the plow. The largest of the boroughs had no more than a few thousands of population, and many of them numbered their inhabitants only by the hundreds. Norwich, which was a large borough, had a population in the neighborhood of 5,500 persons. In appearance, too, the boroughs differed entirely from modern cities. They lacked the paved streets, the stone buildings, the sewage systems, the waterworks, and the multitude of other improvements which we are wont to associate with municipal life. These humble origins of a new urban life were, nevertheless, of great potential importance. From them grew, not long after the Anglo-Saxon period, many towns inhabited chiefly by traders whose accumulating wealth ultimately rendered them an influential class in the community.

In the social system of the later Anglo-Saxons there were still four principal ranks of society, but they had undergone notable changes since the time of the conquest. The eorls, who constituted a nobility of blood, were superseded by the thegns, who formed a nobility based upon service and wealth. The military companions of the king and his principal household servants probably constituted the original element in this class, but by the tenth century it was based largely on wealth. The king's thegns generally received gifts of land from the king, and others might become thegns by the acquisition of sufficient land. The thegns had onerous duties: they were the warriors who constituted the principal element in the army; they had special privileges, such as protection by a wergeld six times that of the ordinary freemen; and they were the possessors of large estates and consequently the lords of other men. Eventually, too, the thegnage became hereditary.

Social organization: 1. The nobility

The ceorls experienced the greatest change. In the period of the conquest they constituted the principal social class; at the end of the Anglo-Saxon period the majority of them had been driven down into the intermediate class of the unfree. They had become praedial serfs; they were bound to the soil. On the other hand, they were not mere chattels. The lord could not sell them apart from his estate, and they were protected by a wergeld smaller than that of a freeman.[6] The serfs owed the lord work for several days of each week on the lands which he cultivated for his own use, and payments mainly in produce. In return they received from the lord small holdings which they tilled to provide for their own sustenance.

2. Ceorls and serfs

A few of the many and complicated economic and social forces which reduced the social status of the ceorl may be indicated. (1) Hard times constituted one of the commonest causes. The free peasant with his crude system of agriculture was often without any surplus to tide him over a period of famine and want. He had to borrow from a wealthier neighbor. He might never accumulate enough surplus to repay the loan, and eventually he would have to surrender his land to his creditor and receive part of it back to hold as a serf. Not infrequently men sold themselves directly into servitude for food, as is told by the chronicler who speaks of "those who bowed their heads for meat in evil days." (2) The Danish invasions spread destruction and caused widespread want. They made men ready to sacrifice freedom in order to secure from their stronger and wealthier

---

[6] This legal definition of the position of the class intermediate between that of the freemen and the slaves is subject to many exceptions, which lack of space makes it impossible to discuss here. In this intermediate class in Anglo-Saxon times there appear to have been so many varying degrees of freedom that they cannot be explained within the scope of a single definition. The above definition is probably true of many cases in the Anglo-Saxon period, and it represents the legal status which attached to practically all members of the class at a later day.

neighbors the protection which their government was not able to give them. (3) The king granted to monasteries and thegns governmental rights over large stretches of territory, which often were converted into lordships. Sac and soc, for example, was sometimes granted. Such a grant gave the recipient the right to the profits of jurisdiction in a certain area. A district would be sliced out of the hundred, in which the freemen, who had before attended the public local court of the hundred, would henceforth attend the private court held by the possessor of the grant. The holder would merely preside at the court; the freemen who attended would find the judgments as they had before in the court of the hundred; the grant itself did not reduce the freemen of the affected area to unfreedom. But the recipient of the royal favor was placed in a position to bring to bear economic pressure, which, in the long run, might result in the depression of the freemen living within his sac and soc. (4) A change in the character of the military service tended to depress the status of the freemen. Originally the fyrd, composed of all the freemen, was the principal fighting force of the Anglo-Saxon state, although the king's *comitatus*, composed of the personal followers who lived at his court and partook of his bounty, was always an important element. As the Anglo-Saxons became more settled after the conquest and more dependent upon their cultivation of the land, service in the fyrd became a greater hardship upon the ordinary peasant. At the same time a change in the mode of warfare made the fyrd a less efficient fighting force. The king came to rely more upon the thegns, who could come to his service well mounted and well equipped with arms and armor, such as the ordinary freeman could not afford. Though the fyrd never ceased to be used for defensive purposes, the thegns came to supply the military force generally employed. To maintain this force, the kings, who had little ready money, gave the thegns generous grants of lands and fiscal rights, such as sac and soc. The thegnage thus became a military aristocracy with economic advantages and legal rights over freemen, which often ended in the economic dependence and social depression of the freemen.[7]

Though the general course of social development in the Anglo-Saxon period was downward, the position of the slaves improved.

[7] Seebohm holds that the Anglo-Saxons began life in England with a mass of serfs who gradually became free. The evidence is largely inferential, but the arguments of Maitland and Vinogradoff for the point of view, which I have attempted to summarize above in broad outline, are so convincing that I have not deemed it necessary to present the other side of the case. Both views are presented at length in the works cited below, p. 832.

The church proclaimed that the slave had a soul, and set its face against the treatment of persons as mere chattels. The economic position of the slave among the early Germans was not notably different from that of the Anglo-Saxon serf. Manumission of slaves seems to have become a common practice. Even without this formality the slaves tended as a matter of custom to be treated like serfs. By the end of the Anglo-Saxon period many slaves had attained the status of semi-free serfs. The class of slaves was small. 3. The slaves

Thus at the end of the Anglo-Saxon period, as at the beginning, there were four principal ranks of society, with degrees and gradations within each rank. There had been, nevertheless, a fundamental change in the social structure. At the beginning freemen predominated; at the end the mass was subordinate to a small aristocracy, and freemen and slaves alike were comparatively few.

In government the general trend of the Anglo-Saxon period was toward centralization. The principal organs of the central government, when England had been unified, were the king and his council, called the witan, an Anglo-Saxon term meaning the wise. The king was selected by the witan, generally from among the members of the ruling house. The king of united England was more powerful than the king of the days of the Anglo-Saxon conquest. The extension of territory under the direct rule of the king, the constant warfare, and the influence of the clergy, who brought with them from Rome ideas of the extent of the royal prerogative which were alien to German thought, all served to strengthen the hands of royalty. The functions of the king were so varied that they do not submit readily to classification. The king was the highest executive authority, and it was regarded as his special duty to maintain peace and order. He commanded and controlled the military forces of the kingdom, summoned and presided over the witan, appointed the principal officials of the state, and actually controlled the appointment of many of the higher officials of the church. The royal authority had few conscious restrictions of a constitutional nature placed upon it, but in practice it was limited in two ways. (1) The centralization did not overcome thoroughly the particularistic tendencies due to the method by which united England had been built from smaller independent parts. The older tradition of local patriotism remained alive until the very end of the Anglo-Saxon period. (2) The king was often largely dependent upon the support of the witan in the exercise of his power. The central government: 1. The king

The witan was an aristocratic body without a trace of popular rep-

resentation in its composition. The ealdormen, local officials named
by the king, the bishops, whose appointment the king generally influenced, and such others of the nobility as the king chose constituted
the membership. The witan advised the king on questions of policy,
acted as a court for the trial of great men and great causes, and assisted the king in the enactment of legislation. "This is the ordinance
that king Edgar, with the counsel of his witan, ordained" begin the
laws of Edgar, and the advice or consent of the witan is mentioned
in the laws of nearly every king who issued any. Such enactments,
however, were probably not regarded as legislation by contemporaries.
Law was custom, and the laws promulgated by king and witan were
probably looked upon as expositions of existing customs, which for
one reason or another needed to be renewed or emphasized, though
occasionally they actually made new law. The modern classification
of a legislature as a body which makes new law, and of a court as
an organ which declares what existing law is, was unknown to Anglo-
Saxon political thought. Legislation and judicial action are regarded
today as properly the functions of different organs of government,
but the king and the witan exercised them both, because as yet no
clear distinction between them existed in the popular consciousness.
The witan contained many of the influential and wealthy men of the
kingdom, whose advice doubtless the king often found it expedient
to follow. Since he controlled the membership in large measure, the
witan can hardly be said to have had a constitutional check upon his
power. The extent of the influence of the witan over the king was
more a question of the personal equation than of constitutional law.
If a king had a strong personality and was a good ruler, he would
dominate the witan; if a king was weak, the order would be reversed.
The customary consultation by the king of such an advisory body,
however, helped to establish a precedent for the demand of a later
day, that the king should not perform certain acts without the advice
of a body of councilors.

The largest division of the united kingdom for purposes of local
government was the shire.[8] The king was represented in the shire
by two officials. The ealdorman (later called the earl) was the older
and more important of the two. His principal functions were to raise
and command the local militia and to preside over the public as-

---

[8] The shires in Wessex probably originated before Alfred's time and often represented
former independent kingdoms or tribal districts. The midland shires probably grew up
around the fortified centers established in the tenth century. In Northumbria there appear to have been no shires until after the Norman conquest.

sembly held in the county, but he might represent the royal authority in many other ways. The office was one of great dignity, and the holder was always a noble. He received in right of his office rich emoluments and a high social status. In the tenth century the number of earls was reduced, and each became responsible for the administration of more than one shire. The other royal official in the county was the sheriff, whose office does not appear to have been instituted until the tenth century. His special functions were to maintain the peace within the shire and to look after the king's revenues. The king derived his income principally from his vast estates, scattered over many counties, which he leased, or had managed by local reeves.[9] The sheriff collected the rents and other payments due the king from these estates and the fines assessed by the courts, and delivered them to the royal treasury. He might be called upon also to carry out any royal orders which required execution locally. After the earls began each to control more than one shire, the sheriffs often acted as their deputies in holding the shire assemblies and even in leading the militia. The sheriffs, however, remained primarily representatives of the royal authority, while the earls tended to become local rulers with more or less independence of the king. Toward the end of the Anglo-Saxon period the sheriffs appear to have been doing most of the actual work of administration in the counties. The most vital organ in the government of the county was the moot (gemot). This was a public assembly held twice a year. Attendance appears to have been confined in practice to the larger landholders of the county, though all freemen may once have been expected to attend. This body constituted a court with both civil and criminal jurisdiction; it could declare local custom, for much of the law in those days was local, differing from county to county; and it transacted a variety of other business of interest to the county. The power of decision rested not with the earl or sheriff, who presided, assisted by the bishop, but with the local residents who constituted the moot. Thus the shire had a large element of local autonomy.

The shires were divided into hundreds. The name is not found in the Anglo-Saxon laws until the tenth century, which has caused some writers to deny the earlier existence of the district as a police and judicial unit.[10] Yet the institution seems to be that called the

2. The hundred

---

[9] A generic term of Anglo-Saxon origin, meaning *official*.

[10] Chadwick, *Studies on Anglo-Saxon Institutions*, pp. 239–262; Liebermann, *Gesetze der Angelsachsen*, ii, 516–522.

pagus by Tacitus, and may have existed in England earlier.[11] The king was represented in the hundred by a reeve, who seems to have become subordinate to the sheriff in the eleventh century. The hundred had a moot, which transacted both administrative and judicial business, being chiefly concerned with the latter. The jurisdiction of the hundred-moot was concurrent with that of the shire-moot. The former was evidently the court commonly used by the ordinary man, since it met every four weeks. The hundred-moot was also more popular in its composition. All free landholders might attend, and probably also the village reeve, the priest, and four men from some of the villages in the hundred.[12] The king's reeve acted as chairman of the meetings, but the local residents in attendance (suitors) found the judgments and transacted the business. The hundred-moot was by far the most active and most popular of the local organs of Anglo-Saxon government. If the germ of later popular liberties of Englishmen is to be found anywhere in the Anglo-Saxon constitution, the hundred-moot appears most likely to have been its seed-plot.

3. The village

Within the hundred was a still smaller territorial unit, the tun, or village, which has been described already in its economic aspects. About the political organization and functions of this unit, the most diverse views exist among modern historians. One distinguished author sees in "the 'talk' of the village moot" "the groundwork of English history,"[13] and those who accept his point of view ascribe to the New England town meeting lineal descent from this venerable institution. Another eminent authority denies to the assembly of the villagers any political or judicial functions, and questions its existence even for the purposes of economic regulation.[14] The difference of opinion is due, as usual, to lack of contemporary evidence, and to the consequent necessity of inference from survivals. It is probably a mistake to think of the village-moot as the place where Englishmen began to obtain the experience in political affairs which enabled them eventually to govern themselves; possibly it is also an error to deny the Anglo-Saxon village any political organization whatever.

The borough was also within the hundred territorially, except the

---

[11] Stubbs, *Constitutional History*, i, §45. For a brief discussion of this question in the light of recent research, see Morris, *Constitutional History to 1216*, pp. 41, 42, 75–81.

[12] The attendance of the reeve and four men, when the lord of the village was absent, is first mentioned in a legal compilation of the twelfth century (Stubbs, *Select Charters*, p. 105). Some of the laws in the collection are derived from the Anglo-Saxon period, but it is not certain that this was one of them.

[13] Green, *Making of England*, p. 188.

[14] Maitland, *Domesday Book*, pp. 147–150.

few instances in which the boundaries of a borough coincided with those of a hundred. The borough was governed usually by a portreeve, who was a royal official, and a popular moot. The moot, however, was rarely local to the borough. It was attended by the freemen who lived within the hundred in which the borough was situated. In other words, those hundreds which were the seats of boroughs held their moots within the boroughs. More distinctive of the boroughs were the markets which were maintained in many of them. The kings required all commercial transactions of importance to take place in these markets, where the sales could be witnessed by local officials appointed for the purpose. Furthermore, the problems of the residents of boroughs which were towns differed in some respects from those of dwellers in rural communities. The national and local laws, because they were designed primarily to meet the needs of a rural population, failed to make provision for many of the needs of the townsmen. The towns consequently developed their own local customs. Few of these customs are known in detail, but their general purpose was to exempt the townsmen from certain types of rents, from tolls, and from other burdens and duties, commonly incumbent upon the community at large, which would have restricted their commercial enterprises.

4. The borough

The primitive character of the Anglo-Saxon political organization is nowhere more clearly apparent than in their judicial system. To the end of the Anglo-Saxon period the right of private vengeance was never entirely discarded, although the state endeavored to limit the occasions when and the methods by which it might be exercised. The Anglo-Saxon laws are filled with detailed assessments of the monetary value of all possible kinds of injuries, from the loss of a toenail to homicide. The fine (bot) was paid to the injured party, or in the case of homicide to the relatives (wergeld).[15] Only in cases where the injured party could not collect the established bot from the transgressor was he at liberty to wage the feud. The enforced acceptance of the bot restricted the right of private vengeance sufficiently to make the courts the generally accepted agencies for the redress of wrongs.

Administration of justice

In the courts the judgment was found by neither judge nor jury. The presiding officer was a royal official who acted only as chairman, and the Anglo-Saxons had no juries. The judgment was found by

Judicial procedure

---

[15] In some cases a fine had to be paid to the state (wite) in addition to that paid to the wronged person, and a few crimes were botless and expiable only by death. Offenses so punished were regarded as breaches of the public peace as well as wrongs to individuals.

the assembled men of the district. It did not settle the question of innocence or guilt, because no evidence was produced in court. The judgment decided merely what mode of proof should be employed to determine innocence or guilt.

The proof   Of several methods available, compurgation or ordeal was generally used. Compurgation means proof by the aid of oath-helpers. The party to whom the proof was awarded, who would usually be the defendant, took an oath that his charge or denial was true, and attempted to secure the number of men prescribed by the court to swear that his oath was a good one. If the defendant were awarded the proof and obtained the required number of oath-helpers, he was innocent. If he failed, he was guilty. For the most serious crimes the appeal to man was insufficient, and an appeal was made to the supernatural. One party was made to undergo an ordeal, which required, in some cases, a miracle to establish innocence and, in others, to establish guilt. It was the theory of the law that God would intervene with a miracle, if it were necessary to maintain justice. When proof was awarded to the defendant, the ordeals worked as follows. In the ordeal of hot iron he carried a piece of red-hot iron in his hand a certain number of paces. The hand was then bound and sealed. If at the end of three days his hand was not discolored, he was innocent. In this and similar ordeals the laws of nature had to be reversed to establish his innocence; in the ordeal of cold water they had to be reversed to establish his guilt. The defendant was bound and thrown into a stream of running water, on the theory that pure water would refuse to receive a guilty person. If he floated he was guilty; if he sank, he was innocent. What satisfaction accrued to the defendants in the occasional instances when they were pulled out innocent but drowned the records fail to relate.

These modes of proof were irrational, but not always quite so irrational as they seem. Though compurgation sometimes developed into a contest in perjury, the oath in those days was a solemn affair. If a man took a false oath, he imperiled the welfare of his soul in the life to come. In the small communities of Anglo-Saxon times, where a man's character was well known to his neighbors, the defendant who had a bad reputation might find it difficult to secure the required number of co-swearers. It was not a risk to be undertaken lightly by honest men. The ordeals were accompanied by solemn and awe-inspiring religious ceremonies conducted by the priest. In a superstitious age they might work upon the mind of the guilty until he would break down and confess. Irrational as these modes of proof were, they probably worked less injustice than might be supposed.

The tremendous influence wielded by the church upon Anglo-Saxon life has been touched upon in the consideration of many previous topics. In all ages religious faith has been one of the strongest motive powers impelling men to action, and the faith of the Anglo-Saxons, once they had been thoroughly converted, was deep. The clergy came to them as mediators between God and man. They had "the keys of the kingdom of heaven." They alone could administer the sacraments which were essential for the salvation of the soul. Receipt of the sacraments did not insure salvation, but failure to receive them insured damnation. Coupled with this universal belief was an otherworldliness of view difficult for us to appreciate. Many of the fathers of the church saw in this life merely a brief period of probation to be ended in everlasting bliss or everlasting woe. The emphasis placed upon the next life as compared with the present was evidenced among the Anglo-Saxons by the popularity of the monastic cloisters. With the average Anglo-Saxon, thought of the future life seems to have been more frequently present than with the average modern man; certainly his thought on the subject was more concrete, for in his imagination heaven, hell, and purgatory were remarkably concrete places.[16] This ever-present, vivid fear of damnation in the next life was a driving force that gave the guardians of the keys a potent influence in every walk of public and private life. They had the exclusive control of the essential means of a highly desired salvation.

This was the fundamental source of clerical influence; it was not the only source. The clergy during the missionary stage displayed unabated zeal for spreading the word. When the conversion of the Anglo-Saxons had been accomplished, Anglo-Saxon missionaries took the lead in the evangelization of the pagan Germans on the continent. The Anglo-Saxon clergy had their share of martyrs for the faith, and the numerous lives of Anglo-Saxon saints testify to the tradition of holy living which they established. They had nearly a monopoly of learning, and the power given by knowledge was even more apparent in that rude age than in this. The respect and veneration which they aroused for the institution they represented brought them wealth and high social standing. Kings and nobles made rich gifts of lands to bishoprics and monasteries. As parishes were established, their churches were endowed with lands from which the priests received the income. In the system of wergelds established by royal enactments the priest ranked with the thegn, and the bishop with the earl.

---

[16] See, for an illustration, Bede, v, 12.

The influence of the clergy depended upon many complex factors, but it rested solely upon moral force in an age when power was generally based upon military strength actual or potential.

The
church in
Anglo-
Saxon life
Though the greatest contribution of the church to Anglo-Saxon life was made in the fields of religious faith and morality, the contribution made in other fields was nevertheless enormous. (1) In the government of the country not only did the church serve as a passive example of unity, but it also took an active part. The bishops sat in the witan, where the business of both state and church was transacted; the bishop cooperated with the earl in the shire-moot; the priest presided at the ordeal, giving to the institution its moral force; and ecclesiastics were often statesmen and the influential advisers of kings. (2) The economic development of the country was also furthered by the church. The emphasis placed upon manual labor by the monks was in itself a wholesome influence. The monasteries, too, were important centers for the development of agriculture and for the practice of industrial arts and crafts. In the management of their estates the monks displayed a skill which made their organization a model for laymen to follow. Several new industries were introduced into England by churchmen. The stimulus given by them to commerce has already been noted. (3) On the foreign relations of England the church had much influence. The early churchmen, who came from the continent, brought with them continental ideas which they spread among the English. The government of the church from Rome necessitated intercourse, and the veneration of saints stimulated many laymen to make pilgrimages to shrines and holy places on the continent. The increase of communication for these various purposes tended to promote the development in England of art, architecture, scholarship, commerce, industry, and civilization in general. (4) The church was the educational institution of the period. When the public and private schools of the empire ceased to exist after the coming of the barbarians, the church took over the task of perpetuating such knowledge as survived from the period of classical antiquity. Aside from the palace-school, all the schools and all the libraries of Anglo-Saxon England were maintained by the church. Thus the Anglo-Saxon church was a many-sided institution with an all-pervading influence upon the life of the time.

Early
schools
The education of the illiterate Anglo-Saxons was begun by the early missionaries, who established schools in the early decades of the seventh century. The range of knowledge accessible in these schools was small. The schools inherited from the classical past a curriculum

consisting of seven subjects called the liberal arts. These were divided into the *trivium*, which included grammar, rhetoric, and logic, and the *quadrivium*, which included arithmetic, geometry, astronomy, and music. In the seventh century, however, these subjects were rarely all taught. Few schools, indeed, advanced much beyond the *trivium*. The subjects were generally taught, moreover, from a few compendiums which had been written in the closing days of the imperial rule in the west or soon after its fall, when a sterile scholarship was no longer equal to the burden of reading longer works. Such a compendium would devote only a few pages to each of the seven subjects. Each subject was more elastic than in our present educational régime. Grammar, for example, might include the study of literature and history, and geometry might be made to cover some geography and natural science; but grammar generally included only reading and writing, while geometry was often not taught at all in this period. The object of the average school was to provide the minimum of knowledge requisite for the clergy, who needed to know how to read and expound the Scriptures, how to write, something of music, and enough arithmetic to compute the date of Easter. The language of the church and of the schools, however, was Latin. Once a student had learned the language, nearly the whole store of the profane and the Christian knowledge of Roman times was open to him, if he could gain access to the writings of the classical authors and of the fathers of the church. But the intellectual atmosphere was too dead to stimulate many to make the attempt. Those who tried encountered great difficulties. The works were preserved only in manuscripts. Since they could be duplicated only by hand they remained scarce, costly, and hard to come by. When schools were first established among the Anglo-Saxons, the way of the scholar was hard.

The Anglo-Saxons received in their schools the best instruction that the age afforded. The intellectual impulse came from two sources. In the south and east the schools were founded by missionaries from the continent. In the north and west the teachers brought the Irish culture, which then probably represented the highest intellectual attainment in Europe. The Anglo-Saxons were influenced by both streams, but the earliest native scholars of note owed their inspiration chiefly to continental teachers. The first school to rise above the general level was that maintained by Archbishop Theodore at Canterbury in the later part of the seventh century. It was one of the few schools in western Europe where Greek was taught at the time. Here several Anglo-Saxons received a thorough training in the limited

Intellectual development

range of knowledge of the day, and were fired with an enthusiasm for intellectual pursuits which found expression in productive literary labors and in the founding of further schools.

Aldhelm of Wessex was the foremost product of this school. His Latin works are grandiloquent in style and far from profound in content, but these failings were characteristic of the literature of the age. His writings display a familiarity with a large number of the Latin authors whose works constituted nearly the whole storehouse of contemporary knowledge. Upon a literary circle composed of Aldhelm's pupils and friends they had a deep influence. Aldhelm was not only "the first of a line of scholars trained in the English monasteries," but he was also the foremost European scholar of his time.[17] Aldhelm was followed and surpassed by Bede, who was the product of the same intellectual influence, though he was never a student at Canterbury. Bede not only made a positive contribution to knowledge in his *Ecclesiastical History*, which is undoubtedly the best historical work of the eighth century, but he also epitomized nearly all the learning of his day. Many of his manuals attained a wide circulation and a long-lived popularity not only in England but also on the continent. From Bede the spirit passed to the school at York, which, in the course of the eighth century, became the most famous school in Europe. By this time the quality of Irish scholarship had declined. When Charles the Great desired a head for his famous palace-school, he obtained Alcuin from the school at York.

While the literary revival called the Carolingian renaissance was thus being begun on the continent under the leadership of an Englishman, English learning was beginning to fall under the blight of the Danish invasions. The efforts of Alfred at the close of the ninth century and the work of Dunstan and his friends in the tenth restored the schools and produced an intellectual atmosphere which may be compared favorably with the continental product of the same century. The English revival, however, did not keep pace with the continental. In the eleventh century English learning declined, just when the schools in Normandy and other parts of northern France were beginning to give to the seven liberal arts such a breadth and depth as they had not attained since the days of the Roman Empire.

The education of the Anglo-Saxons had one result which is found among none of the other German peoples who received from the clergy the classical heritage: it stimulated the production of a national

---

[17] Laistner, *Thought and Letters in Western Europe*, pp. 120, 121.

literature. When schools were first established by the Christian mis- Anglo-
sionaries, the Anglo-Saxons already had heroic poems, such as *Beowulf*, Saxon
preserved in oral form by the bards and minstrels. The coming of literature
letters caused these heathen poems to be written down. It also turned
creative genius into the channel of Christian themes. The connection
between the Latin learning and the national literature is exceptionally
well illustrated by the case of Aldhelm. Latin scholar as he was, Aldhelm never lost his love for the vernacular songs. He wrote in the
tongue of Wessex poems known to Alfred, though they are lost to us,
and tradition has him standing on a bridge as a gleeman, singing English
lays, in order to attract people to his church on Sunday mornings.
With him began an outburst of popular song which lasted till the
Danish ruin. The two great names associated with this verse are those
of Caedmon and Cynewulf. The former was a Northumbrian cow-
herd of the seventh century, whose inspired song won him a place in
a monastery, where he composed religious poems which found many
imitators. Bede has made of Caedmon a living individual;[18] Cynewulf,
who wrote in the next century, is little more than a name. His poems,
however, constitute "the noblest and most finished monuments of Old
English verse."[19] The vernacular literature, when it was revived after
the Danish invasions, took mainly the form of prose. Aside from the
works of Alfred and those inspired by him, such as the *Anglo-Saxon
Chronicle*, the most noteworthy portion of this literature consists of
homilies (i.e., sermons) written mainly between 960 and 1020. The
best of these were written by Aelfric, abbot of a monastery in Oxfordshire. Though he was not an original thinker, he was thoroughly conversant with the knowledge of his day, and he was entirely successful
in his effort to popularize the theological thought of the fathers of the
church. His greatest contribution was to the style of English prose.
When his work was finished, "English had become a literary language."[20] Thus English-speaking peoples have a heritage of national
literature, which is unparalleled for its antiquity by that of any other
European people.[21]

---

[18] *Ecclesiastical History*, iv, 24.
[19] Green, *Making of England*, p. 361.
[20] *Cambridge History of English Literature*, i, 141.
[21] Jusserand, *Literary History of the English People*, i, 79.

CHAPTER V

NORMAN ENGLAND

WILLIAM's coronation gave to his title as king such legality as a conqueror might assume, but it did not give to him undisputed control of all England. Though some of the nobles from central and northern England yielded their allegiance, the acceptance of his rule was not universal outside of those southeastern counties through which the Norman army had marched. Disturbances began in 1067, when the new king was absent in Normandy. In the next year he had to meet local uprisings both in the west and in the midlands and north. He suppressed them without great difficulty, treating the participants, whom he regarded as rebels, leniently. To safeguard against further outbreaks he had castles built in the principal boroughs along his line of march. The northerners, however, were not yet subdued. The aid of troops sent by the king of Denmark made their second attempt in 1069 more formidable. They overwhelmed the local Norman garrison at York, but when the Conqueror arrived, the resistance melted away after comparatively few engagements. Resolving to end rebellion, William meted out a terrible punishment. Between York and Durham he ruthlessly killed or drove out the inhabitants and laid waste the land. This ended serious opposition on the part of the English. In 1070 a small band of Englishmen, led by Hereward, established themselves on the Isle of Ely, where the natural protection of the fens made it difficult to dislodge them. This last isolated bit of national resistance occupies a large place in legend and literature, but it had no important effect on the Conqueror's position. After the northern campaign of the winter of 1069 and 1070 William was the master of England as no English king had been before him.

One of the principal results of the Norman conquest was the establishment of feudalism in England. The lands of Englishmen who had fought against him, William confiscated. They included nearly all the lands in England. Most of them he gave to his followers as a reward for their services. The transfer did not affect the possessions of the mass of Englishmen. Only large estates generally changed hands. Since most of the natives were tenants upon such estates, they remained in possession of their old tenements. To such men the immediately apparent effect was only a change of lords. The change, however, was more than one of mere ownership, for William gave the lands to be held of him upon terms customarily applied to land-holding in Normandy, but nearly, if not quite, unknown previously in England. The few English landowners who were permitted to retain their estates appear to have been required to accept possession on the new terms. These terms constituted the feudal tenure. By their application feudalism became practically universal throughout the kingdom. Since feudalism was destined to remain the basis of English political organization for two centuries and more, and since it had a permanent effect upon English law and society, it demands description.

When feudalism was fully developed, each holder of land from the king by feudal tenure promised to render military and other services in return for his holding. Though he obtained thereby the right to use and enjoy the land, his ownership was not complete. It was limited by the obligations on the land. He had what lawyers term the usufruct. Generally the man who held land from the king undertook to provide the military service of several retainers as well as his own. To obtain them he might sublet (subinfeudate) part of his land on similar terms; the receiver of his grant might do likewise; and so the process of sub-infeudation might continue as long as the land held out. The man who held land from another in this way was the vassal; the man from whom he held was the lord; the land was the fief. The vassal who held directly from the king was a tenant-in-chief; all other vassals were mesne tenants, because they held from the king only mediately. A lord from whom a vassal held only mediately, whether the lord was the king or another, was the overlord or suzerain. If, for example, A held from the king and B from A (king — A — B), the king was the lord of A and the overlord of B. A was the tenant-in-chief of the king and B was the mesne tenant. In practice feudal tenures became highly complicated, for a man might become the vassal of more than one lord. Indeed, a man might have so many lords that he would find it necessary to acknowledge one as his liege lord and swear allegiance to the others only so far as his obligations to them should not conflict with those already contracted with his liege lord. The arrangement of feudal tenures was not symmetrical.

Feudalism, however, was more than a mere method of land tenure; it included also a personal relationship. The lord gave to the vassal protection as well as the use of a fief, and the vassal owed the lord loyalty as well as service. The personal bond was akin to that in the earlier *comitatus*, and it also had similarity to the relationship of patron

[margin note:] Feudal tenure

[margin note:] Personal relationship

and client. The vassal did not become unfree or in any sense a serf; he retained all the political and social rights of a free man; but in some measure he was dependent upon his lord. The strength of the personal tie varied much in individual cases, and it was generally a stronger force in the early days of feudalism than in the later.

Political element

There was also present in feudalism a political element. Feudalism first developed in western Europe largely because governments were so weak that they gave no adequate protection against the prevalent lawlessness and violence. The weak sought from their powerful neighbors protection which the government no longer gave, assuming for that purpose the position of dependency which grew into vassalage. The lords who thus took over some of the duties of government naturally assumed also some of its powers. An individual agreed, for example, to protect a group of persons against attack. In return the group promised to acknowledge the authority of the lord as military leader. Always the lord had military control and fiscal rights over his vassals; often he had a court of justice for them; and he might have other powers which we regard as the attributes of government. When the political aspects of feudalism had free play, as they did in some parts of the continent, the functions of government became divided among a large number of individuals. Much disorder resulted. In France, for example, the greater tenants-in-chief, who held whole duchies or counties, were as powerful as the king whom they nominally acknowledged as lord. The French king could rule effectively only in that small portion of France which remained under his immediate lordship.[1] Vassals like the duke of Normandy, giving him only such support as they chose, were independent in all but name. Among them private warfare was the order of the day. "Legalized anarchy" is a phrase descriptive of feudalism at its worst.

Relations between lord and vassal

The relations between lord and vassal were reciprocal and contractual. Each party had both rights and duties. The relationship was established by the acts of homage and fealty, by which the prospective vassal promised to become the lord's man and swore to perform for the lord certain services. The lord in return gave the vassal a fief, protection, and loyal treatment. The services of the vassal varied with the individual contract, but they were always honorable. Base service, such as manual labor on the lord's land, could constitute no part of a vassal's obligation. The duties of the vassal were of four types. He was morally bound to treat the lord with respect and devotion and

---

[1] See map, p. 122.

pledged himself not to attack the lord's person, his goods, his honor, or his family. His most distinctive duty was to render mounted military service at his own expense. The amount was fixed as to time and distance, the general rule with regard to time being forty days each year. Service of court required the vassal on summons to come to the lord's court in order to give the lord counsel or to assist him in the administration of justice. When the lord's court acted in a judicial capacity the vassal took part with the other vassals in finding the judgment. Pecuniary service involved payments to the lord on various occasions. The feudal aid was due to the lord in emergencies, which generally were defined. In England the most common occasions for the payment of money aids were when the lord knighted his eldest son, married his eldest daughter, or had to ransom his body in war. The other payments constituted collectively the feudal incidents. The relief was a sum paid by the heir of a deceased vassal in order to inherit the estate. When a minor inherited a fief, the lord administered the estate during the heir's minority and took the profits in lieu of the military service which the minor could not render. This was the right of wardship. When the heiress of a fief married, she had to obtain the lord's consent, which became the occasion of a fee. When the vassal died without heirs, the fief reverted to the lord by escheat. If the vassal broke his contract in certain ways, the lord recovered the fief by forfeiture.

Feudalism was brought to England by the Normans because it was the organization with which they were familiar at home. The transition to feudalism was rendered easy by the political and economic conditions existing in England. A weak government and prolonged disorders, such as the Danish invasions, had caused the personal relationship of lord and man to become common before 1066. Private individuals often possessed political rights over other free men. Indeed, fiefs held by definite contract for military and other honorable services seem to have constituted the only significant aspect of feudalism which was absent.[2] William and his Norman followers soon gave organized shape to these formless elements. On the tenurial side feudalism was developed thoroughly. The king gave out lands for a definite amount of military service from each recipient. The tenants-in-chief in turn had to grant parts of their land on similar terms to followers, in order to obtain the number of mounted warriors which they had agreed to supply to the king. The fief which owed the service

Feudalism in England

---

[2] There may have been isolated instances of feudal contracts, but it seems improbable: Stenton, *English Feudalism*, pp. 114–130.

of one fully equipped knight for forty days each year was called a knight's fee. All told, there were in England about 5,000 knight's fees when the process of subinfeudation had been completed. In England the king became almost literally the landlord of the whole kingdom.

William was too strong a king to permit the political side of feudalism to develop freely. Having learned by experience the menace of feudalism to his authority, he placed limitations upon the political powers of his English vassals. (1) He required the mesne vassals to take an oath of allegiance to him superior to that sworn to their immediate lords. Hence a vassal could not conscientiously follow his lord in arms against the king, as could the continental vassal. (2) William kept the old national fighting force, the fyrd. He never became dependent solely upon his tenants-in-chief for an army. In 1075 he used the English fyrd successfully against a group of his Norman vassals who were in rebellion, and the fyrd served his descendants for the same purpose on more than one occasion. (3) The administration of justice, though it fell more largely into private hands, did not become completely feudalized. The old national local courts of the shire and the hundred continued to maintain a vigorous existence. (4) When he granted lands to his tenants-in-chief, rarely did he give to any a large estate composed of contiguous lands. An estate generally consisted of holdings scattered over several counties. This may have been due to accident rather than design, but the result was to make it difficult for any vassal to organize a compact fief so large that it could become practically independent and a serious threat to the power of the crown.

These limitations upon the political side of feudalism were sufficient to check its worst evils. Though the king became a feudal suzerain, he did not cease to wield the royal powers inherited from his Anglo-Saxon predecessors. He was checked sufficiently by the feudal lords to keep him from becoming too despotic; he was strong enough to prevent the feudal lords from seizing enough political power to make anarchy and disorder the rule instead of the exception. Feudalism, as it worked in England, established between the king and the feudal barons a balance which swung now in one direction and again in the other. The struggle to maintain this balance constitutes a large part of the story of the English constitution for many generations after the Conqueror's time.

The government Upon the government of England the ultimate results of the conquest were far greater than the immediate effects. William wrought little organic change in the existing political institutions intentionally.

One of his earliest acts as king was to issue a charter to the citizens of London, guaranteeing to them possession of their local customs. It was typical of the attitude which he maintained throughout his reign. He treated the Anglo-Saxon laws in the same spirit. Of legislation from him only three pieces have been preserved. Two related to the church. The third substituted mutilation for the death penalty and introduced the wager of battle, a bilateral ordeal in which the accuser fought the accused and the victor won his case, presumably as the result of God's judgment.[3] These were not sweeping changes. For the rest he commanded that the Anglo-Saxon laws and customs as they existed in the time of Edward the Confessor should be observed. He retained Anglo-Saxon laws and institutions for the purpose of conciliating his English subjects. Yet the Normans introduced some new institutions, such as the feudal tenure, and they changed decidedly the character of others, such as the offices of the earl and the sheriff. Where the old institutions were preserved, moreover, they were administered by Normans unfamiliar with their working, and thus many institutions which remained much the same in outward form changed in spirit. The final result of the Norman conquest was a great alteration in the English constitution, but the transition was made so gradually that there was no abrupt break with the past. The Norman conquest did not interrupt seriously the continuity in the development of English political institutions; rather it gave to their development a sharp and lasting turn.

Under William the central government was still carried on by the king assisted by his household officials and by a council composed of influential laymen and ecclesiastics. The council contained the same men who would have sat in the Anglo-Saxon witan, but its composition was ruled, nevertheless, by a different principle. William's assembly was made up principally of his tenants-in-chief; it was a court which William held as feudal lord; it was called *curia regis* (court of the king). Its functions, too, were practically the same as those of the witan. The household officials of the king, however, were beginning to give way to more purely administrative officials. The Anglo-Saxon kings had used their household servants, such as the steward and the butler, as their principal ministers and executive assistants. Edward the Confessor imported from Normandy one purely administrative official, the chancellor, who was the king's secretary and attended to

Central administration

---

[3] This enactment also established the murder fine. If a Frenchman was found slain, the people of the hundred in which the body lay had to produce the murderer within a week or pay a heavy fine.

the issue of royal documents. William introduced another, the justiciar, who was the king's chief adviser and head of the royal judicial system. These were steps toward efficiency in government; and greater activities on the part of the older household officials contributed to the same end. This official staff, with the addition of such tenants-in-chief as happened to be in attendance upon the king, constituted a smaller council from which the king sought advice when his feudal council was not in session. This smaller and more permanent council was known by the same name as the larger, and it might perform the same functions as the larger. To contemporaries there seems to have been no distinction between the powers of the two. In order to avoid confusion, the larger body may be called the great council, *curia regis* being reserved for the smaller body.[4]

Local government

In the local government there was even less change in outward form. The shires and hundreds were retained as the local administrative districts, and the public local courts continued to function, although their field of activity was diminished in scope by the increase in the number of private courts. The large earldoms, however, were abolished. William kept earls, but with few exceptions their jurisdictions were smaller and their powers less than those of their Anglo-Saxon predecessors. On the borders or in disturbed areas a few earldoms were left under the control of powerful earls for purposes of defense, but the majority of earldoms became little more than titular dignities which carried more honors and emoluments than powers. The local administrative work of the Norman kings was done mainly by the sheriffs, who were more amenable to the king's will. William also began to hold the local communities of the hundred and the vill more responsible for the maintenance of local order. Another innovation was the occasional despatch of royal commissioners into the different counties to transact royal business locally. This practice served to link the local government more closely to the central.

Domesday Book

The most notable use of royal commissions of this sort was for the compilation of the record known as Domesday Book. William levied the Danegeld as a regular tax on land, and he desired to obtain the information necessary for a new and heavier assessment. After "mickle deep speech" with the great council, he sent his agents on circuit through the counties in 1086. From each hundred they met the Norman settlers, the suitors of the hundred-moot, and the reeve and six

---

[4] There was, of course, no such definiteness in contemporary usage. For an explanation of contemporary nomenclature, see White, *Making of the English Constitution*, second ed., pp. 117–119.

peasants from each vill, whom they required to answer under oath questions concerning the size, resources, and inhabitants of the local estates. The evidence thus obtained was tabulated and recorded to form Domesday Book. Though the record is primarily a valuation, it contains a mass of information about social and economic conditions in England. Despite Pepys' failure to derive therefrom knowledge concerning "the sea and the dominion thereof," it is such a complete record of its kind as exists for no other country of Europe. Probably there was no other European king strong enough to force his subjects to supply such information. Even with all our modern governmental machinery, returns for censuses and taxes are not obtained without sporadic opposition, and in the eleventh century such a public inquisition into the details of men's private business was without precedent. The disgust of William's subjects is reflected in the scornful remark of the Anglo-Saxon chronicler that "it is shameful to relate that which he thought no shame to do." Of grumbling and complaint there was enough; of serious opposition there was none. No better illustration could be found of the increased authority which the kingship had accumulated under William's management.

By the close of William's reign in 1087 the government of England had undergone a pronounced centralization. William retained the powers of the Anglo-Saxon king and added to them the powers derived from his position as feudal overlord. He could call out the old fyrd and a new feudal array; he collected all the revenues which had been received by his predecessors and obtained an additional income from the new feudal dues. With characteristic energy and ability he eliminated the greatest weaknesses that he inherited from both positions. By better organization, by the greater activity of the central administration, by the closer supervision of the local government, and by the more autocratic exercise of the royal authority, William reared upon the solid substructure of Anglo-Saxon local institutions a strong central government. *Centralization*

This result was due only in part to formal legal changes in the organization of the government; in large measure it was merely the expression of William's strong personality. Conqueror and master of men before he was twenty, he was accustomed to exact obedience. He had an inflexible will, and he was determined to succeed. His early hardships left him stern, but he was, on the whole, just. "He was mild to those good men who loved God," wrote an English monk, "but severe beyond measure towards those who withstood his will." William was a keen sportsman, and the great tracts which he reserved for the *William's personality* royal hunting and the strict game laws which he enforced constituted one of the principal grievances which Englishmen felt against him. "He loved the tall stags as if he were their father," said the Anglo-Saxon chronicler. Of his forest laws "the rich complained and the poor murmured, but he was so sturdy that he recked not of them; they must will all that the king willed, if they would live, or would keep their lands or would hold their possessions." "Stark, stern and wrathful," William the Conqueror stands out in bold relief on the canvas of English history; but he was a great king, and he used the power which he acquired to give to England peace and good government.

William and the church

The effect of the Norman conquest upon the English church was no less pronounced than that upon the government, and it was far more direct. William was deeply indebted to the papacy for moral support which had been of assistance to him in the conquest. Though he may have contracted no definite obligation to reorganize the English church, that obviously was what the papacy desired; and the Conqueror was not a man to leave even a debt of courtesy unpaid. Many of the reforms desired by the papacy, moreover, had been accomplished already in Normandy. To William they seemed to be merely a normal part of the ecclesiastical organization. In his settlement of the church, consequently, he seems to have made innovations with conscious intention. In order to appreciate the significance of his changes, it is necessary to glance at the organization of the church as a whole, and to explain the movement of reform which had recently swept over the continental church.

Central government

The government of the church in the eleventh century was becoming highly centralized. The popes had long been the acknowledged heads of the church, but the extent of the control which they exercised over the clergy was the result of a long historical development. Until the tenth century the papal power within the church increased fairly steadily, but during that century and the first half of the eleventh it declined. Near the middle of the century the pope brought to Rome as his friend and influential adviser a monk named Hildebrand, who remained a power behind the throne until he himself became pope with the title of Gregory VII (1073-1085). Under Hildebrand's guidance the papacy placed itself at the head of a movement to reform the evils in the church. It also asserted supremacy over the clergy with an activity and force such as it had not displayed before for centuries. The Hildebrandine papacy in theory was an absolute monarchy within the church. Associated with it in the central government were the cardinals, who constituted an advisory council and an electoral college for the selection of popes, and the papal *curia*, composed of clerks and officials organized in judicial and administrative departments. The papacy also employed with increasing frequency legates, who were agents sent as occasion required to represent and maintain the papal authority in a given locality.

The efficiency of the central government was increased by the hierarchical organization of the clergy. The principal ranks of the secular clergy below the papacy were, in order, archbishops, bishops, and parish priests.[5] Each rank owed obedience to and came under the supervisory control of the rank next above. The local clergy were selected locally. Each archbishop and bishop was elected by a cathedral chapter, consisting of the clergy attached to the cathedral, which was the capital church of the diocese. The parish priest was nominated by a local patron, who, in this period, was usually a lay lord. But the choice of a member of any of these grades had to be confirmed by the next higher ecclesiastical authority before it was valid. The pope could veto the election of an archbishop, the archbishop of the bishop, and the bishop of a priest. The regular clergy were subject to the bishops, except the inmates of exempt monasteries who acknowledged only the commands of the pope.

> Local organization

To complete its governmental organization the church had central and local legislative bodies and a series of courts. Though the pope could decree law for the church, he occasionally called assemblies of the higher officials of the whole church to aid him in the work of governing the church. Such meetings were known as general councils. Similarly each archbishop could hold an assembly of the bishops and principal abbots in his province, and each bishop could hold an assembly of the clergy of his diocese. These provincial and diocesan synods, as they were respectively called, could legislate for the government of the clergy within their respective jurisdictions. To administer the large body of ecclesiastical law which thus developed, there was an ascending series of courts beginning with the archdeacon's and ending with the pope's, with a well-organized system of appeal from one to the next higher in the series.

> Legislative bodies and courts

So centralized and efficient was the governmental organization maintained by Hildebrand and his successors that it often collided with the governments of states. All of the clergy below the pope had a double character. They were officials in a church universal which knew nothing

> Church and state

---

[5] This enumeration omits several grades which are not important for present purposes. Between the bishops and the parish priests, for example, were the archdeacons and the rural deans.

of nationality. They were subordinate to the pope. At the same time they were the subjects of some lay ruler. The English clergy, for example, were subject to two rulers, the pope and the king. When the commands of the two conflicted, the clergy were placed in a difficult position.

Superiority claimed for the spiritual power

In the eleventh century and afterwards the position was rendered particularly difficult by the extreme claims advanced by Gregory VII. He maintained not only that the pope was supreme within the church itself, but also that the pope was superior to all temporal rulers. Since the pope derived his power directly from God, since he was the vicar of Christ on earth, Gregory argued, the power of the pope was higher than that possessed by any lay ruler. Gregory's successors did not cease to advance claims of spiritual superiority. The result was a series of quarrels between kings and their national clergy, who chose to obey the pope when his order conflicted with the royal decree.

Feudalization of the church

Another source of friction arose from the feudalization of the church. The clergy, like others in that age, derived their incomes primarily from land. Higher officials and monasteries often had such vast estates that they could not escape incorporation in the feudal organization. Bishops almost universally became royal or ducal vassals, while abbots held from kings or other lay lords. The king who had such ecclesiastical vassals regarded them primarily as his feudal tenants. He exacted from them as nearly as might be the same services that his lay vassals rendered, except that they were allowed to perform military service by deputy. The clergy felt that the demands of the king often interfered with their spiritual duties. Especially disastrous was the control over the appointment of bishops exerted by the king. From the point of view of the church, such appointments resulted in an evil influence over clerical life, since the king was likely to care more about the feudal loyalty of the incumbent than about his qualifications to be the spiritual head of a diocese. The king, on the other hand, could not allow appointments to places of such power and wealth to be made without his sanction, since vassals of such influence, if they should be hostile to his interests, could do him much harm. It was largely in the effort to break this deadlock that Gregory VII was led to assert the superiority of the spiritual over the temporal authority.

The canon law

A third aspect of ecclesiastical supremacy which caused trouble was the separate jurisdiction of the ecclesiastical courts. The church by this time had an elaborate code of law, known as the canon law, which governed the lives of the clergy and in certain fields the lives of laymen. The courts of the church claimed jurisdiction over all cases in

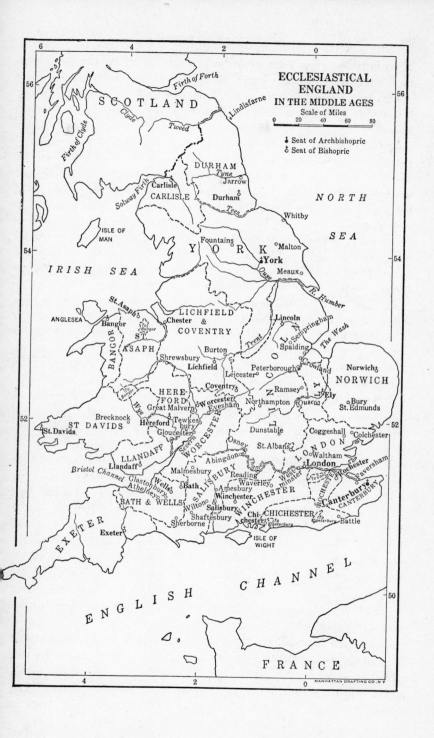

ECCLESIASTICAL
ENGLAND
IN THE MIDDLE AGES

Scale of Miles

0   20   40   60   80

♦ Seat of Archbishopric
○ Seat of Bishopric

SCOTLAND

Firth of Forth

Clyde

Tweed

Firth of Clyde

Lindisfarne

DURHAM

Tyne

Jarrow

Carlisle

CARLISLE

Durham

Solway Firth

Tees

Whitby

NORTH

ISLE OF
MAN

Fountains

YORK

Malton

York

SEA

IRISH SEA

Meaux

Ouse

R. Humber

St.Asaph

LICHFIELD

Lincoln

ANGLESEA

Bangor

Chester &

Sempringham

COVENTRY

The Wash

BANGOR

ST.
ASAPH

*To
Bangor*

Burton

Trent

Spalding

Shrewsbury

Lichfield

Peterborough

Crowland

Norwich

Leicester

Ramsey

NORWICH

HERE-
FORD

Coventry

Northampton

Ely

ST DAVIDS

Great Malvern

Worcester

Ouse

Bury

*To
Bangor*

Evesham

St.Edmunds

Brecknock

Wye

Tewkes-

Dunstable

Coggeshall

St.Davids

Hereford

bury

Colchester

Gloucester

Osney

St.Albans

LLANDAFF

Abingdon

LONDON

WORCESTER

Waltham

Llandaff

Malmesbury

West-

London

Bristol Channel

Glastonbury

Wells

Reading

minster

ROCHESTER

Rochester

Athelney

SALISBURY

Bath

Waverley

Faversham

BATH & WELLS

Amesbury

WINCHESTER

Canterbury

Wilton

Winchester

CANTERBURY

EXETER

Salisbury

CHICHESTER

Exeter

Shaftesbury

Chi-

*To
Canterbury*

Battle

Sherborne

chester

ISLE OF
WIGHT

ENGLISH CHANNEL

FRANCE

MANHATTAN DRAFTING CO.,N.Y.

which a clergyman was a party to the suit, irrespective of the nature of the case, and over all cases concerning marital relations, inheritance, and contracts substantiated by oaths (as most contracts were in the Middle Ages), irrespective of the lay or clerical character of the parties to the suit. If these claims were conceded by a lay ruler, it left him without any authority over his clerical subjects and without authority over his lay subjects in a large and important field of litigation.

When William conquered England, a reformation of the church was at the height of its development on the continent. The movement had been necessitated by a more or less general laxness and corruption in the lives of the clergy. The initiative in reform had been taken by the monastery of Cluny, founded in 910. In England the movement had made itself felt in Edgar's time with only temporary results. On the continent, where the effect had been permanent, monastic life was restored to something like its pristine vigor, but the secular clergy had not yet fallen generally under the influence of the movement, when the Hildebrandine papacy assumed the leadership. It sought to abolish simony, that is, the purchase of ecclesiastical office by bribes, to enforce clerical celibacy, and to centralize the organization of the church in such a way as to make the power of the pope over the clergy supreme. When Hildebrand became pope he attempted further to make the clergy more independent of lay rulers. When William took in hand the affairs of England, the last claim was not yet a part of the program, but the others had won widespread acceptance outside of England. William was expected to apply them to the English church.

The papal program of reform

He began the reorganization of the English church as soon as the conquest was finished. In 1070 ecclesiastical councils were held in the presence of papal legates, who were there to see that the papal program was carried out. Stigand was deprived of his see, and through deposition or death all but two or three of the bishoprics and many of the abbacies were rendered vacant. The vacancies were filled with Norman clergymen, who soon infused the English church with the spirit of moral reform and intellectual activitiy which was prevalent on the continent.

The councils of 1070

The most important of the new appointments was that of Lanfranc to the archbishopric of Canterbury. He was an Italian, who in his youth studied law in the schools of Italy, and for a time practiced successfully. Subsequently he went to Normandy, where he found occupation as a teacher. There he entered the monastery of Bec, of which he eventually became prior. Under his inspiration the monastic school of Bec became one of the most noted in Europe, and during this period Lanfranc himself became one of the most famed theologians of his day. Before

Lanfranc

the conquest Lanfranc had attracted the attention of the duke who sought his advice and showed him favors which included promotion to an abbacy. Lanfranc was an able churchman, a skilled lawyer, and William's trusted friend. In England he became the king's chief adviser in affairs of state as well as in ecclesiastical matters.

The changes in the English church

William and Lanfranc carried out the papal program faithfully up to a certain point. Simony apparently needed little repression in England. Clerical celibacy began to be enforced. The episcopal seats were removed from the small places to more populous centers, where the bishops could exert a greater influence. Cathedral chapters were reorganized and rendered more efficient. The lower clergy were made to conform to the disciplinary requirements of the church. In the monasteries strict observance of the rule was restored, and the purified ascetic spirit of the Cluniac movement was made to prevail. Monasticism, indeed, attained such a renewal of popularity in England that many new monasteries were built. Schools, under the direction of Norman teachers, began a period of activity. Before the close of the Conqueror's reign the whole moral and intellectual tone of the clergy had been greatly elevated.

In the constitution of the church also important changes were made. As a matter of practice the ecclesiastical councils were separated from the lay assemblies, in order to give to the church legislative independence. By royal enactment the bishops were given a jurisdiction separate from that of the lay tribunals. These changes revolutionized the previous Anglo-Saxon customs, in accordance with which the witan had enacted law for the church, and laymen accused of infractions of the ecclesiastical law had been tried in the courts of the hundred; but they made the English practice correspond with the continental and brought the English church more closely into line with the hierarchical organization on which rested Hildebrand's policy of ecclesiastical centralization.

Church and state in England

Beyond this point William and Lanfranc refused to go. When Gregory VII demanded from William an oath of fealty as acknowledgment that England was a fief held of the papacy, he refused to give it. In direct contradiction to a papal decree of 1075 he continued throughout his reign to control the appointment of English bishops and important abbots. William, moreover, placed certain limitations upon the English clergy, which, if enforced, would go far to keep the church dependent upon the state. He allowed no pope to be acknowledged without his consent and forbade the entrance of papal legates or papal letters into England without royal permission. These rules were designed to protect the royal authority in case the commands of pope and

king should conflict. As protection against undue encroachment upon
the royal authority by the local clergy he retained a power of veto over
the acts of English ecclesiastical synods, and he further required that
his consent should be obtained before any of his tenants-in-chief or
officials should be excommunicated. The sentence of excommunication,
which was the principal weapon used by the clergy to enforce its will,
shut a man out from the communion of the church, deprived him of
the sacraments, and meant his eternal damnation if he should die and
the sentence should not be revoked. The sentence might extend to a
prohibition upon his fellow men to communicate with him, and thus
it could be used effectively in a quarrel between king and clergy. These
rules make it clear that William had no thought of surrendering control of the English clergy. But it required a strong king to enforce
them, and by his separation of the ecclesiastical courts and legislative
assemblies William contributed to the growth of a power which was to
wage a mighty conflict with his descendants.

The introduction of feudalism, the centralization of the government,
and the reorganization of the church were the three most striking results of the Norman conquest which became apparent in William's
reign. These innovations were due in large measure directly to the
actions of William, although he probably was not conscious in many
instances of the extent of the changes which his acts were producing.
Other results of the conquest, three in number, were less directly due
to his agency, and their significance was even less fully apparent in
his time; but it was during his reign that they had their beginning.
They were a quickening of the intercourse between England and the
continent, a transformation of the English language, and a stimulation
of intellectual development, which displayed itself especially in the
fields of architecture, literature, and scholarship.

Other
results
of the
conquest

The Norman conquest opened England to the reception of continental influences in all fields of thought and endeavor. The rulers in
state and church and the local nobility became Normans. William
was still the duke of Normandy, many of the English barons retained
their Norman estates, the Norman churchmen in England maintained
an active intercourse with the pope and with the continental clergy,
and Norman merchants brought from the continent the merchandise
that would supply the demands created by the Norman tastes and
fashions gradually spreading throughout England. Englishmen, however, did not remain entirely passive; they were drawn into European
affairs. The rulers of England began to take active part in the political
affairs of the continent; English soldiers fought across the Channel in

Foreign
intercourse

purely French quarrels; and English clerics won promotion to high places in continental churches, became teachers in continental schools, and served as the skilled administrators of the Norman kings of Sicily. The bond between England and the continent became closer and more enduring than it had been before within historic times, and, in contrast with the earlier Scandinavian connection, it brought England into touch with the highest European civilization of the time.

Language
The Norman conquest brought to England a new language. French became the speech of the court and the camp, of the government and the law. The nobility conversed in French, and French was the tongue of the learned so far as they descended to the use of a vernacular. Educated Englishmen learned French as well as Latin, and French was the vehicle of expression necessarily possessed by every ambitious Englishman. For a long time English nearly ceased to be a written language. Yet it remained the spoken tongue of the masses, and eventually the inertia of the masses prevailed over the activities of statesmen and scholars. English survived; but it was a transformed language. The breakdown of inflections, which had begun before the conquest, was hastened by the cessation of the use of English as a literary language. The vocabulary was profoundly modified during the centuries when the two languages were used side by side by the loss of some English words and by the addition of many French words. So great was the alteration that Freeman, with all the pride of his insularity, speaks of the "abiding corruption of our language";[6] but the tongue of Englishmen nevertheless is English.

Intellectual development
In 1066 the intellectual movement, which was to grow into the so-called renaissance of the twelfth century, was well under way in northern France. Many schools had acquired fame and had attracted large numbers of pupils, the content of the *trivium* and the *quadrivium* was being rapidly expanded, philosophy and theology were becoming favorite studies, and the number of original thinkers was multiplying notably. Norman schools were taking a prominent part in the development, and the Norman churchmen soon created a new intellectual atmosphere in England. English schools became more numerous, and many English boys became students in famous French schools. So far and so fast did the intellectual revival go, that Englishmen contributed their full share to the brilliant intellectual achievement of European productive scholarship in the twelfth century.

The literary output of the learned in the Norman period was mainly

---

[6] *Norman Conquest,* v, 547.

in Latin. The *Anglo-Saxon Chronicle* continued to be kept in one Literature
monastery until 1154, but it was nearly an isolated piece of writing in
English. The French poems that the conquerors brought with them
as the favorite literature of society became the models which some
natives of England would begin to follow in the twelfth century, but
they found few imitators in the days of the Norman kings.

Among the Latin works were many which increase our knowledge
of the history of the period. The principal contemporary accounts of Historical
the conquest were written by Normans,[7] but several Englishmen and sources
several Normans settled in England began writing soon after the conquest was over. Florence of Worcester, an English monk, was one of
the earliest.[8] He was little more than a compiler and an annalist.
Eadmer, another English monk, wrote with a better sense of proportion
and a better Latin style of events which he knew intimately. Orderic
Vitalis was a Norman, born in England, who became a monk in
Normandy, but thought of himself as an Englishman. Though his
work is poorly organized, it is an excellent example of the narrator's
skill. Foremost among this group of historians stands William of
Malmesbury in whose veins flowed both Norman and English blood.
It was his ambition to restore historical writing in England to the
pinnacle where Bede had placed it. He succeeded fairly well. In the
critical judgment of his material and in the literary form of its presentation he surpassed all the historical writers of the Norman period.
These works, together with several lesser histories and annals, supply
much fuller information than is to be had from contemporary chronicles for any earlier period.

The artistic aspirations of the Normans found expression chiefly in
architecture. The Normans were great builders. They introduced into Architec-
England the castles which became typical of the feudal régime. William ture
had castles built in many towns of strategic importance, and private
castles were reared as well. They were designed, however, for the
purpose of defense. Their massive walls and square towers gave little
opportunity for the display of architectural art. The churches preserve
the best examples of the Norman style of architecture. Everywhere
the Norman ecclesiastics replaced the existing churches with new
buildings conceived on a grander scale than those previously built

---

[7] William of Poitiers, who was William's chaplain and panegyrist, and William of
Jumièges, a monk about whom little is known, are two of the principal writers. An
anonymous poem attributed to Guy, bishop of Amiens, deals with the battle of Hastings.

[8] His chronicle extends to 1117. It was continued for several years by another monk of
Worcester.

either in England or in Normandy. In the construction of their churches they used a style of architecture marked by round arches, huge supporting round columns or piers, and a general effect of massiveness so distinctive that it is known as the Norman Romanesque. Many cathedrals of England still preserve large portions of their structures as they were reared by their Norman builders. The cathedral of Durham is the best example. The ruggedness of its massive grandeur can hardly fail either to arouse in the observer that spirit of reverence which it was designed to create, or to impress him as a typical product of the Norman genius which was building state as well as church.

Succession of William II

On his deathbed in 1087 the great William made disposition of the succession to his dominions. He desired his eldest son, Robert, who was too weak to make a good ruler of the recently conquered England, to be duke of Normandy, William, his second son, to wear the English crown, and Henry, his youngest, to have a gift of money. Matters were arranged accordingly. The Norman barons of England were dissatisfied. They preferred the easy-going Robert to his younger brother, and they feared the complications likely to result from the division of their allegiance for their English and Norman fiefs. Early in 1088 the majority of them revolted. The new king quelled the rebellion and saved his crown largely by the aid of his English subjects. Though he had to meet another baronial conspiracy later, armed opposition never again seriously menaced his position.

His rule

William Rufus (the red), as he was called, possessed a strong will untempered by the saving grace of a sense of justice. He made such heavy demands on the purses of his subjects that they deemed his rule tyrannical. When bishops or other prelates died, he often kept the vacancies open for a long time, collecting for himself the revenues of the estates attached to the offices. He exacted in payment of feudal incidents sums which his vassals regarded as extortionate. His administration of justice was venal. In 1089 the situation was rendered worse by the death of Lanfranc, who had exerted a restraining influence upon the arbitrary tendencies of the king.

William and Anselm

In his relations with the church the Red King prepared the way for a serious conflict between church and state. After Lanfranc's death he kept the archbishopric of Canterbury vacant in order to secure the rich revenues of the archiepiscopal estates. In 1093, when illness induced repentance, he ordered the appointment of Anselm, whose renown for piety had caused many to urge him for the vacant position. Anselm was an Italian, who, like Lanfranc, had come to Normandy. There he became a monk and eventually the abbot of Bec. He was a distinguished theologian, and he was more interested in scholarship than in administration. He was a mild, gentle, devout scholar who shrank from the burden of executive business which the incumbent of the archbishopric must assume if he would perform his duties conscientiously. Once installed, however, Anselm became the rigid, inflexible exponent of the extreme claims of the church. It is significant of the irreconcilable character of the conflicting claims of church and state that a man of Anselm's temperament should have provoked a struggle between the two powers in England.

Prolonged friction between king and archbishop reached a critical juncture when the latter asked leave to go to Rome to seek the pallium. This request brought to an issue the extent of the royal authority over the English church. For several years two rivals had claimed the papacy. William, exercising the power asserted by his father, allowed the English clergy to recognize neither as the legitimate pope. In order to obtain the pallium Anselm had to acknowledge one or the other. When the king maintained that no pope could be recognized without his consent, Anselm took the position that ecclesiastical law, with its requirement that he should secure the pallium, was superior to the law of the state. It was a clear-cut issue between church and state. Eventually this quarrel was settled in favor of the archbishop through the intervention of papal legates, who outwitted the king in diplomacy. William's defeat increased his ill will, while Anselm became discouraged by his inability to remedy evils in the church in the face of the royal opposition. Finally, in 1097, he sought refuge from further bickerings by going into voluntary exile. Under William the quarrel was not renewed. In 1100, while the unpopular king was hunting in the royal forest, he met his death from an arrow shot by an unknown hand. Anselm's departure and the king's death merely postponed the continuation of the contest. In the next reign it was renewed about another subject, but with the same fundamental question at issue.

The successor of William Rufus was his younger brother Henry. When William died, Robert was absent on the first crusade. Henry, who was a member of the fatal hunting party, rode hard to Winchester, where he secured possession of the royal treasure and the crown. Since his position on the throne had no solid foundation in either primogeniture or election, his first acts were bids for popular favor. The most important of them was the issue of a charter, in which he promised to remedy many of the evils that had been grievances in William's reign.[9]

Accession of Henry I

---

[9] Translated in Adams and Stephens, *Select Documents of English Constitutional History,* no. 7.

By granting liberties to the people, the king voluntarily placed limitations upon his own power. A century later the document became the prototype for the Great Charter, which the barons demanded of John as a right.

Henry and Normandy

By this means the new king apparently won popular support, but he was not to hold his crown without opposition. The English barons had to meet a situation similar to that which they had faced at William's accession. Robert, after his return, was easily persuaded by them to strike for the crown. In 1101 he invaded England, but Henry persuaded him to withdraw without fighting. A few years later the anarchy which prevailed in Normandy under Robert's weak rule caused some of the Norman barons to seek Henry's intervention. In 1106 he crossed to Normandy, won the battle of Tinchebrai, placed his brother in confinement, and took the government of Normandy into his own hands. Thus Normandy was again united to England, but this time England was the leading partner.

Henry and Anselm

Meanwhile Henry had been engaged in a contest with Anselm to maintain control of the church. Shortly after his coronation Henry invited Anselm to return. At their first meeting Henry offered to restore the archiepiscopal estates which William had seized, asking for them the customary homage. Anselm refused to give homage. At Rome in the previous year he had attended a general council of the church, which had formally repeated the Gregorian decrees against lay investiture. Investiture was the formal presentation to an elected bishop or archbishop of the ring and staff which signified the transfer of the bishopric or archbishopric to the candidate designated for the office by election. When Gregory VII became pope, it was customary for kings to confer the ring and staff and thus to control the appointments to purely spiritual offices. Gregory, seeing in this practice the root of simony and the basis of the power of the state over the church, had forbidden it. The attempt to enforce his prohibition against the emperor had occupied so fully the attention of Gregory and his immediate successors, that they had made no serious effort to secure its observance in England. Anselm had accepted investiture from the hands of William II without demur. The council of 1099 had forbidden, under penalty of excommunication of the parties concerned, not only lay investiture, but also the consecration by an ecclesiastic of one so invested, and the performance of homage to a layman by a clerk. Anselm came back to England thoroughly imbued with the spirit of the Gregorian program. He not only declined to do homage

for the fief which he held from the king, but he also refused to conse-
crate the bishops and abbots whom Henry had invested.

Henry could not concede this principle, but he did not wish to come
to an open breach with the archbishop while his tenure of the kingship
hung in the balance. Consequently he temporized. Anselm was allowed
to have the revenues of the archiepiscopal fief, while an embassy was
despatched to the pope to secure an exemption of England from the
decree. When that request was denied, the king prolonged negotiations
without an open break until he had overcome the rebellion against his
rule and was secure upon the throne. Thereupon he seized the archiepiscopal fief and ordered the archbishop to remain in exile until he
was prepared to yield. Further negotiations having failed, Anselm was
preparing to excommunicate the king, when Henry's sister, Adela,
intervened with the suggestion of a compromise. After a discussion of
terms between the two disputants, a proposition was submitted to the
pope which he approved. In 1107 the acceptance of the compromise by
Henry and Anselm brought the controversy over lay investiture in
England to an end.

Though the settlement was called a compromise, it was that in name
only, since the claims of the popes and the English kings were too
fundamentally opposed in principle to admit of any real compromise.
By the terms of the agreement the papacy permitted ecclesiastics to
render homage to the king for fiefs which they held of him. Thus the
king retained his authority as lord over his clerical vassals. The king
on his side gave up the right to invest elected prelates with their offices.
Since this was the main bone of contention, contemporary churchmen
claimed a victory for the church. In reality the king was giving up
only an empty ceremony. His control of the appointments of prelates
he did not lose. He merely pushed his control back to an earlier stage
in the proceedings, and designated to those having the right to elect
whom they should choose. When a vacant bishopric had to be filled, the
choice of the electors was often subject to the influence of the king, and
their election was always contingent upon his assent. To the pope
went the appearance of victory; to Henry, the substance. The outcome
can be weighed only partially, however, by the terms which settled the
issues immediately at stake. In his quarrel with William II Anselm
had not received the sympathy of the bishops, who regarded his claim
as contrary to English custom and opposed to the royal prerogative.
In his contest with Henry a few bishops finally came to his support.
The change in their attitude marked the beginning among the English
clergy of a small party which upheld the papal power in England and

believed that clerical obedience was due to the law of the church when it conflicted with the law of the state.

Henry's government

During the remainder of Henry's reign, which lasted until 1135, England was at peace, though Henry waged small wars in Normandy and Wales. The mere existence of so long a period of peace is sufficiently indicative of the character of Henry's rule; only a strong king could maintain order in those days. Henry was not one whit less masterful than his father, and he was less given to anger. Cool, calculating, and far-sighted in his judgments, he weighed his actions carefully, but he lacked nothing of the force and energy that was characteristic of his house. Government was his business. In order to conduct it well, he laid heavy fiscal burdens upon his people. He did not hesitate to exact feudal incidents which he had promised in his charter to forego. But his government was not as arbitrary as his brother's had been. The poor received the same justice as the rich, and the weak the same protection as the strong. Richly he deserved the title, popularly accorded him, of the "lion of justice." The eulogy pronounced by the Anglo-Saxon chronicler was the highest praise that a contemporary could give to his government. "A good man he was, and there was great awe of him. No man durst misdo another in his time. He made peace for man and beast."[10]

The exchequer

When it comes to an exact enumeration of the changes made by Henry in the government, the sources leave many gaps in our information. It is clear that he carried to a higher state of perfection the process of centralization which William the Conqueror had begun. It was probably in his time that the exchequer took the shape which made it one of the best-organized fiscal departments in Europe. The personnel of the exchequer was same as that of the *curia regis*, except for the addition of a clerical staff. The responsible heads of the exchequer were the treasurer, the chancellor, the justiciar, and the other royal officials who constituted the semi-professional administrative core of the *curia regis*. The exchequer was merely the *curia regis* sitting for financial business. Twice a year, in the autumn and the spring, the exchequer met to audit the accounts of the sheriffs, who collected the larger part of the king's revenues, and to receive the sums due the king. The principal items were the receipts from the royal estates, the fines imposed by the courts, the feudal incidents, and taxes and dues, such as the Danegeld, which the exchequer might order the sheriff to collect in any given year. When the sheriff appeared, his debits

---

[10] Translation by Thorpe, ii, 229.

and credits were set forth by means of counters arranged in columns upon the table around which he and the officials sat, enabling all to see at a glance the balance due the king. This method of accounting gave to the exchequer its name, since the table with its columns and its counters resembled a chessboard.[11] It was probably introduced during the reign of Henry I by members of the *curia regis* who had studied at the school of Laon in France.[12] This was at the time the most famous school in the west, and it specialized in the system of the abacus on which this mode of reckoning was based. Thus did Henry utilize the product of the schools of his day. The regular control by the central government enabled the king to secure the full value of his revenues and to keep a closer watch over the actions of his local officials. It gave his subjects better opportunity to obtain remedy when they were subjected to unjust exactions. It was an important link in the chain forged by the Norman kings to bind the central and the local institutions of government in a unified whole.

Another step in the same direction was the institution of itinerant justices. Under the Norman kings the judicial business transacted by the king's court increased rapidly. Its jurisdiction extended to pleas in which tenants-in-chief were parties, suits which lesser courts had refused to entertain or to decide, and the pleas of the crown. The last consisted of the more serious crimes such as homicide and robbery. In addition to these regular fields of jurisdiction, the king's court might take cognizance of a specific case, which ordinarily would have gone before a local court, by a royal command to that effect issued in the form of a writ. This use of a royal writ to bring a suit before the king's court was in the Norman period an exceptional procedure, reserved mainly for those favored of the king. The judicial writ was to have a long history, until eventually it opened the king's court freely to the king's subjects and became the ordinary mode of beginning a suit; but in the Norman period it was only a notable exception to the normal course of events.

The itinerant justices

When a case came before the king's court it might be decided by the great council or by the *curia regis*. There was no theoretical division of jurisdiction between the two. In practice, however, most of the judicial business tended to get itself done by the *curia regis*. This body was more constantly in session, and its members generally had more or

---

[11] In Latin, *scaccarium*.

[12] This is the view of Poole: *The Exchequer in the Twelfth Century*, pp. 46–57. Haskins thinks its introduction may be placed a few years earlier and connected with the schools of Lorraine: *English Historical Review*, xxvii, 101–106.

less knowledge of the law. They followed their own precedents, and thus developed a uniform procedure. The king's justice, too, was more likely to be impartial and to some extent more rational than that of the local courts. The king's court became popular. The king, on his side, was glad to receive business, because cases meant fees and fines, and such receipts formed an important item of his revenue.

The extension of the activity of the king's court, however, met with one great obstacle. The court followed the king in his constant journeyings, and prospective litigants found it burdensome to travel from parts remote from the location of the court and to follow it on its peregrinations. The Norman kings tried two expedients to meet this difficulty. Occasionally they established in a given locality an official, who was often the sheriff, with a jurisdiction akin to the king's court. This tended, however, to decentralize the system and ran counter to the policy generally followed by William the Conqueror and his sons. The practice which eventually prevailed was to send members of the *curia regis* into the different counties to hold local sessions of the king's court. Apparently sporadic instances occurred during the reigns of William I and William II. In Henry's time royal justices were sent on circuit through many counties of England to hold a court where nearly all cases that came under the jurisdiction of the king's court could be tried.[13] Such justices were called the itinerant justices. They were the *curia regis* on the march (iter). They presided over an extra full session of the county court, which for the time being became the king's court with jurisdiction and procedure entirely different from those of the ordinary session of the county court. The itinerant justices were also utilized by the king to secure the transaction of much of the business of the central government other than judicial. They could negotiate locally for the grant of aids and other taxes or gifts, execute the royal commands hitherto left to the sheriffs who were not so closely bound to the king and not so directly under his observation, supervise the work of the sheriffs, and keep the king better informed of the state of local affairs.

The succession

A question which gave Henry much concern was that of the succession. His only son having died, he persuaded the English barons to accept Matilda, his daughter, as their future ruler. In order to give her a champion, Henry arranged for her marriage to Geoffrey, son of the count of Anjou. When Henry died in 1135 Matilda was not in England, and her husband did little to press her claim. The English

---

[13] Adams and Stephens, *Select Documents*, no. 6.

barons were loath to accept the rule of a woman, for which there was no precedent, and they did nothing to secure the crown for her. Under these circumstances, Stephen of Blois, who was the son of William the Conqueror's daughter Adela, landed in England and claimed the crown. With the aid of his brother, who was the bishop of Winchester, and at the price of grants of privileges to the clergy and to various lay magnates, he induced many barons and prelates to break their oaths to support Matilda and to acknowledge him as king. Three weeks after Henry's death Stephen was crowned.

Although Stephen acquired the crown with ease, he found it difficult to wear. The chief cause of his trouble was his own character. Stephen was courageous, energetic, and conscientious in the performance of his duty, but he was wanting in decision. The barons soon discovered his weakness. Some of them began to enrich themselves by trespassing on the rights of the king or by robbing their neighbors. Widespread disorder and private warfare soon prevailed. In 1138 the situation was further complicated when a group of barons rebelled in behalf of Matilda. The civil war continued almost to the end of Stephen's reign. Many of the English barons used it merely to promote their own selfish interests. Some sold their support to the higher bidder, while others seized the opportunity to plunder and ravage on their own account.

Feudal anarchy

A vivid picture of the woes that England suffered when the barons found that Stephen was "a mild man, and soft, and good and did no justice" is one of the last entries in the *Anglo-Saxon Chronicle.* Then, says the writer, "they filled the land full of castles. . . . When the castles were made they filled them with devils and evil men. Then took they those men that they imagined had any property, both by night and by day, peasant men and women, and put them in prison for their gold and silver, and tortured them with unutterable torture. . . . Many thousands they killed with hunger. . . . They laid imposts on the towns continually . . . ; when the wretched men had no more to give, they robbed and burned all the towns. . . . Then was corn dear, and flesh, and cheese, and butter; for there was none in the land. Wretched men died of hunger; some went seeking alms who at one while were rich men; some fled out of the land. Never yet had more wretchedness been in the land."[14] Thus did England learn what feudalism meant, when the king was too weak to keep its disruptive tendencies in check.

[14] Translation by Thorpe, ii, 230.

The civil war was one of petty sieges and raids accompanied by much ravaging. At one time the rebels captured Stephen, and Matilda practically ruled England. The reversal of fortunes endured for only a few months. Thereafter the war dragged through many years without notable advantage for either side. When her son Henry attained the age of sixteen, Matilda left her claim to him. Under his leadership the war languished for several years. The end came in 1153. Henry, coming to England to lead in person, met with some success, while Stephen was discouraged by the death of the son whom he wished to be his successor. Stephen having lost heart for the struggle and Henry being in no hurry to secure the throne, a peace was readily arranged. Stephen and his followers acknowledged Henry as the heir to the throne, and Henry and his partisans agreed that Stephen should rule for the rest of his life. Property seized during the anarchy was to be restored and the castles built since 1135 were to be demolished. Stephen had scarcely begun the work of restoration when his death in 1154 made Henry of Anjou king of England.

ABBREVIATED GENEALOGY OF NORMAN AND ANGEVIN KINGS

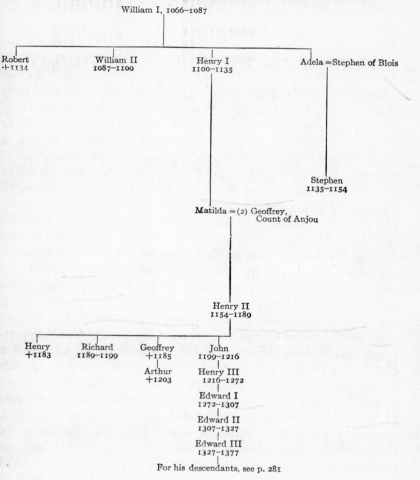

William I, 1066–1087

Robert
✝1134

William II
1087–1100

Henry I
1100–1135

Adela = Stephen of Blois

Stephen
1135–1154

Matilda = (2) Geoffrey,
Count of Anjou

Henry II
1154–1189

Henry
✝1183

Richard
1189–1199

Geoffrey
✝1185

Arthur
✝1203

John
1199–1216

Henry III
1216–1272

Edward I
1272–1307

Edward II
1307–1327

Edward III
1327–1377

For his descendants, see p. 281

CHAPTER VI

HENRY II AND THE ENGLISH CONSTITUTION

Henry II

HENRY II, who reigned from 1154 to 1189, was a man of great physical strength and vitality. Contemporaries, struck by his excessive energy, picture a king who never rested. He was ever on the march, traveling from one part to another of his broad dominions at a rate of speed which drew many a groan from his tired courtiers and more than once confounded his enemies. When time permitted he would hunt all day and return to transact business half the night, standing or pacing restlessly to and fro. He was not handsome. His face was freckled, his hair red, his body short and stout, his arms long, his legs bowed. About his personal appearance he was careless. Yet through these externals men felt the force of a dominating personality. If his appearance was not wholly regal, such was not true of his thought. Henry inherited the kingly ambition of his mother's house. He was not only determined to be a powerful king, but he also loved orderly, well-organized government for its own sake. To the furtherance of this ambition he brought knowledge acquired by an exceptionally good training and natural talents of a high order. He had a store of information derived from books such as was possessed by few contemporary rulers. He also had experience in practical affairs. In 1150 his father had transferred to him the rule of Normandy, where he became familiar with the working of a strong, centralized government before he ascended the English throne. To the knowledge thus obtained he added an ability to rule that was hardly short of genius. He selected efficient subordinates and worked laboriously and patiently with them over details. He delighted in the solution of a knotty legal problem. But with all his care for details he never lost sight of the end to be attained. Preferring diplomacy and tact as the means of carrying his policies in the face of opposition, he did not hesitate to strike when he judged it necessary or expedient; and in action he was prompt, cool, and efficient. With all his ability and wisdom Henry was nevertheless intensely human. Normally working industriously at the business of government, he occasionally gave way to sudden gusts of passion which left him helpless by their very intensity. Pursuing great ends with few scruples about the means employed, he was subject at times to fits of remorse.

A character of marked contrasts, Henry II was a typical man of the Middle Ages and one of the most famous of contemporary kings.

Henry's chief work was the reorganization of the English government. Part of his work was merely that of restoration. The *curia regis,* the itinerant justices, and the exchequer, through which he accomplished his task, had been used by his grandfather. The parts of the English constitution which Henry originated were few. He seized upon powers which had been exercised by his predecessors only tentatively or spasmodically and made their application regular and normal, defined royal rights which had before been vague, increased systematically the royal authority by encroachment upon the powers of the barons, and employed the additional power thus acquired with ever greater efficiency because of the detailed improvements which he was constantly making in the governmental machinery. Henry was not a prolific legislator. He issued few laws, and they were largely in the nature of executive orders, giving directions to his subordinates. Some important changes in the working of the government were brought about apparently by nothing more than oral commands. But the changes which he wrought so informally had an abiding influence upon the English constitution. If Henry took stones which others had quarried, he chiseled them into new shapes and cemented them together into a foundation so durable that parts of it still stand. We owe it largely to him that we are governed by the common law and not by the Roman law, that we are tried by a jury and not by an inquisition. The result of his work which seems most to have impressed contemporaries was the enormous advance made in the centralization of the government. He became the most powerful king that England had yet seen. This served the popular welfare since strong monarchy was at that time the only source from which good government could come. The mass of the people as yet knew little of politics and were unfitted to govern themselves. If the king was weak, the feudal lords waxed strong; and what that signified was sufficiently demonstrated by the reign of Stephen. Henry may have been actuated primarily by his own personal interest, but his interest coincided with the popular welfare. The peace and order that replaced the anarchy of Stephen's reign, the impartial administration of equal justice to all, the suppression of the powers of the feudal nobility—all these reforms added to the royal authority, but they also worked to the advantage of the new nationality that was being formed by the fusion of Anglo-Saxon and Norman blood. Though Henry recognized little constitutional check upon his authority, he was not a tyrant. He used his powers in no spirit of wantonness, but ever for the broad ends of peace and justice. His government was a boon to the rank and file of his people, and wherever groups of English-speaking peoples today rule themselves, they have not yet ceased to derive benefit from it. As a statesman in his own day and generation Henry II deserves to rank among the foremost in the whole line of English kings.

In Henry's reign the sources of information become far more abundant. Of Henry's legislation less than a dozen pieces survive.[1] About his legal changes much may be found in a treatise on the law of England, written probably by Ralph Glanvill who was Henry's chief justiciar.[2] This work is in itself a notable indication of the development of legal knowledge in Engand. It was the first essay to treat scientifically the law of any country. Brief, crude, unsystematic compilations or commentaries were the most that had been attempted previously anywhere in Europe, except for the Roman and canon laws. The book is not only an important source for our information; in its day it was a popular textbook and so helped to unify English law and procedure and to produce a law common to all England. Another source unique in its nature is the "Dialogue concerning the Exchequer,"[3] written by Richard Fitz-Neal, the treasurer. In the form of a dialogue between master and pupil he set forth in detail the working of the financial department. Such a description of an administrative department of a medieval government as this is to be found nowhere else. The work of the exchequer and that of the justices is also illuminated by the pipe rolls,[4] the annual accounts of fiscal transactions kept by the exchequer. These, together with the writs, charters, letters, and other documents issued by Henry's chancery which have been preserved in scattered places, provide the bulk of our information about the constitutional development of the reign.

About other sides of the national life there is a wealth of material. At Henry's court literature and law went hand in hand. In the royal service were some of the most brilliant scholars of the epoch. Roger of Hoveden, the chronicler, and Walter Map, the writer of keen satire, were among the royal justices. Gilbert Foliot, bishop of London, and Peter of Blois, archdeacon of Bath, voluminous writers of letters on

Sources of information

---

[1] Most of them are translated by Adams and Stephens in *Select Documents*, nos. 13–19.

[2] *Tractatus de Legibus et Consuetudinibus Regni Angliae*. Translated by J. Beames.

[3] *Dialogus de Scaccario*. Translated by E. F. Henderson in *Select Historical Documents*.

[4] Most of those for the reign have been printed by the Pipe Roll Society. Only a few extracts have been translated. For these see Gross, *Sources*, pp. 421–422.

contemporary affairs in a polished Latin style, were often at court; and John of Salisbury, the foremost man of letters in Europe, was there at times, though not often in the royal service. The writing of history, too, was passing from the hands of monks into the hands of men of affairs. William of Newburgh was the notable exception. In his quiet monastery in the north of England he wrote a history covering the twelfth century which displays a high standard of critical judgment with regard to the value of evidence. The remaining important contemporary historians of the reign of Henry II belonged to the secular clergy and helped to determine the events of which they wrote.[5] The literary sources as well as the official documents supply a richness and a variety of material for the history of the reign which is of value not only for itself, but also for the indication it gives of the place occupied by scholars in English public life under the rule of Henry II.

For the first decade of his reign Henry's work in England was primarily that of restoration. His aim was to bring back as nearly as might be the good government and the good order of his grandfather's time. At a meeting of the great council, held almost immediately after his coronation, it was decreed that the Flemish mercenaries, who had been an element of disorder under Stephen, should be dismissed, and that castles built without the royal license should be destroyed. As a third part of the program Henry began to revoke royal grants of lands and offices made in Stephen's time. By 1158 these policies had been executed, and the independence which the barons had enjoyed for years past was at an end. Meanwhile Henry had not neglected the reorganization of the government. Soon after his accession he filled the offices of justiciar, treasurer, and chancellor with men who would help him to reconstruct the governmental machinery as it had been in his grandfather's time. The pipe roll of the second year of his reign displays the exchequer reorganized and at work and the itinerant justices again on circuit. Among the new officials none was more prominent than Thomas Becket, the chancellor. He was the son of a prosperous merchant of London. In his youth he attended English schools and later received some training at Paris and Bologna, where the most famous contemporary schools of philosophy and law were respectively located. His education had fitted him for administrative work, and, though he lacked the experience of the older officials, he was familiar with public affairs through his intimate association with

Restoration of order and good government

---

[5] Ralph de Diceto and Gerald of Wales were archdeacons who took part in public affairs. The valuable chronicle which goes under the name of Benedict of Peterborough probably was not written by him or by any other monk.

Theobald, archbishop of Canterbury. As chancellor he displayed such energy and ability in the transaction of public business that he soon became the king's most confidential adviser and trusted agent. The new government worked so well that Henry felt free after 1155 to spend most of his time for several years in his continental dominions. Thus complete success attended the attempt to reestablish a government sufficiently strong to hold in check the disruptive tendencies of feudalism.

Henry II and the church

Before Henry could wield an authority equal to his grandfather's, he had to deal with another opposing force. During Stephen's reign the English church had acquired an independence of royal control such as it had never before enjoyed. Stephen had secured the crown only with the aid of clerical supporters. He paid his debt by the issue of a charter granting to the church privileges which increased its independence of royal control. Though Stephen did not observe all of his promises, the general tendency in his reign was toward the increase of clerical authority. The English clergy, however, did not seek freedom from lay interference merely to exalt their own power; they wished to be more free to yield obedience to ecclesiastical law and papal decree. Bishops on more than one occasion even defied Stephen's commands in order to obey those of the pope. The papal party which originated among the clergy in the time of Anselm had grown into a strong minority. In the early years of the reign of Henry II the clergy did not exercise their increased power in such ways as to cause the new king to attempt to place a curb upon it. Many of the bishops, led by Archbishop Theobald, had supported him against Stephen in the closing years of the latter's reign, and after his accession no issue was raised between the royal and papal claims of authority over the clergy.

Although Henry took no action against the clerical estate in the early part of his reign, he became aware that such action must be taken sooner or later, if he was to fulfill his ambition to consolidate the royal power. The aspect of the increasing clerical power which seems most to have disturbed his legal mind was the jurisdiction of the ecclesiastical courts. A widely awakened zeal for the study of the Roman law produced throughout western Europe a keen interest in the administration of law. Nowhere did this translate itself into action more effectively than in the ecclesiastical courts. Between 1139 and 1142 Gratian, a monk and a teacher of law at Bologna, wrote an orderly and systematic treatise on the canon law, which shortly became known as the *Decretum*. Though Gratian's work was properly a textbook, because it was the first comprehensive survey of the field it came to have practically the value of a codification of the canon law. The work served on the one hand to stimulate the production of a large body of trained lawyers among the clergy, and on the other to define and sharpen the claims of jurisdiction made by the ecclesiastical courts. In England the new interest in canon law not only led to encroachment upon the fields of jurisdiction claimed by the lay courts, but also produced some grave abuses. Clergymen accused of crime were tried in the courts of the church, which could inflict no penalty involving the drawing of blood. Flagrant cases were brought to Henry's attention of clerks guilty of homicide who suffered no heavier penalty than loss of clerical status, fine, or brief imprisonment. It also caused an increase of appeals to the papal court which could not fail to weaken the royal authority.

Henry bided his time until Archbishop Theobald died in 1161. This event gave him the opportunity to place in the highest office in the English church a man who would be disposed to cooperate with him in his ecclesiastical policy, as Lanfranc had with William the Conqueror. Apparently with some such thought in mind, he designated Becket for the post. The king soon discovered that he had placed a wrong estimate on his chancellor. It was Becket's nature to throw himself unreservedly into whatever cause he espoused. Once archbishop, he championed the ecclesiastical cause with all the ardor he had previously displayed for affairs of state. The chancellor's office, which Henry had expected him to continue to hold, he resigned as incompatible with his new duties. When the king began the attempt to curtail the newly acquired powers of the clergy, Becket at once opposed him, and the fundamental question of the superiority of the spiritual to the temporal authority was soon at issue. The quarrel arose over the punishment of criminous clergymen.

Quarrel with Becket

After prolonged controversy between king and archbishop, the quarrel came to a head at a great council held at Clarendon in 1164. Henry, who claimed that his demands represented the ancient customs of the realm, produced a written statement of the customs which he wished the clergy to observe. The document is known as the Constitutions of Clarendon.[6] With regard to accused clergymen, it required that they should be impleaded before the king's court, tried before an ecclesiastical tribunal, and, if found guilty, turned over to the king's justices for punishment. The Constitutions, however, went beyond the original cause of the quarrel. They restated several of the limitations

Constitutions of Clarendon

---

[6] Translated in Adams and Stephens, *Select Documents*, no. 13.

placed upon clerical action by William the Conqueror, claimed jurisdiction for the king's courts over certain classes of cases which the
ecclesiastical forum sometimes tried to usurp, prohibited appeals from
English ecclesiastical courts to the papal court without the royal
consent, asserted the royal right to supervise and control the election of
bishops, and limited the clergy in several other particulars. With few
possible exceptions they represented fairly the customs of the time of
Henry I. From the point of view of the papal claims at that time the
Constitutions represented limitations upon the clerical power. Becket
made no attempt to deny that these were the ancient customs, opposing
them on the ground that secular laws, however ancient, were invalid
when they conflicted with ecclesiastical laws. After several days of debate, however, he gave way, promising to observe the ancient customs.
He seems to have had no intention of keeping his word when he gave
it, and later he obtained a dispensation from the pope, releasing him
from any part of his pledge which bound him to observe customs
conflicting with the liberties of the church. Certainly in practice Becket
did not observe the Constitutions, for he still resisted all attempts of the
king to bring clerics to justice before lay courts. After some months of
opposition he fled to France to escape the consequences of Henry's
anger.

The
murder of
Becket

Subsequently the two negotiated intermittently for six years.
Neither would give way on any essential point. Eventually, in 1170,
Henry met Becket in France and effected a reconciliation which entirely ignored the Constitutions of Clarendon. The archbishop had
no sooner returned to England than he excommunicated some of the
bishops who had taken the royal side in the controversy. The news of
this overt aggression, following immediately upon the reconciliation,
caused Henry to fall into a paroxysm of rage, in the course of which
he cursed the members of his household who, accepting his bounty,
would not avenge him upon this one priest. Four knights, who took
his words more seriously than they deserved, immediately crossed the
Channel, sought the prelate at Canterbury, and murdered him in the
cathedral. Becket served the cause for which he fought better in death
than in life. The shocked public opinion of Europe at once converted
him into a martyr and held the king in some measure responsible for
his death. Henry, in fear of excommunication, forestalled immediate
action by sending to the pope an embassy bearing his promise to
submit to the papal judgment in the matter, and by departing himself
to take part in the conquest of Ireland. In 1172 he made his peace
with the papal legates. By taking his oath that he had no share of

guilt for Becket's murder he was absolved from all sentences of ex-communication directed against Becket's opponents in general. He promised to allow appeals to the papal court, provided he might exact an oath that the parties to an appeal would not infringe upon the royal rights, and to end encroachments upon the liberties of the church introduced in his own time. The Constitutions of Clarendon, which were ancient customs, were not mentioned, and in practice the king was subsequently able to enforce some of their provisions. But the punishment of criminous clergymen he had to forego. For the remainder of the Middle Ages benefit of clergy, by which a clergyman accused of crime could claim trial and sentence in an ecclesiastical court,[7] remained a blot upon the administration of justice in England. In practice, moreover, appeals to the papal court were allowed and made so freely after 1172 that the papal authority in England, which the Constitutions of Clarendon had been designed to limit, became even more extensive than it had been during Stephen's weak reign. Henry met with only partial success in his effort to restrain the growing power of the clergy.

Meanwhile Henry had begun a series of important alterations in the functions of several organs of government. In the relations between the great council and the *curia regis* appeared the beginning of a change which was destined to have important results in time. Judicial business tended to go in ever-increasing amount to the *curia regis*. So much more judicial business was transacted by the central government in Henry's time, and the new forms of procedure rendered it so much more technical, that the judges had to know something more than ordinary laymen knew about the law. In the *curia regis* were several lawyers, trained to their profession, whereas the members of the great council were mostly laymen without special legal knowledge. The mass of litigation consequently drifted into the *curia regis*. Suits in which the interests of the king and the barons were involved continued to be tried before the great council. Other kinds of cases could come there, and sometimes did. Theoretically no distinction was drawn between the jurisdiction of the *curia regis* and the great council, but in practice the smaller body was attaining preeminence as a judicial organ. This was the beginning of a change which would eventually bring about a division of functions between the great council and the *curia regis*. In the reign of Henry II the drift in that direction was as yet barely perceptible.

The great council

---

[7] Eventually treason, on the one hand, and petty offenses, or misdemeanors, on the other, were placed outside its scope.

The *curia regis*

Within the *curia regis* began movements which were destined to end eventually in the breaking away from it of separate courts and administrative departments. In 1178 Henry selected five justices from the *curia regis* who were to do right in every suit. If any question arose too difficult for them to decide, it was to be turned over to the king to adjudicate with the aid of the other members of the *curia regis*. The five may be regarded as a committee of the *curia regis* appointed to transact the judicial business in order that the remaining members of the body might be free for other work, except when difficult cases arose. The establishment of this tribunal was a tentative step toward a set of royal courts which would be separate from the *curia regis*, though the final steps in the process of separation were not taken until later in the Middle Ages. The *curia regis* was also nearing a parting of the ways with the exchequer. Several of the principal officials of the royal household, who were prominent members of the *curia regis*, had in the exchequer no functions which could not be performed by their clerks. Not long after Henry's time most of the members of the *curia regis* ceased to sit in the exchequer, and the men who had been their clerks came to constitute the staff. Thus the exchequer became a separate organ of government.

Royal revenues

The mainstays of the royal revenue were still the income from the royal estates, the feudal incidents, and the profits of justice, which came in steadily year by year. They could be supplemented from time to time by extraordinary levies. One commonly used was the tallage. This was an arbitrary sum levied upon the boroughs and upon the tenants of the king's estates. Each borough or group of tenants paid a lump sum which was agreed upon in the case of each new levy by negotiation between their representatives and the king's agents, who were usually the itinerant justices.[8] The Danegeld, which William I had made a lucrative tax on land, fell into disuse under Henry; but scutage, which had been levied occasionally since at least as early as 1100, was imposed several times during the reign. Scutage was a payment from each knight's fee rendered by feudal tenants in lieu of their military service. Though it was a profitable source of income, it had as much constitutional as fiscal significance. With the income the king could hire mercenaries in place of the feudal array, making himself more independent of the feudal army. Still more important in

[8] Under other names such as *dona* and *auxilia*, Henry II extended levies akin to the tallage in principle to boroughs and rural districts not in the royal demesne, and to the clergy. This extension, however, seems to have had no permanent constitutional significance.

its constitutional significance was the taxation of personal property and income which began during the reign. In 1166 Henry decreed the payment by his subjects of a small tax upon their incomes and personal property in aid of the Holy Land. In 1188 the still more famous Saladin tithe was imposed for the same purpose. This was a tenth of the value of incomes and chattels, and on this occasion the estimates of the contributors could be revised by a local jury of their neighbors. These taxes constitute a landmark in the history of taxation. They signify that England was emerging from the economic stage where the basis of wealth was land. Only where commerce and industry exist is a tax on personal property profitable. In the course of the thirteenth century taxes proportioned to income and to the value of movables became one of the most lucrative sources of supply available to the royal exchequer. The use of the jury of the neighborhood for assessment was also a significant step. Henry had already used this method of valuation once in connection with the Assize of Arms issued in 1181. This was a law which aimed to reorganize the fyrd as an efficient fighting force. Every freeman was required to supply himself with arms and armor to an extent which varied with the value of his personal property. The value of each man's chattels was determined by a jury of his neighbors. This practice of the assessment of taxes by local juries received in later reigns a wider application which helped to prepare the way for popular participation in the government.

Those of Henry's reforms which were destined to have the most lasting results were made in judicial organization and legal procedure. The king's court extended its jurisdiction widely. It continued to be a tribunal for the trial of great men and great causes, of crown pleas, and of cases where justice had failed in the local courts. Its field of criminal jurisdiction was enlarged by extending the list of crown pleas, which could be tried only in the royal court, to include additional crimes. On the civil side business was increased by the extension of the writ process. Under the Norman kings occasionally a party to a suit was able to secure a royal writ ordering his case to be tried in the king's court, but this procedure was distinctly exceptional. Henry introduced a number of writs; each of which prescribed a specific form of judicial action. Any freeman having a suit which fell under one of these forms could obtain from the king by the payment of a certain sum the appropriate writ, which enabled him to secure the trial of his case before the king's court. These new writs provided for suits which

Jurisdiction of the king's court

might arise concerning the ownership[9] or possession of land, and the royal tribunal was thus thrown open to all freemen in a field of litigation of fundamental importance. The law it applied was better and the procedure it used was more rational than anything which could be found in local courts private or public. The king's court gave a surer justice. Naturally it became popular. Men seized eagerly the opportunity to get as a matter of right what before had been a royal boon granted only to the few, and the royal judicial business rapidly increased.

Itinerant justices

An institution which made the royal justice easier of access and supplemented the writ process was that of the itinerant justices. This was not Henry's invention any more than were many other parts of his judicial machine, but its thorough organization and its general and common application were his work. He gave to traveling justices the assured place in the English judicial system which they have occupied ever since. The regular use of the itinerant justices was productive of many advantages. It made the attainment of justice easier and surer for the people by bringing the king's court regularly to every county. It gave to the king a better check upon the sheriffs, who, like most local officials of the central government in the Middle Ages, were disposed to line their own pockets at the expense of the king's subjects. It helped to curtail the power of the barons in their feudal courts, because it contributed to the ultimate production of a single national judicature by the concentration of judicial powers in the king's hands. The system also promoted the attainment of self-government. The justices compelled the freeholders assembled in the county court to aid them in the transaction of the judicial and financial business of the crown. Through this involuntary experience the people learned to participate in the government. More important yet was the uniformity which it tended to give to the administration of the law. In the local courts a variety of customs and laws obtained. The itinerant justices spread throughout the land knowledge of the one set of legal principles used by the central courts. Eventually this legal system prevailed over the local sufficiently to justify its description as the common law. Nowhere else in Europe was there a similar state of affairs. In each province of France and Germany local custom prevailed, and in France and Germany a common law was obtained at last only by the adoption of the Roman law. In England a common law appeared much earlier

---

[9] This usage of "ownership" is held by some to be technically incorrect; but see Pollock and Maitland, *History of English Law*, ii, 2–1

than anywhere upon the continent, and it was English common law, a national common law.

The most important innovation effected by Henry was the introduction of the jury as a normal part of the legal procedure of the king's court. The principle of the jury was not new with him. The germ from which the institution grew was the sworn inquest. A group of neighbors were placed upon oath and required to answer some question which the government wanted answered truthfully. Some of the later Roman emperors used this method to establish locally certain rights of the imperial treasury. The procedure was probably borrowed from Rome by the Frankish kings, who often placed a group of men under oath and forced them to declare what lands in their district belonged to the crown, what wrongs the local royal officials had committed, or whatever else the royal government wished to know. From the Frankish kings the sworn inquest probably passed to the Norman dukes, and Duke William brought it to England. Soon after the conquest he began to use it in order to ascertain the royal rights, and Domesday Book is a monumental example of information derived from the answers to questions given by large numbers of sworn inquests or juries. William's Norman successors continued to employ juries commonly to establish their own fiscal and administrative rights. In a few instances they utilized a jury as a means of deciding a case in a court, but this practice was irregular and exceptional. Under the Normans, moreover, the jury remained, as it had been under the Frankish kings, a royal institution. None other than the king was entitled to use it except by royal permission. Henry II made the jury a regular part of the judicial procedure of the royal courts, and provided that in cases concerning the ownership or possession of land any freeman could have access to trial by jury as a matter of right. Trial by jury in such cases was no longer a matter of special royal favor. This is the innovation of Henry which causes historians to attribute to him the introduction of the jury as a part of English legal procedure. Even this transformation of the exceptional into the normal was not entirely original with him. Recently it has been established that Geoffrey, Henry's father, had made trial by jury freely accessible to the freemen of Normandy in certain classes of cases, when he had ruled the duchy in his son's name.[10] So far as England is concerned, Henry, by establishing the jury as the ordinary procedure in certain classes of cases, laid the foundation of our modern system of trial by jury. With-

Origin of the jury

[10] Haskins, *Norman Institutions*, ch. vi.

out this innovation the sworn inquest in England would never have developed into the modern jury; the instrument monopolized by royalty and the favored few would never have become the palladium of the liberty of the subject.

Henry used the jury in two forms. The antecedent of the modern grand jury was developed to secure a better enforcement of the criminal law. Henry discovered that many crimes went unpunished because none appeared before a court to lay a charge against the known or suspected perpetrators. Usually, in order to bring a criminal to trial, an accusation had to be lodged by an individual, and self-interest was proving to be a motive too weak to secure the suppression of crime. In the Assize of Clarendon (1166) the king ordered that there should be present at the session of the county court assembled to meet the itinerant justices, twelve men from each hundred, and four men from each vill in the county, who had inquired whether any man in the hundred or vill was commonly reputed to be a murderer, robber, or thief, or a receiver of such. Under oath the representatives from each vill presented the names of suspected persons to the twelve representing the hundred, and they presented the names to the justices. This was the accusing, presentment, or indictment jury. Those who were named by the jury were sent directly to trial by the ordeal of cold water. In other words, when the presentment jury was employed, it was substituted for all the preliminary procedure in the older form of trial, the judgment by the assembled suitors was eliminated, and the mode of proof to be applied was determined in advance.

The use of the presentment jury, though it was thus made general, remained under Henry II a royal prerogative. Only the king's courts could employ it. Moreover, a suspect accused by the jury could be tried only in the king's courts. The owner of a private court which had criminal jurisdiction could still try criminals located within the area of his jurisdiction, if they were caught in the act, or were self-confessed, or were impleaded by an individual who had been wronged; but he lost jurisdiction over criminals found within his lands, if they were accused by the presentment jury. The presentment jury, indeed, cut into the privileges of the holders of private jurisdiction in many ways. Men residing within the areas of such private jurisdictions who ordinarily owed no attendance at the court of the shire, and even the owners of privileged jurisdictions themselves had to come to the county court to meet the justices and take part in the work of the juries. When the jury had accused any person, the sheriff could enter private domains ordinarily immune from the visitation of royal officials, if such entrance should be necessary in order to effect an arrest. The presentment jury thus served to limit the powers of the barons in their private courts and to increase the royal authority. At the same time it helped on the one hand to maintain the order essential for the public welfare and on the other to protect individuals against frivolous or spiteful accusations. It is a particularly good example of the double character of most of Henry's constitutional reforms.

Trial by jury was utilized by Henry in certain new forms of legal actions, called assizes,[11] and during his reign its use remained confined almost entirely to the assizes. They were forms of judicial action used to decide a dispute over the ownership or possession of land. To [begin] such an action [it was] necessary to obtain a royal writ. In most [of these actions the] parties were [often] compelled to abide by the award of a jury, and in all of them the decision might be rendered by a jury. The assizes had several advantages. (1) No man could be compelled to defend the possession or the ownership of his freehold by judicial combat, since rational trial by means of a jury could always be had by the defendant who desired it; (2) no man could be dispossessed of his freehold without judgment; and (3) no man could lose his freehold by judgment, unless he had been summoned by a writ. The assizes served to protect the weak against the arbitrary action of the strong, and also to draw a large amount of litigation from the feudal into the royal courts.

In the time of Henry II trial by jury became a regular part of the judicial procedure only in the assizes. In other classes of cases it could still be used only exceptionally as a grant of royal favor. Accused criminals were still tried by the ordeal. The jury had such obvious advantages, however, that it could not fail to supplant the older modes of proof eventually. Its use in civil suits extended so rapidly that within a century the major portion of the field of civil actions in the king's courts was covered by trial by jury. Its extension to criminal trials was brought about by the action of the church. In 1215 a general council at Rome forbade priests to take part in ordeals, and without the solemn ceremonies conducted by the priest the ordeal was valueless.[12] English law temporarily hesitated. In 1219 the king ordered the justices going on circuit in that year to substitute the jury for the ordeal, but subsequently a theory that an accused person could not be

The assizes

Subsequent development of the jury

---

[11] *Assize* was used in the twelfth century with a variety of meanings. It seems most commonly to have been used to designate royal legislative enactments, and thence was transferred to the new forms of legal actions introduced by royal ordinances.

[12] Except judicial combat.

tried by jury except with his own consent cropped up. The obstacle was finally overcome by the invention of *peine forte et dure*. If the accused refused trial by jury, he was placed on the floor of his cell, and weights were piled upon him till he died or accepted trial by jury. By the end of the thirteenth century the jury had almost entirely superseded the ordeal, compurgation, and the other older modes of proof, though not until the end of the Middle Ages did they become obsolete in some of the local courts. Thereafter some of them lingered on in rare and exceptional cases, until they were formally abolished by legislation in the early part of the nineteenth century.

The advantages of the jury

The value of the contribution made to the development of the English constitution by Henry II, when he established the jury as a normal part of the judicial procedure, cannot be easily overestimated. The obvious advantage of the jury is the substitution of a verdict based upon human reason for one based upon chance. The jury was a mode of proof far more likely to result in a just decision than ordeal or compurgation. The jury, moreover, helped to prepare the way for representative government. It contained within itself in crude form the representative principle. The jurors represented their neighbors, and the decision of the jury was the voice of the neighborhood. It also served as a school of politics. The many men who were required to serve on juries received an insight into the king's business which prepared them for participation in public affairs. Finally, the jury, although it originated as an instrument of royalty, became the great protection of popular liberties.

CHAPTER VII

THE ANGEVIN EMPIRE

HENRY's enduring fame rests upon his work as king of England. Yet England was only a small part of the lands he ruled. From his mother he inherited Normandy and Maine, as well as England, and a claim to the overlordship of Brittany. From his father he inherited Anjou and Touraine. In 1152 he married Eleanor, heiress of the duchy of Aquitaine. With her hand he acquired the right to rule the vast territory which stretched from the Loire to the Pyrenees and from the Atlantic nearly to the Rhone. Before he became king of England he controlled more than half of France. As king of England he could claim a more or less effective suzerainty over the larger part of Wales, and during his reign he established a nominal suzerainty over Scotland. In the middle years of his reign some of his Norman-English vassals won a foothold in eastern and southern Ireland, which enabled him to call his son John "lord of Ireland." Aside from the emperor, whose authority was actually or theoretically acknowledged in Germany, Provence, and the northern half of Italy, no European ruler had under his sway anything like so great a sweep of territory.

So vast were the dominions of Henry II that modern writers have fallen into the habit of calling them an empire. They were imperial, however, only in size. In no other sense did they constitute an empire. The different parts of Henry's lands did not form provinces of a single state, nor were all dependent upon a single government. Such authority as Henry exercised in Wales came from his English kingship, and practically that was the source of his authority in Ireland; but he ruled Normandy, Maine, Anjou, Touraine, and Aquitaine each by a separate and independent feudal title. The peoples of these different territories had no common bond other than that of having a common ruler given to them by the accidents of birth and marriage. The inhabitants of Aquitaine differed in racial stock from the men of Anjou and Normandy and they spoke a language hardly more like that of northern France than the tongue of Angevin or Norman was like that of Englishmen. Culturally and economically there were similar diversities in their development. The union of these peoples under one ruler did not violate the principle of nationality because the national feeling did not yet exist, but it lacked any strong cohesive

Henry's dominions

force. The so-called Angevin empire was in fact a strange bundle of heterogeneous and conflicting interests.

The affairs of his French possessions occupied more than half of Henry's time while he was king of England. Ordering the government of one after the other, reducing refractory vassals to submission, and fighting or negotiating for possession of the lordship of fiefs such as Brittany and Toulouse, whose holders desired to acknowledge other lords or no lord at all, filled his days across the Channel with activities not directly pertinent to English history. Henry's relations to his lord, the king of France, however, affected England in important though indirect ways. Though he held his French lands as the vassal of the king of France, the concentration of so much territory in the hands of one vassal was a menace to the authority of the French crown. Henry, moreover, in his capacity as duke of Normandy, inherited a feud with the Capetian kings which had stood since the time of William the Conqueror. Louis VII, the French king, lacking the energy and the resources necessary to wage open war, for a long time contented himself with stirring up Henry's vassals to make trouble for their lord. Only in the closing years of his reign did he begin a mode of attack, which his son, Philip Augustus, was able to carry to a successful conclusion. His new plan was to play the members of Henry's family one against another.

Henry had four legitimate sons who attained manhood. In the order of their age they were Henry, Richard, Geoffrey, and John. Henry had for his sons a deep affection, but his failure as a father was as notable as his success as a king. He "could rule every house but his own."[1] The strong hand with which he restrained his barons was never placed upon his sons. They were spoiled as children and they grew up to become unfilial, selfish, and unruly men. Henry desired to have the inheritance of his dominions arranged during his lifetime. In 1170 he had Henry, the eldest, crowned as his successor in England. Already he had designated him as the heir to Normandy, Anjou, and Maine. He assigned Brittany to Geoffrey to hold of his brother Henry, and Aquitaine to Richard to hold directly of the French king. John, who was only five, had no share in these arrangements and so acquired the appellation of "Lackland." By this division Henry intended merely to indicate how his lands should be divided at his death. He would not risk their unity during his lifetime by giving to his sons real authority in the government of the territories with which he associated

The marginal notes read:

Henry II and the king of France

Henry's sons

---

[1] Haskins, *Normans in European History*, p. 118.

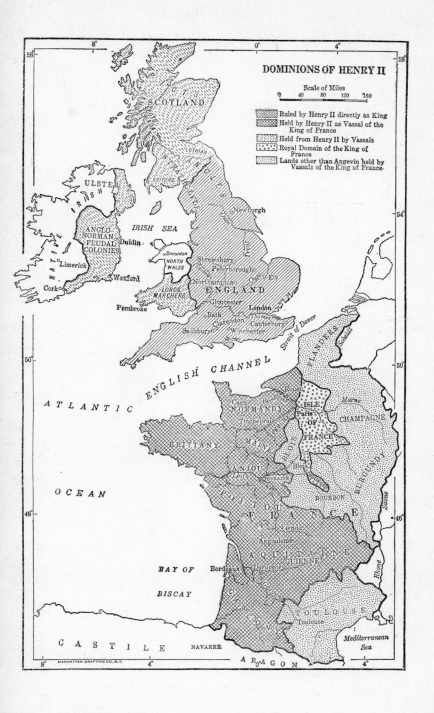

DOMINIONS OF HENRY II

Scale of Miles
0   40   80   120   160

▨ Ruled by Henry II directly as King
▨ Held by Henry II as Vassal of the King of France
▨ Held from Henry II by Vassals
▨ Royal Domain of the King of France
▨ Lands other than Angevin held by Vassals of the King of France

SCOTLAND

LOTHIAN

BRITONS

ULSTER

IRISH

NATIVE

ANGLO-NORMAN FEUDAL COLONIES

Dublin

Limerick

Cork

Wexford

Pembroke

IRISH SEA

Snowdon
NORTH WALES

LORDS MARCHERS

Newburgh

Shrewsbury
Peterborough
Northampton
Ely
ENGLAND
Gloucester
Bath
Clarendon
Salisbury
Winchester
Canterbury
London

Strait of Dover

ENGLISH CHANNEL

ATLANTIC

OCEAN

NORMANDY
Caen
Tinchebrai

BRITTANY

MAINE

ANJOU

POITOU

Loire

TOURAINE

Vienne

Angoulême

AQUITAINE
GUIENNE

Bordeaux

Dordogne

BAY OF

BISCAY

GASCONY

FLANDERS

Scheldt

Rouen

ISLE OF FRANCE
Paris

CHAMPAGNE

Marne

Blois

BOURBON

BURGUNDY

Saône

F R A N C E

Rhone

TOULOUSE
Toulouse

Mediterranean Sea

CASTILE   NAVARRE

ARAGON

MANHATTAN DRAFTING CO., N.Y.

them. His sons were not disposed to live quietly as princes without power. They chafed under restrictions and became eager listeners to the many who had grievances against their father. Their mother, Eleanor, who had long since quarreled with Henry, stirred them to revolt, as did likewise Louis VII. Every dissatisfied baron saw in the restless and undutiful sons an opportunity to strike at the father. One after another Henry's sons rebelled against him. By contemporaries the turbulent offspring were known as "the lion's brood," and Geoffrey openly boasted that "it is our proper nature, planted in us by inheritance from our ancestors, that none of us should love the other, but that ever brother should strive against brother and son against father."[2]

The first rebellion came in 1173. The oldest son fled to the court of his father-in-law, Louis VII, where he was joined by Geoffrey and Richard, and a well-organized rebellion broke out simultaneously in England and in Normandy. The barons on both sides of the Channel joined in large numbers, hoping to shake themselves free from the limitations placed upon them by the old king's régime of law and order. The king of France, with the aid of two of his strongest tenants-in-chief, attacked Normandy, and the king of Scotland invaded England on the north. The rebellion, which drew together a formidable coalition of Henry's principal enemies, for a short time bade fair to overwhelm him. He was saved by the loyal support of the middle classes, who preferred a continuation of the even-handed justice and the orderly government of a strong king to the repetition of the violence and feudal anarchy sure to follow the success of the rebellion. The outcome was a triumphant vindication of the quality of Henry's rule, for only the loyalty of the classes which had benefited the most from it saved the king from defeat.

The rebellions

Though his English subjects did not again rebel, his troubles with his sons did not cease. After 1181 they took up arms against their father on several occasions. After 1186 they had the help of Philip Augustus, who had succeeded Louis VII on the throne a few years before. He was one of the ablest and most astute kings of medieval France. His dominating purpose was to centralize the French monarchy, and the chief obstacle in the path of his ambition was the Angevin empire. Philip was plotting with Geoffrey against Henry, when Geoffrey's death terminated the conspiracy. Subsequently he won Richard to his side. In the summer of 1189 the two defeated

[2] Cited by Green, *Henry II*, p. 209.

Henry in Anjou. The old king, so ill that he could hardly bestride a horse, met them in conference and granted their demands. From this, the greatest humiliation of his life, Henry betook himself to his couch to die. His last hours were rendered still more bitter by the knowledge that John, the one son whom he had believed true, had been engaged with Philip and Richard in the conspiracy against him.

Henry II
and the
British
Isles
outside
England

To the affairs of the British Isles outside of England Henry devoted comparatively little attention; nevertheless he extended his authority more widely than had any previous English king. From the king of Scotland he obtained an unequivocal render of homage, in Wales he maintained all that his predecessors had acquired, and he began the conquest of Ireland. To put these events in their proper setting, it is necessary to review briefly the earlier relations between England and the other parts of the British Isles.

Wales:
1. Anglo-
Saxon
period

During the Anglo-Saxon period the relations between the Celts of Wales and the Anglo-Saxons were generally hostile. In the course of the fighting back and forth across the border, which was more or less perpetual, the Celts had their eastern frontier pushed back permanently some miles to the west of the middle Severn, but they maintained their independence. The acknowledgment of supremacy won from the Welsh princes by the strong kings who united England in the tenth century seems to have been no more than nominal. The Anglo-Saxons made no attempt to conquer Wales for settlement. In 1066 the institutions of the Welsh were still purely Celtic, and there appears to have been little admixture of Anglo-Saxon blood on the Welsh side of the boundary.

2. Nor-
man
period

With the coming of the Normans the relations between England and Wales changed decisively. The Norman lords who settled in the west of England began to conquer southern and central Wales as a private venture. They were aided by the wars and antagonisms among the several principalities and kingdoms into which Wales was divided. Each Norman invader built himself a castle from which he could dominate the surrounding countryside, and the basis for an intermixture of population and culture was thus established. The movement went so far that in the reign of William Rufus it stimulated the Welsh to more united resistance. The Red King and Henry I each made several expeditions to Wales to subdue the native Welsh and to sustain the marcher lords, as these Norman adventurers were called. By the end of the reign of Henry I the marchers were well established on the southern and the eastern slopes of the Welsh mountains. Though they acknowledged allegiance to the English kings, they were largely independent. The power of the southern Welsh, however, was completely broken, and many of their chieftains did homage to the English king after the example of their Norman neighbors. In northern Wales, on the other hand, in a district mainly on the western slope of the mountains, centering around Snowdon, the Welsh remained practically independent under native princes.

When Henry II came to the throne, the situation had altered somewhat in favor of the Welsh. The disorder of Stephen's reign had enabled the princes of South Wales to gain power at the expense of the marcher lords, and the independent Welsh of the north had expanded their territory and increased their strength. Henry made three expeditions to Wales. Though none of them was attended with any signal success, they sufficed to secure nominal homage from the prince of North Wales and to restore the royal authority in South Wales.

3. Henry II

At the close of the Anglo-Saxon conquest the land which we now call Scotland was divided into four kingdoms. North of the Forth, occupying most of the highlands, was the kingdom of the Picts, who spoke Celtic; in the western part of the highlands, centering around the firth of Lorne, was the small kingdom of the Scots, who were Celtic immigrants from Ireland; to the south, holding the estuary of the Clyde and extending beyond Solway Firth was the kingdom of Strathclyde, inhabited by Celts who were closely related to the Celts of Wales; and south of the Forth and east of Strathclyde was land belonging to the Anglo-Saxon kingdom of Northumbria. During most of the seventh century the king of Northumbria bade fair to establish a hegemony over all the other kingdoms, but in 685 the Picts ended that possibility by the decisive defeat of the forces of Northumbria.[3] In the ninth century the king of the Scots secured authority over the Picts; in 1018 the king of these joint peoples[4] defeated the Northumbrians at Carham and annexed the Anglo-Saxon district of Lothian north of the Tweed permanently to Scotland; and in the same year this king established control of Strathclyde, thus completing the political union of northern Britain. Meanwhile the powerful Anglo-Saxon kings of the tenth century had obtained from the kings of the joint kingdom of the Scots and the Picts on several occasions an acknowledgment of superiority, and in 1031 Canute apparently se-

Scotland· 1. Anglo-Saxon period

---

[3] At the battle of Nectansmere. Ecgfrith, the invading Northumbrian king, was killed on the field.

[4] Malcolm II, 1005–1034.

cured a similar admission from the king of the consolidated kingdom of Scotland. What relationship was established legally by these acts it is impossible to say, since feudalism with its clearly defined bond of lord and vassal was not yet known in the British Isles. Actually the superiority was in name only; it gave the kings of England no real authority in the affairs of Scotland; and it appears in each instance to have been temporary in duration. It was during the early years of the united Scotland that Macbeth reigned. He acquired the throne in 1040 by killing King Duncan under circumstances which are not known. Though Shakespeare has made it difficult to believe, contemporaries appear to have regarded him as a good ruler. He was defeated in 1054 by the earl of Northumbria in the battle when Birnam Wood came to Dunsinane, but the earl bought the victory so dearly that he was forced to retire without the accomplishment of any objective, and Macbeth lived for another three years to be slain by Malcolm, the son of Duncan.

2. Norman period

When the battle of Hastings was fought, Malcolm III (1057-1093) was still the king of Scotland. Before he came to the throne, he had acquired English culture during a long residence at the court of Edward the Confessor, and in 1068 he married Margaret, a descendant of the royal house of Wessex. Thus was introduced into Scotland an English influence. One of the important results was a shift of the center of influence in Scotland from the Celtic north to the Anglo-Saxon Lothian, a transference which laid the foundation for the domination of the Celtic highlands by the Teutonic lowlands. Malcolm was ruled by an ambition to extend the boundary south of the Tweed. To further this end he not only made expeditions across the border, but he also gave support and refuge to the Anglo-Saxons who opposed William the Conqueror in the north. In 1072 William invaded Scotland and demanded an accounting. Malcolm appeased him by becoming his man. Whether he did homage for Scotland or only for estates in England which William granted him at the time is a hotly debated question, not settled by contemporary sources. Certainly he allowed his action to place no limitation upon him in practice, for he later continued the attempt to conquer Northumberland. Nor did a similar act of homage to William Rufus put an end to his invasions. Malcolm failed, however, to win any English territory, and in 1092 he lost Cumberland to William Rufus. Henry I rendered relations friendly by marrying Matilda, the sister of the king of Scotland. The dynastic relationship thus established later brought the king of the

Scots into a conflict with Stephen, which ended with the cession of three northern English counties[5] to Scotland.

The policy of Henry II with regard to Scotland was strong and unscrupulous. Though he had agreed to confirm Stephen's grant of the three counties if he should become king, he recovered them early in his reign by threatening war when the king of Scotland was fully occupied with internal rebellion. In 1173, when the king of Scotland joined the rebels against Henry, he was captured. To gain his freedom he agreed to hold Scotland as a vassal and to allow his vassals to render liege homage to the English king as their suzerain. Scotland thus became without equivocation a fief held of the English crown. Moreover, an appreciable Norman influence was making itself felt in Scotland. Already a number of Normans had acquired fiefs in Scotland and positions of influence in the court and army of the Scottish king. The relations established between England and Scotland during the reign of Henry II presented the outward appearance of a connection which might easily have been rendered closer in the course of time; but, as the event proves, either the appearance was deceitful, or Henry's successors on the English throne failed to utilize the opportunity.

3. Henry II

The early development of Ireland shows a decided contrast to that of England. When the light of history dawns, the land was inhabited by Celts who possessed a culture similar in its main characteristics to that of the Celts in Britain. Though the Romans did not conquer Ireland, the Irish had some contact with Roman civilization, for before the fifth century there appear to have been some Christians in the island. In the fifth century St. Patrick converted practically the whole population, and in the same period many scholars seem to have fled before the barbarian invasions from Gaul to Ireland. Subsequently learning and piety progressed hand in hand to a high stage of development. While culture was being destroyed generally in western Europe by the ravages of the barbarians, the undisturbed quiet of Ireland gave opportunity for Christianity and learning to flourish. The harvest was such as only a virgin soil could produce. From the sixth to the ninth century Ireland occupied a place of such preeminence in the religious and intellectual life of Europe that it was known as the "island of saints and scholars." Irish missionaries in this period established the church in Scotland, whence Aidan carried Christianity to Northumbria. They also founded monasteries and spread the faith in many parts of the continent. Irish scholars, too, appeared in many parts of

Ireland: 1. Early development

---

[5] I.e., Northumberland, Cumberland, and Westmorland.

Europe, while many foreigners came to Ireland to study. During the ninth and tenth centuries, however, Irish civilization suffered from the blight of the Danish invasions to such an extent that it never recovered. There was no intellectual revival in Ireland comparable to that which took place in England after the Norman conquest.

The political development of Ireland did not keep pace with the intellectual growth. The tribe and the clan were at the basis of the Irish organization, as they were everywhere among the Celts. As far back as tradition goes, there were five to seven kings, each of whom ruled practically independently, although one of the number usually enjoyed the title of great king. There were, however, many score of lesser kings and chieftains, who were nominally dependent upon the principal kings. The extreme decentralization of the political organization led to endless tribal rivalries and wars. Before the pressure of the Danes political unity was nearly attained under one leader; but when the victories, which cost him his life in 1014, put an end to the immediate danger of further invasion, the intertribal and intratribal warfare became worse than ever.

Economically Ireland was poor. Grazing was the principal industry. The bogs, forests, and mountains were so extensive that native agriculture often did not produce sufficient grain to feed the population. Such commerce as existed was in the hands of the Danes, who had settled principally in a few ports on the eastern and southern coasts. They carried the hides and furs of Ireland to foreign ports and brought back the grain and other articles which Irishmen desired. Without natural advantages for industry and situated at the verge of the known world, Ireland was naturally backward in its economic development.

2. Henry II When Henry II came to the throne, Ireland seemed to supply an easy opening for the satisfaction of his youthful ambition to wage wars of conquest. Intellectually far behind the rest of Europe, weak in resources, and rent by internal dissensions, Ireland seemed to be marked as the prey of the conqueror. Henry acted as William the Conqueror had done under similar circumstances; he sought and obtained the approval of the pope for his expedition. In 1155 he went so far as to broach the subject of an Irish expedition at a meeting of the great council, but subsequently he put the project aside for other business.

The initiative in the conquest of Ireland was finally taken by Henry's subjects. In 1166 one of the principal kings of Ireland was defeated by a coalition of the others and forced to flee. He sought the help of Henry to recover his throne. Though Henry could not go himself, he authorized the petitioner to approach his Anglo-Norman barons.

Richard of Clare, earl of Pembroke, who is generally known as Strongbow, was finally induced to seek the repair of his fortunes in Ireland. Once committed to the enterprise, he easily enlisted lieutenants and troops from among the adventurous Norman population of the Welsh marches. In 1169 the first contingent landed in Ireland. The Irish armies, badly equipped and poorly disciplined, were no match for the Norman troops, and by 1171 the conquest of a strip of territory extending from Dublin to Cork was practically complete. At this point Henry intervened to prevent the establishment of an independent Norman kingdom in Ireland. His hurried visit served rather to assert his authority over the lands already won than to extend the conquest. In the district actually occupied by the English, which subsequently was called the Pale, he established some royal garrisons, gave out earldoms and fiefs to the conquerors, and appointed a justiciar to rule all in the king's name. Before he had completed his plans for administrative organization, he left Ireland, and shortly afterward the royal garrisons were withdrawn. The king's justiciars had such slight authority that the Norman barons were left largely free to pursue their own devices without centralized control. They forthwith conquered, plundered, and destroyed as suited their individual capacities and desires, but, because they could not unite, they could not give good government to the lands they won, nor could they extend greatly the limits of the Pale. In 1177 Henry designated his son, John, lord of Ireland, and in 1185 sent him to his new domain to finish the conquest and to organize the government. John failed to accomplish either task and was soon recalled. So there was left in Ireland a group of Normans, vassals of the king of England but practically free from his control, too small to finish the conquest, organize the government, and spread Norman civilization throughout the country, and yet too powerful to be expelled by the Irish. The result was long-continued strife, which rendered Ireland even more turbulent than before and sowed the seeds of the bountiful crop of hatred which England has not yet ceased to reap.

On the death of Henry II in 1189, Richard, his oldest surviving son, succeeded him without question. Richard was far less of a statesman than his father, finding his chief delight in deeds of war. Brave, reckless, and impetuous, he was a happy-go-lucky person to whom was particularly applicable the contemporary jest about the men of his house: "From the devil we came, to the devil we go." He occupied himself almost exclusively with continental affairs. He cared so little for England that, during his reign of ten years, he visited his island realm only twice. Each visit was of only a few months' duration and

Richard I and England

each visit had for its object the acquisition of money to finance his continental projects. The government of England was left in the hands of his ministers. Since many of them had learned their statecraft in the school of Henry II, the government continued to function in the main without notable alteration. Yet the basis for a change began to be laid in Richard's reign. Though the government remained the same outwardly, public opposition was significantly voiced on several occasions. The advantages of strong government could not be had without attendant burdens. The weight of taxation, which was sufficient to cause much grumbling in the last years of Henry's reign, grew steadily heavier. During Richard's reign the burden of taxation and the feeling of dissatisfaction with his ministers gradually created between the barons and other classes in the community a bond of sympathy which had not existed in the preceding reign. Richard's very absence tended to work a decrease in the power of the crown.

The third crusade

When Richard came to the throne he was already pledged to go on the third crusade. The Latin kingdom of Jerusalem, which had been established in 1099 by the first crusade, was overwhelmed by the Turks in 1187. News of this disaster to the Christian cause stirred the European public to such a pitch of sentiment that it responded readily to a papal call to arms. Early in 1188 Henry II, Richard, and Philip Augustus, in the presence of a papal legate and before a large assembly of their nobles, took the cross. At the conclusion of the war among them, Richard prepared to fulfill his vow. He arrived in the Holy Land in 1191, and soon became the foremost leader of the crusaders. His deeds of valor and his military exploits won him great fame, but they did not recover Jerusalem. Gradually the truth was forced upon him that the recovery was impossible with the forces at his disposal. Late in 1192 he started for home.

Richard's return

Richard's adventures did not end with his departure from Syria. Because he knew that Philip Augustus was plotting with John against him, he feared to land in France. Instead he disembarked at the head of the Adriatic and traveled overland. While passing through the lands of the duke of Austria, whose enmity he had incurred on the crusade, he was apprehended and placed in captivity by the duke. On the demand of his overlord, the emperor, who also had a grudge against Richard, the duke transferred the prisoner to his keeping. The emperor demanded a heavy ransom, which Richard's agents endeavored to raise by the taxation of his English subjects in 1193. Philip and John were trying to purchase Richard's prolonged captivity, but

Richard outbid them. Early in 1194, when a substantial part of the ransom had arrived, he was released.

What effects the crusade had upon England it is difficult to estimate rightly. It was the first time England had supplied a leader of the crusades, and the story of the deeds of their king brought to Englishmen a natural glow of pride. It was also the first time that any large group of Englishmen had taken part in one of these European ventures, and subsequently Englishmen took a larger share in the movement. The principal effects of the crusades upon European civilization were indirect and the most important of them were intangible. Rarely can one seize upon definite things, such as windmills, and say that they were introduced into western Europe by the crusaders. New ideas were the principal fruits of the crusades garnered by the westerners. Men from many sections of Europe were thrown together as they traveled through many lands. They brought back stories of the new things they had observed, and the new tastes they had acquired gradually spread among the people who had remained at home. The interchange of ideas promoted the advancement of civilization in many ways. Commerce and finance, for example, were stimulated. The example and the information of those who returned from the crusades increased the demand in the west for eastern goods. Money circulated more rapidly. Taxes were levied to finance the expeditions, voluntary contributions were large, and the crusaders had to convert much of their personal property into cash and to borrow money in order to equip themselves. Much money and bullion that had been hoarded were brought into circulation, and greater rapidity of circulation always quickens commerce. On learning, too, the crusades had a similar indirect influence. The people who took the journey usually had an intellectual awakening as the result of their experiences. As they came back, they imparted some of their new points of view to those who had remained at home. The intellectual horizon of Europe was necessarily widened. Yet the expansion of commerce and the intellectual development which took place in Europe contemporaneously with the crusades were both under way before the crusades began. It is as impossible to estimate the extent of the stimulus given by the crusades to movements already initiated, as it is to doubt that the crusades produced such a stimulus in some measure. England shared in the common store of such results, but since they were of a kind that might have come to her shores indirectly through the medium of contact with the peoples of France, Germany, and Italy, it is useless to surmise what

England and the crusades

precise part the direct participation of Englishmen in the third crusade had in the production of the general result.

Wars with Philip Augustus

When Richard finally returned to England, he tarried only for the few months necessary to raise money for the war which he had planned to wage for the defense of his possessions in France. During the period of his captivity Philip Augustus had secured the active alliance of John, whom he had enfeoffed with Normandy. John attempted to start rebellions against Richard, but in Normandy he had no support and in England his followers were so few that their incipient rebellion was quelled by the regents before Richard's return. Philip's attempt to invade Normandy had been hardly more successful, although he had acquired a few of the fortresses on the border. Richard pardoned John with contemptuous magnanimity, and in May of 1194 left England, never to return. For the remaining five years of his life he kept up an intermittent war with Philip without decisive results. In 1199 he met his death through the infection of a wound received in combat.

John and the loss of Normandy

Richard's death left the succession to his possessions in some doubt. If the principle of primogeniture had been strictly applied, Arthur, the young son of John's older brother Geoffrey, would have been the legal heir. But the rule was not yet established, and in Normandy feudal custom favored the uncle as a nearer heir than the nephew. John secured the adherence of the Norman barons and was crowned king of England without dissent. In Brittany, Anjou, and Maine, however, Arthur had much support, and Philip accepted his homage and became his guardian. Since John refused to give up his claim to these fiefs, the war begun originally between Philip and Richard continued between Philip and John. Philip, however, had his attention so diverted by a quarrel with the pope that, in 1200, he made a treaty with John. By its terms John was acknowledged as heir to all of the fiefs which Richard had held, and Arthur did homage to John for Brittany. John surrendered only the small territories along the borders of Normandy and Aquitaine which Philip had won from Richard.

John displayed some ability in taking advantage of the situation in these early dealings with his adversary, but he was incapable of holding his own in a prolonged conflict with the astute Philip Augustus. John was easily the worst of the Angevins. He had the vices and meannesses of his house, unredeemed by its virtues. Licentiousness and cruelty were not uncommon characteristics in the men of his family, but John evinced them in an uncommon degree. Others, too, had been false, but none so false as John. He was capable of sudden bursts of energy, but he could not follow out any plan which required sustained effort.

Still worse, his sense of morality was deficient. He not only was guided by low ethical standards, but he often did not comprehend the moral point of view of others. With such mental and moral equipment, he was almost certain, sooner or later, to give the advantage to Philip, who had merely postponed the fulfillment of his ambition. Within a few months of the signature of the treaty John had provided Philip with a perfect *casus belli* from the standpoint of feudal law.

Late in 1199 John secured the annulment of his marriage. He then despatched an embassy to negotiate for the hand of a Portuguese princess. Before its return, he became enamored of Isabella of Angoulême, the daughter of one of his vassals in Poitou. Isabella was already betrothed to Hugh the Brown, another of John's Poitevin vassals, and such a precontract was then held to be nearly as binding as the contract of marriage itself. With the consent of her father, however, John married Isabella regardless of the rights of his vassal. By this act John violated his moral obligation as lord of Hugh the Brown, who appealed to the court of his overlord, the king of France. In 1202 Philip summoned John to appear before his court to answer the charges against him. John, urging one excuse after another, failed to appear. The court therefore adjudged him to have forfeited his French fiefs for failure to perform his service as vassal. Philip promptly renewed the war in order to execute the sentence.

The war went steadily against John, who remained strangely inactive. Once he threw off his sloth long enough to rescue his mother, Eleanor of Aquitaine, who was besieged by Arthur, and to capture her besiegers. John's cruel treatment of these prisoners alienated some of his supporters. When the rumor spread that he had brought young Arthur to his death, the Bretons and the Angevins turned against him. The first rumor was probably false, but before the end of 1203 Arthur appears to have been murdered by John, or at his instigation. Many of the barons of Poitou had been thrown into opposition by John's treatment of Hugh the Brown, and during 1203 treason became rife among his Norman barons. John had ruined his own cause. Philip meanwhile was steadily advancing into Normandy, practically without opposition. At the end of 1203 John left for England, and in the course of 1204 Philip secured complete control of Normandy. Anjou, Maine, and Brittany already acknowledged his allegiance; Touraine was conquered next; and then he proceeded against Poitou. Here his progress stopped. The most of Poitou was occupied easily, but the stubborn resistance of the remainder decided Philip to give up the attempt to advance farther. The independent vassals of southern France, because they believed that the rule of Angevin lords, who would generally be absent, would be milder than that of the Capetians, remained faithful to John. In 1205 Aquitaine, except part of Poitou, was left in John's possession; the remainder of the Angevin holdings in France had been lost.

The loss of his French possessions was a blow to John's prestige. To England as a whole it was a gain, since Englishmen had been heavily taxed to pay for the defense of these French lands from which they received no corresponding benefits. The barons who had possessions both in Normandy and in England were forced to give up their French or their English fiefs. Those who remained in England generally received compensation from the crown for their losses in Normandy. This settlement tended to weaken the power of the crown. The barons, who had previously been as much French as English in their interests, henceforth had only an English horizon. As they took more interest in their English rights, their dissatisfaction with the strength of the English monarchy grew proportionately. The loss of Normandy was one of the causes contributory to the production of the Great Charter.

BRITISH ISLES
PLACES NAMED IN TEXT

Scale of Miles
0   20   40   60   80   100

CHAPTER VIII

THE KING AND THE BARONS

The reign of John may be divided conveniently into three chronological parts. From 1199 to 1205 interest centers primarily in the contest with Philip Augustus; from 1205 to 1213 the dramatic struggle with the pope occupies the center of the stage; and the years from 1213 to 1216 are chiefly important for the production of the Great Charter. The quarrel with the pope grew out of a contested election to the archbishopric of Canterbury held in 1205. When this office became vacant, it had been customary, since the settlement of the quarrel between Henry I and Anselm, for the election of a successor to take place only with the consent of the king. The election was made by the cathedral chapter, and at recent elections the bishops of the province had participated. The monks, who constituted the cathedral chapter of Canterbury, desired to avoid the dictatorial influence of the king and the intervention of the bishops, who had no canonical right to share in the ceremony. A group of the younger monks, therefore, secretly elected a successor and despatched him to Rome to seek the pallium from the pope. Their candidate indiscreetly boasted of his new honor. When the news leaked out, the monks tried to protect themselves by seeking from John, in the customary form, permission to hold an election. At the second election they chose a candidate named by John. A messenger was forthwith sent to Rome to obtain papal approval.

The pope who was thus confronted with two candidates for the archbishopric was Innocent III. He did more, perhaps, than any other pope of the Middle Ages to exalt the power of the vicars of Christ on earth. He was not the pope to let slip the opportunity presented by the disputed election to advance the papal authority. He declared both elections uncanonical and persuaded those monks of Canterbury who were present at Rome to elect Stephen Langton, an English cardinal, to fill the vacancy thus created. The archbishop-elect was a noted scholar and an eminent theologian, who was in every way fitted for the office; but his election violated the custom by which the king controlled the choice of bishops. John refused to accept him as archbishop, confiscated the archiepiscopal estates, and expelled the monks of Canterbury. Innocent replied in 1208 by imposing the sentence of interdict upon England. It suspended public services in the churches

The election to Canterbury

Interdict and excommunication

and deprived the people of some of the most important sacraments. John did not receive the sentence supinely. He confiscated the property of many of the clergy who obeyed the interdict, supplying them with a dole barely sufficient for their subsistence. Some of the clergy gave way, but a sufficient number obeyed the pope to make the strain of the interdict severely felt by laymen. Yet they offered no serious, open opposition to the king. So strong was the Angevin monarchy that the dread decree, which a few years earlier had brought Philip Augustus to terms, failed to move John from his course. When Innocent III found that the interdict was insufficient for his purpose, he excommunicated the king. The sentence not only severed him from communion with the church and damned his soul if he died before it was removed, but it also threatened with the same penalties those who associated with him. Had it been obeyed, the wheels of government must perforce have stopped. John, however, had prepared for the threatened sentence in advance. From the barons whose support he feared might be lost, he had exacted sons or daughters as hostages for their loyalty, and from all freemen he had required a renewal of homage or fealty. When the sentence was issued, he made a terrible example of a clerk in his service, who left for fear of the peril in which continued association with the king would involve his soul. John had him placed in prison and crushed to death beneath a heavy weight. By such expedients he held the support of the nation. The excommunication failed, as had the interdict, to bring the triumph which Innocent III desired.

John, however, was rapidly undermining his own position. The fiscal impositions which had aroused opposition under Richard became more frequent and more burdensome under John. Had John given the same justice as his father, his government would nevertheless have been regarded by his subjects as more oppressive than Henry's, but he substituted his arbitrary and capricious will for justice. In the royal forests where many people lived, he ordered the destruction of hedges and ditches to facilitate his hunting, although they protected the crops from the wild animals which the inhabitants could not kill under penalty of death or mutilation. In several counties he gave the office of sheriff to foreign favorites, who knew nothing of English law and used their positions to increase their own wealth with little regard for their duties. The barons suffered no less at John's hands than other classes in the community. From them John demanded extortionate feudal incidents, enforcing payment often by arbitrary seizure without form of trial or judgment. He increased the royal forests by encroach-

John's
misrule

ments upon their lands. Barons who opposed him took the risk that their relatives, whom he held as hostages, might be subjected to torture. John was hated and detested by all classes. It was only the fear of his arbitrary will, enforced with the aid of hired mercenaries, that prevented the outbreak of revolt. As the number of those who had felt the weight of his tyranny increased, the danger of rebellion grew. Evidence of this ominous state of public opinion was driven home to John in 1212, when he summoned the English feudal army for a campaign in Wales. While it was assembling, he learned from trustworthy sources that the barons were plotting treason against him. Fearing to face them, he dismissed the army.

This knowledge of treason at home made the next move of Innocent against John effective. He declared John deposed, released his subjects from their allegiance, and early in 1213 authorized Philip Augustus to carry out the sentence. Philip was only too glad of an opportunity to wage another war against his ancient enemy. His army was assembled and ready to embark, when John surrendered to the pope in April. John had prepared for defense, but, knowing that he could not rely upon his own followers, he decided to forestall the danger of invasion. At the same time he was bidding for the support of the pope against his barons. He agreed to accept Langton and to give the clergy damages for their loss of property and income. He also did homage for England and Ireland and agreed to pay 1,000 marks a year as evidence that he held these islands as fiefs of the papacy. John's humiliation at the hands of the pope was complete. *Triumph of Innocent III*

The revocation of the papal sentences against John not only halted the invasion of England planned by Philip Augustus, but it also enabled John to begin preparations for an attack upon France. This project John had entertained for a long time. His design was based upon a formidable coalition of Philip's enemies, which he had built up by long negotiations. The count of Flanders, a vassal of the French king, was prepared to strike a blow against his too powerful lord, and Otto IV, the emperor, who was John's nephew, agreed to cooperate, when it became apparent that a rival candidate for the imperial crown had the support of the pope and the good will of Philip Augustus. Philip helped to bring the coalition to a head, when, balked of his intended descent upon England, he turned his army against the count of Flanders. John sent aid to his ally, and prepared himself to attack France from the side of Aquitaine, while Philip was engaged in Flanders. When he summoned his English barons to follow him on this expedition, they almost universally refused. They were now be- *War with France* coming bent upon internal reform, and they regarded John's design to recover his lost possessions in France as hopeless. In 1214, nevertheless, John sailed for Aquitaine, taking with him mainly mercenaries. He could command the service of few of the English barons. A heavy scutage demanded for the expedition further stirred their opposition. Trouble was brewing for him at home, while he was overseas. In France his plans went all awry. His allies were defeated by Philip at Bouvines in one of the comparatively few decisive battles of the feudal age. The count of Flanders was reduced to submission to his lord, Otto IV practically lost his throne to his rival, and the recovery of the lost Angevin possessions in France was relegated to the class of lost causes. John was so powerless against the united force which Philip could now command that he was glad to accept a truce. In the autumn of 1214 he returned to face his irate barons without the victory which might have served to raise his fallen prestige at home as well as abroad.

The winning of the charter

Even before John's departure the barons seem to have begun the formation of a conspiracy to secure reform of the government. Within a few days after his return they held a secret assembly, where the charter of Henry I was produced and each took an oath to make war upon the king, unless he should grant the desired liberties. Early in January of 1215 the barons presented their demands to John. He asked for a delay of his answer until Easter, promising then to give reasonable satisfaction. The interval he used to seek support against his opponents. He granted free elections to the church, hoping thereby to separate the clergy from the barons. He began to exact from all male inhabitants a new oath of allegiance which bound them to "stand by him against all men," but this met with such opposition that he gave up the attempt. He applied to the pope to give aid in his capacity as suzerain. The barons meanwhile assembled in arms and began civil war. They marched upon London, where they were welcomed by the citizens, despite John's attempt to win the support of Londoners by the voluntary grant of a liberal municipal charter. The non-feudal freemen, who had so often turned the scale against the barons in favor of a strong monarchy, had now been alienated by John's tyranny. The clergy, too, were generally hostile. They had suffered greatly during the interdict, and the compensation rendered by John was inadequate. When the open rebellion of the barons brought home to John the universality of the opposition to him, he realized that further resistance was hopeless. On June 15 he met the barons at Runnymede and affixed his seal to a schedule of their demands. The petition was then redrafted to give it the technical form of a charter and issued as the document subsequently called the Great Charter.

In the charter John promised in behalf of himself and his heirs to free the freemen of England and their heirs from abuses listed by the barons. In large part they were violations by John of his powers as feudal lord. He promised to forego the exaction of reliefs above certain specified amounts, to cease the waste and destruction of fiefs which came under his wardship, and to put an end to many other extortionate practices in the exaction of feudal service. Popular interests, including those of both the commercial and the agricultural classes, were protected in a number of clauses. One, for example, secured for the mesne tenants from their lords all the privileges granted by the king to the tenants-in-chief, and another guaranteed a uniform system of weights and measures throughout the kingdom. The right of the crown to seize the property of subjects in order to secure payment of debts was regulated, and, in general, the power of the crown to deprive subjects of their property arbitrarily was limited in various ways. Abuses in the administration of the law of the forest, which weighed heavily on all classes, were reformed, and many evils of recent origin, such as the employment of foreign mercenaries, were abolished. The church received a grant of freedom, which was undefined, except for the specification of freedom of elections and liberty to clerks of egress from the kingdom. In chapter twelve the king agreed that no scutage or aid, excepting the three customary aids, should henceforth be levied without the consent of the great council, and in chapter fourteen the constitution of the great council was defined in detail. These two clauses were used later to help establish the principle of no taxation without representation. In 1215, however, they had no such meaning because they related only to certain specific feudal dues and not to the whole field of taxation, and because the assembly, whose assent was required, was in nowise representative. Among the most important clauses in the charter were those which related to the administration of law and justice. With a few exceptions in a reactionary direction the barons accepted the new judicial system established by Henry II, but they insisted that the king should cease to pervert the system in such ways as to make it render a travesty of justice. Most important of all was clause thirty-nine. "No freeman," it reads, "shall be arrested and imprisoned, or dispossessed, or outlawed, or banished, or in any way molested; nor will we set forth against him, nor send against him, unless by the lawful judgment of his peers and by the law of the land." This did not guarantee trial by jury, as is so often asserted,

Contents of the charter

because trial by jury did not become the common procedure in criminal cases until the reign of Henry III; but it did provide that a freeman should not be deprived of life, liberty, or property without judgment by his social equals, obtained by the mode of trial customarily employed to determine innocence or guilt in the kind of case in question. The clause has almost the same value as the clause in the fifth amendment to the Constitution of the United States which forbids that any person "be deprived of life, liberty, or property, without due process of law." Of more fundamental importance than the guarantee of the chapter itself was the implication that the king was below the law. Certain things the king could not do without the sanction of the courts. The principle appeared again in the sixty-first clause which attempted to provide a means for the enforcement of the charter, if the king should break it. The barons were to designate a committee of twenty-five of their number, to whom complaints of the transgression of the charter could be made. Any four could bring such a transgression to the attention of the king. If he failed to provide remedy within forty days, it was their duty to notify the twenty-five, who could then make war against the king. All the king's subjects were required to take oath to support the barons in such a crisis. This was the great weakness of the charter. The barons could devise no constitutional machinery to secure its enforcement, and they had to resort to the legalization of civil war. But however crude the mode of application may have been, the intent to force the king to exercise his power within the limits prescribed by the charter was clear enough. The essence of the principle of limited monarchy was present in the Great Charter.

Impor-
tance of
the
charter

The constitutional importance of the Great Charter is not readily overemphasized, but its constitutional significance is easily misinterpreted. It has been described more than once as a document comparable to the Declaration of Independence or to the Constitution of the United States, but it is neither a statement of abstract principles of government nor a formulation of general rules for the organization and regulation of a system of government. It is merely a statement of concrete remedies for the concrete abuses of which the barons complained. It is not primarily a piece of legislation, for though it may have made new law in some slight measure, its primary object was to restore what the barons regarded as old law and custom.

Viewed in the historical perspective of the barons, the Great Charter represented an attempt to make the king as feudal suzerain observe his side of the feudal contract. The document gave privileges to classes other than the baronial, and dealt with other than feudal abuses; but it was nevertheless essentially a feudal document which originated with the barons. Since the Norman conquest the king of England had been both a national king and a feudal overlord, but his position as suzerain, which had been emphasized in the actual practice of government, was the side of the royal power which affected the barons particularly and against which the Great Charter was directed. The king's position as feudal suzerain rested upon a contract, actual or implied, between him and his vassals. He gave lands and protection in return for certain specific services. Since the arrangement was contractual the king had duties as well as rights. What those duties were varied from time to time in accord with the content of a fluctuating body of unwritten feudal custom. But from the days of William the Conqueror the tenants-in-chief of the king had been attempting by rebellion or by other means to force the king to keep his side of what they considered the feudal contract to be. Henry II so limited the powers of the tenants-in-chief and so increased his own, that the contractual element nearly disappeared. Richard and John continued to break the contract in ever-increasing ways. In 1215 the barons rose in rebellion and refused to return to their allegiance, until the king should have promised no more to break his contract in those particulars which they specified. The Great Charter revived the nearly extinct theory of the feudal contract, and it was consequently an acknowledgment on the part of the king that the powers of the crown were limited.

The prominence given to the Great Charter in the development of the English constitution was due to the subsequent use made of the document rather than to its specific contents or to its intrinsic merits. The document contained a definite statement of rights which the barons claimed as feudal vassals. Subsequently, whenever the barons wanted to enforce their rights or to limit the powers of the king, they appealed to the Great Charter as a precedent. Later still, when the nation as a whole began to demand rights, though feudalism was long since dead, the same old appeal was made to this document because it embodied the principle that the power of the crown was limited. Henry III reissued the charter three times and confirmed his last issue three times, Edward I confirmed it three times, and his successors during the Middle Ages confirmed it about thirty times more. The frequency of the confirmations was due in large part to the constantly repeated demand for a new confirmation, whenever it was felt that the king was acting arbitrarily without due regard for the interests of his subjects. Often the royal abuses which caused the demands were not mentioned in the Great Charter. Frequently the king could confirm the charter whole-heartedly without binding himself specifically to remedy the abuses giving rise to the popular request for the confirmation; but, because the charter in principle placed limitations on the royal authority, king, barons, and people soon came to understand that a new confirmation was in effect a pledge to rule generally with due regard for the welfare of all classes. Thus the Great Charter became the nation's justification for the assertion of the liberties of the subject against the crown.

Civil war

The barons were the first to break the charter. The more recalcitrant northern barons left Runnymede before the negotiations had been completed, and in defiance of the twenty-five began to harry the king's lands and do violence to the king's men. The twenty-five, moreover, treated John with unnecessary disrespect. John, after observing the provisions of the treaty for about two months, began to prepare for war on his side by sending abroad for mercenaries. He had the support of the pope, who intervened as his suzerain to quell the barons with spiritual weapons. He declared the charter void and placed under sentence of excommunication the barons who should attempt to hold the king to his promise. These events sent some of the barons over to join the few who had remained loyal to John throughout, but the majority determined to resist. To obtain help against the royal mercenaries they invited Louis, the son of Philip Augustus, to become their king. During the winter the barons remained strangely inert, and the war went generally in favor of the king. It took mainly the form of laying waste the country, causing such destruction in the land as had not been seen since Stephen's day. Prince Louis, after his arrival in the spring of 1216, met with temporary success, but his English followers were beginning to display signs of a reaction against him, when John died in the autumn of 1216.

The death of John resulted in an early termination of the civil war, since his personality had been its principal cause. Before his death he designated his older son Henry, a boy of nine, as his heir, and committed him to the keeping of William Marshal, earl of Pembroke. The loyal barons had Henry crowned, and, meeting in council, appointed Marshal keeper of king and kingdom. Hubert de Burgh, the justiciar, assisted him ably; the care of Henry's person was intrusted to Peter des Roches, a French favorite whom John had made bishop of Winchester and tutor of his son; and Guala, a papal legate, occupied an influential place in the counsels of the regency because he was the representative of the king's suzerain. William reissued the charter, omitting a few significant clauses, such as the twelfth and fourteenth, which he promised to reconsider as soon as possible. He also offered amnesty for all previous opposition to the crown. By these acts he deprived the rebels of any just cause for further war, leaving to Louis solely the status of a foreign conqueror. The pressure of ecclesiastical censures, which had long weighed on the barons, was renewed and increased by Guala, and friction with the French followers of Louis further alienated the barons from the prince's cause. Early in 1217 the English barons began to return to the allegiance of Henry III in large numbers. Louis strove to get reinforcements from France with which to continue the war, but, after a defeat on land and the interception of a French fleet bringing aid, he made peace and withdrew with his French followers late in 1217. The rebellious barons were received by William Marshal without the exaction of penalty. Only the English clergy who had supported the barons suffered further for their part in the rebellion. Because they had given the sacraments to men under sentence of interdict and excommunication and had thus disobeyed a papal decree, they were subjected by Guala to heavy punishments.

The rebellion had not been in vain. Shortly after peace was made the Great Charter was reissued for a second time in order to give it all possible sanction. This time the clauses relating to the forests were issued with some revision as a separate charter. Thenceforth the Charters took the place of the original Great Charter. The principles of government desired by the barons in 1215 were now, with a few exceptions caused by minor alterations, a part of the English constitution, accepted loyally by all the parties concerned, including the pope; whereas in 1215 their maintenance had depended upon the ability of the barons to force the king to keep a promise given unwillingly and to defy the spiritual weapons of the pope.

The quality of Henry's rule during the period of his minority depended upon the character of those who controlled the government in his name. As long as William Marshal was at the head of affairs, all went well. This experienced statesman, who was well over seventy, had served three kings of England faithfully before he served Henry III. Unswerving loyalty coupled with a blunt honesty won for him the respect and trust of friends and foes alike. No better man could have been found to restore order out of the chaos which had existed since 1215. The prolonged disturbances had evoked the lawless spirit of feudalism. After the civil war was ended, anarchy threatened to prevail. The regent gradually got the administrative, financial, and judicial systems into working order. By diplomacy or by force he persuaded

The minority of Henry III: 1. William Marshal

barons who were disposed to disregard the legal rights of their king or of their neighbors to hold their peace. The restoration of authority was well under way when he died in 1219.

After William's death no baron stood out as a leader whom the other barons could follow without jealousy and friction. It was recognition of this situation that caused William Marshal during his last illness to commit the keeping of the king to the pope and to the legate who represented him. This arrangement had the sanction of feudal custom, which gave to the lord wardship of the minor heir and the lands of a deceased vassal, and it seems to have been tacitly accepted by the barons. The legate at this time was Pandulph. In practice he ruled in conjunction with Hubert de Burgh, the justiciar, who had the actual management of most of the governmental business, and with Peter des Roches, the tutor of the king, who had no ministerial position. These were the men who took the leadership in shaping the policies of the government, though, like William Marshal before them, they consulted on all important questions the *curia regis*, which was now beginning to be called the king's council when it acted in an advisory capacity. The government thus conducted was weak. The council could not rule with the same authority as a king, and the spirit of disorder engendered by the civil war was ever ready to break out anew. The barons became jealous of one another, and the spirit of rivalry extended to the men who were most influential in the government. Pandulph was opposed by Stephen Langton, and Peter des Roches by Hubert de Burgh. As long as Pandulph remained in office he was able to overcome Stephen's opposition, since as legate he had ecclesiastical powers superior to those of the archbishop, and he appears to have held the balance between Hubert and Peter. In 1221, however, he ceased to be legate. Peter, finding that Hubert, supported by the archbishop, was obtaining the leadership of the council, gave up for the time his effort to control affairs.

Hubert's increased influence brought with it new difficulties. Peter des Roches, himself a Poitevin, had represented to some extent the interests of the foreign favorites who had risen to place and power in John's time, and they remained generally opposed to Hubert. Some of the English barons also resented Hubert's growing authority. The friction was increased by Hubert's efforts to maintain law and order. He attempted to force the unlawful possessors of lands and castles belonging to the crown or to private persons to restore them to the rightful owners. Though he proceeded by judicial process, he was compelled in more than one instance to use armed force in order to get justice done. So much ill feeling did this policy cause that many of the barons threatened civil war if it should be continued; but the moderate councils of Langton, backed by threats of excommunication, prevailed, and the danger of a general conflagration gradually subsided. In 1227 the king's minority came to an end with a formal declaration in the great council to that effect.[1] Subsequently Henry ruled legally in his own name. In actual practice there was little change. The king left the business of government so largely in the hands of Hubert that, after 1227 as before, he was the practical ruler of England.

A chain of events which led to Hubert's downfall began in connection with an expedition to France. During the minority the king of France had taken advantage of disorders in Aquitaine to invade and conquer the northern part. Henry, who was eager to recover his possessions, summoned his English vassals in 1229 to follow him to Aquitaine. They came to the port of embarkation in such numbers that there were not enough ships to transport them, and the sailing had to be postponed. Henry attributed the lack of ships to the deliberate policy of Hubert, who doubted the wisdom of the projected campaign, and he accused the justiciar of being a traitor. On the campaign the king displayed such incapacity as a leader that the costly expedition was without result. Henry was disposed to attribute his failure to his justiciar, who probably was in part responsible for the fiasco.

War with France

Hubert's attitude with regard to papal fiscal exactions was also displeasing to Henry III. In 1199 the papacy for the first time had compelled its clerical subjects to pay a tax of a fractional part of their annual incomes. Taxation, as distinguished from dues, rents, and services, was at that time so rarely levied by any authority that it was generally regarded as good and sufficient reason for resistance. When the imposition was decreed by an authority which had never before attempted to exercise such a right, it was certain to arouse opposition. This first tax was collected with difficulty, although it was levied for a crusade. In 1215 another was raised for the same purpose. In 1229 a tenth was exacted to assist the pope in his war against the emperor. Though the fear of ecclesiastical censures induced the clergy to pay their quotas, the strictness with which the assessment and collection of this levy were made evoked their maledictions, and the sight of English gold going to the support of one party to a foreign war waged for temporal interests in which Englishmen had no concern caused irritation among laymen.

Papal exactions

---

[1] The pope had declared him of age in 1223, but he was nevertheless kept in tutelage so far as the greater portion of his official acts was concerned.

Nor did dissatisfaction with the papal policy stop here. Late in the twelfth century the papacy began to make provisions. The pope provided a clergyman with a benefice, which was the living attached to a clerical office, such as that of the parish priest, by appointing the clergyman to the office. Before that time direct appointments by the pope to offices in the English church had been almost unknown. In the early years of the thirteenth century they became common. They caused opposition for two reasons. The use by the pope of this power in every instance deprived someone else of a right he had previously exercised. Whenever, for example, a parish priest died, his successor was nominated by the person who had the right of patronage, subject always to the approval of the bishop. Whoever had the right lost it temporarily when the pope exercised the right of provision. The priests whom the pope appointed, moreover, were generally Italians, since the pope used the right as a means of providing salaries and rewards for the clerks who served in his household or in his court. The result was unfortunate. Either the recipient appointed an underpaid vicar to perform his duties, put the surplus income in his pocket, and never came near the parish, or a flock of English parishioners found themselves in the charge of an Italian who was ignorant of their language and of their ways.

Hubert's downfall

So great was the exasperation aroused among Englishmen by these practices that in 1232 they resorted to a violent expression of their sentiments. Groups of people, including knights and clergy as well as men of lower degree, robbed and burned the barns containing crops that belonged to Italian clergymen and in some instances maltreated the clerics themselves. The movement appears to have had the tacit support of Hubert, who was generally hostile to foreigners. To the king it represented the culmination of his wrong-doing. The attack was directed primarily against the papal authority for which Henry personally felt the deepest veneration. The protection of the papacy in his youth had unquestionably contributed to the preservation of his throne, and Henry never ceased to feel and to display his gratitude. Hubert's part in these riots sealed his fate. A sharp remonstrance from the pope, coupled with the promptings of Peter des Roches who had recently returned to England after an absence of several years, persuaded the king to dismiss the justiciar from office in disgrace.

Peter des Roches

The fall of Hubert placed the king under the moral domination of Peter des Roches. His old tutor obtained no important office for himself, but he persuaded the king to confer offices upon his relatives, friends, and subordinates, whom he could control. He relied upon his personal friendship with the king to secure the requisite influence in that quarter. The barons soon found they had gone from the frying pan into the fire. Although Hubert's attitude toward the Italian clergymen was undoubtedly popular, the barons were not sorry to see him go. His attempts to maintain law and order had brought him into conflict with the personal interests of many of them, and his long tenure of power was in itself enough to provoke ill will. For the past decade scutages, tallages, or taxes on personal property had been levied nearly every year, and for these and for all other unpopular policies of the crown Hubert took the responsibility and received the blame in popular opinion. But grievances such as these were soon dwarfed in comparison with those which piled up against Peter. The offices great and small were rapidly placed in the hands of Peter's followers, most of whom were Poitevins, and a band of Poitevin mercenaries was imported to be used against opponents. Several Englishmen who incurred Henry's displeasure had their property confiscated without form of legal procedure. The worst days of John's reign appeared to have returned. By 1233 some of the barons, in alliance with the Welsh, broke into open revolt. Henry found that he could count upon few of the remainder for support. In the next year the archbishop, appearing before him with a number of clerical followers, reminded him that through the evil counsel of Peter des Roches John had lost the love of his people. He also threatened to excommunicate the king unless he dismissed the foreign favorites. The threats and exhortations of the archbishop touched a fear of ecclesiastical censures that was deeply ingrained in Henry's mind, causing him to give way. He ejected the foreigners from office, sent Peter away from court, and made peace with the rebellious barons.

The retirement of Peter in 1234 brought to an end the principal influences which had dominated Henry since the beginning of his reign. He did not again give any one adviser an opportunity to control him. In fact, he did not fill the vacancies in the great offices of state with barons or bishops; he either filled them with men of low social rank who would be entirely subservient, or left them vacant and had their functions performed by clerks. To some extent, too, he avoided baronial influence by increasing the authority and functions of officials of his household, such as the keeper of the wardrobe. These more personal attendants were more amenable than such officials as the chancellor and the justiciar. The practice consequently enhanced the royal independence of the barons. The king, in other words, attempted to rule without advisers. He was ill fitted to carry on a government of

Establishment of Henry's personal rule

this type. He inherited few of the evil traits of his father's character, but he was as weak in doing right as John had been strong in doing wrong. Henry was a better man in his private life than any of his Angevin predecessors, he had strong religious feeling, and he was more pious than the average king of the Middle Ages. His personality was rendered attractive by a mild and genial disposition. His intelligence was keen, and he was well educated. But these fine qualities were marred by a fatal weakness of will. He was immediately subject to the influence of any stronger personality with which he came into contact. His actions consequently were capricious. He could be obstinate in a negative way, but he rarely exerted sufficient force and energy to carry any policy to a successful termination before he abandoned it for another. His intellectual ability, moreover, did not extend to the realm of politics; he seemed incapable of distinguishing between wise and foolish policies. Ill suited for the conduct of government at any time, he faced in 1234 a situation of exceptional difficulty. The barons now had their apprehensions thoroughly aroused. They had just received convincing demonstration that a weak king with good intentions might give as bad rule as a strong king with bad intentions, and they awaited the outcome of Henry's experiment in personal rule with a keenly critical spirit.

New foreign favorites

Henry gave causes enough of dissatisfaction. Within a short time he was again surrounded with foreign favorites. With his artistic temperament and aesthetic tastes, he found more pleasure in the company of the polished foreigners who appealed more strongly to his intellectual interests and flattered more successfully his self-esteem than his English barons, and his family relationships necessarily brought many of them to his court. His mother, after John's death, had married her first love, Hugh the Brown, who was a count in Poitou. After Henry's break with the old Poitevin residents in England in 1234, a new group of Poitevins soon arrived from the lands of his stepfather. Early in 1236 Henry married Eleanor of Provence, who was endowed with eight maternal uncles and with other relatives in proportion. A surprising number of them were fortune-seekers who found in England a happy hunting ground, to which they in turn summoned their retainers and friends. Thus was introduced into English public life a new foreign strain consisting of Savoyards and Provençals. Henry showered favors upon them, and they rapidly acquired wealth and positions of influence in church and state. Some of them served him well enough, but they were for the most part actuated by self-seeking interest, and too many of them justified the charges of haughtiness, lawlessness, and greed which Englishmen hurled against them. One and all were odious to Englishmen, and the grievance continued to rankle throughout the period of Henry's personal rule.

A second cause of discontent was the king's extravagance. For an increase of expenditure there was legitimate reason, since prices were rising during the first half of the thirteenth century; but Henry spent large sums in ways that the barons regarded as unnecessary and inadvisable. Between 1234 and 1242 he secured several large grants of revenues from the great council, but thereafter his requests for financial aid were generally denied. As a result he was chronically hard up, often being forced to borrow in order to meet current expenses. His poverty compelled him to be somewhat less lavish in his expenditure. He made no systematic reform, and he steadily declined to accept the grants offered by the barons with the proviso that a committee of their number should oversee the expenditure of the proceeds. The king's frequent demands for money, which the barons regarded as unjustifiable, thus became a standing grievance. *Extravagance*

As the barons gradually found that their protests and criticisms wrought no reform of the government, they began to demand that the king should appoint barons to the great offices of state and to some of the places in his council. They attributed his misrule in large measure to the quality of the advice which he received. To make their case popular with the nation, which was just beginning to be conscious of its nationality, they emphasized their desire to supplant Henry's foreign favorites with English advisers. Their opposition to the foreigners was sincere enough, but they were opposed just as strongly to the Englishmen of low social station who occupied positions of power and influence in the government. They regarded themselves as the natural counselors of the king, and they were actuated rather more by the selfish interests of their class than by any spirit of self-sacrifice for the national welfare. *Advisers*

The cause of baronial discontent which finally led to open revolt developed out of Henry's relations with the papacy. During the period of his personal rule the popular opposition to the papacy waxed strong. The stream of gold which flowed from England to the papal coffers was ever on the increase, and Englishmen believed it was being used largely to further the purely temporal policies of the papacy. The position of the popes as the spiritual heads of Christendom was not assailed; but what popular opinion held to be the greed of the papal court, the corruption of the papacy in its administrative capacity, and its overweening temporal ambitions were subjected to bitter criticism. When *Henry's subserviency to the papacy* the popular feeling of hostility had developed to the point where it translated itself into a desire for action, the clergy and the barons sought the leadership of the king whose dignity and authority were being infringed upon by the papal exactions. Henry, however, could never long shake himself free from his feeling of indebtedness to the papacy. When the baronial pressure was particularly insistent, he protested to the pope, but his leadership of the opposition was never better than half-hearted, and much of the time he openly supported the unpopular papal side. In the years following 1237 a long series of fiscal demands produced a culmination of the anti-papal movement. The residence of a papal legate was attacked by a mob, and a papal collector was expelled from the kingdom. In 1245 and 1246 the great council received the royal support in making spirited protests to the pope. The threat of an interdict, however, caused the king to cease his opposition, and papal taxes continued to be collected from the clergy. The popular temper appears subsequently to have cooled somewhat, but Henry's desertion of the national cause was not forgotten. When the king shortly became involved in a papal enterprise of which the English clergy were asked to pay the cost, the baronial opposition revived and flared into open revolt.

Sicilian venture

In 1254 the pope conferred upon Henry's second son, Edmund, the crown of Sicily. Although the pope claimed the right to dispose of the kingdom of Sicily in his capacity of suzerain, he was not in actual possession. Indeed, he had been for some time waging war against the occupant of the throne, and it was his need for financial and military aid which moved him to bestow the crown on Edmund. As part of the price of this crown, which still had to be won, Henry agreed to pay a debt of over £90,000 previously contracted by the papacy in its prosecution of the war. Part of the money was raised by a tax imposed on the English clergy by the pope, but in 1258 Henry failed to meet one of the installments due. Threatened with ecclesiastical censure by the pope if he delayed the payment beyond a certain time, he appealed to the great council for financial help. The barons, however, had reached the limit of their endurance. They would agree to consider an aid only if the king would allow them to reform the government and the pope would modify the terms of the Sicilian contract. The king, caught between the papal and baronial demands, necessarily gave way, and the barons began a series of experiments in government which made an end of Henry's personal rule and for a time placed power in the hands of a baronial oligarchy.

The first of these experiments was initiated by the Provisions of

Oxford. This ordinance provided for new appointments to most of the administrative offices, and required all royal officials to become responsible to the great council or to a permanent council of fifteen representing the baronial interest. The council of fifteen barons was concurrently established to take the place of the king's council. Some of its members were to be always in attendance upon the king, and he could take no important action without its advice and consent. The effect of its organization was practically to take the government out of the hands of the king and give it to the fifteen barons. The fifteen, however, were required to consult three times a year with a committee of twelve barons, representing the great council, and the great council itself might be summoned at any time. The king could do nothing but submit. The clergy and the middle class generally favored the barons, and even the Savoyards accepted the provisions. The Poitevins who held out were soon forced to leave the realm.

The new government worked badly. The barons, though they were at one in their opposition to the misrule of Henry, could not cooperate to exercise the power which they had obtained. Some were actuated by a national spirit, desiring to wield power for the benefit of all classes; others were moved by selfish interests, seeking only that which was of advantage to their own class. Though the elimination of abuses of which the middle class complained was promised in 1258, it was a year before the great council, under the pressure of the reformers, enacted the Provisions of Westminster, which limited the rights of lords in relation to their tenants and remedied various oppressive practices of the government. The development of factions among the barons gave the king his opportunity. In 1261 he persuaded the pope to release him from his promise and to declare the enactments of 1258 and 1259 null and void. He then dismissed the council of fifteen, putting his own partisans in their places. For a time there was confusion in the government. In some counties the officials appointed by the council of fifteen still received the obedience of the people, and in others the new officers appointed by the king's council. During two years of chaos the baronial party and the growing king's party tried to find some basis of agreement. In 1263 both sides armed, and desultory warfare began.

The acknowledged leader of the baronial cause was Simon de Montfort. Himself a Frenchman, Simon had come to England in 1230 to present claims to the earldom of Leicester, which he inherited from his grandmother. Successful in his quest, he had so far attracted the favor of the young king that in 1238 he was allowed to marry one of the king's sisters. At that time he was regarded by the barons merely as one of the king's unpopular foreign favorites. Henry, however, treated his brother-in-law with his usual inconstancy. As early as 1244 Simon appeared among those protesting against Henry's misgovernment, and eventually he became a trusted and influential member of the baronial opposition. He was the close friend of several contemporary "intellectuals," conversing and corresponding with them at length upon the evils of the time and the possibilities of reform. In the production of the Provisions of Oxford he played a prominent part. He acted with the section of the baronial party which took a national view of the responsibilities of the baronial oligarchy, and he displayed a more patriotic interest than many native-born English nobles. In the period of disorder that followed Henry's repudiation of the Provisions of Oxford Simon's evident sincerity coupled with his ability brought him rapidly to the leadership of the baronial party still opposed to the king. By 1264 many of the barons had gone over to the royalist side; but the younger nobles, the residents of the towns, many of the clergy, and in general the more liberal and progressive elements of the community, who remained loyal to their ideals of reform, were ready to support Simon in civil war against the king. Thus Simon de Montfort became a pioneer in the cause of English popular liberties.

The Barons' War

At the battle of Lewes in 1264 Simon won a complete success. With inferior forces he outmaneuvered the king's army, defeated it in detail, and captured the king. Henry agreed to a new settlement, called the Mise of Lewes, which established a government the same in principle as that set up in 1258. A baronial council of nine, which was dominated by Simon, took the place of the former council of fifteen. In action the government was more liberal than that of 1258, Simon and his followers showing a real regard for the interests of the middle class. In 1265 this class secured recognition by representation at an assembly of the great council. Two knights from every shire and two representatives from every city and borough were summoned. This was by no means the first time the popular element had been represented at sessions of the great council. Simon was not the originator of parliamentary representation, but he was probably the first to bring together at a session of the great council representatives of both the urban and rural elements of the middle class. Previously the townsmen had probably not been represented. The assembly was indicative of the important part which the middle class had come to play in English political life under Simon's tutelage. The barons who seized the government in 1258 had no thought of sharing the exercise of power with other classes, though they reluctantly granted reforms demanded by other classes. For that matter, the time was not yet ripe in 1265 for the permanent acquisition by the middle class of a voice in a national deliberative assembly. The liberal tendencies of Simon had already alienated the majority of the barons, and the assembly of 1265, combined with other evidences of his radicalism, sent over to the king's side many of the baronial minority which had followed Simon in 1264. They united with some of the royalist barons who had refused to lay down their arms after the defeat at Lewes. When Edward, Henry's oldest son, escaped from captivity to become their leader, they became a formidable force. In the battle of Evesham, fought in 1265, Simon was killed, his followers were scattered, and his cause was lost.

The baronial experiments in the art of government were brought to an end on the field of Evesham. The attempt of the royalist reactionaries to take vengeance on their fallen foes prolonged the resistance for two years, but the possibility of any organic change in the English constitution was ended at Evesham. The king immediately resumed the royal authority, the baronial council was removed, the officials appointed by the barons were replaced by royal appointees, and the acts of the revolutionary government were declared invalid. Out of the wreck only the reforms embodied in the Provisions of Westminster were saved. In 1267 the most important of these changes were reenacted in permanent form in the Statute of Marlborough. Yet the effort of the barons had not been entirely in vain. Finding that the Great Charter by itself did not place sufficient limitations upon the king to procure good government, they attempted to reorganize the government in such a way as to place a constitutional check upon the misuse of the royal authority. They overshot the mark by taking the power entirely away from the king and usurping it for themselves. The king was still a necessity in the English government to maintain the balance not only among baronial factions but also among the different social classes. Englishmen did not yet have a sufficient knowledge of politics to work for themselves a government which would not produce a tyranny of class or an anarchy worse than any royal tyranny. Simon de Montfort had a broader vision. He would have given to the middle class a share in the government, which the barons in 1258 would have denied; but, as idealists are likely to do, he went too fast. He, too, found no place for the king; indeed, he substituted himself for the king. But the fundamental constitutional conception developed by the barons in the reign of Henry III survived to bear fruit in later reigns. They sought to make the king rule in closer accord with the will of the baronage. Simon would have substituted the will of the nation for

The failure of the barons

that of a single class. In this broader form the concept finally found application through the gradual acquisition of power by a parliament representative of the nation. Prince Edward, who was Simon's chief opponent, learned much from the conflict. When later he became king, constitutional changes were slowly accomplished, which prepared the way for an effective popular participation in the government of England.

Henry III, for the remainder of his reign, was at peace. Prince Edward in fact, though not in name, took the principal burden of ruling the kingdom, until, in 1270, he departed on a crusade. He was still engaged upon this expedition when his father's death, late in 1272, made him king.

Close of
the reign

CHAPTER IX

INTELLECTUAL AND RELIGIOUS DEVELOPMENT

THE two centuries that intervened between the Norman conquest and the death of Henry III witnessed a notable expansion in the intellectual outlook of Englishmen. The movement was one which England shared with the rest of western Europe. On the continent it began in the eleventh century, came to full fruition in the course of two hundred years, and subsequently went to seed. The interest in intellectual pursuits became more widespread than ever before, and the number of schools multiplied rapidly. The increased activity of the schools was accompanied by an expansion in the area of knowledge and by an improvement in methods of thought. The seven liberal arts remained the basis of the curriculum, but their content grew enormously in bulk. The study of grammar was extended in several schools to include an appreciative study of much classical literature; rhetoric was made to cover a deeper study of law; and logic, or dialectic, gave opportunity for much speculation upon philosophical and theological problems. More attention, too, was given to the *quadrivium*. Most important of all was the new spirit of inquiry that began to actuate students. The thinkers of this period for the most part placed authority above reason. They reasoned only within certain limits prescribed by authoritative expositions of the dogmas of the church. Yet within those limits they began to think independently. They no longer merely put together excerpts from the works of their predecessors; they applied the principles of logic to such subjects as philosophy, theology, and law, and drew their own conclusions. Learning by rote gave place to original thought.

Renaissance of the twelfth century

In the field of classical literature the twelfth century witnessed a notable renaissance. Many scholars became intimately acquainted with the thoughts of the ancients and thoroughly steeped in their diction. Some of the writers of the twelfth century employed a Latin style which was the best written since the classical period. With John of Salisbury, an Englishman, the cultivation of Latin literature reached the highest point attained in the Middle Ages. Before the end of the twelfth century, however, the interest in the classics began to wane. John of Salisbury complained bitterly of those, whom he called the Cornificians, who wanted to shorten the course in arts in order that

Literary revival

the students might advance more quickly to the study of philosophy and theology, the utilitarian studies of that day. Many of the arguments in this controversy have an astonishingly modern sound,[1] and then as now the advocates of a short cut to knowledge had their way. The classics continued to be studied because Latin was an essential tool for the mastery of philosophy, theology, law, or any other branch of learning. As soon as a student had learned syntax and composition thoroughly, he dropped the classics and passed on to the more popular studies. Classical literature was more and more neglected except as a means to an end, until in the thirteenth century the interest in *belles lettres* disappeared.

Scholasticism The field of endeavor which claimed the allegiance of the majority of students north of the Alps was that of philosophical and theological speculation. Here a system of thought was developed so distinctive that it is called scholasticism. It grew out of the attempt to apply the deductive system of logic in the field of religious dogma and developed into an attempt to reconcile the claims of reason with the claims of dogma. Anselm of Canterbury, who is sometimes styled the father of scholasticism, began his speculation with the principle "I believe in order that I may know." Knowledge was to be acquired only in order to support the faith, and reason was not to wander beyond the limits set by faith. Reason was to be used merely to supplement authority. Abélard, whose brilliant formulation and exposition of scholastic principles in the opening years of the twelfth century gave an immense impetus to the movement, started with the assumption "I know in order that I may believe." With him rational insight must prepare the way for faith, since faith without it lacks a foundation in truth. Abélard's method is best illustrated by his work called *Sic et non* (Yes and no). Here he lays down theses, cites the views of opposing authorities, and leaves the solution to the reader. In the eyes of medieval churchmen the method was dangerous because, if carried to its logical conclusion, it might place reason above authority. Abélard, indeed, was convicted of heresy, as were some of his successors who ventured to follow the method of reasoning to conclusions which conflicted with dogma. Abélard's pupils, however, for the most part, modified his method. Peter Lombard wrote a book called *Sentences*, in which he follows the *sic et non* method, but, after he has stated the conflicting opinions of the fathers of the church on a given proposition, he attempts to draw a conclusion which harmonizes the contradictory statements. This type of reasoning came to dominate the scholastic system. It con-

---

[1] See, for example, Krey, "John of Salisbury's Attitude towards the Classics," *Transactions of the Wisconsin Academy of Sciences, Arts, and Letters*, xvi, part ii, 956–964.

fined the spirit of inquiry mainly to the effort to reconcile reason with authority.

The spirit of mental curiosity which found its principal satisfaction in scholasticism also stirred a considerable interest in science. Before Science any great advance could be made it was necessary to add to the stock of knowledge found in Latin works. This task was begun late in the eleventh century and early in the twelfth by westerners who traveled among the Saracens to acquire some of the superior knowledge of the sciences which they had derived in large part indirectly from the Greeks. Some of them also traveled among the Greeks. The result of their researches was the writing of several treatises and the translation into Latin of Arabic and Greek texts. Medicine, mathematics, and astronomy were the subjects especially favored. The scientific knowledge of the men of this period was a strange jumble of scientific truths with fables, myths, and morals. The scientists calculated with Arabic numerals, they knew the use of the mariner's compass, and some of them admitted the spherical character of the earth. But along with accurate knowledge of this sort went much misinformation. The general laws of nature were not worked out satisfactorily, and what was known was not properly systematized. The inquiring mind was there, but the scientific attitude—the ability to distinguish between the true and the false—was generally lacking. All kinds of marvels found in the pages of ancient writers were solemnly repeated as scientific truths without question. Beyond that stage the natural sciences never advanced in the Middle Ages. Later medieval men increased the store of scientific knowledge obtained from antiquity; they made some practical discoveries of their own; but they never wholly disentangled the true from the false, and they failed to crystallize their knowledge in the form of scientific conceptions.

While scholars north of the Alps were devoting their thought principally to philosophy and theology, Italian scholars were giving their Law attention chiefly to the law. Previously, Roman law had been known to most of western Europe only in the form of a few corrupt and exceedingly brief epitomes, consisting mainly of excerpts. The systematic codification of the whole body of the Roman law made by the eastern emperor, Justinian, in the sixth century, was little known in the west outside of Italy, and there it was apparently known only in part and in the form of epitomes. In the twelfth century the whole body of the Roman law preserved by Justinian was studied systematically, its principles were expounded, and elaborate commentaries called glosses were prepared. The field was soon extended to include the law of the church, which was based on Roman law.[2] The study of the civil and the canon law was soon taken up by schools north of the Alps, and it became one of the most popular of the professional courses open to students.

One notable result of this intellectual revival was the rise of the universities. The earliest universities grew up spontaneously in the twelfth century. Schools which had particularly famous teachers attracted students from many parts of Europe, and this cosmopolitan character of the school was the fundamental characteristic in the process of the transformation of the school into a university.[3] By the thirteenth century the principal distinguishing marks of a university had come to be a cosmopolitan student body, one of the higher or professional faculties of theology, law, or medicine, and a faculty containing a considerable number of teachers who had received the master's degree. When the teachers or the students of such an institution organized a gild for the purpose of regulating their common affairs, a university had been created. Once the first universities had been formed and acknowledged as such through custom and practice, new universities began to be established or recognized by charter of pope, emperor, or king.

From the first, one of the principal purposes of the organization of universities was to prevent interference in their affairs by external authorities. One powerful weapon which they commonly employed against the encroachment of local authorities was that of suspending lectures. The medieval university had no campus and buildings. The students lived in hired lodgings, and the lectures were conducted in halls leased for the purpose. When the townsmen trespassed upon rights or privileges which the university claimed on behalf of instructors or students, the suspension of lectures would bring an end to the activities of the university, and the students and instructors would move elsewhere. As the towns were often small and the universities large, the departure of a university would deprive the local tradesmen of a profitable source of income. Through the power of suspending lectures many a university was able to establish a considerable amount of independence as a self-governing community. At an early time, however, the value of the confirmation of their privileges by higher authorities was recognized, and it soon became the common practice for universities to obtain grants of privilege from king, emperor, or pope. The nature of the privileges varied from one university to another, but those

Rise of the universi-ties

Privileges

---

[2] See above, p. 110.

[3] What today we call a university was at this period more commonly called a *studium generale*.

most commonly granted were four in number. (1) The students were treated as clerics and enjoyed the privileges and immunities of the clergy. (2) Members of the university who were accused of any offense could not be tried before ordinary lay tribunals, but had to be impleaded before ecclesiastical courts, or before courts maintained by the university. (3) The right of suspending lectures was formally conceded to them. (4) The candidates upon whom they conferred the degree of master or doctor had the right of teaching in any university without the necessity of undergoing further examinations.

All the work of the universities was conducted in Latin. When a student came to the university, therefore, it was presumed that he was thoroughly grounded in Latin, although there were no entrance examinations to test his ability. The course first taken was that of the liberal arts. This was based on the old curriculum of the seven liberal arts with the addition of a great deal of philosophy. Grammar and rhetoric, which included literature, were generally subordinated, logic was stressed, and the *quadrivium* was expanded. The student obtained his information mainly by attendance at lectures. These took the form of commentaries upon texts because books, which still had to be reproduced by hand, were too costly for the purse of the average student. The lectures were sometimes supplemented by quizzes, or still more characteristically by debates. The daily curriculum of the student who sought a degree was somewhat strenuous, judged by modern standards. He arose at five or six in the morning, attended chapel, and then went to lectures for six or seven hours. The remaining hours of the day he was expected to give mainly to memorizing the lectures he had heard, though there was generally an hour or two after lunch or supper which might be devoted to recreation. The student completed his course and secured his degree by passing examinations and taking part in public debates. These covered the whole work of his course, since there were no examinations in individual courses. In the early days of the universities the length of time required for the course was not prescribed. A student took his examination when he thought he was ready, provided he could swear that he had studied certain prescribed books and had attended lectures and disputations upon them. In the course of time, however, it became the practice to prescribe a minimum requirement of residence. At Oxford in the thirteenth century this was four years for the degree of bachelor of arts and three more years for that of master. After a student had attained the latter, he could continue to study for a degree in theology, law, or medicine, if he so desired.

The course of study in a medieval university represents but one side

The work
of the
students

Student
life

of student life. Then as now men came to the universities with a variety of objects in mind. The serious students who desired a degree may have gone through the prescribed routine more or less faithfully, but there was another class of students who came to the university mainly to enjoy the life. We hear of students who "go to class but once or twice a week, choosing by preference the lectures on canon law, which do not begin till nine in the morning and thus leave them plenty of time for sleep."[4] The problem of discipline was difficult. The students were of all ages, but the average student on entrance was between the ages of thirteen and sixteen, and the undergraduates were consequently more irresponsible than those of a modern university. The universities gave little attention to discipline at first. When they did begin to impose regulations, they frequently condemned all amusements, legitimate and illegitimate alike. There were no athletic sports, either intramural or intercollegiate, on which surplus physical energy might be expended. One result was the devotion of a good deal of energy to the hazing of freshmen and to other forms of rough horseplay. Another was a search for pleasure in reprehensible forms, which included much drinking and brawling. In many respects, however, the life of students has changed but little in the course of 700 years. In their letters they discuss many of the same problems which occupy the attention of students who write to their parents in the twentieth century. The complaint of an Italian father, that "a student's first song is a demand for money and there will never be a letter which does not ask for cash,"[5] finds an echo with many a weary father of this day and generation.

England came into contact with the intellectual revival, when it was in its early stages, as a result of the Norman conquest. Before the end of the eleventh century old schools had been revived and new ones had been founded. Throughout the twelfth century the movement continued unabated in vigor. Large numbers of Englishmen, moreover, sought an education in the more famous schools on the continent. From the early years of the twelfth century onward, the English were intimately associated with the intellectual development which centered in Paris, providing not only many students but also instructors and productive scholars whose works were written at the university. England, however, was not far behind France in the establishment of a university of her own. Before the close of the reign of Henry II a school existed at Oxford which had the essential attributes of a university.

**English
education**

---

[4] Haskins, in *American Historical Review*, x, 23.

[5] Quotation cited by Haskins in *American Historical Review*, iii, 208.

The university of Oxford evidently grew up largely under the influence of men who had been trained at Paris. In many aspects its Oxford
organization was similar to that of Paris. A distinctive feature of
the life at Oxford was the greater prominence given to the organization of colleges within the university. The earliest colleges were
little more than almshouses for poor students. One of the first colleges of the type which ultimately prevailed at Oxford was Merton,
founded in 1264. The donor, Walter of Merton, bishop of Rochester
and at one time chancellor of England, gave an estate, the revenues
from which were used to maintain a community of scholars at Oxford. They lived together in a house under the headship of a warden.
They regulated the conduct of their daily lives in accordance with
the rules established by the founder, but received their instruction
at the lectures conducted by the university. Subsequently many more
colleges of this same general type were founded. Not until late in
the Middle Ages did the practice originate of instruction within the
college, which has developed into the present tutorial system. The
curriculum at Oxford was much the same as at Paris; the faculties
of liberal arts and of theology were the most popular; and the emphasis was placed upon philosophy and dialectic. Oxford, however,
gave rather more attention to grammar and decidedly more to mathematics and science.

Cambridge became a university a few years later than Oxford. It
is possible, indeed, that the access of students and teachers which Cam-
gave Cambridge the characteristics of a university was due to a row bridge
between town and gown at Oxford in 1209. Such incidents were of
frequent occurrence in university towns of the Middle Ages, and
the details of this particular affair are in every way typical. One of
the students at Oxford was so unfortunate as to kill a woman. He
sought safety in flight. The authorities of the town, not finding him
at his lodgings, took some of the students who were fellow lodgers
and put them in prison. They were innocent, a contemporary narrator of the event assures us, but nevertheless they were hanged at
the order of the king. This infliction of penalties upon students by
secular authorities violated the privileges claimed by the university,
and lectures consequently were suspended until remedy should be
had. Meanwhile 3,000 teachers and students migrated, many of them
going to Cambridge to pursue their studies.[6] While this event may
not mark the origin of the university of Cambridge, there is no doubt
of the existence of the university a few years later in the thirteenth
century. The younger university patterned both its organization and

---

[6] The version of the story given by Roger of Wendover, *Chronica*, ed. Coxe, ii, 227.

its curriculum on those of Oxford. During the Middle Ages, however, Cambridge failed to establish that rivalry as an intellectual center which it maintains in modern times, and its intellectual influence was much less than Oxford's both in England and across the Channel.

The results of this intellectual activity on the part of Englishmen may be measured to some extent by the learned men it produced. Several of the most notable of the English scholars of the twelfth century we have met already.[7] They were for the most part men of letters interested in literature. With John of Salisbury at their head, they constituted a group as famous as any that could be found in contemporary Europe. The lure of scholasticism, however, was already beginning to be apparent. Anselm, who was prominent in the development of scholasticism, was archbishop of Canterbury from 1094 to 1109. Subsequently several Englishmen won fame as scholastics in foreign schools. Three of the instructors under whom John of Salisbury studied logic and theology at Paris were Englishmen. In science Englishmen early displayed an interest greater than that to be found elsewhere. In the last decade of the eleventh century and in the first half of the twelfth several Englishmen traveled among the Saracens to acquire some of their superior knowledge of the sciences. The foremost of these early English scientists was Adelard of Bath, who traveled for several years, translated several works, and wrote one of his own setting forth Arabic views on the physical sciences. Later in the century Alexander Neckam wrote a manual which summarizes the knowledge generally current in his time with regard to the sciences. To the Roman or the canon law Englishmen made no important contribution in the twelfth century, though many Englishmen acquired an intimate knowledge of both laws. The only law book of importance produced in England in the twelfth century was Glanvill's, which had to do only with the indigenous law of England.

In the thirteenth century the cultivation of *belles lettres* nearly ceased, and the trend toward philosophy and theology became more pronounced. Two of the most famous scholars of this epoch were teachers at Oxford. Robert Grosseteste, after being a lecturer at Oxford, became bishop of Lincoln and took an important part in the practical affairs of church and state during the reign of Henry III. His wide range of knowledge was remarkable. He wrote upon a variety of subjects, although he was chiefly interested in philosophy

English scholars: twelfth century

Thirteenth century: Robert Grosseteste

---

[7] Above, pp. 108, 109.

and theology. He was one of the leaders in scholastic thought at Oxford, and he did much to promote the study of the physical sciences. His influence upon English thought was widespread, for he had the happy faculty of arousing in others an enthusiasm for intellectual pursuits. It was also deep, lasting until the scholastic system began to give way before the humanistic spirit of the renaissance.

Grosseteste's friend and possibly his pupil, Roger Bacon, who was also an Englishman, had perhaps less influence upon English medieval thought, but modern opinion generally holds him to have been one of the most brilliant of the medieval scholars. His thought, indeed, was so independent and original that it ran counter in many respects to the scholastic tendencies of his age, and consequently was not fully appreciated. He was not free from the scholastic methods of his times, but he saw some of the faults and criticized them. In the philosophical field he opposed many of the views of Thomas Aquinas, the most popular theologian of his day. He condemned the abuses prevalent in the syllogistic form of deductive reasoning used by the scholastics generally and by Thomas in particular, urging the inductive, experimental method, which he employed himself sufficiently to make some important discoveries in science, although he mixed myth and fable with his sound scientific observations like the other scientists of his day. Though he may not have been so far the intellectual superior of his contemporaries as was once thought, none is disposed to place him elsewhere than among the most notable scholars of his age. His work advanced the study of mathematics and science and helped greatly to maintain the preeminence which English scholars had long enjoyed in those fields. **Roger Bacon**

In the field of law Henry de Bracton, a royal justice in the reign of Henry III, wrote a scientific and comprehensive treatise which is of fundamental importance in the development of English jurisprudence. Bracton gained his knowledge of the substance of English common law from his experience in the king's courts. He set forth his knowledge systematically, borrowing his classification largely from the Roman law. He also took some of his material from the Roman law, but generally only when the topic he treated was not covered by the English common law. English law fills nine-tenths of his pages, which constitute not only a thorough textbook, but in some sense also a digest of English common law. Upon the development of English law as well as upon its study Bracton's book had a profound influence. **Henry de Bracton**

The decline of interest in purely literary studies which manifested itself in the course of the twelfth century affected the writing of his-

Historical
writing

tory. The last of the chronicles begun in the time of Henry II[8] was brought to a close early in the reign of John. Thereafter the secular clergy ceased to write history, and historical writing became again nearly a monopoly of the monasteries. These monastic annals are valuable as historical sources, though they have little worth as literature in comparison with the historical productions of the twelfth century. The chronicles written at the monastery of St. Albans constitute a notable exception. The literary impulse was given to St. Albans soon after the Norman conquest by a Norman abbot, who brought to England a love of the new learning. He established a *scriptorium*, a room devoted to the copying and writing of manuscripts, endowing it in order that supplies of ink, parchment, and other essential materials might always be available. A century later another abbot, who was a lover of books, added to the endowment and ordained that a special scribe to write history should always be maintained. Under the stimulus of this tradition the historiographers of St. Albans developed the art of historical writing to the highest level attained in England in the Middle Ages. The first of the school whose work has reached us in its original form was Roger of Wendover. In the range of the topics treated, in the fullness of his narrative, and in the liveliness of his style Roger surpassed any of his contemporaries. He, in turn, was excelled by his successor, Matthew Paris, who took up the work at Roger's death in 1236 and carried it on to the end of his own life in 1259. His chronicle is probably the best product of medieval English historical art and one of the best examples in all Europe. Despite strong prejudices, errors, rhetorical effect, and Latinity of a lower standard than that set by historians of the twelfth century, Matthew had a wide range of valuable information and mastership of the art of telling a good story. Later chroniclers at St. Albans were unable to maintain his high standard, but their works continued to rank among the best of the contemporary histories written during the remainder of the Middle Ages. Although the chronicles written in the thirteenth century generally mark a decline in literary quality, the composition of a few chronicles by laymen is indicative of the wider spread of education. A chronicle concerned primarily with the affairs of London,[9] written by an alderman of the city[10] in 1274, is the first of a series of civic chronicles, while a rhyming chronicle, of which William Marshal is the hero,[11] written in French

---

[8] Above, p. 109.
[9] *Liber de Antiquis Legibus.*
[10] Arnold Fitz Thedmar.
[11] *Histoire de Guillaume le Maréchal.*

by a minstrel, is a good example of the type of work which helped to render history more popular.

Our knowledge of the history of the period subsequent to the reign of Henry II is aided further by the enormous increase in the number of official and private documents written. The most important are the series emanating from the king. Before the close of the reign of Henry II the royal court began to record on rolls of parchment the cases heard before it, and these rolls are extant from the time of Richard I. In the latter's reign the chancery began to register upon various sets of rolls[12] copies of the numerous documents which it issued, and during the thirteenth century the royal exchequer kept an increasing variety of records. While these documents are important chiefly for constitutional and political history, there are few aspects of English history upon which they fail to throw light. Another important series of records came from the clergy. Nearly every monastery kept a cartulary. This was a volume for the registration of charters or deeds concerning the lands and privileges of the community, but it often served as a general memorandum book. In the thirteenth century the bishops began more or less regularly to keep copies of their incoming and outgoing correspondence in registers. These and other ecclesiastical records illumine many aspects of the life of the time other than clerical. Thanks to the spread of learning, the clergy no longer enjoyed a monopoly in the production of written records, and we find many a layman who could write Latin. Two sorts of documents coming from their hands were of special importance. In the course of the thirteenth century the lords of large manors generally began to have accounts kept to aid them in the management of their estates. These place before us the life of rural England. A variety of records kept contemporaneously in the boroughs perform a like service for urban England. From this mere enumeration of only the principal types of documents it becomes apparent that the materials from which the history of England may be gleaned became far more bountiful in the thirteenth century than they had ever been before. Great masses of them have been printed, and many of those in manuscript have been utilized by historians of one subject or another, but it will be many a long day before these records have been made to yield all they can tell us of English history after 1200.

Still another aspect of the intellectual revival was the production of a literature in the vernacular. In England the popular literature

Documentary historical sources

---

[12] The principal sets are the charter, the close, and the patent rolls.

written during the century and a half following the Norman conquest was not in English. Apart from the *Anglo-Saxon Chronicle* and a few homilies, lives of saints, and other devotional works, the vernacular literature written in England was couched in the language of the Norman conquerors whom it was designed to instruct or amuse. English literature, the oldest national literature in Europe, was brought to a temporary cessation, while French literature was just beginning to flow. The latter first assumed the epic form, called *chanson de geste*, intended to be sung or recited by minstrels called *jongleurs*. Its theme was warfare and heroic deeds. It had its home in northern France. In the south a little later the troubadours began to sing lyrics of love and chivalry, which reacted upon the poetry of the north and softened its tone. In the course of the twelfth century the *chansons de geste* "meant for the hall, for Homeric recitation after supper," began to give way to metrical romances "intended to be read in my lady's bower."[13] Their themes were drawn from the past history of France, from the myths and legends of classical antiquity, or from the legends of King Arthur and the knights of the round table. These courtly, fashionable romances were designed mainly to entertain the upper class of society, but, as the widening of the intellectual horizon increased the reading public among the middle class, literature more suited to the tastes of townsmen appeared in the form of the *fabliaux*. These were humorous tales, sometimes coarse in character, which often satirized the foibles and weaknesses of contemporary society. While these were the most typical and popular forms taken by the literature written in the language of northern France, there were many others. Didactic treatises, often in verse, rhymed chronicles, moralizing tales frequently in the form of beast-fables, satirical ballads, and devotional works of all sorts are among the varieties of which there are many extant examples.

In the production of this literature written in French, Anglo-Normans, who wrote in England, took a considerable part. They were the first to utilize as subjects of romance a group of themes derived from legends and folk tales concerned with the Danish period of English history. In the other fields their part was most prominent in that of the Arthurian legends. Arthur, about whom the cycle centers, may have been an historical person who led the Celts in their fierce resistance of the Anglo-Saxon invaders soon after 500. We know nothing of his life with certainty, but early in the twelfth century

---

[13] *Cambridge History of English Literature*, i, 310.

Goeffrey of Monmouth, who lived in the Welsh marches, wrote in Latin a work which he called *The History of the Britons*. Despite the title it is not history. It consists almost entirely of fabulous matter drawn partly from Welsh legends and myths and in some measure from the author's imagination. Arthur and Merlin are the central figures, and the book became one of the fountainheads of the Arthurian romances. It also supplied the material for the earliest rhyming chronicles. A few years later Goeffrey Gaimar, who lived in England, wrote a rhyming French chronicle[14] which purported to be history but was in reality romance woven from the materials found in Geoffrey of Monmouth's work. Gaimar continued his French rhymes, however, in a *History of the Angles*, which deals in large part with historical facts. From these pseudo-historical beginnings arose the legitimate rhyming chronicle, such as that about William Marshal,[15] which helped greatly to popularize history in the later Middle Ages. Writers in England, meanwhile, did not cease to contribute new materials to the Arthurian legends, and several of the metrical romances were composed in England. Nor did the contribution to the French literature of the time by Anglo-Normans whose habitat was England stop there, for their works find place in practically every type of the literature which was produced.

When English again became articulate in literature, the language, the form, and the themes had undergone great changes. The language was middle English, as distinguished from Anglo-Saxon and modern English. During the period after the conquest, when English had been only a spoken tongue, inflections had broken down, syntax had been transformed, spelling and pronunciation had altered, and the vocabulary had received many additions and a few subtractions. Until the middle of the thirteenth century, writing in English was confined almost entirely to religious subjects, though even here much of the form, content, and spirit was borrowed from French sources. The most notable exception was Layamon's *Brut*, a rhymed chronicle written in 1205. Layamon, who was a priest living on the Severn, thus introduced the Arthurian legend into English literature, and at the same time set the example of the rhymed English chronicle. His work has been pronounced "the most valuable single production in English speech between the conquest and Chaucer."[16] About 1300,

English
literature

---

[14] No copy of the work is known to be extant.
[15] Above, p. 164.
[16] Schofield, *English Literature from the Norman Conquest to Chaucer*, p. 350.

Robert of Gloucester, probably a monk in the monastery of that name, produced a metrical chronicle in English which is history and not romance, and thereafter such histories became common. Meanwhile the French metrical romances began to be imitated in English. The imitations, which were usually little more than free translations, were for the most part poor. They were meant for the rude and humble part of society. They are indicative of the greater part which the middle class was coming to take in national affairs. Still more significant from that point of view was the issue of a royal proclamation in English by Henry III in 1258 and the rise during his reign of a political ballad in the tongue of the masses. As literature the English product of this period could not rival the French, but it was gradually assimilating the thought and expression of the French literature at the time when that literature dominated the vernacular literatures of Europe. Thus it was preparing the way for Chaucer, whose masterpiece was to take rank with any produced in medieval Europe.

Architecture

The artistic sense which was seeking one outlet in the vernacular literature found a more perfect expression in ecclesiastical architecture. In the twelfth century the Norman Romanesque underwent many transformations. As the technique became more perfect, the heaviness and massiveness of the earlier structures began to give way to lighter and more ornamental effects. In France contemporaneously the Romanesque was being superseded entirely by a new style of building called Gothic. Toward the end of the twelfth century the new architectural style began to appear in England, and in the course of the thirteenth century it prevailed entirely. It employed pointed arches systematically for both structural and ornamental purposes, substituted clusters of delicate shafts for the ponderous supporting columns of the Norman Romanesque, and reduced the extent of the solid walls by increasing the extent of the openings. The general effect produced is one of lightness, loftiness, and airy grace. In the reign of Henry III the early Gothic style reached the perfection of its development. Henry himself caused Westminster Abbey to be rebuilt in the new style. The purest example of early Gothic to be found among English cathedrals is at Salisbury. The church was built during the reign of Henry III, and apart from the tower and the spire it is in the early Gothic style throughout. The observer of the quiet harmony of the soaring lines of its interior can hardly fail to catch something of the spirit of the people whose lofty aspirations it typifies.

The development of the church after the Norman conquest has

already occupied our attention. Of the relations between church and state and of the secular clergy, as much has been said as space permits; but the regular clergy deserve further notice. For them the Norman conquest marked the beginning of a golden age. The king and his Norman followers had hardly received their lands when they began to found new monasteries. The life of the cloister still appealed to men as the highest type of life possible. Soon it was the fashion for wealthy landowners to establish new monasteries by the creation of endowments in lands, and for the lesser gentry to give from their smaller properties to swell the riches of monasteries already created. For a hundred years after the conquest the religious enthusiasm which found expression in this practical manner was a rising tide. By 1200 more than 500 new monasteries had been founded. Before the end of the century, however, the great era of the monastic revival was past. During the long reign of Henry III only 157 new houses were established,[17] and after 1300 comparatively few new foundations saw the light.

Increase of the monasteries

The monasticism brought by the conquest was in spirit more like that which had prevailed in the age of the English conversion. Essentially it was the spirit of Cluny. In this French monastery the inmates lived by the Benedictine rule, but they followed it with a rigor which was unknown elsewhere at the time. Their reputation for holiness attracted an attention which resulted in emulation. The English monasteries founded after 1066 were at first mainly independent Benedictine houses patterned on Cluny, or houses dependent upon Cluny. By the twelfth century, however, the Cluniacs, in turn, were showing signs of spiritual decay. They had been too successful, acquiring so much wealth that they became concerned too much with the administration of their property and too little with the maintenance of strict discipline and spiritual ideals. As the Cluniacs let the monastic banner fall, new orders arose to bear it aloft. The most important of them was the Cistercian, which was founded in France largely through the efforts of an English monk. The Cistercians adopted a stricter form of the Benedictine rule than the Cluniac, and were still more severe in their asceticism. Soon they began to colonize. In the first half of the twelfth century their houses spread rapidly, many being established in England. The Cistercians had the same kind of influence in the twelfth century that the Cluniacs had had earlier, and their leaven more or less permeated the whole mass of monasticism.

The monastic spirit

---

[17] Bateson, *Mediaeval England*, p. 202.

From the time of the conquest to the closing years of the twelfth
century the monks upheld nobly an ideal of religious life which contemporaries generally regarded as the highest form of Christianity.
In the thirteenth century they began to depart from their high estate.
The monasteries were not notably corrupt. A few cases of grave disorders appear to have been distinctly exceptional. Neither had they
outlived their usefulness. They still contributed largely and intimately
to the national life; they were generally good landlords and good agri-
culturalists; they offered safe deposit for money and treasure, when
bank vaults were yet unknown and robbery was more common than
it is today; they maintained guest-houses in many a spot where the
traveler could have found no other accommodation; and they dispensed charity to all comers at their gates and carried food to the
poor of many a rural district. But they were placing less emphasis
on spiritual and intellectual life and more on the skillful management
of their estates. There was a growing laxness of discipline apparent.
Violations of the strictness of the rule, such as talk at the table or in
the cloister and irregularity in the attendance of services, gave the
inspectors of the monasteries more trouble than carnal lapses. The
monks of the thirteenth century were not gluttons, but they were
more interested in the quality and character of their food than their
ascetic founders ever expected them to be. Little things were these,
but they comported ill with the ideal of monasticism. The intellectual
leadership passed to the seculars, and, while many monks still copied
books, few wrote new ones.[18] Things material had come to take a
place in their interests that should have been occupied by things
spiritual. The religious welfare of many a parish was imperiled by
their greed. In the heyday of their popularity many a noble who
had the power had impropriated to them the revenues belonging
to parish churches. In such cases the monastery provided the parish
with a vicar to whom it paid the lowest possible living wage, taking
the surplus for the use of the monastic community. Before the end
of the century, too, there were instances of the reduction of almsgiving and of the decline of hospitality. The monasteries, in short,
were no longer such prominent centers of spirituality and learning
as they had once been, while their concern with worldly affairs was
becoming ever more apparent. They had not lost their popularity, but
their popularity had passed the flood. Criticism was not yet common; the monks were still respected; but they no longer appealed with

---

[18] *Ibid.*, p. 202.

the same strength to the popular imagination. They still received gifts, but the cartularies display a marked decrease in the amount after the middle of the thirteenth century. Already the popular allegiance was being transferred to the friars, who were rising as a new star in the ecclesiastical firmament.

The first two orders of friars were organized early in the thirteenth century by two men whose ideals were very different. St. Dominic was a learned Spaniard of aristocratic family. He was a skilled debater and an eloquent preacher. For many years he employed these talents in the attempt to end heresy in southern France by converting the heretics. In the course of his mission he gathered companions who lived and worked with him. In 1215 he obtained papal permission to found the Dominican order of friars. He and his sixteen followers lived by rule like monks. There the similarity ceased. The monks lived secluded lives, seeking primarily to save their own souls; the Dominicans went among men to preach, to combat heresy, to arouse the apathetic, to convert the sinner, to save the souls of other men. Almost immediately the followers of Dominic dispersed to spread their missionary spirit in all countries. Within six years their enthusiasm had so impressed their hearers that sixty convents had been established.

The Domini- cans

St. Francis was an Italian of the middle class whose father was a prosperous merchant in Assisi. In his youth he took part in his father's business until he was seized with a serious illness. Upon his recovery he began to devote himself to works of charity. His extravagant liberality alarmed his father, who forced him to leave the business and to renounce his inheritance. St. Francis then became a wandering beggar, devoting himself to a life of good works. His reputation for saintliness soon attracted followers, who necessitated organization. Nearly contemporaneously with St. Dominic, St. Francis obtained papal permission to found a new order. The Franciscans were at one with the Dominicans in the main outline of their organization. They lived by rule, but went forth among men to evangelize the world. Their principles, however, differed from the Dominican. St. Francis believed examples of holy living to be of more importance than sermons. He placed the chief stress upon poverty. His friars were to own no property either as individuals or as a corporation. They were to live from day to day with such food and shelter as they could beg or earn. His thought was to persuade men to lead good lives by placing before them lives patterned as closely upon Christ's as was

The Francis- cans

humanly possible. The poor and humble were to minister to the poor, to alleviate their want, to care for their bodily ills, and to save their souls. St. Francis tended to regard learning as unnecessary, but as his followers saw the success of the Dominicans, they soon began to give more attention to preaching and to prepare for it by a thorough course of training. The Dominicans, on their side, borrowed the principle of poverty from the Franciscans. Learned preaching, however, was ever a more distinctive characteristic of the Dominicans, who were called the friars preachers, and poverty of the Franciscans, who, at the wish of St. Francis, were called friars minors, because none could be less than they.

Development of the friars

The friars were immediately successful. They "came upon Christendom like a revelation—men who had abandoned all that was enticing in life to imitate the apostles, to convert the sinner and unbeliever, to arouse the slumbering moral sense of mankind, to instruct the ignorant, to offer salvation to all."[19] They lived among the poor of the great towns in a spirit of perfect equality; their fare was of the coarsest; their hardships were greater than those of many; but always they brought to others help, good cheer, and a zeal for the faith which was contagious. They stirred the emotions of all classes. Their membership grew rapidly. They became the authors of a revival which made religion again a living factor in the hearts of many to whom it had become a form, or even less. The papacy soon realized the possibilities of the new orders and began to use them as its special agents. They walked among men, having great influence with every rank and class. The popes had but to give an order to the heads of the friars to have it carried out in every corner of Christendom. They used the friars to spread the faith among classes whom both the seculars and the regulars had failed to reach, to carry out policies which the powerful secular prelates would have opposed, and to promote their temporal as well as their spiritual powers. To accomplish these results the papacy conferred upon the friars the most extraordinary privileges. They were allowed to preach, to hear confessions, and to celebrate the mass wherever they might be. They drew parishioners away from their parish priests, eventually competing with the secular clergy for their fees. Papal exemptions placed the friars largely outside the ordinary ecclesiastical jurisdiction and left them responsible chiefly to their own superiors. Such power and popularity were more than human nature could withstand; eventually the friars deteriorated. Their rules about poverty were relaxed suffi-

---

[19] Lea, *History of the Inquisition of the Middle Ages,* i, 266.

ciently to allow others to hold property in trust for them, and they soon had the use of conventual houses and endowments. This diversion of benefactions aroused the antagonism of the monks, who delighted to contrast the real riches of the mendicants with their professed poverty. Wealth, however, was not their besetting sin, for they always remained more or less true to their principles. The properties accumulated for them never rivaled in extent those possessed by the monks. Power unrestrained by adequate responsibility was the evil that undermined their ideals. In the later Middle Ages the friars were still a potent force in the church, and a force that generally made for good, but they no longer retained that buoyant enthusiasm which had rejuvenated the church in the thirteenth century.

In England the friars were received cordially from the first. The Dominicans came in 1220 and the Franciscans four years later. They settled in the towns, where they lightened the burdens and renewed the faith of thousands. Both orders established themselves at Oxford almost immediately after their arrival in England. The Dominicans, as was their custom in university towns, established a school with their own lecturers, which became practically a college of the university. The Franciscans followed their example, and at Oxford it was they who attracted the greatest scholars, despite the higher reputation for learning then possessed by the Dominicans. Not only in England, but also in all of Europe, the dominant minds in the intellectual world of the thirteenth century belonged to friars of one order or the other. Far better educated than the parish priests, trained to eloquence and wit in speech, the bearers of the news of the world, the tellers of stories having both a point and a moral, the friars were welcomed everywhere by rich and poor alike. In a little more than thirty years the Franciscans had established fifty houses in various towns of the English province, and the Dominicans were not far behind. The friars appealed strongly to English popular sentiment, and they acquired an influence which made them a powerful factor in the religious life of England in the thirteenth century. Later their influence declined. Their discipline was observed less scrupulously, they devoted more attention to their buildings, the burden of supplying their material needs impaired their spiritual efficiency and made them importunate beggars, and their quarrels with both seculars and regulars became more bitter. Various were the signs of degeneration, but in England the friars remained more nearly true to their original ideal than they did in many parts of Europe. To the population of the English towns they were still the leading exponents of the faith in the later Middle Ages.

The friars in England

CHAPTER X

LIFE IN COUNTRY AND TOWN

The
village

IN THE thirteenth century the vast majority of the people of England still lived in the country, and the conditions of rural life remained much as they had been in the Anglo-Saxon period.[1] The village was still the typical rural community, and it retained the same economic self-sufficiency and social independence. Its inhabitants had little occasion to travel for business or pleasure, and there was a notable lack of communication with the outside world which rendered the village isolated and unprogressive. The dwellers in such a community received little stimulus from the interchange of ideas with people of other sections, and they continued from generation to generation to do things as their fathers had done them. In the agricultural system there was beginning to be some improvement. In the thirteenth century the two-field rotation was often changed for the three-field, which made the land more productive by bringing it oftener under cultivation, but there was probably no other significant innovation in agricultural technique on any large scale. The open-field system with its wasteful method of intermingled strips still prevailed. Stability was the dominant characteristic of the life of the villagers in the thirteenth century as it had been in the tenth.

The
manor

Though the Norman conquest had wrought no great change in the daily routine of the villager's life, it had provided every village with a lord. Every village now constituted part of an estate called a manor, which was held by a lord. The lord kept part of the estate for his own use. This was known by the Normans as the demesne. It generally included a plot of several acres set apart as the site of the manor house and its outbuildings, gardens, and orchards, a large portion of arable land whence the lord derived the food for the sustenance of his household, and of the meadow land whence came the hay for the lord's cattle. The arable land of the demesne often consisted of strips intermingled in the great fields with those of the tenants, and the pasture and the woodland were usually shared between the lord and the tenants.[2] The arable land in the demesne was cultivated for the lord

[1] Above, pp. 62–64.
[2] A good sketch-plan of a manor may be found in Hone's *The Manor*, p. 42.

174

mainly by the tenants who constituted the population of the village located on the manor. The manor house was not only the home of the lord, or of his agent, but it was also the meeting place of the villagers when they had communal business to transact. The most sumptuous manor houses were beginning to be built of stone, but the ordinary structure was built of wood and clay. The main room, or hall, generally served as the living room of the family and the assembly room of the villagers, though some houses were beginning to have an additional room, called the bower, designed for the use of the ladies of the household. The interior was generally bare and comfortless, though the introduction of occasional chimneys and glass windows is symptomatic of a higher standard of comfort gradually developing among the rich. The remainder of the land in the estate was used by the lord's tenants. On the village street they had their homes, which usually were mere huts thatched with straw, each being surrounded by a small yard. In the arable land each tenant had a number of acre strips which he cultivated for himself, in the meadow land he had a share for his own use, and in the common pastures he could graze a number of cattle proportionate to the size of his holding.

The lords of manors were of many varying degrees of wealth and social influence. They might be great noblemen, owning vast estates, **The lords** or simple country gentlemen with small manors supporting no more than a dozen tenants each. The lord of a manor large or small was a power in the community. Over his tenants he had not only economic but also political rights. His power was far from absolute. His tenants, some classes more than others, were protected in some of their rights by the national law, and in many manors local customs in behalf of the tenants were successfully enforced in the court of the lord against the lord himself. Nevertheless, a harsh or an unscrupulous lord could make life miserable for his tenants, while a good and considerate lord might do much to promote their welfare. A writer on husbandry of the thirteenth century pictures an ideal lord as one who acquainted himself with the complaints which his tenants desired to make against his officials and saw that full justice was done to all classes; but the records of quarrels between a lord and the whole of his tenantry are sufficiently frequent to indicate that some lords fell short of the ideal.

The tenants on the estate belonged to three separate classes. Some were legally free. They generally held free tenements for which they **Free** paid rents of money or produce, although they might owe some service **tenants** in labor. Their tenure of such land was permanent. The lord could not legally remove them so long as they fulfilled the obligations resting on the land. By payment of a fee to the lord a free tenant could sell his holding, and his heir inherited it by payment of relief. Although the rents, fees, and services were burdens upon the land, they bore no relation to the real value of the land. They did not constitute a rent in the modern commercial sense of that term. The free tenant was practically the owner of such a holding, subject only to the restrictions of specified payments and services due the lord. In the thirteenth century tenants who leased lands for a term of years and paid annual sums commensurate with the value of the returns from the land were becoming more common, but tenants of this sort, who were properly leaseholders, were not yet numerous. The free tenant on the manor of the thirteenth century was generally of the first type.

Unfree tenants

The largest class of the tenants consisted of the villeins. They were unfree and they held servile tenures. Each had a holding of arable land, generally about thirty acres in extent, whence he derived the main portion of the subsistence provided for himself and his family. In return for the holding he worked for two or three days each week on the land of the lord. At the seasons of plowing or harvesting he gave for several weeks extra days which were known as boon days. He also made payments of rent to the lord. They were often rendered mainly in kind, consisting of such items as fowls at Christmas and eggs at Easter. The cotters differed from the villeins only in degree. They were usually unfree and owed labor services and payments to the lord, but their holdings were generally of five acres or less and their services were correspondingly lighter. One day of work each week, or sometimes only boon works, usually satisfied the requirements of service placed upon them. The slaves were rapidly disappearing as a class before 1066, and under the Norman régime the few that remained soon became indistinguishable from villeins.

Status of the villein

The unfreedom of the villein was relative. Against his lord he had few legal rights. He was attached to the soil and could not leave the manor without his lord's consent. Freedom might be obtained by a formal grant of the lord, by entrance into the ranks of the clergy, or by living in a town as a citizen for a year and a day. The villein's property was at the mercy of the lord, though it was protected against all others by the lord himself. In practice the lord rarely exercised the full extent of his legal authority. He levied at his discretion heavy and vexatious payments called tallages, and exacted fees and fines on certain occasions. Examples of the latter were the heriot, consisting usually of the villein's best animal, paid upon his death, and merchet, paid when the villein's daughter married.[3] Beyond such exactions as these, which were generally regulated in time and amount by custom, the lord rarely attempted to appropriate the possessions of his villein. Neither did he commonly disturb the villein's possession of his tenement as long as the services and payments due therefrom were rendered. In his person the villein was protected against his lord and all others by the national courts.

If a lord had several manors, or a single large manor, the successful management of his estate was often a complicated business. The lord of a small manor might direct its operation himself, but the lord usually appointed a bailiff to transact the business for him. The lord of several manors would have a bailiff resident on each manor and also a steward to oversee the work of the bailiffs. The steward traveled about from manor to manor, coming to each manor perhaps two or three times a year. It was his function to be well informed on the condition of the lands, houses, tenants, stock, and tools, to direct the general agricultural policies of the estate—deciding, for example, what fields should be cultivated and what crops should be planted in a given year—to keep the manor stocked with necessary supplies, to see that the bailiff performed his duties properly in relation both to the lord and to the tenants, to advise his lord legally, and to conduct the manorial courts. The bailiff looked after the details of manorial administration. He saw that the right crops were planted at the right time and that the plowing, reaping, and other services were performed well by those servants or tenants whose duty it was to do them. On most manors there was a second official called the reeve, who was one of the villeins and was sometimes elected by them. He acted as the foreman of the villagers, it being his principal duty to see that the tenants contributed the amount of services due. The lord kept himself informed through the oral reports of the steward and the bailiffs and by the written accounts of various kinds which these officials were required to render.

Manorial administration

The revenues of the lord were derived mainly from the agricultural produce of the demesne, although by the thirteenth century a few manors could be found where the principal item came from the rents. The produce was chiefly in the form of grain, although dairy products, eggs, meat, poultry, wool, hides, and other products formed a part of the whole which would vary in proportion from one manor to another. The varieties of vegetables and fruits known were few, and of those known the amount raised was small. Lords often derived further

Manorial income

[3] An excellent analysis of the many rents and fees is given by N. K. Neilson in her *Customary Rents* in the second volume of *Oxford Studies in Social and Legal History.*

revenue from the demesne by the sale of hay, pasturage, turf, and wood. Judged by modern standards, the lord's returns from the operation of the demesne were small. The average yield of wheat from an acre was eight or nine bushels in place of the modern average of thirty bushels; but the cost of cultivation was less, since most of the labor was provided by the lord's tenants and fertilization was seldom practiced. The item generally second in importance was that of the rents paid by the tenants partly in money and partly in produce. The fees exacted from the villeins also amounted to a substantial total. The fourth revenue of significance on the ordinary manor was derived from the fines and fees assessed by the manorial court held by the lord. Much of the income from the rents and fees as well as that from the demesne was in the form of produce. In the eleventh century most of this income was consumed directly. Lords who had several manors either traveled from one to the other and resided at each until the year's production had been eaten, or they had the produce from all the manors brought to a permanent residence. Monastic communities necessarily followed the latter method, but the poor roads made transportation by wagon so difficult that it was easier for the ordinary lord to travel to the food. As the circulation of money increased in later centuries, it became possible to market some of the manorial produce. Lords who had more than one manor often found it convenient to buy their food in the markets adjacent to their permanent residences and to sell the produce of demesnes located at a distance in neighboring markets. During the thirteenth century a gradual rise of the price of grain stimulated the sale of produce on most manors. By the end of the century the sale of a considerable portion of the lord's share was common, though generally a portion was still consumed by the owner and his dependents.

Effects of money economy on manorial organization

The introduction of money as a significant factor in manorial economy produced changes of importance in manorial organization. Lords who had cash sometimes found it advantageous to hire labor in place of the forced work of the villeins. On manors where this practice developed, the villeins usually had their labor services commuted for payments in money. The commutation of services in labor to rents in money eliminated one of the most significant characteristics of tenure in villeinage and gave to the holders of such tenures greater economic freedom. The circulation of money also facilitated the lease of lands for rents in money. A lord who did not wish to continue the cultivation of his demesne might find opportunity to lease all or part of it. The growth of these practices was destined ultimately to destroy the characteristic economic aspects of the manor. In the thirteenth century the development was only beginning.

The political power of the lord stood out most clearly in the manorial court. After the Norman conquest every lord had jurisdiction over the free and unfree tenants upon his manor. It extended to civil suits and to lesser offenses such as might be tried in the public local courts. Some lords were also privileged to try serious crimes ordinarily reserved for the royal court as crown pleas. The possession of a private court did not give the lord as complete power over his tenants as might be supposed, because the judgment was usually found by the group of free tenants and villeins in attendance.[4] The manorial court, which met several times a year, was the place where all the communal affairs of the village were aired. In this assembly the transfer or inheritance of the lands of the tenants was acknowledged and recorded, and the appropriate fines or fees were paid to the lord; infractions of manorial customs, such as the failure to perform the services required of the tenement or trespass on the lord's or a neighbor's lands, were punished with fines; those accused of assaults, slanders, and other petty squabbles were adjudged; the reeve and other officials of the villagers, such as cowherds, poundkeepers, and ale-tasters, were elected; and regulations of matters of common interest were established. The joys and the hardships, the tragedies and the comedies of the life of the village, all are set forth in the dry language of the court rolls for those who will read them.

Manorial courts

Upon the towns the Norman conquest acted as a stimulant. It brought England into closer bonds with the continent just in time to give the towns a share in the expansion of European commerce which was beginning. The better protection given to the towns by a stronger central government also served to promote the trade upon which their prosperity rested. The effect upon their growth was marked. By 1300 there were probably some 200 towns. Older towns increased in size and prosperity, though they were still small from the modern point of view. London, the largest, had a probable population of from 25,000 to 40,000, while York and Bristol, the next largest, had about 10,000 each. The average town probably had a population of two or three thousand. The urban population was still a small part of the whole population, but its growing wealth gave it influence, and the townsmen gained in importance in the national life after the conquest.

Growth of the towns

[4] Later in the Middle Ages three separate manorial courts were sometimes held. The court customary disposed of the civil suits of the villeins, the court baron of the civil suits of the free tenants, and the court leet of criminal cases and misdemeanors.

Organiza-
tion of the
towns

During the twelfth and thirteenth centuries the organization of the towns was completely transformed. Before 1066 some of them had established local customs and privileges adapted to their particular needs, but they were not separate jurisdictional units with rights of self-government, and they had no strong sense of communal interest. After the conquest, as the towns grew in prosperity, their inhabitants became more conscious of a corporate spirit of unity, and they began to purchase from their lords charters which granted them special rights and privileges. These charters appeared at the close of the eleventh century and for the next two centuries they increased both in number and in the extent of the privileges granted. The acquisition of charters finally made the majority of towns communities with extensive rights of self-government and helped to make the townsmen a distinct element in the political, social, and economic life of the nation.

The charters which individual towns obtained varied greatly in their content. The boroughs[5] dependent upon lords other than the king usually had to be satisfied with less in the way of privilege, but most of the boroughs in England ultimately received royal charters. Even the royal charters were not uniform, but by the thirteenth century they commonly granted five privileges. (1) *Firma burgi,* or the farm of the borough, meant that the rents, tolls, and other dues owed by the inhabitants to the king were commuted for a lump sum. The community of the town became responsible for the payment to the king of a fixed sum annually, and its officials collected the rents and dues from individuals. The chief advantage was the freedom gained from the intervention of the sheriff in the internal affairs of the town. It gave to the townsmen the management of their own fiscal business. (2) Every borough secured the right to have its own court where the burgesses[6] could transact such judicial business as was not reserved for the royal courts. (3) Freedom from tolls was often given. Tolls, which were charged by every town and by many lords for the privilege of trading in districts controlled by them, were a burden upon trade. A royal exemption from tolls was particularly valuable because it gave freedom from vexatious restrictions in so large a territory. (4) Another common privilege was the right to elect its own officials. This freed the borough from the local executive official formerly appointed by the

---

[5] The term *borough* is used here and subsequently in accordance with present English usage. *Borough* designates an urban unit which is not a city. The title *city* is applied only to a town with a cathedral, or to a town which has been granted the title by charter as an honor. *Town* is the generic term which covers all urban units.

[6] Citizens of a borough.

king and gave it a large measure of local autonomy. (5) The fifth was the right to organize a gild merchant as a means of regulating the trade of the town. Incorporation of the borough, which made it a fictitious person with a common seal and the power to sue and be sued and to possess and convey property, did not become common until the later Middle Ages, but the total of the privileges granted in the charters gave to the boroughs a wide field of free and independent action. Through elected officials the community could act for the welfare of the whole body in dealings with the king, lords, and other boroughs, and its area of home rule was large. The English boroughs, however, were never able to become small independent republics like those in Italy and Germany. Royalty in England developed its strength at an early date, and it was able to hold the municipalities in check from the start. Although extensive liberties of local self-government were granted by English kings, they were held subject to limitations imposed by a strong central government.

The form taken by the government in the different boroughs is rarely defined in the charters. Nearly always there was an executive head, usually called the mayor, who was elected by the burgesses. He, with some assistants, had charge of the administration of the borough, and he presided over the court. Most of the business of the borough was transacted at the court. At the more important sessions, where by-laws would be made and elections held, all the burgesses had the right to be present. In this period the government of the borough was essentially democratic. All citizens could take part. Citizenship was determined usually by the payment of local taxes or by the possession of a house and lot. Before the end of the thirteenth century, however, a tendency toward oligarchy appeared, which later became pronounced. The right to elect officials, to enact by-laws, and to control the finances in many towns passed into the hands of a small council, which, though it might have been originally an elective body, generally became a self-recruiting group. By the end of the Middle Ages instances of popular participation in the government of boroughs were uncommon. *Government of the towns*

One of the most important factors in the internal affairs of the town was the gild merchant. It was an organization composed of those townsmen whose business was selling. Since nearly all townsmen were engaged in some kind of trade, few of the inhabitants were left outside its membership. Its main object was to regulate the commercial affairs of the town in such a way as to give to its members a monopoly of the trade of the town. All outsiders had to pay the tolls from which the gildsmen were exempt, and were subject to other restrictions. Al- *The gild merchant* though farmers from the surrounding district were generally allowed to sell their produce for consumption by the townsmen, and alien retailers of some other articles might be permitted to do business under the regulations of the gild, none except a gildsman could retail certain specified articles or buy any articles to sell them again in the town. When a wholesale merchant came to town he might be required to sell only to gildsmen. To prevent gildsmen who would be purchasers from bidding up the price against one another, a gildsman was generally required to share on demand his purchases with a fellow member at the price which he had paid for them. The gild also had power to settle minor disputes among members, and it attempted to protect members who were subjected to injustice in other towns. With this main object the gild merchant combined a number of fraternal, social, and charitable purposes. It had regular meetings where the officials were elected, by-laws were enacted, and other business was transacted, and these were so regularly the occasions of banquets and merrymakings that the assembly was often called the "drinking." "Among the bibulous brethren of Winchester," says Gross, " 'to drink the Gild Merchant' meant to hold a meeting of the fraternity."[7] Many gilds provided for the visitation of sick members, for the support of indigent members and of widows of deceased members, and for attendance in a body at the funeral of a deceased member. Some, too, dispensed alms to the poor of the town.

The benefits conferred by the gilds merchant have been variously estimated. Their social and fraternal aspects helped to satisfy a desire for association and fellowship which was strong among medieval townsmen, but these were merely incidental objects of the gilds merchant. Such aspirations could be satisfied equally well by the numerous religious gilds which existed solely for charitable, religious, and social purposes and had no connection with business. The gilds merchant should be judged primarily on the basis of their contribution to the development of commerce. Their chief merit was the protection given to their members in a period when the individual trader was likely to encounter much oppression and injustice from local authorities and to receive little aid from the central government. The attempt to monopolize the trade of the town, on the other hand, tended to reduce free competition and to discourage trade. In the twelfth and thirteenth centuries when the gilds merchant were at the height of their development, they probably served a useful purpose. In later centuries, when

---

[7] *Gild Merchant,* i, 33.

the central government began to provide more adequate protection to merchants and the growth of trade made the maintenance of free competition of greater importance, the disadvantages began to outweigh the advantages and the privileges of the gilds became an incubus on trade.

Long before the gilds merchant had run their course the craft gilds were developing alongside of them. A few craft gilds can claim an **Craft gilds** antiquity nearly equal to that of the gilds merchant, but they did not become common until the thirteenth century, and it was only in the course of the fourteenth century that they gradually became more important than the gilds merchant. The craft gild was composed of those residents in a town who were engaged in the production and sale of a certain article. It usually had an industrial element that was lacking in the gild merchant. Each gild included all persons in the town who practiced its craft, and none was allowed to follow the craft in the town who was not a member. It was a common requirement that the members must display a certain degree of competence, but at first little attention was given to the methods by which competence had been acquired. In the course of time, however, it became the general rule that an apprenticeship must have been served before the craft could be followed. The apprentice was bound by contract to work for a master of the trade for a term of years, usually seven. The master provided the apprentice with lodgings, food, and clothes and taught him the trade, while the apprentice gave his work, maintained secrecy concerning the processes of the industry, and governed his deportment according to the instructions of the master. At the end of the period, if the master pronounced him competent, he was free to follow the trade. If he had the necessary capital, he might then become a master who possessed his own shop where he employed apprentices and possibly laborers working for daily wages, manufactured articles, and displayed them for sale. The master's shop was on a small scale both an industrial and a mercantile establishment. If the man who had successfully served his apprenticeship lacked the necessary means to become a master, he would become a journeyman, that is, a laborer at the trade who worked for a master in return for daily wages. As a rule, the masters constituted the most influential members of the gild, and sometimes the other classes had no voice whatever in the affairs of the gild. In the early days of the craft gilds this worked no great hardship, since the capital required to become a master was so small that it was comparatively easy for a journeyman to make the transition. As industry increased in volume, however, the capitalistic gulf between the two classes tended to become wider. There came to be many journeymen who could never hope to become masters. Their interests diverged more and more from those of the masters, often causing friction between the two classes in the later Middle Ages.

The craft gild attempted to regulate within the town both the sale and the manufacture of the particular article which its members produced. By regulations similar to those applied on a wider scale by the gild merchant it sought to preserve for its members a monopoly of the home market in the article manufactured by the craft. It also had social, charitable, fraternal, and protective objects, which it promoted in ways kindred to those employed by the gild merchant. Its most distinctive rules were those concerned with production. Many of them were directed to the maintenance of an honest standard in the products of the industry. Typical rules for this purpose prohibited all kinds of deceitful devices, such as burnishing old spurs and selling them for new. Other regulations were intended to maintain an equality among the masters of the craft. Rules of this type, which were common, limited the number of apprentices and journeymen a master might employ, limited the working time, and limited the quantity of production per master. Some craft gilds also regulated wages and less frequently prices. Such rules as these obviously had as their ulterior object to keep up prices by limiting the amount of production and reducing the amount of competition to a minimum.

The appearance of craft gilds marked a considerable development in the organization of industry. Previously most manufactured articles had been produced in households primarily dependent upon agriculture for their support. Individual artisans here and there maintained themselves solely by the pursuit of some industry other than agriculture, but the rise of the craft gilds meant that in one town several persons gained subsistence from the pursuit of a single industry. A class of artisans, or of industrial workers, had arisen.

Markets Not all of the business was transacted in the shops of the gildsmen; every town and many villages had markets. For the most part they were places where the surplus products of the rural districts were sold to the townsmen. Since the volume of business was not sufficient to maintain a continuous trade, the markets were generally held only once a week. The right to hold a market, which could be acquired only by royal grant, was prized, because the owner, whether town or lord, received tolls on all sales.

Fairs The trade of the markets was essentially local. The opportunity to trade with men of other localities could be found at the fairs. They were held at still greater intervals, usually only once a year, since the extent of the trade other than purely local was still comparatively small. Fairs were held by some private person, such as a lord, a bishop, or an abbot, who had obtained the right from the king. The fair was generally located outside a town where temporary booths and stalls were erected for the use of the merchants frequenting the fair. The owner charged rents for the booths and collected fees on all sales. In order to provide him with a monopoly which would insure his profits, no trading was allowed outside the fair in the immediate locality for the few days or weeks of the duration of the fair. In some instances the sale of food and other articles for immediate consumption was permitted in the neighboring town, but for all other business the townsmen had to come to the fair and pay fees on their sales. The foreigner, on the other hand, was admitted to the fair on a perfect equality with the resident of the locality, being freed from the discrimination maintained against him in the towns. Fairs of this type were held all over Europe. The largest of them were the principal centers of the wholesale trade. To the fairs of eastern France and Flanders, for example, merchants came from many parts of northern Europe to exchange their wares for those of eastern and Mediterranean lands brought mainly by merchants from Italy. The principal fairs were arranged to fall on different dates, and many wholesale merchants traveled from one fair to another on a more or less continuous circuit. Most of the English fairs drew their buyers and sellers only from different parts of England. They were places where bailiffs of manors often came to dispose of the surplus products of the manor and to buy many of the manorial supplies for the ensuing year. Several of the English fairs, however, such as those at Winchester, St. Ives, Northampton, Stamford, and Boston, attracted many foreigners, and were important primarily for their wholesale transactions. At these larger fairs foreigners sold to native merchants a large part of the goods they imported, and bought large quantities of the English staple products, which they exported.

One of the most distinctive features of the fair was the court held by the proprietor. It was known in England as the court of pie powder. The term is a corruption of the French phrase *pied poudré*, signifying that the court was so informal that the traders at the fair could come into the court just as they were with dusty shoes and get their disputes settled promptly. The informal and speedy procedure of the court was its distinctive characteristic. It was designed to meet the needs of merchants who would want to be on their way to the next mart, without

Courts of pie powder

incurring the inevitable delays and inconveniences which the use of the courts of the borough, shire, or hundred with their infrequent sessions and formal procedure would necessitate. Its decisions generally were not based on national law or on local custom, but were more in the nature of equitable findings of what was just and right. The judgment was often found by a group of the merchants attending the fair, who were likely to be guided by a body of commercial laws and customs which the merchants of Europe had developed by their own usage to meet their particular needs. This law merchant appears to have originated among the Italian merchants trading along the coasts of the Mediterranean, who carried it to fairs and markets all over Europe. By the thirteenth century it was an international code of customary law with slight local variations applied in the courts of the fairs and in many of the municipal courts of Italy, Spain, France, Germany, and Flanders. In England, too, its use gradually extended from the courts of the fairs to some of the burghal courts, where visiting strangers could have the advantages of the law merchant at any time. This extension, however, seems barely to have begun in the thirteenth century.

The foreign commerce of England increased rapidly in this period.

Foreign commerce
English exports were mainly raw materials. Wool, which went chiefly to the looms of Flanders, was the principal article of export. In the thirteenth century satirical poets on the continent used the phrase, "to send wool to England," as we now use the phrase, "to send coals to Newcastle."[8] Sheepskins, hides, and tin were also important articles; and lead, salted meats, dairy products, grain, fish, and salt were exported in significant quantities. The only manufactured wares which found a foreign market in large amounts were the coarser woven cloths. The imports consisted largely of manufactured products and of provisions not produced in England, although some raw materials or partly manufactured products used in English manufactures found a place in the trade. Wines from Gascony and the Rhine, furs, tar, wax, linen, silver and other northern products from the Baltic, fine cloths and other manufactured wares from Flanders, silks and fine manufactures from Italy, and spices, drugs, dyes and luxuries from the east constituted the chief imports. This trade was dominated by the foreign merchants, who came from Germany, the lands of the Baltic, Flanders, France, Italy and Spain. English merchants did not yet engage largely in the export trade.

---

[8] Pirenne, *Histoire de Belgique*, third ed., i, 270.

The only important exception was constituted by a group of English merchants engaged in the export of wool, hides, and tin, who appear to have organized sometime in the second half of the thirteenth century to further the interests of their trade, which was chiefly with Flanders. They became known as the Merchants of the Staple, probably because their organization centered about an institution of that name. The name was given to "a depot where traders deposited their wares." It constituted "a continuous mart at which commodities were bought and sold, just as the fair was a periodical mart."[9] Edward I secured for English merchants trading across seas the privilege of having a staple at Antwerp with considerable powers of commercial regulation and self-government. The English merchants who controlled the staple were established as an organized group with an elected mayor at their head and were empowered to exercise quasi-political as well as commercial functions. English exporters trading at this mart enjoyed the special privileges conferred upon the staple, but their business had to be conducted to some extent under the supervision of the English merchants who controlled the staple. English merchants, however, were under no compulsion to trade at the staple. When they had paid duties on their exports at English ports, they could transport their goods whither they would. In 1273 English merchants exported thirty-five per cent of the wool sent out of England, the Italians with twenty-four per cent being their nearest competitors. Other English exports were carried out of the realm mainly by foreign merchants, who bought them from English merchants and producers.

Merchants of the Staple

The foreign trade was conducted upon an intermunicipal rather than upon an international basis. The merchants of London traded with the merchants of Newcastle, Florence, and Bruges; not the merchants of England with those of Flanders and Italy. If a merchant of Paris got into trouble with the merchants of Southampton, he sought aid, not from the government of France, but from the municipal authorities of his home town. Any merchant who came to an English town to transact business, whether he came from a foreign town or from another English town, was subject to all the restrictions imposed by the merchant gild or by other municipal authorities. He generally had to pay local tolls from which the townsmen were free, he could sell

Intermunicipal character of trade

---

[9] Lipson, *Economic History of England,* i, 471. In the reign of Edward I staple was also applied to certain English ports, where Edward decreed, in 1297, that the raw products constituting the staple exports of England, the principal of which were wool, hides and tin, should be assembled for export. The purpose of these staples was to facilitate the collection of the royal customs imposed on these exports.

only at wholesale and only to members of the gild, he had to reside with a local merchant who could keep an eye on his transactions, and he could stay for only forty days. These and other limitations designed to make trade difficult for the foreigners were reduced to some extent by mutual agreements among towns.

In England the greatest exemptions secured by foreigners came from the concessions of the king. In the time of Henry II the merchants of Cologne obtained the special protection of the king for the merchants from that city resident in London. They were allowed to live together in London as a gild or hanse with a considerable amount of internal self-government, and eventually they acquired the right to have their own warehouses, to trade anywhere in England, to be relieved of some of the local tolls, and to engage to some extent in the retail trade. Meanwhile the Teutonic Hanse, as the organization was called, was amalgamated with the Hanseatic League, consisting of a union of German cities which had pooled their commercial interests. The league, which succeeded to the special privileges of the Teutonic Hanse, was under the leadership of the northern German cities, such as Lübeck, Hamburg, and Bremen. It controlled the trade of the Baltic. For the remainder of the Middle Ages the Hanseatic League was a significant factor in the foreign trade of England. Another group of merchants who acquired privileges at an early date came from the cities of Flanders. In the twelfth century they had a Flemish Hanse in London. They do not appear to have acquired such extensive privileges as the Teutonic Hanse, nor did they maintain successfully the monopoly of the Flemish trade. In the course of the thirteenth century the Flemish Hanse declined in importance, until it finally disappeared entirely soon after the close of the century. The French and Italian merchants had no such unions of towns which could negotiate for wholesale exemptions. During the thirteenth century many individual towns and companies of merchants secured from the English crown important relaxations of the restrictions to which foreign merchants were generally subject, and in 1302 the Gascon merchants as a whole received special privileges. A year later Edward I issued the famous *carta mercatoria*. The document decreed the payment of royal customs by foreign merchants in excess of those paid by English merchants. In return it gave the whole body of foreign merchants freedom from certain local tolls and from many of the customary local restrictions on buying and selling. It also guaranteed their contracts, and provided that justice should be administered speedily. Local prejudice, however, created an opposition that was too strong for the crown, and the *carta mercatoria* was subsequently revoked. It required a long struggle between the crown and English commercial interests before a portion of the principal provisions of the concession could be gradually established in the course of the fourteenth century.

One branch of business, the financial, was monopolized by foreigners settled in England. Fluid capital, which could be invested in business enterprises as opportunity offered, or could be borrowed by those projecting new ventures in business, was in the early Middle Ages practically an unknown quantity. The king, however, often wished to borrow money to anticipate his income, and landowners frequently borrowed to meet sudden heavy demands, such as those created by the necessity of paying their expenses on a crusade. Till the closing years of the twelfth century such business was handled solely by the Jews.

Financial business

Although Jews may have been located in England in the Anglo-Saxon period, they first become prominent in English records after the Norman conquest, when considerable numbers came to England from the continent. The Jews were not citizens and they had no rights except such protection as the crown chose to give them. They always constituted an alien element in the community. They did not engage in agriculture or other industries, Christians would have no social intercourse with them, and they lived segregated in the towns. Practically the only pursuit they followed was that of lending money. Medieval men, regarding capital as unproductive, thought it wrong to lend money at interest. The practice was forbidden to Christians by both ecclesiastical and secular laws. The Jews, who were not bound by this Christian teaching, reaped a rich harvest wherever rulers allowed them to operate. Money was exceedingly scarce, and those who wanted to borrow were hard pressed to meet immediate engagements. The Jews consequently could command a rate of interest that varied from forty to eighty per cent. In England the Norman and Angevin kings took advantage of the situation to make profit for themselves. They allowed the Jews to lend money, protected them in the practice, and then mulcted them heavily by means of arbitrary taxes. Among medieval Christians the Jews were intensely unpopular. Their disbelief in Christianity, their social seclusion, and their extortionate practices aroused popular animosity. At the time of the crusades when religious fervor against the infidel was at a high pitch, riots directed against this alien element were of common occurrence. Under Edward I popular feeling against the Jews ran so high that the king gave way before it. He prohibited their usurious dealings and attempted to make them support themselves by industry and trade.

The Jews

When the experiment failed, he ordered them to leave the kingdom, causing a general exodus in 1290.

The expulsion of the Jews was rendered easier because the agents of Italian banking firms, who had been competing with the Jews for a century, were ready to take over the money-lending business of England. The early development of commerce and industry in Italy had produced there a surplus of fluid capital which could be used for investment, before such a surplus came into existence in most of the other countries of Europe. Companies were formed in several Italian cities, which had the capital not only of their own members, but also of depositors. They used this in part to finance ventures in trade and in part to make loans. They were forbidden by law to charge interest, but there were numerous ways of evading the letter of the law. The Italian firms, unlike the Jews, were more than mere money-lenders; they provided some of the facilities of deposit and credit which we associate with modern banking. The largest firms had permanent representatives in the principal commercial centers of Europe, and they transported money and issued bills of exchange. After 1290 the Italian firms constituted the principal financial element in English business.

The central government left the regulation of industry and commerce mainly to the municipalities and the gilds. The legislation enacted by the central government for the purpose of regulating trade begins with the assize of bread issued in the reign of Henry II. This fixed the local retail price of bread on a sliding scale proportioned to the price of wheat in the local market, and required that the bread should be of good quality. Later the price of ale was similarly regulated in relation to the price of barley and a maximum price was established for wine. These assizes had in part the same objects with regard to the quality of the products as our modern pure-food legislation; and in part their purpose was to maintain a just price, which should allow the vendor a sufficient profit to support him and his family comfortably in their station of life, but which should not permit him to make an excessive profit. Beyond this point the central government did not attempt the direct control of prices during the thirteenth century. It legislated concerning the quality of meat, but left the regulation of the prices of that commodity and of others not included in the assizes to the local authorities. Another field of regulation, which the central government entered early, was that of weights and measures. In 1197 the ministers of Richard I issued the assize of measures, which provided a uniform standard of weights and measures through-

The Italian banking firms

National regulation of commerce and industry

out the kingdom. The enactment facilitated commerce by eliminating the uncertainty and confusion inseparable from a variance of standards from one locality to another; it also helped to prevent fraud. In the reign of Henry III the central government also took cognizance of dealers known as forestallers, who attempted to raise prices unduly by cornering a local market, forbidding various practices by which they were accustomed to accomplish that result. The prevention of speculation, however, like the regulation of prices, received much more attention in the detailed ordinances of boroughs and gilds than it received in the enactments of the national government. Between 1275 and 1285 Edward I enacted a series of laws which had the interests of the merchants primarily in view, one of the laws, in fact, being known as the Statute of Merchants. They dealt with the recovery of debts. Previously it had been the common procedure, when a merchant of one town, say Lincoln, failed to pay on time a debt contracted with a merchant of another town, say London, for the merchant of London to recover his debt by the seizure of the goods of any merchant of Lincoln who subsequently came to London. The laws of Edward I forbade this practice, so far as English towns were concerned, and provided a summary legal process by which the goods of the debtor could be seized for the debt. Edward I also prohibited the imposition of excessive tolls by local authorities.[10] The legislation enacted by the central government for the direct regulation of commerce and industry previous to the fourteenth century was thus small in amount, and what there was of it was enforced largely by the local authorities.

---

[10] *Statutes of the Realm,* i, 34.

CHAPTER XI

THE CONSTITUTION UNDER EDWARD I

The man and his work

EDWARD I (1272-1307), unlike his father, was an efficient ruler. He possessed a vigorous personality and executive ability of a high order. The policies which he pursued consistently for large parts of his reign testify to the breadth of his vision. After his return from the Holy Land (1274), he planned to lead another crusade which should include contingents from other European countries as well as England. For this purpose he negotiated successfully with popes to secure the taxation of the English clergy, and attempted to mediate in the quarrels of European princes in order to bring about the general pacification necessary as a preliminary to such a European expedition. Though he devoted to this project much thought and energy, the crusade remained a brilliant dream never realized. After 1294, wars with France, Wales, and Scotland left him no opportunity for ventures in arms farther afield. His spirited foreign policy was paralleled by his effort to bring into existence a united Britain. During the first half of his reign he waged wars which resulted in the final subjugation of Wales, and during the second half he concentrated his energies largely upon the effort to gain control of Scotland. It was in the reorganization of the English government that he displayed his greatest talents and produced the most beneficial results. His innovations were neither great in number nor radical in character. In large part his work was to bring to fruition constitutional germs which had sprouted in his father's reign. The thirty-five years of his reign, however, witnessed constitutional changes so far-reaching in their ultimate consequences that, if we regard Henry II as the founder of the English constitution, Edward I may well be designated as the builder of the first story of the structure.

Edward's legislation

Edward was a more prolific legislator than any previous English king. Some of his enactments did not make new law; they codified with alterations and additions existing laws and customs. Indeed, so much of his legislation was of this type that he is called the English Justinian. Though he did not cover the whole field of law, his lawmaking was so extensive that only a few of its most salient results can be noticed here. Several statutes defined the duties and powers of the royal officials and prohibited administrative abuses. They improved the government and protected the king's subjects against official malpractices such as the levy of excessive fees. Others deprived the feudal magnates of some of the privileges which impaired the royal authority, and also limited the powers of lords over their tenants, prohibiting such unjust practices as the exaction of extortionate feudal aids. One statute reorganized and made more efficient the militia and the crude local constabulary which had been established by Henry III. Laws with regard to the possession and transfer of land influenced the development of the law of real property so profoundly that their effects are still apparent. Most extensive of all was the legislation which dealt with the ordinary law governing the relations between man and man, the criminal law, and the procedure in both civil and criminal trials. "For ages after Edward's day," says Maitland,[1] "king and parliament left private law and civil procedure, criminal law and criminal procedure, pretty much to themselves. Piles of statutes are heaped up . . . but we may turn page after page of the statute book of any century from the fourteenth to the eighteenth, both inclusive, without finding any change of note made in the law of property, or the law of contract, or the law about thefts and murders, or the law as to how property may be recovered or contracts may be enforced, or the law as to how persons accused of theft or murder may be punished."

Although Edward's legislative contribution was particularly important in the field of private law, his work as a whole was no less significant in the field of constitutional law. Much of his legislation served to shape more perfectly the organs of government, to define their powers more clearly, or to settle their relations one to another more definitely. Edward, however, was a skilled administrator as well as a far-seeing legislator. Consequently the process of constitutional reorganization was accomplished largely by means other than statutes. An informal instruction given to an administrative official or a decision of the king's judges might work a constitutional change of permanent character. His influence upon the constitution can best be traced consequently by a survey of English political institutions as they existed during his reign.

Edward and the constitution

In the closing years of the thirteenth century centralization was the road to good government. Edward's experience during the baronial wars of his father's reign had taught him that one of the principal obstacles to improvement was the wide scope of the privileges and

Edward and feudalism

[1] *Constitutional History of England*, p. 19.

exemptions possessed by the feudal magnates. One of his first acts as king was to send itinerant justices throughout the realm to collect evidence concerning the exact extent of such privileges. On the basis of this information he limited the rights of the holders of private courts. He stopped the acquisition by such courts of new jurisdiction of importance and continued the extension of the jurisdiction of the royal courts, which, ever since the time of Henry II, had been narrowing the activities of private courts. By the close of his reign private courts other than those for the trial of villeins were well on the way to decay. On the tenurial side he dealt feudalism a heavy blow by the prohibition of subinfeudation. On its military side feudalism had long since lost its original importance. Edward rendered it still less significant. He required all those having lands worth £20 a year to accept knighthood, whether they were tenants-in-chief or not, and as members of the militia to maintain the military equipment of mounted knights. The foot soldiers for his campaigns in Wales and Scotland were supplied by men enrolled in the militia who were of less than knightly rank. When an army was needed, a royal commission was issued to a local official in each county, authorizing him to select a given number of men from the county for military service under the king. The men so obtained were paid by the king. Thus, out of the militia was gradually developed a competent fighting force, which supplanted the hired foreign mercenaries used by Henry II and his sons, and rendered the king more independent of his tenants-in-chief.

Administrative reforms

Edward did not rest content with a mere increase of his authority at the expense of the barons; he endeavored to wield his power more effectively by the reorganization of the administrative service. He created what amounted to a civil service. Men who served him faithfully for many years in subordinate capacities, such as the clerkships of the wardrobe and the chancery, were gradually promoted to the higher offices, until most of his officials were thoroughly trained administrators. This practice not only improved the quality of the administration, but it also enabled the king to render himself more independent of baronial interference. The men who were willing to go through this long career were for the most part of the middle class. Their sympathies were naturally with the crown rather than with the baronial opposition, and their long service gave them a bureaucratic *esprit de corps* which could never have been created among feudal magnates bound by the prejudices of their class. Many of these officials, too, were dependent upon the royal bounty for the source of their living. Edward, in the second half of his reign when baronial opposition to his policies became strong, relied more and more upon officials of this class, and gave to the barons an ever smaller part in his administrative service and in his counsels. During his reign, too, the wardrobe, a department of the household which was more closely under the personal control of the king than the exchequer and the chancery, was given a more important share in the work of administration. This shift of the center of gravity in the administrative system tended to give the king a more effective control over the whole administrative service. The methods of administrative work were also revised during the reign. In the exchequer, for example, new sets of accounts were established, which served both to improve the work of that department and to render the officials engaged in it more closely responsible to the king. The administrative machine thus built by Edward worked well. It accomplished more efficiently a greater amount of business than that of any previous English king.

In the organization of the judicial system extensive changes took place, though for the most part they merely continued processes which were already well begun. After the reign of Henry II the amount of judicial business transacted by the central courts grew steadily. In part the increase was made at the expense of the courts of the hundred and the shire. By the close of the reign of Edward I these public local courts were left with only a petty jurisdiction in either the criminal or the civil field. They ceased to be important as part of the national judicature, though as popular assemblies they still had a life of usefulness before them. The central courts, as their activities expanded during the thirteenth century, gradually developed a better organization. The work of the itinerant justices was facilitated by a specialization of functions. The early itinerant justices were charged with all kinds of judicial and administrative business which the king wished to have transacted locally. During the thirteenth century it became customary to send out regularly groups of itinerant justices whose duty was to try only one class of cases. The two most important groups had jurisdiction respectively over civil suits (justices of assize) and over criminal pleas (justices of jail delivery). In the same period the three courts of common law became distinct from the parent stem, the *curia regis*. During the reign of Henry III the exchequer became a separate court with its own bench of judges and its own records of the cases tried before it. It was concerned primarily with the royal revenues, but it was also a favorite tribunal for individuals having litigation which involved the collection of damages. The court of common pleas arose out of the desire of the

Judicial system

king's subjects to have a royal court stationary in one place, where they could bring their cases without the necessity of following the king upon his peregrinations. The Great Charter provided for such a court which was maintained at Westminster. In the course of the reign of Henry III this court came to have its separate records, and eventually it came to be called the court of common pleas. The original purpose of its creation was to give facilities for the trial of civil suits arising between subject and subject, and this became the distinctive field of its jurisdiction, though for a long time it entertained some criminal cases as well. During the reign of Edward I still a third court became fairly distinct, though the process of separation from the *curia regis* was not fully completed. The court of king's bench had its distinctive jurisdiction in the criminal field, though it never ceased to try some civil suits. This specialization of functions improved the quality of the justice given by the king's courts, because each court naturally developed the methods of trial best adapted to the attainment of justice in the particular classes of cases that came before it.

The king's council When the three courts of common law had thus been evolved from the *curia regis*, all jurisdiction not belonging specifically to one of the three courts remained in the possession of the *curia regis*. This body, indeed, was still the most important judicial court in the land, but the increasing extent of its action in an advisory capacity gave it more commonly the title of the king's council. It was composed of the king's chief ministers, judges and clerks, and of some additional members who were largely lay and ecclesiastical barons. The official element tended to become dominant, and during the closing years of Edward's reign it had nearly exclusive control. At any time this body might expand to include many barons and prelates who were not sworn of the council. On such occasions the body was known as the great council. The functions of the council increased throughout the thirteenth century, largely because the scope of the work performed by the royal government expanded, but the definition of its functions was still in the remote future. It attended to all the business of the king which no established department, such as the exchequer or the chancery, performed as part of its regular duties. Administrative business of an exceptional character came to it originally or was referred to it by the exchequer or other departments concerned, and a considerable amount of executive work came to it in the course of regular routine; the king sought its advice on all types of policies; it enacted what we should call legislation, many of the statutes of

Edward I emanating from the king and council; and it was active as a judicial body.

In its judicial capacity the council exercised (1) what may best be described as a residual jurisdiction. Ordinary criminal cases and any civil suit instituted by an original royal writ could go before one of the three courts of common law. But large numbers of cases fell into neither of these categories. Such cases went ordinarily to the king's council, which could depart from fixed forms of procedure and, if necessary, decide on grounds of equity and right as distinguished from those of law.[2] (2) The council might also be called upon to try a case which was within the cognizance of the courts of common law. The king could direct such a case to be brought before the council in first instance and was likely to do so when his own interests were involved. (3) Any of the other royal tribunals might refer a difficult case to the council for final adjudication. (4) Finally, the council could hear cases on appeal from a decision of the itinerant justices or of the justices of the court of common pleas which was claimed to be legally at fault.[3]

The council as a court

From shortly before the middle of the thirteenth century the council often exercised this jurisdiction in parliament. The relationship between council and parliament was similar in many respects to that existing between the *curia regis* and the exchequer before the two became separated. Just as the *curia regis* had once been called the exchequer when it held certain sessions each year for financial business, the council in the second half of the thirteenth century was designated as parliament when it met primarily for judicial business in sessions which were normally held one to four times a year.[4] The council which ordinarily sat in parliament was the great council, but on a few occasions only the permanent council appears to have been present. It often happened, moreover, that the magnates who had membership only in the great council would be dismissed before a session of parliament was concluded, leaving the permanent council to transact whatever business was unfinished. The council, however, did not always exercise its jurisdiction in parliament; it tried cases when parliament was not in session. One of the principal reasons for hold-

The council in parliament

---

[2] During Edward's reign cases of this type might sometimes go before exchequer or king's bench, but in such instances the council was always called into consultation. Virtually the residual jurisdiction belonged to the king's council.

[3] The king's bench shared this appellate jurisdiction and eventually retained a part of it.

[4] They could not be held when the king was outside the country because his presence was necessary to constitute a parliament. Sometimes they were not held when war was in progress or other exceptional circumstances intervened.

ing the special sessions called parliaments appears to have been to serve the convenience of suitors and petitioners. The time of each session was announced in advance, and Edward I, early in his reign, decreed that petitions for the redress of grievances or wrongs should be presented to parliament. Some of those received were referred by parliament to appropriate courts or administrative departments for action, and some were settled in parliament by judicial process or other means. Parliament thus became a place where the king's subjects could present petitions, a clearing house for securing action upon petitions, and a tribunal where judicial action could be taken upon those petitions which necessitated it. The functions of parliament did not end with the hearing of petitions and the trying of cases. The king might consult parliament upon questions of policy, seek its approval for projected new laws, or ask its consent for the levy of taxes.

The middle class: 1. Rural

To this institution, which bears little resemblance to parliament as it exists today, was added, by the close of the reign of Edward I, a representative element. The portion of the community represented was the middle class living in country and town. In the rural districts there were many freemen who did not attend the great council. Freeholders who held by other than military tenure and mesne tenants had never been obliged to attend the great council as part of their feudal obligation. The tenants-in-chief, regarding attendance as a burden, generally escaped it when they could. In the thirteenth century only those of the greater tenants-in-chief who were summoned individually by the king commonly appeared at the great council. The lesser tenants-in-chief were usually allowed to remain at home. These three elements in the rural middle class, the non-feudal freeholders, the mesne tenants, and the lesser tenants-in-chief, represented many degrees of wealth and social status, ranging all the way from the humble possessor of a free tenement in a manor to a knight of the shire, who might compare in wealth and local influence with one of the barons. Indeed, in the thirteenth century, when the rule of primogeniture had become commonly applicable to the inheritance of feudal tenures, the younger sons of the barons themselves became members of this middle class. Despite great social differences of this sort, all had the common interests of landed proprietors, and the large amount of governmental work which the Norman and the early Angevin kings required them to do locally in the courts of the shires accustomed them to cooperate in the conduct of public affairs.

The freemen who lived in the towns were of quite another social position. They owned little land, supporting themselves by the pursuit 2. Urban of commerce and industry. Since no gentleman could engage in trade, according to medieval ideas of what constituted gentility, the townsmen did not rank socially with the freemen of the rural districts, whose incomes were derived from land. The townsmen, however, took some part with the freemen of the rural districts in the local transaction of the royal business, being required to send juries to the county courts to meet the itinerant justices. But their influence in the political affairs of the nation was thrust upon them primarily because of their wealth. The townsmen might acquire their wealth in ways deemed less desirable socially than those employed by the landed gentry, but by the thirteenth century they had acquired a great deal of it. Their wealth, moreover, was in a more fluid form than the lands which constituted the capital of the country gentlemen. The townsmen constituted the moneyed class in the community.

For a long time the king did business with these elements locally When he wanted cases tried, taxes assessed, questions answered, or what not, he sent itinerant justices or other agents to the county courts to treat with the assembled knights and freeholders of each county; when he wanted to secure the consent of the townsmen for fiscal exactions, he sent agents to negotiate with the citizens of each town separately. But this method of doing business was clumsy, and eventually English kings began to see that it was more convenient to meet representatives of counties and towns in a central place than to send their agents to all the counties and towns. The idea of representation was not new in itself. It was of the essence of the jury that it spoke with the voice of the neighborhood, and some villages had been represented in the court of the hundred by a reeve and four men from an early time.[5] That which was new was the representation of the middle class throughout England in a central assembly held by the king.

Early development of the representative principle

When the first assembly of this type took place is not known. Possibly Henry II summoned representatives of the middle class to attend the great council which granted the Saladin tithe in 1188,[6] but the first king whose application of the idea can be established with certainty was John. In 1213 he was engaged in the assessment of the damages done to the property of the bishops during the period of the interdict, in order that he might make the promised reparation. The

Early instances of centralized representation

---

[5] **Above,** pp. 72, 120.
[6] *Facts and Factors in Economic History,* by former students of Edwin Francis Gay, pp. 71, 72.

assessment was made by means of juries, and the ambiguous statement of a chronicler seems to imply that John proposed to meet these juries at St. Albans in order to obtain the desired information. If this interpretation of the chronicler's remarks is correct, an early conception of the centralization of representation took the form of a concentration of juries. Much more significant were the writs issued later in the same year by the king to the sheriffs, ordering them to have at Oxford on a certain date four knights from each shire "to deliberate with us concerning the affairs of our kingdom."[7] Since the barons were also to be present, the projected assembly appears like a meeting of the great council with the addition of knights representing the rural middle class of the shires. It is not certain, either that the great council was formally summoned, or that any assembly was held on the specified date, but "certain it is that the idea of calling together representative knights of the shire 'to talk with the king about the kingdom's business' had occurred to John by 1213."[8] During the reign of Henry III resort was had to concentration of representation occasionally, though far from regularly. The most notable of the known instances during the reign of Henry III was the assembly called by Simon de Montfort in 1265,[9] where the urban element of the middle class was first represented.[10] Knowledge of the actual part taken by the representatives of the middle class in the actions of these assemblies is vague, but the advantage to the central government of bringing together at a central place representatives of the middle class for purposes of consultation with the king and council was well recognized by the close of the reign of Henry III. That the practice would become a permanent part of the constitution was not yet settled, however. Simon's assembly had been merely the expedient of an unsuccessful revolutionary party. The instances of representation had been too few and too far apart to have established any certain future for the institution.

The establishment of the representative element as a permanent part of the central government resulted from events which occurred during the reign of Edward I. For a long time Edward experimented with representation. In 1273 and in 1275 representatives of both counties and towns were summoned to meet with the council, as they had been by Simon. From that time until 1295 representatives of the middle

Representation under Edward I

---

[7] Stubbs, *Select Charters*, p. 287.

[8] Levett, "The Summons to a Great Council, 1213," *Eng. Hist. Review*, xxxi, 90.

[9] Above, p. 152.

[10] There is a possibility that boroughs had been represented in a central assembly earlier in the reign of Henry III: White, "Some Early Instances of Concentration of Representatives in England," *American Historical Review*, xix, 745.

class were summoned to appear only at irregular intervals, though more frequently than in the preceding period. The elements represented varied from one time to another. Both rural and urban sections were occasionally present, but more frequently only one of them. In 1295 Edward called one of the most representative assemblies which had yet met. In addition to the great council, it contained representatives not only of the counties and towns but also of the cathedral and parochial clergy. It is commonly styled the Model Parliament, a term which is somewhat misleading, because the meeting did not become the permanent model for later central representative assemblies. Aside from the representatives of the parochial clergy, it contained no group which had not appeared in some of Edward's earlier central assemblies. The lower clergy soon ceased to attend, preferring to grant taxes in their purely clerical assemblies, known as convocations, and to leave other clerical interests to the members of the higher clergy who formed part of the great council. After the Model Parliament the king summoned central representative assemblies nearly every year. In most of them the counties and the towns were both represented. In some instances, moreover, the representatives were associated with the king's council when it was sitting in parliament. By the close of Edward's reign the precedent for the royal consultation from time to time of representatives of the middle class in parliament was firmly established.

How the representative elements would combine with the great council and with each other was not yet settled in the reign of Edward I. In 1295 the knights of the shire acted with the barons, while the burgesses acted by themselves and the representative clergy by themselves in granting money. Had separate deliberation of these three groups continued, the house of commons might never have come into existence, and without it parliament could never have become the guardian of the popular liberties. Though the burgesses represented the wealth of the community, they lacked the social prestige necessary to give a separate house political strength. The knights of the shire, on the other hand, were of the same social class as the barons of the great council. Their ultimate union with the townsmen to form the house of commons gave that body an influence it could not have obtained otherwise. In the reign of Edward I indication of this combination was not yet apparent. Indeed, organization of the representative elements seems to have been notably lacking.

What powers the representatives could exercise were also largely undetermined in the reign of Edward I. When the representatives were present, they took small part in the ordinary work of parliament.

Organization of representative elements

They did not receive petitions and they do not appear to have acted upon them judicially. The king consulted them on the business he wished to put before them and dismissed them, but parliament continued to sit and transact business after they had gone, and it might have begun to do business before they came. Aside from the grant of taxation, there seems to have been no business which parliament could not and did not transact when the representative elements were not present. Many parliaments, indeed, were not attended by any representative elements. When the knights of the shire and the townsmen were present, they might present petitions, and through this channel they eventually acquired a share in legislation. In Edward's time the king might consult them about projected statutes, but he was under no compulsion either to do so, or to take their advice if he did. The parliament had no right to initiate legislation. Only by means of petitions did it gradually acquire the equivalent of that right. The representatives alone, or in conjunction with the magnates, could unite to petition the king for the redress of common grievances. If the king granted the request, the king and council might then draw up a statute ordaining the things sought in the petition. Thus the union of the representative elements with the council in sessions of parliament ended eventually not only in the transformation of parliament into a representative body, but also in the acquisition by that representative assembly of the power which we regard as the most distinctive in the possession of a modern parliament, the power to enact law. In the reign of Edward I neither the one change nor the other had been accomplished, but the first steps in both processes had been unconsciously taken. Another result of the union was to give to the representative parliament, when it had come to be the rule and not the exception, a decidedly judicial cast. The parliament of Edward I was preeminently a judicial organ. The addition of representative elements did not change that emphasis for a long time. Even when the origin of parliament as a court of law had long been forgotten, its judicial character was still apparent, and to this day the house of lords remains the highest court of the land.

In only two of the functions which parliament performed was the cooperation of the representative elements essential. (1) Parliament could not inform the king fully of the state of public opinion without the presence of the representatives. In the closing years of the reign of Edward I such information appears to have been of importance to the king. In that age, when roads were poor, and postal service, newspapers, telephones, and other means of rapid communication unknown, it was difficult to learn the real state of public opinion. The concentration of representatives from all parts of England provided an opportunity to feel the popular pulse, such as was given by no other agency at the king's disposal. (2) After 1297 parliament could not constitutionally grant non-feudal taxes without the consent of the representatives of the middle class. It is probable, indeed, that the representatives possessed the right of consent in practice before that time. The non-feudal tax on personal property became in the thirteenth century the most profitable method by which the king could supplement his ordinary income. It fell upon the middle class as well as upon the barons. During the reign of Henry III the great council sometimes granted the levy of this tax without consultation of representatives of the middle class, but contemporaneously the lower clergy were developing in the separate clerical assemblies called convocations the principle that royal income taxes could not be imposed upon them without the approval of their own representatives.[11] No definite proof exists that laymen of the middle class, borrowing this principle from the lower clergy, asserted that they likewise could not be taxed upon their personal property without the consent of their representatives, but it is significant that Edward I never levied this tax without seeking the assent of representatives of the class. Whether or not the right existed in practice before 1297, it was established constitutionally by the confirmation of the Charters in that year.

The circumstances were these. In 1297 the exigencies of warfare caused Edward to demand heavy taxes on personal property for the fourth consecutive year. Such a demand, even in two successive years, was without precedent. An irregularly constituted assembly granted the request; but the barons, supported by the higher clergy, opposed the levy of the tax, making a display of armed force. The government capitulated and summoned the barons and elected knights of the shire to meet. The assembly, dominated by the barons, sought the confirmation of the Charters in amplified form, and the king consented. The assembly in return approved a new tax on personal property, declaring the old tax void. Its action seems to have been equivalent to an assertion that the king could not levy a tax on personal property without the consent of a properly constituted representative assembly. Among the clauses added to the Charters was one which stated the principle more explicitly. In it the king promised to earls, barons, prelates, and the community of the land that henceforth he would take

Confirmation of the Charters

---

[11] *Persecution and Liberty: Essays in Honor of George Lincoln Burr*, pp. 117–169.

no such manner of exactions as had just been in dispute "but by the common assent of all the realm." Viewed in the light of the circumstances which produced it, this promise may be interpreted as a guarantee to the middle class of a share in the control of non-feudal taxation through their representation in the central assembly.[12] The control may not have extended to the whole field of taxation,[13] but it probably covered the taxes assessed upon personal property, which had become the principal means of supplementing the fixed revenues of the crown. So long as the consent of the landholders of the counties and the burgesses of the towns was needful for the imposition of this tax, the summons of their representatives to the central assemblies of the king from time to time was assured. Control of the purse, moreover, gave to their representatives a lever which they could use to secure from the king desired privileges and powers. The confirmation of the Charters of 1297 is a landmark of fundamental importance in the development of parliament.

Although Edward I gave to the representatives of the middle class a share in the central government which they would one day use to limit the powers of the king, his object seems to have been to increase the efficiency of the government. To him and to his contemporaries the concentration of representation appeared to serve the convenience of the king rather than the interest of the subjects. Representatives who had to make long and expensive journeys to meet the king, and their constituents who sometimes found themselves burdened with new taxes as a result of the journeys, saw little of advantage to be had from the new system. Though the right to participate in the grant of non-feudal taxes gave to the representatives a position which was in some measure independent of the king's convenience and desire, they had not yet discovered the fullness of the opportunity given by the new practice to make their opposition to a royal policy articulate. Though the knights of the shire participated in the assembly of 1297 which secured the confirmation of the Charters, the movement was primarily baronial in its inception and its execution. In the closing years of the reign the representatives of the middle class began to join with the

The value of representation under Edward I

---

[12] This interpretation is open to doubt with regard to both the representative character of the assembly whose consent was required and the non-feudal character of the taxes. For the view contrary to that expressed above, see Pasquet, *Origins of the House of Commons*, p. 237.

[13] "Aids, tasks, nor prises" are the words of the document, and it is impossible to say certainly just what those words meant in 1297. For the view that "aid" included non-feudal taxes of the kind which had just been levied, see Adams, *Constitutional History of England*, p. 190.

barons in framing common petitions for redress of their grievances. Yet it is doubtful if they often took the initiative, and the custom was at most only tentative. There was little about parliament in the reign of Edward I to foreshadow the future greatness of the institution as the champion of the rights of the subject against the arbitrary will of the king.

The active opposition which Edward I had to face came mainly from those classes which had the greatest immunities and exemptions. Of these the barons, whose acts had been chiefly responsible for the disorder of his father's reign, received the chief part of his attention, but he did not overlook the clergy. The popes of the thirteenth century, who never ceased to push the claims formulated by Innocent III, had been particularly successful in England in the time of Henry III.[14] Though the English clergy sometimes had been exploited financially by the popes in behalf of the monarch, they had received papal support for the advancement of the privileges and immunities claimed for their order at the expense of royal authority. Edward was as thoroughly devout as his father, but he would not brook clerical encroachment upon the field of his temporal authority. On several occasions he placed sharp checks on their interference in what he regarded as his sphere of jurisdiction. *Edward and the English clergy*

With the popes Edward was generally on friendly terms. Popular opposition to the papacy waxed stronger because papal provisions increased in number and the weight of papal taxation borne by the clergy grew heavier; but the king derived too much advantage from the papal friendship to sacrifice it readily for the popular clamor. Although papal provisions became more frequent in his reign, the popes interfered with the elections of bishops rather less than they had in the time of his father, and from the papal taxation of the clergy Edward derived much profit. During the first two years of his reign the clergy at the request of the pope paid a tenth to help him and his brother meet the debts incurred for their crusade, and the larger part of the proceeds of several other crusading taxes levied on the clergy by the pope went into the royal coffers. On the other hand, Edward prevented the papal collectors from exacting several new clerical dues which the papacy attempted to institute at this time. *Edward and the papacy*

This opposition, however, was effected without straining friendly relations. Not until the accession of Boniface VIII to the Holy See did a serious rift occur. Boniface asserted the superiority of the spiritual *Clericis laicos*

---

[14] Above, p. 150.

over the temporal authority in extravagant terms. In 1296 he issued the bull *clericis laicos*, which forbade the clergy of any country to pay taxes to lay rulers without the consent of the papacy. The English clergy, who had been hard hit by Edward's severe taxation of the past two years, were happy to follow the papal lead. Under the direction of the archbishop of Canterbury, they refused the royal demand for a fifth in 1296 on the plea of the papal prohibition. The conflict between papal and royal commands they met squarely with the statement that while they owed obedience to both, they owed the greater obedience to the spiritual power. Edward promptly outlawed the clergy, putting them outside the protection of the royal courts. Most of the clergy paid the fifth to escape this sentence. Those who did not had their temporal goods confiscated. Edward's successful opposition together with that of the king of France convinced the pope that he had undertaken more than he could perform. Shortly he modified the terms of *clericis laicos*, and within a year practically annulled them entirely. Though one result of the contest was to throw the clergy on the side of the barons in the struggle for the Charters, it was a complete victory for the king so far as the papacy was concerned.

Despite this and other differences with the papacy, king and pope cooperated to tax the English clergy to their mutual advantage. In 1301 Edward obtained from Boniface the grant of half the proceeds of a tenth imposed on the English clergy for three years by papal order. Edward thus obtained a tax from his clergy without asking their consent. Subsequently the king often found it easier to control the English clergy by securing the aid of the papal mandatory power than by dealing with the clergy themselves. With the accession of Clement V in 1305 the system underwent a notable extension. This friendly pope absolved Edward from his oath taken in confirmation of the Charters, suspended from office the archbishop of Canterbury who had been largely responsible for the clerical and baronial opposition to the king since 1297, and commanded the English clergy to pay to the king a tenth for seven years. In return for these favors Edward allowed the pope to levy a new tax upon the clergy of the British Isles. Annates, as the new tax was called, was a sum which had to be paid by all clergymen newly appointed to benefices in the British Isles within three years. Thus the English clergy found themselves ground between the upper and the nether millstones of the royal and the papal fiscal necessities.

Edward's reign was not to close, however, before an impressive assertion of the popular hostility to the papal financial policies had

Clerical
taxation

been voiced. The levy of annates disturbed not only the clergy, who had to pay them, but also the laity, who feared encroachment on their rights of patronage. At the parliament of Carlisle, held in 1307, the barons and the commonalty petitioned the king to put an end to provisions, annates, and other new fiscal demands of the pope. The papal collector was forthwith indicted before parliament. He pleaded the order of the pope as his justification. Parliament, finding the plea insufficient, forbade him or his agents to exact any of the new payments demanded by the pope. Revenues which the papacy had regularly received from England in the past he was allowed to collect. Edward seems to have been bound by his arrangement with Clement to allow annates to be levied; at any rate, after parliament had been dissolved, he revoked the parliamentary prohibition so far as it related to that tax. The remainder of the parliamentary award he enforced strictly, as did also his son after him. The action taken at the parliament of Carlisle, which was judicial in form and legislative in result, definitely estopped the papal attempt to collect various dues which had been sought without success intermittently for over half a century, though it failed to prevent papal provisions or annates. This legislation marked not only an important turning point in the development of English popular opposition to the papal fiscal policy, but also the beginning of an important series of anti-papal laws enacted by parliament during the fourteenth century.

CHAPTER XII

EXTERNAL AFFAIRS, 1272-1399

Welsh campaign, 1277

WHEN Edward I ascended the throne, he was met by a difficult problem in Wales. During the course of the thirteenth century the prince of North Wales steadily increased the territory under his rule. In 1267 Prince Llewelyn won formal recognition of the enlarged principality. In return for homage to the English king he was acknowledged as prince of virtually all of Wales outside the marches, with lordship of all save one of the native Welsh barons.[1] After the accession of the new king, Llewelyn failed to renew his homage and manifested an intention to hold the principality independent of English control. In 1277 Edward led a large army into Wales. He invested Llewelyn in the north in the inaccessible country around Snowdon and starved him into surrender. The prince agreed to restore the lands and the homage of the Welsh lords which he had acquired in 1267 and to render homage to the English king for the reduced principality of North Wales left in his possession. Edward, in the parts of Wales which were restored to his control, attempted to establish a more settled form of government. English law was substituted in some measure for Celtic tribal custom, and some places were organized like English shires.

Conquest of Wales

The innovations stirred the opposition of the Welsh in the ceded districts, who turned to Llewelyn for leadership. In 1282 he led them against English strongholds. Edward determined this time to end the Welsh troubles once and for all. During the next two years he made a thorough conquest in the course of which Llewelyn was killed and his brother captured. To insure the permanency of his work he built a series of strong fortresses, which commanded the region around Snowdon. In the shelter of these castles towns were established and filled with English settlers to become the centers for the propagation of English civilization in Wales. Edward also provided a new governmental régime by the Statute of Wales enacted in 1284. It declared Wales to have been transferred from the feudal control to the direct dominion of the English king and to be united to the crown of the realm of England "as a member of the same body." The lands which

---

[1] Illustrated by a map at the end of Tout's *History of England from the Accession of Henry III.* The principality also included a few of the marcher lands.

had been subject to the prince were organized like English counties, and English law was established therein, with the exception of certain Welsh customs designated in the statute. The new counties were divided into two groups, each being placed under the central control of a resident justice. Since the courts at Westminster had no jurisdiction in these counties, Wales was treated as a separate part of the realm of England. In the districts controlled by the marcher lords the Statute of Wales made no important change. The lordships of the march had long been ruled by their holders as private jurisdictions, the king having no power over them except that of feudal lord. In the main the private courts of the marchers administered English feudal law, although many local Welsh customs survived. Thus Wales was divided into two distinct parts from the point of view of constitutional and political organization, although the two parts were more or less intermixed territorially. English law prevailed to some extent in both, but the English common law and the royal administration were established only in that part which had constituted the native principality of Wales. This situation continued until the reign of Henry VIII, though during the interval the further expansion of the privileges of the lords of the march was circumscribed, and many of the lordships escheated to the crown through failure of heirs.

The Welsh were not happy under the settlement of 1284. The lords of the march, who had always been a turbulent element, continued to wage private wars and to rule their Welsh tenants with a strong hand. In the former principality the Welsh gave occasional expression to their dissatisfaction with English law and administration by open defiance of authority. In 1294, when Edward had declared war upon France, the Welsh of both the principality and the marches rose in a revolt so formidable that it kept Edward in the field for nearly a year. He had to meet no further serious resistance from the Welsh, though discontent did not cease until long after his day. His settlement, however, laid the foundation for the real incorporation of Wales with England. Though the Welsh still display a certain amount of national feeling based on the survival of Celtic language, literature, and customs, Wales has become legally and politically a more closely corporate part of England than either Scotland or Ireland.

Rebellion of 1294

With Scotland Edward inherited peaceful relations, which for some time he preserved. He left his claim to the overlordship of Scotland in abeyance until a disputed succession to the throne of Scotland enabled him to advance it with fatal success. In 1290 the last member of the royal house of Scotland in direct line of descent died. Among the

The Scottish succession

many descendants of collateral lines, John Balliol, Robert Bruce, and John Hastings had the best claims, but the rules governing the inheritance of the crown were not yet defined sufficiently fully to settle beyond doubt which of the three claims was best. The Scottish nobles split into factions in support of the different candidates, and no authority in Scotland could determine the issue short of civil war.

Edward's intervention

The circumstances offered Edward an opportunity to extend his authority over Scotland. He summoned the magnates of Scotland to meet him at Norham, claiming from them the right to decide the controversy in his capacity as the overlord of Scotland. Edward's claim was of doubtful legality. Before the Norman conquest some kings of the Scots had acknowledged some kind of a political superiority on the part of English kings, but, since the introduction of feudalism had produced well-defined rules with regard to vassalage, only one legitimate king appears to have rendered homage for the kingdom of Scotland. Some of the acts of homage performed by the kings of Scotland to the Norman kings of England may have included Scotland, or they may have extended only to the English fiefs held by the kings of Scotland. The evidence at our disposal makes it impossible to decide with certainty. The homage for Scotland rendered to Henry II[2] had been canceled by Richard I, and no act of homage since performed by a king of Scotland had certainly included the realm of Scotland. The Scots, however, were in no position to protest. The rejection of Edward's claim in all probability would have subjected them both to civil war and to English invasion. The commonalty of Scotland voiced its opposition, but the action went unheeded. Each of the candidates acknowledged Edward as overlord, promising to abide by his award of the crown. Edward then appointed a commission to examine the claims of the several candidates. Pending its report, he took the government of Scotland into his own hands. On the basis of the findings of the commission, Edward, in 1292, decided in favor of Balliol, surrendered to him the government of Scotland, and received from him homage and fealty for the fief of Scotland.

First conquest of Scotland

Having made his claim to the overlordship of Scotland effective, Edward proceeded to exercise his power as no English king had done before him. In his capacity as overlord he heard appeals from the courts of Scotland. In 1294 he ordered Balliol, as his vassal, to provide troops for the English war against France. Balliol was more disposed to obey than were his subjects. His nobles forced him to accept a per-

---

[2] Above, p. 127.

manent advisory committee of twelve magnates, who were practically to control the government. They declared estates held by Englishmen in Scotland to be forfeited. In 1295, at the dictation of the committee, Balliol concluded a defensive alliance with France. Thereby he initiated a policy which was to become traditional during the succeeding three centuries. In 1296 the Scots invaded the northern counties of England. Though Edward was eager to prosecute war in France, he felt it necessary to establish peace in Britain before his departure. In a brief campaign in 1296 he easily carried all before him. Balliol abdicated, surrendering the crown to Edward who forthwith appointed three English commissioners to rule Scotland in his name. In less than five months Edward had conquered a kingdom.

Though Scotland was easily won, it was hard to hold. Many of the Scots refused to take the oath of allegiance to the English king, becoming outlaws. Edward's commissioners failed to move against these opponents. They also displayed toward the rights of the subject people a callous indifference which aroused bitter animosity among the Scots who had accepted the situation and taken the oath of allegiance to Edward. Affairs came to a head when a popular champion appeared in the person of William Wallace. In 1297, after killing an English official, he threw in his lot with the outlaws. His deed became the signal for a popular revolt, which the nobles soon joined. Under his leadership the Scots defeated the English and drove them from the country. Thereupon Wallace was somehow given the title of guardian and for the time being became the real ruler of Scotland. Again Scotland was free and independent. Edward returned to the conquest in 1298. He defeated Wallace, but the opposition of the disgruntled English barons prevented him from following up his advantage immediately. Thereafter he led armies to Scotland nearly every year. The baronial opposition at home and his difficulties with France rendered his campaigns ineffective for a long time. Not until 1305 did the capture and execution of Wallace break the last of the Scottish resistance.

Edward's second conquest, though it seemed to be more thorough, was no more enduring than the first. The Scots were not yet willing to accept dependence. Within the year they were again making armed resistance under the leadership of Robert Bruce, the grandson of the claimant of 1290. Proclaiming himself king, he secured a large popular following, though the nobles were slow in coming to his side. In 1306 the armies of Edward were so victorious that Bruce fled from the country; but the next year he returned and began to reverse the fortune of war. Edward, hastening north at the head of an army, died

Second conquest

Edward's failure

before he reached Scotland. His policy with regard to Scotland was a failure. His desire to unite the two sections of the island had led him to press a technical feudal claim of doubtful legality too far and too fast. When he precipitated a struggle by his arbitrary action, English civilization had already made considerable headway in the lowlands. Many Scottish barons held English fiefs which gave them an interest in English affairs, and during the thirteenth century an English influence had often been strong in the royal court of Scotland. Edward's acts had alienated this English sentiment and united the Saxon lowlands with the Celtic highlands in a common resistance to the foreign invader. A patriotic sentiment had begun to center around Wallace, the national hero, and the consciousness of a common nationality had been aroused. Edward I created between the two peoples a feeling of hostility so pronounced that it became traditional, postponing for centuries the union which he had intended to promote.

Edward II

Though Edward II (1307-1327) continued the war, he had little heart for it. He also lacked ability as a military commander. In fact, he was signally deficient in the qualities which befitted the kingly office. As a youth he took the same attitude toward his father's efforts to give him an education that many a student in our universities still takes. He absorbed as little knowledge of war and statecraft as was possible, devoting himself assiduously to his own amusement. He came to the throne exceptionally ignorant of the business of government, and responsibility failed to improve his attitude. He was not vicious; he was weak-willed and given to idleness and neglect. He was not the man to carry on his father's Scottish policy. Even had he been made of sterner stuff, the obstacles in his path might have proved insurmountable. Edward I left an exhausted exchequer burdened with debt. Partly as a result of his father's policy, too, Edward II had to meet the opposition of the English barons, who were always ready to hinder his preparations for war in order to extort from him concessions of advantage to their class. Under such circumstances his attempt to conquer Scotland was foredoomed to failure.

Bannock-burn

The new king soon gave evidence of his lack of purpose. He led into Scotland the army which his father had assembled, but retired before anything of moment had been accomplished. Thereafter the quarrels forced upon him by the English barons long prevented the organization of a second expedition, had he been disposed to undertake the task. Bruce employed the interval to conquer some of the English garrisons left in Scotland. His successes, together with Edward's indifference, gradually won him the support of many of the Scottish barons who had remained loyal to the English king. A campaign led by Edward in 1310 was singularly ineffective, leaving Bruce free to continue to reduce to submission the English garrisons in Scotland. The news that Stirling, the last important English garrison in Scotland, had agreed to surrender if relief did not reach it before June 24, 1314, caused Edward to make an effort to raise the siege. Even in this crisis the English earls who had been foremost in the baronial opposition to the king refused to serve. Edward nevertheless collected a large army. The English troops, who were compelled to make long marches in order to arrive on time, were tired out when they met the forces of Bruce at Bannockburn, two miles south of Stirling. The English horse attacked the Scottish pikemen, but they were driven back, and the whole English army was soon put to flight. The battle assured the Scots of their independence for the remainder of the Middle Ages. Edward II never formally recognized Bruce as king of Scotland. Only in 1328 did Edward III finally acknowledge by treaty the independence of Scotland, which had been a fact since Bannockburn.

The relations between England and France during the first half of the reign of Edward I centered about the Treaty of Paris, which had been negotiated between Henry III and Louis IX in 1259. The effect of this treaty was to stay temporarily the attempt of the French monarchs to deprive the kings of England of the remainder of their possessions in France. Before that time the kings of England had never renounced their claims to the lands which Philip Augustus had conquered in 1204 and 1205, and the kings of France had never given over entirely the attempt to execute the decree of the French *curia regis*, which had declared the forfeiture of all the Angevin possessions in France.[3] By the terms of the Treaty of Paris Henry III resigned all claims to the former Angevin possessions except Aquitaine, and agreed to render for Aquitaine the homage which he had hitherto refused. Louis IX acknowledged Henry to be the duke of Aquitaine, pledging himself to add to the duchy some of the lands which had recently been wrested from it. The treaty kept a nominal peace during the remainder of Henry's reign, but the promised cession of territory was not made. Edward I, soon after his accession, met the king of France, did homage for his French fief, and set in progress negotiations which resulted in the surrender to him of part of the lands ceded in the Treaty of Paris and in his renunciation of the remainder. Edward's

Early relations of Edward I with France

---

[3] Above, p. 133.

restraint, together with his conciliatory spirit, seemed to have establ lished the basis for a permanent peace.

But no peace could endure which left a large block of French terri tory under English rule. In the twelfth century the Angevin possession in France had been no anomaly, because France was divided into a number of great feudal principalities, which were practically inde pendent of royal control. The kings of France could exert little authority outside the narrow limits of the royal domain. During the thirteenth century, however, the expansion of the royal domain begun by Philip Augustus was continued until the French king ruled directly a sufficiently large part of France to give him control over most of the great fiefs which were still outside the royal domain. The duchy of Aquitaine was an exception which constituted a stumbling-block in the path of centralization, and it was also the seat of a rich trade in wine. Philip IV, who became king in 1285, was strongly intent upon the further consolidation of the royal authority. In any attack upon the English in Aquitaine, moreover, he could hope for support from an incipient feeling of nationality which had been gradually aroused as the administrative centralization, accomplished by his predecessors, had begun to bring home to Frenchmen the community of their interests.

It was under these circumstances that Philip utilized a quarrel between French and English sailors of the Channel ports as an excuse to seize Gascony. The rivalry was of long standing, but in 1293 it took on formidable proportions. A fleet of English and Gascon merchant ships met and defeated a similar Norman fleet in a pitched battle. Because the Gascons had participated, Edward agreed to a temporary surrender of part of Gascony to Philip as a pledge that justice should be done. Once his troops were in occupation the French king declared all of Gascony forfeited. When Edward learned of this treachery, he began war. Expeditions despatched in 1294 and 1296 made little head-way because the need of troops for the Welsh and Scottish wars reduced them to slender proportions. In 1297 Edward, having secured the alliance of the count of Flanders, led an army against north-eastern France without notable result. Subsequently he was too much occupied with Scotland to push the war against France. But Philip, because he became involved in other projects for which he desired a free hand, made peace in 1303 by the restoration of Gascony to its English lord.

Though Philip was compelled by the force of circumstances to release Gascony, he began, when his house was again in order, to

Causes of war

War with France, 1294 1303

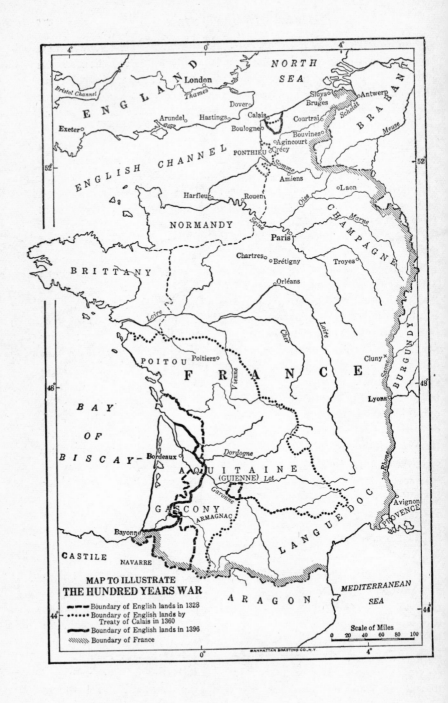

MAP TO ILLUSTRATE
THE HUNDRED YEARS WAR

- - - Boundary of English lands in 1328
······· Boundary of English lands by Treaty of Calais in 1360
▬▬▬ Boundary of English lands in 1396
///// Boundary of France

scheme once more for its recovery. The execution of the treaty of 1303 became the source of new frictions. Reverting to a practice often followed by his predecessors, he attempted to undermine the authority of the English kings in Gascony by encouraging the Gascon vassals to appeal from the court of their English lord to the court of their French overlord and by interfering with the English administration of Gascony. These tactics, which tended to whittle away the authority of the English kings, were provocative of vexatious disputes. Edward II had many controversies with Philip and his successors. They ended, toward the close of his reign, in another war. The French king again conquered Gascony. After Edward II was deposed in 1327, the regents of Edward III (1327-1377), who was a minor, signed a treaty which permitted the king of France to keep the major portion of the lands he had seized.

Gascony under Edward II

This treaty preserved the peace no better than those which had gone before. The usual controversies arose over its execution, the render of homage caused further friction, and the French interference with the English rule of Gascony continued. After Edward III began to rule in his own name, he gradually became convinced that war alone could prevent the ultimate absorption of Gascony by the French. This was one of the principal reasons which actuated him in 1337 to begin against France a war, which is known as the Hundred Years' War because it lasted intermittently for over a century. The war was the culmination of disputes which had been in progress for more than a century. They were ostensibly concerned with boundaries, jurisdictions, and other feudal rights; but the fundamental, underlying cause of war was the incompatibility of the English possession of French soil with the stage of national centralization which the French kings had attained by the fourteenth century.

Culmination of the disputes in the Hundred Years' War

Several other causes helped to provoke Edward III to declare war in 1337. One which seemed at the time to have an even more direct bearing on the issue was the intervention of France on the side of the Scots in a war which Edward III had undertaken against his northern neighbor. Edward saw that the conquest of Scotland would be difficult and probably impossible as long as France should stand ready to aid the Scots by attack upon England. After 1336 he ceased to lead the campaigns against the Scots in person, turning his whole attention to relations with France. Though he continued to negotiate with the king of France concerning their differences until late in 1337, he was seeking allies and preparing for war. These causes of war were primarily political. Another cause was economic. England and Flanders

Other causes of the Hundred Years' War

were economically interdependent. The looms of Flanders could not run without the supply of English wool, and the rich English wool trade found its chief market in Flanders. Politically, however, the county of Flanders was a fief held from the French crown, and in recent years the count of Flanders had become subservient to the king of France, ruling the country in the French interest. This situation, which necessarily affected English economic interests in Flanders adversely, became another reason for the growing animosity between Edward and the king of France. Minor causes were not lacking. The French and English sailors kept up their rivalries, and their attempts to settle their own quarrels from time to time were fruitful sources of international jealousies. In 1336 one of the most powerful nobles of France was sentenced to confiscation of his property and banishment from his country. He sought and obtained refuge at the court of the English king, where he did his utmost to incite his host against the king of France.

Claim to the French crown　　When Edward had finally decided upon war late in 1337, he put forward as a cause a claim to the throne of France. His claim was not without legal justification, though it was a pretext rather than a cause of war. His father had married a daughter of Philip IV. After the death of Philip IV, his three sons had ruled in succession because none of the sons had children other than daughters, and a French court ruled that a woman could not inherit the throne. When the last of the three died in 1328, the question arose whether the throne should go to Edward III, the only grandson of Philip IV, or to the representative of a collateral line.[4] The French court ruled that the law did not permit the throne to descend through a woman, and Philip VI of Valois thus became king of France. At the time, protests had been lodged in behalf of Edward III, who was then a minor, but subsequently Edward rendered homage to Philip VI and allowed the claim to lie fallow. In 1337 it made a good slogan. Its revival was equivalent to a declaration of war.

---

[4] The following genealogical table illustrates the situation:

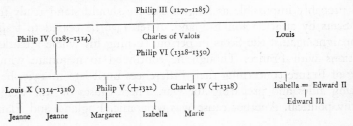

Meanwhile Edward had been seeking allies. The count of Flanders rejected his advances. When he began to sound the Flemish towns- men, the count prohibited commercial relations between Flanders and England. Edward replied by forbidding the export of wool to Flanders and the import of Flemish woven goods to England. The weavers of the Flemish towns were soon thrown out of work, and the merchants lost one of their richest markets. The economic pressure caused them to revolt. In 1338 they secured the renewal of commercial relations with England at the price of their neutrality. Two years later they became the allies of Edward. His first alliance was with the count of Hainault and Holland, his father-in-law. Negotiating from Hainault, he obtained the support of several of the Dutch and German princes of the empire whose lands were located on the northeast of France.

English alliances

Hostilities began on a small scale in 1337, but it was not until 1339 that Edward took up seriously the offensive against France. Invading from the northeast, he ravaged a large section without inducing Philip to risk a battle. When he transported another army from England for a campaign in 1340, his fleet of approximately 150 ships met a some- what larger French fleet off Sluys (Écluse) on the coast of Flanders. The English won a complete victory. The French fleet was almost entirely captured or destroyed, and the highway of English armies to the continent was cleared of obstruction. The victory also freed the English towns on the southern coast from the danger of French raids, to which they had been frequently exposed during the preceding two years. Edward's subsequent campaign on land was even less successful than his first. It was ended by a truce, which was intermittently renewed until 1345. During the interval his German and Flemish alliances broke up. Thus the campaign of 1340 marked the end of the Netherlandish period of the war.

Early campaigns

Thereafter the scene of the war was transferred from the northeast to the northwest of France. In Brittany a contest was begun between two rival claimants of the duchy. When one secured the backing of Philip VI, the other promptly obtained the aid of Edward III. English campaigns in Brittany followed. The first campaign which accom- plished any decisive result took place in 1346. This time Edward landed in Normandy and followed the Seine nearly to the walls of Paris, where he turned and headed for Flanders. Philip, who had retreated before Edward's advance, now began to pursue. At the Somme he pressed ahead of the English, obtaining control of the bridges. Edward appeared to be in a trap, but the timely discovery of a ford enabled him to get his army across the river, where he

Crécy

occupied a position favorable for defense on some hills near Crécy.
The English army, though smaller than the French, consisted principally of paid soldiers, who were better drilled and disciplined than any
feudal army could be. It was constituted mainly of infantry, the archers
outnumbering the mounted knights four to one. The English used
tactics they had learned on battlefields in Wales and Scotland. The
horsemen dismounted and with their pikes made ready to receive the
charge of the feudal cavalry, which constituted the principal element in
the French army. Interspersed with the pikemen were the archers,
whose function was to break the charge of the French cavalry as far as
possible before it struck the English line.

The French began the battle by sending forward their bowmen to
break the ranks of the English defense, preparatory for the charge of
the horsemen. The bowmen were Genoese mercenaries, because the
French had not yet developed that branch of warfare among themselves. Since the bow was not the weapon of a gentleman, the chief
reliance of France was still placed upon the gentlemanly but disorderly
feudal array. In France, where every son of a noble became a noble,
a sharp gulf existed between the knightly and middle classes, which
made it impossible for mounted knights and archers of the middle
class to fight harmoniously side by side as they did in the English
ranks where social distinctions counted for less. The French consequently had to rely on hired archers whose hearts were not in the
fight. They fought, too, under disadvantages. They faced the sun, a
recent shower had wet their uncovered bowstrings, and they used
crossbows which had to be stretched with a rack. The English, who
had kept their bowstrings dry, used the famous English longbow,
which was bent back by hand and could be shot farther and faster
than the crossbow. The Genoese were soon driven back in confusion,
and the ardent but undisciplined French cavalry, refusing to wait for
them to retreat, rode through and over them. This broke the order of
the charge at the beginning. The English archers finished the work.
Every successive wave of charging cavalry reached the English men-
at-arms with its ranks so broken that it was easily repulsed. The
French were overwhelmingly defeated, with losses far in excess of
those of the English. The battle of Crécy demonstrated conclusively
the military superiority of the English.

Calais and
Neville's
Cross
From Crécy Edward advanced to lay siege to Calais, which was
located on the coast near the Flemish frontier. The town, which was
strongly fortified, held out valiantly for a year, yielding only to starvation. Its capture gave to the English control of both sides of the Channel

at its narrowest part, and provided a convenient entrance both for English armies and for English trade. Meanwhile the Scots had attempted a diversion in the English rear. In 1346, at the request of the French king, the king of Scotland invaded England. In the absence of the English king the lords of the northern border organized the local levies and met the Scots at Neville's Cross. They not only inflicted upon them a defeat, but they captured the king, who was kept a prisoner in London. Though the Scottish invasion failed of its purpose, it was an important landmark. For two centuries thereafter the English always had to guard against Scottish invasion in the north whenever they were at war with France.

Elsewhere English arms were no less successful on a smaller scale. In Brittany the English won successes which were crowned by the capture of the claimant to the duchy who was receiving French support. Gascony also was a base of successful English operations. As early as 1337 Philip VI had conquered the larger part of the English possessions in the south, and it was not until 1345 that a serious attempt was made to recover them. During the next two years an English army reconquered many fortified places, extended widely the lands under English control, and made several devastating raids far into French territory. In 1347, when hostilities were temporarily ended by a truce, the tide of English victories appeared to be at the flood.

Other campaigns in France

After 1347 the renewal of the truce maintained a nominal peace until 1355, although fighting still continued to take place occasionally in Gascony, Brittany, and the region around Calais. In 1355 Edward planned to renew the war on a large scale. His own expeditions in that and the next year accomplished little. Expeditions led from Aquitaine by his oldest son Edward, called the Black Prince, had more important results. In his first season he made a destructive raid across southern France. In 1356 he led a similar expedition northward. Near Poitiers he met a French army commanded by John, who had been king of France since 1350. The English army, drawn up on a hill, faced a French army at least three times its size, but tactics similar to those used at Crécy again gave the English the victory. King John was captured, and his army was utterly routed.

Poitiers

France by this time was in miserable plight. All the campaigns had taken place on French soil, causing widespread devastation. In 1348 France, in common with the rest of western Europe, had suffered the ravages of a plague, called the black death, which caused a heavy mortality and hastened the process of social and economic disorganization. Heavy taxation added to the economic burden. Mercenary

Treaty of Calais

soldiers in intervals of unemployment gathered in bands to pillage the countryside, and the government was too weak to reduce them to order. King John was known as "the good," but it was in the sense of "the hail fellow, well met" that the appellation was used, for he was distinctly incompetent as a king. So thoroughly miserable and disgusted were the French people that they began to express their dissatisfaction by open opposition to constituted authority. Rebellions in 1358 and 1359 were repressed with difficulty. France was exhausted, and a fresh campaign, which brought the English king before the walls of Paris, persuaded the regent to make peace. The terms were arranged at Brétigny and subsequently revised at Calais.[5] Edward received Aquitaine, Ponthieu, and Calais to hold in perpetuity, free from the suzerainty of the French king. Aquitaine as defined by the treaty included Poitou and practically all of the other districts which had been within its boundaries in the time of Henry III. England gave up her alliance with Flanders, and France renounced her alliance with Scotland. King John was to be ransomed for the sum of £500,000, an enormous amount for those days. Edward III appeared to have gained with bountiful measure all for which he had entered the war.

Recovery of France

The appearance was deceitful. In reality the fundamental cause of the war was merely aggravated by the increase of English possessions in France. The people of many of the ceded districts accepted their new lord reluctantly and at heart remained faithful to their old allegiance. For some time the kings of France had all they could do to restore order to the distressed and shattered kingdom. In Brittany the war between the rival candidates still continued, and France was infested by bands of marauders composed of both French and English soldiers, whom the cessation of the war had left without employment. John failed to make much headway at the task, but his death in 1364 brought to the throne his son Charles. Not without reason was Charles V called "the wise" by his subjects, for he was one of the ablest of the medieval kings of France. He eliminated corruption in the government, consolidated the royal power, got rid of the companies of freebooters, and gave the French people strong rule and good government. This task occupied him for five years. His work was so well done that at the end of the period he was prepared to make the attempt, which had ever been his ambition, to recover the lands lost to England.

---

[5] The treaty is often called the Treaty of Brétigny, but Calais seems to be its correct designation.

The war with England, in fact, had never ceased, despite the nominal peace. French and English were fighting each other in the armies of the rival contestants for the duchy of Brittany; in Normandy English troops were aiding the cause of a rebellious French nobleman; and the English and the French were supporting rival candidates for the throne of Castile. In this last war, the Black Prince, who was acting as governor of Aquitaine, led an army into Spain which won the day for the English candidate. Nevertheless, the expedition was disastrous for England. Disease caused a heavy mortality in the English host, the Black Prince himself contracting an illness from which he never recovered. The taxes levied in Aquitaine for the expedition added fuel to the discontent with English rule which was already smoldering in many parts of the duchy. In 1369 Charles V took advantage of the situation in Aquitaine to renew the war. When some of the dissatisfied Aquitanian vassals appealed to his court, he cited the Black Prince to answer their charges. When the prince refused, the war between France and England was formally renewed.

Renewal of the war

From the first the renewed war went badly for England. Edward III was already falling into his dotage, and the Black Prince was too ill to lead campaigns. Many others of the ablest English commanders had died. John of Gaunt, duke of Lancaster, a younger son of Edward III, who took the brunt of the leadership after 1369, lacked the military skill of his father and brother. Though Charles V had no great military ability, he knew how to pick men. He chose for the chief command of the French army Bertrand du Guesclin, who, though he was reputed to be the ugliest man in Brittany, was a great general. Charles had already employed him in Brittany and in Spain, where he had discarded the knightly traditions of the French army which had been the undoing of France at Crécy and Poitiers, basing his campaigns on discipline, organization, and strategy. He used free companies and mercenaries in preference to feudal levies, meeting the English on their own terms. Parts of Aquitaine revolted and other parts were soon conquered by the French. The English were unable to repel the French. In 1372 an English fleet, bearing reinforcements, was destroyed by a Spanish fleet equipped by the Castilian king, whom the French had restored to the throne. Ponthieu was also invaded. Brittany was conquered, and the Norman friends of the English were likewise defeated. Meanwhile expeditions sent from England were allowed to raid at will, while French armies hung on their flanks, exacting heavy toll but never coming to an open engagement. In this way one English army after another was worn out and exhausted. By

England's failure

1375 the ports of Calais, Bordeaux, and Bayonne constituted practically all of the French territory left in English hands. The English were sufficiently discouraged to agree to a truce which lasted until the death of Edward III in 1377.

The war
under
Richard II

Edward III was followed by Richard II, whose father, the Black Prince, had died shortly before the old king. Since Richard was still a child, the government came into the hands of incompetent councilors, who accentuated their inefficiency by quarrels among themselves. So weak was the government that England was exposed to serious danger when the war was renewed two days after Richard's accession. Since the naval victory of 1372 the French had controlled the seas. They now began to attack English coastal towns and even to push their raids into the interior. The English expeditions to France continued to be so ill planned and poorly executed that French arms were uniformly successful. In 1380 the situation was somewhat relieved by the deaths of du Guesclin and Charles V. The new king of France, Charles VI, was a minor; and his uncles, who became regents, ruled with more regard for their own interests than for those of the monarchy. The governments of both France and England were weak, internal disorders arose in both countries, and the war languished. The English continued occasionally to send out misdirected and ineffective expeditions against France or her allies, but the French failed either to deprive the English of their last footholds in France or to invade England in force. Since the war was becoming a drawn game, without advantage to either side, both parties gradually became desirous of peace. In 1394 a truce was established for four years, and in 1396 a more permanent arrangement was effected. Richard II married the daughter of Charles VI, and both kings agreed to keep the peace for thirty years. During that interval territorial possession was to remain as it stood at the time of the signature of the treaty. Technically the treaty was only a truce, but it covered so long a period as to be practically equivalent to a peace. The truce left in the hands of the English a strip of the Gascon coast extending from Bordeaux to Bayonne, and Calais. Territorially the Hundred Years' War thus far had yielded Calais to England, but English Gascony was now shrunken within even narrower limits than those of 1337. The territorial settlement measured accurately enough the depth of England's fall from the glory of the Treaty of Calais.

CHAPTER XIII

POLITICAL AND CONSTITUTIONAL DEVELOPMENTS OF THE FOURTEENTH CENTURY

THE political history of the reign of Edward II (1307-1327) centers around a contest between the king and the barons. Edward's weak rule offered the barons excuses for opposition akin to those which they had advanced in the time of Henry III, and they revived methods which had been used to place a check upon the power of Edward's grandfather. The parallelism should not be pushed too far. Though Edward's manifest incapacity as a ruler provided the opportunity for the baronial outburst, and his favoritism for unpopular advisers supplied the immediate occasion, the fundamental cause of the baronial revolt existed before Edward II became king. The barons were protesting against a government which in their opinion Edward I had made too strong and too independent of them.

Baronial opposition to Edward II

A series of quarrels came to a head in 1310, when the barons brought armed followers to a baronial parliament and forced the king to allow them to make ordinances for the reform of the royal household and the realm. They forthwith appointed a committee of twenty-one lay and ecclesiastical magnates, who were called the Lords Ordainers. They completed their work in 1311, when it was submitted to a representative parliament for confirmation. The fundamental purpose of the ordinances was to reorganize the government in such a way that the barons would have a larger share in it. To this end they required the dismissal of many officials whose counsels the barons regarded as inimical to their interests, provided that the principal offices in the royal household and administrative services should be filled only with the assent of the baronage given in parliament, and forbade the king to act on many important subjects without the approval of the same body. Other clauses designed to eliminate existing abuses in the government gave to the ordinances the appearance of promoting the general welfare. Nevertheless, the barons were seeking primarily the advantage of their own class.

Ordinances of 1311

The ordinances worked badly for several reasons. (1) The means provided for their execution proved inadequate. The barons were able to enforce effectively some of the restrictions placed upon the exercise of the royal authority, but, short of coercion, they failed to devise any machinery by which enough of their program could be maintained to

Their failure

produce any significant permanent curtailment of the royal power. The barons never captured the royal household completely. Through the loyal members of that organization the king often worked his will despite the ordinances. (2) The selfishness of the barons soon became apparent. Their failure to support the king in the campaign which ended in the disaster of Bannockburn, to suppress internal disorders, and otherwise to have regard for the interests of the community alienated many of their supporters. (3) Their leaders were incompetent. Thomas, earl of Lancaster, who was the foremost, was unable or unwilling to assume the responsibility placed upon him by the success of his party. He could not wield the power snatched from the king. Under such guidance the baronial group could not long keep a united front. (4) Divisions among the barons eventually gave the king the advantage. In 1322, with more energy than was his wont, Edward attacked Lancaster, whose supporters had fallen away. He inflicted upon the earl a defeat which resulted in his capture and subsequent execution. A representative parliament then repealed the ordinances. The baronial attempt to control the administration by the coercion of the king ended in as complete failure as the baronial experiments of the reign of Henry III.

After this vigorous outburst Edward soon reverted to his former indolence. An irresponsible favorite obtained control of the government. His policy of personal aggrandizement roused anew the jealousies of the barons. When he placed a slight upon the queen, she took the leadership of a conspiracy to depose the king. In 1325 she was sent to negotiate peace with the French king, who was her brother. In France she met Roger Mortimer, a marcher baron who had lost his estates and been driven into exile by the favorite. With him she established a relationship which eventually became adulterous. Around them gathered a band of dissatisfied exiles. Driven from the court of her brother on account of her scandalous behavior, she found refuge with the count of Hainault, who became her ally as the price of a marriage between his daughter, Philippa, and Edward, her son. In 1326 the queen with her followers landed in England, where many Englishmen rallied to her standard. Edward, finding himself practically without supporters, fled to the west. Early in 1327 a representative parliament was called by the revolutionary leaders, where the question was put whether they would have Edward II or his son as their ruler. The parliament declared tumultuously in favor of the son. A formal statement of the reasons for the deposition of the king charged him with incompetence and neglect of his duties. The king of the fourteenth century was ex-

Deposition of Edward II

pected to rule as well as to reign. Parliament did not formally decree his deposition, but by threat of the exclusion of his son obtained his consent to his own deposition in favor of his son. The members of parliament then renounced their allegiance to him. With the deposition of Edward II, his death was a foregone conclusion. After being kept in confinement for several months, he was murdered before the close of 1327.

The deposition of Edward II had some value as a precedent in the later struggle to place constitutional limits on the powers of the English king, but that was not the primary object of the revolutionary leaders who accomplished it. Their motives were largely selfish. They did not wish to limit permanently the royal authority because they anticipated power for themselves through the influence they would be able to wield in the government of Edward's son during his minority. Their ostensible object was merely to rid the nation of a king whose incompetence was universally recognized. Despite the personal weakness of Edward II and despite his deposition, the royal authority survived his reign practically unimpaired.

Constitutional significance

Yet the foundations on which a representative parliament would one day rear a structure of limited monarchy, begun in the time of Edward I, continued to be laid during the reign of Edward II. Parliament under Edward II was still primarily a court which acted generally without the attendance of popular representatives. When the barons provided for frequent parliaments in the ordinances of 1311, they had in mind assemblies of the magnates to hear pleas, receive complaints against the royal officials, and provide remedies for petitions. The commonalty had no place in the parliament envisaged by the ordinances.[1] Nevertheless, representatives of the counties and towns were summoned to central assemblies in nearly every year of the reign. The frequent observance of the custom served to give it steadily a more binding force. What was still more significant, the representative element was present on every occasion when parliament had to consider a crisis between the king and the barons. When the ordinances were issued in 1311, when they were repealed in 1322, when the king was deposed in 1327, and on other occasions of less importance popular representatives took part in the actions by which parliament ratified the various changes. Their participation in these events was more or less passive, but they were active enough in other directions. Their consent was asked for every levy of a tax on personal property during the

Parliament under Edward II

[1] Davies, *Baronial Opposition*, p. 511.

reign, and in 1309 the grant of such a tax was made conditional upon a favorable reply to a petition in which they stated their grievances. This action marked the beginning of a process of bargaining for grants of taxation by which representative parliaments in later reigns limited the royal power. The petition of 1309 and another formulated by the knights of the shire and the burgesses in the parliament of 1320 resulted in the enactment of statutes. They were definite steps toward the acquisition, by the representatives, of an initiative in legislation, and statutes soon came to consist mainly of petitions of the representatives as modified by king and council. In 1322 the revocation of the ordinances of 1311 enacted by a representative parliament contained the statement that "the matters which are to be established for the estate of our lord the king and of his heirs, and for the estate of the realm and of the people, shall be treated, accorded and established in parliaments, by our lord the king, and by the assent of the prelates, earls, and barons and the commonalty of the realm; according as it hath been heretofore accustomed."[2] This has been interpreted by some as a promise that the commons should have a share in all legislation, and by others as a concession to the commons of the right to a voice in legislation fundamentally constitutional in character. It is doubtful if it meant one or the other, since legislation was still hardly distinguishable from judicial action. More probably it was merely a vague acknowledgment by the king of the right of a representative parliament to a consultative voice in affairs of importance to all classes of the realm. Interpreted even in this limited sense, the enactment was not subsequently observed with any regularity. The tacit acknowledgment that non-feudal taxation could not be imposed without the consent of a representative parliament, the demand for the redress of grievances in return for the grant of a tax, and the use of common petitions to secure a virtual initiative of legislation constituted precedents of far greater value for the subsequent acquisition of political power by the representative element, than the open assertion contained in the enactment of 1322.

During the regency necessitated by the youth of Edward III the political situation changed little. Nominally the council responsible for the government was controlled by a group of magnates representing the tradition of the Lords Ordainers; actually the government was managed by a group of courtiers, belonging mainly to the royal household, who took their orders from Mortimer and Queen Isabella. The

The regency, 1327-1330

---

[2] Adams and Stephens, *Select Documents*, p. 97.

domination of these two was gradually rendered unpopular by the shameful character of their personal relations and by the greed and double-dealing of Mortimer. In 1330 the young king secured the condemnation and execution of Mortimer, deprived his mother of her influence in the government, and brought the regency to a close.

Under the leadership of Edward III the factional disorder which had so long disturbed the realm gradually died out. In his council the baronial and the household elements were so fairly balanced that the government functioned without undue friction until the outbreak of the Hundred Years' War. For some time previously Edward had been reviving the administrative position of the household, and the necessity of raising large quantities of military supplies brought the wardrobe prominently to the fore. The officers of the household again came into their own. The more independent departments, such as the chancery and the exchequer, were made subordinate to the household administration. The worst days of Edward II appeared to have returned. But this experiment was of short duration. In 1340 Edward III caused the resignation of his chancellor, Archbishop Stratford, who had previously been his chief adviser. Stratford represented the public administration and the baronial tradition as opposed to the more efficient but more irresponsible household officials and courtiers. The barons promptly rallied to his cause. With the support of the representative element in the parliament of 1341, they forced the king to restore the archbishop to his favor, and to sanction a statute providing that all ministers should be selected by the king after consultation with a representative parliament and should be answerable to parliament at each session. Within a few months Edward declared the statute repealed, stating bluntly that he had given his consent as the only means of securing the needed taxation. But though ministerial responsibility to parliament was not established by these events, the predominance of the courtiers in the administration was effectively checked. Within a few years the balance between the baronial and the household elements had been restored.

By this time Edward had achieved such popularity that the conflict between royal and baronial policy, which ran through the reigns of his grandfather and father and into the early years of his own, had largely disappeared. His personality, in which majestic qualities were combined with graciousness, courtesy, and affability, won the regard of the increasing numbers of all classes who came into contact with it. Though he probably did not possess great intellectual capacity, he was richly endowed with energy and ambition. The pursuits of peace

The rule of Edward III

did not attract him in the same measure as did deeds of chivalrous daring and warfare, but he was not neglectful of the internal welfare of his people. The wars which delighted him, moreover, gradually aroused the national sentiment of the English, causing him to stand forth as the national leader and hero. He cared so much more for the pursuit of his military ambitions than for his kingly prerogatives that he was prepared to placate the possible opponents of his policies with concessions. The nobles were generally as happy as he to have the opportunity for military exploits. Nevertheless, he took pains to keep their good will by numerous grants of privilege. The middle class found him so responsive to the petitions which its representatives presented in increasing numbers at the parliaments of his reign, that it acquired a significant influence in the affairs of the central government.

In the closing years of the reign these happy conditions changed for the worse. After the war was renewed in 1369, Edward fell into his dotage. He lost interest in the government, falling under the sway of his mistress and of unscrupulous advisers. The war was mismanaged, and the tide of defeat accompanied by renewed taxation caused popular dissatisfaction akin to the social and religious unrest which was manifested concurrently. Weak monarchy brought with it the inevitable accompaniment of aristocratic factions, each seeking to secure control of the government in its own interest. In 1377 the reign ended in the midst of political conditions similar to those which had obtained at the beginning, and which were destined to continue throughout the greater part of the next reign.

Edward III and parliament

In the development of parliament the reign of Edward III was an era of fundamental importance. The representative element, using such control of taxation as it had acquired, began to bargain. When the king asked for taxation, it made the grant dependent upon the remedy of grievances or upon the grant of privileges sought in the common petitions, which were now being formulated with ever greater frequency. The first steps in this policy were probably taken by the representatives with little consciousness of the strength of the weapon which they had in their hands; but the war placed the king under a financial strain so much heavier than any experienced by his predecessors, that the representatives began consciously to barter with him for those things which they desired for themselves or for the classes which they represented. The king, whose heart was in the war, conceded their demands freely as the only means to secure the essential taxation. When he broke his promises with almost the same freedom and geniality with which he gave them, the representatives persistently renewed their demands. By this process they secured for themselves an assured place in parliament, and for the parliament of which they were a constituent part a more active and extensive share in the government. By the close of the reign the union of the knights of the shire and the burgesses in the commons had taken place; lines of cleavage, which would result finally in the establishment of the house of lords, had begun to develop between the council in parliament and the council out of parliament; and parliament had increased its control of taxation, secured a large share in legislation, and made occasional efforts to control the executive policy, which, though less successful, had resulted in one precedent of constitutional significance.

In its formal organization parliament remained the same in the time of Edward III as it had been under his father and his grandfather. All of the members met in a common session. Only the work of such common sessions is recorded officially in the "Rolls of Parliament" as the acts of parliament. So large and heterogeneous a body, however, could transact nothing more than formal business. From an early time parliament broke into separate groups to debate the matters put before the whole body in the king's speech. The council remained in the parliament chamber, while the other elements went elsewhere. How the other elements would combine was for a long time uncertain. The representative clergy soon dropped out, preferring to deal with temporal affairs in convocation. The knights of the shire deliberated sometimes by themselves and sometimes with the burgesses. In the course of the reign of Edward III, probably in the decade between 1339 and 1349, the latter became customary. About this time the knights and the burgesses began to be designated in official records collectively as the commons,[3] they had a common place for the conduct of their deliberations in the precincts of Westminster Abbey, they had a common clerk, and before the end of the reign they had begun to elect a speaker to voice in the parliament chamber the decisions which they reached in their separate proceedings. Practically the house of commons had been formed, though technically the commons did not yet form a separate house of parliament.

The council in parliament was beginning to assume the form of the house of lords. The house of lords would not be an institution entirely distinct from the council until members of the council had ceased to sit in parliament by virtue of their membership in the council. The process of separation was virtually accomplished by the gradual dis-

Organization of parliament:
1. The commons

2. The lords

---

[3] Gray, *The Influence of the Commons on Early Legislation*, p. 208, n. 9.

appearance from the council in parliament of royal officials, who constituted the influential element in the council out of parliament, leaving in the council in parliament only lay and ecclesiastical lords. The process was well begun during the fourteenth century. In the time of Edward I the official element of the council, which was more subject to the control of the king, took an equal part with the baronial element in the work of the council in parliament. Indeed, it probably took the leading part. During the reign of Edward III the predominating element in the council in parliament was coming to be the baronial, which was more independent of the king and more likely to oppose his wishes. The baronial group, moreover, was in the process of having its membership definitely fixed. Certain barons and their sons after them were being summoned and others omitted time after time. Attendance was becoming practically an hereditary duty attached to certain baronies. All of the bishops were summoned regularly, but the number of abbots and priors, like that of the barons, was being reduced by this selective process. By the end of the fourteenth century not only was the council in parliament well on the way to become the house of lords, but the developments which were to make the membership of that house an hereditary peerage were also far advanced.

Functions of parliament: 1. judicial

The functions of parliament were increased and defined during the fourteenth century. The judicial power developed by means of differentiation between parliament and council. In the time of Edward I the council out of parliament could transact the same judicial business as parliament. The jurisdiction of the two bodies ceased to be identical during the reign of Edward III. Parliament established the right to hear appeals on writ of error from the common law courts, and to try peers accused of crimes.[4] The summary modes of trial developed by the council evoked much opposition, and parliament strove to handle the petitions of private persons in order to prevent their adjudication before the council. But the task was too great for infrequent and short-lived parliaments. The larger part of the judicial work tended to pass to the council, although the development was not completed until the fifteenth century.

2. Taxation

The growth of the power of parliament depended primarily on its control of taxation. The control of the grant of taxation, which had been acquired in large measure by the confirmation of the Charters in 1297, was extended and improved during the reign of Edward III. In 1340 parliament, at the initiative of the commons, secured the con-

---

[4] It also prevented the trial by council of cases which would force a man to answer for his freehold.

sent of the king to a statute which forbade the levy of an aid or a charge of any kind without the consent of the magnates and the commons given in parliament. The phraseology of this statute would appear broad enough to prohibit all non-feudal taxation without the consent of a parliament containing the representative elements, but the king continued from time to time to raise new customs with the consent only of the merchants or of the council. Parliament kept up its protests until the king practically accepted the principle of parliamentary control of the grant of taxation. For the next century the principle was rarely violated. Parliament further attempted to control the expenditure of money raised by taxation, but its successes were too occasional to establish any precedent of permanent importance.

In the reign of Edward III parliament also became more active in the enactment of legislation, and the commons acquired a prominent part in this work, including the power practically to initiate legislation. The growth of the legislative function hinged upon the use of the common petition. In the reign of Edward I the mass of petitions came from individuals. They were settled by judicial or quasi-judicial action. The few common petitions were initiated by the magnates or the clergy, though the commonalty sometimes joined in their presentation. These resulted generally in acts of parliament which were judicial in form but legislative in effect. They were very few indeed. Nearly all of the acts of parliament, which we should deem legislative, obviously originated with the king or his council. This prominence of the council in the legislative work of parliament ceased during the reign of Edward II, as a result of the attempt of the barons to reduce the influence of the official element in the king's council. The official councilors were still called upon by the king and by parliament itself to draft or frame statutes, but they no longer made the law enacted in parliament.[5] Contemporaneously with this development, the knights and burgesses began for the first time to present common petitions. In 1325 they complained because their petitions were treated like the petitions of individuals. In the first parliament of the reign of Edward III they asked to have their petitions made statutes in parliament and held good.[6] During the course of the reign, by wielding the club of finance, the commons secured the essence of this petition. Time after time their common petitions were transformed into acts and placed on the statute-rolls. By the end of the reign of Edward III a considerable amount of legislation had been enacted by parliament, and far more

3. Legislation

---

[5] Baldwin, *King's Council*, pp. 313–316. See also above, pp. 202, 230.
[6] Pollard, *Evolution of Parliament*, pp. 117–120.

of it had been initiated by the commons than by the king. Parliament, indeed, was no longer the purely judicial body it had been in the time of Edward I; its center of interest was being transferred from the individual petitions to the common petitions; it had become a legislative body.[7]

4. Control of policy

Another field where parliament sporadically sought some control in this period was that of governmental policy. In the fourteenth century kings still sought advice from parliament. Sometimes they followed the advice given; often they did not; more frequently they sought no advice at all. Through the common petitions backed by control of the purse, parliament could sometimes force unwelcome advice upon the king. The principal method by which parliament consciously attempted to obtain control of the executive policy was by forcing the king's ministers to become responsible to parliament for their official acts. In 1341, at the time of the crisis between the barons and the courtiers, parliament appeared to have established nearly complete ministerial responsibility.[8] The repeal of the statute by the king and the subsequent acquiescence of parliament would indicate that the attempt was premature.

Impeachment

Another such attempt was not made until the closing years of the reign of Edward III, when the weakness of the government, the partisan politics of opposing baronial factions, the weight of taxation, and the repeated military failures had combined to produce popular irritation. The two baronial factions striving for control of the government, which Edward III was too weak longer to guide, were led by two sons of the king, Edward, the Black Prince, the eldest son, and John of Gaunt, duke of Lancaster, the fourth son. In 1376 John of Gaunt was supreme through his influence over the king's mistress and over a group of the royal officials of the courtier type. Since 1370 parliaments had been protesting with increasing vehemence against the misgovernment. In 1376 the commons, under the patronage of the Black Prince, made a vigorous and determined onslaught. Two of the foremost of the courtier ministers were accused of malversation by the commons before the lords, and convicted. They were deprived of office, fined, and imprisoned. Several courtiers of lesser importance were also convicted and driven from office. Parliament also enacted such extensive reforms that it became known as the Good Parliament. In the main its work was not destined to endure. The Black Prince died in the midst of the session, leaving as his heir, Richard, a boy of ten. In the next

---

[7] Gray, *The Influence of the Commons on Early Legislation,* ch. viii.

[8] Above, p. 227.

year John of Gaunt, by successful influence at elections, secured a packed house of commons and undid the work of the Good Parliament. But the precedent established by the trial of the king's ministers on the accusation of the house of commons could not be wiped out. It was the precedent for the form of trial called impeachment, and it was an important step in the development of parliamentary control of the executive. It was based on the principle that a minister of the king must answer to parliament for his conduct in office. If he acts illegally, it is no defense to plead the order of the king for his act. The king can do no wrong, and the minister must take responsibility for his own acts. When ministers learn that they may suffer penalties if they carry out the royal command in opposition to the will of parliament, the king, who of necessity must act through his ministers, is likely to find himself hampered in any attempt to rule arbitrarily. As a means of enforcing ministerial responsibility, impeachment was a clumsy weapon because it could be invoked properly only when a minister had acted illegally; but as a parliamentary check upon the arbitrary power of the crown, impeachment subsequently proved to be of great value.

When death closed the long reign of Edward III in 1377, the throne passed to Richard, the son of the deceased Black Prince.[9] The reign of Richard II (1377-1399), from the point of view of political and constitutional development, may be conveniently divided into three periods: the minority (1377-1389),[10] constitutional rule (1389-1397), and absolutism and tyranny (1397-1399).

Reign of Richard II

The minority was a period of popular discontent and political strife. Richard was too young to rule, and the advisers who conducted the government in his name labored under the disadvantage of counsels divided by the spirit of faction. The mismanagement of the war continued, the heavy and badly distributed taxation caused strong popular dissatisfaction, and the growing social unrest reached its climax in the Peasants' Revolt of 1381. In the early years of the minority the government was controlled by parliament to an extent never witnessed before. In this work the commons took an active and important share, which, by contrast with their passivity under similar conditions during the reign of Edward II, gives measure of the progress they had made during the reign of Edward III. Parliamentary control, however, proved ineffective. The council which managed affairs was reasonably responsive to parliamentary guidance, but it was weak and divided, parlia-

The minority

---

[9] See genealogical table on p. 281.

[10] He attained his majority in 1387, but his political tutelage did not end till two years later.

ment was really incompetent to direct it, and no leader rose to the occasion. Richard, when he grew older, surrounded himself with a circle of friends who supported his ambition to throw aside the superintendence of parliament and take the government more largely into his own hands. In 1385 he made his intention manifest by refusing to change his ministers at the request of parliament. The opposition came to a climax in the parliament of 1388, when five nobles accused five of the noble supporters of Richard's personal rule of treason, and secured their condemnation. The five accusers, who were known as the Lords Appellant, were actuated partly by selfish motives, but their triumph was nevertheless a noteworthy vindication of the power of parliament to limit the will of an arbitrary king.

Constitutional rule

The victory, like most of the events of this confused period, was of slight consequence. In 1389 Richard declared himself of age and entitled to a share in the administration. He secured parliamentary approval of his assumption of the right to appoint ministers and councilors by announcing his intention to rule with regard for the wishes of parliament. Eight years of constitutional rule followed. The king restrained his petulant temper, concealed his despotic tendencies, and worked harmoniously with parliament. Long truces brought a cessation of the war, and England was more quiet and prosperous than it had been since 1369. Richard did not oust the faction of the Lords Appellant from his council and administration, but he gradually balanced them by new appointees. The danger both of oligarchic and of royal tyranny seemed to be removed.

Tyranny

In reality Richard had been gradually rebuilding the old household bureaucracy on a royalist basis and introducing into the council a large section of this courtier element. In 1397 he struck for vengeance on the Lords Appellant and for freedom from the shackles of parliament. The first indication of his change of attitude was a typical outburst of rage in 1397, caused by a parliamentary petition which criticized the expenses of his household and sought their reduction. He demanded from the speaker the name of the originator of the petition and had the author, Thomas Haxey, tried by the lords for treason. Haxey was convicted though he was not executed. This was an attack upon the foundation of the power of the commons, for if a petitioner could be condemned to death when he introduced a resolution displeasing to the king, the house could not protect popular liberties against a tyrannical king. Later in the same year Richard called another parliament. The house of commons was filled with his nominees and the house of lords contained a number of new and younger peers who favored the king. Richard had the Lords Appellant arrested and accused of treason before the lords for their acts of 1388. They were condemned, and, along with many of their adherents, were executed, exiled, or imprisoned. In 1398 the same packed parliament voted Richard a revenue for life and delegated the most important of its powers to a small committee which was filled with the king's adherents. Richard had rid himself of the baronial opposition and of parliament at the same time. No check remained on his arbitrary will. Despite the overthrow of constitutional checks, he might conceivably have ruled long, had he ruled well. But he ruled rashly. He imposed pecuniary burdens on his subjects at will, imprisoned critics and opponents without trial, boasted publicly of his unlimited power, and placed his subjects in fear of their lives and property. Meanwhile Henry of Lancaster, son of John of Gaunt, whom Richard had exiled, organized a plot to overthrow his cousin. In 1399, while the king was in Ireland quelling a revolt, Henry landed in England, where followers rallied to his cause in large numbers. Richard, on his return, finding himself without supporters, was forced to abdicate. Parliament, which was then summoned, accepted his abdication, and thereupon declared Henry of Lancaster to be king of England as Henry IV.

The revolution of 1399 vindicated the principle that the sovereign must rule subject to the limitations of his power established by parliament. It assured the position which parliament had acquired during the fourteenth century, because Henry IV was labeled "made in parliament." He was the descendant of the fourth son of Edward III, and the descendant of the third son had the legal claim to the throne by hereditary right. Henry IV owed his throne to parliament; if he would hold the crown, he must acknowledge parliament. The revolution also affected profoundly the royal administrative organization. It did not end the household system, but it did establish the baronial element as a permanent part of the administration, and it "rendered futile any attempt to set up an interior royal cabinet of confidants against the accredited ministers of state."[11] That all this was not an unmixed good the rule of the house of Lancaster was still to demonstrate. But the fundamental principle had been established that the king who would keep his crown must give some heed to the voice of the nation expressed in parliament.

The revolution of 1399

Before leaving the constitutional history of the fourteenth century it is necessary to trace certain other institutional developments. The

[11] Tout, "Some Conflicting Tendencies in English Administrative History during the Fourteenth Century," (Reprint from *Bulletin of the John Rylands Library*, viii), p. 19.

The king's council

king's council has often been introduced into the narrative, but a few supplementary words are necessary to summarize its development in the fourteenth century. What the council was to become was hotly contested between the magnates and the king on several occasions during the period. The magnates wanted it controlled in their interest by a permanent membership of nobles, while the king sought a council that should be royalist and bureaucratic. Until the reign of Richard II the nobles always lost, because, when they had forced or persuaded the king to admit a large permanent baronial element into the council, they had never succeeded in finding individual members of their order who were willing to persevere in the arduous duty of constant attendance at the council board. Their effort in the reign of Richard was slightly more successful, but further baronial experiments under the house of Lancaster would demonstrate that the council was to be primarily a royal agency. The magnates claimed to be the counselors of the king on questions of policy, but the work of the council was in so much greater measure executive and judicial in character that it must perforce be filled largely with trained administrators and jurists. The house of lords was coming to be the place where baronial policies were formulated and expressed. The struggles of the fourteenth century, however, did much to define the membership of the council and contributed somewhat toward the delimitation of its functions.

The functions of the council were still the same in kind as they had been in the time of Edward I,[12] but they were greater in amount because the business of the government was increasing. Aside from its work in an advisory capacity, the functions of the council were largely residual in character. It transacted administrative or judicial business which did not fall within the acknowledged sphere of established departments or courts, or which was referred to it by them. During the fourteenth century some of these departments and courts increased the scope of their activities, with the result that the functions of the council were decreased by that much. How parliament cut into the legislative and judicial fields previously occupied by the council has already been related.[13]

The court of chancery

Another differentiation which was beginning to carry away some of the judicial work of the council was that growing up between the chancery and the council. During the reign of Edward I it became a practice to refer some of the cases arising under the residual jurisdiction to the chancellor. When the chancellor tried such causes, however,

---

[12] Above, pp. 196, 197.
[13] Above, pp. 230, 231.

he was required to have associated with him some of his fellow councilors. During the fourteenth century the portion of the residual
jurisdiction exercised by the court of chancery grew steadily. The
chancellor's court developed forms of procedure different from those
used by the council, and the attendance of councilors tended to become
perfunctory. By the end of Richard's reign the court of chancery had
taken over a large part of the judicial business of the council in the
field of civil jurisdiction, and it was nearly independent of the council.
Since most of the cases which came before it were not covered by the
common law, the chancery decided them by principles of equity. It
thus became the principal court exercising an equitable jurisdiction.

The further changes made in the central judiciary during the fourteenth century, which it is important to note, have been mentioned in
connection with parliament.[14] It remains to deal with the innovation
in the local judiciary made by the creation of the justices of the peace.
They developed out of the conservators of the peace who, in the thirteenth century, were concerned with the keeping of the peace in every
county, but had no judicial functions. Before 1327 they were empowered
by statute to receive indictments against suspected criminals, but the
persons indicted before them had to be delivered to the itinerant
justices for trial. Further extension of powers came with the growth of
social disorders. In 1329 the conservators were converted into justices
by commissions which authorized them to hear and determine felonies
and trespasses. These commissions were later superseded, but after
several years of experimentation the appointment in each county of
justices of the peace selected from the local gentry became the permanent practice. The justices, once established, were utilized for an
increasing variety of work. Not only did their judicial functions
expand, but they became the principal agents of the king for the
conduct of local affairs. In 1388 they were required to hold judicial
sessions four times each year, whence came the quarter sessions that are
still in use. In the fifteenth century they were given a summary police
jurisdiction over a large number of petty offenses. After the justices had
been established, the greater part of the legislation which required local
enforcement was given to them to administer. They enforced statutes
regulating wages, prices, conditions of labor, and many other things.
By 1485 the amount of administrative work done by the justices of the
peace was in excess of that previously performed by any other local
officials. They had nearly superseded the sheriffs. As judicial officials

*Justices of
the peace*

---

[14] Above, p. 230.

they had supplanted the old local courts of the shire and the hundred. They became, indeed, practically the local rulers of the counties.

The justices of the peace were originally established to extend the control of the central government over local affairs. The justices were appointed by the king, but they were not royal officials sent down from the center to administer the law locally. In each shire a local lord was associated with a few other residents of high social standing who were men of substance and legal knowledge. Their quality gave them influence and authority among the fellow residents of their bailiwicks, and they were generally efficient officials. They did not, however, become a bureaucracy. In France similar royal agents were appointed at about the same time, but they were royal agents, sent out from Paris, whose interests remained solely those of the king. The English justices accumulated great authority, but their sympathies remained largely with the people among whom they lived, and their social standing gave them a certain independence even against the king. So free from the bureaucratic spirit were the justices of the peace that they did much to carry the liberties of Englishmen safely through the troubled period of the sixteenth and seventeenth centuries, when the Tudors and the Stuarts threatened to wipe them out completely.

CHAPTER XIV

SOCIAL, ECONOMIC, AND RELIGIOUS DEVELOPMENTS OF THE FOURTEENTH CENTURY

THE life of the English people in the fourteenth century presents great contrasts. The Treaty of Calais appears to mark the height of Social life the medieval glory of England. Edward III, supported by the English national feeling, had led his people in a series of victories so brilliant as to make English arms the most renowned in Europe. Yet Edward III lived to see his broad possessions in France reduced to coastal strips and his people depressed by the gloom of a losing war. Feudalism to outward seeming reached its climax in the chivalry of the fourteenth century. The knightly deeds, the tournaments, the pageants, and the feasts, which the chroniclers loved to record, give glittering testimony to the medievalism of the period. But modern conceptions which were incompatible with the feudal social structure were taking root. The war brought the feeling of nationality to a most unmedieval pitch. Under its stress knights and burghers learned to work harmoniously in the house of commons and yeomen archers and mounted knights temporarily leveled distinctions of class in order to win Crécy and Poitiers. Intermarriage began to take place between the richer merchants and the landed gentry. In the chivalrous society of the fourteenth century birth counted for much; yet wealth was beginning to break through the social wall. More breaches were being made, too, through which laborers could pass into the lower section of the middle class. The lower ranges of society, indeed, were beginning to stir in a most modern manner. In the towns the artisans frequently opposed tumultuously the conditions of life and labor imposed upon them by their rich employers; in the country the rural wage earners displayed a kindred spirit, while among the villeins bitter resentment grew against the restrictions of their bondage. The life of the nobility and the wealthy section of the middle class was characterized by luxury and display; that of the workers by dissatisfaction, unrest, and rebellion.

In the middle of the century the lives of all classes were temporarily affected disastrously by the visitation of a plague, now called the black Black death death. Many authorities believe it to have been the bubonic plague. The disease was highly contagious and generally fatal. It originated in the east, whence it followed the trade routes to Italy, France, and the

British Isles. In England the black death first appeared in the west in the summer of 1348. In London it raged during the next winter. Thence it passed up the east coast in 1349, extending its ravages to Scotland and Ireland in the next year.

Mortality

The havoc wrought by the black death was frightful. The sanitary conditions under which people lived in the Middle Ages were such as to favor the spread of any contagious disease. In the towns the narrow, crowded streets were often filled with filthy refuse. Everywhere the dwellings of the poor were squalid and unhealthy, and those of the better classes were often poorly ventilated and dirty. The food was coarse and frequently unwholesome. Under such conditions the epidemic could not fail to cause a heavy mortality. No statistics were then kept, but the chronicles and various other documents provide many concrete illustrations of the deadly effect of the contagion. In some places the existing cemeteries could not accommodate the dead, and new ones had to be hurriedly opened. Individual graves could not always be dug, and the dead had to be buried promiscuously in trenches. Whole families were sometimes wiped out. The mortality appears to have been as heavy in the rural districts as in the towns. At the manor of Hadeston sixty-eight out of a population of less than four hundred died; at the manor of Winslow three out of five adult males died; at Cornard Parva, where there were about fifty heads of families, sixty people died and twenty-one families disappeared completely. Among the clergy the mortality was especially heavy. Among the secular clergy, who were particularly exposed to the disease because of their faithful ministrations to the sick and the dying, the death rate was from five to fourteen times as heavy as in ordinary years. In Buckinghamshire and Worcestershire nearly a half of the parish priests died. Nor could the monasteries with their life in common escape their toll. At Ely twenty-eight out of forty-three inmates died, and at Meaux only ten out of fifty monks were left alive.

How large a part of the whole population of England was carried away by the black death it is impossible to say in the absence of any complete statistics. Contemporary chroniclers make estimates that vary all the way from one-third to nine-tenths, but the notorious inaccuracy of medieval chroniclers with regard to figures was doubtless accentuated in this case by the prevalent terror. Modern investigators have multiplied many times the concrete evidence of the types cited in the preceding paragraph, and on that basis have estimated the death rate at one-third to one-half. Cardinal Gasquet, on the basis of the records preserved in episcopal registers, has established a probability that such a figure would hold good for the secular clergy.[1] But their duties exposed them in exceptional measure to infection, and the examples relating to the rest of the population are too few and too scattered to justify the same proportion for laymen. How easily such evidence may be exaggerated is illustrated by the events which accompanied the epidemic of influenza which swept over many cities and towns in the United States in the autumn of 1918. In many places the hospitals could not accommodate a tithe of the patients who applied for entrance; whole families were ill at once, deserted by their servants and with no nurses to be had; coffins could not be supplied in sufficient numbers to house the dead; stories were current that sometimes the dead had to be buried in trenches; and more than once whole families became extinct. Yet this scourge, which aroused the horror of all who came into contact with it, increased the annual death rate in Philadelphia, to take a concrete example, from 17.10 in a thousand in 1917 to only 24.37 in a thousand in 1918. To those who witnessed the devastation, the fatalities seemed to be far greater in number. The normal death rate of medieval England was unquestionably much higher than that of Philadelphia in 1917, and the mortality caused by the black death far in excess of that in 1918; but the recent experience gives force to the conjecture that the estimate of one-third to one-half takes insufficient account of the horrified exaggeration which would inevitably affect the point of view of the survivors in 1348 and 1349.[2]

Though the vexed question of the extent of the mortality must be left in abeyance, there is little doubt that it was sufficiently large to have had pronounced social and economic effects. For the moment the whole material and moral life of the people was upset. Like other overwhelming disasters, the black death temporarily loosened the morals of the community. Trade and industry in some centers were disrupted. The export of manufactured cloth fell off during the next few years by over fifty per cent, and the production of tin by approximately sixty per cent. In the country some farms were abandoned, here and there a whole village was left deserted, cattle wandered in the fields with none to claim them, and crops rotted in the fields with none to harvest them. The secular clergy were decimated to such an extent that untrained and even ignorant candidates had to be promoted to the priesthood in order to fill the vacancies. The resulting decline in the

General results

---

[1] *The Black Death, passim.*

[2] That 33⅓ to 50 per cent is an overestimate seems to be the consensus of opinion of recent investigators. See, for example, Usher, *Introduction to the Industrial History of England,* pp. 92–97; Levett and Ballard, "The Black Death" in *Oxford Studies in Social and Legal History,* v.

personnel of the priesthood was evident for many a day after 1349.
The depopulated monasteries were many of them unable ever again
to attain their old quotas; their discipline relaxed; their property shrank
in value; and thus the plague contributed to the permanent decline of
their influence in the community.[3]

Effect on rural life

Of the permanent effects the most important was the change wrought
in rural life. The number of manors to be cultivated was not reduced.
The amount of labor available to cultivate them was materially smaller.
The inevitable result was an increase of wages. They went up often to
double their previous amount. Many landlords stared ruin in the face.
Death had deprived them of the customary services of many of their
villeins. It had also deprived them of many of their tenants and reduced their rent-rolls. The revenues they received from mills, courts,
and many other sources were likewise reduced by the decrease in the
number of their tenants. At the same time the cost of many of the
articles they had to buy soared. Producers of manufactured articles
could more easily add the additional cost of labor to the price. The
prices of grain and meat which the landowners produced did not increase in proportion. The landowners promptly sought the help of the
government.

Statute of Laborers

The Statute of Laborers was the result. In 1349 the king and council
issued an ordinance to regulate wages and prices, and at the next meeting of parliament in 1351 the ordinance, with some revisions, was made
a statute. It required every workman, who was not bound to a lord
or exercising a craft, to take work when it was offered to him. Work
both in country and in town must be done at the rate of wages customary before the pestilence under penalty of fine to be paid both by
those who paid and those who received higher rates. Prices of the
necessaries of life were to be kept reasonable. It was legislation enacted
in the interest of the classes which controlled the government, but it
was not unjust from the contemporary point of view. When the laborers took advantage of the situation to demand higher wages, they were
running counter to the theory of the just price.[4] But the statute could
not be enforced. The laborers refused to accept the lower wages, though
many were punished, and the landlords, rather than let their crops
spoil at the time of harvest, generally paid what the laborers demanded.
For a time wages may have been kept lower than they would have

[3] Mode, P. G., *Influence of the Black Death on the English Monasteries* (Chicago,
1916).

[4] See above, p. 190.

been without the intervention of the government, but they could not be maintained "at the statutory level."[5]

With the failure of the Statute of Laborers, some landlords found it unprofitable to continue their old practices and were forced to make many adjustments. In some districts the villeins were so reduced in numbers that they were able sometimes to secure reductions in their services or commutation of their services to money payments. The lords were sometimes constrained to make concessions or lose their villeins, for so much land lay idle and wages were so high that the villein who ran away had an excellent opportunity either to get a new holding on better terms, or to improve his condition by working for hire. Hired labor was hard to obtain under conditions that were not prohibitive of profit. So difficult did it become for the lords of many manors to work their own demesnes, that they gave up the attempt and leased their demesnes to tenant farmers for money rents. This change also facilitated the commutation of the services of the villeins to money rents, since the lord who had leased his demesne no longer had any use for the services. Neither practice was new,[6] but both were now followed on a large scale.

Demesne leases and commutation

These changes generally worked temporarily to the economic disadvantage of the landlords during the stage of transition; to the villeins and the rural wage earners they were immediately and permanently beneficial. The conversion of labor services to money rents gave the villein economic freedom with opportunity to take advantage of the high wages in his spare time. The rural wage earners were not only benefited by the increase in wages, but they were made an important class in the rural community. This class, which was recruited mainly from cotters, emancipated villeins, and the younger sons of villeins, had first become of significance in the rural community in the thirteenth century, when transactions in kind began to give way to transactions in cash.[7] With the steadily increasing use of cash in the manorial economy the demand for hired labor grew, and the ranks of the rural wage earners were constantly enlarged. The black death and the subsequent acceleration of commutation and of demesne leases probably increased the proportionate size of this class; certainly it placed a premium on its services which rendered its position better economically and socially.

The improved condition of the working classes only served to arouse their discontent. The peasants of the second half of the fourteenth cen-

---

[5] Putnam, *Enforcement of Statutes of Labourers,* p. 221.
[6] Above, p. 178.
[7] Above, pp. 178, 179.

Discontent of the peasants

tury were economically in a position to live more comfortably than their ancestors. But the advantages they had gained merely whetted their appetite for more. They became impatient with the restrictions that held them back from further progress. *Piers Plowman,* the contemporary poem, though generally in sympathy with the peasants, tells us that landless laborers scorned to dine on cabbage a day old, nor were they suited with penny ale and a piece of bacon, but they must have fresh meat or fried fish, and that hot or hotter for the chill of their maw.[8] The peasants soon discovered their power, and began to form combinations for securing higher wages, reducing their rents, or bettering the conditions of their service. Their frequent successes fostered their confidence and raised their contentious spirit. Finally, in 1381, they put their power to the supreme test of revolt.

Economic and social causes of the Peasants' Revolt

Though the grievances which stirred the working classes to rebel were of such varied nature that in many instances they were peculiar to one locality, it is possible to sort out a few that were fairly universal. The wage earners were particularly aggrieved by the attempt to execute the Statute of Laborers, which they considered unjust. The villeins as a class were dissatisfied with their bondage. Among them a feeling was widely prevalent that there ought to be social equality, that all men had been born with equal rights, and that it was wrong for them to be bound to the soil. The couplet,

> When Adam delved and Eve span
> Who was then the gentleman?

became the watchword of the rebellion.

The reformers

The flame of discontent was fanned by the preaching of reformers. They were of different types. John Ball was a priest who was active in and around London. He harangued the peasants on the iniquity of bondage and finally took a prominent part himself in the organization of the rebellion. The rugged eloquence of such fiery talks as the following was not lost on his discontented audiences. "My good friends," he is reported by the chronicler Froissart to have said, "things cannot go well in England, nor ever will until everything shall be in common; when there shall be neither vassal nor lord and all distinction levelled, when the lords shall be no more masters than ourselves. . . . They have handsome seats and manors, when we must brave the wind and rain in our labours in the field; but it is from our labour that they have wherewith to support their pomp."[9] Other poor priests preached

---

[8] Paraphrased from Passus VI, lines 309–313.
[9] As quoted by Trevelyan, *Age of Wycliffe,* p. 197.

similar doctrines to smaller audiences. Some of the wandering friars also may have taken part in setting class against class. At least they were accused of it by their enemies.

Another reformer who probably had some influence unintentionally was John Wycliffe. He was a famous scholar, who as a reformer was concerned wholly with the evils in the church. His doctrines on that subject were extremely radical and might be easily misinterpreted. Consider, for example, the following free translation of one of his typical statements. "Every man," he says, "ought to be a Christian (in gracia), and if he is a Christian, he is the master of the world with its contents; therefore every man must be master of the world. Since a man can not be master of the world with a multitude of men, unless all those should have all things in common: therefore all things should be in common."[10] It is an excellent illustration of the syllogistic obscurity of scholasticism, but the conclusion is clear enough to suit the most radical socialist of the present day. In this extract Wycliffe is arguing about the church. Neither here nor elsewhere did he intend to apply his philosophic radicalism to social conditions. But less learned disciples, who, without his sanction, spread his views about the country, made no such fine distinctions. They applied his doctrines to the landlords, and thus added fuel to the flame.

The principal grievances of the peasants were social and economic in character, but in some measure the revolt was a political protest. The prevailing dissatisfaction with the mismanaged government pervaded the ranks of the peasants. A political cause, moreover, was the immediate occasion of the outbreak. In 1377 a poll tax was levied for the first time. It reached many of the poor who had never been subject to the taxes on property and incomes previously levied. It was highly unpopular with the very class that was inoculated with the virus of social revolution. Two years later a second poll tax was levied, and in 1380 a third was imposed. This was intended to be heavier on the rich than on the poor, but it was apportioned with such ignorance that in many communities the poor had to pay at a heavier rate than ever before. As a result false returns were made on a large scale. When the returns were sorted, the evasion was discovered. In 1381 commissioners were sent out to investigate the frauds and to collect from the evaders. The commissioner for Essex was resisted by force, and the villagers who participated in the riot at once aroused all Essex. Messengers were sent to Kent, but the Kentishmen had already risen. The

The poll taxes

[10] *Tractatus de Civili Dominio,* ed. by R. L. Poole, i, 96.

word was rapidly passed to other sections of the country. The attack on the commissioner took place in the last days of May. Within two weeks southeastern England was in revolt, and before the end of June the movement had spread as far north as York and as far west as Somerset.

The attack on London

The rebels in Essex and the southern counties began at once to converge on London. As they went along they entered manor houses, destroyed the court rolls containing the evidence of serfdom, and murdered the most unpopular landlords. In the towns they pillaged and destroyed some buildings. On June 12 the rebels from the south, under the leadership of Wat Tyler and John Ball, encamped across the river from London, and the rioters from Essex approached the northern and eastern sides of the city. On the next day the gates were opened to them by sympathizers within the city, which was undefended. On the first day the mob was restrained by its leaders from indiscriminate pillage. On June 14 the king granted an interview which the leaders of the rebels had requested. In a tumultuous parley which often threatened to become a riot, he granted the demands of the leaders, the principal of which were that the villeins should be made free tenants, and that the rents paid in place of customary services should be reduced. Meanwhile the mob in London captured and killed several of the king's advisers and officials. As the mob spirit rapidly rose, widespread murder, robbery, and destruction of property took place. The king's clerks worked throughout the day engrossing the charters which had been promised. As the rebels received them, many went home. Enough remained, however, to render certain a repetition of violent scenes on the morrow. The king, therefore, on the advice of his councilors, sought another interview with the leaders, in the hope that they might be induced to withdraw their followers. Contradictory accounts make it impossible to say just what took place at the conference held outside the city. For some reason Wat Tyler drew his dagger in the presence of the king and was struck down by the king's followers. It was a tense moment. The horde of rebels began to draw weapons, and a rush on the king and his handful of followers appears to have been imminent, when Richard rode forward and offered to be their leader. His bold act carried the day. After momentary indecision they began to follow, and Richard led them away from the city. The mayor of London, meanwhile, returned to the city, where the announcement of the king's peril served within the hour to collect an armed force of several thousand citizens. The mayor and his force soon caught up with the king. With an army at his back the king did not take vengeance, but gave the rebels permission to disperse, which they promptly accepted.

The departure of the peasants from London practically ended the revolt. The movement was confined almost entirely to the counties south and east of the Exe-Tees line. Though it spread rapidly the peasants were not well organized. The only strong concentration of forces outside of London was in East Anglia. There the backbone of the rebellion was broken by local magnates, led by the bishop of Norwich. The peasants had no common object, they were poorly armed, and after the revolt had been quelled in these two centers, it was easy to put it down in detail elsewhere. By autumn the last embers of the rebellion had been smothered. The revolt elsewhere

The revolt was a complete failure. The royal charters of liberation were revoked. So far as it is possible to tell, villeinage remained after 1381 as it had been before. The attempt to enforce the Statute of Laborers was maintained, and labor troubles of the types common before 1381 continued, though they seem gradually to have subsided in the next century.[11] During the fifteenth century services in labor and personal villeinage practically came to an end, though a few villeins could still be found in the sixteenth century. But the disappearance of villeinage was the result of those transformations of agrarian organization which were already producing commutation on a large scale before 1381. The revolt appears to have done nothing greatly to hasten or to retard the working of these economic causes. The results

The spirit of lawlessness in the fourteenth century was not confined to the workers. The prolonged warfare with its alternation of active service and idleness created a kindred spirit among the upper classes. Its growth was promoted also by the prevailing system of livery. This "was originally the allowance in provisions and clothing which was made for the servants and officers of the great households, whether of baron, prelate, monastery or college."[12] The emphasis later came to be placed on the clothing, which in the fourteenth century took the form of uniforms. Wealthy magnates issued these not only to household servants but also to large numbers of retainers. Such uniforms were no longer mere badges of service; they had become marks of honor and power. Their wearers contributed to the magnificence and local influence in which the households of the great rivaled one another, receiving in return the patronage and protection of the lord. This was given sometimes by force of arms, but more commonly in the form of Livery and maintenance

---

[11] Trevelyan, *Age of Wycliffe*, p. 253.

[12] Stubbs, *Constitutional History*, iii, 531.

influence used with officials and with courts to further the interests or the suits of individual retainers. Often such influence was exerted upon the courts in a way that perverted the course of justice. Maintenance, as this practice was called, was a growing evil throughout the fourteenth century. The Hundred Years' War enhanced the evil of livery. Edward III commonly filled his armies for foreign service by contracts with the nobles. Each noble supplied his own services and those of a large number of followers for a fixed wage. The noble's followers wore his livery and were paid by him. Bands of retainers thus came to be constituted largely of soldiers, who found it difficult to settle down as law-abiding citizens in the intervals between their campaigns. Depredations by the members of such bands became common, and the injured parties often found it impossible to secure justice in the courts because of the maintenance of the lords, who frequently resorted to bribery, intimidation, and force. In some instances the possessors of such bands used them to plunder, rob, and terrify the surrounding countryside. The evils of this system early caused protest from the commons, who presented many petitions on the subject during the century. Prohibitory statutes failed to stop the spread of the practice. The dependence of the king upon the nobles for his armies made it impossible for him to eliminate maintenance and liveries, and the influence in the government acquired by the nobles in the time of Richard II rendered the situation still more hopeless. At the turn of the century the government was powerless to check the growth of these pernicious practices which were nullifying the administration of justice, spreading disorder, and placing the weak at the mercy of the strong.

The
merchants

Notwithstanding the growth of internal disorder and the strain of external war, industry and foreign commerce expanded in the fourteenth century. During the second half of the century, while the landlords were experiencing an economic depression and the laborers were dissatisfied with the conditions of their life and labor, a class of wealthy merchants was coming to the fore. When the Hundred Years' War began, Edward III borrowed freely from the Italian merchants and such other foreign sources as he could tap. His failure to pay his debts ultimately dried up these sources and contributed largely to the failure of two of the great Florentine banking houses which did business in England. The king was forced to fall back on the English merchants for loans. It gives evidence of the capital developed among them, that they were able to take over a large part of the financial business formerly transacted by the Italian bankers. Before the end of the century English capitalists were "conducting in English towns much of the business which had hitherto been done by aliens at fairs,"[13] and they were beginning to push the English trade in foreign markets.[14] With the acquisition of capital on a larger scale, the native merchants were becoming influential socially and politically. Some merchants were ennobled during the century. Piers Plowman testifies to their improved social status in his plaint that soap-sellers had been made knights.[15] In London and most of the other towns they secured virtual control of municipal affairs, and they had strong influence in the national government, not only through the municipal representatives in parliament but also directly because of the king's dependence upon them for loans. Their national importance by the time of Richard II is well attested by the numerous laws enacted to regulate the foreign commerce of England in their favor.

The regulation of commerce by the central government in this century was greater in amount than it had been previously, enactments being particularly numerous during the reign of Edward III. They represent in the main an opportunist policy dictated by the circumstances of the moment. The central government continued sometimes to grant to foreign merchants privileges of the type conferred by the *carta mercatoria*, but it was compelled to abandon or modify many of them by the pressure exerted by Londoners and other jealous English townsmen. The staple, through which the trade in exports was largely regulated, was thoroughly reorganized. In 1313 it was given a monopoly by the requirement that all staple exports should pass through it, subject to the regulations established by the Merchant Staplers for the conduct of business therein. The Merchant Staplers thus became a quasi-official organization as well as a commercial company. In the reign of Edward III the compulsory principle was abandoned, only to be restored after a few years. Abuses of the renewed monopoly led to legislation in 1353 and 1354, which regulated its exercise more carefully. For a time thereafter the staple was placed under the management of royal officials, but its control was returned eventually to the Merchants of the Staple. The location of the staple shifted several times. Sometimes it was in English ports and sometimes in towns across the Channel. In 1363 Calais, which was already the staple for some products, was made the staple for wool. There, except for a few brief intervals, the staple remained for the rest of the Middle Ages.

Regulation of commerce to 1377

[13] Cunningham, *English Industry and Commerce during the Early and Middle Ages,* p. 373.

[14] Gras, *Early English Customs System,* p. 111.

[15] Chadwick, *Social Life in the Days of Piers Plowman,* p. 51.

The most radical departure in the regulation of industry by the central government was the attempt to fix wages and prices inaugurated by the Statute of Laborers. This constituted a vast encroachment on the field hitherto left almost exclusively to towns and gilds. In practice, however, the central government had scant success in the regulation of wages and still less in the regulation of prices. Some effort was also made to encourage native manufactures. It may best be illustrated by the policy pursued with regard to the manufacture of woolens, which was the foremost English industry of the period. In the early years of the fourteenth century this industry, which had been the only one to provide wares for export in any quantity before 1300, seems to have suffered a decline. In 1326 the use of imported woolens of the cheaper grades was prohibited in order to provide a better home market. This stringent measure was twice repeated by Edward III, and once the exportation of wool was prohibited; but none of these measures was enforced for more than a short period. Edward III encouraged the immigration of skilled Flemish weavers, though it is doubtful if they came in sufficient numbers to produce any marked development in the native manufacture of woolens. The greatest stimulus was given unintentionally by the heavy taxes placed on exported wool after 1337 for financing the war. After the middle of the century both the production of and the export trade in woolens expanded enormously, while the amount of wool exported gradually declined. The central government attempted to maintain certain qualities and standards of measurement in the woolens produced, just as it laid down rules with regard to the qualities of certain foodstuffs.[16] To manufactures other than woolens the central government gave less attention. Its intervention in the industrial field was much less in amount and importance than in the commercial.

The policy of regulation pursued by the central government during the reign of Richard displays the influence of the newly made capitalists. A series of statutes excluded foreign merchants from the retail trade and secured the internal trade of the country to Englishmen. In 1381 the first Navigation Act was passed. It required Englishmen shipping goods into or out of England to employ English ships. After brief experience demonstrated that English ships were too few to handle the trade, the statute was amended to the effect that English ships, when they were available, should be preferred to others. With

[16] Above, p. 190. The requirements concerning woolens were not left to local enforcement, like those concerning food, but were enforced by a royal inspector called the aulnager.

the intention of providing a larger amount of the circulating medium for a business necessarily transacted mainly by means of cash, the export of bullion was prohibited except by the government for the maintenance of its foreign possessions. Collectively the legislation of Richard's reign seems to reflect a clearer consciousness of a national policy of regulation than any which had gone before, and to presage the maxims of the mercantile system of economic thought,[17] which was destined to govern the policy of national regulation, when the growth of national consciousness had finally caused the decay of the old local system of regulation. In 1399 the signs of the approaching decline of the particularistic system are manifest only in the light of the events of the next century. The towns and the gilds still regulated commerce and industry locally to suit their own selfish ends to a far greater extent than the central government regulated them in the national interest. Nevertheless, the national point of view was more influential in economic regulation than it had been a century earlier.

Both the national spirit and the prevalent feeling of unrest found expression in the religious life of the English people during the fourteenth century. The former took the form of an outburst of anti-papal sentiment, while the latter gave rise to an anti-clerical movement. The English opposition to papal provisions and to papal taxation of the English clergy, which had been manifested frequently during the thirteenth century, reached a climax with the Hundred Years' War. For many years the papacy had been located at Avignon, just across the Rhone from France. The popes were French, and the cardinals and other members of the papal court predominantly so. Englishmen naturally assigned French sympathies to a French papal court. As the war produced a rising tide of nationalism, they came to believe, whether rightly or wrongly, that some of the gold which went from England to Avignon found its way eventually into the coffers of the French kings and was used against English arms. The belief resulted in action. In 1351 parliament enacted the famous Statute of Provisors, which decreed that those who accepted papal appointments to English benefices should be subject to imprisonment until they paid fines and renounced their provisions. Two years later parliament attempted to strengthen the royal courts in a contest which was being waged with the papal court for jurisdiction. The appeal to the papal court of cases cognizable in the king's courts was regarded as prejudicial to royal authority and burdensome to defendants summoned outside the realm.

Anti-papal legislation

---

[17] See below, pp. 363, 364.

For half a century or more this practice had been forbidden, but the prohibition often proved difficult to enforce. The Statute of Præmunire established a new legal procedure designed to render the prohibition more effective.[18] It did not affect the wide field of jurisdiction claimed by the ecclesiastical forum in matters which the royal courts acknowledged to be outside the scope of their jurisdiction.[19] The most significant expression of the national feeling against the papacy was made by the parliament of 1366. The pope was pressing for the payment of the thousand marks of annual tribute promised by King John, which was more than thirty years in arrears. Parliament, when consulted by Edward, replied that none could place the realm in such subjection without the consent of the lords and commons, which John had never had. The payment subsequently ceased.

This noteworthy series of acts gives weighty evidence of the popular dissatisfaction with some of the papal policies. Apart from the advice given in 1366, however, their effect was largely on parchment. The king found papal provisions too useful for his own purpose to bring them to an end. In the fourteenth century bishoprics had become the rewards which the king conferred regularly on his faithful ministers and chief officials. He found it easier to secure their appointment from complacent popes than to force their election from cathedral chapters. Benefices were obtained in the same manner for clerks and lesser officials in his service. Since the pope aided the king practically to provide salaries for his servants from the revenues of the church, the king could hardly oppose the use of papal provisions to confer lesser offices and benefices upon others. So little effect did the Statute of Provisors have, that it was enacted again in 1390 with more severe penalties attached. The second statute seems to have succeeded in placing some limits on papal provisions, for it was invoked successfully in the king's courts from time to time, but it certainly failed to bring them to an end. How the Statutes of Præmunire were enforced is less well known. It has usually been taken for granted that the enactment of a third Statute of Præmunire in 1393 was caused by failure to enforce the earlier legislation. A more careful interpretation of the statute, which is loosely phrased, makes it appear to have been merely supplementary to the earlier legislation in intent. Its legal interpretation half a century later gave it a scope far wider than its original meaning, making its severe penalties apply to any who should procure or bring into England papal letters or sentences derogatory to the king or the

[18] In 1365 a second Statute of Præmunire further elaborated this principle.
[19] See above, pp. 90, 91, 110, 111.

realm.[20] Possibly præmunire was enforced better than provisions, but it seems probable that the anti-papal legislation was more important for its expression of popular opinion than for its actual accomplishment in the fourteenth century.

The anti-clerical movement found its best expression in the career of John Wycliffe (c. 1328-1384). He first acquired fame as a teacher at Oxford, where he became the leading exponent of the scholastic philosophy. Early in his career he became interested in the clerical abuses which he saw about him. His prolific Latin writings of this period, although they are addressed to scholars in the complicated and tiresome style of contemporary scholasticism and deal primarily with theology and philosophy, contain a deal of vigorous criticism of the clergy and suggest drastic remedies. The theory which he developed at greatest length in this period was that of "Civil Dominion," which maintained that the civil authority had the power and the duty to confiscate the property of clerics of high or low degree who failed in their duties or abused their powers.

John Wycliffe at Oxford

His fame gradually extended beyond academic walls. His advocacy of depriving the clergy of some of their endowments appealed to many of the nobles to whose advantage it would work, and his criticism of the clergy touched a responsive chord in many laymen. In 1374 he was drawn into politics. Under the patronage of John of Gaunt, duke of Lancaster, he soon began to preach his doctrines from the pulpits of London. Anti-clerical feeling was already rife among laymen. The duke by his support of Wycliffe hoped to win for his faction the popularity which the Good Parliament demonstrated that it lacked. Wycliffe proved to be as effective with popular audiences as he had been with his students. His success disturbed the clergy. In 1377 the bishops summoned him to appear before them at St. Paul's to answer for his teachings. At the hearing he was ostentatiously supported by John of Gaunt, but the proceedings were ended abruptly when the Londoners burst into a riotous demonstration against the duke. That Wycliffe did not share his patron's unpopularity was shown when the reformer was brought to trial a second time in the next year. On this occasion the initiative was taken by the pope, who ordered certain of the English bishops to try Wycliffe for heresy. The trial was held in 1378. The bishops were now acting not in their own behalf but as papal commissioners. The government and the people arose to Wycliffe's defense. The queen mother forbade the bishops to pronounce

His wider appeal

[20] Waugh, "Great Statute of Præmunire," *Eng. Hist. Rev.*, xxxvii, 173-205.

sentence, and a London mob interrupted the proceedings soon after the trial began. The bishops adjourned the hearing for what proved to be *sine die*.

Clerical
abuses

Meanwhile Wycliffe had begun to extend his popular appeal by writing copiously in English. In a long series of pamphlets and sermons he attacked the evils of the church in hard, stinging English, which could be read by many to whom his Latin works were sealed books. The evils of which he complained had evidently stirred popular indignation deeply. Bishops too frequently gave to affairs of state the attention that should have been bestowed upon their spiritual duties. The monks and other wealthy ecclesiastics occupied themselves too largely with the care of their property. Penance was being corrupted by the practice of substituting money payments for actual penances, which spread abroad the notion that pardon for sins could be bought, though the church never sanctioned any such belief. The ecclesiastical courts, which enforced the payment of tithes and had a jurisdiction of sins that gave them inquisitorial rights over a man's most private affairs, often exercised their powers oppressively and corruptly. The parish priests, who brought the church most intimately into the lives of laymen, were too often underpaid, ignorant, and careless of the welfare of their flocks. Such were typical evils against which Wycliffe inveighed before 1378. He stood forth as a reformer, striving to eliminate abuses and to secure the reform of the church from within. In the articles of heresy charged against him at the trial of 1378 only one concerned a matter of doctrine, and that was of minor importance. His attack of abuses, his program of disendowment, and his denial of the temporal power of the clergy were the principal charges against him. So long as Wycliffe did not deny the spiritual authority of the clergy and sought only the remedy of manifest abuses, he was voicing the convictions of many laymen.

Heresies
of
Wycliffe

After 1378 the character of Wycliffe's teachings began to change. The papal attack caused him to question the authority of the Holy See. The papal schism of 1378 shook his belief to its foundations. Two years earlier the seat of the papacy had been restored to Rome, but the French cardinals, disliking the Italian pope who was chosen in 1378, seceded, and elected a French pope, who set up his establishment at Avignon. For many years thereafter the world was treated to the extraordinary spectacle of two rivals, each claiming to be the vicar of Christ on earth and the supreme head of the church. Wycliffe's doctrinal beliefs, already weakened by his disgust with the concrete abuses produced by the existing ecclesiastical system, gave way before the shock. He soon attacked the sacramental system, which was the basis of clerical power. He denied the cardinal doctrine of transubstantiation. This was the belief that in the sacrament of the Eucharist the bread and wine partaken by the communicants were converted into the actual body and blood of Christ without any change in the external appearance of the bread and wine. He also belittled all the sacraments as a means of salvation compared with the efficacy of an upright life. He denied the authority of the pope and set up the Bible as a sufficient rule of conduct. In order to make this needful authority available to laymen he and his assistants translated the scriptures into English. In this period, too, he began to send out disciples to travel the length and breadth of England preaching his views.

When Wycliffe ceased to be merely a reformer and became a revolutionist, he lost much of his popularity. The discontent of the English **Last years** people with existing religious conditions was great, but it was not sufficient to cause them to desire the complete overthrow of the church. In 1382 John of Gaunt repudiated his connection with Wycliffe, and a convocation of the province of Canterbury condemned several of Wycliffe's doctrines as heretical and secured the banishment of the reformer from Oxford. He was allowed to spend the remaining two years of his life at his rectory in Lutterworth, where he continued his writings and his organization of a missionary force.

His followers, who soon became known as the Lollards, were less fortunate. The government was not ready to support the spread of **The** heresy. Convocation persuaded the king's council to enact an ordinance **Lollards** which ordered the sheriffs to assist the bishops in the arrest of those accused of heresy. With the aid of the secular arm several of Wycliffe's lieutenants were arrested, tried in the ecclesiastical courts, and condemned of heresy. All recanted or escaped. When parliament next met, however, the commons protested against the ordinance, enacted without their consent, and forced its withdrawal. The anti-clerical feeling among the commons was still too strong to allow the state to aid the church even to suppress doctrines subversive of the faith. For some years the poor priests, as Wycliffe's missionaries were called, spread their master's teachings with comparative impunity. They won a large number of converts, among whom were wealthy townsmen and country gentlemen, who helped to protect them against the bishops and favored their cause in parliament. In 1401, however, the bishops secured legislation from parliament, which authorized the state to assist the church in the apprehension of heretics and to burn at the stake those who should be condemned.[21] For some years the statute was not stringently enforced. A few suffered the extreme penalty; more recanted. In 1414 Sir John Oldcastle, a knight who was a friend of the king, was tried and condemned. He escaped from prison, led an abortive Lollard uprising, and was hanged as a traitor along with thirty-six of his companions. His fate gave others of the Lollard gentry pause. A vigorous persecution for the next ten years sent Lollardry into a marked decline. The sect did not disappear entirely, but it was driven under ground. Martyrs cropped up occasionally during the remainder of the fifteenth century. Even in the sixteenth Wycliffe's heresies seem still to have had disciples who were preparing the way for the spread of the Reformation.[22] Wycliffe's doctrines, moreover, were carried from Oxford to the university of Prague in Bohemia, where they had a profound effect on John Hus, whose writings, in turn, strongly influenced Luther. John Wycliffe not only gave expression to the anticlerical feeling of his day, but in his later years went far ahead of the spirit of his age and became the precursor of the Protestant Reformation.

English literature

The nationalism and the unrest which pervade so many aspects of English life in the fourteenth century are reflected in the literature. In the first half of the century the literary trend evident at the close of the thirteenth century[23] pursued its course. The copious flow of religious and didactic manuals, sermons, and poems continued unabated and reached a high level in the devotional poetry of Richard Rolle of Hampole; Robert Mannyng of Bourne produced a rhyming English chronicle; and an endless stream of romances still slavishly imitated the French models. In this period, too, rudimentary drama made its appearance with the more definite formulation of the cycles of miracle plays, which amused the townsmen of that day. By the middle of the century the toilsome study of the French metrical romances began to produce its fruit. Several anonymous poems were written, which rival the French in power and in originality of thought and expression.[24] In the second half of the century English became the favorite language

---

[21] Statute *de haeretico comburendo.*

[22] It is a debatable and debated question whether Lollardry lived on *sub rosa* into the sixteenth century as a sufficient force to affect the Reformation. The actual evidence available is scanty, but a movement that necessarily ran in secret channels would leave little trace. Moreover, some of the most promising sources of evidence have not yet been thoroughly explored. For a statement of the two points of view, see Trevelyan, *Age of Wycliffe,* ch. ix; Gairdner, *Lollardy and the Reformation in England,* vol. i; and Gasquet, *Eve of the Reformation,* pp. 185-187.

[23] Above, pp. 167, 168.

[24] Such, for example, as "Gawain and the Green Knight."

of courtly literature, which culminated in one of the great poems of the English language. In 1362 a statute ordered the use of English in the courts of law. In this period, too, English supplanted French as the language of instruction in many of the schools. Romances continued to be written in French, it was still the current speech of many Englishmen, and lawyers still transacted their business in that language despite the statute. But French was on the rapid wane. Chaucer's great poem and *Piers Plowman* were written in English. Gower, of lesser fame, who wrote his first poem in French, later deserted it for English, Wycliffe turned from Latin to English to become a father of English prose, and the French of the lawyers rapidly became a hopelessly technical jargon. Latin remained the language of the church, the university, and the official record, but the literature of the English people had again become English.

In much of the English literature of this period the prevailing spirit of dissatisfaction with existing conditions finds expression. Wycliffe's **Critical** prose works were written to give tongue to the religious unrest. The **spirit** critical spirit appears also in literature that was intended primarily to amuse and entertain. The trend is well displayed in the two great poems of the period. *Piers Plowman* is essentially the people's poem. It describes the life of common men, the life of the laborer. Throughout the whole poem runs a stringent criticism of the evils and abuses of the times. The corruption of the clergy, the oppressions practiced by the rich, the misery of the poor, the social wrongs, the misgovernment, all are depicted. Peace, Wrong and Reason are personified. Peace and Wrong have a quarrel and bring it before the king to settle. Reason, the adviser of the king, is asked to have pity on the offender, Wrong, but he declared "that he would not 'till all lords and ladies love truth, . . . and clerks and knights are courteous, and priests practice what they preach, till the custom of pilgrimages and of carrying money out of the land ceases. . . . Were I king, no wrong should go unpunished or get grace by bribes. Were this rule kept, Law would have to become a labourer, and Love should rule all.' "[25] In this sad tone the poet characterizes the society of his time. Chaucer, who appears to have been the son of a rich London merchant and was a member of the king's household, wrote for the upper classes in very different vein. His *Canterbury Tales* portray the pleasant side of life, and their joy and gaiety contrast strangely with the gloom and sadness of *Piers Plowman*. But Chaucer none the less sets forth the evils of his age. He

[25] As paraphrased in *Cambridge History of English Literature*, ii, 12.

touches them with light and gentle satire, the spirit of moral reproach prevalent in *Piers Plowman* is lacking, but his geniality does not conceal the spirit of adverse criticism which is the spirit of his times.

The universities

The national literature of England in this period takes rank second to none; the same is true of the speculative thought which had its home at the universities. For the most of the century the universities were materially prosperous and intellectually vigorous. At Oxford five new colleges were endowed, and at Cambridge seven. Oxford increased her independence of both lay and ecclesiastical control, as did Cambridge in lesser degree. Academic freedom bred independent thought. In the fields of science and mathematics Oxford retained the preeminence she had acquired in the previous century,[26] and in the field of scholasticism no other European university can rival the list of famous names on Oxford's roll. John Duns Scotus (1265-1308), who taught at Paris and Cologne, as well as at Oxford, won European fame for his acute reasoning which gave him the title of the "subtle doctor," but led him into a web of fine-spun distinctions such as brought scholasticism into disrepute a century later. William of Ockham (1280-1347), who was trained at Oxford, taught at Paris, served the emperor, and won a cosmopolitan reputation embodied in his epithet of the "invincible doctor." With the outbreak of the Hundred Years' War the supplementary course at Paris, which had served to give so many English scholars European distinction, became impossible, but the intellectual activity which kept Oxford at the front of the scholastic world did not cease. Wycliffe, in whom the scholastic movement at Oxford culminated, and several of his predecessors received their training at Oxford, pursued their careers north of the Channel, and won universal recognition of their scholarship. The influence of Oxford, moreover, was not confined to the academic world. The speculations of Oxford teachers were often carried from the lecture rooms to the outside world, where they sometimes swayed public opinion strongly. Ockham lent his pen to the emperor to uphold his temporal power from papal encroachment, and Wycliffe entered the English political forum for a similar purpose. More than one English statesman of the day was educated at Oxford. But the intellectual greatness of Oxford was not destined to outlive the century. Wycliffe was the last of the schoolmen. When his followers were driven from the university, freedom of thought temporarily departed with them. Keen speculation gave way to the repetition of empty formulae, and a period of intel-

[26] Mansbridge, *Older Universities of England,* p. 40.

lectual torpor followed. So far did the decline go, that not only did Oxford lose its European prestige to Paris, but it also lost the greater part of its influence on national affairs. Cambridge, which had not risen so high, did not fall so far, but its curriculum was no less bound up with the outworn scholasticism. The intellectual glory of the universities passed with the century.

Historical writing in the fourteenth century failed to keep pace either with literature or with learning. The historical work of the monks, like many other of the services they had performed for society, suffered a marked decline. The St. Albans school continued to produce throughout nearly the whole of the period, but its products attained nothing more than mediocrity until Thomas Walsingham, near the close of the century, revived somewhat of the spirit of Matthew Paris in his histories, which cover the closing years of the reign of Edward III and extend into the fifteenth century.[27] Of the few other chronicles which emanated from monasteries, some two or three contain material of historical value presented in a literary form that is not unreadable. The remainder are of little worth as literature or as history. The greater part of the historical writing was done, however, by secular clerks. From their pens came a number of narratives which contribute substantially to our knowledge of the reign of Edward II and of the first forty years of the reign of his son, though they represent but a modest literary attainment. In the last years of the reign of Edward III there is a surprising dearth of native historians, and we have to rely mainly on the work of a native of Hainault who was in the service of Queen Philippa. Jean Froissart is less trustworthy than some of his duller predecessors, and he is full of prejudice. But the vividness of his portrayal surpasses that of any other historian of England who wrote in the fourteenth century. While the literary quality of the historical writing of the period was poor, the historical value of the works designated customarily as literature exceeds that attached to similar compositions in any earlier period of English history. The pages of Wycliffe, Chaucer, Gower, and others fairly teem with information about the life of the different classes of the English people. But the history of the fourteenth century, in even greater measure than that of the thirteenth, is better told in official records than in historical narratives or in other literature. Other than the rolls of parliament, which are of fundamental importance for the history of that institution, the records of the fourteenth century are sufficiently

Historical sources

---

[27] The histories are *Chronicon Angliae* and *Historia Anglicana*. There is some doubt about Walsingham's authorship of the first, but it came from St. Albans.

like in kind to those of the preceding century to require no additional description. In copiousness they increased so enormously, however, that only a small portion of them has yet been utilized adequately. Our knowledge of the fourteenth century must be held subject to much revision in the light of fuller evidence.

CHAPTER XV

LANCASTER AND YORK

THE rule of Henry IV (1399-1413) was dominated by his ambition
to make his tenure of the throne secure. Made king by parliament, **Internal**
without hereditary right, he could hope for security only when he had **difficulties**
convinced the nation that his rule would be good. It was no easy task.
To placate the clergy he legislated against heretics and to win popular
approval he made concessions to parliament. Nevertheless, opposition,
which became rebellion, arose in many quarters. Rebellion was favored
during the early years of his reign by a variety of circumstances.
(1) The internal disorder was so great that a friend reported to the
king: "thefts, murders, and adulteries abound, oppression of the poor,
quarrels and contentions." These conditions not only bred desperadoes
ready to take part in any venture, but they also caused the people "to
grouch against King Harry" for the lack of governance which permitted such evils to endure.[1] (2) Insurrections nourished in this
friendly atmosphere could always focus upon the person of one whose
hereditary claim to the throne was better than Henry's. The deposed
Richard, after a few months in prison, met his death, probably at
Henry's command; but an impostor appeared at the hostile court of
Scotland, where he could always be invoked to arouse popular sympathy for an armed demonstration in favor of Richard II by any English faction momentarily dissatisfied with Henry. Plotters who found
this fiction too transparent bid for popular favor in the name of the
young Edmund Mortimer, earl of March. His descent from Lionel,
the third son of Edward III, gave him a better hereditary title than
that of Henry.[2] (3) Malcontents might always hope for support from
France, Scotland, or Wales, where there existed varying degrees of hostility toward the new dynasty.

The French king, whose daughter was the wife of Richard II, refused
to acknowledge Henry and held the long truce arranged with his **External**
predecessor to be nullified. Internal dissensions among the French **dangers**
prevented the organization of formidable attacks upon England, but
disaffection was encouraged in Gascony, the English coasts were raided
sporadically, and French cooperation with Henry's enemies was always

[1] Wylie, *England under Henry IV*, i, 200, 265.
[2] See the genealogical table on p. 281.

a possibility. In the north the Scots were raiding the border and threatening more serious invasion. Wales soon broke into open rebellion. Owen Glendower, a Welsh gentleman who deemed himself wronged by a lord of the march, extended the scope of his private quarrel to embrace a national rebellion designed to secure Welsh independence. Surrounded by these dangers, the new king was forced to tax his physical energy and his political ability to the utmost to keep the scepter in his grasp.

Rebellion began when Henry celebrated his first yuletide. The lords who had been the abettors of Richard's tyranny plotted to gain secret entrance to the castle of Windsor and assassinate the king and his sons in their sleep. So well was the conspiracy laid that they gained admission to the castle, but their victim, warned at the eleventh hour, escaped. During the next two years war had to be waged against Scotland and Wales. The latter, carried on by the king in person and by his eldest son, was notably unsuccessful. At home disaffection caused several local disturbances, and open talk of rebellion reached proportions that led to executions. At the end of 1402, Sir Edmund Mortimer, uncle of the earl of March, espoused the cause of Owen Glendower, and proclaimed his nephew lawful king. A few months later the Percies, father and son, cast their lot with Mortimer and Glendower. The elder Percy, who was earl of Northumberland, and his son, Harry Hotspur, controlled vast resources in the north of England. Their support had been an influential factor in Henry's acquisition of the throne, and they had since been his most trusted adherents. They had defended the northern border against the Scots, winning in 1402 a considerable victory. A dispute between them and the king over custody of the prisoners, who were valuable for purposes of ransom, accentuated a rift already begun over other financial claims of the Percies. It ended in their rebellion in 1403. The king, who was taken unawares, rushed to the west an army which he was assembling for a Scottish campaign. Hotspur was on the march to join Glendower, who now controlled the greater part of Wales. Their junction might well have been fatal. Henry intercepted Hotspur at Shrewsbury and won a victory by a close decision. Hotspur fell on the field. Northumberland, who took no part in the battle, was deprived of some of his power and pardoned. The victory freed the king from the most pressing of his dangers, but the Welsh revolt was further complicated by French aid, while disorder and petty conspiracies continued at home.

In 1405 rebellion again openly reared its head in England. Northumberland raised the northern counties in what threatened to become a

(margin note: Rebellions)

serious insurrection. Prompt action overcame the rebels before they were thoroughly organized. This time Henry showed no mercy to the leaders, but Northumberland escaped the block by timely flight to Scotland. This triumph proved to be the turning point in Henry's fortunes. Thereafter internal discontent gradually subsided. Three years later, when Northumberland unfurled the standard of revolt for the third time, so few rallied to his cause that the local levy sufficed to stay his course and end his career. After 1405, too, Henry's eldest son, Henry, began to make headway against Owen Glendower. Scotland was rendered harmless by a stroke of fortune. In 1406 English pirates accidentally captured James Stuart, heir to the throne of Scotland, and delivered him to the English king. Though James shortly became king, Henry kept him in captivity as hostage for the good behavior of the northern kingdom. In the next year the French, who were now rent by the rivalries of noble factions, made a truce with Henry. This deprived the Welsh of all hope of aid from that quarter. In 1409 Sir Edmund Mortimer died. By that time the English had reconquered the castles captured by Glendower, and only the dying embers of the Welsh rebellion were left alive. In England sedition was extinct. For the remainder of his reign Henry enjoyed the political quiet which he had earned at the cost of a physical breakdown.

"Henry IV, striving lawfully, had made his own house strong; Henry V, leading the forces with which his father had striven, made England the first power in Europe."[3] When Henry V came to the throne in 1413 he was only twenty-five, but for more than a decade he had been commanding soldiers in the field. His thoughts naturally turned to feats of arms. He soon made manifest his ambition to restore the military grandeur which England had enjoyed in the days of Edward III and to win glory as the conqueror of France. His project was favored by conditions both at home and abroad. Henry V, thanks to his father, had behind him a nation contented with Lancastrian rule and a people sufficiently prosperous to bear the cost of foreign war. In France, on the other hand, all was discord. Charles VI, who had been king since 1380, had ruled weakly. A long minority had given rise to feuds among the nobles who strove to secure control of the government. Thereafter the king displayed signs of a mental weakness which ended in insanity, and the factious rivalries continued. The principal contest came to be between a party led by the count of Armagnac and another led by the duke of Burgundy. The bitter rivalry of Burgundians and

Renewal of the Hundred Years' War

---

[3] Stubbs, *Constitutional History*, iii, 73.

Armagnacs gradually forced the French nobles to espouse one side or the other. Eventually the spirit spread downward throughout the nation, until the French were divided into two hostile camps. No national interest or no real principle was at stake, but in 1411 the strife broke into civil war, which was only nominally ended by a peace patched up in 1414. Henry V took advantage of the situation to ally himself with Burgundy, and in 1415 he invaded France.

He landed at Harfleur, took the town by siege, and started to march thence to Calais. Near Agincourt he was intercepted by a French force greatly superior in numbers. The French forgot the lessons of du Guesclin, resorted to the old feudal tactics of Crécy and Poitiers, and suffered an overwhelming defeat. In 1417 Henry renewed the attack, making a war of sieges. By the beginning of 1419 he had captured the principal Norman towns and strongholds and was in practical possession of Normandy. Meanwhile the Burgundian duke wavered in his support. His assassination by the Armagnacs in 1419 caused his son to seek revenge with the aid of the English. The alliance that followed gave Henry such an advantage as he could never have hoped to win by military campaigns. The result was the Treaty of Troyes in 1420. By its terms Henry agreed to marry Katharine, the daughter of Charles VI, and was acknowledged as regent of France and successor to Charles. The son of the French king was disinherited. The treaty gave Henry control of the northern half of France. Except a few strongholds, only France south of Paris remained loyal to the son of Charles VI and refused to abide by the Treaty of Troyes. After the treaty Henry began the conquest of Armagnac territory. In 1422, while engaged in this task, he died of dysentery contracted during the campaign.

Henry's heir, of the same name, was only a few months old. Both in England and in France the royal business had to be conducted by advisers. The inevitable factional disputes which followed were more disastrous than usual. Not only did they weaken the English position in France, but eventually they grew into a civil war at home. Before his death Henry V designated his brother John, duke of Bedford, to take charge of affairs in France and his brother Humphrey, duke of Gloucester, to manage affairs in England. The latter, who had been acting as regent during the absence of Henry V in France, had already created many enemies among the councilors with whom he had worked. They secured from parliament an act which subjected Gloucester to restrictions in the council, where he was strongly opposed. The leadership of the opposition was taken by the Beauforts, his half-uncles, who were sons of John of Gaunt, born out of wedlock, but legitimated by act of

The side notes in the left margin:

Agincourt and Troyes

The regency

parliament. Throughout the period of the regency the quarrels of the factions of Gloucester and Beaufort weakened the government of England and handicapped the conduct of the war in France.

The duke of Bedford, in decided contrast to his brother Humphrey, ruled and commanded with hardly less ability than his deceased brother, Henry V. Under his direction the war in France was continued successfully. Before the close of 1422 Charles VI also closed his life, making the infant, Henry VI of England, the king of France. The son of Charles VI refused to acknowledge the Treaty of Troyes, claimed the throne as Charles VII, and with the aid of the Armagnacs kept up a resistance to English arms. He was at this time a weak leader, influenced by selfish and unwise counselors. His defense steadily crumbled before the vigorous onslaught of Bedford. In 1429 the English had pushed the Armagnacs back of the Loire and were besieging Orléans, the key to the country still held by Charles, when the tide of war was turned by the appearance on the scene of one of the most dramatic figures in history, Joan of Arc. She was a young peasant girl, inspired by the belief that she had received a mission from God to save France. She came to the court of Charles VII, pierced his torpor with her enthusiasm, and was allowed to lead troops to the relief of Orléans. Among the soldiers Joan created a patriotic fervor which knew no bounds. She led them successfully in assaults on English redoubts which had been regarded as well-nigh impregnable. Within a short time the English were forced to raise the siege of Orléans and withdraw. Subsequently the maid inspired the French in several successful battles against the English, but in 1431 she was captured by the Burgundians, who turned her over to the English. The English soldiers had come to look upon her as a witch, and had become thoroughly demoralized in consequence. In the hope that the morale of his soldiers might be restored, Bedford had her tried by a French ecclesiastical commission, which condemned her as a heretic. Thereupon she was burned at the stake.

Though Joan's career was brief, she accomplished her mission. When she first appeared, the spirit of French patriotism was nearly extinct. For years the country had been split by internal rivalries which Charles VII seemed too weak to heal. The English had been so steadily victorious that even those Frenchmen who still supported Charles VII were beginning to feel it impossible to stem the tide. The French national spirit was obscured in a fog of apathetic gloom. Joan swept away this indifference of despair and kindled anew the spirit of French nationality. Her ideal lived after her death and continued to stir the French

Joan of Arc

Close of the war

people. Henceforth Bedford could do no more than retard the French advance; he could not stop it. In 1435 Burgundy deserted Henry VI for Charles VII. In the same year Bedford died, and none could take his place. The dissensions, which only Bedford had been sufficiently influential to allay, still rent the council. In 1437 Henry VI was declared of age, but he was too weak to command the situation. The council retained practical control of the government, and the quarrels of factions continued unabated. Under these conditions the English cause was hopeless. In 1436 Paris was lost. In 1444 the earl of Suffolk, an ally of the Beauforts, who had finally deprived Gloucester of influence and won control of the council, secured a truce of two years in return for a marriage between Henry VI and Margaret of Anjou, whose aunt was the queen of Charles VII. The marriage was followed by the cession of Maine to France. In 1449 and 1450 Normandy was regained by the French. In 1451 the last English stronghold in Gascony was captured. When an English expedition sent to recover Gascony was disastrously defeated in 1453, the Hundred Years' War came to an end. England was stripped of all her possessions in France except the single city of Calais. The loss was a blow to the pride of the English, but it was in reality beneficial to England as well as to France. In the fifteenth century the consciousness of nationality had become so strong among the French that England could no longer hope to hold blocks of French territory, as she had done in the Middle Ages. The attempt had produced only a useless waste of men and money, and the stoppage of the drain was a positive advantage.

Internal disorder

The close of the Hundred Years' War saw England on the verge of civil war. The strife of factions had long been preparing the ground for the conflict. The quarrels of the nobles rendered the government inefficient and promoted disorder in the realm. Livery and maintenance, fostered by the renewed wars and encouraged by the lack of governance, throve mightily in the time of Henry VI. Powerful nobles not only had their own tenants and retainers, but they could also command the adherence of the smaller landowners for miles around. In whole districts people went in fear of their lives and property. Robberies, abductions, murders, and oppressions of all kinds were practiced with impunity.[4] In such districts it was generally useless and often dangerous to seek justice. In some instances the justices of the peace and the sheriffs were the henchmen of the powerful offenders; in others they were bribed or intimidated. Injured parties often refrained from

---

[4] Fortescue, *Governance of England*, ed. by Plummer, p. 24.

bringing before a court the retainer of a great lord for fear of placing their lives in jeopardy. Private wars between nobles were of common occurrence. During the minority remedy was hopeless, since some of the worst offenders were among the lords of the council. They also controlled the house of lords, and by means of their retainers they often dictated the election of knights of the shire and through their nominees dominated the house of commons as well. A strong king who could repress the factions among the nobles and compel them to keep the peace seemed to be the one possible remedy; but Henry VI, when he came of age, proved to be a gentle, well-meaning, weak-minded man who, with the best of intentions and most generous of impulses, promoted the evils of a situation which he abhorred. On one occasion two nobles waged a private war to secure possession of an office which the king with his accustomed generosity and forgetfulness had granted to both of them. In a land where violence was the order of the day and the magnates, who strove for control of the government, possessed large bands of armed followers, it was easy for their feuds to develop into a civil war.

The story of their bickerings is a dreary chronicle of self-seeking which it would be profitless to relate further than is necessary to explain the background of the war. In the days of the minority, when the quarrel was between Humphrey, duke of Gloucester, and Henry Beaufort, bishop of Winchester, such right as there was appeared to be on the side of the latter. However selfish the bishop may have been, he had political ability, which Gloucester lacked. In the main Beaufort was successful. Except for brief intervals Gloucester was held in check, though he always retained sufficient power to force upon the bishop quarrels which made the work of government difficult. After the king was declared of age in 1437, the balance swung more decidedly in favor of the Beauforts. They succeeded in making the king their puppet, acquiring such ascendency that they were able to eclipse Gloucester. The victory of the Beauforts made possible the promotion of some of the younger members of the house. Within a few years Edmund Beaufort, the duke of Somerset, and his close friend and ally, the earl of Suffolk, were the most influential men in the government. After the king's marriage, which was arranged by Suffolk, Margaret of Anjou dominated the king, and she worked hand and glove with Somerset and Suffolk. Neither duke nor earl had the ability to wield wisely the power they had acquired, and their failures soon rendered them unpopular. In 1447 they arrested the discredited Gloucester on the charge of treason, and five days later he died in confinement. Rightly or wrongly,

Political dissensions

they were suspected of causing his death, and public opinion began to turn against them. Soon afterward the terms of the truce with France became generally known, and they aroused widespread criticism. The prolonged losses of English arms had caused profound discontent which was ready to vent itself on anyone whom popular fancy should deem responsible. The cession of territory still occupied by English troops for what was generally esteemed no adequate return was commonly attributed to Suffolk and was regarded as little better than treason. When the English in Normandy, commanded by Somerset, were conquered so suddenly and so completely in 1449 and 1450, the nation could find no adequate explanation except treason. Thereupon the popular indignation boiled over.

Death of Suffolk and Cade's rebellion.

The first result was the impeachment of Suffolk in the parliament of 1450. Henry VI, who could see no wrong in his friends, would not allow the earl to be tried, and banished him from the realm for five years. The people, however, refused to let him go. The ship on which he had embarked for the continent was intercepted and he was seized and beheaded. This deed of violence was followed almost immediately by Cade's rebellion, a popular outbreak in Kent and Sussex, called after its leader. The rebellion was not a peasants' revolt but a political protest. It was joined by many small landholders and men of substance, and its immediate occasion was the news of the final defeat in Normandy. The demands of the rebels were mainly political in character. They complained of the maladministration of justice, the packing of parliament by means of armed retainers, the failure of the government to protect the possessions of landholders against powerful neighbors, the treachery which had lost Normandy, and the murder of Gloucester. Lack of governance was the burden of their refrain. What they wanted was a change of ministries and reform of the government. The rebels were well organized and observed military discipline. The army raised by the lords of the council to meet them mutinied, the king fled from London, and the rebels entered without opposition. For a time they kept order, while they wreaked vengeance on such of the king's ministers as they could lay hands upon. When they began to pillage, the citizens expelled them from London. Subsequently they were easily dispersed.

Dynastic rivalries

Thus in 1450 the ground was thoroughly prepared for civil war. The government was weak and popularly discredited, the king was a figurehead, parliament had failed to maintain order, resort to armed force was of almost daily occurrence, and strife among noble factions contending for political power had become traditional. It required only a spark to fire the explosion of this loose powder and to cause the contest of factions to develop into a civil war. This was supplied by the claim of Richard, duke of York, to the throne. On his father's side Richard was descended from the sixth son of Edward III, but his mother was the sister of Edmund, earl of March, the heir of Lionel, the third son of Edward III. When Edmund died in 1425, Richard inherited his title to the throne. For many years he said nothing of his claim. Meanwhile he took a leading part in politics. He was a supporter of Gloucester's faction in the council, becoming its leader after Gloucester's death. The removal of Gloucester also made him the natural heir to the throne so long as Henry VI remained childless. Content with this position, he did not assert his claim. As leader of the opposition to the Beauforts, however, he came into conflict with Suffolk and Somerset. In 1450, taking advantage of Suffolk's downfall, he collected retainers from his estates, marched to London, and practically forced the king to admit him to his council. His avowed purpose was to reform the government. When his endeavor to oust Somerset failed, he resorted to armed force. In 1452 his army met the king's, but the impending battle was avoided by the king's concession of York's request. If Henry promised to dismiss Somerset, as York was led to believe, he belied himself; but, on the other hand, he did not punish York, as he was urged to do by Somerset. Shortly afterward the king became insane, York was appointed regent, and Somerset was imprisoned. At the end of 1454 the recovery of the king again reversed the situation. York lost his office and Somerset was restored to power. On this occasion the queen gave evidence of her intention to be rid of the Yorkists. Meanwhile the birth of a son to Henry had deprived York of his position as the natural successor to the throne. He still made no claim to supplant Henry. He raised the standard of rebellion ostensibly to defend the Yorkists from the anticipated attack of Somerset and the queen. But the dynastic question was now in the background of all political thought, and eventually it became the principal issue in the contest.

The wars that followed came to be known later as the Wars of the Roses because of the tradition that the white rose was the badge of York, and the red that of Lancaster.[5] No great principles were at stake. When the main object of strife came to be dynastic, the people at large had little direct interest in the outcome. The wars were fought mainly by the nobles, supported by their tenants and retainers. They were rather an expansion of the earlier factional fights of the reign than a

Wars of the Roses

---

[5] The tradition of the white rose was true, but the badge of the red rose did not appear till the time of the Tudors.

manifestation of popular feeling. In 1455 York won the battle of St. Albans, where Somerset was slain. For two years thereafter York controlled the government, and during part of the time was regent while the king was again temporarily insane. In 1456, however, the king's recovery enabled the queen to resume the ascendency. Three years later, when she felt her position sufficiently strong, she began to assemble troops. York immediately armed, but his followers were outnumbered, and he was compelled to flee. In 1460, however, his followers defeated the king at Northampton, and thereafter he claimed the crown. Because many of his own supporters were unwilling to accept his claim, it was finally compromised by an agreement that he should inherit the throne after the death of Henry VI. Meanwhile Queen Margaret, who had no thought of allowing her son to be disinherited, was raising the Lancastrian henchmen. Near the end of the year the duke of York met them in battle at Wakefield, where he was defeated and lost his life. The queen then marched to the south and defeated the Yorkists in the second battle of St. Albans, where King Henry was released from his Yorkist captors. The Lancastrians, however, were not strong enough to take London and turned north. Edward, son of Richard of York, pursued, and at Towton, near York, inflicted upon them a decisive defeat. Henry VI and Margaret were compelled to seek safety in Scotland, while Edward returned to London to be crowned king and to begin the rule of the house of York.

Parliament under the Lancastrians

Though the Lancastrian period ended in civil strife, it witnessed a remarkable expansion of the power of parliament. Henry IV could hardly do otherwise than seek the advice of parliament. His very accession by parliamentary action was an acknowledgment of his dependence upon parliament, the insecurity of his hold upon the crown made the retention of parliamentary support essential, and the constant warfare thrust upon him made necessary frequent appeals to parliament for financial aid. Parliament soon discovered the advantages of the situation and began to demand privileges and powers. Henry IV felt constrained to concede one petition after another, until parliament acquired such power and influence as it had never wielded before. The renewal of the Hundred Years' War made Henry V financially dependent on that body, and those responsible for the administration during his long absences necessarily sought parliamentary support. The long minority of Henry VI, his weakness and lack of decision after he became of age, and the continuance of the war produced similar conditions during the greater part of his long reign. With the outbreak of disorder and civil war in 1450, the government nearly ceased to function, and parliament became hardly more than the agent of the faction temporarily in control. Until that time, however, the power acquired by parliament in the reign of Henry IV was not only maintained but was even further defined and expanded.

The legislation of the period continued to emanate principally from the commons, and only in a few instances were their petitions changed in any important particulars by the king before they became statutes. The commons also kept their control of the grant of taxation, and used it effectively to secure the legislation and the royal concessions which they desired. Once Henry IV threatened their control by obtaining the consent of the lords to a proposed tax before consulting them, but their prompt protest became a precedent for the establishment of the custom that grants of money should originate with the commons. *Legislation and taxation*

In their attempts to influence the king through his council and ministers the Lancastrian parliaments were highly successful. In 1404, when internal disorder was at its height and disaffection was still rampant, parliament freely attacked the king's government. It complained of mismanagement of the king's household, and secured the dismissal of several officials, and the promise that others should be appointed in parliament. The members of the council were also named in parliament. The lords appointed were not sufficiently regular in their attendance to constrain the king greatly in his action, but the commons evidently expected that the designation of councilors in parliament would make them responsible to parliament in some measure. In 1405 the commons voted taxes "not only by fear of God and love for the king," but also "by the great confidence which they had in the lords elected and ordained to be of the continual council."[6] When the events of 1405 convinced them that their confidence had been misplaced, they secured the appointment of a new council and a provision that all the important documents issued by the king should be approved by the council and no significant royal action taken without its advice. "The demands of the commons and the concessions of the king almost amounted to a supersession of the royal authority."[7] They were not literally enforced, but they were maintained with sufficient rigor to limit the royal discretion during the greater part of the remaining years of the reign. *Relations with the council*

With the accession of Henry V parliament lost much of its control over the council, but the council necessarily remained powerful in the

---

[6] Stubbs, *Constitutional History*, iii, 248; Baldwin, *King's Council*, p. 155.
[7] Stubbs, *op. cit.*, iii, 56.

absence of the king. Henry V kept it filled with lords, and it worked harmoniously with parliament. During the minority of Henry VI an autocratic council wielded the whole royal executive power. It was named originally by the lords of parliament. Subsequently the lords of the council dominated parliament and kept the two bodies in harmony. When the king's minority ended, no substantial change in the situation occurred. The weak king was practically ruled by the council until Suffolk acquired the ascendency in the decade of the forties. The earl disregarded the council and through the favor of the king generally managed affairs alone. It was largely this which lost him the confidence of parliament and led to his impeachment. Subsequent attempts to revive the council had only temporary results. Confidence was gone, the lords generally ceased to attend, the council lost its power, and parliament lost its control.[8]

So ended a premature constitutional development. It was a striking display of parliamentary power while it lasted. Under Henry IV it went so far that it seemed to foreshadow the modern system of government by a cabinet responsible to parliament; but the elaborate constitutional machinery on which rests the responsibility of the modern cabinet was beyond the ken of the Lancastrian politicians. The relationship established between parliament and council in the time of Henry IV fell into desuetude in the last years of the Lancastrian period and lost all significance as an institutional precedent.

During the reign of Henry IV the commons established precedents which helped them eventually to secure the privileges of freedom of speech and freedom from arrest. The former, when it was finally established, gave to the members of the house of commons immunity outside of parliament for utterances made in the transaction of parliamentary business. Without it the commons could not act independently as the representatives of the rights of the nation, because speeches displeasing to the king might subject their author to penalties. The principle was involved in the case of Thomas Haxey in 1397.[9] Though he was not a member of the commons, he was condemned as the author of a petition which the commons had accepted and presented to the king as their own. In 1399 the commons vindicated their right to express their opinion freely to the king by securing from Henry IV a reversal of the judgment against Haxey. Henry IV also acknowledged the right of the commons to reach their decisions free from royal pressure. The privilege of freedom from arrest in civil actions

Privileges
of the
commons

---

[8] Baldwin, *King's Council*, pp. 190–208.
[9] Above, p. 234.

while attending parliament was useful to protect members against the king or other powerful persons whose wishes they might oppose. This privilege had existed for a long time, its original purpose having been to prevent interference with those who consulted upon the king's business; but it was of importance to have Henry IV confirm the privilege when it was becoming an aid to the commons in maintaining their independence of the royal influence. These privileges constituted a bulwark behind which the commons could safely voice the sentiments of the nation, however displeasing these might be to the king. In the fifteenth century, however, the limits of these privileges were vaguely defined, and they did not pass unchallenged. In 1453 the duke of York, who was in power, secured the arrest of Thorpe, the speaker of the commons, who was a strong Lancastrian partisan, and the commons sought in vain to obtain his release on the ground of privilege. In later reigns also parliament was not able always to maintain its privileges in practice, but the later claim that such privileges existed probably goes back to the precedents of the reign of Henry IV.

As parliament increased its influence in the government, representation came to be more highly valued, and the commons began to demand its regulation. One of the first manifestations of this attitude was the resentment evoked by the interference at elections, by means of which packed parliaments were obtained frequently after 1376. Early in the reign of Henry IV remedy was sought by laws requiring that the sheriffs' reports of elections should be certified by some of the voters, and imposing heavy fines on sheriffs who made false returns. In 1430 interference was further guarded against by a statute which restricted the right to vote for knights of the shire to those who possessed freehold estates yielding a profit of forty shillings a year. Previously the elections had taken place at public sessions of the county courts, which apparently any freemen might attend. In the fifteenth century the nobles were using their retainers to secure the election of their henchmen at the county court. The statute excluded these and other undesirables from the franchise, since the possessor of land which yielded forty shillings clear yearly value in the fifteenth century was a man of moderate wealth. This statute governed the franchise in the counties until 1832. While the elections in the counties were thus being regulated, the boroughs were left free to settle their own electoral procedure. Much variation resulted in the burghal franchise. In one group of boroughs practically all owners of real estate could vote,[10] in another

Composition of the commons

---

[10] I.e., holders of burgage tenures.

all payers of local taxes, in a third freemen, who in the fifteenth century were mainly the members of the gilds, and in a fourth only members of the governing bodies of the towns. But the lack of central control of the right to vote in the boroughs did not mean that the townsmen were notably slower than the rural landowners to recognize the value of participation in the work of parliament, for toward the middle of the fifteenth century unrepresented boroughs began to petition the king for the privilege of representation. After 1445 eight boroughs were enfranchised by Henry VI, and more were added in later reigns.

Failure of parliament

The Lancastrian period as a whole was one in which parliament made much progress. It did not acquire many wholly new powers, but it secured from the Lancastrian kings definite recognition of powers already claimed in the fourteenth century. It was a period of the fixation of the powers of parliament. At the same time the experiment proved that parliament was not yet prepared to assume too much responsibility. The evils of the later part of the reign of Henry VI were due mainly to the inability of the government to repress social and political disorders. A powerful parliament could not yet maintain order without the aid of a strong king.

Early years of Edward IV

Largely for this reason the people acquiesced in the assumption of the crown by the Yorkist dynasty in 1461. They were ready to pay any price for the peace and order that would enable them to resume the prosperous conduct of industry and commerce. They wanted a king who could restrain the warring factions of the nobles, maintain order, and give an adequate administration of justice. These things Edward IV attempted to provide with only partial success in the early years of his reign. Such widespread plundering as had marked the recent years of the war was ended, but maintenance and liveries with their attendant evils continued unabated; plots, riots and disturbances of various sorts were frequent; justice was still difficult to obtain, though the king attempted to secure its better administration; and in the north the Lancastrians maintained war until they were decisively defeated in 1464.

Edward IV and Warwick

Even this victory failed to end the disturbances, for new troubles arose from the estrangement by the king of the earl of Warwick. The latter was the cousin of the king and the wealthiest and the most influential noble of the realm. His initiative and leadership had won the victories which made it possible for Richard of York to claim the throne in 1460, his help had enabled Edward IV to mount the throne, and until 1464 he dictated to the king much of his policy. The rift between the friends began with the king's marriage, which took place early in

1464. The bride was Lady Elizabeth Grey, a widow with two children. Her father, Richard Woodville, Lord Rivers, was a peer of recent Lancastrian creation, and her whole connection was Lancastrian. Politically and socially the marriage was so indiscreet that the king kept it secret until the tentative negotiations of Warwick with the king of France for the disposal of Edward's hand forced him to announce it. The earl was chagrined to find that he had been allowed to discuss alliances based on the king's marriage when the king was already married. The marriage soon touched him more closely. The new queen had eleven brothers and sisters, whose interests the king promoted. Many of them were married into the families of great nobles, much to Warwick's displeasure, and the earl soon found that his influence with the king was being lost to the Woodvilles, whom he regarded not only as political opponents but also as social upstarts. The ensuing coolness between the king and the earl was brought to a crisis by a difference of opinion on foreign policy.

Burgundy and France were both bidding for England's alliance. The duke of Burgundy, who controlled the Low Countries and other territories as well as Burgundy, was richer and more powerful than many contemporary kings. To Louis XI, the astute and wily king of France, he appeared to be a menace to France, and the rivalry between the two was becoming intense. At the beginning of Edward's reign Louis XI had given open support to the cause of his kinswoman, Margaret of Anjou. He soon discovered that he had supported the losing side, and after 1464 he sought the alliance of Edward IV. Warwick, who saw in the alliance security from the danger of Lancastrian attacks and the general advantage of Edward IV and England, advocated it warmly. The traditional spirit of hostility toward France was still alive in England, however, and England's principal trade was still with Flanders, now controlled by Burgundy. Edward IV, moreover, was becoming resentful of Warwick's tutelage. In 1467 he accepted the offer of an alliance to be cemented by the marriage of his sister Margaret to Charles the Bold, duke of Burgundy, and to result in a joint attack on France by Burgundy and England. *[margin: Burgundy and France]*

To Warwick this was the last straw. On receipt of the news he left court and retired to his estates, where he began to nurse plans for the recovery of his power. During 1468 Edward IV was kept busy with the repression of Lancastrian plots, stirred up largely by Louis XI, and Warwick was left free to mature his project. In 1469 his followers rose in rebellion. Edward IV was taken completely by surprise. A large group of his supporters was defeated, some of the Woodvilles were *[margin: Warwick's rebellion]* executed, and he was captured. Warwick was actuated only by the desire to recover his lost influence over the king. He had no dealings with the Lancastrians, but, to the contrary, repressed a Lancastrian uprising which took place contemporaneously with his own. He was soon forced by public opinion to release the king, who began at once to plot the overthrow of the earl.

Restoration of Lancaster

Edward found that Warwick was not supported by all of the Yorkists, and he soon gathered a sufficient force to proclaim the earl a traitor and to put him to flight. Warwick then allied himself with Margaret of Anjou, secured the support of Louis XI, and started a Lancastrian rebellion which forced Edward IV to seek safety in Burgundy. Again Warwick had made a king. For a few months in 1470 and 1471 Henry VI reigned while Warwick ruled. His tenure of power was brief. Edward obtained the help of Burgundy, and he was secretly assured of the support of many Yorkists who nominally followed Warwick. Most important of these was the king's own brother, the duke of Clarence, who, having deserted Edward for Warwick, was now ready to betray the earl. The issue was decided at Barnet, where Edward won a complete victory and the king-maker lost his life. In a later battle the son of Henry VI was killed and Margaret of Anjou was captured. Shortly afterward Henry died in the Tower of London. The line of Lancaster was ended, the male line of the Beauforts was also extinct, and the only surviving representative of the Lancastrian claim was Henry Tudor, earl of Richmond, a boy of fourteen, whose mother was a Beaufort. His title was too remote to be a menace. Edward IV was thus freed not only from the domination of Warwick, but also from the danger of Lancastrian revolt.

Closing years, 1471–1483

The remaining years of Edward's reign were comparatively peaceful. In 1475 he transported a large army to France, intending to make war upon Louis XI. Finding his ally, the duke of Burgundy, too fully engaged with warfare on the German side of his dominions to render any efficient aid on the French side, he accepted the offer of Louis XI to pay a lump sum and an annual pension for peace. Later a short war with Scotland conducted by his brother, the duke of Gloucester, netted the recovery of Berwick. These expeditions had little effect upon the internal affairs of England, which followed a quieter course than at any time since 1450. Edward's security upon the throne, the popularity won for him by his geniality, and the general desire for peace and order gave him the opportunity to wield great power. His rule was strong by contrast with what had gone before, though it was not tyrannical. He indulged in occasional high-handed acts, as when he secured from parliament the attainder of his brother Clarence, who perished in the Tower, men knew not how, though tradition soon had it that he was drowned in a butt of malmsey. But "false, fleeting, perjur'd Clarence" deserved no better fate, and Edward's few despotic acts generally had no significant effect upon the interests of the mass of his subjects. To them his rule was a boon. Though he did not suppress disorder and violence entirely, he fostered the commercial interests of his people and maintained a better administration of justice than had been known for years.

The extent of the increase in the power of the king is made apparent by an examination of his relations with the council and with parliament. Under Edward IV the council ceased to be the master of the king and became his servant. Parliament had no control whatever over its composition. Few great lords, other than those who held offices of state, were appointed to it, and the number of the members of lesser estate was increased. The official element dominated the council, and the king dominated his officials. The council did not cease to be an advisory body, but the king consulted it less and was less bound by its decisions when he asked for them. As an administrative and a judicial organ, on the other hand, it become more active; but here also it became more dependent upon the king, acting primarily as an instrument to secure the better execution of the royal will.

The king's council

During the course of the fifteenth century the jurisdiction of the council was more clearly defined in custom and practice. Throughout much of the century parliament continued to display jealousy of the judicial work of the council with its summary procedure, but the attempts to limit its vague field of jurisdiction were ineffective. In the reign of Henry VI, moreover, parliament gave up the effort to deal with all the petitions of individuals, and at the close of each session turned over the unanswered petitions to the council. This tended to bring the greater part of the residual jurisdiction of first instance to the council. Although parliament did not cease entirely to hear civil suits in first instance, its jurisdiction in practice became mainly appellate, except impeachments and the trial of peers. By this time, however, the petitions were more than the council could handle. It in turn gave over its unanswered petitions to the court of chancery. This court, which exercised a wide field of jurisdiction in equity, had become practically independent of the council. Nearly all of the petitions presented to the council which involved judicial procedure on the civil side were transferred to it, unless they were referred to the courts of common law. The council, in other words, allowed most of its civil jurisdiction to

Jurisdiction of the council

pass to the court of chancery. Original cases on the criminal side, which for some reason the courts of common law could not handle, occupied most of the time which the council devoted to judicial business. Since the council ordinarily sat in a chamber of the palace which had a starred ceiling, the council, when it exercised this jurisdiction, came to be called commonly the court of star chamber. With the growing disorder of the fifteenth century such cases became increasingly frequent. The breakdown of the system of trial by jury caused many petitions to the council for justice which could not be had in the courts of common law. The growth of anarchy forced parliament to recognize the need of some such jurisdiction, and in 1453 it gave its sanction to the exercise by the council of this jurisdiction in cases of riot and other crimes of violence typical of the disorder of the period. By this time, however, the council was experiencing the inertia common to the other branches of the government, and it failed to accomplish more than the other courts. Under Edward IV the judicial power of the council gradually revived. After 1468 cases of riot and violence were brought before it in steadily increasing numbers. But the council hesitated to inflict adequate penalties on the great lords brought before it. The council in star chamber was still a defective instrument for the suppression of maintenance and livery with their attendant evils.

Of parliament Edward IV rendered himself more independent than the Lancastrian kings had been. In some instances he influenced the elections and secured houses of commons which were favorably disposed toward him, and the commons during his reign exercised much less influence upon legislation than formerly. His greater freedom from parliamentary control, however, depended mainly upon the infrequency with which parliament met. Only six parliaments assembled during his reign, and with one exception their sessions were short. He was able to do without frequent parliaments because he secured revenues from other sources than parliamentary grant. His first parliament provided for the resumption of royal lands which Lancastrian kings had alienated and for the forfeiture of the lands of the Lancastrian nobles. A later parliament granted him tonnage and poundage[11] and other customs revenues for life. Only four of his parliaments granted him direct taxation. Edward IV used forced loans to some extent, as Henry

---

[11] This was a tax of so much on each pound of the value of certain exports and imports and of so much on each tun of wine imported. In the fourteenth century parliament granted it for specified terms and in the course of the fifteenth century it became customary for parliament to grant the revenue for the remainder of the king's life.

VI had done, but he generally paid his debts. His most important non-parliamentary revenue came from forced gifts called benevolences. These Edward IV sought from his wealthier subjects with great success. A foreign observer thus described his methods: "I have frequently seen our neighbours here who were summoned before the king, and when they went they looked as if they were going to the gallows; when they returned they were joyful, saying that they had spoken to the king and he had spoken to them so benignly that they did not regret the money they had paid. From what I have heard, the king adopted this method: when anyone went before him he gave him a welcome as if he had known him always; after some time he asked him what he could pay of his free will towards this expedition; if the man offered something proper, he had his notary ready, who took down the name and the amount; if the king thought otherwise, he told him 'such a one who is poorer than you, has paid so much; you, who are richer, can easily pay more,' and thus by fair words he brought him up to the mark."[12] But behind the affability of the king lurked the unspoken threat of the royal displeasure, which few cared to incur. Edward derived much profit from the courts by using them to extract heavy fines for small breaches of the law. He also became a trader, employing many ships and deriving considerable profit from his mercantile ventures. During the later years of his reign the pension which he received from the king of France was an important item of revenue. From these sources he accumulated so large a fortune that with the practice of thrift he was able not only to run the government for many years of peace without parliamentary grant, but also, what was still more remarkable, to pay the wages of an army of 20,000 despatched to Scotland. The control of the purse, on which rested the power of parliament to limit the king, was badly impaired in the days of Edward IV. With the king it was probably a mere policy of financial expediency. But while no conscious institutional change may have been intended, the balance of constitutional power shifted decisively in favor of the king.

Edward IV left as his heir a boy of twelve named Edward. The reign of the young king opened with a struggle for the regency between the queen-mother representing the Woodville faction, and Richard of Gloucester, the brother of Edward IV. The latter had been named protector by the deceased king, but the Woodvilles, who had the young king in their keeping, seem to have plotted to get control of the government. By treachery Richard seized and imprisoned the ma-

Edward V and Richard III

---

[12] Quoted by Scofield, *Edward the Fourth*, ii, 105.

ternal relatives of Edward V who had the boy in their charge, obtained possession of the king's person, and secured acknowledgment as protector. Not satisfied with that position, he began to conspire with the leading nobles and members of the council to usurp the throne. Having won the support of the more unscrupulous, he secured the execution or imprisonment of his chief opponents. He then advanced the absurd claim that the children of Edward IV were illegitimate, and secured acknowledgment as king from an irregularly constituted parliament filled with his supporters. Shocking as these deeds were, they might possibly have passed muster in that age of bloodshed and violence if he had not proceeded to extinguish the male line of Edward IV by having Edward V and his brother smothered in the Tower. Even the callousness produced by the Wars of the Roses could not view that deed with apathy. Many of the Yorkists found themselves united with the Lancastrians in secret opposition to Richard III. If the tyrant was to be overthrown, someone had to be put in his place. The opposition quickly focused upon Henry Tudor. His claims to the throne were remote, but he was nevertheless the nearest male representative of the Lancastrian line. His leadership was made acceptable to the discontented Yorkists by his projected marriage to Elizabeth, the eldest daughter of Edward IV.

Bosworth Field

When the crisis came, Henry Tudor was living in Brittany, where he had found refuge for many years. Before he could be notified and given time to mature his plans, a rebellion which broke out prematurely in 1484 was quelled by Richard III. Subsequently Henry secured troops and money from the king of France, and, when he finally crossed the Channel in 1485, his followers in England were better prepared for the occasion. The two armies met on Bosworth Field, where Richard III was slain and Henry won a complete victory. He promptly secured parliamentary ratification of his occupation of the throne, and the rule of the house of Tudor was begun.

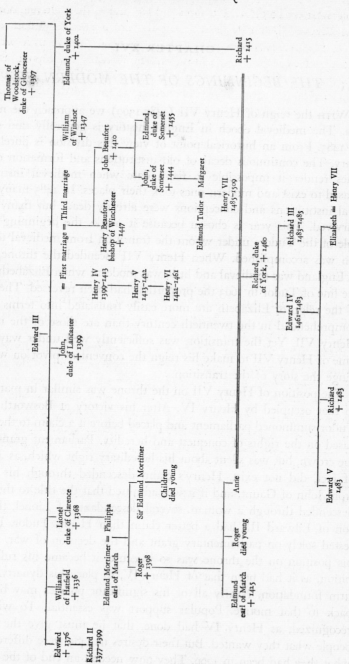

ABBREVIATED GENEALOGY OF THE
HOUSES OF LANCASTER AND YORK

Edward III

William
of Hatfield
✝ 1336

Edward
✝ 1376

Richard II
1377–1399

Lionel
duke of Clarence
✝ 1368

Edmund Mortimer = Philippa
earl of March

Roger
✝ 1398

Sir Edmund Mortimer

Children
died young

Roger
died young

Edmund
earl of March
✝ 1425

Anne

John,
duke of Lancaster
✝ 1399

= First marriage = Third marriage

Henry IV
1399–1413

Henry V
1413–1422

Henry VI
1422–1461

John Beaufort
✝ 1410

Henry Beaufort,
bishop of Winchester
✝ 1447

John,
duke of
Somerset
✝ 1444

Edmund,
duke of
Somerset
✝ 1455

Edmund Tudor = Margaret

Henry VII
1485–1509

William
of Windsor
✝ 1347

Edmund, duke of York
✝ 1402

Richard
✝ 1415

Richard, duke
of York, ✝ 1460

Edward IV
1461–1483

Edward V
1483

Richard III
1483–1485

Elizabeth = Henry VII

Richard
✝ 1483

Thomas of
Woodstock,
duke of Gloucester
✝ 1397

CHAPTER XVI

THE BEGINNINGS OF THE MODERN ERA

Transition
from
medieval
to modern

WITH the reign of Henry VII (1485-1509) we approach the modern era. The medieval epoch in English history is generally said to end at 1485. From an historical point of view this division is purely arbitrary. The continuous decay of old institutions and formation of new ones render it impossible to fix a date when medieval institutions ceased to exist and modern ones took their places. In 1485 many medieval institutions and conceptions were already dead, but many others survived. This year is chosen because it marks the beginning of the rule of the Tudors under whom the transition from medieval to modern was accomplished. When Henry VII ascended the throne, much in England was medieval and little was modern; when Elizabeth ended the line of Tudor in 1603 the proportion had been reversed. The events of the reign of Elizabeth are more easily translated into terms readily comprehended in the twentieth century than are those of the reign of Henry VII. Yet the transition was sufficiently well under way in the time of Henry VII to make his reign the convenient pivot on which to hinge the story of the transition.

Position of
Henry
VII on
the throne

The position of Henry VII on the throne was similar in many ways to that occupied by Henry IV. After his victory at Bosworth Henry Tudor summoned parliament and placed before it a claim to the throne based on the rights of conquest and heredity. Parliament granted him the crown, but was silent about his hereditary right which, as a matter of fact, did not exist. Henry's claim descended through his mother from John of Gaunt, and if it was admitted that the title to the throne descended through a woman, several descendants of Lionel, the third son of Edward III, had a better claim than Henry Tudor. His title rested solely on parliamentary grant and the decision of war. Because his position on the throne was so insecure, it became his ruling ambition, as it had been that of Henry IV, to place his dynasty upon a firm foundation. Nearly all of his significant policies may be traced back to that motive. Popular support was essential. To win it he recognized, as Henry IV had done, that he must give the English people what they wanted. But their desires in 1485 were different from what they had been in 1399. They now needed an end of the dynastic quarrels that had disturbed the peace of England since the middle of the fifteenth century, fostering care and protection for an expanding commerce, and most of all freedom from internal disorder. These things Henry VII endeavored to provide. As a further prop to his position he sought to win recognition of his house from foreign rulers, who were by now generally disposed to fish in the troubled sea of England's dynastic waters.

To end the dynastic troubles Henry's first step was to marry Elizabeth, the eldest daughter of Edward IV, who was the most direct descendant from Lionel. When she bore Henry a son, in whose person were united the claims of Lancaster and York, Henry's position on the throne was strengthened. Nevertheless, he had to meet the attempts of several aspirants for the throne who were supported by discontented Yorkists and sometimes had the help of foreign rulers. The first serious rebellion was led by an impostor. Lambert Simnel, who had good manners and grace of carriage though he was the son of an artisan, was coached by Yorkist leaders to impersonate a member of the house of York descended from Lionel. When he was finally educated in demeanor, he was taken to Ireland, where Yorkist sympathizers were powerful. Many Irish leaders pledged themselves to his cause, and he also had the support of Margaret, the sister of Edward IV and dowager duchess of Burgundy, whose court had become the refuge of discontented Yorkists. In 1487 he landed in England with an army of 8,000 made up of German mercenaries supplied by Margaret, and of Irishmen. In the short but stubbornly contested battle of Stoke the conspirators were defeated and Simnel was captured. Henry, considering him beneath the dignity of execution, made him a scullion in the royal kitchen, but while he might make merry over the rebellion, it had been a serious menace.

Though this rebellion did not end the conspiracies of the Yorkists, it temporarily halted their activities, leaving the king free to give his attention to foreign affairs. Acknowledgment of the equality of his house by the ruling dynasties of Europe was what he particularly desired. His purpose could best be accomplished by a marriage alliance, and so Henry began to seek a marriage for Arthur, his eldest-born. He looked first to Spain, where the recent union of the kingdoms of Castile and Aragon by the marriage of Ferdinand and Isabella had created a unified state. The Spanish sovereigns saw in Henry's offer an opportunity to further a project which they entertained against France. They desired to recover two Spanish provinces located in the eastern

Rebellions

Medina del Campo

Pyrenees, which had fallen into the hands of Louis XI,[1] but they were
too occupied with a war against the Moors in the south to undertake
the project unaided. They demanded of Henry, therefore, that he should
invade the north of France while they attacked in the south. It was a
high price to pay for the alliance, for peace and economy were necessary for the restoration of order within England. But the marriage
alliance was so essential for the welfare of the house of Tudor that
Henry took the risk. In 1489 he signed the Treaty of Medina del
Campo, agreeing to attack France in return for the marriage alliance.

Étaples

The war with France was of brief duration. In 1489 Henry sent
troops to assist the duchess of Brittany, who was resisting French invasion, and others to assist Maximilian, heir of the king of Germany[2]
and guardian of his son's rights in Burgundy, against whom the Flem-
ings were rebelling with the aid of the French. Maximilian changed
sides with a characteristic fickleness that was typical of the diplomacy
of the age, and the duchess made peace with France. Left in the lurch,
Henry extricated himself by brilliant diplomacy. Charles VIII, the
king of France, had so set his heart upon an invasion of Italy that he
was ready to pay a high price for the peace which would enable him
to depart. In 1492 he made the Treaty of Etaples, wherein he agreed
to pay Henry a large indemnity to withdraw his army from France.
A later treaty gave Spain possession of the contested provinces in the
south. For Henry it was a notable diplomatic triumph. He obtained the
marriage alliance, did little fighting, and secured an advantageous peace
that covered his expenses.

**Perkin
Warbeck**

His European success came just in time to be of aid against a second
pretender. In 1491 the Irish Yorkists picked up Perkin Warbeck, a
Flemish apprentice of goodly outward mien, and persuaded him to
impersonate an heir of the house of York. The support of Charles VIII
was speedily secured. By the Treaty of Étaples, however, the French
king agreed not to harbor pretenders to the English throne, and Perkin
was forced to take refuge with Margaret of Burgundy. There he received the support of Maximilian, who in 1493 became king of Germany, and of Philip, Maximilian's son, who was the duke of Burgundy.
He had already been acknowledged by the king of Scotland. Perkin thus
became the center for the union of all of Henry's enemies. In 1495,
when Perkin finally got an expedition under way with ships and
men furnished principally by Maximilian, the English shore was so
vigorously defended that he sailed on to Ireland. Subsequently Henry

---

[1] I.e., Cerdagne and Roussillon.
[2] More correctly, king of the Romans.

deprived him of most of his foreign support. Charles VIII met with such surprising success in Italy that in 1495 the League of Venice was formed to oppose him. Venice, Milan, the pope, Maximilian, and Spain united to drive him from Italy and keep him out. For the latter purpose they desired the alliance of Henry. Maximilian accordingly made peace with the English king. In return Henry agreed to do little more than not to help France. This diplomatic victory deprived Perkin of all foreign aid except from Scotland. In 1496 a Scottish invasion of England failed, but in the next year internal disorder in England gave Perkin a new chance. The collection of a tax in Cornwall started a rebellion joined by 15,000 men. The king of Scotland invaded the north and sent Perkin to land in Cornwall. It was "a dangerous triplicity to a monarchy," says Bacon, "to have the arms of a foreigner, the discontents of subjects and the title of a pretender to meet."[3] The movements failed to come simultaneously, however. The rising in Cornwall was suppressed and King James was driven back across the border before Perkin landed in England, where he was easily captured.

This event marked the fruition of the policies which Henry had followed so long. He had won recognition from foreign powers, repelled foreign invasion, subdued internal rebellion, and removed the threat to his position on the throne which had caused him keen anxiety for many years. The ambassador of Milan, reporting to his government at this time, wrote: "This present state is most stable, even for the king's descendants, since there is no one who aspires to the Crown," and the Spanish ambassador reported: "Henry is rich, has established good order in England, and keeps the people in such subjection as has never been the case before."[4] It was the turning point in his reign. He never again had to face a serious plot against the throne. Conspiracies still cropped out occasionally, but they received little support and never came to a head. Henry succeeded in making the position of his house secure.

Henry's security

Meanwhile Henry insured peace with Scotland by the marriage of his daughter Margaret to James of Scotland, and prepared the way for the eventual union of the crowns of England and Scotland. In 1503 the Spanish alliance was renewed by a treaty which arranged for the marriage of Katherine of Aragon, the daughter of Ferdinand and Isabella, whom the premature death of Arthur had rendered a widow, to his brother Henry, who was now the heir to the throne. For the remaining years of his reign Henry's friendship was generally sought

Foreign affairs

[3] Cited by Temperley, *Henry VII*, p. 149.
[4] Pollard, *Reign of Henry VII*, i, 171, 196.

by European powers without significant diplomatic result. Henry's foreign policy as a whole was highly successful. He secured ample recognition of the Tudor dynasty and notably increased England's prestige in European politics.

Ireland

In large measure Henry's foreign policy was dominated by the exigencies of diplomatic situations created by the pretenders. Another of Henry's policies affected by the pretenders was that which he pursued with regard to Ireland. Since the time of John no English king except Richard II had gone to Ireland, and for the most part English kings had neglected it. They made sporadic attempts to keep control of the English in Ireland, which were neither prolonged nor effective. Since early in the fourteenth century the Pale had been shrinking. Many of the Anglo-Irish, moreover, sank their civilization to the level of that of the native Irish, who remained in the sixteenth century, as they had been in the twelfth, a half-savage people, organized in turbulent clans, practically impossible to control. The English in Ireland who retained their English traditions were generally hostile to the native Irish, but they had become impatient of English control and were likely to oppose any English government which attempted to regulate their affairs too closely.

Henry's Irish policy

Henry had to face the Irish difficulty because the majority of the Anglo-Irish were Yorkist, and Ireland became the favorite hatchery of Yorkist plots. The government of Ireland was given nominally to an English viceroy, who never went near Ireland. Such government as existed in Ireland was administered by a lord deputy, who was usually a member of the Anglo-Irish community within the Pale. For a long time the award of this office had been mixed up with a family feud, which for generations had been waged with as much bitterness and disorder as the tribal wars outside the Pale. For some years before Henry's accession the earls of Kildare, who were heads of the victorious family, had been lord deputies. Since the family was Yorkist, Henry deprived the earl of his deputyship, and in 1494 sent Sir Edward Poynings, an Englishman, to take his place. Sir Edward secured from the Irish parliament the enactment of several statutes for the better governance of Ireland, usually designated as Poynings' Acts. One required that before a parliament assembled in Ireland, the lord deputy and the Irish council should notify the king of the proposed agenda. The parliament could be held only if the king consented, and it could transact only such business as the king approved. Another established in Ireland the laws enacted by the English parliament previous to 1495. This legislation made the control of the king over Ireland closer. The new deputy, however, did not stop the quarrels of the rival families. In 1497, when the danger of Yorkist plots was removed, Kildare was restored because the influence of his family was essential to maintain order.

Henry VII not only established his house but he also won for it the loyal support of a wealthy and influential class in the nation by his commercial policy. During the fifteenth century the export of woolens, the principal article produced by English manufacturers, increased in relation to the export of wool, the staple raw product of foreign trade. English foreign commerce was ceasing to be passive and was becoming active. Some English merchants were doing business on a sufficiently large scale to enable them to build their own ships and market their own wares, and the number of English merchants engaged in foreign trade mounted steadily. They carried on their business under many risks and difficulties, to obviate which they sought the help of the central government. During most of the century the seas about England were infested by pirates, who together with England's enemies made even the shores and harbors of England unsafe. When English merchants penetrated new markets, they were restricted by the protective measures of the native merchants, and they found it difficult to secure justice in foreign courts. They had to compete with foreign merchants who were well established in control of large branches of English trade. Italian cities handled most of the trade between England and the Mediterranean, which since the Hundred Years' War had gone largely by sea through the Strait of Gibraltar. The Hanseatic League dominated the trade of the Baltic and of part of the North Sea. These foreigners, who were settled in England with special privileges, tried to exclude English merchants from the fields whence they came. The need of aid from the central government was becoming the more pressing because trade was shifting from an intermunicipal to an international basis. The recent centralization of France, Spain, Burgundy, and other states made it almost essential for central governments to treat together concerning the commercial rights and privileges of their nationals. The municipal basis of trade had not disappeared entirely, but individual English towns could no longer arrange their commercial relations with individual towns of Flanders as profitably as their king could settle them with the duke of Burgundy.

The aid given by Lancastrian and Yorkist kings had been comparatively small. Under the pressure of parliament the Lancastrians permitted the expansion of the restrictions imposed in the later years of the fourteenth century on foreign merchants trading in England. In

Foreign commerce

general these were merely the application on a national scale of regulations which towns and gilds had long enforced locally. Laws required from foreign merchants heavier tolls, limited the duration of their stay in the country, prohibited them from dealings with other aliens, excluded them from the retail trade, and denied them permanent residence in England. Such legislation was difficult of enforcement, and the attempts to enforce it were never consistently maintained for any long period. The most important groups of foreigners, moreover, such as the Hansards, were exempted by their privileges from the greater part of these restrictions. English merchants trading abroad received even less help. Commercial treaties were negotiated with several powers. Merchants trading to the Baltic and to Flanders secured from Henry IV the right to organize associations for mutual protection. They elected governors who could arrange disputes between English and foreign merchants, secure redress for their injuries from foreigners, and to some extent regulate locally the English trade in these parts. Such groups were often styled Merchant Adventurers, and their organization was analogous to that of the Merchants of the Staple, who continued to flourish at Calais. From time to time the Hansards were threatened with loss of privileges in England if they did not make concessions to English traders in the Baltic; but at the end of the period the position of the Hansards in England was little impaired, while the trade of English merchants in the Baltic had declined so greatly that the groups of Merchant Adventurers trading there had ceased to exist and the Merchant Adventurers trading to Flanders constituted the only association left with the name.

Henry VII was fully awake to the needs of English merchants. He wanted the support of the rich and powerful mercantile class for his dynasty, and he saw the wisdom of expanding English commerce in order to secure the national strength which would render England influential in the international relationships just struggling into existence. Consequently he conceived a comprehensive program of encouragement and applied it vigorously. He renewed the principle of the obsolete Navigation Act of Richard II. He took every opportunity to negotiate favorable commercial treaties. From foreign merchants who had privileges in England he demanded reciprocal privileges for English merchants trading abroad. So strong was his international position in the latter half of his reign that his commercial negotiations and policies were highly successful. They gave English merchants decided advantages in such branches of trade as the Flemish, enabled them to break some part of the monopolies of trade previously maintained by the Hanseatic League and Venice, and reduced the privileges of the Hanseatic League in England.

The importance of trading companies as agencies for the expansion of English foreign commerce Henry recognized fully. The central government as yet gave English merchants trading abroad little protection against pirates, injuries inflicted upon them by foreigners, and restrictions imposed upon them by foreign governments. Only by organization among themselves could English merchants meet foreign competition and protect themselves against piratical attack and foreign commercial jealousies. To perform these functions successfully, such organizations needed governmental powers and commercial privileges which only the central government could confer upon them. The Staplers, who had long possessed such privileges and powers from the government, occupied an established position which Henry took pains to preserve. The Merchant Adventurers, who had their mart at Antwerp and dealt chiefly in woolens, received from him much fostering care and protection. They were organized as a regulated company. Any English merchant gained entrance by payment of a fee. The members elected officials who protected members of the company trading in Flanders, excluded from the trade English merchants who did not belong to the company, and laid down rules which each member of the company had to observe in the transaction of his business. They regulated, for example, such things as the price of goods and the amount one merchant could sell. Each member of the company, however, made his own private ventures. Because Henry saw that the expansion of the growing trade in cloth was to the interest of England, he imposed a heavy duty on exported wool and a light duty on exported woolens, thus encouraging the woolen industry and the Merchant Adventurers. He allowed the company to reorganize and gave it increased and better-defined powers of regulating the trade. The Merchant Adventurers justified Henry's judgment by winning much of the English foreign trade that had previously been in the hands of foreigners.

The Merchant Adventurers

Thus Henry consistently attempted to further the interests of the new mercantile class. He favored the English merchant against the alien in England and at every point he tried to assist Englishmen in penetrating new fields of commercial activity. His policy was an immediate success. An Italian resident in England commended Henry for having made England rich by the support he accorded commerce. His work was even more important for the future because he laid down the lines of policy followed by later Tudors.

Henry's success

Henry's most important industrial legislation had to do with the

Craft gilds craft gilds. They had passed the zenith of their influence and were beginning to be supplanted by the domestic system. Industrial organization in England has passed through four phases. First came the family or household system where work is carried on by members of the household for the use of the household. Then followed the craft gild. A master employs a few workmen in his own house or shop to produce goods for sale, usually directly to the consumer. Organization in gilds was superseded by the domestic system, under which work is carried on by families in their homes or by masters in their shops, but it is no longer done with economic independence. The worker often receives his raw materials from a merchant capitalist and always sells to him. A middleman is introduced between the actual producer and the consumer. Last of all appears the factory system, still in vogue, where workmen are gathered in large groups under the direct control of the capitalistic employer. These stages are neither rigidly distinct nor exclusive, but during the second half of the fifteenth century there was a perceptible drift away from the gild organization toward the domestic system. The causes were many. Most important, perhaps, was the capitalistic control of the gilds. As the masters acquired wealth, they made the terms of apprenticeship harder, and made it increasingly difficult for a journeyman to become a master. The workmen in some industries were already revolting against the exclusiveness of the masters in the fourteenth century, and in the fifteenth some of them began to migrate to the rural districts, where they could carry on work unrestricted by the regulations of the gild. This movement was made possible by the appearance of capitalistic merchants who could supply the workers with raw materials and take the finished products, paying the workers for their labor. In the woolen industry particularly this transformation was well developed by the time of Henry VII. Another cause of the decline of the gilds was their local selfishness. Their attempt to exclude all competition in their immediate localities caused stronger opposition, as the shift of commerce from an intermunicipal to an international basis made it more apparent that the local privileges of the gilds often conflicted with the national interest. Before 1485 the central government began to regulate the craft gilds in some details, and Henry expanded this control. In 1504 it was enacted that no ordinance subsequently decreed by a gild should be binding until it had been approved by certain of the king's judges or ministers. Thus he made the future policy of the gilds subordinate in some measure to the central government and assisted the decline already begun.

In the field of agriculture Henry's attempts at regulation had little effect. Agrarian organization was well on the road to a revolution being wrought by the practice of enclosures. During the fifteenth century this practice became common. Landlords or large tenant-farmers were throwing together the small tenements on their lands and converting the whole into one large area of tillage or sheep pasture. The latter was the more common because the increasing demand for wool was making it more profitable to raise sheep than grain. This change was disastrous for the small tenants who were ejected from their holdings. They found it extremely difficult to settle again because the care of sheep required less labor per acre than the cultivation of the soil, and hence the demand for rural labor was falling off coincidently with the ejections. By the time of Henry VII the movement was causing bitter complaint and was presaging the social disorder which became rife in later reigns. Parliament imposed restrictions on the practice of enclosures without success. Enclosures were the result of a natural economic development which legislation proved powerless to stop.

Although Henry VII failed in this one particular, both external commerce and internal industry waxed prosperous during his reign. His regulative legislation, however, would have been without effect, had he not also ended internal disorder. The restoration of law and order was the most important of Henry's tasks. To it he devoted so much attention that he has been dubbed the Big Policeman.

One of the principal forces that had made for disorder was the nobility. The nobles had been the leaders in the Wars of the Roses, and it was they, with their bands of retainers, who constantly menaced the orderly administration of law and justice. The wars, however, had left them weak. Their numbers had not been greatly decreased, but "the tallest heads were gone."[5] None arose to take the place of the leaders who had perished during the wars. Moreover, their estates had shrunk in many cases and their wealth was diminished. The nobles were not in a position to offer strong opposition to a king whose determination to rule them with a heavy hand commanded the approval of the influential middle class.

From the first Henry excluded the nobles from a share of political power. The offices of state and household were given mainly to men drawn from the middle class, whose interests were so dependent on those of the king that they served him faithfully. They also constituted the influential element in the council. Men of this stamp, who could not oppose the royal will with impunity, were selected by Henry as

Enclosures

The Big Policeman

The nobility

[5] Pollard, *Reign of Henry VII*, iii, 319.

the fitting agents of the strong government which he was engaged in building. The position of the nobles who attended the royal person was reduced to that of courtiers. In the house of lords Henry worked his will through the spiritual lords, among whom were several of his former supporters. The upper house appears never to have opposed the royal will. The great part which the nobles had played in politics was over.

Maintenance and liveries

With the nobility politically weak, it was easier to enforce against them the many laws enacted to secure the preservation of the peace. This legislation applied to all classes of society, but, since the nobles had been the chief promoters of discord, it hit them the hardest. At his first parliament the new king forced the lords to take an oath against maintenance and livery. Of course the evil did not disappear immediately. When Henry once visited the earl of Oxford, he found him keeping a band of retainers. The earl's hospitality did not bar Henry from exacting punishment. In farewell he said: "My lord, I thank you for my good cheer, but I may not endure to have my laws broken in my sight; my attorney must speak with you." The speech cost Oxford £10,000.[6] Despite such exceptions, the bands of retainers gradually disappeared until they reached the vanishing point.

Administration of justice

Another obstacle was the maladministration of justice. Trial by jury seems frequently to have been a "contest in perjury,"[7] and juries that were not bribed were overawed. Frequently criminals were not apprehended and never came before a court. Numerous acts aimed to eradicate these evils. Those accused of murder were to be brought before a court within a year; townships which failed to apprehend a murderer were fined; and coroners who held an inquest were paid for it, while those who failed to hold one were fined. Juries were dealt with severely. From a civil jury appeal could be had to a special jury of twenty-four. If the second jury reversed the first, each member of the first jury was fined. If a criminal jury acquitted an accused person wrongfully, the council could review its verdict and inflict penalties upon the jurors.

The most notable of Henry's judicial reforms was his use of the court of star chamber. This court was not created by him. It was simply the council exercising jurisdiction which it had long possessed.[8] His

---

[6] Bacon, *Works* (London, 1824), v, 168.

[7] Pollard, *Reign of Henry VII*, i, xxxix.

[8] Above, p. 278. A statute of 1487, later called the statute of star chamber, authorized three principal officers of state, a spiritual and temporal lord, and two justices to try seven offenses typical of the régime of disorder. The court does not appear to

innovation was to employ the court in a vigorous campaign to bring to justice those accused of livery and maintenance, riots, bribery of juries, and similar deeds of violence which were the sources of the prevalent disorder. The court was better adapted to the purpose than were the courts of common law which had failed so long and so lamentably to punish adequately those guilty of such offenses. Its procedure was more elastic, and it could use many methods of obtaining the necessary evidence which were denied to the courts of common law. It tried cases without a jury, and even the most influential could not hope to bribe or intimidate it. The rigorous enforcement of justice through the agency of this court gradually compelled the powerful lawbreakers to desist from those practices which had imperiled the rights of the king's subjects and set at defiance the royal authority throughout the fifteenth century. As employed by Henry VII, the court of star chamber was a boon to his people. Wrapped in this court was a threat to popular liberties, because it tried cases without a jury and, on account of its personnel, was more amenable to the royal influence than were the courts of common law. But not until the abuse of the court by the Stuarts did it acquire that ill-favored repute which has made it synonymous with tyranny; it served Henry as the most effective instrument at his disposal for the restoration of law and order.

Court of star chamber

Although Henry did not abuse the court of star chamber, it was his intention nevertheless to rear a strong monarchy. This appears most clearly in his relations with parliament. After the early hectic years of his reign, Henry followed the example of Edward IV and did without parliament. Of the seven parliaments which he summoned, six sat before 1497. Financial independence of parliamentary grant gave him freedom from parliamentary control. This he secured in far greater measure than Edward IV. He soon discovered that grants of taxation from parliament not only subjected him to parliamentary checks but also endangered his popularity. On two occasions the levy of taxes granted by parliament provoked local rebellions. From his seven parliaments, therefore, he sought but five grants of direct taxation. The revenues which he enjoyed practically independently of parliamentary grant were the same as those of Edward IV, but their yield was greater. His first parliament authorized the resumption of crown lands which had been alienated since 1455 and gave him tonnage and poundage for life. The increase of foreign commerce rendered the latter a fruit-

Parliament

have been independent of the council, and it was given no jurisdiction which the council did not already possess. Apparently the main purpose of the statute was to strengthen the council in star chamber in the exercise of the jurisdiction which it already possessed.

ful source of supply. Henry also raised benevolences, despite their prohibition by the parliament of 1484. In the later years of his reign he employed the criminal law as a means of extortion, prosecuting under obsolete laws or false charges, and obtaining fines sometimes through conviction by packed juries. All of these sources were insufficient to render independent of parliamentary grant a king who indulged in wars or in lavish expenditures, but Henry practiced economy with a rigidity that gave him the reputation of a miser and accumulated a large surplus above his needs.

When parliament met, the king usually succeeded in managing it. This was easier in the sixteenth century than it would be in the twentieth, because the lack of easy means of communication made it difficult for any common public opinion to formulate itself on specific issues. The representatives could rarely secure the opinions of their constituents on measures presented to them in the course of the session, they came to parliament with no common purpose, and the shortness of the sessions hindered the formation of an *esprit de corps* after the house had met. Under these conditions the speaker became an instrument of management, and the king generally secured the election to the office of a member of his council, who would expound the royal views. Parliament was the more amenable, because Henry so manifestly ruled in the interest of the middle class which constituted the backbone of the house of commons. Such acts as that providing for the trial of certain classes of cases without indictment by jury manifestly threatened the popular liberties, but they were of obvious and immediate practical benefit to the king's subjects. It is indicative of the extent of the royal control that the greater and more important part of the legislation of the reign originated with the king and his officials, though the commons did not cease to initiate legislation.

The result of Henry's rule was to increase greatly the royal authority. He gave the English nation what it most desired. At his death the new dynasty was securely established on the throne with a title undisputed at home and "safeguarded from external attack by a series of alliances with foreign powers,"[9] the important and growing commercial interests had received much encouragement, peace and order had been restored, and the realm was free from the danger of civil disturbance. In the process "England became the prize of that Tudor dynasty which had brought her deliverance."[10] *De jure* the constitution had been changed but little, but *de facto* the king was far more powerful.

Henry's power

[9] Fisher, *History of England, 1485–1547*, p. 124.
[10] Busch, *England under the Tudors*, i, 291.

The council placed no check on his will, parliament was not a serious obstacle, and the administration of justice could be controlled or perverted to suit his ends, if needs be. Henry's people were not unaware of the increase in the royal authority, but they acquiesced because the parliamentary experience of the fifteenth century had made it evident that the only road to law and order was through a strong executive. The very means by which Henry increased his power worked to the advantage of his subjects. Henry's personal ambitions coincided with the popular interests. Henry, moreover, used his power wisely. He was rarely guilty of a wanton or capricious act, and he displayed real solicitude for the welfare of his people. Furthermore, the extent of his power was somewhat concealed from the popular view because the outward form of the constitution underwent so little change. Thus Henry laid the foundation of the strong monarchy which was characteristic of the Tudors, and secured for it the popularity on which it rested.

The reign of Henry VII was manifestly a period of great changes. The alteration in the character of the government, the remarkable expansion of commerce, the agrarian revolution, and the decay of the gilds were signs of a vast transformation that was in the making. Another movement which assumed importance in his reign, though it began before and continued after, was the Renaissance. It began with a renewed interest in classical antiquity, which first manifested itself in Italy in the fourteenth century. The study of classical literature was not new, but the spirit with which men approached its study was new. They sought the truth. They soon developed a critical faculty and cast aside the trammels of authority which had restricted the speculative thought of the schoolmen. They applied their new ideas to actual life and began to act upon them. Literature and learning were the first to feel the impulse, but eventually art, architecture, politics, religion, and every other field of human endeavor were affected. The most significant aspect of the new spirit was its individualism. This did not originate solely in the revival of classical antiquity, but the revival strengthened the concept, for individualism is writ large in the classics. The right of the individual to think and act for himself independently, a concept alien to the point of view of the average medieval man, became the watchword of students of the new type (humanists), and from them spread gradually but widely to the rank and file. The Renaissance has been aptly defined as the rebirth of the individual.

In England the earliest trace of the Renaissance is found in Chaucer, who was influenced in some measure by the pioneers of the movement

The Renaissance

in Italy. It proved to be merely a fleeting impression. During the fifteenth century English literature fell from the high pinnacle where Chaucer placed it. Poetry continued to be written in large quantities, but it consisted for the most part of poor and feeble imitations of Chaucer's work. Prose fared somewhat better. "The thing to be remembered for the moment is that the number of prose-writers increases. They write more abundantly than formerly; they translate old treatises; they unveil the mysteries of hunting, fishing, and heraldry; they compose chronicles; they rid the language of its stiffness."[11] Prose was being popularized. But not yet was English the language of the learned or prose the form taken by literature designed to entertain. Malory's *Morte d'Arthur* is the brilliant exception. Utilitarian, didactic, or devotional are adjectives applicable to most of the prose, and rarely does it rise above the mediocre in technique.

Historical writing went the way of the other literary efforts of the century. In this period the monastic annals dwindled away. Walsingham continued his work until 1422. Thereafter few monasteries kept up the historical tradition. Those which did produced only meager annals covering brief periods and containing little of other than local interest. History was being written elsewhere than in the cloister. Latin, moreover, was ceasing to be the language of historians. Two lives of Henry V written in Latin follow classic models and display a departure from the medieval annalistic tradition under the influence of the Renaissance,[12] but the greater number and the most important of the histories were written in English. The only chronicle which was continuous and contemporaneous for any large part of the period was an English work called the *Brut*.[13] The number of editions still extant testifies to its popularity. Even more indicative of the changing times is the considerable number of civic chronicles written in English. They were of no great literary merit, but those written in London were of much historical value.[14] There is significance "in the fact that through the London Chronicles and the *Brut* a narrative written in English speech for popular use for the first time takes rank as a leading contemporary authority."[15] The writing of history was passing from the monks to the burghers, and the reading of it from the learned few to

---

[11] Jusserand, *Literary History*, i, 521.

[12] For editions of these, see Gross, *Sources*, no. 1814.

[13] Edited by Brie for the *Early English Text Society*, 1906–8.

[14] Good examples may be found in Kingsford, *Chronicles of London* (Oxford, 1905); Flenley, R., *Six Town Chronicles of England* (Oxford, 1911), and Gairdner, J., *Historical Collections of a Citizen of London*, Camden Society, 1876.

[15] Kingsford, *English Historical Literature in the Fifteenth Century*, p. 135.

the large middle class. The transition was not productive of the best type of historical work. Nothing in the fifteenth century can compare with the chronicles of William of Malmesbury or of Matthew Paris. But history was being popularized, and the way was being prepared for the historian who would apply the critical spirit of the Renaissance to the materials which he utilized for the narrative intended for popular consumption. With the work of Polydore Vergil that stage was reached. He was an Italian scholar who came to England as collector of the papal revenues in 1501. After long study of English chronicles he wrote a reasoned history of England[16] based on evidence selected with some critical judgment of its value. It was a readable narrative which broke completely with the dreary, annalistic form of presentation. Vergil wrote in Latin, which was the language of the humanists, but his book was soon translated, and it became popular. His method influenced many later historians, and in the sixteenth century the historical art attained a higher level.

The history of the fifteenth century, however, is told inadequately in contemporary narratives. More than ever it is necessary to rely on other sources. Official and semi-official documents of the types previously described supply the most important information, and legal treatises again become significant.[17] Literature other than historical is of less value for history than the literature of the preceding century. But a new source is provided by private letters. These became more common in the fifteenth century than ever before, because so many more people could read and write. They not only give intimate glimpses of everyday life, but they also contain many allusions to public affairs. Private correspondence in those days often supplied the news now gleaned from newspapers. Of the several collections of letters which have survived the ravages of time the largest, the most instructive, and the most amusing are the Paston letters.[18] They were written by and to three generations of a Norfolk family which had recently entered the ranks of the gentry. The business and the diversions of the family, the disorder and corruption of the times, the social customs, the political affairs of the kingdom, and other aspects of life infinite in variety pass in a naïve review which is as entertaining as it is informative. Probably no other source gives to the reader as vivid an impression of the life of the fifteenth century.

The higher learning suffered the same decadence as literature. At

Other historical materials

---

[16] *Anglica Historia.* For editions, see Gross, *Sources,* no. 1854.
[17] Namely, the works of Fortescue and Littleton. See Gross, *Sources,* nos. 1873, 1876.
[18] The best edition is that by James Gairdner, 6 vols., London, 1904.

The
univer-
sities

Oxford and Cambridge several new colleges were founded, but the material resources of the universities were generally inadequate for their educational needs. The number of students declined substantially. The higher degrees were rarely taken. The universities were intellectually stagnant. With the final suppression of Wycliffism at Oxford early in the fifteenth century, scholasticism lost its life. Syllogistic reasoning became an empty form which merely preserved the distorted tradition of a brilliant intellectual past. It no longer provided a stimulus to intellectual activity. In the fifteenth century, before the Renaissance began to quicken the thought of the universities, England produced neither a great scholar of European fame nor any great leader of European public opinion.

Spread of
education

Though the intellectual attainment of England in the fifteenth century was on a lower level than in the preceding centuries, education was becoming more widespread. The sons of noblemen were still generally educated in the castle, as they had been in the heyday of chivalry, but the sons of the country gentry and the sons of prosperous merchants who did not intend to follow the clerical calling were beginning to attend the universities in small numbers and the grammar schools in large numbers. The value of an education in school as a training for the ordinary pursuits of life was beginning to be appreciated, and education was being secularized. It was ceasing to be a clerical monopoly. New grammar schools were founded up and down the land, and in many instances they were maintained by lay authorities. While higher education was on the decline, elementary education was spreading rapidly.

Begin-
nings
of the
literary
Renais-
sance in
England

The intellectual atmosphere of England in the fifteenth century was so unfavorable to the spirit of the Renaissance that the movement made little impression until the end of the century. Isolated individuals displayed an interest in the new thought which found such brilliant exposition beyond the Alps, but they had small influence upon contemporary Englishmen. One of the first of these was Duke Humphrey of Gloucester, the brother of Henry V. Selfish and erratic as he was in politics, he was nevertheless the patron of letters and the friend of Oxford, when its slender endowments placed it in sore need. His interest in the intellectual movement led him to bring to England Italian humanists to instruct him in the new interpretation of the classics and to arouse in England an interest in the revival of letters. Not long after Duke Humphrey's death Englishmen began occasionally to go to Italy to study under the leaders of the new movement. They brought back to England the spirit of the literary Renaissance, but they appear to have done comparatively little to spread it abroad. They did not establish in England the study of the humanities on the Italian model.

That was the work of the next generation of English scholars who sought the light in Italy. The first who began to teach in England the new views he had acquired in Italy was William Selling, an Oxonian and a monk. He went to Italy in 1464. After his return he became prior of Canterbury, where he made the monastic school a center of the new learning. Among his pupils was Thomas Linacre, who went from Canterbury to Oxford and thence to Italy, where he studied the classics and science, taking a degree in medicine. Another Oxonian, William Grocyn, who had been a friend of Linacre's in college, went to study in Italy contemporaneously. Early in the last decade of the century these two returned to Oxford and began to lecture. They were profound scholars who acquired European reputations, and they practically established humanism at Oxford. Linacre later became the tutor of the sons of Henry VII and eventually was appointed physician at the royal court. Among the students of Grocyn and Linacre was John Colet, who, following in the footsteps of his teachers, went to Italy, and returned to teach at Oxford in 1497. His lectures on the epistles of St. Paul cast aside the allegorical interpretation inherited from the Middle Ages and attempted to arrive at their meaning by putting them in their historical setting. Later he became dean of St. Paul's in London, where he introduced the new educational methods in a school for boys. Such fame did these teachers acquire that Erasmus, a Dutchman, who later became the most prominent figure in the northern Renaissance, came to Oxford to study with them.

The result of the work of these and other lesser scholars was to set up a new conception of scholarship in England. The systems of thought which had been imposed by medieval scholasticism did not give way without a struggle. At Oxford the opponents directed their attack against Greek as the typical study of the new régime, and the "Trojans," as they called themselves, tried to ridicule and bully the "Grecians" out of Oxford. The Grecians, however, secured the support of the king. Henry VIII had been trained in the new culture, and he was easily persuaded by Sir Thomas More, who held a place of high favor at court, to lend his influence to the suppression of the Trojans. More had studied under Grocyn, Linacre, and Colet, and, though he had never been to Italy, was thoroughly imbued with the scholarly spirit of the Renaissance. His *Utopia*, in which he pictures an ideal society, so at variance with existing political and social conditions as to be a severe criticism of them, is a typical product of the freedom of thought

Literary revival

Effect on scholarship

inspired by the new learning. Thanks largely to his influence, the Trojans were silenced, and the new studies were enabled to take root at Oxford. Cambridge was still more thoroughly inoculated with the virus of the new system; and from the universities the movement spread to the schools.

Broader
results

The results, if judged by the scholarly product, were disappointing. The number of great scholars at the universities remained comparatively few and the literary product of the classical Renaissance in England was not of great importance. By the middle of the sixteenth century attendance at the universities had again fallen off perceptibly. But the influence of the Renaissance in England was not primarily literary. The chief result was to provide a new conception of life, and this gradually permeated all classes of society. Though the universities declined, schools continued to increase in number, and the new point of view passed from the schools to the home and the market place. Though derived from classical writings, it was translated into English action, and the actions of men in the Tudor age were long of more importance in other fields than they were in literature. When the new conceptions finally found glorious expression in the literature of Elizabeth's day, the literature which they produced was distinctively English. The important results of the revival of letters in England were indirect. "The real revelation of the Ancient World was later felt by those who, unable to construe a simple Latin sentence, yet saw before them the living figures of antiquity."[19] What men wrote about life was less affected than the life that men lived.

Printing

The popularization of the ideal of the Renaissance was promoted by the invention of movable type which made it feasible to print books. The new process appears to have been used first at Mainz in 1454. It was brought to England by William Caxton, who set up a press at Westminster in 1477. Within three years he printed editions of thirty different books. Other presses were soon at work, and a stream of literature began to issue from them. The new books, produced cheaply by mechanical means, could be bought by many who had been unable to afford the cost of manuscripts copied laboriously by hand. The printed page brought to the multitude the opportunity to acquire knowledge at just the time when the spirit of the Renaissance was arousing among them the desire for it.

Another manifestation of the Renaissance which affected England profoundly was that of geographical discoveries. These were so great

[19] Einstein, *Tudor Ideals,* p. 317.

that they were tantamount to a revolution. Until the Scandinavian peoples began to sail the seas in the ninth and tenth centuries, European knowledge of the world was hardly wider than that possessed by the Romans. The vikings discovered Iceland and Greenland and in all probability reached America, but the area of commerce was little expanded thereby. Commercial ventures on such a scale were impracticable when fluid capital, the protection of centralized states, and the stimulus of a broad intellectual horizon were lacking. With the later growth of the overland trade with the far east, Europeans began to travel in Asia. Beginning in the thirteenth century some of these travelers wrote accounts of their experiences which were read with keen interest. Marco Polo's marvelous narrative circulated widely. The popular imagination was thus being kindled when the conquests of the Turks began to cut off the established trade routes between east and west. By this time the trade of Europe with Asia was of great importance. These conditions stimulated men in the fifteenth century to seek for a route to the east by sea. They looked in two directions. The Portuguese began to sail down the western coast of Africa, until in 1498 Vasco da Gama reached India by the way of the Cape of Good Hope. Under the auspices of Spain Columbus sailed west and discovered America in 1492.

Geographical discovery

The spirit of discovery was not lacking in England. The earliest ventures were financed by merchants of Bristol who were then among the wealthiest and most progressive merchants of the kingdom. In 1480 two ships sailed to the west in search of land. The expedition failed in its quest, as did several others undertaken in subsequent years; but in 1497 John Cabot, an Italian resident of Bristol, was successful in reaching the mainland of North America. Cabot's expedition was another private venture, though Henry VII granted Cabot a monopoly of trade in any lands he should discover and bestowed on him a pension after the successful issue of the voyage. Cabot's sons and other merchants of Bristol continued the voyages of exploration for a few years, but, as the barren lands which they had found yielded none of the profitable trade they sought, while the patronage of the king provided little in the way of financial support, they became discouraged and abandoned the project. Between the explorations of the reign of Henry VII and the first expeditions which yielded immediate commercial returns, half a century elapsed. But while these early voyages were without immediate tangible results, they did something to fire the imagination of contemporary Englishmen and helped to create the

English voyages

spirit which later sent Englishmen forth into all parts of the newly discovered world to seize their share of the world's commerce.

Though Englishmen were slow to realize it, the result of the new discoveries was to place England in an entirely new commercial position. In the course of the sixteenth century the area of commerce expanded enormously and the main routes of trade changed entirely. England, which had been in a side eddy of the world's commerce, was now placed in the center of its main stream. Few Englishmen grasped the full significance of the change immediately, but in the second half of the sixteenth century they began slowly to reap the advantages of their new geographical situation. Before the last Tudor was laid to rest they had built the enduring foundation of England's sea power and prepared the way for her colonial empire.

Effects of the discoveries on England

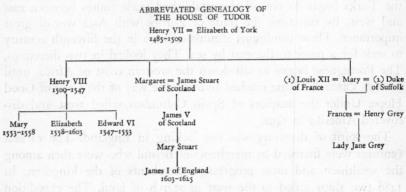

ABBREVIATED GENEALOGY OF
THE HOUSE OF TUDOR

Henry VII = Elizabeth of York
1485–1509

Henry VIII   Margaret = James Stuart   (1) Louis XII = Mary = (2) Duke
1509–1547   of Scotland   of France | of Suffolk

Mary   Elizabeth   Edward VI   James V   Frances = Henry Grey
1553–1558 1558–1603   1547–1553   of Scotland

                                       Mary Stuart   Lady Jane Grey

                                    James I of England
                                        1603–1625

CHAPTER XVII

HENRY VIII

WHEN Henry VIII ascended the throne in 1509 his position was as different from that occupied by his father in 1485 as can well be imagined. Danger from rival claimants to the throne was gone; the feuds of York and Lancaster were laid to rest; peace and order had been maintained long enough to produce a tradition of strong government; the rising commercial class was loyal to the house of Tudor; and no foreign ruler could longer shake the throne by threat of pretender and internal rebellion. By his people Henry's accession was hailed with joy. At eighteen he was open, genial, and generous. In sharp contrast to the old, crafty, and suspicious Henry VII, who was respected and feared, the young king could be loved by his subjects. He knew how to share himself with his people, how to be familiar with his subjects without sacrifice of the royal dignity. He had a magnificent physique, was fond of sports, and was reputed the best archer in his kingdom. He had all the popularity that today would go to a king who was the best bat in England. Henry VIII also attracted to him the learned of his kingdom. From his tutors he had imbibed the spirit of the Renaissance, and his court was the resort of men cultured in the new learning. Position of Henry VIII

Henry further increased his popularity by his early acts. He pardoned most of the offenders condemned during the last years of his father's reign, and canceled the obligations of those who had been forced by extortion to agree to pay the king money. He married Katherine of Aragon, and forthwith his court became the scene of never-ending pageants, revels, and tournaments. The treasure piled up by Henry VII fast disappeared, but the gorgeous display did its part in making Henry VIII beloved of his people. During the first years of his reign the government ran smoothly in the channels fixed by Henry VII. Internal tranquillity was not disturbed. Finding little to occupy his attention at home, Henry VIII turned to foreign affairs. Early acts

There the new king soon found scope for his youthful ambition to win glory and renown. Europe was still in the throes of the Italian wars which had begun in 1494. These wars were caused chiefly by the national consolidation of France and Spain at the close of the fifteenth century. As these states began to feel their national strength, they The Italian wars

wanted to try it out, just as most small boys pass through a period
when they want to fight all the other small boys in the neighborhood.
Italy, divided into several petty states jealous of one another and torn
by dissension, offered the obvious field for conquest. Twice France won
and lost the southern kingdom of Naples, which finally fell to the
crafty Ferdinand of Spain. With Milan in the north the French had
better luck. They conquered it in 1499 and were still in possession.
The year before Henry VIII came to the throne Italian affairs had
passed through one of the kaleidoscopic changes common at the
period. Someone turned the wheel and the pieces fell into the League
of Cambrai. The pope, Louis XII, king of France, Ferdinand, king
of Spain, and Maximilian, the emperor, joined to attack Venice. In
1509 the French defeated the Venetians, and all shared the spoils. The
Italians then did what they had often done before. When the foreigner,
whom they had invited to enter, had served his turn, they united to
drive him out. The pope soon allied with Venice, secured the aid of
Ferdinand, who changed sides with no more scruple than he changed
his coat, and invited Henry VIII to join the Holy League against
France.

To Henry the invitation was welcome. He desired to emulate the
War with France, 1511–1514 martial deeds of Edward III and Henry V; England was no longer
forced to refrain by internal disorder; and France was the traditional
enemy when fighting was to be done. In 1511 he satisfied his ambition
and displayed his loyalty to the church and his respect for his father-in-
law, Ferdinand, by joining the league. His aim was to secure a slice
of French territory, and his allies allowed this to stand as his ostensible
object. What they really wanted was a diversion in France while the
French were driven out of Italy and ousted from Spanish Navarre.
In 1512 an English army was sent to Spain to cooperate with Spanish
troops in southern France. It was so placed as to serve as a screen for
the Spanish operations in Navarre and given nothing to do. After
several months of inactivity and insubordination the English army
returned home without orders from the king. It was "a breach of
discipline, unexampled in the military annals of England,"[1] and a
severe blow to Henry's pride. By now it was becoming apparent even
to Henry that he was being used by Ferdinand as a cat's-paw. The
league's chestnuts were out of the fire, since the French had been
driven out of Italy and the Spanish were in occupation of Navarre,
but Henry felt he must retrieve the ridiculous position in which his

[1] Brewer, *Reign of Henry VIII*, i, 20.

army had placed him. In 1513 he led an army into northeastern France, won the Battle of the Spurs, and captured two cities. It was a brilliant and futile campaign. While Henry was in France, the Scots, following an ancient tradition, invaded England, only to be overwhelmingly defeated on Flodden Field in a battle that cost their king his life. Ferdinand, meanwhile, had made a truce with France practically withdrawing from the league; a new pope favored peace; and Maximilian soon deserted the alliance. Left in the lurch by his allies, Henry had no recourse but peace. In 1514 a marriage was arranged between Louis XII of France, who was worn out and decrepit at fifty-two, and Henry's younger sister Mary, aged seventeen. The king of France agreed to pay the English king an annual pension and allowed him to keep Tournai as a pledge for its payment. Henry was well out of a difficult situation. His principal gain was a thorough knowledge, acquired by bitter experience, of the lying and deceitful methods of contemporary diplomacy.

The war had one other result of importance; it brought Thomas Wolsey to the fore as Henry's chief minister. By birth Wolsey belonged to the middle class. He received a good education at Oxford and rose to be one of the chaplains of Henry VII. Under Henry VIII he occupied a position of minor importance in the household, until he became the leading spirit in the organization of the war. He assembled troops, provisions, and transports for the largest expedition England had ever made against France, he helped to plan the campaign, and the successful negotiation of peace was largely his work. In 1515 Henry VIII made him lord chancellor, he was already archbishop of York, and he was soon a cardinal and papal legate. From this time until his downfall in 1529 Wolsey was mainly responsible for the policy of the government. The young king gave his time to tennis and the dance, to music and the chase, while Wolsey worked. Henry kept his finger on the pulse of public affairs. He was a bright young man, and he managed to keep informed of much that transpired while he pursued his pleasures. When he gave orders they were obeyed, for Wolsey early discovered that, despite his youth, he "would be obeyed, whosoever spake to the contrary." But for the most part he left Wolsey a free hand. His confidence was not misplaced. Wolsey was an able statesman. At diplomacy he could beat Ferdinand and Maximilian at their own game. When he wanted to lie on a grander scale than usual, he could speak "as it becomes a cardinal, on the honor of the cardinalate." He had one great fault. As his power grew, so did his pride. The Venetian ambassador records that when he first arrived

Thomas Wolsey

in England, Wolsey used to say "his majesty will do so and so"; soon it became "we shall do so and so"; and finally it took the form "I shall do so and so." His arrogance made him unpopular. The nobles regarded him as an upstart who had deprived them of their just share in the king's counsels, and the people tended to fasten on him the policies they did not like, while Henry received credit for popular policies.

Habsburg-Valois rivalry

For many years Wolsey's attention was given chiefly to foreign affairs. In 1515 Louis XII died, dissolving the marriage alliance with England and bringing to the throne of France Francis I of the house of Valois. The new monarch, who was only twenty-one, was eager to restore the prestige of France, and before the year was out he reconquered Milan. In 1516 Charles of Habsburg, who was the duke of Burgundy, became king of Spain by the death of Ferdinand.[2] His first step was to make peace with France in order that he might be free to strengthen his position in Spain. But his acquisition of the Spanish crown made war between Habsburg and Valois well-nigh inevitable. Charles was even younger than Francis and no less ambitious. The causes of the rivalry of France and Spain in Italy still existed; as duke of Burgundy Charles inherited a tradition of hostility to France; and his rich possessions on both sides of France were a menace to French power. In 1519 the death of his grandfather, Maximilian, brought to Charles the ancestral lands of the Habsburgs, which centered in Austria, and resulted in his election as holy Roman emperor. With that event the outbreak of open hostilities between the dynasties of Habsburg and Valois became only a question of time. In 1521 began the war which was destined to last intermittently for nearly forty years. It was chiefly a dynastic struggle waged for territorial possessions and power with utter disregard for the interests of peoples, but it dominated the international relations of European rulers.

English diplomacy

The keen desire of his master to profit from the situation to advance his own fame led Wolsey to enter upon a long career of tortuous diplomacy. During its course he seems to have glimpsed the theory of the balance of power which later became a cardinal principle of European diplomacy. It was the necessary complement of the development of the nationalistic principle that no one state should be allowed to

---

[2] The following abbreviated table displays the extraordinary heritage of Charles V:

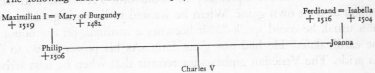

Maximilian I = Mary of Burgundy
+ 1519   + 1482

Ferdinand = Isabella
+ 1516   + 1504

Philip
+1506

Joanna

Charles V

become so powerful as to threaten the independence of all the others. Therefore, if one state became too powerful, others should ally against it. If Wolsey saw the principle, he failed lamentably in execution. In 1519, when war impended, both Francis and Charles began to bid for Henry's support. After the new emperor had visited England, Henry went to France to hold with Francis the famous interview in the Field of the Cloth of Gold, where all the pomp and circumstance of chivalry were revived. The most important event was a wrestling match in which Francis threw the English king and thus heaped fuel on the bitter jealousy which Henry felt for his brother monarch. Henry then went to see Charles in Flanders, where he secretly displayed his preference for the cause of the Habsburgs. After the war began, Wolsey went to Calais to mediate between Francis and Charles. While he was presiding over the arbitration proceedings, he negotiated an offensive alliance with Charles. This was published early in 1522, when Henry was ready to take part in the war.

The war went badly. Expeditions sent to France in 1522 and 1523 accomplished little, and the inevitable invasion of England by the Scots was turned aside more by good fortune than by design. Henry learned, moreover, that the war was not popular with his subjects. In order to obtain the necessary supplies, a forced loan was raised in 1522, and in 1523 parliament, which had not met in eight years, was summoned to grant taxation. Wolsey demanded for the king a huge subsidy. When the commons hesitated, he came down in state and attempted to overawe them. They refused to debate in his presence. Eventually they granted less than the desired sum, but in the course of the debate some of the speakers criticized sharply the policy of war. For the tax Wolsey received the blame, but the king saw that he could not ask for further grants without risk to his own popularity. As a consequence England marked time in relation to the war. In 1525 the whole situation was altered by a victory won by Charles at Pavia. The French were overwhelmingly defeated and their king was taken prisoner. Charles appeared to be the dictator of Europe. Henry's first impulse was to join with his ally to invade France and divide the spoils, but for a year past he had contributed practically no aid, and Charles naturally declined to share with him the fruits of victory. Henry found, moreover, that he could not get money to finance such a policy. Mindful of his recent experience with parliament, Wolsey in 1525 tried to raise the amicable loan. It was in reality a heavy tax assessed against each man who would have been required to pay a tax had parliament granted one. The Londoners resisted payment, and in

The war

Suffolk it caused open rebellion. Wolsey then withdrew the demand for a fixed quota and permitted each to contribute what he would. The Londoners retorted that benevolences had been illegal since the reign of Richard III. Eventually the demand had to be withdrawn entirely. It was Henry's first rebuff, and he learned his lesson well, as later events were to prove. The worst of the immediate consequences he escaped by throwing the blame on his minister, but his martial ambitions had to be abandoned. He turned, therefore, to Wolsey's policy, and made an alliance with France, designed to help restore the badly disturbed balance of power. After the release of Francis the arrangement was expanded into an offensive alliance against Charles, but before England had taken any aggressive action under it, the whole situation was complicated by Henry's desire to secure the annulment of his marriage with Katherine of Aragon.

Causes of the divorce

Henry's desire for a divorce[3] arose from mixed motives. One influential factor was his desire for a male heir. Of several children born to him and Katherine, all except Mary had died at birth or shortly after. For a reigning queen on the English throne there was no precedent. It seemed likely to mean a disputed succession and a return of such evils as England had suffered in the fifteenth century. The situation caused the king apprehension long before he began action in 1527, and there were many who shared his fears. Henry's affection for Katherine had been cooled somewhat by her partisanship for Spain. Katherine could never forget that she was a Spanish princess, and she was importunate in behalf of Spain at inopportune times. As far back as 1514 she had so angered her husband by her championship of her father's interests, when Henry had just cause to believe that Ferdinand had betrayed him, that he had threatened her with divorce.[4] The cause that probably was the immediate occasion of Henry's attempt to secure a divorce was his passion for Anne Boleyn, one of the ladies attendant on the queen. He probably fell in love with Anne early in 1527, though the event is obviously of a type which it is beyond the power of the historian to date specifically. At any rate Henry made manifest his intention to seek a divorce in April of 1527.

He based his action on a technicality. Katherine was his brother's widow, and the law of the church forbade the marriage of a deceased brother's wife. To make the marriage possible, the pope had issued

---

[3] The use of this term is loose but convenient. The church did not grant divorces, and what Henry wanted was known technically as a *separatio ab initio*. Its effects were the same as modern divorce, except that it illegitimated any issue of the union.

[4] *Letters and Papers*, i, 5718; *State Papers, Venetian*, ii, 479.

a decree which dispensed with the law in this particular case. Henry Early proceed-ings contended that the dispensation was invalid. It was his first thought to secure a judgment in an English ecclesiastical court, marry Anne, and later obtain the confirmation of the pope. This scheme was stopped by events in Italy. In May, 1527, the troops of Charles sacked Rome and made the pope, who was the ally of Francis, a prisoner. With the head of the church in the power of Charles, who was the nephew of Katherine, it became too great a risk to contract a second marriage before the papal court, the highest court of appeal on marital law, had dissolved the first marriage. It became necessary to deal directly with the papacy. Henry therefore asked that power to try the case should be delegated to Cardinal Wolsey. This the pope refused, but he commissioned Wolsey and Campeggio, an Italian cardinal, jointly to try the case in England. He instructed Campeggio secretly to delay the decision, because he wanted to be sure whether France or Spain would win in Italy. The court began to sit in the spring of 1529, but, before it reached a decision, the case was summoned to Rome. Shortly afterward the Treaty of Cambrai ended the war between Francis and Charles, leaving the latter the dominant power in Italy. The pope could not afford to antagonize Charles. Henry could not hope for the papal annulment of his marriage unless he could bring pressure to bear on the papacy to counterbalance that exerted by Charles.

In England the failure of the court to grant the divorce had two results. The first was the fall of Wolsey. He had failed to secure what Change of policy Henry had set his heart upon. For that his property was confiscated and he was dismissed in disgrace, though nominally he was punished for violation of the Statute of Præmunire. His years of faithful service did not condone the one failure with a king who was colossally selfish and utterly heartless. The second was that Henry took the lead of the forces in England that were opposed to the papal and sacerdotal power and began an attack on the papal jurisdiction that resulted in the abolition of the papal control of the English church and placed it under the headship of the king.

To obtain the help of the nation Henry called parliament in 1529. Before it was dissolved seven years later, it had ended the papal juris- The Reforma-tion Parlia-ment diction in England. For that reason it is called the Reformation Parliament. How far it represented popular opinion is an important question and one impossible to answer beyond the shadow of a doubt on the basis of the evidence so far brought forward. There are those who would have us believe that Henry by his control of parliament forced the separation of the Anglican church from the Roman communion upon an unwilling people; others assert with equal force that Henry merely allowed a strong popular feeling against the administration of the church to take its course under his guidance. The truth is probably somewhere between the two extremes. Henry used his influence to secure some members of the house of commons who would favor his policies, but the evidence is not sufficient to justify the conclusion that the house of commons was systematically packed with subservient royal henchmen. When the house had come together Henry on occasion exerted remarkable political skill to secure favorable action on his measures, but the house occasionally asserted its independence with a good, round negative. Absolute as Henry may have been, he could hardly have forced so great a novelty upon a whole nation unalterably opposed to it. To a considerable group the innovation was not fundamentally displeasing, though the group may or may not have constituted a majority of Englishmen.

Renais-
sance and
Reforma-
tion

The nation was in some measure prepared for the acceptance of such a change. For a long time there had existed in England both an anti-clerical and an anti-papal feeling. In the thought of the sixteenth century there were many currents which tended to quicken these antagonisms. The Renaissance let loose a critical spirit which placed many existing institutions on the defensive. The leaders of the English Renaissance were particularly interested in the church. Colet by precept and example emphasized the need for critical study of the Bible and laid the foundation for one of the chief tenets of the later reformers. He cast aside much that had been regarded as authority on the Bible in the Middle Ages. He also criticized vigorously and fearlessly the corruption in the lives of the clergy about him. Erasmus essayed a critical text of the New Testament, and, while it was not very critical according to modern standards, it was a dangerous tampering with authority. Erasmus also attacked many abuses in clerical life and in the practices of the church, holding them up to keen satire in his *Praise of Folly*. More made his protest against intolerance and poked his milder fun at the clergy in his *Utopia*. None of these men wanted to overthrow the existing ecclesiastical system. All desired a reform from within. Colet died before the Protestant revolution on the continent waked an echo in England; Erasmus would have nothing to do with the Protestant leaders; More used his pen strenuously to defend the clergy against the attacks of those who would overthrow the established order, and finally gave his life rather than give up his faith that the pope was the head of the church. Actions speak louder than words. Yet these men and their like supplied the Protestants with a method of attack and an arsenal of weapons, and gave new vigor to anti-papal and anti-clerical tendencies.

Another current of thought that influenced a section of English opinion came from Germany. In 1517 Martin Luther nailed to the door of the church at Wittenberg the ninety-five theses which attacked the abuses in the administration of papal indulgences. They brought him into a controversy that caused him to advance to a denial of some of the doctrines of the church. Within a few years he denied the papal headship and the necessity for the intervention of the clergy between man and his maker to secure salvation, and proclaimed the right of every Christian individual to interpret the scriptures for himself and the doctrine of justification by faith alone. He won a large following in Germany, where his movement became known as the Protestant Reformation. In reality it was a revolution, since he had advanced beyond the stage of reform and demanded the overthrow of the church. Luther's writings soon began to find readers in England, and they exerted some influence on English thought before 1529, though it is impossible to tell how many disciples they had won. *The Lutheran movement*

These seeds of criticism fell on a fertile field of discontent. Before Luther's books began to be imported, a good bit of heresy existed in England. In seven years of the reign of Henry VII twenty-five heretics were condemned in London alone. But there is no indication that large numbers were yet dissatisfied with the doctrines of the church. With the administration of the church it was otherwise. Long before the time of Henry VIII, opposition to papal intervention in English affairs other than spiritual had become traditional in England. In the early years of the sixteenth century the feeling was sharpened by the growth of the national sentiment and by the ever more prominent part taken by the popes in the filthy arena of international wars and politics. Some of these worldly-minded popes, moreover, were guilty of such scandalous personal conduct that the moral influence of the papacy as the spiritual head of the church was sadly impaired. Against the clergy complaints of the type made by Wycliffe in the fourteenth century were frequent in the opening years of the sixteenth, and such abuses as benefit of clergy and the corrupt administration of ecclesiastical courts caused several outbursts of popular indignation. There was developing in the sixteenth century some measure of popular antipathy toward the clergy as a caste. *English popular opinion*

Henry's plan was to utilize this state of public opinion to secure from parliament an attack on the papal power which would force the pope to grant his personal desire. The first act of parliament, passed in

Attack on
the pope,
1529–1532

1529, prohibited non-residence of the clergy and other abuses, and inflicted penalties even on those who had dispensations from the pope authorizing them to commit the abuses. The real significance of the act rested in the assumption that a papal dispensation was not valid against a lay statute even in a purely ecclesiastical affair. When this threat to the papal power failed to move the pope, Henry proceeded to take further steps with the object of intimidation. At this time he seems to have made up his mind, probably under the influence of Thomas Cromwell who soon became his chief adviser and his principal agent in the execution of his ecclesiastical policy, to carry the policy to the limit of repudiation of the papal jurisdiction, should it become necessary. In 1531 the king accused the whole clergy of breach of Præmunire because they had recognized Wolsey as legate. The charge was probably legal, but it was unjust, since the king himself had licensed Wolsey to act. The clergy, reading the writing on the wall, voted in convocation to pay the king a huge fine. When Henry further demanded acknowledgment of the king as supreme head of the English church, they reluctantly agreed to it with the proviso, "as far as the law of Christ allows." Early in 1532 parliament again took a hand in the game, petitioning the king to remedy many clerical abuses such as excessive probate and mortuary fees.[5] The king turned it over to convocation, and, to secure the protection of the king from further attack, that body made the submission of the clergy. It agreed that existing ecclesiastical law should be revised by a commission controlled by the king and no new laws enacted without the royal consent. These acts gave Henry control of the clergy. He then secured from parliament the Act in Conditional Restraint of Annates. It forbade the large payments customarily made to the pope by bishops and archbishops when they received their offices. The act was conditional, because it was left to the discretion of the king to retain annates at a reduced rate if he could reach an understanding with the pope within a year. Henry waved it over the head of the pope without result. Coercion had failed.

Separation
of the
Anglican
church

Henry then set out to end the papal jurisdiction in England, in order that he might secure the annulment of his marriage in an English court having supreme jurisdiction. Events followed fast and furiously. In 1532 Henry secured the appointment of the subservient Cranmer to the vacant archbishopric of Canterbury. This gave him control of the highest ecclesiastical court in England. In January of

---

[5] Later it enacted a statute against several of them.

1533 he married Anne; in May Cranmer handed down his decision that Henry's marriage with Katherine had never been valid; and in June Anne was proclaimed queen. Meanwhile parliament was at work. Before the close of 1534 it enacted legislation prohibiting appeals to the papal court, stopping all payments from the English clergy to the pope, arranging for the king to exercise the power of confirming ecclesiastical appointments and other powers previously wielded by the pope, and declaring the king without qualification to be the supreme head of the English church. No change was made in the doctrines of the Anglican church, except those concerning the headship of the pope. Parliament, indeed, took occasion to assert its orthodoxy in one of its legislative enactments. But the breach with Rome was complete. The issue between church and state that runs athwart the whole of the Middle Ages was now settled: the state was supreme.

Henry had won his cause. He still had to secure his new position against the danger of attack, for it did not sit well upon many Englishmen. In 1534 he had parliament pass the Act of Succession, which entailed the crown upon his heirs by Anne, declared it treason to slander the marriage with Anne by writing or by deed, and required all subjects to take an oath to observe the statute under penalty of misprision of treason. Few refused, but among those who did were Sir Thomas More and Bishop Fisher of Rochester, two of the most prominent men in the kingdom. They were ready to support the succession but not to deny the primacy of the pope. They were put in prison and eventually executed for treason, though refusal to take the oath did not carry with it the extreme penalty by the terms of the act. The very prominence of these men made the greater impression on the popular imagination of the determination of the king to have his way. This was followed by a new Act of Treason, extending the definition of that crime enormously. To call the king a heretic, schismatic, or tyrant became treason. So broad was the definition that the utterance of almost any criticism of the king could be brought within its scope. With the aid of these acts a reign of terror was instituted. The oath of supremacy was administered widely and the few who refused to take it were executed. Informers and spies were located throughout the country to watch for disaffection, and several who were reported to be critics of the king were executed. Such opposition as was felt was suppressed by this reign of high-handed tyranny.

Henry needed more than the mere suppression of opposition; he needed the active support of an influential class in the community. This he secured by dissolving the monasteries and sharing the spoils

Succession and treason

with the landed gentry. The dissolution was managed by Cromwell. He sent out agents to visit the monasteries and make inquiries concerning the conduct of the inmates. It seems clear that his agents were expected to make a case against the monasteries that would seem to justify their dissolution. Without doubt, evils existed. Episcopal inspections of monasteries in the fifteenth century disclosed much laxity of discipline. Since life by rule was the essence of monasticism, continued carelessness in the observance of discipline was likely to breed corruption. Unprejudiced evidence concerning conditions in preceding years makes it appear highly probable that some immorality existed among the monks in 1535, but the amount reported by Cromwell's commissioners was unquestionably an exaggeration. The dissolution of the monasteries was due less to their corruption than to their failure to fill the place in the society of the sixteenth century that they had occupied in the society of the Middle Ages. They were no longer centers of learning; they produced no chronicles worthy of the name; they could not act as pioneers in the capitalistic enterprise of the sixteenth century; and they no longer appealed universally to the highest religious ideals of the age. They still served as inns, and they still distributed alms. Their charitable expenditures, however, represented only a small part of their incomes; and though they constituted the only organized charity, they were utterly inadequate to cope with the huge mass of poverty caused by the economic transformations of the period. In the sparsely settled north the hospitality and alms of the monasteries were still important factors in the life of the community, but in the more thickly populated, commercial south they had ceased to hold a high place in public esteem, and their landed possessions were the object of growing envy.

These conditions made the dissolution possible; the evidence gathered by Cromwell supplied the pretext for action. In 1536 parliament passed an act ordering the dissolution of monasteries with incomes of less than £200 annually and conferring their property upon the king. During the next three years the greater part of the remaining monasteries were suppressed without parliamentary sanction. Most of the abbots were persuaded to surrender their abbeys voluntarily. The abbot of Reading, who refused, suffered a fate designed to give pause to those who contemplated opposition. He was brought before a judicial commission previously instructed by Cromwell that the abbot was "to be tried and executed."[a] In 1539 a packed parliament sanctioned

---

[a] Merriman, *Thomas Cromwell*, i, 175.

the surrenders already made and authorized the dissolution of the few that remained.

The dissolution brought to the king great wealth. He kept enough to make unpopular taxation unnecessary for the nonce, but the greater **Results** part of the monastic lands he gave away or sold at a low price to the landed gentry of the neighborhood. The recipients, who constituted an influential class, became the loyal supporters of the house of Tudor, and they were bound to the new ecclesiastical organization because the restoration of papal authority might force them to disgorge their plunder. It also strengthened the new order in other ways. The regular clergy were more closely attached to the papacy than were the secular, and their suppression removed one of the most dangerous sources of opposition to Henry's leadership. The disappearance of the abbots from the house of lords rendered that body more amenable on ecclesiastical questions. Twenty-eight abbots dropped out in 1539. Six new episcopal sees were created from a portion of the spoils, and their holders became members of the upper house, but the spiritual lords were henceforth in a minority.

One result of the change was less pleasing to Henry. In the north the dissolution caused the outbreak in 1536 of a rebellion called the **Pilgrimage** Pilgrimage of Grace. It was a time of economic distress in the rural **of Grace** districts, when the elements of discontent were easily aroused. Economic and social forces contributed to the production of the movement, but it was primarily a protest against the dissolution. The chief demands of the rebels were the restoration of the monasteries and of the old faith and the dismissal of Cromwell and other advisers whom they regarded as responsible for the recent ecclesiastical policies. To the king they proclaimed their loyalty. The rebels were mainly peasants, though some gentlemen joined. The king, having no standing army, was forced to temporize. He treated with the leader, granted some of his demands, and promised pardon to all except ten ringleaders. When the radicals among the rebels refused to accept the terms, the rebellion was repressed and the rebels punished with much cruelty. To secure the district against future disturbance the king established the council of the north. It consisted of royal appointees and was given wide discretionary power of an arbitrary character. It made the royal power far more effective than the local magnates on whom the king had previously relied.

Henry did not intend to sacrifice any of those ecclesiastical changes which had been necessary to accomplish his personal ends. On the **Doctrine** other hand, he was not prepared to permit more innovations than were necessary for that purpose. Though the conservative rural districts might oppose the changes already wrought, an urban element which desired doctrinal change was beginning to appear. The Protestant ideas brought from the continent were beginning to appeal to some Englishmen. Indeed, Cranmer, one of Henry's chief advisers, was influenced by them somewhat. But Henry would have none of it. In 1536 he called upon convocation to define the cardinal doctrines of the church, but he dictated the ten articles which convocation promulgated for that purpose. Traces of the Protestant point of view appear, as, for example, in the article which permits the retention of images but condemns their superstitious veneration. But the doctrines expounded are those of the church before the separation. In 1539 Henry went still further in the Six Articles Act passed by parliament. This laid down six fundamental Catholic doctrines and imposed penalties of the utmost severity for their denial. Henry was now persecuting those who were not sufficiently orthodox Catholics and those who were too orthodox. In 1540 six men were drawn together to Smithfield to be executed. Three were loyal Catholics who denied Henry's supreme headship and were punished under the act of 1534; three were heretics who denied Catholic doctrines set forth in the Act of the Six Articles.

One innovation which Henry authorized tended to promote the spread of Protestant views. In 1537 he licensed the publication of an English translation of the Bible. Two years later he allowed another translation to be printed, and ordered a copy to be placed in every church where people could consult it. A few years later he commanded the translation of certain parts of the service followed regularly in the churches. These translations made knowledge of the holy writ readily accessible and tended to promote popular discussion of religious questions and speculation on the doctrines of the church. While Henry was insisting that his subjects should take his view of ecclesiastical doctrines, he was putting in their hands the evidence on which they could base their own judgments. The later translation of the Bible, moreover, though Henry did not know it, was in large part the work of Tyndale, who was a pronounced Lutheran. He was a scholar of the new type, who translated from Greek and Hebrew originals. On many critical words he departed far from the Latin of the Vulgate, which was the version authorized by the church, giving to his translation a decidedly Protestant tone. Unwittingly Henry helped the Protestant cause and promoted the divergence of opinion which he sought to prevent, though the effect did not become apparent in his own day.

Thus Henry established his headship, used it to define the doctrines

Bible and
services in
English

of the English church, and forced his people to accept them. Outward The work
uniformity of belief he would have. It is a striking illustration of the of Henry
pitch of his absolutism, but it was probably an advantage to the nation. VIII
Toleration was an unknown principle in the sixteenth century. If the
nation had split between Catholic and Protestant, civil war or persecution on a far larger scale than that maintained by Henry would have
been the result. Such, at least, seems to be the lesson taught by the
experience of continental peoples. Henry's executions are writ large
on the page of history because they were so often manifestations of a
despotic will and because so many of the victims were men of high
station. Yet the bloodshed was far less in England than in any country
on the continent which passed through a similar change. In forcing
the whole nation to face the religious question as he faced it, Henry
exercised such tyrannical power as no English king before his day
had wielded; but he tided the nation over a dangerous crisis, and only
a strong monarch could have accomplished that result.

Meanwhile Henry was trying further matrimonial experiments. The
birth of Elizabeth in 1533 was a disappointment, and as Henry's hope The other
of an heir waned he lost interest in Anne. In 1536 she was accused of four
incest and adultery, tried, pronounced guilty, and beheaded. Her
brother and four other men shared her fate. Her guilt is problematical.
The conviction by a court of one whose removal from the scene was
desired by Henry is no evidence of guilt, but the gratuitous execution
of four men seems more than enough to have satisfied even Henry's
sense of propriety. However that may have been, Cranmer promptly
held a court which declared the marriage with Anne invalid and
placed Elizabeth's claim to the throne in the same category with
Mary's. A few days after the execution of his second wife Henry
married Jane Seymour. Her character and reputation were considerably
better than those of Anne, and she was probably happier than most
of Henry's queens. In 1537 she died after giving birth to a son, the
future Edward VI. Thereafter Henry remained in a state of single
misery for over two years, though it was hardly his fault. In these
years the possibility of attack from Catholic Europe loomed so large
that Henry felt constrained to use his hand as a pawn in the diplomatic
game. Early in 1540 he married Anne of Cleves to secure an alliance
with that small German state. According to all accounts, Anne was
something less than fair to look upon. After Henry had seen her, he
fulfilled the terms of the treaty with reluctance. Almost immediately
he found that the alliance was more of a burden than a help. This
time Henry took out his spite on Cromwell, who had negotiated the
treaty. Since the minister could not well be accused of his crime,

which had been to carry out the will of the king, he was charged with favoring Protestant doctrines, which served as well to bring him to the block. Anne was quietly divorced. She was given a generous alimony, and died many years later with her head on her shoulders. Thus Henry rid himself of an unpopular minister, an ugly wife, and a dangerous foreign alliance. Parliament immediately besought Henry "for the good of his people to enter once more into the holy state of matrimony." Nothing loath, he married Katherine Howard, who was fair of face and dark of reputation. Apparently he was enamored of his new bride. When he was informed of her past indiscretions he seemed inclined toward clemency, but when he received proof of her violation of the seventh commandment, she was sent to accompany Anne Boleyn. A year later, in 1543, he married Katherine Parr, who was twice a widow. She must have had tact in abundance. She won not only the affection of the choleric old king but also that of his two daughters. She had the extraordinary good fortune to have her third marriage dissolved by Henry's death in 1547.

Foreign policy, 1529–1547

Foreign affairs after 1529 interested Henry chiefly from the point of view of their effect on the internal situation in England. After Wolsey's fall the king was his own foreign minister. Until the separation he clung to the French alliance, hoping that Francis would help to press the pope for the divorce. After the abrogation of the papal power his foreign as well as his internal policy was directed to the maintenance of the accomplished fact. It was threatened by a new pope who became active against heretics and attempted to unite Charles and Francis against England. To meet this danger Henry kept up his alliance with France until the renewal of hostilities between Habsburg and Valois in 1536 rendered its continuance unnecessary. The death of Katherine of Aragon in the same year made possible a reconciliation with Charles, and Henry reverted to a policy of neutrality. The cessation of the war in 1538, however, renewed the danger of a Catholic crusade against England. It was the pressure of this situation that led Henry into his ill-fated marriage alliance with the little duchy of Cleves. Hardly had it been completed when the probability of a renewal of hostilities between Francis and Charles caused both monarchs to bid for his favor. Eventually Francis, becoming fearful that Henry would ally himself with his rival, began to urge the king of Scotland to attack England. Henry anticipated the move by taking the aggressive against Scotland in 1542. He then allied himself with Charles, sending troops across the Channel to cooperate in an attack upon northeastern France. The English captured Boulogne, and after Charles made peace with Francis (1544), Henry was able to use it as a lever to secure peace (1546) on the basis of the payment of an indemnity by France. The war with Scotland served only to bind the Scots to the French more closely than ever. It failed to win the permanent adherence of the Scots to the English plan of a marriage between Mary, heiress to the throne of Scotland, and Edward, heir to the English crown. When Henry died (1547), he left the relations between England and Scotland more strained than ever.

The closing years of Henry's reign provide less striking examples of the royal absolutism than the period of Cromwell's ascendency, though arbitrary executions by no means ceased. After Cromwell's fall Henry ruled with the advice of his privy council as a whole, with no one adviser predominant. During these years Henry experienced much physical discomfort. He grew corpulent and unwieldy, and at times suffered great pain from an ulcer in his leg. Through all his years of power his egotism and selfishness had grown upon him, and his lack of health now rendered him highly irascible. A less lovable character can hardly be imagined. Yet Henry remained popular to the end. The amiable qualities which had attracted the popular fancy in his youth had long since departed, but the old king had led the nation successfully through difficult times, and if he may have lost the love of his people, he still commanded their loyalty.

The judgments on Henry VIII are as diverse as the story of his reign appears to be paradoxical. None would deny that he was selfish, gross, and cruel. His policies were dictated by his selfish personal aims, and they were carried out by arbitrary means. But they brought results which were not at variance with the national will. The separation, for example, could not have been accomplished had it not met the wishes of a large part of the nation. The extent of his power, moreover, was largely concealed. He cloaked his acts with the guise of legality, and he preserved the outward forms of the constitution when he worked the greatest injustice. His judicial murders affected comparatively few individuals, while the rank and file received from his courts an even-handed justice that could not have been obtained from a weaker king. His despotic leadership carried England through the ecclesiastical revolution with a minimum of bloodshed. His strong rule assured the continuance of the material prosperity of his people. How much Henry may have violated the moral sentiment or the political ideals of his age may be debatable, but the results of his rule were judged by contemporaries to be conducive to the welfare of the nation. Only thus can be explained the maintenance of such an absolutism not only without the force of arms but even without serious protest from any large part of the nation.

CHAPTER XVIII

PROTESTANT AND CATHOLIC

The
minority

IN 1547 England's king was once more a child. Edward VI, Henry's heir, was only ten. For the six years of his reign England experienced again the evils of a royal minority. Faction reared its head, and plot, counterplot, intrigue, and rebellion became the order of the day.

Creation
of the
protec-
torate

The council of regency consisted of sixteen persons named by Henry VIII. Acts of parliament had authorized him to dispose of the succession to the crown by will and to arrange for the organization of the government during a royal minority. The council as first planned by Henry balanced the leading partisans of the new and the old religious ideas, but events of the closing years of his life upset the balance in favor of the new. The earl of Hertford, the brother of Jane Seymour and the uncle of Edward VI, who leaned toward the Protestant doctrines, soon obtained the leadership. He secured from the council appointment as lord protector and had himself created the duke of Somerset. At his persuasion Edward VI abrogated the will and granted supreme power of government to the lord protector and a council of twenty-six. The new council, which owed its authority to the live king and not to the dead one, was so constituted that Somerset soon obtained complete power. He retained this authority for nearly three years.

Foreign
policy

In the field of foreign affairs Somerset inherited from Henry VIII a difficult situation. The war with France had exhausted the treasury and left it burdened with debt. Relations with Scotland were still unstable, and the French were dissatisfied to leave Boulogne in English hands. Neutrality, which had been the keystone of Henry's foreign policy whenever it had been successful, seemed to be unattainable by Somerset, had he been inclined in that direction. In Scotland he resumed Henry's attempt to eliminate French influence. He only made bad matters worse. His successful invasion of Scotland caused the Scots to arrange a marriage between Mary Stuart, their infant queen, and Francis, heir to the throne of France, and forthwith to despatch Mary to France. This ended the plan to unite England and Scotland by the marriage of Mary to Edward VI, and left French influence supreme in Scotland. Nor did the continuance of a desultory war improve the situation. With France, Somerset had much friction about Boulogne, which ended in a declaration of war by France in 1549.

With regard to internal affairs Somerset's attitude was more liberal than that of his age. One of his first steps was to secure the passage of legislation which pruned the Treasons Act of its worst features and rescinded the Act of the Six Articles and other legislation against heresy. He soon advanced in the Protestant direction. More of the services of the church were ordered to be read in English, and parliament passed acts permitting the marriage of the clergy and authorizing other practices which savored of Protestantism. Doctrinal innovations followed. In 1549 the first Act of Uniformity became law. It required the use in all churches of a new prayer book which had been produced by Archbishop Cranmer. It was modeled largely on old English service books and retained much of the form of worship of the old church, but Cranmer was so far influenced by continental divines of the new faith that in places it leaned toward Protestantism. The cardinal doctrine of transubstantiation, for example, seemed to be practically denied in one place, where the communion was treated as a pure memorial, though the language was so obscure that different readers could derive from it totally different opinions of its meaning. The prayer book represented the first step in the introduction into the English church of Protestant doctrines, though it did not go far in that direction. Clergymen who failed to use the new prayer book incurred heavy penalties, but no penalty fell upon laymen who chose not to attend the new services. *Religious changes*

Concurrently with these novelties, changes begun in the time of Henry VIII were being pushed rigorously to a conclusion. In 1545 parliament had decreed the dissolution of chantries and many other religious endowments, conferring them upon the king. A chantry was a perpetual endowment established to pay a clerk to sing masses at an altar for a departed soul. Endowments for this and similar purposes were numerous, and, though individual endowments were not large, their total was enough to excite the cupidity of the king when the greater wealth of the monasteries had been swallowed up. The work of confiscation was hardly under way when the death of Henry caused the act to lapse. Under Edward it was renewed and its scope was extended to include the greater part of religious endowments other than those attached to cathedral and parish churches, colleges, and certain schools. Many of the endowments were used in part for charitable, educational, or social objects. The non-industrial gilds, for example, used their endowments, which had been established by the small contributions of generations of members, for the help of indigent members, solemnities at the funerals of deceased members, pageants, and other *Dissolution of the chantries* purposes, as well as to pay for prayers for the souls of deceased members. But prayers for departed souls, according to the statute, perpetuated belief in purgatory and tended to promote superstition and errors in religion; and the funds of the gilds had to go. With them necessarily went the gilds themselves. Persons of moderate circumstances, who in many a town and village had enjoyed the social pleasures and the pecuniary benefits of these gilds, felt directly the injustice of the act. Nor were they compensated by the promise of the statute to use the confiscated property to endow schools and provide for the poor, for the promise was not kept. Comparatively little of the proceeds got further than the pockets of the king and the gentry. The dissolution of the chantries touched closely a much larger number of laymen than did the dissolution of the monasteries.

Contemporaneously with the dissolution, the government was waging

Destruction of relics

a war of destruction against relics, images, and shrines, which shocked the sentiments of many who still found their comfort in the old faith. The work of iconoclasm had begun under Cromwell's leadership. His plea that the popular veneration accorded such objects bred superstition was supported by some loyal Catholics, such as Erasmus; but when Henry VIII had the bones and relics of St. Thomas the Martyr burned and his festival discontinued, the desecration of the most popular shrine in England produced among the rank and file of the faithful a profound feeling of horror. With the accession of Edward the pace of the devastation was accelerated. In the towns Protestant mobs, quick to reflect the altered spirit of the government, began to break into churches and to demolish the images without authorization. The government soon extended the ban to pictures and stained windows, and cheerfully wrought the destruction of priceless treasures of medieval art. The distinction kept by Henry between images associated with superstitious practices and those which were not was abandoned, and all were given indiscriminately to the hand of the spoiler.

These and similar changes wrought in the old order by the govern-

Popular opinion

ment under Somerset produced a great divergence in popular opinion. To large numbers they were acceptable. Despite the Six Articles the tenets of the new faith spread fast in the closing years of Henry's reign. But there were also large numbers to whom the innovations were sacrilege. In the rural districts of Cornwall and Devon the first use of the new prayer book provoked a rebellion which ran through the summer of 1549. It caused disturbances also in Oxfordshire and neighboring counties. Thence the spirit of rebellion spread to other parts of

England, where, though contemporaneous, the rebellions were due to economic and social rather than to religious grievances.

To the common people the sixteenth century had brought much economic distress. The large body of contemporary literature devoted to England's woes reflects much prejudice, and some of it is merely the product of the human habit of comparing the present with the good old times. But the possibly heated language of disgruntled contemporaries receives sufficient confirmation in the cold words of official documents to justify the conclusion that misery was widespread. The stories of whole villages destroyed by the process of enclosures, of towns depopulated by the transfer of industry to the domestic system, of men thrown out of work without chance of new employment, of rising prices, and of paupers, vagrants, and criminals ever on the increase had ample foundation. Contemporary literature pictures the middle years of the sixteenth century as a period when the times were out of joint.

Social distress

The causes of the distress were numerous and complex, but three, at least, may be distinguished as fundamental. The most significant was the influx of precious metals from the mines of Mexico and Peru. After the decade of the twenties, when Spain began to reap her harvest of treasure from this source, the receipts steadily mounted. As this bullion gradually circulated through the rest of Europe, it caused the value of gold to depreciate, which expressed itself to the consumer in the form of a rise in the prices of commodities. The process was so gradual that its greatest effect was not felt until the second half of the century, but it had gone far enough by the reign of Edward to cause hardship. As is ever the case when the currency depreciates, commodities respond earlier than wages or salaries, and the consumer feels the pinch when he gradually finds that his income, though nominally the same in amount, will buy for him much less of this world's goods than in former years. Such statistics as have been gathered for England in the sixteenth century are fragmentary, but they indicate that by the middle of the century the cost of living had increased while wages had not. The purchasing power of wages had decreased decidedly. The rise in prices was seen clearly enough by contemporaries, who realized that it was the cause of many of their ills. But they failed to see the principal causes of the inflation. They ascribed it to bad harvests, monopolies, increasing luxury, enclosures, and similar causes, which in some cases may have been contributory in slight measure and in others were wide of the mark, but were in no case fundamental.

Increased supply of precious metals

Another cause of the hard times was the debasement of the coinage.

Debase-
ment of
the coinage

This was begun by Henry VIII in 1543 as an easy way to make money. He introduced more alloy into each coin and also reduced the weight. Gold was rendered worth only ten times the value of silver, while in France the ratio was 11.82 and in Germany 11.38. Gold began to be exported to the continent in large quantities. In 1545 still further debasement brought gold to the ratio of five to one, and gold coins nearly disappeared from circulation in England. The silver coins left were so debased that they would not pass current at their face values. Prices fluctuated rapidly and business was demoralized. The burden was particularly heavy on the poorer classes because they were generally forced by economic pressure to accept payment at the face value, while they could buy commodities only at the real value. Somerset endeavored to improve the condition of the coinage, but found the treasury too poor to stand the reform. The evil remained without mitigation throughout Edward's reign, and in his later years it was enhanced by still further debasement. This was practically the only important cause which was not a natural economic development beyond legislative control, but contemporaries generally failed to appreciate the significance of debasement as a cause of their troubles, and those who understood preferred debasement with all its evils to taxation, which was the alternative.

Capital-
istic
enterprise
in
agriculture

The cause to which contemporaries generally ascribed their sufferings was the growth of enclosures. Since the reign of Henry VII this movement had continued to progress rapidly. On contemporaries its ill effects made a strong impression, partly because they were obvious and striking, and partly because they were felt principally by the rural populace which still constituted by far the largest element in the population. Enclosures, however, were merely the principal manifestation of a more fundamental transformation which was taking place in agrarian organization. During the Middle Ages the land was worked primarily for the support of the immediate group that lived upon it. The typical community of the Middle Ages was the self-sufficient village.[1] When a local market with its small and steady demand was the only market available, it was impossible to work the land primarily for a profit. With the growth of the demand for wool, which could be more easily transported to distant markets than most agricultural products, and with the growth of towns, which provided markets for adjacent rural districts, capital began to be invested in land for profit. The appearance of lands leased at commercial rents and the development

---

[1] Above, pp. 63, 174.

of enclosures in the later Middle Ages testify to the growth of capitalistic agriculture.[2] The movement, which was comparatively slow until near the beginning of the sixteenth century, was accelerated in the time of the Tudors as the growth of commerce and the consequent rise of new markets gave greater opportunities for the profitable investment of money in land at the same time that the increase of fluid capital provided the means. Large landowners and occupiers, who could command the capital, and merchants, who were beginning to invest in land some of the profits of trade, began to work estates in the ways which would produce the most profit or to demand rents which could be paid only by those who exacted from the land its full yield. Either practice worked hardship on the small tenants who constituted the bulk of the rural population. To work the land at the greatest profit required its agglomeration in large estates. The small tenant generally could not pay the increased rent demanded and continue to make a living from his tenement. Often he was given no opportunity. The landlord evicted him in order to throw a number of small holdings into a more profitable large whole. The fundamental change which wrought havoc in rural England of the sixteenth century was the substitution on a large scale of capitalistic enterprise for the prevailing method of working the land for bare subsistence.

Enclosure became the principal manifestation of capitalistic agrarian enterprise because the improvements necessary for profitable production could not be made under the open-field arrangements. The enclosure might include the common lands of the villages or the arable fields; it might be made for the purpose of more extensive pasture, more intensive agriculture, or for the creation of parks and hunting preserves. In the sixteenth century the object generally was to provide great ranges for sheep, which could be most profitably managed in large flocks. That the sheep eat up the people is the burden of the popular plaint. The restrictive legislation of Henry VII[3] did naught to stay the movement, and numerous acts in the reign of Henry VIII accomplished little more. How much land was enclosed cannot be stated exactly. Contemporary complaints give the impression of an enormous amount, but incomplete statistics indicate that the amount was but a small percentage of the land even in those counties where the most enclosure took place. Even so, it was on a grander scale than had ever occurred before, and on a sufficient scale to cause suffering and want in many parts of England.

Enclosures

---

[2] Above, pp. 178, 243, 291.
[3] Above, p. 291.

The hardships produced by enclosures fell with greatest force on the customary tenants and the rural laborers. They took a variety of forms. One was a sharp rise of rents. Though this was due in part to the depreciation in the value of money, the initial cause was the capitalistic use of the land which put rents on a competitive basis. If a landowner did not enclose his land and evict his tenants, he wanted a rent that would correspond to the profit he could obtain from enclosure. The new commercial rents, which were called rack rents, represented a significant advance over the old rents fixed on a customary basis. The tenants, who were adversely affected economically, were the more disgruntled because they regarded the increase as a purely arbitrary use by the landlords of a power which they happened to possess. "Consider you," says Brinklow, "what a wickedness is commonly used throughout the realm unpunished, in the inordinate enhancing of rents."[4] Where the common lands were enclosed the smaller tenants were deprived of the pasturage which enabled them to keep cattle. To many a village laborer the loss of his cow was enough to push him over the brink of poverty. When the intermixed holdings of the tenants in the arable fields were enclosed, the possessors of small tenements were often cast adrift. Many of them held land originally in villeinage, which was protected only by custom. If they could not be evicted legally, they often found it practically impossible to obtain redress against the use of force and fraud. These evictions of whole groups of tenants constituted one of the most striking results of the movement, because their huts of flimsy structure were easily torn down, or, if merely left unoccupied, would soon be leveled to the ground by the action of wind and weather. The universal outcry of contemporaries over this desolation[5] finds verification in official records.[6] The tenants who were thus deprived of their homes had to find new homes and often new occupations. The transition was a period of hardship and poverty. For a time, if not permanently, they swelled the ranks of the army of paupers and vagabonds which was being recruited also by the other economic and social transitions of the period.

Somerset felt real sympathy for the sufferings of the common people. In 1548 he issued a proclamation ordering the previous legislation against enclosures to be enforced and announcing the appointment of

---

[4] *Complaynt of Roderyck Mors*, p. 9.

[5] E.g., Brinklow, *Complaynt*, pp. 48, 49; *Discourse of the Common Weal*, ed. Lamond, p. 15.

[6] E.g., Leadam, *Domesday of Inclosures, passim*. Tawney evaluates the evidence excellently in his *Agrarian Problem*, pp. 253–265.

a commission of investigation. The commission performed its labors under difficulties. The enclosers put their henchmen on some of the juries that gave evidence before it, intimidated others, and secured the presentment of much fraudulent evidence. Honest evidence was hard to obtain because the governing classes sympathized with the enclosers. The country squires and the rich burghers who attended the house of commons profited from the enclosures. Even Somerset's fellow councilors were in large part enclosers and opposed to his policy. One man could not drive the majority of the governing class to execute a policy which affected its own interests adversely. When his inability to obtain results became apparent to the sufferers, they lost hope of any legal redress of their wrongs and rose in revolt. Somerset, the reformer

The rebellion began in Somerset in 1549, and spread toward the east. The most important center was in Norfolk, where some 16,000 peasants were led by Robert Kett. They tore down the hedges and leveled the ditches which marked the enclosures. They plundered the landowners and shared the provisions thus obtained, but refrained from bloodshed. The gentry who were caught by the rebels were brought before a court maintained by Kett in their camp, but the punishments inflicted were never worse than imprisonment in the camp. The rebellion ran through the summer, partly because the government was busy with the religious revolt in the west and partly because Somerset was loath to take drastic action against rebels whose just grievances and orderly proceedings did much to excuse their illegal methods. When his attempts to secure the peaceful dispersion of the peasants failed, he finally sanctioned the use of the armed force necessary to suppress the revolt. Kett's Rebellion

The rebellion was the occasion of Somerset's downfall. Many of the council had opposed his policy. To them the rebellion was conclusive demonstration of the protector's folly. The general dissatisfaction with Somerset gave to the earl of Warwick an opportunity to advance his personal ambitions. With a number of his fellow councilors he plotted to oust the protector from the council and secure the leadership for himself. Somerset, finding himself without support other than that of the powerless peasants, submitted to his deposition from the protectorship. A few years later Warwick had him tried under an *ex post facto* law of treason and secured his execution. Somerset's fall

With the downfall of Somerset the experiment in liberty and toleration came to an end. Warwick, though he had himself created duke of Northumberland, never held the title of protector, but he wielded power as great as any ever possessed by Somerset. He came to power Reaction on a program of reaction, and a reactionary policy continued best to serve the selfish ends which ever constituted his chief guide. Under his direction the definition of treason was again enlarged in scope. The agrarian disturbances were met with a new act which reversed the previous policy of the Tudors. It authorized landowners to enclose their commons provided they left enough for their tenants. Since the tenants were given no voice in the determination of what sufficed for their needs, the landlords were practically left free to enclose as much of the commons as they pleased. If twelve peasants met to break down an enclosure they committed felony; if forty met for the purpose, they were guilty of treason. Such acts were typical of the new régime.

Reversal
of foreign
policy

In his foreign policy Northumberland cringed. Though peace was rendered necessary by an empty exchequer, it did not have to be purchased at the highest price. Northumberland needed to be free from foreign entanglements in order to devote his attention more fully to his personal aggrandizement. He surrendered Boulogne at the end of four years for half the price France was to have paid for it at the end of eight, and gave up all claim to the arrears of the French pension. He recognized the betrothal of Mary Stuart and Francis, practically giving his sanction to the Franco-Scottish alliance. To secure a quick peace with Scotland he surrendered the places occupied by English troops without any compensation. English prestige in European affairs was completely eclipsed.

Religious
changes

In religion Northumberland's policy was more radical and less tolerant than Somerset's. In 1552 a second Act of Uniformity established a new prayer book, more distinctly Protestant in tone than the first. The order of communion, for example, was treated as a memorial in such terms that the communicant could make little else of it. Imprisonment was meted out not only to priests who used other services but also to laymen who attended other services. Even failure to attend the authorized worship on Sundays subjected a layman to excommunication. In the next year the doctrine of the church was further defined by the forty-two articles issued by the council. They asserted the typical Protestant doctrine of justification by faith, denied transubstantiation, and abandoned five of the seven medieval sacraments, though they were otherwise moderate toward Rome.

Northum-
berland's
plot

Meanwhile Northumberland was plotting to secure the succession to the throne for his own family. By 1552 it was manifest that the king would soon die of tuberculosis. The succession was conferred by the will of Henry VIII upon Mary Tudor, Edward's half-sister. The daughter of Katherine of Aragon had remained staunch in her mother's faith, and her accession would certainly mean the downfall of the Protestant Northumberland. Nor was this the worst he had to fear. The duke had led the council unsuccessfully in a petty persecution of Mary to force her compliance with the established form of worship. If Mary, in the day of her power, should elect to take revenge in the Tudor way, the loss of his head was like to follow hard upon the loss of his power. In such a contingency he could hope for no help, for his arbitrary acts and domineering ways had rendered him thoroughly unpopular. To forestall these unpleasant possibilities Northumberland conspired to exclude Mary from the succession. His control of the government enabled him to take the initial steps with entire success. By 1551 he had ousted his principal opponents from the council and supplanted them with his own supporters. From this compliant council he obtained authority for the king to dispense with the requirement that the royal acts should be attested by the signatures of six councilors. Since his domination over the young king was complete, this virtual abolition of the minority practically placed the royal power in Northumberland's hands. He had little difficulty in persuading Edward to carry out his policies. In this instance the desired act was the more readily obtained because Northumberland appealed to the king's religious sentiments, which were sincere. He asked Edward to devise the crown by will in order to keep it on a Protestant head. The young king accordingly left the crown to Lady Jane Grey, the eldest granddaughter of Mary, the younger sister of Henry VIII,[7] and to her heirs male. The councilors, who also had heads to lose, hesitated long over the endorsement of the document, but finally confirmed it. The will of the dying but reigning king, as expounded by Northumberland, held greater terrors than the displeasure of a queen who might never rule. Meanwhile Northumberland's eldest son, Guildford Dudley, had married Lady Jane Grey. It remained only to secure the necessary popular support when the death of the king should bring the crisis. Here Northumberland counted on the Protestants to rally to the cause of the Protestant succession. Foreign help might also be forthcoming. In 1552 the Protestants drove Charles V in headlong flight from Germany, and the French king renewed the Habsburg-Valois conflict. Mary's cousin had too many troubles of his own to come to her rescue, while the king of France, who did not wish to have Charles's relative and admirer on the English throne, looked with favor on the candidacy of Lady Jane

---

[7] See genealogical table on p. 302.

Grey. When Edward finally died in July of 1553, all seemed favorable to the accomplishment of Northumberland's design.

Its execution proved to be another matter. The first act went according to the schedule. Lady Jane Grey, though she had no personal desire to wear the crown, played the part assigned to her and was proclaimed queen. Mary was less ready to accept her rôle. When Edward's end was near, she responded to a summons to come to his bedside, where Northumberland planned to seize her; but before her arrival she learned of her brother's death, whereupon she fled to Norfolk and issued a call to arms. Still more disastrous was the failure of the Protestants to take their cue. Their difficulty was the obvious illegality of Edward's will. Parliament had authorized Henry VIII to settle the succession by will, but Edward had no such sanction. They disliked the prospect of a Catholic ruler, but they feared Mary and Catholicism less than Northumberland and more wars of the roses. When Northumberland set out to meet the large army that had rallied to Mary's banner, his own troops melted away. When he returned to London, he found that the city with the council in its wake had gone over to Mary. Shortly she entered London and was crowned queen. Lady Jane was sent home and Northumberland to the Tower *en route* to the block.

When Mary Tudor came to the throne, her outlook on life had been warped by her unhappy past. After the marriage of Henry VIII and Anne Boleyn, when Mary was only a young girl, she had been separated from her mother, deprived of the company of her friends, subjected to petty annoyances and humiliations inspired by the jealousy of Anne, abused, and sometimes in danger of death. During Northumberland's span of power she had been outrageously treated because of her persistence in the observance of the Catholic worship in her own house. All these sufferings had not broken her spirit. She inherited enough of the egotism and imperiousness of her father and enough of the determined obstinacy of her mother to carry her through. But the experience left its mark of bitterness and harshness on her spirit. Her policies as queen were also dominated by the past. She had been born years before the breach with Rome had been contemplated, and she had been trained in the faith by her Spanish mother. In the years of her tribulation she had found her only consolation in religion, until she had become inspired with the belief that the evils which had fallen upon her and upon the kingdom were alike attributable to the departure of England from the ancient faith. She came to the throne with the firm conviction that it was her mission to restore the faith, and the

Mary Tudor

fact that its restoration would establish her own legitimacy served to strengthen her purpose. In the field of foreign relations her past likewise dictated her policy. During the long period since 1533 few Englishmen had dared display friendship for Mary. She had become accustomed to seek advice and protection from the Spanish ambassadors to England who represented the power of her cousin, Charles V. As queen she continued the friendship the more readily, because the help of Spain would also further her religious policy.

With regard to religion Mary made her intentions manifest at once. The bishops who had been imprisoned in Edward's reign for their opposition to the religious innovations were released and appointed to the privy council. Bishop Gardiner, who had been the leading champion of the old faith, was made lord chancellor and became her chief adviser. When her first parliament met in 1553, she demanded the restoration of the Catholic church. By the repeal of nine acts passed in the preceding reign parliament restored the Catholic doctrine and service as they had stood at the close of the reign of Henry VIII, but it refused Mary's request to rescind the act of the royal supremacy, and it would entertain no proposal for the return of the confiscated lands. It also declined to impose a penalty for non-attendance at mass. The nation might be willing to follow Mary back to the Catholic worship, but it was not ready for the restoration of the papal authority.

Restoration of Catholic worship

Mary was not content, but for the moment she held her peace because she was intent upon the arrangement of her marriage with Philip of Spain, the son of Charles V and the heir to his broad possessions, except the ancestral domains of the Habsburgs which centered about Austria. Mary desired the marriage for both personal and political reasons. She thought it would further the Catholic cause in England, and her Spanish blood, her respect for Charles, and her admiration for Philip moved her in the same direction. In reality the marriage was a political error because it was bound to be tremendously unpopular in England. Time and again in the sixteenth century Englishmen had displayed a strong prejudice against foreign intervention in English affairs, and Mary's marriage to Philip aroused the popular fear that England would be subordinated to Spain. Gardiner, as staunch a Catholic as Mary, saw the danger, and warned Mary that she would do more harm than good to the Catholic cause by associating in the popular mind the restoration of Catholicism with foreign intervention in English affairs. But Mary had the Tudor will without the Tudor tact, and she determined to go her own way. Gardiner made the best of a bad bargain, and in the treaty of marriage protected the political

The Spanish marriage

independence of England as far as was possible. Nevertheless, the marriage was so unpopular that its announcement immediately provoked no less than three rebellions.

Rebellion

One in the west and one in the midlands were of small importance. The third, organized chiefly in Kent and led by Wyatt, menaced Mary's position seriously. The troops sent against the rebels deserted and joined the uprising. Mary was left unprotected in London, and if Wyatt had attacked at once, she might have been easily captured. But his delay gave Mary time to assemble more troops, which defeated the rebels when they finally penetrated London. The first sufferers for the rebellions were innocent of any connection with them. Lady Jane Grey would not have profited by the rebellion had it succeeded; but she, her husband, and several adherents, who were under sentence of treason adjudged in 1553, were now executed. Elizabeth, Mary's half-sister, was released. Though some of the rebels professed to act in her name, no proof of her complicity could be found, and public opinion ran strongly in her favor.

Restoration of the papal headship

The rebellion did nothing to stay Mary in her course. Her second parliament was asked to ratify the treaty of marriage and to renew the statutes against heresy and the Six Articles Act. Parliament sanctioned the treaty, but failed to pass the legislation. Mary then summoned a third parliament, instructing the returning-officers to admonish the electors to choose members of a Catholic sort. The warning apparently had effect, for this parliament proved more amenable. It repealed the legislation of Henry VIII which had wrought the separation, and restored the papal jurisdiction in England, though even this parliament had to be assured by the pope that restoration of the confiscated monastic and chantry lands would not be demanded, before it would abolish the royal supremacy. This parliament also renewed the laws against heresy.

Persecution of Protestants

By this time Mary had placed a heavy strain on the popularity which was the basis of the Tudor absolutism. However the majority of the queen's subjects may have felt about the restoration of Catholic doctrines and ceremonies, they did not like the Spanish marriage or the return to the papal jurisdiction. Heedless of the state of public opinion, Mary proceeded with what she conceived to be her duty and began the persecution of heretics. The first trials were held early in 1555. Of six accused, only one recanted and the remainder were burned at the stake. This was quite contrary to Mary's expectations. She had anticipated many recantations which would weaken Protestantism, whereas the persecutions only served to stiffen resistance. The spirit of the Protestant martyrs was that expressed by Latimer to Ridley, when they were led together to the stake. "Be of good comfort," said he, "we shall this day light such a candle, by God's grace, in England, as I trust shall never be put out." But Mary failed to understand. For the remainder of her reign the fagots continued to burn, and nearly 300 perished at the stake. The persecution lost to Mary her last vestige of popularity and defeated her very end. It made impossible the endurance of the reunion with Rome. Many who had accepted the papal restoration loyally revolted at these methods. Local mobs and uprisings, starting generally from some fresh burning, became frequent. Though it was unlike a Tudor to profit so little from public opinion, there is no reason to doubt Mary's sincere belief that she was serving the interests of Catholicism. From the first she had displayed her willingness to sacrifice political power for the sake of religion, and she may have thought that she was now sacrificing popularity for the same end.

Throughout the period of the persecution the discontent grew and the criticism of Mary became more bitter and outspoken. A climax came when Philip, her husband, persuaded her to send English troops to help him in his war against France. The pope, who was allied politically with France, visited his displeasure on Mary. She learned that the pope cared not a whit for her sacrifices and her loyalty when his political interests happened to differ from hers. To her that was the bitterest pill of all. The mental attitude of Philip's troops, who prayed for the pope every night and fought against him every day, was not attainable by Mary. As the nation saw it, the greatest misfortune was the capture of Calais by French arms in 1558. This was a stinging blow to the pride of the English. It was a convincing demonstration that the marriage had subordinated England to Spain, and it alienated public opinion still further from the papacy. A few months later Mary died. Her last days were rendered bitter by the knowledge that her sacrifice of power and popularity had been in vain. With Mary fell the last hope of Catholicism in England. *The loss of Calais*

Elizabeth followed Mary on the throne in accordance with the terms of her father's will. Though the daughter of Henry VIII and Anne Boleyn could hardly be other than a Protestant, she was accepted by the Catholics as Mary had been by the Protestants. Yet the prospect for a successful reign was not bright. The national support of Elizabeth had as yet no enduring foundation. It was produced in part by fear of the alternative civil war, and it represented no settled conviction on the part of the English people. Five years before Mary had occupied *Elizabeth's position* the same position, but no ruler of the house of Tudor had died so universally disliked. Elizabeth's task, moreover, was more difficult than her sister's had been. The popularity which was the essential foundation of the Tudor strong monarchy had cracked under the weak rule of Edward VI, and under the misrule of Mary it had crumbled away completely. But the danger of internal dissension, the threat of external attack, and the social and economic disorders made more essential than ever the good government which could be given in the sixteenth century only by a strong monarch.

England in 1558

To the English people the evils were more apparent than the remedy. The religious question was now a burning issue which might easily provoke civil war. The violent oscillations of recent years rendered difficult the attainment of any settlement sufficiently satisfactory to a majority to have stability. The social and economic evils which had produced rebellion in the reign of Edward VI were still operating as powerful stimuli to popular discontent. Mary's government had done nothing to allay the resultant disorder, and the "lack of governance" was nearly as great as it had been in Lancastrian days. Before England's house could be set in order, foreign intervention had to be eliminated. In the time of Northumberland Spanish and French agents had been leaders in the plots for and against Mary, and in Mary's time Philip had attempted to subvert England to the Habsburg interests, while the French ambassadors had continually incited rebellions designed to prevent it. But the removal of foreign influence was not a simple problem. England was engaged in foreign war, Philip was not likely to resign his pretensions without a struggle, and the king of France could menace England through his nearly complete control of Scotland. In England the royal treasury was poor, the fortifications were decayed, the supply of arms and ammunition nearly exhausted, and the few troops demoralized. Abroad English prestige had departed. "Steadfast enmity, but no steadfast friendship"[8] was in sight. Never since the beginning of the reign of Henry VII had England's plight appeared so hopeless.

Elizabeth

To this problem Elizabeth brought a thorough education, a knowledge of men and affairs acquired by experience, the Tudor shrewdness, and a tact such as only the fortunate members even of her sex possess. During Mary's reign she had carried herself circumspectly through rebellion and plot aimed to place her on the throne, when a single false step would have meant her death. The experience had brought her

---

[8] Contemporary memorandum cited by Creighton, *Queen Elizabeth*, p. 44.

confidence and self-reliance. She had all the love of power and all the egotistical selfishness of her father, but she recognized that the desired absolutism must be based on the popularity disregarded by Mary and must be wielded subject to limitations unknown to Henry VIII. The low ebb of popular confidence in the monarchy forced her to cultivate the popularity which had come to her father largely without his conscious effort. She ever listened for the rumble of popular opinion, discriminating with nicety between that which must be taken into account in drawing the line of monarchical policy and that which was ephemeral. She often won her will by skillfully formulating the public opinion which she professed to follow; she knew when to make minor concessions in order to save larger ones; when she would have her way despite public opinion, she overcame opposition in a secret, underhanded manner; and when she yielded she did it as ostentatiously as possible. With these qualities of a great politician Elizabeth combined the petulancy of a spoiled child, the vanity of the vainest of women, and the ingratitude of a Tudor. But these traits of her character were generally visible only to her intimates, and even there she rarely indulged them at the expense of policy. She was ready to subordinate the woman to the queen and even to utilize her womanly heritage to further her interests as queen. Flirtation was to become a powerful weapon in her diplomatic armory. Power was her ruling ambition, and to attain it she was prepared to restrain her meannesses and her passions, to promote the popular welfare, and to exert political ability of a high order.

The first question to receive Elizabeth's attention was that of religion. She approached it from the point of view of expediency and with a spirit of moderation. She continued to attend mass, forbade changes in the service, and kept the Marian clergy in office until parliament should legislate upon the subject. Meanwhile she prepared in her council the measures to be placed before parliament. In this body were eleven who had sat in Mary's council and only six new members. Seven of the eleven, however, had also sat in councils of Henry VIII and Edward VI and were not tarred with Mary's brush of fanaticism, while among the six were Cecil (later Lord Burghley) and Sir Nicholas Bacon, who were staunch Protestants and Elizabeth's chief ministers and advisers. The parliament came together in 1559. No evidence indicates that it was systematically packed. The official element which would voice the policies of queen and council was influential, as it was in all the parliaments of the Tudors, but it constituted only about

Eliza-bethan settlement

one quarter of the commons.[9] The alacrity with which this house enacted the legislation prepared by the council would seem to indicate a popular willingness to return to Protestantism.

The settlement was effected by two laws. The Act of Supremacy settled the constitutional position of the English church. Practically it restored the situation which had obtained at the close of the reign of Henry VIII. It repealed Mary's acts which had revived the papal jurisdiction and established the persecution; revived the eleven acts of Henry VIII which had accomplished the separation, except the Statute of Supremacy; conferred upon the crown the powers of the supreme head but not the title; required all holders of office in church and state to take an oath acknowledging the queen's headship and denying the spiritual jurisdiction of any foreign prince; and imposed severe penalties on those who should maintain any foreign authority against that of the queen. The Act of Uniformity fixed the form of worship and in some part defined the doctrine of the church. It established the prayer book of 1552 slightly modified, and enjoined its use throughout the kingdom. The alterations were in the direction of moderation and designed to make it acceptable to the moderate elements. The penalties for failure to use the new services were heavy, but laymen who failed to attend them were required only to pay one shilling a Sunday, and nothing was said against attending other services. Later the doctrine of the church was further defined by the thirty-nine articles,[10] which were the forty-two articles of Edward VI revised to be less extremely Protestant. The settlement was not satisfactory to the extreme Catholics on the one side or to the extreme Protestants on the other, but it placed the English church on broad middle ground.

---

[9] Bayne, "First House of Commons of Queen Elizabeth," *Eng. Hist. Rev.,* xxiii, 455–476, 643–682.

[10] Accepted by convocation in 1562 and enacted by parliament in 1571.

CHAPTER XIX

EXTERNAL RELATIONS UNDER ELIZABETH

IN THE field of foreign relations Elizabeth faced at the outset a delicate situation. Mary Stuart, the queen of Scotland, was now married Philip II
to Francis, heir to the throne of France. Scotland was being ruled by
her mother, Mary of Guise, with French troops and in the French
interest. Mary, moreover, claimed the throne of England. According
to the law of the Roman church, Henry VIII had not been married
to Anne Boleyn because his marriage to Katherine of Aragon had
not been legally annulled. Elizabeth consequently was illegitimate.
Granted this claim, Mary Stuart was the lawful queen of England
because of her descent from Margaret, the sister of Henry VIII. The
claim appeared morally sound to Catholic Europe and seemed fair
to have the political backing of France. The prospect disturbed Philip
II as well as Elizabeth. He did not wish England lost to Catholicism,
but he did not wish it restored to the political advantage of his French
rival. In 1559 he sought to avert both calamities by suing for Elizabeth's hand. This forced upon Elizabeth one of the most critical decisions of her reign. Her acceptance would bring protection against
the Franco-Scottish danger, but it would also place England under a
Spanish Catholic domination which would be distasteful to Englishmen. Her rejection of the offer was likely to cause Philip to stand aside
should France carry out any hostile project against England, and
might bring about a Habsburg-Valois alliance against England. Elizabeth, deciding between a government based on national support and
one sustained by foreign aid, declined the honor.

A few months later the Franco-Scottish danger became acute. In
1559 a treaty terminated the war between France and Spain, leaving Franco-
France free to aid Mary Stuart in her projects against Elizabeth. In Scottish
the same year Francis II, Mary's husband, became king of France. danger
Since he was only fifteen, his advisers controlled the government. Two
of the most influential were members of the house of Guise, brothers
of the regent of Scotland and uncles of the queen of France. Under
their aggressive leadership the danger of a French invasion of England
by land from Scotland in behalf of Mary Stuart's claim to the English
crown became imminent.

From this danger Elizabeth was saved by an anti-Franco-Catholic movement in Scotland. The leader of the Reformation in Scotland was the rigid and austere John Knox, who stamped the movement with Calvinism. Alongside of this religious manifestation there developed a national sentiment directed against French domination. Since the French government of Scotland was intolerant of Protestantism, the opposition united. In 1559 the Scots rose in rebellion and sought aid from Elizabeth. The invitation offered to Elizabeth escape from a grave danger, but it was not without risks of its own. Its acceptance would make England stand out as the champion of the Protestant cause, and might provoke Catholic retaliation. So far Philip II had remained neutral, but this might throw him into the arms of France. Elizabeth also hesitated to establish the precedent of rendering aid to subjects in rebellion against their ruler. She finally agreed in 1560 to help the Scots drive the French from Scotland but not to overthrow their sovereign. The combined English and Scottish army was successful against the French troops of the regent. The French king meanwhile found himself occupied at home with the premonitory outbreaks of the religious wars that were to devastate France for years to come. Mary Stuart was forced to treat. By the Treaty of Edinburgh her agent agreed that the French should be withdrawn from Scotland except 120 soldiers, and that Francis and Mary would omit the arms of England from their quarterings. Subsequently a Scottish parliament abolished the papal power in Scotland and established a Protestant church.

So far as England was concerned, the result of chief importance was the creation of a feeling of common interest between the peoples of England and Scotland as opposed to the nations of the continent. It lessened but did not end the French danger, because Francis and Mary refused to ratify the treaty. Near the close of 1560, however, Francis II died. He was succeeded by his brother from whose councils the Guises were temporarily excluded. A French attack upon England in their interest was no longer a possibility. Mary Stuart found herself in France merely a helpless widow, and early in 1561 she therefore returned to Scotland to occupy the throne as ruling queen.

Elizabeth, freed from any immediate danger of attack from France, soon took the aggressive in that quarter. In 1562 the French Protestants rose in rebellion and appealed to her for help. Influenced by the hope of weakening the Catholic party in France which was hostile to England and by the dream of recovering Calais, she sent English troops to France. They were of little help to the French Protestants, and Elizabeth's claim to Calais became a source of embarrassment to them.

War with France, 1562–1564

They were so dissatisfied, indeed, that after the war was ended by a compromise which conceded to the Protestants a certain amount of toleration, they united with the Catholics to force the English to leave the country. The attempt to conquer French territory was a serious mistake.

Soon after this disastrous war was ended by treaty in 1564, Mary Stuart became for the second time a menace to Elizabeth. When she first came back to Scotland, such a possibility seemed remote. She came to rule a turbulent and half-rebellious people whose sympathies were Protestant and English. She was, however, endowed with a brilliant and talented mind and with a beauty which fascinated and captivated all with whom she came in contact. For a time she devoted herself to winning the good will of her subjects. She kept her religion a private matter, and by playing skillfully on the national feeling and on differences among the Protestants she secured some measure of success. At the same time she was arranging for her marriage with Lord Darnley which took place in 1565. He was a Catholic subject who had the royal blood of England in his veins. The marriage strengthened Mary's position as a claimant to the English throne, and it was a bid for support from the Catholic nations of the continent. That such support might be forthcoming was beginning to appear highly probable. After 1559, when the war between Habsburg and Valois ended, religion began to take the place of dynastic considerations as the basis of groupings of powers. Europe began to divide into Protestant and Catholic camps. The Catholics, moreover, were being moved toward a militant union by the spirit of the Counter-Reformation. If they should form such a combination, England, the most powerful Protestant state, would be the enemy, and Mary Stuart would become the instrument by which England might be brought back to the faith.

Mary Stuart

The Counter-Reformation was a reform of the Catholic church from within. Though it did not culminate in militant Catholicism until the decade of the sixties, it had been growing for a long time. Contemporaneously with the Lutheran revolt many devout Catholics who saw the abuses of which the Protestants complained sought to eliminate them without departing from the church. They made little progress until the papacy took the leadership of the movement. Beginning in 1555 the popes were reformers. Some were mild and conciliatory and some were bigoted and unyielding, but all were leaders of the project to clean the Catholic house and to force its departed occupants to return. The movement was given its charter by the Coun-

The Counter-Reforma- tion

cil of Trent. The assembly had been summoned originally at the instigation of Charles V to effect a compromise with the Lutheran Protestants. Interrupted by wars and the plague, it sat intermittently from
1545 to 1563. So far as its original purpose was concerned it was a
complete failure. It defined the doctrines of the church in such a way
as to make them more unacceptable to the Protestants than ever. It
declared the tradition of the church to have equal authority with the
Bible, denied faith alone to be sufficient for salvation, and reasserted
the doctrine of the seven sacraments more strongly than before. It
did, however, accomplish the reform of the church by decrees to improve the discipline of the clergy and to remedy the abuses. In its
closing years an aggressive spirit pervaded its sessions. As a result of
its work the church stood forth reformed, under united leadership, as
the militant foe of Protestantism.

The
Jesuits

The war against the Protestants was waged in part by propagandist
and missionary methods. In this field the papacy received efficient aid
from the Jesuits. The Society of Jesus had been established in 1540
by Ignatius Loyola. He was a Spaniard whose successful career as a
soldier had been ended by a wound in his leg. During a long con-
valescence he became interested in devotional literature, began to
follow ascetic practices, resolved to become a monk, and eventually
decided to establish a new order of his own. The Jesuits took the oath
of chastity, poverty, and obedience like the monks, but like the friars
lived in the world among men. Their primary object soon came to
be the propagation of the faith among the infidels, the Protestants,
and the wavering among the Catholics. The spirit of the order, given
to it by the soldier who was its founder, was essentially militant. It
was organized with military precision and practically with military
discipline. The head of the order had absolute power, and every member owed unquestioning obedience to the orders of the superior next
above him. In Europe the order worked with the upper rather than
with the lower social classes, and its members were carefully selected
for that object. Only men of intellectual ability, physical fitness, and
strong personality were taken. Every member had to have the best
education obtainable before he could enter the most active service.
During the second half of the sixteenth century the Jesuits became
influential in all of the Catholic countries of Europe. They not only
became the principal moving force in the church, but they also won
places in royal courts and exerted a profound influence on the political
affairs of Europe.

The leaders of the Counter-Reformation, however, envisaged more than propaganda against the Protestants. Since it was still deemed possible to change the religion of a people by changing the religion of a ruler, wars for thrones appeared to offer the most effective means of recovering the lands won by the Protestants. The secular leadership needed for this task was sought in Spain. Centuries of warfare against the Mohammedans had given to the Spaniards a reputation as perpetual crusaders, and they had been the first of the Catholic nations to reform the abuses in their own church. The Spaniards accepted with pride the position of the instruments of God chosen to defend the Catholic religion in Europe. Philip II, their king, found the lay leadership of the Counter-Reformation so congenial that eventually it became more important to him than all his dominions. Before he could stand forth in that capacity, however, a diplomatic revolution had to be accomplished. The first step toward it was taken in 1565 at a conference held at Bayonne between Catherine de' Medici, queen regent of France, and an agent of Philip. What took place at the interview was kept secret, but it was accepted generally in Europe as marking the termination of the Habsburg-Valois rivalry and the beginning of a Franco-Spanish alliance directed particularly against Protestants, English, French, and Dutch. To England the interview seemed to portend the union of France and Spain in armed support of the claims of Mary Stuart.

Diplomatic revolution

From this possibility Elizabeth was saved by events which occurred in three different countries. In the Netherlands the popular opposition to Philip and to his policy of religious persecution broke into revolt in 1566. Philip had to despatch Spanish troops, and his attention was diverted from England. In the next year the religious wars were renewed in France, and they continued intermittently until 1570. Most spectacular and most important was the downfall of Mary Stuart in Scotland.

Protestant revolts

Mary's disaster was the result of her own weakness. After her marriage she threw off the mask and began to play the Catholic game openly, alienating many of her Protestant subjects whose support she had won by her earlier policy. But Darnley proved to be a broken reed. He was a vain, dissolute, idle, and jealous fool. He treated Mary brutally, helping no whit in her negotiations with Catholic powers. Mary, forced to rely on some other adviser, came to depend on David Rizzio, her secretary, and one of the few Catholics in her entourage. Darnley, rendered insanely jealous and spurred to the act by the Protestant lords of Mary's court, murdered Rizzio almost before Mary's eyes. A hollow reconciliation followed. During the interval of peace

The fall of Mary Stuart

Mary gave birth to a son, the future James VI of Scotland. Darnley, however, did not cease his disgraceful behavior, and Mary began to seek help from one of her council who was a loyal supporter, the earl of Bothwell. Abused by her husband, she fell violently in love with the bold, reckless nobleman. There were obstacles in the way of a marriage, for Mary had a husband and Bothwell had a wife. The first was removed by murder. Darnley's house was blown up and he was found strangled. Of Bothwell's participation there was no doubt, and, while Mary's complicity has never been proved, her subsequent protection of Bothwell served to strengthen the widespread popular belief in her guilt. Shortly afterward Bothwell seized Mary, taking her to a refuge, where she remained until he had completed the process of divorce from his wife. They then returned to Edinburgh where they were married by Protestant rites.

These events ended Mary's career. She could no longer expect help from Catholic Europe, and the Scots were turned against her almost to a man. The Protestant lords easily defeated Bothwell's forces, put him to flight, and captured Mary. She was forced to abdicate in favor of her infant son and placed in confinement. In 1568 a conspiracy enabled her to escape, but she failed to recover the throne, and sought refuge in England. Elizabeth did not wish to surrender Mary to her Protestant foes and still less did she wish to aid her rival against them. Eventually she placed the deposed queen in a guarded castle, where she remained imprisoned for the rest of her life. Thus Elizabeth was saved from the gravest danger she had yet faced.

Flight to England

Mary Stuart proved to be hardly less dangerous in prison than she had been when free. Her captivity was followed in 1569 by a rebellion of the English Catholics who sought to arrange a marriage between her and the duke of Norfolk, to place him and Mary on the throne, and thus to restore Catholicism in England. The earls who were its leaders were dissatisfied with their small share in the government and the overweening influence of Cecil, whom they regarded as an upstart, but they were actuated mainly by religious motives, and these served as the only inspiration of their followers, who came mainly from the northern counties. Philip's ambassador in England encouraged the plotters, who hoped for the support of Spanish troops from the Netherlands. The rebellion hardly came to a head before it collapsed. Many Catholics refused to rise against their lawful ruler, the rebels failed to release Mary, and Spanish help did not materialize. The leaders fled, leaving their followers to Elizabeth's vengeance. They were hunted down in every village of the north and executed. Nor

Rising of the Earls

did the leaders escape the same fate, for the regent of Scotland captured them and turned them over to Elizabeth. Thus ended the last of the reactionary rebellions of the English Catholics begun with the Pilgrimage of Grace.

In 1570 the Catholics struck another blow. The pope excommunicated Elizabeth and secured the publication of the bull in England. Had he taken the action earlier, it might have had more serious consequences, since the bull declared Elizabeth deposed and absolved Catholic subjects from their allegiance to her. As it was, the act served only to embitter the English feeling against the Catholics. It was followed in the next year by the Ridolfi plot. Ridolfi was an Italian banker in England, who was secretly an agent of the pope. The plan was much the same as that of the preceding rebellion. Norfolk, who had saved his head by deserting the rebels, was to marry Mary, and they were to be placed on the throne by armed intervention from abroad. The pope and Philip II gave their adherence. Cecil discovered the plot in its early stages, allowed it to mature till he had all the threads in his hands, and then struck. The Spanish ambassador was dismissed and Norfolk and other implicated nobles were executed. Parliament, convinced that Elizabeth's life was not safe so long as Mary lived, clamored for her execution also, but Elizabeth held back. Thereafter plots temporarily ceased, and for a time Elizabeth was able to keep Philip busy on the continent.

Excommunication and plot

During the period which lasts from 1570 to about 1584 Philip gradually emerged as England's chief enemy. For many years the hostility was kept under cover because neither side was prepared to come to open war. In 1572 the Dutch again revolted, and Philip desired to recover control of the Netherlands before he attacked England. As long as Mary Stuart lived, moreover, it always seemed possible that she might be placed upon the throne of England by the simple process of Elizabeth's assassination, and England restored to the Catholic fold without the necessity of a war of conquest. Elizabeth held back largely because she dreaded war. Time and again her councilors urged her to take advantage of a favorable diplomatic situation or of Philip's embarrassments to unite the Protestants in a war against Spain. But Elizabeth went her own way. She used her diplomatic arts to detach France from Spain, gave secret aid to the Dutch rebels, and damaged Philip's interests wherever she could do it in an underhanded manner without giving to Philip an actual *casus belli*.

Rise of the Spanish enemy

Elizabeth's relations with France depended upon the rise and fall of factions at the court of the French king. One group, led by the

Guises, sought the suppression of Protestantism in France and favored close relations with Spain. The Protestants were opposed to Spain and favored England and the Dutch. In 1570 a peace caused a temporary cessation of the religious wars in France, giving the leaders of the Protestants opportunity to gain the ear of the king, who was beginning in his weak way to resent the Spanish influence in the internal affairs of France. With the rise of the Protestant influence the danger of a united attack upon England by France and Spain waned. Elizabeth took advantage of the situation to flirt with one of the king's brothers, whom she kept dangling until 1572, when she secured from France a treaty of defensive alliance. The restoration of Catholic influence in the council of the king and the revival of the religious wars soon rendered this diplomatic victory temporarily valueless, but the rise of a third party made possible a more successful attempt to detach France from Spain. A group of French Catholics, who cared more for France than for militant Catholicism, organized to oppose the Guises and the Spanish influence. In 1578 Elizabeth began a flirtation with the duke of Anjou, another brother of the king, who was influential with this group and favorable to French intervention in behalf of the Dutch. She played the game so well, that she persuaded Anjou to accept the governorship of the Netherlands and to commit France to the Dutch cause against Philip.

To the Dutch rebels Elizabeth was friendly because the continuance of their rebellion was the chief safeguard against a Spanish attack upon England. She helped them secretly, but was not prepared to come openly to their aid lest she should provoke Philip to attack England. In 1579 the Dutch cause was rendered critical by dissension among themselves. The southern provinces, which were Catholic, formed one union, and the northern provinces, which were Protestant, another. This was the expression of a division that resulted eventually in the modern Belgium and United Netherlands. The immediate result was to restore Spanish control in the Catholic south. Only the seven northern provinces of the United Netherlands were left to keep up the struggle against Spain. They seemed doomed to failure unless they secured outside aid, and it was this crisis which caused Elizabeth to flirt so desperately with Anjou. The French aid which he was finally induced to bring proved of little worth, and in 1584 his death deprived Elizabeth of the last hope that France might pull her chestnuts out of the fire. In the same year, William of Orange, who was the heart and soul of the Dutch resistance, was assassinated. Deprived both of his leadership and of French aid, the Dutch cause seemed hopeless.

By this time Philip's score against Elizabeth was so long that his conquest of the Netherlands was almost certain to be followed by the invasion of England. Elizabeth therefore abandoned her policy of peace. In 1585 she sent English troops to aid the Dutch.

While these continental developments had been bringing the enmity between Elizabeth and Philip into the open, popular feeling against Spain in England had been brought to fever heat. In this development the English Catholics had no small part. Beginning in 1569 they became active against Elizabeth politically. During the next decade they fell under foreign influence to an extent that branded Catholicism in the popular thought as anti-national. Seminaries were established on the continent to train English Catholics for the priesthood. Several Englishmen availed themselves of the opportunity. Later they returned to England to strengthen the Catholics in their resistance and to win Protestants back to the fold. They were not a serious political menace until 1580, when two Jesuits came to England and began to plot with the Spanish ambassador under the aegis of Philip and the Guises to place Mary on the throne. From that time Catholic plots were continually being hatched. Some had as their method a rebellion aided by foreign invasion, while others sought their object by the simpler mode of Elizabeth's assassination. None of the plots succeeded because of the watchful care of Walsingham, Elizabeth's secretary. Through a secret service he laid bare the plots, and in 1583 and 1584 he arrested several of the conspirators. The news of the plots, coming together with the report of the successful assassination of William of Orange, stirred Englishmen to a fury. They formed a voluntary association to protect the queen and to avenge attempts on her life. The association was legalized by parliament in 1584. As Philip stood forth ever more clearly as the head of militant Catholicism in Europe, this rage against the Catholics mingled with the growing hatred of Spain, until patriotism became nearly synonymous with a desire to fight Spain.

The plots culminated in one led by Anthony Babington. Walsingham, who knew of the plot soon after its inception, let it develop until he had full proof of the guilt of the leading conspirators. Philip had approved the plan, and among the plotters was Mary Stuart. The announcement was made in 1586. It was accepted as a convincing demonstration of the national opinion that Elizabeth's life could not be safe as long as Mary lived. Parliament requested Elizabeth to order Mary's execution. She vacillated long, but finally signed the warrant in 1587. The council then executed the warrant, without making the time known to Elizabeth for fear she would countermand it. With

Marginal notes:

Catholic plots

Execution of Mary Stuart

characteristic meanness Elizabeth tried to throw responsibility for the act on the secretary of the council, whom she dismissed. To England the execution of Mary Stuart meant the climax of the national feeling in favor of Elizabeth and against Spain. To Philip II it meant that the only way left to recover England for Catholicism was to resort to arms.

The Tudor seamen

Still another reason which made war with England desirable to Philip was the necessity of protecting his sea route to the wealth of the Americas. The Tudor seamen had broken the monopoly of trade which Spain attempted to maintain with her colonies, plundered and pillaged Spanish settlements in the new world, and robbed and sunk the Spanish galleons that bore the rich treasures of the new world to the old.

Maritime enterprise under Henry VIII

England's sea power had developed slowly. In the initial voyages of discovery the Cabots gave England a share, but these beginnings were not followed up immediately. The failure of these early voyages to yield profit discouraged private ventures, and Henry VIII was too busy with other affairs to give much attention to oceanic enterprise. Early in the day, moreover, Portugal and Spain, with papal sanction, claimed monopolies of the exploration and trade of the most desirable portions of the newly discovered lands in the east and the west.[1] Since the rich trade of the far east was the goal of all voyages of discovery in this period, the possession by Portugal of the route by way of the Cape of Good Hope and by Spain of the routes to the west and southwest tended to retard English attempts at exploration. In the reign of Henry VIII, however, two expeditions sought to discover a new route to the east by sailing to the northwest, and William Hawkins and other sea captains made voyages to Brazil, where they traded profitably with the natives in defiance of the Portuguese monopoly. On one of these voyages a Spanish ship laden with gold and precious stones was attacked and captured. Thereby a precedent was set which the Elizabethan seamen did not allow to fall into oblivion.

The northern explorations

About the middle of the century English capitalists began energetically and persistently to seek a share of the trade of the lands beyond Europe. In 1553 a strong company was formed to seek a new route to the east by sailing northeast. A fleet of three ships was fitted out and placed under the command of Sir Hugh Willoughby, with Richard Chancellor second in authority. Willoughby and his whole crew were caught in the arctic winter and perished of cold, but Chancellor

---

[1] For a critical treatment of the line of demarcation between the Portuguese and Spanish monopolies, see Harrisse, H., *Diplomatic History of America* (London, 1897).

entered the White Sea, landed near Archangel, and established profitable commercial relations with Russia, which was then a land little known to western Europe. In the reign of Elizabeth a further effort was made to reach Asia by the northeast, and the project of a northwestern passage was revived by the voyages which left the names of Frobisher and Davis prominent on the map of North America. These voyages did much to develop the skill, hardihood, and courage of English sailors, but they demonstrated that ice blocked the route to the east by way of the north.

Long before the exploration of the northern routes was abandoned as hopeless, English merchants and sailors had begun to seek the greater profits to be derived from an invasion of the monopolies of Portugal and Spain. William Hawkins had pointed the way, and in the reign of Edward VI English expeditions began to trade with the natives of western Africa. The Portuguese offered armed resistance to this invasion of their monopoly, and before the close of the first decade of Elizabeth's reign the warfare necessary to conduct the trade so reduced the profits that it ceased to attract adventurers. Meanwhile, Sir John Hawkins, the son of William, had begun the invasion of the Spanish monopoly of the west. In 1562 he collected a cargo of Negroes on the western coast of Africa, carried them to the West Indies, and sold them as slaves to the Spanish colonists. The first venture was so profitable that others followed. When the Spanish government forbade the trade, Hawkins began to overawe the colonial governors by display of armed force, in order to dispose of his cargoes to the colonists who were eager to buy them. In 1568 his fleet, while in a port on the Spanish main, was treacherously attacked by a larger Spanish fleet, whose commander had guaranteed his peaceful departure. The pitched battle which followed inflicted great injury upon both fleets, and it put an end to the attempt to trade peacefully with the Spanish colonies in America.

The English sailors, however, did not cease to seek the wealth which they had discovered was to be had on the Spanish main. They merely changed their tactics and began to seize Spanish treasure by armed force in reprisal for the monopoly maintained by Spain. They soon learned that they were superior to the Spaniards in naval skill, and with daring recklessness they plundered treasure-ships and sacked the Spanish colonies in America. Most remarkable of all were the exploits of Sir Francis Drake, whose deeds of boldness culminated with his voyage around the world. Starting from England in 1577 with five small ships, Drake sailed through the Strait of Magellan and up the

Marginal notes:

Invasion of Portuguese and Spanish monopolies

Warfare of armed reprisals

western coast of America, where no Englishman had been before. He took one Spanish port after another, robbed it of its accumulated treasure, and sailed away. When he reached the coast of California, he dared not return the way he had come. Sailing west, he circumnavigated the globe, returning to England in 1580 with one surviving ship laden with fabulous wealth. Expeditions of this type were pure piracy judged by modern standards, and some were no better when measured by the vaguer definitions of the sixteenth century. But they were not regarded as reprehensible by contemporary Englishmen. Elizabeth, striving to avoid war, did not sanction them openly, but she countenanced them secretly, while Englishmen generally looked upon them with increasing glee as the national hatred of Spain mounted. Philip II resented them deeply, but until he was ready to make war openly upon England, he could retaliate only in kind. When the Spaniards caught the English in their territory, they punished them for their infringement of the Spanish monopoly and turned them over to the inquisition to be tortured as heretics. The sufferings inflicted on English sailors by Spaniards was a favorite theme of the pamphleteers who were stirring to the dregs the cup of English bitterness against Spain. The English sea dogs themselves were actuated to undertake these piratical ventures by love of adventure and lust for gold, but they were moved also by a feeling that they were advancing the cause of their queen, their country, and their religion. "To break through the Catholic monopoly of the New World, to kill Spaniards, to sell negroes, to sack gold-ships, were in these men's minds a seemly work for the 'elect of God.' "[2] "For Queen and Country they would go anywhere and attempt anything."[3] Such were the men who, during Elizabeth's reign, were building England's power on the sea.

The results   Long before Elizabeth and her councilors were ready to fight Spain, the sea dogs had come to hate and despise the power of Spain on the sea, and they longed for the chance of open and avowed war. Their activities had produced a large body of thoroughly trained seamen ready to hand when the time should come. Their exploits had bred in the minds of Englishmen new conceptions of the importance of sea power, stimulated the growth of a new national spirit, and aroused a bitter hatred of Spain. Their success had been so great that Philip II had to conquer England or yield control of the sea.

Philip began in 1586 to prepare a fleet for an attack upon England.

---

[2] Green, *History of the English People*, iii, §801.

[3] Raleigh, *English Voyages of the Sixteenth Century*, p. 53.

The Armada was so large that it could not concentrate in one port.
Drake seized the opportunity to attack the portion in the port of
Cadiz, where he destroyed thirty-seven Spanish ships. He was anxious
to continue the process, asserting that he could prevent the Armada
from leaving Spain; but Elizabeth, who was still vacillating between
the necessity for war and her desire for peace, withheld her consent.
The Armada was finally ready to sail in the summer of 1588. It was
commanded by a landsman, who was a good general but knew nothing of naval tactics, because Philip II desired a commander who would
not oppose a knowledge of the sea to the detailed orders which he
wished to give. The fleet numbered 131 ships, but only 120 of them
reached the English Channel, and of these one-half were victualers
which took no part in the fight. Their tonnage was 60,000, and they
carried 25,000 men, though the effective fighting force was only 10,000
to 12,000.

To meet the Armada the English had 197 ships of about 30,000
tons burden. The majority of them were small ships supplied by
private enterprise. Only thirty-four belonged to the royal navy. Of
these ships some fifty never took part in the fight. The smaller English ships could be maneuvered more easily, and they offered less
easy targets than the high Spanish galleons. The commander was
Lord Howard, appointed in part because of his title, but he was assisted by experienced commanders like Frobisher, Hawkins, and
Drake from whom he did not scorn to take advice. The crews numbered only seven to eight thousand, but they were better sailors and
better gunners than the Spaniards. Their spirit was indomitable. Many
of them had fought and conquered Spanish ships. In their opinion,
"twelve of her majesty's ships were a match for all the galleys in the
king of Spain's dominions."

The fight began as soon as the Armada entered the Channel. The
purpose of the expedition was a combined attack by sea and land.
The Armada was under orders to sail through the Channel to Flanders, embark the Spanish troops there, and convey them across the
Channel to England. Consequently, when the English attacked, the
Armada maintained a running fight which lasted from Sunday to the
following Saturday, when the Spanish fleet reached the narrowest part
of the Channel and cast anchor. The English did not destroy many
of the Spanish ships, but they inflicted much damage, and their evident superiority gradually weakened the Spanish morale. When the
English sent fire ships among the anchored Spanish fleet, the Spaniards fell into such a panic that they did not stop to weigh anchors,

but cut their cables and ran before the wind. Their commander finally got a group of them up into the wind, and off Gravelines fought with the English the only significant battle of the whole series. Six Spanish ships were disabled or sunk and 4,000 Spaniards killed before the Armada fled north before the wind. The English fleet pursued until a storm arose ending all danger, whereupon Elizabeth, in a typical fit of parsimony, recalled it. The storm, however, finished what the fleet had begun. Many of the Spanish ships sank or ran aground, and only 65 of the 131 ships ever returned to Spain.

The victory was fraught with consequences of tremendous import. Upon Englishmen themselves the defeat of the foremost power in Europe had a profound influence. They ceased to look upon themselves as upon the defense and began to regard themselves as a chosen people. It called forth the spirit of a nation which had found itself, and this exuberant, aggressive national spirit is characteristic of Englishmen after 1588. Before Europe, England stood forth as the successful champion of Protestantism against Catholicism. It was a decisive defeat of the Counter-Reformation movement in its militant aspects, and everywhere in Europe it gave courage to the Protestant cause. It opened to Englishmen the road to commerce and to empire. None could now dispute their right to travel the oceanic highway. The humbling of the greatest power in America meant that North America was to be colonized by Englishmen and not by Spaniards. The day of Spain as a world power was done; the dawn of England's day was breaking.

The victory over the Armada decided England's supremacy, but it did not end the war. Burghley, who would have let well enough alone, naturally appealed to the queen, but Drake and many others of Elizabeth's court wished to follow the victory with an offensive against Spain. Under their urgent persuasion the queen gave way. In 1589 an expedition was sent to Spain to damage Spanish shipping and to attack Spanish ports. Its organization and despatch were thoroughly typical of Elizabeth's methods of business. Though the expedition was a national undertaking, two-thirds of the expense was borne by the commanders, of whom Drake was one, and such adventurers as they could persuade to subscribe. Elizabeth delayed its departure for weeks while she debated with her council the advisability of countermanding it, and the troops were forced to eat a large hole in their scanty store of supplies before they got under way. The expedition inflicted some damage on Portuguese and Spanish ports, but it ac-

Later
naval
warfare
against
Spain

complished much less than it might have done, had it not been short of ammunition, artillery, and equipment through the niggardliness of the queen. The fault was Elizabeth's, but with her usual ingratitude and inconsistency she visited the consequences on the commanders. The few prizes should have been distributed to the subscribers, according to the original agreement, but Elizabeth seized them all for herself and left Drake under a cloud of disfavor, until he was allowed to make the West Indian expedition that saw his death in 1595. After this fiasco no expedition was undertaken on the same scale for several years, but every year a small fleet was sent out to prey on Spanish commerce. Sometimes ships of the royal navy constituted the fleet; more often they were the ships of private adventurers. This sort of warfare was more congenial to Elizabeth, because it cost little and might bring large profits. It was on such an expedition that Sir Richard Grenville in command of the *Revenge* off the Azores fought single-handed against the whole Spanish fleet the battle famous in story and song. It was the only English vessel lost in all the naval warfare against Spain. In 1596 a naval expedition organized on a large scale burned Cadiz and destroyed the shipping in the harbor. Though the naval war continued into the reign of James, this was the last significant action. It was a forceful demonstration of England's naval superiority.

Throughout this period Elizabeth not only maintained naval warfare against Philip II, but she also assisted his enemies in the Netherlands and in France. The 6,000 soldiers whom she had sent to the aid of the Netherlands in 1585 were maintained with more or less regularity. Though their lack of training rendered them inefficient at first, in the course of time they developed into veterans and contributed to the ultimate attainment of Dutch independence.

War against Spain in France and Holland

In France the group of Catholics headed by the Guises and supported by Philip II began a war to exclude from the succession Henry of Navarre, the Protestant heir. In 1589, when Henry inherited the throne, he had little money and few troops. Elizabeth responded to his appeal for help in order to prevent Spanish domination of France. Every year thereafter until 1595, when Henry IV was securely established on the throne, Elizabeth sent English troops to France, though Henry's conversion to Catholicism in 1593 strained relations somewhat. Aid "was given by Elizabeth grudgingly, followed up inadequately, its value diminished by delay, vacillation, poor equipment, and unwise restriction; its morale was low and its support from home indifferent."[4] Even so, it came at a critical time, and was of no small importance to the national cause of France led by Henry IV.

The final attempt of Philip II to retaliate for the many blows given by England was made through Ireland. To estimate its significance it is necessary to review the Irish policy of the Tudors after Henry VII. Henry VIII ended the rule of the Irish Pale by the earls of Kildare and placed it under English deputies. Though he made no attempt to conquer lands outside the Pale, he made agreements with several of the tribal leaders, and he tried to extend English customs to the native district by law and precept. The reigns of Edward VI and Mary saw the institution of a new policy which ultimately had important effects on Irish history. Early in Edward's reign some native Irish tribes on the border of the Pale broke into revolt. When they had been subdued, it was suggested that the territories of the rebels be colonized with English or Anglo-Irish as a means of Anglicizing the native Irish. An act passed by the English parliament in 1557 confiscated the land of the rebels to the crown and provided for its regrant to English settlers and to native Irish in the proportion of two-thirds and one-third. This was the small beginning of a policy subsequently followed on a large scale.

Irish policy, 1509–1558

Elizabeth attempted to maintain in Ireland the policy of her father. But Henry VIII had found it difficult to finance his policy, and Elizabeth's income was more slender than his. The Irish revenues did not suffice to maintain the small armed force kept for purposes of police in time of peace. During her reign, consequently, the governors of Ireland instituted a new mode of taxation called cess. The lord deputy would issue orders to the officers of the army, authorizing them to seize provisions and supplies at prices fixed by the officers below the market values. Eventually cess was extended to include the quartering of soldiers on the country. The Anglo-Irish of the Pale resented cess as taxation imposed upon them without their consent. They were also aggrieved at their exclusion from the government of the Pale. Thus, while the policy of colonization was arousing hostility among the native Irish, the imposition of cess and their exclusion from the government were evoking the complaints of the Anglo-Irish.

Elizabeth's policies

These grievances were producing among the native Irish and the Anglo-Irish a spirit of opposition to English rule, but they were not sufficient to overcome the traditional hostility between the native Irish and the Anglo-Irish and produce common action against England. The bond of a common interest was supplied by a common grievance

Religious grievance

---

[4] Cheyney, *History of England from the Defeat of the Armada,* i, 305.

about religion. The religious changes in England previous to Elizabeth's reign awakened but faint echoes in Ireland. The successive alterations were introduced into the Pale, but beyond that they did not extend, and even there they were not thoroughly established. They caused no strong opposition until they were seized upon by the papacy as a means to embarrass Elizabeth. In 1561 the pope sent an agent to Ireland to arouse zeal for the faith and opposition to Elizabeth's ecclesiastical policy. The response was so enthusiastic that other agents followed, and a systematic propaganda was maintained in behalf of the Catholic faith and against the Protestant government of England.

In 1569 the movement culminated in rebellion. The leader of the Anglo-Irish rebels alleged as the reason for his rebellion the command of the pope to deprive Elizabeth of her kingdom. Before the warfare was ended, he formed alliances with several tribes of the native Irish. He also had the support of the pope and received some aid from Philip II. The rebellion lasted intermittently until 1583. It never seriously threatened the English supremacy in Ireland, because some of the Anglo-Irish fought against the rebels. But the union of Anglo-Irish with native Irish under the protection of a foreigner, made possible by the displacement of political grievances by religious, was an alarming portent. To foreign powers Ireland offered a weak spot in England's armor. Philip's early attempt to utilize it was an additional cause for the war with Spain.

Rebellions, 1569-1583

After the victory over the Armada the danger from Ireland became acute. Philip II began to plot with the many dissatisfied Irish leaders, and in 1598 the discontent broke into rebellion. The insurrection, which was led by the O'Neills of Ulster, was national in its scope. England had never before had to meet such widespread and well-organized resistance in Ireland. The Spanish were so slow in sending assistance that the back of the Irish revolt was broken before 5,000 Spanish troops arrived in 1601. The English consequently were able to settle separately with the Spanish, and then to quell the natives in detail. The last of the rebellion was crushed only in 1603, just after the death of Elizabeth. The result was the first real conquest of Ireland by the English. So extensive was the scope of the war that it cost Elizabeth during the last four years of her reign one-third more than her revenues. It also prepared the way for a wholesale extension of the policy of colonization in the time of her successor, James I. Elizabeth carried the policy of Irish conquest further than any of her predecessors, but in her reign were planted the seeds of Irish nationalism which were to bear bitter fruit in the seventeenth century.

The rebellion of 1598–1603

CHAPTER XX

ELIZABETHAN ENGLAND

Internal develop-ments

THOUGH it was in Elizabeth's time that England faced triumphantly manifold dangers of foreign attack, smote the might of Spain, made the sea her own, and opened wide the highroad to empire, these are but the half that make her reign notable in the annals of English history. Under Elizabeth's guidance the new church, established by the government, was adopted as its own by the nation. For long radical Protestants and Catholics did not cease their opposition, but in the closing years of the reign religious controversies were tempo-rarily stilled. Anglican and Separatist were destined at a later day to carry their dispute to the field of battle, but that day had not yet dawned when Elizabeth's reign closed, and the danger of warfare between English Protestant and English Catholic, with which the reign opened, had long since passed away. The economic depression that ushered in her reign slowly lifted. When the queen ended her work, commerce and industry were thriving and wealth had increased enormously. New and better houses, furniture, clothes, and material comforts of all sorts were becoming evident on every hand. Before the national prosperity the social disorder gradually subsided. During her reign the Renaissance ripened such fruits as had never previously grown in the garden of English literature. Under the queen's wise direction the nation was brought back from the brink of anarchy where Mary had placed it, popular confidence in the monarchy was restored, and Englishmen developed a national feeling of such depth and strength as they had never experienced before.

Penal laws against Catholics

The salient characteristic of the Elizabethan religious settlement was its moderation. The government did not grant freedom of wor-ship, though the penalties for non-conformity were mild, but it did not attempt to coerce the religious beliefs of laymen. Only those who aided foreigners against England were heavily penalized. As the reign progressed, the lines dividing the established church from the Cath-olics on the one side and from the extreme Protestants on the other tended to become more sharply defined. The severity of the legisla-tion against the Catholics increased as the political danger from the Catholics grew. Moved to anger by the rising of the earls, the bull of excommunication, and the Ridolfi plot, parliament in 1571 made it treason to declare that the queen was not or ought not to be queen, or to bring into England a papal bull. Importers of articles blessed by the pope were subjected to severe penalties, and Catholics who had fled to the continent were ordered to return within six months under pain of confiscation of their property. These laws were directed against the political activities of the Catholics. Cecil could still maintain that "there shall be no colour or occasion to shed the blood of any of her Majesty's subjects that shall only profess devotion to their religion without bending their labours maliciously to disturb the common quiet of the realm."[1] The activities of the secular priests in the decade of the seventies, followed by those of the Jesuits and the resultant outbreak of new plots, roused the nation to a frenzy that brought a crop of savage laws. In 1581 it was made treason to attempt to convert a subject of the queen to the Catholic faith, the saying or hearing of mass was forbidden under severe penalties, and Catholic recusants —that is, those who did not attend the established church—were fined £20 a month. These laws constituted the first serious attack on the Catholic religion as such. Four years later Jesuits were banished from the realm on pain of death. The series was completed in 1593 by acts requiring poor Catholic recusants to abjure the realm, and requiring those wealthy enough to pay the fine not to travel more than five miles from their homes.

In this penal legislation Elizabeth had her hand forced by the nation. Her general attitude toward the Catholics was lenient. The exigencies of political dangers compelled her to accept these stringent measures, but council and parliament forced her farther and faster than she desired to go. She tempered the wind to the Catholics, moreover, by enforcing the penal legislation laxly. During her reign the Catholics who suffered the extreme penalty were with few exceptions guilty of opposition to the government which might well be adjudged treason under the modern definition of that term.[2] Not a tithe of those who incurred the extreme penalty under the legislation of 1581 were executed. Neither were the laws against Catholic recusants executed strictly. The letter of the law was harsher than the practice, and the government remained more tolerant toward the Catholics than did the nation.

Though the Protestants were less dangerous to Elizabeth than were the Catholics, they became during the reign a menace to the established church and to the power of the crown. At the outset many

---

[1] Quoted by Klein, *Intolerance in the Reign of Elizabeth*, p. 39.
[2] *Ibid.*, pp. 50–52.

**Puritans
and
Separatists**

Protestants felt that the settlement did not depart far enough from
the Roman church. They wanted to purify the church of those aspects
of its ritual or organization which savored of Catholicism and were
not justified by their interpretation of the Bible. Foremost among
them were the Protestants who had gone into exile in Mary's reign.
Across the Channel they had come into contact with Calvinism and
had come to regard the prayer book of Edward VI as far too mod-
erately Protestant. These radical Protestants, who sought what they
deemed greater purity, began early in Elizabeth's reign to be called
Puritans. In the course of the reign two groups developed among
them. The members of one remained in the new church and endeavored to secure the alterations in its service and organization which
they desired. The members of the other attempted to set up separate
congregations where they could worship as they pleased independently
of the established church. Those of the latter group were also called
Separatists.

**Vestiarian
contro-
versy**

In the early years of Elizabeth's reign the Puritans belonged almost
entirely to the former group. They directed their attention primarily
to outward forms and ceremonies which they thought retained too
much from the unreformed church. The vestments of the clergy and
such practices as the use of the cross in baptism and kneeling at communion evoked their criticism. In 1563 those who sought reform were
defeated in convocation by a single vote. Subsequently it became common for each priest to conduct the service in his own church as he
saw fit. The practice, which was contrary to the Act of Uniformity,
caused Parker, archbishop of Canterbury, to issue a set of rules for
the conduct of worship. The attempt to enforce them secured general
outward conformity without causing the resignation of great numbers of the clergy, but it embittered the Puritans. Unable to reform
the church or to remain in it without conformity, some of the Puritans
took to more radical courses.

**Presby-
terians
and
Separatists**

Some began to hold assemblies, called conventicles, where they
worshiped by rites other than those prescribed in the prayer book.
Another group, whose leading exponent came to be Thomas Cartwright, at one time a professor at Cambridge, began to oppose the
episcopal organization as Catholic, and to advocate the adoption by
the English church of the Calvinistic or Presbyterian system. Both
of these movements threatened the established church. The latter was
also a serious menace to the control of the church by the state, for
it was characteristic of the Presbyterian organization to attempt to
manage the state. To meet these manifestations Elizabeth issued a

proclamation against conventicles (1573) and stirred up the prelates to greater zeal in the enforcement of the Act of Uniformity. With the appointment of Whitgift to the archbishopric of Canterbury in 1583, the policy of suppression was accelerated. Though he was partial to Calvinistic doctrines, he had no sympathy for the Presbyterian ecclesiastical organization, and he believed in rigid conformity. He began to use the court of high commission, which Elizabeth had appointed to exercise her powers of supreme headship, to carry out a vigorous repressive policy. By that time not only were some of the Presbyterians beginning to maintain separate assemblies for worship, but there had also appeared a still more radical group of Separatists, called after their leader, Robert Browne, who were the forerunners of the Independents. The Brownists preached that each congregation should have power to settle its own ecclesiastical government and observance. Such doctrine was utterly subversive of a state church. Indeed, it was too democratic for the safety of the monarchical principle itself. With the increase of radicalism on one side and of intolerance on the other the controversy became so violent that sober men were alarmed. Parliament, which had generally favored the Puritans, came to the support of the queen. In 1593 it passed an act against conventicles. Frequenters of such meetings were to be imprisoned for the first offense and banished for the second. If any who were banished should afterward appear in England they were to be executed as felons. This act accomplished its purpose temporarily. Some of the Separatists were punished, some went into exile, and the remainder subsided. Even those Puritans whom the act did not affect held their peace. In Elizabeth's last years there was a lull in the controversy between the church and the extreme Protestants, though it proved to be the calm that goes before the storm.

In economic and social affairs Elizabeth faced the same problems that had baffled the government in the reign of Edward VI. Prices still soared, debased coins circulated, enclosures increased, and poverty, vagabondage, and crime continued. Elizabeth and her advisers saw no less clearly than Henry VII that the popularity essential for a successful strong monarchy was dependent upon the economic welfare of the people, and they understood full well that the fleets, the armies, the fortifications, the armament, and the equipment necessary for the successful repulse of the ever-impending foreign invasion could be obtained only through such taxes and contributions as a prosperous people could pay. Both choice and necessity led Elizabeth and her ministers to grapple with the pressing problems of industry, com-

National regulation of economic and social affairs

merce, and social welfare. The national regulation of economic and
social conditions was favored by still other factors. The local regulation of the gilds was by now quite thoroughly broken down. The
decay of the gilds had been aided by the dissolution of the chantries[3]
which deprived some of the industrial gilds of part of their funds,
but in the main it was caused by the continuance of economic and
social conditions already evident in the time of Henry VII.[4] Had
the craft gilds retained their pristine vigor, they could hardly have
coped with the new conditions of business. They had no place in a
new economic order based on large-scale capitalistic enterprise, far-
flung markets, and keen competition among rival nations. The nation, moreover, was alive to the situation. The inadequacy of local
regulations was apparent, and the growing consciousness of a national
unity of interests disposed men to seek the aid of the central government. Under these circumstances Elizabeth's government undertook
the regulation of the economic and social affairs of the nation on an
unprecedented scale.

Recoinage

The first problem was the currency. The debased coinage was a
cause of high prices and economic distress which the government
could remove at the cost of some temporary loss and inconvenience
to the nation. In 1560 a special mint was established and the project
was announced to the public. The debased silver coins were called
into the mint, melted, and converted into coins of standard fineness.
The possessors of the old coins had to take the loss. Each received
of the new coins only the actual value of his old coins and not their
face value. A small bonus was paid to those who brought the base
money to the mint before a certain date. After certain dates the bad
coins ceased to be legal tender and the mint no longer accepted them
for recoinage. The details of the difficult transaction were so well
planned and executed that it was completed within a year.

Statute of
Appren-
tices

Three years later the government attempted to stabilize the conditions of labor. These were more or less chaotic. The growth of enclosures, the consequent displacement of the population in some
rural sections, and other causes had produced a large number of
tramps and vagabonds, while in other districts there was a scarcity of
rural wage earners. The exodus of artisans from the towns to escape
the tyranny of the gilds had resulted in the decay of many towns,
while the rural artisans were often inadequately trained and subject
to no supervision. The Statute of Apprentices covered the whole of

[3] Above, pp. 321, 322.
[4] Above, p. 290.

this broad field. It required artisans who followed a trade to have served an apprenticeship for a minimum of seven years. Able-bodied men who were not skilled artisans or apprentices were required with certain exceptions to serve as agricultural laborers on demand. Ordinary workmen either in trades or in agriculture were to be hired for at least a year and could leave or be dismissed on notice of no less than three months. Hours of labor and wages were regulated. Wages were fixed not at a definite and universal rate, but annually by the justices of the peace in each locality in accordance with local conditions, though the justices acted under the central supervision of the privy council. The statute appears to have accomplished some of the results sought and to have contributed to the improvement of industrial conditions.

Another problem inherited from the past was poverty. During the Middle Ages the care of the poor had been left to the voluntary ministrations of the church. The monasteries were the principal dispensers of charity, and though they could not cope with the growing poverty of the sixteenth century, their dissolution removed the one source whence extensive relief might come. The government, having confiscated their wealth, felt some responsibility for the services they had performed for the community, but little was done beyond enacting laws against vagabonds and beggars. Elizabeth began in 1563 with legislation empowering civil authorities to collect weekly payments from those who did not give alms voluntarily. From this first experiment she advanced step by step, until in 1601 a long series of acts was codified in a law which remained the basis of the relief of the poor by the state until 1834. It provided for the appointment in each parish of overseers of the poor, who were empowered to levy a local tax (rate) on the owners of property in order to provide funds for the support of the poor. Assistance of this sort, however, was not to be given to able-bodied paupers. The overseers were directed to provide work for them. Those who could work and would not were whipped or kept in houses of correction. The systematic assistance of the poor and the detailed regulation of conditions of work and employment by the state in Elizabeth's reign unquestionably helped to eliminate much of the suffering and distress so characteristic of the first half of the century.

The poor law

Industries were encouraged by the grant of patents of monopoly. They gave to the recipients a monopoly of the sale of a certain article for a specified term of years. The earliest patents were issued to stimulate certain mining and manufacturing industries that were necessary

Monopolies

to provide munitions of war. Later they were granted to those who would agree to develop new manufactures in England. These patents of monopoly served their purpose well. Several new manufactures were established in England by their means. Before the close of the reign, however, they began to be abused. They were given to favorites or sold for profit. They were extended to the sale of articles which were not the product of new industries, and to some of the necessaries of life. The high prices produced by monopolies in such articles caused a popular outcry. Parliament demanded their abolition, and public opinion ran so strong that in 1601 Elizabeth, much against her will, promised to revoke the existing patents and to grant no more. She withdrew only the most unpopular, however, leaving many still in force at the close of the reign.

Alien immigrants

The introduction of new industrial processes from abroad, where they were more highly developed than in England, was further aided by the considerable influx of religious refugees from the continent. Many of them were skilled artisans who brought new trades and improved some of the methods in those already established. The foreigners often aroused the local opposition of English artisans and manufacturers, but the central government encouraged their immigration and gave them protection. They were rightly regarded by Lord Burghley as a means of promoting his policy to increase the industrial resources of England. In several instances the new industrial arts which they brought became permanently domiciled.

Agriculture

Agriculture, which was still the fundamental industry of England, profited more from natural economic developments than from legislative regulation, though it was not neglected by the government. In Elizabeth's reign the price of grain rose higher comparatively than the price of wool, with the result that the land under tillage expanded considerably. This served to redress the balance, and complaints about enclosures became less numerous. Enclosures did not stop, but more of the enclosed lands were used for agriculture. In some measure the government stimulated the increase of tillage by lightening the restrictions on the export of grain and thus improving the market for agricultural products. The rural community, moreover, had by this time accommodated itself to the new conditions created by the capitalistic utilization of the land, and the distress and suffering inseparable from the stage of transition abated.

Foreign commerce

The encouragement of Englishmen engaged in foreign commerce was a primary consideration with Elizabeth's government. What they needed particularly was help in securing new markets. During the three preceding reigns the broad lines of commercial policy laid down by Henry VII had been followed, though they had been subordinated more or less to political considerations. The foreigners who still controlled large branches of the English foreign trade in the time of Henry VII had been largely superseded. The diversion of the far eastern trade to the oceanic route and the advance of the Turks gradually ruined Venice, and the last Venetian fleet came to England in 1532. The Hanseatic League lost many of its privileges in the reigns of Edward VI and Mary and was reduced to the position of other alien merchants trading to England. On the other hand, many of the markets which Englishmen had held or secured with the aid of the commercial treaties of Henry VII were lost or being lost by the beginning of Elizabeth's reign. The Merchants of the Staple had ceased to be of importance, largely because the wool which was their principal export was now used by English manufactures. The loss of Calais, the home of the staple, was the final blow to their business. Political rivalries and religious antagonisms had put an end to the prosperous Spanish trade acquired by Englishmen after the commercial treaties arranged by Henry VII and had greatly depressed the trade with Flanders, though the Merchant Adventurers still kept their mart at Antwerp. In the Mediterranean also the policy of Henry VII had borne good fruit, but the English traders had gradually found it impossible to cope with the chaotic conditions produced by Mediterranean warfare and piracy, and no English trading ventures to that part of the world had been made since 1553.

Since the principal need of English merchants was to recover old markets or secure new ones, Elizabeth's government aided them chiefly by strengthening old companies or chartering new ones. Now that Englishmen were beginning to push their trade to the ends of the earth where the English government could give them no adequate protection, such companies were more necessary than ever.[5] In India, for example, the English traders had to meet the armed rivalry of the competing companies of other nations, establish residents to deal with the natives, build forts, and maintain their own protection at an effort and expense beyond the scope of isolated individual enterprises. Companies organized on a sufficiently large scale to provide protection and to deal with the natives or with foreign governments provided the only means by which Englishmen could take advantage of the new commercial openings to be found in many parts of the

Chartered trading companies

---

[5] See above, p. 289.

world. The recent failure of private enterprise in the Mediterranean seemed to offer convincing demonstration of the need of chartered companies. Such a company, in return for its onerous burdens of regulation and protection of the trade, demanded and received power to exclude from the trade Englishmen who were not members of the company. The monopoly might become a hindrance when the trade had been fully established, but without this incentive English commercial enterprise probably would have expanded much less rapidly under the conditions existing in the sixteenth century.

When Elizabeth's reign began, three companies of this type already existed. The Staplers were on their last legs, and a new charter granted by Elizabeth failed to revive their fortunes. The Merchant Adventurers were more successful. By shifting their depot from Flanders to northern Germany and later opening a branch in the Netherlands, they more than recovered the lost ground. The Muscovy Company, formed in 1553 to seek the northeastern passage, had developed a profitable trade with Russia and was seeking to establish trade with Asia by the overland route across Russia. This was the first company to be organized on the principle of joint stock. The members of the company bought shares and elected a governor and directors, who conducted the business and paid dividends to the shareholders. This organization corresponded much more nearly to the form of a modern corporation than did the regulated company in which each purchaser of a share transacted his own business.

The issue of charters to new companies began as a result of further difficulties with the Hanseatic League. In 1579 the privileges of the Hanse were further curtailed and a regulated company of English merchants, called the Eastland Company, was given a monopoly of the trade with the lands of the Baltic. Two years later the Turkey Company was organized by joint stock to revive the trade with the eastern Mediterranean. In 1583 this was followed by the Venice Company. Both companies were successful, and after a few years they were amalgamated and reorganized as a regulated company under the name of the Levant Company. With the promoters of companies, as with the explorers, the ultimate goal was generally the rich trade of the far east. The attempts of the Muscovy and the Levant Companies to connect with it by indirect routes were not particularly successful, new routes by sea failed to materialize, and Englishmen were gradually forced to the conclusion that the only feasible route was the one by way of the Cape of Good Hope. The war with Spain stimulated Englishmen to try this route, because the conquest of

Old companies

New companies

Portugal by Spain had made this route nominally a Spanish monopoly. After several private ventures had found the difficulties too great, a joint-stock company was formed. In 1600 the East India Company received its charter from Elizabeth and began the career destined to make it the greatest of all English trading companies.

The development of the English merchant marine was held by Burghley to be of fundamental importance. Not only was it the desirable adjunct of an expanding foreign commerce, but it was also the essential training school whence sailors could be drawn for the navy, that was now coming to be regarded as England's main defense against attack. He did not favor particularly the policy of the Navigation Act passed in the time of Henry VII,[6] though it was retained in a modified form; but early in the reign he secured the passage of a law which required the consumption of fish in place of meat on Wednesdays and Fridays. It was designed to stimulate the fishing industry and provide a larger number of trained sailors. The policy seemed to be justified by results, for a few years later the number of ships and mariners in England had increased greatly.

Merchant marine

This extensive body of regulative enactments was actuated largely by a new set of economic theories which were beginning to be the vogue during the reign of Elizabeth. These theories, called collectively the mercantile system, developed from the growth of the national idea. As the different nations of Europe became fully conscious of their nationality in the sixteenth century, they began to test their strength by wars with other nations. One of the first instincts of a new consciousness of nationality is a readiness to meet any challenge to its interests by war. The wars of the sixteenth century gave demonstration that the days of feudalism had departed, and that success in war was determined largely by the length of the purse. So the new nations began to see in economic prosperity and self-sufficiency the essential foundation of political strength and national security. Men began to speculate keenly on the principles of economics, but the ultimate purpose in view always remained political rather than economic. The welfare of the state, which was above all the groups and individuals composing it, was the object sought by the mercantilists. Consequently they justified the regulation of economic affairs by the government in ways that affected adversely the interests of groups or individuals, provided the nation as a whole benefited. The theory centered upon a conception of nationality that was new, but

The mercantile system

[6] Above, p. 288.

it took its start from ideas that were old. The protectionist, monopolistic past of the gilds and boroughs gave to the thought of the present its direction and something of its form and content. The basis was widened from the group or locality to the nation.

The mercantilist deduced his system from the premises that wealth constituted the economic basis of the political strength of the state, and that the most desirable form of wealth was treasure (i.e., the precious metals). Today we are wont to think of money as a measure of wealth and a means of exchange. We put the emphasis on the commodities we can buy with money rather than on the money itself; but the mercantilist point of view was not unreasonable in a money market where forms of credit were still in their infancy and both the government and private merchants had to have actual cash with which to transact their business. Granted these premises, the conclusion seemed to follow that trade should be regulated in such a way as to bring specie into the country. If a nation could sell more goods to other nations than it bought from other nations, the balance, they reasoned, would have to be paid in treasure. "To sell more to strangers yearly than we consume of theirs in value"[7] became the object of mercantilist reasoning. With this point of view and these principles almost any amount of regulation by the government can be justified. Exports may be stimulated by bounties and imports discouraged by tariffs. To sell more than it buys, a nation must have manufactures, and so the regulation of internal industries becomes a factor. Since an increase of the numbers which take part in manufactures and commerce will increase the foreign trade, the promotion of foreign immigration by legislation is justified. The theory may be spun to a thread of any fineness needful to secure governmental intervention in any desired field. With Elizabethan statesmen the mercantile system had not yet assumed its later extravagant form, but its fundamental principles dominated their point of view and found expression in their legislation.

Changes in industrial organization

The organization of industry underwent some significant changes during the second half of the sixteenth century. While the trend away from the control of the gilds and toward the domestic form of industrial organization continued, several industries became organized on a large capitalistic scale, and some of them developed plants or factories in which scores—or even hundreds—of laborers were employed. Some of the industries established by means of patents of

---

[7] Thomas Mun, *England's Treasure by Foreign Trade*, ed. 1903, p. 7.

monopoly required plants with equipment which often included heavy machinery run by water power. Among them were paper and gunpowder mills, alum and copperas factories, sugar refineries, saltpeter and brass works, and cannon foundries. An alum factory which contained large furnaces, cisterns and boiling-pans represented an investment of several thousand pounds, and the annual cost of materials might run to £1,000. In such a factory sixty men might be employed inside and many more outside. A cannon foundry employed 200 men, and a paper mill gave work to a still larger number. The development of enterprises which needed extensive amounts of capital and numerous employees was also extended to some of the older industries through the discovery of new technical methods of production. In the conversion of metallic ores to metals and the preparation of the metals for the use of the workers who made them into nails, hardware and other finished products, the small forge, which cost little to build and was operated by a master with a few helpers, was superseded to some extent by the blast furnace operated with bellows driven by water power, which necessitated the construction of a large plant with a considerable outlay of capital and the concentration of a large group of laborers. The growing scarcity of wood and the consequently increased difficulty of obtaining charcoal as a fuel for the furnaces, ovens and kilns used in various industries led to the invention of new types in which coal could be used for fuel. The greatly increased demand for coal and ores produced by this industrial change caused the mining shafts to be sunk deeper than they had been before. At the lower levels the mines were flooded by water and the dangers from gas became greater. The elimination of these difficulties resulted in the investment of much capital in the construction of drains, the erection and maintenance of drainage engines driven by water or horse power, and the building of ventilation shafts. A few factories were erected in established industries where no fundamental improvements of technique were made, such as the production of salt from the sea, the boiling of soap, and the brewing and textile trades. The rise of these factories and plants did not bring the gild and domestic systems to an end. At the close of Elizabeth's reign the great majority of industrial laborers still worked in the small shops of the gild masters or in their own homes. Labor in factories was still the exception, but the appearance of "capitalistically owned mines and manufacturing establishments" marked the beginning of changes in industrial technique and of the concentration of capital in industry which was destined to lead in the course of two centuries to the greater and faster transformation known as the industrial revolution.[8]

Domestic system

In the domestic system, which continued to be the prevailing form of industrial organization, there was also an extensive development of capital. The workers under this system usually lived in rural cottages and derived some portion of their living from land attached to the cottage. Toward the end of the sixteenth century many cottagers became almost wholly dependent upon industry because its expansion was providing them with greater opportunities of employment in that field. In Lancashire, for example, the introduction of the cotton industry had that effect. Another result of the growth of capital employed in domestic industries was the dependence of more laborers upon a capitalist employer. The domestic worker might himself be a small capitalist. He owned his tools, and he might buy the raw material, work it up, and sell the finished product in a neighboring market. In the case of some materials, such as wool, he could employ the labor of the members of his family in some of the processes of production, and he might hire the help of some of his neighbors. In Yorkshire the woolen industry was generally organized in this manner. It was more common, however, for the worker to obtain the raw material from a capitalist to whom it belonged, return to him the manufactured article, and receive from him wages for the work performed. This form of organization gave a large degree of control of the industry to capitalists and made the workers dependent. It was common in the woolen industry in the west of England, where it had developed so far that some of the larger capitalists gave employment to several hundred domestic laborers, and one of the richest of them left at his death a fortune of £40,000.

National prosperity

These developments in industry and commerce produced during the later years of Elizabeth's reign a remarkable period of prosperity. Prices were high, but money was plentiful. The old prejudice against interest gave way, and banking and commercial lending became important factors in business. Commercial and industrial enterprises organized on a comparatively large capitalistic scale became common. The rapidly growing wealth was distributed inequitably. Wages still advanced so much more slowly than prices that the ordinary laborer had small share in the general good fortune, but even his position appears to have been more comfortable at the end of Elizabeth's reign

---

[8] Paragraph based principally upon J. U. Nef's "Progress of Technology," *Economic History Review*, v, 3–24.

than at the beginning, if the descriptions of contemporaries are to be trusted. The merchants and the tradesmen, the country gentry and the small independent landed proprietors (yeomen) lived in such comfort as they had never known before. The cramped and cheerless manor houses gave way to the stately, many-windowed country houses of the type still designated as Tudor, which were designed for beauty and enjoyment rather than for defense. Smaller houses were no longer built of wood and clay but of timber, brick, or stone. Even cottages commonly displayed chimneys and glazed windows. Rare was the village where new buildings were not reared in Elizabeth's day, and the overwhelming majority of the new buildings were homes. The furnishings increased accordingly in richness and comfort. Even in humble homes straw pallets gave place to comfortable bedding, wooden platters were exchanged for pewter, and wooden spoons for silver or tin. Food on the average table became greater in variety and abundance. Among the prosperous the expenditure on fine clothes was so lavish as to arouse the scorn of the Puritans and the apprehensions of the government. The literature of Shakespeare's time reflects a material prosperity which contrasts so greatly with what had been known only a generation before that contemporaries deemed it luxury.

Hand in hand with the growth of prosperity went the spread of learning. The interest aroused in education by the Renaissance bore **Learning** a full crop of grammar and elementary schools in Elizabeth's reign. The older mode of education in the castle went out of fashion, and the sons of gentlemen mingled with the sons of tradesmen and farmers who thronged the schools. Education became the privilege of classes to whom before it had been unattainable. The instruction of the schools perpetuated the classical tradition, but Latin remained a complementary language which served primarily to emphasize the value of the mother tongue. An appreciative reading knowledge of English became widely diffused. Histories of England's past were sold in large quantities, translations of the classics issued from the press frequently, pamphleteers began to mold public opinion, and plays began to be presented regularly before large popular audiences. An educated public came into being, and it demanded knowledge.

The depth of Elizabethan learning did not correspond to its breadth. In that respect the early promise of the Renaissance was not kept. **Scholar-** The intellectual restlessness that pervaded the nation lacked the normal **ship** complement of scholarship at the universities. There the Reformation created an atmosphere unfavorable to scholarship. Each change of religion during the century brought to the universities royal commissions which ordered educational policies to suit the religious views of the moment and removed the instructors who were not in accord therewith. The Elizabethan settlement ended the oscillations but not the control. Settled conditions and economic prosperity doubled the number of students at Oxford, but the invasion of academic freedom was enough to militate against the highest type of independent thought. There were good scholars, steeped in the classical literary tradition, but no group of scholars stood forth preeminent. To train men for service in church and state was becoming a principal function of the universities. Parker, Whitgift, Walsingham, and Burghley were Cambridge men whose careers illustrate the union of learning with action that was typical of Elizabethan England.

Poetry

The intellectual glory of the Elizabethan epoch was its literature. There the spirit of the Renaissance found expression in a series of masterpieces. Poetry had enjoyed many disciples since the reign of Henry VIII, when a group of young courtiers made it fashionable to compose sonnets and other verses. Their quality was good, bad, and indifferent; but until 1579, when Edmund Spenser published his *Shepherd's Calendar*, there was no certain indication of the greatness that was to mark the Elizabethan literary product. Spenser's poem was the best produced in English since Chaucer's death, and it was surpassed a few years later by his *Faerie Queene* which is generally accorded rank as one of the great poems of the language.

The drama

Meanwhile the drama had begun to attract poetic genius. Interest in dramatic representation had been growing since late in the thirteenth century. To the miracle plays of that age crude farces and masques had been added in the late fifteenth century and the early sixteenth. The Renaissance aroused an interest in the Roman drama, and after the middle of the sixteenth century comedies and tragedies began to be written on the classic models. In the early years of Elizabeth's reign plays of these sorts became so popular in London that the first theaters were built in 1576. Previously the plays had had scant literary value, but thereafter a group of university men, among whom the most prominent was Christopher Marlowe, improved upon these sources and developed a distinctively English drama. It had faults innumerable. It was filled with bombastic blood and thunder, it rarely had unity, and it presented impossibilities as normal human acts. "The most chaotically improbable action, the least carefully adjusted characters. the wildest rant of dialogue, the most shocking impropriety of incident and phrase meet one at every turn."[9] But it had vigorous originality, it was couched in blank verse, which with Marlowe sometimes attained majestic effects, and it pleased contemporary audiences. It prepared the way for the masterpieces of Shakespeare.

Prose was not yet the medium chosen by literary artists. Lyly's *Euphues,* published in 1579, marked a turning point of some importance in the use of English prose as a vehicle of literary expression. It was intended to be a moral treatise for the instruction of courtly circles, but it was designed also to entertain, and thus became unintentionally an early antecedent of the English novel. Its style, though labored and mechanical, was nevertheless an effort to make the English language a medium of polished expression. Stranger still, it accomplished some of its purposes. It was popular in the circles for which it was written, where it did much to dispel the current tradition that true literature in the form of prose could be expressed worthily only in Latin. A few years later Sir Philip Sidney, courtier, diplomat, and soldier, demonstrated that greater beauty of style might be attained with less affectation. His works[10] were highly regarded by contemporaries and did much to advance the cause of prose, though their reputation proved to be ephemeral. Hooker's able defense of the position of the Anglican church,[11] in a style rarely rivaled for dignity, is the only piece of prose which literary critics generally accept as a masterpiece, though Sir Francis Bacon expressed the practical philosophy of his *Essays* with a terse pithiness that still wins the approval of critics and charms a circle of intelligent readers. In prose it was essentially a period of experiments. They gave to prose for the first time a recognized place in English literature, but for the most part they were so far surpassed in later ages that they are no longer read primarily for their literary merits.

The historical writing of this period hardly attained the rank of literature. The growth of the national feeling produced many writers who sought to glorify England's past, and provided for their works a ready sale. But the public demanded of historians, as it does of newspapers today, sensations rather than the truth. The historians continued to use the form of chronicles, they accepted credulously the statements of older chroniclers, and in their narratives of contemporary events they mingled gossip with facts, gave undue space to the abnormal, and waxed discursive on trivialities. On contemporary affairs their works

Prose (margin)

Historical works (margin)

---

[9] Saintsbury in Traill's *Social England,* iii, 517.
[10] *Apologie for Poetrie* and *Arcadia.*
[11] *Ecclesiastical Polity.*

are storehouses of information for the student who would know the lives lived by Tudor men. Edward Hall's *Chronicle*, the first of the series, is contemporary with Henry VIII. Holinshed's *Chronicles*, a cooperative work, was published first in 1578. It contained not only a history but also Harrison's *Description of England* which gives a remarkable picture of the changing society of the day. John Speed, John Stow and William Camden were the historians of the later years of Elizabeth's reign, and the last two particularly collected valuable historical material. They were also antiquaries who were moved by their pride in England to describe her glories as they saw them. Camden in his *Britannia* "carried his readers along the highroads, through the towns and cities of his native country, revealing, as he went, her natural scenery, her antiquities, her learning and her strength,"[12] while Stow performed a like service for London.[13] Actuated by a kindred spirit, Richard Hakluyt became the historian of the exploits of Englishmen on the sea. He sought high and low for accounts of voyages made by Englishmen and edited these tales that were stranger than fiction in his *Principall Navigations*. Though these works and the many like them of lesser importance lack the artistic design that is the prerequisite of classical and modern historical literature, they preserve a record of events of great value and they had a profound influence on their contemporaries. Their authors were actuated by the ambition to inspire in their readers pride in the greatness of England. They succeeded. Their books were popular. The facts which they collected fired the imaginations of other men. Marlowe interpreted the imperialistic dreams and visions of Englishmen with the aid of Hakluyt, Shakespeare derived materials for his historical plays from Holinshed, and countless men found in the pages of the chroniclers some of that enthusiasm for queen and country which motivated their actions.

Other historical materials

The student of the present day who seeks to reconstruct the England of the Tudors must rely primarily on documents and writings not intended to be historical. These increased enormously in abundance and variety. Two of the important new types of official documents were the journals of the houses of lords and commons and the register of the privy council, while among private documents diaries began to appear. With the development of printing men began to write for publication on current questions. Broadsides and pamphlets became a significant part of the wares on display in Elizabethan bookstalls, and many a book was issued to convince the public that this or that was

---

[12] *Cambridge History of English Literature*, iii, 373.
[13] *Survey of London*.

right or wrong. Social evils, such as enclosures, became the subject of complaints and the object of reforms,[14] economic questions were discussed pro and con, and religion furnished the theme for endless partisan and controversial writing. Foxe's *Actes and Monuments*, published early in Elizabeth's reign, is a notable example of the last type. It is a martyrology, written with a bitter Protestant bias and a love of gruesome details, but with dramatic power. It seems to have supplied a contemporary lack of both devotional and light literature, and it had an extraordinary and persistent popularity. Of another type were the pamphlets issued in the Marprelate controversy. This was waged between Puritan and Anglican and takes its name from the Puritan pseudonym of Martin Marprelate signed to a series of the pamphlets that began to appear in 1588. The dispute was violent, and both sides descended to scurrilities, though the tracts written by Martin achieved a satirical style not without influence on English literature. The legislation of 1593 decided the controversy against the Puritans, but not before it had made the pamphlet the accepted means of appealing to popular opinion on partisan questions and an important historical source from that time to the age of the newspaper. The writings that crown the literary achievement of the Elizabethan age are likely to disappoint the seeker for historical material. Shakespeare, for example, does not set his scenes in contemporary England, and his historical plays have little value for the times they portray; but his characters from foreign lands or from England's past voice the sentiments of Elizabethan England. Consider the bold, defiant patriotism of the last lines of *King John*:

> This England never did, nor never shall
> Lie at the proud foot of a conqueror,
> But when it first did help to wound itself.
> Now these her princes are come home again,
> Come the three corners of the world in arms,
> And we shall shock them. Naught shall make us rue,
> If England to itself do rest but true.

This is not the patriotism of the men who refused to follow John's banner to France and wrung from him the Great Charter; this is the patriotism of Elizabethan men. It is the spirit that pervades all kinds of Elizabethan literature, the spirit that made it influential among contemporaries, and the spirit that confers upon it something of that quality which has made it live to appeal to the men of our day.

---

[14] See, for example, the works mentioned above, p. 326.

CHAPTER XXI

THE GOVERNMENT OF THE TUDORS

Fact and theory of the constitution

THE monarchs of the house of Tudor actually wielded far greater power than their medieval predecessors. Yet the framework of the constitution did not change greatly. Some new organs of government appeared and some old organs lost old powers and acquired new ones, but the transformation was not so great in the machinery of government as it was in the way the machinery was worked. The court of star chamber was not invented by Henry VII, but it was used in a new way to reduce the power of the nobles and to enhance the power of the crown. In the early years of the Tudor rule parliament lost some of its control of taxation, but this did less to increase the royal authority than did the conscious support which parliament gave to the absolute policies of the ruler. The constitution was altered by the Tudors more in practice than it was in theory.

Hallam, in a famous passage, enumerates five checks on the royal authority established during the Middle Ages, and ascribes the Tudor strong monarchy to their violation. His point of view embraces some truth and much fiction. The checks which protected the liberties of the subject, in Hallam's estimation, were parliamentary control of taxation and legislation, arrest only on a warrant specifying the offense and no prolonged imprisonment without trial, trial by jury in a public court, and the responsibility of royal officials to stand suits for damages or impeachments for their illegal acts.[1] Undoubtedly some of the Tudors obtained revenues unconstitutionally without parliamentary grant, but the other checks either did not exist legally or were not violated notoriously. The king had never lost completely the power to legislate in council without reference to parliament,[2] and the council had tried cases without jury by processes unknown to the common law long before Henry VII came to the throne. The right of impeachment was not violated in the sixteenth century; it simply was not used. The wide extension of the definition of treason and the arbitrary executions under Henry VIII constitute as flagrant examples of tyranny as can be found in the sixteenth century, but the definition of treason was expanded

---

[1] *Constitutional History*, i, 2 (ed. of 1897).
[2] McIlwain, *High Court*, pp. 313–320; Holdsworth, *History of English Law*, ii, 366–368; iv, 99–104.

by act of parliament, and the executions rarely took place until arrest had been authorized by warrant and guilt had been pronounced by a jury or by the peers of the accused. The executions were no less arbitrary because the forms of law were observed, but they were seldom illegal. The spirit of the constitution changed far more than its outward form.

The increase of the royal authority was rendered possible by a variety of circumstances. When the first Tudor came to the throne, the principal social force which had maintained limits on the royal power during the Middle Ages was weak. The feudal nobles could offer no effective opposition when an able ruler deprived them of the greater part of their power. This gave to the king the opportunity to secure full control of the council and other organs of government, which Henry VII was quick to seize. He augmented his authority largely by the use of powers which these organs had possessed legally under his predecessors, but which his predecessors had not utilized fully in practice. Either the nobles had blocked the attempt, or they themselves had exercised the powers, as they did during much of the fifteenth century, when they dominated both council and parliament. The middle class, which might have attempted to limit the power of the crown through its representation in Tudor parliaments, preferred its exercise by a king sensitive to their interests and desirous of their support rather than by a selfish nobility. One tyrant was better than many. This attitude the astute Henry VII took pains to cultivate. By his zeal for the interests of the middle class he cemented firmly its alliance with the monarchy. His successors who had the longest reigns, Henry VIII and Elizabeth, were also the possessors of great political acumen. They continued and expanded his policies. The executions of Henry VIII fell with particular weight on the nobility, and those which followed the Rising of the Earls and the Ridolfi plot marked the passing of the last of the nobility of the old feudal type. The surviving nobility had been created by the house of Tudor and was loyal to its creator. Henry VIII, moreover, removed once and for all the possibility of the clerical opposition which had so often balked his predecessors. The only source left whence opposition to the royal power might come was the middle class, and Henry VIII and Elizabeth took pains to forge new links in the chain of interest that bound this class to the throne. The Tudors were able to erect a strong monarchy because the governmental breakdown of the fifteenth century provided the opening for a reorganization, and they had the ability to take advantage of it.

Yet the exceptional character both of the ability of the Tudors and

Establishment and maintenance of strong government

of their opportunity is insufficient alone to explain their great power. The strong rule of the Tudors was virtually based on popular support. Neither Henry VIII nor Elizabeth kept a standing army to enforce their commands, and the most arbitrary acts of Henry VIII were sanctioned by parliament. Manifestly popular opinion favored a powerful monarchy. Two currents of thought contributed to the production of that point of view. As the Renaissance with its emphasis on Roman antiquity spread, it popularized knowledge of a ruler whose will had been law and tended to idealize strong government. The growth of the national spirit produced a consciousness of common aims and needs which could best be served by a centralized authority. So far did this go, that in the reign of Elizabeth the queen became practically the symbol of nationality. The point of view was sustained by the practical consideration of the need of a strong government. This was obvious during the greater part of the period. When Henry VII came to the throne the desire for a powerful executive was nearly universal. When the restoration of peace and order had lessened the need, Henry VIII rallied the national support by an attack on the papal jurisdiction. The divorce was not popular; this or that detail of the religious change was disliked by one group or another; but the elimination of foreign control from England was deemed so desirable that Englishmen sank their differences and gave their approval to the absolutism essential for the accomplishment of the separation. The unpopularity of the policies followed by the government in the reigns of Edward VI and Mary nearly wrecked the royal authority, but with the accession of Elizabeth the constant threat of foreign invasion revived the national consciousness of the wisdom of strong leadership. With the victory over the Armada the pressure ceased. A reaction followed, but it was not strong enough to overcome the feeling of loyalty to the queen who had led the nation through so many difficulties. Hence it was not until the time of the Stuarts that the strong executive was seriously attacked.

The chief instrument of the Tudor government was the council. Throughout the period it remained the supple instrument of the royal will which Henry VII had made it. The nobles did not disappear from the council, but they remained in the minority. Beginning with Henry VIII they were with few exceptions of the Tudor creation. Men of the middle class, chosen for their administrative ability, constituted the influential element. Wolsey, the son of a wool merchant, and Thomas Cromwell, who was the son of a Putney blacksmith and had followed the trades of trooper, merchant, accountant, and solicitor before he became a statesman, dominated the council of Henry VIII, while Cecil (later Lord Burghley) and Walsingham, both of the middle class, were the leading members of Elizabeth's council. Men of such a stamp could not oppose the king's will. They might and did influence the royal policies by their advice, but if the king did not accept their views, they did what the king commanded; and they did it faithfully, even when the mandate was at variance with their better judgment. On the other hand, these trained councilors could handle efficiently a much larger amount of business than the incompetent feudal barons. Their duties became so multifarious, indeed, that they produced a reorganization of the council. In the reign of Henry VIII a small group of councilors was selected to attend the king, while another group remained at work at Westminster, whether the king was there or not. Individuals might pass from one group to the other, and the two groups might meet together at times. Either group was the king's council, but the group about the king, which naturally became the more influential, was commonly called the privy council.

The work done by the council was enormous in both amount and variety. It deliberated on all affairs of state and, when the ruler gave discretion, decided them. It was active in foreign affairs, receiving foreign diplomatic representatives and giving directions to English diplomatic agents abroad. It framed many of the bills which were brought before parliament. It frequently enacted ordinances with the consent of the king. Legislation in council, indeed, was typical of the Tudor régime. During the period the power was further defined. In 1539 parliament passed the *lex regia* which gave to proclamations made by the king in council the force of law, provided they did not destroy the force of existing law or impose punishment extending to forfeiture or loss of life or limb. This has been called the worst example of the servility of Tudor parliaments. As a matter of fact it seems merely to define a right which the king and council had always possessed, and states what before had been a somewhat vague doctrine, namely, that statutes are superior to proclamations. Its very enactment implies, moreover, that parliament delegates to the council a legislative power. In 1547 the act was repealed, but royal proclamations continued to be issued as they had been before the passage of the act. In Mary's reign the question came before the court. The judges gave the opinion that a proclamation could not impose fine, forfeiture, or imprisonment, or make new law, but could only confirm or ratify an old law. The decision went unnoticed. Throughout Elizabeth's reign conciliar proclamations, carrying penalties for their infraction, were issued freely and were upheld by the courts. The council saw that laws and proclamations were enforced, and this occupied a large part of its time. It supervised with an astonishing amount of detail the work of local officials charged with the execution of the large mass of Tudor legislation that required local administration. It still received numerous petitions from subjects seeking redress of grievances. Most of them it referred to the appropriate courts. It might hear evidence on them, but it rarely imposed punishment. It investigated charges of treason, and it might and did use torture for the purpose of extracting evidence or confession. The hard work of the council was primarily responsible for the efficiency of the government of the Tudors.

Council and parliament The relations of council to parliament changed significantly under the Tudors. Though the official element in the council had become less influential in parliament during the fourteenth century,[3] the members of the permanent council continued to sit in parliament. In 1539 this connection was practically ended by a statute which deprived councilors of a vote in parliament by virtue of their offices. The treasurer, the secretary, or any other official, however prominent he might be in the council, could sit in parliament, but he could not vote there unless he had a peerage that qualified him to vote in the house of lords or had been elected to the house of commons. The separation of the house of lords from the council, which had been begun in the fourteenth century, was practically completed by this act. A privy council sitting in parliament without a vote was a poor mouthpiece of the royal wishes. Henceforth councilors who were commoners, as most of them were, sought election to the house of commons. The electors were generally glad to be represented by an official who stood high in the royal favor, and the councilors became prominent and influential members of the commons. Through these elected councilors the king continued to influence parliament, as he had done before when the councilors acted in parliament as his appointees, but the influence was now exerted directly on the house of commons. The change helped to effect an alliance between the king and the commons which tended to increase the influence of the lower house of parliament as compared with the upper.

Local councils The tendency of the Tudors to govern by conciliar action is seen also in the use of local or subsidiary councils to rule parts of the country liable to disorder. Of these local councils the most important were the council of Wales, established by Edward IV, and the council of the north, charged with the government of the five northern counties after

---

[3] Above, pp. 229, 230.

the Pilgrimage of Grace in 1536. They had criminal jurisdiction and extensive administrative powers, which they exercised under the direction of the privy council. They kept order where the arm of the central government did not reach, but their necessarily extensive discretionary authority was a menace to individual liberties. Under the Tudors, when they were closely supervised by the privy council, the order they maintained outweighed the disadvantage of their occasional arbitrary acts. Under the Stuarts, when the outbreaks which gave rise to them had ceased and the control of the privy council over them had become loose, they were regarded as the peculiar agents of despotism and became a popular grievance.

Akin to the local councils were the many special courts created by the Tudors. The court of requests, which was established to hear the civil suits of men who were too poor to sue in the ordinary courts, the court of high commission, which enforced the Acts of Supremacy and Uniformity and exercised other ecclesiastical jurisdiction, the court of star chamber—not new but more active under the Tudors—the councils of Wales and of the north, and several other courts of similar type encroached extensively on the province of the courts of common law. All of these courts were more or less connected with or subject to the council. They were consequently more dependent upon the will of the king than were the courts of common law. They all had summary procedures unknown to the common law and based more or less on the Roman law, which was especially adapted to emphasize the absolutism of the monarch. Most of these courts did and all of them could act without a jury. Since every one of them was established to meet a special set of circumstances, each contributed substantially to the maintenance of law and order in the early years of its development. But however great an advantage they may have been temporarily, they were capable of grave abuse. Individual liberties and rights had no protection against such arbitrary courts other than the wisdom and discretion of those who controlled them. The Tudors made these courts one of the principal institutional props of their authority, but they used them wisely without great abuse. In the closing years of Elizabeth's reign, when the special circumstances that had evoked these courts had ceased to exist, their arbitrary powers were beginning to arouse popular apprehension, but it was not till the Stuarts converted them into engines of tyranny that they fell before a storm of popular obloquy.

The judicial system of the Tudors also included the use of martial law in time of peace. In the sixteenth century martial law gave power

Martial
law

to punish with death or milder penalties without form of trial. It seems to have been the theory that such power should be used only in the field in war time,[4] but Mary and Elizabeth used it to punish without trial those who had taken part in rebellions, and the latter used it as justification for warrants ordering the execution of some participators in mere riots in London.

Law of
treason

A tyrannical manifestation of the Tudor monarchy occurred in connection with the law of treason. It affected both the legal conception of the crime and the method of procedure at trials for treason. The definition reached its widest limits under Henry VIII. The basis of the law previously had been the statute of 1352, which made it treason to plan to kill the king or immediate members of his family and display the intention by an overt act, to levy war on the king, or to aid his enemies. The statute extended the crime to a few other acts, the courts had stretched it somewhat by constructive decisions, and its scope had occasionally been expanded temporarily by parliamentary enactment, but these remained the principal acts constituting treason until the time of Henry VIII. In his reign nine statutes enlarged the scope of the crime, until it was practically treason to speak ill of the king. When his minister, Cromwell, had his system of spies spread over the country, harmless persons were punished for casual remarks. A notorious instance is that of a farmer, over eighty years of age, who was walking home in the rain with a companion. He remarked, "It is long of the king that this weather is so troublous or unstable. I ween we shall never have better weather while the king reigneth, and therefore it maketh no matter if he were knocked or patted on the head."[5] He was haled into court, where he confessed that he might have uttered something of the sort when he was intoxicated. His fate is not recorded, but death was often the penalty for no worse. It was literally dangerous to pass remarks about the weather. Such a definition of treason was enough to make any government a despotism. In 1547 this act was repealed and subsequent definitions were much less severe, though they continued to be far broader than that of 1352.

Trials for treason were notably unjust. To be accused in the time of Henry VIII was nearly equivalent to execution. In 1552 safeguards for the accused were provided in the mode of procedure. The most important was that he should be confronted with two witnesses of the act. The law was not observed, however, and to the end of Elizabeth's reign the accused often was not confronted with witnesses, or

---

[4] Smith, Thomas, *De Republica Anglorum,* ed. Alston, p. 59.
[5] Cited by Merriman, *Thomas Cromwell,* i, 117.

even allowed counsel to plead for him. Sometimes, indeed, suspects were subjected to torture to extract confessions. Trials for treason remained notably unfair to the end of the period.

Yet, if the few years when the enforcement of the statutes of treason were left to the tender mercies of Cromwell be excepted, the injustice of trials for treason touched few except political offenders. Ordinary justice was rendered between man and man and ordinary crime was punished far better under the Tudors than in any previous century. The special courts generally gave good justice, though they may have imperiled the principles on which English justice was based. In the reign of Henry VIII, indeed, there seems to have been some danger of the introduction of Roman law. The code of Justinian, with its emphasis on the authority of the monarch, could not fail to please Henry VIII, and this was the time when the Roman law, under the impetus of the Renaissance, was acquiring new influence all over Europe. The danger of a reception of the Roman law in England may not have been imminent, but it seems to have been a possibility. With the second half of the century even the possibility passed. In that period it was largely the summary procedure of the Roman law used by the special courts that provoked the jealousy of the courts of common law. However much the perversion of justice in individual cases may have endangered the liberty of the subject, the general results of the administration of justice by the Tudors were beneficial for the time to the people they ruled. *Administration of justice as a whole*

The relations of king to parliament in the sixteenth century assumed in practice a new aspect. The experience of the fifteenth century had convinced the people and the king that they had a common enemy in the nobility, and in the course of the sixteenth century other common enemies arose, such as the pope and Spain. Both king and people generally looked upon parliament as the instrument by means of which the cooperation essential for the welfare of both could be effected. Henry VIII pronounced himself emphatically on the importance of parliament to him when he said, "We at no time stand so high in our estate royal as in the time of parliament; when we as head and you as members are conjoined and knit together into one body politic."[6] The generalization to the effect that the Tudors ruled without parliaments or with packed parliaments contains just enough of the truth to make it misleading. The last years of the reign of Henry VII and the early years of the reign of Henry VIII, when parliament was rarely called, *King and parliament*

---

[6] Quoted from McIlwain, *High Court,* p. 338.

constitute a chapter apart in the parliamentary history of the Tudors, and the number of parliaments successfully filled with royal nominees is easily exaggerated. Henry's statement describes far more accurately the normal attitude of the Tudors. The people, on their side, felt the need of royal participation in order to make the action of parliament effective.[7] Harmonious cooperation was the ideal, and if the Tudors were the more influential partners in the firm, they generally had the tact to conceal somewhat the extent of their influence. The representatives of the people in parliament were seldom tempted to assert the leadership of the combination. But the dependence of the ruler on parliament for a century had the inevitable result that parliament gradually became conscious of its power. In the seventeenth century, when the pressing reasons for cooperation had departed, the popularity of the monarch had been lost, and the Stuarts asserted openly a superiority in the partnership, parliament countered with a similar claim. Thus the effect of the Tudor strong government on parliament was, curiously enough, to increase its relative importance in the government.

Another result of the alliance between king and people was to enhance the power of the house of commons in relation to that of the house of lords. The upper house was reduced to political insignificance in the time of Henry VII,[8] and there it remained under the Tudors. In part this was accomplished by the creation of new peers loyal to the monarchy and in part by the ecclesiastical changes. The dissolution removed the abbots, and the abolition of the papal jurisdiction gave the king complete control of the appointment of the bishops. Since they constituted a third of the house, control of their votes made it necessary to command the votes of only a few lay peers in order to have a majority. After the separation, the crown rarely encountered any serious opposition from the house of lords.

House of lords

The growing importance of the house of commons is attested not only by the care with which Henry VIII and Elizabeth cultivated its good will but in many other ways. "Before 1529 there is hardly a reference to its proceedings in the dispatches of any foreign diplomatist or observer; from that time onwards the correspondence of French, Venetian, and Spanish ambassadors becomes one of the main sources of parliamentary history."[9] Representation in the body began to be so highly prized that many boroughs petitioned for it. During the sixteenth century the membership increased by fifty per cent. Election to

House of commons

---

[7] Above, pp. 373, 374 and citations given by McIlwain, pp. 336–338.
[8] Above, p. 292.
[9] Pollard, *Evolution*, pp. 321, 322.

membership came to be esteemed; the eldest sons of peers sought it; bribery appeared; boroughs with a small electorate began to be bought by those who desired to control seats in the house and the rotten boroughs had their beginnings. The house of commons was beginning to offer a career; membership was becoming the object of ambition.[10] These are the straws that show how the wind of prestige blew on the house of commons in the sixteenth century.

The increased influence of the house of commons was due largely to the deliberate policy of Henry VIII. In the early years of his reign he continued his father's plan. He met parliament so infrequently that it seemed to be fairly on the way to desuetude. That it did not arrive at that destination was due to a change in Henry's attitude, caused by his discovery of the extent of his financial dependence on parliament and of the effect of popular opposition to his policy. His first parliament granted him tonnage and poundage for life. This, together with the treasure left by his father and the income from the royal estates and feudal dues, carried him through two years of peace. As soon as he indulged his fancy for war, he had to have more money. Between 1512 and 1515 three parliaments were called to grant the necessary taxes. When he went to war again ten years later, he tried to do without parliament by means of a forced loan. His subjects were required to lend a certain percentage of their incomes to the king. Repayment was promised, but was not forthcoming. When this proved inadequate, parliament was summoned. The successful opposition of this parliament to his fiscal demands and his foreign policy apparently taught Henry something of the force of public opinion and of the significance of the house of commons as its mouthpiece.[11] In 1529, when popular support became essential for the success of his attack upon the pope, he reversed his previous attitude toward the commons. Thereafter he met parliaments frequently, and endeavored to bend the commons to his will by more adroit methods.

The means by which he manipulated the house of commons were varied. In the parliaments of 1536 and 1539 the royal influence was used to secure a subservient majority in the house. To some extent this was done through friendly nobles, who, by their local prestige, by the purchase of boroughs, or by the bribery of electors, controlled the election of several members. In part it was done by direct pressure on the electors. Thomas Cromwell, for example, wrote to the electors of Canterbury, stating that the king *"desired"* them to elect the candidates

[10] *Ibid.,* pp. 158, 159, 322, 323.
[11] See above, pp. 307, 308.

whom he named. They ventured to elect others, whereupon Cromwell wrote *"requiring"* them to cancel their election and hold a new one, where the king's candidates should be named "as ye intend to avoid his highness's displeasure at your peril." Needless to say, the burgesses of Canterbury met again and *"freely, with one voice,"* elected as their representatives the men named by Cromwell.[12] At other elections also Henry expressed his wishes to nobles or directly to constituencies with regard to individual candidates, but apparently no other parliaments of his reign were packed in such a wholesale manner as these two assembled under the auspices of Cromwell. Henry relied more on his ability to influence the commons after they had met than he did on the exertion of pressure at elections.

The speaker, though nominally elected by the house, was practically appointed by the king, whose views he was expected to represent before the house. The councilors and other royal officials who were elected to the lower house also began at this period to exert a strong influence in behalf of the king. Most of all he relied on his own ability to secure the cooperation of the commons, for it was this he sought rather than servility. He often took the house into his confidence instead of dealing with it at arm's length through others. When an independent member proposed that the commons should ask him to take back Katherine of Aragon, he issued no command to them to be silent, as even the tactful Elizabeth did later when they attempted to discuss her marriage. Henry VIII sent for the speaker and explained to him just why Katherine could not be restored. The explanation of the royal views was sufficient. The commons dropped the question. His methods were sometimes more imperious. When the commons rejected Henry's bill in conditional restraint of annates by a vote of ayes and noes, he went down to the house and had a division taken. The members went into the lobby, the ayes returning through one door and the noes through another. On this vote the bill passed. Henry issued no commands, but, as Stubbs says, "partly by promising that there should be no more acts against the pope, partly by the terror of his majestic eyes, he obtained a majority; men could not comfortably vote in the presence of the definer of all præmunires."[13] These incidents illustrate the skill with which Henry VIII managed the house of commons. He was not always successful, for some of his measures were rejected by the house, but he secured the enactment into legislation of all his important policies. That he thought it wiser to manage

[12] Merriman, *Thomas Cromwell*, ii, 13; *Letters and Papers*, x, 852, 929.
[13] Stubbs, *Seventeen Lectures*, p. 281.

the house of commons than to do without it, however, was an acknowledgment of its importance which tended to exalt it more than the
king's manipulation tended to degrade it.

The successors of Henry VIII generally attempted to maintain the
same relations with the house of commons by more or less the same
methods. Somerset made no effort to tamper with the elections. He
relied primarily on his influence with the commons. It was insufficient,
and the commons were decidedly more independent than they had
been under Henry VIII. Northumberland found that popularity was
necessary even to pack the house. When he made the attempt, the resulting house of commons was so refractory that parliament had to
be dissolved. Mary also was unfortunate with her parliaments. The
house of commons in each parliament enacted some of the legislation
she demanded, but never all of it. Four of her five parliaments were
dissolved on account of the opposition of the commons. Even the use
of the royal influence in two of the elections did not produce houses of
commons which did all that the queen's government asked of them.
The experience of these two reigns indicates that something more than
royal efforts at packing was needed to secure compliant houses of
commons.

Elizabeth's position in relation to the house of commons was in
some ways more advantageous than that of Henry VIII and in some
ways more difficult. Until 1588 the impending danger of foreign invasion tended to make the disposition of the commons favorable to
cooperation with the queen. On the other hand, the house was becoming more conscious of its strength, and public opinion was making
itself more strongly felt. The house of commons that Henry VIII had
put in the saddle was beginning to reach for the reins. Elizabeth met
parliament as infrequently as possible, but she had to call it at fairly
regular intervals to get money. For supplies she was more dependent
upon parliament than her father had been. The proceeds from the
confiscation of ecclesiastical property, which had swelled his coffers,
were not available to her, nor did she venture to use benevolences or
forced loans. Government, on the other hand, cost more in her day.
Faced with the necessity of controlling the house of commons if she
would have her way, she did it with a skill that rivaled her father's.
During the first half of her reign no great effort seems to have been
made to interfere with elections; but during the last two decades,
when the commons were becoming too independent to submit readily
even to her tactful management, her privy councilors undertook, apparently with some success, to influence elections by ordering sheriffs

Edward
VI and
Mary

Elizabeth

to promote the election of specified candidates or of men well affected to the government. In her last years, however, it was only her popularity that kept the house of commons from becoming more recalcitrant than it did.

The growing importance of the house of commons in the sixteenth
Parlia-
mentary
privileges
century is reflected also in the increase of controversy over parliamentary privileges. These constituted its chief protection against outside interference, and made it possible for the house to voice the nation's wishes when they conflicted with those of the ruler. Freedom of speech was vindicated in 1512 in the case of a member who was prosecuted in a court for bills he had introduced into parliament. In 1542 the speaker included it for the first time among the ancient privileges of the house that he demanded of the king at the beginning of each session, and thirty years later it became the regular form to demand freedom from arrest, freedom of speech, and freedom of access. By the last was meant the right of the house to have audience with the king through its speaker. Under Elizabeth freedom of speech fared badly. She forbade the commons to debate her marriage or ecclesiastical matters which had not previously been considered in convocation. A member who subsequently moved a committee on ecclesiastical affairs was excluded from the house, and another was imprisoned. Freedom of debate was far from an established fact at the close of Elizabeth's reign. Freedom from arrest, on the other hand, was vindicated on several occasions, though it was still to be the question of debate under the Stuarts. One new right of importance which the house acquired in this period was that of settling the validity of the elections of its own members. This had previously been done in chancery or in council. In Mary's reign the house once exercised the right, and in Elizabeth's they secured a possession of it that was not contested until the time of James I. Though none of these privileges was established beyond dispute, the importance of the precedents set in the sixteenth century comports ill with the point of view that the house of commons was subservient to the Tudors, however tractable it may have been.

The strong central government of the Tudors maintained internal
Local
govern-
ment
peace and order largely because it was based on strong local institutions. These became much more active than they had been in the Middle Ages. New duties and powers were given to them by statutes, and they underwent an extensive reorganization.

The most notable change was the substitution of the parish for the
The parish
vill or manor as the local unit of civil administration. The vill had never been of great importance as part of the government. The parish,

which generally coincided with the vill, but might be larger or smaller, was the unit of ecclesiastical organization. It was the territorial charge of a priest. On the administrative side of his duties he was assisted by two churchwardens elected by the parishioners. They looked after the maintenance of the buildings and property of the church and kept order in church. They had the power given by canon law and sanctioned by the common law to levy taxes from the parishioners for the repair of the church. They were more active than the constables, the only officials of the vill, and the early statutes of Elizabeth that required local execution designated the churchwardens as the local agents of enforcement. Thus they became civil as well as ecclesiastical officials. When the new overseers of the poor were established, their unit of administration was made the parish. In Mary's reign a surveyor of the highways was appointed in each parish to secure an improvement in the hopelessly inadequate local system of the repair and maintenance of the roads. The constables were the only local officials whose bailiwicks were the vills, and many of the functions they had previously performed were transferred to the new officials of the parish. By the close of the century the parish had practically superseded the vill as the local administrative unit, and it was far more active and important in that capacity than the vill had ever been.

In the counties no such extensive reorganization took place. Lords lieutenants were created in the reign of Edward VI whose functions were to levy and command the militia in each county, using it at their own discretion in the case of a local rebellion. Otherwise no new officials were created. The justices of the peace had their powers greatly amplified. Practically every statute that required local execution thrust new duties upon them. They not only were the judges of the local courts, both criminal and petty, but they exercised extensive police functions, oversaw the building and maintenance of public works in the county, fixed wages and prices, enforced penal laws against Catholics and Puritans, superintended the administration of the poor law, and performed a host of other functions. They were practically the local rulers of the counties. *The counties*

Local government became far more important under the Tudors than it had ever been before, but it was not local self-government. These local officials were merely agents to assist the central administration. All of them, except the coroners, the churchwardens, and the constables, who were locally elected, were appointed by the central authority or by the centrally appointed justices of the peace. The pivot on which the system swung was the justice of the peace. In the county the *Relation to the central government* justices themselves did most of the administrative and judicial work, and all of the other officials of the county, except the lords lieutenants, were more or less responsible to them. In the local units the constables and churchwardens, though popularly elected, were under the direction of the justices in many things and subject to their supervision in all. The overseers and surveyors were appointed by them as well. The justices in turn were under the direction of the privy council, which might direct their work in general terms or order them to do specific acts. The council kept itself informed of their actions by means of records of their proceedings kept by a deputy of the keeper of the rolls, who was named in the commission of the peace and was independent of their authority. Individuals who deemed themselves wronged by the justices could complain to the council or to chancery.

Legally the system was highly centralized. The justices of the peace were responsible to central authority, and other local officials to the justices of the peace. In actuality the system was not so completely centralized as it appears on paper. The control of the central government was fairly close under the Tudors, but the country gentlemen who held commissions of the peace were not amenable to the same discipline as clerks whose livelihood depended on the pay of the crown. Their social position among their neighbors caused them to have regard for the interests of the people they ruled as well as for those of the government they served, and the large discretionary powers which necessarily went with such multitudinous functions gave them a certain degree of independence of both. The result was an administrative system sufficiently centralized to secure the good administration of the law and sufficiently responsive to local needs to prevent the formation of a bureaucracy as the basis for an unpopular despotism.

CHAPTER XXII

KING VERSUS PARLIAMENT

JAMES I, who came to the throne in 1603, represented the natural
order of hereditary succession. Elizabeth was the last of the legitimate
descendants of Henry VIII. Her death left the descendants of the
sisters of Henry VIII the only claimants to the throne.[1] The will of
Henry VIII preferred the heirs of his younger sister Mary to those of
his older sister Margaret, but Elizabeth's councilors had long looked
upon James as her successor,[2] the privy council immediately proclaimed
him king, and he was accepted whole-heartedly by the English people.
His right to the throne was never seriously questioned, but his ability
to rule faced a severe test. The nation was beginning to fret under the
tight rein of the Tudors. The need for it was gone. There was no longer
danger from a disputed succession, the nobles had been suppressed,
the Reformation was securely settled, and the defeat of the Armada
had ended the danger of foreign invasion. England was peaceful and
prosperous. Now that a strong monarchy was no longer essential for
the popular welfare, the nation was beginning to recognize some of
its disadvantages. Toward the close of Elizabeth's reign parliament
displayed a growing disposition to oppose the royal will. With the
accession of James the check imposed by the bond of loyalty to the old
queen was removed. A wiser king than James would have found
England difficult to govern in 1603.

James's position

James did not anticipate difficulty. He came to the throne with a
background of experience acquired as king of Scotland and with a
theory of monarchy in accord with the prevailing European tendency
toward absolute forms of government. In Scotland he had never been
able to put theory into practice, but he looked upon his English inheritance as a centralized monarchy which would give free play for
his theory. Neither his practice nor his theory gave him knowledge of

Person-
ality and
ideas

[1] The following table is abbreviated:

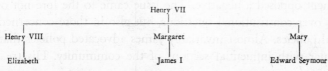

[2] Read, *Mr. Secretary Walsingham*, iii, 339.

the English constitution or of the English people. He assumed that he could rule more wisely than Elizabeth. He possessed no mean ability. His abstract thoughts on government were often keen, but he rarely understood when they would bear practical application. He stood firm where concession would have been the better part of wisdom, and gave way in the wrong place. As a judge of human nature James was often at fault. He took advice from empty-headed favorites like Buckingham, who appealed to his fancy, and allowed the opinions of a great statesman like Sir Francis Bacon to go a-begging. He possessed none of the tact that had been so characteristic of Elizabeth. Nor did he possess his predecessor's skill in the evaluation of public opinion. When it differed from his, he was too apt to treat it with contempt. It was a bit difficult for him to comprehend that he might be mistaken. With such a personality popularity was out of the question for James, had he sought it. He did not seek it, nor did he see that it had been one of the main supports of the Tudor monarchy.

Divine right

Popularity was superfluous to a ruler whose rights were what James conceived his to be. In his estimation his subjects had no rights; they might have privileges granted by royal favor; otherwise they had only duties.[3] His theory of kingship was that of divine right. Monarchy, this theory holds, is a divinely ordained institution. A king is consequently accountable only to God. He is not responsible to parliament or to the nation. Indeed, parliament and all the other organs of government derive their power from the king. Subjects owe this divinely created institution active obedience, and resistance is a sin. It is the king's duty to rule for the welfare of his subjects, but he is the only judge of what constitutes their welfare. If he fails in his duty, however, his subjects have no redress. Even against a tyrant they have no right of rebellion. Such a theory places the king above the law, above parliament, and above the nation.

James I and parliament

James not only acted upon this theory, but he flaunted it before parliament. The commons, already chafing under the restraints of the Tudors, met the attempt of a Stuart to increase the royal power still more with opposition. The fundamental issue soon came to be the extent of the royal authority. To the king's claim that it was unlimited, parliament opposed a negative. The issue came to the fore not only in debates over constitutional questions, but also in those concerned with national policies. Almost invariably James advocated policies that were unpopular with influential sections of the community. His treatment

---

[3] Prothero, *Select Statutes*, p. 313, n. 1.

of the Puritans, his relations with the Catholics, his attempted union of England with Scotland, and his foreign policy brought the adverse criticisms of parliament. James took no heed of the popular wishes. When parliament sought to press them upon him, he informed the members of the house of commons that it was not their place to discuss questions of policy; these were "king's craft" "far above their reach and capacity."[4] At first the commons were merely irritated, but, as one quarrel between king and parliament followed another, vexation gave place to alarm. The house of commons finally became intent upon the assertion of the rights of the subject, and determined to place constitutional limits on the power of the king. The efforts of James to increase the royal authority served only to promote a contest between king and parliament which led eventually to civil war.

One of the first issues that the new king had to meet was that of religion. Soon after his arrival in England he was presented with the millenary petition, so called because of its reputed signature by one thousand Puritan divines. It requested reforms in the service of the church and the discipline of the clergy, but sought no significant change in the government of the church. James replied by inviting representatives of the Puritans to debate with the bishops in his presence at the palace of Hampton Court. In the course of the conference one of the Puritans suggested the subsequent reference of contested points of worship to the bishop and his presbyters. At that James burst out: "If you aim at a Scottish presbytery it agreeth as well with monarchy as God and the devil."[5] Of Presbyterianism James had had enough in Scotland. He frankly opposed Presbyterians and Separatists because their tenets were not in accord with the monarchical principle. As a result of this attitude, James denied nearly the whole of the petition, though he approved the request for a new translation of the Bible, and appointed a commission which produced the King James Version of it a few years later. The expression of his general disapproval of the Puritans did not stop, however, with the denial of their petition. In convocation he obtained the enactment of canons designed to secure the more rigid application of uniformity. During the remainder of his reign many of the Puritans were forced out of the church into the ranks of the Separatists, and those who remained cherished no love for the royal authority.

With the Catholics James was no more fortunate. When he came to the throne the savage penal laws of Elizabeth still obtained, though

The Puritans

---

[4] *Ibid.*, pp. 294, 310.
[5] Montague, *History of England*, p. 11.

they had long been enforced laxly. Even before James left Scotland some of the Catholics had obtained from him what they believed was an assurance that he would not maintain the penal code. After his accession no notable change in Elizabeth's practice appeared. Some of the Catholics, angered because the recusancy fines continued to be levied, formed a plot to capture the king and force him to grant their demands. Other Catholics betrayed the plot, and James out of gratitude allowed the fines to be almost entirely remitted. The increase in the number of those who ceased to attend church was so great that James became alarmed. After a few months he began to collect the fines again. This weak and vacillating policy caused a group of Catholics to attempt the Gunpowder Plot. When parliament met in the autumn of 1605, they planned to blow up the chamber where king, lords, and commons would be assembled, and to secure control of the government in the resulting confusion. The plot was discovered and the plotters apprehended, but it revived the popular fear of the Catholics which had been lulled since the victory over the Armada. Parliament enacted a still more stringent law against the Catholics. James sanctioned the legislation, but openly allowed it to remain unexecuted. His leniency toward the Catholics displeased the Protestants generally and the Puritans in particular.

With parliament James came into conflict at its first session in 1604. He made no attempt to control the composition of the house of commons, the number of privy councilors and royal officials who were members was notably smaller than it had been under the Tudors, and though the speaker was still a royal nominee, James made little effort to manipulate the house. Such precautions seemed unnecessary to a king who thought he had only to make known his will to be obeyed. The house of commons had other views. Almost immediately it took issue on a question of privilege. Despite the precedent of Elizabeth's reign,[6] the returns of the election were made to chancery. In one constituency the return of Goodwin as elected was disputed by the defeated candidate, Fortescue, who was a privy councilor. The chancery declared Goodwin was not entitled to a seat because he was an outlaw, and ordered a new election, which seated Fortescue. The house maintained that Goodwin was not outlawed, that outlawry did not disqualify him if he was, and that his election was valid. James, instead of settling the individual case on its merits, raised the constitutional question of the right of the house to determine disputed elections, informing

---

[6] Above, p. 384.

the members that "he had no purpose to impeach their privilege, but since they derived all matters of privilege from him and by his grant, he expected that they should not be turned against him. . . . By the law, the House ought not to meddle with returns, being all made into Chancery, and are to be corrected or reformed by that court only into which they were returned."[7] This threatened the independence of the house. As one member put it in debate: "By this course the free election of the country is taken away, and none shall be chosen but such as shall please the King and Council."[8] The house accordingly took up the struggle in earnest. The king finally acknowledged the right of the house to determine the elections of its own members, but obtained the seat for his candidate by asking for it as a personal favor. The whole incident was typical of James. He had gone out of his way to assert that parliamentary privilege depended on his favor, had raised the constitutional principle unnecessarily, and then had sacrificed it to win the individual case.

Another divergence arose over James's project of union with Scotland. Though the countries had the same king, their institutions still remained entirely separate. James sought to unite the two sufficiently to enable him to take the title of king of Great Britain. The tradition of hostility between the countries proved to be too strong to be overcome in a moment, and the commons declined to enact the necessary legislation. The most they would do was to appoint a committee to discuss terms of union with representatives of the parliament of Scotland. The refusal to comply with his wishes made James very angry. In a later session parliament agreed that each nation should repeal the laws hostile to the other and arrange for the mutual extradition of criminals, but free trade and English citizenship for the Scots they would not grant. The courts served the king better than parliament. A suit yielded the decision that Scotsmen born after James's accession to the English throne were English citizens, and with that James had to rest content.

Scotland

Before the first session was prorogued, James and the commons disagreed on still another question. The commons, who were in sympathy with the Puritans, began to debate mild reforms of the church similar to those suggested in the millenary petition. James, taking umbrage, addressed to them a rebuke for their interference in religious affairs, which was an attack on their freedom of speech. The commons thereupon drew up a document which they called an apology to the

Apology of the commons

[7] Gardiner, *History of England*, i, 168.
[8] Protnero, p. 327.

king for their actions, but which was in reality a defense of them. It traversed the doctrine of divine right, as James had expounded it in the course of his controversies with them, and laid down the platform of parliamentary rights. They told the king that he had been misinformed. Their privileges, on which depended the liberties of the subject, they asserted to be theirs by right and not by any grace of his; particularly they claimed the right "that in parliament they may speak freely their consciences without check and controlment"; they warned the king that he could make no laws concerning religion or other subjects except by consent of parliament; they suggested that his majesty forsake his present misinformants "to receive public information from your Commons in parliament"; and finally they capped the "divinity" that "doth hedge a king" with the divine quality of the voice that doth issue from the people.[9] The issue of limited monarchy versus absolute monarchy was squarely joined.

Bate's case

Two years later the issue was again raised on the fundamental question of control of taxation. In Elizabeth's reign an import duty, called an imposition, was levied on currants, which James continued to exact. In 1606 a merchant named John Bate imported some currants without paying the imposition, and the crown sued in the court of exchequer. Counsel for Bate took the ground that the imposition was an illegal tax because parliament had never sanctioned it. The judges decided in favor of the king on the ground that a king could not exist without revenues and therefore he could take revenues at his discretion.[10] As the judges elaborated their argument, they limited the king's power to treat his subjects as he pleased only by his own forbearance. Of other limits they knew none. The decision in favor of the crown was not in itself of great importance because it probably could have been justified by precedent. But if the grounds alleged by the judges were accepted, parliament would be left without any control of taxation and with no means to restrain the king. James would have legally the unlimited power that he claimed.

The great
contract

James promptly took advantage of the judgment to increase the number of impositions. Fortunately for the nation, the increased revenues still fell short of the expenditures. The rising prices and the growing functions of the central government had forced upon Elizabeth an economy that verged on parsimony, and the Irish war of her closing years had left heavy debts to James. He rapidly increased the deficit by his extravagance. England by contrast with barren Scotland

---

[9] *Ibid.,* pp. 286–293.
[10] Adams and Stephens, *Select Documents,* p. 329.

appeared to James to be a land flowing with milk and honey, where economy had no place. By 1610 income and expenditure were so far apart that he called parliament into session and asked for a grant of taxes. This presented to the house of commons the opportunity to secure the redress of their grievances. Prominent among them were feudal dues and purveyance. The former were the vexatious remnants of an antiquated institution, and the latter, which was the right of the king to seize provisions and some other articles at an appraised value, had always been the object of popular dislike. The commons proposed to the king that he should forego these revenues in return for a parliamentary grant of a permanently fixed annual sum. They haggled long with the king over the bargain, which came to be known as the great contract, and eventually they tried to obtain the redress of other grievances before making the appropriation. In the course of the debates the king set forth the theory of divine right in terms more extreme than any he had yet employed before parliament. Members of the house began to cite precedents from the Lancastrian period, which seemed to substantiate their view that the king was below the law. Finally the house began to debate impositions. James then sent a message to the commons, announcing his willingness to listen to complaints arising from any particular imposition, but ordering them not to discuss the right to levy impositions, which was his by law and by judicial decision in the case of Bate. They replied that the decision, if it were sound at common law, enabled the king to levy all taxes without parliamentary consent, and demanded freedom to debate the power of the crown if they chose. The royal officials in the house appealed in vain to Tudor precedents and cited the similar prohibitions placed on the freedom of the speech of the house by Elizabeth. The house insisted until James revoked his prohibition. Before legislative action on the impositions was completed, however, James, deciding that he would prefer economy to such dependence on parliament as the commons aimed at, dissolved the parliament and allowed the great contract to fall through.

Thus, early in 1611, came to an end the parliament which had first been summoned in 1604. In the course of its five sessions the question of the powers of the king had been debated with ever-increasing acrimony. Cooperation had given place to opposition between king and parliament. The result was to get well under way the contest between king and parliament that was not finally settled until the revolution of 1688.

Result of the first parliament

The king's program of fiscal reform was so far from successful that in 1614 he resolved to summon parliament again. On this occasion he attempted to influence the elections. He found that this expedient of the Tudors could no longer be used successfully. Public opinion had been so stirred by the results of the first parliament that the agents who undertook to secure the return of nominees of the crown failed miserably. They acquired the epithet of "the undertakers," and the commons assembled with an attitude more hostile than ever. To the royal demand for supplies they paid no attention, beginning at once to air their grievances. The parliament met on April 5, 1614. The debates grew ever more bitter. On June 5 James threatened to dissolve it if supply was not granted at once, and two days later he carried out his threat. Not a single bill became law, and the parliament became known as the Addled Parliament. After the dissolution several of those members who had opposed most emphatically the royal views of the absolute character of the royal authority were arrested and put in the Tower. Thus James demonstrated his disregard for freedom of speech.

From 1611 to 1621, with the exception of the Addled Parliament which did no business, the king ruled without parliament. During this decade the rights of the nation found a new champion in the courts of common law. On several occasions cases involving the constitutional questions in dispute between king and parliament came into these courts, where the judges, led by the great lawyer, Sir Edward Coke, gave decisions unfavorable to the king's claims. Coke believed that the courts of common law should hold a position independent of king and parliament, except so far as their decisions were subject to review by the high court of parliament, in which the king shared with the lords the right of judgment. To Coke reverence for the common law was a fetish, and from his wide knowledge of medieval law he drew numerous precedents for opposition to absolutism. He probably opposed the implications of divine right not so much because he believed abstractly in the liberty of the subject as because he worshiped the medieval precedents which placed limitations on the crown. Whatever his reasons, he maintained the principle vigorously, and he could and did on occasion tell James to his face that the law was greater than the king.[11]

James held that the courts were dependent on the king. His point of view received ample confirmation from the sixteenth century, when so much judicial work was done by special tribunals acting without jury; nor did all medieval precedents support Coke's view. The best

---

[11] On this incident see the critical discussion of R. G. Usher in *Eng. Hist. Rev.*, xviii, 664–675.

exponent of the thesis that the courts ought to be limited by the executive was Sir Francis Bacon, who held office under both Elizabeth and James and eventually became the latter's lord chancellor. "Let the judges be lions, but yet lions under the throne, being circumspect that they do not check or oppose any points of sovereignty"[12] was Bacon's famous *dictum* on the subject. He thought that to let the judges decide broad political and administrative questions by the narrow technicalities of the common law would be against the best welfare of the state. In cases involving constitutional questions the judges ought to defer to the opinion of the executive. Bacon's point of view has so much justification that today only in the countries where the common law prevails can judges of the ordinary courts submit public officials to the same rules of law that govern the relations of private individuals one to another. In France and other continental countries administrative tribunals exist for the enforcement of public law, and officials can be sued for their official acts only before these special courts. In the seventeenth century Bacon was unfortunate in having his theory applied concretely by a king whose conception of the welfare of the state was utterly at variance with that held by a large part of the nation.

Led by Coke, who became chief justice of the common pleas in 1606, the judges attacked repeatedly in one particular or another the jurisdiction claimed by the special courts, such as chancery and the court of high commission. In 1610 parliament petitioned against the use of proclamations by the king. James referred the question to the judges. He received a reiteration of the decision of Mary's reign, that by proclamation the king could make no new law nor add to the penalties of an old one, with the gratuitous opinion, particularly applicable to James's practice, that no proclamation could make an offense punishable by star chamber that was not already so by law. In 1613 Coke was promoted to be chief justice of the king's bench, where it was hoped the nature of the cases would give him less opportunity to oppose the king. He was soon at it again. In 1614 the government wished to convict a man of treason. Before proceeding, it consulted the judges individually to make sure the prosecution would be successful. Coke objected to the consultation of the judges singly, but it was an old practice, and the other judges gave way. Further disputes followed, until finally a case came before king's bench that involved the power of the king to appoint to certain offices. The court was ordered not to proceed further without consulting the king. To admit this principle would have made

---

[12] Gardiner, *History of England,* iii, 2.

the courts entirely dependent on the king, since he could intervene whenever he thought his interests were at stake. The chief justice and his colleagues consequently disregarded the order. Thereupon they were summoned before the king, and all except Coke promised henceforth to obey such an order. Coke was forthwith dismissed. The courts could no longer protect the rights of the subject against the will of the king.

Meanwhile James was further arousing the ill will of the nation by his partiality for unworthy favorites and by an unpopular foreign policy. Royal favorites were not new. Elizabeth had always had them at her court without arousing strong popular animosities. James's first favorites were unpopular because they were Scotsmen. He squandered a good deal of wealth on them, and worst of all he took their advice. After 1612 he depended largely on the advice of a Scotsman whom he raised to the English peerage and eventually created earl of Somerset. The king still consulted his privy council, but gave it little heed. The business of state was often settled in private conversations with Somerset, whose abilities as a statesman English councilors distrusted. This was bad enough; worse followed. Somerset desired to marry a lady who already had a husband. When she sued for divorce, the king used his influence with the judges to secure a decision in her favor. The lady apparently manufactured some of her evidence, and later she procured the death of a man who threatened to expose the fraud. Both Somerset and his wife were tried and convicted of murder. James commuted the sentence, but he had to forego the pleasure of Somerset's company. The scandal combined with the apparently utter disregard of justice caused widespread popular criticism of the king. James learned nothing from it. Already a young chap named Villiers was high on the road to royal favor; before long he became duke of Buckingham and slipped into Somerset's shoes. Under James the government was fast becoming a despotism of the worst type: a despotism controlled by irresponsible favorites.

In foreign policy James's first step was wise but unpopular. In 1604 he made peace with Spain. England had long since demolished Spanish power on the seas, France and the Netherlands no longer needed English help against Spain, and continuance of the war seemed profitless. James felt none of that hostility toward Spain which had almost become part of the religion of many Englishmen. He had been reared a Protestant, but his mother, Mary Stuart, had been a Catholic and his wife favored Catholicism. James himself was tolerant on the religious question, and he respected Spain as a great power. The treaty

The
favorites

The
Protestant
alliance

failed to obtain for English merchants the right to trade with Spanish colonies, which Elizabeth had demanded, and ended a prosperous trade in which much English capital had been invested while the war kept open the ports on the Spanish main. Subsequently James's policy was led in a more popular direction by his advisers, who favored alliances with Protestant powers. At that time the danger of a religious war in Germany loomed upon the horizon. The settlement of 1555, which left the ruler of each German state free to fix the religion of his people, had led to great friction between Protestant and Catholic states. Early in the seventeenth century this became so sharp that a union of several Protestant states was formed under the leadership of the elector Palatine, ruler of the Palatinate, a strong and prosperous state on the Rhine, and a Catholic league was organized in opposition. James once came to the help of the German Protestants when they contested with the Catholics the control of a small state. His intervention led in 1612 to a permanent alliance based on the marriage of James's daughter, Elizabeth, to Frederick, elector Palatine. With this policy Englishmen were in sympathy.

It was after 1612, when James veered toward friendship with Spain, that his foreign policy became thoroughly unpopular. The new departure was brought about by the death of the minister who had been chiefly responsible for his foreign policy, and by the influence over James acquired by the ambassador who came to represent Spain in 1613. The new ambassador, who is generally called by his later title of Gondomar, was one of the most astute diplomats of the age. He soon learned James's weaknesses, and by a combination of flattery and firmness he became nearly as influential with the king as were his favorites. Spain sought the alliance of England for two reasons. If a religious war developed in Germany, Spain was almost certain to engage on the Catholic side. The Spanish king still posed as the champion of Catholicism. In any religious war in Germany, moreover, the branch of the Habsburg house which held Austria and the imperial title was bound to take part on the Catholic side, and the Spanish and Austrian Habsburgs maintained a close alliance on religious and political issues. Spain sought, therefore, to wean England from the German Protestant alliance. The Spanish government hoped also to recover England for Catholicism. War having failed, the next expedient was royal marriage, which would make the ruler of England in a later generation a Catholic. Gondomar proposed, therefore, in behalf of his master, that Charles, the heir to the English throne, should marry a daughter of the king of Spain. James was pleased to negotiate. When Spain pro-

Relations
with Spain

posed as part of the alliance that the children of the marriage should be educated as Catholics by the mother and that the English penal laws against the Catholics should be suspended, he hesitated. He knew that these proposals would be entirely unacceptable to the nation. The negotiations were secret, but Gondomar's influence over the king, which was patent to all, was a source of much popular dissatisfaction.

Thirty
Years'
War

While the negotiations hung fire, the whole situation was complicated by the outbreak in Germany of the religious wars that were destined to last for thirty years. They began with the revolt of the Bohemian Protestants against their Habsburg king, who was a bigoted Catholic. At first success accompanied the Bohemian arms. Spain was quick to see that she would probably be called to the aid of the Austrian Habsburgs. With this possibility imminent, the position of England became of great moment. James's son-in-law, Frederick of the Palatinate, the head of the German Protestant league, was likely to be involved, and James had with him a defensive alliance. Spain suggested, therefore, that James should act as mediator. James, who was highly flattered, accepted. While he studied the question Frederick accepted the kingship of Bohemia tendered to him by the rebellious Bohemian nobles, and with it the leadership of the Protestant cause. Spain, meanwhile, was preparing for war, and in 1620 a Spanish army occupied the Palatinate, the ancestral domain of James's son-in-law. James at last awoke to the fact that Spain had duped him. By the suggestion of mediation and a renewal of the negotiations for the marriage alliance he had been restrained from giving aid to his son-in-law, while Spain was preparing to attack him. When he finally comprehended the trick, he became thoroughly angry, and resolved to intervene in behalf of Frederick.

Benevo-
lences

His first problem was finance. War could not be fought without money. Since 1614 he had been fairly successful, with the aid of an efficient minister of finance, in making both ends meet. After the dissolution of his last parliament he had resorted to a benevolence, which had not been used since the time of Henry VIII. Despite a good deal of pressure, which included a heavy fine imposed by star chamber on a gentleman who ventured to criticize the policy, the benevolence yielded only £66,000. The nation was now too fearful of the suppression of parliament to assist the king to deprive parliament of its one guarantee of existence. It was mainly by the reorganization of the fixed revenues and the establishment of economies in the spending departments that the budget was made to balance. These would not suffice to finance campaigns. Since James did not wish to meet parliament, he tried another benevolence. From the members of the privy council and the city of London he obtained £28,000, but from the rest of the nation he received only excuses. Pressure was brought to bear; prominent country gentlemen who refused to contribute found themselves appointed sheriffs and lord lieutenants to serve without pay; others received an unfair apportionment when the militia was mustered. It was all to no purpose. The people favored war because their bugbear, Spain, threatened the Protestant power on the continent. They felt that England, the champion of Protestantism, ought to come to the rescue. But the desire to have parliament summoned was even stronger. Seven years of government by favorites without parliament had given rise to fears of the establishment of an irresponsible despotism. James could obtain for a popular cause from the nation at large only £6,000. He was compelled to summon parliament to meet in 1621.

When parliament convened, it was an astonishingly loyal body. Before its assemblage news had come that Frederick had been de- **Supply** feated and driven a fugitive from Bohemia, while Spanish troops were overrunning the Palatinate. The nation was so desirous of war that parliament was ready to drop discussion of the old constitutional grievances and rally to the support of James who was momentarily bent upon war. With his usual lack of insight James missed the opportunity of reconciliation with the nation. He asked for the grant of a large sum, but made no explanation of his plans for the war. In his thought the conduct of war was no business of the house of commons. But the commons desired to know how the troops were to be used before they authorized their levy. They granted a small tax in order to display their good will toward a policy of war, and awaited further information from the king before granting more.

While they waited, they naturally fell to debating the national grievances. Their first attack was upon monopolies. These had in- **Monopo-** creased in number under James and they were greatly abused. It was **lies and** evident that their grant was controlled largely by the royal favorites. **impeach-** Indeed, several of them were held by Buckingham's relatives. A blow **ments** at the monopolies was indirectly a blow at the royal favorites. Under the leadership of Sir Edward Coke the commons accused before the house of lords the holder of one of the worst abused monopolies and a magistrate who had used his authority corruptly to support the extortionate practices of the holder. The defendants were tried in accordance with the forms of impeachment. Technically the case was not an impeachment, but for practical purposes it was a revival of the weapon which the house of commons had not used against the king since the fifteenth century. James, recognizing it as such, tried without success to prevent the action. The two men were condemned. The house then impeached Lord Chancellor Bacon, who was an important royal official. The real reason for the attack was the support given by Bacon to the extreme claims of power advanced by James, though the charge against him was the acceptance of bribes in his capacity as judge. Technically he was guilty, and so pleaded, though it is probable that he had never allowed the justice of his decisions to be affected by bribes. His condemnation, however, placed in the hands of the house of commons a potent instrument to use in their struggle with the king. It was a warning that those who advised the king in courses regarded by parliament as unconstitutional would have to reckon with parliament. Before the house of commons completed its work by a bill abolishing monopolies, James prorogued the session, but its warning was heeded. The king subsequently revoked eighteen of the most obnoxious monopolies by proclamation.

Great
Protes-
tation

When parliament met for its second session later in the same year, James asked further supply, still without explanation of its intended use. The commons wanted war against Spain, they distrusted Gondomar, and they were fearful of the king's intentions with regard to the Spanish marriage. They therefore granted a small subsidy and prepared to petition the king to go to war against Spain, to marry Charles to a Protestant, and to enforce the laws against recusants. Gondomar saw a copy of the petition before it was despatched to the king. Forthwith he wrote to James a letter, "the like of which," says Gardiner, "had never before been placed in the hands of an English sovereign." Among other things the ambassador said that did he not depend on the king to punish the house of commons, he would have left England already. "This it would have been my duty to do, as you would have ceased to be king here, and as I have no army to punish these people myself."[13] James did not order Gondomar to leave the kingdom; he wrote an angry letter to the house of commons.

The royal missive attacked freedom of speech in two particulars. It commanded members of the house not to meddle with affairs of state in general and Charles's marriage in particular, and informed them that the king would punish those who spoke against him in parliament. The commons thereupon requested the king to withdraw or explain away those parts of his letter which appeared to threaten their right to debate those questions which might properly be the subject

---

[13] Gardiner, *Prince Charles and the Spanish Marriage,* ii, 136.

cf their debate and their undoubted ancient right to liberty of speech. In his reply James again harped upon their meddling with things far above their reach. He guaranteed to the present house its freedom of speech, but he did it in terms which denied that freedom of speech was their right. The house determined to cease bickering with the king, but to define its constitutional right. The Great Protestation was accordingly framed and entered on the journal of the house. It declared affairs concerning the king, the state of the realm, and various other matters to be proper subjects for their debate, and that every member had of right freedom of speech to treat such questions.[14] A few days later, when parliament had been adjourned, James, in the presence of the privy council, tore the record from the journal. Parliament was then dissolved. The last word in the controversy rested with the king, but the Great Protestation had asserted such a right of the commons to initiate and debate important policies as had not been exercised by them under the Tudors, and James's petulant action did not erase the record from the memory of the house.

This burst of temper left James with a body of ill-equipped volunteers on his hands but without the money necessary to send them to the Palatinate. This had been Gondomar's object. Now that he had James where he could not fight, it was easy to persuade him to resort again to negotiation. James was made to hope that Spain would withdraw its troops from the Palatinate for the sake of a marriage alliance with England. Gondomar classed James in the category of those who could be fooled all the time. Charles meanwhile conceived the idea that it would be a lark to go to Spain and woo his bride in person. Supported by Buckingham, who would be his companion, he won the consent of his father and started for Spain in 1623. When Charles arrived, the Spaniards set the priests to work to convert him to Catholicism. Between theological discussions Charles found little time to press his suit. On the one occasion when he circumvented the etiquette of the Spanish court and sought to carry on his courtship in person, he accomplished it only by jumping over a garden wall. He was rewarded by the shrieking flight of his intended bride, who made little distinction between this heretic and the gentleman of the cloven hoof. In the course of time Charles discovered that the marriage was not likely to take place unless he became a Catholic, and that if it took place, the Spanish troops would not move from the Palatinate.

Charles a-wooing goes

---

[14] Documents in Prothero, *Statutes,* pp. 307–314; White and Notestein, *Source Problems,* pp. 210–225.

Charles and Buckingham returned to England with rage in their
hearts against Spain.

When Charles returned a bachelor, England went wild with joy.
The dissolution of the parliament of 1621 had stirred the popular
opposition to the king as never before. When, on top of that, it became
known that James had let the prince go to Spain to contract a marriage
alliance, talk that was little short of treason became common.[15] The
reaction of popular opinion was equally strong. When it was noised
abroad that Charles and Buckingham wanted war with Spain, enthusiasm knew no bounds. James tried to stem the tide, but Charles,
Buckingham, and popular opinion forced him to call parliament.
When it met in 1624, James passed into the background. The nation
thought at last it had leaders for its anti-Spanish policy, and Charles
and Buckingham had the real power in the parliament of 1624.

This time the king asked the advice of the commons as to what he
should do, having Buckingham explain the situation to them. James
wanted a war against Spain by land in the Palatinate, while the
commons wanted war by sea. They dreamed of a war of the Elizabethan
type, when Englishmen of the present generation could emulate the
deeds of Hawkins and Drake and cripple Spain sufficiently to force
the withdrawal of Spanish troops from the Palatinate. They made a
liberal grant, though it was less than half what James asked, and made
clear their desire for naval war, though the specifications of the grant
did not prohibit war in the Palatinate. All the while James was being
held to the course only by the browbeating of Charles and Buckingham.
On one occasion the Spanish ambassador nearly persuaded James to
give up the policy of war. When Charles and Buckingham discovered
it, they instigated the commons to impeach the treasurer, Middlesex,
who was the one councilor still in favor of Spain. It was done forthwith. He was convicted of maladministration, but his real offense was
to advise the king contrary to the wishes of parliament. It was a dangerous game for Charles to ally himself with the commons against an
institution which he must soon uphold as divine. James saw it clearly
enough when he said to Charles with prophetic insight, "You will live
to have your bellyful of impeachments."[16] But the impeachment accomplished its immediate object. Though James soon prorogued the
session, he promised that he would call parliament again when he had
ascertained what alliances could be made against Spain.

The principal alliance that James sought was one with France. He

[15] *Somers Tracts,* ii, 470–473, 552, 553.
[16] Gardiner, *Duke of Buckingham and Charles I,* i, 66.

proposed that Charles should marry Henrietta Maria, the sister of King Louis XIII, in return for French aid against the Spanish in the Palatinate. The French demanded the exemption of English Catholics from persecution, which James had promised the commons he would not grant.[17] They were ready to help against the Spaniards only by the payment of a subsidy for six months. They were not willing to send French troops into the Palatinate. James was disposed to hesitate, but Buckingham, who was beginning to dream of the glory to be won by waging a brilliant war on the continent, urged him to concede step by step what France asked. By this means he was finally persuaded to accept a secret clause binding him to allow his Catholic subjects to exercise their religion without persecution, while French assistance against Spain was guaranteed only by an oral promise and was so limited in character and time as to be valueless. James fulfilled his part of the contract. The imprisoned Catholics were released, and an arrangement was made whereby the Catholics paid their recusancy fines publicly and received them back secretly. This deception was almost the last act of James. Early in 1625 he died.

The first of the Stuarts had succeeded only in undermining the royal power of which he loved to boast. Not only had he created such a hostile public opinion as had never existed under the Tudors, but he had also allowed the control of the house of commons to slip into the hands of leaders who were ready and able to give effective parliamentary expression to that opinion. When James neglected to keep in the house either councilors who could manage it or a group of members who were amenable to conciliar management, the leaders of the opposition grasped the reins. Under their guidance the house began to transact much of its important business in committees, where councilors could exert less influence. The adoption of other new modes of procedure promoted the same end. Important bills no longer emanated solely from the council; some of them were framed in committees of the house. Grievances were formulated and urged systematically and aggressively. Policy was ceasing to be "king's craft." By the close of the reign the opposition was so deeply intrenched behind parliamentary procedure, so ably led by members of ability, and so strongly supported by a considerable section of public opinion, that the council could never again wield such control of the house of commons as it had exercised in Elizabeth's day. The commons were no longer merely "a ratifying body, with the right of occasional refusal"; the initiative,

---

[17] Prothero, *Statutes*, p. 320; Gardiner, *The Duke of Buckingham and Charles I*, i, 59.

which had been largely in the hands of the council under the Tudors, was rapidly becoming theirs.[18]

Foundation of the empire

While Englishmen at home were preparing to wrest constitutional liberties from the king, Englishmen abroad were laying the foundations of colonial empire. During the reign of Elizabeth, when Englishmen first began to think of the sea as their own domain, men of vision began to dream of empire, but the attempts of Sir Humphrey Gilbert to colonize Newfoundland and of Sir Walter Raleigh to colonize Carolina failed. The first successful colony was planted in the reign of James. In 1606 the king chartered two Virginia Companies. One, made up of merchants of London, was given the right to trade and colonize in what is now Virginia and the neighborhood. The other, constituted mainly of merchants of Plymouth, received similar rights in what is now approximately New England. In the next year the first company founded Jamestown in Virginia. At first the enterprise nearly failed because the company and the colonists looked for immediate returns from discoveries of gold or from trade with the natives. When the problem was seen to be one of the slow development of agriculture, the fortunate discovery of the suitability of the region for the culture of tobacco assured the future of the colony. The other company planted a colony on the coast of Maine, but soon abandoned the project. The next successful colony was established at Plymouth by a group of Separatists who had left England and gone to Holland in 1607 and 1608 because they desired to be free from James's requirements of conformity and to worship as they pleased. They found life in a foreign country economically hard, and they discovered that their children would be likely to lose their English nationality and culture. Finally they decided to go to America. They obtained help from the Virginia Company of London, which was then controlled by Puritans, and set sail in 1620 to establish a new colony in Virginia. Their accidental landing at Plymouth north of the Virginia grant caused them to found the first permanent colony in New England. During the reign of James settlements were also made in Newfoundland, Bermuda, and one of the smaller islands of the West Indies, and the companies which colonized several other islands during the early years of Charles's reign were in the process of formation. By the close of the reign of James a colonial empire in the west was in the making.

India

In the east the problem was not one of colonization. The East India Company sought only to secure a share of the rich trade which had

---

[18] Paragraph based mainly on Notestein, *Winning of the Initiative by the House of Commons.*

ever been the goal of maritime enterprise. They turned their attention first to the islands. There were the spices which were the most profitable wares of the eastern trade. They found the Dutch just ahead of them. The Dutch attempted to exclude the English, and their company had so much greater resources and was so much better supported by the home government that they carried the day. The last act in the contest was the massacre of Amboina in 1623. Twelve of eighteen English-men who held this trading post for the English East India Company were captured and judicially murdered by a superior force of Dutch. The incident aroused intense irritation in England, but James I was too occupied with his Spanish policy to do anything about it. The English East India Company subsequently withdrew to the mainland of India. There it had already established a factory at Surat on the western coast near Bombay. In 1639 it acquired a station at Madras on the southeastern coast and a year later it located a trading post in Bengal near the site of the later Calcutta. These became the three great centers of English influence in India, the sources of a profitable trade, and the bases of empire, but the East India Company as yet had no imperial ambitions.

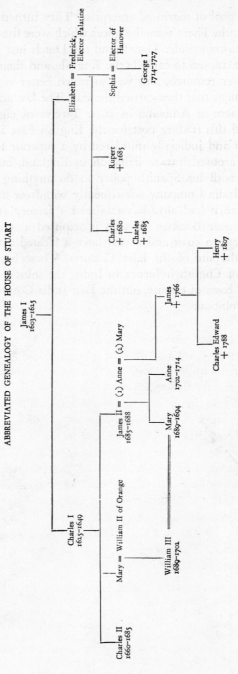

ABBREVIATED GENEALOGY OF THE HOUSE OF STUART

James I
1603–1625

Charles I
1625–1649

Elizabeth = Frederick,
Elector Palatine

Charles II
1660–1685

Mary = William II of Orange

James II = (1) Anne = (2) Mary
1685–1688

Rupert
+ 1685

Sophia = Elector of
Hanover

William III
1689–1702

Mary
1689–1694

Anne
1702–1714

Charles
+ 1680

Charles
+ 1685

George I
1714–1727

James
+ 1766

Henry
+ 1807

Charles Edward
+ 1788

CHAPTER XXIII

THE ROYAL AUTHORITY VERSUS THE LIBERTIES OF THE SUBJECT

CHARLES I inherited from his father certain topics of divergence from parliament. (1) Despite the wishes of the house of commons, James had undertaken extensive warfare on the continent. He had sent troops to Holland and to the Palatinate. The latter expedition had been badly mismanaged. The troops were poorly supplied and equipped because James lacked sufficient funds, and many of them had died of exposure and disease. (2) The French treaty was unpopular. Though the secret clause was not yet known, England obviously got little compensation for the risk of a Catholic queen. (3) Charles was burdened with Buckingham. He was generally thought to be responsible for the treaty with France and for the policy of the war. When Charles retained the favorite in a position of influence, the fear of irresponsible despotism was kept alive. (4) The underlying constitutional issue was likely to crop out on the slightest occasion. Parliament was now sensitive about the rights of the subject, and it was ready to oppose any and all claims of the king to superior power.

Political heritage of Charles I

These problems might cause grave dissensions, but Charles had an excellent opportunity to prevent the widening of the breach with parliament. What little the people knew of Charles was to his advantage. He had won great popularity by his return from Spain without a bride and by his subsequent anti-Spanish policy. He was young, and his princely mien was a pleasing contrast to his father's uncouth appearance. He was temperate, and he banished from his court some of the vices which had sullied his father's. His previous agreeableness to the commons led them to believe that he would recognize their position. Had Charles been willing to meet parliament affably, he might have averted a crisis. This was precisely what he could not do. He had his father's view of the sanctity of a king, being prepared to sacrifice his life for his ideal of kingship.[1] He was even less able to gauge the

Charles's personality

---

[1] In 1645, when the civil war was going against him, he wrote to his son, Charles: "My late misfortunes remember me to command you that which I hope you shall never have occasion to obey; it is this: if I should at any time be taken prisoner by the rebels, I command you (upon my blessing) never to yield to any conditions, that are dishonourable, unsafe for your person, or derogatory to regal authority, upon any considerations whatsoever, though it were for the saving of my life." Clarendon, *History of the Rebellion* (Oxford, 1827), v, 2090.

significance of public opinion, having no notion of the effect of his acts upon popular sentiment. In his opinion opposition was error. Once he had taken a position he clung to it with an obstinacy nothing could shake. His high ideals of honor forbade the sacrifice of a cause which he had made his own, even to promote his own personal advantage; but they were not sufficient to render his word reliable when it was pledged to his opponents. With such a personality Charles could not have remained a popular king had events been more favorable to him. To meet the delicate situation existing in 1625 he was unfitted by character, ability, and training. Trouble began in his first parliament, which was summoned a few days after his accession.

Supply in 1625

Charles opened parliament with a demand for money to carry on the business begun in his father's time. He gave no information of his plans with regard to the war, no explanation of what had been done with the money granted in 1624, and no statement of the amount he needed. He apparently assumed that it was the business of the house to grant money without consideration of its expenditure. The commons wanted to know at least who the enemy was. As one member put it, "The promises and declarations of the last parliament were in respect of a war; we know yet of no war nor of any enemy."[2] In their indecision they adopted the expedient previously tried with James. They granted taxation far short of the amount needed for the projected preparations for aggressive war. Charles consequently asked for a further grant, and on this occasion let it be known that he proposed to aid the Netherlands with 6,000 soldiers, send an army into Germany, and pay large subsidies to the king of Denmark and to Count Mansfeld, who was the commander of a mercenary army engaged in Germany on the Protestant side. The commons, who still favored a naval war against Spain, found this a far more extensive program than they desired to undertake. They were not accustomed to talking in such large sums, and they were feeling the pinch of a serious depression in the wool trade. In the ensuing debates Buckingham was named as the adviser responsible for this ambitious policy, and the session bade fair to develop into an attack upon the favorite. To avoid this possibility Charles dissolved parliament without further grant.

Religious issues

The house had observed a conscious restraint with regard to grievances because it seemed unfair to saddle the new king with the misdeeds of his father. Religious issues, however, were causing such grave concern that the commons could not refrain from an expression of

---

[2] *Debates in the House of Commons in 1625* (Camden Soc.), p. 31.

their views on that subject. During the reign of James the Puritans had increased in numbers, while the strength of their sentiment had been intensified by the harshness of the treatment accorded them by the government, by James's contempt for their position on morals, and by his leniency toward the Catholics. James had no quarrel with them theologically, nor did he object fundamentally to their desire for the simplification of ceremonies; he thought they threatened his ascendency in church and state. His attitude had produced in the house of commons a close connection between opposition to divine right and support of Puritanism.

In 1625 the discussions of the commons developed a threefold object. They petitioned Charles, in the first place, to enforce the penal laws against the Catholics more strictly than had been the custom in his father's time. Though their fears of the Catholics appear somewhat unreasoning to the dispassionate judgment of the twentieth century, they were very real to the English Protestants of the seventeenth century. In the days of Elizabeth all Catholics had been feared as the political enemies of England, the Gunpowder Plot had revived the fear, James's dealings with Spain had aggravated it, and Charles's marriage to a Catholic in 1625 gave it new life.

The Catholics

The commons also asked that the salaries attached to the smaller pastorates might be increased and kindred reforms undertaken, in order that ministers of higher intellectual and moral types might be secured; and that ministers should be allowed greater freedom of speech in preaching. To secure a ministry which should place more emphasis on a moral and upright life and less on ceremony was a primary object of the Puritans. It may perhaps be designated as the main aim of the Puritans who were not Separatists. They had much justification. Among the clergy were ignorant or careless priests who merely read the services, did little or no preaching, and neglected the morals of their flocks. Examples of pastors who were drunkards or led immoral lives were not unknown.[3] On the other hand, the Puritan point of view of morals was becoming so rigid that it held the pursuit of business or recreation on Sundays to be positively immoral. Many devout Christians of that period saw no evil in the games and pastimes which from time immemorial had taken place on the village green on Sundays when the services in the church were over; but to the Puritans they were anathema.

Moral reform

They sought further to silence the utterances of a new school grow-

[3] Gardiner, *History of England under the Duke of Buckingham and Charles I*, i, 211; Usher, *Reconstruction*, i, book ii, ch. x.

ing up within the Anglican church, which attacked the Calvinistic doctrines dear to the Puritans, recognized the Roman Catholic church as a true church though corrupt and unsound in its doctrines, leaned toward the elaborate services of the Roman church, and tended to uphold the doctrine of divine right. It sought a middle way between Puritans and Catholics. To Puritans of that age moderation was an untenable position in religion; they saw in it only a dangerous drift toward Catholicism. The point of view of the new school had begun to be expounded in the closing years of Elizabeth's reign, and during James's reign it had won a number of advocates. Though the group was still small in 1625, it was influential. Many of its supporters were theologians of ability. James had promoted several of them to important official positions in the church primarily for that reason. He had not favored the new school particularly. His own theological inclinations were more or less Calvinistic, but he was broad-minded enough to tolerate the new views and learned enough in theology to recognize the intellectual worth of their exponents. The commons in 1625 attacked the new school by having their sergeant take into custody Richard Montague, a rector, who had written pamphlets expounding the doctrines favored by the new school. Charles responded by appointing Montague one of his chaplains. By this act he stood forth as the patron of the new school.

The parliament of 1625 left Charles with a war on his hands and with no money in his pockets. Since he did not wish to abandon the war, he summoned another parliament to meet in 1626. Before it came together, two fiascoes in foreign policy had aroused strong popular criticism. The first arose out of the marriage treaty with France. By its terms the king of England had agreed to lend the king of France on demand eight ships to use against his enemies. It was the expectation at the time that they would be employed against Spain. Soon afterward war broke out between the French king and his Protestant subjects, who held the port of La Rochelle. In 1625 Louis XIII demanded the ships. Charles and Buckingham knew that their use to help reduce La Rochelle would antagonize the English people, and they feared that failure to send them would endanger the French alliance. In the effort to avoid the dilemma they embarked on a long career of duplicity. On one occasion they despatched the ships with secret orders to the commander to organize a mutiny in his own fleet. In the summer of 1625, deceived by a rumor that peace had been made in France, they let the ships go. The rumor was false, and knowledge that English ships were likely to be used against the French Protestants caused much indignation in England.

Buckingham, however, had another card to play. He planned to send the fleet against Spain to damage Spanish ports and shipping and plunder Spanish treasure ships. He counted on this Elizabethan exploit to arouse English enthusiasm for the war to a pitch which would induce parliament to grant the subsidies promised to Denmark and Count Mansfeld for the war in Germany. The expedition against Spain did not work out quite as Buckingham planned. It was poorly supplied and equipped because the king had no money. One ship was said to have had sails that had been used in the fleet which defeated the Armada. The fleet had poor commanders and ill-disciplined troops because Buckingham awarded the command on the basis of favoritism. After a badly mismanaged action in the harbor of Cadiz, the fort was taken and troops were landed. After twenty-four hours without food, they marched inland, captured a quantity of wine, and got drunk in a body. The expedition returned disgraced without treasure or prizes. The whole affair was a monument of mistaken policy, bad management, poor organization, stupidity, and cowardice.

The expedition to Cadiz

With these examples of incompetency before them the commons met in 1626. They shelved the king's request for supply, and proceeded at once to institute an inquiry into past disasters. Their object was to impeach Buckingham. They still had confidence in the king, ascribing the fault to his advisers. To show their good will to him they passed supply in the form of a resolution which they proposed to enact as a bill when their grievances had been redressed. They then drew up charges for the impeachment of Buckingham and presented them to the house of lords. Buckingham was their grievance. Charles, however, was loyal to his minister. He imprisoned Sir John Eliot and Sir Dudley Digges, the leaders of the house, hoping to stop proceedings. When the house refused to transact business until they were released, he yielded the point, but ordered the house to cease other business and consider supply at once. The house failed to comply, and Charles then dissolved his second parliament.

Parliament of 1626

Again Charles and Buckingham had to face the problem of waging war without money. The non-parliamentary income of the crown was insufficient to run the government adequately in time of peace. From parliament Charles had received only two subsidies (£140,000). He had mortgaged some of the royal estates and pawned the crown jewels; Buckingham had spent generously from his own personal fortune; it was not enough. Mansfeld had been driven from the Palatinate

The forced loan

and in the summer of 1626 the king of Denmark was decisively defeated. The disasters were due in part to the failure of Charles to supply the contracted subsidies. To add to the difficulty, France was rapidly becoming hostile. Under this pressure Charles resolved to appeal from parliament to the people, for he did not yet believe that parliament truly represented national sentiment. He therefore ordered the justices of the peace to ask the inhabitants of their respective counties to make a free gift to the king. When this met with almost universal refusal, he tried a forced loan. The collectors were instructed to demand from each taxpayer the amount he would have had to pay had parliament granted five subsidies. It was taxation without parliamentary grant. In the first few counties the attempt had some success, but opposition from an unexpected quarter turned the scale against the monarch. Charles asked the judges to sign a document declaring the forced loan legal. Though the judges had paid their quotas without a murmur, they refused to declare the principle legal. Charles thereupon discharged the chief justice, carrying a step further his father's contention that the judges should be subservient to the crown. By such a policy he risked undermining the respect of the people for all law and order. Nor did he further the cause of the loan. The action of the judges encouraged the spirit of opposition, and the collectors soon met with resistance everywhere. "Lincolnshire," says a contemporary letter, "did little better than rebel. . . . Shropshire hath utterly denied, and so hath Devonshire, and the gentlemen of Warwickshire, that are sent for up, do refuse to come."[4] Some who refused payment were arrested, but the whole nation could not be consigned to prison. The attempt to collect the remainder had to be abandoned.

From this constitutional grievance sprang another. Among those imprisoned by the order of the king were five knights who appealed to the court of king's bench for a writ of habeas corpus. This writ orders the keeper of the prison to bring the prisoner before the judges and show cause why he should be detained. The reason given on this occasion was the order of the king. Counsel for the prisoners maintained that, unless the king gave his reasons, the prisoners should be released. Without cause shown the prisoners could have no trial, and chapter thirty-nine of the Great Charter, guaranteeing that no man should be imprisoned "except by the legal judgment of his peers and by the law of the land," would be of no effect. If the king could ignore this right of his subjects, he could arbitrarily commit all of

Five knights' case

---

[4] *Court and Times of Charles the First*, i, 190.

his opponents to prison and keep them there indefinitely. None could have rights against the king. Though the bench refused to commit itself definitely on the principle of law involved, it refused to release the prisoners.

Added to these constitutional grievances was another failure abroad. The hostility of France increased, until Buckingham decided to aid the French Protestants against the French king. He led an expedition to the relief of the French Protestants besieged in La Rochelle and attempted to take the Isle of Rhé, which guarded the harbor. Buckingham displayed personal courage and some ability as a leader, but the difficulties caused by lack of money and lack of popular support were too great to be overcome. The troops were the riffraff of creation brought together by the press gangs; they went unwillingly; and they were cowardly and disobedient. Buckingham had to accept defeat, returning without the triumph that he hoped would revive the waning royal cause. The Isle of Rhé became his "Isle of Rue."[5]

Expedition to Rhé

Out of this expedition grew new constitutional grievances. Charles had no money with which to pay his troops or to provide them with quarters and provisions. Before embarkation and after the return the troops were quartered on the inhabitants. Nominal compensation was supposed to be given, but the quartering was compulsory and payment was often not forthcoming. Not only was this another extra-constitutional method of extracting money from the English subject, but it also led to great friction. The soldiers, drawn from the lower social stratum and left without pay, not only created great disorder in the homes where they were placed, but they also committed many depredations in the neighborhood. When citizens tried to obtain redress, their claims were adjudged by martial law administered by army officers.

Quartering of soldiers

When Charles summoned his third parliament in 1628, these events had a profound influence upon the elections. In many constituencies those who had opposed payment of the forced loan were elected, and a large majority opposed to the recent unconstitutional policies was returned. Charles failed completely to gauge the popular temper. He opened parliament with his customary short demand for money. He vouchsafed no explanation of its intended use, and the tone of his speech was contemptuous. The commons went at once to grievances. They quickly decided to disregard the questions of poor advisers and bungled expeditions and to concentrate on the attempt to protect the liberties of the subject against unconstitutional attacks of the type

Petition of Right

---

[5] *Ibid.*, i, 317.

recently made upon them. In the famous Petition of Right they asked the king henceforth to observe the rights of his subjects as set forth in four particulars. They cited precedents to show what these rights were. The petition demanded that "no man hereafter [should] be compelled to make or yield any gift, loan, benevolence, tax or such like charge, without common consent by Act of Parliament," and that there should be no imprisonment without cause shown, no enforced billeting of soldiers, and no martial law in time of peace. When Charles agreed to the petition, he acknowledged by implication that he had acted unconstitutionally. The importance of this document is second only to that of the Great Charter. It placed the first important constitutional restrictions on the strong monarchy which had been built by the Tudors and abused by the Stuarts.

Tonnage and poundage

After the grant of their petition the commons voted taxes. They then turned to other grievances. In the course of debate the opinion was expressed that the king's promise to levy no tax without parliamentary consent included tonnage and poundage. This had not yet been granted to Charles by parliament because he had never given that body time to make a desired revision of the schedules of rates. He had collected the duty, however. When he prorogued parliament in 1628, he took occasion to say that the Petition of Right did not extend to tonnage and poundage. Legally he may have been right, but he seemed to the commons to be disregarding the promise he had just made.

Three resolutions

When Charles called this parliament for its second session in 1629, a long-standing grievance had been removed. Buckingham had been assassinated. The commons turned to questions of policy and began at once to air their grievance concerning tonnage and poundage. Before they reached any conclusion, they wandered to the question of religion. By this time it was clear that Charles favored the new, ritualistic, anti-Calvinistic school within the Anglican church. Laud, who was its leading light, had practically become his chief ecclesiastical adviser. The archbishop of Canterbury, who was in sympathy with the Puritans, had no influence with the king. Only members of the new school were being promoted to ecclesiastical offices by the king, and they dominated the ecclesiastical policy of the government. Since the group constituted only a small minority in the church, its control of the policy of the church under royal patronage antagonized not only the Puritans but also many members of the church who were not Puritans. In 1628 the king issued a proclamation to stop the bitter war being waged by polemics. He declared the thirty-nine articles to be the doctrine of the church of England, ordered their literal acceptance by laymen without debate, and provided for the settlement of any obscurity of meaning by the clergy, acting with the consent of the king. To the Puritans the thirty-nine articles were not particularly unacceptable, but the command for silence was gall and wormwood. It was this proclamation and the innovations of the new school in the service that the commons began to discuss in 1629. By this time the likelihood of any grant of tonnage and poundage was remote, and, since Charles objected to the criticism of the commons, he determined to dissolve parliament. He ordered the speaker to put to the house the question of adjournment, intending subsequently to declare the dissolution. When the speaker put the question, contrary to the usual procedure, the house voted "no." The speaker then started to leave the chair, in order to end the sitting. He was held down by force. The doors were locked to exclude the king's messenger sent for the mace, the removal of which would have ended the sitting. Three resolutions were then brought forward. When the speaker refused to read them, they were read by a member. They were adopted with shouts of approval as the king's messengers were beating at the doors to gain admission. The resolutions declared anyone a capital enemy of the kingdom who should introduce an innovation in religion, advise the levy of tonnage and poundage, or pay it. The resolutions were opinion, not law, but the opinion was that of a large part of the nation. Charles's subsequent disregard of it led directly to the civil war.

After the dissolution of 1629, Charles determined to rule without parliament. By this time it was clear that the joint exercise of power by king and parliament, which had been typical of the Tudors, was no longer possible. The parliamentary opposition to the effort of the king to make himself preponderant in the government was developing into a contest for supremacy. The parliaments of the seventeenth century had attempted to control the actions of the king to a far greater extent than had those of any earlier period. The parliaments of Charles's reign had made it manifest that he could secure their cooperation only by yielding powers which he counted as his own. He preferred to do without parliament, of which he had come to abhor the very name. Charles's personal rule lasted for eleven years. During that period many of his subjects began to fear the creation of a permanent, irresponsible despotism. Charles did nothing to make his government popular. He expected his opponents to change their attitude, because he could not conceive that his own position was wrong. While he waited for the transformation to take place he ruled with-

Personal rule

out regard for public opinion, trespassing further and further upon the liberties of the subject. Year by year the popular antagonism to his rule grew more bitter.

Charles's first act was to arrest nine of the leaders of the parliamentary opposition, charging them with "notable contempts against the king and his government and the stirring up of sedition against the state." Since what they had said in parliament was the basis of the accusation against them, they claimed parliamentary privilege and refused to plead before any other court than parliament. The court of king's bench, before which they were tried, sentenced them to fine and to imprisonment until they would acknowledge themselves wrong and give surety of future good behavior. Six of them secured their release by compliance, but the remainder declined to deny their right to voice opposition to the king in parliament. Two of them were detained in prison for ten years. Sir John Eliot, the one of the three who had been the foremost leader and organizer of the opposition in the house of commons, contracted tuberculosis in his cold, damp prison. When his petition for more healthful quarters was rejected by Charles, liberty became essential to save his life. Still he refused to buy freedom by approval of the doctrine that parliamentary opposition to the king was wrong, the one price at which the king would sell it. In 1632 he died in prison, a martyr to the cause of popular liberties. The fate of these men moved the leaders of the Puritan opposition profoundly and strengthened them in their course. Though the Petition of Right may not have been violated technically, it obviously gave no protection against arbitrary imprisonment to those who should venture to criticize or oppose the actions of the king.

After this ominous beginning of his personal rule, the acts of Charles which did most to arouse opposition and to prepare the way for the civil war had to do with taxation and religion. Charles faced a difficult financial problem. He was already heavily in debt, and the existing non-parliamentary revenues were not enough to run the government in time of peace. He immediately made peace with France and Spain, endeavoring to keep himself free from all external complications "and especially from those which might involve additional expenditure."[6] Thereby he brought England into disrepute. The king's poverty forced inaction in European affairs and caused England's prestige to wane steadily, while France under Richelieu was forging ahead to occupy the position of predominance that Spain had held in the sixteenth

Margin notes:
Imprisonment of parliamentary leaders

Royal finance and foreign policy

---

[6] *Calendar of State Papers, Venetian,* xxiii, 17.

century. So little was England considered in international affairs that, when the ministers of Charles threatened war against Spain, the Venetian ambassador to England assured his government in a cipher despatch that they were "cackling."[7] The many Puritans who cherished the Elizabethan tradition of a bold foreign policy and wanted to see England strike a blow in behalf of the Protestant cause, which was still at stake in the Thirty Years' War, watched the decline of England's international influence with dismay.

Even peace did not fully retrieve the king's financial situation at home. Nor did the continued levy of tonnage and poundage without parliamentary sanction suffice. New sources of revenue had to be devised. By reviving obsolete practices Charles increased his income in ways that were probably legal, but they seemed to break the spirit of the Petition of Right. They were, moreover, of a nature to produce a feeling of unjust treatment among those who were compelled to pay them, and a feeling of exasperation among those who feared that they would render the king independent of parliament. *New revenues*

The first experiment was the compulsory distraint of knighthood. Every person whose income from land was £40 or more annually was compelled to accept knighthood or pay a fine. Since acceptance involved greater expense than the fine, the second alternative was generally chosen. This had been a common practice in the thirteenth century, but it had not been used since the reign of Henry VII. Its revival caused an irritation out of proportion to the profit to the crown. A kindred exaction was the forest fine. Vast areas, including in some instances the whole of a county, which had once belonged to the royal forest, had been sold centuries before by Charles's predecessors. In 1634 they were inhabited, cleared, and cultivated by men who believed themselves the owners. Charles claimed the sales to have been illegal and demanded return of the lands. The possessors, who could hope for no protection in courts controlled by the king, were obliged to pay heavy fines to keep their estates. A third expedient was less obsolete but no less vexatious. New monopolies, which doubled the price of necessities such as soap, were granted to companies. The last parliament of James had prohibited monopolies, but only to individuals. The new monopolies broke the spirit but not the letter of the law. To such "devices and subtleties" did Charles have recourse rather than meet parliament.

The significance of the financial makeshifts, which these examples

---

[7] *Ibid.,* p. 529.

sufficiently illustrate, was estimated by the Venetian representative at the royal court with penetrating judgment. In reporting to his government the death of a prominent councilor, who had been responsible for the invention of many of them, he described the work of the deceased as follows: "By his quibbles he brought great relief to his Majesty in the present scarcity of money, by inventing various methods of extortion, though under the pretense of the breach of ancient and obsolete laws, with this reservation, however, that he only attacked those who could support the pecuniary penalty, both because of the gifts of fortune which they possessed, and because it did not affect a great number, which might lead to a rising, prejudicial to interests of state. He studied to leave the generality of the people apparently exempt, although actually they suffered from the consequences."[8] Among those who bore the burden directly, moreover, were many of the country gentlemen who were leaders among the Puritans.

Ship
money

The levy which provoked the strongest feeling of oppression was ship money. When it was necessary for the defense of the realm, the Plantagenet sovereigns had been accustomed to call on the port towns to supply ships manned and equipped for the navy. In 1634 royal writs ordered the port towns to provide ships of a size to be found only in London, or to pay the equivalent in money. At the time England was threatened with no invasion, but Charles explained the need by the statement that English commerce on the North Sea was in danger of attack by all powers. Though this claim seemed to many to be mere sophistry, the tax was paid without open opposition. The next year ship money was levied again, being extended on this occasion to the inland districts as well as to the ports. Thereby, in the opinion of a contemporary, "the liberty of the subjects of England received the most deadly and fatal blow it had been sensible of in five hundred years last past."[9] Ship money had become nothing more or less than a tax imposed without the consent of parliament. In this form it violated the letter as well as the spirit of the Petition of Right. When the kingdom appeared to be at profound peace, the emergency did not impress the taxpayers as so pressing that parliament could not be summoned to vote taxation. To combat this opinion Charles appealed to the judges. He asked them if the king could compel his subjects to contribute to ship money for the defense of the realm in time of an emergency, and if the king was not the sole judge as to the existence of such an emergency. They replied in the affirmative, and the collec-

[8] *Ibid.*, p. 265.
[9] d'Ewes, cited by Henderson, E. F., *Side Lights on English History*, p. 75.

tion progressed without serious open opposition. But the tax was not paid willingly. "In all my life," said the observer previously quoted, "I never saw so many sad faces in England as this new taxation called ship-money occasioned; nay, the grief and astonishment of most men's hearts broke out into sad and doleful complaints, not only under the burthen they felt at the instant, but with ominous presage of the issue; for many refused absolutely to pay, and most that did pay it, yielded out of mere fear and horror of greater danger."[10] The people, the Venetian ambassador recorded, "are well aware that this opening for the royal authority cannot be allowed without a momentous restriction of their liberties. They exclaim aloud and lament the violation of their privileges." It seemed to them that they were "spending their liberty more than their cash."[11] When a third levy was made in 1636, still more refused to pay. In the next year a test case was made of John Hampden. His attorney argued that the tax could be levied only with the consent of parliament. The king had no discretion to impose it unless the danger was so imminent that he had no time to call parliament. The attorney-general claimed for the king the absolute right to judge of the emergency. The judges decided seven to five for the king. The judgment strained the nation's forbearance nearly to the breaking point. Even those who believed that the king ought to have discretionary power to act where the law was silent and to override the law when a crisis should make it necessary for the welfare of the nation, began to realize that Charles Stuart was not a man who could be trusted with such discretion. He was attempting to rule England on the theory of a perpetual emergency.

The second of Charles's policies which rendered his rule unpopular was his use of power to force upon Englishmen a form of worship favored only by a minority. Soon after the dissolution in 1629 the court of star chamber began to inflict heavy punishments on Puritans who criticized the existing tendencies in the church. A typical penalty was that of fine, imprisonment, and loss of ears inflicted upon the author of a book inveighing against the bishops. In 1633 the new school was given complete control of the church by the appointment of William Laud to the archbishopric of Canterbury. Laud's ideal was rigid conformity to the service prescribed in the prayer book as interpreted by the new school. Between 1633 and 1637 he conducted a visitation of the parishes of England to investigate the mode of worship followed. Clergymen who differed from his views in the slightest

Religion

[10] *Ibid.*, p. 76.
[11] *Calendar of State Papers, Venetian,* xxiii, 315, 346.

degree were discharged. The communion table could not remain in the center of the church, where the Puritans wanted it; the east end was the proper place in Laud's opinion; and there it must be, though to the Puritans it might smack of Rome and idolatry. Within the church uniformity was enforced with a severity never known before. Laymen who dared to attend other services were prosecuted, and conventicles were sought out and broken up. Men could find relief neither within nor without the church. Many believed, moreover, that Laud was preparing the way for the reunion of the Anglican church with Rome, and the lax enforcement of the recusancy laws by Charles heightened their fears. Popular feeling was stirred to the depths. Its intensity was demonstrated by an incident which took place in 1637. William Prynne, an acute, learned, long-winded, and pedantic Puritan lawyer, was well known to popular fame through a savage sentence imposed on him by the star chamber in 1632. For writing a book which attacked the stage he had been sentenced to be pilloried, to have his ears cut off, to pay a fine, and to undergo imprisonment. On that occasion the crowd jeered. Five years later he with two companions received a similar sentence for writing against the bishops. This time an immense crowd gave an impressive demonstration of sympathy. In four years Laud had set nearly the whole nation against Charles. In 1629 there had been a moderate group between the Laudians and the Puritans; in 1637 there were no longer any moderates; an overwhelming majority was bitterly hostile to the ecclesiastical policy of Laud and Charles.

The first Bishops' War

When ship money and Laudianism had thus strained the patience of the opponents of the personal rule almost beyond endurance, Charles precipitated a crisis by attempting to force the English ecclesiastical system upon the Scots. They were ardent Presbyterians. James had foisted bishops upon the Scottish church, but their power was little more than nominal. In 1637 Charles ordered the use in Scotland of a prayer book modeled upon the Anglican. Resistance began at the first service where the new form was used, and it rapidly became universal. The Scots bound themselves by the National Covenant to defend Presbyterianism against the bishops and the prayer book. Charles had to accept defeat or fight. Under the strain of war his system broke down. When he tried to exact forced loans and raise money by other expedients, he met with nearly universal resistance. Of the army which he impressed and took to Scotland one of his household who accompanied him wrote, "I dare say there was never so raw, so unskilful and so unwilling an army brought to fight. If we fight with these forces . . . we shall have our throats cut."[12] Since his resources were too slender to provide an army sufficiently large to meet that of the Scots, he ignominiously yielded what the Scots demanded.

When Charles gave his word to the Scots, he had no thought of keeping it if he could find any way to reduce the Scots to submission. In his extremity he called upon Wentworth, Lord Strafford, to become his chief counselor. Wentworth had been one of the leaders of the house of commons in the movement that produced the Petition of Right. Even then he seems to have believed that the king ought to be decidedly superior to parliament in general. Later he broke with the leaders of the popular opposition entirely, whereupon Charles began to utilize his services. He employed him successively as president of the council of the north and lord deputy of Ireland. Both offices were of a nature to sharpen his tendency toward arbitrary government. In Ireland particularly he won an unenviable reputation by the high-handed and ruthless methods with which he reduced the turbulent Irish to order. Lord Strafford came back to England in 1639 prepared to advise Charles to treat the English as he had treated the Irish. "Black Tom Tyrant" the nation dubbed him, as soon as his bent became evident. Lord Strafford

His first advice was to call parliament. Since the Scots were in rebellion, the English nation ought to come to the king's assistance. If it did not, the king would be justified in overriding the law. So argued Wentworth. The nation elected for the most part not only Puritans but those Puritans who in the past had shown the most boldness in opposing the royal decrees. When parliament convened on April 13, 1640, Charles demanded supply before grievances. Parliament, composed of men whose ardor to redress the national wrongs had been burning ever more fiercely for eleven years, insisted on the reverse order. After three weeks it was dissolved. The dissolution caused "so great a defection in the kingdom" as "hath not been known in the memory of man."[13] In London it produced a mob which threatened the lives of unpopular royal advisers. In several counties the soldiers of the militia, when they received news of the dissolution, refused to obey the commands of their officers, not being willing to serve against the Scots. Violent demonstration, however, was a transitory phase which soon passed. The principal result of the Short Parliament was to bring home to the people of different localities for the first Short Parliament

---

[12] *Memoirs of the Verney Family during the Civil War,* i, 306, 307.
[13] *Ibid.,* p. 332.

time common knowledge that opposition to the financial and religious policies of the king was unyielding in character and national in scope.

Charles was alarmed by the threats of the mob, but failed to understand the depth of the popular feeling of which violence was merely the ebullient symptom. When it had subsided, he returned to his project of a campaign against the recalcitrant Scots. Taking Strafford's advice, he threw the constitution to the winds and rode the prerogative. An army was impressed which included "all the arch knaves of the kingdom," but vigorous effort through forced loans and other financial expedients failed to provide for its proper equipment. Charles's army met the army of the Scots on the border, but it would not fight. When the Scots advanced into England, the English retreated. The Scots occupied the northern counties, and there seemed to be no obstacle between them and London. Charles had to treat to stop the progress of their invasion. They virtually refused to make a permanent agreement which was not ratified by parliament. Charles perforce capitulated. After arranging an armistice by promise of an indemnity to the Scots, he summoned the English parliament.

The parliament which met on November 3, 1640, was destined to be known as the Long Parliament. The members were thoroughly united in the purpose of placing limits on the absolutism which had rendered the king independent of parliament for so long. The events of the past eleven years had reached their climax in the arbitrary acts since the dissolution of the Short Parliament. The large majority in the house of commons found leaders in Hampden, of ship-money fame, and Pym, on whom had fallen Eliot's mantle. Under their leadership a series of constitutional reforms was undertaken immediately. The first task was to rid the king of his evil advisers. They were regarded as responsible for the king's tyrannical government, and in Strafford's case, at least, it was feared that he would influence the king to use force against parliament if he should be left at liberty. Accordingly Strafford and Laud were apprehended, while several others escaped by flight. Strafford was impeached at once. He was accused of treason, of which he was not technically guilty. When the commons saw that they could not prove their charge to the satisfaction of the lords, they dropped the impeachment, and proceeded by bill of attainder. When the lords hesitated to pass the bill, they were brought into line by the production of evidence which seemed to demonstrate that the foreign and Catholic queen, Henrietta Maria, had attempted to secure an army to use against parliament. Pym's manipulation of mobs helped in overawing the lords. Charles, who had prom-

(margin notes)

Second
Bishops'
War

Attainder
of
Strafford

ised Strafford protection, was induced to consent to the bill by a mob of Londoners which occupied the yard of the palace and threatened the death of the queen if he should use his veto. To save his queen Charles consented. His action wrung from Strafford the bitter exclamation: "Put not your trust in princes!" Strafford died, not because he had been guilty of treason, which was legally an attack upon the person of the king, but because he had advised the king to disregard the fundamental laws which protected the liberties of the subject. Back of the action of the commons was the conception that the king was below the law and that the minister who advised him to override the law was guilty of treason. Strafford's attainder was part and parcel of the effort of parliament to protect the liberties of the subject by placing constitutional limits on the royal authority; but however statesmanlike the view of treason as a crime against the nation may have been, it worked injustice in the individual case of Strafford, because it was an *ex post facto* definition.

Meanwhile the Long Parliament had begun its second task, which was to eliminate constitutional abuses by the enactment of legislation. (1) The regular meeting of parliament in the future was assured by the triennial act. It provided that parliament should come together at least once in three years and arranged for its assemblage in case the royal summons failed to appear at the proper time. (2) To insure against royal dissolution before its work of reform had been completed, it enacted that the existing parliament could not be dissolved without its own consent. (3) Further acts abolished the special courts,[14] which had become the main props of Stuart tyranny. The courts of star chamber, high commission, council of the north, and council of Wales were swept away. The privy council was deprived of all except appellate jurisdiction over places outside of England. (4) Other acts prohibited the levy without parliamentary consent of ship money and of the other arbitrary exactions employed recently by Charles. (5) By resolution parliament declared that judges should be appointed for good behavior and should not hold office at the mere pleasure of the king. To all these measures Charles gave his consent.[15] He had no option. All classes of the nation were so united in these demands that he was powerless to resist.

The third question which parliament attempted to settle was that of religion. On this issue developed a decided difference of opinion, whence arose a party that came to the support of the king. Opposi-

Constitutional reforms

Religion

[14] See above, p. 377.
[15] Except the last, which was not in the form of a bill.

tion to the Laudian system was general, but there was lack of agreement on what to put in its place. The more radical wished to abolish episcopacy; but a large party, which was thoroughly attached to the episcopal system, desired only to remove the innovations of Laud and to leave the organization of the church fundamentally unchanged. This divergence, which appeared early in the session, became pronounced in debates which took place in the summer of 1641. Soon afterward parliament adjourned. During the recess local disorders occurred in several parts of England which were accompanied by outbreaks of religious fanaticism. Groups began to worship God as they pleased, and fantastic styles of worship appeared here and there. The moderate members of parliament began to grow conservative. Further attack upon the royal authority seemed to them to threaten law and order. At the same time the preservation of episcopacy and the prayer book began to appear to them as synonymous with the preservation of orderly government. The Episcopalians were on the way to become Royalists.

Irish
rebellion

Their conversion was completed by a constitutional issue that arose in connection with a rebellion in Ireland. Under James there had been great friction between the Protestant rulers of Ireland and the Catholics. James, though he vacillated somewhat, tended to treat the Irish Catholics leniently so long as they did not attempt to worship publicly. The English governors of Ireland went further than the spirit of James's instructions and kept up a more or less unauthorized persecution of the Catholics. James, moreover, though he did not generally favor persecution, desired to convert the Catholics to Protestantism, and some of his efforts in this direction caused the Irish great dissatisfaction. His most unpopular policy was the colonization of northern Ireland with Protestants. The policy was not new with James, but he carried it out more thoroughly than any previous sovereign. Early in his reign, large areas which belonged to those who had taken part in the last rebellion of Elizabeth's reign were confiscated. They were given to Scottish and English Protestants. The former particularly were induced to settle in large numbers. So extensive was the colonization that much of Ulster in the north of Ireland remains to this day strongly Protestant. At the time the colonization aroused the opposition not only of the native Irish, who were deprived of their lands, but also of the Anglo-Irish of the Pale, who thought it a scheme to make Protestantism predominant in Ireland. Charles granted the Catholics greater privileges, but Strafford, when governor, disregarded them, as he did all other liberties of Irishmen. The harshness of his rule left all Ireland bitter in spirit. The experience of the Irish during the reigns of James and Charles taught them to expect greater leniency from the king than from his agents. When the success of the Long Parliament appeared to threaten a Puritan domination, they became hopeless. In the late summer of 1641 they revolted against English rule.

The news reached parliament soon after it assembled in the autumn for its second session. The commons were anxious to quell the rebellion, but they were afraid to place under the king's command an army which might be turned against themselves. They proposed to ask the king to accept ministers approved by them, unless he wanted them to take the control of the army out of his hands. This was a greater encroachment upon the royal authority than many who had supported the earlier constitutional reforms were prepared to make. Men like Hyde wanted the king reduced to an equality with parliament, but they were not prepared to make parliament superior to the king. Pym and the more radical felt that they could not stop where they were. They believed that the reforms already accomplished could be maintained only by seizing additional powers that would make parliament the stronger partner in the firm. The resolution passed the house of commons but stuck in the house of lords. The strength of the two parties was shortly put to a better test by the vote on the Grand Remonstrance. This resolution summarized the popular grievances against Charles, reviewed what parliament had done to remedy them, and stated the further reforms which the radical party held to be necessary. It was a manifesto of the party that followed Pym. It was carried in a large house by a majority of only eleven. The Episcopalians had become Royalists; the king had a party.

Appearance of the Royalists

With the nation divided nearly equally on fundamental constitutional and religious questions, civil war soon became inevitable. Early in 1642 Charles came to the house of commons with troops and tried to arrest in person five of the leaders of the radical party who, forewarned, had sought safety in flight. This attack on parliamentary privilege caused some of the recent converts to the royal cause to waver, but in the spring parliament acted so unconstitutionally as to drive them back. It passed the militia bill, giving to parliament the power to appoint the commanders of the militia. When the king refused his consent, parliament declared it to be law without. For this there was no precedent. If the power of parliament to enact law without the consent of the king was accepted, it left the king without any power except what parliament should choose to give him. By the end

Outbreak of war

of April it was becoming extremely doubtful whether the disputes could be restricted to "the tongue and the pen." In June parliament carried the principle of parliamentary supremacy still further in the nineteen propositions which it submitted to Charles as a basis for the reconstruction of the government. Privy councilors, the principal officers of the crown, the heads of the courts, and peers were to be appointed only with the approval of parliament, and the church was to be reformed as parliament should direct. Acceptance by Charles would have made him as great a figurehead as the king is in the English government today. His refusal settled the fact that there was to be a civil war, though the war did not actually begin until Charles unfurled his standard at Nottingham on August 22, 1642.

Though the personal rule of Charles ended in civil war, it had the good result of stimulating English colonial enterprise in the new world. Before the opposition to the royal policies became articulate in 1640, many of Charles's subjects so despaired of the preservation of their civil and religious liberties in England that they sought escape from misrule by emigration to the colonies. In 1632 Lord Baltimore, a Catholic, received from the king the grant of Maryland. Two years later he established a colony where religious toleration and many civil liberties were enjoyed by the settlers. The Puritans developed a well-organized movement to obtain relief from the tyranny of Charles's personal rule. In 1628 a group of them secured a grant of land from the successor of the Plymouth Company[16] and founded the Massachusetts Bay Colony as a bulwark "against the kingdom of Anti-Christ, which the Jesuits labour to rear up in all quarters of the world."[17] After the sudden dissolution of parliament in 1629 "divers were so fearful what would follow so unaccustomed an action, some of the principal .of those liberal speakers being committed to the Tower, others to other prisons—which took all hope of reformation of Church government from many not affecting Episcopal jurisdiction"[18]—that the exodus was greatly accelerated. The subsequent activities of Archbishop Laud against the Puritans rapidly increased the numbers who sought refuge from oppression. In 1630 a thousand Puritans went to Massachusetts, and by 1640 the number of settlers had reached twenty thousand. During the same period many Puritans sought new homes in other colonies. It was, indeed, a Puritan migration.

Effect of the personal rule on colonization

---

[16] Called the Council for New England.

[17] White, cited by Newton, *Colonizing Activities of the English Puritans*, p. 41.

[18] F. Gorges, cited *ibid.*, p. 82.

Adverse economic conditions in some parts of rural England also stimulated emigration. Before the civil war began, the four New England colonies were well established, Maryland was on its feet, Virginia was in thriving condition, and many of the smaller islands of the West Indies had been settled by Englishmen.

CHAPTER XXIV

THE CIVIL WAR AND THE INTERREGNUM

The
combat-
ants

THE causes which determined the selection of sides in the civil war were highly complex. In a general way the north and west supported the king, and the south and east parliament, but there were numerous exceptions. It was not a war of sections. Neither was it a war of classes. The nobles and the gentry with their dependents and their followers generally fought for the king, while the townsmen, who were generally Puritans, fought in larger numbers for parliament. But a considerable minority of the gentry, such as Oliver Cromwell, fought for parliament, and there were townsmen in the armies of the king. Principle was the main dividing line. Those who believed in episcopacy generally fought for the king, and those who believed in its abolition, for parliament. But even this was not a clear-cut line of cleavage. Some who were half-hearted in their support of the bishops fought against parliament because of their dislike of rebellion, and some who desired the episcopal system fought for parliament because they distrusted Charles. A smaller number were actuated primarily by constitutional considerations. Those who believed whole-heartedly in the superiority of parliament could oppose the king readily, but few on the Royalist side believed in a royal authority as extensive as Charles desired. Principle was the deciding factor, but the principle which was the primary consideration of one man might be of secondary importance to his neighbor. Not only were districts and classes split, but in several instances brother fought against brother and father against son.

Resources

At the outset the king possessed a slight advantage. Neither side had a well-disciplined army, but the king's forces contained more of the gentlemen who were accustomed to handle the sword and to command. They infected the troops with their own high spirit. Oliver Cromwell was among the earliest of the Parliamentarians to recognize this superiority of the royal armies. "Your troops," he wrote to Hampden, who was fighting for parliament, "are most of them old decayed serving men and tapsters, and such kind of fellows, and their troops are gentlemen's sons and persons of quality. Do you think that the spirits of such base and mean fellows will ever be able to encounter gentlemen that have honour, and courage, and resolution in them?

You must get men of a spirit . . . that is likely to go on as far as a gentleman will go, or else you will be beaten still."[1] The king also had more men on horseback. Cavalry was relatively more important than it is in modern warfare. The weapons of the infantry were clumsy, making it an unwieldy force that often could be broken by a charge of cavalry. Neither side possessed great leaders until the war brought Cromwell to the front among the parliamentary commanders. The earl of Essex, who was the chief commander of the parliamentary forces at the beginning of the war, was steady and plodding without a spark of genius. Most prominent among the Royalists was Prince Rupert of the Palatinate, the king's nephew. He was a brilliant, dashing leader of his own troop of cavalry, but gave small thought to the interests of the Royalist army as a whole. Parliament had the more favorable geographical situation, the center of its operations being London. Control of the well-drilled militia from London gave it an advantage in infantry. Parliament, moreover, secured the navy which Charles had built up with ship money. Control of the sea enabled the Parliamentarians to cut Charles off largely from outside supplies, and helped them to maintain a foreign trade of primary importance to their commercial constituency. But so much time was required to develop the value of the navy as an asset, that it gave no signal advantage in the initial stages of the war. So it was also with the financial superiority of parliament. The southeast, of which parliament had military control, was much richer than the northern and western districts controlled by Charles. Eventually parliament established an orderly system of heavy taxation. In addition to fruitful forced loans and confiscations it levied the old subsidies on a new, more remunerative, and fairer assessment, and imposed for the first time an excise on the sale of several articles of common consumption. So well did the last two expedients work that they were retained after the close of the war to become a permanent part of the national fiscal system. When the parliamentary financial machine was finally perfected, it produced annually more than three times the revenue received by Charles in 1635, when ship money swelled his income.[2] At the beginning of the war, however, these resources could not be tapped immediately. Both of the contestants had to rely largely on voluntary gifts and loans, which the gentlemen who followed the royal banner supplied as liberally as the burghers who supported parliament.

[1] Cited by Gardiner, *History of the Great Civil War*, i, 47.
[2] Scroggs, "English Finances under the Long Parliament," *Quarterly Journal of Economics*, xxi, 482, 483.

Cam-
paigns of
1642–1643

During the first two years the war went generally in favor of the king. It began with a series of skirmishes and isolated conflicts all over the kingdom between neighbors who hastily took up arms for one side or the other. Charles's main army was generally victorious, but when the attempt was made to march down the Thames valley to London the parliamentary army was large enough to bar the way. Charles retreated, taking up winter quarters at Oxford. When the campaign was renewed in the spring of 1643, Charles had three armies in the field. One was in the southwest in Cornwall and Devon, another in the northeast in Yorkshire, and the main army at Oxford. The general plan was to concentrate the three armies along the radii reaching from the circumference, where they were located, to London, the center of parliamentary power. The Royalist armies in the northeast and the southwest won complete victories over the armies opposed to them, opening wide the way to London. Charles was unable to take advantage of the situation because the local feeling in his armies was too strong. The Parliamentarians held three fortified places, Hull in the north, Gloucester in the west, and Plymouth in the southwest. Charles's troops were unwilling to march to London and leave these parliamentary forces in their rear to work havoc on the unguarded countryside. Charles had to turn aside from his concentration to take these strongholds. They were able to hold out for the rest of the season, and by that time the Parliamentarians had under way a better organization. By the spring of 1644 the opportunity to concentrate on London had passed.

Cromwell
and
Marston
Moor

In 1644 parliament brought into the field new forces which turned the scale. In the preceding year negotiations with the Scots resulted in the Solemn League and Covenant, whereby parliament practically agreed to establish Presbyterianism in England, and the Scots in return for this and a subsidy undertook to aid the Parliamentarians with an army. The treaty led to the establishment by parliament of the Committee of Both Kingdoms as an executive with power to "order and direct" the war.[3] It was composed jointly of Scots and of twenty-one members of the Long Parliament. The latter in large majority favored an energetic prosecution of the war. Under their guidance the parliamentary armies became more effective. A second army was drawn from the eastern counties of England. During the past year several local regiments had been drilling there in accordance with the parliamentary plan of organizing groups of counties to meet

---

[3] On the formation and significance of this committee, see Notestein, "Establishment of the Committee of Both Kingdoms," *Am. Hist. Rev.*, xvii, 477–495.

the local armies of Charles. One regiment in the association consisted of men picked by Oliver Cromwell, who recognized the need of soldiers whose martial spirit should equal that of the gentlemen who fought for the king. He organized, drilled, disciplined, and inspired it, until it became a crack regiment. When he became second in command of the whole army of the Eastern Association, the spirit and efficiency of his regiment gradually permeated the whole body of troops, which became known as the Ironsides. In the campaign of 1644 the Ironsides joined the Scottish army, which came down from the north. At Marston Moor Cromwell snatched victory from what appeared to be disaster and enabled the Parliamentarians to inflict a decisive defeat on the Royalist army commanded by Rupert. "God made them as stubble to our swords," wrote Cromwell. The victory gave parliament control of the northeast and placed the king on the defensive for the rest of the war.

Following the campaign of 1644 the parliamentary forces were completely reorganized. For some time a rift had been growing between those Parliamentarians who desired peace by means of accommodation with the king and those who wished to push the war vigorously to a conclusion and defeat the king utterly. Essex and the other older commanders belonged to the former group. The results of the campaigns which they had conducted during 1644 had been far from satisfactory. Opportunities to inflict upon Charles a decisive defeat had been missed by failure of the generals to push their military advantages, and one of the armies had been defeated by the Royalists. The utterance of one of the generals, "if we beat the king ninety-nine times, yet he is king still, and so will his posterity be after him, but if the king beat us once we shall all be hanged, and our posterity made slaves," reflected a spirit of such extreme caution as made victory hopeless. Those who desired to win the war saw that their purpose could be accomplished only by the removal of the half-hearted commanders and a reorganization of the army. Cromwell, whom the events of 1644 had rendered the most prominent among them, took the lead in the house of commons of an attempt to secure the dismissal of the incompetent commanders. When his project aroused such bitter animosities that they threatened to weaken the parliamentary cause by a division of its supporters, Cromwell compromised on the Self-Denying Ordinance, which required all members of parliament to resign their commands. It removed not only the generals whose dilatory tactics had lost the fruits of victory in 1644, but also Cromwell himself. His retirement proved to be only temporary. The

Reorganization of the parliamentary forces

ordinance was followed by a thorough reorganization of the army in accordance with a plan worked out by the Committee of Both Kingdoms, of which Cromwell was a member. Except for local levies the divided armies were given up. In their place one picked, well-paid army, called the New Model, was established. Of this army Fairfax, who had taken no prominent part in the recent controversy, was made commander-in-chief, but Cromwell became commander of the cavalry and the moving spirit. Under his inspiration the whole New Model became an efficient military machine, just such as the army of the Eastern Association had been on a smaller scale. "Fear God and keep your powder dry" became the watchword of an army that fought with confidence in itself, its leaders, and its cause.

Naseby and the end

In the summer of 1645 the New Model, led by Fairfax and Cromwell, nearly annihilated the main Royalist army at Naseby. Before the end of the year the subsidiary Royalist armies were cleaned up, and Charles was left practically without an army. Early in 1646 the Parliamentarians captured the few strongholds left to Charles. The king, who was now little better than a fugitive, surrendered to the Scots. Cromwell, leading with true military genius well-paid and well-equipped troops who were inspired with the belief that God was on their side, had defeated the gentlemen who fought without adequate supplies for an ecclesiastical system and for an ideal of kingship which the king who led them did not practice.

Presbyterians and Independents, 1642–1646

When the surrender of the king brought to an issue the problem of reconstruction in church and state, the opponents of the king could not agree among themselves on the terms to be presented to him. The attempt to formulate a constructive settlement brought to a head a divergence which had been developing since 1642. When the war began, parliament ceased to represent a united nation. During the course of the war it ceased to represent fairly the party opposed to the king. The difference of opinion in the parliamentary party began with the question of religion. Practically all who fought against the king desired the abolition of episcopacy, but they disagreed on what should take its place. One group wanted a Presbyterian state church, which would be no more tolerant than the Episcopal state church it was designed to supplant. In 1643 parliament became morally bound to this policy by its acceptance of the Solemn League and Covenant. Outside of parliament was a strong party which thought this to be merely the substitution of one form of ecclesiastical tyranny for another. The Independents, as the members of this party were called, wanted freedom for each group of Puritans to worship as it pleased.

To them the Presbyterian minister upheld by the state was merely "old priest writ large." The Independents grew in numbers, and they were particularly influential in the army after the formation of the New Model. Parliament was utterly disregardful of the opinions of those who were winning its victories, and it calmly went ahead with plans for the establishment of the Presbyterian system.

The open breach came soon after parliament submitted to Charles the Propositions of Newcastle as the basis of peace. They demanded the establishment of a Presbyterian church in England and Scotland and control of the militia and navy by parliament for twenty years, a period long enough to cover the probable remainder of the reign of Charles. The proposed constitutional settlement would have left the situation virtually as it had stood in the summer of 1641, for parliamentary control of the army was to be only temporary. Meanwhile parliament passed bills establishing a Presbyterian church and imposing severe penalties on those who worshiped otherwise. This attack on the liberty of conscience, dear to the Independents, was followed early in 1647 by an order to the New Model to disband without its arrears of pay. Since obedience meant the loss of toleration as well as pay, the army refused. Thereupon the soldiers organized and elected leaders to formulate a plan of action. Parliament, threatened with the revolt of the army, sought to unite with the king and the Royalists. Charles having rejected the Propositions of Newcastle in the hope that he could profit by the dissensions among his enemies, parliament now offered to restore him without further limitation on the royal authority than had existed in August of 1641, if he would establish a Presbyterian church for only three years. This reactionary movement of the Presbyterians toward the Royalists led to the second civil war in 1648 and eventually to the restoration in 1660. In 1647 the army forestalled the possibility of an alliance between king and Presbyterians by taking possession of the king's person.

On the same day that the king was captured, Cromwell threw in his lot with the army. As a member of parliament and the favorite commander of the army, he had striven for conciliation between the two, though his sympathies were with the Independents. He could no longer hope to stay parliament in its arbitrary career by peaceful debate, but his influence in the army might be sufficient to restore order and discipline, prevent the impending outbreak of anarchy, force parliament to accept reasonable terms, and secure a settlement without further civil war. Such seem to have been some of the considerations that motivated his action.

Marginal notes:
Breach between parliament and the army

Cromwell's position

While parliament was still thinking in terms of 1640, the soldiers had been developing radical political theories. In the democratic debates which they held for the purpose of deciding upon their policies, they developed in its essentials the theory of the natural rights of man, which later had a profound influence upon the political institutions of the United States. Legitimate government, they said, rests upon the consent of the governed. Eventually they followed the argument to its obvious conclusion, that government ought to be by a parliament of one house elected by universal manhood suffrage. Democratic religious ideals were yielding their fruit in political democracy. Cromwell was no believer in these theories. He saw that the majority of Englishmen did not want democracy, however good it might be in abstract theory, and he understood that it was impossible to govern a people with a government better than that which they themselves desire. He persuaded the army to offer to the king a settlement in a document called the Heads of Proposals. Under these heads they asked for religious toleration and parliamentary control of the militia and offices of state for ten years. No man was to be forced to accept Presbyterianism and the bishops were to have no coercive power. They also demanded the dissolution of the Long Parliament and the election of a new parliament based on more equal constituencies and a broader franchise. When Charles rejected the proposals, he placed Cromwell in a difficult situation. The radicals, known as the Levelers because they desired to make all men politically level or equal, got the ear of the army, and it required all of Cromwell's authority and tact to prevent a revolt. The soldiers, under the influence of the Levelers, drew up the draft of a constitution, called the Agreement of the People, on which they demanded a popular referendum. They proposed to brush aside king and parliament and appeal to what they regarded as the source of all authority, the people. The Agreement abolished the kingship and the house of lords and placed government in the hands of a parliament of a single chamber elected by universal manhood suffrage. It placed limitations even on this popular assembly by a bill of rights setting forth certain liberties of which the subject could not be deprived by parliament. Cromwell saw that the first thing to consider was "whether, according to reason and judgement, the spirits and temper of the people of this nation are prepared to receive and to go along with it."[4] To him the impossibility of the practical use of the constitution was more important than the theoreti-

---

[4] Cited in *Clarke Papers,* ed. Firth, I, lxxii.

cal merits of its provisions. Believing that such a radical departure from previous governmental practice could not win the general approval of Englishmen, he and the other officers by long debate persuaded the army to moderate its demands and to present the amended Agreement to parliament instead of holding a popular plebiscite upon it. In these debates were expressed for the first time many of the democratic theories and practices which now form part of the constitution of the United States.

Cromwell labored to save the monarchy, but he could not save Charles Stuart. The negotiations with the king convinced the army of his duplicity. "He gave us words," said one of the officers who conducted the negotiations, "and we paid him in his own coin, when we found he had no real intention to the people's good, but to prevail by our factions, to regain by art what he had lost in fight."[5] When Charles refused new proposals submitted by parliament after the rejection of the Heads of Proposals, even parliament lost its faith in him. Clarendon, the chief adviser of the king, records the ominous character of the change of opinion. "Upon the receipt of the king's answer," he writes, "there appeared a new spirit and temper in the house of commons; hitherto, no man had mentioned the king's person without duty and respect, and only lamented 'that he was misled by evil and wicked counsellors; who being removed from him, he might by the advice of his parliament govern well enough.' But now, . . . 'every man's mouth was opened against him with the utmost sauciness and license; each man striving to exceed the other in the impudence and bitterness of his invective. Cromwell declared, that the king was a man of great parts, and great understanding . . . but that he was so great a dissembler, and so false a man, that he was not to be trusted.' "[6] In the opinion of the army his wrongdoing culminated when he made a treaty with the Scots which precipitated a second civil war. The Scots agreed to restore him to the throne without stipulation as to the form of government in return for a Presbyterian church for three years. The Scots invaded England, many Royalists rose for the king, and some Presbyterians joined. In the face of this danger the army healed its differences and went forth in 1648 to put down the new rebellion. It accomplished the task in a few months. While the army was thus occupied, parliament tried to make peace with Charles on terms which did not provide for religious toleration. This action settled the fate of the king. It so frightened the inde-

Second civil war

---

[5] *Memoirs of Colonel Hutchinson,* fifth ed., p. 305.
[6] *History of the Rebellion* (Oxford, 1827), v, 2199.

pendents "that it made them as violent in their zeal to pull down, as the others were in their madness to restore, this kingly idol."[7] The army, when it had finished the war, was thoroughly disgusted with the Long Parliament, and it was implacable in its hatred of Charles. The first civil war might be attributed to Charles's ministers, but for the second the obstinacy and double-dealing of Charles himself were responsible. Consequently the army marched back to London determined to take affairs into its own hands.

Pride's Purge

On December 6, 1648, Colonel Pride stationed a detachment of troops at the door of parliament and excluded Presbyterian members from entrance. Pride's Purge left only the remnant of a remnant of a parliament that had been representative eight years before. In 1642 nearly two-fifths of the 504 members had left to fight for the king. In 1648 nearly three-quarters of the remainder were expelled. Only ninety members remained, and no more than fifty or sixty ordinarily attended sessions. Because they constituted the sitting part of parliament, they were promptly dubbed the Rump. They represented only the army. England was now governed by a military despotism thinly disguised.

Execution of Charles

The first fruit was the execution of Charles. Early in January the commons sent to the lords an ordinance, creating a commission to try Charles Stuart. The lords rejected it. The commons then passed it without the consent of the lords, accompanying it with three resolutions. They declared that the people have all just power; the commons represent the people and thus have supreme power; what the commons declare law is law, though the consent of the king and the lords be not had. The destruction of Charles necessitated the destruction of the monarchy. However true the principles may have been, their declaration did not justify the act of the Rump, because it did not represent the people. Charles was executed in 1649. His violent death shocked the public and foredoomed the republican experiment to failure. The noble manner in which he left the world caused his bad deeds to be forgotten, and he soon came to be regarded as a martyr. The republican government always had the stigma of his death upon it. Charles did more to preserve the monarchy by his death than he had ever done during his life.

With the execution of Charles it became necessary to set up a government in place of that which had been destroyed. The Rump proceeded to abolish the kingship and the house of lords and to declare

---

[7] *Memoirs of Colonel Hutchinson,* p. 331.

England a commonwealth. It created an executive council which was to be appointed annually by parliament, and was intended to be the mere creature of parliament. Religion was settled by the grant of toleration to all except Catholics and Episcopalians. Parliament thus followed out the broad lines of the Agreement of the People. The Commonwealth so constituted found support with few Englishmen outside the army. They did not care for a republic forced upon them with the sword. Indeed, the army itself was not quite satisfied. It desired the dissolution of the Rump and the election of a new parliament. For the time being the army did not urge dissolution too strongly because the new republic was threatened by too many dangers. To the danger of internal disorder was added the possibility of hostility from France and the Netherlands which had been bound to Charles by family ties, and the actuality of rebellions in Ireland and Scotland in behalf of Charles II, the son of the deceased king. Under these conditions the retention of the Rump was the only way to avoid open military rule.

Since 1641 the Irish had been left largely to their own devices. Neither parliament nor the king had many troops to spare for the Irish rebellion. Charles, indeed, when the war began to go against him in England, negotiated with the Irish rebels for an army to use against his English foes, and granted to the Irish toleration of Catholicism and a parliament free from the restrictions of Poynings' Act.[8] The English Puritan parliament was the enemy of the Irish, and the parliamentary victory was regarded as a great disaster by the Irish. They joined in the rebellion of 1648, and on this occasion the Irish Protestants united with the Irish Catholics. In 1649 they proclaimed Charles II king, and attacked the small parliamentary force in Ireland. Cromwell came promptly to the rescue with reinforcements. He stormed Drogheda, one of the centers of the rebels, allowing every man in the garrison, including priests, to be put to the sword. It was a savage outburst of the Puritan hatred for the Irish Catholics. In the same way one town after another fell before Cromwell's onslaught, until, by the summer of 1650, only isolated bits of resistance were left. The Cromwellian settlement of Ireland, established by act of 1652, was extremely harsh. The first five clauses excepted five categories of rebels, amounting perhaps to 80,000 persons, from any pardon for life or estate. The remainder of the act established the policy of transplantation. Rebels not included in the first five

The Commonwealth

Ireland

---

[8] Above, p. 286.

clauses were to forfeit two-thirds of their lands and receive the equivalent of the remaining third in a different part of the island from that in which they had previously lived. Their original estates were given to English settlers. For the remainder of the Cromwellian régime the policy of transplantation and colonization was carried out, and the penal laws were vigorously enforced against the Catholics. So oppressively did his Puritan minions carry out his policies that the name of Cromwell has remained a term of reproach in Ireland to the present day.

Scotland

From Ireland Cromwell went to Scotland, where Charles II was present in person. At Dunbar, in 1650, he defeated a veteran Scottish army twice the size of his own, and a year later at Worcester he defeated overwhelmingly another Scottish army which had invaded England. Since the Scots could not raise another army, they had to accept the government established by Cromwell. It was a contrast to the severity of the Irish settlement. The Scots received free trade with England, the Presbyterian church was allowed to stand, and the government of the English officials was more efficient than that to which the Scots were accustomed. But the settlement was unpopular. It was an alien government, which violated the national feeling, and the requirement that Protestant sects other than the Presbyterian should be tolerated was exceedingly irksome to the Scots.

Colonial policies of James and Charles

The Commonwealth government, thus freed from the danger of rebellion, maintained a vigorous colonial and foreign policy. During the reigns of James and Charles the home government had paid little attention to the colonies. In 1623 James had the Virginia Company of London dissolved, and placed the government of Virginia directly under the crown. The extensive colonial self-government, which had been developing under the patronage of the company, was little affected thereby. Charles I found it so difficult to maintain divine right in England that he troubled little about stifling democracy in the colonies. The great Puritan emigration was so like a secession that it aroused the apprehension of the government. In 1634 Charles appointed a commission for foreign plantations, which was intended to rule the colonies in general and Massachusetts in particular more strictly, but the colonists in Massachusetts resisted the attempt to interfere in their internal affairs, until the trend of events in England gave Charles abundant occupation at home and left the colonists free to conduct their affairs much as they pleased. The external trade of the colonies was regulated but little before 1640, largely because there was little of it to regulate. The export of tobacco, the only product yet grown in large quantities, was confined to England in order that the crown might profit from a levy on the trade; Lord Baltimore's charter of 1632 required all exports from Maryland to be sent to or through England; Charles I revived the old Navigation Acts; and various regulations of detail demonstrated an intention to confine the trade of the colonies to England; but there was not yet any comprehensive system of imperial control of colonial commerce. "Under the first two Stuarts, there was gradually evolving a more or less definite scheme of controlling both the economic and the political development of the empire,"[9] but it was far from completion either in theory or in practice, when the civil war left the colonies nearly free from central supervision.

When the Puritans took control of the English government in 1649, they gave a new impetus to maritime and colonial activities. They were interested in the affairs of the many Puritans who had found refuge in the new world. The English Puritans were largely townsmen whose interests were commercial; and they were the true inheritors of the Elizabethan spirit of aggressive nationalism which had had its birth in the struggle with Catholicism and found its most glorious expression on the sea. When Virginia and the Barbadoes declared for Charles II, parliament forbade them to carry on external trade, except in English ships or in foreign ships licensed by the Commonwealth to trade with them. Legislation was backed by a display of naval force which persuaded the rebellious colonies to acknowledge the Commonwealth. The restriction of trade was only temporary, but it had one aspect of permanent importance. The limitations placed on foreign ships engaged in the colonial trade were expanded into a policy of complete exclusion by the Navigation Act of 1651. The act prohibited the importation into England or its dependencies of goods from Asia, Africa, or America carried in ships not owned by Englishmen or English colonists and manned by crews of like nationality. It was not solely colonial legislation, for the same rule applied to European countries except that foreign ships could carry the goods of their own countries into the ports of England. The act was designed to give to English and colonial ships a monopoly of the carrying trade and was aimed chiefly at the Dutch. The Commonwealth thus returned to the policy of centralized imperial control, but it left to the colonies great freedom in the management of

(margin note) Trade and colonies under the Commonwealth

[9] Beer, *Origins of the British Colonial System*, p. 340.

their internal affairs, and it did little to restrict colonial exports to the English market.

One immediate result of the Navigation Act was a war with the Netherlands. During the first half of the seventeenth century the Netherlands had become the foremost maritime country in Europe. Spanish sea power had declined rapidly since the Armada, and Portugal had perforce followed the fortunes of Spain. England had been too intent on internal affairs to maintain its position on the sea, and France had devoted its attention too exclusively to wars of aggrandizement by land. The Dutch, who had no other resource than the sea, had concentrated their attention on commercial expansion with remarkable success. They had the lion's share of the rich herring fisheries of the North Sea, they monopolized the spice trade, the richest trade of all, and they controlled the carrying trade of the world. This last fact was the chief inspiration of the Navigation Act. The Puritan Commonwealth, whose support came from traders and townsmen, set out vigorously to revive English commerce and to contest the supremacy of the Dutch merchant marine. The Navigation Act would deprive the Dutch of a large share of their prosperous carrying trade and throw it into the hands of the English. The Dutch were too dependent for a livelihood on their maritime supremacy to let it go by default. The Navigation Act, moreover, was merely the culmination of a long series of frictions which the rivalry of the past fifty years had produced. The English and Dutch fishermen were always coming to blows off the English coast, the massacre of the English traders at Amboina in the Dutch East Indies in 1623 and the rivalry in the east still stuck in the English crop, and the Dutch found no joy in the English claim that Dutch ships should dip their flags to English warships in the Narrow Seas as a sign of English supremacy. The English still recalled with bitterness the unredressed violation of neutrality in the battle of the Downs, where, in 1639, a Dutch fleet had shot to pieces a Spanish fleet which had taken refuge in English waters within sight of an English fleet. The Dutch would not expel Royalist supporters of Charles, and the government of the Commonwealth had received no satisfaction for the murder of its ambassador by English Royalist refugees in Holland. The Navigation Act merely filled the cup, as it was intended to do. Early in 1652, when a Dutch fleet refused to lower the flag to an English fleet, a fight ensued which marked the beginning of hostilities.

Naval experts call the war that followed one of the great naval wars of history. Nine pitched battles took place in two years. In

1652 the Dutch had the better of the contest. The Channel was swept Dutch war clear of the English, the Dutch established a superiority in the Mediterranean which put English trade at their mercy, and they persuaded Denmark to close the entrance of the Baltic to English ships. In the next year the tide turned. An English victory forced the Dutch admiral to retire to his home ports, and the English blockaded the Dutch coast. The Dutch finally broke the blockade, but in the process their fleet was too badly damaged to take to sea again for a long time. For the two years the war was a draw, but the Netherlands could less easily stand the strain than England. Their whole prosperity rested on their sea trade, which was halted. The Dutch were anxious for peace, and the English were not averse. The Dutch agreed to salute the English flag in the Narrow Seas, to pay compensation for the massacre of Amboina, to make good the losses inflicted on English shipping by Denmark, and not to harbor the exiled Stuarts. The commercial rivalry was not ended, but England had the better of the treaty and temporary naval superiority.

Despite the success of its aggressive imperialistic policies, the Commonwealth was not popular at home. In 1653 it fell because it was Downfall of the Commonwealth unrepresentative. Though the Rump no longer represented even the army, it clung to power with tenacity. When the army returned from its victories in Ireland and Scotland, it was disposed to dismiss the Rump, but Cromwell deemed it wiser to request parliament to dissolve itself. Though he recognized the unrepresentative character of the body, he also realized that the ghost of constitutionality which hovered over the Rump was the only thing between England and open military rule. When parliament fixed the date of its dissolution in 1654, he was inclined to wait, but the radical army forced his hand. Early in 1653 he drove the members out of the house and declared parliament dissolved. That left the rule of the army patent to all, and necessitated the substitution of some other form of government. A freely elected parliament, for which the army professed a desire, was an impossibility. It would have meant the restoration of the monarchy and the end of toleration for the Independents. Yet the semblance of representative government was essential if Englishmen were to be educated to the ideas of democratic government and religious toleration held by the army. The sword makes a poor political primer. In this dilemma Cromwell called the Little Parliament, commonly known as the Barebone Parliament, after the name of one of its Puritan members, Praise-God Barebone. It consisted of 140 members selected by the officers of the army from a list of nominations made by Independent congregations throughout the country. As might have been anticipated, it proved to be an assembly of reforming fanatics, and the officers soon rid themselves of it. After the failure of this experiment, the officers outlined a plan of government in a document called the Instrument of Government. Cromwell's acceptance of this constitution late in 1653 ended the Commonwealth and began the Protectorate.

Instrument of Government

The Instrument of Government was the first written constitution of the modern type. It had no permanent influence on the English constitution, but it was the prototype of the Constitution of the United States. By its provisions the executive power was assigned to a lord protector, subject to the advice of a council of state. The first incumbents were named, and Cromwell was made lord protector. The legislative power was vested in an elected parliament of 460 members, of whom sixty were equally divided between Ireland and Scotland and the remainder allotted to England. The seats were apportioned roughly according to population, but the suffrage was far from universal. Catholics and those who had fought against parliament received no vote. Parliament was given control of legislation, being empowered to pass a measure over the protector's veto by a simple majority. The protector was provided with permanent revenues, estimated to be sufficient to maintain a civil list, an army of 30,000, and a navy. All additional revenues had to be voted by parliament. An embryo bill of rights was instituted by the guarantee of religious liberty to all except Catholics and Episcopalians.

War with Spain

While Cromwell awaited the election of the first parliament under the Instrument, he launched a war against Spain. The nominal grievance was the Spanish seizure of English ships in West Indian waters, for, though England now had colonies there, Spain still claimed a monopoly. The real reason was the possession of a large and efficient navy which lay idle, when it might be upholding Protestantism and the Elizabethan tradition. The fleet sent to attack San Domingo failed miserably, but it conquered Jamaica, which became the nucleus of English empire in the West Indies. Later the navy won a brilliant victory over the Spanish, and the army, in alliance with France, captured the port of Dunkirk in Spanish Flanders. The successful results of this war added to those of the war against the Netherlands restored the European prestige which England had lost through its long period of absorption in internal affairs, and revived the glorious Elizabethan naval tradition which had been well on the way to oblivion. The cost in taxation and in disturbance of trade was so heavy that the wars alienated the support of the commercial class from the Protectorate; but they developed a professional navy, which from that day to this has been the pride of Englishmen.

The exploits of the navy, however, could not win popularity for the government of the Protectorate. The Instrument of Government, which was designed to establish the government of a parliament controlled by the people, fell far short of this ideal in practice, because it was the government of a minority maintained by force. Even the minority was not satisfied, for the new parliament, elected under the auspices of the army and purged of nearly a hundred undesirable members by Cromwell,[10] demanded the revision of the Instrument. It could not rest content with a constitution framed by the army. Cromwell consented, provided the members would not alter certain provisions which he regarded as fundamental for the preservation of religious tolerance and the prevention of parliamentary tyranny like that of the Rump. But these were precisely what parliament wanted to change. "Oliver was determined to save England from religious intolerance and from the omnipotence of an irresponsible Assembly. The members were determined to save her from despotism and military rule."[11] Cromwell ultimately broke the deadlock by dissolving parliament, just as James I and Charles I had dissolved their obstinate parliaments.

Shortly Cromwell was driven into a still more arbitrary position by his attempt to force upon the people democratic ideals which they did not want. Two judges sent to the north to hold trials for treason refused to act, saying that the ordinance constituting treason, issued by Cromwell and the council without parliamentary consent, was null and void. They were forthwith supplanted by subservient judges. Finally, resistance to the government and several petty local uprisings forced Cromwell to unmask the military character of his government. He divided England into districts and in each placed a major general with a detail of troops to enforce the law. The major generals, in the estimation of a Puritan who was not friendly to Cromwell, "ruled according to their wills, by no law but what seemed good in their own eyes, imprisoning men, obstructing the course of justice between man and man, perverting right through partiality, acquitting some that were guilty, and punishing some that were in-

Government of the Protectorate

---

[10] He was empowered to exclude members from the first few parliaments by the Instrument itself.

[11] Trevelyan, *England under the Stuarts*, p. 307.

nocent as guilty."[12] Though this description may contain some exaggeration, the government of the major generals was the rule of the
army pure and simple brought home to every man's door. The natural unpopularity of military rule was enhanced by the strictness with
which the major generals enforced the "blue laws" which Cromwell
had enacted. Dueling, cockfighting, and swearing were forbidden, and
the Puritan sabbath was upheld in all its severity. On that day shops
could not be opened, traveling was permitted only in case of a necessity certified by a justice of the peace, "and persons 'vainly and pro-
fanely walking on the day aforesaid' " were punished.[13] The irritation
which such laws inevitably cause was increased many fold when they
were executed by squads of soldiers. The sword is not a good weapon
for waging a moral crusade.

In 1656 Cromwell, because he needed money, as kings had done
before him, summoned another parliament. Again he excluded a
hundred members who were opposed to the government, and again
those who were permitted to sit sought to revise the constitution.
Cromwell allowed them to frame a new constitution, which they
called the Humble Petition and Advice. Its principal innovations were
to make Cromwell king with the power to nominate his successor
and to establish a second chamber in the parliament, called the "other
house" and consisting of members nominated by Cromwell for life.
Its purpose was to rid England of the detested military rule. It was
becoming clear that the only way to restore civilian rule was to return to the old form of government with a king and a bicameral
parliament. The title of king Cromwell declined, estimating it as
"only a feather in a hat," but the remainder of the constitution he
accepted. The government established by the Humble Petition and
Advice found no more popular support than its predecessors. When
parliament met again, early in 1658, forty of Cromwell's staunchest
supporters had been appointed to the "other house," and the Presbyterians and republicans, who had been excluded from the previous
session, were admitted to swell the ranks of the opposition. The house
of commons began immediately to attack the "other house," becoming
so refractory that the protector dissolved parliament. Before another,
which he summoned, had assembled, he died in 1658.

After Cromwell's death the Protectorate soon crumbled. Oliver's
personality had given to the system its only cohesive force. His son

Humble
Petition
and
Advice

---

[12] *Memoirs of Colonel Hutchinson*, p. 371.
[13] Firth, *Oliver Cromwell*, p. 351.

Richard, who succeeded him, lacked the strength of his father's personality. He "was a peasant in his nature, yet gentle and virtuous, but became not greatness."[14] The army soon obtained his retirement and took charge of the government. The Rump was recalled to provide the appearance of respectability, but when the assembly with its old arrogance began to dictate to the army, it was again dismissed. These rapid changes crystallized the popular opinion, which had been forming for some time, that the only way to end military despotism was to restore the Stuarts. The man who brought about the restoration was George Monk, commander of the troops in Scotland. When the army in London expelled the Rump, he marched south with his army and restored it. He then ordered the Rump to dissolve itself. When it refused, he brought back the Presbyterian members who had been excluded by Pride's Purge in 1648. Parliament then ordered a new election and voted its own dissolution. The new parliament, called a convention because it was not properly summoned by royal writs, met in 1660. It immediately invited Charles II to occupy the throne. The Protectorate was at an end.

End of the Protectorate

Though Englishmen hailed the restoration of the monarchy with joyful acclaim, the experiments of the Commonwealth and the Protectorate had not been in vain. Without them Englishmen could not have arrived peacefully at that consensus of opinion which made the restoration possible. In 1649 disunion had been so great that military rule had been the only alternative to anarchy. By 1660 Englishmen had been convinced by the trial of other forms of government that monarchy suited them best. The experiments of the Commonwealth contributed astonishingly little to the permanent constitutional machinery of the English government. Of republican forms and methods of government Englishmen had had enough. But to the constitutional ideals of Englishmen Cromwell and the Puritans made a contribution of fundamental importance. Within a few generations religious toleration and the sovereignty of the people became essential parts of the English constitution, though the monarchical form was not changed. These were the ideals of Cromwell and the army, and it was their administration of the Commonwealth and the Protectorate that first brought them home to Englishmen.

Contribution of Commonwealth and Protectorate

For the outcome of the civil war and the conduct of affairs during the interregnum Oliver Cromwell was responsible more than any other one man. He belonged to the class of country gentlemen which

Oliver Cromwell

[14] *Memoirs of Colonel Hutchinson*, p. 370.

was supplying the leaders of the Puritan party and winning such a share in the government as it had never had before. He served without particular distinction as a member of the parliament which secured the Petition of Right. In the early days of the Long Parliament he impressed fellow members as a bold, vigorous, even intemperate supporter of the extreme party led by Pym, but he was not then one of the foremost leaders. One of the first to see the kind of army that was necessary to win the war, he organized the force that made parliament victorious. Beginning his military career at the age of forty-three, he learned to fight as he went along. So well and so rapidly did he assimilate the teachings of observation and experience, that he became the greatest military leader produced by the civil war. At the close of the first civil war Cromwell's dominating personality became steadily more influential among the divided opponents of the king. After he decided in 1647 that the way to save the results of the civil war was to cast his lot with the army against parliament, he became the most powerful man in England. In 1653 he became the ruler of a nominal republic, which he converted into a government more absolute than the Stuart despotism had ever been. Contemporary estimates of him in the last phase of his career were harsh. To Royalists he appeared merely to be satisfying a lust for power, and many republicans judged him to have "sacrificed the public cause 'to the idol of his own ambition.' "[15] More dispassionate modern critics absolve him of hypocrisy. They accept as sincere his profession that he sought only to carry out God's will and served no personal ends. Believing that the Puritans were God's chosen people, he acted as the head of the Puritan party. Because he believed the tenets of that party to be the best for the nation, he did not hesitate to make himself a military dictator in the effort to force them upon the nation. As a statesman he was inconsistent. "One year he was foremost in pressing for an agreement with the King, another foremost in bringing him to the block; now all for a republic, now all for a government with some element of monarchy in it."[16] He met difficulties as they came and altered his policies as the promotion of his ends amid rapidly changing circumstances seemed to demand. Though he failed of his main purpose, he was not merely "damned to everlasting fame." The man who, in the "general wreck of powers and parties," "saved the British Empire from partition, the civil liberties of England from

[15] Firth, *Cromwell*, p. 475.
[16] *Ibid.*, p. 478.

Royalist reconquest, the Free Churches and free-thinkers from destruction by those of the narrow way"[17] conferred lasting benefits upon the nation. Measured by the extent of his achievement, without regard for the meteoric character of his career, he must still be accorded the greatness deserving of perpetual fame.

[17] Trevelyan, *England under the Stuarts*, p. 327.

CHAPTER XXV

THE RESTORATION AND THE REVOLUTION

Political settlement

WHEN Charles II saw the trend of events in England in 1660, he issued at Breda, his place of exile in Holland, a declaration of his policies. He offered to pardon all rebels except those whom parliament should designate; to leave to parliament the question of the restoration of the lands of the Royalists; to pay the wages of the army; and to allow parliament to make the religious settlement, with the proviso that no religious belief should be persecuted unless it should disturb the peace of the realm. This Declaration of Breda became the basis of the political settlement effected by the legislation of the convention parliament, which the Long Parliament had ordered to be summoned. An act of amnesty pardoned all except some of the regicides and two others. The confiscated lands of the king, the church, and the Royalists were ordered to be restored, but Royalists who had been forced to sell their lands received no compensation. The army was paid and disbanded, except 5,000 troops which were retained as a standing army. This parliament also abolished feudal dues and purveyance. In return it imposed permanent taxes intended to yield £600,000 annually. In addition it granted to Charles for his life taxes designed to produce a further annual income of £600,000. The total was meant to be sufficient to cover the royal expenses in ordinary times, but the income from the taxes proved to be only about one-half what was anticipated. Charles was left far more dependent on parliament than the convention intended.

Constitutional situation

The constitutional situation created by the restoration was a balance of power between king and parliament. The convention declared the reign of Charles II to have begun in 1649 on the death of his father and invalidated all parliamentary enactments passed since 1641 without the assent of the king. The sweeping constitutional reforms effected by the Long Parliament before September, 1641, were retained to become permanent parts of the constitution.[1] The monarchy no longer had the arbitrary courts of star chamber and high commission; it could no longer levy taxes without parliamentary consent; nor could it legislate by proclamation. The absolute monarchy of

---

[1] The triennial act was repealed, but the essential principle that parliament should meet at least once every three years was preserved.

Charles I was ended. The control of the king by parliament, on the other hand, was far from complete. The king still had a veto over legislation, he retained command of the militia, and he was the executive over whom the legislature had no adequate means of control. By its hold of the purse strings and its power of impeachment parliament could secure the remedy of any serious abuses of the executive power, but it lacked the means to hold the king responsible for failure to carry out its will, unless he should overstep the legal limits of his discretionary authority, which were still large. On the occasion of a war with the Dutch (1665-1667) parliament decreased these limits somewhat. It renewed the practice of granting taxes for specific purposes and of demanding an audit of accounts. After 1667 this procedure became regular. By making its appropriations sufficiently detailed, parliament could confine the discretionary power of the executive within very narrow limits, though this possibility was not grasped for many years. The restoration left king and parliament with approximately equal constitutional powers. This might work well as long as the two cooperated harmoniously, but if one differed from the other, neither had a constitutional right to decide the issue. The location of ultimate authority was left unsettled. The final determination of this issue was the constitutional development of chief importance during the reigns of Charles II and James II.

The religious settlement was not accomplished by the convention parliament. This assembly contained large groups of Presbyterians and Anglicans, with a small group of Independents holding the balance. The Presbyterians wanted the establishment of a broad church which would be acceptable to both Presbyterians and Anglicans. The defeat of this policy by a combination of the Royalists and the Independents left the religious settlement to the next parliament. It was elected in the spring of 1661, when the reactionary spirit in favor of royalty was running strong. A substantial majority was Royalist and ardently Anglican. The Royalist proclivities of this parliament gave it the name of the Cavalier Parliament and caused the king to keep it in session until 1679. Its radical Anglicanism led it, between 1661 and 1665, to enact legislation which made the established church narrowly Anglican and ended toleration. (1) The Municipal Corporations Act required members of the governing bodies of municipalities to renounce the Solemn League and Covenant, to take oath that it was unlawful to resist the king, to take the oaths of allegiance and supremacy, and to take communion in the church of England. Few Dissenters, as Protestants who were not members of the Angli-

Religious settlement

can church were now beginning to be called, could conscientiously fulfill all these tests. The Anglicans secured control of the municipal corporations which returned many members to the house of commons. (2) The Act of Uniformity required all incumbents of livings in the church, the universities, and the schools to subscribe to the prayer book. Between 1,200 and 1,800 pastors resigned. Toleration within the church ceased. (3) Freedom of worship outside the church was then stopped by the Conventicle Act, which imposed harsh penalties on those who should take part in religious worship conducted elsewhere than in an Anglican church, when five or more persons other than the members of a family were present. (4) The code was completed by the Five Mile Act. It required the ministers who had refused to take the tests prescribed by the Act of Uniformity to take an oath not to resist the king and not to attempt any change of government in church or state. Those who declined were forbidden to approach within five miles of a town or of any parish where they had previously taught or preached.

In the settlement Charles II gave parliament free rein, intervening actively only to seek greater toleration for rebels, Catholics, and Dissenters than parliament was inclined to bestow. He left the management of the government in this period largely to his advisers. Upon his return from exile he had selected a privy council in which the Royalists and Presbyterians were fairly evenly balanced. Since the council was too large to be an efficient advisory body, Charles took his advice mainly from an inner circle, which came to be known as the cabal or the cabinet. In this group Hyde, now created Lord Clarendon, who had advised Charles I since 1641 and Charles II since 1649, was the most influential. Charles II soon gave himself over to a life of licentious ease, and let Clarendon do the work, though he did not fail to keep sufficiently in touch with affairs to make his influence felt when he was interested. He was the ablest of the Stuart rulers, affable, witty, a keen judge of men, and a good politician. When he chose to exert himself, as he sometimes did later in his reign, he was capable of the effective direction of the government, but, being guided neither by high principles nor great ambitions, he rarely made a sustained effort. His attitude with regard to the royal prerogative was sufficiently typical. He entertained a desire to increase it and eventually took some steps in that direction, but he never went very far. He was not prepared, on the one hand, to apply himself steadily to the fulfillment even of that ambition, nor, on the other, to risk arousing opposition strong enough to send him

Character of Charles II

again into exile and deprive him of the pleasures afforded by residence in Whitehall.

One of the places where Charles frequently exerted his influence was in foreign affairs. When he was restored to the throne, England was in alliance with France and technically at war with Spain. At first he was undecided whether to let this heritage from the Protectorate stand or to change it for an alliance with Spain. While he was in exile, he had been expelled from his refuge in France as a consequence of the French alliance established by Cromwell, and he had since that time been friendly with Spain. It was his natural impulse to continue this friendship, and several of his counselors thought this the wiser policy for him to pursue. France, on the other hand, was the strongest power on the continent, Louis XIV was his cousin, and Charles admired his cousin's strong government unfettered by any parliament, and coveted his wealth. The ultimate decision of the question was determined by the offer of an alliance with Portugal which was to be established by Charles's marriage to Catharine of Braganza, a princess of the royal house of Portugal. The Portuguese were ready to pay a large dowry and to cede Bombay, an important trading post in India, and Tangier, a valuable naval station near the entrance of the Mediterranean. What they wanted in return was an English army of 10,000 men to aid them in the war which they were waging against Spain for their independence. These terms were attractive to Charles. The inadequacy of the revenues granted by parliament placed him in sore need of money, and he was interested strongly in the advancement of England's imperial power. It was soon learned that this alliance would also promote friendly relations with France. Although Louis XIV had just concluded a victorious war with Spain by a treaty which provided for his marriage with the eldest daughter of the king of Spain, he was desirous of keeping Spain weak. His wife had renounced her right to inherit the Spanish throne, but her renunciation had been contingent upon the payment of a dowry which had not been made. Since her brother, the Spanish king's only son, was an invalid, whose early death was expected, Louis saw in the situation an opportunity to further the ambitions of territorial aggrandizement which he already entertained. It was his secret ambition to claim in behalf of his wife at the appropriate time the Spanish Netherlands on one side and Spain on the other. With this encouragement from France, Charles accepted the proposed alliance with Portugal in 1661.

The community of interests thus established between Charles and

Early relations with France

Louis was further strengthened by the sale of Dunkirk. This Channel port, which Cromwell's troops had captured from Spain, was desired by the king of France. His offer of a large sum for it was accepted by Charles in 1662. The sale was highly unpopular in England, where Dunkirk was looked upon as a second Calais. Clarendon, however, received the blame, it being the popular conception that he had been bribed by Louis to advise his master to sell. Charles derived from the transaction the idea of looking to his cousin for the money which he could not obtain from the English parliament.

Before these contacts led to a definite alliance, England drifted into another war with the Netherlands. The commercial rivalry of the two nations continued to produce friction after 1654 as it had done before. In English commerce Charles was keenly interested. In 1664 he allowed ships of the royal navy to be used to seize a Dutch trading post on the west coast of Africa and the Dutch colony of New Amsterdam in America. These acts of aggression provoked a naval war which lasted until 1667. The English had rather the better of the warfare, though in the winter of 1667 a Dutch fleet sailed up the Thames, doing a little damage to English shipping and a great deal to English pride. Soon after, peace was made at Breda. England abandoned her last claims to the Spice Islands in the east and secured New York in the west.

The Anglo-Dutch war was followed by a complete reversal of alliances. In 1667 Louis XIV put forward a fantastic claim to the Spanish Netherlands in the name of his wife, invading them with a large army. For some years his aggressive attitude had aroused the vague fears of his neighbors, but this flagrant attack for the sole purpose of aggrandizement fully awakened Europe to the fact that France had superseded Spain as the bully of Europe. The Dutch saw at once that the success of Louis would threaten their independence. Though they had had the nominal alliance of France in their recent war against England, they now sought the alliance of England, the other power which had most to lose by French expansion in that direction. Charles was nothing loath. He had agreed in advance not to oppose French aggression in the Spanish Netherlands in order to detach France from the Dutch alliance; but now that his war against the Dutch was ended, he wanted from Louis XIV a larger price for his non-intervention. Early in 1668, after he had failed to obtain as much as he desired, he entered the Triple Alliance of the Netherlands, England, and Sweden, formed to prevent the further extension of the conquests of Louis XIV. Since the king of France had the best generals, the largest armies, and

Second
Anglo-
Dutch war

The
French
alliance

the greatest resources in Europe, it is doubtful if the Triple Alliance could have stopped him, had he chosen to continue; but he thought it discretion to accept the terms of the Triple Alliance, subsequently break it up by diplomacy, and renew his war of aggression under more favorable circumstances. Charles had made it quite evident that he was for sale, and in 1670 Louis arranged with him the Treaty of Dover. He agreed to pay Charles an annual pension, and to provide him with troops whenever Charles thought the time ripe to make England Catholic. Charles undertook to aid France in some future war against the Netherlands. The treaty was kept secret from all except a few of Charles's intimate advisers, and to conceal it still further, other ministers were allowed to negotiate a sham treaty which covered the alliance against the Dutch but omitted mention of the Catholic part of the plot. Whether so astute a politician as Charles was momentarily deceived by the belief that it would be possible to restore Catholicism in England, or whether he suggested this part of the treaty merely as one means of inducing Louis to pay the money which undoubtedly was one of his chief objects in negotiating the treaty, it seems impossible to say.[2]

If he really thought it feasible to establish Catholicism, he soon discovered his mistake. In 1672 he issued a Declaration of Indulgence which suspended the operation of the penal laws against the Catholics and the Dissenters. It was intensely unpopular. The beginning of the war against the Netherlands in the same year made necessary the assembly of parliament to secure funds. When it came together, it objected to the Declaration of Indulgence, offering the king a large grant if he would withdraw it. Charles complied. Parliament, to make assurance doubly sure, then passed the Test Act. It required all holders of office under the crown to take communion in the Anglican church and to make a declaration against transubstantiation, a typically Catholic belief. It excluded Catholics from office, and also most of the Dissenters. It was so convincing as a demonstration of the strength of the popular feeling against the Catholics that Charles dropped the Catholic side of his policy.

Declaration of Indulgence

The French side was maintained longer, though it was no more popular. Though the secret Treaty of Dover was not known, Charles's manifest friendship for France, taken in conjunction with the Declaration of Indulgence, raised suspicions of his intentions. The war begun against the Netherlands in 1672 was not popular. Though the commercial rivalry with the Netherlands had not subsided, Englishmen

Relations with the French and the Dutch

---

[2] See Feiling, *British Foreign Policy, 1660–1672*, pp. 267–275; Ogg, *England in the Reign of Charles II*, i, 338–355, 362.

were not prepared to wage a war designed to fill their pocketbooks at the cost of advancing the cause of absolutism and Catholicism represented by Louis XIV. French dominance on the continent would ultimately endanger any material gain from a Dutch war. After 1673 parliament would grant no more money for the war, and in 1674 Charles was forced to withdraw. For a time he retained his French pension because Louis XIV was fearful that parliament would make any grant of taxes dependent upon English aid to the Dutch against the French. In 1677 parliament did express such an opinion, and this threat enabled Charles to obtain more money from the king of France. Despite the payment, Charles followed the suggestion of parliament so far as to begin negotiations for a Dutch alliance, which resulted in the marriage of his niece Mary, the daughter of his brother James, to William of Orange. With this evidence of good will toward the Netherlands, parliament voted money for a war against France, but it failed to appropriate enough for an effective campaign. The majority which desired war was still distrustful of Charles's intentions, though it was not yet known that Charles had been receiving French money to prevent parliament from committing England to hostilities against France. The danger was sufficiently imminent, however, to cause Louis XIV to agree to renew the payments which he had stopped after the marriage, in return for an undertaking by Charles to keep England at peace. From this final piece of double-dealing Charles failed to profit because he did not keep his part of the bargain. England was beginning to come to the help of the Dutch, when the war was ended in 1678 by a treaty between them and Louis XIV.

Internal political situation in 1678

These external policies had a strong repercussion upon internal politics. Ever since the Declaration of Indulgence the suspicion that Charles sought to build a Catholic despotism had been growing. His persistent anti-national policy of friendly relations with Louis, the most powerful Catholic and the greatest despot in Europe, increased English suspicion, though nothing was definitely known of the Treaty of Dover or of the duplicity of Charles's subsequent negotiations with Louis. It was this situation which created a strong minority of opposition in the loyal Cavalier Parliament and led to the formation of the political parties which ever since have been a prominent part of the English parliamentary system.

Opposition to 1667

Opposition, of course, had never been entirely lacking, but before 1672 it had been either factious or short-lived. As early as 1663 the Cavalier Parliament refused the request of the king to be allowed to set aside freely the penal clauses of the acts on religion. Political opposition began with the Dutch war of 1665-1667. Though England was on the whole successful, the disgrace of the Dutch exploit on the Thames was remembered and the earlier victories were forgotten. Clarendon, though he was blameless, was held responsible in public opinion, and in parliament this point of view was diligently spread by courtiers who sought to supplant Clarendon as the chief adviser of the king. Charles, who had tired of Clarendon's lectures upon his evil ways, anticipated an impeachment, dismissed the minister, and sent him into exile.

After 1667 no single minister was again given as much power as Clarendon had exercised. Charles advised with the committee of the privy council on foreign affairs. To this committee he might call whom he pleased, but there were five who had the chief influence.[3] Since their initials spelled "cabal," which already had a sinister meaning, the group was soon known popularly as *the* cabal. The five agreed on no one policy except that of religious toleration, and they supported that for different reasons. Two were Catholics and three were Protestants, but no one of the five believed in the parliamentary policy of letting the Anglican church persecute Dissenters. Charles used the cabal's unity on toleration to secure their support for his Declaration of Indulgence. On other policies he played them one against another secretly. The period of the cabal was one of secrecy, intrigue, and duplicity. It prepared the way for the rapid growth of popular fears and apprehensions concerning the royal policies after 1672. The opposition which smashed the cabal arose over the Declaration of Indulgence. The Test Act caused the resignation of one of the Catholics. The Protestant earl of Shaftesbury, who was beginning to suspect that Charles's policy of indulgence was designed merely to promote Catholicism, was dismissed by the king.

After the break-up of the cabal Charles took as his chief adviser the earl of Danby, who was the leader of the intolerant Anglican group in parliament. Danby built up a regular party of supporters whose chief tenets were intolerant Anglicanism and a wide royal prerogative. Opposed to this party was a group which believed in toleration for Protestant Dissenters and in the supremacy of parliament. Shaftesbury soon became the leader of this group, giving it an organization like that of a modern political party. Within a few years Danby's followers were called the Tories, and Shaftesbury's the Whigs. The Tory principles were more popular with the rural gentry, their tenants and dependents, and the clergy. The Whig party comprised a majority of the nobles,

The cabal

Formation of parties

---

[3] They were Clifford, Arlington, Buckingham, Ashley (Lord Shaftesbury) and Lauderdale.

the commercial classes of the towns, and the Dissenters. Since Shaftesbury's party was stronger in the country than it was in parliament, he sought to force Charles to dissolve the Cavalier Parliament, hoping that a new election would produce a Whig majority.

The Catholic Terror

Two events played into his hands in 1678. The first was the Catholic Terror. This was produced by Titus Oates, who, apparently in search of notoriety, concocted a series of lies about Catholic plots to dethrone Charles, seize the government, and establish the Catholic church. These specific charges, though false, were "taken for gospel." They fanned into flames the smoldering fears of Catholic plots which had haunted the popular mind for many years. The public, indeed, flared into a state of unreasoning panic. "I never saw . . . the nation in more apprehension and consternation," wrote Evelyn, the diarist.[4] Parliament enacted a law requiring its members to express their disbelief in several Catholic doctrines. This act excluded Catholics from parliament until 1829. Several innocent people were convicted by the courts and executed. When Oates finally accused the queen of an attempt to poison the king, it was more than even a gullible populace would swallow, and Oates and his gang began to decline in favor.

Impeachment of Danby

Shaftesbury utilized the popular frenzy to build up the Whig party and bring it to power. He put forward the program of exclusion of the Catholic succession, disbandment of the army, and the impeachment of Danby. He had not accomplished any one of the three, when the popular excitement began to cool. His chance came, however, through the action of Louis XIV. Convinced of the double-dealing of Charles, the French king procured the publication in parliament of a letter, written by Danby at the order of Charles, in which Charles offered to help Louis secure peace for a sum of money at the time when parliament was granting him money to make war upon France. Danby made it appear that he had written the letter at the order of the king, but the commons would not allow him to shift the responsibility. He was impeached, and Charles, in order to save his minister, dissolved the Cavalier Parliament.

Catholic exclusion

Charles was forced to call a new parliament in 1679 because he had no money. One of the officers of the exchequer declared "that there was not money sufficient for bread for the king's family."[5] The election, fought on party lines, gave the Whigs a majority. They introduced a bill to exclude Catholics from the succession to the throne. The nearest heir was James, the brother of Charles, who openly acknowl-

---

[4] Ed. by Dobson, iii, 25, 26.
[5] Reresby, *Memoirs and Travels*, p. 196.

edged himself a Catholic. To save his brother, Charles dissolved the parliament before it granted supply. Two other parliaments summoned in the next two years had similar results. Subsequently Louis XIV began again to subsidize Charles, making him temporarily independent of parliamentary grant. By this time Charles had won the fight for his brother. The fear of Catholic plots had subsided. The Whig party had alienated some of its support by its attempt to vest the succession in the duke of Monmouth, the king's illegitimate son, who was a frivolous fop. James had a mind of his own, and was notably serious. The attitude of parliament, moreover, had aroused a fear that departure from the hereditary line of succession would result in civil war, and Englishmen had had their fill of civil war.

So far did the reaction go that Charles was able to take revenge on the Whigs. He failed to secure the conviction of Shaftesbury, who sought safety in flight after his acquittal; but two other Whig leaders were accused of connection with a plot to seize the person of the king, convicted, and executed; and the duke of Monmouth was exiled to Holland. The Whig party for the time was leaderless, unpopular, and thoroughly discredited. The Tories enjoyed a complete ascendency. To maintain it permanently Charles had *quo warranto* proceedings instituted against boroughs which still had Whig governments despite the Corporation Act. A town receiving the writ had to prove in court that it exercised specified powers by virtue of its charter. If proof satisfactory to the court could not be produced, as it rarely could, the charter was forfeited. The king then granted a new one in terms that guaranteed control of the municipal government by the Tories. The result was to give the Tories control not only of the municipal governments but also of the house of commons. Charles did not reap the fruit of his efforts. He died in 1685 before another parliament met. *[Last years of Charles II]*

James II was accepted as king without significant protest. Slight rebellions in Scotland and in western England never seriously threatened his position. With most Englishmen the memory of the recent internal strife was so green that their fear of civil war was next to their fear of Catholicism. The latter the new king allayed by announcement that he would maintain the government and the Anglican church as they were by law established. Protestants, assured that the king would keep his religion a personal matter, expressed their relief in a saying which went the rounds: "We have now for our Church the word of a king, and of a king who was never worse than his word."[6] The heir, *[James II and the nation]*

---

[9] Macaulay, *History of England* (Boston, 1855), i, 350.

moreover, was a Protestant. By his first marriage James had two daughters, Mary and Anne, both of whom were Protestant; and though his second wife was a Catholic, there were no children by this marriage. Since a Protestant succession seemed assured, a temporary period of Catholic rule was better than civil war. So reasoned many of James's subjects.

The new monarch made a good impression by his gravity and his industry. "The change upon the face of the English court," wrote a contemporary, "is very remarkable: in the last king's time mirth, plays, buffoonery, etc., domineered, and was incouraged; now there is little to be seen but seriousness and business."[7] Observers of the transformation predicted "much happiness to the nation, as to its political government."[8] But James was also unlike his brother in that he understood the popular temper no better than his father. For a few months he ruled with the good will of his people. He called parliament at once, obtaining from a subservient Tory majority elected as the result of the *quo warranto* proceedings, the grant of a large income for life. But loyal as the parliament was on political questions, it refused the royal request to suspend the Test Act. As a consequence James prorogued it after two short sessions in 1685 and never met it again. Thereafter he entered upon a career of senseless despotism, which soon brought about his downfall.

Already his policies with regard to the rebellions had begun to cause

Military despotism popular misgivings concerning his promise not to seek "arbitrary power." In the west the "ignorant, cruel," subservient Judge Jeffreys, sent on a judicial circuit to try the rebels, imposed such severe sentences in so brutal a manner that his circuit was given the name of the "bloody assizes." This judicial reign of terror impressed the nation unfavorably. It was followed by the news that the army of 30,000, raised to crush the rebellion, had been retained as a standing army. The ostentatious display of 16,000 of these soldiers encamped outside of London aroused the fear of a military despotism.

Catholic despotism James soon made manifest his intention to force Catholicism upon the nation. Though parliament had opposed the policy, James declared his power to dispense with the penalties of the Test Act, and began to appoint Catholics to the privy council and to offices of state. Having dismissed the judges who disagreed with this doctrine and packed the bench, he had a test case made of Hales, a Catholic, who had

---

[7] Fountainhall, *Memoirs* cited by Cheyney, *Readings in English History*, p. 535.
[8] Evelyn, *Diary*, iii, 181.

accepted appointment to office from the king and had not fulfilled the requirements of the Test Act. Hales pleaded a dispensation from the king, and the judges upheld the royal power to dispense with the law. James then began to confer offices freely upon Catholics, introducing them not only into civil positions but also into places in the church and the universities. The appointment of many Catholic officers caused the Protestants to fear an intention to suppress their religion by means of the army. Opposition to some of the appointments made to instructorships at Oxford was suppressed in a high-handed fashion. James furthermore created a court of ecclesiastical commission, which, under another name, was practically the old court of high commission. His purpose may have been to delegate the powers as head of the church which, as a Catholic, he did not wish to exercise,[9] but his action defied the act of the Long Parliament which not only abolished the court of high commission but also forbade the establishment of any similar court in the future. The court was suspected to be designed as an instrument to aid the king in overcoming the opposition of the Anglican clergy to his Catholic policies, and it was used for that purpose.

By this time popular dissatisfaction was so strong and so general that James began to recognize the need of more supporters. In 1687 he sought to win the favor of the Dissenters for his Catholic policy by the issue of a Declaration of Indulgence which suspended the penal clauses of the laws on religion and authorized Protestants and Catholics to worship in public. A similar declaration in 1672 had been declared unconstitutional by parliament. It aroused further opposition and did not help James. Most of the leaders of the Dissenters, despite their persecution by the Anglicans, preferred alliance with them to alliance with James and Catholicism. They generally refused to avail themselves of the declaration. In 1688, nevertheless, James issued a second declaration and ordered the Anglican divines to read it on a stated Sunday. Seven bishops promptly presented a petition to the king, pointing out that parliament had declared the suspending power illegal and requesting that the order be rescinded. Though James refused, on the fatal Sunday the order was almost universally disobeyed by the clergy. The defiance meant that the clergy had turned against the doctrine of non-resistance which they had so long preached in their sermons on divine right.

James retaliated by having the seven bishops charged with the publication of a seditious libel. This action aroused all England. Public

---

[9] Clark, *Later Stuarts*, p. 118.

The crisis | interest centered on the proceedings at the trial, and excitement reached fever heat. The judges were under the influence of the king, and an attempt was made to pack the jury. But James's unconstitutional acts and the fear of Catholicism had united the whole nation, Tories and Whigs, Anglicans and Dissenters. One of the judges boldly declared the Declaration of Indulgence illegal. The jury, after a session through the night, pronounced the bishops not guilty. Crowds in the courthouse and all over the city went wild with joy. In the provinces similar demonstrations followed on the heels of the horsemen who bore the glad tidings from one end of England to the other.

Rebellion | The trial was the signal for the end of passive resistance. Shortly before it took place, a son had been born to James. That meant that the heir to the throne was a Catholic. There was no prospect that James would ever rule constitutionally, and Catholic rule could no longer be regarded as merely an episode. James, moreover, had been making preparations to secure a packed parliament, and many leaders of the opposition feared that, by this means, he might make the monarchy absolute and work his will with regard to Catholicism. Faced with these circumstances, they decided upon rebellion, but they were not ready to begin the movement without outside help because the standing army might enable the king to quell any purely English insurrection before it could become effectively organized. On July 30 seven prominent leaders of both the Whigs and the Tories accordingly united to address to William of Orange an invitation to come to England in arms for the purpose of leading an English uprising in behalf of the popular liberties. William was the ruler of the Netherlands; but he was selected largely because he was the husband of Mary, the elder daughter of James, the Protestant nearest in the line of succession to the throne.

William, who had previously been sounded informally, had already intimated his probable acceptance of such an invitation. Before he could take troops to England, however, he had to be sure of Dutch support. It was not to be had merely for the asking, because the Dutch feared that Louis XIV might attack them while their army was absent in England. Louis XIV himself helped William out of this difficulty. By announcing that he would treat a Dutch invasion of England as an attack upon himself, he caused the Dutch to assume falsely the existence of an alliance between France and England against the Netherlands and to favor William's project as a means of breaking it up. Then, by attacking Germany on the Rhine frontier, he relieved the Dutch apprehension of any immediate French invasion of their own country. William was thus able to complete his preparations and sail for England in November.

James, meanwhile, had failed in an attempt to recover popular support by revoking at the eleventh hour some of his acts which had roused the opposition, but he had a fleet and an army with which to repel the foreign invader. Fortune favored William. He decided not to engage the English fleet and to take the serious risk of having his line of retreat by water cut off, because he feared that any warfare between the Dutch and the English before Englishmen had rallied to his standard might revive old animosities and make him appear to the English as a foreign conqueror rather than as the leader of an English rebellion. He therefore sailed through the Channel before a favoring breeze and landed in the west of England. The English fleet, which was stationed near the mouth of the Thames, was unable to reach the Channel until the wind changed, and once it was there, it was first becalmed and then driven into harbor by a gale. William's initial success was due in no small measure to the "Protestant wind." After William was safely ashore, James led his army toward the west to meet him, but so many of his followers deserted and he became so distrustful of the loyalty of his army that he returned to London. The retreat was followed by negotiations in which William demanded only that Catholics should be excluded from office and that a parliament should be summoned to make the needful provisions for the maintenance of the liberties of the subject and of the Protestant religion. To save these was the published purpose of William's coming to England; and had the parliament been called, James would still have had a good chance to remain upon the throne, though with his powers strictly limited. He did not remain to finish negotiations, but fled to France and sacrificed his opportunity.

His flight left England without a government. William called together all those who had sat in a parliament of Charles II and sought their advice. They suggested that he should temporarily assume charge of the government and issue writs inviting the constituent bodies of the kingdom to elect representatives to a convention. When the body met on January 22, 1689, it was for practical purposes a parliament, though legally it was only a convention because it had not been convened by the king's writs. The members of the convention were nearly unanimous in their opinion that the king had deserted his post and

The crown

should not be restored,[10] but the Tories and the Whigs were not agreed upon the new type of government which should be established. The Tories, who had emphasized the royal power and in large part had accepted the theory of divine right, found it difficult to abandon the principle of hereditary succession to the throne. The Whigs, who believed in a powerful parliament and had made the exclusion bill their policy in 1679, were merely following their accepted political tenets when they proposed to select a new king by act of parliament. The latter, who, with the support of some of the Tories, had the majority in the house of commons, adopted a resolution to the effect that James had broken the original contract between king and people, had violated the fundamental laws, and, by his withdrawal from the kingdom, had abdicated the throne, leaving it vacant. In the house of lords, where the majority was Tory, this resolution stuck, because it disregarded hereditary right completely. A motion to create a Protestant regency to rule in the name of James failed, on the other hand, because enough of the Tories recognized the unstable and dangerous character of such a government. Yet the majority of the Tories could not bring themselves to accept the principle that the throne was vacant. They claimed that when James abdicated, the throne passed to the nearest heir; and since James's son, they asserted, was supposititious, Mary was the rightful queen. This would have left William subordinate to his wife, and it was no more satisfactory to Mary than it was to him. This deadlock between the principles of hereditary right and election was broken by an announcement from William that he would serve neither as regent nor as consort. If they did not want him as king, he would return home. The Tories were forced to face squarely the issue of James II, king by divine right, or William and Mary, rulers by act of parliament. A small group of irreconcilables clung to divine right. They soon became known as Jacobites.[11] They constituted a discredited though dangerous party, because their success meant the overthrow of the government established by the convention. The greater part of the Tories united with the Whigs to offer the crown to William and Mary. The tender was accompanied by a declaration of the rights of the nation (later enacted in the form of a bill) which became a constituent part of the terms upon which parliament granted the crown. These acts settled the crown on William and Mary and their heirs, provided for its transfer to Anne, Mary's sister, and her heirs, if the first line should fail, enumerated the arbitrary acts of James II, and declared them illegal.

---

[10] A small group of the Tories still desired to bring back James with limited powers.
[11] From *Iacobus*, the Latin form of James.

William and Mary by their acceptance of the offer settled the question of the crown.

These events of 1688 and 1689 constituted the revolution of 1688. James II had not legally forfeited the throne, and he was the only authority who could call a legal parliament. It was a bloodless revolution, but it effected a fundamental change in the constitution. This was not contained in the Bill of Rights. Important as that document was constitutionally, the declaration that standing armies were illegal was probably the only wholly new constitutional principle enunciated. The abolition of the dispensing power, of the ecclesiastical commission and similar courts, of taxation without parliamentary consent, of excessive bail or fines, and of cruel and unjust punishments was not novel, nor was it an innovation to declare that subjects had the right to petition the king, that elections to and speech in parliament should be free, that parliament ought to be held frequently, and that juries should be fairly drawn. These matters enumerated in the Bill of Rights the nation claimed before 1688. Because Charles II and James II had violated them, it was an advantage to have them stated specifically in written form. They were so valuable, indeed, that some of them were incorporated in the first ten amendments of the Constitution of the United States in nearly identical language. But the great change wrought was in the security of the guarantee that these principles would be observed in the future. The revolution of 1688 settled finally the contest between king and parliament for sovereignty. Since parliament had made a king, it could unmake one. Henceforth there could be no doubt of the superiority of parliament. The framework of the constitution was not greatly altered, the king was still left extensive powers, and time was to demonstrate that parliamentary control of the royal authority was distinctly limited; but thereafter no king who so far transgressed the limitations placed upon him by law as to arouse the determined opposition of his subjects could hope to retain the throne. The theory of divine right as a working principle of government was dead in England.

Some changes in the framework of the constitution brought about by legislation after the revolution may be regarded as part of the revolutionary settlement. (1) The Mutiny Act (1689) declared standing armies and martial law unknown to the common law of England, and then proceeded to give the king power to raise an army and rule it by martial law for six months. Subsequently the act was renewed at frequent intervals, usually each year. The need to have this legislation reenacted so often helped to assure frequent meetings of parliament,

The constitution

Additions to revolutionary settlement

though the necessity for annual grants of taxation was the primary factor which rendered yearly parliaments necessary. (2) The Toleration Act (1689) practically allowed all sects to worship freely except Catholics and Unitarians. The civil disabilities imposed for religious belief were not removed. The Test Act still remained in force. (3) A Triennal Act (1694) limited the duration of parliament to three years, preventing a repetition of the Cavalier Parliament which was kept in session so long that it entirely ceased to represent the nation. (4) The Treasons Act (1696) provided safeguards for the accused which made it impossible for the king to rid himself of mere political opponents by accusing them of treason. It required that the accused should see the indictment, be permitted to have counsel, and be faced with two witnesses of the overt act. The Act of Settlement (1701) was rendered necessary by the death of Anne's son, leaving her the only representative of her line. Since William and Mary had no children, the crown would revert to the line of James II on the death of Anne, unless other provision should be made. The act conferred the reversion of the crown on the Electress Sophia of Hanover and her heirs.[12] It was made the occasion to correct some of the minor defects and omissions of the revolutionary settlement. The most important was the provision that judges could be removed only on the address of both houses of parliament.

The revolutionary settlement in Scotland was more difficult to accomplish. When William became king of England, he did not thereby become king of Scotland. The Stuart line was Scottish and the Scots felt more personal loyalty to James II than the English. Yet a majority of the Scots cared more for a Protestant than for a Scottish ruler. Consequently a group of representative Scotsmen invited William to call a convention in Scotland similar to that held in England. The convention offered the crown to William and Mary. The minority still loyal to James was large, however, and the highlanders, among whom Stuart sentiment was strong, refused to acknowledge William. In 1689 they defeated a small army of William's in a minor engagement at Killiecrankie. The highlanders soon tired of the offensive. When William offered them favorable terms, clan after clan accepted. The Macdonalds of Glencoe failed to take the oath of allegiance before the date set by William, though they tried to take it a few days later. It was not the fault of the clan, but that was not known to William, who, in 1692, ordered the punishment of the clan, as he had previously announced that

Revolu-
tionary
settlement
in
Scotland

---

[12] See above, p. 406.

he would. The order was carried out more infamously and brutally than William intended. The soldiers sent to execute it were received as guests by the clansmen of Glencoe, who had no knowledge of the order. After the soldiers had been entertained for several days, they were ordered to kill their unsuspecting hosts, sparing neither women nor children. A large part of the clan was slain in cold blood.

The massacre of Glencoe ended the warfare in Scotland, but William subsequently experienced many difficulties in the government of the country. To gain the country he made large concessions. The established church, which had been made Episcopalian at the restoration, was restored to Presbyterianism, and parliament was made more independent of the king than it had been since the union of the two crowns under James I. The latter change forced William to ride two horses accustomed to pull in different directions. Great friction arose between England and Scotland over trade. When a rising commercial class in Scotland sought to expand foreign trade, the English parliament not only excluded the Scots from the English and colonial trade but it also tried to wreck the trading companies which the Scots formed to develop their own foreign commerce. A crisis came with the formation of the Darien Company under a charter from the Scottish parliament. It proposed to establish a colony on the isthmus of Darien to carry on an overland trade between the Atlantic and Pacific, with the ultimate object of gaining a share of the eastern trade. The colonists sent out in 1698 were attacked by the Spaniards and driven out. At this time, when some of his subjects were at war with Spain, William was attempting to negotiate a partition treaty[13] which was designed to keep England at peace with Spain in Europe. The Scots attributed the failure of the company to the jealous enmity of England. These complications determined William to bring about the union of England and Scotland. Before he had gone far with the project, he died (1702), and Anne came to the throne.

Friction with Scotland

Meanwhile friction between Scotland and England continued. In 1703 the Scottish parliament passed an act making the succession to the crown of Scotland different from that to the throne of England. The English parliament retaliated with new restrictions on trade. The war of retaliation between parliaments bade fair to end seriously, but wiser councils prevailed. A committee of both kingdoms was appointed to decide on the terms of a union. Its work was consummated by the Act of Union in 1707. Scotland received generous terms. Though it lost

Union

---

[13] See below, p. 473.

own parliament, it was given sixteen peers and forty-five members the house of commons in the British parliament. This was one-venth of the representation, but it assumed only one-fortieth of the financial obligation. It received complete free trade with England and was allowed to keep its local political, legal, and ecclesiastical institutions. The union was of great advantage to both countries. It relieved England from the imminent danger of a hostile country on her borders, and it gave Scotland a needed opportunity to secure foreign commerce. The union, however, was long unpopular, especially with Scotsmen. They were not generally reconciled to it until the middle of the eighteenth century, when the effects of the new prosperity became apparent.

War with Ireland

Ireland presented the most difficult problem William had to meet. Cromwell's settlement left approximately three-quarters of the land of Ireland in the hands of Protestants, though probably five-sixths of the population was Catholic. Charles II restored only a small portion of the confiscated lands, but he permitted the Catholics to enjoy practical toleration. This was so much better than the situation left by Cromwell, that Charles was generally popular in Ireland. James II maintained the same policy and was himself a Catholic. When he called on the Irish Catholics from his refuge in France for their support, they arose at once. James came to lead them in the spring of 1689, bringing with him French gold, ammunition, and troops. The Irish parliament proceeded to confiscate the lands of Protestants and to restore the Catholic church to an equality. William had to allow Ireland to become independent or fight. He came with troops in 1690, and won the important battle of the Boyne. James distinguished himself chiefly for the speed with which he left the battle-field and got back to France. Though their Stuart ruler failed them, the Irish Catholics were still sufficiently united in their opposition to Protestant rule to continue the war. They had little success. Place after place fell into the hands of the English, until Limerick, the only important center left to the Irish, capitulated in 1691. William, who was now engaged in a war with France, was anxious to transfer the troops engaged in Ireland to the French front. His general, who was in charge in Ireland, consequently gave lenient terms to secure the surrender of Limerick and end the war in Ireland. He allowed the Irish who wished to emigrate to France to join the French service, agreed that the Irish Catholics should exercise their religion as in the days of Charles II if the Irish parliament would ratify the arrangement, and promised to restore to the rebels the greater part of their estates as they had stood in the time of Charles II. William's power was thus established in Ireland in 1691.

After the rebellion Ireland settled down to a long period of peace which might have been a comparatively prosperous and happy period if England had kept the terms of the Treaty of Limerick. But the Protestants in Ireland protested, and the English parliament adopted their view. Soon after the capitulation of Limerick the English parliament enacted a law requiring the members of the Irish parliament to make a declaration against transubstantiation. It debarred Catholics from the Irish parliament for the first time. This was only the beginning. A long series of acts against the Irish Catholics followed during the reigns of William and Anne. Most of them were in direct violation of the Treaty of Limerick. Catholics were excluded from office. In order to split up Catholic estates it was enacted that the lands of a Catholic must be divided equally among his children. If one son became a Protestant, however, he received the whole estate, leaving his Catholic brothers landless. No Catholic teachers were allowed in schools or private homes, nor could Irish children be sent abroad to be educated. Heavy penalties were placed on the intermarriage of Protestants with Catholics. Catholic worship was not forbidden, but it was hedged about with intolerable restrictions. Burke's dictum with regard to these laws describes their character justly. He called them "a machine of wise and elaborate contrivance, and as well fitted for the oppression, impoverishment, and degradation of a people, and the debasement in them of human nature itself, as ever proceeded from the perverted ingenuity of man."[14]

Persecution of Catholics

But the penal laws did not end the ills of the downtrodden Irish. Instigated by English traders who feared the competition of the Irish, the English parliament enacted a series of laws which not only excluded the Irish from participation in English commerce, but also suppressed a large part of the trade and industry which Ireland already possessed. In the reign of Charles II the export of live stock to England was prohibited. This had been a staple trade, but the Irish avoided the worst effects by slaughtering their own animals and exporting the beef. They were developing a profitable trade with the colonies when another act forced the Irish to import staple colonial products by way of England. This so increased the price that the trade was no longer profitable. Meanwhile the Irish developed the manufacture of woolens into a staple industry. In 1699 the export of woolen goods to any coun-

Laws of trade

---

[14] Quoted by Lecky, *Leaders of Public Opinion in Ireland*, p. 123.

try except England was prohibited, and the English duties on imported woolens were so high as to be prohibitive. This deprived Ireland of her staple industry and left her only the trade in provisions. These had no market among the northern countries, which had the commodities that Ireland wanted to buy, and such trade as Ireland had left was with the nations of the south. "From hence," says Swift, "we get wines, brandy and fruit very cheap and in great perfection; so that though England has constrained us to be poor, they have given us leave to be merry."[15]

To Ireland the revolution of 1688 was a misfortune. While it brought to England political liberty and to Scotland prosperity, to Ireland it brought political and religious tyranny, moral degradation, and economic depression.

---

[15] *Prose Works*, ed. Scott, vii, 161, 162.

CHAPTER XXVI

THE LAST OF THE STUARTS

THE revolution not only changed the English constitution fundamentally, but it also involved England in a foreign war. William
sought control of England with the hope that he might secure its aid
in the war already begun against France. After Louis XIV attacked
the Netherlands in 1672, William became the leader of the European
opposition to France. When the Dutch war was ended in 1678, the
French king continued to add to his territories on the eastern frontier
of France by pretense of judicial decree backed by military force. In
this way the remainder of Alsace and most of the Saar basin were
secured. Strassburg and a part of Luxemburg were occupied without
a pretense of right other than force. These aggressions in time of peace
threatened the independence of all the neighbors of France, and they
robbed independent powers of portions of their territory. The lands
seized by the king of France had acknowledged the sovereignty of
various German princes, Sweden, and Spain. The powers affected
finally ceded the seized territories on condition that further aggression
cease, but Louis did not keep his agreement. In 1686 the powers determined to resist further attack by force. The emperor, the kings of
Spain and Sweden, the Netherlands, and several of the German princes
formed the League of Augsburg, which was subsequently joined by
Savoy and even by the pope. The political aggressions of the French
king had temporarily united Protestant and Catholic Europe against
the common enemy. The members of the league agreed to maintain
the boundaries as they then stood and to keep an army of 60,000 prepared to resist their violation. Two years later Louis precipitated war
by sending an army of invasion into the Palatinate. When William
sailed for England, the War of the League of Augsburg had already
begun.

Situation on the continent

William III, who was the heart and soul of European opposition to
France, sought to attach England to the league as soon as he was
established on the throne. To do this he had to convince parliament
of England's interest in the war. In some measure public opinion was
already favorably disposed. Throughout the reigns of Charles II and
James II the English people had evinced more or less antagonism toward the aggressive policy of Catholic France. On one occasion the

English religious feeling

feeling was so high that only the friendship of Charles II for his cousin Louis kept parliament from joining the Netherlands in a war against France.[1] In 1685 this latent hostility had been sharpened by the revocation of the Edict of Nantes. This ended toleration of the Protestants in France and caused many of them to seek refuge in Protestant countries. The tales of persecutions and sufferings brought by those who came to England were still fresh in 1688. Still, the War of the League of Augsburg was not primarily a religious war. On the continent Protestant and Catholic powers were united against Louis XIV by their common fear of political aggression, and in England the establishment of a Protestant dynasty removed the immediate dread of a Catholic despotism backed by the arms of France. English religious feeling was a strong incentive for war, but it alone might have been insufficient.

Imperial interests

Another cause of England's entrance was her interest in colonies, commerce, and sea power. During the second half of the seventeenth century these had become a primary interest with the commercial classes. In America twelve of the thirteen continental colonies had been founded, and they contained a thriving population of over 250,000. In the West Indies the British colonists numbered approximately 90,000. The trade of these colonies with the mother country grew steadily. By the time of the revolution of 1688 it represented more than twelve per cent of the total external trade of England.[2] In the east the East India Company was thoroughly established in its three chief centers of influence in India, and its trade was highly profitable. The growing significance of this commerce to England is amply attested by the amount of legislation enacted to regulate it after 1660 and by the creation of various boards and commissions to administer commercial and colonial affairs.[3] The tenets of the mercantile theory, moreover, were now the commonplaces of economic thought. As the theory had developed in the seventeenth century, it placed undue emphasis on England's external trade as the foundation of national economic prosperity, and regarded the empire as the basis of England's commercial prosperity. Naval power was necessary to protect commerce and to hold the empire. Hence the trinity of colonies, commerce and sea power influenced English thought and played their part in determining the English policy toward Louis XIV in 1689.

France had become England's most dangerous competitor for commerce and colonies. In the western world Spain still held the largest

[1] Above, p. 454.
[2] Beer, *Old Colonial System*, i, 14, 15, 39–44.
[3] See below, pp. 494–496.

and the richest empire, but Spain was a decadent power. In the east the
Dutch were still the chief competitors of England, but, while they
kept their monopoly of the trade of the Spice Islands, they were not
formidable competitors for the trade of the mainland. The Navigation
Acts, moreover, had largely excluded the Dutch from the British carrying trade and had made their rivalry in this field of less importance.
France, meanwhile, had been pursuing a vigorous policy of colonial
and commercial expansion. In America the French colonists numbered only 12,000 or so, but they held the valley of the St. Lawrence on
the north, they had established friendly relations with the Indians, and
they were constantly ranging the interior behind the Alleghenies on
trading and exploring expeditions. Their activities had already raised
the fear that the English colonists would be confined to the Atlantic
seaboard if the expansion of the French was not brought to a halt. In
1664 the French East India Company was formed. Within a few years
it had established trading posts to rival those of the English on the
eastern coast of India. In 1689 the French company was still weak, but
its policies were indicative of an aggressive attitude, which made it
the greatest potential danger to the commercial monopoly which the
English company sought to maintain. France, moreover, was increasing its navy with rapidity. To the English commercial classes France,
with its great resources, its apparently aggressive colonial and commercial policies, and its expansive naval program, seemed to be a far
greater menace to England's sea power, commerce, and colonies than
the Netherlands or Spain. The merchants were Whigs, and the revolution of 1688 brought the Whigs to power in parliament.

Rivalry
with
France

A third reason that induced parliament to declare war was the attitude of Louis XIV toward James II. He not only gave the fugitive king
a home, but he also continued to recognize him as king of England
after parliament had declared William III to be king. In the spring of
1689 Louis provided James with men and money for his Irish venture.
It was an act of open hostility which stirred anew the fears that Louis
would foist upon England a Catholic despotism.

Louis XIV
aids
James II

In May of 1689 parliament declared for war. William forthwith
united with the other hostile powers in an offensive and defensive
alliance against France. It was a momentous decision. It marked the
return of England to the European position she had held in the time of
Elizabeth as the head of the defense against the Catholic power which
threatened to destroy the balance of power and dominate Europe. Then
it had been Spain; now it was France. It also marked the beginning
of a long duel with France. For the next century and a quarter, when-

England's
entry

ever England went to war, France was on the other side, and during half of that period England was at war. In every war colonies, commerce, and sea power were involved, and they generally constituted the chief interest of England in the war. The aggrandizement of one power or another on the continent did not often contain a serious threat to England herself, nor could England hope to gain lands in Europe to her profit; but by fighting her principal colonial rival on the continent England strengthened her colonial empire, expanded her commerce, and maintained her supremacy on the sea. The entry of England into the war in 1689 begins the age in which the shopkeepers dictated the foreign policy of England.

Scope of the war

The War of the League of Augsburg, like the European conflicts that followed in the eighteenth century, was fought in many parts of the world. There was a naval war in the Narrow Seas, war by land in the Spanish Netherlands and on the Rhine, war by land and sea in southern Europe and the Mediterranean, war in the American colonies where it was called King William's War, and small engagements in India and Africa.

Narrow Seas

For the first two years after England joined the league, the principal scene of the war was in Ireland and on the English Channel. When Louis XIV was surrounded on all sides by the allies, he evacuated the Rhenish Palatinate after laying it waste, and stood on the defensive on his own frontiers, except for the invasion of Savoy. He saw that William was his chief enemy and that William's weakest spot was Ireland. So long as Ireland held out, William could not take an English army to the continent and leave England undefended against an enemy in the rear. Louis aided James, but he failed to coordinate the work of his fleet. If William could have been kept from Ireland until James had had time to organize the resistance, English troops might have been kept from participation in the continental war for a long time. In 1690 the French fleet defeated the English and Dutch near Beachy Head, but it was a victory of slight consequence because William was already in Ireland. Two years later the decision was reversed in the battle of La Hogue, which gave England command of the Channel for the remainder of the war.

Eastern front

In 1691 William was able to cross and take charge of the campaigns against Louis XIV in the Spanish Netherlands. Here the French had already won some successes. In 1692 they took the important town of Namur and defeated William in a pitched battle. Thereafter the war continued to go in favor of France, without decisive victories, until William won his first success against France by the recovery of Namur.

On the Rhine operations were unimportant, but a French army was held on the defensive and kept from participation in the main French offensive in the Spanish Netherlands.

Meanwhile Louis XIV began operations against Savoy and Spain. The French navy was drawn into the Mediterranean to support the army, and the French arms were making good progress, when they were checked by the English fleet. It blocked the French ships in the harbor of Toulon, deprived the invading armies of their support, and broke the force of their attack upon Spain. The campaigns in the south resulted in no decisive conflicts, but they held a French fleet and army useless while the forces of Louis XIV in the Spanish Netherlands received the first decisive check inflicted on a French army for many years.

The Mediterranean

By this time France was becoming exhausted financially. The loss of Namur was a blow to French renown which inclined Louis XIV to peace, while the defection of Savoy in 1696 and the consequent release of a French army for operations on the northeastern front cooled the ardor of the allies. The war was ended in 1697 by the peace of Ryswick. France restored all the territories acquired since 1678 except Strassburg, the Dutch were allowed to garrison some of the fortresses on the French frontier of the Spanish Netherlands, and Louis XIV acknowledged William III as king of England. The settlement was indecisive. The prestige of France as the greatest power in Europe was shaken, but it was not destroyed. Events were soon to demonstrate that France could recuperate.

Peace of Ryswick

After an interval of only four years a new war arose from the disputed succession to the Spanish throne. Charles II, the king of Spain, had stood on the verge of the grave for forty years. He was childless, and the question of the succession had long disturbed Europe. His aunts and his sisters had married into the houses of the Austrian Habsburgs and the French Bourbons. If either house should secure Spain and its possessions, the balance of Europe would be completely upset. William III was particularly concerned to prevent the union of France and Spain. After the peace of Ryswick he negotiated with Louis XIV a treaty providing that the Spanish possessions should be divided among the claimants. When the premature death of one of the candidates invalidated the treaty, another was arranged. It had no more effect than the first. The king of Spain did not agree to it, and, when he finally died in 1700, he left the throne of Spain and the Spanish dominions by will to Philip, a grandson of Louis XIV. The latter threw the partition treaty to the winds and accepted the terms of the bequest

Partition treaties

in behalf of his grandson. The emperor, who was the head of the Austrian branch of Habsburg, had never ratified the partition treaty because he claimed the whole Spanish inheritance for his son. He denied the validity of the will, and sent an army into Italy to take Milan, a Spanish possession. He then despatched an ambassador to William III to secure the support of England and the Netherlands against France. On the attitude of England depended the question whether the war should remain local in Italy or become another great European conflict.

English attitude

Of William's attitude there could be no doubt. He had been the chief opponent of Louis XIV for too long to let such an opportunity go by. But he could not lead England into the war without the consent of parliament, and the English nation was divided. The Tories, who represented the agricultural section, were only lukewarm in their support of imperial expansion. They were quite willing to let slip an opportunity to further England's imperial interests rather than to resort to war. To them the succession to the Spanish crown was merely a complication of European politics which had no direct bearing on English affairs. Philip was not the immediate heir to the French throne, and the imperial interests of England did not seem to them to be threatened. The Whigs needed no prodding from William to view the succession of Philip as fraught with menace to the British empire. They believed without question that Spanish colonial policy would be dictated by France, which was already England's chief colonial rival. If France controlled both her own and the Spanish colonies and could combine the French and the Spanish navies, England's maritime power, the basis of her national prosperity, would be placed in dire jeopardy. But the Tories had the majority in parliament, and William was in despair of obtaining parliamentary sanction of the war, when the acts of Louis XIV made it clear that the Whig view was correct and united the nation in the support of William and his policy of war.

Decision cast for war

Louis XIV publicly reserved the right of the new king of Spain to inherit the throne of France, if it should fall to him, depriving the Tories of their chief argument. He seized the barrier fortresses on the French frontier of the Spanish Netherlands. They had been defended by garrisons half Dutch and half Spanish, and their arbitrary seizure by the French was an act of open hostility. This was followed by the news that commercial companies were being formed in France to exploit the Spanish colonial possessions, which seemed to confirm the chief Whig contention. These events were a threat to England's imperial power. They caused popular opinion to veer so strongly that even a Tory parliament finally authorized the king to make an alliance against France. In 1701 he formed the Grand Alliance in which the principal parties were the emperor, the Netherlands and England. Meanwhile Louis XIV did the one thing necessary to unite English public sentiment in favor of the war. When James II died, he acknowledged his son as king of England. English anger knew no bounds. A new parliament elected in the autumn of 1701 supported the policy of war to the hilt, voting to maintain an army of 40,000 men.

At the beginning of the war the forces of the two combatants were not unequally matched. The allies had Prussia and many other German states added to their numbers, while France and Spain had Portugal, Savoy, and Bavaria for allies. England and her allies could eventually produce greater armies and their financial resources were greater. The French armies were the better trained, and at the beginning of the war they were larger. France had the central, compact position from which to operate, and she had unity of policy, the lack of which seriously hampered her opponents. On the other hand, the allies had the greatest general of the war in the duke of Marlborough, and the next best in Eugene of Savoy, who was a commander in the service of Austria. Early in 1702 William III died and the throne passed to Anne (1702-1714). She placed Marlborough at the head of the English army, giving him a free hand in dealing with the allies and in the conduct of the war. During the seventeenth century the French had produced the ablest military commanders, but during the War of the Spanish Succession they had none to compare with Marlborough and Eugene.

Resources

The campaigns of the war have to be followed in Italy, the Spanish Netherlands, Spain, the empire, and on the sea. When England entered, the Austrians, commanded by Eugene of Savoy, were already at war with France in northern Italy. Eugene was successful until 1703, when the French drove him out. A French and Bavarian army awaited him on the Austrian side of the mountains, and with a French army in his rear he appeared to have small chance of escape, when the desertion of the duchy of Savoy to the allies forced the French army in his rear to turn back to secure its own communications. The French and Bavarian army in Austria was met by Marlborough early in 1704. He had been leading the allied armies against the French in the Spanish Netherlands. When he saw that Austria could not withstand the French attack without help, he slipped away secretly to join Eugene and intercept the French before they could overrun Austria. He met

Italian, Austrian, and Flemish campaigns to 1706

them at Blenheim, where, in a battle which displayed his military genius to the full, he inflicted upon them an overwhelming defeat. It broke the French attack on Austria completely and lowered French military prestige. It was the first pitched battle lost by French troops for a long period, and it was the greatest English victory on land before Waterloo. For the remainder of the war Marlborough confined his campaigns to the Spanish Netherlands. In 1706 the victory of Ramillies drove back the French to the defense of their own borders. In the same year Eugene of Savoy defeated the French at Turin, occupied Milan, and forced the French to evacuate Italy.

Spanish campaigns

The only bright spot left to France in 1706 was the situation in Spain. The campaign in Spain had begun with naval operations which yielded England sufficient success to detach Portugal from her French alliance. In 1703 the English ambassador, named Methuen, negotiated two treaties which initiated a long friendship between Portugal and England. The first established an offensive and defensive alliance; the second arranged for the importation of Portuguese wines into England at a duty less than that imposed on French wines in return for the like favorable treatment of English woolens in Portuguese ports. In the next year the English took Gibraltar. The allies then attacked on both the east and the west, forcing their way to Madrid, where Archduke Charles, son of the emperor, was proclaimed king. The Spanish people, however, wanted Philip V as their ruler. They rose against the allies, making it impossible for them to hold the country. In 1707 the French completed their discomfiture by a defeat which rendered further progress in Spain impossible. The only subsequent success of the British in this region was the capture of the island of Minorca, which gave them a needed naval base in the Mediterranean.

Closing campaigns

Outside of Spain the war went steadily in favor of the allies. Though there were few important naval engagements, the English navy kept the French fleets where they were practically useless. In America the colonists finally conquered Acadia (1710). In the Spanish Netherlands Marlborough broke the French defense almost completely at Oudenarde in 1708. A year later at Malplaquet he defeated the French army which a last, despairing effort of Louis XIV had put in the field. The road to Paris lay open to Marlborough. He was prevented from traveling it by the advent of his political opponents to power at home. In 1711 they secured his dismissal and began negotiations which ended in the peace of Utrecht in 1713.

The treaties established at Utrecht settled the balance of power in

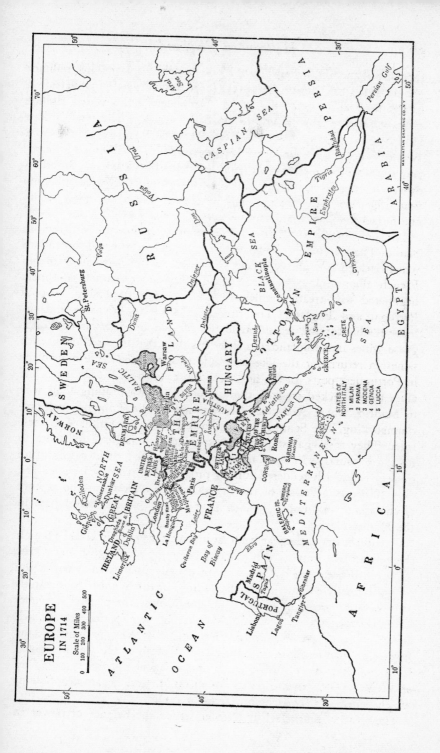

EUROPE
IN 1714

Scale of Miles
0 100 200 300 400 500

ATLANTIC

OCEAN

NORTH SEA

GREAT BRITAIN

IRELAND

Dublin
Limerick

Glencoe
Killiecrankie
Culloden
Dunbar

Drogheda
London

La Hougue

Quiberon Bay

Bay of Biscay

FRANCE

Paris
Loire

Madrid

SPAIN

PORTUGAL

Lisbon
Lagos

Tangier
Gibraltar

BALEARIC IS.
MINORCA
MAJORCA

MEDITERRANEAN

AFRICA

NORWAY

SWEDEN

BALTIC SEA

DENMARK

UNITED NETHER-LANDS

Hanover

Berlin

PRUSSIA

POLAND

Warsaw

SILESIA

THE EMPIRE

AUSTRIA

Vienna

HUNGARY

Danube

St. Petersburg

RUSSIA

Volga

Don

Dnieper

Dniester

BLACK SEA

Constantinople

OTTOMAN EMPIRE

GREECE

Aegean Sea

CRETE

CYPRUS

CASPIAN SEA

PERSIA

ARABIA

Tigris
Euphrates
Baghdad

Persian Gulf

EGYPT

Adriatic Sea

NAPLES

Rome

STATES OF THE CHURCH

CORSICA

SARDINIA

STATES OF NORTH ITALY
1 MILAN
2 PARMA
3 MODENA
4 GENOA
5 LUCCA

MANHATTAN DRAFTING CO. N.Y.

Europe for the next generation. Philip V was recognized as king of Spain and the Spanish colonies with the proviso that the crowns of Spain and France should never be united. Austria secured Milan, Naples, and the Spanish Netherlands. The Dutch were given control of the barrier fortresses. Savoy was given Sicily and assured of an independent position in northern Italy, free from French control. Great Britain secured Gibraltar, Minorca, the Hudson's Bay region, Nova Scotia and St. Kitts in the way of territory; the *asiento*, giving England a monopoly of the importation of slaves into the Spanish colonies for thirty years; an agreement allowing the British to send annually one ship of 620 tons burden to trade with the Spanish colonies; and the acknowledgment of the succession to the British crown as arranged by parliament. The principal advantage gained by Great Britain was the increase of her colonial empire and the strengthening of her naval and commercial power. The struggle had exhausted both her rivals, the Netherlands and France. The former was entering upon a permanent decline. The latter could recover some of the ground lost, but not all of it. For the time the British navy was supreme and the British merchant marine the foremost in the world. When trade revived immediately after the war, Great Britain secured many branches of it that had previously been in French or Dutch hands. Between 1710 and 1714 the tonnage of the ships which cleared from English ports doubled. The war stimulated British trade in all its branches and provided a basis for the maintenance of the commercial supremacy thus obtained.

Peace of Utrecht

The internal political development of England during the period of these wars centered in the strife of political parties. The revolution transferred the balance of power to parliament, and the parties strove for the control of the house of commons which would enable the party in possession of a majority to influence the policies of the government. To the voters the parties became the agencies by which they could secure the expression of their opinions, and they returned a majority of Whigs or Tories, as one party or the other appeared better to reflect the popular sentiment of the moment. With this political situation, the like of which had never existed before in any country of Europe, William III found it difficult to cope. Few of the Tories could support William whole-heartedly, and the more extreme were secretly Jacobites, who favored the return of James. His natural alliance seemed to be with the Whigs, whose party principles were exemplified by the revolution. The Whigs, however, wanted William to become a party leader, while he conceived his duty to be the

William III and the parties

leadership of the nation irrespective of the bickerings of parties. The Whigs, moreover, were committed to the principle of the limitation of the royal prerogative, which naturally did not appeal to William. The situation was summed up neatly in the reputed conversation of the king with his secretaries. " 'Every Whig,' said the Tory Secretary, 'is an enemy of your Majesty's prerogative.' 'Every Tory,' said the Whig Secretary, 'is an enemy of your Majesty's title.' "[4] His difficulties were accentuated by his personal unpopularity. He was naturally taciturn, his ill health prevented the maintenance of a popular court like that of Charles II, and he was a foreigner. Few Englishmen ever knew him intimately. To the rank and file he made no personal appeal as a ruler; he was merely the abstract personification of the principles of Protestantism and political liberty.

King and parliament
The result was the development of so much friction between king and parliament that it made the operation of the government difficult. The Whigs, who had the majority in his first parliament, determined to take revenge on the Tories for the persecutions the Whigs had undergone in the days of Charles II. William, who desired the support of the whole nation for the war, felt that it was a mistake to keep many of the leaders of the Tories in constant fear of punishment for acts committed in previous reigns. He sought from parliament an act of indemnity that would relieve the Tories of responsibility for past political misdeeds. The house of commons debated it for two sessions, but the Whigs made so many exceptions that it was becoming a bill of pains and penalties, when William dissolved parliament in 1690. The violent partisanship of the Whigs had so alienated the people that the election resulted in the return of a majority of moderate Tories. For a time the relations between parliament and the king were harmonious; but after a few years the commons began to grumble about the grant of further supplies for the war and endeavored in various ways to obstruct the administration. Finally the Tories opposed the continuance of the war so strongly that popular sentiment swung back to the Whigs, who obtained a majority in the third parliament. Though this party favored the war, it criticized and obstructed the royal policies hardly less than the Tories. When the war was ended, the Tories again came to power. They reduced the army to 7,000, when William requested 30,000, and revoked grants of land which he had conferred upon some of his Dutch favorites. To William it appeared to be rank ingratitude from a na-

---

[4] Macaulay, *History* (Boston, 1859), iii, 51.

tion which he had rescued from the arbitrary rule of James II and had led successfully in a European war. It was this parliament which also opposed the entry of England into the War of the Spanish Succession. The change of popular opinion forced the Tory parliament to enter the war, and the new parliament, which was Whig, was supporting the king loyally when he died. But on the whole William fared badly with his parliaments.

Queen Anne, who came to the throne in 1702, was deeply and sincerely pious and she enjoyed a quiet family life. These homely virtues endeared her to her people. She had the great advantage of being English. Her strong feeling for the church made her more acceptable to the Tories than her predecessor had been. Anne, however, had had so little experience with affairs of state that she necessarily allowed many of her policies to be framed for her by others. She had some strong prejudices to which she clung with a true Stuart obstinacy; otherwise her opinions were formed largely by the friends who had her ear at the moment. Since her friendships were personal, her political judgments were formed largely on the basis of her personal likes and dislikes of those with whom she came into contact. Throughout her reign the political situation was profoundly influenced by a set of intrigues which centered about the control of the queen's political acts through her intimate friends.

Anne, like William, professed herself to be independent of parties, but her strong feeling for the Anglican church caused her to have the more personal friends among the Tories. She soon dismissed most of the Whig ministers who held over from the preceding reign, putting Tories in their places. The two leaders were Marlborough and Godolphin. The former inclined toward the Tories, though he felt no strong partisanship. He had great political skill, and, what was more important, the duchess of Marlborough, who was a lady of opinions, was lady of the queen's bedchamber and had a monopoly of Anne's ear. Godolphin was a moderate Tory who accepted the revolution loyally and was not averse to toleration for Dissenters. The policy of the two was to concentrate the national attention on the war and keep peace in party politics. It was easier said than done. The new parliament elected in Anne's reign had a large majority of Tories, who, though content to carry on the war, were bent on giving expression to the partisan spirit of the day and wreaking vengeance on the Whigs who had held office before them. In one way or another Godolphin and Marlborough defeated several such attempts, but they finally decided it would be necessary to throw over the extreme Tories

Queen Anne

Marlborough and Godolphin

and rely on the support of the moderate Tories. This was done in 1704 and 1705, but it was done too late. The violence of the Tories had rendered them unpopular. In the election of 1705 the Whigs secured a majority. In order to keep the support of parliament for the war, Marlborough and Godolphin then allied with the Whigs. They found it difficult to persuade the queen to supplant Tories with Whigs. On one occasion they threatened to resign unless she would dismiss from the cabinet a Tory who was her friend. Placed on the horns of this dilemma, Anne wept, but refused to give way. Eventually the resignation of the minister settled this particular difficulty, but it was only after the strong objections of the queen to one Whig after another had been overcome, that the cabinet became entirely Whig in 1708.

Downfall of the Whigs

The combination with the Whigs did not work well. In return for their majority in the house they demanded more offices than Marlborough and Godolphin were disposed to award them. More disastrous still was the loss by Marlborough's wife of her influence over the queen. The duchess was superseded in the queen's affections by a lady who served the Tory cause and whispered in the queen's ear the advice dictated by a leader of the Tory opposition. Worst of all, the Whig policy of war was becoming unpopular. The voters were beginning to count the cost and not the victories. It needed little to turn the tide of popular sentiment decisively, and that was supplied by the trial of Sacheverell in 1710. The gentleman, even among high churchmen, was an extremist, who delighted to preach bitterly polemical sermons in condemnation of the principles of the revolution of 1688. The commons consequently impeached him. The Tories promptly proclaimed him as a martyr, a hero, and the champion of the church. The trial created a popular furor all over the country. The Whigs dared not give him a heavy sentence in the state of public opinion. When they gave him a light one, the Tories hailed it as a victory. Anne interpreted it the same way. She dismissed Godolphin and the Whigs from the cabinet and gave their places to Tories. An election held forthwith justified her action and gave the Tory cabinet a Tory majority in the house.

The Tories, 1710–1714

The purpose for which the Tories were elected was to make peace. This they accomplished with reasonably satisfactory results, though it was done with a perfidy to England's allies that was a national discredit. But the Tories sought election in order to bring woe to the conquered Whigs. This they did admirably by three legislative enactments. The Property Qualification Act required a member of the house of commons to have a landed estate of £600 annual value if he represented a rural constituency, and of £300 if he represented a borough. Since the Whigs were townsmen, whose wealth was generally invested in business, while the Tories were landed proprietors, the purpose of the act is obvious. The Occasional Conformity Act required holders of office to take communion with the church of England regularly, putting an end to the practice by which Dissenters had complied with the Test Act by taking the Anglican communion once a year. The Dissenters, needless to say, were Whigs. The Schism Act required all teachers to be licensed by a bishop, to attend only the Anglican church, and to teach only the Anglican catechism. It was nicely designed to compel the children of Whigs to grow up in ignorance or in the Anglican faith. Such were the tender mercies dictated by the contentions which governed party strife in the good old days. But all their machinations availed the Tories nothing. When Anne died in 1714, she was succeeded, in accordance with the Act of Settlement, by George I of Hanover, whose sympathies were with the Whigs.

The bitterness of the party strife in these two reigns and the difficulties experienced by William III and Anne with parliaments, which preferred to indulge in factious quarrels rather than to cooperate with the ruler in the conduct of the national business, were due in large part to a defect in the constitution left by the revolutionary settlement. The revolution established the superiority of parliament to the king, but it provided no constitutional machinery by which that superiority could be maintained adequately in detail. Parliament could now prevent flagrant breaches of the constitution by the king, but the king was still the chief executive with wide discretionary power. In the daily work of government the king was still largely independent of parliamentary control. He might fail to carry out the wishes of the majority in the house of commons or even thwart the will of the house of commons, without leaving any opening by which the commons could secure redress. The ruler was personally irresponsible to parliament, his ministers could be successfully impeached only for flagrant breaches of trust, and the wheels of government could not be tied up by withholding supplies every time the commons desired to secure the dismissal of an efficient Dutch captain whom they disliked merely because he was Dutch, or to obtain the king's consent to a bill of comparatively small importance. The majority in the house of commons was constantly fretted because it could not direct the policies of the government in detail; the king was continually handicapped in the conduct

Defect of the revolutionary constitution

of the war and in the execution of other policies which he regarded as of primary importance for the welfare of the nation, because he could not secure the necessary legislation from the majority in the house of commons.

The remedy

In the course of the eighteenth century this difficulty was obviated gradually and almost unconsciously by the introduction of new methods of working the machinery of government. The structure of the government was not changed, but old parts came to perform new functions, and the relations of the different parts to one another were altered completely. This transformation was brought about as the result of practice and custom and not as the result of any definite plan embodied in legislation. It was largely the result of the new significance of parties. The whole change centers in the development of the cabinet.

Cabinet government today

Before the steps in this development can be traced intelligibly it is necessary to have an understanding of the salient characteristics of cabinet government as it now exists. Contemporaries generally failed to grasp the constitutional significance of the early steps, and only in the light of later events does it become clear. The cabinet of the present is practically a committee composed of the leaders of that party which has a majority in the house of commons. The head of the cabinet is the prime minister. He is nominally chosen by the king, but in practice the king must select the acknowledged leader of the party. The prime minister chooses his colleagues, but the freedom of his choice is restricted by the practical necessity of awarding places to the other leaders whom his party follows. The members of the cabinet are the heads of the most important administrative departments and control the administration. They also control and direct the legislative work of parliament. In both capacities they are responsible for all their acts to the house of commons. If they fail to introduce important legislation desired by a majority of the house, if they introduce legislation that the majority does not favor, if they follow a foreign policy displeasing to the nation, or if they permit the public vaccinator in Bermondsey to charge too high fees for vaccinations, the house of commons can bring them to account. The machinery by which the house enforces this responsibility is nicely adjusted to secure the remedy of small grievances without the upheaval attendant upon the resignation of the cabinet, and to cause the resignation of the cabinet when it has failed to interpret popular opinion on a major issue. If the latter alternative is adopted, a cabinet which represents the victorious majority is then formed. In this arrangement the king is little more than a figurehead. Though nominally the executive power is still his, he can perform no executive act except through one of his ministers. Since the minister must take the responsibility for the act, he will not perform it unless he thinks it will meet the approval of the majority in the house of commons. If the king should insist, the cabinet would resign. The king could obtain no other cabinet to run the government, since the majority in the house of commons would support only its own leaders, and no other cabinet could obtain the legislation and the appropriations necessary to transact the governmental business. The king would be forced to yield to the wishes of the cabinet, since it would return to power and start the motionless wheels of government on no other terms. The outward form of the government today is the same as it was in 1689; actually the powers wielded by the king in 1689 are now in the hands of the cabinet, which is responsible to the house of commons, which in turn is responsible to the electors.

The cabinet in 1689 was a fairly definite institution. During the reign of Charles II, it had become an established practice for the king to have an inner group within the privy council which he consulted on important affairs. After a subject had been discussed by the small group it might be placed before the larger group of the privy council, or it might not. The king might still consult the privy council formally in the first place, but after 1689 in practice the king generally took his advice from the cabinet. In all other respects the cabinet of the seventeenth century differed from the cabinet of the twentieth. (1) The members were not necessarily leaders of the majority in the house of commons. Indeed, they were not necessarily members of parliament, though in practice they usually were. They were regarded merely as the personal servants of the king without any constitutional relation to parliament. (2) The cabinet felt no need of acting as a unit, as it does today, on all important business. The opinions expressed to the king were merely those of individual members. (3) The king was under no compulsion to accept the advice of the cabinet, or even to seek it. (4) The cabinet was not responsible to parliament individually or collectively, unless one of their number committed a crime or a misdemeanor that made him liable to impeachment. *The early cabinet*

During the reigns of William and Anne the cabinet became in some slight degree dependent upon the house of commons. In the reign of the former a tentative step was taken in that direction unconsciously. William's first cabinet was chosen from both parties in order to secure the support of the whole nation; it worked quite in the contrary fashion. His ministers quarreled among themselves and failed to obtain from parliament the legislation the king needed to carry out his *Relations of the cabinet to parliament under William III* policies. Eventually one of his advisers suggested that smoother relations with parliament might be obtained by the selection of his cabinet from the party which had a majority in the house of commons. Acting on the suggestion, between 1693 and 1696 he gradually supplanted the Tories with Whigs to make the party complexion of the cabinet correspond with that of the house of commons. Thus William discovered almost by accident that king and parliament would work more harmoniously if the advisers of the king were the influential members of the majority in the house of commons.

Neither the king nor the house of commons recognized, however, that the experiment exemplified an important constitutional principle. William had no notion that it was necessary or even expedient to change his cabinet whenever the majority shifted from one party to the other in the house of commons. He did not see clearly that a cabinet of the party in the minority could not influence the majority as well as a cabinet of the party in the majority. He still regarded his advisers primarily as his personal servants. Consequently he looked upon the opposition of the house of commons as directed against himself, when in reality it was often directed against his ministers. The balance of parties in the house of commons changed twice after 1696, but William altered the composition of his cabinet to match only once. He never fully understood that much of his friction with parliament was due to the lack of harmonious relations between his cabinet and the majority in the house of commons.

But if William failed to see clearly the opportunity to influence the house of commons through the cabinet, the house of commons was still more blind to the possibilities of influencing the policy of the king through the cabinet. A cabinet composed of the influential members of the party in control of the house of commons could hardly fail to influence the king in accordance with the wishes of that party, but the house still looked upon the cabinet as a group of secret advisers over which it lacked control other than that given by impeachment. This distrust of the cabinet went so far that the house gave expression to it in the Act of Settlement (1701). One clause provided that after the accession of the house of Hanover "all matters and things relating to the well governing of this kingdom, which are properly cognizable in the privy council by the laws and customs of this realm, shall be transacted there; and all resolutions taken thereupon shall be signed by such of the privy council as shall advise and consent to the same." This would have killed the cabinet and made the privy council the only legal advisory body of the king. Another clause, which forbade holders of office under the crown to occupy a seat in the house of commons, was aimed at the use of offices to bribe members; but it would have prevented the cabinet from becoming responsible to the house of commons, since the members of the cabinet were the heads of the important administrative departments. Both provisions demonstrate that the commons saw none of the possibilities of cabinet government in 1701.

In the reign of Anne some of the possibilities of the cabinet as a link between the queen and the house of commons began to be recognized by both parties. The house repealed the first clause of the Act of Settlement directed against the cabinet and altered the second in such a way as to permit the principal officers of state, who were likely to be in the cabinet, to sit in the house of commons, provided the members so appointed should stand for reelection. Anne was persuaded by Marlborough and Godolphin to change the personnel of her cabinets to keep them in consonance with the party situation in the house; the change to the Whigs made between 1705 and 1708 was practically forced upon her against her wish. She dismissed the Whigs at the first opportunity, but she waited until the Sacheverell trial gave the opportunity. Moreover, she immediately dissolved parliament and held a new election, which returned a Tory majority to support her Tory cabinet. Anne recognized that it was no longer possible for a Tory cabinet to obtain from a Whig parliament the legislation necessary to run the government. Thus in Anne's reign it became clear that the cabinet must be of the same party as the majority in the house of commons. The ruler could no longer choose his advisers solely to suit his personal fancies; he was limited with regard to party. The cabinet was not yet responsible to the house of commons, but in a measure, as yet ill defined, it was dependent upon the house, and the sovereign was in some measure dependent upon the cabinet.

The reign of Anne also saw the first tentative, unconscious step toward the unanimity of the cabinet. William throughout his reign felt free to consult any members of his cabinet without consulting the whole group. He acted as his own minister of foreign affairs, often initiating important policies without consultation with his cabinet. Under such conditions there was little opportunity for the cabinet to act as a unit. The cabinet could not well develop a collective responsibility for acts about which it was not consulted. Anne with her slight knowledge of affairs was more dependent on advice than William had been. She took advice freely from her friends, whether they were in the cabinet or out of it, but her incompetence forced her to rely on

Anne limited in choice of cabinet

Unanimity of the cabinet

her ministers far more than William had done. Anne's tendency to be governed by impulse rather than by reason made it so difficult for them to deal with her that they dropped into the occasional practice of debating questions informally among themselves before they discussed them with her. When they presented to her a united front on an important matter, she rarely dared to reject their advice. The practice appears to have been dictated by no other purpose than convenience, but it was destined to have an important future development. When later it hardened into a custom, the king no longer had full knowledge of the differences of opinion among his advisers, and his opportunities to influence the decisions of the cabinet were greatly limited thereby. Later, too, the unanimity of the cabinet would aid the development of its responsibility to the house of commons. But the uncertain, tentative steps taken toward unanimity in the reign of Anne affected mainly the relations between the cabinet and the queen, tending to make the cabinet more independent.

Last use of the royal veto

The development of cabinet government was further promoted in Anne's reign by two events which seemed to have little direct connection therewith. In 1708 Anne used the royal veto for the last time. As contemporaries could not foresee that it would be the last time, the event had no significance for them; but we, who look back, see in it one of the indications that the cabinet was becoming more responsible for the legislative program of parliament. If the cabinet guided that successfully, the royal veto was not needed; if it failed, the remedy was not a veto but a new cabinet, because the passage of a bill unsatisfactory to the cabinet would mean that the existing cabinet no longer controlled the majority in the house of commons. It was long after Anne's time before this principle was established, but the disuse of the veto indicates the strength of the drift toward the irresponsibility of the queen and the fuller responsibility of the cabinet.

Creation of peers in 1711

The second event was the creation in 1711 of eleven Tory peers in order to make the majority of the house of lords of the same party as the majority in the house of commons. When the election of 1710 provided the new Tory cabinet with a majority in the house of commons, the house of lords still remained Whig. The Tory cabinet soon discovered that the legislation which it secured from the house of commons could not be passed through the house of lords. The creation of peers to prevent a deadlock between the two houses settled the principles that the representative house of commons was more important than the hereditary house of lords, and that the cabinet was to be responsible to the more popular chamber.

CHAPTER XXVII

ECONOMIC, SOCIAL, AND INTELLECTUAL ASPECTS OF STUART ENGLAND

THE economic conditions of life during the seventeenth century remained substantially the same in their broad aspects as they had been in the closing years of the sixteenth. Agriculture was still England's mainstay. In 1696, when the total population was approximately five and one-half millions, about four millions lived in the country, and the greater part of these were dependent primarily upon rural pursuits.[1] In the technique of agriculture the seventeenth century witnessed a certain amount of progress. Successful experiments were made here and there with fertilizers which increased the productivity of the soil, and with improved rotations of crops which made it possible to cultivate the land every year and to eliminate the waste of allowing it to lie fallow periodically. This development became more marked after the restoration. The civil war with its devastation and heavy taxes imposed great burdens upon landholders. Some of them were forced to sell their lands, and the confiscation of the estates of the royalists by the government threw still more land upon the market. The purchasers often sought to make as much profit from the land as possible, and apparently this helped to accelerate the trend toward improved methods of agriculture, though the new landlords were not the only ones who tried experiments. The improvements, however, remained scattered in different sections of the country and won no widespread adoption. Despite much writing on agriculture, exact knowledge of the capabilities of different kinds of soil and of the properties of different kinds of fertilizers was still lacking. A new method which worked well in one type of soil might fail entirely in another. As long as advance depended so largely upon the method of trial and error, it was naturally slow. Before the experimentation could have any universal effect, moreover, it was essential for the scattered strips of the old open-field system to be converted into single compact holdings

Agriculture

[1] More exact figures for the county of Gloucester indicate that the proportion of the population in that county primarily dependent upon agriculture was not much over fifty per cent: A. J. and R. H. Tawney, "An Occupational Census of the Seventeenth Century," *Economic History Review*, v, 36, 39. But many whose principal work was industrial still lived in the country and were not wholly detached from the land.

by the process of enclosure. Where they survived, they necessitated the retention of the wasteful and extravagant methods of cultivation inherited from the Middle Ages. In some measure this change was being wrought during the seventeenth century. In the first half of the period enclosures still caused complaint and opposition, though the situation was not as acute as it had been in the middle years of the preceding century. In the second half of the seventeenth century public opinion began to be more favorable to enclosures. Attention became centered less upon the sufferings of the peasants and more upon the increased income which resulted from the technical improvements in cultivation made possible by enclosures. The government, had it been disposed to hinder the process, no longer had at its disposal the special courts by which the Tudors and the early Stuarts had sometimes placed obstacles in the way of particular enclosures. The enclosures caused less disturbance of the population than in the sixteenth century because they were used more for tillage and less for pasture; and it seems probable, moreover, that the growth of industry enabled peasants who were cast adrift by the enclosures to find other employment more easily than had been possible in the early days of the movement. It is difficult to estimate the extent of the enclosure which took place during the period of the Stuarts, because it was accomplished mainly by private agreements which left little trace in written records. Probably more land was enclosed in the seventeenth century than in the sixteenth, but in 1714 more than half of the arable land was still unenclosed. By that time, however, the views of progressive farmers and writers on agricultural problems were making an impression, and the opinion was spreading that enclosure was a desirable innovation. The amount of land under cultivation was being extended by the reclamation of the fens and other waste lands. Agriculture was stimulated by the action of parliament, which, in 1689, passed a corn law giving a bounty on grain exported when the price was less than six shillings a bushel in the English market. In the early years of the eighteenth century landlords were finding it possible to raise their rents, and agriculture seems to have been in a generally prosperous condition.

Those who derived their living from the land were divided into several social classes. Most influential was the class of gentlemen, often designated as the gentry or as country squires. They owned large estates producing annual incomes of hundreds or thousands of pounds. In the first half of the century they lived on their estates, finding pleasure in the improvement of the beautiful and comfortable manor houses which were their homes, in the management of their lands, in the

Country squires

patriarchal oversight of their tenants, in the hospitable entertainment of their friends and neighbors, and in the pursuit of such diversions as hunting, hawking, and horse-racing. During the reign of Charles I a large number of country gentlemen who were courtiers lived in London during much of the year, and after the restoration it became fashionable even for those who had no place at the royal court to come to London to enjoy the social pleasures of the winter season. Though country squires were sometimes boors, many of them were men of culture who possessed good libraries which they used with enjoyment and appreciation. After the restoration gentlemen seem to have been less given as a class to making companions of books; certainly they were no longer interested in the same books, for the tremendous emphasis placed upon religious thought by the country squires of the earlier period gives place to rationalism and materialism among their descendants. Politically the squires were the most influential class in the nation during the seventeenth century. Under the Tudors they were already supplying the justices of the peace who were the local rulers of the shires. During the reign of James I they acquired control of the house of commons; in the civil struggle they produced the leaders; after the restoration they furnished the bulk of the members of parliament and of the officials and advisers of the king; and after the revolution of 1688 they became the governing class.

In rural society of the seventeenth century the yeomen were of fundamental importance. They were the owners of smaller estates, though the wealthiest of them possessed incomes equal to those of the poorer country gentlemen. They formed a prosperous, industrious, sturdy, independent element in the population. They exercised their right to vote with pride and took an intelligent part in national affairs. The yeomen, for example, formed a large part of Cromwell's Ironsides. They seem to have been diminishing in number, but at the close of the century they were estimated at 160,000. Tenant farmers who held their lands by lease or other tenures were increasing in number, though they were probably not yet quite as numerous as the yeomen. They were generally somewhat less wealthy and less influential than the yeomen. The rural wage earners constituted a large class. Their wages were usually low, though the majority of them did not live in dire poverty. The married laborer usually had a cottage and a few acres of land which he occupied as tenant, and the unmarried laborers were often boarded by the farmers who hired them. The standard of comfort among them was low compared with that of the present, but their living conditions relative to those of other classes of society were per-

Other rural classes

haps less hard than they are now. They probably had greater economic independence and led a more enjoyable outdoor life than the average laborer does today.

Industry continued until 1642 to develop along the lines which had been laid down during the second half of the sixteenth century. The spread of the new technological processes, and particularly the substitution of coal for charcoal in several industries, caused the growth of further factories and large-scale enterprises. During the civil war business suffered a severe depression, from which it did not recover during the interregnum. After the restoration, the general trend of industry appears to have been toward an increase of output, though some brief depressions intervened, and some industries did not share in the general prosperity. The Yorkshire woolen trade remained stagnant until near the close of the seventeenth century because it had to compete in foreign markets with newly developed foreign manufactures of cheap woolens; and the iron industry declined because the supply of charcoal necessary for smelting the ore was giving out. New inventions and improvements of technical processes continued to be made in this period. Just before the close of the century Thomas Savery invented an atmospheric or fire engine which could pump water out of mines, and a few years later Thomas Newcomen produced a much more efficient model. It made possible the rapid development of the coal industry and facilitated the mining of ores. The decline of the iron industry caused attempts to smelt iron ore with coal. In 1621 Dud Dudley secured a patent for the production of iron with coal, and he claimed to have been successful. His product probably was not of merchantable quality, and his experiments certainly had no general effect upon the iron industry. Nearly a century later, shortly before the close of Anne's reign, Abraham Darby, in his celebrated iron works at Coalbrookdale, succeeded in smelting iron ore into pigs of cast iron by using coke derived from coal. The smelted iron was so much more liquid when it came from the furnace that he was able also to run it into small molds and produce directly small cast iron wares such as previously had been cast from the pigs by a second smelting. His cast iron produced with coke, however, could not be converted into a good quality of the tougher malleable iron which was essential for the manufacture of many kinds of wares, and his process did not come to be employed generally in the iron trade for several decades. In addition to these major inventions, many of a minor character were perfected. Thus the process of technological development and the concentration of capital in industry continued after 1660, but it seems probable that people were drawn into large-scale industry at a less rapid rate than they had been during the century preceding 1640, and it is certain that the large majority of workers still performed their labors under the domestic system.

In the governmental regulation of industry a change of principle occurred during the period of the Stuarts. The centralized, paternal control of industry established in the time of Elizabeth was maintained by her two immediate successors, but under the strain of the civil war it collapsed. After the close of the war, the governments of the inter-regnum attempted to revive some parts of the traditional system, and others were allowed to lapse. Nearly all of the existing industrial monopolies were canceled, and thereafter new ones were granted only for limited periods in behalf of those who made new inventions. An effort was made to regulate wages according to the terms of the Statute of Apprentices, and it was sustained in some counties until the early years of the eighteenth century. After 1660 parliament expressed itself on several occasions in favor of the law of apprenticeship, and new regulations concerning the quality of industrial products, such as woolens, were enacted, but all of this legislation was enforced laxly. The older laws for the regulation of industry and the newer laws of the same type tended to fall into disuse for two reasons. The privy council, which had supervised the regulation of industry under the Tudors and the early Stuarts, ceased to exercise control after the restoration, and the justices of the peace, left to their own devices, enforced these laws spasmodically or not at all. Public opinion began to favor the freedom of industry from governmental restrictions, and after the revolution parliament was largely influenced by capitalists who naturally favored the new point of view.

While the old type of industrial regulation, which was based upon the theory of promoting the interests of the several classes in the community, was declining, a new type, which had for its purpose to promote a maximum production, to assure the stability and prosperity of staple industries, and to provide them with markets and raw materials, was growing up. The laws of the new type put more emphasis upon commodities and less upon persons. To enumerate these legislative enactments would be dreary and profitless, but the types may be illustrated. (1) Some laws sought to provide an adequate supply of cheap raw materials for the use of manufactures. The prohibition on the exportation of wool was maintained, and some raw materials which were not produced in England were admitted free of duty. (2) The importation of finished manufactured wares was discouraged

Regulation of industry

by high customs duties, which extended in some instances to prohibition. In 1701, for example, the East India Company was forbidden to sell in England the silks, muslins, and calicoes which it imported in large quantities from the east. (3) The home consumption of internal manufactures was encouraged by sumptuary laws such as that which ordered that buttons and buttonholes should be worked with woolen thread instead of silk. (4) The exportation of manufactured wares was promoted by the grant of bounties on exports, and by other means. (5) The immigration of foreign artisans was encouraged because they introduced new industries, helped to increase the industrial output, and thus swelled the economic wealth of the country. In 1709 the law of naturalization was modified to make the process much easier of accomplishment.

The
artisans

For the artisans the seventeenth century was, on the whole, a period of material betterment. Prices of commodities continued to rise until the middle of the century, when they reached the peak. Thereafter they tended to fall off a little. Evidence with regard to wages is inconclusive, but they appear to have risen slowly throughout most of the century. It was a period when the standard of comfort of the working classes was probably improving. How far the laborers had become solely dependent upon their wages seems impossible to determine. The growth of capitalism in the domestic system was probably forcing more of the workers in the cottages to sell their labor rather than the product of their labor, but most of them probably maintained subsistence farming and thus escaped complete dependence upon wages. Yet the rise in the early years of the eighteenth century of combinations of employees to secure better wages from their employers testifies to the existence of a class which had become primarily dependent upon wages.

Trading
companies

In the field of foreign commerce a strong tendency developed to abandon the organization under the control of monopolistic trading companies in favor of individual enterprise. English merchants not included in the companies objected ever more strenuously to these monopolies, and the invasion of the monopolized fields by interlopers, who had no membership in the companies, became more frequent. In the later years of the seventeenth century the tide of popular opinion began to run against the companies. Laws were passed to break down the monopolies of some companies and to limit or undermine those of others. An attack on the East India Company demonstrated to the satisfaction of the prevailing public opinion of the time that a monopoly was still necessary to promote English trade in the far east to the best advantage; the Hudson's Bay Company fell in the same category; otherwise the trading companies were doomed by the early years of the eighteenth century. Though they lingered throughout the eighteenth century, they had outlived their usefulness as the pioneers in the development of new fields of trade. During the century the foreign trade became steadily more freely open to individual initiative.

The encouragement of external commerce was the ultimate object of the greater part of the economic legislation enacted under the influence of the mercantile system. The development of a favorable balance of trade stood so far in the forefront of mercantilist thought that even the regulation of industry was undertaken with a view to the effects on commerce. After the restoration the attempt to encourage external trade became much more pronounced. Charles II, despite his general attitude of carelessness with regard to affairs of state, gave more attention than his predecessors to the encouragement of commerce. After the transfer of the balance of power to parliament in 1689, the Whigs were keen to advance the commercial interests of the kingdom. Charles appointed a committee of trade composed of administrators and merchants to investigate the conditions of trade and to make reports and recommendations to the privy council, and subsequently committees or boards of the sort were much in evidence as the promoters of regulative legislation. Charles also negotiated several favorable commercial treaties, and the series was continued by such treaties as the Methuen and the *asiento*.

Encouragement of commerce

The legislation enacted after 1660 to encourage external commerce, like that concerned with industry, needs to be passed in review only so far as regards types. (1) A series of acts regulated various industries in ways designed to decrease imports and to increase the supply of articles for export. (2) Duties on imports and, to a less extent, bounties on exports were established to accomplish the same ends. (3) Laws intended to promote the prosperity and the efficiency of the mercantile marine were enacted. (4) More attention was given to the development and maintenance of the navy which was necessary to protect merchant shipping and to hold the empire together.

Regulative legislation

The practical application of the mercantile theory in detail may best be illustrated by the regulation of imperial trade. In the development of the colonies the first half of the seventeenth century was a period of beginnings when comparatively little attention was given to colonial trade.[2] By that time the trade was coming to be of some significance,

Imperial commercial policy

---

[2] See above, p. 438.

and the growth of the colonies in the second half of the century rendered their trade continually of more importance. With the restoration began a prolonged series of legislative enactments designed to control the trade of the colonies in ever greater detail. When the mercantile theory was applied to the colonies the ideal of English statesmen was a self-sufficing empire. They had in mind an empire which should produce within its borders all the raw products and manufactured articles consumed by its inhabitants, carry its own trade in its own ships, and be independent economically of all other empires and countries. The ideal did not always prevail with the legislators, who sometimes saw the interests of England large and those of the colonies small; but much of the legislation was intended to promote the interests of the empire as a whole, and some of it actually gave the colonies an advantage at the expense of England.

The three main objects which the acts of trade sought to promote were to strengthen the navy and the merchant marine, to make the colonies a source of the supply of raw materials and of products not produced in England, and to make the colonies a market for the manufactured products of the home country. The main methods of application were five. (1) Goods could be carried to and from the colonies only in English or colonial ships. (2) The export trade of the colonies was to a large extent confined to the English market. (3) Goods produced in England received a partial or total monopoly in the colonial market. (4) Colonial goods received preferential treatment in the English market. (5) Some colonial manufactured wares which would compete with those of England were not allowed to be exported from the colonies of their origin.

Acts of trade

The acts of trade which applied these principles to the commerce of the colonies began with the Act of Navigation of 1660. This repeated with some alteration of details the earlier act of 1651. In the early days of its application this act caused some hardship by raising the cost of freight, but it fell on Englishmen and colonists alike. In New England, moreover, it helped to stimulate a prosperous shipbuilding trade. In the same act the principle of the enumerated articles was laid down. Tobacco, sugar, cotton, and dyewoods could be shipped from the colonies only to England.[3] Later the list was increased. They were for the most part staple products of the southern continental and West Indian colonies which were produced in England in small quantities or not at all. In 1663 another act required that European commodities

---

[3] The original act permitted exportation to Ireland also, but this was soon revoked.

destined for the colonies must be shipped to England and put on shore there before they could be transported to the colonies. This was designed to increase the cost of transportation and give English goods an advantage in the colonial market. This act and the enumerated articles placed restrictions on colonial trade. They prevented the colonists from buying in the cheapest market and selling in the dearest. The hardship was less than it appears on paper, since the course of American trade after the American Revolution indicates that England was a natural clearing house for much of the trade between America and the continent of Europe. The English legislators, moreover, offset the restrictions in some measure by preferential treatment of some colonial products in the English market and by exceptions when the restrictions were found to work serious damage. Colonial tobacco, for example, could be imported into England at a lower duty than tobacco from other places, and when naval stores were placed on the list of enumerated articles a bounty was offered for their importation into England. In 1730 rice, which had been placed on the list, was allowed to be exported directly to southern Europe, its natural market, on payment of a colonial export duty half the amount of the import duty levied in England.

The acts which limited colonial manufactures were passed so obviously in the interest of English manufacturers and merchants, without regard for the welfare of the colonists, that they have received the harshest criticism. In 1669 the colonies were forbidden to export manufactured woolens, and some years later their transportation from one colony to another was forbidden. In 1732 similar prohibitions were placed on the manufacture of hats. In 1750 the colonists were forbidden to manufacture iron beyond the pig or bar stage even for local use. The last was more than balanced, however, by permission to import iron in these stages of manufacture into England free of duty. The disastrous effects of the other acts in the series, moreover, can be easily exaggerated, since the colonies were still in an agricultural stage of development where manufactures on an extensive scale had not become generally profitable.

One act in the series, which caused much irritation in the northern continental colonies, gave no advantage to England. It merely benefited one group of colonies at the expense of another group. In 1733 the Molasses Act placed a prohibitive duty on molasses and sugar imported into the continental colonies from other than the British West Indies. The northern colonists had developed a brisk trade with the West Indies in these articles, which they secured in exchange for the lumber and provisions that constituted their staple products. The molasses and sugar, which were manufactured into rum, could often be secured cheaper in the French or the Dutch West Indies, and eventually the demand became so large that the British West Indies could not supply the whole of it. The Molasses Act was a heavy handicap to an important branch of the commerce of the northern colonies.

These acts undoubtedly placed serious limitations on the freedom of colonial trade, but they also gave to the colonists some advantages, and they damaged some English interests. English taxpayers bore the whole expense of the necessary naval defense of the empire, English consumers paid higher prices for the colonial products given preferential treatment in the English market, and various other English interests complained of one disadvantage or another put upon them by the system. The disadvantages were by no means all on one side. This was entirely in accord with the mercantilist theory, which justified interference with trade which worked harm in some quarters, provided it was thought to promote the interests of the empire as a whole. The colonists, however, felt little community of interests with England. They did not feel themselves to be a sufficiently constituent part of the empire to endure restrictions which harmed their economic interests, however much they benefited theoretically the empire in general.

The acts of trade, however, did not bear heavily on the colonists
Adminis- because they were not effectively administered. Those of the reign of
tration Charles II were for the most part self-executory. The informer of a
of the violation of the acts received part of the fine inflicted as a penalty. The
acts English committees and boards concerned with the oversight of trade were more advisory than executive in character, and the officials of the customs were the most active of the English officials engaged in the enforcement of the acts. In the colonies the colonial governors had a general responsibility for their execution locally, and a few collectors of customs were stationed in the colonies. The royal officials in the colonies, however, were not provided with adequate assistants and equipment, and they obtained little help from the colonists in the way of information or otherwise. When they brought an offender before a court, the colonial jury would rarely convict. Under William III the attempt was made to hold the colonial governors more strictly accountable for the enforcement of the acts, and courts of admiralty were established in the colonies to try without a jury alleged violations of them. Even with these aids the few royal officials in the colonies were able to accomplish little. They lacked adequate support and assistance

from the English government, and they had a united colonial opposition to face. The honest officials rarely cared to stir up a hornet's nest by attempting to enforce the acts, and the dishonest were content to let them be disregarded so long as their pockets were lined. In the eighteenth century, previous to the Seven Years' War, official inaction was more or less disregarded by the home government, which was generally content to let sleeping dogs lie. As a result the colonists violated with impunity those acts of trade which interfered with their interests, and they never felt the full force of the restrictions placed upon them on paper.

The growth of commerce in the seventeenth century finally resulted in the establishment of the Bank of England in 1694. After the restoration, the need of a bank was generally felt by men engaged in business. Because business was on too large a scale to be transacted on a basis of cash, an adequate system of credit was becoming a necessity. The goldsmiths of London performed some of the functions of banks, but their services did not keep pace with the demand for facilities of credit and places of deposit. The immediate occasion of the creation of the bank, however, arose from the necessities of the government. The inadequacy of the royal revenues after 1660 made loans necessary in increasing volume. Until the time of William III such loans were contracted for definite terms; but in 1692 the expenses of the war were so great and the prospect of immediate repayment so small that a loan was made which was intended to be a permanent interest charge on the exchequer. It marked the beginning of the permanent national debt. The people did not yet have sufficient confidence in the government to lend readily, even at ten per cent. When another large loan became necessary in 1694, the government was glad to arrange with a group of merchants for the establishment of the Bank of England. The merchants subscribed £1,200,000 to a loan, which became their capital for a bank. For this the government paid them £100,000 annually, and gave them a charter authorizing them to receive deposits, make loans, and issue bank notes. For several years the bank had to struggle for existence. Since it was originated by a group of Whigs, the Tories took several opportunities, created by political or financial conditions, to embarrass it; but its value for making capital available for an expanding business finally became so apparent that it rose above the petty machinations of party politics and came to be regarded as a national institution.

Social life under the first two Stuarts was influenced profoundly by the Puritans. They were of many types. The moral earnestness that

The Bank of England

was characteristic of them all affected them in many different ways. Some wished to persecute those who did not see eye to eye with them, while others advocated religious toleration. George Fox, who later founded the Society of Friends and gave to its members their tenet of peace and their mystical tendency to seek communion with the divine by the quiet process of inner contemplation, was as much a product of Puritanism as William Prynne, who felt it his bounden duty to censor the sins of his neighbors. Puritanism had not yet assumed that terrible sternness which it manifested in the period of the civil wars. Some of the Puritan gentry still wore hair, clothes, and adornments which were in style, enjoyed the dance, hunted with neighboring squires, and found pleasure in music and in works of art. They were inclined, indeed, to ridicule the eccentricities of garb which some of the townsmen affected as a protest against the time and money wasted on dress by ladies and gentlemen of quality. But however much Puritans might differ among themselves on many points, they were at one in the emphasis which they placed on the importance of the individual's moral uprightness. There was a "moral grandeur" in their lives which could not fail to affect the social tone of the community.

On social classes Puritanism acted as a leveler. Spiritual equality was a Puritan ideal so far practiced as to make the distinctions of social rank of less moment. It gave to the Puritans of the lower social grades a new sense of dignity, and to the gentlemen and the merchants a greater spirit of kindness and courtesy toward their social inferiors. The Puritan gentleman who "never disdained the meanest nor flattered the greatest"[4] typified the spirit that produced theories of social and political democracy among the Puritans in their day of power. Yet, though the Puritans paid less attention to social gradations based upon birth, their "gospel of hard work" tended to set up new distinctions based upon a man's success in his chosen calling. Puritan thought regarded "industry and diligence" as every man's duty. It was a view which, on the one hand, produced scant sympathy for those of the poor whose troubles were due to their own idleness or thriftlessness and, on the other hand, created respect for those whose assiduous pursuit of their occupations brought success in the form of worldly wealth.

Not all of the Puritans were content to influence social life only by example. Though many led pious and devout lives in fellowship with their neighbors of like mind, without attempting to force their opinions

---

[4] Quoted by Green, *History of the English People*, section 881.

upon others, some were driven to become social reformers by a conviction that it was their duty to reprove sin. In the life about them they found objects of legitimate criticism. It is difficult to believe that social standards in the time of James I were generally corrupt. Society was still simple and rural. The gentry, who were its leaders, came within the orbit of the royal court only in small numbers, and the London season had not yet begun. Yet increasing wealth and luxury may have brought with it a wave of dissoluteness. Puritan complaints were not entirely without foundation. The court of James I was profligate, and though Charles, by his more dignified example, improved the tone of the court, the morals of many courtiers still fell considerably short of a moderate Puritan ideal. The country houses of a few of the lords and gentry were perhaps no better. Among all classes intemperance and profanity were common. In their crusade against such evils as these, some of the Puritans became so censorious that they aroused the enmity of the worldly against Puritans in general.

Puritans and social reform

Still greater antagonism was evoked by the Puritans who did not stop with the effort to reform public morals. To the extremists pleasure and sin were nearly synonymous. They attacked the stage, dancing, card-playing, fashionable dress, and many kinds of sports. "Many sports which as sports they did not condemn have ceased to exist, because the Puritans condemned their use on Sundays, the only day on which working people could practice them regularly." Those whose pleasures were criticized or interfered with naturally entertained bitter feelings against the Puritans. Between the sinners on the one side and the saints on the other was a great mass of moderates who had no strong sympathies with either, but were gradually forced to take sides. Thus the reigns of James I and Charles I witnessed a social struggle which, no less than the political and the religious struggles, constitutes part of the background of the civil war.[5]

The extremists

When the Puritans came to power they clamped down the lid on public immorality and on many popular forms of amusement. Plays, bear-baiting, and cockfighting were prohibited early in the career of the Long Parliament. Games were forbidden on Sunday. When Christmas fell on a weekly day of fast appointed by parliament, the fast was enforced. In 1647 parliament prohibited the observance of Christmas and saints' days. Under the Protectorate punishments were imposed for swearing, gambling, betting, and drunkenness, the drinking of healths was forbidden, and horse-races were suppressed. To have a hole bored

Rule of the saints

---

[5] Paragraph based mainly on Miss Bateson's article in Traill, *Social England*, iv, 167–172.

through their tongues was a penalty inflicted on many who were convicted of swearing. The rigorous enforcement of these blue laws by Cromwell's major generals greatly intensified the growing desire of the nation to be rid of the Puritan ascendency.

With the restoration the pendulum made a full swing. The social democracy of the Puritans was promptly overthrown, and the old social dictatorship of the lords and the gentlemen of birth was restored in town and country. Puritanism was discredited. The upper classes for the most part deserted it, and it became the religion of the middle and lower classes. Fashion ruled supreme, and nearly all the social conventions that the Puritan despotism had imposed at the point of the sword became unfashionable. The Puritan sabbath was the one notable custom which survived the reaction that for a generation went to excess in the search for pleasure. Charles II set the pace in a court notorious for its licentiousness. Evelyn notes that Charles "brought in a politer way of living," but led "a voluptuous and sensual life, which a vicious Court had brought into credit."[6] It seems probable that moral standards declined temporarily among the upper class which gave to society its tone. In 1675 the commons voted "that the atheism, debauchery, and impiety of the present age be inserted, as grievances to be redressed."[7]

But the whole nation did not confuse social liberty with social license, and those who did were not permitted long to hold sway without protest. Puritans were silenced, but all sober and moderate persons were not Puritans. Though William and Mary were not saints, they lent their influence to the reform of manners and morals. The court in their reign had little social influence, but the quiet and sober tastes prevalent at Anne's court modified social customs considerably. After the revolution of 1688, moreover, social reform became the subject of popular agitation. In 1692 a society for the reformation of manners was founded. The members agreed to inform the authorities of cases of cursing, drunkenness, violation of the sabbath, disorderly houses, and things of like nature, because the existing laws against such practices operated only when private persons brought an accusation before a magistrate. For several years the society flourished, though eventually it declined because, as Defoe had predicted, the convictions were obtained mainly against persons of the lower orders of society. The upper class was content to force the lower classes to be good, but had no thought of taking its own medicine. Still more influential in the production of a refinement of manners were the essayists of Anne's reign. The idea of

Gravity becomes rebellion

Sobriety finds tongue

---

[6] *Diary,* iii, 141, 183.
[7] Reresby, *Memoirs and Travels,* p. 156.

publishing a non-partisan paper, devoted entirely to essays, originated with Steele, but it was Addison who wrote the most influential essays. The new journals were popular, and the ideals of conduct and demeanor held up in such essays as those on Sir Roger de Coverley, which display an ideal country gentleman, helped to disseminate more polished manners and healthier social conventions.

In intellectual development the restoration marked a change in the direction taken by speculative thought. In the first half of the seventeenth century scholarship was devoted in exceptional measure to theology. The emphasis placed on the Bible by the Puritans led to its intensive study both by the Puritans and by their opponents. The literature produced was largely controversial, but it was no longer merely a question of skill in debate. Both sides believed that the truth would prevail; each side thought the truth was its monopoly, and sought to convince in argument by expounding its truth. To have greater knowledge than the other side became the goal of each side. The controversialists were not only conversant with the store of knowledge of classical antiquity accumulated by their predecessors in the sixteenth century, but they often acquired a thorough knowledge of Greek and Hebrew, and they established many of the canons of textual, historical, and literary criticism which are followed by research students of the present day. The erudition which centered upon the Bible and on the subsidiary classical, oriental, and patristic fields was far above any similar previous achievement of English scholarship. *Theology*

Though the search for the truth by the newer and more accurate methods was pursued mainly by the students of the Bible in the first half of the seventeenth century, it spread in some measure to other fields. Historians began to recognize the value of documents. Several writers on contemporary events filled their pages largely with documents, and several of those interested in England's past published great collections of documents which have been of service to historians ever since. Writers of historical literature, moreover, began to give much more attention to the search for materials and to weigh more critically the evidence which they discovered. *History*

In the field of science, the initial steps of a fundamental change in the method of approach were taken. In the reign of Elizabeth scientific methods had changed but little since the Middle Ages. The increase of scientific knowledge in England was still dependent primarily on the discovery and study of the works of the ancients. Francis Bacon spoke for the inductive method, and, though he practiced it little himself and was by no means the first to announce it, he influ- *Science* enced others to observe and record natural phenomena, and may be said to have heralded the transition to modern methods of scientific study in England. During the first half of the century the methods of observation and experiment were applied to the natural and physical sciences by an increasing number of students, though the greatest discovery in the scientific field, that of the circulation of the blood, was made by William Harvey, a contemporary of Bacon. The practice of medicine and knowledge of public sanitation did not make great progress, however. In 1665 London was visited with a plague which exacted a frightful toll of death and caused great consternation.

Learning after the restoration

After the restoration learned scholars did not cease to study the Bible, but secular fields of study became the more popular. Charles II accentuated the trend by the display of an intelligent interest in art, music, literature, and science, which made it stylish for gentlemen to be informed on such subjects. Charles was particularly interested in science. In 1661 he became a member of a society which subsequently was known as the Royal Society. It consisted of a group of men engaged in scientific experiments who had been meeting irregularly since 1645, and it gave a strong impulse to scientific investigation. In the following years English scholars contributed largely to scientific knowledge, particularly in the fields of chemistry, physics, and astronomy. The greatest results were achieved by Sir Isaac Newton, who is still universally associated in popular thought with the discovery of the law of gravitation. The members of the Society were also interested in the application of scientific discoveries to the problems of industry and agriculture, and this union of interest between science and business eventually led to great practical results in the eighteenth century.

Rational-ism

On the modes of thought which governed the attitude of Englishmen of culture toward politics, religion, and life in general, perhaps no one man had so great an influence as John Locke, who published most of his works in the decade following the revolution of 1688. He was primarily a philosopher, but he also wrote works on political theory and religion. In all these fields he interpreted the fundamental beliefs of his day and formulated them with such success that they dominated English thought for the next century. The essence of his teaching was the application of the test of rationality. The emphasis on common sense as the proper guide to thought and conduct began with the restoration. Of ideals men had had their fill. Sham and cant were to be shunned like the plague. Plain, unadorned, prosaic common sense was the standard maintained by the fashionable set at the court of Charles II, whence it spread rapidly throughout the intellectual circles of London and more slowly to the provinces. The nature of the change is well illustrated by the difference in the sermons that were popular at the beginning and at the end of the seventeenth century. The divines who delighted their audiences when the fervor of Puritanism ran high addressed their hearers from above and made ostentatious parade of their truly great learning; the popular preacher at the end of the century appealed in simple terms to the reason of his audience which was composed of laymen of average intelligence. "Politically, the change means toleration, for it is assumed that the vulgar can judge for themselves; intellectually, it means rationalism, that is, an appeal to the reason common to all men; and, in literature it means the hatred of pedantry and the acceptance of such literary forms as are thoroughly congenial and intelligible to the common sense of the new audience."[8]

The development of literature during the period of the Stuarts proceeds from the heroic age of Shakespeare to the prosaic age of the essayists. It is a transition not only from poetry to prose but also from antique to modern. Shakespeare has more in common with Chaucer than with Dryden, the outstanding literary figure of the restoration, "and Dryden has less in common with Shakspere than with countless other writers of sound prose who have illustrated the reign of Queen Victoria."[9]

Literature

During the reign of James I the literary product was still of the Elizabethan type. Shakespeare wrote some of his best plays in this period, and the best of his contemporaries and successors were also active. Poets kept the Spenserian tradition on a high plane, and some new masters appeared. Bacon was still writing English prose, and this was the time of the authorized version of the Bible, than which no single book has ever had a greater influence on English literature.

Early years of seventeenth century

With the reign of Charles I a decline began. It became apparent first in the drama, and it had gone a long way when the Puritans closed the doors of the playhouses in 1642. In poetry it began later and was never so marked. Poetry ultimately became conventionalized, but it did not become decadent like the drama. Prose ran for the most part into controversies on the political and religious questions that agitated the nation. Many of the works produced display deep learning, but few have literary qualities that make them attractive to the reader of the present. To the general trend there were exceptions, chiefly in the form of devotional and autobiographical productions. Far above

Middle years

---

[8] Stephen, *English Literature and Society of the Eighteenth Century*, pp. 44–51.
[9] Wendell, *Temper of the Seventeenth Century*, p. 8.

all rises Milton, generally ranked second only to Shakespeare. Before the outbreak of the civil war he was writing poetry that placed him in the front rank of English poets. During the next two decades he deserted the muse for controversial prose in behalf of the beloved Puritan cause, and during the interregnum he acted as secretary to the republican government. While serving in this capacity he lost his sight. At the restoration he narrowly escaped punishment, but he was finally allowed to go into retirement where he composed *Paradise Lost*, the greatest epic in the language.

Restoration period

That contemporaries generally failed to recognize the greatness of the poem is indicative of the complete change of literary ideals that had taken place since the beginning of the century. The poem enshrined the spiritual meaning of the Puritan faith, and the writers of the restoration were concerned with a public which did not care to be reminded of Puritanism. They knew not Joseph. Equally apart from the main stream is *Pilgrim's Progress*, in which John Bunyan, an unlettered lay preacher who suffered long imprisonment under the Clarendon code for his steadfastness in dissent, set forth his conception of the Puritan belief in such vivid allegory that even in this age many are still familiar with the difficulties of Christian's journey.

Milton and Bunyan made the ideals of a past age live for men of the future. Those who wrote contemporaneously with them after 1660 sought to please a fashionable circle which preferred something after the order of what today we are wont to call realism. In the first outburst most of the literature dealt with unpleasant aspects of life. When the theaters were reopened in London, their patrons came from the royal court and its entourage. The dramatists wrote to please this audience, and witty but coarse comedies were the result. The poets wrote of trivialities more or less vicious in a form of rigid politeness which developed into the couplet, later carried to the height of its possibilities by Pope. Prose became more commonly a vehicle of artistic expression. Style was emphasized as never before, though it became stilted somewhat as it became polished. Satire became popular. Samuel Butler's *Hudibras*, a satirical poem on the Puritans published soon after the restoration, acquired a vogue which gave satire an important place in literature subsequently. The dean of letters in this era was John Dryden, who demonstrated his superiority in all the forms of literature that were popular during the period. In his early plays he catered to the prevailing corruption of taste, but the work done shortly before the end of his life, which came in 1700, displays a more wholesome spirit. The revolt against ideals still runs strong, but the facts which appeal are no longer only those concerned with the baser side of life. Common sense has been rescued from the slough where it fell in the early restoration, and is ready to be put to the service of the essayists, whose message was sane if it was not profound.

The reign of Anne saw a remarkable development of English prose. The style became clear, incisive, graceful, and polished. The two most characteristic forms were the political pamphlet and the essay. With the development of the system of parties the leaders of parties began to subsidize the writers of political pamphlets as a means of molding public opinion. The electorate was small, and the reading part of it, which formed the opinion of the whole electorate, could be reached by the pamphlet. This type of literature probably had a greater influence on political issues than at any other time before or since. Most of the authors of the time wrote some political pamphlets, but the ablest came from the pens of Defoe and Swift. The great essayists were Steele and Addison. Since the civil war periodical newspapers had been published, and in 1702 the first daily newspaper was established. Two years later Daniel Defoe began to publish a periodical which, though devoted mainly to news, contained an occasional essay. In 1709 Steele launched the *Tatler*, a periodical given mainly to essays. It was followed by the still more famous *Spectator*. Steele had the cooperation of Addison, and several other writers contributed. The essays not only became patterns of style that were long copied, but they also gave a cleaner tone to the literature and improved the public morals and culture of the period.

Essayists and pamphleteers

In historical literature the old annalistic form of compilation gave way to reasoned narratives which give due attention to the relation of cause and effect and have more regard for literary finish. Lord Bacon's *Henry VII* has been called the first historical monograph. This may be an exaggeration; but it represents a critical study of some of the sources and it has merit as a literary essay. Historians of contemporary events also began to give more weight to documents and more attention to style. Of these the best example is the earl of Clarendon's *History of the Rebellion and Civil Wars in England*. Hardly less interesting is Bishop Gilbert Burnet's *History of His Own Time* which deals with the period after the restoration.

Historical literature

A new type of historical source which becomes common during the seventeenth century is the personal narrative in the form of memoirs, autobiographies, and diaries. Burnet's narrative partakes largely of the character of memoirs, and there are many others which convey valuable historical evidence in a most entertaining manner. Most lively of

Memoirs

all is Pepys' *Diary*, which sets forth the intimate thoughts and experiences of an extremely curious man during the first decade after the restoration. It gives a vivid glimpse of life in London during an interesting social epoch. Evelyn's *Diary*, though more sober in tone, is scarcely less interesting and is more enlightening about political affairs.

Other historical sources

Other new types are the newspapers and periodical publications, works on political theories, and writings on political economy. Older types such as public documents, letters, and pamphlets become far more abundant. The literature reflects contemporary life more closely than does the literature of the previous century, and it consequently yields more to the historian. The wealth of the materials, indeed, becomes almost overwhelming to the historian who seeks a thorough knowledge of the period.

CHAPTER XXVIII

WALPOLE AND PITT

GEORGE I was fifty-four when he became king of England. His habits, which were already fixed, were those of the simpler court of Hanover. He came without a queen, but he brought two German mistresses and a small retinue of Germans whom he kept about his person. He was reserved, awkward, and slow. He did not speak English, and he did not try to learn. His tastes were coarse. He had a good fund of common sense and a strong sense of fair-dealing. In Hanover George had been an absolute ruler, but he recognized that the English constitution was different and restrained himself accordingly. At first he displayed strong attachment to his German favorites and to Hanover, but he soon learned to trust his English ministers and to keep his Hanoverian interests in the background. His bad qualities were more patent than his good ones; his indifference, his coldness, his German court, and his love of Hanover were the first to impress the nation; he was promptly unpopular. *George I, 1714–1727*

These first impressions helped in no small degree to produce a rebellion in 1715. George appointed a cabinet composed almost entirely of Whigs, under the leadership of Lord Townshend. An election held early in 1715 returned a large majority of Whigs to the house of commons. The Tories, bitter over their loss of power, were driven to despair when the Whigs with the customary partisan vindictiveness impeached the leading Tories. Some of them determined not to accept the new dynasty and threw in their lot with the Jacobites, who plotted rebellion. The situation seemed favorable. The despatch of an English fleet to the Baltic to make a demonstration against Sweden gave rise to the suspicion that England was being subordinated to Hanover, since the latter state was at war with Sweden. The new dynasty was not popular. Riots and demonstrations for James, who was the son of James II and was called the Pretender, caused the Whigs to pass the Riot Act, an important constitutional measure, which is still in force. It empowered a justice of the peace to read the act whenever twelve or more persons assembled to disturb the peace and to order them to disperse. Failure to comply within an hour rendered the members of the assemblage guilty of felony. Many of those who did not favor the Pretender appeared to be indifferent. A *Jacobite rebellion* well-organized Jacobite rebellion would have been a serious danger to the house of Hanover.

Nevertheless, the rising failed. The Pretender was too incompetent to plan a campaign and act as leader. He would give no assurance of the maintenance of the established church, and few even of the Jacobites were willing to risk a restoration of Catholicism. On the eve of the outbreak Louis XIV, who had promised help, died. His successor, Louis XV, was a child, necessitating the appointment of the duke of Orléans as regent. The new ruler found that Philip V, the Bourbon king of Spain, despite the peace of Utrecht, had designs on the throne of France. This put the regent in a glass house where it seemed unwise to throw stones at George I, and the Pretender to the British throne lost his French support. Consequently, when the earl of Mar rashly began a rebellion in the highlands of Scotland without adequate plans or resources, few of the English joined, and it was easily quelled.

Whig
ascend-
ency

The principal result was to establish a Whig ascendency, which lasted until the reign of George III. Enough Tories were tainted with Jacobitism to give point to the Whig contention that the return of the Tories to power meant a change of dynasty and a revolution. The Whigs seized the opportunity to dismiss the last of the Tories, making the administration entirely Whig. They also passed the Septennial Act, which lengthened the life of parliament from three years to seven and gave them four additional years in which to establish their domination securely.

Whig
schism

The Whigs settled themselves so firmly, indeed, that the leaders could afford to quarrel. The divergence arose over foreign policy. Townshend was apprehensive of the complications which the position of George I as the elector of Hanover might produce for Great Britain; Stanhope was more adventurous and more ready to embroil Great Britain on account of Hanover. Europe was restless. The peace of Utrecht had left dissatisfaction in many quarters. Spain objected to the Austrian predominance in Italy, and Philip V schemed to secure the French throne; Charles VI of Austria coveted Sicily which had gone to Savoy, and still dreamed of the throne of Spain; and the northern nations were at war with Sweden. This was roughly the situation in Europe which led George I, under the guidance of Stanhope, to make two alliances in 1716. By the Treaty of Westminster Great Britain and Austria agreed to help each other defend their existing possessions. A treaty with France arranged for mutual help against their respective pretenders. The latter ran counter to the policy pursued by England steadily since 1689, and it could not be a permanent policy because France was still Great Britain's chief colonial and commercial rival. For those reasons Townshend opposed it. Stanhope favored it because the chief threat to the peace of Great Britain came from the Pretender, and Great Britain needed the peace which friendship with France would promote. For his opposition Townshend was superseded by Stanhope as leader of the cabinet, and later dismissed. The king was now dependent on a cabinet of the party in the majority in the house of commons, but he was still free to choose his advisers from among the leaders of the party.

Stanhope's leadership of the cabinet was important chiefly for foreign relations. His object was to extend the network of alliances in such a way as to maintain the peace of Europe and the stability of the Hanoverian dynasty. The chief threats of disturbance came from Sweden and from Spain. The former was met by a naval attack on Sweden; the latter, by the Quadruple Alliance. In 1717 Spain attacked Austria in Italy. That caused Austria to join with France and Great Britain to keep the European peace. The Netherlands had previously adhered, and thus the Quadruple Alliance was formed in 1718. Its purpose was to force Spain to keep the peace. When Spain refused, France invaded Spain by land and a British fleet destroyed the Spanish fleet in the Mediterranean. Spain was forced to withdraw from Italy and to settle outstanding differences at a congress of the European powers. The congress began in 1722. In the previous year the war of the northern powers had been ended by a treaty which removed that source of disturbance. Stanhope's policy was a great success. He secured the temporary stability of the Hanoverian dynasty, and helped to restore peace in Europe.

Stanhope's foreign policy

Meanwhile internal affairs passed through a financial crisis when the South Sea Bubble burst in 1721. The South Sea Company was organized in 1711 to trade with South America and was given a monopoly of the trade. It took up a large portion of the public debt in somewhat the same way as the Bank of England had done earlier. Subsequently it was favored by the government with the grant of additional commercial privileges. The *asiento*, for example, obtained from Spain at the close of the War of the Spanish Succession, was awarded to the company. The capital of the company was so large, however, that the whole of it was never used in commercial ventures, and profits were sought by manipulating the stock market. In 1720 a gigantic scheme was floated. Holders of government obligations of indebtedness, other than the Bank of England and the East India

South Sea Bubble

Company, were allowed to convert their bonds or other evidences of governmental indebtedness into the stock of the South Sea Company. The company agreed to pay the government a bonus for the privilege of the conversion and ultimately to accept a lower rate of interest on the bonds and other obligations of the government which came into its possession by means of the transaction. The company made its profit by giving out its stocks at the market value, which was high, and accepting the governmental evidences of indebtedness at par or below. Thus it required stock of the face value of only £3,250,000 to acquire governmental obligations of the face value of £9,500,000. Partly because the government seemed to be behind the company and partly because the company made unscrupulous promises of high returns upon its stocks, a wave of speculative mania sent its stocks soaring from £128 a share to over £1,000. In 1721 the inevitable crash came, ruining many investors. The public anger was directed against the cabinet. The support of the company by the government had given the public confidence, and some members of the cabinet had accepted bribes from the company. The popular indignation ran so high that the Whig party was threatened with loss of power. It was saved by Sir Robert Walpole.

Walpole was the younger son of a Norfolk squire, destined originally for the church. While he was at Cambridge in pursuit of the necessary education, his elder brother died, making him the heir to the rich estate. His father at once removed him from the university to teach him to manage the estate. Education at a university was superfluous for a squire's heir. His father molded him into a typical country squire. He became a keen, shrewd man of business, coarse in his manners and morals, open-hearted, free, and easy in his intercourse with men, a good sportsman, and a hard drinker. These characteristics, which would made it difficult for their possessor to become more than a ward politician today, did not hinder Walpole's political career in the age in which he lived. Walpole came to parliament in 1700, sitting for a borough controlled by the family. By hard work and ability he put himself in line for promotion, and, when the Whigs were in power under Anne, he held several minor offices in the ministry. During this period he acquired the reputation of having the best head for figures of any man of his day. In 1714 he was made a member of the cabinet, but three years later, following the fortunes of his brother-in-law, Lord Townshend, he resigned and went over to the opposition. A few months before the bubble burst, he and Townshend healed their differences with Stanhope and were taken

Early career of Walpole

into the cabinet in subordinate positions. When the crash came, Walpole was free from all connection with the company, and his reputation for figures made him just the man to salvage the wreck. He was put in charge of the exchequer, Stanhope died soon after, the ministers guilty of the acceptance of bribes died or resigned, and the cabinet was reorganized. As a result Walpole became practically the head of the cabinet.

Walpole kept his leadership for twenty-one years. During this long tenure of office he displayed the qualities of a statesman. He was not an idealist. His ministry had nothing of the sublime that seemed to attach to Pitt's later leadership. Walpole's point of view would commonly be judged materialistic. He sought to give England a good government reared on a solid foundation. His chief means were common sense, hard work, and persistency. He followed his object steadily and purposefully without the *beau geste* or the fanfare of oratory, but his wide grasp of the facts of public business and his sound and penetrating judgment impressed contemporaries in an age of rationality. He was a manager rather than a leader of men, but he managed with great skill.

Walpole's
statesman-
ship

Any estimate of his contribution is difficult because it was negative rather than positive. His chief purpose was to prevent the Hanoverian dynasty from being overthrown. When he came to power, the Hanoverian king was still far from popular, riots and disturbances were common, Jacobite plots had not ceased, and a rebellion was always a possibility. Walpole strove to avoid any policy which might arouse the dormant popular opposition. Parliament was so constituted that Walpole was not directly dependent on popular support for his position, but he sensed public opinion and heeded it as did few statesmen of his time. When a reform of taxation that he proposed in 1733 proved unpopular, he gave it up, though it was a wise measure and he had the votes to put it through parliament. What Walpole refrained from doing displays his political wisdom as well as what he did. In foreign policy his attitude was the same. He saw as clearly as any Whig leader that Great Britain's interests were opposed to those of France and Spain, her chief colonial and commercial rivals; but he sought their friendship because peace seemed to him essential for the prosperous economic and political development of England internally. He accomplished his object. When he left office, the Hanoverian house was secure upon the throne and prosperity ruled. It was not a brilliant contribution, but it was solid.

The internal policies to which Walpole gave his chief attention

Economic
policy

were economic. Though he was a mercantilist, he placed more emphasis than was customary on the promotion of internal industry as a means of supplying commerce with products for foreign exchange. To this end he revised the existing complicated system of customs duties. Export duties were removed from manufactured articles and import duties were canceled or reduced on many raw materials used by English manufacturers. The popular opposition to his excise bill of 1733, which was intended to simplify the collection of some other import duties to such an extent that they could be decreased in rate without reduction of the amount received from them by the government, prevented the complete execution of his plan, but his program went far enough to cause one contemporary writer on economic subjects to assert that "he found the book of rates the worst and left it the best in Europe."[1] His ministry was certainly a period of economic prosperity when industry, shipping, and commerce increased materially. Without much doubt his able financial and commercial policies contributed to the production of that result.

The
cabinet

Under his leadership the principles of cabinet government developed notably. The cabinet became much more independent of the king. George I, after the early years of his reign, rarely attended meetings of the cabinet because he did not speak English; under George II (1727-1760) the custom hardened into a precedent. This procedure made it possible for the members of the cabinet to iron out their differences before they approached the king with advice, and left the king with less opportunity to influence the decisions of the cabinet. The king found it ever more necessary to have a cabinet which could command a majority in the house of commons. In 1727, when George II came to the throne, he was loath to accept Walpole as his adviser. While crown prince, George had quarreled with his father, and his antagonism had extended to Walpole, his father's chief minister. Experience of a few days with another chief adviser soon convinced the new king that Walpole was the one leader who could manage the house of commons and decided him to sacrifice his personal predilections to the necessities of state. The cabinet, on the other hand, was still dependent partly on the favor of the king. Walpole recognized the need of the royal support, taking pains to win the ear of Queen Caroline, whose influence on the political opinions of George II was profound.

In the principle of the unanimity of the cabinet the developmen:

---

[1] Coxe, *Memoirs of Sir Robert Walpole* (1798), i, 749.

of this period was pronounced. Before 1716 the cabinets had rarely been entirely uniform in their party structure. A Whig cabinet generally contained a few Tories, and *vice versa*. In 1716 the cabinet became completely Whig and remained so. Furthermore, under Walpole all of the members were expected to support publicly any general policy which the cabinet decided to adopt. If any disagreed with the general policy, they could keep quiet or resign. If they opposed the policy of the cabinet in parliament, Walpole forced them to withdraw from the cabinet. Carteret retired in 1724, and Pulteney was kept out for this reason, though they were among the brilliant leaders of the Whig party. Townshend departed in 1730, and three years later several members who opposed Walpole's excise bill were dismissed. On this occasion Walpole consulted the king and queen. They gave their approval, realizing that Walpole was introducing a new principle of cabinet government. From that time the principle of the solidarity of the cabinet was well recognized in the reign of George II. In practice, too, the principle of solidarity under the leadership of one man became fixed. The name of prime minister had been applied to the leading minister before Walpole's time, but no minister had ever maintained such a domination over his colleagues as Walpole established.

At the same time that the cabinet was becoming less dependent upon the king, it was becoming more dependent upon the house of commons. Walpole knew that his influence with the king and his control of the policy of the government depended on his ability to command a majority in the house of commons. Walpole's majority rested partly on corruption, but it was due in part to his skillful management. He recognized that his policies must secure the approval of the majority. When he lost the support of the majority, he resigned. The political dependence of the cabinet on the house of commons was more clearly appreciated by Walpole than by any of his predecessors.

Thus the cabinet took a long stride in its development toward the modern form under Walpole's guidance. The theory did not keep pace with the practice. Walpole seemed to realize the constitutional significance of the position he was giving the cabinet better than did many of his contemporaries. In 1741, when the parliamentary attack opened that led to Walpole's downfall, the lords protested that "a sole or even a first minister, is an office unknown to the law of Britain, inconsistent with the Constitution of this country, and destructive of liberty in any government whatsoever."[2] The modern theory of cabinet government did not yet prevail, nor was the practice firmly fixed. The successors of Walpole sometimes ignored the principles of Walpole's system, but they usually found it necessary to revert to them. The broad outlines of cabinet government had been laid down in practice. Though they were still vague in many particulars, they were far more clearly traced in 1742 than they had been in 1721.

Electoral
corruption

Walpole kept the support of a majority in the house of commons largely by means of corruption. Many members of the house of commons did not represent the voters who nominally elected them; they voiced the sentiments of the Whig aristocrats who really secured their elections. Corruption of the electorate was by this time widespread among the boroughs. In many of them the right to vote was possessed by a mere handful of inhabitants. In some this was due to a decline of the population, effected by economic causes working during the centuries since the boroughs had been enfranchised; in others it was due to local limitations on the franchise, which confined the right to vote to a small part of the whole population. It has been estimated that only one out of ten adult males had the suffrage in the eighteenth century. The classic case of Old Sarum, where there were no inhabitants and the seven owners of certain tenures in the place elected two members of parliament, is at the extreme, but many a borough returned two members elected by less than one hundred voters. In such boroughs one of two situations prevailed. In some a neighboring landowner, through his powers as landlord, through family influence, by purchase of the votes, or by other means, obtained permanent control of the votes and at every election named the candidates for whom the electors voted. In others the voters were bribed at each election. These rotten or pocket boroughs had appeared as early as the sixteenth century, when they were used by their patrons to supply members favorable to the crown. In the first half of the eighteenth century the number had increased and was increasing, and the greatest patrons were the Whig nobles. In rural districts and in towns where the suffrage was not thus restricted, bribery and mob violence were common. The protests of a defeated candidate who lost an election through his opponent's bribery of the electorate were adjudged by a committee of the house of commons which had a majority of the party having a majority in the house. Disputed elections were consequently decided

---

[2] Cited by Blauvelt, *Development of Cabinet Government*, p. 224.

generally by a purely party vote, irrespective of the evidence presented. Through the corruption of the electorate the votes of a large group in the house of commons were controlled by a small number of Whig nobles, who would support only a Whig cabinet.

Within the house of commons political morality was on an equally low plane. The corruption of members of the house became common in the time of Charles II, when the king bought the votes. After the revolution the leaders of parties practiced it on a steadily increasing scale. The votes of members of the house were not usually bought for cash, though such transactions were not unknown. Party loyalty was more often assured by the grant of profitable offices or sinecures under the crown. "It is on record that out of 550 Members there were in the first Parliament of George I no less than 271, in the first Parliament of George II no less than 257, holding offices, pensions, or sinecures."[3] Sometimes social favors and distinctions which the influential Whig nobles could confer kept wavering Whigs in line. Walpole, who was above the acceptance of a bribe, cynically used the means at hand to secure a majority in the house of commons; and so far did political corruption go in his day that it was hardly regarded by public opinion as a breach of public morals.

Parliamentary corruption

Despite Walpole's skillful management of the house of commons and the extent of his corruption, the opposition gradually gained strength. Though the center of the opposition was the Tory party, the bitterest and most brilliant of Walpole's opponents were the Whig leaders, Carteret and Pulteney, who were kept out of the cabinet by the prime minister. They were joined by lesser Whig leaders in like position, and in the closing years of Walpole's régime a small but influential group of younger Whigs joined the opposition on their entry into the house. Though they bought their seats in the house, they posed as the champions of the people against the corrupt administration of Walpole. To the prime minister, who dubbed them the "boy patriots," they gave no little trouble. Among them were George Grenville, later of Stamp Act fame, and William Pitt, than whom the house of commons has probably never known a greater orator. It was a heterogeneous group, but, as Walpole's ascendency alienated one Whig leader after another, it grew constantly in strength. Aside from the Tories it was a factious opposition without fixed principles. Its object was to defeat Walpole, and it seized upon any cause which offered an opportunity to make popular capital.

The opposition

---

[3] Lecky, *History of England*, i, 472.

Walpole's foreign policy

The attack which was finally successful was made on Walpole's foreign policy. After 1722 the ambitious rulers of Spain continued to threaten the peace of Europe from time to time. Walpole succeeded in building up alliances which forced Spain to keep the peace. The central pivot of his policy was a continuation of friendly relations with France. In 1733 this policy was weakened by the formation of the Bourbon family compact, in which the ruling houses of France and Spain agreed to act together to advance their colonial and commercial interests in opposition to those of Great Britain. The compact was secret, and for the time it had no results because France was occupied with a war over the succession to the crown of Poland (1733-1735). In this war Walpole kept Great Britain neutral, much to the displeasure of the king whose Hanoverian interests were involved, and he took the lead in intermediation that brought the war to an end and restored the peace of Europe. Subsequently he strove for peaceful relations with France and Spain, even though he seems to have learned of the family compact.

Grievances against Spain

Walpole's policy with regard to Spain ultimately gave the opposition its opportunity. Against Spain many Englishmen felt that they had grievances of a commercial nature. Spain preserved a monopoly of the trade with her American colonies, but by the Treaty of Utrecht she had allowed Great Britain to break this monopoly at two points. Great Britain was allowed to supply the Spanish colonists with slaves and once a year to import such other commodities as could be freighted in a ship of 620 tons burden. These rights had been conferred on the South Sea Company, which abused its privileges by importing goods in excess of the amount allowed. Private British traders, moreover, were smuggling large amounts of goods into the Spanish main. To defend herself against this invasion of her rights Spain licensed patrol ships (*garda costas*), which searched British ships found in Spanish waters, seizing them if evidence of illicit trade appeared. That the Spaniards had this right was undisputed, but the British complained of the way it was used. Several British ships not engaged in smuggling were condemned, some of their crews were maltreated, and sometimes the *garda costas* searched British ships on the high seas. Though these were real grievances, the Spanish had a bigger one. The British government made no attempt to stop the smuggling by her nationals, as did the governments of other maritime countries such as France and the Netherlands. The British public took no account of the Spanish side of the case but saw only the British grievances.

The attempt of the British government to secure redress began in 1731, when the tale of Jenkins's ear came to England. Jenkins was an English trader who asserted that a Spanish pirate had captured him and cut off his ear. The story stirred so much public sentiment in England that the government sought satisfaction from Spain for that and other grievances. The negotiations brought no results, and in 1738 the opposition seized on this question for an attack upon Walpole. It staged a debate in which the keynote was the obligation of Great Britain to uphold British mercantile interests and to avenge the sufferings inflicted on British seamen by Spaniards. Various seamen were examined before the bar of the house of commons, and their assertions of Spanish atrocities were spread broadcast. Friend Jenkins was reported to have brought his severed ear in a box for the house to inspect. When asked by a member to relate his experience, he supplied a popular catchword in the phrase, "I recommended my soul to God and my cause to my country." So much influence did his narrative exert on public opinion that a contemporary writer alludes to "Spanish depredations on our estates, persons, and ears."

Jenkins's ear

The jingo tactics of the opposition fell on fertile soil. The influential commercial interest had already aroused a strong feeling against Spain. Stories of British sailors tortured by the inquisition, confined in chains in prisons crawling with vermin, or worked to death as slaves, did the rest. The martial fervor ran high. Walpole's attempt to settle the differences by negotiations did not please the opposition, which represented him as wielding the pen when he should have drawn the sword. In 1739 Walpole, against his better judgment, yielded to the popular clamor and declared war on Spain.

The outbreak of war put Walpole in a false position. Since he opposed the war it was naturally thought that he would not be a good leader. He wanted to resign, but remained at the request of the king. He felt free to do so because he still had a majority in the house. In 1739 the war went well. A British fleet captured Porto Bello in the West Indies. But in the next year all went wrong. Naval expeditions to the West Indies were ineffective. What was worse, the war with Spain threatened to become merged in a European conflict which arose over the succession to the Austrian dominions. The accession of Maria Theresa, who was the first woman to inherit the lands of the Austrian Habsburgs, rendered Austria weak. Frederick the Great of Prussia, seizing the opportunity to aggrandize his possessions, claimed the province of Silesia and invaded it. France, hoping to dis-

Downfall of Walpole

member its old rival, allied with Prussia and invaded Austria. Popular sentiment in England appeared to favor the traditional policy of an alliance with Austria against France and Spain, but George II, fearing for Hanover, declared its neutrality for a year, placing a stumbling block in the way of negotiations. The old cry went up that Great Britain was being subordinated to Hanover. The elections of 1741 went against Walpole, leaving his majority so small and unstable that he resigned early in 1742.

The War of the Austrian Succession

Meanwhile Great Britain had practically become one of the allies against France, though formal declaration of war was not issued until 1744. In 1743, an army, consisting mainly of British and Hanoverian troops under the leadership of George II, won the battle of Dettingen against the French. Two years later, under command of the king's son, it lost the battle of Fontenoy in Flanders. Concurrently Charles Edward, the grandson of James II, came to Scotland. With the support of a few highlanders, he began a rebellion to obtain the English throne. He won a slight victory, but the English did not come to his aid, and in 1746 he was decisively defeated at Culloden. Subsequently Great Britain won some naval victories, but the war as a whole was now dragging along indecisively. The allies on both sides had conflicting interests, there were no common objectives, and general aimlessness was the result. By 1748 all parties were so weary of the fruitless struggle that peace was made at Aix-la-Chapelle. A return to the status before the war was the general principle of the peace. Great Britain accordingly gave up Louisburg, a strong French fortification in America which the American colonists had captured, and received back Madras, which had been lost to the French in India. The right of Spanish search, which had brought Great Britain into the war originally, was not mentioned. The principal exception to the general rule was the retention of Silesia by Frederick of Prussia. This exception helped to breed another European war in the near future.

The cabinet, 1742–1754

When Walpole resigned, the leadership of the cabinet went to Carteret,[4] who had been in the opposition. He brought in a few of the other discontented Whig leaders, but only two or three Tories. Several of Walpole's colleagues remained in the new cabinet. It was still a Whig administration. Not much more than the headship changed. At first his conduct of the war won approval, but in 1743 public opinion became dissatisfied, and in the next year his colleagues, led by Henry Pelham, forced him to resign. The downfall of Carteret

---

[4] Lord Wilmington was the nominal head.

was aided by his failure to manage the majority in the house of commons. Henry Pelham and his brother, the duke of Newcastle, possessed the control that Carteret lacked, largely because the duke was the largest boroughmonger in the kingdom and looked carefully after the distribution of offices and favors to the members of the house.

After the resignation of Carteret, Henry Pelham became the head of the cabinet, retaining the position until his death in 1754. The new prime minister was a follower of Walpole, but the cabinet retained a few Tories and some of the leaders of the Whig opposition. A few of the "boy patriots" were also included, though William Pitt, the ablest of the group, was kept out because of the king's dislike. Pelham shared his power with his brother, the duke of Newcastle. The latter, who was much ridiculed by contemporaries, possessed little administrative capacity; but he was an excellent politician who attended carefully to the maintenance of a majority in the house of commons. Henry Pelham, who framed most of the policies, is thus dismissed by Lecky: "A timid, desponding, and somewhat fretful man, with little energy either of character or intellect, he possessed at least, to a high degree, good sense, industry, knowledge of business, and parliamentary experience; his manners were conciliatory and decorous, and he was content to hold the reins of power very loosely, freely admitting competitors to office, and allowing much divergence of opinion."[5] After the conclusion of the war his administration was quiet and comparatively unimportant.

Before the war closed, however, an incident occurred which displays the strength already attained by the cabinet system. George II did not like the duke of Newcastle, and he detested Lord Chesterfield, who was in the cabinet. In 1746 Pelham suggested some changes in the cabinet, including the admission of Pitt. To George II Pitt was anathema because he had voiced the public opinion that Great Britain was being subordinated to Hanover in the war. The king refused to make any changes, whereupon the cabinet resigned in a body. The king gave the seals to Pulteney (now Lord Bath). He failed to obtain enough colleagues to form a cabinet because it was recognized that, as long as the retiring cabinet controlled the majority in the house of commons, no other cabinet could get support. Pulteney's failure compelled the king to accept Pelham's terms, though he did succeed in relegating Pitt to the ministry and keeping him out of the cabinet. Evidently, when the cabinet chose to exert the power,

---

[5] *History of England,* i, 446.

it could force the king to accept its policies if it controlled a majority in the house of commons.

In 1754 the death of Henry Pelham left the leadership of the cabinet to the weak and incompetent duke of Newcastle, just as England was drifting into the Seven Years' War. The war grew out of the colonial rivalries of England and France.

In India the French and the British had become keen competitors during the course of the eighteenth century. Previous to 1754 the French had the advantage. Their superiority was due largely to the ability of Dupleix, who came to India as an official of the French East India Company in 1720 and later became its governor. Under his guidance the French began to intervene in native politics in order to extend their own commerce and limit that of the British. The political situation in India favored the policies of Dupleix. In the closing years of the seventeenth century and early years of the eighteenth the great mogul empire, which had been established by a foreign conqueror from the north in the time of Elizabeth, broke up. The mogul still resided at Delhi, the capital of the empire, but many of the states of India which had acknowledged his rule either revolted and became independent, or acquired independence while still acknowledging a nominal allegiance to the mogul.[6] The sudden acquisition of liberty was followed by many petty wars among the native states over boundaries, successions, and kindred causes of dispute. Both the British and the French intervened in these quarrels. Dupleix at first was the more successful. By assisting one side or the other he acquired friends and allies among the native rulers, extended the influence of the French, and curtailed that of the British. After the treaty of Aix-la-Chapelle compelled him to return Madras, which he had conquered from the British during the War of the Austrian Succession, he strove to drive the British from Madras through his influence with the natives. He nearly succeeded when he established as the nabob of the Carnatic, the native state in which Madras was located, a native claimant who was friendly to the French and hostile to the British. This threat to Madras finally roused the representatives of the British company to resist. Led by Robert Clive, a clerk who abandoned the ledger for the sword with phenomenal success, the British seized the capital of the Carnatic, held it against the French, and restored the native rival of the claimant supported by Dupleix. Thereafter French prestige rapidly declined among the natives of southern India. In 1754 Dupleix was

---

[6] See map below, p. 682.

recalled because his costly policies, which were not appreciated at home, were not bringing immediate returns in trade. Hostilities between the French and the British being thus suspended, a provisional treaty was arranged, though it had not been ratified when the Seven Years' War was declared in 1756.

Meanwhile the rivalries of French and British colonists on the other side of the world had reached proportions that were destined to involve the mother countries in hostilities. Rival claims to the basin of the Ohio became the immediate occasion of the friction. From the first the methods of colonization followed by the English and the French had been different. The English settled on the seaboard in comparatively compact groups. During the seventeenth century they were content to remain east of the Appalachians, where they established themselves on a solid agricultural foundation. The French entered by way of the St. Lawrence. Without pausing to build colonies on an enduring basis, they followed the waterways into the interior. During the seventeenth century explorers, fur traders, and missionaries pushed along the lakes and down various rivers that flowed into the Ohio and the Mississippi. By 1750 the French were settled along the St. Lawrence and in Louisiana, while their trading posts, missions, and forts dotted the map here and there in the region of the Great Lakes and in the basins of the Ohio and the Mississippi. During the first half of the eighteenth century British fur traders began to penetrate the region of the Ohio, diverting some of the Indian trade from the French; but before 1750 the British had done little to occupy the district, though the old claims were still maintained that the colonies on the coast included all the lands to the west.

English and French in America

The chain of events in the contest for possession of the valley of the Ohio which led immediately to the outbreak of war began in 1749. In that year the governor of Canada sent an agent to make formal claim to the Allegheny and Ohio territory for France. In the same year the king of Great Britain chartered the Ohio Company, giving it 200,000 acres on the Ohio. In the next year the company despatched an agent to explore the grant with a view to settlement. This active policy on both sides soon produced a clash. In 1752 the Canadian governor sent an expedition to build forts along the route from Lake Erie to the Mississippi by way of the Ohio. The governor of Virginia thereupon sent George Washington with a written protest, warning the French to keep off British territory. He was politely received and courteously disregarded. Meanwhile the governments at London and Paris encouraged their colonial representatives to uphold

Armed hostilities in the Ohio region

their respective claims. In 1754 the governor of Virginia sent Washington to build a fort at the fork where the Allegheny and the Monongahela unite to form the Ohio. He found the French already in possession. After two engagements, he surrendered and retired. Open war had begun in the colonies.

When the news of these events reached England, the duke of Newcastle vacillated. While he made half-hearted preparations for war, he apparently tried to make himself and others believe that war could be avoided. In 1755 he sent a British fleet to intercept French transports bearing troops to Canada. The fleet committed an act of war by the capture of two French ships, but allowed the greater part of the transports to escape. In the same year he sent General Braddock with two regiments of British troops to drive the French from the Ohio, and Braddock with his army was destroyed by the French and their Indian allies. Though war had not yet been declared between France and Great Britain, these events made such a war so nearly inevitable that the duke began to cast about for allies. Advances to Austria did not meet with a favorable response. Since George II was anxious to protect Hanover against France, an alliance was concluded with Frederick of Prussia early in 1756. Austria had long been waiting for an opportunity to recover Silesia and already had an alliance with Russia designed to serve that purpose. Austria had also sought the alliance of France. When Prussia deserted the French alliance for the British, France reversed the policy of centuries and formed an alliance with Austria. Thus in 1756 Europe divided into two armed camps and the Seven Years' War began.

For the first two years the war went almost uniformly against Great Britain. In America Oswego was lost to the French in 1756. In the next year British plans of campaign failed through the inability and sluggishness of the commanders. The commander of a British fleet of seventeen ships declined to attack a French fleet which had eighteen ships and a greater weight of metal. From India came the news of the Black Hole. In 1756 the native ruler of Bengal, Surajah Dowlah, attacked and captured the British post of Calcutta. The one hundred and forty-six survivors were confined over night in a small room with insufficient ventilation, where all but twenty-three suffocated or were trampled to death before morning. On the continent Great Britain lost Minorca (1756) through the failure of the navy to cooperate with the defenders. The French defeat of the Hanoverian army, led by the son of George II, was followed by the disbandment of the army and the occupation of Hanoverian possessions by the

Outbreak of war in Europe

The war, 1756–1757

NORTH AMERCA
1754

British Territory
French Territory
Spanish Territory
Hudson Bay Co's Territory

French (1757). Prussia, Great Britain's ally, was in no better plight. This little state, with a population of 5,000,000, was pitted against Russia, Austria, and France, with a combined population of 90,000,000. In 1756 Frederick won notable victories, but in the next year he lost hard-fought battles both to Austria and to Russia.

The news of these disasters threw the nation into a state of despair. The incompetence of the government and the inefficiency of the commanders of the armed forces were all too apparent. So hopeless appeared the case that Englishmen nearly lost faith in their cause. Chesterfield, who was thoroughly conversant with affairs abroad, wrote: "Whoever is in, or whoever is out, I am sure we are undone both at home and abroad. At home by our increasing debt and expenses; abroad, by our ill-luck and incapacity. . . . We are no longer a nation. I never yet saw so dreadful a prospect." Pitt wrote: "The day is come, when the very inadequate benefits of the Treaty of Utrecht, the indelible reproach of the last generation, are become the necessary but almost unattainable wish of the present, when the empire is no more, the ports of the Netherlands betrayed, the Dutch Barrier Treaty an empty sound, Minorca, and with it the Mediterranean, lost, and America itself precarious."[7] Horace Walpole felt it was time "for England to slip her own cables, and float away into some unknown ocean."[8]

This state of public opinion forced the king to bring Pitt into the cabinet and give to him the conduct of the war. The people had long wanted the Great Commoner, but the king's antipathy was so strong that he would not accept Pitt until no other alternative was possible. In 1754, when Pelham's death made Newcastle prime minister, he needed a member of the cabinet who could lead the debates of the house of commons, since he belonged to the upper chamber. Henry Fox and William Pitt were such influential speakers in the house of commons that only one or the other could manage the majority. Newcastle offered a place to Fox on terms he would not accept; Pitt was ignored because of the prejudice of the king. The leader picked by Newcastle was unable to lead, and Fox and Pitt united in baiting him. Thus the Whig house was divided when the war began in America. The obvious solution was to give office to both, but the duke feared to admit them on an equality with himself lest he should be overshadowed. The latter would come on no other terms; the former was finally persuaded. Pitt, left alone to maintain the attack on New-

Marginal notes: English public opinion

Reorganization of the cabinet

---

[7] Both citations from Lecky, *History of England*, ii, 531, 532.
[8] *Letters*, iv, 92.

castle, decided to supersede him. During 1756 he assailed the weak policies of the cabinet with inconsistency but with telling effect. Though his attacks did not affect the votes of the house of commons, they put their author forward as the man in whom the country believed. As the news of one defeat after another arrived, the public distrust of the cabinet grew. Fox, refusing to face the music, resigned. Left without a leader who could control the house, Newcastle necessarily turned to Pitt. He refused to serve with the duke. Yielding to necessity Newcastle resigned, and the king finally consented to the formation of a cabinet in which Pitt had the real power though not the nominal headship. This was in entire accord with public opinion, but in those days of political corruption the votes of the house of commons did not reflect popular sentiment. Newcastle still controlled enough votes to block Pitt. The king, who fretted under Pitt's control, finally took affairs into his own hands and dismissed the cabinet. There ensued eleven weeks of negotiations in 1757, while Great Britain remained headless in the midst of war. Eventually the king found that Pitt was too strongly intrenched in popular esteem to be omitted. Since the popular statesman was not strong enough in the house of commons to act alone, the king, after exhausting every expedient to keep him out, called upon him and Newcastle to act together. The alliance was made on a basis which enabled Pitt to say without much exaggeration: "I borrow the Duke of Newcastle's majority to carry on the public business." In the new cabinet Pitt was practically a dictator with regard to the conduct of the war.

William Pitt

William Pitt came to power without rank, fortune, or important political or social connections. This in itself was an extraordinary accomplishment in the political arena of that day. Though he soon won attention by his powerful oratory, he refused to travel the accustomed road to office. He kept himself free from any taint of corruption when political morality was at a low ebb. From the first he opposed Walpole and the Whig machine. He often made himself the mouthpiece of the unrepresented masses, carrying his championship on occasion to the point of demagogy. This gave him the confidence of the nation, but it did not win him friends in a house composed largely of the representatives of rotten boroughs. In the house his influence was based almost entirely on his oratory, which moved his hearers profoundly. He was so great a master of invective that few cared to oppose him in debate. Because he was too proud, dictatorial, and reserved to manage a party, he needed Newcastle to keep the votes in line. Nor did his weaknesses end here. He was a born actor, even in daily intercourse with friends studying the effect of pose and gesture to the point of affectation. His self-confidence was so great as to amount to egotism. He was at times supercilious, passionate, irritable, and inconsistent. In his long career before and after the Seven Years' War he accomplished comparatively little. But in 1757 he was the right man in the right place. He was actuated by a lofty, fiery patriotism, and he had the rare power of inspiring his hearers and his subordinates with the same spirit. His genius turned the tide of defeat and made the war one of the most glorious fought by Great Britain during the eighteenth century. He was a great war minister.

Pitt promptly set to work to rouse the nation and to direct its energies. He completely reorganized the service. He recalled the commanders whose incapacity had been demonstrated, disregarded the custom of promotion by seniority, and picked young officers of ability, like Howe and Wolfe, for places of responsibility. The troops were reorganized and strengthened and immense supplies provided. Throughout the service energy, efficiency, and enthusiasm reigned.

Pitt's reorganization

The campaigns Pitt himself planned in broad outline. His great aim was to break France through her colonial empire. America naturally became the chief object of his attention, and here he even gave instructions concerning the details of expeditions. His general plan was to break the long line from the St. Lawrence to the Mississippi, which the French had to hold in order to confine the British colonists to the seaboard, and then to converge on the center of French power in Canada. In India he left the plans to the genius of Clive, taking care only to send a fleet to prevent French reinforcements from reaching India. On the sea two British fleets were detailed to guard the French Atlantic and Mediterranean squadrons, while other expeditions were sent against French colonies in the West Indies and in Africa. On the continent, Pitt, repudiating all his former utterances, helped Frederick to the utmost, saying that he would win America in Germany. He paid Frederick subsidies large for that day. The Hanoverian army was reorganized, strengthened by the addition of British troops, and set to work to keep France too busy on the Rhine to permit the junction of French troops with the Austrian and the Russian against Frederick. While France was kept busy on land, Pitt sought the opportunity to crush her colonial and naval power.

Pitt's reorganization, which took place in the last half of 1757, resulted in successful campaigns during the next two years. All over the world, on land and sea, British arms turned back the tide of defeat and won magnificent victories. So greatly did the story change

The tide of victory

that Horace Walpole wrote: "One is forced to ask every morning what victory there is, for fear of missing one."[9]

In America in 1758 the fortress of Louisburg, which guarded the entrance to the St. Lawrence, was taken, and the line was broken by the capture of forts Duquesne (Pittsburgh) and Oswego. In the next year three expeditions were planned to converge on Quebec. One was to take Niagara and come down the St. Lawrence, another to take Ticonderoga and reach Quebec by the same route, while Wolfe was to come up the river. The first two expeditions took their immediate objectives but were prevented by the difficulties of the terrain from reaching Quebec. Wolfe alone, by the magnificent feat of daring that cost him his life and won him undying fame, captured the fortress. After the fall of Quebec, Montreal was helpless. In 1760 it, and with it Canada, passed to the possession of the British.

In India Clive went to Bengal to deal with Surajah Dowlah. In 1757 at Plassey, with an army of 3,000, of which two-thirds consisted of sepoys (natives trained in European modes of warfare), he defeated an army of 50,000 led by Surajah, restoring English prestige in the north. In the south the French were hard pressed. The new governor had lost many of the native alliances established by Dupleix, and he was short of arms, food, and money. In 1759 the French fleet was driven from Indian waters by a British squadron, leaving the French in India to their fate. In 1760 the British defeated them at Wandewash, and in 1761 Pondicherry, the principal French factory in India, surrendered. With its fall French dominion in India came to an end.

On the continent Frederick was fighting the bloodiest battles of the war against tremendous odds. During 1757 and part of 1758 he won some victories. Thereafter he suffered crushing defeats. Only the genius of Frederick and the failure of his enemies to cooperate to the best advantage saved his armies from annihilation. In 1760 he had a slight measure of success, but at the end of the year he was still in a desperate plight, with his armies depleted and his money gone. The combined Hanoverian and British army meanwhile had twice defeated the French and in 1760 were still holding the French armies on the Rhine.

On the sea the fleets took some of the French colonies in the West Indies and trading posts in Africa, and captured many warships, privateers, and merchantmen. In 1759 they defeated the French Mediterranean fleet off Lagos and the Atlantic fleet in Quiberon Bay. By

---

[9] *Ibid.*, iv, 33c.

1760 nine-tenths of the French navy had been captured or destroyed. In that year, when George II died, Pitt had France completely at his mercy.

When it came to the negotiation of peace, however, Pitt was at a disadvantage. Though Great Britain could win little more from **Pitt's** France, Frederick, whom the minister had pledged himself not to **downfall** sacrifice, was in a bad position. The French, the Austrians, and the Russians each occupied parts of Prussian territory, and to keep Prussia intact Pitt would have had to yield some of the British gains. Hence he continued the war primarily to aid Prussia. This policy gradually became so unpopular in England that in 1761 he held conversations with France concerning peace. When France demanded the redress of several grievances of Spain, negotiations fell through. Up to 1759 Spain had remained neutral, but a change of sovereigns in that year was followed by a reversal of the Spanish policy. The interjection of Spanish demands into negotiations between France and Great Britain made it clear to Pitt that a dangerous intimacy existed between France and Spain, and a few months later he learned that an agreement existed between the two countries, though he was ignorant of its terms. As a matter of fact, it was the third family compact by which Spain agreed to declare war on Great Britain in 1762 if peace had not been made before then. Pitt felt confident enough of Spain's hostile intent to demand of his colleagues in the cabinet a declaration of war against Spain. His colleagues refused to support him. Some were jealous of his great power, others doubted the expediency of the policy, and others were influenced by the new king, who wished to recover the power which the king had lost to the cabinet under his two immediate predecessors, and sought the elimination of the influential director of the war as the first step in breaking the power of the cabinet. Pitt resigned.

While Pitt had been negotiating, he had continued to prosecute the war vigorously. He had also prepared for the anticipated war with **Peace of** Spain. A few months later it became so evident that Spain planned **Paris** to enter the war that the cabinet, now led by Lord Bute, the former tutor and the personal friend of George III, declared war. Pitt's plans were carried out. In 1762 Havana was taken from Spain in the West Indies, and Manila in the Philippines. In the same year Frederick's fortunes, which had continued adverse during 1761, were reversed. A change of rulers resulted in the withdrawal of Russia from the war. Frederick was able to defeat an unaided Austria. Under these conditions Bute found it easy to negotiate the Peace of Paris, which was concluded in 1763.

The treaties gave Great Britain much less than she might have obtained had she pushed her advantages. Bute was so anxious to conclude peace quickly, in order to promote the political projects of George III at home, that he made no attempt to stand out for the most that Great Britain could get. Nevertheless, the peace was a glorious one for the British. In America Great Britain secured Canada and undisputed possession of the continent as far west as the Mississippi. From Spain she received Florida in exchange for Havana, Spain being compensated by the receipt of Louisiana from France. In the West Indies four of the islands which Great Britain had captured from France, including the most important, were returned and the rest were retained. France was also allowed to fish off Newfoundland and given the islands of S. Pierre and Miquelon where the fish could be cured. Except for these few islands the French empire in the west was ended. In India the conquests made since 1749 were mutually restored, but France was forbidden to erect fortifications in Bengal. In Africa Great Britain kept one of the French posts on the coast of Guinea and restored the other. In Europe Great Britain recovered Minorca. France came out of the war bankrupt and deprived of her empire and her navy. The peace left Great Britain the foremost colonial power in the world.

ABBREVIATED GENEALOGY OF THE HOUSES OF HANOVER
AND SAXE-COBURG AND GOTHA (WINDSOR SINCE 1917)

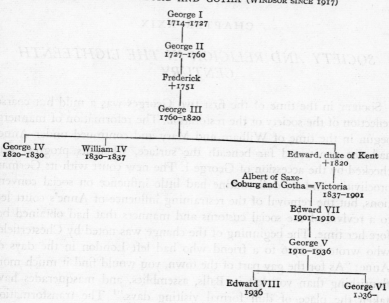

George I
1714–1727

George II
1727–1760

Frederick
+1751

George III
1760–1820

George IV   William IV   Edward, duke of Kent
1820–1830   1830–1837   +1820

                Albert of Saxe-
            Coburg and Gotha = Victoria
                                1837–1901

                    Edward VII
                    1901–1910

                     George V
                    1910–1936

            Edward VIII   George VI
              1936   1936–

CHAPTER XXIX

SOCIETY AND RELIGION IN THE EIGHTEENTH CENTURY

Social
development

SOCIETY in the time of the first two Georges was a mild but coarse reflection of the society of the restoration. The reformation of manners, begun in the time of William and Mary and continued under Anne, had not penetrated far beneath the surface, when its progress was checked by the accession of George I. The new court with its German proclivities and its dull routine had little influence on social conventions, but the removal of the restraining influence of Anne's court led to a revival of the social customs and manners that had obtained before her time. The beginning of the change was noted by Chesterfield, who wrote in 1716 to a friend who had left London in the days of Anne: "As for the gay part of the town, you would find it much more flourishing than you left it. Balls, assemblies, and masquerades have taken the place of dull formal visiting days."[1] The transformation was rapidly consummated. English society became in many ways brilliant and fascinating, but, judged by modern conventions, it was in many aspects coarse and vulgar, and in some of its standards immoral. The court of George II tended to promote these characteristics. George III, who had a fine sense of social rectitude, made the royal court a place of greater social decorum and higher moral standards. Its influence on the middle class was marked, but it was near the close of the eighteenth century before the leaders of fashion began to affect careless simplicity in dress, to frown on coarse language, and to regard such things as gambling and excessive drinking as bad form. The social life of the epoch of the first two Georges consequently is typical of the greater part of the eighteenth century.

Social
strata:
The
gentle-
men

In the eighteenth century society was still divided into fairly well-defined classes. The class which looms largest in the world of fashion was composed of gentlemen. In the eighteenth century the term did not have its present connotation. A man was born a gentleman. Without the accident of birth no amount of good breeding could make a gentleman, while the most boorish country lout was a gentleman if he had been born such. "Our modern Acceptation of a *Gentleman*

---

[1] Chesterfield, *Letters,* ed. Mahon, iii, 12.

then," says Defoe, "and that in spite of defeated Reasoning, is this, A person BORN (for there lies the Essence of Quality) of some known, or Ancient Family; whose Ancestors have at least for some time been rais'd above the Class of Mechanicks."[2]

The gulf between the gentlemen and other orders of society was still wide. Throughout the literature of the period this distinction of class appears as the accepted order of things. Gentlemen of assured birth expected and generally received from other classes that sort of treatment which superiors often demand of those whom they regard as inferiors. Those with riches newly acquired, who had not yet proved their superiority by having a sufficiently long line of ancestors acknowledged as gentlemen, attempted to secure deferential treatment from poorer classes in ways that provided the novelists, Fielding and Smollet, with opportunity for the exercise of some of their choicest bits of humor.

The gentlemen were of various degrees and gradations. At the top were the various ranks of the nobility. More numerous were the gentry. They consisted of those who had reasonably large incomes from landed estates, and of their descendants. It made a vast difference whence the income was derived. The merchant with ever so large an income and ever so good manners was not a gentleman. On the other hand, many gentlemen had slender incomes. To maintain the income of landed estates it was necessary to observe the rule of primogeniture; otherwise the basis for the proper distinction of a gentleman would soon have disappeared. But the younger sons, though they inherited no estates, were received into the society of gentlemen as long as they did not demean themselves by working for a living. The clergy, the army, and the navy were open to them, and so long as they remained within one of these professions, they could drink themselves to death at the best clubs in town.[3] In the lower ranks were many who were in a transitional stage between the middle class and the ranks of the gentlemen. A wealthy merchant, for example, might retire and buy estates. If he asserted his right to the title of gentleman with sufficient persistency, his grandson might win an acknowledged place in the ranks. The class of gentlemen was by no means a closed corporation, and wealth now opened fairly easily back doors into the august assemblage.

Another fairly distinct social group consisted of the merchants. The

---

[2] *Compleat English Gentleman*, p. 13.

[3] An old gentleman, telling his recollections in 1814, said that formerly "there were a thousand clubs for one now, and almost all drunken." Broughton, *Recollections*, i, 101.

The
middle
class

accumulation of large fortunes in business was becoming common, and the moneyed class was coming to have so much political influence that the old stigma on trade was beginning to break down. A foreign observer records that "in England commerce is not looked down upon as being derogatory, as it is in France and Germany. Here men of good family and even of rank may become merchants without losing caste."[4] Younger sons occasionally went into trade to revive the family fortunes, and the marriage of a "city fortune" was looked upon with complacency. The older view that classed all tradesmen as mechanics still produced many Will Wimbles "bred to no business and born to no estate," but the social prejudice against wealth acquired in business was decreasing in the eighteenth century. The importance of this group in the social structure is well attested by Burnet. "As for the men of trade and business," he says, "they are, generally speaking, the best body in the nation, generous, sober, and charitable: so that, while the people in the country are so immersed in their affairs, that the sense of religion cannot reach them, there is a better spirit stirring in our cities; more knowledge, more zeal, and more charity, with a great deal more of devotion. There may be too much of vanity, with too pompous an exterior, mixed with these in the capital city; but upon the whole, they are the best we have."[5]

The men who followed business or professions in the towns constituted the most influential element in the middle class. Of corresponding social status in the country were the yeomen. During the first half of the century they formed a significant social class. Though they generally traveled little and were often ignorant of affairs falling outside the narrow orbit of their own experience, they displayed a high degree of practical intelligence and they gave to rural society a wholesome spirit of sturdy independence. During the course of the century their numbers suffered a marked decline. By the end of the century they had largely given place to farmers who worked their lands as the tenants of great landowners.

The
laborers

The remainder of the population, which constituted the largest part, consisted mainly of the artisans in the towns and the rural wage earners. Until late in the eighteenth century, when the industrial revolution affected the modes of life of many of them profoundly, their economic and social position in the community did not change notably from what it had been in the closing years of the seventeenth

---

[4] de Saussure, *Foreign View of England*, p. 215.
[5] *History of His Own Time*, vi, 215.

century. They impressed a foreign observer as efficient and generally prosperous in comparison with the same classes across the Channel.

The royal court of the eighteenth century which probably was most in harmony with the prevailing manners and morals of the times was that of George II. While still prince of Wales he quarreled with his father and set up a separate establishment. Because his father's court was Hanoverian, the prince took pains to make his distinctively English. When he became king his court was consequently more typical and more influential socially. The personalities of the three chief figures at the court give an index to its character. The court of George II

George II possessed several bad qualities and a few good ones. He was not quite as phlegmatic as his father, and he could entertain the strongest likes and dislikes. He appears to have been a fussy, pompous, irascible little man, who suspected that he had no great ability but sought to make others think that he had. He possessed great personal courage, and his standards of veracity and honor were higher than those generally current. He was assiduous about business, but worked on the details rather than on the main substance. He was methodical with a mechanical regularity which drove those about him almost to distraction. His finer emotions were blunted, and as he had quarreled with his father, so he quarreled with his son. George II

The queen, Caroline of Anspach, had the greater ability of the two. She had a speculative temperament and keen intellectual curiosity, but her training had been superficial, and, as the king did not like to read or to have her read, she found little opportunity either to cultivate her own intellectual interests, or to patronize and reward the genius of others. Caroline had a firm grasp of political affairs, and her greatest ambition was to rule the king. In this she succeeded at the cost of much personal unhappiness. She had to devote herself to the king's whims and pleasures. He spent with her several hours every day, and, though he snubbed and scolded her outrageously, he seems to have cared more for her than for any other person. The queen spent hours in his society when she would have preferred to be with her books, humored his caprices, accepted his snubs, and joked him about his mistresses for the sake of power. She controlled the king, and Walpole and the court knew it. The king also knew it, but he appeared to think no one else did. Queen Caroline

Walpole was as coarse-grained in social intercourse as he was in political life. "That he lived for many years in open adultery, and indulged to excess in pleasures of the table, were facts which in the early part of the eighteenth century were in themselves not likely to Walpole excite much attention; but his boisterous revelries at Houghton exceeded even the ordinary license of the country squires of his time, and the gross sensuality of his conversation was conspicuous in one of the coarsest periods of English history. When he did not talk of business, it was said, he talked of women; politics and obscenity were his tastes."[6]

Coarseness
of the
court

The court in which three people of this stamp were the leading figures was not a place where refined tastes and manners reigned. Queen Caroline, despite her intellectual tendencies, set the pace in coarseness. The duchess of Marlborough, writing after the queen's death, characterized her conversation in the drawing-room as "generally very improper discourse for a public room."[7] Common sense was the prime qualification for popularity at the court of George II. Sentimentality and affectedness were so out of fashion that frankness was cultivated to a point which the present generation would deem vulgar, coarse, and indecent. "The world improves in one virtue to a violent degree," says Lady Mary Montagu, fresh from an evening at court, "I mean plain-dealing. Hypocrisy being, as the Scripture declares, a damnable sin, I hope our publicans and sinners will be saved by the open profession of the contrary virtue. I was told by a very good author, who is deep in the secret, that at this very minute there is a bill cooking-up at a hunting-seat in Norfolk [i.e., Walpole's] to have *not* taken out of the commandments and clapped into the creed. . . . Honour, virtue, reputation, etc., which we used to hear of in our nursery, is as much laid aside and forgotten as a crumpled riband."[8] When the trend of fashionable life in town was in this direction, such a court served merely to give it greater momentum.

Coffee-
houses

The life of a gentleman of leisure about town was largely a round of pleasure. His day was likely to begin with a walk in the park, where he could join the parade of fashionable society. Thence he might proceed to a coffee-house, "for 'tis a rule with the English to go once a day at least to houses of this sort."[9] These had become in London a social institution. The introduction of coffee, chocolate, and tea as common beverages had led to the establishment of the first coffee-house near the middle of the seventeenth century. Coffee-houses rapidly became centers for the discussion of news. The coffee-house kept copies of current newspapers, and many patrons attended merely

---

[6] Lecky, *History of England*, i, 394, 395.
[7] Cited in Traill, *Social England*, v, 138.
[8] *Letters and Works of Lady Mary Wortley Montagu*, i, 350.
[9] Baron de Pöllnitz, cited by Thackeray, *Four Georges*.

to read the latest news. They naturally became centers of political discussion, and particular houses became associated with habitual groups. The literary men and the wits could be found at certain houses, others were the resorts of politicians, while others attracted the dandies. Early in the eighteenth century a contemporary estimated the number in London at 3,000, and they long continued to be centers of "news, politics and fashion."

Of the time left on his hands some would probably be spent at cards. The spirit of gambling was rife among all classes, and in polite society both men and women were much addicted to it. "The English at this time," says Fielding, "were so addicted to gaming that several of the great men used to make it the sole business of their lives; and not only the messrs. but also their dames used to spend whole days and nights at their cards."[10] In the early years of the reign of George III "society . . . was one vast casino. On whatever pretext, and under whatever circumstances, half a dozen people of fashion found themselves together . . . the box was sure to be rattling, and the cards were being cut and shuffled."[11]

Gambling

In the evening our friend might go to the theater, the opera, or a masquerade. The stage was no longer as popular or as immoral as it had been, but popular taste was still coarse, and the plays were for the most part on a low literary and moral plane. In the fashionable world the opera was more popular than the play. The Italian opera had been introduced in the reign of Anne, and in the time of the first two Georges it was maintained by several famous Italian singers and by the musician, Handel, whose greatest contribution was made in the field of sacred music. At the opera the man about town could come into contact with real art, though it was not a native product. The most immoral place where he could spend the evening was the masquerade. Introduced in the reign of George I, "the masquerade soon became more than a figurative leveller of society; for sharpers, and women of ill-repute, and others, gained admission, and the consequence was nightly scenes of robbery, and quarrels, and scandalous licentiousness. The general agreement of contemporary writers on this subject can leave no doubt on our minds of the evil effects of masquerades on the morality of the day."[12]

Theaters, operas, and masquerades

Wherever the gentleman spent his evening, he would probably bring home a considerable load of liquor. Heavy drinking was nearly a

[10] Paraphrased from Fielding, *Covent Garden Journal*, no. 17.
[11] Trevelyan, *Early History of Charles James Fox*, p. 77.
[12] Wright, *Caricature History of the Georges*, p. 68.

Drinking universal vice. "Debauch runs riot with an unblushing countenance" is the dictum of a foreign observer. "It is not the lower populace alone that is addicted to drunkenness; numbers of persons of high rank and even of distinction are over fond of liquor."[13] To provide plenty of drinkables was an essential part of any host's duty. "Can there be any thing more barbarous," wails Burnet, "or rather treacherous, than for gentlemen to think it is one of the honours of their houses, that none must go out of them sober."[14] "No one can study the public or personal history of the eighteenth century without being impressed by the truly immense space which drinking occupied in the mental horizon of the young, and the consequences of drinking in that of the old."[15]

Life in town To imply that such was the daily life of the majority of the town dwellers would probably be a gross exaggeration. "Civil and sober gentlemen" were common enough even in London, but coarse and vicious tastes prevailed in fashionable society, and were common in other social sets. Social conventions were so lax that excesses did not place one outside the pale; rather they gave, in some sets at least, a certain kind of social distinction. Swearing, vulgarity, drinking, and gambling, moreover, were sufficiently common to give the tone to society. Few of those who avoided such conduct themselves criticized it in others, for to appear priggish was a sure road to Coventry when hard common sense ruled all.

Country gentlemen Of country gentlemen there were many types. Sir Roger de Coverley is an ideal rather than a type, but there were Squire Allworthys, beloved of their tenants, who were kind and thoughtful friends, neighbors, and landlords. But the Squire Westerns, ignorant and hard-drinking, interested only in their horses and their dogs, appear to have been a large company. Such a country gentleman, as described by Defoe, "enjoys his espous'd brutallity, hunts, hawkes, shootes, and follows his game, hallows to his dogs, dams his servants, dotes upon his horses, drinks with his huntsman, and is excellent company for two or three drunken elder brothers in his neighbourhood; and as here is his felicity, so here is the utmost of his accomplishments."[16] Lady Mary writes peevishly of her life in the country: "The consequence of which is, the poor female part of their family being seldom permitted a coach, . . . their lords and masters having no occasion

---

[13] de Saussure, *Foreign View*, p. 191.
[14] *History of His Own Time*, vi, 212.
[15] Trevelyan, *Early History of Charles James Fox*, p. 83.
[16] *Compleat English Gentleman*, p. 39.

for such a machine, as their mornings are spent among hounds, and the nights with as beastly companions, with what liquor they can get in this country."[17] The observation of a foreigner corroborates these harsh English judgments. "A great number of these gentry," says de Saussure, "have neither the manners nor the politeness which real gentlemen are supposed to possess, and their education is often very limited. Debauch and hunting form their principal occupations. Naturally there are several noted exceptions to this rule. I know of some men who have travelled, and of others who take a particular interest in science and literature, but they are certainly in the minority."[18] The manners and the habits of the country squires differed from those of their town brethren, but their morals were evidently about the same.

Of the lives of the laborers, as is ever the case, contemporary literature tells us far less. It was with them an age of material comfort,[19] but their manners and their morals were largely influenced by those of their social superiors. Their amusements and their vices were merely a degree coarser. They were no longer contented with the beer that had long been the national drink, but sought more violent spirits. "Drunk for 1 d.; dead drunk for 2 d.; straw for nothing" was the sign which appeared over a gin shop in 1736.[20] The city populace is usually described as brutal and insolent. "The populace," says de Saussure, ". . . has no education and no fear of God. I am even persuaded that many of this class never go to church, and have no notion of religion, and are addicted to all manner of debauch. I am speaking of London; in the country it is different."[21]

The commonalty

The hard drinking and the immorality prevailing among the lower orders produced a large amount of lawlessness. In towns a mob could be collected on any pretext, and on any occasion of a public celebration the mob was always likely to take a hand. Robberies were of common occurrence. In London the streets were never safe at night, and in the country highwaymen often operated in the full light of day. If a thief was caught, he was hanged, but that was only a path to glory. The hangings at Tyburn were public spectacles, and those who kicked their last without showing fear won great applause from the London multitude.

Lawlessness

---

[17] *Letters and Works of Lady Mary Wortley Montagu*, i, 30.
[18] *Foreign View*, p. 212.
[19] Burnet, *History of His Own Time*, vi, 205; de Saussure, *Foreign View*, pp. 218–220.
[20] Traill, *Social England*, v, 136.
[21] *Foreign View*, p. 220.

Education

The state of society, as many contemporary observers pointed out, was due in large part to ignorance. So strongly did common sense rule the day that the need of an education was not recognized. The children of the workmen had small chance to acquire an adequate education had they desired it. The state maintained no schools, and the schools supported in part by endowments were inadequate. But those who could afford to pay for the education of their children often neglected it. The merchants of the towns generally availed themselves of the opportunity, but among the gentry an education was often held to be a useless bit of polish. It was all very well for younger sons who must earn a living to attend the university; but the heir, whose chief needs were to know how to hunt and manage an estate, had no need of the brand of learning to be had at Oxford or Cambridge. The heir usually had a tutor at home for a few years, under whose guidance he might learn to read, write, and figure. If his parents were of liberal mind and not hidebound by the general English prejudice that all things foreign were trash, the heir might be sent on the grand tour to travel abroad for two or three years. Sometimes it supplied him with polished manners and generally it provided him with some amount of affectation and with a few new vices.

The clergy

When such was a prevalent view of the value of an education, it is not strange to find that the general note sounded in the literature of the period with regard to the clergy is contempt. In large measure this was merely the natural defense of a corrupt society against the preachers of a moral and an upright life. But the clergy were not without grave faults. Beyond preaching their weekly sermons many clergymen made no attempt to uplift the spiritual life of their parishioners.[22] The great number of underpaid clerical positions, moreover, resulted in the introduction of many men of inferior knowledge and ability into the ranks of the clergy. The richer livings, on the other hand, were frequently given to younger sons, by whom they were often regarded merely as sources of revenue. Such appointments did not tend to win respect for the calling. The profession was not without many good, pious, and able members. In the theological controversies of the day the clergy more than held their own. Nevertheless, the clergy manifestly failed to have any noteworthy effect upon the lax morality of the times.

Church and state

In part this may have been due to the handicap placed upon the church by its relation to the state and to politics. When William III came to the throne the clergy were placed in a difficult position. They

[22] See, for example, the emphatic complaint of Bishop Burnet, *History of His Own Time*, vi, 195.

had generally preached the doctrine of divine right. With William's accession they had to abandon their principle and take the oath of allegiance, or lose their positions. The large majority took the oath, suffering some disrepute thereby. But that did not end their troubles. William's religious views were broad and he had little sympathy with the narrow Anglican church. He appointed latitudinarian bishops, like Burnet, the historian, and thus estranged the clergy from their natural leaders.

Under Anne the situation was somewhat relieved. She was in thorough sympathy with the Anglican clergy and she was a sincerely pious woman. She used her influence to promote religion. Her practical help is illustrated by Queen Anne's bounty. Since the Reformation the crown had received considerable revenues from the clergy. Anne gave all these to augment the salaries of underpaid livings. In her time, too, the building of churches was promoted and religious societies were formed. The members of such societies attempted to lead a more devotional life than the average members of the church, and met oftener for the purposes of religious discussion and observance. But even under Anne the church suffered from its political associations. The clergy were generally Tories, and the victory of Sacheverell was the triumph of the Tory party rather than of the church. The high church cry of the mob was political in its significance.

The superficiality of the change in Anne's reign came to light with the accession of George I. Both he and his son deserted Lutheranism for Anglicanism at the behest of the Act of Settlement, but neither had any sincere interest in religion. Soon afterward the building of churches ceased and the religious societies began to fall into desuetude. After 1717 convocation, the legislative body of the church, ceased to meet. Whig ministers, as part of the system of spoils, gave the bishoprics to Whigs, who were out of touch with the rank and file of the Tory clergy. For the time the church fell into a state of torpor.

During this period the only notable activity of the clergy was in intellectual fields. Among the upper social class there was beginning Deism to be scepticism about the truth of religion. Walpole was a sceptic in private, though publicly he professed to support the established church because he thought it essential to secure the obedience of the masses. This attitude was common among the governing class; and no point of view could have harmed the spiritual life of the church more. This intellectual opposition the church met, and met successfully as far as logic is concerned. The principles of this intellectual opposition are collectively designated as deism. It is difficult to define, because it never became an organized system of philosophical thought.

Its essence was the denial of the supernatural in religion. The deists endeavored to establish religion on a purely rational basis. They omitted faith, the strongest element in religion. The clergy took up the challenge, and clerical writers placed revealed religion on a solid intellectual basis which the deists did not shake.

All this intellectual controversy, however, had no effect on the average citizen. A moral life may be brought about by an appeal to the mind, but a religious life must come also from the heart. To sentiment the church in this period made no appeal. The clergy adopted the prevailing point of view. Plain, prosaic common sense was the proper thing. Any appeal to sentiment or emotion was to be decried. Despite the brilliant defense of its principles, the church, so far as its practical work was concerned, became thoroughly permeated with the spirit of rationality. The preacher feared to approach superstition on the one side or fanaticism on the other, and any trace of enthusiasm might be interpreted by his audience as one or the other. The only resort was to abstract reasoning or to dull common sense. "Don't get drunk or you will ruin your health; nor commit murder for you will come to the gallows; every man should seek to be happy, and the way to be happy is to be thoroughly respectable"; such platitudes were the essence of such sermons. They presented truths that none was disposed to deny, but they were somewhat lacking in inspiration to do better. "Dull, duller and dullest are a sufficient critical vocabulary," says Sir Leslie Stephen, "to describe their merits."[23] Without spiritual influence the church neither moved the upper class from its scepticism and immorality, nor provided comfort for the masses. Its cold, prosaic rationalism made no appeal to the heart that would stir emotions and revive religious faith.

This lack was supplied by the Methodist movement led by John Wesley. Though Methodism led to a separation from the church of England, it was begun by leaders who were ordained ministers of the Anglican church. The movement had its origin in a society at Oxford to which Methodist was applied in derision. It was a small group of about fifteen members, modeled on the religious societies of the reign of Anne. Private prayer, visitations of the poor and needy, and a general strengthening of piety and religious devotion among its members were its objects. The ridicule directed against it is a commentary upon the public attitude toward any sign of religious fervor.

Rationality in the church

The Methodist Society

---

[23] *History of English Thought in the Eighteenth Century,* ii, 335–338.

In the organization were the brothers, John and Charles Wesley, and George Whitefield, the three great leaders of the Methodist movement. Of the three, John Wesley was the most influential both in the society and in the broader movement. The Wesleys were the sons of a country clergyman. They were reared in poverty, but they received the training befitting the sons of gentlemen, since they were descended from the gentry. From their early youth their minds appear to have been filled with a fiery piety which took complete possession of them. They were trained for the priesthood in the established church, and they had no thought of reforming the church till John Wesley began to preach to the masses in 1738. Whitefield came from a lower social class and was a man of different type. He was temperamental and erratic. He lacked ability as an organizer and leader, but he was a great orator and moved the masses even more powerfully than John Wesley. His fervent appeals, however, would have had little permanent effect, had they not been accompanied by the organizing ability of John Wesley.

The Wesleys and Whitefield

A turning point in John Wesley's career came between 1735 and 1738. In 1735 he went to a pastorate in Georgia. Religion was already the single object of his life, but he was steeped in the formalism of the highest church party of his time. In that new community he endeavored to enforce rigid forms of observance which would have brought protest even in England. He was domineering and quarrelsome, winning the hearty dislike of his parishioners. His ministry in Georgia was a dismal failure, and in 1738 he returned to England. At this time he became acquainted with some of the sect of the Moravians, through whom he was inspired with the belief in justificacation by faith. This was no new doctrine in the church of England, but it had long since ceased to be emphasized. It furnished Wesley's intensely religious nature with the spark necessary to kindle the flame of religious devotion in the hearts of others. As Wesley preached the doctrine, it became a belief that faith would cause the divine spirit to manifest itself suddenly to the individual and supply him with a conviction that his sins had been forgiven and his salvation secured. Wesley, with all the depth of his strong nature, felt that his soul had thus been suddenly saved, and he immediately sought to save other souls. Thus the Methodist movement began in 1738.

Beginning of the Methodist movement

John Wesley was soon joined by his brother Charles and by Whitefield. They went forth to preach the gospel of faith throughout the land. They still regarded themselves as ordained ministers of the church of England, and they preached from the pulpits of churches

Its growth

wherever the regular clergy would permit. But the clergy looked askance at the movement. The sermons of the Methodists were enthusiastic to the verge of fanaticism; they were designed primarily to stir the emotions. The clergy naturally recoiled and began to exclude the Methodist preachers from their pulpits. The Methodists then began to build separate chapels, and Whitefield began field preaching. Nothing daunted these leaders. They traveled the length and breadth of the land, endured privations and hardships, and faced mobs in order to spread religious feeling among the people. They succeeded. Thousands who had never been to church heard them and were moved. Thousands who received no satisfaction from the empty rationalism of the established church found relief in the doctrine of faith. Disciples multiplied, societies were formed, and lay preachers under the direction of John Wesley helped to spread the new gospel.

The results

The Methodist movement resulted ultimately in the foundation of a new sect. John Wesley always maintained that he was a member of the Anglican church, and Whitefield left it only with keen regret. The doctrines of Methodism were not in conflict with those of the Anglican church, but its spirit was utterly different. Wesley, moreover, found it necessary to establish a separate organization. It began with the building of separate chapels. Eventually a conference of the leaders of the movement was organized for the government of the Methodists. So long as the Methodists professed to be within the church, this was an *imperium in imperio*. When the connection finally had to be given up, the Methodists became a separate sect.

The most important result of the movement was its effect upon the masses. Methodism made little appeal to the upper social class, but it permeated the middle and the lower classes and aroused among them a strong religious spirit. This gradually improved the moral tone of the community. By the end of the eighteenth century the uplift was pronounced. The movement initiated by John Wesley had been a potent factor in the accomplishment of the result.

Eventually the movement had a reactionary effect upon the established church. In the later part of the eighteenth century a movement developed within the church, called the evangelical revival, to make a stronger spiritual and religious appeal to the community. Under its impulse the established church recovered the spiritual character which it lacked earlier in the century. By the closing years of the century religion held a place in English life which rendered England impervious to the wave of scepticism that swept over so many parts of the continent in that period.

CHAPTER XXX

THE KING, THE CABINET, AND THE EMPIRE

WHEN George III came to the throne in 1760, he began a systematic attempt to break down the system of cabinet government. It had become so strongly intrenched in practice that George II once declared: "Ministers are the king in this country."[1] This objective had been given to George III through his mother's influence. The death of his father when he was a child had left the direction of his education to his mother. She had come from a small German court where the power of the king was absolute, and this was the ideal she endeavored to impart to her son. His tutors were carefully chosen to promote the point of view of a strong kingship. They had George read such works as Blackstone's *Commentaries*,[2] which enumerated the extensive legal powers of the crown and assigned them to the king, despite their exercise in practice by the cabinet,[3] and Bolingbroke's *Patriot King*, which developed the thesis that a national king, who has the welfare of the nation at heart, should break down the tyranny of the party system and rule above parties, though the limitations placed on the king by the cabinet rested on the party system. The substance of his training is summed up in his mother's exhortation: "George, be a king!"

George III employed two principal means to achieve his end. He attempted to disrupt the existing parties, and more particularly the dominant Whig party. For the cabinet to work at its best it is necessary to have two parties and only two. The issues are then clear cut. The members of the majority must support the policy of the cabinet, unless they disagree with its principles to such an extent that they prefer those of the other party. If the cabinet has to rely for its support on groups having diverse views, it has to follow a weak and colorless policy to avoid the alienation of any group of its supporters. Even then a coalition cabinet is apt to be short-lived, because its defeat does not necessarily mean a decisive change of policy. If George III could break up the parties, the resulting weakness and instability of the cabinets would give him more opportunity to exert an influence. The second means employed by him was to weaken his cabinets by dividing them

George III and his object

His methods

---

[1] Cited by Blauvelt, *Development of Cabinet Government*, p. 181.
[2] They were not published until 1765, but George read them in manuscript.
[3] See book i, ch. vii.

internally. With cabinets that were not homogeneous the king could often play on the differences to accomplish his will.

His
personal-
ity

The situation on the accession of George III was favorable for the execution of these policies. The new king was popular. He was the first of the line of Hanover to be English born and bred, and his "glory in the name of Briton," which he inserted in the first speech from the throne, received a hearty response from the nation. George, moreover, had many homely virtues which had been conspicuously lacking in his immediate predecessors. He was an affectionate son, a faithful husband, sincerely pious, and strongly opposed to many of the vicious social customs of the time. These endeared him particularly to the stolid middle class. His popularity did not endure, because traits of his character, which became apparent as the nation became better acquainted with him, were less admirable. He was narrow-minded, ignorant, arbitrary, and obstinate. He had a high sense of duty, and devoted himself assiduously to the business of government, but he lacked the ability to rule well. He frequently seized upon the wrong policy, made it distinctively his own, and pursued it with a pig-headed obstinacy that no amount of reason could shake. His unwise exercise of power, when he finally obtained it, soon brought him unpopularity which defeated his system. But at the beginning of his reign these qualities were not in evidence, and his personality was an asset.

The
party
situation

The Whig party, moreover, was already divided into factions. The members of the house of commons were not subject to the same pressure of public opinion in the eighteenth century that meets them today. Public opinion was more apathetic, it had less opportunity to formulate itself, and the narrow franchise and corrupt electoral system rendered the members more or less independent of such opinion as was expressed. In these circumstances the members tended to group themselves under leaders whom they found personally congenial, or from whom patronage might be expected. The Whigs were already broken into several cliques of this sort in the house, and Pitt's cabinet was divided against itself when George III came to the throne.

Lord Bute,
1761–1763

To rid himself of Pitt under these conditions was easy. Lord Bute, the personal friend of the king, was introduced into the cabinet; he informed the king of the differences of opinion within the cabinet; and George III played on them until Pitt's colleagues opposed his policy and caused him to resign. Lord Bute, a Tory, was soon made prime minister, though the cabinet remained mainly Whig. Meanwhile the king was building up a personal following in the house of commons. He took the patronage of the crown away from his ministers and distributed it himself. He kept careful watch of parliamentary debates and votes, rewarded those who supported his policies, and deprived of their offices and pensions those who opposed. The group which he obtained by these corrupt means came to be known as the King's Friends. At his order they supported the cabinets which accepted his dictation and voted against the cabinets which opposed the royal wishes. With their support, by setting Whig factions against one another, and by the purchase of votes for cash Lord Bute secured the approval of the house of commons for the peace of Paris in 1763. His success ended his political career. The peace proved to be so unpopular that Bute resigned in order to take the responsibility upon himself and shield the king.

His resignation forced the king to give the leadership to a Whig, since there was no other way to obtain a majority in the house of commons. George Grenville, who was out of harmony with the old Whig organization, was given the office, and the duke of Bedford was induced to join the cabinet and bring his faction to its support. Several of the other Whig factions now agreed to act together under the leadership of Pitt. They had a sufficient majority to have defeated the cabinet, but Pitt, who did not believe theoretically in the party system, vacillated and failed to lead them. The Grenville cabinet consequently remained in power until 1765, when it secured the passage of a bill which displeased the king.

Grenville, 1763–1765

Aside from imperial policies, the business which occupied the chief attention of Grenville's cabinet was the prosecution of John Wilkes. This gentleman was the publisher of a paper, called the *North Briton,* which attacked Bute's administration vigorously. In number forty-five Wilkes published a sharp criticism of the king's speech to parliament, which was concerned with the peace made in 1763. Wilkes, who was the author, took care to designate the speech as the work of the ministers, it being already a well-recognized dictum that the king's speech should be written by the cabinet and as such be subject to criticism. But the king's large share of the responsibility for the peace was so well known that the criticism was regarded as an attack on the king's attempt to assume power. The king, taking it as a personal affront, insisted on the prosecution of Wilkes. The cabinet proceeded to employ the most arbitrary methods. By a general warrant specifying no name, which was afterward declared illegal, Wilkes' abode was searched. Wilkes was subsequently arrested in violation of his privilege as a member of the house of commons. By *habeas corpus,* however, Wilkes

The Wilkes affair

established his right to freedom from arrest. The first round in the courts went against the king.

George III, however, was not ready to let the matter drop. The cabinet had a majority in the house, and its votes were now swung into line. The commons ordered the forty-fifth number of the *North Briton* to be burned by the hangman, voted that the privilege of the house did not cover the offense of Wilkes, and expelled the critic from the house. Meanwhile a former minister, whom he had criticized, forced a duel upon him and wounded him seriously. On his recovery he went to France, whence he did not return to plead in the judicial proceedings instituted against him by the cabinet. The result was his outlawry.

Popular
feeling

The second round went to the king, but it was a victory of questionable value. The peace had been decidedly unpopular. The attempt to suppress public comment by such arbitrary methods at once created a strong sentiment in behalf of the liberties of the subject. Wilkes, though his moral standard was low and his private life vicious, became a popular hero. Many public demonstrations were made in his favor and against the king, who was generally recognized as responsible for the persecution of Wilkes. The first exercise of power by George III roused an ominous spirit of popular opposition.

Rocking-
ham,
1765–1766

The cabinet, despite its success in the persecution of Wilkes and its adoption of an imperial policy pleasing to George III, was in other ways too independent to suit. In 1765 it capped the climax by the passage of a bill[4] which aroused the king's resentment so deeply that he threw himself into the hands of the Newcastle connections and the old Whig organization. To be free of Grenville, he accepted a cabinet led by Rockingham. Though George III appeared to have given up the attempt to control the cabinet, in reality Rockingham's position was weak. The Whigs were still disunited, and Pitt refused to give the cabinet his support. The king regarded it as a makeshift to fill the gap until he could arrange a more satisfactory cabinet, and the King's Friends constituted an important element in the cabinet's majority. When the cabinet adopted measures which met the royal displeasure, its majority soon dwindled. Within less than a year George III was able to dispense with its services.

At this juncture Pitt finally came to the king's rescue. Several times since 1763 George III had sought his help, because the Great Commoner had come to disbelieve in the party system. His reasons were

---

[4] It was a regency bill, necessitated by George's illness, so framed that it omitted the king's mother from the regency.

very different from those of the king. Pitt saw the evils of the party system of his day and sought to rise above them; George III understood that his control of the cabinet depended upon the disruption of the Whigs. Though Pitt had previously declined the king's invitations, in 1766 he accepted office and formed a coalition cabinet. It included Whigs, Tories, and King's Friends, who constituted a heterogeneous and uncongenial group. The old Whigs would have nothing to do with it. Pitt probably saw the dangers, but apparently he expected to dominate the king and the cabinet as he had done once before. If this was his intention, he failed. The result of his second ministry was to assure the fulfillment of the king's wish to rule as well as to reign.

Pitt's coalition cabinet

From the first the cabinet was weak. Pitt assumed such a domineering tone with his colleagues that the existing divergences of opinion were accentuated. George III, who learned of the differences through his friends, utilized them to his own advantage. Pitt, moreover, made the mistake of accepting the title of the earl of Chatham, which excluded him from the house of commons, where his influence rested on his oratory. His cabinet rapidly became unpopular. A foreign alliance which he attempted to negotiate failed. In 1766 the cabinet, in order to avert an impending famine, prohibited the exportation of grain by order in council and was severely censured in debate in the commons for its arbitrary conduct, though it was not outvoted. In the next year the cabinet, for the first time since the revolution of 1688, was defeated on a money bill. But the most difficult problem of the cabinet was in the field of imperial policy. Should conciliation or coercion be applied to the American colonies? Pitt wanted conciliation, the king and the opposition wanted coercion, and the cabinet seems to have been thoroughly divided in sentiment. The prime minister did not face the issue. He retired to the country ill, either in fact or in name, with the gout. The cabinet was left practically headless, and each member was free to run the business of his department as he pleased. The result was that the king generally had his way, and the cabinet pursued imperial and domestic policies which were thoroughly uncongenial to Pitt.

Pitt's failure

Meanwhile a series of changes took place in the cabinet that added further to its weakness. In 1767 Lord North, a Tory, was appointed chancellor of the exchequer. In the next year the septennial election occurred. Royal money was spent freely and successfully to swell the ranks of the King's Friends in the house. Subsequently Pitt resigned. The prime minister who followed was only a nominal leader, and the cabinet remained weak and divided.

Ministerial disorganization

During this period of ministerial disorganization the personal sys-

Renewal
of the
Wilkes
affair

tem of the king underwent a severe test. In 1768 Wilkes returned from France, stood for election from Middlesex, and was returned. Subsequently he went to prison to serve the sentence imposed upon him by the court in 1764. Wilkes was regarded as the exponent of the popular liberties, and his election was a protest against the corrupt government maintained under the personal rule of the king. The election had been accompanied by the demonstrations of a violent mob. Later, when Wilkes was taken to prison, and again, when he took his seat in parliament, huge mobs collected to bear witness to the strength of the popular feeling in his favor. The king finally induced the cabinet to have the house expel Wilkes, but a few days later he was again elected from Middlesex. Thereupon the house again expelled him and without legal right declared him incapable of holding a seat in the existing parliament. Again the king had triumphed over Wilkes by the use of arbitrary, illegal, and corrupt methods. It was a costly success. It engendered a radical spirit directed particularly against the corrupt house of commons, which did the bidding of the cabinet against the manifest will of the people. It also enhanced the unpopularity of George III, who was regarded as responsible in some measure for the policy of the cabinet.

Lord
North

The cabinet meanwhile underwent a reorganization under the leadership of Lord North. George III had found him thoroughly congenial. He was a good debater, a tactful manager of the house of commons, and of no mean ability. But what pleased George III particularly was North's acquiescence in the royal views. When North's advice was not adopted by the king, North accepted the king's policy, though it might not accord with his better judgment. In the house North was soon able to construct a substantial majority. The Tories rallied to his support, and together with the King's Friends bought by royal patronage and bribes, they constituted a dependable majority. By becoming the manager of a party and by using the corrupt political methods of his day, George III had succeeded in his effort to secure power. From 1770, when North completed the reconstruction of the cabinet, until 1782, when he resigned, George III was able to obtain the policies which he desired. The system of cabinet government which seemed to have been established in the reign of George II was temporarily overthrown.

Need for
reform of
imperial
policy

The question which chiefly occupied the government while George III managed affairs was that of the American colonies. The imperial control of the colonies was forced upon the attention of the government at the close of the Seven Years' War. The war had roused a keen interest in imperial problems among Englishmen, and it had made evident the need for changes in the imperial policies previously pursued. The new acquisitions of territory made necessary many adjustments with regard to such questions as boundaries, relations with the Indians in the newly acquired territories, defense, and trade. The crisis of the war, moreover, had brought into a glaring light the inefficiency of the existing system of imperial administrative control. The need of reforms could not be ignored in the light of recent experience and in the prospect of an expanded and vastly more important empire.

What the cabinets did with regard to imperial policy after the close of the Seven Years' War was motivated largely by the difficulties which had been experienced during the war and before. One great obstacle to the successful administration of the colonies had been the lack of coordination among the central organs through which the crown exercised its executive control. In the eighteenth century the privy council, the secretaries of state, the lords of the treasury, the commissioners of the customs, and the board of trade had important parts in the colonial administration, but their respective spheres and their relations to one another were exceedingly ill defined. Nor was there any single central authority responsible for the correlation of their work. The colonists did not know where to go when they wanted to transact business. Often they were bandied about from one office to another. When one department obtained enough power to be efficient, the others became jealous of it; when affairs went wrong, each tried to shift the responsibility to another. In 1763 it was stated by a member of the government that the issue of conflicting orders from different central organs to the royal officials in the colonies was of common occurrence.

Central imperial control

The board of trade, created in 1696, had been designed to bring harmony into the system. It fell short of this ideal, but it kept the system from working as badly as might have been expected. Usually the other authorities referred their colonial business to the board of trade for information. The board thus reviewed the greater part of the colonial policy of the government. The secretary of state for the southern department, who was the secretary concerned with colonial affairs, could do much to correlate the work of the most important organs of central control, because he was *ex officio* a member of the board of trade and also a member of the committee of the privy council charged with colonial affairs. But the secretary often did not bother. The board of trade could accomplish little in the way of unity because its consultation by the other departments was often not compulsory, and its advice, when sought, might be ignored. It could recommend action to the committee of the privy council, but it possessed no power of final decision.

Board of trade

The efficiency of the board consequently depended upon its personnel and upon its relations to the other central authorities engaged with colonial affairs.

From this point of view the development of the board of trade may be divided roughly into three periods. From 1696 to 1714 the active members were conscientious in the performance of their duties. Though the offices changed hands frequently because they were regarded as political, nevertheless the board was vigorous and fairly efficient. During the greater part of the period the privy council and the secretary for the southern department consulted it and accepted its advice. From 1714 to 1748 the board was lethargic. The personnel deteriorated because the board was used to provide adherents with sinecures. Burke's description, though written of the board at a later date, is applicable to this period. "This board," he says, "is a sort of temperate bed of influence, a sort of gently ripening hothouse, where eight members of parliament receive salaries of a thousand a year for a certain given time, in order to mature, at a proper season, a claim to two thousand, granted for doing less, and on the credit of having toiled so long in that inferior, laborious department."[5] The interposition of a committee of the privy council between the privy council and the board weakened its influence with the council, and it also lost functions to the secretary. Newcastle, who was secretary from 1724 to 1748, took over much of the important business previously initiated by the board and transacted it without consultation with the board. From 1748 to 1761 the board was under the leadership of a more aggressive president, who rendered it more active and authoritative. After his resignation in 1761 the board slipped back somewhat, but it did not again become as inactive as before.

Local royal officials

The control exerted by such central administrative organs over the colonies was necessarily loose and inefficient. The evils of the system were further increased by the weakness of those who represented the royal authority in the colonies. The most important of the local agents of the British government were the colonial governors who constituted the local executives.[6] The governors generally had to face the opposition of the colonial assemblies, and since the division of authority rendered their support from home precarious, they often disregarded their instructions from London and yielded to the colonists. The general depend-

---

[5] *Works,* ii, 340.

[6] The governors of Connecticut and Rhode Island, who were chosen by the colonists, constitute exceptions. The governors of the proprietary colonies, Pennsylvania and Maryland, were not appointed by the crown, but their appointments were subject to royal approval, and they were responsible to the crown for the administration of the acts of trade.

ence of the governors on the assemblies for their salaries gave to the colonial legislatures a power over the governor and his agents which orders from England could not counterbalance. During the long period of salutary neglect under Newcastle the colonists exercised an actual control over their internal affairs, which they had come to regard as their right. *De jure* the colonial assemblies were subordinate to both the British executive and the British parliament,[7] but *de facto* the colonists regarded their local legislatures as independent both of parliament and of the local representatives of the British executive. The colonists acknowledged a dependence on the central British executive, but experience had taught them to anticipate a lax control from that source.

The poor enforcement of the acts of trade in the colonies had been brought to the attention of the British government during the war through its effort to stamp out the illicit commerce between the continental American colonies and the French West Indies. These tropical colonies had never raised their own food, and the British colonies had long been their chief source of supply. With the outbreak of the war, their French source of supply was cut off by the British navy. The consequent scarcity of provisions gave to the British a great advantage in the war against the French in the West Indies. It also made the trade in provisions so highly profitable that the American colonists continued to engage in it despite laws declaring it illegal. The colonists were interested only in the reduction of French power in Canada; and the help given the French in Canada by the provisions they sold to the French in the West Indies was too indirect to be apparent to the colonists. No imperialistic sentiment hindered them, for they had no feeling for the empire as a whole. This trade with the enemy was regarded by the British government as little short of treason, for without these supplies many of the French West Indies could have been starved into surrender. The British navy broke up the trade intermittently, but it was never able to stop it permanently because many of the royal officials in America connived at it. The illegal trade with the French brought home to the cabinet the weakness and corruption of the colonial administration.

Illegal trade with the enemy

The illegal trade with the enemy also called attention to the lax enforcement of the acts of trade. Since the provisions sent to the French West Indies were purchased mainly with molasses and sugar, Pitt tried to end the trade by giving orders in 1760 for the better enforcement

Lax enforcement of acts of trade

---

[7] For a contrary view, see McIlwain, *American Revolution.*

of the Molasses Act of 1733.[8] The order was carried out sufficiently well to evoke from the merchants of Boston an organized resistance and to cause serious friction with the colonies of Massachusetts and New York.

Imperial defense

Another problem which reached a critical stage during the war was that of imperial defense. In the previous practice the whole cost of the essential naval defense of the colonies had been borne by the British taxpayers. For military defense in time of peace the colonies had been responsible, except for a few British garrisons kept in the most exposed or outlying colonies. When the empire was at war, the colonies which were not actually attacked were often backward in supplying troops and supplies to aid those which were, orders from England assessing the quota of each colony had little effect, and troops always had to be sent from Great Britain. Just before the Seven Years' War the colonies made an unsuccessful attempt to agree among themselves on their respective quotas. During the war the British government had great difficulties in persuading some of the colonies to do their part. The existing system of military organization was obviously in need of reform, and it seemed clear that the initiative could not come from the colonies.

Proclamation line

The cabinet which first faced these problems was that of George Grenville (1763-1765). The newly conquered territory was taken under direct imperial control in 1763 by the issue of a royal proclamation which forbade settlement west of a boundary established along the Appalachians. The purpose was to protect the Indians, who occupied the territory, from exploitation by unscrupulous settlers, traders, and land-grabbers, until the imperial government could make satisfactory arrangements with the Indians for cessions of parts of the territory. To the colonists the frontier, which they called the "proclamation line," was a galling restriction. It disregarded settlements which had already been made on the other side of the mountains, ignored the long-standing claims of several of the colonies to the interior, and aggrieved many colonists who planned to settle in the new country or to exploit its riches.

New policy of imperial defense

Another duty which the British government decided to assume was that of imperial defense. The outbreak of an Indian war in 1763 seemed to indicate the need of permanent garrisons to protect the colonial settlements and to keep control of the interior. The cabinet also had in mind the ultimate need to be prepared for the anticipated attempt

---

[8] Above, p. 495.

of France to obtain revenge. A standing army of 10,000 men was deemed a necessity by responsible British statesmen. Since past experience made it evident that the colonies could not cooperate among themselves to supply and maintain such a force, the cabinet determined to establish a British standing army.

The application of these new imperial policies involved heavy expenditures; and so it became a third object of the imperial reorganization to make the colonists help defray the cost. The British taxpayers would still bear the whole cost of naval defense and the larger part of the cost of the new military defense; but since the colonists would receive a large part of the benefits, it seemed just to ask them to relieve the heavily burdened British exchequer by the contribution of taxes which would pay part of the cost of the standing army. The methods employed by the imperial government to raise the desired colonial revenues aroused among the colonists an opposition which developed into the American Revolution. `Colonial taxation`

One method employed to obtain a larger income from the colonies was to attempt the better enforcement of the acts of trade. If the duties already established by those acts could be collected, the revenues would be swelled materially. Extensive changes of detail were made in the local administration. The navy was employed to prevent smuggling; customs officials who were appointed to go to the colonies were forbidden any longer to remain at home and fill their places by deputies; the jurisdiction of the courts of admiralty was strengthened and expanded; and many other improvements were instituted. The colonists watched these reforms with dismay. The innovations tightened the reins of imperial control and damaged colonial commercial interests. They did not notably improve imperial administration from the point of view of the better government of the colonies. The fundamental evils produced by the perpetual muddle among the many organs of central control continued with little alteration. `Enforcement of the acts of trade`

In 1764 the Sugar Act was passed. It placed new customs on several articles. The most significant item was the new duty on molasses. The act of 1733, which placed a prohibitive duty on the trade, was about to expire. The act of 1764 renewed the duty but reduced it by one-half. The purpose was to make it less profitable to smuggle and thus to increase the revenues. In form the act of 1764 was similar to the older acts of trade, but in purpose it was different. They were designed primarily to regulate commerce; the Sugar Act was passed in order to raise a revenue. `The Sugar Act`

Grenville's financial policy culminated with the Stamp Act of 1765.

A year before its enactment Grenville announced his intention to frame such legislation. When the colonial agents in London discussed the project with him, he was reported by one of them to have said: "I am not, however, set upon this tax. If the Americans dislike it, and prefer any other method of raising the money themselves, I shall be content."[9] Some of the colonial agents notified their colonial governments that they might tax themselves if they preferred,[10] but colonial assemblies took no other action than protestation. When the agents presented the colonial objections to taxation of the colonies by the British parliament and urged that the revenue should be obtained by requisitions on the colonial assemblies, Grenville asked, "Can you agree on the proportions each colony should raise?" Since they admitted the impossibility of agreement, Grenville proceeded with his legislation. It required that stamps purchased of the government should be used on practically all legal documents, many commercial papers, such as ships' clearance papers, newspapers and pamphlets, and some other articles. The tax was to be paid in silver, of which there was none too much for colonial commerce and industry.

In America the act raised a storm. The colonists refused to pay the tax. In some places the royal officials were attacked by mobs, agreements not to import British goods were formed among the merchants, and delegates from the majority of the colonies came together in the Stamp Act Congress (1765) to protest the measure. The resolution of the Congress was expressed in moderate terms, but it raised the fundamental issue of taxation without representation. The opposition to the previous acts had taken economic grounds. The damage done to business was the principal complaint. The opposition of the Stamp Act Congress was more serious, because it brought forward the question of the constitutional power of parliament to tax the colonies. Grenville had reasoned excellently in the abstract, but he had failed to understand practical conditions in the colonies.

After this outburst on the part of the colonists the imperial government could either settle the question of parliamentary supremacy by an appeal to force, or it could withdraw the demand. It could not execute the act with the existing administrative machinery available in the colonies. When the decision had to be made, Grenville had been replaced by Rockingham. He had not approved of the act originally, and the cabinet was further influenced by the protests of English

[9] Cited by Lecky, *History of England*, iii, 347.
[10] *Ibid.*, especially note 1. Compare Van Tyne, *Causes of the War of Independence*, pp. 140, 141.

merchants who had experienced losses as a result of the non-importation agreements. In 1766 the Stamp Act was repealed, though it was accompanied by the Declaratory Act, which asserted the constitutional right of parliament to tax the colonists. The repeal for the time conciliated the colonists, but if it was to have a permanent effect, the principle of the Declaratory Act would necessarily have to remain dormant.

Continuity of policy was impossible while the political intrigues of George III were producing constant changes of cabinets. When Pitt followed Rockingham, the fate of the colonies in the headless cabinet fell into the hands of Charles Townshend. He revived the policy of taxing the colonies to help defray the cost of imperial administration. The Stamp Act Congress had made a distinction between acts regulating trade and those imposing taxes on the colonies. Since the former, which imposed taxes on imports, had been in effect for over a century, it was only the latter which the Congress claimed to be unconstitutional on the ground of taxation without representation. The taxes levied by the acts of trade were regarded by the colonists as designed primarily to regulate commerce and not to raise a revenue. Unfortunately, responsible British statesmen, among whom was Townshend, received the impression that it was primarily a distinction between forms of taxation which the Stamp Act Congress intended to make.[11] They understood that the colonists objected to the levy by parliament of internal taxes but not of external taxes. To meet this distinction Townshend imposed new duties on glass, paper, lead, paint, and tea imported into the colonies. He also continued the reorganization of the customs service begun by Grenville. His reforms were so effective that they were equivalent to the reenactment of many of the acts of trade. From 1760 to 1768 the American customs had yielded about £2,000 annually; from 1769 to 1774 the revenue was £30,000 and more yearly. Whatever theory the Americans may have had with regard to external taxation, they resisted Townshend's acts. The new act might be like the old acts in kind, but the purpose of the old acts of trade was to regulate trade, and that of the new was to raise a revenue. The opposition took much the same forms as that to the Stamp Act, but it was more violent and more prolonged.

Again the cabinet had to face the problem of withdrawal of the obnoxious legislation or coercion. It vacillated. Coercion was tried for two years. Troops were sent to Boston to help the customs officials en-

Townshend's acts

North and coercion

---

[11] See the questions and answers in the record of the evidence given by Benjamin Franklin before a committee of the house of commons which examined him in 1766, quoted in the *Life of Franklin* by J. Bigelow, i, 477–481.

rorce the law. But in 1770 the cabinet decided by a majority of one to withdraw the Townshend duties, except that on tea. That was left in order to maintain the principle that parliament could tax the colonies. The adoption of a partially conciliatory policy helped the situation for a time, but violent opposition did not subside entirely. Many of the colonists were determined to fight the principle which the tax on tea represented. In 1773 a group of those who were so minded held the Boston tea-party and dumped cargoes of tea into the harbor. The news of this event aroused much indignation in England. Lord North determined to resort to coercion again. In 1774 he secured the passage of legislation which the colonists designated as the intolerable acts. These acts closed the port of Boston, extended the royal power in the government of Massachusetts, limited the right of public meeting, provided that persons accused of capital offenses should be removed from Massachusetts for trial, and imposed new requirements for the quartering of the soldiers in Massachusetts. They served to unite the colonists under the leadership of the radical element, which had wanted revolt from an early stage of the controversy. In 1774 the first Continental Congress was held, early in the next year came Lexington and Bunker Hill, and in 1776 the Declaration of Independence announced that the American Revolution had begun.

The policies of the British government which produced the revolt were the result of inefficiency and ignorance. They were not intended to be tyrannical. Grenville's view that the colonies ought to contribute to the cost of their own defense seems just enough. He had parliament tax them only after he had given them the opportunity to tax themselves.[12] From any past experience of England, or from that of any other colonial power, there seemed to be no reason to anticipate opposition on constitutional grounds. Grenville knew that the colonists would object to new taxes but so would Englishmen object to a new tax in England; no one welcomes additional taxation. What he and his successors failed to see was that the colonies had for too long enjoyed a large degree of practical independence and had become too populous and too wealthy to submit to a radical departure in imperial policy which seemed to the colonists to affect their interest adversely. He and his successors generally lacked intimate knowledge of the problems of these pioneer communities on the other side of an ocean that the sailing vessels of that day took months to cross. Nevertheless, this information should have been theirs before they embarked on new

Inexpediency of imperial policy

---

[12] Above, pp. 553, 554.

imperial policies or became responsible for critical dealings with the colonies. The results were policies that were inexpedient and unwise.

In some measure the mistakes were due to the mediocre ability of the statesmen whom the chances of party politics in England made responsible for imperial administration in this period. But the statesmen were handicapped in serious ways. The lack of any proper coordination among the many organs of the central government concerned with imperial control worked with fatal success to prevent any unified and efficient policy. In the critical years after 1768 the policies of different organs conflicted even on such fundamental questions as conciliation or coercion. Moreover, until Lord North became prime minister in 1770 and the policy of the cabinet became that of the king, no harmonious cabinet was in office long enough to develop a consistent policy. Either conciliation or coercion pursued steadily and efficiently would probably have been more successful than the alternation of kicks and caresses that followed the rapid changes of cabinets brought about by the machinations of George III. The policy of vacillation irritated the colonists, helped the colonial radical minority to make converts, and gave the colonists confidence in their ability to oppose the British government successfully.

But inexpediency is not tyranny. When the colonists resisted by violence the execution of laws enacted by parliament, it was not tyrannical to attempt to maintain them by force, unless the constitutional claim of the colonists, that they could not be taxed without their own consent, was right. This hardly any Englishman admitted. Many English statesmen believed it better to repeal the Stamp Act than to maintain it by force; but Pitt was almost the only statesman of note to deny the power of parliament to tax the colonies internally. Even he asserted the power of parliament to tax the colonies externally and to legislate on every other internal subject. The prevailing English view seems probably to have been constitutionally correct.[13] The colonial contention of "no taxation without representation"[14] rested on the assumption that the colonial legislatures were coordinate with parliament and not subordinate to it. The colonists acknowledged the executive headship of the king, but denied the legislative supremacy of parliament. The position of the colonial assembly, in their view, was analogous to that of the parliament of Scotland before the union. The precedent of a century and more was against their claim. In 1650

(margin notes: Responsibility therefor; Tyranny)

---

[13] For a learned exposition of the contrary view, see McIlwain's *American Revolution*.

[14] After 1767 generally expressed more broadly in the form, "no legislation without representation."

the parliament of the Commonwealth asserted its right to legislate for the colonies in words very similar to those of the Declaratory Act of 1766, and thereafter parliament often did legislate for the colonies. After the revolution of 1688 changed the balance of power in the constitution, the legal right of parliament to legislate for the colonies became still less assailable. The proper legal analogy was between the colonial assemblies and the English municipal corporations, which, though they received charters from the king giving them powers of local self-government, were in all things subordinate to parliament.

Representation

Yet, though the colonial contention was probably without constitutional or legal foundation, it was not without justice. Englishmen had little sympathy with the constitutional position of the colonists, because in practice "no taxation without representation" meant to the average Englishman no taxation which parliament had not sanctioned. Representation in the colonies and in England meant two different things. In most of the colonies taxes could be voted only by representatives in whose election the taxed had had an opportunity to take part. In England this had never been the theory or practice of representation. In England only one out of approximately ten adult males voted, but the other nine did not escape taxation. Every Englishman, whether he resided in England or in the colonies, was theoretically represented in parliament. In constitutional theory the colonists had no basis for their claim that they were unrepresented; but as a practical question the balance of right would appear to have been on their side, because the nine Englishmen who paid taxes without a vote had the same political, social, and economic interests as the one who could vote, while the interests of the colonists in a new country three thousand miles away were utterly different from those of the Englishmen who had the franchise.

Legislation

In practice, moreover, the legislation which parliament had enacted for the colonies before 1763 related mainly to the regulation of trade. The few acts which interfered with the internal affairs of the colonies were concerned with such subjects as the post office, Indian trade, currency, and other matters which the colonists were generally disposed to recognize as falling properly within the sphere of imperial control. In its essentials the distinction of the Stamp Act Congress between taxation for raising revenue and taxation for regulating trade was sound. Actually parliament had not enacted before 1764 any significant legislation which had for its primary purpose the taxation of the colonists. Granted that parliament had the power, its failure to use it for so long a period rendered reasonable the colonial view that its application after 1763, however legal, was arbitrary.

Whether the constitutional claims of the colonists were right or wrong constitutionally or abstractly, there can be little doubt that they appeared to be wrong on both grounds to the average contemporary Englishman. To him the colonies appeared to be dominions, which should be subject to the British executive and to the British legislature. The colonial cry of tyranny left him cold. The attitude of the colonists appeared to the British taxpayer to be unconstitutional and ungrateful. For a long time the controversy seems to have made little impression on British public opinion. The gravity of the situation was little appreciated. The Stamp Act riots appeared to be much like the riots which often occurred in England, and until 1774 the average Englishman probably had little reason to think much about the situation in the colonies. When the events of 1774 made it clear that a crisis had arrived, the general attitude seems to have been unfavorable to the colonies. In the house of commons only a small faction of Whigs, led by Rockingham and Charles James Fox, maintained a hopeless opposition to the government, and the house seems on this occasion to have reflected public opinion fairly. *English public opinion*

In America the military problem faced by Great Britain was difficult. The territory of the colonists was so large and so sparsely settled that it was well-nigh impossible to occupy it effectively. The coastal towns were occupied easily, but the occupation accomplished little. The colonists in the hinterland continued peacefully about their affairs. To meet and conquer a colonial army gave the English no control of the country because nearly every colonist knew how to handle a rifle, and, whenever the interior was threatened, large numbers of militia and irregular troops gathered on short notice. To wear the colonists out with armies required enormous forces and the construction of fortifications. To Great Britain, just recovering from the burden of the Seven Years' War, the expense of such a policy was prohibitive. The alternative of a naval blockade appealed neither to the king nor to the military leaders, whose familiarity with the European methods of warfare caused them to underestimate the difficulties in the colonies. *The military problem*

War by land appeared more feasible than it proved to be. The colonists lacked unity, and England counted on the support of large numbers of colonists who did not believe in separation from England. The difficulties of the colonists at times seemed insurmountable. The colonists paid taxes for the support of the Revolutionary army with but little better grace than they had contributed to the cost of the British standing army. The Continental Congress had to issue paper money that was worthless. The colonists sold supplies to British troops for gold, while American troops with paper money starved. It was hard to obtain or to hold sufficient recruits for the American army. Some of the colonies that were not invaded were loath to send troops to those that were. At no time was the American army strong enough to meet the main force of the British successfully in pitched battle without foreign aid. To the British it always looked possible to overcome the American army and beat down the last bit of resistance.

At the beginning of the war the colonists were successful in compelling the British troops to evacuate Boston. Thereafter the British occupied New York, and during 1776 and 1777 the middle colonies were the principal area of warfare. Near the end of 1776 Washington was forced to give up the attempt to defend New York and to retire into Pennsylvania. His surprise of Trenton and subsequent victory at Princeton across the Delaware in New Jersey revived American hopes, but the following winter was one of great hardship and discouragement for the American army. In 1777 the British planned to secure control of the Hudson-Champlain route and isolate the New England colonies. An army under Burgoyne was to march down from Canada and an army under Howe to march up from New York, until the two effected a junction. Howe muddled the plan by stopping to attack Philadelphia. He took it easily and held it against Washington, but the delay was fatal to Burgoyne, who was met by an American army and forced to surrender at Saratoga in the autumn of 1777.

The surrender of Burgoyne was of vital consequence because it induced France to come openly to the aid of the colonies. The French were still smarting from the Seven Years' War, but the desire of revenge had not been strong enough to bring them into the war as long as it appeared possible that the colonies might be conciliated or easily reduced to submission. France did not want to take the risk of being left in isolated opposition to Great Britain. France lent the Americans money and allowed them to buy ammunition, but went no further until the capitulation of Burgoyne gave evidence that the colonial cause had a prospect of success. Early in 1778 France allied itself with America and thereafter gave effective assistance. Nor was France the only power to become hostile. Great Britain's overwhelming commercial and naval superiority had aroused the apprehension of other European maritime powers, just as France had earlier set all Europe against her by her predominance on land. In 1779 Spain joined with

Campaigns to 1778

Entry of other powers

France. Because the Netherlands were treating with America, Great Britain, anticipating their open hostility, declared war in 1780.

In the same year the position of Great Britain was further weakened by the League of Armed Neutrality. It was led by Russia and included all of the northern maritime powers. Its object was to protect neutral shipping against seizure by British privateers. It did not make good all its claims regarding the rights of neutral ships to trade with the belligerents, but it forced Great Britain to be more careful in its treatment of neutral commerce and weakened an important means of British offense.

League of Armed Neutrality

With the entrance of France into the conflict the war assumed a new character. Great Britain was vulnerable through the very extent of her empire, and the necessity of defense elsewhere weakened her offensive in America. In 1778 the British and the French each took an island in the West Indies, the British took S. Pierre and Miquelon and the French posts in India, and fought an indecisive battle against the French fleet in the Channel. But Great Britain could not keep the pace. The cost of the war was excessive. Not only did British troops have to be transported to America, but also a large part of their supplies. As Great Britain's enemies increased, the national income decreased, because Great Britain lost more foreign markets and her enemies captured more of her shipping. With the accession of Spain the navies of Great Britain's opponents became superior in numbers. Between 1779 and 1781 Great Britain's enemies incited the natives of India to attack the British, took British stations on the African coast, two islands in the West Indies, most of Florida, and Minorca. They besieged Gibraltar and at times controlled the English channel. Great Britain obtained a few victories, but they were far from enough to offset the failures.

World war, 1778–1781

In America the principal seat of the war shifted to the southern colonies after 1778. Here the British had some success. Working up from Georgia, they defeated several colonial armies, but they were eventually forced by guerilla warfare to give up most of the interior and keep to the seaboard. Finally, in the summer of 1781, Cornwallis with the main British army in the south retired to Yorktown in Virginia. Washington came down from the north with an American and French army and closed the exit on the landward side. The only British fleet in American waters that could come to the aid of the army was defeated by the French fleet. Lord Cornwallis, recognizing the hopelessness of his situation, surrendered.

War in the colonies, 1778–1781

This surrender practically ended the war. Great Britain, losing everywhere, seemed to be in a desperate plight. English public opinion would no longer support the war. From 1774 to 1778 the popularity of the war grew in England. But the news of Burgoyne's surrender brought realization that the subjugation of the colonies was not to be such a simple matter as had been anticipated. After France joined, the war spirit revived, but the attitude toward the colonies changed. The feeling grew that the attempt to conquer the colonies should be abandoned and attention concentrated on Great Britain's European enemies. The enormous cost of the war in America, the lack of any decisive victory there, the additions to the allies against Great Britain, their victories, and the threat of a French fleet in command of the English Channel in 1779 had worked their effect by the end of that year. Popular desire for the termination of the war with the colonies was so strong that North's majority declined notably.

As this opinion gained strength, it became apparent that the chief obstacle to its adoption was George III. Since 1770 the American policy had been mainly guided by the king. He had previously used his influence in behalf of coercion, and his counsels favored extreme policies in the conduct of the war. North really disliked many of the policies which he advocated in the house of commons at the instance of the king. In 1779 he desired to resign rather than to continue the war against America. He remained only at the insistence of the king, who knew that the loss of North would end his personal power. The extent of the king's personal influence in the government had been fairly well understood by politicians for some time. The failure of the government to respond to popular opinion in the conduct of the war after 1778 made it manifest to all. The view that the American war was secondary in importance to the subversion of the constitution by the king gained currency. In petitions formulated at various public meetings held in 1779 and 1780 the reform of parliamentary corruption, on which the king's system was based, and the conclusion of the American war found a joint place. In 1780 Dunning carried in the house of commons by a majority of eighteen his famous resolution, "that the influence of the crown has increased, is increasing and ought to be diminished." People were beginning to believe what the leaders of the Whig minority had long preached, that the success of the royal policy in America would result in the establishment of a tyranny at home.

The king, however, still controlled a majority. In the election held in 1780 the government used bribery freely and came back with an increased majority. But it could not survive the news of Yorktown. That event convinced a majority that the war with the colonies must be ended. The majority of the cabinet dwindled so rapidly that early in 1782 Lord North resigned despite the protests of the king. It meant the defeat of the king's system. The parliament had been so recently elected that renewed appeal to the electors was useless. George III had only the choice between the appointment of a Whig cabinet and abdication. So bitterly did he feel his own personal defeat that he is said to have contemplated the latter alternative, but he finally called on Rockingham to form a Whig cabinet. Thus the American Revolution not only established a new republic in America but it also helped to preserve popular government in England.

The reestablishment of the cabinet system of government did not take place without a struggle. In 1782 all seemed lost to the king. Rockingham represented the old Whigs, whom George III abhorred, and Rockingham himself had been forced upon the king once before in the days when he was building his system. George III had to take not only the hated party but also the most obnoxious leader of it. Rockingham, moreover, insisted on the king's assurance that he would oppose neither the grant of independence to the American colonies nor laws to eliminate much of the bribery and corruption of parliament which lay at the root of the king's influence. George III soon discovered, however, that the Whig party was not yet united. The faction formerly led by Pitt and now guided by Shelburne had a number of seats in the cabinet nearly equal to that occupied by Rockingham's old Whigs. The king, falling back upon his old game of promoting dissensions, had some success in setting Shelburne against Rockingham.

Disunity of the Whigs

When the divergence finally developed into an open breach between Fox and Shelburne, the king scored a momentary triumph. Charles James Fox had become an influential leader among the Whigs while the party was in opposition. His position had been established despite serious handicaps. The excessive indulgence in vicious amusements which marred his private life alienated many who might have been attracted by his political principles, he lacked first-rate capacity for the management of a party, and his passionate love of liberty led him to champion unpopular causes, such as that of the American colonists between 1776 and 1780. But his exceptional brilliance and skill in debate brought him recognition in the house of commons; his kindly, great-hearted, and lovable disposition cemented strong personal friendships even among those who could not condone his conduct in private life; and his unselfish advocacy of political liberty won him zealous, high-principled followers. In Rockingham's cabinet he received recognition by his appointment to the secretaryship of state concerned with

Fox-Shelburne quarrel

foreign affairs, which made him responsible for the negotiation of peace with France. Shelburne, being the secretary responsible for the colonies, claimed control of negotiations with them. From the first the two disagreed about their respective spheres and about the conduct of negotiations. In Paris their representatives gave conflicting information on the attitude of the cabinet to the plenipotentiaries of France and of the colonies. Since the French and colonial diplomats were working together, they soon discovered the split in the cabinet and took full advantage of it. When Fox learned what was taking place, he demanded the recall of Shelburne's representative, who had committed several indiscretions. He resigned when the cabinet refused to uphold him. Rockingham had died the day before. The consequence was a reconstructed Whig cabinet led by Shelburne (1782). The king had come to his own again.

Peace of Versailles

The effect of the quarrel on the negotiation of peace was necessarily somewhat adverse to Great Britain's interests. The astute American commissioners took full advantage of the situation to secure from Shelburne all that was possible. The negotiations with France were helped somewhat by a British naval victory over the French in the West Indies in 1782, but the peace finally concluded at Versailles in 1783 was necessarily humiliating to British pride. By the treaty with France and Spain, France recovered S. Pierre and Miquelon, exchanged islands with Great Britain in the West Indies about equally, secured the lion's share of the trading posts in Africa, and received back her posts and trading privileges in India. Spain secured Minorca and Florida, ceding only the Bahamas. By the other treaty the colonies received their independence to be exercised in a territory reaching west to the Mississippi and north to approximately the present boundary. They also secured the right to fish off Newfoundland. In return they promised no more protection to colonists who had supported Great Britain during the Revolution than a recommendation of the Continental Congress that justice should be given to them. In England the desertion of the Loyalists was the most criticized aspect of a peace naturally none too popular.

Fox-North coalition

The triumph of George III was short-lived. Fox soon took his followers over to the opposition led by North. In 1783 the coalition carried a vote against the cabinet, Shelburne resigned, and North and Fox formed a cabinet. George III was furiously angry over the result. He had no great fondness for Shelburne, but Fox he hated. Not only was Fox now the leader of the most detested section of the Whigs, but he also had hurt the king nearer home. He was the boon companion of the prince of Wales, whose debauchery George III attributed largely to the evil influence of Fox. Lord North George III regarded as a traitor. His return to power in alliance with the Whigs was beyond the royal endurance. The king determined to be rid of this combination at all costs. After Fox had passed a bill for the reform of the government of India through the house of commons, the king gave a peer a card authorizing him to say that whoever voted for the bill "would be considered by the king as an enemy." The lords rejected the bill, and George III made it the occasion to dismiss the cabinet. The act was unconstitutional. The house of commons, indeed, passed a resolution to the effect that it was a high crime to report the king's opinion on any question pending in parliament with a view to influence votes.

Though George III took an unconstitutional way to rid himself of the cabinet, his action was eventually supported by the country. He gave the formation of the new cabinet to William Pitt, the second son of the deceased earl of Chatham. Pitt was then only twenty-five, and he had been in parliament only four years. Old politicians laughed at an untried boy who dared to fight against experienced leaders like Fox and North, when they had an overwhelming majority. Only with great difficulty could Pitt bring a cabinet together. Fox played into his hands. He tried to force Pitt not to dissolve and hold an election. That aroused the voters, who were none too fond of the Fox-North coalition, which many of them regarded as organized only to secure the spoils of office. Fox and North, moreover, carried the fight to the extreme of holding up supplies. The country became interested in the spectacle of a youth contesting against such odds. The feeling grew that he was not receiving fair play. For three months Pitt was defeated on every measure. Only when the opposition was finally reduced to a majority of one, did he dissolve. The election, held in 1784, returned Pitt with a good working majority. It seemed to be another victory for the king, but it turned out otherwise. The new minister was personally more congenial to the king than the defeated leaders, and his opinions often coincided with those of the king, but when they differed, the minister had his way. Pitt was the master. The attempt of the king to rule was finally defeated. Henceforth the cabinet system was an established part of the British constitution.

The younger Pitt

CHAPTER XXXI

THE INDUSTRIAL REVOLUTION

Signifi-
cance

WHILE the American Revolution was taking place, England was in
the midst of economic changes so fundamental that they eventually
revolutionized the life of the English people. They have long been
designated collectively as the "industrial revolution," but since they extended to agriculture, some writers draw a distinction between the
industrial and the agrarian revolutions. Recent researches have caused
some to doubt even the revolutionary nature of the movement, and
they are inclined to substitute for "industrial revolution" such phrases
as "the transition to industrialism" or the "unprecedented social and
economic development." This difficulty with regard to nomenclature
need not trouble us, because the usage of "industrial revolution" seems
destined to endure, but the reasons for the difficulty are sufficiently
important to require explanation. When the term first became current,
the movement was thought to have begun about 1760 and to have been
completed in its essential outlines early in the nineteenth century. It
now appears that the development of capitalization and of improved
technical methods in agriculture and industry, which marked the revolution, did not begin abruptly in the second half of the eighteenth century, but had behind it a gradual and continuous evolution running
through two centuries.[1] At the other end, it has been pointed out that
no single industry had yet passed through a complete technical revolution in 1830. Though "revolution" may thus imply a sharper and more
sudden change than actually occurred, it is not entirely a misnomer.
Not only did the speed and extent of the changes increase enormously
beginning approximately at 1760, but also within the next century the
open-field system of agriculture disappeared and an industrial organization in which the domestic system was predominant gave way to one
in which the factory system prevailed. If the changes be judged by their
effects upon society, and not by their cataclysmic quality, they were
without question revolutionary. So profound were the consequences,
indeed, that only with great effort can we who live among them today
visualize the manner of lives men lived before the revolution took
place. Many of the economic, social and political problems which we

---

[1] Above, pp. 324–326, 364–366, 487, 488, 490, 491.

now face had their origin in the economic transformations which began in England in the second half of the eighteenth century.

We have already seen how an agrarian revolution began in the six- teenth century, when rich men, seeking to gain profit, invested money in land on sufficient scale to unsettle the older system under which agriculture was practiced "by a community for its own maintenance on cooperative conditions."[2] The principal manifestation of the change was the growth of enclosures, and this process continued without notable alteration of speed until about the middle of the eighteenth century. Even at that late date the open-field system still prevailed in the larger part of England. During the second half of the seventeenth century a growing interest in the improvement of agricultural methods began to display itself, and in the first half of the eighteenth much scientific and technical progress was made. The rapid development of these two processes after the middle of the eighteenth century con- stituted the final and decisive portion of the agrarian revolution which had begun in the sixteenth century.

The experiments in agricultural technique were conducted mainly by wealthy landholders who could afford the cost of failures. One of the first of these pioneers to win enough fame to have his methods copied widely was Jethro Tull, who published the results of his experi- ments in 1731. His chief contribution was to sow field crops in drills instead of broadcast, in order to make it possible to cultivate the soil frequently while the crops were growing. He discovered that frequent disintegration of the soil improved the crop, though he misunderstood the reason. He invented both a horse-drill to drop the seeds in rows and a horse-hoe for cultivation. The refusal of his laborers to use the new machines at first was typical of an attitude toward improvements which was widespread. His system of husbandry, however, was adopted widely in the course of time because it made sowing more economical and increased the yield. Another innovator was Lord Townshend, Walpole's brother-in-law, who devoted the leisure ob- tained by his retirement from political life to the betterment of his estates in Norfolk. So notable was his success that he acquired from his friends and neighbors the appellation of "Turnip" Townshend. His most useful experiments were with the rotation of crops. By a four-course rotation of turnips, barley, grasses, and wheat he made it possible to use the land every year and eliminated the waste of fallow land one year in three. The value of his experiments is illustrated by

Nature of the agrarian revolution

Early experiments

---

[2] Hammond, J. L. and B., *Rise of Modern Industry,* p. 82.

the experience on one farm, where their adoption increased the annual returns from £180 to £800 in a period of thirty years. A third great name in the agricultural annals of the period is that of Bakewell. He specialized in the breeding of cattle. Before his day cattle were not raised primarily for food. Sheep were grown for their wool, and cows for dairy products. Little attention was given to breed, and sheep and cattle were gaunt and of small value for their meat. Bakewell began his work in 1750. He succeeded in producing a breed of sheep of much heavier weight. His efforts with cattle were less successful, but here his numerous imitators obtained better results. Before the end of the century the average weight of the carcass sold to the meat markets had more than doubled.

Obstacles to progress   While the introduction of these new methods improved English agriculture during the middle decades of the century, their adoption could not be widespread until certain obstacles to change had been removed. The open-field system hindered the practice of new methods, because the necessity for communal management of the great fields rendered individual initiative difficult, and because most of the new methods could not be pursued with profit on the scattered strips. Dissemination of the knowledge of the improvements was slow and difficult, because the average farmer was prejudiced against new ways and preferred to do things as his father had done them. The prevailing form of lease, which was terminable at the will of either the landlord or the tenant, made the leaseholder unwilling to sink capital in the permanent improvement of his land, lest his lease should be revoked before the expiration of the term of years necessary to reap the returns. The lack of facilities for reaching a market made costly improvements useless in some parts of England. These obstacles were overcome in the second half of the century.[3]

Progress of enclosures   The open fields were ended by a notable acceleration of enclosures. From 1700 to 1760 over three hundred thousand acres of land were enclosed, between 1761 and 1801 well over three million acres, and during the next half-century nearly as many more. The underlying cause of this spread of enclosures was the increased pressure of the population on the supply of food and the consequent growth of the demand for agricultural products. Between 1700 and 1760 the population probably increased absolutely by about a million. The increase of the proportion of the urban population to the rural was still greater. In 1696 a contemporary estimated that not much more than a fifth of the population

---

[3] Prothero, *English Farming Past and Present,* ch. ix.

was urban, while Arthur Young, writing in 1769, placed one-half the population in towns. Though neither of these estimates is exact, they establish the probability of a large growth of the element of the population engaged primarily in commercial and industrial pursuits and dependent upon the rural element for its supply of food. The statistics with regard to the exports and imports of grain tell the same story. Until about 1770 England exported more grain than she imported, for the next decade or so the imports about balanced the exports, and after 1790 the imports decidedly exceeded the exports. The growing demand for food which these figures demonstrate made agriculture more profitable and hastened the processes of reclaiming waste land and of increasing the productivity of land already under cultivation. Large landowners, who began to see the possibilities of applying such improvements as had been introduced by Tull, Townshend, and Bakewell, used their influence to secure the enclosures without which the application was unprofitable. They were actuated largely by their desire to secure greater financial returns from their lands, but this motive was partially concealed by an enlightened public opinion which regarded enclosures as progress toward the increase of the resources of the country.

After 1760 enclosures were ordinarily accomplished by acts of parliament. The first step was a petition to parliament asking for the lands of a village to be enclosed. This was formulated by the larger landowners, and it naturally asked for methods of enclosure which would favor their interests. After 1775 notice had to be posted in the parish before a petition was sent to parliament, but even if the small proprietors of land in the village opposed the project, ordinarily they could not stop it. Parliament required that the owners of three-fourths or four-fifths of the land to be enclosed should consent to the measure, but often a few of the larger owners who wanted the enclosure represented that portion of the land, and occasionally one landowner alone possessed enough of the land to initiate a petition. If parliament gave leave, as it usually did, the petition would be formulated as a private bill and acted upon like other private legislation. At the committee stage of the procedure petitions against the projected enclosure might be heard. If they were presented by other large landowners of the district, they might result in amendments or even in the defeat of the bill, but if they were presented by the poorer members of the community, they rarely had any effect, because the signers could neither interest a member of parliament to uphold their case nor afford to hire a lawyer to represent them before the committee. The landowning mem-

Process of enclosure

bers of parliament supported the landowning petitioners, and seldom did the private bill fail to become law. The act provided for a commission to survey the lands of the parish and to redistribute them in single compact holdings, in accordance with the terms of the act, to those who had rights in the lands. The small farmer or cottager often did not know just what his legal rights were, and he could not pay a lawyer to put his case before the commission. Even if the commissioners allowed his claim, they might award him "inferior land, or land in an inconvenient position."[4]

Effects   On the effects of enclosures both contemporaries and modern scholars have differed widely. That they improved the agricultural system and brought great profits to the large landowners few are disposed to deny. To the small owners and leaseholders they were disadvantageous in the long run. It is probably a mistake to ascribe the disappearance of the yeomen to enclosures, because they seem to have declined greatly in numbers before 1760, when the process of enclosure first became rapid. But the enclosures, combined with the new methods of farming, required large investments of capital to produce profits, and such of the yeomen and small leaseholders as were left were generally unable to meet the competition of their wealthier neighbors. To the poorer classes in the villages enclosures were a disaster. Cottagers who had no legal rights to the land which they used, or had none which they could prove to the satisfaction of the commissioners, lost their all. Those who received allotments had to bear their portion of the heavy cost of the enclosure and were required to fence their new holdings. Many could not meet these expenses and were forced to sell their plots at such prices as are usually obtainable at forced sales. A cottager who could meet the charges might find his new plot so small that, deprived of the rights to pasture a cow, some pigs and some geese on the common and to gather fuel from the underbrush in the wood, which he had previously possessed, he could not maintain himself. He, too, would find it necessary to sell his land. Some had holdings so small that they were awarded only a sum of money, which did not last long. The result was the disappearance of peasant proprietors from the countryside. This large class which had previously been dependent on wages only in part lost their homes and became solely dependent on their wages. The more intensive cultivation adopted on the enclosed estates increased the demand for rural wage earners, and the growth of industry provided ample opportunities of work in the towns; but the transition was neverthe-

---

[4] Hammond, J. L. and B., *Village Labourer*, p. 59.

less difficult, and the living conditions of the new classes of wage earners appear to have been far less comfortable than those of the cottagers under the old system.

The ignorance and prejudice which prevented the adoption of the new methods devised by men like Tull, Townshend, and their disciples were broken down largely by the work of Arthur Young. He failed twice to manage farms successfully, because he was interested in the theoretical rather than the practical side of agriculture. Between 1766 and 1775 he traveled extensively, observing agricultural methods and writing about them. He first made generally known the system developed in Norfolk as the result of Townshend's example. His writings were widely read and his advocacy of the new methods had much influence. Largely as the result of his endeavors the government in 1793, when it was entering a war against revolutionary France, established a board of agriculture of which he became the first secretary. The board surveyed the country systematically and continued the diffusion of knowledge by means of publications. This propaganda helped to bring about the wide adoption of the improvements developed earlier in the century.

Partly as a result of this agitation the old leases at will were gradually superseded by leases for definite terms of years. Such a lease relieved the tenant of the fear that he might be evicted before he had reaped the profits from his permanent improvements on the land, and made capital more readily available for investment in costly improvements.

In manufactures the results of the revolution were still more extraordinary. The fundamental change was the substitution of mechanical power for human exertion. A long series of mechanical inventions and improved technical processes rendered the application of human energy more efficient, or made possible the use of water power or steam to perform labor formerly done by hand. A result was the displacement of the domestic by the factory system, which altered completely the conditions of the life of the industrial workers, developed a new group of industrial capitalists who became influential in politics and society, and affected more or less the living conditions of all classes of society. The application of the mechanical inventions began in the first half of the eighteenth century, but it became rapid and extensive only in the second half. Before the close of the century the movement had gone far enough to make many of its results apparent, though the whole process was not completed until far into the nineteenth century.

The mechanization of industry began and was developed most fully

Marginal notes:

Diffusion of knowledge

Improved leases

Nature of the industrial changes

Silks

in the textile trades. The first of them to have its organization affected significantly by the introduction of machinery run by power was the silk industry. Though it had existed in England in the Middle Ages, it did not amount to much until the closing years of the seventeenth century, when a prohibition of the importation of French silks and an immigration of French Huguenot silk workers caused it to grow rapidly into an important industry. In 1718 a patent was granted to Thomas Lombe for the use of a machine "designed to give the final twist to silk thread that has already been formed by the combination of several filaments loosely twisted together."[5] The machine carried a large number of spindles and thus spun many threads at once. The patentee did not invent the machine, but imported it from Italy, where it had been in use for a century or more. Because it had to be run by water power, the new machine was set up in mills, and by 1765 several of them, each employing several hundred workers, were operating in different parts of England. The principal significance attached to this development is that "the modern factory system had its beginnings in the silk industry."[6]

Growth of cotton industry

Inventions which transformed every process in an industry are best exemplified in the production of cotton goods. This industry was introduced into Lancashire by the beginning of the seventeenth century. Its growth was slow. Since all of the raw material had to be imported, its development may be measured by the importation of cotton. In 1701 this amounted to two million pounds, and fifty years later it had increased to three million. Another yardstick is provided by the exports of the finished product. At the beginning of the eighteenth century the value of the average annual exports of woolens amounted to £2,000,000, while that of cottons was just over £23,000. In 1751 the exports of cottons had increased only to £46,000. About that time the fashion set toward cotton goods, and by 1764 the annual exportation had mounted to £200,000. The spinning and weaving were still carried on almost exclusively by hand in the homes of the workers, but the increasing demand helped to stimulate the invention of machines, and these soon caused its transfer to factories.

Weaving

The first invention was John Kay's flying shuttle, which was patented in 1733. The shuttle carried the cross thread through the warp, which consisted of the lengthwise threads upon the loom. When the warp was broad, two men were required to throw the shuttle to and fro. Kay's device, by the use of a lever and springs, enabled one weaver

[5] Usher, *History of Mechanical Inventions*, p. 240.
[6] Lipson. *Economic History*, ii, 103.

to perform the whole operation. It did not require artificial power and was applied to the hand loom. It was adopted first by the weavers of woolens and was not utilized generally by the weavers of cotton until about 1760.

Even before that time the principal difficulty in the trade had been the lack of a sufficient supply of spun yarn to keep the weavers con- Spinning tinuously occupied. This problem led to several attempts to find a method of mechanical spinning. Between 1745 and 1760 at least four different men invented spinning machines, but none of them was commercially successful. Apparently all of them were imperfect, and the inventors lacked either the capital or the ingenuity to make their machines practical and market them. Two men finally solved the problem at about the same time by different methods. Between 1764 and 1767 James Hargreaves, a poor weaver near Blackburn, invented the spinning jenny. It was so arranged that a worker by turning a wheel caused several spindles to revolve at once, spinning several threads in place of the one thread which could be produced by the old spinning wheel. Hargreaves tried to keep his invention secret, and used it only in his own home to provide yarn for his loom, but it met a fate which was common to many other inventions of the period. News of it leaked out, and a mob of spinners, who feared that it might come into common use and deprive them of work, invaded the house and destroyed the machine. Hargreaves then moved to Nottingham, where he acquired partners whose capital enabled him to establish a small factory. The spinning jenny was patented in 1770, and it soon came into general use. Meanwhile Richard Arkwright had begun to experiment with spinning by rollers, and in 1769 he patented a machine which was called the water frame. It reduced the cotton, which had previously been twisted into a loose and coarse thread of the size of a small rope, known as a roving, to a fine thread by pressing it between successive sets of revolving rollers, and gave the necessary twist by whirling spindles which drew the thread from the last set of rollers. The water frame was based upon the same principle as an unsuccessful machine which Lewis Paul had patented in 1738, and contemporaneously with Arkwright's experiments two other men were working on the construction of a similar machine. Claims were later advanced that Arkwright borrowed his ideas from one or the other of these sources. The evidence is so confused that it is impossible to say certainly whether he was the true inventor of spinning by rollers, but he was undoubtedly the first to apply the method with practical success, and it was his machine which spread throughout the industry. Ten years after Arkwright secured his patent, Samuel Crompton produced a machine called the mule, which combined the best features of the jenny and the water frame. The one spun a finer thread, but did not give it the hard twist which made it firm. The mule did both. It was so far superior to the earlier machines that eventually it replaced both of them.

Other processes

All three of these spinning machines took the cotton only after hand processes had converted the material to the form of rovings. The next steps were to invent machines which could perform these earlier stages of the work. The initial process in preparing cotton for spinning was carding, which straightened the fibers and interlaced them sufficiently to produce a continuous ribbon or sliver. Paul secured a patent for a carding machine in 1748, but it never worked well. The principal improvements which brought the carding machine into general use were devised by Arkwright between 1775 and 1785. In the same period he also invented two machines which rolled and spun the slivers into rovings. The inventions of Arkwright made it possible to perform by machinery all the processes necessary to transform the raw cotton into yarn which the weaver could use.[7]

Cotton factories

Another result of Arkwright's inventions was to make cotton spinning a factory industry. Both the jenny and the mule could be run by hand, but Arkwright's machines were too large and heavy for use in the home, and they required more power than the human arm. Since water power was needed to run one machine, it was economy to group a large number of them in one factory, where they could be run by one source of power. Factories began to become common in the decade following 1770. They were for the most part small, poorly organized, and confined to one process in the industry, such as carding or spinning. Better factories were largely due to the example set by Arkwright. He established several factories in which the whole sequence of operations from carding to spinning was carried on under one roof.[8] He also attained extraordinary success "in co-ordinating all the various parts of his vast industrial structures; in organizing and disciplining large bodies of men, so that each man fitted into his niche and the whole acted with the mechanical precision of a trained army," and "in combining division of labour with

---

[7] Before the cotton could go into the carding machine, the seeds had to be removed by hand until Eli Whitney, an American, invented the cotton gin in 1792.

[8] Wadsworth and Mann, *The Cotton Trade,* p. 492.

effective supervision from a common centre." His business enterprises became models which were copied far and wide.[9] Another impetus toward large factories was given by the application of steam as the motive power, which first took place in 1785. Thereafter the growth of factories was so rapid that within the first three decades of the nineteenth century the carding and spinning of cotton had practically ceased to be household industries.

The last process in the industry to come under factory organization was weaving. The invention of a power loom was finally stimulated by the increase of the production of yarn to such an extent that the hand weavers could not use all of it. Edmund Cartwright, a clergyman, who heard casually of the difficulty, was tempted to essay the task, and in 1785 he was so far successful that he secured a patent. Since he had never seen a hand loom in operation when he constructed his machine, it gives no cause for wonder that his invention did not work very well. It also evoked the determined opposition of the weavers, who were receiving high wages because the demand for their work was so heavy. They went so far as to burn one of the mills in which the new loom was being tried. Before the power loom could make progress, however, extensive improvements had to be made in its structure. These began to be produced by other inventors early in the nineteenth century, though it was not until 1822 that the perfection of the power loom reached a stage which made it a commercial success, and not until 1841 that it attained an approximate approach to its modern form. How long the weaving industry remained under the domestic system, while the remainder of the cotton industry was being converted to the factory system, is indicated by the slow growth of the number of power looms in use in England. In 1813 there were only 2,400; in 1820 only 12,150; in 1829, after the improved loom had come on the market, 45,500; and in 1833, when the value of the new loom had been proved, 85,000. By that time the domestic weaving of cotton was well on the way to extinction.

Weaving

The effect of the mechanical inventions upon the productivity of the cotton industry can also best be told by figures. In 1781, when many of the new machines had been invented and some factories had been built, the value of exported cotton goods was £355,000. Twenty years later, when the use of the new machines had become widespread, it was £7,000,000. In 1841, when the power looms had

Increase of production

---

[9] Lipson, *History of the English Woollen and Worsted Industries*, p. 153.

become common and the transition of the industry to the factory system was virtually completed, it had mounted to £23,400,000.

Woolens

In the cotton industry the transformation from the domestic to the factory system was more rapid than it was in other industries. In woolens, the other great textile trade, the transition was much more gradual. The greater part of the machines used in the manufacture of cottons could be used in the making of woolens, but some of them required extensive alterations, and some new machines had to be invented for processes which were lacking in the cotton industry. Kay's flying shuttle was adopted by many weavers in Yorkshire during the lifetime of the inventor, but it was not employed extensively in the west of England until the closing years of the eighteenth century and the early years of the nineteenth. In Yorkshire the carding and spinning of woolens and worsteds passed gradually into the mills between 1790 and 1825. Combing, a process which was used in place of carding for certain types of wool, did not become a machine industry until after 1840. Cartwright invented a combing machine, but, like his loom, it required many improvements by later inventors before it could be of practical use. The power loom also was not employed extensively for worsteds until the same period, and its general use for woolens still had to await the solution of several technical difficulties. Even after 1850 a substantial number of hand looms were still operating in the woolen industry. Thus the industrial revolution in woolens had only its beginning in the eighteenth century and was accomplished mainly during the first half of the nineteenth.

Decline of the iron industry to 1750

The production of iron in the first half of the eighteenth century was divided into three main operations. In the foundry the iron ore was smelted in blast furnaces, and the resulting liquid iron was run out into furrows, where it cooled into pigs of cast iron. In the finery the pigs were heated at a forge and hammered by large hammers run by water power. This process reduced it into bars of malleable iron which had greater tensile strength and could be used for many purposes for which the more brittle cast iron was not suitable. If the bars produced at the finery were to be used by smiths for the manufacture of nails, tools, or other small wares, they were sent through a slitting and rolling mill. "The slitting wheel, which was worked by water, broke or cut up the cold bar into short lengths; these lengths were then heated and when hot put under the rollers, also worked by water, and rolled flat."[10] The manufacture of this

[10] Hammond, J. L. and B., *Rise of Modern Industry*, p. 133.

product into wares was not in the main a part of the iron industry, but constituted a branch of the metal trades. The first two of the three processes in the iron trade were declining during the period on account of the increasing scarcity of charcoal. The pigs which the first Abraham Darby produced by the use of coke were not of sufficiently good quality to be refined into commercial malleable iron. Cast iron, on the other hand, was not used extensively, and his successful use of coke to produce cast iron does not appear to have become generally known until about 1750. At that date no method of using coke or coal in the fineries had yet been discovered. The rolling mills and the metal trades did not share this decline, because they could import bar iron from Sweden and America and use coal for heating it. In the two earlier stages of production the sulphurous fumes of coal damaged the quality of the iron, but after the iron had been refined, coal did not cause it to deteriorate.

After 1750 the iron industry began to recover from its depression, chiefly as the result of two developments. One was an extension of the use of cast iron products. They were much cheaper than the wares of malleable iron, because they were run immediately from the foundry furnace into finished products, while the wares of malleable iron had to go through the finery, the mill and the smithy. A few years after 1750 the knowledge of Darby's process of smelting with coke became generally known, and the iron masters increased greatly the variety of cast iron products and created a demand for them. The other development was the discovery by the second Abraham Darby of a method of producing with coke pigs which could be converted into good malleable iron at the finery. The process was perfected around 1750, and within a few years other iron masters were using it. Both developments depended primarily upon the use of coke in the blast furnaces of the foundries. They did not cause a sharp rise of production. During the third quarter of the century the increase of output probably did not average more than one per cent a year. *The recovery of the foundries*

The perfection of methods which made possible the use of coal in the fineries is associated with the name of Henry Cort. In 1783 and 1784 he received patents for the processes of puddling and rolling. In puddling the pig iron was melted in a furnace burning coal before it went to the forge. While the iron was liquid, it was stirred or puddled, and the motion caused the sulphurous gases to escape. When it had cooled sufficiently, it was hammered, and finally it was heated again and run through rollers which squeezed out the re- *The use of coal in the fineries* maining impurities. Cort was not the first to employ coal in refining iron, the type of furnace used for puddling was not his invention, and other phases of his process may have been partially anticipated by others; but he "was the first to combine and co-ordinate these fragmentary improvements into a single new process."[11] Cort's inventions revolutionized the industry. Coal was not only cheaper than charcoal, but it was also far more plentiful. Its use made possible a rapid expansion of production and a reduction in the price of the product. The new process was so much quicker than the old that fifteen tons could be produced in the length of time required to produce one ton under the old system. The puddled and rolled iron was, moreover, of superior quality to any malleable iron made by the former method. Another advantage was that the rolling mills could produce variously shaped bars of iron suitable for structural purposes, and large sheets which could be used for the construction of such things as tanks, boilers, and ships. In 1788 the output of pig iron in Great Britain was 68,000 tons, by 1796 it had nearly doubled, and ten years later it had doubled again and stood at 250,000 tons.

Organization of the industry

The effect of these developments upon the organization of the iron industry was to convert it into a series of large-scale enterprises. Organizations of this type had existed since the seventeenth century, but in the eighteenth they became the rule. With the use of coal the industry moved to the neighborhood of the coal mines in the midlands, the north and the northwest. "Furnace, forge and mill" were more commonly combined in a single plant, and some firms purchased and worked the iron and coal mines which supplied their raw materials. Iron became a far more heavily capitalized industry than cotton. The metal trades, on the other hand, remained under the domestic system far into the nineteenth century. In 1840 the cutlery workers in the vicinity of Sheffield, and the makers of locks, nails, tools and other small products of iron in the region around Birmingham still labored mainly in their own homes or in small shops. They represented many varying degrees of dependence upon their employers, but they were not yet generally congregated in factories, though some factories had been built.

Steel

A new process of making steel was discovered by Benjamin Huntsman shortly before the middle of the eighteenth century. Previously, malleable iron had been converted into steel by a slow process of heating in which charcoal was applied to increase the content of

---

[11] Ashton, *Iron and Steel*, p. 93.

carbon. If a better product was desired, this steel was heated again and hammered. Huntsman mixed both qualities and smelted them by a new method which removed the impurities. The crucible steel produced in this manner was much harder, and it was soon in demand for the manufacture of such products as tools requiring a sharp cutting edge, and watch springs. It became a thriving industry, but it grew in the eighteenth century upon no such scale as the manufacture of iron. Crucible steel was far too costly to be used for structural purposes, and it was not until after 1859, when Bessemer completed a new process of making steel, that steel became one of the fundamental heavy industries.

The mining of coal during the eighteenth century experienced no such sensational changes as occurred in the cotton and iron industries, but it made steady progress. The pits went deeper, the scale of working grew, and the methods gradually improved. As the underground galleries became longer, the difficulty of getting the coal to the foot of the shaft increased, and in the later part of the century iron rails were laid on which small cars could be run. They were also employed on the surface to transport the coal to the canal or other shipping point. "These rails gave a great impetus to the moving of coal."[12] As the shafts went deeper, the hoisting of the coal to the surface presented new problems which were met late in the century by means of water power or steam and the development of better hoisting apparatus. The production of coal probably increased less than fourfold during the century, but the use of the steam engine in factories and the inventions of Cort did not come until a few years before the end of the century. When their effect was finally felt in the nineteenth century, the output of coal expanded more rapidly, though it was the second half of the century before coal became the foundation of British industry.

Coal

In all of the industries which have been mentioned and in many others the invention of the steam engine had a revolutionary influence. James Watt, the inventor, was a trained maker of mathematical instruments, who was allowed to establish a shop within the precincts of the university of Glasgow. The demands for the construction of scientific apparatus developed his mechanical skill and inventive genius, and intercourse with the brilliant scientists of the faculty and his own studies gave him scientific knowledge. His attention was first called to steam engines in 1759, and four years later he began

The steam engine

---

[12] Knowles, *Industrial and Commercial Revolutions*, p. 71.

to study a model of Newcomen's engine in the possession of the university. In this engine steam was forced into the cylinder to push the piston up, it was then condensed by cooling the cylinder in order to create a vacuum, and the atmospheric pressure pushed the piston down. By experiment Watt discovered that three-fourths of the steam was being wasted, and his first problem was to avoid the waste. His solution was to keep the cylinder always hot and to build a separate cold condenser connected with the cylinder. When the piston was pushed up, the steam would rush into the separate condenser, leaving a vacuum in the cylinder without cooling it. When he built his first model, however, he improved upon his original idea by using steam to push the piston down as well as up. In the building of a model he experienced great difficulties. He could not make the heavy parts himself, and the making of machine parts according to specifications was then an unknown trade. He had to rely upon a smith whose productions were so inaccurate that they often had to be done over. As he advanced, he kept making improvements in design which caused further delays. He was unable to finance the building and marketing of engines, and in 1767 he went into partnership with John Roebuck, the principal owner of the Carron Iron Works. In 1769 he obtained a patent and began to build a trial engine. He soon found that even the skilled mechanics of the Carron works could not make the parts true. The special difficulty was to obtain a cylinder into which the piston would fit exactly. If it fitted loosely, the steam would escape and the engine would run badly or not at all. The consequence was that the construction of the engine was still dragging along when Roebuck failed in 1772. Watt was then taken into partnership by Matthew Boulton, a hardware manufacturer who had a large factory near Birmingham. Boulton had more sympathy for Watt and understood his problems better than Roebuck had done. He gathered workmen who could make the more delicate pieces of machinery, and he obtained from John Wilkinson, an iron master who had invented a new boring process for making cannon, an iron cylinder which was bored accurately. The trial engine was completed in 1774, and the manufacture was begun in 1776.

The engines found a ready market. Several mines in Cornwall were preparing to suspend operations because the mines had become so deep that the cost of pumping out the water with Newcomen's engine was prohibitive. Watt's engine, by saving the waste of heat, saved coal, and it was also more powerful. Once it had been tried, many orders followed. It was also used for running the bellows of iron works. It could not be employed to provide power for factories because it only worked a vertical rod up and down, and a rotary motion was needed to run machinery. Between 1780 and 1782 Watt solved that problem, and during the next few years made extensive improvements over his first solution. In 1785 the first steam engine was installed in a cotton factory, and by 1800 cotton factories were using 92 engines and other textile factories were using 22 more. The significance of the steam engine may be illustrated by its relation to the iron trade. It was substituted for water power not only to blow blast furnaces but also to work the forge hammers and to run the slitting and rolling mills. It made the industry independent of water power, the lack of which in a dry summer had often forced a foundry to close. It made possible the development of a stronger blast, which caused the iron to melt better and at the same time saved coal. "The use of steam, which made it easier to produce iron, increased at the same time the demand for cast iron goods, since they were needed for the manufacture of steam engines, and also for the machinery in the cotton and other industries which was worked by steam engines."[13]

The difficulties which Watt experienced in obtaining accurate parts for his first engine were typical of the obstacles which all makers of machinery encountered at the time. They were accentuated in Watt's case, because the steam engine was more complicated and required greater accuracy than other contemporary machines. The maker of a machine had to employ smiths, cabinet makers, clock makers, instrument makers and skilled mechanics of various trades as necessity dictated. The parts were made by hand, and since "the dexterity of hand and correctness of eye" varied not only from man to man but also at different times in the same man, the products were subject to variations and inaccuracies. After the parts were made, it usually required much alteration and adjustment to assemble them into a machine which would work. Watt, or some of his employees, usually set up his early engines, and, with all their knowledge and skill, they often found it necessary to tinker with an engine for a long time after it had been erected, before it would run satisfactorily. "After easing her here and screwing her up there, putting in a new part, and altering an old one, packing the piston and tightening the valves, the machine would at length be got to work."[14] What was needed was the development of machine tools for the making of machines. This

Machine tools

---

[13] Hammond, J. L. and B., *Rise of Modern Industry*, p. 141.

[14] Smiles, *Industrial Biography*, p. 181, cited by Usher, *Industrial History of England*, p. 328.

did not come until the nineteenth century, but the first steps were taken in the closing years of the eighteenth. In 1794, for example, Henry Maudslay devised an addition to the lathe known as the slide rest. The lathe turned the article upon which work was to be done, and, before the invention of the slide rest, the workman accomplished the work by holding a tool against the turning article. When the object was metal, accuracy was nearly impossible. The slide rest held the tool against the revolving object, and, when it had been perfected, attained accuracy. In such a simple thing as a screw it made the difference between a faulty and a true thread. Further development of machine tools was slow. By 1820 a few firms were making the construction of machines their sole business, and during the next thirty years many important inventions were made in machine tools. By that time machines, which once could be made only by the most skilled craftsmen with many imperfections, were being manufactured with a high degree of accuracy by machines tended largely by unskilled laborers. The new machines were much cheaper, and, being made principally of iron, they were also more durable than the old machines, which had many wooden parts.

The significance of this development is brought out by the contrast between the experiences of Watt and Bessemer. The latter invented a process for making bronze powder which he wished to keep secret. He distributed specifications of the parts of machines which he needed to several machine shops in such a manner that no one shop made all the parts for any one machine. In 1843 the parts were delivered to the factory, and Bessemer with two helpers assembled the machines and installed them without any serious trouble. The development of machine tools was necessary before the steam engine and the other mechanical inventions of the eighteenth century could be made with sufficient accuracy and cheapness to produce that rapid increase in the use of machinery which established the machine age. As late as 1835 about 1,300 textile factories were using water wheels and only about 1,900 were employing steam engines. The development of machine tools also illustrates particularly well another important aspect of the industrial revolution, and that is the interdependence of the whole movement on its various parts. An invention in one industry often made possible the improvement of a process in another industry. The machine tool industry was dependent for its existence upon the improved methods of refining and working iron discovered late in the eighteenth century and steadily bettered thereafter, and the reason for its existence was the demand created by the mechanical inventions begun in the same period and multiplied thereafter.

The potteries supply an example of an industry in which the factory system developed without the aid of artificial power or sensational mechanical inventions. The trade was confined to a small portion of Staffordshire, where there were convenient supplies of clay, coal and lead. At the beginning of the eighteenth century it was conducted in many small, primitively equipped units, each employing from six to ten men and boys. During the first half of the century many improvements were made in the materials employed. In order to secure white ware, white sand and clay began to be imported from Devon. In 1720 the practice of adding ground flint to give a still purer white was begun. The dust from the flint gave the workers diseases of the lungs, and between 1726 and 1732 a method of grinding flint under water was patented. Soon afterward liquid lead began to be used in place of salt for glazing. It gave a smoother surface and was cheaper. On the technical side a lathe was introduced to give a better finish to an article after it had left the potter's wheel, and after 1730 the potter's wheel was largely superseded by the use of molds into which the clay was run or pressed to give it the desired shape. By the middle of the century the market for the potteries had expanded so greatly that the advantages of production in units of larger size began to be seen. Owners of small plants began to add one baking oven to another, and in the course of the second half of the century several of these expansionist movements grew into factories. The largest and most famous of them was owned by Josiah Wedgwood. On the technological side he improved the baking ovens and experimented with the measurement of high temperatures which was essential for controlling the quality of the wares produced. Methods of enameling the better wares and printing designs on the cheaper were discovered by others, but Wedgwood carried the artistic side of decorating and shaping his ornamental wares to a degree of excellence that made them famous. Within his factory labor became highly specialized, and his discipline and control of the workers were comparable to those maintained by Arkwright. He was also very successful in the organization of the commercial side of the business. In the last years of the century two processes developed by others helped to expand enormously the manufacture of cheaper wares. One was a method of printing an object before it was glazed. It worked particularly well with blue, and the willow ware design manufactured in Staffordshire by Josiah Spode won a popularity which has not yet departed. The other was the introduction by the second Josiah Spode of bone paste into the body of china. It made possible for the first time the production of cheap china, the earlier cheap pottery having been the coarser earthenware. Despite the growth of the industry promoted by these many improvements, the factories remained independent of mechanical power. In 1793 a steam engine was introduced into the flint and glaze mills, but the remainder of the work continued to be done by hand. Not until after 1870 was mechanical power commonly used for pressing the clay into molds.

Transportation: roads

A fundamental aspect of the industrial revolution was the improvement of transportation which made larger markets available. The establishment of the local surveyors of the highways by the Tudors had failed to produce good roads, and in the early years of the eighteenth century the roads were very bad. In some regions such articles as pottery and coal were carried on the backs of horses because there were no roads suitable for wagons. The roads which could be used by wagons were generally in such a state of disrepair that transportation was very slow. These evils were finally remedied by the establishment of toll roads. Parliament would authorize a private company to charge tolls on a specified piece of road, and in return the company would build or repair the road and maintain it in good condition. The first parliamentary act of this type was passed in the reign of Charles II, but such acts did not become common until the second half of the eighteenth century. Several of the companies employed engineers, of whom the most famous was Macadam. He surfaced roads with angular fragments of granite which packed down to form a hard roadbed and prevented the formation of ruts and holes such as had rendered the older roads so difficult of passage. The value of this mode of construction is attested by its continuous use to the present day. By the early years of the nineteenth century regular coach services enabled travelers to accomplish in a day or less a journey which had taken several days before the turnpikes were built. The transportation of commodities was also rendered much easier and faster, and regular wagon services were organized between London and such manufacturing centers as Leeds and Manchester.

Canals

Contemporaneously with the improvement of the roads an era of canal construction began. The first canal was completed in 1761. It ran from Worsley to Manchester, and its chief purpose was to reduce the cost of the transportation of coal to the manufacturing center. Though the canal was only eleven miles long, it was a difficult feat of engineering. Its successful termination was the signal for a boom which covered England with a network of canals. The canals not only rendered new markets accessible, but they also reduced the cost of carriage. The canal from the coalpits of Worsley reduced the price of coal in Manchester by one-half immediately, while the cost of transportation from Wolverhampton to Liverpool was reduced from 100 s. to 25 s. a ton. Before the rise of the railroads in the nineteenth century 2,600 miles of canals had been built at a cost of $50,000,000.

These profound changes in economic practice were accompanied by a reversal of economic theory. The new theory was formulated by Adam Smith, who published his *Wealth of Nations* in 1776. It was a declaration of independence in economic thought. He denied the main principles of the mercantile system. In his view the most important form of wealth was consumable goods, since one nation could always buy gold from another with goods. Granted that premise, it becomes more important to encourage production than commerce. The mode of encouragement represents the most vital difference of Smith's theory from the old. The national welfare could best be promoted, he thought, by giving to each individual the freest possible scope to work out his own self-interest. Under such a régime each man would find it to his interest to produce what other men want. Production and trade would be directed into the most profitable channels, while competition would keep prices at a reasonable level. The less regulation of industry and commerce by the government the better the economic situation, since external regulation is bound to interfere with the working of natural economic laws. As Smith expresses the principle, "the patrimony of a poor man lies in the strength and dexterity of his hands; and to hinder him from employing this strength and dexterity in what manner he thinks proper without injury to his neighbour, is a plain violation of this most sacred property."[15] Again, he says: "Every individual is continually exerting himself to find out the most advantageous employment for whatever capital he can command. It is his own advantage, indeed, and not that of society, which he has in view. But the study of his own advantage naturally, or rather necessarily leads him to prefer that employment which is most advantageous to the society. . . ."[16] It was, in short, the economic system of *laissez faire* (let alone).

The influence of Adam Smith's teaching was immediate and widespread. It gave systematic expression "to ideas towards which the

Economic theory

[15] *Wealth of Nations*, ed. Cannan, i, 123.
[16] *Ibid.*, p. 419.

leaders of industry had long been feeling their way."[17] His book went through five editions while he was yet alive. The new capitalists who owned the factories desired to work out the new problems of business free from governmental interference, and they used their influence to promote the new doctrine. Pitt was an acknowledged disciple of the new theory. The book was well known to legislators, who frequently mentioned it in parliament after 1783. By the end of the eighteenth century *laissez faire* was the economic doctrine prevalent in English thought with regard to the governmental regulation of industry. Its chief influence before 1800 was negative. Few new laws were enacted for the further regulation of industry and commerce. Not until the nineteenth century did the government begin to repeal rapidly much of the regulative legislation previously enacted.

Results
The results of the industrial revolution probably cannot be enumerated with entire accuracy within brief compass. They were so complex that some of them have defied analysis, and competent scholars disagree over important details. Chronology presents a serious problem. In the early years of the nineteenth century the effects were becoming apparent, but the use of machinery was still limited to certain industries, and within those industries to certain processes or certain regions. In some industries and districts the domestic system held its own far into the nineteenth century. While one may say without serious fear of contradiction that the industrial revolution made the factory system the predominant form of organization, that result had not yet been attained in the opening decade of the nineteenth century, and was not attained until the second half of the century. Another disturbing factor is the war with France during the closing years of the eighteenth century and the early years of the nineteenth. Economic and social ills in that period have sometimes been attributed too readily to the industrial revolution without sufficient consideration of the war as a contributory cause.[18] Yet the effects of the industrial revolution upon daily life were so profound that the difficulty of brief explanation does not justify silence. The difficulty is mentioned primarily for the purpose of warning the reader that the following summary is somewhat tentative and may stand in need of qualification.

The most direct material result was an enormous increase of the industrial output. A primary factor in the production of this result

---

[17] Lipson, *Economic History*, iii, 266.
[18] Some of the economic and social effects of the war are noted in chapters xxxii, xxxiii.

was the increased efficiency given to the application of human energy by the use of machines and artificial power. Each worker, with the same expenditure of physical and mental energy, could produce a greater amount of the manufactured product. This, of course, was not the only factor. In the potteries the increased production was due mainly to improved technical methods and better management. The use of new mechanical inventions and artificial power in some industries increased the demand for the products of other industries not yet transformed by these means. The improved means of communication contributed to the increase of production in no small measure by rendering new markets available and old ones more easily accessible. The economy of labor, the better technical processes, the more efficient management and the cheaper transportation rendered the products of the transformed industries cheaper or better, and often accomplished both results. Many of the domestic industries were also affected, since they obtained from the transformed industries cheaper materials with which to work. The lower prices of products stimulated a demand for them, and commerce experienced a growth which may be illustrated by the figures for foreign trade. From 1700 to 1783 the annual value of the combined exports and imports increased gradually and fairly steadily from ten to twenty-eight millions of pounds. In the next seven years it jumped to thirty-nine millions, and during the decade from 1790 to 1800 it reached the huge total of seventy-three millions. The tonnage of the ships which cleared from British harbors corroborates the story. In thousands of tons the figures are 289 for 1709, 647 for 1760, and 2,130 for 1800. The revolution took place in England before it did in other European countries, and for a long period the superior quality and greater cheapness of British manufactured wares gave them an immense advantage in the competition for the markets of the world. The wealth of England was increased many fold.

The increase of wealth eventually benefited all classes, but the capitalists gained the largest share in the distribution at the beginning. The concentration of capital in industry began long before the period of the mechanical inventions, but it was greatly accelerated during that period. In order to use the new machines to the best advantage it was necessary to group a large number of them in one factory where they could all be run by one unit of artificial power; the equipment of an efficient plant for the production of iron required a larger investment of capital than had formerly been necessary; and even in industries like the potteries, which were not mechanized, the savings

The margin notes: Industrial production; The capitalists

which could be attained by production upon a large scale, when the market was large, became apparent. With the constant development of circumstances such as these, capitalistic organization, which before the industrial revolution had been exceptional, became normal. The capitalists eventually dominated industry, and long before that time arrived they were becoming influential in politics and society. As early as 1785 the manufacturers were exerting a strong influence upon the policies of the government which were likely to affect their industries, and before the first quarter of the nineteenth century had expired, the industrial capitalists constituted practically a new and important class in society.

Labor

The effects of the industrial revolution upon labor were both good and bad. Eventually the rise of the factories in one industry after another caused cottage labor to be superseded. Once a branch of industry had been successfully mechanized, the product could be manufactured so much more cheaply by machines than by hand that the cottage laborers could not maintain competition. Their earnings gradually dwindled until they were too small to provide a living, or even to provide those who still retained small plots of land with the supplementary income necessary to eke out that derived from agriculture. They gradually joined the great mass of factory operatives or the group of rural wage earners. The transition was often difficult to make and it was the cause of much suffering while it was taking place. To skilled laborers by hand who were too old to acquire skill in tending the new machines the change was particularly disastrous. They were frequently forced to sacrifice their cottages, accept the wages of unskilled workmen in the factories, and live in less comfort in the dreary, crowded tenements of a town. The transition did not take place in all industries at the same time, and a period of adversity for the domestic workers in one industry might be a period of prosperity for those in another. In the early years of the nineteenth century, when the weekly earnings of spinners by hand in the cotton industry were declining, those of the domestic weavers of woolens in the north were increasing. It was merely a postponement of the evil day, for the weavers by the hand loom were later forced to make the same transition which the domestic spinners had made earlier, but the prolongation of the movement prevented it from assuming disastrous proportions at any one time. The number of workers who suffered from the transition was always in a distinct minority at any given stage in the course of the industrial revolution.

Even if those who were caught in the transition be left out of account, the supersession of the domestic by the factory system was not an unmixed blessing for the laborers. On the other hand, some modern writers, who have idealized the life of the cottage workers, have depicted the conditions of labor in the early factories in colors which are too dark. Many contemporaries believed that the introduction of labor-saving machinery would decrease the demand for labor, and laborers were so convinced of it that they often attacked factories and destroyed machinery. The fact is, however, that the machinery so reduced the prices of wares that the demand for them grew sufficiently to provide increased opportunities for employment. It is probable also that large groups obtained better wages in the factories than they had received before, and it is certain that the lower prices of commodities enabled the workers to enjoy a variety of material comforts such as their ancestors had never known. Unskilled laborers, moreover, found in the factories such opportunities to better their positions by the application of energy and ability as had not existed in the domestic system.

The conditions of labor in the factories were in some respects better and in others worse than those which existed in the homes. Many of the early factories were full of dust and dirt, but the same was true of the homes in which the same kind of work was performed. Those who labored in the factories did not have to eat and sleep with the refuse of their work. Some of the machines, moreover, eliminated hand processes which had been most unhealthy. Most of the work in the factories was monotonously dreary, but that was also true of much of the work done in the homes. The division of labor which caused a workman to perform over and over only one of the several processes needful for the production of any article was intensified by the mechanical inventions, but it had already gone so far in the homes that few workers experienced any longer the joy of creation. It was, indeed, more of a physical strain to tend a hand loom than a power loom. The employment of women and children in the factories finally evoked an outcry from the humanitarians, but the situation was inherited from the domestic system. In the homes, however, most of the children worked under the friendly eyes of their parents and not under the direction of an overseer. That to which the laborers themselves most objected was "the tyranny of the factory bell." For the long hours during which the power kept the machines in motion, the workers had to tend them without intermission, under the discipline established by the employer and enforced by his foreman. Many domestic laborers had to maintain equally long hours in order to earn a bare subsistence, but they were free to begin, stop and rest when they pleased. The operatives in the factories felt keenly a loss of personal independence.

The factory system also increased largely the number of laborers who were completely dependent upon their employers economically. It did not create the wage system. When domestic workers no longer owned the means of production, they were selling only their labor. The number of those so circumstanced was large in the eighteenth century, but some of them were preserved from entire dependence upon their industrial employers by subsistence farming or by agricultural by-employment. The laborers in the factories were solely dependent upon their employers for wages. If the wages were too low or if employment ceased, they could fall back upon no other resource. The result was to intensify the quarrels between labor and capital, which had already begun under the domestic system. Early in the eighteenth century combinations of workers similar to trade unions were being formed in the domestic industries, and in the second half of the century strikes for better wages were common. In such contests the concentration of labor in factories gave to the workers the advantage that they could form more closely knit and more efficient unions for bargaining collectively with their employers.

Movements of population

The new organization of industry caused a notable change in the distribution of population. The coal was mainly in the north and west, the iron plants moved to the neighborhood of the coal fields, and the new factories were located largely in the same regions. These industrial centers drew their laborers at first mainly from the surrounding countryside, and no large direct migration of workers from the south of England to the north appears to have taken place. Nevertheless, the balance of the population between the south and the north was altered decisively. The most densely populated counties of England outside of London and its neighborhood, which had always been in the south, came to be in the north. The industrial revolution also brought about a concentration of the population in urban units. The industrial plants were grouped where there was water power, easy access to a supply of coal, or other facilities; and the workers necessarily settled in the neighborhood of the industrial establishments. England, which had been predominantly rural for centuries, became in the nineteenth century predominantly urban.

The sudden concentration of the population in towns produced serious problems of housing, sanitation, paving and lighting, with which the existing municipalities were unprepared to cope. A large part of

the working population of the manufacturing towns in the early
years of the nineteenth century lived in overcrowded, unsanitary tenements, with an inadequate supply of pure water, on streets and alleys
rendered unsanitary by poor pavements and lack of a proper system
of sewage. Discomfort, disease and misery came to be the lot of too
many operatives in the new factories. In the small amount of time
which the urban workers had at their disposal for amusement, recreation and education, there was scant opportunity to obtain them. Many
of the rural domestic workers, to be sure, lived in homes which were
neither comfortable nor sanitary, and found little time for amusement
or education, but they could at least enjoy the fresh air and the
natural beauties of the countryside in their moments of leisure. The
congestion of population in the towns increased the dangers arising
from the lack of proper sanitation, and also added to the dreariness
of the life of the workers, who at best could walk into the country
only on Sundays and holidays. "The new town was not a home
where man could find beauty, happiness, leisure, learning, religion, the
influences that civilize outlook and habit, but a bare and desolate
place, without color, air or laughter, where man, woman and child
worked, ate and slept."[19]

The industrial revolution contributed indirectly to the production
of important political changes. With the growth of industry Great
Britain became dependent as never before upon the outside world
for markets and supplies of raw materials. Most significant of all was
the dependence upon external sources for a supply of food. This was
due to an increase of population which probably may be attributed
only in part to the industrial revolution. It was the consequence partly
of a decreased death rate brought about by the advance of medical
science, but it seems probable that it was caused partly by an increase
in the birth rate stimulated by the demand for child labor and by the
administration of the poor law.[20] The dependence made it vital for
Great Britain to control the sea, in order to keep her people from
starvation, and affected profoundly her international relations. The
economic revolution helped ultimately to bring about the reform of
parliament. The shift of the population brought out glaringly the inequalities of representation. In 1821, after the change in distribution
was well under way, the twelve coastal counties from Norfolk to
Somerset, where the population had been thickest in the Middle Ages,
had a population of about 3,700,000 out of a total of approximately

Life in the new towns

Political effects

---

[19] Hammond, J. L. and B., *Rise of Modern Industry*, p. 232.
[20] On the poor law, see below, pp. 650, 651.

12,000,000, but they returned to the house of commons 115 out of a total of 203 representatives of boroughs. Less than one-third of the population returned more than half of the urban representatives. Populous boroughs in the north, like Leeds and Manchester, had no representation at all, while Old Sarum with no inhabitants and Boroughbridge with 86 sent two members each to the house of commons. The rotten boroughs, moreover, were in the main controlled by the landed aristocracy. The new industrial capitalists resented the control of parliament by the landed interests, and eventually they used the influence of their great wealth to secure the reform of a system which perpetuated the power of the landlords and deprived business of an adequate representation. An immediate result of no small importance was to give to Great Britain the economic advantage in the war which began with France in 1793. The possession of the longer purse was largely responsible for Great Britain's victory in this great war, which closed the duel waged intermittently between England and France for a century and a quarter.

CHAPTER XXXII

WILLIAM PITT THE YOUNGER

WILLIAM PITT, who came to power in 1784 and remained at the head of English affairs continuously for eighteen years, was the second son of the earl of Chatham. When he became prime minister he was only twenty-five. He had studied with the design of a political career, making it a practice to haunt the galleries of the house of commons, where he obtained the precocious knowledge of the ways of the house which enabled him to become its leader at an age when few members succeed in winning its serious attention. Political talents of a high order helped him to retain the office of prime minister for an exceptionally long period. In parliamentary debate he towered head and shoulders above all his contemporaries except Fox, though he could not rival the power of his father's oratory. In the management of men, on the other hand, he displayed much more tact than Chatham, becoming a remarkably skillful manipulator of party politics despite a "correct, decorous," and somewhat reserved deportment. His enduring fame as a statesman rests upon his accomplishment during the period of peace between the close of the American Revolution in 1783 and the outbreak of war with France in 1793. As a war minister he was much less successful than his father. Yet, despite his mistakes, his administrative capacity, political uprightness, whole-souled patriotism, and "heroic endeavor" so impressed contemporaries that the nation felt more confidence in his leadership than it did in any of his successors during the period of the war. Pitt takes place with his father in the small group of England's great parliamentary statesmen.

Pitt's most notable policy was his reorganization of the public finances. Great Britain emerged from the American war heavily indebted and with the public credit badly impaired. Despite Rockingham's reforms, many sinecures were still left in the public service, and many of the officials who were concerned with the public revenues were not held to any proper accountability. Malversation and peculation were rife. The revenues were so extremely complicated that their collection involved a large waste. Many legitimate branches of trade were overburdened, and smuggling was thus encouraged. By a large number of detailed measures Pitt reduced the financial system to order. Many of the sinecures were abolished, and the remaining officials were

The man

Financial
reform

593

rendered responsible. The revenues were reduced in number and simplified in their administration, with the result that their collection cost less and their total yield increased. Duties on articles that received the chief attention of smugglers were so reduced that smuggling ceased to be profitable in proportion to the risks. Smuggling consequently decreased. Under Pitt's wise administration the public income grew steadily, the public credit was restored, and commerce was encouraged.

Reciprocity with France

Pitt also promoted commerce by the application of the principles of Adam Smith to foreign trade. In 1786 he negotiated a treaty with France which provided for a mutual reduction of duties on all except a few specified imports. This reciprocal arrangement evoked a strong opposition in England, because it ran counter to the mercantilist theories which had governed the regulation of foreign commerce for centuries. In practice it proved to be advantageous to British industry and commerce until its operation was interrupted by the war with France. Pitt thus took the first tentative step toward the introduction of free trade and became the pioneer statesman in that field, though the intervention of the war with France delayed the second step for many years.

Parliamentary reform

Pitt further demonstrated his liberal views by his advocacy of the reform of the house of commons. During the first half of the eighteenth century the unrepresented masses had been apathetic with regard to the inequalities of representation and the narrow franchise. When the policies of George III caused strong popular opposition, it could not be expressed by constitutional means for lack of adequate representation. The opposition consequently expressed itself by means of huge demonstrations, which often took the form of violent mobs. The extent and the violence of the manifestations in behalf of John Wilkes gave evidence of the strength of the public feeling in favor of electoral reform and served to stimulate a popular agitation in its behalf. At first the movement had little organization and found no favor with statesmen, but in the course of time societies began to be formed to maintain propaganda, and a few liberal statesmen, like Chatham, pronounced in its favor. In 1785 Pitt introduced a bill to deprive the worst of the rotten boroughs of their representatives and redistribute them to counties and populous towns. He was not very insistent upon its passage. Apparently he feared to risk pressure upon his supporters lest it should split the majority. Too many members of his party owed their seats to the patrons of decayed boroughs. Consequently the bill never became law.

While the evils of the electoral system continued under Pitt, the corruption of parliament, by which the Whig aristocracy and George III in turn had maintained a majority, was nearly given up. The reforms of the Rockingham administration had eliminated many of the sinecures and pensions that had constituted the backbone of the system. Pitt refused to use those that were left, nor did he resort to other forms of bribery to secure votes in the house of commons. He thus put a final end to the system of direct bribery of the members of the house of commons which had been a growing evil for a century. On the other hand, he did not hesitate to pervert to his own advantage the electoral system which he had failed to reform. He created new peers more liberally than any of his predecessors, conferring the honor particularly on the patrons of rotten boroughs.

Parliamentary corruption

One urgent problem which Pitt had to solve was the control of British affairs in India. The problem resulted from the conquests of the East India Company during the Seven Years' War. Clive, after his victory at Plassey, set up a complacent native to take Surajah Dowlah's place as nabob of Bengal. The arrangement gave the representatives of the company practical control of the large native population of Bengal. The power of the native ruler was sufficiently nominal to leave him subject to a large amount of dictation from the British. When he finally attempted to assert his independence in order to protect his native subjects from British graft, he was driven out and forced to seek refuge with the native ruler of the neighboring state of Oudh. The British thereupon attacked and defeated the nabob of Oudh, capturing both him and the mogul whom he protected. The hesitancy of the company to seize spoils in the form of territory caused its representatives to take the *dewani* instead. This was a grant which empowered the company to collect the revenues of Bengal and certain adjacent provinces, pay a fixed sum to the nabob, maintain the native military establishment, and retain the surplus. Thus the company acquired a large degree of actual power to govern the natives of Bengal without any corresponding legal responsibility for their government. The agents of the company, isolated far from home, with opportunities for illicit gains on every side, and without adequate salaries, entered upon careers of plunder and graft.

Indian affairs

Eventually the situation was brought to the attention of the British government by the resulting financial straits of the company. In 1772 a committee of the house of commons investigated conditions and reported many evils to the house. Corruption was rife among the company's agents in Bengal. Lawlessness reigned unchecked among the

Regulating Act, 1773

natives because the British, who collected the revenues, did not maintain the police and the courts. The management of the company was poor. The directors at home could not control adequately their officials in India. In India unity was lacking. The independence of the three presidencies of Bombay, Madras, and Calcutta of one another caused confusion and conflict in their relations with the natives. On the basis of this report Lord North secured the passage of the Regulating Act in 1773. It made the government of Calcutta superior to the other two, and, to secure responsibility, made the governor of Calcutta largely dependent upon a resident council of four. The first governor and councilors were named by parliament, but in five years the appointment was to revert to the company, subject to the approval of the government. The British government was to be kept informed of the political and military policies of the directors of the company. Though the act prescribed how the company should exercise some of its powers, it left the company still primarily responsible for the management of British affairs in India.

The Regulating Act worked badly. Warren Hastings, the first gov-

Warren Hastings ernor sent out, was an able and energetic proconsul. When it was necessary to act quickly, he was so often met by the factious opposition of his council that he sometimes disregarded its advice, contrary to the terms of the act. He engaged in wars with the natives in order to maintain the frontiers of Bengal and to protect the position of the British against the machinations of the French among the natives during the war of the American Revolution. To obtain the funds necessary to finance some of these costly wars, he practically forced certain weak native rulers to provide him with treasure. The deeds of Hastings demonstrated that the Regulating Act was insufficient and finally convinced English statesmen that willy-nilly the problem of India was one of territorial responsibility.

Since Fox had been ousted by the defeat in the house of lords of

Pitt's India Act his policy of Indian reform, Pitt became responsible for the introduction of some measure designed to improve conditions in India. His act, passed in 1784, provided for a dual control. The British government was to have the superior direction of political and military affairs, and the company the management of commerce. To exercise this power a new board was created, headed by a secretary of state. The company's board of directors was required to submit to the governmental board all papers bearing on political and military matters, and its orders on these subjects could be changed or nullified by the governmental board. The company still appointed the officers resident in India, except the governor-general, but they could be removed by the governmental board of control. The act also enlarged the power of the presidency of Calcutta over the other presidencies and modified the unworkable features of the Regulating Act. The act was the first to acknowledge squarely the responsibility of the British government for the government of the natives in the area controlled by the company. The dual control worked well enough to cause its retention until the Indian mutiny of 1858.

Pitt's foreign policy before the outbreak of the war with France was also reasonably successful. Great Britain emerged from the war in 1783 without an ally and with her prestige badly shaken. His first important step was the formation of the Triple Alliance with Prussia and the Netherlands. The people of the Netherlands were divided at the time into two hostile parties, composed of the supporters of the stadtholder, who was the executive authority, and of the republicans who opposed his rule. France took advantage of the situation to extend her influence. In 1781 Austria, by setting aside the Barrier Treaty of 1715, caused the Dutch to withdraw their garrisons from the fortresses on the French border of the Austrian Netherlands and opened the way for French aggression. In 1785 France formed an alliance with the republican party. The object of the alliance was to prevent the opening of the Scheldt to navigation, which Austria had decreed in the previous year contrary to the terms of the Treaty of Westphalia. Great Britain also desired the Scheldt closed, since Antwerp on an open Scheldt might become, in the possession of a great power, a great trading port and a naval station of sufficient strength to threaten Great Britain's position on the Channel. But Great Britain viewed with apprehension the extension of French influence in this direction. The king of Prussia was concerned, because he was related by marriage to the stadtholder. These and other common interests brought Great Britain and Prussia together. They united to eliminate French influence in the Netherlands by the restoration of the stadtholder to power. In 1788 Great Britain, the Netherlands, and Prussia formed the Triple Alliance, by which they guaranteed one another in their territories. The treaty of 1785, which closed the Scheldt and was guaranteed by France, was now guaranteed also by Great Britain and Prussia. Pitt thus checkmated France and put an end to Great Britain's isolation.

A further action of the Triple Alliance was directed against Russia's policy in the Near East. For a generation Russia had been attacking Turkey intermittently to secure territory around the Black Sea. It was becoming clear that her ultimate goal was control of that sea

Triple Alliance

The Near East

and of Constantinople and the straits to the Mediterranean. Previously during the eighteenth century Great Britain had been friendly to Russia and had interposed no obstacle to her expansion in the Near East. Pitt saw in Russia's aggressions upon Turkey a menace to Great Britain's position in the Mediterranean and to her dominion in India. When Russia and Austria united to attack Turkey in 1788, Russia was hindered by an attack from Sweden in the rear. Russia thereupon instigated Denmark to attack Sweden. Under the influence of Pitt the Triple Alliance forced Denmark to withdraw from the alliance against Sweden and thus put a spoke in Russia's Near-Eastern wheel. This action was the first step in Great Britain's reversal of policy with regard to Russia. The English public, however, was not yet ready to follow Pitt further. In 1791, when he desired to employ the threat of force to keep Russia from wresting more territory from Turkey, parliament refused to support him. Nevertheless, Pitt's policy ultimately prevailed. During the nineteenth century Great Britain with a few aberrations was friendly to Turkey and hostile to Russia's expansion in the Near East.

Nootka Sound

With Spain Pitt was more successful. In 1789 the Spaniards seized an English ship in Nootka Sound off Vancouver, where the British had made a settlement. Spain claimed possession of the western coast of America as far north as 60° by right of discovery. The confiscation of the ship was a protest against the invasion of her monopoly. Pitt denied the claim, because Spaniards had made no effective settlement. Spain began to prepare for war, but, when she found that the French Revolution had rendered the Bourbon family compact of no avail, she recognized her weakness and surrendered her claims to the territory in dispute.

Causes of the French Revolution

Meanwhile there had begun across the Channel events which were to involve Great Britain in a war with France, affect profoundly internal affairs of England, and let loose in Europe new conceptions of liberty and nationality destined to dominate European international relations throughout the nineteenth century. The French Revolution was more properly a European revolution that had its origin in France. It was directed against inherited social and political conditions which had become obstacles to the well-being and the advancement of the individual citizen and of society as a whole. The despotic royal governments, in league with the comparatively small number of people constituting the nobility and the higher clergy, kept down the mass of their subjects. As the members of the upper social classes possessed something like two-fifths to one-half of the land, monopolized nearly all of the important and well-paid positions, frequently drew large incomes from the national treasuries for which they gave no services in return, and usually paid only a small percentage of what should have been their proper share of taxes, they enjoyed a disproportionate and mainly unearned share of wealth and influence at the expense of the people as a whole. Their domination was rendered the more intolerable by the manifest contempt of their regard for those outside their own circle. The most successful and highly educated business and professional men, if unable to buy their way into the nobility, were compelled to acknowledge their inferiority by their very ways of dressing and living. Unfortunately the evil did not stop even there, for the middle class displayed much of the same pride and selfishness toward those still lower in the social scale, monopolizing trade and industry so far as they were able. Although open-minded and generous individuals were not lacking in any class, and though a man endowed with exceptional talents might make a career for himself, the man born into Europe in the eighteenth century—be he peasant, artisan, merchant, or the follower of a profession—usually found advancement for himself or his children blocked for lack of opportunity and his lot rendered uncomfortable by the scorn and insolence of the treatment accorded him by those born more fortunately than himself.

Such a man could hope for no improvement of his situation because of his inability to influence the action of his government. Almost **Political** without exception the governments of continental Europe were theoretical despotisms in which the ordinary citizen had no share. Though many of the rulers of the later eighteenth century were intelligent men and women of good intentions who tried to remedy some of the many evils, no one of them either would or could introduce what we should call self-government. The average individual could hope for no redress when the government took away a large part of his income by taxes, wasted the money that was collected, forced him to submit to courts that were often unjust, expensive, and dilatory, placed harmful restrictions on trade and commerce, persecuted him for his religious belief, and in general sacrificed his interests to those of the nobles and higher clergy.

Men submitted to these conditions for centuries because they were believed to be natural and inevitable; but during the eighteenth century an increasing number of people came to think of them as un- **Intellec-** natural and avoidable. One of the reasons why the Revolution began **tual** in France and always had its center there was that some of the French were among the first to arrive at this new point of view. In France many prosperous members of the middle class, through study of the works of writers on government and political philosophy from the ancient Greeks down to Locke, were persuaded that changes should be made. The study of history, and especially the history of England, convinced them that changes could be made. Illustrious writers and thinkers, such as Voltaire, Rousseau and Montesquieu, popularized the idea that the existing evils were ridiculous and unnecessary. The American Revolution, in both its principles and its success, seemed to the reformers a final demonstration of their ideals.

Beginning of the Revolution

There was also another reason why the Revolution commenced in France. The French government, thanks to the careless and extravagant handling of the national revenues and to the money spent in the war of the American Revolution, was bankrupt. After the attempts of several ministers to reform the financial system had been defeated by the opposition of the upper classes, it was decided to call a meeting of the estates general. This body consisted of the representatives of the three estates, the nobility, the clergy, and the common people. After an early development somewhat parallel to that of the English parliament, it lost its opportunity to control taxation in the fifteenth century and gradually fell into desuetude. When it was summoned in 1789, it had not met for 175 years. The resurrection of the only organ of government in which the common people had any voice raised high the popular hope that grievances were at last to be redressed. The representatives of the people, known as the third estate, came to the assembly filled with this spirit and resolved not to accept the minor part assigned to their predecessors in former sessions of the estates general. Being equal in number to the representatives of the nobles and the clergy combined, they insisted that the three estates should sit in one house instead of in the customary three, and that the single chamber should have power to reform social conditions and to frame a new constitution. Largely because of the support of the city of Paris and the infection of the royal army with the new ideas, the members of the third estate had their way. Thus the Revolution was begun.

Beneficent Revolution

The first two years of the Revolution constituted a period of reform when the most lasting and important results of the whole movement were accomplished. With all the zeal of emotional theorists the members of the national assembly attempted to destroy and rebuild the whole social and political structure of France. The destructive part of their work, which included the abolition of the royal despotism, the privileges of the nobility and clergy, the onerous and debasing remainders of the manorial and the feudal systems to which the peasants had been subjected, the unequal administration of justice, the confused system of laws, the division of France into separatistically inclined provinces, the huge accumulation of landed property by the nobles and clergy, and many other abuses, has been in the main of permanent benefit. But on the constructive side the members of the national assembly, while highly successful in some of their tasks, made some serious, not to say fatal, mistakes. In their inexperience and their passion for democracy and symmetry they constructed a government which could not last. The king was made responsible for good government without being given sufficient power to secure it, while he and the single-chamber parliament were likely at any time to reach a deadlock from which there was no constitutional outlet. This situation widened the breach between the well-meaning and incompetent king and the party of reform. A second attempt at reconstruction turned him still more against the movement and rendered hostile a large and important section of the people as well. Not only was the church deprived of all its property and regular sources of income, but its bishops and priests were to be elected like any officials of the government, made dependent for their salaries on the state, and compelled to swear an oath approving changes which most of them, like the pious king, could not conscientiously take. The limitation of suffrage and officeholding to taxpayers indicated that it was a middle-class movement and that the proletariat had yet to win a place in the new order. Nor could the government deal with the discontent and opposition which this constitution provoked. The units of local government had been made so independent that it was hard for the central government to raise the money and troops necessary to maintain order. The king was unwilling to play the rôle assigned to him and was appealing secretly for outside aid. The result of all this opposition and weakness was that men, who were in some cases sincere democrats and in others mere self-seeking politicians, organized the mobs of poorer people in opposition to the government.

After the failure of the king's attempted flight the whole nature and course of the Revolution changed. Beginning with the autumn of 1791, radical leaders, working mainly through clubs of which the Jacobin was the best known, rapidly came into control both within the assembly and outside. They overthrew the constitution, established a republic, and imprisoned and executed all who opposed them. In January of 1793 the king was sent to the guillotine. The dominant faction put down internal dissensions and opposition with vigor and ruthless-

Reign of Terror

ness. Threatened by internal revolt and foreign invasion, it became the policy of the extremists to rule by terrorizing all opponents. They executed great numbers not only of the nobles and clergy but also of moderate reformers of the middle class. The inevitable reaction came in the summer of 1794, when the end of civil war and of the fear of foreign invasion robbed the terrorists of any reasonable excuse for continuing their extreme policy. Robespierre, the most prominent of the leaders, was sent to his death by his colleagues, who were in fear of their own heads as long as he lived. Control passed to those who were weary of bloodshed. In 1795 they secured a reorganization of the republic. The executive power was vested in a committee of five, called the Directory, which retained authority for the next four years. The Directory proved to be aimless and corrupt, but it restored the revolutionary movement to the control of the middle class and ended the reign of excessive violence.

The Revolution and Europe

The Revolution early involved France in war with a large part of Europe. The first feeling of most of the continental rulers was one of satisfaction. They were inclined to take a favorable opportunity to cut down the power of France. Their complacency soon gave place to alarm lest the Revolution spread to their own countries. After the change in the character of the Revolution in 1791, the kings and the more conservative classes in other countries regarded the movement as a terrible and contagious disease from which their own territories must be guarded. The Austrian emperor was the first to become involved in war with France. He was interested a very little because his sister was the French queen, and very much because the German princes who were neighbors of France appealed to him for protection against the extension of revolutionary principles to their own feudal domains. In 1791 he addressed a blustering remonstrance to Louis XVI, which played into the hands of the anti-monarchical war party in France and led to a declaration of war against Austria by the French assembly in April, 1792. Prussia joined its ally, Austria. The French army, which had been completely demoralized by the Revolution, failed to repel the invaders. During the summer volunteers were enlisted and drilled. The tide turned in favor of France at Valmy in September. By November the French armies occupied Savoy, several provinces on the Rhine, and Belgium. The last was won by the defeat of the Austrians in a pitched battle. The French politicians soon demonstrated that their ambitions included not only the propagation of popular rebellions in adjacent countries but also the continuance of the old monarchical policy of the extension of French frontiers. Revolutionary France, which had set out to liberate, remained to occupy, oppress, and annex. In each of the occupied districts the French supported a party which professed the revolutionary principles. At the request of this party in Savoy the country was annexed to France. In Belgium this party organized a government under French tutelage. In November the French legislature offered assistance to all peoples who were "harassed for the cause of liberty." It also declared the Scheldt open for navigation in defiance of the treaty of 1785 and the British guarantee of 1788. The aggression of revolutionary France looked to Europe little different from that of Louis XIV. It seemed much more dangerous, because it was more successful when propagated by rebellion and supported by a national army.

The first judgment of the English public on the Revolution appears to have been favorable. Since the restoration of the Stuarts Englishmen had been wont to regard France as the home of tyranny. The revolutionists were consequently regarded as engaged in the resistance of unjust oppression. Until the summer of 1790 public opinion in England generally approved the results of the Revolution, if the contemporary newspapers fairly reflect popular sentiment. Before the end of the year a rift appeared in public opinion. In October Burke published his *Reflections on the French Revolution* in a pamphlet. He dwelt upon the evils of the movement and sounded a note of alarm lest these principles spread to Great Britain. Seldom has a pamphlet influenced public thought so profoundly. Mild approval changed to distrust, and, as the Revolution became steadily more violent, distrust gave place to horror and aversion. This change of view had important results. It altered the balance of parties, repressed for a generation all movements for reform whether moderate or revolutionary, and produced a public opinion favorable to a war against France.

The Revolution and English public opinion

The first indication of the effect on parties appeared in 1791. In a debate in the house of commons, Burke, who was a prominent Whig, aired his views. Fox, who was the leader of the Whigs and an enthusiastic believer in the French Revolution, opposed him hotly. This breach between the two leaders of the Whigs subsequently spread to the party. The more conservative Whigs began to fear that the revolutionary principles were spreading to England. Pitt played on their fears until they decided, at the end of 1792, to depart from the radical leadership of Fox and throw in their lot with Pitt and the Tories, who represented law and order and the repression of all liberal tendencies.

The party situation

The policy of severe repression of movements for reform adopted

Repression by the government in 1792 had little excuse other than public hysteria, unless it was in part a deliberate game played to frighten the conservative Whigs into the ranks of Pitt's followers. The example of the Revolution stimulated English reformers to new activities. Old societies became more active in their agitation for reforms, new ones were formed, and much ephemeral literature urged reforms of various kinds. Among the reformers were a few radicals who preached revolution. An occasional pamphlet was inflammatory and seditious. Thomas Paine, who had poured oil on the flames of the American Revolution with his pamphlet, *Common Sense,* wrote the most radical of them. His *Rights of Man*, which was a reply to Burke, decried the monarchical form of government, and advocated its overthrow. The Corresponding Society, formed in 1792, had its constituency among workingmen, corresponded with the radical leaders in Paris, and talked the jargon of the Revolution, but it had little influence and its actual proceedings were more foolish and fantastic than violent. Riots and disorders took place in several towns, but with one or two exceptions they were caused by the scarcity and the high price of food. In the second half of 1792 the French assembly sent secret agents to England to stir up revolution. All of these things taken together gave scant evidence of any widespread feeling in favor of revolution, but the popular apprehension created by Burke's pamphlet served to magnify and distort them, until every advocate of legitimate reform was deemed to be a revolutionist. Pitt and his colleagues, who had little excuse for the acceptance of such exaggerated views, acted in a way to increase the popular fears. In the spring of 1792, Grey (later earl Grey) gave notice in the house of commons of a motion for the reform of the house. Pitt objected that such a motion was likely to become the beginning of revolutionary propaganda and insinuated that the Society of the Friends of the People, composed of highly respectable gentlemen whose sole object was parliamentary reform, entertained revolutionary designs. By these tactics he completely confounded legitimate reform with revolutionary propaganda. When this loose idea of what constituted sedition had become current in 1792, the cabinet issued a proclamation against seditious writings. Later in the year it called out the militia. This action could be taken by the executive without the consent of the legislature only when actual insurrection existed. There was no insurrection, but in the excited state of public opinion it was believed that one impended, and the alarm was widespread. It brought the conservative Whigs into Pitt's camp, killed the cause of legitimate reform for the duration of the war, and aided the formation of a national sentiment in favor of war with France.

The French invasion of Belgium in November of 1792 gave rise to the events that brought Great Britain into the war. The occupation of Belgium by a power like France was in itself a cause of apprehension. In the judgment of English statesmen, it also threatened the independence of the Netherlands, the ally of Great Britain. The opening of the Scheldt violated a treaty which Great Britain had guaranteed. The actions of the French menaced British strategic and commercial interests in the Low Countries, the maintenance of which had become traditional. The decree of the French legislature offering to help any people who would undertake rebellion, constituted an insult, if not a menace, when French secret agents were known to be inciting revolution in England. The French policy of territorial aggrandizement roused anew the spirit of rivalry which had existed between Great Britain and France for a century. The martial ardor of the English was stimulated, moreover, by a feeling of horror engendered by the radical and violent course which the Revolution had taken since September of 1792. After the opening of the Scheldt the British cabinet informed the Netherlands that Great Britain was ready to fulfill its engagement to keep the river closed, if the Netherlands so desired. In the negotiations which followed among the three powers, the new French legislature became convinced that British feeling was hostile to France, and the British cabinet lost all faith in the French protestations of peaceful intent. Early in January of 1793 France delivered what was tantamount to an ultimatum, a few days later the British cabinet requested parliament to vote an augmentation of the armed forces to protect British dominions, assist British allies, and oppose France, and on February 1 France declared war on Great Britain. It began twenty-two years of almost continuous warfare between the two rivals.

Causes of war

Pitt at once formed the other countries at war with France into the First Coalition. British subsidies were paid to Austria, Prussia, Sardinia, and Spain. The Empire, Portugal, and Naples also joined the allies, and Russia promised to cooperate with her fleet. In the early part of 1793 the war went generally in favor of the allies. The French army which invaded the Netherlands was defeated and driven out, and the armies of the allies crossed the frontiers of France at several places. Before the end of the year, however, the French, keyed to an intense pitch of patriotic fervor by the invasion of their own land, applied universal conscription and raised a large army, while

The war, 1793–1795

the allies were split by jealousies. The eastern powers had their attention diverted by the partition of Poland, and the British scattered their energies disastrously in several small campaigns. The allies were almost universally defeated and French soil was cleared of enemies with one insignificant exception. The British navy captured a few French ships and some small colonies; otherwise the tide of war had turned completely. On land the French continued to be universally successful. Early in 1795 they occupied the Netherlands. Soon afterward the First Coalition broke up. Prussia made the first treaty of peace with the new revolutionary government and was followed by Spain. The only important powers left in the war against France were Great Britain, Austria, Sardinia and Russia, and Russia never sent any armies.

Since this left Austria and Sardinia the principal opponents of France on the land, the scenes of the war shifted to the Rhine and **Rise of** to Italy. In the Italian campaigns, which took place in 1796 and 1797, **Napoleon** the genius of Napoleon Bonaparte first displayed itself. Napoleon, a Corsican by birth, had attended military schools in France and he had friends among the officers of the French army. In 1793 he returned from Corsica to France to fish for a career in the troubled waters of the Revolution. He talked liberty, fraternity, and equality with such good effect that he won the sobriquet of "the little Robespierre," but his democratic ideals were a mere pretense assumed as a means to further his ambition for power. In the campaigns of 1793 and 1794 he secured the opportunity to display something of his military ability, and in 1795 he won the gratitude of the legislative assembly by saving it from the mob by means of cannon placed in the streets of Paris. His reward was command of the French armies sent to operate in Italy in 1796. The rapidity with which he defeated the Austrians and Sardinians was phenomenal even in that day of French victories. By skillful strategy and speedy operation he split the Sardinians from the Austrians, forced them to sign an armistice, and then drove the Austrians out of Italy. In 1797 Austria was compelled to make a peace which surrendered the Austrian Netherlands to France, sanctioned the French frontier on the Rhine, and acknowledged the republics, nominally independent but really controlled by France, which Napoleon had formed largely out of Austrian possessions in northern Italy. Napoleon's campaigns left Great Britain the sole surviving opponent of France.

While the last of Great Britain's allies were being overwhelmed, Great Britain was experiencing the darkest days of the war. At home

the burden of taxation, a financial crisis, and a rise of prices were causing widespread distress, while the navy nearly lost control of the sea.
The fleet acquired the Cape of Good Hope, Ceylon, and several of
the Dutch East Indies during 1795 and 1796, though the French recovered some of the West Indies. In 1796, when insurrection threatened in Ireland, the French were prevented from landing an efficient
army only by a storm, and a small body of troops actually escaped
the Channel fleet and disembarked in Wales. In the Mediterranean the
failure of the British fleet to cooperate properly contributed to the success of Napoleon. Early in 1797 the British naval record reached its
nadir, when the sailors of two fleets in home waters mutinied. The
year, however, saw a revival of naval efficiency, which came just in
time to avert the danger of a French invasion of England. The French
project was made feasible by additions to the French fleet. The conquest of the Netherlands in 1795 gave France control of the Dutch
fleet, and an alliance with Spain in 1797 placed the Spanish fleet at
her disposal. After the defeat of her other enemies, the union of the
French fleets for the invasion of England was the next logical step.
It was prevented by two British victories. Early in the year the Mediterranean fleet defeated the Spanish off Cape St. Vincent, largely
through a brilliant maneuver of Nelson, who was the commander
of one of the ships. Later the Channel fleet defeated the Dutch at
Camperdown. The British stood alone, but their naval supremacy was
restored.

The
British
navy

Napoleon soon discovered the significance of the British victories.
After his return from Italy, he was placed in command of an army
in the north of France, designed for the invasion of England. Conversation with the Norman sailors convinced him that a stronger
navy was essential for success. Since he could not attack England, he
decided to strike at the bases of her power. They were sea power,
commerce, and empire. In 1798 he transported an army to Egypt,
where successful conquest would embarrass Great Britain's position
in the Mediterranean and the Red Sea and provide a base for the attack of Great Britain's rich dominion in the east.[1] Again he learned
the significance of Britain's navy. In the summer Nelson defeated the
French fleet in the battle of the Nile (Aboukir Bay) and destroyed
Napoleon's line of communication with France. Though he was bot-
tled up, he continued his campaign by an advance into Syria, but,
when he besieged a coastal town of primary importance, the British

Napoleon's
Egyptian
campaign

---

[1] These probably formed part of Napoleon's designs: Dennis, *Eastern Problems at the
Close of the Eighteenth Century*, pp. 173–184.

fleet forced him to raise the siege. Having marched his men up hill, he had no choice but to march them down again. When he returned to Cairo, he learned that a Second Coalition had been formed and that the Directory was hopelessly weak and unpopular. The time had come to strike for power. Leaving his army, he arrived in France in the autumn of 1799.

Napoleon and the Second Coalition

The Second Coalition had been organized by Pitt and cemented with British gold early in 1799. It had been rendered possible by the aggressive policy of France against her neighbors. As one encroachment after another made evident the intention of France to disregard the peace of 1797, the European powers joined with Great Britain to prevent the further extension of French imperialistic designs and republican principles. Russia, Austria, and several smaller states became Great Britain's allies. The Directory was so demoralized that the renewed war went in favor of the allies, though their progress was hampered by the lack of proper cooperation. When Napoleon returned, he was hailed as a conquering hero by a people which knew nothing of the real situation in Egypt. He seized the opportunity to overthrow the Directory and establish the Consulate. The new government had a specious appearance of popular representation, but was so arranged that power resided in an executive body of three consuls, which Napoleon as first consul dominated. Subsequently the policy of France was the policy of Napoleon.

Napoleon launched a program of law and order at home and set forth early in 1800 to break the Second Coalition. Russia had already deserted because of friction with Austria. Napoleon duplicated Hannibal's feat, went over the Alps into Italy by the high passes, took Austria by surprise in the rear, and won a decisive victory. Another French army defeated the Austrians in southern Germany. These two victories forced Austria early in 1801 to make a second peace, which ended the Second Coalition.

Great Britain meanwhile had accompanied success on the sea with the usual blunders on land. A joint Anglo-Russian expedition against the French in the Netherlands was defeated in 1799 with a heavy loss of men and money because of poor plans and incompetent leadership. In 1798, however, British control of the sea prevented France from giving to rebels in Ireland the aid which would have rendered the insurrection formidable; during the next two years the navy conquered more of the Dutch possessions in the East Indies; and in 1800 Malta in the Mediterranean was taken from the French.

These events left a situation similar to that which had existed at the close of 1797. Great Britain was bereft of allies, but she was still supreme on the sea. On this occasion Napoleon was able to strike an indirect blow at Great Britain's sea power. The British navy, just as in the American war, had angered neutral powers by its searches and seizures of their vessels. The northern powers were the most affected. In 1800 Denmark appealed to Russia. The reigning tsar was swinging from coalition with Great Britain to friendship with Napoleon, who naturally urged him in the same direction that Denmark wished him to take. Toward the close of 1800 the northern powers, led by Russia, declared an armed neutrality and demanded that Great Britain observe with some modifications and additions the rules proclaimed by the league of 1780.[2] Though this action brought the northern powers to the side of France, Great Britain was unwilling to forego the advantage given by control of the seas and allow neutrals to supply France with naval stores. In the spring of 1801 a British fleet, which met with success largely because Nelson disregarded the orders of his superior officer, attacked the Danish fleet and batteries in the harbor of Copenhagen. The contemporaneous accession of a new tsar less hostile to Great Britain made possible a compromise. Great Britain conceded some of the demands of the league, but established her contention that a neutral flag should not protect from seizure the property of belligerents, and secured a more favorable definition of contraband of war. Great Britain thus overcame a serious menace to her naval power and deprived Napoleon of an offensive weapon.

League of Armed Neutrality

The naval expedition to the Baltic was planned by Pitt's cabinet, but before its successful outcome Pitt had resigned on the Irish question. During the course of the eighteenth century the harsh restrictions placed upon the Irish in the closing years of the seventeenth century and early years of the eighteenth[3] were somewhat ameliorated. By smuggling in some directions and by developing new commerce in others, the complete paralysis of Irish industry was removed. The position of the Catholics became better in practice than it appeared in the statutes, because many of the penal laws were practically ignored. But while the evil effects of these policies were reduced they were not eliminated. Ireland still had a host of wrongs which she wanted redressed.

Ireland in the eighteenth century

The American Revolution brought to Ireland its opportunity. In

---

[2] See above, p. 561.
[3] Above, p. 467.

the early stages of the war Ireland supported the British policy. When France entered the war, the Irish raised large bands of volunteers to protect the country, which had been denuded of regular troops for the war in America. Once large numbers of Irishmen had acquired arms and discipline, Irish leaders saw an opportunity to obtain the redress of grievances while Great Britain was weak. In 1780 the implied threat of armed force induced the British parliament to withdraw many of the restrictions on Irish trade. Two years later the Irish parliament, led by the orator and patriot, Henry Grattan, demanded and obtained legislative independence. Poynings' Act[4] was repealed and also a later act which authorized the British parliament to legislate for Ireland.

Many elements of friction remained in the situation thus established. The cabinet still appointed the Irish executive, over whom the Irish parliament had no control. It also retained the power to veto the acts of the Irish parliament. Yet the Irish parliament was sufficiently independent to give the cabinet a great deal of trouble. Another difficulty was caused by the unrepresentative character of the Irish parliament. Though four-fifths of the Irish were Catholics, no Catholic could be a member of the parliament or vote for a member. The Presbyterians of Ulster were in a like situation. The Irish parliament represented only a narrow, Anglican minority. Even that representation was vitiated by electoral and parliamentary corruption similar to that which prevailed in England.

The inclination of the Irish and the British parliaments to pull in different directions on common questions was manifested several times during the early years of Pitt's ministry. The development reached a crisis in 1788, when George III became temporarily insane. The British parliament, after a long wrangle over the constitutional issues involved, named the prince of Wales regent, placing limitations on his powers. The Irish parliament invited the prince to become regent without limitations. The recovery of the king ended the divergence, but it had made evident the possibility that the head of the state in Great Britain might have powers different from those of the head of the state in Ireland, or might even be a different person. The difficulty of ruling the empire with two independent parliaments in action, which had previously been experienced in the case of Scotland,[5] was now demonstrated in the case of Ireland.

The events which finally convinced Pitt that the parliamentary

[4] Above, p. 286.
[5] Above, p. 465.

union of Great Britain and Ireland was the remedy were set in mo- French
tion by the outbreak of the French Revolution. The spirit of unrest Revolu-
loosed in Ireland found expression in two directions. In 1791 the Pres- tion and
Ireland
byterians of the north founded the society of United Irishmen to
agitate for parliamentary reform. In order to secure the support of
the Catholics, it declared for the removal of the civil restrictions placed
upon them and for their admission to political rights. Among the
Catholic peasants of the south the first result was a series of agrarian
outrages directed against the landlords. As the two movements tended
to coalesce, they soon became of sufficient importance to attract Pitt's
attention. In 1793 he secured the enactment of a measure which admitted the Catholics to the suffrage. The result was not entirely happy.
It flooded the constituencies with ignorant voters, but still excluded
the educated Catholics from seats in parliament. As evidence of Pitt's
good intentions, however, it sufficed to allay some of the Irish discontent. The stay was only temporary. Agitation for further reforms
failed, the mistakes of the viceroy of Ireland made Pitt appear in
popular conception as more opposed to further reform than he was,
and the radical Irish leaders became influential. Their solution was to
plot rebellion in alliance with France. Eventually the rebellion broke
out prematurely in 1798. It never threatened Great Britain seriously;
it was quelled easily and cruelly; but it convinced Pitt that the arrangement of 1782 did not solve the Irish question. Consequently he
began to prepare for the legislative union of Great Britain and Ireland.

In 1799 a measure providing for the union was defeated in the
Irish parliament. The Protestant ascendency did not intend to lose Irish union
its graft voluntarily. The Irish government then set out to buy a
majority with peerages, offices, pensions, and cash. Meanwhile Catholics were won to the project by an intimation that it would be accompanied by Catholic emancipation. In 1800 the Act of Union passed
both parliaments. The separate Irish parliament ceased to exist on
January 1, 1801. Ireland received representation in the British parliament by thirty-two peers and one hundred commoners. The Act of
Union eliminated some of the causes of friction between England and
Ireland and lessened the danger of the disruption of the empire. It
was, however, unpopular with many Irishmen, and it remedied few
of Ireland's grievances.

Pitt, who recognized its shortcomings, planned to complete the
pacification of Ireland by giving to the Irish Catholics emancipation
from some of their civil disabilities and enabling them to sit in parliament. When Pitt brought the question before the cabinet in 1801,

Failure of
Catholic
emancipation

some of his enemies informed the king before the cabinet had settled the terms of the projected measure. It was easy to work on the anti-Catholic prejudices of George III until he came to believe that the terms of his coronation oath bound him to refuse to consent to such legislation. Pitt, who felt that he was practically pledged to the measure, informed the king that he must offer his resignation unless he could have the royal approval. He was not prepared, however, to force the resignation of the whole cabinet by making it a party issue, fearing apparently that he might drive the obstinate king into another fit of insanity. Pitt therefore resigned early in 1801. Those of his colleagues who had had the largest share in the direction of the war followed their leader, but a number of his colleagues remained in office. Addington, the new prime minister, was the friend and understudy of Pitt. Pitt's resignation placed the direction of the war in the hands of inexperienced ministers, but it did not change the party in control.

Pitt's
repressive
policy

In England Pitt had effectually suppressed all agitation for reform. The proclamation against sedition in 1792 urged local authorities to seek out and prosecute the authors of seditious works. In the excited state of public opinion this was enough to cause a large number of trials. During the next two years many persons who were wholly innocent of any intention to overthrow existing institutions were convicted by judges who were too prejudiced and juries who were too panic-stricken to distinguish between reform and revolution. During 1794 the juries, becoming more temperate, gave the policy of the government a check by refusing several convictions. In 1795, however, the government was back to the charge. Several riots, caused chiefly by economic distress, were ascribed to political causes by the cabinet, which made them the ground for an act temporarily suspending *habeas corpus*. The provisions of this law, which by renewal was kept in force until 1801, enabled the cabinet to imprison opponents and critics without giving them any opportunity for trial. Nor did Pitt's reactionary policy stop there. Two acts followed. The Seditious Meetings Act prohibited public meetings for discussion without the approval of a magistrate who should attend and who might dismiss the meeting and arrest any person speaking derogatorily of the king, the government, or the constitution. This legislation deprived that large part of the population unrepresented in parliament of any opportunity to express its opinions on public affairs, and left the ruling caste free to use the treasure and man power of the country for the war as it pleased. The Treasonable Practices Act was still

worse. It made it treason to plan an act of treason or to utter words
inciting to an act of treason. No overt act was necessary to constitute
treason. A criticism of the government could readily be construed
as treason under this definition. Needless to say, these acts suppressed
all but sporadic instances of agitation for reform and of public criticism of the government. Pitt and the borough-owners were left free
to carry on the war to suit themselves, for Fox and the Whig oppo-
·ition were in a hopeless minority. In all probability the majority of
·he people favored the war, but they had no way to make their
opinions effectively articulate.

The economic situation in England during the war had been somewhat anomalous. Foreign commerce increased in value between 1792 Economic
and 1801 from forty-four to seventy-three millions of pounds. This conditions
prosperity, moreover, was on a sound basis. It was due to no speculative expansion but to the substantial products of the economic revolution. Yet it was a period when the poor experienced much distress
and misery, and when financial crises were common. The total wealth
of England had increased, but it had not yet been evenly distributed.
The distress of the poor was acute in the winters of 1794-1795 and
1800-1801, when failures of the crops caused an unprecedented strin-
gency in supplies of food. But aside from the years of scarcity, prices
of commodities increased much faster than the prices of wages, while
the demand for labor fluctuated widely. When these evils reached a
crisis, they often caused riotous outbreaks like those of 1794-1795.
The demands of the rioters were generally political in character,
because, failing to understand the economic causes of their distress,
they believed that a voice in the government was the only way to
obtain the supposedly necessary remedial legislation. The ruling class,
swayed by the theory of *laissez faire*, was deaf to any remedy other
than suppression. In 1799 and 1800 parliament added to the legislation against political agitation the Combination Acts, which imposed
severe penalties on laborers who combined to secure better conditions
of employment. They made universal restrictions upon labor which
had been applied earlier in the eighteenth century only to specific
industries.

Though labor suffered most, capital did not have an entirely easy
time. A financial crisis in 1793 was tided over by using the credit of
the government to sustain the credit of individuals whose capital was
tied up. A second crisis in 1797 was more serious. The bank was
forced to suspend payment of gold for its notes, and the government
authorized the continuance of the suspension. The notes of the bank

were thus rendered inconvertible. The action relieved the crisis temporarily, but its ultimate results were unfortunate. Because the power of the bank to issue paper currency was not properly limited, too much was issued. The consequent depreciation of the notes below their face value caused prices to rise still further and produced much inconvenience and difficulty in the transaction of business. Under the stress and strain of war Pitt's management of internal affairs was no more brilliant than his conduct of the war.

CHAPTER XXXIII

THE NAPOLEONIC ERA, 1801-1815

WITH the dissolution of the League of Armed Neutrality the war again became a drawn game. In the Mediterranean a French fleet was defeated. In Egypt an expedition, planned before Pitt left office, forced the French to agree to evacuate. But Great Britain was in no position to invade France without allies, and Napoleon could not deliver any significant blow at England for lack of naval power. Under these conditions negotiations for peace became possible. They resulted in the Treaty of Amiens, ratified early in 1802. France agreed to withdraw from Egypt and some of the territories occupied in Italy. Great Britain gave up Malta to be placed under the protection of the European powers and restored all of her many conquests, except Ceylon and Trinidad.

The treaty was received with delight by the English, who were weary of the privations of war. Londoners reflected the rejoicing of the nation when they greeted vociferously the bearer of the ratification of the preliminaries and drew his carriage in triumph through the streets. Nevertheless, the treaty was soon the subject of severe criticism. Though Great Britain had the equal if not the better of the situation at the close of the war, she surrendered far more territory than France. The treaty left the French in Belgium, the very situation which had brought Great Britain into the war; placed no limitation on French aggression in Europe; and failed to secure the abrogation of French laws which prohibited the sale of British goods in the territories controlled by France. A settlement which left considerable portions of Europe closed to British commerce could not long satisfy a people preeminently industrial and commercial. Napoleon's utterances and acts after the treaty kept British statesmen on the anxious seat. He not only aroused their apprehensions by extending his control over territories adjacent to France, but also gave to them the impression that he intended to attack the British Empire. He initiated a naval building program, acquired Louisiana, reconquered San Domingo in the West Indies, and sent to the east a nominal commercial mission, which reported primarily on the possibilities of military conquest. His retention of garrisons in the Netherlands gave rise to the conjecture that he planned to control the Cape of Good Hope, which by the treaty Great Britain had restored to the Netherlands, and with it Great Britain's principal route to India. In the face of this evidence the cabinet believed that maintenance of the peace merely gave Napoleon time to prepare for war. Great Britain, after giving a technical *casus belli* by a refusal to surrender Malta, declared war in the spring of 1803.

The war did not result in important campaigns until 1805. Meanwhile "Pitt's gold" formed the Third Coalition, in which Russia and Austria became the chief allies of Great Britain. Napoleon, who now had assumed the imperial title, made elaborate preparations to invade England, massing his armies in the north, building transports, and strengthening his navy. None knows certainly whether he was from the first using this demonstration as a cover for his preparations against Austria, or whether he planned to invade England, altering his intention only when he found that his navy could not escape from Nelson to secure the necessary control of the Channel. It was only after his fleet had failed to reach the Channel at the appointed time that he set his army in motion for Austria. A few days later Nelson defeated the combined French and Spanish fleets in the battle of Trafalgar. His own death in the hour of victory was England's heaviest loss. The victory gave Great Britain control of the sea during the remainder of the war.

Napoleon, however, was already on the way to Austria. By the rapidity of his movements he surprised the combined armies of Austria and Russia at Austerlitz in 1805 before they were ready to meet him. Austria was overwhelmed. She made a humiliating peace and dropped out of the coalition. The consequent reorganization of the German states so extended Napoleon's influence beyond the Rhine that Prussia became alarmed. The king of Prussia also learned that Napoleon had deceived him. Hanover had been promised to Prussia by Napoleon, who was generous with the continental possessions of George III. In 1806 Napoleon offered to give Hanover back to the English king. This was too much, and Prussia rushed headlong into war. At Jena in 1806 she was wiped out as a European power. In the next year Russia was hammered into submission at Friedland. The subsequent Treaty of Tilsit marked the apex of Napoleon's fortunes. The tsar abandoned the coalition to become the ally of Napoleon. He received a free hand to expand in the east, with a promise of French aid under certain contingencies. In return he agreed to support Napoleon's control of central Europe and to assist him in an attack upon Great Britain's commerce. The treaty left Napoleon the master of nearly all of continental Europe.

Napoleon had once more isolated Great Britain, but his supremacy on the continent would never be secure with Great Britain undefeated.

After Trafalgar, an attack on British colonies or sea power was hopeless, but commerce, the third prop to Britain's power, seemed vulnerable. By extending to a continental scale the policy of exclusion of British goods, which already had been applied for years to a smaller area, Napoleon hoped to ruin British commerce. This policy was known as his continental system. It was inaugurated by a decree issued at Berlin in 1806. Napoleon had previously extended the exclusion to the ports of northern Germany, evoking from Great Britain retaliation in the form of a blockade of the northern ports under Napoleonic control. The decree of Berlin forbade all peoples under his sway to have commerce with the British Isles and declared all merchandise exported from Great Britain to be lawful prize. It also declared the British Isles in a state of blockade. It was a paper blockade, since Napoleon had no ships with which to enforce it. In 1807 Great Britain issued orders in council, which practically declared all French and allied ports to be in a state of blockade. Neutrals, however, might call at a British port for a license, which, if granted, permitted them to proceed to French ports free from molestation by the British. Napoleon replied with his decree of Milan (1807), declaring any ship sailing to or from a British port lawful prize, should it subsequently enter a port under his control.

The success of Napoleon's system depended on the universality of its application. As long as any continental ports were open to British ships, British goods could be smuggled across the land frontiers in sufficient quantities to impair the value of the restrictions. By the end of 1807, however, Napoleon controlled nearly all the ports of Europe. Russia joined the system by the Treaty of Tilsit and agreed to help force it upon Sweden, Denmark, and Portugal. Denmark was driven to adhere by Great Britain's high-handed and unfriendly act. In 1807, fearful lest Napoleon should acquire the Danish navy, the British bombarded Copenhagen for the second time, obtaining the surrender of the Danish navy. Portugal was occupied by French troops soon after. Turkey was hostile to Great Britain. Sweden was left outside, only to be forced into the system two years later. For a time the boycott of British goods bade fair to be successful. During the next few years it cramped British commerce sufficiently to aid materially in the production of a severe commercial depression which began in 1811.

In reality the continental system was a boomerang which contributed to Napoleon's downfall. The superiority of some British manufactures and the British control of the supply of some foodstuffs, such as coffee and tea, deprived the continental peoples of some of the necessities of life. Growing dissatisfaction among some of the subject and allied peoples aroused a national feeling of opposition to the Napoleonic yoke so strong that it culminated in their revolt. The continental system was largely responsible for the abandonment of the French alliance by Russia in 1812, and the desertion led Napoleon to make his fatal campaign to Moscow. The attempt to enforce the continental system, moreover, was one of the causes of the expansion of the Napoleonic empire to an unwieldy size. The Iberian peninsula, which Napoleon occupied almost solely for this purpose, became his weakest spot.

Peninsular campaigns, 1808–1813

After the occupation of Portugal, Napoleon sought to strengthen his grip upon Spain. Although Spain was his ally, in 1808 he sent a large army into the country, declared the king deposed, and placed his own candidate upon the throne. The Spaniards revolted as the Portuguese had done before them. They could not stand against Napoleon's armies, but the nature of the country favored a guerilla warfare, which Napoleon with all his armies could not quell. The British government took the opportunity to make its first effective intervention on the continent. British troops were sent to Portugal. They were soon placed under the command of Wellesley, later the duke of Wellington. In a series of hard campaigns, known collectively as the Peninsular War, he drove the French armies out of the peninsula. In 1813 his army followed the French across the Pyrenees, and during the next year kept a French army busy in the south, while British allies were invading France from the east and bringing Napoleon to terms.

Downfall of Napoleon

While these operations were taking place Napoleon had trouble in the east. In 1809 Austria entered the war again, only to be forced into a still more shameful peace by the decisive battle of Wagram. In 1812 his failure to conquer Russia, which had deserted the continental system, marked the beginning of the end. When he invaded Russia, the Russians lured him to Moscow, which he found deserted and denuded of supplies. He was forced to retreat through the Russian winter at the cost of an army. At this juncture the Prussian nationalist spirit expressed itself in an alliance with Russia, which Austria later joined. By conscription Napoleon raised a new army and invaded Germany, only to be disastrously defeated at Leipzig in 1813. Thereafter nearly all Europe rose against him. In 1814 the allies marched into France from the east, forced Napoleon to abdicate and retire to Elba, and sanctioned the restoration of the house of Bourbon to the throne of France. In the next year Napoleon escaped and returned to France for the famous Hundred Days, which ended at Waterloo in

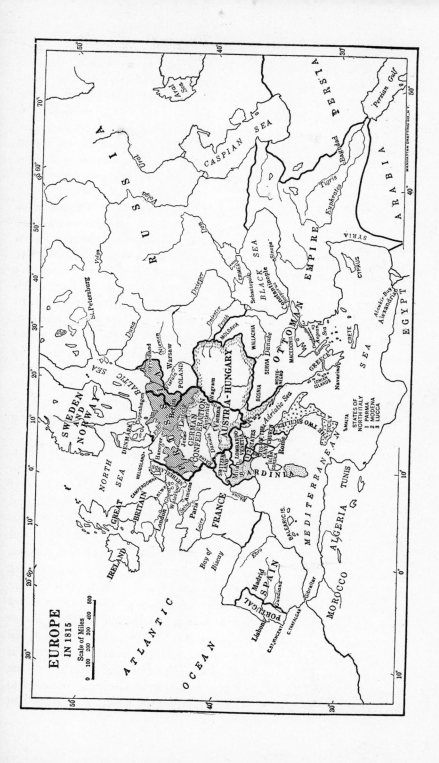

EUROPE
IN 1815

Scale of Miles
0 100 200 300 400 500

EUROPE

1815. Thereafter he was banished to the island of St. Helena in the middle of the Atlantic, and Europe saw him no more.

When Napoleon was finally conquered, the settlement of Europe was a difficult task. For almost a generation Europe had been at war. The revolutionary armies and Napoleon had overthrown the whole system previously existing. New states and new governments had been created, while old states and old dynasties had disappeared. Moreover, the liberal principles of the French Revolution had found acceptance with many of the peoples under Napoleon's sway, and the spirit of nationality had been evoked in many quarters. To these newfangled notions the sovereigns and diplomats who reconstructed the map of Europe gave little heed. The contemporary who described them as "crowned scoundrels cutting up Europe like carcass-butchers, and cruelly maltreating their subjects who rescued them from Napoleon,"[1] was driving a tack with a sledge hammer; but it was true that most of the gentlemen at Vienna still thought mainly in terms of the diplomacy of the eighteenth century, which disregarded the aspirations of peoples in order to satisfy the ambitions of monarchs. "Legitimacy," by which was meant the restoration of the dynasties which had ruled before the upheaval, "equilibrium," or a balance of power in Europe, and the "containing" of France by a ring of states sufficiently strong to offer obstacles to possible aggression by France were their major guiding principles. Their failure to recognize the strength of the new national sentiments was responsible for many subsequent disturbances of Europe.

Peace with France was made by treaties negotiated at Paris in 1814 and 1815, and the rest of Europe was reorganized at the Congress of Vienna in 1815. Largely through the influence of Great Britain France was accorded generous treatment. Lord Castlereagh, the secretary for foreign affairs, and the duke of Wellington, who represented Great Britain, believed it wiser to leave France strong and contented than to provoke a desire for revenge by dismemberment such as Prussia urged. The boundaries were left nearly as they had been in 1789, and the colonies which had been captured by Great Britain were returned, with the exception of Mauritius, Tobago, St. Lucia, and the Seychelles. An indemnity and allied troops stationed within the borders to guarantee Europe against further French aggression were the only significant penalties imposed upon France for the havoc Napoleon's armies had wrought in Europe. Another settlement favored by Great Britain was

Peace of Vienna (marginal note)

---

[1] Sheridan, cited in Broughton, *Recollections,* i, 206.

the union of Belgium (Austrian Netherlands) with Holland under the rule of the Dutch king. By the establishment of a larger state it was hoped to prevent the extension of French influence to a part of the coast regarded as vital in relation to British maritime interests. In the continental arrangements elsewhere Great Britain was interested less directly. The Holy Roman Empire and the numerous petty German states which had disappeared were left in abeyance. The thirty-eight states which survived were joined in a confederation so loose that each state was practically independent. Italy was again divided into the old separate states with a few exceptions. Norway was taken from Denmark and placed under the same king as Sweden. Russia, Prussia, and Austria secured considerable additions of territory. The British territorial gains were colonial. In addition to the French colonies, Great Britain received Heligoland in the North Sea, Trinidad in the west, Malta and a protectorate of the Ionian Isles in the Mediterranean, and Ceylon and the Cape of Good Hope in the east. By these additions Great Britain became the greatest imperial power in the world.

In order to preserve their work the diplomats at Vienna organized the Quadruple Alliance. The members were Great Britain, Russia, Austria, and Prussia. The purpose of the alliance was to maintain the peace of Europe. To further this object the four powers agreed to hold occasional conferences to consider the measures necessary for the promotion of their design. For several years the alliance not only regulated the international relations of Europe but also intervened in the internal affairs of several countries to suppress liberal movements from which the three eastern autocratic members feared contagion.

Meanwhile, during the closing years of the struggle with Napoleon, Great Britain had been at war with the United States. The causes of the war were the impressment by the British navy of sailors on American vessels and the seizure of American ships engaged in trade with the French. Since deserters from the British navy sometimes found refuge on American ships, the British claimed and enforced a right to search American ships and to seize such sailors as they alleged were deserters from the British navy, disregarding the principle that American ships constituted American soil. The right of search for contraband goods the British used with moderation during the early years of the war. Occasional seizures of American boats caused some irritation, but they did not interfere seriously with the American merchant marine, which grew until it was the largest in the world. A branch of the American trade on which its prosperity rested in large part was that between the French West Indies and Europe. After 1793 Great

War with the United States: causes

Britain for some years did not attempt to stop the trade, provided the voyage between the French colonies and France was broken by landing the goods in the United States. In 1805 the decision of a British admiralty court authorized the seizure of American vessels engaged in the carrying trade between France and her colonies notwithstanding the broken voyage, and within a few months "a prodigious number" of American ships was brought into British ports by British cruisers. In 1806, while negotiations were in progress on these points of difference, Great Britain declared a blockade of the ports under French control, and British ships of war enforced it off Sandy Hook and the capes of the Delaware. When Napoleon's continental system and the retaliatory measures of the British were put into effect soon afterward, they threatened to ruin the thriving commerce of the United States. Neutral ships became liable to seizure by the one power, if they observed the rules of the other. Resentment was felt in the United States against both powers, but the hostile feeling gradually focused on Great Britain. Before 1807 Great Britain had caused more friction, particularly after her abrupt, wholesale attack on American shipping begun in 1805, and after 1807 British enforcement of the decrees against neutrals was more effective than the French. The confiscations of Napoleon seemed small compared with those of Great Britain. In 1812 the United States finally declared war.

The war was fought on a small scale. To Great Britain it seemed a subordinate part of the struggle against Napoleon, and the United *Course* States was too poorly prepared to undertake extensive operations. Nevertheless the warfare was violent, engendering bitterness on both sides. On the Canadian frontier, where the principal encounters on land took place, both participants won and lost several engagements, but neither was able to effect the permanent occupation of any significant portion of the territory of the other. On the sea the initial advantage went to the United States. Her navy won notable engagements in single conflicts with ships of the British navy, and American privateers did much damage to British shipping. But as the war in Europe progressed favorably for Great Britain, more ships of the royal navy were released for service against America. The American victories declined, and the effective blockade of American ports practically stopped American commerce. In 1814 troops which had been released by the end of the Peninsular War were sent to America. One army captured Washington and burned it; another was decisively defeated by General Jackson at New Orleans.

Before the latter engagement was fought, peace had been made.

Peace

The defeat of Napoleon in 1814 placed the United States at a great disadvantage in the contest, and the damage to her trade had already disposed her statesmen toward peace. The close of the war, moreover, automatically ended the practice of the abuses of which the United States complained. Great Britain, being apparently free to give her whole attention to the war with the United States, was at first disposed to demand stiff terms, but Wellington convinced the cabinet that the situation in Europe was less settled than it appeared (as later events fully demonstrated). It was also deemed expedient to settle affairs with the United States before they should become complicated with the impending European settlement. With both sides disposed to accept reasonable terms, it became possible to conclude the Treaty of Ghent late in 1814. It arranged for the surrender of all conquered territories, but it left disputes about boundaries and fisheries to subsequent settlement, and the original causes of the war, the impressment of American seamen and the restrictions on neutral commerce, were not mentioned.

Pitt's second cabinet, 1804–1806

During the Napoleonic struggle many changes in the personnel of the cabinet took place. Of Addington, who became prime minister when Pitt resigned in 1801, Canning's squib,

> Pitt is to Addington
> As London is to Paddington,[2]

expressed caustically and brutally the general estimate. He would do to make "a peace which every one would be glad of, but no one would be proud of,"[3] but he could not be followed into war without hesitation. As war became imminent in 1803, his majority dwindled. When Pitt finally abandoned him and went into opposition, he resigned. In the crisis the nation wanted the leadership of "the pilot that weathered the storm." Pitt desired to make a cabinet of the best men of both parties, but George III would not hear of a cabinet which would give Fox so much power. Pitt's new cabinet, therefore, was weak because some of the strongest of his former colleagues, who had worked with the Whig opposition under Addington, refused to join any except a coalition cabinet. His slim majority finally became undependable, when the house voted to impeach a colleague who was his dearest friend. To a minister who had had his own way for many years, it was a bitter humiliation. It was followed by news of the disaster at Austerlitz. Pitt, whose health was already undermined by hard work, did not

---

[2] Quoted by Brodrick and Fotheringham, p. 28.
[3] *Memoirs of the Life of Richard Brinsley Sheridan,* ed. T. Moore, ii, 300.

rally from these blows. Early in 1806 he died. His last words, "My country! How I leave my country!"[4] expressed not only the sincere patriotism which had actuated him, but also a heartrending sense of failure. "He may have err'd, but his Transcendent talents were an honour to England and will live in posterity"[5] is a contemporary judgment which stands the test of time.

The death of Pitt rendered the cabinet so weak that the king was forced to accept a coalition. Though known as the cabinet of all talents, its chief was Fox and the majority of its members were Whigs. The two chief policies of Fox were the abolition of the slave trade, which had long been agitated, and peace with France. The first he secured by the passage of appropriate resolutions, which were later enacted into a law prohibiting commerce in slaves after January 1, 1808. The way for this action had been prepared by a long parliamentary agitation in its behalf, led by William Wilberforce, who, throughout his long career in the house of commons during the late years of the eighteenth century and the early years of the nineteenth, was a leading advocate of philanthropic and humanitarian causes. His second policy Fox failed to accomplish. He began negotiations with Napoleon, but he could not obtain acceptable terms, and he became convinced that the war must continue. Early in the autumn of 1806 Fox died, and his colleagues soon came to grief. They attempted to remove the restrictions which prevented English and Scottish Catholics from holding military commissions, but met with so much opposition from parliament and the king that they resigned early in 1807. This brought to an end the only Whig administration which held office during a period of forty-three years.

All talents

The real leader of the new cabinet was Spencer Perceval, who won a reputation as a "gallant fighter" in the house of commons. "He is not," said a member of the house, "a ship-of-the-line, but he carries many guns, is tight built, and is out in all weathers."[6] He took up the war at a particularly difficult stage and never wavered in its prosecution. He was, however, narrow and reactionary in his views and gave that tone to the cabinet until his assassination in 1812. His successor, Lord Liverpool, whom a later Tory minister designated as "Arch Mediocrity," held office till 1827. Though he was more moderate in his opinions than Perceval, he was generally opposed to innovations. His

The cabinet after 1807

[4] Rose, *Pitt and the Great War*, p. 558. Compare Lord Gower, *Private Correspondence*, ii, 170.

[5] W. Lamb, quoted in Lord Gower, *Private Correspondence*, ii, 162.

[6] Lord Holland, *Further Memoirs*, p. 133.

attitude was probably due more to indolence than to conviction. He found it easier to do nothing. With two notable exceptions the other influential members of the cabinet during this period were of a like illiberal turn of mind. George Canning was unquestionably the most brilliant of the younger generation of leaders who became prominent among the Tories after the death of Pitt. He was an eloquent speaker, a literary light, and an administrator of marked ability. His sarcasm, egotism, and "pettishness" made him a difficult colleague and won for him so much dislike in the house of commons that a member, without contradiction, spoke of his qualities as "talents without character."[7] In 1807 he was the most liberal member of the cabinet. In 1809, however, a quarrel with Castlereagh caused his resignation. From 1816 to 1820 he held an office of minor importance, but he did not again become an influential member of the cabinet until 1822. Lord Castlereagh, who belonged to the same generation, was also a statesman of exceptional ability. "Put all their other men together in one scale and poor Castlereagh in the other—single he plainly weighed them down" was the obituary judgment of a political opponent. In parliament he won a reputation for "good judgment, good manners and bad English."[8] On one occasion, "when he had spoken for an hour tediously and confusedly, he declared, 'I have now proved that the Tower of London is a common-law principle.'" He advised the country gentlemen "not to turn their backs upon themselves," and it gave him no qualms to end a long oration with the little word "its."[9] The unfortunate quarrel with Canning forced him out of the cabinet in 1809, but after his return in 1812 he remained in office until his death ten years later. His highly successful conduct of foreign affairs during the critical closing years of the war won him the gratitude of the nation and the respect of Europe. Subsequently his strong desire to restore normality led him either to concur in repressive policies or to stand aside and allow them to be formulated without opposition. After he became the leader of the party in the house of commons, he guided the debates in behalf of many reactionary measures which were primarily the work of his ministerial colleagues who sat in the house of lords. Thus he acquired a popular reputation for exceptional illiberality which was not deserved. Nevertheless, he did little to stay the reactionary trend of his colleagues. The cabinet which came to power in 1807 and held office

[7] Hobhouse, cited by Halévy, *History of the English People, 1815–1830*, p. 156.
[8] Brougham, cited in *Creevey Papers*, pp. 386, 391.
[9] Russell, *Recollections and Suggestions*, p. 22.

with some reorganizations until long after the war was generally illiberal in its policies.

The cabinet was not rich in ability, and from time to time it was disturbed by dissensions such as that which caused the resignation of two of its ablest members in 1809. In 1810 a minister wrote, "We are all, I think, on the *kick and the go*, but have probably a month to run."[10] On several other occasions the government was so weak that it appeared about to fall. It was preserved from that fate largely by the divisions among its opponents. The Whigs were split by the rivalries of individual leaders, such as had dissipated the strength of the party ever since 1760. Still more fundamental was a division between a liberal wing which desired reform and a conservative group which regarded the liberal members of the party as too radical. "There is," said a leader of the party in 1811, "a want of popular feelings in many individuals of the party. Others are exasperated with the unjust and uncandid treatment they have received, and are every day receiving, from the modern Reformers. Another set are violent anti-Reformers, and alarmed at every speech or measure that has the least tendency towards reform. There is but one measure on which the party are unanimously agreed, and no one man in the House of Commons to whom they look up with that deference and respect to his opinion which is necessary to have concert and cooperation in a party."[11]

The internal policy of the cabinet during the closing years of the war is well illustrated by two of the many prosecutions which it instituted. Sir Francis Burdett was the leader of a small group of reformers in the house of commons, who were called Radicals. They were more progressive than the advanced Whigs and they acted independently of both parties. When the president of a debating society was imprisoned for the publication of a debate which criticized the action of the house of commons, Burdett protested in a public letter. Perceval had the house commit him to the Tower. Burdett resisted arrest. He barricaded his house, and the mob rallied to his defense, hailing him as the protector of the popular liberties. When the officers finally forced an entrance, they found him instructing his young son in the principles of Magna Carta. The incident created a great furor, giving to Burdett in popular esteem the place of a second Wilkes. William Cobbett was the publisher of a paper, called *Cobbett's Weekly Register*, which had become the mouthpiece of radical opinions outside of parliament and

The opposition

Revival of repression

---

[10] Palmerston, quoted by Walpole, *Perceval*, ii, 172.
[11] Lord Holland, quoted in *Creevey Papers*, p. 144.

was destined to become in future years one of the principal agents in the creation among the masses of a public opinion favorable to reforms. In 1810 he was tried for publication of a criticism of the cabinet and condemned to imprisonment for two years. These two cases indicate the revival of popular agitation for reform, which had almost died out after Pitt's repressive measures, and display the cabinet placing itself on the side of severe and unreasoning opposition to all popular movements.

The economic conditions which prevailed from 1801 to 1815 brought prosperity to some and hardship to many. The volume of business conducted by manufacturers and merchants grew steadily, if the expansion of exports provides a true index. The advantages of the industrial revolution were beginning to be felt in Great Britain, while as yet no similar development had taken place on the continent. Despite the continental system, the superiority of British goods in price or quality and the British control of the seas made possible the rapid expansion of British foreign trade during most of the period. The one drawback to the prosperity was the speculative character of business due to the sudden and unexpected fluctuations of demand caused by the fortunes of war. Often a manufacturer who had borrowed capital to produce a large supply of goods for a given market was deprived of access to his market. He was caught with a surplus without a market and forced to sell where he could at a loss. His factory was closed, his hands idle, and his debts unpaid, until a new market was found. On several occasions such happenings were sufficiently common to produce financial crises and commercial depressions. The most severe of all was the depression which took place between 1811 and 1813. Many failures occurred, many factories closed, and business generally experienced great difficulties.

Agriculture was generally prosperous. The limited foreign supply of foodstuffs kept the price in the British market high in most years. But the agricultural prosperity rested on an artificial basis. The average high price tempted farmers to cultivate much land which would not produce grain at a profit when the price of grain was at an ordinary figure. The farmers invested in the improvement of poor land large amounts of capital, which they would lose if prices dropped before enough crops had been raised to recompense them for the original outlay. Lord Brougham, a contemporary, estimated that the production of grain had increased forty-eight millions of bushels, while the permanent demand had increased only sixteen millions. For four successive seasons, from 1809 to 1812, the crops were badly damaged, and

Margin notes:
Economic conditions: manufacturers and merchants

Agriculture

the agricultural interest was depressed at the same time as the industrial.

Labor While the capitalists were generally prosperous, though with many vicissitudes, wage earners were almost uniformly in distress. The dislocation of labor caused by the shift from the domestic to the factory system was still in progress; wages did not rise in proportion to prices of food; the speculative character of business made employment unsteady and uncertain; and the poor law was administered so badly that it encouraged the idler and handicapped the laborer who honestly attempted to earn his living. During the depression from 1811 to 1813 the suffering was acute. Unemployment was common, while the price of food was inordinately high. Riots were of frequent occurrence. Those which attracted most attention were the so-called Luddite riots directed against machinery. In Nottinghamshire, where the knitting of stockings was an important industry, a type of machine, which had previously been applied to other purposes, began to be used for the production of cheap stockings of an inferior quality. They soon captured a large part of the market which had been held by stockings of better grade and higher price knitted by another kind of machine. Many of the workers on the latter type of machine, who were thrown out of employment, went about the country in well-organized groups smashing the machines of the other type, to which they attributed their misfortunes. The practice spread also to the woolen industry of Yorkshire and the cotton industry of Lancashire, where skilled laborers by hand in some instances had suffered from the competition of the new machines and in others feared it. In these three counties machinery was destroyed on a large scale during 1811 and 1812.

In addition there were many burdens that affected all classes alike. National taxation increased from £1 2s. a head to £4 1s., and the enormous growth of pauperism added heavily to the weight of local taxation. The stoppage of payments in gold by the bank caused a depreciation of paper money, which eventually reached thirty-five per cent. In 1811 the paper currency was made legal tender. To the average man it meant that he could buy far less with the same amount of money. Walpole estimates that a man who had a fixed salary of £1,000 annually throughout the war found his salary in 1815 worth only three-quarters of the commodities which it had been worth at the beginning. The income tax took ten per cent, and the remaining £900 would purchase no more than could have been bought with £750 before the war.[12]

Common evils

---

[12] Walpole, *History of England*, i, 50.

CHAPTER XXXIV

THE END OF THE TORY RÉGIME, 1815-1830

Transition from war to peace

DURING the years immediately following the close of the Napoleonic struggle, the transition from war to peace caused great difficulties and disturbances in England. Unemployment, poverty, and distress were widespread. The evils of the situation were rendered more acute by the failure of both the government and the people to grasp the magnitude of the problem of post-war reconstruction. The cabinet, failing to understand the full significance of the extraordinary economic readjustments which were taking place, did comparatively little to assist the transition and to alleviate the popular suffering. The people hardly realized that a problem existed. They expected peace to be followed immediately by the blessings of prosperity. The peace was the occasion of excessive popular manifestations of joy. Cobbett said of the celebration, "One boundless scene of extravagance and waste, and idleness and dissipation pervaded the whole kingdom, the people appeared to be all raving drunk, all raving mad."[1] The demonstration was a natural reaction from the prolonged strain of war. It was also an expression of the popular belief that relief from the inconveniences and hardships which had been borne for years with enduring fortitude was finally in sight. When this anticipation remained unfulfilled and the situation grew worse instead of better, the bitterness of the disillusionment caused a violent reaction. People attempted to express their grievances and secure redress by means of mass meetings and mobs, the only means available. The government, striving to maintain order, repressed such demonstrations with severity. The clash between the reactionary tendencies of the cabinet and the popular desires for reforms became pronounced.

Economic depression, 1815–1820

That the cessation of hostilities had failed to bring prosperity was clear by the early part of 1816. During the next two years the people of Great Britain experienced the worst depression they had yet known. Manufacturers found no market for their goods, and prices fell. Iron, for example, dropped from £20 to £8 a ton. Factories closed, throwing thousands out of work. The grain crops of both years failed on account of cold, wet seasons, causing the prices of foodstuffs to soar.

[1] *History of the Regency,* section 277.

Renewal of manufacturing in 1818 brought only temporary relief. In 1819 conditions were again as bad as ever. Only in 1820 did the revival of industry and commerce begin which was destined to endure for several years.

The distress caused an unprecedented number of disturbances and riots. The laborers, attributing their starving condition to various **Disorder** causes, attempted to remove the causes by physical violence. In the south and east the agricultural laborers considered their sufferings due to a monopoly of the landlords. They went about in mobs burning barns which often contained grain already scarce. The Luddite riots were renewed on a large scale. In the iron and coal districts there were many strikes accompanied by violence and destruction of property. In several large towns bread riots became common.

The causes of the depression were not far to seek, though they were far from obvious to contemporaries. In 1815 the manufacturers and **Causes of** merchants were heavily overstocked with goods in anticipation of the **depression** opening of the continental market. When it was opened, the continental peoples had no money with which to buy. The demand of the government for military supplies, which amounted to £56,000,000 or so annually, ceased suddenly, leaving the invested capital to be transferred to new fields of endeavor. Over 400,000 men were demobilized and thrown into the large group of the unemployed. In short, the resumption of peace caused a complete dislocation of the national economic organization which had existed for twenty years. The years from 1816 to 1820 constitute the period when the most difficult part of the transition from war-time to peace-time organization was taking place. During these years, moreover, taxation remained heavy and the depreciation of the currency continued.

Though the fundamental causes of distress could not have been removed by legislation, the misery might have been alleviated by that **Remedial** means in some measure. The cabinet was more given to repression **legislation** than to relief, but it did secure the passage of three measures designed to be remedial. In 1815 the corn law was revised to give greater protection to British-grown grain against grain imported from abroad. Corn laws, which placed a protective tariff on imported grain, had been on the statute book since the closing years of the seventeenth century. They were designed to give native growers a high price in the national market. The later laws imposed a prohibitive duty on imported grain until the price in the home market reached a famine figure, when the duty was lowered or dropped entirely. When four-fifths of the population lived in the country and England raised a surplus of grain for exportation, such laws were not unreasonable. In the closing years of the eighteenth century, when the agricultural population ceased to be in a majority and the importation of grain exceeded the exports, the corn laws increased the price of bread consumed by all to benefit one class in the community. During the war the price at which grain could be imported free or at a nominal duty was raised on the plea that Great Britain must grow as much of her own supply of food as possible in time of war. The corn law of 1815 raised this high price still further in the attempt to benefit agriculture. The Tories, who were in power, represented the landlords and naturally voted for legislation favorable to their class, despite a number of petitions against the measure perhaps larger than ever before known in parliament. In 1816 the income tax was repealed, because an adverse majority in the house of commons forced the action upon the cabinet. In 1819 the currency was deflated by a provision for the resumption of the payment of specie by the bank. This reform, also, was more or less foisted upon the cabinet by a committee which unexpectedly shed its prejudices and reported, on the basis of reason, in behalf of resumption.

The
cabinet

The small amount of remedial legislation and the manifest unwillingness of the cabinet to undertake that much bred widespread popular dissatisfaction. The attitude of the cabinet was due in part to its inexperience in the conduct of government in time of peace. The ministers who led the cabinet in 1815 had learned their business in time of war. But the reactionary tendencies of the cabinet seemed to justify the popular feeling that its members had little sympathy with the sufferers and less understanding of the causes of their distress. Nor could the suffering laborers see much greater hope of help from a house of commons so constituted that a foreign observer could describe it as "the most aristocratic assembly in the world."[2] Radical leaders like William Cobbett, whose primary object was parliamentary reform, spread this point of view assiduously. They asserted, with some truth and much fiction, that all the evils of the time could be remedied by legislation; that the parliament as constituted would not give the desired relief, because it did not represent the distressed laborers; that the first step toward all other reforms was the reform of parliament. The masses were in such misery that they were willing to accept any explanation of the causes of their condition; *Cobbett's Weekly Register*

[2] Broughton, *Recollections*, ii, 188.

became their gospel and agitation for parliamentary reform their chief activity.

At first the radical movement flowed in quiet channels. Clubs were formed, corresponding societies sprang up, mass meetings were held, and petitions were presented to parliament. Soon it became confounded with the disturbances caused by economic distress. Unscrupulous radical leaders seized upon the disorders promoted by social and economic causes and converted them into political demonstrations. As a result, the radical movement, in the thought of the middle classes, became connected with physical violence. Between 1816 and 1820 the agitation was carried to such unjustifiable lengths that a public, more or less discontented with the reactionary ministry, was driven to support it as the lesser of two evils. "All the tinsel and lace" rallied round the cabinet.[3] The moderate spirit of reform, which might have received support from the influential middle classes, was killed for the time being by the violence which extreme leaders inspired among the masses.

Spirit of the movement for reform

The first riot associated with political principles took place in Spa Fields in London in 1816. A huge crowd, which gathered to hear an address on parliamentary reform, was inflamed by unprincipled speakers to commit some depredations. The cabinet, seizing upon it as evidence of a seditious movement, passed two acts of coercion which were called by a liberal the "liberticide acts."[4] One suspended *habeas corpus* for the last time in English history; the other amplified the law against seditious meetings. The debating society of the university of Cambridge was closed, as were likewise several literary and scientific societies. Force begat force. After the passage of the acts plots of insurrection actually began to be formed, and a minor local rebellion came to a head. But the attempt of the government to magnify such riots as that of Spa Fields into rebellion failed. Juries refused to convict its leaders of treason. They also refused to convict critics of the government whom the cabinet prosecuted. The repressive policy of the cabinet reached its climax with the "Peterloo massacre" of 1819. At St. Peter's Fields in Manchester a huge crowd gathered to hear an oration on parliamentary reform. The local magistrates ordered the soldiers to charge the crowd in order to arrest the speaker, and several were killed or injured. The cabinet congratulated the blundering magistrates, and secured the passage of a whole code of repressive legislation, commonly known as the Six Acts. The act which forbade meetings for

Riots and repression

[3] *Creevey Papers*, p. 257.
[4] Mathieson, *England in Transition*, p. 187.

military drills and exercises was not objectionable. Those which made the law against seditious libel more stringent, limited the freedom of the press, and further increased the restrictions on the right of public meeting were of a more arbitrary type. The public generally condemned the action of the magistrates, and the Six Acts rendered the cabinet unpopular. But once more the violent radicals turned the tide of popular opinion. In 1820 a group of them planned to assassinate the whole cabinet when it met for dinner on a certain evening. The conspiracy was discovered and the conspirators arrested at their rendezvous in Cato Street. This event aroused anew the old fears of radicals as violent and dangerous persons. It seemed to justify the arbitrary measures of the cabinet. At an election necessitated by the death of George III and the accession of his son, George IV, in the same year, the Tories held their own. The cause of reform was for the time completely crushed. With the return of economic prosperity, however, violent demonstrations ceased, and the supporters of moderate reform began to obtain a hearing.

Foreign
policy

To the British public the foreign policy of the cabinet seemed to be at one with its internal policy. Several times between 1815 and 1820 the Quadruple Alliance held conferences to discuss the affairs of Europe. The three eastern powers displayed a strong inclination to intervene in the internal affairs of various states in order to check the growth of popular liberal movements. In many countries where liberal constitutions had been established during the revolutionary and Napoleonic era, absolute governments were restored after 1815. The peoples of these countries became restless and gave signs of revolt in behalf of more liberal constitutions. To the rulers of Russia, Austria, and Prussia, who were the most autocratic in Europe, these liberal movements appeared to threaten the peace of Europe. They judged the suppression of such disorders to be a proper function of the Quadruple Alliance. Castlereagh, the British foreign minister, maintained that the only purpose of the alliance was to prevent such aggressions by one state against another as might provoke war; internal changes in any state gave no cause for action by the alliance. In a conference held in 1818 Castlereagh's view prevailed over the other urged by the tsar; but in 1820, when popular revolts against despotic governments broke out in Naples, Spain, and Portugal, a conference decided to intervene. The rebellion in Naples was quelled and the ruling house restored along with the illiberal constitution. A similar movement in northern Italy was also suppressed. The three allies announced it to be their policy that no legislative or administrative changes ought to take place in any

European state without the consent of the ruling sovereign freely given. This attempt to set back the clock received no sanction from Great Britain. Castlereagh kept Great Britain officially aloof from the action of the other powers, and his answer to the announcement of the allies stated that their principles could not be accepted by the British government. Castlereagh, however, did not break with the Quadruple Alliance, because he still believed it necessary to maintain peaceful external relations among the states of Europe. The British public failed to understand Castlereagh's attitude. Popular feeling was generally in sympathy with the liberal movements, and, despite Castlereagh's disavowal of the policy of intervention in the internal affairs of other states, his failure to break with the alliance gave the British public the impression that the British cabinet was in sympathy with the repressive policy of the eastern powers. Somewhat unjustly the foreign policy of the cabinet was deemed to be part and parcel of its program of reaction.

The event which finally turned the balance of public opinion strongly against the cabinet and helped to prepare the way for a liberal reorganization was the attempt of the cabinet to obtain a divorce for George IV. The new king was a fat man whom all the world did not love. Though he could be gracious and charming and was not without political acumen, his shameless debauchery and his treacherous and unfeeling treatment of his friends and relatives had lost him the respect of the nation before he came to the throne. In 1795 he married Caroline of Brunswick in accordance with an arrangement made by his father. She was so thoroughly uncongenial to the prince that within a year the pair separated. For a time the princess lived in seclusion in England. Later she took up her abode on the continent. When her husband inherited the throne, she returned to demand her rightful position as queen. The king, who refused to live with her, persuaded the cabinet to begin proceedings for divorce before the house of lords. Though the queen had been indecorous and indiscreet in her conduct, the public immediately championed her cause. The question of her innocence or guilt of the improper conduct charged against her gave the enthusiastic crowds which welcomed her back to England no concern. Her conduct did not win popular approval, but she was pitied as a woman abused by a worthless husband who was an unpopular king. From her landing at Dover to her arrival at London large, sympathetic crowds made her journey a triumphal procession. At Dover she was greeted by a salute from the cannon at the fort. The crowd removed the horses from her carriage and drew her to the hotel. "At Canterbury the officers of a

Divorce proceedings against Queen Caroline

cavalry regiment came in uniform to salute her. At Chatham she was received by surpliced clergymen." In London the mob ordered an illumination to celebrate her coming and smashed the windows of houses which displayed no lights.[5] For several months popular demonstrations in her favor and against the king and the ministers continued with unflagging zeal. So strong was public feeling in her behalf that a bill of pains and penalties to be inflicted upon her passed the Tory house of lords by a majority of only nine. To pass the bill through the house of commons was so obviously hopeless that the cabinet dropped it. So far as the king and queen were concerned the dilemma was cut by the death of the queen a few months later, but the popular condemnation of the cabinet for its participation in the quarrel remained unabated. A bit of scandal had weakened the position of the cabinet more than its repressive internal policy or its supposedly reactionary foreign policy.

In 1822 the cabinet repaired its weakness by a change of personnel
and a consequent change of policy. The suicide of Lord Castlereagh
resulted in the appointment of Canning as secretary of foreign affairs
and leader of the house. Canning was popular because he had resigned
from the ministry rather than take responsibility for the proceedings
against the queen. He was more liberal than many of his colleagues,
and he was sufficiently influential to lead the cabinet in a more liberal
direction. He was ably supported in his liberalism by two of his colleagues who were brought into the cabinet nearly simultaneously. A few months before Canning's appointment the reactionary secretary for home affairs had resigned and been succeeded by Robert Peel. The latter was so typical a product of the industrial revolution that he was sometimes called by his political opponents the "Spinning Jenny." His father was a self-made factory owner, who sent his son to Oxford to fit him for a political career. The son arrived in parliament in 1809, fresh from honors at the university. His maiden speech, which the speaker pronounced "the best first speech since that of Mr. Pitt,"[6] made so good an impression that he was soon given subordinate office by Perceval. Though associated with illiberal colleagues, Peel kept his mind open to conviction. He cared more for principles than for party affiliations, and he was ready for reform, if he became convinced of its advantage. At this stage of his career he seemed to be "as deeply bitten by 'liberality' in every way but on the Catholic question, as any of his

Change of personnel in the cabinet

---

[5] Halévy, *History of the English People, 1815–1830,* pp. 91, 92.
[6] *Creevey Papers,* pp. 122, 386.

fellows."[7] Early in 1823 Huskisson, a liberal friend of Canning's and an exceptionally able financier, was added to the cabinet. The accession of these three caused a change of policy as decisive as if an entirely new cabinet had taken office. Subsequently the liberal spirit dominated the cabinet. Between 1822 and 1830 the liberal wing of the Tories carried through a number of moderate but important and progressive reforms.

The new spirit first displayed itself in the field of foreign affairs. Canning, as a matter of fact, did not change greatly the fundamental principles of Castlereagh's policy. He also was the champion of non-intervention. But he so altered the emphasis that contemporaries thought he had wrought a reversal of policy. Though Castlereagh refused to participate with the eastern allies in their policy of intervention in the internal affairs of other states, he did not oppose them strongly and publicly. Since the liberal cause seemed to be the one most likely to disturb the peace of Europe, Castlereagh was too cautious to break with the Quadruple Alliance, which seemed to him to be the principal safeguard of peace. Canning's opposition to the repressive policy of the allies was more pronounced. He did not hesitate in behalf of non-intervention to break up the system of congresses and to strain severely the bonds of the Quadruple Alliance. He believed that the interests of peace could be better promoted by the championship of nationalities. His methods were revolutionary. To the horror of European diplomats and to the consternation of some of his Tory colleagues he resorted to "open diplomacy." " 'Our influence,' he said, 'if it is to be maintained abroad, must be secure in the sources of strength at home; and the sources of that strength are the sympathy between the people and the Government; in the union of the public sentiment with the public counsels.' "[8] By taking the nation into his confidence he won national support for a bold, independent British policy.

When Canning joined the cabinet, the powers were entering a conference to consider suppression of a popular revolt in Spain. The British representatives, acting upon Canning's orders, took so decided a stand against intervention that it was given up as a joint policy of the allies. In 1823 France, which now had membership in the conference, entered Spain to end the rebellion and restore the Spanish king. Since the eastern powers approved the expedition, the British minister of foreign affairs was unable to prevent it. France having upset the balance of power in the old world, Canning redressed it in the new.[9]

Foreign policy

---

[7] *Ibid.*, p. 442.
[8] Cited by W. A. Phillips, *George Canning*, p. 120.
[9] Speech of Canning, cited *ibid.*, p. 138.

The suggestion from France and the eastern powers, that a congress should meet to consider the suppression of revolts in the Spanish-American colonies, threatened British commercial interests recently established there. Canning not only refused to take part in a congress but also defied any power other than Spain to restore the colonies to their allegiance. It was virtually a declaration that the allies must confine their system to Europe. Since Great Britain controlled the sea, it was effective. The action of the United States, taken at the same time, completed the discomfiture of the alliance. In his famous message President Monroe announced that the United States would regard any action of the allies "to extend their system to any portion of this hemisphere as dangerous to our peace and safety" and an unfriendly act toward the United States. In the next year Great Britain ranged itself definitely on the side of liberalism by acknowledgment of the independence of several South American republics. In 1826 Canning even abandoned the policy of non-intervention. British troops were sent to Portugal to prevent the invasion of the country by a Spanish army. Great Britain, to be sure, was bound by treaty, as Canning alleged, to defend Portugal against attack by another state; but the result was once again to bring Great Britain to the support of a liberal uprising against an aristocratic constitution which Spain had intended to uphold. Meanwhile a war which had arisen between Greece and Turkey split the interests of the eastern allies. Canning wrecked the Quadruple Alliance and gave to the British foreign office nationalist and liberal sympathies which it retained long after his day. His policy was in accord with British popular opinion, and it was the first step in making the Tory program accord with the liberal views of the British public.

In internal affairs the new spirit first found expression in a reform of the criminal law. It was, moreover, one of the first reforms actuated by a humanitarian motive that was just beginning to take hold of the public imagination and was during the next two decades to actuate the passage of a large amount of social and economic legislation. The criminal code was a product of long growth. In the course of centuries one capital offense after another had been added to the list, while few had been removed. Many had been established to meet an exceptional set of temporary circumstances. In 1823, when the circumstances had long ceased to exist, the penalties were still there. Over two hundred offenses were punishable by death, and many were extremely petty. Picking a man's pocket, stealing fish, or stealing five shillings from a shop were capital crimes. Not only was the system

Criminal
law

barbarous, but it was bringing the law into disrepute. Juries often failed to convict those obviously guilty of minor offenses, because the penalty was death. Crime was on the increase because misdemeanors so often escaped with no punishment at all. A crusade to end this anomalous system was begun in 1808 by Sir Samuel Romilly, a lawyer whose sympathies had been stirred by observation of the cruelties and injustices which it inflicted. In that year he introduced into parliament and carried a bill to reduce the penalty for the picking of pockets from death to transportation. For the remaining ten years of his life he continued to bring similar measures before parliament, but few of them became law. After his death, Sir James Mackintosh assumed the leadership of the movement. He ceased the attempt to remove the death penalty from one offense at a time and sought to obtain a comprehensive law which would reform all the evils at once. In 1819 he secured the appointment of a select committee to investigate the whole subject, and on the basis of its report he secured the passage of some further legislation. He was still far short of the general revision which he desired, when Peel, the new home secretary, became interested and undertook to carry on the work. The support of the cabinet assured the systematic reform for which the work of Romilly and Mackintosh had prepared the way. In 1823 Peel obtained the enactment of laws which abolished the penalty of death in the case of harmless offenses— such as appearance in the road with the face blacked—and of those punishable as misdemeanors at common law. The acts abolished the death penalty for about one hundred offenses. Subsequent legislation continued the reform until only three crimes remained punishable by death, and the other penalties for crimes had been classified on the rational basis of making the punishment approximately commensurate with the offense.

Under Huskisson's leadership the initial step was taken toward breaking the shackles with which the mercantile system had bound British commerce. The restrictions placed on the carrying trade of foreign ships by the navigation acts were removed from the ships of countries which maintained no restrictions against British ships. The duties placed on the importation of several articles were reduced. They included a number of raw products used by manufacturers, such as silk, wool, and iron, articles of consumption not produced in England, such as wines, coffee and sugar, and a few manufactured wares, such as cottons and woolens. The reductions were not extensive, but they constituted a reform of significance. Among the articles were some which had been fostered by protective legislation for centuries. The

Steps toward free trade

prohibition on the exportation of wool, for example, was removed entirely, and the duties on imported wool and imported woolens were reduced. The reduction of such time-honored duties as these gave to Huskisson's changes a greater influence in the direction of free trade than their bulk and extent might indicate. The alterations were introduced in the budgets from 1823 to 1825. Thereafter a severe industrial crisis caused Huskisson to discontinue the further extension of his policy, and changes in the cabinet resulted in his resignation in 1828. No further progress toward free trade was made for many years.

Repeal of the Combination Acts

The repeal of the Combination Acts[10] was of much benefit to the laborers. During the eighteenth century workers who formed unions or combinations and attempted by strikes to force their employers to grant better wages, hours, or other conditions of labor laid themselves open to legal prosecutions by their employers, which, if successful, subjected them to terms of imprisonment or other penalties. The courts, beginning as early as 1706, decided in many cases that workmen who struck for better wages were guilty of the common law offense of conspiracy in restraint of trade. Another snare for the workmen was the masters and servants clause in the Elizabethan Statute of Apprentices which was kept alive long after most of the other clauses had become obsolete. It forbade persons who had undertaken to do a piece of work to leave before it was finished, under penalty of fine and imprisonment. Since in many industries, as they were organized in the eighteenth century, the laborers never finished their work in the sense of the statute as it was interpreted by the courts, they left their work unfinished and became liable to the penalties of the statute if they struck for better wages. Early in the century parliament, at the instance of the employers, began to enact statutes imposing penalties upon workers in individual industries who combined to secure better conditions of labor, and the employers in many industries could invoke such laws, before the acts of 1799 and 1800 extended the principle to all industries. In the early years of the nineteenth century combinations of laborers were successful in obtaining better wages by strikes on several occasions, but it was because the employers chose not to invoke any of the several laws against them. In other instances laborers were prosecuted and punished for participation in strikes, and no laborer could ever engage in a strike without taking serious risk of ending in prison.

Huskisson and Peel were persuaded to remedy this injustice largely by the evidence produced by Francis Place. He was a master tailor who

---

[10] Above, p. 613.

remembered the days when he had been a journeyman and retained his sympathy for the laborers. After he had collected a large amount of information concerning the hardships and injustices inflicted upon the workers by the Combination Acts, he interested Joseph Hume, a Radical member of parliament, in his cause. In 1824 Hume secured the appointment of a select committee to investigate the working of the acts. The workingmen were ignorant and afraid to give their evidence, and the governing class was prejudiced and without desire to understand the difficulties of the laborers. Place picked the witnesses whom Hume called before the committee, coached Hume on the questions to ask and the laborers on the answers to give, and produced such a mass of evidence of the injustice of the acts that the committee reported in favor of repeal.[11] Huskisson and Peel were convinced, and in the same year not only the Combination Acts but also the clause of the Statute of Apprentices were repealed, and the interpretation of the common law which made strikes for better wages or hours conspiracies in restraint of trade was nullified. The laborers, however, made unwise use of their liberties. Many strikes took place immediately, and in several instances they were accompanied with violence and destruction of property. In 1825 a new law forbade the laborers to act in combination except to secure the regulation of wages and hours of employment, and it revoked the protection given by the preceding act against the masters and servants clause and against charges of conspiracy. The result was to legalize trade unions for certain purposes and to give them greater freedom than they had possessed before 1824, but to leave them handicapped in many ways.

These reforms were not passed without much friction in the cabinet between the new liberal members and the narrow, reactionary Tories, who were not fully aware that the Napoleonic era had passed. In the commons and in the nation the reactionary Tories received support mainly from the landed class, while the progressive wing found favor with the commercial and industrial classes, and particularly with the new capitalist class created by the industrial revolution. The cabinet held together largely because Lord Liverpool, the prime minister, was a past master in the art of smoothing over the differences between the factions. When he was incapacitated by a stroke of apoplexy in 1827, the balance was completely upset. Canning became the next prime minister, whereupon the narrow Tories resigned. Since the liberal Tories alone were not strong enough to provide a majority, Canning

Reorganizations of the Cabinet

---

[11] Wallas, *Place*, ch. viii.

gave office to several moderate Whigs. But Canning was hardly under way when he died. An attempt to secure as prime minister a peacemaker,[12] who could hold the balance as Liverpool had done, failed, and in 1828 the duke of Wellington was appointed. The man who had won the war was to the people "the Duke," as if there was no other. But he was too "dry, cold, self-contained"[13] to become a popular politician. He was, moreover, opposed to the liberal movement. He promptly dropped the Whigs and brought back the reactionaries. The liberal Tories, who had followed Canning, soon found themselves uncomfortable and resigned. Thus in 1828 the cabinet became composed almost exclusively of narrow Tories.

While these changes were weakening the cabinet, it had to face

The Near East

three difficult problems. The question of the Near East had first attracted the attention of Europe when the Greeks revolted against the Turks in 1821. Great Britain at first did nothing except to watch Russia. Since Pitt's day it had become British policy to guard against further acquisition of territory by Russia at the expense of Turkey. English politicians suspected Russia of "a fixed intention to make Constantinople a seat of her power."[14] When Russia began to display intentions of intervention, Canning, seeking to avoid the necessity of British intervention, began tortuous negotiations to keep Russia out. Meanwhile the sympathy of the British public was raised to a quixotic height by the romantic deeds of Byron, who went to aid the cause of the oppressed Greeks and for it sacrificed his life. So strong did the sentiment become, that Canning found it difficult to maintain friendship with Turkey, when the war began to go against the Greeks. As relations developed with Russia, moreover, joint intervention with Russia seemed to be the most effective way to prevent an undue extension of Russian influence. In 1827 therefore he signed the Treaty of London, in which Great Britain, Russia, and France agreed to demand an armistice and a permanent settlement on the basis of Greek self-government under nominal Turkish suzerainty. If Turkey refused, the allies agreed to maintain a peaceful blockade against the Egyptian fleet, which was aiding Turkey against Greece. When Turkey refused, the commander of the British squadron was instructed to carry out this policy, using force if necessary but committing no act of hostility. Just what such orders meant may well have puzzled the commander. He used the British and allied ships to draw a cordon across the harbor where the Egyp-

---

[12] Namely, Lord Goderich.
[13] McCarthy, *History of Our Own Times,* i, 416.
[14] *Creevey Papers,* p. 476.

tian fleet was anchored. When it attempted to come out, the allied fleet conquered and destroyed it in the battle of Navarino. The event took place late in 1827 after Canning's death. Wellington's cabinet consequently had to settle the problems raised.

Because the narrow Tories who favored friendship with Turkey had never approved Canning's policy, Wellington did not follow up the intervention. Neither did he publicly abandon the policy by making the reparation demanded by Turkey. He drifted. Meanwhile Russia alone sent an army into Turkey and forced the cession of Greek independence in 1829. Russia extended her influence in the great provinces of Moldavia and Wallachia, which were made practically independent of Turkey, though left nominally dependent, and secured the friendship of Greece. Great Britain lost the friendship of Turkey and dimmed her prestige in Greece. Wellington forfeited much that Canning had won. The result weakened the cabinet, for the public had followed the Greek question more closely than it watched most foreign diplomacy. All liberals, Tories as well as Whigs, were disgusted. Even the reactionary Tories did not relish Wellington's complete failure. The outcome of the eastern policy served to discredit the cabinet with all parties in 1829.

Another policy which lost the cabinet more supporters than it gained was that of a new corn law. The law of 1815 had not helped the agricultural class as much as had been anticipated, and it had proved most harmful to the consumers. In 1826 a scant harvest threatened such widespread distress that the cabinet secured parliamentary authority to permit the importation of grain before the famine price of the act of 1815 had been reached in the market. This action demonstrated so forcibly the injustice of the act to the consumers, who had no interest in the land and constituted approximately two-thirds of the community, that the act of 1815 had to be revised. When Canning undertook it in 1827, Wellington secured the defeat of his bill in the house of lords. When the duke became prime minister, he was forced by the divisions in his cabinet to introduce the same bill with slight modifications. The new act allowed grain to be imported at any time, but fixed the duty on a sliding scale, making it high when the price in the English market was low and reducing the duty as the price in the English market advanced shilling by shilling. The price at which grain came in free was lowered from 80 s. to 73 s. The act alienated some of the landlords, and won the duke no credit with the liberal element, which recognized that the measure was essentially Canning's.

The last question that rent the cabinet was the removal of civil

New corn law

disabilities imposed on various religious sects. In 1828, at the initiative of a Whig, who was not a member of the cabinet, the restrictions of the Test and Corporation Acts, which excluded Protestant dissenters from office, were removed without particular difficulty. The Protestant dissenters had long been exempted from the penalties of these acts by the periodical passage of acts of indemnity. But Catholic emancipation aroused tremendous prejudices. This issue was forced on the cabinet in a curious manner. When the liberal Tories left the cabinet in 1828, one of their successors had to stand for reelection in his constituency, which was the county of Clare in Ireland. At the election he was defeated by Daniel O'Connell, who, being a Catholic, could not sit in parliament. The election was conducted in an orderly manner. The Catholic voters, led by their priests, marched up to the polls and voted without a single untoward incident. To have so orderly a demonstration in Ireland of all places was convincing evidence of the thoroughness of the organization of the Irish Catholics in behalf of emancipation. The Irish Catholics had been agitating for emancipation ever since 1801, when Pitt's resignation had deprived them of the relief anticipated as a part of the union. Daniel O'Connell had been organizing the movement for many years. The Clare election demonstrated that his work had been effective.

The two leaders of the cabinet, Wellington and Peel, were bitterly opposed to Catholic emancipation, but the Clare election convinced them that failure to grant it would produce civil war in Ireland. They persuaded the cabinet to introduce a bill to relieve the Catholics of their disabilities and to give them, among other things, the right to sit in parliament, though the value of the concession to the Irish Catholics was diminished by another bill, which required a voter to own a freehold producing an annual income of £10 a year and reduced greatly the number of Irish Catholic voters. English popular opinion did not favor the bill, the king disliked it, and its authors did not believe in its principle; but Wellington drove the Tories into line and forced it through parliament in much the same way that he had pushed the French out of Spain. He thought it his duty to prevent civil war at the cost of sacrificing his own and his party's convictions. Catholic emancipation in 1829 brought the climax of the unpopularity of Wellington's cabinet. The good old bred-in-the-bone Tories lost faith in human nature when their leaders forced them to swallow Catholic emancipation. They began to suspect that Wellington and Peel were traitors to the cause.

The weakness of the cabinet prepared the way for its downfall on

the issue of parliamentary reform. In 1830 the death of George IV
brought to the throne his brother William. The accession of a new
king necessitated an election. In the campaign the reform of the house
of commons became for the first time a party issue. When the violent
agitation for reform gradually subsided after 1820, moderate reformers
began to obtain a hearing for their doctrine of a reform that should go
no further than the abolition of the most rotten constituencies and the
extension of the suffrage to the middle class. As it became possible to
contemplate a reform which would not transfer the government to the
ignorant masses, the movement for reform became divested of its
radical associations and came into the realm of practical politics. In the
decade between 1820 and 1830 individual Whigs, among whom the
most prominent was Lord John Russell, began to advocate it. By the
election of 1830 the movement had gained such an impetus that it
crept into the campaign. Public opinion in its favor was stimulated by
the revolution of July in France. Because the restored monarchy of the
house of Bourbon had set itself against the liberal constitution established after the downfall of Napoleon, the French people, in a practically bloodless revolution, overthrew the house of Bourbon and established a "citizen king" in the person of Louis Philippe. This apparent
victory of liberal institutions in France occurred just in time to arouse
the sentiment of English electors in favor of reform. Some fifty seats
changed hands, which was a large turnover in the days when the greater
portion of the seats was controlled by patrons. In nearly every instance
of change an opponent of reform was defeated and a liberal put in his
place.

The Whigs meanwhile had healed the dissensions which had so
long rendered the party powerless. When the new parliament met,
they held a caucus and adopted reform as a party principle. In a speech
at the opening of parliament Wellington put the Tories at the other
pole. He described the British electoral system as the most perfect ever
devised by the hand of man. "I am fully convinced," said he, "that the
country possesses at the present moment a Legislature which answers
all the good purposes of legislation, and this to a greater degree than
any Legislature ever has answered in any country whatever. I will go
further and say, that the Legislature and the system of representation
possess the full and entire confidence of the country. . . . I will go
still further, and say that if at the present moment I had imposed upon
me the duty of forming a Legislature for any country . . . I do not
mean to assert that I could form such a Legislature as we possess now,
for the nature of man is incapable of reaching such excellence at once;

but my great endeavour would be, to form some description of legislature which would produce the same results."[15] Such extreme reaction aroused every element of opposition. In two weeks the cabinet was forced to resign. Thus was ended a Tory régime which had lasted, with one brief interval, for nearly half a century.

[15] Quoted in Kendall, *Source-Book of English History*, p. 383.

CHAPTER XXXV

AN EPOCH OF REFORM, 1830-1846

THE Whig cabinet which took office in 1830 was headed by Earl Grey. Though he was a conservative Whig, essentially aristocratic in his views, he had been an advocate of parliamentary reform all his life. His aristocratic leanings were reflected in his choice of colleagues. With two exceptions they were peers or the sons of peers. Some, such as "honest Jack" Althorp, who, as a leader of the house of commons, was loved and trusted by all sections of the Whigs, were of like moderate mind with their leader. But the more radical Whigs were represented. Henry Brougham, who voiced the desire of the middle class for reform, was lord chancellor. The young earl of Durham, whom his tenants called "Radical Jack," and Lord John Russell, the advocate of reform, who was in the ministry but not in the cabinet, were intrusted with the framing of the bill. Several followers of Canning, who henceforth acted with the Whigs, were also included. The cabinet was representative of nearly all shades of liberal opinion and exceptionally well endowed with talent.

The Whig cabinet

The reform bill was introduced in the house of commons by Lord John Russell. It provided for a reform so much more extensive than had been anticipated that it won widespread popular approval. In the house, however, it passed the second reading, when the general principles were in debate, by a majority of only one. In the stage of committee, when the details were considered, the bill was amended out of shape. The cabinet lacked a sufficient majority to secure the passage of the measure. Grey therefore advised the king to dissolve parliament and hold a new election. The election was bitterly fought in the midst of great excitement. Throughout the country a cry went up for "The Bill, the whole Bill, and nothing but the Bill." Wherever public opinion could find expression, it was unanimous in favor of reform. The new house passed the bill by a substantial majority. The house of lords rejected it. A tremendous popular agitation followed, frequently accompanied by mob violence. In Bristol the rioters had possession of the city for three days and destroyed a large section of it by fire. Everywhere unions and associations were formed to prepare for armed resistance, if the bill should not ultimately pass. The opposition in the house of commons wilted. As a staunch opponent

Passage of the reform bill

of the measure in that house put it, "The four M's, the Monarch, the Ministry, the Members and the Multitude all against us."[1] In the next session the bill was passed again by the house of commons. The lords did not reject it a second time, but they began to discuss amendments that would destroy its principle. The cabinet recommended the appointment of enough new peers to give a majority in favor of the reform. Since the number required was large, William IV refused. "As the king repeatedly said . . . (perhaps being the only poetry he ever made)—'I consider dissolution Tantamount to revolution.' "[2] The cabinet resigned, and Wellington, called by the king, tried to form a Tory cabinet. So strong was popular opinion and so determined and well organized were the popular organizations formed to support the bill, that this crisis brought the country within measurable distance of civil war. There were no more riots, but men prepared soberly and seriously to fight for the popular rights. The danger was avoided by the failure of the duke to form a cabinet. Since a Tory majority was lacking in the house of commons and obviously could not be obtained by a new election, he could not find a sufficient number of colleagues foolhardy enough to accept office. The king was forced to take back the Whig cabinet and accept its advice. When the Tories saw that new peers would be created, enough of them remained away from the house to give the Whigs a majority without additions to their ranks. Thus the first reform bill became law in 1832, and the principle was vindicated that the house of lords could not block legislation on which favorable popular opinion had been expressed strongly.

The act reformed the electoral system in three main particulars. (1) The constituencies were not equalized, but the worst evils were removed. The smallest boroughs lost both of their representatives, and several of intermediate size lost one member each. The seats thus gained were distributed to the populous towns, previously represented inadequately or not at all, and to the counties. (2) The worst anomalies of the franchise were swept away. The forty-shilling freeholder, who resided on his freehold, kept the right to vote. Owners by other tenures and leaseholders for long terms of estates of the yearly value of £10, and leaseholders for short terms or tenants-at-will whose tenements were worth £50 a year were added to the voters in the rural constituencies. In the boroughs the old qualifications[3] were abolished

---

[1] *Croker Papers*, i, 528.

[2] *Ibid.*, p. 530.

[3] See above, pp. 273, 274.

with one unimportant exception. Otherwise the franchise in boroughs depended solely on occupation of premises. The occupier of a house or a shop worth £10 estimated annual rental could vote, subject to certain qualifications with regard to length of residence and payment of taxes. (3) The conduct of elections was improved by provisions for a more adequate system of registration of the voters, the reduction of the days for voting from fifteen to two, and the reduction of expenses at elections. The reform stopped far short of equal constituencies or universal suffrage. The electorate established under the new system was not greatly wider than that under the old. After 1832 only one out of thirty persons in the population had the right to vote, while universal manhood suffrage gives the right to one out of about four and a half persons. But the grip of aristocratic patrons was broken, and the middle class obtained a strong influence upon elections. The workingman still had no share in politics.

After the reform of parliament other reforms were bound to follow. Public opinion had been prepared for changes by a variety of influences. Prominent among them was the utilitarian philosophy first propounded by Jeremy Bentham. It assumed that utility was the main purpose of government, and utility was defined as "the greatest happiness of the greatest number." It was to be accomplished by legislation. This point of view, which was propagated by many publicists and politicians, by 1832 exerted a profound influence on public opinion. By that time, too, Adam Smith's system of *laissez faire* no longer gave universal satisfaction. Though it had been applied to industry for years, a huge mass of the population was still living in abject poverty and in unsanitary conditions, earning wages barely sufficient for existence, forced to work unreasonably long hours under adverse conditions, and subject to acute suffering whenever there was a scarcity in the wheat market. John Stuart Mill asserted that the fallacy of the theory was its assumption that the chief object of economic development was to increase the amount of material wealth possessed by the nation. A higher and better end, he maintained, was to obtain the equitable distribution of that wealth. Wealth that went only into the pockets of the capitalists did little good to the great number. In practice the laborers were unable to secure the economic liberty of selling their labor, which the system of *laissez faire* assumed, and the capitalists had the advantage in bargaining for their labor. Regulation was justified, therefore, to that extent which would enable labor to deal with capital on equal terms. Mill began to propound his views in the decade of the twenties. Eventually his opinions in-

Public opinion and reform

fluenced the economic legislation of the nineteenth century profoundly, though it is difficult to say how far they had affected popular thought by 1832. Strongest of all the motives behind the popular desire for reforms was probably the humanitarian. For many years a few philanthropically-minded persons had been calling the attention of the public to the distressing conditions in which a large element of the population lived. They had created a strong popular feeling that these conditions constituted a blot on civilization and should be wiped out, whatever philosophical and economic theories might be.

Factory Act

The regulation of the labor of children in factories was one of the first fruits of the humanitarian spirit. The agitation for this reform had long been growing. Dr. Percival of Manchester was the first to bring to the attention of the public the deplorable conditions of labor in the factories. Having occasion to investigate the causes of a local epidemic of fever, he traced its origin to the children employed in the cotton factories. That led to a study of the conditions of their labor and the submission of a report to the local board of health in 1796. Employment in large factories, he asserted, was generally injurious not only to the health of the children but also to their intellectual and moral development. The long hours of work left them no opportunity for either recreation or study. The ruin of one generation of children after another, he prophesied, would cause serious economic loss to the nation by the wastage of man power. So impressive was the report that the board of health brought it before parliament. Sir Robert Peel, a factory owner and the father of the statesman, took the matter up and secured the passage of an act to regulate child labor. It was limited in scope to apprentices, who constituted a small part of the children employed, and it was never adequately enforced.

The question was again brought to the attention of parliament by Robert Owen. He had worked his way from the ranks of the operatives to the ownership of a cotton factory. When he was receiving only a meager salary, he gave one-third of it to promote the cause of education. After he attained success, he retained his strong philanthropic and humanitarian interests. As an owner he convinced himself by experiments that the children employed in his factories could be given shorter hours, better conditions of employment, and more time for education at little or no loss of profit to the owner. He then began a crusade to make the application of his reforms universal. He interested members of parliament, who secured the appointment of a select committee which assembled valuable evidence of the appalling conditions existing in most factories in 1816. An act to regulate the age of children employed in cotton factories and the hours of their labor followed. It became almost immediately a dead letter because it was left to the justices of the peace to enforce. They were estimable country gentlemen, but they were unfamiliar with the conditions of urban labor, and there was none with the interest or the responsibility to require them to execute the legislation. Owen's work was important, nevertheless, for it first brought the matter to the attention of the general public.

Subsequently the matter was kept before the public. In 1830 a renewed vigor in the agitation for reform succeeded in arousing widespread sympathy. Another parliamentary committee was appointed to collect evidence. Its researches merely confirmed those of the earlier committee. The children commonly began work at the age of eight or nine and sometimes younger; they worked twelve to fourteen hours a day or even longer, often under unsanitary conditions; in some factories they were driven with whips when they became exhausted during the late hours of the day; they had no opportunity for recreation or education; and the health of many of them was permanently undermined. On the basis of this evidence Lord Ashley (later the earl of Shaftesbury) introduced a bill to regulate the labor of children. Popular approval was so strong that the cabinet finally came to the support of the measure. Thus it became law in 1833. The act applied to all textile factories with a few exceptions. Children below nine years of age could not be employed, between the ages of nine and thirteen their hours were limited to nine a day, and between thirteen and eighteen to twelve. It also made some slight provision for better sanitary conditions. The most important aspect of the act, however, was the establishment of inspectors appointed by the central government. This insured the enforcement of the act. The law was he first indication of a tendency, which later became pronounced, to .ake the control of local affairs away from incompetent local officials and give them to the central government.

After the passage of the first effective act, further regulation was merely a question of agitation and time. Lord Ashley continued to promote the movement in parliament. Acts passed in 1844 and 1847 reduced the hours of labor for children from nine to thirteen years of age to a half-day, or to alternate days, with the requirement that the other half be given to school; placed women in the same category as young persons from thirteen to eighteen years of age, and reduced their working day to ten hours; made provisions for the protection

Further legislation

of dangerous machinery; and improved the older act in many details. In 1842 the principles of the factory acts were extended to the mines. By this time the principle of the regulation of the conditions of labor by the government was almost universally accepted. Subsequently it was extended broadly.

Abolition of slavery

In the same year that the Factory Act was passed, slavery was abolished. The group of reformers which had finally secured the abolition of the slave trade in 1807 regarded that as merely the first step. Thereafter they began to appeal for the abolition of slavery itself. Their literature and their tales of cruelties gradually found a response, and public opinion steadily became more favorable. At the same time the parliamentary influence of the West Indian planters, who were the chief slave owners in the empire, declined. In 1814 the trade with the West Indian colonies had constituted nearly one-sixth of the whole of British external commerce; in 1833 it was only a fifteenth. In 1830 Brougham, an erratic but brilliant and liberal Whig leader, pledged himself to his constituents to support abolition. When he became an influential member of the Whig cabinet, the cause was assured. Since the measure affected only the colonies, it was introduced by Lord Stanley, the colonial secretary. The act provided that slavery should cease in 1834. In order to make the transition easier for both the owners and the slaves, the former slaves were to remain as apprentices, owing a part of their time to their former masters for several years before they became entirely free. The owners of slaves regarded the act as a righteous gesture by the mother country at their expense, but the British public was sufficiently sincere to contribute taxes amounting to £20,000,000 to help defray the losses to the owners.

Poor law

In 1834 the cabinet proceeded to the reform of the poor law. The distress of the laboring classes and the constant growth of pauperism had been a matter of grave public concern since the beginning of the war with France. The wretchedness of a rapidly increasing mass of the population obtrudes itself into nearly every historical aspect of the period. Among many causes of the misery,[4] the maladministration of the poor law was fundamental. The principles of the law in force before 1834 were still those of the Elizabethan act of 1601,[5] but they had become vitiated in the practice of administration. The justices of the peace, who had large powers to supervise and interfere with the parochial overseers who administered the act, were no longer controlled effectively by the central government. The squires of this

---

[4] See above, pp. 613, 627.
[5] Above, p. 359.

period were often not of the type to exercise administrative discretion intelligently.[6] At the same time the burden of administrative work thrown upon them was ever on the increase. Their work was bad enough in the eighteenth century when their problems were mainly those of a simple agricultural community; when they had to face the complex set of economic and social conditions created by the economic revolution, it became hopeless. The portrayal by Dickens[7] of a justice of the peace as entirely and absurdly dependent on his paid clerk for a knowledge of his duties and powers hardly seems a caricature in the light of sober history.

What the justices had done to the poor law may be illustrated. A justice could issue an order to an overseer compelling him to give relief to a specified inhabitant of his parish. In the eighteenth century such orders became common. A loafer, who could get no aid from the overseer who knew him, could generally find in another part of the county some justice who could be deceived sufficiently by a story of hard luck to induce him to issue an order for relief. The distinction between the able-bodied and impotent poor dropped entirely out of sight. In 1795 the justices of Berkshire, assembled at Speenhamland, all unconsciously ushered in a new epoch in the history of the poor law. Possessed of larger hearts than heads, they were moved by the manifest inability of the laborer with ordinary wages to earn enough to buy the necessary food for his family to declare an administrative policy so important in its effects that it has become known as the Speenhamland Act. Fixing a scale of relief proportioned to the price of wheat and the size of the applicant's family, they offered to give relief to every laborer who applied. The system was widely copied with disastrous results. Since able-bodied men could obtain relief, some employers fixed their wages so low in relation to the prices of commodities that their employees had to supplement their wages with poor relief. The laborer who tried to be independent found it impossible to compete with the laborers subsidized from the poor relief. All sense of independence was being lost by the laborers, providence and thrift were ceasing to be virtues, and the moral fiber of the community was being undermined. Taxation for the relief of the poor tripled between 1783 and 1834, and in some sections the increase was far above the average. The extreme case cited in the report was that of a village where the tax increased from £10 11 s. in 1801 to £367 in 1832.

---

[6] See above, pp. 536, 537.
[7] *Pickwick Papers*, ch. **xxv**.

The new law provided that no relief should be given to able-bodied persons unless they resided in the poorhouse. As a pronounced social stigma attached to such residence, the remedy proved harsh but effective. The act also reorganized the administration, giving a central board a large degree of control over the work of local administrators, and making poor-law guardians, elected by the local taxpayers, the influential element in charge of the local disbursement of relief. The act worked so well that the rate of taxation for relief of the poor dropped notably within a few years.

Municipal Corporations Act

In 1835 the government of the towns was reorganized. Before the reform, the municipal governments in the vast majority of cases had fallen into the hands of an unrepresentative oligarchy. In two-thirds of the boroughs the members of the governing council served for life, the membership was renewed by cooptation, and the council made the appointments to the administrative offices. Only in a minority of boroughs did the municipal corporation retain any representative character, and in many of them the franchise was extremely narrow. In Plymouth, where the population was more than 75,000, the number of voters was 437, of whom 145 were non-resident. "In Norwich," says the report of the commissioners appointed to investigate, "the great majority of the inhabitant householders and ratepayers[8] are excluded from the corporate body; while paupers, lodgers, and others, paying neither rates nor taxes, are admitted to the exercise of the functions of freemen [i.e., voters], and form a considerable portion of the corporation."[9] Such governments, having no responsibility to the people, handled the corporate property and the municipal taxes to suit their personal advantage. Banquets for members of the corporation and large salaries paid to sinecure officeholders absorbed the funds, while the pressing needs of waterworks, sewers, paving, lighting, and police, created by the large increase of the urban population, went without provision. In this problem the new parliamentary voters of the middle class created by the act of 1832 were particularly interested. They were largely manufacturers and merchants who lived in the boroughs and paid municipal taxes. They wanted to eliminate the corruption and secure efficient governments, which would provide the needed police and public works. Consequently it was one of the first reforms undertaken, though legislation was delayed until a commission had had time to study and report.

[8] Namely, payers of local taxes.
[9] First Report of the Commissioners appointed to inquire into the Municipal Corporations in England and Wales, *Parliamentary Papers* (1835), p. 33.

The act deprived a large number of the smallest boroughs of their municipal charters. In the remainder, except London, it created uniform governments. The government was placed in the hands of a council elected by the resident ratepayers. The councilors served for three years, one-third retiring every year. Excepted were one-third of their number, whom the councilors elected to serve for six years, of whom one-third retired every two years. In this manner the council always preserved an element of experienced members. The council was made responsible for the whole government of the borough. It elected the mayor annually, and it appointed the salaried officials, who actually ran the waterworks and performed the other municipal functions under its supervision. The reform worked remarkably well. The corruption and inefficiency of the old system were almost entirely eliminated. The fundamental organization of British municipal government is still that established in 1835, though its powers and funccion have been greatly enlarged.

Athwart the domestic issues of this period ran the Irish question. Catholic emancipation had settled only one of the many grievances of the Irish. After 1829 they demanded vociferously the redress of two further wrongs. The first was the existence of a Protestant established church to which the Catholics were compelled to contribute support in the form of tithes. The Catholics objected not only to the compulsory support of another church but also to the payment of salaries to rectors who had only one or two parishioners and sometimes none at all. "The Church of Ireland," said a contemporary, "in a very great degree consists of bishops without clergy, churches without clergymen, and clergymen without churches."[10] The Irish demanded the abolition of the tithe. The second complaint was the complete ascendency of the Protestants in official places in Ireland. The viceroy and the secretary, who occupied the castle at Dublin, whether Whig or Tory, gave all the patronage to Protestants. The police, the local judiciary, and even the juries were Protestant. The success of Catholic emancipation had taught the Irish that the best instrument with which to pry favors from the British parliament was violence or the threat of violence. Their agitation took the form of agrarian outrages. By 1831 large parts of Ireland were in open anarchy, controlled by irresponsible secret societies. The government found it impossible to discover and punish offenders because juries would not convict and witnesses feared to tell the truth.

Irish problems

---

[10] *Wellesley Papers*, ii, 82.

Slight modifications of the mode of collecting tithes brought no cessation of violence. In 1833 Lord Stanley, who was then secretary for Ireland, brought in two bills, which mark the beginning of a "quick alternation of kicks and caresses" with which Great Britain attempted to govern Ireland during much of the nineteenth century. A coercion bill provided for the military rule of the disturbed districts by martial law. A second measure provided for a reorganization of the Anglican church in Ireland, calculated to reduce expenses by £120,000. Half of the saving was to be used to lighten the fiscal burden imposed on the Catholics for the church and the other half was to be placed at the disposal of the government. The last clause raised a hot contest. To O'Connell, the leader of the Irish in parliament, it was the one satisfactory aspect of the bill, because it implied the possibility of disestablishment of the Irish church and the end of tithes. If the government could take £60,000, it could take the whole. For that very reason it roused so strong an opposition from the supporters of the established church that it had to be dropped in order to get the bill through the house of lords. Stanley subsequently was transferred to the colonial office, and a new Irish secretary in the next year tried a bill to reduce the tithe and convert it to a tax on land payable by the landlords. This, it was hoped, would remove the irritation of the Catholic peasants, who would no longer pay tithes directly. The bill split the cabinet. Lord John Russell "upset the coach" by advocating in debate the principle of the appropriation clause dropped from the preceding bill. Once the issue had been raised, a difference of opinion became apparent in the cabinet. Lord Stanley thereupon resigned. In the next year he went over to the opposition bench, and later, as the earl of Derby, he was destined to become three times a Tory prime minister. Three colleagues followed Stanley. The cabinet was patched up, but the cracks were still there. Further altercations within the cabinet resulted finally in the resignation of Earl Grey in 1834. He had consistently supported the reform of parliament throughout his career; in the great fight for the passage of the reform bill he had stood firm for the whole measure, when many of his colleagues favored compromise; but the rapidity of the reforms which followed the act of 1832 had made him afraid of the consequences. With his radical colleagues he was like a hen with a brood of ducklings, and he was glad of the excuse to resign.

The king chose as his successor Lord Melbourne, an old Canningite, who had acted with the Whigs for some years. He was an affable, courteous, indolent man whom everyone liked. Entertaining moderate opinions, and being without strong convictions, he was able to hold the balance between moderate and radical Whigs somewhat as Liverpool had held it among the Tories. Aside from the leadership, the cabinet changed little. Melbourne's cabinet found a solution of the Irish difficulties. In 1835 Melbourne made with O'Connell the "Lichfield House compact." The Protestant ascendency in Ireland was to be broken up and O'Connell given part of the patronage, the bill of 1834 was to be introduced again, and a milder coercion act passed. In return O'Connell was to bring to the support of the cabinet the Irish votes in the house of commons. These he controlled so completely that they were called his tail. The compact was loyally kept on both sides. Between 1835 and 1841 O'Connell's tail saved the cabinet from defeat many times. The cabinet appointed a new secretary for Ireland, who gave O'Connell the promised places for Catholics and held the balance impartially between Protestants and Catholics. When the Protestant justices of Tipperary demanded a special force to put down the disorder in that county, the secretary refused because the trouble was due to the unjust treatment of the tenants by the landlords. He suggested pointedly that "property had duties as well as rights." The tithes bill failed in the house of lords, but it was finally passed in 1838. In the same year the principles of the new poor law were extended to Ireland, and in 1840 Irish municipal corporations were reformed in such a way as to give Catholics a share in the municipal government. The period of Melbourne's cabinet was one of the most peaceful in the annals of the British control of Ireland during the nineteenth century. {.marginnote}

Policy of Melbourne's cabinet

When Melbourne assumed the headship of the cabinet, it was already weak. There had been divergences not only on the Irish question but also between the moderate and the radical Whigs on questions of reform. The reforms alienated some of the supporters whose interests were affected adversely. In the autumn of 1834 the situation of the cabinet seemed so doubtful that Melbourne suggested that the king seek advice from the Tories. Peel accordingly formed a cabinet and held an election. During the campaign he made an address to his constituents at Tamworth, announcing his loyal acceptance of the reform of parliament and his willingness to reform any institution, provided the need of reform was demonstrated. "If," he said in his famous address, "by adopting the spirit of the Reform Bill, it be meant that we are to live in a perpetual vortex of agitation; that public men can only support themselves in public estimation by adopting every popular impression of the day,—by promising the instant

Weakness of the Melbourne cabinet

redress of anything which anybody may call an abuse; . . . if this be the spirit of the Reform Bill, I will not undertake to adopt it. But if the spirit of the Reform Bill implies merely a careful review of institutions, civil and ecclesiastical, undertaken in a friendly temper, combining, with the firm maintenance of established rights, the correction of proved abuses and the redress of real grievances,—in that case I can for myself and colleagues undertake to act in such a spirit."[11] The Tamworth manifesto was part of Peel's effort to change the Tory party from one of mere reaction to one of moderate progress. In large measure he was successful. A large section of the Tories accepted his point of view, and some of the more moderate Whigs were attracted by it. The transition of such Whigs to the ranks of the Tories was made easier by the use of the term Conservative in place of Tory, a usage which became common in the following years. In the same way the radical Whigs and the Radicals were tending to coalesce under the designation of Liberals. In the election of 1834, however, Peel failed to obtain a majority, and after a few weeks of office he resigned. Lord Melbourne returned to power with a cabinet little stronger than before. Sometimes it would have lacked a majority without the aid of O'Connell's followers. It was too weak to strike out on any great constructive policy. After the passage of municipal reform in 1835, it did little more than to supplement the reforms already enacted.

The colonies, 1783–1830

The one exception to the general inertia was the reform of the Canadian government, which was forced upon the cabinet by a rebellion in Canada. In the decade after 1830 the colonies occupied the attention of English statesmen to a larger extent than at any time since 1783. After the loss of the American continental colonies only the fragments of empire were left. Few envisaged the vast dominion soon to be built in India, Canada was regarded as of little worth, and Newfoundland, the British West Indies, Gibraltar, two small posts on the western coast of Africa, and St. Helena constituted the insignificant remainder. The loss of the keystone of the arch was a blow to English pride, and for a time Englishmen seemed content to consider their imperial policy a failure. For many years no conscious effort was made to expand the empire, and no attempt was made to remove the imperfections of the imperial system of government which had contributed to the loss of the American colonies.

Notwithstanding this indifference, some expansion took place. In

---

[11] Peel, *Memoirs*, ii, 62.

1786 parliament began to seek for a place to which convicts could Expansion
be transported in order to relieve the congestion of English prisons.
It decided upon Australia, which Captain Cook had partially explored several years before in the interests of a scientific expedition.
In 1787 the first lot of convicts was despatched under military escort.
Thus was begun without the slightest intention on the part of the
government a colony destined to become one of the most important
in the empire. The war with France resulted in the rapid growth of
the empire.[12] The expansion was intentional, but the new conquests
did not immediately arouse any general enthusiasm for the development of the empire. After 1815, as before, statesmen generally felt no
great responsibility for the colonies, and the public took slight interest
in imperial problems.

About 1830 the attitude of thinkers and statesmen toward the colonies began to change. A few never lost faith in Britain's imperial Change in
mission, but the majority regarded the colonies as a burden. They imperial
thought that no advantages of trade acquired by the possession of policy
the colonies could offset the cost of their maintenance and defense. after 1830
Some of the latter desired to be rid of the colonies as soon as possible;
but more of them, like Russell and Grey, believed that Great Britain,
having assumed the burden of the colonies, should promote their welfare in every way, until the time was ripe for them to assume independence. These new currents of thought helped to bring about important action with regard to the colonies after 1830. (1) The abolition
of slavery was dictated by British moral sentiment rather than by
imperial considerations, but its effects were felt chiefly in the colonies.
(2) As a part of Huskisson's fiscal policies the existing restrictions of
the mercantile system which most hampered the colonies were in
some part removed, while many of the restrictions on British importa-
tions which gave the colonies an advantage for their products in the
British market at the expense of the British consumer were retained.
(3) In 1830 a society was founded at the initiative of Gibbon Wakefield to promote systematic colonization. Wakefield, who was the
guiding spirit of the society, believed that emigration to places like
Canada and Australia would improve social and economic conditions
in England by relieving the congestion of population and would develop an empire of great value. The society did much to awaken
public interest in imperial problems. Under Wakefield's influence the
government adopted a new policy of promoting emigration of free

---

[12] See above, p. 620, and below, p. 681.

colonists to Australia, which laid the foundation for the remarkable development of that colony. (4) Most important of all was the inauguration of the system of colonial government which developed eventually into self-government in the great English-speaking colonies.

Since 1783 no significant change had been made in the methods of colonial government. Subject to variations of detail, there were two main types of government. In colonies like Gibraltar or Malta held mainly for military purposes, and in tropical colonies where the white population was small and the native element large, a governor appointed by the crown had all the power. He might have an appointed council, but he was little restricted by it. In colonies where the population was largely or entirely white, such as Canada, an appointed governor and council and a locally elected assembly constituted the government. This type of government always caused friction, as it had done in the American colonies before 1776, because the governor and the assembly frequently disagreed, and neither could control the other adequately. In 1837 the defects of the system caused a crisis in Canada, which induced the cabinet to take the first step toward responsible colonial government.

After the conquest of Canada in 1763, it was for some time governed without a popular assembly. This type of government was the best when the problem was one of adapting British rule to French subjects. In 1774 the Quebec Act made this system permanent. It gave to the French Canadians freedom of worship and preserved to them their French code of law. Under this régime the French Canadians were loyal to British rule. The large emigration of the loyalists after the American Revolution created a new problem. The English colonists could not be governed by the same law as the French. In 1791 the Canada Act divided the country into two provinces. Upper Canada (Ontario), inhabited by the English, and Lower Canada (Quebec), inhabited by the French, were each given an elected assembly. Thereafter the experience with the thirteen colonies was repeated. Both assemblies quarreled interminably with the governors. The situation was aggravated by racial jealousy in Lower Canada, as the English began to settle there more numerously. In the decade after 1830 the governor and the assembly were at a deadlock most of the time. In 1837 Canadian dissatisfaction found expression in open rebellion. In Upper Canada the revolt amounted to little, but in Lower Canada the French Canadians had to be suppressed by force of arms.

The cabinet, seeking a remedy, sent to Canada as a special commissioner to examine conditions and report, Lord Durham, a bril-

Colonial government

The Canadian problem

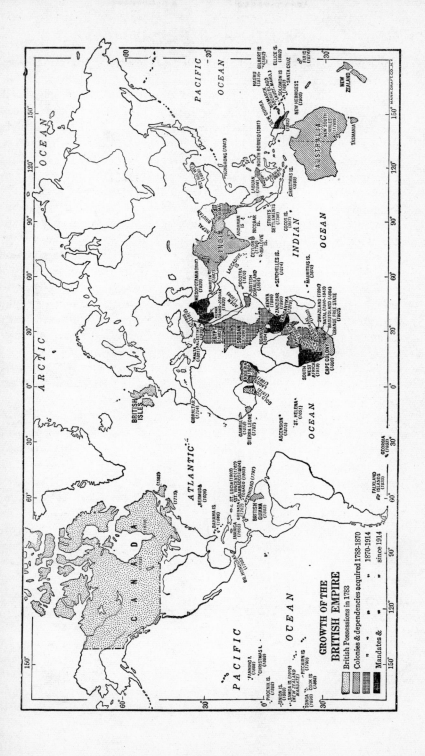

GROWTH OF THE
BRITISH EMPIRE

liant, erratic, radical Whig. His report is designated by Egerton as Lord
"the most valuable document in the English language on the subject Durham's
of colonial policy."[13] It recommended two principal changes. The first report
was the union of Upper and Lower Canada under one legislative
assembly. The second read: "The responsibility to the United Legislature of all officers of the Government, except the Governor and his
Secretary, should be secured by every means known to the British
Constitution. The Governor, as the representative of the Crown, should
be instructed that he must carry on his government by heads of departments, in whom the United Legislature shall repose confidence;
and that he must look for no support from home in any contest with
the Legislature except on points involving strictly Imperial interests."[14]
In other words the colonial governor, appointed by the British cabinet, was to become, like the British king, a ruler who reigns but does
not rule. From this principle purely imperial policies were to be excepted, but on questions of local government Canadian ministers responsible to the Canadian assembly were to have the executive power.
Their relation to the governor of Canada was designed to be analogous
to that of the British cabinet to the king.

The first recommendation was embodied in an act of parliament in
1840. The second was accomplished mainly by the instructions given Reforms
by the British cabinet to the governors. Since it was largely a matter adopted
of practice rather than of law, it took longer to accomplish. It was
undertaken, moreover, with more or less hesitancy, since colonial self-
government seems logically incompatible with control by the crown.
The first set of instructions were far less emphatic than Durham's
recommendation, and the early governors under the new system could
not free themselves from the dilemma that they could not take orders
from both the British cabinet and their local advisers. Nevertheless,
these instructions constituted the first step toward self-government.
It became an accomplished fact when Lord Elgin became governor in
1846. His instructions were more explicit and his belief in the principle sincere. He succeeded finally in the establishment of responsible
government in Canada without sacrifice of the prestige of the crown
represented in the governor's person.

Long ere the consummation of Durham's policy, Melbourne's cabinet had departed from office. In 1837 William IV died. He was suc- Defeat of
ceeded by his niece, Victoria, a girl of eighteen. In the ensuing par- the Whigs
liamentary election the Whigs lost several seats, coming back with a

---

[13] *Short History of British Colonial Policy,* p. 304.
[14] *Report of the Earl of Durham* (ed., 1902), p. 241.

majority of only thirty-eight, which was too small for dependable support. In 1839, when the cabinet was able to carry a measure by a majority of only five in a full house, it took the opportunity to resign. Peel was asked to form a cabinet, but the queen refused to change some of the ladies of her bedchamber from Whigs to Tories at his request, and he declined to take office otherwise. The queen regarded these ladies as her personal attendants, while Peel, fearing their influence on the mind of the young queen because they belonged to Whig families, insisted on counting them as holders of political offices which should change with the ministry. Out of deference to and sympathy for the inexperience of the queen, Melbourne agreed against his own wish to return. His position was no stronger than before. After several defeats, a new election in 1841 resulted in a victory for the Tories, and Peel became prime minister.

During the period between 1835 and 1841, while the weakened Whig cabinet was marking time with regard to internal affairs, various sections of the public were actively discussing the desirabilty of further reforms. Among these currents of public thought three gradually assumed the proportions of well-defined movements.

Among the laborers the desire for further parliamentary reform became widespread, developing into the movement called Chartism. For a few years after the act of 1832, satisfaction with what had been accomplished was general. Though the working classes had not obtained the vote, they were economically prosperous, and the reformed parliament seemed to be meeting their desires for economic and social reforms. The ruling classes were naturally content "to let well enough alone." Russell won the epithet of "Finality John" by a declaration that the changes made in 1832 were sufficient for all time. The small group of Radicals in parliament continued to make annual motions for universal manhood suffrage, but none expected them to pass. As one reform followed another after 1832, however, the laborers began to feel that they were receiving no great benefits therefrom. The poor law, which deprived them of outdoor relief, they regarded as a positive hardship. When they were coming to the conclusion that the reform of 1832 was insufficient, a commercial depression which threw many out of work in 1837 produced the pressure of distress necessary to set in motion an agitation. Though the movement was of the old type—fundamentally economic and social in its causes, but seeking the remedy of a voice in legislation—it received the new name of Chartism. The appellation was derived from a document called the People's Charter, in which the popular demands were set

Margin notes:

Popular movements

Chartism

forth under five heads (later extended to six). They included annual parliaments, universal manhood suffrage, equal electoral districts, and other reforms equally extravagant at the time.

The workers first made their wants known by means of petitions which were circulated at mass meetings and presented to parliament. In 1839 delegates from the manufacturing towns met in London and prepared a monster petition. When it was disregarded by the house of commons, the violent element, never lacking in such movements, was stimulated. In 1841 the physical force party, as this group was called, engineered riots and armed uprisings that had to be quelled by military force. The rank and file, however, accepted their defeat with sullen gloom, and Chartism subsided. In 1847 another commercial crisis revived it for a last manifestation. In 1848 a monster procession, which was planned to escort a petition to parliament, was given up when the government forbade it. The petition, when it arrived in a normal way, was found to have some three million less signatures than had been advertised, and of the two million signatures attached, many were shown to have been forged. The resulting ridicule killed Chartism effectively. After 1848 popular agitation for parliamentary reform ceased for many years.

The Anti-Corn-Law League was an organization founded in London in 1836 by the principal Radical leaders in the house of commons. Its purpose was to rouse public opinion against the corn law. It had little effect until a similar association formed in Manchester came under the leadership of Richard Cobden. The son of a yeoman, he had carved his own way in life, even to his self-education, until at the time he was a prosperous merchant in Manchester. He had a gift for organization and the rare ability of rendering abstract principles popular. He was later joined by John Bright, a self-made manufacturer, who had less ability for argument, but possessed a power of fiery, persuasive declamation which stirred the popular imagination. Under the leadership of Cobden assisted by Bright, the league rapidly won the masses by a campaign of lectures and pamphlets. The laborer was told that much of what he paid for his bread went into the pockets of the English landlords, who were enabled to charge more for their wheat because the tariff protected it from competition; rural tenants were informed that the corn law did not benefit them, since their profits went to the landlords in the form of higher rents; and the industrial population was showered with statistics designed to demonstrate that its output was restricted because great markets like Germany and the United States could pay for British manufactures only

Anti-Corn-Law League

with grain, which was excluded from Great Britain by the corn law. In 1841 the league redoubled its activities, and Cobden was sent to parliament to lead the fight there for "untaxing the poor man's loaf." [15] When Peel became prime minister, the Anti-Corn-Law League was exerting a strong influence on public opinion.

Oxford Movement

The Oxford Movement was a development of profound importance in religious thought. It was begun about 1833 by a group of Oxonians who sought to arouse greater spiritual enthusiasm within the church. In part their object was to save the church from attack by the state. By that time the evangelical movement had lost much of its momentum, and the spiritual tone of the church seemed to be dropping back. The proposal in 1833 to confiscate some of the revenues of the established church in Ireland raised fears of further secular reform, which were well justified. When Peel held office in 1834, he acknowledged the need of the reform of the church by the appointment of an ecclesiastical commission. Its recommendations were enacted into legislation by the Whigs between 1836 and 1840. The revenues of the church were redistributed in such a way as to produce more adequate salaries for the worst-paid positions, the absenteeism of rectors was restricted, and the collection of tithes was simplified. The members of the Oxford group desired to forestall such interference on the part of the state by raising the morale of the clergy. They were influenced by love of tradition and interest in the medieval lore of the church to emphasize the sacraments, the ritual, and the doctrines of the Middle Ages. As a result they drifted toward the Roman Catholic church. In 1845 John Henry Newman, a prominent leader of the movement, went all the way over to join the Roman communion. Many others followed. The movement accomplished much good. The standards of the clergy improved and the Anglican church became more effective. But the ritualistic Roman tendencies of the leaders evoked opposition from many laymen, and the conversions to Catholicism roused a strong popular prejudice.

Lord Palmerston

The foreign policy of the Whig cabinet from 1830 to 1841 was directed by Lord Palmerston. He began his political career as a Tory, first holding office in the ministry of 1807. In 1828 he joined the group of Canning's followers who seceded from Wellington's administration, going eventually clear over to the Whigs. His foreign policy was in many ways a continuation of Canning's. He sympathized with the liberal and national movements, and asserted the interest and honor

---

[15] Morley, *Cobden,* p. 124.

of Great Britain boldly whenever international complications arose. His methods, however, were his own. Canning could display the mailed fist when necessary, but he was generaly suave and diplomatic. Palmerston usually scolded and blustered, if he did not become actually insolent. He intervened in many European affairs where British interests were not directly involved. It was a policy which eventually won for Great Britain the active dislike of many foreign chancelleries, but from 1830 to 1841 it had immediate successes.

The problems which Palmerston faced when he came to the foreign office arose from the outbreak in several parts of Europe of the same spirit which produced the revolution of July in Paris. Despite the repressive policies of the great continental powers, the liberal and national movements had not been broken. The revolution of July served as a spark to light the flame of rebellion in Belgium, Poland, Spain, Portugal, and parts of Italy. Palmerston intervened diplomatically in Spain, Portugal, and Belgium. It was the movement in Belgium which affected Great Britain most vitally, and it was here that Palmerston's diplomacy had its greatest success and the most important effect on later history. His problems in 1830

The Belgians revolted against the Dutch rule. The union of Belgium and the Netherlands was one of the arrangements made at the Congress of Vienna for which Castlereagh was largely responsible and of which Great Britain was most proud. It was believed that a strong barrier had been erected against the revival of French ambitions to extend the frontier in that quarter. In reality it was one of the worst settlements made at Vienna, because it disregarded the feeling of nationality. The Belgians differed linguistically and religiously from the Dutch, and their economic interests were also at variance. The entire disregard of these differences by the Dutch king served to increase the intensity of the Belgian nationalistic antipathy, which was already strong in 1815. When the Belgians struck for independence in 1830, British foreign affairs were still in the hands of Wellington, who had been one of the statesmen responsible for the settlement at Vienna. To him the union of Belgium and the Netherlands still seemed desirable from the point of view of British interest. But the pronounced sympathy of the French for the French-speaking and Catholic Belgians made French intervention on the side of Belgium nearly a certainty, should another power attempt to coerce Belgium. So Wellington agreed to refer the matter to a conference in London of the five powers, Great Britain, France, Prussia, Austria, and Russia. This was the situation when the duke left office. Belgium

Palmerston was no less determined to protect the British interest in the opposite coast, but he approved of the national aspirations of the Belgians. He consequently found it necessary to work with France against the three eastern powers, which favored the Netherlands, and at the same time to prevent the extension of French influence in Belgium. To persuade the conference to sanction the separation of Belgium was not difficult, because it seemed to be the only way to avoid a general European conflict. But the bases of separation fixed by the conference were so favorable to the Netherlands that Belgium refused to accept them. After long negotiations the powers altered the terms in favor of Belgium. The Netherlands refused the new arrangement and renewed the war. The Belgians asked and received French aid. This development threatened a general war, because the other powers, and particularly Great Britain, were not willing to let Belgium fall under French control. Palmerston saved the day. He obtained another armistice, told France that she could remain in occupation of Belgium only on pain of war with Great Britain, and by skillful diplomacy obtained from the powers revised terms of separation. When the Netherlands rejected them, Great Britain united with France to drive the Dutch out of Belgium. In 1832 both powers withdrew, leaving Belgium independent on the basis of the third arrangement of the powers. The Netherlands offered no further armed resistance, though not until 1839 did it make a treaty with Belgium. The treaty, which gave Belgium independence and perpetual neutrality, was guaranteed by the five powers participating in the conference. The British interest that the Belgian coast should not fall into the hands of a great power was thus amply guarded by Palmerston under critical circumstances without a European conflagration.

The Near East

Palmerston's diplomacy also had a significant effect on later events in the problem of the Near East. Twice while he was at the foreign office, the ruler of Egypt, whose dependence on Turkey was purely nominal, attempted to wrest Syria from Turkey by force. On each occasion Palmerston came to the rescue in order to prevent Russia from becoming the sole protector of Turkey. He obtained the cooperation of other powers in joint intervention to force Egypt to keep the peace. Eventually Turkey was placed under the joint protection of the five powers, Great Britain, France, Prussia, Austria, and Russia. Palmerston's success, however, did not obliterate entirely the British apprehensions of Russian designs which these events had renewed.

The second crisis provoked serious tension with France, which the British cabinet believed had designs on Egypt. When the restless ruler of Egypt began to prepare for a career of conquest in 1839, France joined with the other four powers to urge both parties to keep the peace. But after Egypt had successfully attacked Turkey, France declined to join with Great Britain to put pressure upon Egypt in order to preserve the integrity of the Turkish dominions. France did not wish to forfeit the friendship of Egypt. Palmerston, however, obtained the help of the other three powers, leaving France isolated. The French were so mortified as momentarily to talk of war, though saner counsels soon prevailed. France accepted the diplomatic defeat and signed the final treaty with the other four powers. Thus Russia was kept out of Turkey, France out of Egypt, and Palmerston won what contemporaries regarded as a resounding diplomatic triumph.

Tension with France

In the Far East Palmerston's ministry was marked by the initiation of a war which produced the first significant breach in the Chinese policy of the exclusion of foreigners from her trade. The war was fought primarily to force China to acknowledge Great Britain's diplomatic representatives and to advance Great Britain's commercial interests, and for those reasons it received Palmerston's hearty support. The war was finally provoked in such a way that it appeared to be waged to sustain the illicit importation of opium into China. Thus it became known as the Opium War.

The Far East

Before 1840 China adhered to a policy of isolation. A few licensed foreigners were allowed limited privileges of trade in Canton. Until 1833 the British portion of this trade was in the hands of the East India Company. Its officials were required to deal with an organization of Chinese merchants and were not allowed to approach the Chinese government directly. When the British parliament revoked the monopoly of the company and opened the trade of other British merchants, the British government sent to China accredited agents to represent the interests of British merchants and to help the Chinese government prevent the smuggling into China of opium, which was grown in India in large quantities. The Chinese government treated these officials as inferiors, as it had before those of the company. When the British officials demanded to be received as the accredited representatives of another government, the Chinese government subjected them to humiliating discourtesies and indignities. To enforce recognition of their diplomatic status Palmerston sent gunboats to China. The display of force had no effect. Meanwhile the quantity of opium entering China was growing. Finally, in 1839, the Chinese government forced the British commissioner to order the confiscation of opium owned by the British in China, and the order was carried out by British officials. Soon after this act a war began which lasted until 1842. It went in favor of the British, who used their advantage to obtain diplomatic status for British representatives, the opening of five additional ports to British trade, and the cession of the island of Hong Kong. China paid a heavy indemnity for the confiscated opium and secured no alteration of the complacent attitude of the British government toward the illegal trade in opium.

When Peel defeated the Whigs in 1841, the policy at issue was fiscal. For five years the blundering finance of the Whigs had produced an annual deficit. Since a reorganization of the system of taxation was a prime necessity, Peel undertook it in the budget of 1842. The measure contained two remarkable features. The first was the imposition for three years of an income tax. This was a form of taxation previously used only in time of war. The second was a sweeping simplification and reduction of the schedules of the tariff. His object was in part to increase the revenue by decreasing the duties, but it was also his design to take a tentative step toward free trade. His revision of the tariff was based on the report of a commission which had investigated the subject in 1840 under the guidance of Joseph Hume. The report claimed that the existing protective tariff was on most articles a burden to the consumer, without being a source of profit to the government. It demonstrated that ten-elevenths of the whole receipts from the customs were produced by 82 of the 1,200 articles protected, and six-sevenths of it by nine articles. Peel lowered the duty on 750 of the 1,200 articles taxed. His general principle was to remove all prohibitions on imports and levy a duty of five per cent on raw materials imported, twelve per cent on partly manufactured products, and twenty per cent on manufactured wares. It was a continuation of Huskisson's policy on a grand scale.

Peel's free trade budgets

With Peel the reduction was experimental. He waited three years to see how it would work. When the expiration of the income tax forced him to decide, he pronounced in favor of free trade. In his budget of 1845 he retained the income tax for three additional years to cover the period of transition, abolished the duties entirely on the 430 items which produced the least revenue, removed all duties on exports, and lowered the duties still further on several of the remaining articles. This budget produced something like consternation among the country gentlemen who followed Peel, but, since they could not well unite with the Whigs and Radicals who wanted still more free trade, they gave the budget their grudging support.

Peel, moreover, had not favored free trade in the item which touched the interests of the Tory landlords most directly. In the corn law, which imposed a high duty on imported grain, he made no material reduction of the duty. His attitude was somewhat inconsistent, but maintenance of the corn law was essential to keep the support of his party. Nevertheless, he was open to reason, and the arguments of Cobden and his followers gradually convinced him. In the session of 1845, after a speech of Cobden's, the prime minister said to one of his followers: "*You* must answer this, for *I* cannot."[16] The event which moved him to take action was a famine in Ireland. In 1845 a blight destroyed the crop of potatoes, which constituted the principal food of the Irish. It meant starvation to a large portion of the Irish in the autumn of 1845 and the winter of 1846. To ameliorate the rigor of the famine it was necessary to make food as cheap as possible. Suspension of the corn law was an obvious method. Peel saw that temporary suspension would demonstrate conclusively that the tax on food was a burden to the whole community, imposed for the benefit of a minority composed of the landlords. With that acknowledgment once made, he believed the restoration of the corn law would be impossible in the existing state of public opinion. The Anti-Corn-Law League had done its work. The British public was converted to free trade. Peel decided therefore to propose the permanent repeal of the law. When several members of the cabinet refused to support him, he resigned. Lord John Russell was called to form a Whig cabinet, but Earl Grey refused to serve with Palmerston at the foreign office and Palmerston declined to serve elsewhere. Russell gave up in despair. Peel returned with a slightly reorganized cabinet pledged to the repeal of the corn law.

Peel and the corn laws

Peel introduced his bill in 1846. It provided for a gradual reduction of the duty until it became merely nominal at the end of three years. The bill also included further relaxations of other duties. It meant complete free trade, for grain was the last bulwark of protection. In 1849 the navigation acts were finally repealed, and subsequent legislation completed the revision of the tariff, until duties were levied on imports for the purpose of revenue only. Peel practically made free trade the policy of Great Britain.

Establishment of free trade

In the process he smashed his party beyond repair. When he brought forward his bill in 1846, the Tory landlords were temporarily stunned. They were ready to give opposition to the bitter end, but they had no leader. At the crisis a leader offered himself. Back in 1837 a dream-

Split of the Tories

[16] Morley, *Cobden*, p. 213.

ing Hebrew had come into parliament. Benjamin Disraeli was blessed with a vivid imagination, a supreme nerve, and great ability. Though his father provided him with worldly wealth and inspired in him a love of literature and culture, he was not socially of quite the same kind as the members of the best club in London. Indeed, he appeared so hopeless in this respect that his brilliant speeches won him scant political recognition. At first he displayed somewhat radical tendencies, but he soon drifted to the support of Peel. After he was passed over in the appointments of 1841, he began to criticize his leader. He made much capital out of Peel's change of front on protection, and voiced the feelings which the dumb country squires could not express. They wanted the guidance of the man who in debate said of Peel, he "caught the Whigs bathing, and he walked away with their clothes," and described him as "a political burglar of other men's ideas."[17] In 1846 Disraeli organized the Tory backwoodsmen, but he knew them too well to put himself forward as their leader. They wanted his brains, but they must be led by their kind. So a popular member of the party became the puppet leader and Disraeli pulled the strings. It was hopeless to defeat the bill; Irish, Radical, Whig, and many Tory members would vote for it; but what Disraeli and the landlords wanted was revenge on Peel, who had ignored Disraeli and had betrayed the cause of protection. Their opportunity came quickly. As was ever the case, relief for Ireland went hand in hand with coercion. The famine had caused an outburst of disturbances, and an Irish coercion bill was being sent through the house contemporaneously with the repeal of the corn law. On the same night that the repeal passed its final reading in the house of lords, the protectionist Tories united with the Whigs and the Irish to vote against the coercion bill in the house of commons. Peel was defeated, the cabinet resigned, and the Tories long remained divided into two groups which refused to work together.

Foreign policy

The foreign policy of Peel's cabinet was directed by Lord Aberdeen. He was as conciliatory as Palmerston had been aggressive. Under his supervision Great Britain ceased to interfere without warrant in the internal affairs of other countries, and British claims, which had no apparent basis in justice, were no longer pressed. He was occupied largely with the attempt to smooth the feathers of some of the foreign chancelleries which Palmerston had ruffled. The most tangible results of his administration were two treaties negotiated with the United

---

[17] McCarthy, *History of Our Own Times,* i, 266, 272.

States. Relations with that country were thoroughly strained when he sent a special envoy to Washington. His agent reached an agreement about the boundary between the United States and Canada. The question had been in dispute since 1783, and during the past few years had caused much friction. The Webster-Ashburton Treaty signed in 1842 took away from the United States a strip claimed by Maine, and ceded to the United States territory north of Vermont and New York claimed by Canada. Four years later a still sharper crisis over the Oregon territory nearly precipitated war, but a conciliatory spirit finally prevailed. Aberdeen, shortly before he left office, was able to conclude a treaty which established the forty-ninth parallel as the northern boundary of the United States, but left the whole of Vancouver to Great Britain.

CHAPTER XXXVI

AFFAIRS CHIEFLY FOREIGN AND IMPERIAL, 1846-1865

Party situation

FOR many years after the resignation of Peel, parties were in a state of unstable equilibrium. The Tories remained separated into two groups: the protectionist Tories among whom Disraeli was the moving spirit, and the free trade Tories led by Peel (Peelites). The Whigs, though nominally a united party, often failed to work in harmony. The differences between the conservative Whigs of the old school and the more progressive group still continued. The Whigs, moreover, could not always count on the votes of the Radicals among whom the strongest element was now the so-called Manchester school led by Cobden and Bright with policies of "peace, retrenchment and reform." The division of the Whigs was not as open and bitter as that of the Tories, but there was always the danger that it would split the vote of the party on any definite piece of legislation. In the course of time a new alignment of parties took place, but the elimination of factions and the reconstruction of strong Liberal and Conservative parties was not finally completed until 1868. During the interval, if a cabinet was homogeneous, it generally had to secure support from some group besides its own followers in order to obtain a majority. The alternative was a coalition cabinet. In either case the cabinet had to straddle issues to avoid the offense of either group of its supporters. It could undertake no great constructive policy. The cabinets generally did little more than mark time. The period is singularly destitute of important domestic legislation compared with either the preceding or the succeeding epoch. The cabinets changed frequently. Since a new cabinet rarely meant a decisive change of policy, the house turned out the cabinets with a light heart.

Russell and his cabinet

After Peel's defeat Lord John Russell, who had successfully led the Whigs in the house of commons for many years, was the logical choice for prime minister. The inheritor of the traditions of a liberal Whig family, he made "the cause of civil and religious liberty all over the world"[1] his own thoroughout a long and distinguished political career. Though not an orator of the first rank, "languid Johnny glowed to

---

[1] Russell, *Recollections and Suggestions*, p. 174.

glorious John"[2] when a rare occasion stirred him sufficiently, and he was always a resourceful debater. His political and moral courage was so great in contrast to his diminutive stature, that he was sometimes called "our little giant."[3] By 1846 these qualities had won him universal respect, though he was too reserved to arrive at such popularity as later fell to Palmerston's lot. Too self-confident and sometimes too impulsive, he failed to attain after 1846 that fame as a statesman of which his previous career seemed to give promise. In the formation of his cabinet he sought the alliance of the Peelites. They declined to take office, though they generally voted with the cabinet in order to save free trade. To the Manchester Radicals, against whom the old Whigs were strongly prejudiced, he offered no place. His cabinet, consequently, was purely Whig, and it had to frame weak and colorless policies in order to win the support of the Peelites and to avoid the alienation of the Radicals.

The most pressing problem was Ireland. When Peel came to power in 1841 the alliance between O'Connell and the cabinet was broken. O'Connell and Peel were personally antagonistic, and the Tories restored the Protestant ascendency. O'Connell reverted to his former demand for the repeal of the union and began to organize the Irish in associations similar to those which had won Catholic emancipation. Peel, becoming alarmed, prohibited a monster demonstration which O'Connell had planned to hold in 1843. The Irish leader, forced to decide between obedience and rebellion, countermanded his order for the meeting. This gave dissatisfaction to the more hot-headed of O'Connell's followers and served to check the force of the agitation for repeal. The famine, however, produced both distress and turbulence. The suspension of the corn law, the employment of the people on public works, and the distribution of free food only partially alleviated the misery, which continued until a normal crop was raised in 1847. The deaths caused by starvation and fever were numerous. The passage of a coercion act similar to the one on which Peel had been defeated did not end the disorder. Driven by desperation, and filled with bitterness by a calamity attributed by them to the British government, the young Ireland leaders revolted from O'Connell's moderate leadership just before his death in 1847. Inspired by the liberal and nationalistic revolutions, which began in France and spread to other parts of Europe in 1848, they plotted rebellion. The movement was successfully nipped in the bud by the arrest of the leaders, but the bitter discontent of the Irish

Irish policies

[2] *Dictionary of National Biography*, xlix, 462.
[3] *Later Correspondence of Lord John Russell*, i, p. xviii.

still simmered. The one permanent remedy tried by the Whigs did more harm than good. In 1849 the Encumbered Estates Act made it possible, on the petition of the creditors, to sell estates encumbered with debts by cutting any legal intricacies involved. The purpose was to improve the position of the tenants by facilitating the introduction of more efficient landlords; the result was to transfer many estates to capitalists who took advantage of the tenants and rendered their position worse than before.

Other policies of the Whigs were of a piece with that pursued in Ireland, but the cabinet was allowed to blunder along, largely because no union of opposing factions could be made. Peel kept his followers in line in order to save free trade from the attack of the protectionists. In 1850, however, Peel died, his followers became restless, and the cabinet came to grief. The motion of a private member for further reform of parliament was opposed by the cabinet, not on principle, but because it wished to frame its own measure of reform. The Peelites abstained from voting, and the Radicals, caught by the principle, voted for it. The cabinet was defeated and resigned. The result was farcical. Lord Stanley, soon to become the earl of Derby, who was now the leader of the protectionist Tories, declined to form a cabinet because his followers numbered only one-third of the house. Russell then attempted to form a coalition between the Whigs and the Peelites. He was in a fair way to succeed, when negotiations were wrecked by the Ecclesiastical Titles Bill.

This bill was primarily of importance against the background of the Oxford Movement. In 1850, when English public opinion was still excited by controversy over the Anglican drift toward Rome, the pope issued a rescript dividing England into dioceses for the government of the Catholic church. Previously the Catholic church in England had been treated as in the missionary stage and governed by vicars apostolic bearing titles derived from foreign lands. The rescript was published in the summer, when the cabinet was scattered. Russell, with characteristic impetuosity, wrote, without consultation of the cabinet, a public letter, denouncing the act of the pope as an insult to the queen, and intimating that it was intended as a step toward the union of the Anglican church with Rome. At the next session of parliament he brought forward the Ecclesiastical Titles Bill, which forbade the assumption of titles derived from the United Kingdom by priests of the Catholic church, under penalty of voidance of their acts. The bill was still before the house when the cabinet resigned. It prevented the projected coalition, because the leaders of the Peelites opposed it. They felt, as Glad-

Fall of the cabinet, 1851

Ecclesiastical Titles Bill

stone later said, that the spiritual dangers to the Anglican church could not be met by "temporal legislation of a penal character."[4] Russell refused to withdraw the bill, negotiations fell through, and Russell came back to power at the head of the Whig cabinet which had resigned. Such was the ridiculous political situation. The fate of the bill was hardly less ludicrous. It passed, but remained a dead letter until it was repealed several years later.

The cabinet soon fell as the result of a quarrel between Russell and Palmerston on the conduct of foreign affairs. As a rule, no department is more closely supervised by the prime minister than that of foreign affairs, but under the easy-going Melbourne Palmerston had been allowed to do much as he pleased. Under Russell he continued to take important steps without consulting his chief or his colleagues. As his policies were often rash, Russell began to fear that he would involve Great Britain in war if he were not restrained. Bright, who thought his policy "dangerous," described it as "meddling everywhere, advising, controlling, encouraging, menacing, as he pleases, in every country not of first-class power in Europe."[5] In 1848, for example, Palmerston instructed the English ambassador at Madrid to lecture the Spanish queen on her illiberal principles and to advise her to take some liberal ministers into her cabinet. Since the internal affairs of Spain were distinctly not Great Britain's business, the queen dismissed the English ambassador. Palmerston was justly criticized; in a normal house he would probably have been defeated. In the same year, without the knowledge of the queen or his colleagues, he authorized a contractor to the British government to supply the insurgent Sicilians with arms. On this occasion his prank cost him a public apology to the king of Naples. Palmerston and his colleagues

Despite these vagaries Palmerston's policy was popular. The British public liked his breezy way and his almost insolent assertion of British superiority in European affairs, and it was in sympathy with his support of the liberal and national movements on the continent. British liberals rejoiced in the leadership of a foreign minister who could so stir the enmity of continental reactionaries as to evoke from them the couplet: Palmerston and the public

> If the devil has a son,
> He surely is Palmerston.[6]

[4] Morley, *Gladstone*, i, 411.
[5] Trevelyan, *John Bright*, p. 190.
[6] *"Hat der Teufel einen Sohn*
So ist er sicher Palmerston." —Strachey, *Queen Victoria*, p. 211.

To many of his countrymen Palmerston appeared to be the champion of justice and right, whose guidance in the perplexing field of international affairs they could accept with confidence and enthusiasm.

With the queen it was otherwise. Queen Victoria at this time probably overestimated her constitutional power, and she had decided views on foreign affairs. Her family and dynastic connections with continental rulers gave her greater sympathy with the monarchs than with their peoples. In these views she was inspired by her husband, the prince consort, Albert, a prince from a small German state, whom she had married in 1840. The queen not only disliked much of Palmerston's policy, but she also objected to his methods. His frequent embarkation on a policy without consultation with her aroused her indignation.

Palmerston laughed at the fears of his colleagues, disregarded the queen, whose preference, he said to a colleague, "does not signify a pin, after all,"[7] and plunged into a venture which nearly cost him a censure from parliament, brought him a rebuke from the queen, but made him more popular than ever. A Portuguese Jew, who had acquired British citizenship at Gibraltar, moved to Greece, where his house was plundered by a mob. He sought the help of the British government to obtain redress. Palmerston, taking up the case, made diplomatic representations to Greece. When they failed, he had a British fleet seize Greek ships, forcing the Greek government to acknowledge the claim. Meanwhile he repulsed a French offer of mediation with so much rudeness that the French ambassador was withdrawn from London.

This venture was rather high-handed even for parliament. In the house of lords Palmerston was censured. In the commons, however, he obtained a vote of confidence by his able defense of his own policy in a speech which an old member thought "the most effective and extraordinary"[8] he had ever heard. In his conclusion Palmerston caught the popular ear when he asked the question, "whether, as the Roman in the days of old held himself free from indignity when he could say *'civis Romanus sum,'* so also, a British subject, in whatever land he may be, shall feel confident that the watchful eye and strong arm of England will protect him against injustice and wrong?"[9] The house of commons supported him because he turned attention from his methods to his aims and results. With the public it was a triumph for Palmerston.

The queen could not forget the danger of his methods. Russell, too, was nervous. He helped to defend the foreign minister in the house,

Palmerston and the queen

Civis Romanus sum

[7] Broughton, *Recollections,* vi, 236.
[8] *Ibid.,* p. 257.
[9] Cited by Marriott, *England Since Waterloo,* p. 205.

and then tried unsuccessfully to persuade him to exchange the foreign office for another. Thereupon the queen sent to Palmerston a famous memorandum in which she demanded (1) to be informed of what he proposed to do before he did it, in order that she might express her opinion on new policies, and (2) that he would not without her knowledge alter the terms of despatches which she had approved. This memorandum is popularly supposed to have defined the relations ever since deemed correct between the ruler and the foreign office. Palmerston promised to abide by the arrangement, but soon disregarded it.

The queen's memorandum

In December of 1851 Louis Napolean made the *coup d'etat* by which he overthrew the French republic established in 1848 and prepared the way to make himself emperor. The cabinet decided on strict neutrality, but Palmerston nevertheless expressed his approval unofficially. Russell, although he had done the same thing, had been for so long under pressure from the queen to get rid of Palmerston, that he decided to end his difficulties, and seized upon this issue to demand the resignation of his foreign minister.[10] The cabinet thereby lost its most popular member and was greatly weakened. Before the close of 1852 Palmerston caused its defeat, whereupon he wrote to his brother: "I have had my tit-for-tat with John Russell and I turned him out on Friday last."[11] Russell might humiliate Palmerston temporarily at the wish of the queen, but when the public began to reason that behind the queen was a German prince, who was her consort, the prime minister could not make Palmerston stay put.

Defeat of the cabinet

Stanley, now the earl of Derby and leader of the opposition, consented to form a cabinet, in which Disraeli became chancellor of the exchequer and leader of the house of commons. The new cabinet was weak, for few men in the protectionist party had previously held office. "The fact is," said Palmerston, "that this Government has only two real men in its ranks . . . Derby and Disraeli. The rest are all cyphers as to debate."[12] Before making a pronouncement on protection, Derby held an election in order to learn the opinion of the country on the question. The election of 1852 left the cabinet still in a minority and constituted a decisive popular mandate for free trade. On the introduction of the budget Disraeli announced the acceptance by his party of the amount of free trade already established. It was hoped that the removal of the issue that had originally split the Tories might bring the

First Derby-Disraeli cabinet

[10] Bell, *Lord Palmerston*, ii, 46-50.
[11] Cited from Low and Sanders, *History of England during the Reign of Victoria*, p. 94.
[12] Ashley, *Life of Palmerston*, i, 348.

Peelites back to their old allegiance. Gladstone proved intractable. He had a personal antipathy to Disraeli, which induced him to speak against the budget. This caused its defeat and the resignation of the cabinet late in 1852.

The new cabinet was a coalition of Whigs and Peelites led by Lord Aberdeen, a Peelite. Though remarkably strong in individual talent, it was weakened by internal differences of opinion. Russell and Palmerston came to loggerheads on parliamentary reform, and Aberdeen opposed Palmerston and Russell on foreign policy. Aberdeen, though very learned and by no means timid, was too gentle to keep his colleagues in their places. In 1853 Russell had a project of parliamentary reform before the cabinet at the critical period of the negotiations which led to the Crimean War. Palmerston, who objected to reform, was forced by Aberdeen to resign, nominally on that issue, but really because the queen and the prime minister resented the influence which he wielded in the cabinet on the Turkish question. This time his punishment lasted only for a week, because popular sympathy for him was demonstrated so strongly that his recall to the cabinet was demanded and obtained by some of Aberdeen's colleagues. At this juncture Palmerston's knowledge of foreign affairs was considered essential. In 1854 Russell introduced his bill into the house. The country, intent upon war, was so apathetic on reform that the bill evoked little interest. Palmerston refused to support it, and the cabinet was consequently so lukewarm in its behalf that Russell resigned. Eventually he was persuaded to drop his bill and return. But a cabinet with such internal dissensions as these was not the cabinet to lead the country in war, and in 1855 it went to pieces on that issue.

The immediate occasion of the Crimean War was a dispute over the control of the holy places in Jerusalem. In 1740 Turkey had conceded this right to France in behalf of the Roman Catholics, but a century later, the Greek Catholics, who made many more pilgrimages to these shrines, had practical control of them. In 1852 Napolean III demanded of Turkey the rights granted by treaty. The tsar opposed the grant of the request. He regarded himself as the protector of the Greek Catholic church which was the national church of Russia. Turkey tried to satisfy both parties by the issue of two decrees that said one thing to the Greek Catholics and another to the Roman. This duplicity satisfied neither the tsar nor the emperor, who both began to press for a favorable decision. In 1853 the tsar further demanded a protectorate over the members of the Greek church in the Turkish empire. This overshadowed the earlier Russian claim. Its cession would have been a serious encroach-

Aberdeen coalition

Crimean War: causes

ment on the sovereignty and independence of the Turkish state. The British ambassador advised the Turkish government to refuse.

The attitude of Great Britain was affected by the fears of Russian expansion in the east, which had been aroused during the first half of the century. The tsar had expected the Aberdeen cabinet not to oppose his aggression. He was personally acquainted with Aberdeen, whose administration of the foreign office under Peel had demonstrated his thoroughly peaceful disposition. The tsar traded upon it so far in 1853 as to renew his famous proposal that, since Turkey was the sick man of Europe, Russia and Great Britain had better agree on the division of his possessions when he should have died. Aberdeen disavowed any desire for territorial aggrandizement at the expense of Turkey, but the tsar still expected him to keep the cabinet from adopting an attitude hostile to Russia. But the cabinet was a coalition, and Palmerston and Russell favored opposition to Russian aggression. Moreover, they had the support of British public opinion.

British attitude

The previous aggressions of Russia and the attempts of British statesmen to check them had implanted in the popular mind an abiding suspicion of Russian designs against British dominion in India. It had been fed not only by the clashes over the Near East[13] but also by rivalry in the Middle East. The latter region includes, roughly speaking, Persia and Afghanistan. Russia bordered the district along the Caucasian Mountains and round the Caspian. Persia was lifeless, and Afghanistan controlled passes which made it the gateway to India. It was a feasible road for a conqueror of India to travel. Napolean, indeed, had once proposed such an invasion to the tsar. At that time British statesmen had recognized the danger sufficiently to arrange a defensive alliance with the ruler of Persia; but in 1827, when Persia called upon Great Britain to help her repel Russian invasion, the British government bought release from its obligation. A Russian menace in that quarter was not yet apprehended. Ten years later British opinion had veered. Persia attacked Herat, supposed to be the key to Afghanistan, and did not raise the siege until the British navy made a demonstration in the Persian Gulf. The British, attributing the activity of Persia to Russian intrigues, became more apprehensive than ever of Russian designs.

The Middle East

In 1853, when Turkey on the advice of the British ambassador refused the Russian demand, Russia occupied Moldavia and Wallachia. An attempt of the four powers, Great Britain, France, Austria, and Prussia, to bring Russia and Turkey to terms failed. The tsar accepted

Outbreak of war

---

[13] See above, pp. 597, 598, 640, 664.

the settlement suggested by the four powers, but the Turkish government, fearing rightly that its terms, as interpreted by the Russians, did
not deny Russia's right to protect the Greek Catholics in Turkey, rejected it. The Turks then proceeded to take matters into their own
hands. They ordered the Russians to evacuate the occupied provinces,
and when the order went unheeded, they declared war. Russia, having
announced that it would undertake no offensive against Turkey, nevertheless fell upon the Turkish fleet at Sinope and sank it. The English,
dubbing it the "massacre of Sinope," went wild for war. They thought
of it as a war for freedom, because the Russian government was a
despotism; they forgot that the object of their solicitude was no less a
despot.[14] With this spirit abroad in the nation, the war party in the
cabinet prevailed. In 1854 Great Britain joined with France to prevent
the establishment of Russian control of Turkey.

Before the French and British aid arrived, the Turks had driven the

**The war in
the Crimea**
Russians from the occupied provinces, but the British and French
governments had already decided to carry the war into Russian territory and attack the fortified port of Sebastopol in the Crimean peninsula. The combined British and French forces were expected to take
the place by assault, and it probably could have been carried when the
allies arrived in September. The French commander, however, deem-
ing the project hopeless, refused to cooperate in an attack. The allies
settled down to a siege, which gave the Russians time to rush troops
into the undermanned fortifications. During the autumn another Russian army forced the allies to fight several heavy battles. With the
coming of winter it withdrew, leaving the severe climate to deal with
the besieging troops. The British army, having come equipped for an
assault, lacked proper protection against the cold. The commander,
failing to anticipate the difficulties, did not have a road built from the
harbor to the camp. The existing road became impassable for wagons,
and the soldiers were compelled to carry the supplies on their backs as
well as to dig trenches. A storm which wrecked a fleet of provision
ships added to their miseries. The war office, becoming snarled in the
red tape which had been woven in the long period of peace, failed to
rush supplies to meet the emergency, sent some supplies that were useless, and omitted some of the things most urgently needed. The army
suffered greatly from exposure. Thousands of the soldiers were incapacitated by illness, and the death rate from disease was high.

At home the sufferings of the soldiers raised a popular outcry. The

---

[14] Paraphrased from the statement of John Bright: Trevelyan, *Bright*, p. 226.

war was the first of which the public was kept currently informed through the agency of special correspondents. The harrowing pictures drawn by the *Times* wrought public opinion to such a pitch that it demanded a scapegoat. Though the war office was by no means solely responsible, it was not blameless, and a parliamentary attack upon the cabinet was the only constitutional means by which public dissatisfaction could express itself. In 1855 a motion in the house of commons to appoint a committee of inquiry caused the resignation of Russell on the ground that he could not honestly oppose the motion. When the motion was carried, the remainder of the cabinet resigned. The nation felt rightly enough that Aberdeen, who opposed entrance into the war, was not the man to lead the nation through it. The nation wanted Palmerston, but the queen did not. Only when she had tried unsuccessfully to find another head for the cabinet, did she confer the seals upon Palmerston. His cabinet was still a coalition of Whigs and Peelites, with Aberdeen and a few of his friends omitted. Within a short time the remaining Peelites dropped out, leaving Palmerston the head of a straight Whig cabinet.

Change of cabinet

The administration of the war, which was already improving, was infused with new life by Palmerston. At the front the return of spring remedied the worst difficulties, and the siege was conducted with renewed vigor. The British and the French, reinforced by Italian troops, took the fortifications late in the summer. The British public desired to continue, dreaming of great victories under Palmerston, but the French desired peace. The cabinet consequently entered negotiations which ended in the Peace of Paris in 1856. By its terms Turkey and Russia mutually restored their conquests; Turkey promised to protect its Christian subjects; the independence of Turkey was guaranteed; the Black Sea and the Dardanelles were closed to ships of war and coastal fortifications; the navigation of the Danube was placed under control of an international commission; and Moldavia, Wallachia, and Servia were given internal autonomy under Turkish suzerainty guaranteed by the powers. Russia had made no gains, but that was poor compensation for Great Britain's heavy expenditure of money and life. One of the French diplomats, who helped to negotiate the treaty, exaggerated little when he said of it, "There is nothing to show which is the conqueror, and which the conquered."[15]

End of the war

After the resignation of the Peelites Palmerston's majority became precarious. In 1857 the Peelites and several of the radical Whigs threw

---

[15] Quoted by Low and Sanders, *History of England during the Reign of Victoria.* p. 125.

Cabinets, 1855–1865 their votes with the opposition, leaving the cabinet in a minority. Palmerston dissolved and held an election in which the real issue was public confidence in Palmerston, though the nominal issue was a war with China in which the opposition held that Great Britain was in the wrong.[16] The answer appeared decisive. Several of the Manchester school and several of the Peelites who had voted against the cabinet lost their seats. Palmerston obtained the first clear majority that any cabinet of one party had had in this troubled period. The majority did not mean, however, that new lines of party cleavage had been found. Indeed, it had so little significance with regard to party that the majority was unstable. In 1858 Palmerston was again defeated on an insignificant question. This time Derby and Disraeli formed their second cabinet. Their tenure of office was brief. Failure to win an election in 1859 caused them to resign after little more than a year of power. Palmerston then formed a cabinet, which Gladstone joined as a Liberal, practically putting an end to the separate organization of the Peelites. This cabinet, the longest lived since Lord John Russell's, remained in office until Palmerston's death in 1865.

Indian policy after 1784 Soon after the close of the Crimean War the British had to meet an uprising of the natives of India. The movement had in its background the rapid expansion of British dominion in India. This policy was carried out by the British rulers of India more or less in opposition to the wishes of the directors of the company and the British government. One of the chief causes of the passage of Pitt's India Act, the recall of Hastings, and his subsequent impeachment was the career of conquest upon which the governor-general had embarked. His wars were regarded by a considerable section of popular opinion as wantonly waged for the mere sake of conquest. His successor was forbidden to declare war or enter into treaty for making war without the consent of the British government, unless it should be necessary to defend British or allied native territories against attack. The new governor kept the letter of the law, but he made war contrary to its spirit. His experience demonstrated that with the best of intentions a policy of non-intervention in the affairs of the natives who were independent of British rule would not work. The responsibilities for the rule of some of the natives, already assumed as the result of the policies of Clive and Hastings, rendered necessary occasional participation in native wars. An offensive against hostile native rulers who had not actually attacked British possessions was sometimes deemed necessary in order

---

[16] Below, pp. 685, 686.

to defend British possessions. To the northwest of Bengal, for example, the valley of the Ganges supplied an easy road to any enemy coming from that direction. Step by step the British rulers of India were induced by attack, or the menace of impending attacks, to expand British control to the headwaters of the river far to the northwest, in order to protect Bengal. After 1793, moreover, the French began to stir up the native powers against the British. When such dangers arose, time rarely permitted the exchange of messages with London before taking action. Ambitious governors would not stand by and watch quietly the loss of British prestige and power in India for lack of instructions from London. So the process of expansion continued despite the opposition to the policy at home.

The governor-generalship of the marquis of Wellesley[17] (1798-1805) resulted in a vast extension of British territory in India. In 1798 Napoleon was in Egypt, apparently with designs on India; and Tippu, the ruler of Mysore, who was a fanatical enemy of the British, was arming, under French instigation and with the alliance of strong native neighbors, to drive the British power from India. The French danger having caused the cabinet to sanction a forward policy, Wellesley did not wait for Tippu to mature his plans. He detached the ruler of Hyderabad from alliance with Tippu and arranged with him a subsidiary alliance. Such alliances had been used temporarily by Clive and Hastings, but Wellesley made them the means of the permanent extension of British power without annexation. The usual terms of such an alliance rendered Great Britain responsible for the defense of the allied state against attack, gave to the British command of the native army paid by the native government and control of the external affairs of the native state, but left the native ruler free to manage the internal affairs of his state. Wellesley then conquered Mysore, annexed large portions along the coast, and placed the remainder under a subsidiary alliance. Two other states[18] in the south he annexed outright. In three years his additions extended British dominion over the whole of southern India. On the northwest of Bengal Wellesley forced the ruler of Oudh to cede to the British a large part of his state, including Delhi, the old capital of the mogul empire, and to increase the extent of British control over the rest. The greatest native power left in India was a confederacy of the Marathas, which controlled a large section of central India. They also were under French influence. When they fell to quarreling among themselves, Wellesley allied himself with one of their

Rapid expansion, 1798–1805

---

[17] An elder brother of the duke of Wellington.
[18] I.e., the Carnatic and Tanjore.

number against the others, broke the backbone of the Maratha power, and secured the surrender of important coastal areas on the east and west. In 1805 the policy of intervention was ended by his recall. The directors of the company had long been protesting, and he went so far and so fast that his friend Pitt finally became alarmed. Before he left, however, he had made Great Britain so overwhelmingly the dominant power in India, that subsequent governors found it difficult to escape the assumption of responsibility for the maintenance of order in the rest of India.

Gradual expansion, 1805–1848

After 1805 the policy of intervention alternated with that of non-intervention, as the necessities of the moment or the ambitions of successive governors-general dictated. Continual disorder in the portions left under native rule menaced the welfare of the sections under British rule or protection. In the attempt to maintain order in these sections and protect them from aggression, the governors were constantly lured farther on the road to empire, despite the protests of the government and of the directors of the company at home. In 1818 another war with the Marathas and their allies resulted in the annexation and subjugation of large sections in central India. In 1825 and 1826 a war with Burma ended with the acquistion of extensive Burmese territory to the east of Bengal.

By this time Great Britain controlled in some measure nearly the whole of India except Sind and the Punjab in the northwest. The British suspicion of Russian designs against India through Persia and Afghanistan, which developed in the decade of the thirties, made possession of these territories appear highly desirable as a defense against attack from central Asia. Sind was conquered and annexed in 1843 without excuse and in defiance of its rights held by treaty with the British. "Peccavi, I have Sind" was the brilliant epigram with which the conqueror announced the literal truth. Prolonged internal disorder was the reason assigned for the invasion of the Punjab, which was concluded in 1846 by the annexation of some territory and a partial control of the rest.

Dal-housie's administration, 1848–1856

With the appointment of Lord Dalhousie in 1848 began a new period of rapid expansion and consolidation of British power. When the natives of the Punjab revolted, the new governor-general subdued them thoroughly, annexing the whole state. He reorganized the government with such good results that within a few years the natives of the district were among the most loyal supporters of British rule. At the other end of the Indian empire Dalhousie later waged a war that resulted in the annexation of Lower Burma. These were the only important conquests

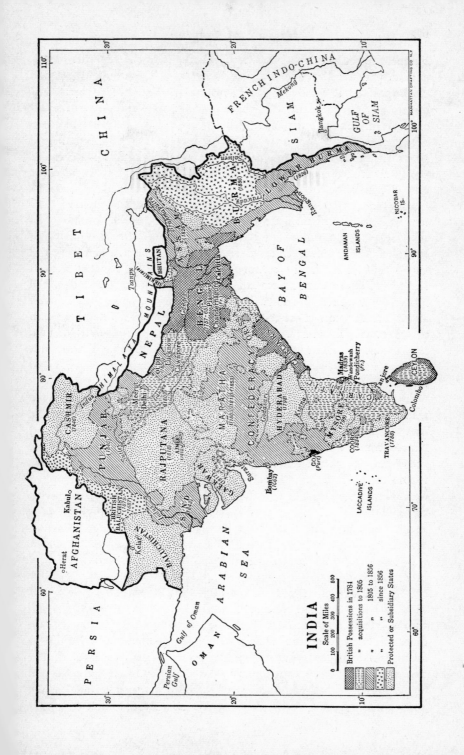

of Dalhousie, but he placed under British sovereignty much territory in central India which had been only under British protection. His purpose was to give the states better government by substituting British for native rule. Most of his annexations of this sort were made by application of the doctrine of lapse. The ruling dynasties of several small states in subsidiary alliance with Great Britain came to an end during Dalhousie's administration. Native custom allowed a ruler without heirs to adopt one. Dalhousie prohibited the practice, claiming the rule for Great Britain by lapse. Oudh, which had faithfully fulfilled its treaty obligations since 1765, but was one of the worst-governed states in India, he arbitrarily annexed without even the excuse of lapse.

This forceful annexation of peaceful allied states was first applied extensively by Dalhousie. Before Wellesley's time the British, by making treaties with native states on equal terms, established a ring of friendly native buffer states around their possessions. In the struggle with the French this system proved inadequate, and Wellesley developed a system of subsidiary alliances which subordinated the native states that were not annexed. The system of subsidiary alliances, however, gave the British government little right to interfere in the internal affairs of the allied states, and Dalhousie felt more keenly responsible than his predecessors for the good government of peoples for whom the British government already had undertaken a limited amount of responsibility. So he proceeded to annex them. To the natives of the states thus annexed Dalhousie's action seemed arbitrary. Their dissatisfaction became one of the causes of the rebellion which broke out in 1857 under Dalhousie's successor.

There were many other causes of native discontent. The innovations made by Dalhousie and his immediate predecessors for the purpose of improving living conditions among the natives violated native customs which were sanctified in some instances by religion or superstition. The rapidity of recent changes caused the natives to fear that their religion and their civilization would be swept away. The principal causes of the revolt, however, were the conditions in the army. The movement began as a mutiny among the native troops, and throughout its course it was confined to the north center and northwest of India, where the sepoys from Oudh and Bengal were located. In those regions it was joined by sympathizing civilians, but the center of its strength was in the revolting troops. Since the days of Clive India had been conquered and held by native troops drilled by British officers. The extended conquests of recent years had resulted in large additions to the native contingents. In 1856 they numbered more than

Causes of Indian mutiny

230,000 men. The British troops, always small in number compared with the native troops, had been reduced by the necessities of the Crimean War to less than 45,000. In 1857 the native troops were thoroughly discontented. The governor-general had recently issued an order that the company should enlist no soldiers who would not serve beyond the seas. The order was caused by the experience of the recent Burmese War, when a regiment of sepoys refused to travel on transports for fear of losing their caste. Many of the sepoys belonged to a Hindu military caste. The new order excluded their sons from the one trade they could follow. Recently a new cartridge had been introduced. It was encased in greased paper and sometimes the lubricant employed was derived from the fat of cows and hogs. A Hindu could not touch the former without losing caste and the latter was forbidden to Mohammedans. The sepoys, believing that a deliberate attack upon their caste was intended, were terrified. The unrest grew steadily until May of 1857, when the sepoys of Meerut mutinied, marched on Delhi, the ancient capital, and gave the signal for a general insurrection.

The mutiny
The three chief centers of the mutiny were Delhi, Lucknow, and Cawnpore. At the last the Europeans were massacred in cold blood by a signal deed of treachery. At Lucknow they fortified themselves in the residency and held out for three months against overwhelming numbers. Relief came slowly because the British were unprepared. The few troops in India were so widely scattered that it took a long time to bring them to the scene of action. Reinforcements were summoned from England and from Persia; British troops on the way to China were commandeered by the governor-general; but for a long time the British troops in India were contending against hopeless odds. In September a force finally fought its way to Lucknow, only to arrive too depleted to raise the siege. It could only aid the besieged until a larger force arrived in November. Meanwhile the assailants of Cawnpore had been defeated and Delhi had been recovered. These victories broke the backbone of the revolt, though it required another year to stamp it out completely. On the mutineers the British inflicted a terrible punishment.

Effect on the government
The Indian mutiny was the final blow to the old system of dual control by the company and the government established by Pitt in 1784. The need to send papers back and forth between the directors of the company and the governmental board of control caused delays when quick decisions were needed. The division of authority made it difficult to bring responsibility home definitely to anyone. As the empire had grown, the anomaly of leaving part of the responsibility for the

government of subject peoples to a company interested primarily in gainful trade had become more apparent. At every interval of twenty years, when the company's charter was renewable by parliament, the powers of the company had been reduced. In 1813 the company lost its monopoly of trade with the exception of the trade to China; in 1833 the last vestige of its monopoly was swept away; and in 1853 its charter was made terminable at the will of parliament, and appointments on the basis of a competitive civil service were substituted for its patronage. The mutiny brought public opinion to the conclusion toward which it had long been drifting. The British people had come to feel that the responsibility for the government of so vast an empire was theirs, and the mutiny convinced them that the power, single and undivided, should also be theirs.

A bill to accomplish this object was introduced by Palmerston in 1857, but he made his exit before its passage. Disraeli made the question non-partisan, and its urgency was so great that an act was passed in 1858, despite the lack of a Tory majority. It transferred the political powers of the company to the crown. The government of India was given to a secretary of state, who was to be a member of the cabinet directly responsible to parliament. He was required to seek but not to take the advice of a board of fifteen experts, of whom a majority must have resided in India for at least ten years. The act also made some modifications in the local government of India. But the fundamental change accomplished was the establishment of a unified responsibility for the government of the Indian empire.

India Act, 1858

Meanwhile British arms were engaged in another war in the Far East. The Chinese government had never carried out fully the treaty of 1842. It also continued to treat the accredited agents of the British government as inferiors. These causes of friction prepared the way for a war which the British representative forced upon China as the result of an incident in which Great Britain appeared to be in the wrong. In 1856 the Chinese authorities at Canton boarded a ship flying the British flag and arrested a Chinese member of the crew. The ship had a British master and once it had had a British register, but it was "Chinese built, Chinese owned, Chinese manned"[19] and at the time had no right to fly the British flag. The British representative, however, demanded reparation. When it was refused, he summoned warships to attack Canton. Subsequently he added a demand that the treaty of 1842, which gave the English free entrance to certain ports,

Second war with China

[19] Bright, *History of England*, iv. 289.

should be better observed. To a majority of the house of commons the war appeared so unjustifiable that Palmerston was defeated on the question in 1857. In the ensuing election the voters evinced a confidence in Palmerston rather than a knowledge of Chinese affairs, but the result was the continuance of the war. During the period of the mutiny the war languished because the troops intended for China were diverted to India. By 1860 China was bullied into submission. It ratified the earlier treaty and made further concessions. The chief results were the actual opening of the ports ceded in 1842 and the acknowledgment of the right of Great Britain to maintain in China accredited diplomatic representatives, who could safeguard the interests of British subjects in China by the diplomatic methods customarily employed among the nations of the west.

Japan

Two years later Great Britain entered into a brief war with Japan. In 1858 friendly negotiations had obtained entry for British trade in five ports of Japan and the establishment of diplomatic and consular representatives. A few years later native jealousy resulted in the murder of a member of the British embassy. When the compensation demanded was not paid, the British employed force to secure its payment. As a result of these forceful proceedings, which in the case of China were high-handed as well, Great Britain obtained an advantageous position in the trade of the Far East, which was destined soon to become of great importance in the commercial world.

Internal affairs 1859–1865

Internally the period following the Indian mutiny was one of political torpor. Lord Palmerston, at the head of the cabinet after 1859, was as conservative on internal changes as he was radical in foreign affairs. Though he was the leader of a Liberal cabinet, he was opposed to all organic reform. His influence, combined with the unstable balance of parties, rendered the house averse to innovations. With the nation Palmerston was popular, and prosperity rendered the working classes contented. There was no significant popular agitation for legislation, and the period from 1859 to 1865 was one during which both parties marked time with regard to internal affairs.

European policies

In foreign affairs the cabinet was more active, but outside the Far East its policies with few exceptions failed to advance British prestige notably. The British attitude was less forceful and arbitrary than it had been under Palmerston previously, partly because Palmerston was growing old, and partly because Russell was in charge of the foreign office. In their aims, however, Palmerston and Russell were in sympathy. Their first venture was to use British diplomacy in behalf of the Italian national and liberal movement. In 1859 the Italians, with the aid of

France, ousted the Austrians from large parts of northern Italy. Napoleon proposed to leave Italy divided into separate states, ruled in some instances by despots; but the Italians started a movement to unite the separate states under a single liberal rule. To this development France and all the other great continental powers were inimical. The British pronouncement that the Italians ought to be permitted to settle their own internal affairs served to restrain other powers from hostile intervention and to promote the successful outcome of unification. In 1863 the cabinet again demonstrated its liberal principles by the voluntary cession to Greece of the Ionian Isles at the request of their inhabitants. The last gesture in behalf of liberalism in Europe ended in a fiasco. Possession of Schleswig and Holstein, two provinces adjoining Denmark on the south, occupied partly by Danes and partly by Germans, came into dispute between Denmark and the German Confederation. It was a complicated question about which Palmerston said "that only three persons in Europe were completely acquainted with the truth, the Prince Consort who was dead, a German professor who was in a lunatic asylum, and himself—and he had forgotten it."[20] The sympathies of Palmerston and Russell were with Denmark. When they failed to negotiate a compromise, they threatened war. But when Prussia, in alliance with Austria, attacked Denmark in 1864 to obtain possession of the provinces, popular opinion was not strong enough to justify British participation in defense of the weak. Thus the last display of the Palmerstonian mailed fist served only to win the derision of Europe for Great Britain's foreign policy.

In its relations with the United States during the civil war from 1861 to 1865, the cabinet helped to create a long-abiding feeling of bitterness toward Great Britain in a considerable section of American public opinion, without winning any compensating advantages for Great Britain. The American civil war affected Great Britain disadvantageously. The great cotton factories were almost solely dependent on the cotton which the southern states could no longer supply, and thousands of the operatives were thrown out of work. Despite their suffering, however, they sympathized with the north, which John Bright taught them to believe had espoused the cause of freedom. This opinion was entertained generally by the working class, but it was not articulate. The ruling class, whose opinion found expression in the newspapers, generally favored the planters of the south. The southern states were opposed to the protective tariff maintained by the United

Relations with the United States

---

[20] Robertson, *Bismarck*, p. 16.

States. British statesmen thought that a victorious south would establish
free trade, to the great advantage of British commerce. In 1863, when
Lincoln's proclamation of emancipation had demonstrated that slavery
was a dominant issue of the conflict, and it had become clear that the
south probably could not win, the friendly feeling for the Confederacy
cooled. The cabinet maintained officially a position of neutrality, but
the sympathies of most of the members were those of their class, and
not all of them refrained from the public utterance of their views.
Gladstone in particular eulogized the southern cause in a public speech
which he afterwards acknowledged was a mistake. This attitude failed
to produce in the north the friendly feeling that impartial neutrality
might have evoked, and words that were not followed by action soon
lost their effect on the south.

The first diplomatic crisis aroused strong popular feelings of hostility
on both sides and left an extraordinary bitterness in the United States.
In 1861 two agents, whom the government of the Confederacy despatched to interest the governments of Great Britain and France in its
cause, were seized from a British ship on the high seas by a ship of
the United States. This was probably a violation of neutral rights as
they had been previously interpreted by the United States, though it is
doubtful if it was more than a technical violation of them as they had
been interpreted by Great Britain.[21] The American public, however,
was so irritated by the contemptuous attitude of the British press toward
its cause that the seizure was received with acclaim as a twist of the
lion's tail. This attitude provoked in Great Britain an outburst of
popular indignation which the cabinet heeded. The British government
declared the seizure to be a violation of neutral rights, demanded redress,
and began to prepare for war. The cabinet was disposed to couch the
demands in stiff terms, but Prince Albert, on his deathbed, used his
influence to secure a modification of the despatch which softened its
tone. The government of the United States disavowed the action of
its captain who had acted without instructions, released the envoys,
and ended what had threatened to become a disastrous crisis.

In another instance the action of the British government was less
satisfactory to British public opinion. The government of the United
States suspected that the Confederate government was obtaining in
British shipyards ships which it used as privateers. In the case of one
ship, subsequently named the *Alabama*, the ambassador of the United
States informed the British foreign office of his belief that it was being

---

[21] Adams, C. F., *The Trent Affair* (Boston, 1912).

built for the Confederate government. Russell neglected to investigate until the ship had left Liverpool. Subsequently the ship did much damage to northern commerce, providing the basis of claims for compensation put forward by the United States after the war had ended. Later Russell by vigorous action prevented the departure of other ships intended for the Confederacy and put an end to what he designated privately as a "kind of neutral hostility."[22] Eventually he acknowledged his failure to detain the *Alabama* to have been a fault.[23]

[22] *Later Correspondence of Lord John Russell*, ii, 334, 335.
[23] *Recollections and Suggestions*, p. 235.

CHAPTER XXXVII

GLADSTONE AND DISRAELI, 1865-1885

Gladstone   PALMERSTON's death in 1865 marked the end of an epoch in political affairs. Earl Russell was his successor, but Gladstone became the real leader of the Liberal party. The earl was old and he was in the house of lords, while the real fight was in the house of commons. Though Gladstone was new to the leadership of the party, his parliamentary career was already long and distinguished. He entered parliament in 1833 at the age of twenty-four, where he early displayed an extraordinary capacity for hard work, a powerful intellect, and exceptional eloquence in debate. In 1853 the speech with which as chancellor of the exchequer he introduced the budget won him general recognition as one of the few great parliamentary orators. A contemporary said justly of the speech, it "has raised Gladstone to a great political elevation, and what is of far greater consequence than the measure itself, has given the country assurance of a *man* equal to great political necessities and fit to lead parties and direct governments."[1] Meanwhile his opinions were becoming steadily more liberal. Though he changed his mind slowly and decorously with much inner communing, he began as a high Tory, followed Peel into the moderate wing of the Conservative party, and by 1865 had arrived "unmuzzled" in the advanced wing of the Liberal party. Palmerston merely voiced the general recognition of what the change from his own to Gladstone's leadership of the Liberals would mean when he said, near the close of his life, "Gladstone will soon have it all his own way; and, whenever he gets my place, we shall have strange doings."[2] In 1865 Gladstone was just entering upon that portion of his career when his extraordinary talents seemed to be developed to their fullest capacity. "He was unquestionably the most efficient and eloquent speaker" in parliament,[3] and his high moral tone appealed strongly to large groups of Englishmen. In later years, as a tendency to convince himself by his own oratory grew upon him in sufficient measure to give a sting to Disraeli's characterization of him as "a sophistical rhetorician inebriated by the exuberance of his

---

[1] Greville, quoted by Morley, *Gladstone*, i, 470.
[2] Quoted by Trevelyan, *John Bright*, p. 344.
[3] Hamilton. *Parliamentary Reminiscences*, p. 62.

own verbosity,"[4] and his attitude, which a political opponent described as "that of a very good man struggling with wickedly minded opponents,"[5] became stereotyped, his influence and popularity passed their zenith; but to the very end he remained the "Grand Old Man."

On the Conservative side Derby was in like situation with Russell. Disraeli in the house of commons was the real leader of the party. Though his parliamentary career was five years shorter than Gladstone's, he had been the leader of his party in the house of commons for many years. His brilliance and his ability to lead had completely overcome the suspicion with which his Tory colleagues had regarded him during the earlier and more erratic part of his career.[6] What had been viewed as "insolence" and "impudence" in his early speeches[7] was now accepted as the boldness of genius. He had nearly attained that preeminence which the unfriendly John Bright described as "a great triumph of intellect and courage and patience and unscrupulousness."[8] His intellectual processes, methods of leadership, ideals, and policies were nearly the exact antithesis of Gladstone's. He reversed his policies to suit the needs of his party with a careless disregard of the charge of inconsistency, though the taunt that he altered his policies without changing his opinions stirred his anger. Wit and epigram were more prominent in his speeches than weight of argument. "Gladstone once described him as 'the greatest master of Parliamentary sarcasm and irony for the past two centuries.'"[9] Though possessed of a vivid imagination, he pushed a pose of practicality to the verge of cynicism. Yet he wrote far less important legislation upon the statute book than Gladstone, while the ideas and ideals to which he gave expression lived long to influence the political thought of his countrymen.

Before these two giant statesmen could lead parties united on clear-cut principles, a new alignment was necessary. Men who could unite on Palmerston's do-nothing policy could not all follow Gladstone in a progressive policy. The reorganization was accomplished by the debates on the reform bills of 1866 and 1867.

Russell's cabinet, in 1866, introduced a bill for the further reform of parliament. Since 1848, when the Chartists made their last demonstration, there had been no strong demand for such a measure. Yet during this quiet interval both parties pledged themselves to further

Marginal notes: Disraeli | New alignment of parties | Parties and reform

[4] Meynell, *Disraeli,* p. 466.
[5] Hamilton, *op. cit.,* p. 62.
[6] Above, pp. 667, 668.
[7] Broughton, *Recollections,* v, 112, 283; vi, 39, 40, 115.
[8] Quoted by Trevelyan. *John Bright,* p. 389.
[9] Hamilton, *Parliamentary Reminiscences,* p. 143.

reform. The act of 1832 destroyed a system which was the product of centuries of development. It put in its place purely arbitrary qualifications for the suffrage. The occupation of a house worth a rental of £10 annually represented neither a traditional nor a logical settlement. If it drew a line below which it was expected that no educated person would be found in 1832, the line had changed in twenty years. In 1852 many of the superior artisans who paid £6 or £7 a year for their houses were intellectually competent to enjoy the suffrage. In 1852 both Russell and Disraeli acknowledged that the intelligent laborer ought not to be excluded from the suffrage, and before 1860 these leaders had carried their parties with them. Yet so anomalous was the grouping of parties in the house and so apathetic was the public, that nothing was accomplished until 1867.

Reform bills in parliament

Lord John Russell introduced the first party measure on the question. In 1851 he proposed a new bill to the cabinet, but the opposition of some of his colleagues caused him to drop it. When a private member introduced a measure later in the same session, he opposed it, with the explanation that the cabinet would undertake legislation on the subject. If further reform was to come, the father of reform wanted the credit for it. He accordingly brought forward a bill which reduced the household qualification in boroughs from £10 to £5 and was designed to give the better workingmen the vote. Before it had advanced to the second reading Palmerston had his "tit-for-tat" with Lord John.[10] Nothing daunted, Russell brought the question before the coalition cabinet in 1853 with results which have been related.[11] Palmerston, when he was prime minister, promised to take up parliamentary reform, but he was less than half-hearted in his interest, and before the engagement was fulfilled, he went out of office. Disraeli, hoping to bolster up the conservative minority with the votes of the liberal Whigs, introduced a bill in 1859. Russell, however, objected to the bill because it extended the franchise in the rural districts where the Conservatives were strong, and did nothing for the artisans of the towns. It was consequently defeated. The Conservatives went to the country without success, but even Palmerston recognized that a victorious party, which had voted against a reform on the ground that it was not sufficiently liberal, was bound to produce another bill. In 1860 Russell accordingly brought forth a bill framed on the same principle as his earlier measures on the subject. The fate of the bill was peculiar. John Bright made fervid speeches round the country in behalf of reform without stirring

---

[10] Above, p. 675.
[11] Above, p. 676.

popular interest. In the house the discussion was formal and languid. Even to Russell it seemed useless to drag the bill through a reluctant parliament and force it upon an uninterested country. He therefore withdrew the bill.

Circumstances seemed more favorable in 1866, when Lord Russell had become the head of the cabinet, Gladstone had been converted, and Palmerston, the chief stumbling block to reform, had been removed. The recent triumph of the northern states in the American civil war had demonstrated that the opinions of the laborers might be more sound than those of the ruling class. It had also shattered the belief, entertained by many of the ruling class, that a democratic government was bound to fail in the end. What was more important, the workingmen had finally formed large and efficient associations to agitate for reform. After the chartist movement with its revolutionary spirit subsided, many workingmen who desired manhood suffrage continued to work for it in a less spectacular manner. Some of their leaders recognized that, having failed to force the reform upon parliament and having no representation there, they needed the help of the radicals and liberals in parliament. Some of the members of this parliamentary group were in partial sympathy with the movement and offered it some support, but it was difficult for the two groups to work in harmony. The laborers wanted representation for the ultimate purpose of obtaining economic and social legislation of benefit to their class, while most of the radicals and liberals believed so firmly in *laissez faire* that they were more or less opposed to legislation of that type. The workers who had supported the crusade against the corn laws found that Cobden and other leaders of it tended to oppose legislation which would limit the freedom of employers in order to give advantages to employees. The radicals and liberals who were willing to support an extension of the suffrage were not prepared to go to the limit of manhood suffrage. Not only did the two groups fail to cooperate effectively, but even the laborers were unable to unite among themselves upon political reform. The bills previous to 1866 attracted no strong popular demonstrations in their favor partly for this reason and partly because they fell so far short of the manhood suffrage which the workingmen demanded. Several factors combined to end the indifference of the laborers. In 1857 John Bright began an attempt to unite the radicals and the workers in behalf of an extension of the right to vote, which, though it fell short of manhood suffrage, would give the franchise to many laborers. About the same time new organizations of workingmen began to be formed to agitate for the reform of parliament, and by 1866 two of

Popular moveme[nt]

them had become large, active and influential. Another factor was the support given to the movement by the trade unions. Since 1842 many unions had improved their organization and efficiency, but they had not previously attempted to exert political influence. In 1866 many of them were associated with one of the large organizations engaged in propaganda for electoral reform.

Gladstone responded to this new state of public opinion with a bill which provided for a moderate extension of the suffrage to the urban laborers. It was advocated in moderate terms and received without enthusiasm. The indifference disappeared when a group of the Whigs organized to oppose further reform. A reference of John Bright to one of the leaders as having retired to his cave of Adullam and called about him everyone in distress and everyone who was discontented gave the group the name of the Adullamites. United with the opposition, this wing mustered enough votes to defeat the bill and force the cabinet to resign. The queen called Lord Derby to form a cabinet. The Conservatives were in a minority and a proffered alliance with the Adullamites was declined. Nevertheless, Derby and Disraeli organized their third cabinet. While the negotiations were taking place, the dead horse of parliamentary reform was suddenly brought to life. The laborers, who had failed to give effective public expression of their views on the previous bills, were now prepared to be articulate. In the debates on the bill, moreover, the leader of the Adullamites had raised the issue of class. "If you wanted venality, ignorance, drunkenness—if you wanted impulsive, unreflecting, violent people— where do you look for them? Do you go to the top or to the bottom?" was his utterance on one occasion. Such phrases not only stirred the masses but they also caused Gladstone to become warmer in his advocacy of reform. "But," said he, "the persons to whom their remarks apply are our fellow-subjects, our fellow-Christians, *our own flesh and blood.*"[12] Bright went forth and applied the lash of his fiery declamation. The people responded with huge demonstrations in London and elsewhere. A general popular desire for reform was manifested for the first time since the days of Chartism.

Disraeli was prompt to seek credit for his party by meeting the popular demand. Lord Derby described the maneuver as "dishing the Whigs" and "taking a leap in the dark." Disraeli's first bill was too moderate for the more radical Whigs. A section of his own party and the conservative Whigs would not support any measure of reform.

---

[12] Morley, *Gladstone*, ii, 202, 203.

Disraeli decided, therefore, to seek the votes of the radical Whigs. He withdrew his first bill and substituted a second. Gladstone insisted that it be made still more liberal by amendments, and the left wing of the Whigs wanted to go even further than Gladstone. Disraeli was forced to accept one amendment after another, until the bill became by far the most radical measure that had been proposed by any government. An opponent described it as "the result of the adoption of the principles of Bright at the dictation of Gladstone."[13] The liberal elements in the Whig and Conservative parties, however, were strong enough to pass it, and it became law in 1867.

The change in the constituencies followed the principle laid down in 1832. Seats were transferred from small boroughs to large boroughs and counties. These changes were few in number. The radical departure was in the franchise. In the boroughs the vote was given to every adult male who occupied as owner or tenant a dwelling house on which he had paid the local tax for the poor, or who occupied lodgings worth £10 a year unfurnished. In the counties the annual value of the property by the ownership of which one could qualify to vote was reduced generally from £10 to £5, and a new mode of qualification by the occupation of premises worth £12 a year was established. In the boroughs the suffrage became so broad as to be nearly universal. Between 1832 and 1867 the number of voters had increased from one in thirty of the population to one in twenty-two. The act of 1867 nearly doubled the last figure. The rural wage earners were still largely excluded from the franchise, but the largest part of the working class had been admitted.

The act of 1867

In the same year parliament enacted the British North America Act, which created a federal government in Canada and marked another milestone in the progress of colonial self-government. The movement for federation originated in Canada. After the acquisition of self-government which followed Lord Durham's report, friction still continued between the French of Lower Canada and the English of Upper Canada, making it difficult for the new government to function. The leaders of both parties in the Canadian parliament finally agreed that the best solution of the problem was to establish a federal form of government with a division of powers between the central and the provincial governments. A plan for such a government was adopted by the Canadian parliament and received the adherence also of New Brunswick and Nova Scotia. It differed from the federal organization

Federation of Canada

[13] *Ibid.*, ii, 235.

of the United States in that the central government was to have all the powers not specifically conferred upon the provincial governments. The legislation passed by the British parliament was little more than a ratification of the constitution proposed by the Canadians. The act provided for the admission to the federation of the other portions of British North America, and the dominion of Canada later came to include them all except Newfoundland.

Reorganization of parties

After the passage of the reform bill the unstable equilibrium of parties soon came to an end. Early in 1868 Derby retired, leaving Disraeli prime minister. Gladstone was now the real leader of the Liberals. This concentration of the leadership of each party so decisively in the hands of one man, and the bold, clear-cut policies which these great leaders adopted, united their parties and restored the two-party system. The unification of the Liberal party, which had now completely absorbed the Peelites, was brought about on the Irish question.

Fenian movement

Irish problems were once more projected into politics by the Fenian outrages. The Fenian movement, unlike most violent outbreaks in Ireland, was primarily neither agrarian nor religious in its nature. It was stirred up largely by Irish Americans who had emigrated at the time of the great famine and after. They believed that England was the cause of Ireland's woes and that England's policy was the real cause which had forced them to leave their native land. They nursed their bitterness and inspired with it their relatives and friends in Ireland. Throughout the period of peace that followed the young Ireland rebellion of 1848 the gall was spreading. In 1865 it produced open revolt. The government was forehanded. It captured or drove to flight many of the leaders, preventing any concerted rebellion; but during the next two years the Fenians planned and executed a number of senseless and dastardly outrages both in Ireland and in England. Once more Ireland's wrongs were forced upon the attention of Great Britain.

Disraeli's defeat

Gladstone saw in the situation an opportunity to unite the Liberal party. The government offered only a policy of repression. Gladstone maintained that a quiet Ireland could be obtained only by the redress of Ireland's wrongs. He announced a policy of Irish reforms, chief of which was the disestablishment of the Irish church. His party rallied to his support, and before a united Liberal party the Conservatives were in a hopeless minority. An election resulted in an endorsement of Gladstone by the new electors, and in 1868 he formed his first cabinet.

Gladstone began his program of reform with a bill to disestablish and disendow the church in Ireland. The justice of a measure to relieve the Irish of the support of a church which claimed the allegiance of only eight to twelve per cent of their number could hardly be denied, but it was opposed strenuously by those who feared that its principles might be extended later to the English church. The opposition, however, was not strong enough to stop a reform on which the recent election had been fought. The bill passed in 1869. It provided that after 1870 the church in Ireland should cease to be a part of the government and be placed on a voluntary basis like other churches. It could no longer, for example, force laymen to pay tithes. The greater part of the property of the church was confiscated, but the churches and the larger part of the income were transferred to the new voluntary church. The remainder, amounting to approximately £7,000,000, was appropriated by the government to relieve suffering in Ireland. By this legislation Gladstone removed a long-standing grievance of the Irish.

Disestablishment and disendowment

Another Irish grievance of equal antiquity which Gladstone attempted to remedy arose from the methods of landholding prevalent in Ireland. The land was generally leased in small parcels of thirty acres or less. In most parts of Ireland the tenant by the custom descended from old Irish tribal law had greater rights in his tenement than those of a tenant-at-will, but the law enforced by the courts gave him only the rights of a tenant-at-will. Since it was the custom for the tenant to make his own improvements, an unscrupulous landlord could by ejection or by an increase of rent deprive the tenant of his improvements without compensation. Such an act might violate local custom, but the law gave the wronged tenant no protection in the courts.

Irish land law

Gladstone met the difficulty in 1870 by an act which virtually applied to the whole of Ireland a principle of the tenant-custom of the province of Ulster, and made it law. The most important provision forbade the eviction, without compensation for his unexhausted improvements, of a tenant who had made improvements in his tenement, unless he had failed to pay the rent or had committed other specified faults. It was an attempt to legalize the system of double ownership of the land which practically existed in fact. It accomplished some good, but fell far short of its purpose because it failed to limit the rents which the landlord could charge. The landlord could still take the profit of the improvements by raising the rent, or he could increase the rent to such a figure that the tenant could not pay and then eject him without compensation. The tenants soon found that the act gave them but slight protection against unscrupulous landlords.

Another great reform was accomplished in the session of 1870 by

Education
Act, 1870

the passage of an act which revolutionized the system of elementary education. Previously the elementary schools had been managed almost exclusively by private persons and financed by endowments, private contributions, and fees paid by the pupils. The greater part of them, moreover, were controlled by a religious society. These schools, however, did not satisfy the Dissenters because they gave religious instruction in the doctrines of the church of England. The Dissenters consequently had established some non-sectarian schools. Until 1833 the national government did nothing whatever to promote elementary education. In that year the reforming Whigs appropriated the munificent annual sum of £20,000 to aid elementary education. Subsequently the size of the appropriation was increased from time to time, and inspectors of schools were appointed. But the system was wretchedly inadequate. In 1869 nearly one-half of the children old enough to go to school were not in attendance.

The legislation of 1870 authorized the local government in any locality where the voluntary (i.e., private) schools did not offer adequate facilities for the education of the children to set up a school board for the purpose of establishing and maintaining public schools. The expenses were to be paid partly from local taxes, partly from national taxation, and partly from fees received from the children. Attendance at school between the ages of five and thirteen could be made compulsory by the local authority in any district, and the fees of poor children could be remitted.[14] The bill was nearly wrecked on the question of religious instruction which had previously dominated elementary education. It was finally settled by compromise. The Cowper-Temple clause required religious instruction to be non-sectarian in schools receiving support from local taxation, and the "time-table conscience" clause ordered the period given to religious instruction in all schools to be scheduled at the first or last period of the day, when parents could withdraw their children if they so desired. On the other hand, the aid given by the central government to the voluntary schools, which were left free to give what religious instruction they pleased, was further increased.

Adminis-
trative
reforms

By sweeping administrative reforms the cabinet increased the efficiency of the government. In 1870 an executive decree placed the civil service on the basis of competitive examinations. The order was applicable to each department only with the consent of the head. The foreign office alone chose to remain outside its scope. This reform

---

[14] Ten years later attendance was made uniformly compulsory, and in 1891 the fees of all children were abolished.

secured the administrative service against the danger of a system of spoils which the recent increase of democracy, judged by the experience of democracies elsewhere, seemed to threaten, and it provided a permanent corps of trained administrators who gave stability to the policies of departments of which the heads were frequently changing. The army was increased in size, and its administration and that of the war office were thoroughly reorganized. One aspect of this change which produced strong opposition was the abolition of the purchase of officers' commissions in the army, in order to make possible promotion on the basis of merit. This abuse, which enabled young men of wealth to buy promotion over the heads of their elders in the service, was of particular value to the sons of peers who sought military careers, and the house of lords blocked the bill which embodied the reform. The cabinet thereupon abolished the purchase of commissions by the issue of a royal warrant. This exercise of the executive authority was authorized by statute, but its use after a failure to accomplish the result by legislation raised a storm of criticism.

The protection of the new voters enfranchised by the act of 1867 was the purpose of the Ballot Act passed in 1872. It provided for the use of the Australian ballot. The secret vote, which was thus established, had been part of the program of a society formed for the promotion of parliamentary reform in 1780, and one of the six points in the People's Charter. It protected the voter against intimidation, and made more difficult the use of pressure by employers to influence the votes of their employees. It was a significant promotion of clean politics. **Ballot Act, 1872**

The Judicature Act of 1873 reorganized the procedure and jurisdiction of the central courts. They had become so complex and technical that many abuses throve. Often simple cases could not be decided without long delays and immense costs. The well-known tirade of Dickens on the court of chancery[15] does not exaggerate the evils at their worst, and they were vexatious and costly at their best. The act established one supreme court of judicature, divided into a high court of justice and a court of appeal. The high court is divided into the three branches of (1) chancery, (2) king's bench, and (3) probate, divorce, and admiralty. It hears both civil and criminal suits in first instance, and it can apply both law and equity. The act intended appeals from this court to the court of appeal to be final, but this was modified a few years later. In civil suits appeal lies to the court of appeal, and thence, under certain conditions, to the house of lords, **Judicature Act, 1873**

---

[15] *Bleak House*, ch. i.

which is still the highest court of the land. In criminal cases appeal only on writ of error went directly to the house of lords. Subsequent acts improved the organization of the upper chamber for the performance of judicial functions and placed a court of criminal appeal between the high court and the house of lords. The act of 1873 swept away a mass of anomalies in procedure, simplified the confusion of jurisdictions, and rendered the attainment of justice easier, more certain, and less expensive.

A piece of legislation in behalf of trade unions was conceded by the cabinet as a consequence of the influence attained by the trade unionists through their better organization and through the voting power given to them by the act of 1867. After the repeal of the combination acts, trade unionism declined. Many of the laborers hoped to secure through an amalgamation of unions a general adjustment of their social and economic ills, and, when they were disabused of this utopian ideal, they lost some of their interest in the unions and turned to the political Chartist movement. Some of the unions applied themselves to the more practical purpose of obtaining better wages and conditions of labor, but they met with more failures than successes. Even after the reform of 1832 the ruling class had scant sympathy for the unions, and the employers often broke strikes by lockouts and secured the punishment of strikers by invoking against them charges of conspiracy or of breaches of contract under the masters and servants laws. In some instances men who attempted only peaceful collective bargaining were convicted of some breach of the law. When the Chartist movement first collapsed in 1842, the trade unionists were disillusioned and discouraged.

Trade unionism, 1825–1867

This attitude of despair gradually gave way before attempts to make trade unions more practical both in their organization and in their aims. Unions began to employ paid officials to manage their affairs, they devoted more attention to the education of their members on the problems which concerned the laborers, they obtained more permanent members, and they collected from their members funds which they used to hire lawyers to defend members who were prosecuted by employers and to finance strikes. Though most unions remained local, federations of unions on a national scale were formed in some trades, and one influential amalgamation of unions in associated trades was established. These and other kindred developments rendered the trade unions so much stronger and influential that in 1867 they not only helped to bring about the extension of the suffrage but they also secured the enactment of a law which removed the worst abuses in the application of the laws of masters and servants against workmen.

Contemporaneously with these successes, two events threatened the very existence of the trade unions. In 1866 a series of violent acts against non-unionist employees committed by unions in Sheffield aroused a public feeling against trade unionism and led to the appointment of a royal commission of inquiry. The other event was a judicial decision in the case of Hornby versus Close. A union was seeking to recover from its secretary a sum of money which belonged to it. Its claim rested upon a law of 1855 which, as previously interpreted, protected an association "established for a purpose not illegal" against defalcations by its officers. The court decided that the act did not apply to a trade union, because such an association, though not criminal, was so far in restraint of trade as to be illegal. The judgment left the trade unions not only without legal protection for their funds but also without the legal standing which they had previously believed themselves to possess. The danger from the commission of inquiry was averted by leaders of the labor movement whose evidence convinced the commissioners that the Sheffield incidents were not typical of the whole trade union movement and caused it to render a report which was not particularly unfavorable to trade unionism. The legalization of the unions was accomplished in 1871 by legislation which declared that a trade union was not illegal solely because it was in restraint of trade and granted protection to their funds in accordance with the terms of the act of 1855. The victory of the unions, however, was far from complete, for another law strengthened and extended the law of conspiracy by imposing penalties for intimidation, picketing, molestation and many other acts which were commonly employed in strikes. The act seemed to make it impossible to strike even in the most orderly manner without committing criminal acts.

Legislation of 1871

In foreign affairs the cabinet, though prepared to represent British interests firmly, was opposed to the domineering and provocative methods which had been used by Palmerston. The first event of importance was the outbreak of the Franco-Prussian war in 1870. Great Britain endeavored to bring about a settlement of the differences between the two powers by negotiation, but it was impossible to stop the war when Napoleon III and Bismarck, the Prussian chancellor, both desired it. Though the foreign office failed in the hopeless attempt to preserve the peace of Europe, it protected British interests by obtaining from each of the belligerents a fresh guarantee of the neutrality of Belgium. Before the war ended with the victory of Prussia in 1871 and the subse-

Foreign policy

quent formation of the German empire, British diplomacy received a notable check. Russia, urged by Bismarck who wished to prevent any British sympathy for France from finding expression, seized the opportunity, while France was engaged, to declare itself freed from the observance of those clauses in the Treaty of Paris of 1856 which neutralized the Black Sea. Great Britain could only protest, unless it was prepared to wage war against Russia with the sole aid of Turkey. Eventually it entered a conference of the powers signatory, which formally abrogated the clauses that Russia had refused longer to observe. This renewed the popular apprehension of Russian aggressive designs which had begun to subside after the Crimean War, and gave currency to a popular view that the cabinet weakly surrendered to Russia. The sentiment was further strengthened by subsequent Russian activities in the direction of Afghanistan. The government guarded adequately against Russian absorption of Afghan territory by direct diplomatic negotiations with Russia, but the public interpreted the cabinet's policy of non-intervention in Afghanistan as a weakness. Thus the relations maintained by the cabinet with European powers were somewhat unreasonably a cause of much popular dissatisfaction.

Still more unpopular was Gladstone's arbitration of the *Alabama* claims with the United States. Since the close of the civil war the United States had been demanding compensation for the damages inflicted on her shipping by the *Alabama*[16] and other raiders which had been built in Great Britain for the Confederacy. The British government had been willing to negotiate or arbitrate these claims, but it had refused to acknowledge additional constructive claims for indirect damages, which it regarded as extravagant. Gladstone finally reached an agreement with the government of the United States to submit the claims to a tribunal of arbitration, consisting of representatives of the king of Italy, the president of Switzerland, and the emperor of Brazil, in addition to those of Great Britain and the United States. The tribunal, which sat in 1872, ruled out the indirect claims, but awarded large damages for the destruction wrought by the *Alabama* and similar ships. It was a valuable precedent for the settlement of international disputes by arbitration. In Great Britain the decision was received unfavorably by the public, which judged it to be unfair. Thus in 1872 the foreign policy of the cabinet was popularly condemned in all of its principal aspects.

By this time its internal policies were also producing dissatisfaction. For a time the constructive policies of Gladstone had made his admin-

---

[16] Above, pp. 688, 689.

istration appear to be a golden age for liberalism, but the policy of reform had been pushed ahead so fast that it was losing momentum. The government had carried through not only the far-reaching reforms enumerated, but also many others of lesser importance. As Goschen said, the ministers "had spent their majority like gentlemen."[17] In 1872 Disraeli referred to the ministers on the treasury bench as a "range of exhausted volcanoes."[18] The new reforms served to alienate one group after another. As the opposition put it, the cabinet had "harassed every trade, worried every profession, and assailed or menaced every class, institution, and species of property in the country."[19] With the growing weakness of the cabinet, some of the old dissensions in the Liberal party began to come to life. In 1873 Gladstone was defeated on a bill to reorganize the Irish system of higher education, the last of his three measures designed to pacify Ireland. He resigned, but Disraeli refused to take office because he wanted Gladstone to hold the election in order to make the issue what Gladstone had done. Gladstone resumed office, but, as Disraeli anticipated, the ministry became daily more discredited. By 1874 the situation was so embarrassing for the cabinet that Gladstone dissolved and held an election.

Weakness of the cabinet

Disraeli meanwhile had been building up the Conservative party with great success. In his famous Crystal Palace speech of 1872 he laid down the policies of a rejuvenated Tory party and forecast a program which the party followed for the next thirty years. He announced it to be the business of the Conservatives to protect the existing institutions of the country. Since the progressive reforms of the Liberals had excited alarm among the moderate elements, this proved to be a popular cry. The timid were beginning to fear that the Liberal zest for change threatened not only the established church but also the house of lords and even the monarchy.

Conservative program

But Disraeli was too wise to make the appeal *ad hominem* solely on a negative issue. In the debates on the second reform bill he predicted that many of the enfranchised workingmen would become Conservatives. He was laughed to scorn. Five years later, at the meeting of the national organization of the Conservative party, which was the occasion of the Crystal Palace speech, the chairman said: "A few years ago everybody said that if a Conservative workingman could be found, he ought to be put in a glass case. We have found for him the largest

[17] Walpole, *Twenty-five Years*, iii, 203.
[18] Buckle, *Disraeli*, v, 191.
[19] *Ibid.*, v, 262.

glass case in England to-night,"[20] a reference to the fact that the Crystal Palace was full of laborers. The workers, in fact, had not split so unevenly between the Liberals and the Conservatives. So Disraeli proclaimed as the second object of his party legislation which would improve the social and economic position of the workingmen without causing the upheaval attendant upon the cataclysmic methods of the Liberals. Thus was begun the so-called "Tory democracy," which has been an important element in the party ever since.

The most progressive of Disraeli's views, however, were those on imperial affairs. Here he was far more radical than Gladstone. For a generation the general tendency had been to regard the colonies as burdens. Disraeli gave to the Conservatives the watchword of maintenance of the empire. As a forecast of the policy of his party for the next generation his utterance on this subject was remarkable. "Self-government," he said, "when it was conceded, ought to have been conceded as part of a great policy of Imperial consolidation. It ought to have been accompanied by an Imperial tariff, . . . and by a military code which should have precisely defined the means and the responsibilities by which the Colonies should be defended, and by which, if necessary, this country should call for aid from the colonies themselves. It ought, further, to have been accompanied by the institution of some representative council in the metropolis, which would have brought the Colonies into constant and continuous relations with the Home Government."[21] In the forthcoming election his utterance had weight, for Gladstone had pushed the policy of non-intervention abroad and economy in the military service further than was pleasing even to many of the liberals.

With these constructive principles the Conservatives went into the fight better equipped with popular policies than was usual. The National Union, an organization which had been formed within the party in 1867, did efficient work in winning the votes of the workingmen. The interests which had been offended by Gladstone's reforms did the rest. The Conservatives returned from the election with a clear majority for the first time since 1841.

Internal reforms

Disraeli's administration for the next six years emphasized those things which Gladstone had subordinated. On internal reforms Disraeli went slowly, as he had promised. Yet he fulfilled his pledge to the workingmen by a number of moderate, beneficent laws designed to improve the conditions of their life and labor. In 1875 a Public Health

[20] Cited by Lowell, *Government of England*, i, 538.
[21] Buckle, *Disraeli*, v, 195.

Act, which formed part of Disraeli's *sanitas sanitatum, omnia sanitas* program and was dubbed by the Liberals "a policy of sewage,"[22] codified and consolidated the previous legislation on the subject and reorganized the sanitary administration. An Artisans' Dwellings Act gave local urban authorities the power to condemn buildings, or even whole congested areas, as unfit for human habitation, have the buildings torn down and new dwellings built, or to have existing dwellings improved. Another law repealed Gladstone's act of 1871 against the trade unions, legalized peaceful picketing, and established the principle that the acts of a combination of persons engaged in a trade dispute were not criminal if the same acts were not criminal when committed by an individual. It was accompanied by an act which removed from the unions the last of the restrictions imposed by the masters and servants laws. This legislation finally legalized collective bargaining and gave to the trade unions their charter of freedom. In 1878 the Factory and Workshop Act codified the legislation with regard to the hours and conditions of labor. Since the act of 1847 further legislation had applied the principles of the earlier acts[23] to industries other than the textile, and amplified the earlier measures. The act of 1878 was a complete code, which revised the previous laws and added to them much that was new. The extent of the detail which the regulation attained is indicated by the fact that the text filled sixty-five pages of folio.

These and other lesser reforms of similar nature constituted a policy of "honest humdrum" which aroused no such apprehensions as the reforms of Gladstone. Since most of Disraeli's reforms merely expanded policies begun in previous administrations, they appeared less radical than the innovations of Gladstone. They were, moreover, in accord with what was coming to be the popular opinion with regard to the proper function of the government in the regulation of the economic and social affairs of the nation. The individualistic theory, which held that the only business of the government was to protect the individual from violence and fraud, and the *laissez-faire* theory, with its emphasis on the economic freedom of the individual, were losing the places which they had occupied in popular esteem during the early years of the nineteenth century.[24] The first breach had been made by the Factory Act of 1833, justified chiefly by humanitarian motives,[25] but by 1868 Mill's leaven had done its work. Public opinion was swinging

Legislation and public opinion

---

[22] *Ibid.*, v, 362.
[23] See above, pp. 649, 650.
[24] Above, pp. 585, 586, 647, 648.
[25] Above, pp. 648–650.

away from the older theories toward socialism and collectivism. The swing was more or less unconscious, and it was not pronounced. The legislation contemplated was for the most part of a type which could be supported by one who conceived himself to be either a broad-minded individualist or a moderate socialist. A socialistic state which should control all the means of production was the last thing that Englishmen desired in the mid-Victorian era, but it was coming to be the general consensus of opinion that the failure of individualism and *laissez faire* justified a certain amount of legislative regulation of industry, commerce, and social conditions. Differences of opinion with regard to the proper extent of such regulation were coming to be questions of degree rather than of kind. Disraeli by these laws made his party the mouthpiece for those who would advance more slowly. For the remainder of the century both parties advocated regulative legislation in more or less opportunist fashion to win the votes of the workingmen, but the Liberals were generally inclined to be more radical than the Conservatives.

Imperial policies

In contrast to his quiet internal policy Disraeli's external policies impressed contemporaries as brilliant. His first step was startling. In 1875 he purchased for the British government the shares in the Suez Canal held by the ruler of Egypt. The canal, which had been opened in 1869, was of fundamental importance to Great Britain because it controlled the shortest route to India. The shares purchased by Disraeli gave Great Britain control of nearly half of the stock and a voice in the management of the canal. The shares were being offered for sale in France, where their purchase would have made the canal a French monopoly. In order to forestall France, Disraeli negotiated the purchase with the aid of London bankers on the responsibility of the cabinet, seeking the subsequent sanction of parliament. The transaction struck the popular imagination as a masterly stroke of imperial policy. After public attention had thus been drawn to India, Disraeli further emphasized its importance by asking parliament in 1876 to confer upon the queen the title of empress of India. Though it was regarded by many as a mere *beau geste*, it served to rouse the loyalty of the natives of India and to give strength to the bond of imperial sentiment.

The Near East

By this time the situation in Turkey was giving the cabinet grave concern. The promise of the Turkish government to accord its Christian subjects better treatment after the Crimean War had not been kept. This, together with Turkish misgovernment, caused the two provinces of Bosnia and Herzegovina to revolt in the summer of 1875. The three eastern powers, Russia, Austria, and Prussia, intervened unsuccessfully to secure peace. Disraeli supported this effort, but when the same powers invited Britain to join in putting pressure on Turkey, he declined because Britain had had no voice in framing the policy. In 1876 Bulgaria revolted. Here Turkey let loose irregular troops which committed horrible atrocities. All Europe was stirred, and Gladstone made England ring with his demand that Great Britain should no longer support the terrible Turk. Shortly after, Servia and Montenegro came to the help of the rebel peoples. The blaze had spread until it threatened to involve all of Europe. The strength of public opinion after the Bulgarian massacres caused Disraeli to send a representative to negotiate with representatives of the other powers at Constantinople. They agreed upon a program of reform which would have satisfied the rebels and restored peace, but the Turkish government, believing that Great Britain would not join with the others in the use of force, refused all the demands. Russia thereupon intervened alone. War was declared early in 1877, and by 1878 the Russian troops were threatening Constantinople. The Turks consequently capitulated, and peace was made at San Stephano. The treaty enlarged Bulgaria and gave it autonomy under nominal Turkish control; made Montenegro, Roumania, and Servia independent; and secured autonomy for Bosnia and Herzegovina. The treaty left to Turkey only a small strip of territory in Europe, for though Bulgaria was still nominally under Turkish suzerainty, it was expected to become a sphere of Russian influence, and it included a large part of Macedonia at the very gates of Constantinople.

The aggression of Russia revived in Great Britain all of the old fears of Russian ambitions. Early in 1878 the cabinet warned Russia that the occupation of the Dardanelles would endanger friendly relations with Great Britain, and demanded that any treaty between Russia and Turkey which altered the terms of the treaties of 1856 and 1871[26] should have the assent of the powers signatory to those treaties. These threats were accompanied by a request in the house of commons for a large appropriation to increase British armaments. After the signature of the treaty, Disraeli insisted that it departed from the earlier treaties and must be revised by the signatory powers. When Russia refused, he continued preparation for war. The jingo spirit began to run high in England. Before this threat of hostilities Russia gave way. Having reached an understanding with Great Britain on some of the principal revisions to be made, Russia agreed to enter a congress at Berlin. Dis-

Congress of Berlin

---

[26] See above, pp. 679, 702.

raeli dominated the congress and secured his principal demands. Bulgaria was reduced in size. Macedonia was restored to Turkey, and the remainder of the big Bulgaria was split into two autonomous parts. Disraeli hoped by this device to reduce the extent of Russian influence. Bosnia and Herzegovina were placed under the administrative control of Austria, though they remained nominally parts of Turkey. Great Britain took control of the island of Cyprus and guaranteed the integrity of Turkey's Asiatic dominions. Disraeli had accomplished the ends of Great Britain without war. He seemed to have scored a great diplomatic triumph, and his dictum of "peace with honour" was generally accepted at home. In the light cast by later events this estimate needs revision. The settlement at Berlin left much soreness and many causes of friction. The independent Balkan states objected to the return of Macedonia, which was inhabited by their fellow Slavs and Christians. Their machinations to recover it later became a cause of much trouble. The rule of the Serbs in Bosnia and Herzegovina by Austria led to endless friction between Austria and Servia. But this light was lacking to contemporaries, and they generally hailed "Dizzy's" diplomacy with acclaim.

Imperial wars: Afghanistan

Though Disraeli avoided war in the Near East, his aggressive imperial policy led Great Britain into petty conflicts elsewhere. The advancing influence of Russia in Afghanistan caused Great Britain to demand of the native ruler of that state the acceptance of a resident British adviser. When the demand was refused, British forces invaded Afghanistan, forcing the native ruler to acquiesce in the British control of his foreign relations. Soon after the British troops were withdrawn, the British agent and his companions were slain by the natives. A British punitive expedition was in occupation of Afghanistan when Disraeli's administration closed.

South Africa

In southern Africa the government rushed into a high-handed policy and was involved in a native war by its local representatives. After the acquisition of Cape Colony by the British in 1814, much friction developed between the Dutch inhabitants, called Boers, and the British government. It came to a head with the abolition of slavery, which affected the interests of the Dutch farmers adversely. In the next few years a general exodus of the Boers took place. They migrated to regions north of Cape Colony where they founded the virtually independent states of the Transvaal and Orange Free State. At first the British government in South Africa claimed sovereignty over the Boers in their new homes, but in 1852 the Sand River Convention conceded to the Boers of the Transvaal practical independence. Two years later the Orange Free State secured like treatment. Subsequent troubles with the natives led the British government to advocate a confederation of the states of South Africa. The colonial secretary in Disraeli's cabinet eventually determined to annex the Transvaal, if local circumstances "rendered it in any way possible."[27] An agent so instructed found it possible to declare the Transvaal annexed, and the cabinet subsequently ratified his action. Later, another representative, contrary to the wishes of the cabinet, rushed into a war to protect the Boers against the native Zulus. Though ultimately successful, British arms suffered some disastrous defeats through the incompetency of the commanders.

By this time Disraeli's vigorous imperial policy was causing a popular reaction. Though spirited and brilliant, it had entangled Great Britain in costly wars of doubtful utility, which did not redound to the credit of British arms. The connection with the Suez Canal had also involved Great Britain in the internal affairs of Egypt. Disraeli's imperialism did not prove as attractive in practice as it had appeared in prophecy. Many, too, regarded his policy as too unscrupulous, and great impetus was given to this opinion by Gladstone, who, though he had formally resigned the leadership of the Liberal party, was still regarded as its popular oracle. "The infamy of Lord Beaconsfield's [i.e., Disraeli's] policy is only equalled by the villainy with which he has carried it out" was said by a political opponent to be the gist of Gladstone's numerous speeches during the campaign.[28] Though Disraeli endeavored to make the Irish question the dominant issue in the election held in 1880, Gladstone's plea that the imperial idea was being carried too far prevailed. The Liberals won the election, and Disraeli resigned without awaiting the meeting of the new parliament.

Election of 1880

Though Gladstone had retired from the leadership of the Liberal party, his speeches had started the Liberals on the road to victory. No Liberal cabinet could succeed without him. Since he would take no subordinate place, he became prime minister for the second time. Under his leadership the reversal of Disraeli's foreign and imperial policies necessarily occupied a prominent place among the policies of the cabinet.

Gladstone, 1880–1885

In South Africa Gladstone had to deal with a revolt of the Boers of the Transvaal who objected to annexation. The Boers had the better of the warfare with the British troops opposed to them. Finally they defeated a small detachment of them in a pitched battle. The

South Africa

[27] Buckle, *Disraeli*, vi, 414.
[28] Hamilton, G., *Parliamentary Reminiscences*, p. 172.

news of the disaster excited the British public to demand retribution, but Gladstone, who believed that the annexation of the Transvaal had been morally wrong, refused to prolong the war merely for the purpose of revenge. He offered peace on the basis of the internal independence of the Transvaal under British suzerainty. These terms were accepted in 1881. In 1884 they were modified by deletion of reference to suzerainty, though Great Britain kept control of the external affairs of the Transvaal. Though the parliament led by Gladstone had been elected to right the wrongs done by Disraeli, this reversal, apparently at the dictation of the Boers, was unpopular. Nor did it secure permanent peace in South Africa.

Afghani-stan

In Afghanistan Gladstone reversed Disraeli's policy immediately. Though British arms were successful in this quarter soon after the appointment of the new cabinet, evacuation was ordered. Gladstone was opposed not only to the policy of conquest but also to the difficulty and cost of maintaining British power among the warlike tribesmen of this mountainous state. The withdrawal was completed in 1881, leaving Afghanistan an independent state. The wisdom of this policy was brought into question before the close of Gladstone's term of office, when Russia began once more to advance the frontier of her empire from the north toward Afghanistan. In 1885 Russian troops occupied Penjdeh, which was claimed by the ruler of Afghanistan. The occupation not only led to a battle in which the Afghans were defeated, but it also opened to the Russians the road to Herat. Since the English government could obtain from the Russian government no definite assurance that the advance would stop at Penjdeh, even Gladstone regarded war as necessary. The cabinet announced to parliament its intention to ask for the grant of the money necessary to prepare for war, and the tension became so acute that "in every capital in Europe war was considered inevitable."[29] The danger was avoided by a British proposal to arbitrate the question, which was accepted by the Russian government. This ended the crisis, and Gladstone's successor concluded the negotiations which delimited the frontier, but the region still remained a potential source of friction between the two powers. The incident also brought home to the English government its complete lack of friends among the powers of Europe, when it discovered that all of them were likely to oppose the passage of the Dardanelles by British ships in the event of war.

In Egypt Gladstone not only failed to reverse Disraeli's policy but

[29] Gooch, *History of Modern Europe*, p. 31.

he even extended it. The khedive of Egypt had been forced by his own **Egypt**
extravagance to sell his shares in the Suez Canal. Subsequently his
prodigality continued, to the alarm of his English and French creditors.
In 1876 the French and the British sent representatives to Egypt, who
eventually assumed charge of the national finances in order to secure
payment of the debt. In 1881 a group of Egyptians, who objected to the
native misgovernment and the intervention of foreigners, rose in rebellion with the war cry of "Egypt for the Egyptians." Eventually the
movement became fanatical and resulted in the death of many Europeans. The British government invited France and Italy to join in
intervention, but both declined. In 1882 Great Britain entered Egypt
and put down the rebellion alone. Subsequently British agents assumed
responsibility for a large part of the government of Egypt. No protectorate was declared, and Gladstone announced his intention to withdraw as soon as order and good government should have been restored.

Gladstone soon discovered that the assumption of power carried
with it responsibilities that he had not foreseen. A rebellion in the **The**
Sudan involved the British government in Egyptian affairs far more **Sudan**
deeply than he had intended. The Sudan was an Egyptian province
to the south of Egypt. It had never been thoroughly conquered, and it
had always been subject to misrule. In 1883 the native tribesmen rose,
drove the Egyptian troops into the fortresses, and cut to pieces an
Egyptian army commanded by British officers sent against them by the
khedive. The resident British officials advised the cabinet that the
Egyptians could not hold the Sudan without help. The cabinet decided
that it was no business of Great Britain's. At the same time, the Egyptian garrisons cornered in the Sudan could hardly be left to their fate.
In 1884 General Charles Gordon, who had previously acted as the
governor of the Sudan under the Egyptians, was sent to Khartum, the
capital of the Sudan, to facilitate the evacuation. Whether he was to
take charge of the evacuation or merely to report on what was necessary to be done was perhaps not made entirely clear in his orders, but
he went beyond the intention of the cabinet when he settled at Khartum and attempted to restore order. He was soon cut off. A relief expedition was necessary if he was to be saved. The cabinet delayed, since
a British expedition would bring upon Great Britain responsibilities
which the cabinet had tried to avoid. The delay was fatal. The expedition, which it eventually despatched, arrived at Khartum two days after
Gordon and the garrison had been annihilated by the Sudanese. When
the news reached England it caused an outburst of popular indignation. Gordon was something of a popular idol, and his death was at-

tributed to the criminal negligence of the cabinet. The popular verdict was reached in ignorance of Gordon's orders, but the manifestly weak and vacillating policy of the cabinet left it with little claim on popular esteem. A vote of censure was avoided in the house of commons by only fourteen votes, and it was the disaster in the Sudan that was largely responsible for the defeat of the cabinet a few months later in 1885. So far as the Sudan was concerned, the result was negligible. The expeditionary force had hardly begun to attempt to quell the rebellion, when it was recalled. The Sudan was left to go its own way.[30]

Beginning of African colonial expansion

The occupation of Egypt was but one step in a scramble for possession of African territories which was begun by the European powers in this period. The new spirit of aggressive imperialism, of which Disraeli was the apostle in England, found expression also in France and Germany. When these powers began to look abroad for colonies, Africa offered the largest area of desirable lands still uncontrolled by white men. The bacilli which gave them the African fever came from the Congo. Interest in this region was stimulated by the explorations made by David Livingstone, a Scottish missionary, between 1858 and 1873, and by Henry M. Stanley, an American journalist of British birth, during the next few years. The latter, in 1878, after he had tried without success to interest Disraeli in the region, entered the service of King Leopold of Belgium, who, in the next year, organized an international association which laid the foundations of the Congo Free State that later became a Belgian possession. France was quick to follow suit. In 1881 the raising of the French flag on the north bank of the Congo prepared the way for the development of the colony of French Congo, and the occupation of Tunis in northern Africa was begun. In the next year the French proclaimed a protectorate over part of Madagascar, and a year later extended this claim to embrace the whole island. During the same period they established footholds on the west coast from which they pushed rapidly into the interior to form the huge colony of French West Africa. Germany came into the field late, because Bismarck, the German chancellor, for a long time opposed colonial expansion. He felt that the German empire formed in 1871 needed to concentrate upon internal development and the stabilization of its position in Europe. Only in 1883 did the growth of German popular sentiment in behalf of colonies and a favorable international situation cause him to begin the attempt to secure colonies. In the next year, Germans, acting with his sanction, asserted rights to terri-

---

[30] On this vexed question see Allen, *Gordon and the Sudan,* and Knaplund, *Gladstone's Foreign Policy,* ch. viii.

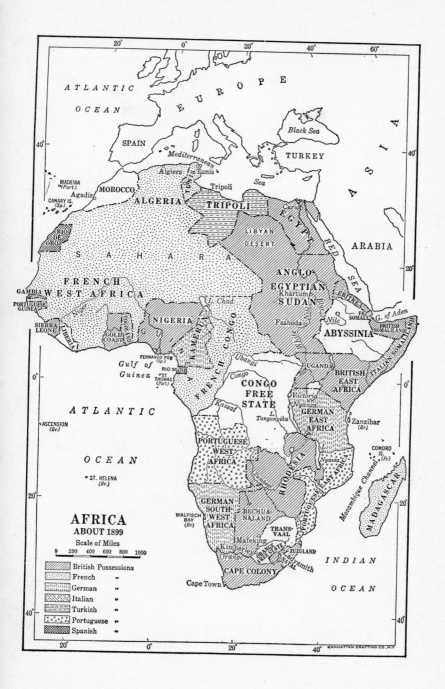

ATLANTIC
OCEAN

E U R O P E

A S I A

SPAIN

Mediterranean
Algiers Tunis
Tripoli
Cairo

Black Sea

TURKEY

MADEIRA
(Port.)
Agadir
CANARY IS.
(Sp.)

MOROCCO

ALGERIA

TRIPOLI

EGYPT

RED SEA

ARABIA

RIO DE
ORO

S A H A R A

LIBYAN
DESERT

ANGLO-
EGYPTIAN
SUDAN

ERITREA

G. of Aden

FRENCH
WEST AFRICA

L. Chad

Khártum

FR.
SOMALI.

BRITISH
SOMALILAND

GAMBIA
PORTUGUESE GUINEA
SIERRA
LEONE
LIBERIA

Niger

NIGERIA

KAMERUN

FRENCH CONGO

Fashoda

Nile

ABYSSINIA

ITALIAN SOMALILAND

GOLD
COAST

FG

FERNANDO POO
(Sp.)
RIO M.
ST.
THOMAS
(Port.)

Gulf of
Guinea

Ubangi

Congo

Kassai

CONGO
FREE
STATE

L.
Tanganyika

Victoria
Nyanza

UGANDA

BRITISH
EAST
AFRICA

GERMAN
EAST
AFRICA

Zanzibar
(Br.)

ATLANTIC

ASCENSION
(Br.)

OCEAN

ST. HELENA
(Br.)

PORTUGUESE
WEST
AFRICA

Nyasa

PORTUGUESE EAST AFRICA

RHODESIA

COMORO IS.
(Fr.)

Mozambique Channel

MADAGASCAR

AFRICA
ABOUT 1899

Scale of Miles

0 200 400 600 800 1000

GERMAN
SOUTH
WEST
AFRICA

WALFISCH
BAY
(Br.)

BECHUA-
NALAND

Mafeking
Kimberley
Orange
ORANGE
FREE STATE

TRANS-
VAAL

ZULULAND
Ladysmith
NATAL

INDIAN

OCEAN

British Possessions
French   "
German   "
Italian   "
Turkish   "
Portuguese "
Spanish   "

CAPE COLONY

Cape Town

MANHATTAN DRAFTING CO., N.Y.

tories which became the colonies of German Southwest Africa, Kamerun and Togoland, and in 1885 German East Africa was taken under the protection of the German government.

The British government was still more tardy in entering the competition for African territories, if its Egyptian venture be left out of account. Gladstone regarded the existing empire as a heavy burden of responsibility and had no desire to add to it by further annexations. As late as 1882 the cabinet rejected an opportunity to establish a protectorate over Kamerun. But all of Gladstone's colleagues were not of like mind with him, the influential leaders of opinion in Cape Colony wanted expansion in South Africa, and British explorers, merchants and missionaries were establishing relations with the natives of various regions which sometimes forced the hand of the government. All of these groups became excited when Germany and France began to seize territories in the neighborhood of British lands or interests, and they succeeded in persuading the British government to take action in several areas. When the French and German attempts to secure portions of West Africa began, the British government was already represented in the region of the Niger delta by a consul, and a private British company controlled most of the trade with the natives of the area. When a French company was established to compete for the commerce of the district, the British company met the competition successfully and forced the French company to sell out. When the German threat became apparent in 1884, the head of the company, with the help of the consul, arranged treaties with the native chieftains placing their territories under British protection. An agent sent into the interior to make the last of them, when he was returning down the Niger with the signed treaties, passed a German agent going up the river just too late to acquire the territories for Germany. The British government acknowledged the established facts, secured recognition of the claim to Nigeria from the Berlin conference, and declared a protectorate in 1885. In Kamerun, on the other hand, the British consul, whom the government sent to make treaties with the natives in 1884, arrived just after a German agent had taken possession of the territory. In South Africa, the government, after holding back for a long time, was finally induced by a missionary in the region and by the politicians of Cape Colony, among whom Cecil Rhodes was influential, to send troops into Bechuanaland to protect the natives from exploitation by white settlers and raiders and to prevent the occupation of the territory by the neighboring Boers or Germans. The action resulted in the proclamation of a British protectorate soon after Gladstone's resignation. In

British
expansion
in Africa

East Africa Gladstone also opposed expansion, only to give way in the end. Here the British had much influence in the island of Zanzibar, where the government maintained a consul. In 1884 several members of the cabinet formulated with the consul and a British explorer a plan to keep control of the opposite mainland for the British. Gladstone persuaded the cabinet to shelve the project; but after the Germans established themselves in East Africa, the cabinet obtained the approval of Bismarck for the development of East Africa to the north of the German protectorate by a British trading company, and so the colony of British East Africa had its beginning.

New Guinea

The acquisition of a portion of the island of New Guinea in the neighborhood of Australia was made in the same spirit. The Dutch were in possession of the western end of the island but the remainder was free from European control. The Australians desired the annexation of the eastern part before it should fall into the hands of a power which might become an undesirable neighbor. Since the colonial office turned a deaf ear to the proposal, the colony of Queensland finally took possession of it in 1883. This action was repudiated by the home government, but it caused the cabinet to consider what should be done with regard to New Guinea. In 1884, while the cabinet was still undecided, Germany occupied the northern part, leaving open only the southern portion, which Great Britain promptly claimed in 1885. Thus Gladstone, against his inclination, was pushed along the path of imperial expansion.

Friction with Germany

This sudden and rapid imperial expansion necessarily brought Great Britain into controversies with some of the other powers involved. The most serious of them was with Germany. The friction began over the territory which became German Southwest Africa. Late in 1882 a German merchant asked protection of the German government for a trading post which he proposed to establish there, and received promise of it, provided no other government claimed the region. Although Great Britain had refused two years before to take responsibility for the protection of German missionaries in that section, except in Walfisch Bay, which the British occupied, Bismarck asked the British government if it exercised authority in that region, and stated that, if it did not, Germany proposed to protect its own subjects there. The British reply postponed a definite answer until it should be known where the post was to be established and the government of Cape Colony should have been consulted. The German post was established in the spring of 1883, but the British delayed their definite answer until autumn. They then claimed that any settlement in the region would infringe British rights, though British sovereignty had not been proclaimed there. The German chancellor protested this application of a Monroe doctrine to Africa, and on December 31, 1883, demanded to know by what right Great Britain claimed sovereignty of the area. Previously the German official communications appear to have given no clear indication that Bismarck wanted to establish a colony in Southwest Africa, and the cabinet labored under the delusion that the chancellor was still opposed to colonial expansion. The note of December 31 should have made the German intentions obvious, but the colonial secretary professed to believe that it left to Great Britain the choice of annexation or of acquiescence in German annexation. Since the British government was not prepared to assume the expense for the upkeep of a new colony, and it was Cape Colony which desired protection from foreign neighbors, he asked the government of the Cape if it would annex the district. By this time Bismarck believed that the British begrudged the Germans any share in the colonial field, and he suspected that the home government was plotting with Cape Colony to forestall German annexation of Southwest Africa. He therefore announced that the German merchant would receive protection from the German government, and proceeded to bring pressure to bear upon the British government. He hinted broadly that he would withdraw his support of the British position in Egypt, unless Great Britain ceased to oppose the legitimate acquisition of colonies by Germany. Since the British responsibilities for the Egyptian debt to the European powers were such that the withdrawal of German support would place Great Britain in a hopeless situation, the cabinet agreed, on June 21, 1884, not to question the German protectorate proclaimed in Southwest Africa. Gladstone, though he disliked Bismarck's methods of accomplishing his end, had no objection to Germany as a colonial neighbor, and the foreign and colonial secretaries, Lords Granville and Derby, appear to have been chiefly responsible for the serious blunders made by the British in the course of the negotiations.

After this experience, Bismarck not only made no further attempt to pacify the British government, but he even went to the extent of deceiving it with regard to the purposes of the agents whom he sent to take possession of Togoland, Kamerun, East Africa and northern New Guinea. Early in 1885 the British government acknowledged Germany's right to these colonies. It could not do otherwise, for the Egyptian situation was as bad as ever, the disaster at Khartum had just occurred, and war with Russia over the Penjdeh incident appeared to be imminent. Even these concessions do not tell the whole story of

Bismarck's application of the screws. Before he became brusque with Great Britain, he had reached an understanding with the French government that Germany and France should work together to promote their colonial ambitions against Great Britain. In 1884 the British foreign office made a treaty with Portugal which recognized some old Portuguese claims to control the mouth of the Congo. France, supported by Germany, protested the treaty and forced Great Britain to enter with other powers the Berlin conference on African questions, where the Congo Free State was recognized, the Congo river was declared free for the navigation of all nations, and the possibility of a Monroe doctrine for Africa was estopped by the provision that territories claimed must be effectively occupied. The conference ended early in 1885. By that time Bismarck had secured from Great Britain full recognition of Germany as a colonial power, and he realized that the development of the new empire would be better served by friendship than by enmity with Great Britain. At the same time the French cabinet which had cooperated with him went out of office, and the new cabinet was less friendly. Before Gladstone's cabinet resigned, he became conciliatory in his attitude, and with Gladstone's successors he worked harmoniously on colonial issues. But his change of heart did not erase from the slate the record which had been written there. Long after these negotiations, the British foreign office still treasured the belief that the German policy on imperial questions was one of deceit, bullying and blackmail; while the German foreign office was equally distrustful of British aims and preserved the tradition that Great Britain, despite her vast colonial empire, was selfishly opposed to all German imperial expansion. Though these views were due in part to misunderstandings caused by blunders on both sides, they were never eradicated, and they remained in the remote or the immediate background of all subsequent negotiations of the two powers on imperial problems as long as Germany retained a colonial empire.

The internal policies of Gladstone's second cabinet were less striking than those of his first. Legislation was enacted to secure a number of minor social and economic reforms, but the most radical change was the third reform of parliament accomplished by acts passed in 1884 and 1885. The qualifications for voting which had been established for urban constituencies by the act of 1867 were extended to the counties. The chief result was to give the suffrage to the agricultural laborers, who had constituted the only large class still excluded. The ratio of voters was increased to one in six of the population, attaining approximately manhood suffrage, though the right to vote still depended

Parliamentary reform

on the ownership or occupation of property. In the distribution of seats the act applied the new principle of representation in proportion to population. Earlier redistributions had simply taken representatives away from the less populous districts to give them to more populous ones. The legislation of 1885 created single-member districts, which were intended to be equal by a rough approximation. The principle was not applied uniformly. A small number of two-member constituencies survived, and also a few single-member districts with a population below the general average.

A problem which Gladstone found no easier to solve than the Egyptian was the Irish. From the time of the union to 1880 the imperial parliament had legislated for Ireland with many beneficial effects, but the legislation had been given only when the disorder in Ireland compelled the attention of British statesmen. In this legislation little regard was had for the opinions of the Irish people. The program of Gladstone's first cabinet, for example, was introduced into parliament without consultation of the wishes of the leaders of the Irish members of the house of commons. Irish representation in the British parliament amounted to little because the Irish members were in a hopeless minority. They could make no impression on legislation intended for Ireland. The inability of the Irish to influence the imperial parliament to treat Irish problems from an Irish point of view led them to demand the right to manage their own affairs. Under O'Connell this demand took the form of repeal of the union. After O'Connell's day this issue was for a long time dormant. When it was revived, it took a different shape. In 1870 the Home Rule Association was formed. It did not ask for a separation as complete as repeal of the union implied, but advocated control of the internal affairs of Ireland by the Irish people. In the next year, at by-elections, Butt, who became the parliamentary leader of the movement, and four other Home Rulers were elected to the house of commons. The advocates of home rule secured fifty-eight out of one hundred Irish seats at the elections of 1874, and sixty at the election of 1880.

Under the leadership of Butt the demand for home rule was placed before parliament in the ordinary way. Nothing came of it. In 1879 the death of Butt transferred the leadership of the party to Charles Stewart Parnell, who had been responsible for much of the policy of the party for the past two years. He was of English descent, the landlord of an Irish estate, a graduate of Cambridge, and a Protestant; but he inherited and nourished a hatred of the English. After his entry into parliament in 1875, he soon rose high in the councils of the Home

Irish home rule

Irish agitation

Rule party; he also came into touch with the Fenians; and in 1879 he became president of the Land League of Ireland, which had just been organized for the purpose of improving the position of the Irish tenants. Parnell was all that Butt was not. "Mr. Butt was genial and expansive; Mr. Parnell was taciturn and reserved. Mr. Butt admitted no force but argument; Mr. Parnell believed in no argument but force."[31] With cold logic devoid of passion Parnell incited his followers to violence, since that was the only method which had yet been used successfully to wring from the leaders of parliament concessions to Irish demands. He proposed to end the parliamentary indifference to Irish questions exemplified in Disraeli's answer to a colleague who sought his advice as to what he should say in answer to an Irish member. "'Speak,' replied Disraeli, 'for fourteen minutes and say nothing.'"[32] Shortly before the close of Disraeli's administration the Irish began to employ obstructionist tactics in parliament and to incite agrarian outrages in Ireland. Parnell advised Irish tenants to offer a fair rent, and, if the landlord refused, to pay none. Whoever took a farm from which a tenant had been evicted was to be sent to Coventry. So thorough was the campaign, that the word "boycott" was added to the language from the name of Colonel Boycott, who was the first to receive such treatment. In the early months of Gladstone's administration the campaign reached huge proportions. In parliament the obstructionist tactics of the Home Rulers were so successful that they forced an extensive revision of parliamentary procedure. In Ireland the agrarian outrages against the landlords jumped from 304 in 1878 to 863 in 1879 and to 2,590 in 1880.

Gladstone met the situation in the customary manner. He passed a coercive act to strengthen the Irish executive, and legislated on the land which appeared to be the immediate cause of disorder. He was not yet converted to home rule. In 1881 he passed a new land act, based on the principle of "the three F's," fixity of tenure, protection against the arbitrary increase of rents (fair rents), and freedom of sale of the tenant's rights. A land commission was appointed, which as a court could fix a judicial rent that could not be changed for fifteen years. During that term the tenant could sell his rights in the land. The act expanded the principle of the act of 1870, recognizing more fully the dual ownership of the landlord and the tenant. The act of 1881 accomplished some good, but it left room for an enormous amount

Gladstone's policies

---

[31] May, *Constitutional History*, ed. Holland, iii, 149.
[32] Churchill, *Churchill*, i, 84.

of friction between landlord and tenant. It failed to satisfy the Land League, and agrarian outrages continued.

The next step was the arrest of Parnell and a stringent application of coercion. In this policy, however, Gladstone weakened. In 1882 he made an agreement with Parnell, promptly dubbed the "Kilmainham treaty" from the name of the jail in which the Irish leader was confined, to release the Irish suspects held in confinement in return for the influence of Parnell and his colleagues against the agrarian outrages. Just after this compromise with the forces of disorder the new Irish secretary and another official, who was his companion, were stabbed to death in Phoenix Park in Dublin. For this act Parnell was not directly responsible. Consequently Gladstone kept his agreement. Parnell was left free, and the land act was amended to meet Parnell's wishes. Simultaneously the coercive power of the Irish executive was increased. The combined policies secured a notable reduction of the disorder in Ireland, but they left the Irish still thoroughly dissatisfied with British rule. The necessity for further legislation was obvious, but the cabinet could reach no decision on what it should be. The dissension contributed to the weakness which caused the cabinet to resign in the summer of 1885.

CHAPTER XXXVIII

THE GROWTH OF IMPERIALISM, 1885-1905

Salisbury

IN 1885 the Conservative took office under new leadership. Disraeli had finished his long career. In 1876 ill health caused him to seek relief from the burden of duties in the house of commons by entering the house of lords as the earl of Beaconsfield, and five years later he died. His successor was the earl of Salisbury. The new leader was a man of resolute character with strong convictions, who was distinguished for his practicality. Though so caustic and rash in debate as to be named "a master of flouts and jeers" and to be accused of "blazing indiscretions," he was in office prudent and cautious. Quick to grasp the import of any business which he had to transact and a hard worker, he made an exceptionally able executive. Aristocratic in his tendencies, he did not attain such popularity as went to Gladstone or Disraeli, but his reputation for sound judgment won respect.

Conservatives and Ireland

In 1885 he was loath to accept office because a decisive election could not be held until the new voters enfranchised by the recent act had been registered, and during the interval he would be without a majority. Gladstone's position was so embarrassing, however, that he agreed not to block the Conservative legislation. Thus Salisbury was able to develop a Conservative policy with regard to Ireland. By the passage of the Ashbourne Act the Conservatives applied to the Irish agrarian problem the principle of creating the single ownership of the tenant. The idea was not wholly new. It originated with John Bright, who secured the insertion in the Disestablishment Act of 1869 of provisions to assist the tenants on the glebe-lands of the church to purchase their tenements. The government would lend them three-quarters of the purchase price on a long term at low interest. Some 6,000 tenants availed themselves of the act. The idea had been extended by the acts of 1870 and 1881 to landlords generally, but the procedure had been made so complicated that only 1,600 tenants had borrowed money for the purpose. The act of 1885 extended this principle so broadly that it had all the effects of a new policy. The full purchase price would be advanced by the government to the landlord and charged to the tenant, who could pay the government in small sums extending over a long series of years. The administration of the act was simple. It became popular immediately. In two years the sum appropriated by the act was exhausted, necessitating a new appropriation. Subsequently the Liberals accepted the policy, and a series of acts kept it in continuous operation. By 1909 nearly one-half the land in Ireland had been transferred to the ownership of the tenants. The difficulty over land, which had been such a constant source of irritation, had been largely removed.

Despite the ultimate success of this policy, it did not satisfy the Irish desire for home rule. The election of 1885 made this the leading issue of British politics. The Liberals returned from the election with more votes than the Conservatives, but the Home Rule party, which increased its membership in the house to eighty-six, held the balance of power. Gladstone, though he had been converted to home rule, kept silent during the election, partly because he did not wish to bid for the Irish votes and partly because he thought that home rule was more likely to succeed if the Conservatives proposed it. In his effort to keep it free from the rancor of party politics, he went so far as to offer to support any adequate measure which the Conservatives might introduce. His plan was defeated by the indiscretion of his son, who allowed his father's change of opinion to become public. Since Gladstone could not deny the fact, he had no choice except to acknowledge it. Early in 1886 Salisbury was defeated by the combined votes of the Liberals and the Irish, and Gladstone returned to office pledged to home rule. His bill provided for an elective Irish parliament of two houses with general power to legislate for Ireland on all subjects not expressly reserved for the imperial parliament. The principal subjects thus reserved were the crown, the army and navy, foreign and colonial affairs, trade and navigation, coinage, weights and measures, copyright, and the endowment or establishment of any religion: a list comparable to the powers conferred upon the federal government by the Constitution of the United States. The executive was to be a viceroy appointed for a term of years and no longer a member of the cabinet. He was apparently intended to hold about the same position as the governor-general of a colony with responsible government. He would be the executive of the acts passed by the imperial parliament, but a cabinet of ministers responsible to the Irish parliament would be the real executive of the Irish parliament. Imperial control was to be maintained by the power of the crown to veto an act of the Irish parliament, and the question whether any act of the Irish parliament was beyond its competence could be tested by judicial appeal to the British privy council.

The chief arguments advanced in favor of home rule were three.

Gladstone and home rule

(1) The Irish, on account of common traditions, race, and religion, constituted for purposes of government a nation. Since they were in a minority in the imperial parliament, without power to influence its decisions on Irish policies, they would always be discontented with the legislation enacted by that body. The separation by water would prevent the destruction of that nationality, and home rule would maintain a sufficient connection to avoid the danger of a separate Ireland on Britain's flank. (2) The British government of Ireland had been a constant and a complete failure. (3) Home rule would relieve the British parliament of the obstruction of the Irish members and of the burden of Irish business, which would be a great advantage in the crowded state of the parliamentary docket. The chief objections brought against the bill were also three. (1) Home rule would endanger the union. An Ireland so far independent would be dangerous to Great Britain in time of war. (2) Ireland was not fitted for self-government. Its people were not sufficiently advanced to govern themselves, as was witnessed by their recent turbulence. (3) It would subject the Protestant minority to the tyranny of the Catholic majority. Protestant Ulster would not be safe from a vengeful Catholic Ireland. "Ulster will fight and Ulster will be right" was the jingle with which the Conservatives caught the popular imagination.

The chief result of Gladstone's effort to enact home rule was a split in the Liberal party. A large group of Liberals, among whom the most prominent was Joseph Chamberlain, refused to support the measure and voted against it. They called themselves Liberal Unionists. For several years they held aloof from both parties, but eventually they were absorbed by the Conservatives. When Gladstone was defeated by the votes of his own party, he held a new election in the summer of 1886. The election confirmed the popular opposition to home rule. Gladstone's third cabinet came to an end when it had been in office only a few months.

Salisbury's second cabinet, 1886–1892

Salisbury's second cabinet lasted for six years. He endeavored unsuccessfully to secure the permanent alliance of the Liberal Unionists by the offer of seats in the cabinet to their leaders. The period was a quiet one, except in Irish affairs. The development of Tory democracy moved forward a pace, and the moderate social and political reforms of the period were numerous and beneficial. In the field of foreign affairs delicate situations developed, but Salisbury, who acted most of the time as his own foreign minister, successfully kept out of war.

In Ireland the guidance of affairs fell to Arthur Balfour, Salisbury's nephew. He ruled with a strong hand. Instead of a temporary coercive act, such as had previously been customary, he secured the passage of Irish policy permanent legislation on the subject. But while he repressed disorder with force, he attempted to remove some of its permanent causes. He secured an extension of the policy of the Ashbourne Act and designed several measures to relieve the poverty which lay at the root of Ireland's discontent. The policy was in large measure successful. By 1892 Ireland was more orderly than it had been for many years.

For the Home Rule party, however, the period was one of stress and strain. In 1887, when Irish affairs were still in a disturbed state, Home Rule party the London Times published several letters, purporting to have been written by Parnell, which condoned the Phoenix Park murders. Parnell asked for the appointment of a parliamentary committee to investigate the authenticity of the letters, claiming that he could not secure an unprejudiced jury in Middlesex. The plea was sufficiently plausible to induce parliament to appoint a special commission of judges. In 1890 this body pronounced the letters forgeries. The incident redounded greatly to the credit of Parnell and the cause of home rule. It was scarcely over when Parnell was named co-respondent in a suit for divorce. His evident guilt cost him his leadership. Gladstone was just planning a fresh campaign in which he had decided to make home rule once more the leading issue. His supporters were ruled too thoroughly by Madam Grundy to allow him to continue to work with Parnell and keep his own following. Under pressure from Gladstone the Irish members, after long wrangles, split in two. Forty-four deserted Parnell, chose another leader, and kept their alliance with Gladstone. In 1891 Parnell died. With his removal the healing of the breach became merely a matter of time. It was accomplished in 1899 by John Redmond, Parnell's successor; but during the interval the movement for home rule was greatly weakened.

The most striking internal reform carried out by the Conservatives was that of local government. In 1888 the County Councils Act trans- County Councils Act ferred the administration of the counties from the centrally appointed justices of the peace to locally elected county councils. The justices of the peace retained their judicial functions, but their autocratic control of local administration was supplanted by a democratic régime.

The complications of foreign policy which gave Salisbury the most difficulty were caused by the forward imperial policy of Great Britain. Growth of imperial sentiment The seed of imperialism planted by Disraeli began to take root in the decade of the eighties, despite a temporary setback in the closing years of his administration. In 1887 the queen held a jubilee in celebration of the completion of the fiftieth year of her reign, which was attended by representatives from all parts of the empire. It did much to emphasize the importance of the empire in public thought. In the same year members of the cabinet held a conference with representatives of the self-governing colonies and of some others. The conference had few concrete results, but it helped to strengthen the bond of imperial union.

Salisbury's first action in the imperial field after he became prime minister in 1885 was an attempt to decrease Great Britain's imperial responsibilities. He sent an agent to Turkey to negotiate for the British evacuation of Egypt, and in 1887 a convention was formulated whereby British troops should be withdrawn in three years unless the Egyptian administration should not have been adequately reorganized by that time. This effort to remove the millstone which had weighed so heavily upon Gladstone's cabinet in its recent negotiations with Germany failed, because France and Russia objected to the possibility of British occupation beyond three years and persuaded Turkey not to ratify the convention. Not long afterward the appearance of French designs upon the Sudan convinced Salisbury not only that Egypt ought to be retained but also that the Sudan ought to be occupied.

This attempt to stay the march of British imperialism was not typical of Salisbury's general attitude. While his first cabinet was still in office, Upper Burma was added to the empire. The reason for the expansion was the rivalry of the French. They had been established for a long time in Cochin-China and other provinces on the eastern side of the Indo-China peninsula, and they were beginning to compete successfully with the British for concessions from the king of Burma. Protestations of the British government to the French government went unheeded, and in 1885 a British army conquered the country. The king was deposed, and Upper Burma was annexed to India.

The colonial rivalries which gave Salisbury the most trouble were in Africa. While Gladstone's cabinet of 1886 was still in power, a new method of advancing British imperialism in Africa was adopted. The private trading company which operated in the Niger region was made officially a representative of the British government by giving it a royal charter. The company was empowered to govern the districts claimed by Great Britain and to acquire treaty rights from the natives which would add to them. The policy had the advantage that it relieved the government of the heavy expense of providing the administration of the territory. Salisbury's cabinet followed this precedent. In 1888 the private company in East Africa was chartered as the Imperial East Africa Company, and in the next year

Imperial policies: Egypt

Upper Burma

Africa

a charter was given to the British South African Company, which was organized by Cecil Rhodes to occupy the huge territory later known as Rhodesia. All of the companies were successful in the work of imperial expansion, but their government of the natives eventually raised problems which forced the British government to take over the territories acquired by them. The most pressing problems created by them for Salisbury's solution were, however, the clashes with the African agents of other European powers who were also players in the game of expansion. Salisbury's chief work as foreign minister was to negotiate treaties which established recognized boundaries of the territories claimed by the several powers and so brought an end to some of the rivalries which had attained dangerous proportions in several regions. Portugal, which contested the occupation of Rhodesia in the hinterland of Portuguese East Africa, was forced to forego its claims by the use of the strong hand. In 1890 Salisbury demanded the withdrawal of Portuguese troops from the territories claimed by Great Britain. Portugal was obdurate, but the issue of an ultimatum caused it to give way. In the same year a treaty with France secured recognition of British claims in the interior of the Niger region and a protectorate over Zanzibar, in return for acknowledgment of a French sphere of influence in Northwest Africa and a protectorate over Madagascar. An agreement concluded with Germany in 1890 delimited favorably to Great Britain the German protectorates in East and Southwest Africa, recognized the British control of Zanzibar, which was the coastal outlet for the trade of German East Africa, and acknowledged the British right to Uganda, although a German expedition had recently established a claim to the region and defeated a British project to acquire it. In return for all this, Great Britain ceded to Germany the little island of Heligoland in the North Sea. The territories involved were so absurdly disproportionate that Salisbury was said to have acquired a suit of clothes in exchange for a trouser button; but Heligoland was of strategic importance to Germany in relation to the Kiel canal which was then being built, and it became of still greater significance when Germany began to build a navy.

When Salisbury took office in 1885, he was so profoundly impressed by the isolation of Great Britain that he asked for and received informal assurance of Bismarck's friendship, particularly in disputes with France. He spoke of his policy as keeping in step with Germany, and the treaty of 1890 was one of its fruits. Another was a secret agreement made with Italy in 1887 and later extended to include Austria. The general purpose was to protect each of the powers against encroach-

Other foreign relations

ment by another power upon its rights and interests in the Mediterranean. It was aimed, on the one hand, against possible French attack
upon the English in Egypt or the Italians in Italy or northern Africa,
and, on the other, against Russian aggression in the eastern end of
the Mediterranean, which Austria and England wished to prevent.
Germany was not a party to the alliance, but it was to her advantage,
because both Russia and France were in an aggressive mood at the
time, and if either attacked Germany or her allies, it would be helpful
to have England committed against the two powers in the Mediterranean. Bismarck's intervention in the negotiations with a threat
to withdraw German support in Egypt, if Great Britain continued
to remain isolated, undoubtedly influenced Salisbury's decision. The
treaty did not definitely commit Great Britain to war in behalf of her
allies, but it was a dangerous entanglement, and Rosebery, when he
became foreign minister in 1892, allowed the agreement to lapse. Thus
Salisbury kept in step with Germany chiefly to protect the British
position in Egypt against the French, but in 1889, when Bismarck
suggested a public alliance between Great Britain and Germany, he
declined. His nominal reason was that the government was too dependent upon the uncertainty of a parliamentary majority to contract
such an alliance, but his real reason seems to have been that the
dangers of a definite commitment to a continental power outweighed
the advantages of protection against France.

In 1892, when parliament had nearly run its legal life, Salisbury
dissolved. The election left the Conservatives in a minority against
the combined Liberals and Irish Nationalists (Home Rulers). Salisbury
was immediately defeated by their united votes and resigned. Gladstone then formed his fourth cabinet. It labored under several disadvantages. Even with the support of the Irish its majority was only
forty. To form a cabinet, Gladstone had to give office to men who
differed widely from him on some questions. Lord Rosebery, for example, supported imperialism as ardently as the Conservatives. But
the greatest burden of the cabinet was the Newcastle program. The
Liberal Caucus, unlike other British party organizations, professed to
express the popular desires of the Liberal party on questions of policy
as well as to help win elections. Before 1886 this had caused no great
difficulty. The split on home rule, however, caused Joseph Chamberlain, who had created and managed the Caucus, to leave the party.
Thereafter Gladstone thought it wise to court the Caucus more or
less. In 1892 consequently he felt bound to carry out the reforms
which the Caucus in its platform had demanded. These reforms were

**Glad-
stone's
fourth
cabinet,
1892–1894**

legion. With the happy irresponsibility of a party out of power the Caucus proposed and adopted new planks of reform at each annual meeting. In 1891 at Newcastle they were all incorporated in a single platform, called the Newcastle program. It was a program which might well have occupied a cabinet with a dependable majority for a decade. With a small majority it made progress impossible, for not only was there conflict of interests as to what reforms should be taken first, but also there were groups in the party opposed to many of the projected reforms. Behind the difficulty over the Newcastle program and explaining its adoption was a significant change in the composition of the Liberal party. A large group of the more conservative members of the party had joined the Liberal Unionists in 1886, and they had carried with them a large section of the voters belonging to the upper class and the upper section of the middle class. Along with them had gone Chamberlain, the most influential radical leader, whose support of the Conservative party and ultimate union with it gave a new impetus to Tory democracy. But the desertion of the conservative element rendered the Liberal party more dependent upon the radical voters who did not follow Chamberlain, and they were largely laborers and members of the lower section of the middle class.

Gladstone insisted on home rule as the first venture. The second bill was similar in outline to the first, the most important difference being the retention of eighty Irish members in the imperial parliament. This bill passed the house of commons, but was rejected by the house of lords. Gladstone chose to ignore the defeat, and proceeded with other legislation. The only important measure which he pushed through parliament was the Parish Councils Act of 1894, providing for self-government in the smallest areas of local government. Immediately afterward he resigned. His eighty-five years, of which he had served the last sixty-two in parliament, were weighing upon him. Both his vision and his hearing were defective. But old age was not the sole cause of his resignation. He could not control his colleagues. The leaders of the party who believed in expansion insisted on large naval estimates, and Gladstone would not countenance a militaristic policy.

Legislative program

With the retirement of the Grand Old Man, the queen had the exceptional opportunity to make a real choice of the prime minister. Gladstone had dominated the party for so long that it was not clear which of the younger leaders was foremost in the councils of the party. She selected Lord Rosebery, who headed the group of im-

Lord Rosebery, 1894–1895

perialistic Liberals. He led a troubled existence for a few months, borne down by the weight of the Newcastle program. In 1895 he took the occasion of an unimportant adverse vote in the house of commons to resign from a position which the differences within the party had rendered embarrassing.

Imperial policies

The three years while the Liberals were in power witnessed no decline in Great Britain's imperial aggressiveness. Lord Rosebery, who was foreign secretary in Gladstone's cabinet and exerted a large degree of control over foreign affairs in his own cabinet, seemed, indeed, to carry an imperial chip on his shoulder. In 1893 he insisted that Uganda, which controlled the headwaters of the Nile, should not be evacuated. To the majority of his colleagues, who looked forward to the abandonment of Egypt, this was rank heresy. "Harcourt stormed, Gladstone expostulated, Morley, and even Asquith were in dismay,"[1] but Rosebery had his way, and a protectorate over Uganda was maintained. During the same year Great Britain came close to the verge of war with France over Siam. This kingdom was a buffer state between the British and French possessions in Indo-China, and both powers were playing the game of extending their influence there. On June 30 news came that two British gunboats stationed at Bangkok to protect British residents and property during a French blockade of Siam had been ordered to leave. Rosebery telegraphed them to remain, and inquired of Germany and Italy what their attitude would be in the event of war between Great Britain and France. The danger was avoided when it was learned that the officer in charge of the gunboats had misunderstood the French admiral. Tension with France, however, continued to be the Liberal order of the day. Early in 1895, when rumors were heard that the French had designs upon the Sudan, Sir Edward Grey, under-secretary for foreign affairs, declared in a parliamentary speech that the whole valley of the Nile was a British sphere of influence, and gave warning that a French advance into that region would be "an unfriendly act."

Salisbury's third cabinet, 1895–1902

After Rosebery's resignation, Lord Salisbury formed his third cabinet. This time the Liberal Unionists joined forces with the Conservatives. Among their leaders who accepted office, Joseph Chamberlain was the most notable. An election yielded the Conservatives a substantial majority. The majority of the voters did not favor home rule, and it was recognized that the aggressive imperial policy of the recent cabinet did not represent the ideas of the majority of the Lib-

---

[1] Spender, *Great Britain,* p. 62.

eral party. The remarkable growth of imperial sentiment helped the conservatives to win the election.

The cabinet intended to undertake extensive legislation upon internal affairs under the guidance of Chamberlain, who had long been an ardent advocate of social reforms. Chamberlain, however, was appointed to the colonial office, where he soon became engrossed with pressing imperial concerns, and the only important reform accomplished was the Workmen's Compensation Act of 1897. For a long time after machinery became common, the only recourse of a laborer injured in the course of his employment was to sue his employer for damages. As the courts interpreted the common law on the subject, damages were rarely obtainable. In the case of Priestly versus Fowler, decided in 1837, the court declared that damages were not due from the employer when the injury was due to the carelessness of a fellow employee. Since the foreman was a fellow employee, it was rarely possible to hold the employer himself legally liable. In 1880 this doctrine of common employment was in large part abolished by statute. The act failed to give the workman adequate remedy because he could rarely afford the costs of a suit. Less than seven per cent of those injured or killed obtained compensation. The legislation of 1897 made employers in most industries liable for compensation to injured workmen according to rates fixed by the act, unless the employer could prove the injury due to the "serious and wilful misconduct of the injured." The burden of proof was thrown on the employer, and injured employees received compensation automatically except in the rare cases when the employer could prove "serious and wilful misconduct" to the satisfaction of a court.

Though this was the only important piece of social reform enacted by the Conservatives under Salisbury, in 1901 they made a new codification of the factory laws which had been expanded enormously by legislation since Disraeli's Factory Act of 1878. The minuteness of detail with which the code regulated labor was remarkable. A child could be employed in a factory or workshop only when he had reached the age of twelve and had presented a certificate of physical fitness from a physician and a record of a minimum of work in school passed with a certain standard. He must, moreover, continue to attend school for half his time. Young persons between the ages of fourteen and eighteen and women could work no more than fifty-five and one-half to sixty hours a week, between certain hours on each day, and with certain minimum hours for meals. The sanitary regulations alone became a whole code, providing for cleanliness and proper

Employers' liability and workmen's compensation

Regulation of hours and conditions of labor

ventilation. The provisions for the proper fencing and protection of dangerous machinery were also numerous. The system of regulation had been extended in some measure also to protect the clerks in shops and stores, the miners, the railway employees, and the children working in the streets outside of school hours—such, for example, as newsboys. Nearly every field of labor was more or less regulated with regard to the hours and conditions of work.

The **empire**

The very auspices under which the Conservatives won the election caused the cabinet to emphasize the empire. Salisbury, though he was strenuous and sincere in his efforts to avoid complications with foreign powers, favored imperial expansion, and Chamberlain was fertile with plans to promote the unity of the empire. In 1897 the Diamond Jubilee of the queen gave occasion for an enthusiastic parade of imperial sentiment and for the second of those imperial conferences which have now become a permanent and influential part of the imperial organization. Suggestions of a federated empire with an imperial parliament representing the self-governing dominions as well as Great Britain went beyond practical possibilities, but the discussion of imperial defense and imperial trade was fruitful. Canada granted preferential customs duties to British imports, and it was agreed that efforts should be made to extend the policy to other dominions. Two years later the extent of the voluntary aid given to Great Britain by the self-governing colonies in a war waged to promote imperial designs gave eloquent testimony to the strength which the imperial bond had assumed without the aid of a formal constitution.

Australian federation

In 1900 a federal government for Australia was authorized. The act was passed by the British parliament in response to a demand from the Australians, just as the legislation for the federation of Canada had been enacted earlier upon the initiative of the Canadians. The two movements for federation, however, were not parallel, since federation resulted in decentralization in Canada and in centralization in Australia. After convicts began to be sent to Australia, free Englishmen soon began to go voluntarily, and the migration of free settlers was greatly stimulated by Gibbon Wakefield after 1830. The free colonists eventually outnumbered the convicts, and their complaints caused the home government to cease using Australia for penal settlements after the middle years of the century. In 1850 several of the separate colonies which had been formed were given a large degree of self-government in accordance with the spirit of Lord Durham's report, and later the right was extended to the remaining colonies. As the colonies grew in the second half of the century, they began to feel the need of cooperation in many of the problems which were common to them all. They wanted to end the restrictions imposed upon trade by the separate tariffs of each colony, they were fearful of the expansion of European powers and of the United States in the Pacific, and they desired a common policy to prevent Asiatic immigration and keep Australia a white man's country. At the same time, they hesitated to surrender their independence, and it required a long period of agitation in the closing years of the century before they agreed upon the form of common government which received the sanction of the British parliament in 1900. The new federation was called the commonwealth of Australia. Like Canada it retained the cabinet type of government in both the central and the state governments, but its federalism was patterned more closely upon that of the United States. The separate states retained all the powers which were not attributed specifically to the federal government.

In several instances Great Britain's imperial interests produced difficult relations with foreign powers. The new prime minister had been in office only a few months when the United States threatened war. Salisbury had declined a request of the United States to arbitrate a dispute over the boundary between Venezuela and British Guiana. President Cleveland thereupon declared the refusal of arbitration a violation of the Monroe Doctrine and asked congress for power to appoint a boundary commission and to impose its decision on Great Britain "by all the resources of the United States." The martial spirit ran high in the United States, but Salisbury kept his head. He laid the British case before the American boundary commission and finally consented to submit to arbitration. The decision of the tribunal was almost entirely favorable to the claims of Great Britain. The final outcome was a more friendly feeling between the United States and Great Britain. The people of the United States learned that Great Britain was more "anxious to avoid offense" than in the days of the civil war, and both peoples came to realize that they did not want a war with each other.[2] The arbitration served to lift the disfavor with which the British public had viewed that mode of settlement since the arbitration of the *Alabama* claims. The initiation of an era of good feeling was completed by the attitude of the British when the United States went to war with Spain in 1898. The continental peoples generally favored Spain, but the British sympathy was given to the cause of the United States. The rising generation on both sides

Relations with the United States

---
[2] Trevelyan, *British History in the Nineteenth Century*, p. 419.

of the Atlantic began to dwell more upon the common heritage of speech, traditions, and ideals and less upon the outworn hatreds based on events long since past.

Fashoda

Imperial expansion soon produced other crises. As the British possessions in Africa grew, the value of the basin of the upper Nile as a link between the holdings in the north, the center, and the south became more apparent, and the Rhodesian vision of a "Cape to Cairo" railway became more attractive. The rumors of French designs on the Sudan led the government to reverse Gladstone's decision. In 1896 Kitchener, in command of an Egyptian army led by British officers, was despatched by the Anglo-Egyptian government to conquer the Sudan. The expedition was successful, finishing a thorough conquest with a decisive victory over the natives in 1898. A few days later Kitchener learned that a French officer with a small detail of troops had marched across from the west and raised the French flag over Fashoda, higher up the Nile. A sharp diplomatic crisis ensued. Kitchener claimed the place for the British. The French commander refused to retire without orders from the French government. Salisbury presented a demand for withdrawal to the French foreign office. When compliance was delayed, war became imminent. After several weeks the French government gave way, surrendering any claim to the Sudan. A joint Egyptian and British rule was established. The route from Egypt to British East Africa was secured, but British relations with France were badly strained.

The Far East

During the closing years of the century Great Britain's position in the Far East was threatened. Great Britain had exercised a predominant influence in that part of the world ever since the second Chinese war had forced China to open her doors partially to foreign commerce. A war between Japan and China, fought in 1894 and 1895 for possession of Korea, began a scramble of the western powers for possession of parts of China, which changed the Far Eastern situation entirely. Japan's decisive victory first made the European powers aware of the rise of a new power in the east. Japan secured Port Arthur and other territorial concessions which were inimical to the Russian advance across northern Asia. Russia, with the help of Germany and France, forced Japan to restore her conquests on the mainland. Great Britain refused to be a party to the transaction, and thus won a friendship which later proved of great worth for the maintenance of British interests in the Far East. Two years later the murder of two German missionaries gave the opportunity for Germany to execute a seizure which had been planned two years earlier. In 1898 China leased the port of Kiaochow in the Shantung peninsula to Germany. In the same year Russia arbitrarily seized Port Arthur, which she had forced Japan to return under the plea of maintaining the integrity of China. Since the British interest in China was commercial and not territorial, the British government opposed diplomatically the partition of China. When diplomacy failed, however, Salisbury made haste to secure the lease of Wai-hei-wai, a port so placed as to give Great Britain strategic equality with Russia and Germany in relation to Peking. Salisbury followed this with treaties defining spheres of interest and protecting the Chinese provinces of greater interest to Great Britain from alienation to foreign powers.

Meanwhile Great Britain had been drifting into war in southern Africa. The rapid expansion of British power in that quarter had aroused the apprehensions of the Boers in the Transvaal for the partial independence guaranteed to them by the treaties of 1881 and 1884.[3] The situation was further complicated by the discovery of rich gold fields in the Transvaal in 1885. So many foreigners rushed into the gold fields that the Dutch population became fearful of their domination of the government. The Boers excluded the foreigners from the franchise, made it difficult for them to acquire citizenship, taxed them heavily, and placed other disadvantages upon them. The foreigners protested, and those who were British sought the aid of the British government. In Cecil Rhodes, who was premier of Cape Colony and the managing director of the British South African Company which controlled Rhodesia, they found a sympathetic listener. It had long been his ambition to consolidate the South African territories. The existing régime in the Transvaal was the chief obstacle to its accomplishment. Eventually he agreed with a group of the foreigners resident in the Transvaal to promote a revolution against the government of the Boers, in order to bring the Transvaal under British rule. He stationed Dr. Jameson with a troop of the British South African Company's forces so that he could assist the foreigners when they should summon him to their aid. The foreigners quarreled among themselves and failed to rise, whereupon Jameson invaded the Transvaal in 1895 without awaiting their summons. Unaided, his position was hopeless. He was easily defeated and captured by the Boers. The British government investigated the circumstances and punished the leaders of Jameson's raid with imprisonment. Their sentences were light, however, and Rhodes, though he resigned his posi-

Background of the Boer War

---

[3] Above, p. 710.

tion in Cape Colony, was never punished for his share in the plot. The report of a parliamentary committee censured him and exonerated the colonial office of knowledge of the impending raid; but incomplete evidence seems to indicate that Chamberlain, the colonial secretary, was not unaware of the intended use of Jameson's troops, though not of the use which actually was made of them.[4] The Boers, believing that the British government was cognizant of the conspiracy, treated foreigners more harshly than ever. They also began quietly to prepare for war with Great Britain. Attempts of the British government to obtain better conditions for the British in the Transvaal failed. In 1899 the failure of a series of conferences increased the tension. Finally the British government intimated that it would dictate the terms of settlement, whereupon the Boer government issued an ultimatum, and upon its rejection invaded Natal and Cape Colony. The Boers of the Transvaal were joined by those of Orange Free State.

The war

In the early days the war went entirely in favor of the Boers. Though they were lacking in military discipline, they were trained fighters and they were well equipped. The British, who had underestimated their foe, had adopted roughshod diplomatic methods without adequate military preparations. In the northern triangle of Natal, exposed to attack on both sides, a British army was defeated and finally shut up in Ladysmith. Several attempts at relief failed. The larger part of the remaining British forces were besieged at Kimberley and Mafeking on the other side of Orange Free State. The news of these disasters stiffened the attitude of the cabinet and roused imperial sentiment throughout the empire. Lord Roberts was sent as commander-in-chief with Lord Kitchener as his chief of staff. Within a year they had at their command an army larger than the whole population of the Boer republics, and the largest British army which had ever been assembled. It was composed not only of regulars but also of many volunteers, and it included contingents contributed voluntarily by Canada, Australia, and New Zealand. Early in 1900, under the direction of the new commander, Kimberley was relieved, the Boer states invaded, the armies of defense defeated, and the capitals of both states occupied. Ladysmith meanwhile had been relieved. Before the end of 1900 the power of the Boers appeared to be completely broken. Orange Free State and the Transvaal were both declared annexed to Great Britain. Appearances were deceitful. The Boers continued a guerilla warfare which was extremely difficult to combat.

---

[4] Spender, *Great Britain*, pp. 91-99; Ensor, *England*, pp. 233-236; Garvin, *Chamberlain*, iii, chs. xlix-li.

Kitchener, now left in command, gradually occupied the country, building blockhouses as he advanced, and guarding his communications with long lines of troops. Because the Boers fought out of uniform, he found it necessary to destroy farms and bring the families of the farmers, who were his opponents, into concentration camps, where mortality of the children was heavy. Eventually these stringent measures wore down the resistance and peace was made in 1902. Great Britain added the two Boer states to the empire, but gave their new subjects generous terms. The Boers received a large sum of money to rebuild and stock their farms, were permitted to keep Dutch beside English in schools and courts, and were promised self-government in the near future.

During the war strong manifestations of anti-British sentiment in several continental countries confirmed some of the leaders of both parties in the belief, which they had begun to entertain shortly before the war, that Great Britain could no longer afford to maintain the traditional policy of "splendid isolation." All of the great continental powers were divided into two alliances. The Triple Alliance, which was formed in 1882, included Germany, Austria and Italy. Bismarck's primary purpose in entering the alliance was to strengthen Germany against the possible attempt of France to seek revenge for the humiliation of 1871. Germany also had an eastern frontier to defend, and Bismarck protected this by an alliance of the three emperors of Germany, Russia and Austria. In 1887, when the tsar allowed this treaty to lapse because Russian and Austrian interests conflicted in the Balkans, Bismarck succeeded in establishing a dual alliance between Germany and Russia to last for three years. In 1890, shortly before the expiration of the treaty, the new emperor, William II, dismissed Bismarck and announced that German foreign policy would steer a new course. One of the first landmarks of the new course was the failure of Germany to renew the treaty with Russia. The consequence was that Russia and France, moved by apprehension of danger from Germany and the Triple Alliance, formed in 1891 an entente which ripened into the binding Dual Alliance in 1894. The existence of these two alliances soon began to affect the attitude taken by the several European governments on foreign and imperial policies, and British statesmen discovered after 1894 that the policy of isolation had disadvantages when the other European powers were divided definitely into two camps. The main advantage of isolation had been the avoidance of commitments which might have landed Great Britain in war: but when British ministers found that under the new circum-

Marginal notes:

Causes of change of opinion on isolation: Triple and Dual alliances

Relations with France

Relations with Germany

stances they could rarely obtain the friendly cooperation of any European power on the foreign and imperial questions of interest to them, they began to wonder if an alliance was still too high a price to pay for a steady friendship. They also began to feel more keenly the danger of an attack upon the empire by a combination of powers. The intense imperial and commercial rivalries which had developed since 1880 contained ominous possibilities of the outbreak of war, and the huge but scattered British Empire presented many fronts which appeared easy of attack and difficult of defense.

Relations with France and Russia

The experiences which brought home to British statesmen the need of friendship abroad were in the field of imperial affairs. Friction with France continued until it culminated in the Fashoda incident of 1898. Relations with Russia concerning the Near East were not as strained as they had sometimes been in the past. Salisbury eventually reached the opinion that Great Britain in her support of Turkey "had backed the wrong horse," but Great Britain and Russia still remained at odds over various aspects of the question. The old rivalry continued in the Middle East, where Russian commercial and financial influence was expanding in Persia; and a new rivalry developed in the Far East, where the Russian advance, which menaced the British commercial interests in China, reached a climax with the seizure of Port Arthur in 1898.

Relations with Germany

The final determining factor was a change in the relations with Germany. While Bismarck remained in office, the relations between Great Britain and Germany on imperial problems were generally friendly, except in 1884 and 1885, when Germany acted with France against Great Britain. After Bismarck was dropped in 1890, it became impossible to keep step with Germany. In Egypt Germany continued to support the British position usually, but elsewhere she began to obstruct British claims and to press her own with vigor. Disputes over boundaries in West Africa, the British rights in Zanzibar, German fears that Great Britain might acquire parts of the Portuguese colonies in Africa, German claims in Samoa and other issues became the sources of much petty friction between the two foreign offices. The German foreign office became suspicious of all British designs, and the old complaint was raised that the British "always grudged everything to Germany and treated her as if she were of no account."[5] It fell into the habit of badgering the British foreign office in order to obtain concessions. Just German demands were sometimes made in

---

[5] *British Documents on the Origins of the War*, i, 325.

a provocative manner. It was, perhaps, the form as much as the content of German diplomacy that irritated the British. The German foreign office also began to work upon the theory that, since diplomacy on African questions was conditioned by the existence of three interested powers, Germany, France and Great Britain, Germany should be free to combine with France or Great Britain against the other as the advancement of her own interests might demand at any juncture. The effectiveness of this policy was illustrated in 1894, when Rosebery arranged a treaty with Congo State which ceded to Great Britain, among other things, the lease of a narrow strip of land adjacent to German East Africa. It established a connection between Rhodesia and British East Africa, and was necessary if a Cape to Cairo railway should ever be built. France opposed the lease and Germany joined with her in bringing such diplomatic pressure to bear upon King Leopold of Belgium that the British government finally allowed the concession to be withdrawn. When Salisbury came to office in 1895, the momentary hope that relations with Germany might be improved was shattered by an interview which he had with William II at Cowes later in the year. The details of the conversation are unknown, but the Near East was the subject, and Salisbury had previously hinted to the German ambassador that the time had come to divide Turkey among the powers of Europe. The result of the interview was to alienate the emperor and Salisbury personally, and the effect of Salisbury's suggestion concerning Turkey was to raise suspicion in the German foreign office that Salisbury was attempting to embroil Germany in war. The climax of this friction was reached in 1896, when William II sent to the president of the Transvaal, on the occasion of the Jameson raid, a telegram congratulating him "that without appealing to the help of friendly powers" he had repelled the armed bands invading his country and had maintained the independence of his country "against foreign aggression."[6] It was at best a gratuitous insult to Great Britain, and at worst a threat of war. Eventually the significance of the telegram was belittled, and relations between the foreign offices settled back to normal, though British public opinion remained incensed for a long time.

The experience which finally determined the cabinet to seek the friendship of one of the continental powers was the Russian advance into China. Early in 1898 Salisbury proposed to the Russian government that the two powers should come to an understanding with re-

---

[6] Cited by Low and Sanders, p. 436.

gard to their respective policies in China and Turkey. The suggestion was not well received, and Russia subsequently occupied Port Arthur. It was then decided to approach Germany. Salisbury was not yet convinced that the abandonment of isolation was wise, but there can be little doubt that Chamberlain had the sanction of the cabinet for entering into discussions with the German ambassador for the purpose of establishing a closer connection with Germany. What he proposed was a defensive alliance "based upon a mutual understanding as to policy in China and elsewhere."[7] The German government declined the offer. It felt doubtful about the possibility of ratification of such a treaty by parliament in the existing hostile state of British public opinion. It also regarded the risk as greater than the gain. What Great Britain obviously wanted was help against Russia. If the alliance should result in war, Germany would have to take the brunt of the Russian attack, and all she would receive in return would be concessions in China and Africa. It seemed impossible, moreover, that Great Britain could attain a friendly understanding with either Russia or France, and Germany seemed to be in a strategic position to obtain what she wanted from Great Britain by opportune threats of support of France or Russia without undertaking the responsibility of an alliance with Great Britain. The door to future consideration was left open, however, by the statement that the German government regarded the plan as premature. The British tried again in 1899, when the emperor accompanied by Chancellor Bülow visited England and gave Chamberlain the opportunity to renew his proposal; but the idea of a German alliance thrown out by Chamberlain in a public speech was received without favor in England and with opposition in Germany, where public feeling was strongly against the British on account of the Boer war. The question was opened for its final discussion in 1901 by the initiative of Eckardstein, the first secretary of the German embassy, who was acting during the illness of the ambassador. He spoke to Lord Lansdowne, the British foreign minister, but since he was violating the instructions of his government in opening a discussion of the question, he represented to his foreign office that Lansdowne had begun the conversations. He also deceived each government concerning the views of the other. The German government wanted Great Britain to join the Triple Alliance, but the British government did not discover this condition, which it was not prepared to accept, until Salisbury had an interview with the

---

[7] Langer, *Diplomacy of Imperialism*, ii, 495.

German ambassador, after the one returned from a vacation and the other returned from a long illness. The result of this final discussion of an alliance was to leave "both sides distrustful and suspicious. The Berlin government believed that the British had made the first overtures and had then dropped them unceremoniously. . . . In London, on the other hand, it was thought that the Germans wanted the alliance and had offered it, only to follow up the offer with what seemed like impossible conditions."[8]

Meanwhile the British public was beginning to feel resentment against Germany not unmixed with apprehension. The negotiations for an alliance had been secret, but the telegram of 1896 and the repeated anti-British demonstrations made by the German press, the German people, and German statesmen gradually stirred British indignation. So far did this go, that the cooperation of Great Britain and Germany in 1902 and 1903 to force Venezuela to acknowledge claims for damages done to their nationals was distinctly unpopular with a considerable section of British opinion. The display of this opinion was so notable, indeed, that it had some influence on the decision of the cabinet to decline an invitation extended by Germany in 1903 to join with Germany and France in the construction of the Bagdad railway. Germany for some years had been becoming the chief commercial competitor of Great Britain. Colonial rivalries with Germany had given British statesmen less trouble than those with France and Russia; but under the guidance of William II and his advisers Germany sought her "place in the sun" with a display of aggressiveness that aroused some popular apprehension of German designs against the British empire. This was accentuated by the immense naval building program adopted by Germany in 1898 and 1900. Great Britain had long followed the standard of a fleet as powerful as any two in Europe. The Germans evidently intended to end that supremacy. The British public was not excited about the situation, but it gradually began to think of the possibility of German aggression.

Growth of coolness between Germany and Great Britain

The failure of negotiations with Germany merely emphasized the need to find friends elsewhere, and the opportunity was at hand. Japan had already begun conversations looking toward an alliance between the two countries to protect their respective interests in the Far East. What Japan wanted was to keep Russia out of Korea. It was ready to meet any Russian advance in that direction with war, but it needed an ally in case the Dual Alliance was a bond strong

Alliance with Japan

---

[8] *Ibid.*, ii, 742.

enough to bring France to Russia's help in the event of a Russo-Japanese war. Great Britain had first suggested a German alliance chiefly to secure help against further Russian aggression against China, and though the Russian position in China had now been reasonably well defined, Japan would be a friend in case of need. Perhaps the main incentive to the British cabinet was the knowledge that Japan was negotiating concurrently with Russia for an agreement on their respective spheres of influence, and the consequent fear that an alliance between the two powers which would render Great Britain's position in the Far East hopeless might be formed. The negotiations between Japan and Great Britain were carried to a successful conclusion early in 1902 by the formation of a defensive alliance. It was agreed that if the interests of the contracting parties in China and Korea caused one of them to be attacked by another power, the other contracting party should remain neutral; if one contracting party was attacked by two powers, the other contracting party would come to the aid of the attacked party. Thus the British took the first step away from isolation.

Death of
the queen

Before the close of the Boer War, the death of Queen Victoria in 1901 ended the longest reign in English history. During her reign the constitutional power of the monarch had probably declined, but her personal influence had apparently grown stronger and the monarchical form of government had been strengthened in popular affection. In the closing years of her reign particularly the crown was becoming the symbol of the new empire in which she had taken an unaffected though seemly pride. In her old age she was dictatorial and often dour and grim; but her fundamental kindliness, her sincere sympathies with the joys and sorrows of her people, her middle-class attitude toward social conventions, her devotion to duty, and the very simplicity of her character endeared her to the rank and file. Her career did much to build up an ideal of monarchy which still lives in British dominions.

Retire-
ment of
Salisbury

Soon after the accession of Edward VII, as soon as the Boer War was finished, Lord Salisbury, who was in failing health, retired. He died a year later. His resignation of the leadership meant no change of party, for the Conservatives still had a substantial majority obtained by an election held in 1900, when the vote was practically an expression of the popular desire to carry the war to a conclusion. He was succeeded by Arthur Balfour (later Lord Balfour), who for some years had been the leader of the party in the house of commons.

One of the most important accomplishments of this cabinet was

the formation of an entente with France. The treaty with Japan left
Great Britain still desirous of friendship with a European power,
and since advances to Russia and Germany had both failed, France
was the logical candidate. The French people had not forgotten
Fashoda, and their feeling toward England was decidedly cool; but
Edward VII, who liked the French, did much by a visit to Paris in
1903 to end the coolness between the two peoples and to promote a
spirit of good will. Delcassé, who had been French foreign minister
since 1898, had given way on Fashoda in the face of a strong hostile
sentiment in France, and had otherwise displayed a desire for accommodation with Great Britain on colonial questions. He realized
that if France was ever to recover Alsace-Lorraine, it could not have
a hostile England on its hands. Under these circumstances an entente
cordiale was established between Great Britain and France in 1904.
A series of conventions settled the outstanding disputes between the
two countries on imperial questions the world over, extending from
Newfoundland to Siam and from Madagascar to the New Hebrides.
The kernel of the nut was an agreement about Egypt and Morocco.
The French gave the British a free hand in Egypt, and thereby removed the incubus which had long hampered British diplomacy.
They received from the British recognition of their special interest
in Morocco, and secret clauses contemplated the French occupation
of that country and its division between France and Spain. No alliance was made, but the whole purpose of the entente was to end
the danger of war between Great Britain and France and to establish
the basis for friendly cooperation in the mutual advancement of their
imperial interests in the future.

The
entente
cordiale

In the social field Balfour's cabinet secured the enactment of two
significant measures. A change in the system of public education was
forced upon the government by a judicial decision which declared
that essential powers used by the school boards were not conferred
upon them by the act of 1870 or by subsequent legislation. This necessitated a new law, and Balfour took the opportunity to make an extensive educational reform. The act, which was passed in 1902, abolished the school boards and placed the local control of elementary,
secondary and technical schools in the hands of the governments of
the boroughs and counties. The greatest change, however, was to bring
the voluntary schools under the new authorities as far as their educational methods were concerned. The managers of the voluntary
schools had to provide the buildings and maintain them, but the cost
of education was to be paid from the local rates. The act secured a

Internal
reforms

better standard of education in many of the voluntary schools, but it aroused strong animosities on the religious issue. The voluntary schools were left free to give denominational religious instruction, but under the "time-table conscience clause," which made it possible for parents to withdraw their children during the period of instruction. Many non-conformists, however, resented the use of public funds to maintain schools in which the beliefs of the church of England were taught, and some of them went so far by way of protest as to refuse to pay the rates and to endure the term in jail which such refusal entailed.

The Licensing Act of 1904 was designed to promote temperance, a cause which was growing in popular favor. One method of promoting it was to decrease the number of licensed houses permitted to sell liquor, and the local licensing authorities in some areas where there were too many public houses were refusing to renew the expired licenses of some of the houses. To many it seemed unfair to deprive of his business a publican whose premises were properly managed without giving him compensation. Because the law did not permit this to be done, the reform was proceeding slowly. The new legislation authorized compensation to be given, from a tax levied on the liquor trade, to those who lost their licenses not for misconduct but for the advancement of the public interest.

Balfour's resignation

By this time the majority of the Conservatives was beginning to break up. Early in the day criticism of the conduct of the war alienated some support, and dissatisfaction with the meager Conservative program of social reform became more pronounced. When the outlook of the party was thus becoming obscured by light clouds, Chamberlain rolled up a thunderhead. In 1903 he pronounced publicly in favor of an imperial preferential tariff. His thought was to establish a protective tariff which would give colonial products a preference over foreign goods in the British market and to obtain the like treatment of British goods in British colonial markets. This was further than the imperially-minded conservatives could go as a body. The colonial secretary and some of his sympathizers resigned from the cabinet, but the leaven began to work within the party. The division of Conservative opinion grew so rapidly that Balfour withstood the parliamentary attacks of the Liberals only by the most adroit political management. Eventually his cabinet became so weak that it could obtain the enactment of no important legislation. Thereupon it resigned without awaiting a vote of censure.

CHAPTER XXXIX

OTHER PHASES OF ENGLISH LIFE AND THOUGHT IN THE NINETEENTH CENTURY

IMPROVEMENTS in means of transportation during the nineteenth century caused extensive changes in British commercial and industrial organization and affected profoundly the lives of all classes. The beginning of the modern railway is marked by the opening of a line between Liverpool and Manchester in 1830. Before that time rails had long been used by the coal mines, early in the nineteenth century locomotive engines had been invented, and several years before 1830 the locomotives and the rails had been associated, but a successful railway had not been built because it had not been recognized that steam locomation would work well only on a roadbed free from steep gradients. George Stephenson, who discovered this principle, applied it in the construction of the railway from Liverpool to Manchester, and he was also one of the chief designers of a new type of engine which attained a speed of twenty-nine miles an hour. These factors made the railway an immediate success. During the next fifteen years many other short lines were built, and thereafter the consolidation of existing lines went along with new construction. By 1875 the main trunk lines had been established.

Though the steamship was invented early in the nineteenth century, it did not become a practical oceanic carrier of freight until after 1860. The chief difficulty was that the amount of coal which had to be carried did not leave enough room for cargo. This was overcome by several developments. New types of marine engines which consumed less coal were invented. In the fifties came the double expansion engine, in the seventies the triple expansion, and in the nineties the turbine. In the sixties iron began to be used commonly in place of wood for building the hulls of ships. Since the displacement of an iron ship was less, more freight could be taken on board before the load line was reached. In the eighties steel, which was lighter than iron, began to be employed. After 1860 the new ships constructed in Great Britain were chiefly steamships, and they rapidly superseded sailing ships. In 1913 the tonnage of the sailing ships registered in Great Britain was only 850,000, compared with a tonnage of steamships amounting to more than 11,000,000.

Railway

Steam-ships

Late in the century electric tramways began to operate in the towns. They made it possible for many to improve their living conditions by moving into the suburbs. Before the close of the century the internal combustion engine had been utilized to produce automobiles, and in 1897 the Diesel engine, using crude oil for fuel, was invented. Neither of the last two inventions had any effect upon the life of the nineteenth century, but they transformed the life of the twentieth very rapidly. The last horse bus disappeared from the streets of London in 1911. Concurrently with these means of more rapid transport, methods of speedier communication were developed. The first telegraph line was established in England in 1843; the first cable across the Atlantic was laid in 1866; the telephone was invented in 1876; and the sending of messages by wireless was begun in 1896.

Some of the principal results of these speedier means of transportation and communication may be indicated. The increased amount of the communication of the British among themselves and with the other peoples of the world stimulated the interchange of ideas and promoted the rapid development of civilization and culture. The ease of communication rendered possible a centralization of the British government which became notable in the second half of the nineteenth century. It also helped during the later years of the century to create within the empire a much closer bond. The fast and cheap transportation of commodities made available to all classes of the community an increasing variety of material comforts. An illustration is provided by the many new articles of diet which appeared in the market. Perishable goods could be shipped much longer distances, and, with the invention of refrigerator cars and ships, the meat, butter, eggs and fruits of the world made their appearance upon the British dining tables. The railways and the steamships made possible for the first time the transportation of bulky and heavy goods, such as coal, iron and machines, in large quantities over long distances. Buyers in any part of the world could deliver their orders to British firms and obtain delivery of the goods with despatch and regularity. The improved transportation was a factor of primary importance in producing the enormous expansion of British industry and commerce which took place after 1850 and made Great Britain for the next quarter of a century "the workshop of the world." It prepared the way for the creation of the large organizations of business characteristic of modern times. The successful combination, under one management, of many geographically separated units was necessarily dependent upon rapid communication and transportation. The railways themselves created a large demand for iron and steel, and they gave temporary employment while they were being built, and permanent employment after they had been built, to a large number of workers. After steam superseded sails, Great Britain became not only the foremost builder of ships in the world but also the principal carrier of the world's commerce. Not all the results were advantageous to Great Britain in the long run. Before 1870, for example, Great Britain had nearly a monopoly of carrying goods from the north of Europe to the Mediterranean, because they went by sea. After Germany completed her trunk lines of railway, much of this freight was shipped overland. Before the railways were built, iron could be manufactured profitably only where it was found in proximity to coal, unless one product could be brought to the other by water transport without any long haul by land. As long as this situation obtained, Great Britain led the world in the manufacture of iron. After 1870 the development of railways in Germany and the United States made it possible for these countries to become strong competitors of Great Britain in the iron and steel markets of the world. These illustrations, taken from the large number which might be presented, are perhaps sufficient to demonstrate that the changes made in the fields of transportation and communication during the nineteenth century left few aspects of life untouched.

For twenty years after the close of the Napoleonic wars agriculture did not recover from the slump caused by the fall in the price of grain, and in 1846 the repeal of the corn laws gave it another temporary setback. Before that date, however, the extensive application of improved systems of drainage to inferior types of soil was adding to the amount of land which could be cultivated at a profit, and after 1846 progress was made by the invention and general use of new or better types of agricultural tools and machines, and by the development, through chemical experiments, of new fertilizers and of a more scientific knowledge of the most advantageous use of all kinds of fertilizers. At the same time the railways were opening new markets to the farmers. These developments contributed to the production of a period of agricultural prosperity extending from 1853 to 1873, but it was followed by an extremely severe depression which lasted for the remainder of the century. The cause of the depression was American wheat. New railroads which connected the western prairies of the United States with the seaboard made it possible to ship wheat to Great Britain and sell it at a price with which the British growers could not compete. Soon wheat began to come also from Canada and

Agricul-
ture

other countries, and grain was followed by meat from the United States, Australia and Argentina. The larger part of the British people benefited from the cheaper price of food, but the farmers, who were protected from the competition by no tariff, faced ruin. The area planted to wheat contracted, much land was allowed to revert to rough pasture, improvements such as drainage ceased, and the rents of the landlords and the wages of the agricultural laborers declined. Beginning in the nineties, some progress was made in the development of truck, dairy and fruit farms. The government promoted this movement somewhat by giving assistance to those who wished to acquire small holdings,[1] which are better adapted to diversified farming than large farms. In the early years of the twentieth century agricultural conditions improved to some extent, but they still remained far from satisfactory.

Industrial organization

The growth of industry during the nineteenth century was a continuation of the industrial revolution on an intensive scale. New technical processes and new machines continued to be invented and old ones continued to be improved. Factories grew both in number and in size. The scale of capitalization of industrial enterprises increased. A law enacted in 1862 authorized the formation of joint-stock companies in which the liability of the investors was limited. One company could collect the capital of many small investors and increase its business far beyond the scope attainable by an enterprise dependent for its capital upon an individual, a family or a partnership. The change had the unfortunate effect of widening the gulf between labor and capital, because the investors in such a company ordinarily left its management to salaried executives and did not themselves come into personal contact with the employees of the company. As companies increased in capitalization, they expanded their markets, and the competition with other firms became keener. This led in the later years of the century to the formation of trusts and combinations which brought all the enterprises engaged in one line of production within the country or within a given area under common control or into common agreement. They effected economies of production, and they also tended to eliminate competition and produce monopolies. In some fields the combinations became international in scope.

Though these developments indicate that British industry was generally prosperous during the nineteenth century, progress was far from uniform. By 1820 business had recovered from the prostration

---

[1] Below, p. 771.

which followed the Napoleonic wars, but it was not until 1835 that the value of British exports increased notably over the figure to which it had been reduced by 1819. Until 1850, moreover, financial panics and commercial depressions, with their attendant closing of factories, unemployment and distress, occurred frequently. In 1825 and 1826, for several years beginning in 1837, and again in 1847 large numbers of laborers could find no employment, and their sufferings left their memento in the phrase, "the hungry forties." From 1850 to 1873 industry was almost uniformly prosperous, the only notable exception being the cotton industry while it was deprived of raw material by the American civil war. In this period Great Britain was able through her supplies of the basic commodities, coal and iron, her superior industrial organization, and the transformation in the means of transportation to secure the trade of the world. She "was the forge of the world, the world's carrier, the world's ship-builder, the world's banker, the world's workshop."[2] British exports expanded enormously, and employment was plentiful and steady. This golden era was followed by a depression which lasted intermittently until 1886. In those years the depression of agriculture caused a loss of income which seriously curtailed the internal industrial market, and simultaneously Germany and to some extent the United States began to become serious competitors of Great Britain for the markets of the world. After 1886 Great Britain recovered from the slump, though, with the rest of the world, she had to pass through another in 1893 and 1894. In 1900 the exports of Great Britain still exceeded those of any other country in value, but she had ceased to be the workshop of the world after the depression which began in 1873. In 1900 the production of steel in both Germany and the United States far exceeded that in Great Britain, and the British exports of many staple manufactured articles were remaining stationary or declining, while those of Germany and the United States were increasing. Great Britain's exports of coal, machinery and ships were still growing, and she was still the principal carrier of the world's trade, but her supremacy in manufactures was gone, and the leadership in technological inventions, which had so long been hers, had passed to other countries.

The depression which prevailed during the greater part of the period between 1873 and 1886 played an important part in the development of imperialism. It was common to other European countries, and it caused men in Germany and France as well as in Great Britain

Trade and imperialism

[2] Knowles, *Industrial and Commercial Revolutions*, p. 139.

to think of ending what seemed to be an overproduction of commodities by obtaining new markets. When the need was felt, the recent development of transportation seemed to offer the opportunity for its fulfillment. The interiors of backward countries could be opened up by building railways, and steamships had brought the coastal regions of the world nearer in point of time. Africa could be utilized for a market and a source of raw materials to an extent which had never been possible before, and when the need brought realization of the opportunity, the scramble for the continent followed. Great Britain not only took part in the quest for new territories and new commercial and financial concessions in backward countries, but she also sought to make closer her commercial bonds with the existing empire. It was not without significance that the first imperial conference was held in 1887, the year after the depression ended.

Wages

The general trend of wages during the nineteenth century was upward. After the Napoleonic era they dropped below the high level of the war, but remained higher than they had been before the war. From 1820 to 1850 they remained fairly stable, and thereafter they rose fairly steadily except for a lag during the depression from 1873 to 1886. During the whole of the period from 1820 to 1900 the prices of commodities were falling, except during the period of prosperity from 1852 to 1873. The real value of wages increased throughout the period, becoming stationary in the opening years of the twentieth century. This development was not uniform in all industries. During the period from 1820 to 1850 the wages of hand-loom weavers were going down, and during the last quarter of the century the wages of agricultural laborers decreased. In the earlier years depressions caused much unemployment. After the depression which ended in 1886 a group of unemployed appears to have been permanently in existence, the workers in the sweated industries were not earning a living wage, and many laborers had only casual employment. At the end of the century the group of laborers who were in poverty and distress was sufficiently large to have aroused a strong public belief in the need of further reforms, but the working class in large majority was far more prosperous than it had been in the first half of the century.

Living conditions of laborers

The living conditions of the workingmen also improved greatly during the course of the century. Beginning with the Public Health Act of 1848, steadily expanding legislation and growing knowledge of the principles of public sanitation gradually eliminated many of the causes of disease which wrought havoc in the industrial towns and took their toll even in the rural districts during the early years of the century. Proper paving, sewage and water supply, systematic disposal of garbage and refuse, and the removal from congested areas of trades dangerous to the public health were practically universal requirements by the close of the century. The medical profession, at the same time, made vast strides in its knowledge of both the cure and the prevention of disease. The effect of these developments was to lower the death rate to such an extent that the population of Great Britain increased steadily, although the birth rate increased only slightly from 1848 to 1877,[3] and actually decreased thereafter. The average worker was also better housed at the end of the century. His home may not have been beautiful, but it was comfortable. Slums and overcrowded homes still existed in some towns, but several of the larger municipalities had exercised their powers under the housing acts to improve large areas. Workingmen, moreover, generally had more time which could be given to recreation and enjoyment. The daily hours of labor decreased during the century, and during the last three decades of the century the half-holiday on Saturday became common. The opportunities to enjoy this additional leisure also increased. More attention was given to the preservation of parks and open spaces in the towns; and the railways, which began to offer cheap excursions on Sundays late in the century, made possible a day in the country or at the shore. The spread of education, the growth of free libraries, the rise of cheap newspapers, the opening of art galleries and museums to the public on Sundays, and other kindred developments provided the workingmen with advantageous means of spending their hours of leisure, which had been lacking to their predecessors earlier in the century. The standards of living among the working class improved greatly during the course of the century.

Despite the growing wealth of the manufacturers, merchants, bankers, lawyers and followers of other businesses and professions, the social distinction between them and the gentlemen whose incomes came from the land survived into the Victorian period. The country gentlemen were, however, very different in type from their predecessors of the eighteenth century. "In morals and intellect they were not disturbingly above or below the average of their countrymen, who regarded them with some truth, as being in all bodily gifts the finest stock in Europe. By exercise, temperance and plebeian alliance, the spindle-shanked lord of Fielding had become the ancestor of an in-

Social classes

---

[3] The apparent increase may not have been real, but may have been due to better methods of registration of births: Ensor, *England*, p. 103.

vigorated race. They had shed their brutality and extravagance; their eccentricities were of a harmless sporting kind; they were forward in good works; they habitually had family prayers."[4] Though they were more worthy of it, their social dominance continued largely because the other classes acknowledged it. As the period progressed, the members of the upper middle class, who lived in the suburbs of the great towns, developed their own social groups and paid less attention to the social pattern set by the country gentlemen. At the same time the upper social class tended to become less exclusive, as is evidenced by the admission for the first time to some of the London social clubs of distinguished members of the middle class. The social leadership of the gentlefolk was finally undermined seriously by the agricultural depression which, by the curtailment of their rent-rolls, attacked its economic foundation, though even at the close of the century it had by no means disappeared.

Social standards and customs

The social life of both the middle and the upper classes in the Victorian era was characterized by its domesticity. In the towns outside of London one might occasionally enjoy a concert, a theater or a ball, provided his religious scruples did not prohibit the last two; many gave an evening a week to religious meetings and perhaps an evening a month to a literary society. "Seriousness, few amusements, religion and work were the hall-marks of the middle class in the new towns, where all that was not labour was middle class."[5] In London the amusements were more diversified, but even there they were very limited when contrasted with the present. The Victorians preferred to entertain their friends and neighbors in their homes. The homes which were built during the period were generally not attractive on the outside, and they were often filled with heavy furniture and a superabundance of inartistic ornaments on the inside, but they were comfortable and hospitable homes, in which one met refined manners and pleasant social intercourse. The country gentlemen had at their disposal few forms of diversion in the evenings other than the entertainment of guests. Their hospitality was no longer of the boisterous order of the Georgian era, for the squires of this period were cultivated gentlemen whose view of the proprieties of social intercourse did not differ notably from that of the townsmen. Toward the close of Victoria's reign, the view that it was wrong to devote too much time to pleasure began to break down, and in the "gay nineties" more diversions were sought outside the home.

---

[4] *Early Victorian England*, ii, 485.
[5] *Ibid.*, i, 238-243.

Recreations which took the form of healthy exercise out-of-doors were naturally much more plentiful for the country gentlemen than **Sports** for the townsmen. Few members of the middle class could leave their occupations long enough to fish, hunt, shoot or ride with any regularity, had the opportunities to follow these sports been available to them. As early as the middle years of the century, groups of the middle class in the towns began to organize rowing and cricket clubs, but it was not until the last two decades of the century that the participation of suburbanites in games and sports became widespread. The game of lawn tennis was invented in 1874, and it spread rapidly. Golf had been imported from Scotland a little earlier, but it became popular only in the eighties. In the same period the invention of the bicycle made it possible for townsmen who could not keep horses to reach golf and tennis clubs more easily and to make more frequent trips to the country. By the close of the century sports had become a normal part of the social life of the urban middle class.

In order to appreciate fully the outlook of Victorians on society, politics, business or almost any other aspect of life, their strong re- **Religion** ligious convictions must be taken into account. Their beliefs were at bottom evangelical, but they were not confined to low churchmen. They were shared by high churchmen and by non-conformists, and they were common also to all classes of society. There was nearly universal belief in the literal acceptance of the Bible and in a future life of eternal bliss or woe. A man's future reward or punishment was determined in part by his faith, but above all it was determined by his conduct. So nearly universal was this point of view that it imposed upon all alike a code of moral conduct which could be broken only at the risk of strong social disapproval. Duty, self-restraint and self-improvement were regarded as outstanding virtues. Pleasure was not banned, but it was not to be pursued as an end nor should it occupy too large a place in the scheme of life. It was well "to be serious, to redeem the time, to abstain from gambling, to remember the Sabbath day to keep it holy."[6] This religious outlook produced some absurdities. It was so strongly Sabbatarian that "the Victorian nobility would walk rather than drive to church, so as not to infringe the resting of their grooms and horses,"[7] and many a man whose childhood fell under its influence must still be puzzled to understand the principles of right and wrong by which it was determined for him what he might and might not do on Sunday. The danger that

[6] *Ibid.*, ii, 414.
[7] Ensor, *England*, pp. 309, 310.

a picture or a word might produce evil results led to pruderies which it is easy enough to hold up to ridicule. No doubt the outward acceptance of the code by some who dared not reject it led to hypocrisies. Yet a commonly accepted religious belief which inspired men to find pleasure in doing their duty was a force which affected profoundly the thoughts and actions of Victorian men and women.

In the last two decades of the century the universality of this belief began to disappear. As scientific knowledge increased, the educated classes found it more difficult to accept the literal interpretation of every statement in the Bible. The rise of week-end holidays and parties is but one indication that the strict observance of the Sabbath was passing. Many were the signs that a growing group of persons were beginning to give less attention to religion than their parents had done.

Romantic school in literature

In literature the romantic movement was just getting under way when the nineteenth century opened. The romanticists had their harbingers in the eighteenth century, but for the most part literature during that century followed the canons set by the writers who flourished during the reign of Anne. Samuel Johnson, who was the leading light among a large group of literary men in the second half of the eighteenth century, still upheld the orthodoxy established by Addison and Pope. The classics supplied the models for style and ruled largely the content of literature. Reason and common sense were the proper literary guides. Johnson, whose views are preserved in the conversations which Boswell, his friend, incorporated in his biography, was opposed to cant, sentiment, unreality and new literary fashions generally. Yet Oliver Goldsmith, though he was Johnson's friend and a member of the literary club in which Johnson was the dictator, and though he followed the established forms in his writings, displayed sympathies with social movements and philanthropic reforms which were not in the classical tradition. Horace Walpole, who is remembered primarily for his witty letters, had a pronounced interest in the Middle Ages and produced a romance in his *Castle of Otranto* which, with its horrors and improbabilities, had nothing in common with "the cold and well-disciplined merit of Addison" or "the sober and correct march of Pope."[8] An interest in older English and Scottish poetry, ballads and legends produced a crop of poetic compositions which departed far from the ideals of classicism in one direction or another. Some writers were more or less unconscious of their violation of the classical conventions, others broke them intentionally but

---

[8] Walpole, cited by Phelps, *Beginnings of the English Romantic Movement*, p. 107.

apologetically, and only a few were forerunners of romanticism with design and without shame.

During the first quarter of the nineteenth century the prevailing trend was romantic. A large variety of new forms took the place of those favored by the classicists, and the change was made deliberately. In the preface to the *Lyrical Ballads*, which Wordsworth and Coleridge published in 1798, the former announced that the poems were written in the simple language of common men because it was better adapted to poetic diction than the artificial diction of recent writers. The fields in which the romanticists found their subjects were many and varied. The beauties and mysteries of nature, the history of periods other than that of Roman classical antiquity, distant and little-known portions of the world, and man in his natural state as distinguished from man bound by existing social conventions supplied the greater part of the themes which were popular with both writers and readers. Wordsworth exerted the foremost influence in creating a new appreciation of nature which has never since been lost, and Keats found in nature an inspiration which resulted in rich poetry of a very different type from that written by Wordsworth. Coleridge "revived the supernatural as a literary force" and gave new impetus to medievalism and distant lands as sources of romance.[9] Sir Walter Scott popularized historic poems and novels, and Byron, who superseded Scott as the most popular poet of the period, took his readers through many ages and many lands. Shelley combined a love of nature with philosophic speculation.

These and other famous authors of the period not only influenced profoundly the literary development of the nineteenth century, but many of them also affected thought on political and social aspects of life. Wordsworth and Coleridge lost their original sympathies with the French revolution, but both were the advocates of liberty, and Wordsworth did much to promote the spirit of national patriotism which Canning applied to British foreign policy, and which became distinctive of the nineteenth century. Wordsworth and Coleridge both arrived eventually in the Tory camp, and the former opposed the reform bill of 1832. Robert Southey, who was the friend of both, traveled the same road, but he always retained a strong humanitarian spirit. Byron and Shelley were both rebels against society, but the intellectual revolt of the latter was much more complete. Byron's passionate pleas and actions in behalf of the oppressed disseminated a

---

[9] Mair, *Modern English Literature*, p. 224; Osgood. *Voice of England*, p. 406.

liberal sentiment throughout Europe, while Shelley, who had less vogue in his day, has become the accepted poet of socialism.

Literature of the Victorian era

Few of the romanticists survived and continued to write in Victoria's reign, though the romantic influence affected much of the literature produced after 1837. Victorian literature was so diversified in style and content that no single label will cover all of it, or even indicate the main trend. It was written largely to entertain or instruct the new middle class, and it reflected more fully and accurately than in most periods the intellectual and moral outlook of those whom it informed or amused. It is a good mirror. An exceptionally large amount of it also portrayed one aspect or another of the life of the period in which it was written, and some of the imaginative literature advocated social reforms. To the historical student Victorian literature brings abundant fruit.

Poetry

Though poetry no longer towered so far above other forms of literature as it did during the romantic period, it never ceased to hold an important place. Throughout nearly the whole of the reign Tennyson was the most popular poet, because he embodied in his poetry the aspirations of his age. Robert Browning, whom some critics hold to have been the better poet, won recognition much more slowly, because he did not appeal to the prevailing sentiments until he had educated a public to understand him. A comparison of the works of the two poets provides a pleasant road to an appreciation of some of the ideals of the era. Mrs. Browning gave poetic expression, among other things, to humanitarian feelings, and her *Cry of the Children* was influential in behalf of the reform of child labor. Dante Gabriel Rossetti and William Morris, who belonged to a slightly younger generation, turned back to the Middle Ages for inspiration. Their explorations of the period were so much more thorough than those of the romanticists had been that they found a far greater wealth of material. Both were also interested in art. Rossetti was a leader in a school which gave new aims to English artists. Morris turned to the decorative arts and did much to arouse in the public a feeling for more beautiful furniture and fittings in the home. He also gave his pen to the promotion of the new socialistic movement for a period in the eighties. Swinburne, who upheld in his poetry the principle of "art for art's sake," is naturally more noted for his form than for his substance, but his ideas ran counter to currently conventional religious views and were prophetic of the doubts which developed late in the century. Kipling, who began to write his vigorous poems and stories in the eighties, gave voice to the imperial sentiment of the period.

The novel attained a position of such importance in literature as it had never enjoyed before. From 1837 to 1870 Dickens made England laugh and commiserate with him over his intensely human caricatures of a wide variety of human types. His novels struck hard against abuses and preserved for us intimate glimpses of the English life of the period. Thackeray, who was writing at the same time, is the complement of Dickens for the historical student. "Dickens gives us the England of the 'masses' and the *bourgeoisie*, the life of the slum, the inn-parlour, the lodging-house; Thackeray shows us the club, the mansion, the manners and customs of the genteel world, and of the world that would be genteel if it could."[10] The Brontë sisters, Mrs. Gaskell, and Mary Evans, who wrote under the name of George Eliot, won fame contemporaneously with Dickens and Thackeray. The Brontës give less insight into contemporary life and manners than the other two. Both Mrs. Gaskell and George Eliot enrich our knowledge of rural life, and the former, in her *Mary Barton*, made a powerful plea against the evil economic and social conditions among which the laborers in the new towns lived in the forties. Charles Kingsley, who was a Christian socialist and gave active help to the workingmen, also devoted novels to the social miseries of the same period, and Charles Reade wrote several works of fiction which were little more than interesting propaganda for various social reforms. Anthony Trollope, whose fiction began to be popular in the fifties, made his novels accurate pictures of the respectable aspects of the life of his time. The principal novelists of the last three decades of the century tell us less of contemporary English life. Meredith, who excelled in the analysis of characters and had a pronounced influence in the production of the movement for the liberation of women, wrote philosophic novels. Hardy utilized an intimate knowledge of the English peasants for the production of pessimistic effects which were philosophical in outlook and had no vital association with the economic depression which was ruining the peasants at the time. Robert Louis Stevenson told tales of romance and adventure in settings remote in place or time from the England of his day. Those of us who are unversed in the canons of literary criticism are thankful that Stevenson passed the critics and that contemporaneously the unsung Arthur Conan Doyle, by the creation of Sherlock Holmes, provided still another avenue of escape from the 'ologies and the 'isms which began to invade the novels of the closing years of the century. Among the other less renowned writers of prose fiction, Mrs. Hum-

[10] Low and Sanders, *History of England*, p. 464.

phrey Ward gave good descriptions of the manners and interests of the upper classes, and W. E. Norris provided portraits of country society akin to those of Trollope for earlier decades, but the Victorian novel as a key to the understanding of contemporary life had its great days during the first half of the reign.

The "enthusiasm" of Victorian literature "for social truths as an instrument of social reform," of which a Victorian literary critic complained,[11] is for the historian of the period a piece of good fortune. This spirit not only found expression in fiction and in poetry, but it also actuated several writers who criticized the complacency and the apathy of the middle class. They tell us much concerning contemporary ideals both by the aspects of society which they criticized and by the profound influence which they exerted upon the thought of the time. Carlyle, who published his best works between 1831 and 1845, was most influential as a preacher of moral and social reforms, though he was also an historian who enunciated the doctrine of hero worship and exemplified it by rehabilitating Oliver Cromwell. By the strength of his convictions and the extraordinary language in which he clothed them, he caused many Englishmen to share his dissatisfaction with the materialism of the age and to give more thought to moral and social issues. Ruskin, who began to write in the forties, was concerned with art and architecture, but he popularized the gospel of beauty and aroused public consciousness of the external ugliness which the machine age was producing. As he gave more thought to the ugliness of the conditions in which the poor lived, he was so strongly moved by their misery that in 1859 he began to write in behalf of economic and social reform. On these questions he affected potently the thought not only of the middle class but also of the laborers. Matthew Arnold devoted the first part of his literary career to the production of poetry, which, though it won the approval of the critics, was not popular. After 1867 he gave his attention almost entirely to literary criticism. He stirred many of his countrymen to a higher regard for culture and an appreciation of good literature by ironical criticism of the indifference produced among them by their absorption in and contentment with material progress and by critical guidance to what was best in literature.

The progress of thought which was particularly characteristic of the nineteenth century, and which most impressed contemporaries, was in the scientific field. The advance was most obvious to the ordinary

---

[11] F. Harrison, *Studies in Early Victorian Literature*, pp. 12, 13.

observer in the application of the sciences. The telegraph, the telephone, electric light and power, the part taken by chemistry in the development of the steel industry and of agriculture, and the production of synthetic aniline dyes are merely examples of a multitude of changes which brought home to Victorians the wonders of man's conquest of nature. This increased power of man over natural resources was based upon the extension of the knowledge of the principles of nature gained by the steady development of experiments and theories. The public was naturally less aware of the steps in this growth of pure science, for little of it was as spectacular as the scientific discoveries of the twentieth century, and Darwin's theory of evolution was the only advance comparable to the discoveries of Newton in its revolutionary effects upon thought. Yet the total accomplishment at the end of the century was so vast that it was collectively the object of popular amazement, and more or less unconsciously and indirectly the thought of everyone had been affected by it. When, for example, the doctor cheerfully informs his patient that he may get up but had better live on carbohydrates and avoid the proteins for a few days, the patient is likely to have a more or less definite idea of what foods he may eat, but he may not be familiar with the theory of organic chemistry upon which this classification is based, nor associate its establishment with A. M. Williamson, an English chemist. We are all aware that the scientific discoveries of the nineteenth century have a tremendous influence over our lives, but most of us have no real conception of the extent of it. Within brief compass it is impossible to trace this rapid development, or even to convey any adequate impression of the part which British scientists took in it, but a few illustrations may serve to give some indication of its place in English thought of the nineteenth century.

In the fields of physics and chemistry British scientists made notable contributions. In 1808 John Dalton converted "a vague hypothesis" concerning atoms into "a definite scientific theory,"[12] which made possible the subsequent development of the analysis of chemical compounds and the establishment of formulae for chemical substances. Atoms were long considered as symbols; but with the rise of the kinetic theory of gases based upon the movement of molecules, and the consequent study of molecular structure, they began to be regarded as real substances. To this development the English scientists, J. P. Joule and J. Clerk Maxwell, made significant contributions between 1857 and 1879. The way to the divisibility of the atom was partially prepared by

Physics and chemistry

---

[12] Dampier-Whetham, *History of Science*, p. 228.

Joseph Thomson near the close of the century, but the theory of electrons, which has wrought great changes in both physics and chemistry, was not worked out until the present century. The fundamental laws of valance, which is the combining power of an atom of one element for atoms of other elements, were established during the middle years of the nineteenth century by experiments conducted partly in England but mainly abroad. This new knowledge became particularly important in the field of organic chemistry for the production of synthetic compounds, which is now done on a huge commercial scale. The view that sound was due to waves was accepted in the eighteenth century, but it was early in the nineteenth before Thomas Young laid the foundation upon which others built a real physical theory of light waves, making possible an enormous increase in the knowledge of optics. Subsequently electromagnetic waves were established theoretically by Michael Faraday, mathematically by Clerk Maxwell, and experimentally by a German (1887). This was the road which led to wireless and radio, among other things. The first exact methods of spectrum analysis were devised by Germans, but British scientists utilized them to advantage. In 1868 Norman Lockyer deduced from a spectroscopic analysis the existence in the sun of a new element which he called helium. In 1895 Sir William Ramsay obtained from a rare mineral a gas which gave the same line in the spectrum as helium. The existence of an element was thus discovered in the sun twenty-seven years before it was found in the earth. New principles with regard to heat constituted one of the most important discoveries made during the nineteenth century. At the close of the eighteenth the old view that heat was an imponderable liquid was overthrown. Between 1840 and 1850 Joule conducted experiments which led to the conclusion that heat was a form of energy, and established the amount of work necessary to produce a given amount of heat. His work supplemented by that of others established the principle of conservation of energy, according to which energy cannot be created or destroyed. A few years later William Thomson (later Lord Kelvin) announced the principle of degradation of energy. In every transfer of energy, some escapes into heat and becomes less available. Thus, although the total energy of the universe remains constant, the amount of available energy steadily decreases. This unifying theory opened new fields of investigation which proved very fertile not only in physics and chemistry but also in biology and physiology. One of the advances which most impressed laymen was in the field of electricity and magnetism. Knowledge of these phenomena was beginning to be acquired in the later years of the eighteenth century, but it was the experimental work begun by Faraday in 1831 which laid the foundations of several branches of electric science. By carrying further experiments begun a few years before by Sir Humphry Davy he established the laws of electrolysis. This process, by which an electric current is used to decompose chemical compounds, is employed commercially to produce a large number of standard products. The dynamo and most of the other electric machinery of commercial importance depend upon another principle which he established. "Faraday's discoveries were so far-reaching that they have even been coupled with the law of the conservation of energy and Darwin's theory of descent as the greatest scientific ideas of the latter half of the century."[13] Clerk Maxwell was another English scientist who added largely to the knowledge of electricity and magnetism by the reduction of the phenomena to mathematical laws. During the last five years of the century X-rays and radium were discovered by continental scientists, but their development took place in the next century.

The advances made in medicine and surgery impressed laymen as being little short of marvelous. They were based largely upon the steady march of knowledge in all of the organic sciences such as anatomy, organic chemistry and physiology, the use of many new instruments to aid in diagnosis such as the stethoscope and the clinical thermometer, the discovery of anaesthesia, and the proof that many diseases were caused by microbes. The first practical use of anaesthesia was made by American doctors between 1844 and 1846, but James Simpson, a professor of medicine in the university of Edinburgh, was the first to employ chloroform. The use of an anaesthetic not only reduces the pain suffered by the patient, but it makes possible the performance of operations which previously had been impossible. A few years later Louis Pasteur established specific microbes as the causes of certain diseases. Before that time the causes of most diseases had been a mystery. Once they were known, tremendous strides were taken toward the prevention of diseases. The principal British contributor in this field was Lord Lister, a surgeon. He introduced the antiseptic treatment of open wounds by destroying the germs with antiseptics such as carbolic acid, and in 1867 he established aseptic surgery by demonstrating that wounds would not become septic if they were protected against all living germs. Between 1879 and 1889 the bacilli which caused several diseases were isolated by German scientists, making possible both general protective measures by better sanitation and preventive medicine. When, for ex-

Medicine and surgery

[13] Sedgwick and Tyler, *Short History of Science*, p. 354.

ample, it was found that the germs of malaria were carried by a certain type of mosquito, it became possible to reduce or eliminate the danger of infection by destroying the breeding places of the mosquitoes. The identification of the bacilli also made possible further progress with inoculation. Edward Jenner, an English doctor, had introduced the process of vaccination which gave immunity against smallpox late in the eighteenth century, and Pasteur had extended the process to some other diseases; but after the discovery of the bacilli and their culture, vaccines were prepared which gave partial or complete immunity against several diseases. These developments not only prolonged human life, but they also reduced greatly the amount of physical pain and suffering which the average individual has to undergo.

Geology

The science of geology was practically created in Great Britain. In 1785 James Hutton published *A Theory of the Earth* in which he upheld the view that the formation of the earth's surface should be explained by natural operations still in progress such as the transfer of soil by rivers to the bed of the ocean. For a long time this thesis won little recognition, and the older view that the explanation was to be found in a series of catastrophes including the flood of Noah continued to prevail. British scholars, however, began to study the sequence of strata exemplified in the rocks of Great Britain, and in 1830 Charles Lyell published the first volume of his *Principles of Geology*. In this work he collected what he and others had discovered, and gave a systematic and comprehensive exposition of the theory that the history of the earth could be traced by the record of the rocks and of the fossils contained in them, interpreted in the light of the natural forces which were still active. The demonstration that the surface of the earth had been formed gradually through millions of years was so conclusive that it put an end to the theory of sudden formation by special creation, and placed geology on a sound scientific basis. A few years later Louis Agassiz, a native of Switzerland, developed the theory that boulders had been deposited by glaciers, and not by the deluge or by volcanoes sending out showers of rocks. The theory of general glaciation which he finally proposed proved extremely fruitful in the explanation of geological phenomena, and one of the foremost scholars in developing it was the Scotsman, James Geike. Meanwhile, the discovery of flint implements and of the remains of man and animals in association with geological strata had enabled Lyell in 1863 to assign to man much greater antiquity than had hitherto been imagined, and the study of prehistory was begun.

In biology the event of foremost importance was the establishment of the theory of organic evolution. The conception of an evolutionary Biology process in nature is as old as the days of the Greek philosophers, and philosophers were still playing with it in the nineteenth century, but scientists paid little attention to it for lack of convincing evidence. This was supplied by Charles Darwin, a naturalist, who spent twenty years collecting the evidence on which he based his theory. In 1858 he received from Alfred R. Wallace a paper which contained the essence of his own theory. Fortunately he had written an abstract of his theory in 1844, and had spoken of it in a letter to a friend in 1857. He therefore arranged to have these data made public simultaneously with Wallace's paper, and in 1859 he produced his book on *The Origin of Species by Means of Natural Selection*. Starting from his observation that living forms of all kinds tend to vary in some particulars from their parents, he reasoned that if pressure of numbers in any race renders it impossible for all members of it to survive, any variation which is of use in the struggle for existence gives the individuals which possess it a better chance to arrive at maturity and to rear offspring which will inherit it. The variation tends to spread throughout the race by the gradual elimination of those not possessing it. When the whole race finally has been changed, a new species has been established. He thus suggested natural selection, or the survival of the fittest, as the main cause of the origin of species, though not the only one. The theory of organic evolution soon won the acceptance of scientists, and later research has tended to confirm it, though natural selection alone has come to be regarded as an inadequate explanation of it, and some of Darwin's assumptions with regard to heredity appear to be untenable. The theory affected all of the many sciences which have to do with organic matter, and the science of anthropology practically arose from it.

Organic evolution also had a profound influence upon many fields of thought other than scientific. Some theologians opposed it because it conflicted with the story of special creation as told in the book of Genesis. For the same reason it shook the faith of some of the laymen who had been reared on the literal interpretation of the Bible. Eventually theologians saw that it left plenty of room for theology, because it did not explain such things as consciousness, will, morals or even the origin of life; and laymen, as they became more familiar with the theory, generally recognized that it left intact the fundamental beliefs of Christianity, but for a generation it caused many to struggle with bitter doubts. Meanwhile another school was applying evolution to explain religion, and aspects of Darwin's theory had found their way into sociology, ethics and philosophy, and were being reflected in

762

novels, such as those of Meredith. Perhaps no other one scientific concept has had so much influence upon popular thought within so short a period.

Philosophy   In the field of philosophy the effect of Darwin's theory was to intensify a type of thought based upon science which was already influential. This philosophy may perhaps be described collectively as naturalism. Its general trend was to make man appear to be merely a mechanism or a machine, and it omitted such things as God, the soul and the will. Herbert Spencer was the English philosopher whose thought was most influenced by science, and he had many readers, though he was somewhat scorned by other philosophers. He, however, acknowledged the existence of a higher power which is beyond our knowledge. On the whole, the philosophy of naturalism did not find a particularly congenial home in England. In the seventies Thomas H. Green was laying at Oxford the foundation of an idealist school of philosophy. Many English scientists, moreover, were well aware that the laws of science were in reality only working hypotheses, and they found no joy in philosophic systems which accepted them as fundamental truths. Their position has affected popular opinion as the scientific discoveries of the present century have progressed, but these could not be foreseen at the close of the nineteenth century. At that time naturalistic philosophers were approaching the height of such popular influence as they attained in England, and were taking their place among the many cross-currents of thought which were shaking Victorians from the complacency enjoyed by them earlier in the century.

CHAPTER XL

THE ROADS TO UTOPIA AND ARMAGEDDON

THE Liberals, led by Campbell-Bannerman, accepted office at the end of 1905, holding the election early in 1906. The result was a land- Election of slide for the Liberals. They came back with a majority over all other 1906 parties combined. In addition they could count generally on the vote of the Irish Nationalists, and on most measures they could secure the vote of the Labor party. The appearance of this new group in the house of commons was one of the most significant aspects of the election. The members of the house who had previously represented labor constituencies, advocated the interests of labor, and called themselves labor members had for the most part accepted membership in the organization of one or the other of the two great parties. Those holding themselves independent of both parties had been too few to have any separate organization.

The success of the new Labor party at the polls constituted a land- mark in the growth of the influence which labor had exerted upon Growth of national affairs since trade unions had received their charter of liber- trade unions ties in 1875. For a few years after that event an economic depression since 1875 caused the trade union movement to decline. When it revived, it became more aggressive. The older unions were composed mainly of skilled workers, they charged high dues, and they had accumulated funds to provide benefits for their members in cases of illness or other misfortunes. As a consequence, they tended to be cautious and conservative. After 1880 the unskilled workers began to organize unions, and a successful strike of the London dockworkers in 1889, which won widespread popular attention, gave impetus to the movement. The new unions charged small dues, provided no insurance for their members, and accumulated funds only to finance strikes. They were radical and aggressive in their attitude. Both the new and the old unions added to their numbers until by 1900 they had two million members. Aside from the successes and failures of individual unions in collective bargaining with employers, the collective influence of the unions upon public opinion and upon legislation for the welfare of the workers grew steadily. This was exercised largely by the Trades Union Congress, which was an annual assembly of delegates from trade unions, where common aims and policies were debated and formulated.

Socialism

During the last twenty years of the nineteenth century socialism became a factor of importance in the working-class movement. The failure of the utopian socialistic schemes of Robert Owen to obtain immediate practical benefits for the laborers caused a reaction against socialism after 1835. Although Karl Marx came to England in 1849 as a political refugee and lived there the rest of his life, the doctrines of his famous work on *Capital*, of which the first volume was published in 1867, had slight effect upon English thought until they had become influential in continental countries, whence they returned to England. The first society for the propagation of Marxian socialistic principles was formed in 1881, though it did not declare definitely for governmental ownership of the principal means of production until two years later. It was followed by the formation of other societies which had for their principal object to spread knowledge of socialism. They gradually converted many workingmen to belief in socialistic principles, though the effort of one society to persuade trade unions to adopt socialism officially was a failure. The socialistic societies, however, did not stop with the advocacy of theoretical socialism; they also proposed immediate practical reforms, which often appealed to the trade unions. The demand for a legal working day of eight hours, for example, originated with a socialistic society, and was finally endorsed in 1890 by the Trades Union Congress. Theoretical socialism, with its appeal to class prejudice, seemed to the larger portion of the British workingmen revolutionary and impractical, but the agitation for immediate reforms obtained a far better response. This was conducted by socialists who hoped to lead the working class gradually along the road of socialistic reforms to socialistic principles; and the Fabian Society, composed mainly of intellectuals who were sympathetically interested in the labor movement, was particularly successful in arousing interest in socialistic reforms. By 1906 the influence of this moderate type of socialism upon the thought not only of the laborers but also of the general public was profound.

The Labor party

The socialist movement also helped to bring about the formation of the Labor party. The Trades Union Congresses for many years tended to keep the trade unions out of politics. They passed resolutions in favor of the election of trade unionists to parliament, but no attempt was made to establish a separate party to represent the laborers. When trade unionists were elected, they usually joined the Liberal party. The socialists advocated a separate party from the first, and many of the new unionists also became desirous of a labor party. The presentation of their views in the Trades Union Congress year after year wore down the majority opposed to it, but failed to change it to a minority. In 1892 a group of the new unionists who were also socialists became impatient and formed the Independent Labor Party. It announced as its purpose "to secure the collective ownership of all means of production, distribution and exchange," and also a large program of immediate reforms.[1] The party could not become influential politically without the support of the trade unions, and this it sought to obtain through the Trades Union Congress. In 1899 the Congress finally adopted a resolution which authorized the summons to a special congress of representatives from cooperative, socialist, trade union and other working-class organizations to make plans for increasing the number of labor members in the next parliament. When the congress met in the next year, it voted in favor of the establishment of a distinct Labor group in parliament, pledged to "cooperate with any party which, for the time being, may be engaged in promoting legislation in the direct interest of Labour."[2] It also appointed a permanent committee to direct the affairs of the new party, which had the support both of many trade unions and of the socialists. It was this party which elected twenty-nine members to parliament in 1906, and at that time took the name of the Labor party. The members organized themselves as a separate group in the house of commons, and announced their intention, as long as they lacked a majority, to vote with the party which should offer the more radical social legislation. Two years later the annual conference of the party declared itself in favor of the control by the state of the means of production, distribution and exchange, but the parliamentary members continued their practical plan of working for the most advanced legislation in behalf of their class which they could obtain.

The Liberals soon provided them with an abundance of legislation of this type. The desire for social reform was not confined to the laborers, but it had widespread popular approval as well, and the Liberals had won the election largely on that issue. They proposed to depart from the opportunist attitude of the past and undertake an organized policy of comprehensive social reconstruction. They were no longer contented with remedies merely palliative in character, but sought by legislation to remove some of the causes of poverty and distress. During the next eight years they enacted legislation which carried Great Britain far away from the ideals of individualism and *laissez faire* which had prevailed a century earlier. Indeed, they landed Great Britain among

Liberal social program

---

[1] Cole, *Short History of the Working Class Movement*, ii, 168.

[2] *Ibid.*, ii, 183.

the most advanced of the socialistically paternal states of the twentieth century. With the objects of many of the Liberal plans of social reform the Conservatives had no fundamental quarrel. Some of the new measures, indeed, merely pushed to greater lengths reforms previously advocated by the Conservatives themselves. They consequently accepted in principle several of the important Liberal bills and confined their criticism to the details of the application. But their opposition to other measures, which bore more distinctively the stamp of the Liberal party, went to an indiscreet length. In the first few sessions of parliament they used the huge majority of the Conservative party in the house of lords to block several bills which had passed the house of commons. The answer of the Liberals was to limit the power of the house of lords, and thus make a fundamental constitutional reform.

The lords and the commons, 1906–1908

The trouble between the houses began in the first session. The election had been fought on a great variety of issues. One of the questions to the fore was free trade or protection. Here the Liberals stood for free trade and the existing order. In other fields they had pledged themselves to a large number of reforms. They began with education because the non-conformists who objected so strongly to the education act in 1902 were mainly Liberals. The bill of 1906 provided that schools supported by public taxes should be under public management and could maintain no religious tests for teachers. After passage through the house of commons, the bill was so altered by amendments in the house of lords that the commons dropped it upon its return.

In this first issue between the two houses, the position of the lords was essentially this. They maintained that education had not been one of the prominent questions in the recent campaign. They claimed that the majority of the people did not favor it. If the cabinet thought otherwise, it could dissolve the house of commons and hold an election on that policy. If the cabinet received a popular mandate, the house of lords would give way. The Liberals believed the house of lords had no right to force a referendum when they had just come fresh from an election with a huge majority. They interpreted the victory as a popular approval of their general program. The objection of the Liberals was not to the conservatism of the house of lords. To hold up hasty and ill-considered legislation is the essential function of a second chamber. But the Liberals felt that the second chamber in this instance had been actuated not by true conservatism but by the Conservative party.[3] A large majority of the peers belonged to this party. The suspicion had

---

[3] All these arguments may not have been used at one time, but they appeared in the course of the controversy.

been entertained by Liberal cabinets before. Gladstone particularly had grumbled about the partisan spirit with which the lords had rejected his Home Rule Bill in 1893. In 1906 the cabinet took notice of the action. When it was announced in the house, the prime minister, Sir Henry Campbell-Bannerman, said: "The resources of the British Constitution are not wholly exhausted. The resources of the House of Commons are not exhausted, and I say with conviction that a way must be found, a way will be found, by which the will of the people expressed through their elected representatives in the house will be made to prevail."[4] This was a pronouncement by the cabinet that the time had come to "end or mend" the house of lords.

The partisan attitude of the lords was reflected on other measures during the session of 1906. The Plural Voting Bill, which had as its object to allow a man to vote in only one place, was rejected by the upper chamber. It was not a radical reform, but it was a policy which had been advocated by Liberals and opposed by Conservatives for years. The Trades Disputes Bill was of much more radical type. It had for its purpose to free the trade unions from the restriction placed upon them by a judicial decision in the Taff Vale case. In 1900 the striking employees of the Taff Vale Railway were supported by the Amalgamated Society of Railway Servants in which they had membership. In the course of the strike individual strikers damaged the property of the company. The company sued the Amalgamated Society for damages and secured £23,000. This decision placed upon the unions disabilities which made it almost as difficult for the laborers to strike as it had been before the acts of 1871 and 1875. The Liberals introduced a bill to give a union exemption from liability for damages committed by strikers, unless the acts were authorized by the union. It did not satisfy the unions, and they secured the introduction of a private bill which freed trade unions from any legal liability for civil wrongs committed by them or on their behalf. The cabinet, finding many Liberals pledged to its support, substituted it for their own measure. This bill, which gave to the trade unions such exemption from the law as no individuals or corporations enjoyed, might well have been changed or rejected in a truly conservative body, but the lords passed it promptly. It was not so distinctively a Liberal policy.[5] The king's speech at the beginning of the next session announced that the ministers had the relations of the two houses under consideration. Before any result followed, the houses came to a deadlock in 1908 over the Licensing Bill. It pro-

---

[4] Hansard, *Parliamentary Debates,* 4th series, clxvii, p. 1740.
[5] Lowell, *Government of England,* i, 409.

posed to revoke 30,000 licenses for the sale of liquor in fourteen years and compensate the holders of such licenses for the loss of their vested interests from taxes levied on the liquor trade. At the end of fourteen years local option was to come into effect. The object was to promote temperance, but the Liberal measure went much faster than the legislation enacted by the Conservatives six years before, and in the end it went much further. The house of lords rejected it.

The controversy reached a crisis on the budget in 1909. Lloyd George, the chancellor of the exchequer, faced a deficit of over £16,000,000, caused chiefly by the cost of the Liberal social reforms and the policy of a greater navy. The new taxes with which he proposed to meet the deficit embodied some of the principles of social reform maintained by the Liberals. They bore heavily on the lords individually. They fell with greater weight on the rich than on the poor, and they placed new burdens on the great estates of which the lords were the chief possessors. Since much of the proceeds was to be used to pay old age pensions, it was virtually taxation of the rich to support the poor. It also embodied the principles of some reforms which the lords had already rejected. Some of the purposes of the Licensing Bill of 1908, for example, would be accomplished by the passage of the budget. When the budget came before the lords, it placed them in a difficult situation. Their control of finance was limited. They could not constitutionally initiate or amend money bills. Since 1860 they had not rejected one. Their right of rejection was doubted, because such action would leave the cabinet without money to run the government and thus thwart the will of the people completely. But the lords maintained that this was more than a budget. "This is not a budget," said one opponent, "it is a revolution." To insert in the budget reforms which the lords had previously vetoed, it was said in debate, deprived the lords of their right of a voice in ordinary legislation. The social changes involved were so great that the lords insisted on putting the budget to a popular referendum. They rejected the finance bill by a large majority in an exceptionally full house.

In the opinion of the Liberals this was the culmination of the wrongdoing of the house of lords. The house of commons declared it to be a "breach of the constitution." Mr. Asquith, who had become prime minister after the death of Campbell-Bannerman in 1908, dissolved the house and held a new election. The campaign was one of the bitterest in years. As a popular mandate it was not entirely satisfactory. The Conservatives gained sufficient seats to equal the Liberals. Only the votes of the Irish Nationalists and the Labor group gave the Liberals

Margin notes:

Budget of 1909

Reform of the house of lords

cabinet a majority. It secured the passage of the budget, and then introduced resolutions on the reform of the house of lords. They proposed to deprive the house of lords of power to control financial legislation and to leave to it no power over other legislation except to compel deliberation. Meanwhile the house of lords had seen the light. It adopted resolutions with regard to its own reform. Its program was to improve the personnel and leave its powers alone. At this juncture Edward VII died, being succeeded by George V. It seemed advisable, if possible, to avoid embarrassment of the new king with so difficult a question. Conferences of the leaders of the two parties were held in search of a compromise. They failed, because the plans were too diametrically opposed. One confirmed the system of two chambers and sought to make the second chamber worthy to exercise power; the other condemned the dual system and practically ended the power of the house of lords.

In the autumn of 1910 the prime minister introduced a bill framed on the lines of his earlier resolutions. It passed the house of commons, to be rejected by the house of lords. Thereupon a new election was held on the sole issue of the house of lords. In the new house the parties remained of nearly the same strength as in the old. In 1911 the Parliament Bill passed the commons. This time it was so amended by the lords as to destroy its principle. Asquith then announced that he had the consent of the king to create enough new peers to pass the bill. As several hundred would have been required, it would have meant a social revolution. Before this threat the lords gave way. When the bill came before the upper chamber a second time, enough of the Conservative peers remained away or voted with the Liberals to enable the Liberal peers to carry the bill. The Parliament Act authorized the speaker of the house of commons to decide what were money bills. Such measures were to go to the king for his assent at the end of a month, even if the lords did not pass them. Other bills were to go to the king for assent if they had passed the house of commons in three consecutive sessions, provided two years had elapsed from the date of the first introduction. The house of lords can now delay legislation, but it cannot stop any on which the house of commons insists.

Meanwhile the Liberal government had been proceeding steadily with its program of social reform. In the improvement of the conditions under which labor was carried on, the Liberals found it necessary to do comparatively little except to amend and expand existing legislation. In 1906 they passed a new Workmen's Compensation Act which included many occupational diseases among the injuries for which the employers must give compensation, and extended the principle of the

Conditions of labor

act of 1897 to many additional industries, such as household service. The act protected thirteen millions of laborers in place of the seven millions protected by the earlier legislation. Two years later the government secured the enactment of a law making a working day of eight hours compulsory in the mines.

The one radical innovation of the Liberals in this field was their

Sweated
industries
and the
minimum
wage

legislation on sweated industries. Sweating was defined by a committee of the house of commons to mean "that work is paid for at a rate which, in the conditions under which many of the workers do it, yields to them an income which is quite insufficient to enable an adult person to obtain anything like proper food, clothing, and house accommodation."[6] For the most part it is done by workers in their homes, though it may be conducted in workshops, or even in factories. The laborers in such industries are unskilled, they are usually so situated that they must submit to the forced sale of their labor, and combinations of laborers for collective bargaining are virtually impossible. The problem had attracted the attention of several recent governments without legislative result. In 1909 the Liberals passed the Trade Boards Act, which established a minimum wage in certain specified industries, such as ready-made tailoring and paper-box making. The board of trade was empowered to appoint a trade board in any of the specified industries, and the trade board could establish for the industry a minimum wage which the employers must pay under penalty of a fine. This act protected a section of labor which had scarcely been touched by previous legislation.

The Liberals also sought to promote the health and well-being of

Public
health

the worker in his home. Since the public health code of 1875[7] there had been legislation on other lines to help accomplish this result. The Liberal legislation in this field for the most part merely carried further what earlier laws had begun. A series of small allotments acts culminated in 1907. Their purpose was to remedy the divorce of man from the land which the factory system had produced. They empowered local authorities to buy land and let it on easy terms in small lots of an acre or less to laborers who desired to have gardens. A series of housing acts[8] was expanded and consolidated in the House and Town Planning Act of 1909. Their object was to relieve the overcrowded tenements and the evil sanitary conditions of the homes of many workers in the

[6] "Report of the Select Committee on Home Work," *Parliamentary Papers*, 1908, viii, p, iii.

[7] Above, p. 704.

[8] For the first one, see above, p. 705.

large cities, which constituted one of the chief causes of ill health. Collectively they empowered local authorities to condemn and tear down buildings unfit for human habitation, to build model cottages and tenements for workingmen, to remodel whole areas of slums, and to establish plans for the systematic growth of towns. Much good was accomplished by the acts, but they were never carried out thoroughly, partly because their execution by local authorities was left too largely permissive, and partly because some of them were hedged about with too many restrictions. To the series of acts designed to preserve open spaces in towns for parks and recreation grounds the Liberals made no significant legislative addition, though they continued to increase these important aids to health under the acts already in operation.

Some of these acts passed by the Liberals benefited the rural wage earners, but they had in view primarily the artisans in the industrial centers. The movement for small holdings sought the betterment of rural conditions. It was the thought of its early advocates that the restoration of the small agricultural holdings, which had disappeared with the enclosures, would improve social and economic conditions of life in the country. The movement was aided by an economic development, which, after 1880, made it less profitable to grow wheat in competition with America and Russia. The large farm, which was the best unit for wheat, was less well suited to some of the more diversified forms of agriculture than the small one. In 1892 the first Small Holdings Act empowered local authorities to purchase land and sell or lease it in small farms of from one to fifty acres. The act did not work well. In 1907 the Liberals placed the initiative in the purchase of such land with the central government, and made it possible to acquire the necessary land by compulsory process, should the owner refuse to sell. *Small holdings*

The greatest innovations of the Liberals were their legislative enactments designed to prevent destitution. The poor law of 1834 had worked well in many respects. During the second half of the nineteenth century the number of paupers had decreased relative to the population. The absolute number, however, was still large. The act of 1834, moreover, was primarily palliative in character. The more scientific study of social problems in the closing years of the nineteenth century was producing a public demand that the government should not be content merely to relieve destitution, but should do more to remove its causes. In response to the demand a royal commission was appointed at the close of 1905 to investigate poverty. It made thorough studies, presenting an elaborate report of over forty volumes in 1909. The Liberal program was based largely on this report. *Poor law commission*

Old age
pensions

Legislation was begun on old age pensions before the report was completed. The act was placed on the statute book in 1908. It provided that every person seventy years of age, who had not been a criminal or an habitual loafer,[9] should receive a pension from the central government, provided he had been a British subject for the past twenty years and a British resident for the past twelve, and received an annual income of no more than £31 10 s. The pension varied from 1 s. to 5 s. a week, depending on the size of the recipient's income. The class protected was to contribute nothing directly to the cost of its own protection. The cost was to be met by general taxation. The law virtually provided that poor relief should be given to a large class under another name without stigma, disqualification, or discomfort attached to it. The plan avoided the insidious dependence intentionally created by the old poor law, and was readily accepted by the aged workers. When the law had been in operation only a short time, more than three-quarters of a million persons were receiving pensions.

Labor
exchanges

In the next year labor exchanges were established to facilitate the mobilization of labor and thus prevent one of the causes of unemployment. The act provided for the establishment of 350 labor exchanges in urban centers, grouped in eleven districts, under the central control of the board of trade. Information of any vacancies was to be supplied to all the bureaus and passed over to applicants for such vacancies. If the position should be in another place, the bureau could advance traveling expenses to the prospective applicant. The bureaus were also to compile statistics which were expected to help in the classification of the causes of unemployment.

Working-
men's
insurance

The final act in the series provided for the compulsory insurance of workingmen. Against sickness, which Lloyd George estimated was the cause of thirty per cent of the poverty, the insurance of manual laborers was made nearly universal. In nearly all cases the employer was required to contribute three pence a week, the male employee four pence, the female three pence, and the government two pence. The benefits included free medical treatment, special treatments or payments in certain cases, and weekly payments, varying in amount with the age and sex of the recipient, during an illness which was not prolonged over twenty-six weeks. Insurance against unemployment was regarded as experimental. It was applied only to specified trades where unemployment was common. The insurance was compulsory within those trades. The principle of contribution was the same as for insurance

---

[9] Paupers were excluded at first but were later included.

against sickness, and the benefits consisted of weekly payments during unemployment for a period of fifteen weeks.

In the same year provision was made for the payment of an annual salary of £400 to the members of the house of commons. This was done to satisfy the members of the Labor party. For the most part they were unable to give their attention to parliamentary duties and at the same time to support themselves. Until 1909 they had received aid from the funds of their trades unions, but in that year the court, in the Osborne case, declared such use of the funds of a union to be illegal. The act of 1911 rendered it possible for a man who had no independent income to sit in the house of commons. It was another step toward more representative government.

Payment of members

Despite all this legislation in behalf of the laborers, numerous strikes took place during 1911 and 1912, and in several of them the government intervened. Some it was able to settle by conciliation, but others were accompanied by so much violence that troops were used to keep the peace, and a few people were killed. Two of the strikes were on a more extensive scale than Great Britain had previously witnessed. A strike of the railway unions tied up all but one of the railways in the kingdom. It caused a complete paralysis of industry; but at the end of two days the government, by promising an investigation of their grievances, persuaded the strikers to go back to work and leave the settlement of the issues to boards of conciliation. Early in 1912 the Miners' Federation called out the miners in all the coal fields of Great Britain in order to secure a minimum wage, and over a million men stopped work. The government proposed a minimum wage in each district, to be established by a conference of owners and miners in the presence of a representative of the government who should fix the rate in case agreement could not be reached. Two-thirds of the owners accepted the plan, but the other third and the leaders of the miners rejected it. The government, nevertheless, enacted its proposal into law. The Miners' Federation then took a ballot of its members. A majority opposed the settlement, but it was so small that the Federation declared the strike ended, and the men returned to work.

Labor unrest

In 1912 the Liberal government introduced a third Home Rule Bill. Since 1909 the Liberals had been dependent on the Irish Nationalists for a majority. Home rule was probably the price they had to pay for the Irish votes. In the two decades which had elapsed since the second Home Rule Bill, conditions in Ireland had changed considerably. The Conservatives, who had been in power for nearly the whole of the two decades between 1886 and 1905, had done much to improve the eco-

Irish home rule

nomic and social conditions of the country and to give the Irish greater popular control of their local organs of government. These policies, together with the land acts, seemed to have placed the Irish question upon a different footing. Disorder had decreased until it had nearly disappeared; Ireland appeared to be more contented; certainly it was far more prosperous. The argument that Ireland was not fitted for home rule appeared to have lost its force.

The bill passed the house of commons three times, only to be rejected by the house of lords. By the time it came to the king for signature, Great Britain was involved in the World War. To both parties it seemed unwise to take the risk of internal conflict which the execution of the act would involve. While the bill had been before parliament a tremendous opposition had developed in Ulster. In the debates on the Parliament Act of 1911 the Conservatives often insisted that the Liberals had no popular mandate in favor of home rule, while the Liberals implied that the question was before the voters in the election of 1910. The Conservatives were probably right, since the reform of the house of lords dominated that election almost to the exclusion of other issues. Whether they were right or wrong, the Conservatives waged a bitter partisan warfare on the bill. They easily stirred the Ulsterites to extreme measures. Before the close of 1912 the covenant was being circulated in Ulster for signatures. The signers agreed not to recognize the authority of a home rule parliament, if one should be instituted. It was incipient rebellion. The Ulsterites followed this with the purchase of arms and the establishment of military drills. Early in 1914 several officers of the army stationed in Ireland expressed a preference to be dismissed rather than to serve against the Ulster volunteers. It was not mutiny, as it was popularly thought at the time, because the question of their preference had been put to them by the commander-in-chief; but the mere putting of such a question to the officers was a sign of serious lack of discipline in the army, which made the Irish situation extremely dangerous. Meanwhile the Catholics took up the challenge of the Ulsterites and began to arm for the support of home rule. In July, 1914, shots were exchanged between them and the forces of the crown, resulting in the death of a few persons. This event might have marked the beginning of a civil war had not the outbreak of the European conflict temporarily stilled internal differences. Lest they should be revived, the approval of the Home Rule Act by the king was accompanied by the passage through parliament of a Suspensory Act, which rendered the Home Rule Act inoperative for the duration of the war. Before the time came for it to be put into effect, it was superseded by other legislation.

Before the shadow of the war fell upon Great Britain the Liberals secured the passage of one other important reform. In 1912 the cabinet introduced a bill to disestablish and disendow the Anglican church in Wales. The majority of the Welsh were Non-conformists, but they were required to contribute to the support of the Anglican church. Their position was similar to that of the Irish Catholics before the disestablishment of the Anglican church in Ireland. They had long protested, and their complaints were finally heeded by the party which represents the interests of the Non-conformists. The parliamentary history of the bill paralleled that of the measure for home rule. It was thrice passed by the commons and as many times rejected by the lords. It came to the king for his sanction soon after the outbreak of the war in 1914. It was approved with a suspensive provision, but after the war its principles were incorporated in a new piece of legislation. The four Welsh dioceses, which had been part of the province of Canterbury from time immemorial, were separated from the established church and placed on a voluntary basis. The endowments received before 1662 were confiscated and the income transferred partly to the university of Wales and partly to the county councils for purposes of local government.

Welsh disestablishment

Though the Liberal cabinet was strenuous in its pursuit of internal reforms, it found time to initiate important imperial policies. The most striking imperial development under its direction was the union of South Africa. After the close of the war with the Boers the Conservative cabinet did much to facilitate the restoration of the conquered states. When it went out of office, it was preparing to give the Boers representative government in accordance with the terms of the treaty of 1902. The Liberal cabinet decided not to go through the intermediate stage of representative government, which was similar in principle to the type once used in the American colonies, but to grant the Boers complete responsible governments at once. Self-government was granted to the Transvaal in 1906 and to Orange Free State in the next year. The experiment worked well. It soon led to a desire for union among the South African colonies. Geographically and economically they constituted a unit. Common regulation of such factors as railways and tariffs would obviously be a great advantage. The numerical preponderance of the native population also created a problem which could be better met by a common policy. Eventually a convention assembled and drew up the draft of a constitution which was accepted in 1909 by the par-

Union of South Africa

liaments of Cape Colony, the Transvaal, and Orange Free State, and by popular referendum in Natal. The British parliament approved the constitution with slight changes, and the Union of South Africa was established in 1910. Unlike Canada and Australia, its government is not a federation; it is a unified state in which the four formerly independent states have become provinces. Its relations to the British government, on the other hand, are essentially the same. Thus it has become one of the great self-governing dominions.

India

In India the Liberal cabinet took a step destined to be of decisive importance in the reorganization of the government. At the opening of the twentieth century the government of India was still autocratic. More than half of the territory and four-fifths of the population of India were contained in fifteen provinces directly under British rule. In these sections the natives had no voice in the government and no control over it. The remainder was divided into native states, which, with two small exceptions, were controlled, some in greater degree and some in less, by British residents appointed by the British Indian government. In the closing years of the nineteenth century a nationalistic movement began among the natives. The Hindus were back of the movement in the early stages, and it was led largely by educated natives, who recognized the benefits conferred upon India by British rule and sought not to overthrow British control but to secure a voice in the government for the natives. In 1906 the Mohammedans began to organize to agitate for similar ends. For a few years after 1905 the situation was complicated by an outburst in Bengal of fanatical opposition to British rule which found expression in assassination and the use of bombs. But the British government did not confound the two. Under the influence of John Morley, a radical Liberal, who was secretary of state for India after 1906, the cabinet was disposed to concede something to the nationalistic movement led by the moderate leaders.

What could be granted was a difficult decision. Any approach to self-government seemed to be out of the question. The vast population of India, which comprised one-sixth of the human beings on the globe, was so heterogeneous racially, linguistically, and religiously that a sense of common nationality sufficiently strong to provide an adequate basis for unified self-government seemed impossible. Nor was the great mass of the population sufficiently well educated to exercise the franchise intelligently. Morley consequently sought to satisfy the educated moderates by giving them some influence in the government without giving them control of it. The executive councils of the secretary, the viceroy, and the governors of provinces were thrown open to natives, and a few were appointed to office. In 1909 the Indian Councils Act opened the legislative councils to natives. The viceroy and each of the governors of provinces had one of these. Previously they had consisted of officials and others appointed by the executive. The official element predominated and safeguarded the control of the executive. The law of 1909 enlarged the councils and introduced an element elected by the natives. The electorate was extremely narrow. Only something like 30,000 of the better educated received the vote in a population of over 250,000,000. Nevertheless, a variety of classes and interests were represented. In the viceroy's council the official element remained in a majority, but in the provincial assemblies the elected element had a majority. The councils were given ample opportunity to discuss, criticize, and advise, and they brought the British executive in touch with native popular opinion, but they had no direct control over the government. "They could not stop supplies of money or turn out the administration on a question of policy." The officials responsible for the government of British India were still responsible to the British parliament. The new councils "were not intended by their authors to be the prelude to parliamentary government, a basis for which did not, in Lord Morley's opinion, then exist in India."[10] For a time they contented the native leaders, but before long dissatisfaction with their limited character became uppermost. Soon the natives began to agitate for a larger share in their own government, and after the war further concessions were made. Thus the step taken in 1909 proved to be merely of a preliminary character.

In the field of foreign affairs the Liberal cabinet had to meet a series of critical situations which finally culminated in the war of 1914. They began with an issue over Morocco which arose shortly before the cabinet took office. When the Anglo-French agreement concerning Morocco was made in 1904, the French government failed to provide the German government with official notification of its terms, and it made no suggestion, such as was more or less customary at the time, that France would not object if Germany should seek imperial gain in some other part of the world. The German government naturally felt that it had been treated cavalierly. Germany possessed commercial rights in Morocco guaranteed by an international convention of 1880, and the extension of French influence there would be likely to curtail those rights. Consequently, when France began early in 1905 to negotiate with the sultan of Morocco to secure reforms in that country, the

Algeciras

[10] *These Eventful Years,* ii, 312.

German government, fearing that it might be the first step looking toward French control, took action to prevent that outcome. The kaiser was sent to Morocco, where he made a declaration in favor of the independence of the country, and the German government then proposed a conference of the powers signatory of the treaty of 1880. The French government, feeling itself menaced by Germany and being fearful of war, gave way, and agreed to a conference to meet at Algeciras in 1906. This was the situation when Sir Edward Grey superseded Lord Lansdowne at the foreign office. He thought that Germany was attempting to test the strength of the entente cordiale, and both he and his chief promptly announced that they would maintain the principal aspects of the foreign policy of their predecessors and remain loyal to the entente. Great Britain accordingly supported France diplomatically in every move both before and during the conference. The result of the conference was to give Germany the appearance and France the substance of victory. A police was established in Morocco which was nominally international but was really under French control.

This crisis made the entente cordiale a far stronger bond than it had been in the beginning. A rupture between France and Germany seemed for a time to be so probable that conversations were begun between French and British military and naval experts on the military problems which would arise if Germany should make unprovoked attack upon France and Great Britain should support France. The naval conversations began under Lansdowne in 1905. The military conversations began in 1906 as the result of questions addressed by the French ambassador to Grey soon after his accession to office. The ambassador wished to know if Great Britain would support France in case of an unprovoked attack by Germany over the Moroccan question. Grey gave no promise. Support would depend, he said, on British public opinion, but he thought it would be favorable. The French government then asked that the military and naval conversations should take place. Without them, it urged, Great Britain could give no effective help, should it wish to do so in the time of a crisis. Grey agreed to the conversations with the understanding that they would not bind the action of either government, should occasion for a decision arise. Grey made his reply after consultation with Campbell-Bannerman, Asquith, and Lord Haldane, but without consultation of the cabinet. The conversations continued from 1906 until 1914. Before they were finished, they had settled how Great Britain could land 160,000 men in France in twelve days, the French fleet had been concentrated in the Mediterranean, and the British fleet was located in the North Sea.

The naval and military conversations

The Atlantic coast of France was unprotected unless the British navy should guard it. The cabinet did not know of the conversations for a long time. The French government recognized formally that the conversations committed the British government to nothing, but they served to raise French hopes of British help in case of trouble and made some British statesmen feel that Great Britain was under moral obligation to France.

Meanwhile conversations with Russia, which resulted in an understanding in 1907, had been begun. Till 1905 the spirit of antagonism between Great Britain and Russia continued to run high. Russia, however, needed friends. She had just been defeated in the Russo-Japanese War (1904-1905), her army was disorganized, and her debt was heavy. German and French friendship could not be had concurrently. The foreign office at London was desirous of removing Russian enmity, on account of the suspicion of German designs engendered by the Moroccan crisis and by the growing German navy. From the British point of view, moreover, circumstances favored a Russian entente. Great Britain was relieved of fears of Russian machinations in the Far East by the success of Japan in the recent war. The Near East had ceased to be as great a cause of friction between Great Britain and Russia as it had once been, because Teutonic influence in the Balkans and the beginning of the Bagdad railway made Germany a greater menace to British interests in that quarter. Only the Middle East remained as a source of serious friction. With both countries favorably disposed, the conversations begun in 1905 led to a convention in 1907. It arranged for a sphere of Russian influence in the north of Persia, a British zone in the southeast, and a neutral district between. Russia acknowledged the preponderant influence of Great Britain in Afghanistan. The agreement produced a rather unsavory chapter in British foreign relations. The Russians employed intrigue and aggression to extend their control within their Persian sphere at the expense of the independence of the Persian government. Grey protested repeatedly to the Russian government, but when his protests had no effect, he had to stand aside, and sometimes even to support the Russian designs, because he did not dare to sacrifice Russia's friendship. The Russian entente of 1907 practically created a Triple Entente beside the Triple Alliance. It meant that all of the great powers were included in the two armed camps, and Great Britain could not risk destruction of this balance of power. As time progressed, it became more apparent that any action by one power which seemed inimical to the interests of any power in the other group might easily become the cause of war.

Russian entente

German
attitude

The German government at first expressed no disapproval of the accord between Great Britain and Russia, but in 1908 the kaiser began to talk about the British attempt to "encircle" Germany. Since 1903 the British had begun to oppose the German project of the Bagdad railway, they had often tried to obtain from Germany a mutual limitation of naval building programs which would leave the German navy permanently inferior to the British, and the understandings among Great Britain, France and Russia seemed to be consolidating into an entente directed by Great Britain against Germany. Though the last fear was as exaggerated as were Grey's suspicions of German designs, the German public gave all these views ready credence. As far back as 1898 many Germans believed that the big British navy was maintained for their particular disadvantage. When Great Britain began to build to keep ahead of the German naval program, they felt sure of it. Public opinion in Germany was prepared for the appearance of the kaiser "in shining armor."

Bosnian
crisis,
1908–1909

The Bosnian crisis gave the opportunity. In 1908 Austria took advantage of the crisis in Turkey, caused by the successful revolution of the young Turks, to declare the annexation of the provinces of Bosnia and Herzegovina. The act caused little practical change in the status of the two provinces, which had been administered by Austria since the Congress of Berlin.[11] Technically, however, it violated the treaty of Berlin, just as Russia had earlier broken the treaty of 1856.[12] Russia, Great Britain, and France asked Austria to bring the annexation before a conference of the powers signatory, but Austria disliked the proposal. The German government, though it regarded the Austrian annexation as hasty and ill-considered, felt that failure to support Austria would weaken the Triple Alliance disastrously in the face of the supposed encirclement policy of the Triple Entente. It therefore suggested that the annexation should be ratified by an exchange of notes. When Russia delayed her answer, Germany demanded an immediate "yes or no," with an intimation that a delay or a negative might bring dire consequences. Since Russia was not prepared to fight, and Great Britain and France gave her no strong support, she gave way.

Servia

The crux of the situation had been in Servia. The provinces of Bosnia and Herzegovina were inhabited chiefly by Slavs of the same branch as the Serbs. The annexation placed a definitive check on Servian nationalistic aspirations. Servia in desperation sought at least to obtain an outlet to the sea, and for a time Servia and Austria appeared to be

[11] Above, p. 708.
[12] Above, p. 702.

on the verge of war. The powers of the Entente gave no help to Servia, and Austria replied with a demand that Servia should undertake henceforth to live in neighborly relations with Austria and cease to stir up trouble for Austria in the two provinces. When Russia, Servia's protector, gave way, Servia was forced to swallow the bitter pill. The blow to Russia's prestige in the Balkans was stiff, and the Russian public felt that Russia had been deeply humiliated. The threat of force gave Germany a diplomatic triumph.

In a diplomatic crisis which came in 1911 Great Britain took a leading part. France sent an army into Morocco ostensibly to quell insurgent tribes. Spain and Germany chose to regard it as the beginning of French occupation and a breach of the Algeciras agreement. Spain occupied the share given her by the secret treaty of 1904; Germany sent a gunboat to the port of Agadir ostensibly to protect the lives and property of Germans in Morocco but in reality to intimate to France that Germany was determined in her opposition to French expansion in Morocco. Germany then sought to secure compensations elsewhere in Africa for giving France a free hand in Morocco. Grey, being uninformed of the German purpose, became alarmed. He feared the Germans sought a naval base at Agadir and that Germany would force France and Spain to divide Morocco with her without consultation of the other powers signatory to the Algeciras agreement. Consequently Lloyd George, in a speech at the Guildhall, announced that Great Britain would not stand aside where her interests were vitally affected merely to avoid war. This threat caused a brief period of extreme tension, which relaxed only when the German government explained that it sought compensations elsewhere than in Morocco. It revived in lesser measure from time to time as negotiations between Germany and France progressed, but eventually an agreement satisfactory to France was reached. Germany acknowledged the special interest of France in Morocco and ceded a small portion of Kamerun, receiving in return a large slice of French Congo. This time Great Britain had taken a hand in the diplomacy of threats.

After 1911 the tension never wholly disappeared. In 1912 Lord Haldane, the secretary of war, was sent to Germany to negotiate a mutual reduction of the naval building programs which had become extremely heavy financial burdens upon both countries. The German government still retained the view, which had prevailed when it had begun to build the fleet, that Great Britain would cooperate with Germany only when she had been taught to respect Germany's power, and failed to recognize that the German naval threat was steadily forcing Great

Agadir, 1911

Relations with Germany and France in 1912

Britain into closer friendship with France. It therefore wanted a ratio of two German to three British keels, unless a political understanding could be reached between the two countries. Great Britain stuck to the ratio of two to one, and was not prepared to assume the responsibility of an alliance such as Germany desired, because it would have meant desertion of the entente with France and Russia. In the same year the entente with France was more clearly defined. During the Agadir crisis some members of the cabinet had become fearful that the military conversations had encouraged France to count too certainly on British assistance in making her military plans. In 1912 a discussion in the cabinet produced a demand "that the fact of the military conversations being non-committal should be put into writing." A letter was then drafted in the cabinet which Grey gave to Paul Cambon, the French ambassador with whom he had had the original conversation in 1906.[13] Cambon wrote a reply of similar tenor. The Grey-Cambon letters have been represented by some as creating an obligation of honor hardly less binding morally than an alliance, and interpreted by others as designed to prevent such a construction being placed on the military and naval conversations.[14]

Balkan Wars, 1912–1913

Meanwhile a new menace to the peace of Europe had appeared in the Balkans. In 1912 Servia, Montenegro, Bulgaria, and Greece formed an alliance and took a favorable opportunity to attack Turkey. Their chief object was to free Macedonia, which Disraeli had restored to Turkish misrule.[15] They met with extraordinary success. The great

---

[13] Above, p. 778.

[14] The letter of Grey to Cambon, dated November 22, 1912, reads as follows:

"From time to time in recent years the French and British naval and military experts have consulted together. It has always been understood that such consultation does not restrict the freedom of either Government to decide at any future time whether or not to assist the other by armed force. We have agreed that consultation between experts is not, and ought not to be, regarded as an engagement that commits either Government to action in a contingency that has not arisen and may never arise. The disposition, for instance, of the French and British fleets respectively at the present moment is not based upon an engagement to co-operate in war.

"You have, however, pointed out that if either Government had grave reason to expect an unprovoked attack by a third Power it might become essential to know whether it could in that event, depend upon the armed assistance of the other.

"I agree that, if either Government had grave reason to expect an unprovoked attack by a third Power, or something that threatened the general peace, it should immediately discuss with the other whether both Governments should act together to prevent aggression and to preserve peace, and, if so, what measures they would be prepared to take in common. If these measures involved action, the plans of the general staffs would at once be taken into consideration, and the Governments would then decide what effect should be given to them." Grey, *Twenty-five Years,* i 94-95.

[15] Above, p. 708.

powers then intervened to secure a settlement, calling a conference in London. The negotiations were made in a tense atmosphere. Servia demanded the outlet to the Adriatic which she had been denied in 1909. Austria was opposed, fearing not only Servian economic competition but also a potential base for a Russian fleet. Russia was disposed to advocate the cause of her protégé. The feeling between Austria and Russia was bitter. At the conference Sir Edward Grey did not support the Servian claim and did much to restrain Russian demands. Germany supported the principal Austrian contention, but used persuasion to make Austria conciliatory. Under these circumstances a settlement satisfactory to Austria was obtained and serious danger of a general European conflict was avoided. Sir Edward Grey was largely responsible, and he was aided effectively by the German representative.

The last turn of the Balkan wheel went against Austria. After the treaty, which was signed on May 13, 1913, the Balkan allies soon quarreled among themselves over the division of the spoils. Servia and Greece conquered Bulgaria, and in August forced upon her the treaty of Bucharest, which gave them the lion's share. The outcome was a sharp decline of Austrian prestige in the Balkans. Austria had long supported Bulgaria, which had been the strongest of the Balkan states. The new situation left Bulgaria weak, while Servia, where the "greater Servia" agitation stimulated disorder in Bosnia and Herzegovina and seemed to threaten the disruption of Austria-Hungary, was rendered stronger and more influential than before.

Such was the situation when the assassination of the archduke of Austria and his wife in Serajevo, the capital of Bosnia, on June 28, 1914, set in motion the events which led directly to the Great War. The assassins were Bosnians who received arms and incitement to the deed from Servians.[16] The Austrian government determined to take the favorable opportunity to deal with Servia. On July 2 the Austrian government sent to William II a statement of its proposed policy in the Balkans, which included the elimination of Servia "as a factor of political power in the Balkans."[17] The kaiser, recognizing that it probably meant Austrian military action against Servia and possible war with Russia, expressed his approval on July 5. On the next day the chancellor, speaking officially, said to the Austrian agent: "Austria must

Serajevo and the Austrian ultimatum

[16] Whether or not the Servian prime minister knew of the plot and took no steps to stop it or to notify the Austrian government seems to be impossible to decide certainly on the basis of the evidence so far uncovered. At the time the Austrian government was able to establish no connection of the Servian government with the plot.

[17] *German Documents Collected by Kautsky*, tr. by Carnegie Endowment, no. 13.

judge what is to be done to clear up her relation to Servia; whatever Austria's decision may turn out to be, Austria can count with certainty upon it, that Germany will stand behind her as an ally and friend."[18] Virtually Austria was told to do whatever she pleased, and that, whatever she did, Germany's armies were at her disposal in case of need. With Germany tied to her apronstrings Austria prepared to force a war upon Servia. On July 23 she presented to Servia an ultimatum designedly so stiff as to render acceptance impossible. It demanded the extirpation of the "greater Servia" movement and prescribed the ways in which it should be accomplished. An answer was required within forty-eight hours. On July 25 Servia's reply conceded practically all the demands, except only those which violated her sovereignty. If her reply should be judged unsatisfactory by Austria, she offered to submit the whole question to arbitration. Within a few minutes of its receipt, Austria declared the answer insufficient and her ambassador withdrew from Belgrade. The same evening Servia mobilized, and presently Austria mobilized against Servia.

Efforts to maintain peace

After the murder, the British government watched events with anxiety. Though Great Britain was not directly involved, the possibility of a critical situation in European politics was manifest. If Austria attacked Servia, it was probable that Russia would come to Servia's protection. Though the definite commitment of Germany to aid Austria in that case was not known to Grey, the probability of that outcome was obvious. When the publication of the ultimatum made it appear that Austria was likely to provoke a war with Servia, Grey began efforts to prevent the outbreak of hostilities. He asked Germany to use its influence with Austria to secure an extension of the time limit, asked Russia not to mobilize before he had had time to work for peace, and urged moderation upon Servia. On July 26 he asked Italy, France, and Germany to join with Great Britain in a conference to discover "an issue which would prevent complications."[19] Austrian consent, which was a *sine qua non* for such mediation, could be had only through German initiative. Germany replied on July 27 that such a conference would be tantamount to a court of arbitration, which could be called only at the request of Russia and Austria. Meanwhile the Russian foreign office had suggested direct conversations between the Russian and Austrian governments as a better means of reaching an understanding.

These events occurred before the text of the Servian reply to the

---

[18] Cited by Fay, in *Am. Hist. Rev.*, xxv, 627.
[19] *Cambridge History of British Foreign Policy*, iii, 490.

ultimatum reached the foreign offices of Great Britain, Germany, and Russia. When it arrived on July 27, it produced at all three courts the impression that no sufficient cause of war was left. Sir Edward Grey immediately had a conversation with the German ambassador. He maintained that Servia, because of pressure from Russia, had yielded such an unbelievable amount of the Austrian demands that Austrian failure to accept the reply as a basis for peaceful negotiations could be interpreted only as an intention to seek an excuse to crush Servia. Since he had used his influence for moderation with Russia, he requested Germany to urge Austria to accept the reply as a basis for a conference. After the report of this conversation and the receipt of the text of Servia's reply, the German government seems to have changed its attitude somewhat. Later in the day it suggested to the Austrian government, apparently for the first time, that it might be well to consider the possibility of peaceful conversations before resorting to war. During the next three days the German government bombarded Vienna with telegrams urging Austria to enter upon negotiations with Russia. In one telegram the German pressure even went to the verge of a threat.

The action came too late. On July 28 Austria declared war on Servia "chiefly to frustrate any attempt at intervention."[20] Two days later the Austrian government professed itself willing to listen to some of the suggested projects of mediation. Had its profession been sincere, it had been delayed too long to prevent European conflict. The previous evening Russia had begun to mobilize. Russia mobilized slowly. When news reached the Russian capital on July 29 that the Austrian guns were bombarding Belgrade, a partial Russian mobilization on the Austrian frontier was ordered. Russia feared that delay of mobilization for further discussion would enable Austria to overwhelm Servia before Russian help could arrive. Since mobilization was recognized by Germany as practically the beginning of war, the maintenance of the general peace was rendered next to impossible. During the night of July 30 Russia ordered general mobilization, and on the next day Austria began mobilization against Russia. Since the Russian mobilization was now publicly directed against the German frontier as well as the Austrian, Germany, on July 31, declared the "threatened state of war" which was preparatory to German mobilization. At the same time Germany sent to Russia an ultimatum demanding within twelve hours a promise to demobilize, and to France

Outbreak of war

---

[20] *Am. Hist. Rev.,* xxv, 637; Kautsky, *Documents,* nos. 257, 313.

an ultimatum demanding within eighteen hours a promise of neutrality. Failing to receive satisfactory replies, Germany declared war against Russia on August 1 and against France on August 3.

Entry of
Great
Britain

Whether Great Britain would enter the war or remain neutral was not decided definitively until August 4. On July 27 the seriousness of the diplomatic situation was placed before the cabinet and before parliament. The cabinet reached no conclusion on what its action would be in the eventuality of a general conflict. It was so thoroughly divided in opinion that a decision would have caused its downfall. In parliament the difference of opinion was equally great, and it ran athwart the lines of party. The nation spoke with no more certain voice. Grey felt that Great Britain was not definitely committed to support France in the event of war, and that, in the existing state of public opinion, he must give no pledge. Repeated requests from France and Russia for a pledge were met with a negative, the last being issued as late as August 1. Even when France asked, in accordance with the agreement of 1912, for a definite answer, the cabinet replied on July 31 that it could make no engagement. To a request from the other side for British neutrality Grey gave a like answer, though he intimated to the German ambassador that Great Britain would be quickly drawn in if Germany and France should become involved. On July 31 he asked the French and German governments to respect Belgian neutrality. The acceptance of France and the evasion of Germany created a strong feeling in the cabinet. On the next day Grey proposed to the cabinet that, since the French fleet was in the Mediterranean, the British fleet should oppose the German fleet if it came through the North Sea or the straits of Dover to attack France. On the day following, the cabinet, having before it a statement of the leaders of the opposition that they would uphold the government in the support of France, sanctioned Grey's proposal, subject to parliamentary approval. Though the liability was as yet limited, the cabinet was practically committed to war. Two of the members, who opposed war, resigned. Parliament and the nation, however, were still free to decide. Grey presented the question to the house on August 3 in a powerful speech. The interests of the empire were at stake, as Grey freely stated. If France should be crushed, the nicely adjusted balance of power would be destroyed, and the very existence of the empire would be imperiled. All this influenced public opinion, but it was the German ultimatum to Belgium that turned the tide definitively. News that it had been issued on the previous day was confirmed while the house was sitting. The attack on little Belgium, whose neutrality

Prussia had guaranteed, caused a revolution in public opinion, bringing into line the doubters and the waverers. The house of commons supported war without a division. On the next day news arrived of the actual violation of Belgian neutrality by Germany. The cabinet, now united, despatched an ultimatum to Germany. At midnight, when no answer had been received, Great Britain was at war with Germany.

At the beginning of the war the powers of the entente had a numerical superiority of armed forces available. Their armies outnumbered those of the central powers by approximately thirty-five per cent.[21] The British navy gave the allied powers control of the sea, keeping open a field of supply far greater than that available to the central powers. During the course of the war these factors became of decisive importance; at the beginning they were of less value. At that time, moreover, the central powers had the advantage in nearly every other particular. They had the central position, which enabled them to transfer their armies wherever they were needed. They possessed the more centralized command, the better-equipped armies, and the better communications. At the outbreak of the war they sent against France armies which outnumbered those of their opponents, relying on their unified control and their facilities of transport to transfer some of them to the Russian front, should it become necessary. The armies of the entente were on two widely separated fronts. On the western front the three armies of Belgium, Great Britain, and France lacked the single command necessary for efficient operations. On the eastern front the Russians could not utilize all of their man power for lack of adequate means of transportation. The Russian armies placed in the field were often short of arms and ammunition. Great Britain, despite the control of the sea, could not supply the deficiency, because Germany dominated the Baltic and soon obtained control of the Danish straits, leaving the northern route, which was icebound during a large part of the year, the only one open. The initial advantage rested with the central powers.

The war began with the German invasion of Belgium. The German plan was to attack before the armies of France were fully organized, put them out of the war, and thus secure freedom to pit the whole force of Germany against Russia with her greater but less mobile resources. The Belgian route was selected for two reasons. The French frontier of Germany was protected by the terrain, by defenses, and by French troops far better than the French frontier of Belgium.

Resources of the combatants

Invasion of Belgium

---

[21] Based on Maurice's statement in *These Eventful Years*, i, 229.

Frontal attack was likely to cause fatal delay. The French mobilization, moreover, was concentrated against the German frontier. If the German armies went through Belgium as speedily as planned, they would strike the main French force on the flank, or in the midst of the confusion attendant upon a change of front undertaken during the process of mobilization. The success of the German campaign depended upon the rapidity of its execution. Belgium resisted invasion. The little Belgian army could not stop the mighty German hosts, but it compelled them to take eighteen days in place of six to cross Belgium.

Invasion of France

The delay gave Joffre, the commander of the French armies, time to make new disposition of his forces and enabled the British to transport an army of 90,000 and place it on the Belgian frontier. French troops also came up. Neither arrived in time to help the Belgians. The Germans had captured the last fortified place between them and France, when the British and the French advanced. Met by superior numbers, the French line broke, and the British had to retreat rapidly. The Germans advanced, sweeping all before them, until they reached the line of the Marne, where Joffre had prepared for the main defense. The battle of the Marne lasted several days, ending in German defeat. The Germans retreated to the Aisne, where they stopped the French and British pursuit and intrenched themselves. The battle of the Marne was a decisive victory. It destroyed the German hope of the immediate elimination of France, and settled that the war would be long. The decision was an advantage to the allies, who needed time to organize and utilize their resources. Great Britain had put practically its whole available force in the field, but with more time at its disposal it was able to raise, drill, and equip millions of soldiers. Time fought on the side of the allies. In the north, meanwhile, the Germans took Antwerp and began a drive to secure the coastal towns on the Channel. The Belgian, British, and French lines held until the arrival of British and French reinforcements from the south finally forced the Germans to give up their attempt. Had they reached Calais and Boulogne, which were their objectives, the communications between Great Britain and France would have been rendered far more difficult and dangerous. With the end of this campaign both sides intrenched. The battle line, extending 600 miles from the coast to Switzerland, became an intricate series of trenches and defenses, which could be broken only by a tremendous sacrifice of life. For a long time the line remained nearly stationary.

The Russians took the offensive early in August. From the salient of Russian Poland one army invaded eastern Prussia, while another invaded Austrian Galicia. The Russian army in Prussia was defeated by Hindenburg in one of the most overwhelming victories of the war. More than 80,000 Russians were taken prisoners. Against the Austrians the Russians were successful. They won one center of importance by a great battle and were before another when a counter-offensive, organized by Hindenburg, forced them to withdraw to defend Russian Poland. Having compelled Hindenburg to retire, they returned to Galicia, where, in the early spring of 1915, they took their second objective. Hindenburg meanwhile launched a second counter-offensive, which established the Germans in trenches in Russian Poland, but did not divert the Russian attack on Galicia. This was the climax of Russia's success. The trench warfare having released many German troops from the western front, a huge army of over 2,000,000 Germans and Austrians was assembled to overwhelm the Russians. Mackensen drove them out of Galicia in the late spring, and Hindenburg followed with an invasion of Poland. Warsaw was captured and the Russians were forced to withdraw their line far behind their own frontier. Not only to the Russians who had lost millions of men, but to the whole allied cause, it was a terrible disaster. Russia still possessed an immense reservoir of man power; but with a corrupt government, inadequate supplies, poor means of transport, and a badly shattered morale, the Russian preponderance in man power counted for little. The war had to be won in the west.

Meanwhile the British had taken over control of the sea. At the outbreak of the war the German navy sought safety in home ports, where most of it stayed throughout the war. A few German cruisers remained on the ocean, doing damage to British shipping, until the last of them was sunk in 1915. Early in the war Japan entered in alliance with Great Britain and besieged and took Kiaochow, the German possession in China. Since this had served as a base for several of the German cruisers, Japanese aid released a part of the British navy for work in other parts of the world. The British navy fought few important engagements because the Germans gave no opportunity. An attack on a German fleet stationed at Heligoland sank four German ships (1914), and a German fleet, which raided the coast of England, received extensive injuries, though only one cruiser was sunk (Dogger Bank, 1915).

The uncontested control of the seas was an advantage to the allies. Their ships could range the world for supplies and transport troops from Great Britain and from the British colonies to the front without let or hindrance. The resources of the world were at the disposal of the allies. The central powers, on the other hand, were confined to their own resources. Within a week German merchant ships were swept from blue water. Great Britain also limited greatly the supplies which Germany could obtain from neutrals by extending the list of contraband, searching all ships bound for Germany or adjacent neutral states, and seizing therefrom contraband goods. At the end of 1914, when the German government placed the food supply of Germany under public control, the British government declared contraband all foodstuffs destined for Germany, throwing the central powers on their own resources for food. Early in 1915 Germany replied with a submarine campaign. The submarines lurked off the British coast and torpedoed such British ships as they could intercept. What the campaign meant was brought home to the world when the *Lusitania* was sunk with nearly 2,000 passengers, of whom 100 and more were citizens of the United States. The U-boats did such damage to British shipping that they caused grave apprehension. Great Britain was utterly dependent upon an outside supply of food. If Germany could cut off that supply, Great Britain would be helpless. The campaign of 1915, however, fell far short of that result. Food, ammunition, and troops still moved across the waters with only a small percentage of loss.

German colonies

Another result of the British naval superiority was the easy conquest of the German colonies. Those in the Pacific were taken with the aid of Japan during the first few months of the war. The colonies on the Guinea coast of Africa required a greater effort, but the last one was conquered by an Anglo-French expedition early in 1916. In southern Africa difficulties were encountered. An expedition sent against German Southwest Africa had to be recalled because a small group of discontented Boers started a rebellion in the South African Union. The majority of the Boers remained loyal and assisted the British to put the rebellion down. It lasted only for a few months. In 1915 the delayed expedition returned to the charge and took German Southwest Africa. Only in German East Africa did the Germans offer successful resistance. There British arms did not finally triumph until 1918.

The Near East

Aside from the Russian campaigns, the most important developments in 1915 took place in the Near East. To the central powers control of this section was vital. Deprived of commerce by sea, the Near East was the one place where they could obtain the necessary additional supplies and establish a route to the east which would provide their industries with markets. To the allied powers its possession was not of such fundamental importance, but its control by the central powers would threaten the Russian position on the Black Sea and in central Asia, and the British empire in Egypt and India. Turkey, where German influence was strong, joined the central powers soon after the outbreak of the war. The central powers could not reap the full benefits of Turkish adherence to their cause unless a continuous route of communication between Austria and Turkey could be established. The support of Bulgaria, Roumania, and Greece came to be of crucial importance, and both groups of belligerents made strenuous diplomatic efforts to secure it.

The allies, moreover, attempted to obtain control of the Straits and thereby render the Turkish alliance valueless. Early in 1915 a fleet bombarded the fortifications in the Dardanelles and an expeditionary force was landed on the peninsula of Gallipoli. The campaign was perhaps misconceived; it was certainly mismanaged. It ended in failure. Several ships were lost in the bombardment, the troops were decimated, and nothing was gained. The attack was at a standstill by the summer of 1915, though the troops were not withdrawn until the next winter. **Gallipoli**

During 1915 two new nations joined the groups of the antagonists. Italy entered on the side of the allies in the spring. The Italian people evinced a sympathy for the allied cause, but the Italian government sold to the highest bidder. The Italian diplomats sought to recover the portions of Austria inhabited by Italians, long designated as "Italia irredenta." Austria was willing to cede them as the price of Italian support, but naturally sought to confine the districts within as narrow limits as possible. The allies, bargaining with lands not their own, could afford to be more liberal. By the Treaty of London they promised to Italy districts on the north of Italy and on the eastern side of the Adriatic, which went far beyond the limits of any Italian population and included the lands of many Germans and Jugoslavs. The accession of Italy had no immediate result of importance. Her geography forces Italy to mobilize her military power slowly. Her attention was directed to the conquest of the lands ceded by the Treaty of London, where the terrain rendered attack difficult and defense easy. The only immediate result was to divert a part of the Austrian army to the new front. The entrance of Bulgaria on the side of the central powers in September of 1915 had more striking immediate consequences. **Italy and Bulgaria**

The first was the conquest of Servia. During the first year of the

Conquest
of Servia

war. Servia, with an heroic ability that exceeded expectations, repelled three invasions of the Austrians. In the autumn of 1915 a large Austro-German army invaded from the north and a large Bulgarian army from the east. Servia was overwhelmed. Only a small remnant of her forces escaped. The Austro-German army, continuing its advance, conquered Montenegro and Albania. The allies had hoped for Greek help, but Greece remained neutral. When it was too late, they landed an inadequate force at Salonika, a Greek port, which controls the southern entrance of Servia. It not only accomplished nothing, but it was saved from dire peril only by the transfer of the troops on Gallipoli to Salonika.

Asiatic
Turkey

With communications between the central powers and Turkey established, the significance of Teutonic control of the Near East soon became manifest. Turkish troops were sent over the Bagdad railway to meet a British expedition which was working toward Bagdad from the Persian gulf. The British troops were soon besieged in Kut-el-Amara. Relief expeditions were defeated. A large Russian force, which came down upon Asiatic Turkey from the north, had some success, but not enough to divert the Turks from the siege. In the spring of 1916 Kut-el-Amara fell. Subsequently the invading Russians were put on the defensive in Armenia.

Western
front,
1915–1916

On the western front it was slowly demonstrated in 1915 and 1916 that victory in the system of trench warfare would depend ultimately on superiority in numbers of men and amounts of munitions. In the spring of 1915 the Germans withdrew large forces for their attack on Russia and stood on the defensive in the west. The British, who now numbered half a million or more, took the offensive, as did the French in two other places. None of the drives yielded their objectives. In the counter-attack against Ypres the Germans, though they surprised the allies by the use of poisonous gas, likewise failed of their objective. The chief difficulty of the allies was the lack of sufficient shells to destroy the German trenches and entanglements in the area where an attack was projected. By early autumn this handicap was overcome, but two offensives attempted by the British and the French in September yielded small results and fell far short of their objectives. Early in 1916 the Germans, having settled with the Russians, returned to the attack on the western front. In the sector of Verdun they massed large forces and made a determined attack for several months. They advanced their lines for some distance, but they did not take Verdun or break through. Virtually it was a French victory. In the summer the allies attempted a similar drive on the

Somme with a similar result. They advanced for a few miles, but failed of their objectives. The losses in such attacks were enormous on both sides, but the allies could better stand the wastage of men. In 1916 Great Britain adopted compulsory military service, and fresh troops continued to come from the dominions. Germany and Austria had already passed the peak of their effective fighting strength. In 1916, moreover, the allies equaled, if they did not surpass, the enemy in their equipment of munitions, gas, planes, and other engines of trench warfare.

In 1916 Germany risked an encounter with the British navy for the first and only time during the war. In the spring protests of the United States caused the German government to modify its policy with regard to submarines. It promised not to sink merchant ships without warning. Since this limited the effectiveness of the submarine offensive, Germany apparently decided to take issue with the British fleet. On May 31 the German fleet steamed into the North Sea, where it was discovered by an advance squadron of the British fleet commanded by Admiral Beatty. Though the British fleet was smaller than the German, it engaged at once in order to hold the German fleet until the main British force, commanded by Admiral Jellicoe, could come up. When it arrived, the British fleet endeavored to encircle the German to prevent its return to German ports. The maneuver was unsuccessful. During the night the German fleet escaped. The losses of the British fleet were considerably more than those of the German, but only the escape of the German fleet during the darkness saved it from destruction. The Germans were well aware of their plight. They never dared to risk another encounter. The British control of the seas was left more secure than ever.

Battle of Jutland

On the eastern front Russia surprised the central powers by the force with which she returned to the charge after her disaster of the year before. Along a front of 250 miles the Russian armies pushed back the Austrians for a distance of from twenty to sixty miles, occupying a large amount of Austrian territory. The Austrians were compelled to give up a drive begun against the Italians and to withdraw all available troops for use on the eastern front. The Italians, who had been pushed down the slopes of the Alps, were making a desperate and successful stand. They followed the retreat of the Austrians with a forward movement which yielded Gorizia, the first stage on the road to Trieste. Late in the summer Roumania entered on the side of the Allies. Russia failed to support her, and the allied army at Salonika, which had now swelled to 700,000, did nothing.

Other fronts, 1916

The central powers put in the field a large army which overran Roumania and occupied two-thirds of it.

Changes
in the
cabinet

The spectacular victory of the central powers in Roumania was partly responsible for a change of cabinet in Great Britain. When the war began in 1914, it became unpatriotic to oppose the government. It was agreed to drop all contentious legislation. An official opposition practically ceased to exist. Though Asquith began to consult the leaders of the opposition informally, the feeling grew among the Conservatives that their support should be acknowledged by the inclusion of some of their leaders in the cabinet. The claim was given point by the signs of weakness which the Liberal cabinet had shown before the outbreak of the war. When the leaders of the opposition let Asquith know that they would offer criticisms of the conduct of the war, he formed a coalition cabinet in May, 1915. It was composed mainly of Liberals and Conservatives, but included also a member of the Labor party. During 1916 the failure to win any decisive result so frayed the nerves of a public weary of war that criticism of the cabinet became strong. It was felt that Asquith was handicapped in the vigorous prosecution of the war by his regard for the constitutional liberties of the subject. Much power had been centralized in the hands of the cabinet, as is inevitable in time of war, but the public thought the cabinet used its power somewhat hesitantly. A supreme effort to win the war regardless of the liberties of the subject became a popular desire. Lloyd George seemed better adapted for such a part. In the coalition cabinet he had held the new office of minister of munitions. He had administered with enthusiasm and success the Munitions Act, which interfered more with the liberties of civilians than any act up to that date. He was always the keen exponent of the popular sentiment of the moment, and he was a foremost preacher of the gospel of the sacrifice of all else to the winning of the war. In December of 1916 the popular demand became so strong that Asquith resigned to make way for Lloyd George at the head of a new coalition cabinet.

The war
cabinet

The change went beyond one merely of personnel. A constitutional reorganization of the cabinet also took place. Long before the war the cabinet appeared unwieldy to keen observers. Twenty intelligent men sitting around a table must necessarily have differences of opinion. With unity an essential principle of cabinet government, agreement sometimes became difficult. Decisions by the full cabinet meant loss of time and effort in discussion, and they might easily result in half-hearted compromises. Heads of administrative departments might have to give to discussion time needed for the work of their departments. A tendency was evident to form a circle within a circle. On some policies the prime minister apparently substituted the advice of a few of his colleagues for that of the whole cabinet. The strain of war brought the development to a climax. The number of the cabinet was increased by the inclusion of the heads of new departments, such as the ministry of munitions; agreement became more difficult when prompt action was more imperative; more meetings of the cabinet were necessary when it was more important than ever that the heads of departments should devote their attention more largely to their departments. The cabinet of 1916 was designed to overcome these handicaps. It consisted of only five members, though the number was later increased to seven. It was responsible for the general policy, particularly with regard to the war. The other heads of departments, who had previously been included in the cabinet, were relegated to the ministry. They were still jointly responsible for the general policy and would resign if the cabinet did, but they no longer had an authoritative voice in the decisions. The heads of departments were left freer to give attention to the complex problems raised by the steadily increasing control of industry and commerce by the government.

The Germans were nearly as disturbed by the failure to obtain a decision in 1916 as were the allies. They held large territories belonging to their enemies, but the possibility of increase grew smaller as the war of wastage continued. The German government consequently tried to induce the allies to negotiate a peace while Germany was in an advantageous position to dictate the terms. The allies declined. Germany then determined to let loose her submarines in an attempt to destroy British commerce and starve Great Britain into surrender. On January 31, 1917, the German government announced that all ships, enemy or neutral, within a certain distance of Great Britain, France, or Italy, would be sunk on sight. The United States was offered lanes which could be traveled at times and under conditions such as no independent power could accept. The campaign of ruthlessness bade fair for a time to be successful. The amount of British shipping sunk by the submarines had grown steadily for the past two years. In 1917 the tonnage of British ships destroyed in the first six months nearly equaled the loss of the whole of the preceding year. British ships were being destroyed faster than they could be replaced. The acceleration of the destruction of allied and neutral shipping was even greater. In the second half of the year, however, the rate declined. The allies used convoys successfully for protection

Unrestricted submarine warfare

against the submarines, and they devised many new methods of defense. The rate was still alarmingly high, but it was more than offset by the further result of the unrestricted submarine warfare, which was the entry of the United States into the war in April, 1917. President Wilson had protested immediately against the proposed policy of sinking neutral ships. As soon as ships of the United States were sunk, the United States declared war. Though troops from the United States did not arrive in France in sufficient numbers to have a significant effect upon the outcome until the next year, ships and supplies were available at once in quantities more than sufficient to defeat the purpose of the unrestricted submarine campaign.

Russia's exit

Just as the United States was entering the war Russia was leaving it. In March of 1917 a revolution gave a stupid and corrupt autocracy its deserts. For several months "confusion worse confounded" reigned in Russia. Power finally lodged with radical Bolshevists. The army was necessarily infected with the disorder. During the summer the Germans pushed it back at will, releasing the greater part of their eastern divisions for use on the western front. In the spring of 1918 the Germans dictated the terms of the Treaty of Brest-Litovsk, which gave them practical control of a large part of Russia. They were rapidly extending their influence in the remainder by gradual penetration, when the allies sent to northern Russia a sufficient force to enable the groups opposed to the Bolshevist régime to place a check on German aspirations.

The Near East, 1917

While this misfortune to the allied cause was developing, the British began for the first time to make headway in the Near East. The army in Mesopotamia recovered Kut-el-Amara, took Bagdad, and pushed the Turks nearly out of Mesopotamia. Later in the year another expedition went from Egypt through Syria and captured Jerusalem. These campaigns got well under way the movement which finally caused the collapse of Turkey. The situation in the Near East was further improved by the entrance of Greece on the side of the allies. The allied army at Salonika was thus enabled to operate more freely, though it accomplished nothing of significance until 1918.

Caporetto

To Italy 1917 brought disaster. Some of the Austro-German divisions, freed from the eastern front, were transferred to the Italian front, where they began an offensive in the autumn. At Caporetto, where the Italian line turned west from south, two Italian corps allowed the Germans to come through. Only by an extremely rapid retreat were the Italian armies saved. They fell back all the way to the Piave, where they finally held. Though it was a great disaster, Italy was not put out of the war, as the central powers had hoped.

On the western front the season of 1917 opened favorably for the allies. The Germans retired for several miles on the front of the Somme, which had been rendered untenable by the allied drive of the previous season. The retreat shortened their line and gave them a new system of superior trenches called the Hindenburg line; but it yielded to the British a significant amount of territory. Subsequently the story was less happy. The allies, who now had superiority in numbers, took the initiative. An army, mainly French and under French command, sought to end the slow work of nibbling, break through the German lines on an extended front, and force a war of movement. It failed disastrously. The losses were so great and the disappointment so keen that the British had to attack the Germans to keep them occupied in Flanders, while the French recovered their morale. Though the British drive yielded little territory, it served its purpose. Late in the summer the French renewed the offensive with some success. The results obtained by the allies in 1917 were small compared with the high hopes with which the campaigns had been begun in the spring.

Western front, 1917

In the spring of 1918 the numerical superiority of the British and the French had been lost. The German divisions brought from the east had practically equalized the numbers. The Germans, however, had practically their whole force in the field, while the allies had a fresh source of supply in the American troops, which now began to arrive rapidly. The Germans consequently staked their all on an effort to win the war before the Americans could be placed in the front line in large numbers. In March the Germans went through the thinly held British trenches in front of Amiens and many miles beyond. They were held short of Amiens, a critical center in the allied line of communication, but they made one of the greatest advances so far accomplished on the western front. They followed with a second successful drive to the north, and a third to the south which brought them to Chateau Thierry on the Marne. Their territorial gains constituted deep and dangerous salients in the allied line.

German offensive

But the turn of the tide had come. The German casualties, which had been tremendous, could be replaced only to a very limited extent. Their troops, moreover, were displaying signs of war weariness. The British, on the other hand, received considerable reinforcements from home, and by July more than a million American soldiers had reached France. Two divisions were employed in the army which

Allied offensive, 1918

checked the German advance at Chateau Thierry, and subsequently they were utilized in rapidly increasing numbers. Moreover, the great danger had finally produced unity of command under Foch. In July, when the Germans began their fourth thrust, it was stopped quickly. The allies then launched a counter-offensive. In the second battle of the Marne they wiped out the salient which the Germans had established by their third attack. The allies then attacked at several places with uniform success. At the end of September the British broke through the Hindenburg system of defenses in Flanders. This finally convinced the German command on the western front that the war must be ended.

The German government hesitated. The news from other fronts helped it to reach a decision. During the summer the allied army with its base at Salonika overwhelmed the Bulgarians, who signed an armistice on September 29. In Turkish Asia the British armies in Syria and Mesopotamia both continued to advance, until the Turks signed an armistice on October 30. In Austria-Hungary the subject nationalities revolted on a widespread scale during 1918. When the Italians took the offensive in October, they found the Austrian army demoralized and soon put it to complete rout. On November 3 the Austrians signed an armistice. Bereft of allies, with their opponents advancing steadily and rapidly on the whole length of the western front, the Germans had no option. On November 11 they signed the armistice dictated by the allies, bringing the war to an end.

The internal affairs of Great Britain during the war were managed by the government primarily with a view to the necessities of the war. The organization of the community for that purpose was a triumph of legislative and administrative skill, but it was necessarily of an ephemeral character. The only important permanent changes wrought by legislation were the reform of elementary education by act of 1918 and the fourth reform of the house of commons enacted in the same year.

The crying need of better facilities for elementary education was driven home by the strain of the war. Great numbers of children never continued their education beyond the low minimum required by law.[22] Between the years of twelve and fourteen they joined the ranks of unskilled workers, losing all prospect of improving their lot in life. Too many of them eventually became unemployables because they never learned to do anything well. For once the department

Margin notes: End of the war — Reforms of 1918 — Education

---

[22] Above, p. 729.

of education was headed by an educator, H. A. L. Fisher, who treated the problem from an educational rather than a religious point of view. The act required attendance at school for full time from the ages of five to fourteen and attendance for part time in continuation schools until the age of eighteen. It also attempted in a variety of ways to improve the quality of the instruction given in elementary schools. The cost was so heavy that the clause with regard to continuation schools never went into effect.

The genesis of the reform of parliament is probably to be found in the movement for women's suffrage. During the twentieth century British women had been agitating for the right to vote, and during the years immediately preceding the war a radical group had indulged in violent demonstrations of one sort or another. With the outbreak of the war the agitation ceased, but British women contributed so magnificently to war work that opposition to their participation in the franchise practically disappeared. The act of 1918 conferred the right to vote upon every woman thirty years of age, who occupied a house or other property worth a rental of £5 a year, or whose husband occupied such property. It also made a sweeping change in the male franchise. A man twenty-one years of age may now qualify by residence, by occupation of business premises worth £10 annually, or by a university degree. Plural voting was restricted. A voter may not vote in more than two of the constituencies where he may be qualified. The act also redistributed the seats. It increased the membership of the house of commons to 707[23] and apportioned the seats one to a district. The approximate population of the district in Great Britain was 70,000, and in Ireland 43,000. A few boroughs with a population slightly below the average kept a single member and a few two-member constituencies were preserved. The act increased the electorate two and a half times.

Reform of parliament

---

[23] Reduced to 615 in 1922 when the Irish Free State was established.

CHAPTER XLI

INTERNAL AND IMPERIAL DEVELOPMENTS, 1918-1944

Election of 1918

As soon as the war was finished Lloyd George went to the polls. The condition in parliament was anomalous. Since 1916, when its life expired, parliament had several times prolonged its own existence in order to prevent an appeal to the electorate in the midst of war. During the war an official opposition did not exist, but signs of dissatisfaction had not been wanting. Despite the huge program of social reform enacted by the Liberals before the war, much social discontent remained. The irksome restrictions necessitated by the control of industry and food and the strain of distress and suffering caused by the war had a cumulative effect in the production of a desire for reform. As long as the war lasted, patriotism restrained any attempt to express this opinion, but the vague desire that a better England should follow the war took possession of many people. The leaders of the Labor party, who abandoned the coalition, met this situation with an attractive program of post-war reconstruction. At the same time, they made it much easier to affiliate with the party; and the dissatisfied, whether they were laborers or not, displayed a pronounced tendency to join the ranks of the Labor party. At the polls, however, past evils and future reforms were alike forgotten. The election became a vote of gratitude to the cabinet which had won the war. In the campaign Lloyd George worked with the Conservative leader, Bonar Law, to favor Conservatives and oppose Liberals in many constituencies in order to preserve the balance between the two parties in the coalition upon which the two leaders had agreed. The result was to split the Liberal party beyond repair. One wing followed Lloyd George into the coalition with the Conservatives, while the other went into opposition. The coalition secured 526 seats, a majority over all. Labor, though it returned with only sixty-one seats, became the official opposition because it had more seats than the independent Liberals.

Cabinets 1918–1944; the coalition

Lloyd George remained at the head of the coalition government until October, 1922. It was a troubled period. Not only did the settlement of Europe present extremely difficult problems, but Great Britain and the empire also provided hectic experiences. The cabinet met disturbances in Ireland, Egypt and India with policies which were reasonably successful. In Great Britain the difficulties of the transition from war to peace were enhanced by numerous strikes, and after 1920 the inevitable depression caused a huge amount of unemployment. The attempts of the government to cope with the situation failed to bring about the utopia of which men had dreamed during the war, and some of the resulting discontent was directed against the government. Lloyd George's management of foreign relations also evoked criticism, and it was the Near-Eastern situation which became the immediate occasion of his fall. The Turkish nationalist party, refusing to accept the treaty presented to Turkey at the close of the war, set up a capital in Asia Minor and began to reconquer some of the territory which the treaty had assigned to the Greeks. Great Britain continued to support the Greeks, while France advocated a revision of the treaty in favor of the Turks. In 1922 France made a separate treaty with the Turks, the Greeks were overwhelmed, and Great Britain was left in a position where it had to go to war in behalf of Greece or concede what the Turks demanded. British support of the Greeks had been a mistake from the beginning, and the outcome was too much for the Conservative followers of Lloyd George. The majority of them announced their abandonment of the coalition, causing Lloyd George to resign.

Bonar Law formed a Conservative cabinet, and an election, fought on the slogan of tranquillity, gave the cabinet a majority. After a few months the new prime minister was forced by failing health to retire, and Stanley Baldwin was chosen as his successor. He was not satisfied with a do-nothing policy, and desired to relieve the unemployment which continued on a large scale. What was needed was better industrial conditions, and he judged the remedy to be a protective tariff. During the war import duties had been placed upon several articles. Their primary purpose seems to have been fiscal, but some of them were so arranged as to give preference to goods imported from the colonies. After the war these duties were increased, and in 1921 duties were imposed to protect certain key industries. The amount of protection was not large, and Baldwin proposed the comprehensive application of preferential protection. In the election held on this issue popular opposition to the taxation of food caused the Conservatives to lose their majority. They still possessed more seats than any other party, but no party had a majority. Since the country had decided against the cardinal policy of the Conservatives, the king turned to the party with the next largest number, which was

The Conservatives, 1922–1924

the Labor party. Early in 1924 Ramsay MacDonald formed a Labor cabinet.

Labor, 1924

Though the Labor party was avowedly socialistic, many of its members did not believe in real socialism. Many of the trade unionist members regarded the party primarily as the means of attaining the practical ends which the unions desired, and many of the newer members were dissatisfied with both the older parties and regarded Labor merely as the party of progress. The cabinet attempted no approach to state socialism, and its dependence for a majority on the votes of the Liberals rendered impossible even the enactment of legislation of a distinctive party type. It abolished most of the protective duties enacted since 1915, and it passed a successful housing act which was no more radical than its predecessors in the field; but its internal policy was comparatively unimportant. It did not end unemployment, and it displayed no more genius than previous cabinets had done in the settlement of the many labor disputes which confronted it. Its greatest triumph was in the field of foreign affairs, where MacDonald succeeded in persuading France to accept a new and promising settlement of German reparations. The Labor cabinet was finally turned out in the autumn of 1924, when the Liberals deserted it in a critical vote on the question of the recognition of Soviet Russia.

Conservatives, 1924-1929

At the following election the Conservatives obtained a majority. They won more from Liberals than from Labor, and the Liberals came back a thoroughly broken and discredited party. Baldwin became prime minister for the second time. This cabinet brought back the amount of protection which the Labor government had swept away, met and conquered a general strike, and enacted a goodly amount of important legislation. Much of its legislation was not progressive enough, or else it did not improve existing economic and social conditions sufficiently, to satisfy the country. When parliament had run its legal life in 1929, Baldwin campaigned on "safety first," while the Labor party presented a program which contained many reforms but roused little fear of pure socialism. Many Labor candidates promised also to end unemployment. The Labor party came back from the election with more seats than any other party in the house, though it did not have a majority over both the Conservatives and the Liberals.

Labor, 1929-1931

Soon after MacDonald formed his cabinet, the admonitory symptoms of an economic depression began to appear. Before they were recognized, the government enacted a law which increased the sum disbursed for unemployment insurance. The greater part of the remaining bills designed to carry out the pledges made in the campaign failed of passage, and the promises to abolish unemployment resulted in nothing but talk. Some of the duties established by the previous cabinet were removed, but others were so profitable financially that the chancellor of the exchequer could not dispense with them when the income of the government was diminishing. In 1930 the economic situation became serious. The number of unemployed had more than doubled, placing such a financial strain upon the exchequer that a royal commission was appointed to seek a remedy. This was followed early in 1931 by a committee to investigate possible economies. Both reported in the summer that the financial situation of the government was grave. The committee claimed that the government faced a huge deficit which must be met if bankruptcy was to be avoided. It recommended that half of the deficit be obtained by reduction of expenditures, and half by additional taxation. On this issue the cabinet split. MacDonald and some of his colleagues wished to follow the recommendations of the committee; but the remainder, supported by the majority of the party, refused to contemplate economies which would reduce the amounts paid by the government to the unemployed. By that time the reports had alarmed foreigners who had money in England, and they were withdrawing gold from the Bank of England at such a rate that a complete collapse of the British system of credit was threatened. MacDonald consulted with the leaders of the opposition parties, secured the resignation of the cabinet, and waited upon the king. He was authorized by the king to form a national cabinet to meet the emergency.

The new cabinet contained leaders of all three parties, but the greater part of the Labor party went into opposition and support came mainly from Conservatives and Liberals. The cabinet secured the passage of a budget framed in accordance with the report of the committee, and, in order to retain what gold was left in the country, abandoned the gold standard, which had been restored in 1925 after departure from it during the war. The cabinet then went to the polls and won an overwhelming victory. The election was taken as a mandate for protection, and in 1932 a general tariff was established, preferences were negotiated with the dominions, and the quota system, by which Great Britain permits the importation of only a specified amount of certain commodities from another country in return for a similar concession from that country, came into use. Agriculture was regulated to increase the prices of products by reducing the amount of production, and farmers were helped to a certain extent by subsidies.

National cabinet, 1931-1944

A large part of the national debt was converted to bonds on which the rate of interest was lower, and payments on the war debt to the United States were first reduced and then dropped. By 1934 Great Britain had turned the corner. Unemployment was receding, and the taxes began to yield enough to enable the chancellor of the exchequer to restore the reductions made in unemployment benefits in 1931 and to reduce the income tax slightly.

The headship of the cabinet changed in 1935. Both in the cabinet and the house the Conservatives constituted the largest element in the coalition, and recognition was given to this fact by making Baldwin prime minister, though the cabinet retained the title of a national government. An election confirmed the reconstructed cabinet, and Baldwin remained in office until 1937, when he resigned on account of advancing years. He was followed by Neville Chamberlain, who also was a Conservative. Chamberlain was occupied mainly with an attempt to keep European peace which was threatened by Germany, and, when his effort failed, with the war which began in 1939. After the outbreak of hostilities he organized an inner cabinet in accordance with the precedent set in the preceding war. As a leader in war he did not arouse the enthusiasm of the British people. He had gone so far in his endeavors to appease Germany that doubts were entertained as to his capacity to meet the crisis. They found expression in open criticism after British attempts to prevent the German occupation of Norway in the spring of 1940 had failed. The British wanted a more resolute and aggressive leader. Recognizing the trend of public opinion, Chamberlain resigned. He was followed by another Conservative, Winston Churchill, who reorganized the cabinet extensively, bringing in members of the Labor party and also Conservatives who, like himself, had opposed the policy of appeasement. He has proved to be a great war minister.

Kings George V died early in 1936. When he came to the throne in 1910, he was not well known to his people. As he faced the grave problems created by the reform of the house of lords, Irish home rule, the war, and one further difficulty after another, he bore himself in such a manner that he gradually won the admiration and esteem of his subjects. He came to be regarded popularly as the ideal of what a constitutional monarch should be. In 1935 the celebration of the twenty-fifth anniversary of his accession evoked expressions of loyalty and affection throughout the empire. He was followed by Edward VIII, who abdicated before the close of the year. The cause of his action was his desire to marry Mrs. Simpson, the American wife of one of his subjects. The king's interest in Mrs. Simpson had been the subject of comment in the American newspapers for some time, when Baldwin, acting somewhat unconstitutionally without previous consultation of the cabinet, went to the king and advised him that such a marriage would create a scandal dangerous to the prestige of the crown. No law prevented the king from marrying the lady of his choice after she had obtained a divorce—which she soon did—but the prime minister advised him that "in the choice of the queen the voice of the people must be heard," and asserted that popular opinion would be adverse. Edward then asked the cabinet formally to secure the enactment of legislation authorizing a morganatic marriage which would not make his wife the queen. The cabinet, after consultation, replied that it would be impossible to obtain such legislation either in the British parliament or in the dominions. When Baldwin presented this information to the king, he added that the king now had left only the alternatives of abdication or abandonment of the marriage project. When the act of abdication was introduced into parliament, Baldwin explained what advice he and the cabinet had tendered, and received the support of an overwhelming majority. Apparently the British people were sorry to lose a popular king, but felt that abdication was the only solution if he insisted upon an unpopular marriage. Edward was followed upon the throne by his brother George VI.

One of the first problems which the government had to face after the conclusion of the war was demobilization both of the army and of the internal organization of the country built up during the war. The war had vastly accentuated the trend toward centralized paternalism which had already become apparent in the early years of the twentieth century, and it was desirable for the government to end its extensive regulation of the daily affairs of British citizens. In some spheres the change was relatively simple to make. In 1919, for example, the cabinet was restored to the form which it had had before the war. The governmental control of industries, on the other hand, could not be ended suddenly without a risk of economic dislocation which would cause hardship to many. This process was stimulated, however, by the economic slump which began in 1921. As wages and prices fell, the government found itself responsible for the payment of large subsidies to industries in which it had guaranteed a certain level of wages or prices during the war, and this hastened the process of decontrol of industry. In 1921 the government divested itself of control of the mines and railways and revoked its undertaking of the previous year to guarantee minimum wages and prices for grain in agriculture. The necessity for economy also served as a spur to reduce

Internal affairs: demobilization

more rapidly the size of the bureaucracy which had been developed during the war. Yet the process of decontrol was never carried far enough to limit the government to the functions which it had exercised before the war. It has had to intervene several times between mine operatives and the miners. The railways remained organized in four great systems as they had been during the war, the control of railway rates by the government was more complete than it had been before the war, and a national wages board was established to decide questions of wages. In 1924 the Labor government restored minimum wages in agriculture, and during the depression which began in 1929 the government assumed a larger control of agriculture than ever before. These are merely illustrations of a steady drift toward a more paternalistic government which became pronounced after 1918.

Several other significant constitutional changes have taken place. The paternalistic trend has tended to increase the strength of the executive at the expense of the legislature, and this growth of executive power has been augmented by the growing habit of enacting statutes in an extremely general form, leaving to the executive branch wide discretion in working out the details of their application by means of rules and orders. "This is, in effect, to transfer the legislative function to the Bureaucracy, who under powers conferred upon them by Parliament not infrequently perform, like the absolute monarchs of olden time, the threefold function of legislator, executor and judge."[1] In 1932 parliament delegated to the executive extensive powers to impose taxes in association with the new import duties. Important innovations in the procedure of the cabinet have taken place. The practice of the war cabinet of maintaining a secretariat has been retained, and minutes of the business transacted at cabinet meetings are kept and copies are distributed to the ministers. Much of the secrecy of cabinet meetings has gone. In 1932 the principle of unanimity was abandoned when the national cabinet announced that ministers who did not agree with the decision of the majority of the cabinet on import duties would be free to express their variant opinions without the obligation to resign. A final extension of the franchise was accomplished in 1928, when the age at which women might begin to vote was reduced from thirty to twenty-one.

After Great Britain went to war in 1939, the cabinet was granted a vast increase of power. The Emergency Powers Act of that year gave the government authority over all aspects of industrial production and

Other constitutional changes

---

[1] Marriott, *Modern England*, p. 444.

further legislation the next year placed in its hands complete control over all persons and property. The government did not plan to use this power except as far as was necessary, but it could "direct any person to perform any service required" with the remuneration, the hours and the conditions of labor fixed by the government, and it could take over the management of any business. By means of orders issued under these acts and with the aid of supplementary legislation the people and resources of Great Britain were thoroughly and comprehensively mobilized for the war effort. This autocratic power was established by democratic processes because the British recognized the need of centralized control to meet the dangers which they faced. It is a safe assumption that when the war is over, the government will divest itself of these powers and restore the normal constitution.

Contrary to general expectation, after the first world war was concluded at the end of 1918, two years of prosperity followed. Prices and wages rose, and the demand for labor was so extensive that the greater part of the demobilized soldiers and munition workers found work. The laborers saw in the situation an opportunity to better their condition. Membership in the trade unions increased rapidly, and after the war measure of compulsory arbitration was repealed, an exceptionally large number of strikes took place. The demands had to do mainly with wages and hours, but behind the movement was also a general belief in economic democracy. In 1919, for example, the miners demanded not only shorter hours and higher wages, but also the public ownership of the mines and a democratic control of them in which the miners should have a share. The government intervened in many of the strikes with varied success. When the miners made the preceding demands with the threat of a strike, the cabinet secured the postponement of the strike until a commission appointed by the government had had time to investigate the situation. On the basis of the commission's report the miners obtained an increase of wages and a reduction of hours from eight to seven a day, and the strike was averted, though nothing was done about nationalization. When the railwaymen struck in 1920, on the other hand, it appeared that the government, which was then still responsible for the management of the railways, had been rather peremptory in its negotiations with the representatives of the union. The strike, which lasted nine days, failed to plunge the community into the chaos which was anticipated. The government utilized the Defense of the Realm Act to organize volunteers who prevented the development of a serious food shortage in any locality. The strike was ended on the basis of the renewal of negotiations, and these

Labor unrest

resulted in establishing wages upon a sliding scale in relation to the prices of commodities, a settlement which was satisfactory to the strikers. In addition to intervention of these types in many trade disputes, the government also established in 1919 the national industrial conference, consisting of representatives of many organizations of employers and trade unions. Their discussions, which lasted until 1921, produced no legislation, but they did much to relieve the tension between capital and labor. The outcome of the many strikes was not uniform, but the general effect was to improve the wages, hours or other conditions of labor of a large number of workingmen. From these strikes arose two pieces of legislation of permanent significance. The Industrial Courts Act established a permanent court to which labor disputes might be referred voluntarily for arbitration. It also authorized the minister of labor to appoint a court of inquiry to investigate the causes and circumstances of a dispute and prepare a report for submission to parliament. This court can require witnesses to appear and give evidence under oath. Its findings in several disputes have not only helped the government to define its attitude but also provided the basis for the formation of an intelligent public opinion. The Emergency Powers Act gave the government authority to take any special measures necessary to prevent the deprivation of the community, or any large part of it, of the means of life, such as food, water or light, when any proposed action threatens to produce such a result.

With the coming of the depression in 1921, the strikes became defensive rather than offensive, seeking to prevent the fall of wages rather than to secure their increase. The number of strikes decreased, but they were still frequent, and they continued until the general strike of 1926 marked a turning point. The strikes which most affected the general public and which were typical of the fortunes of labor in general were those of the miners. Late in 1920, when the price of coal was high, the miners demanded both better wages and a reduction of the price of coal. A brief strike secured a small advance in wages to remain in effect until March 31, 1921, when a permanent settlement was to be negotiated. By that time the price of coal had fallen greatly, and the employers insisted on a reduction of wages arranged district by district. The miners not only refused the decrease but wanted wages arranged on a national scale, as had been the custom during the war when the government controlled the industry. The miners struck and sought a sympathetic strike from the railwaymen and the transport workers, who with the miners constituted the triple alliance. This organization had been formed originally with the intention that each of these powerful unions should present its own demands and strike simultaneously. On this occasion the two other unions had no demands of their own to make, but they agreed to call a strike, and the country faced what would be tantamount to a general strike. When the appointed day came, the leaders of the two unions refused to order the strike because the miners had refused to follow the advice of the other unions in conducting their negotiations. The desertion was a heavy blow to the cause of labor, causing the workers to designate the day on which it took place as "black Friday." The miners continued their strike until June, when they accepted both lower wages and district settlements. This complete defeat of the miners was followed by reductions of wages in many other industries and by a marked decline in trade union membership.

In 1926 the initiative of the miners finally produced the general strike which had been threatened for so long. In 1923 the production of coal in the Ruhr was so reduced by the French occupation that the demand for British coal increased. The industry became so prosperous that the miners were able to negotiate an advance of wages in 1924. After the French left the Ruhr, the foreign demand for British coal declined, and in 1925 the operators announced a reduction of wages. When the miners rejected the terms, the government tried to bring the two parties together, and finally offered a subsidy to maintain wages for nine months while a commission made a study of the industry. The commission recommended a reorganization of the management of the industry along lines desired by the miners, to be carried out preferably by the owners but by the government if necessary. It also approved a reduction of wages less than that proposed by the owners. The government accepted the report, but the miners rejected it and struck against any reduction of pay or increase of hours. The Trades Union Congress supported the miners and ordered a strike in several vital industries, including transport services and the printing industry. The government organized volunteers to maintain transportation and prevented a food shortage or any notable increase of prices. The strike thus failed of its object, and after nine days it was called off. The miners continued their strike for several months. The government enacted into law several of the recommendations of the commission with regard to the reorganization of the industry, and revised the law of 1919 to enable the miners to work eight hours a day. The owners in most districts offered pay for an eight-hour day as good as that existing before the strike, and eventually the miners came back on those terms. The general strike, which Baldwin characterized as an unconstitutional attempt to coerce the government, alienated public opinion, and in 1927 the government secured the passage of the Trade Disputes and Trade Unions Bill, which limited the power of the trade unions. It declared general strikes or large sympathetic strikes to be illegal, rendered the right of picketing innocuous by making illegal the intimidation of workers who desire to work, and protected the members of unions against any compulsory contributions for political purposes. By that time the workers themselves were becoming weary of the prolonged industrial unrest, and an era of comparative calm followed.

Unemployment

The brief boom following the war prevented the anticipated development of unemployment on a large scale, but it came with the slump which began in 1921. By 1923 the amount of unemployment had declined, but thereafter more than a million were always idle, and for several years following the depression which began in 1929 the number was greatly enlarged. The principal remedy which the government applied to the situation was unemployment insurance. In 1920 the act of 1911, with slight revision, was extended to all workingmen except those in domestic service and agriculture, tripling the number who were entitled to insurance. In order to meet the crisis of 1921, a new act swept away the limitations on the payment of benefits. Unemployed who had not made the requisite number of payments were to receive the weekly benefits, and the period of the benefits was increased beyond fifteen weeks. Since the payments made by employers, employees and the government could not meet this strain, the government had to provide the additional funds required. A large number of unemployed, instead of receiving unemployment insurance for which premiums had been paid, actually received under that name charity from the government. Insurance and relief were completely confounded. Many further acts dealt with the subject. The benefits practically became continuous and were increased in amount. Additional sums were allowed for the dependents of a recipient of benefits. The limitation of benefits to a man who had made reasonable efforts to obtain work was interpreted so liberally at times that the incentive of those who were receiving benefits to seek work was undermined. The improvement of these unfortunate conditions was begun in 1929. The Labor government provided that those who had exhausted their claims to insurance benefits should receive aid from the exchequer. Insurance and the dole were thus separated. The national government reduced the amount of the benefits for several years, and in 1932 it also began to demand a more careful examination of the means of support possessed by the unemployed who had used up their insurance benefits and were seeking the dole. Further legislation enacted in 1934 completed the separation of insurance and relief, and placed the administration of both on a more sound and rational basis. In 1936 unemployment insurance was extended to agricultural workers, and in 1940 the benefits received during unemployment were increased in amount. By that time the demand for labor created by the war was reducing unemployment rapidly. In 1942 less than one hundred thousand were unemployed.

A field of social reform in which extensive progress has been made since the first world war is the housing of the working class. During that war the building of houses nearly ceased, and at its close the shortage of homes for workers was causing difficulties. The coalition cabinet began to subsidize the building of houses for laborers and secured the erection of a goodly number before the need for economy in governmental expenditure forced the abandonment of the program in 1922. It was revived by the Conservatives in 1923 and expanded by the Labor cabinet in 1924. Under the programs of the two cabinets, which supplemented each other, nearly a million homes were constructed. The reforms culminated with a plan for the clearance of slums, instituted in 1933. This provided for the demolition within five years of about 300,000 homes, and the building of new houses or apartment buildings for the accommodation of the families displaced by the clearance. The project was to be financed three-quarters by the national government and one-quarter by the local governments. When this act expired in 1938, new legislation arranged for the continuation of financial aid by the national government to local projects for building new houses for the purpose of clearing slums and eliminating the overcrowding of homes. In 1943 the government announced that it was formulating a plan for building and town-planning, designed to continue for twelve years and to employ 1,250,000 men, to be put into effect after the war.

The legislation on old age pensions, like that on unemployment, has been revised for the benefit of the workers. A few years after the first world war the maximum pension was increased to 10 s. a week and the annual income below which one qualified for a pension was raised to £49 17 s. 6 d. The age limit was reduced from seventy to sixty-five years, but in order to meet the additional cost those who would receive pensions at the lower age were required to contribute weekly from their wages, and their employers and the government were required to supplement these contributions as they did for workingmen's insurance. The non-contributory pension at the age of seventy

Housing

Other aspects of social security

was, however, allowed to continue. Recently the pensionable age for contributing women was placed at sixty years, and pensioners who could prove need were granted an increase in their pensions. During the present war the whole program of social security has received thorough study with a view to its expansion. In 1942 a governmental committee, of which Sir William Beveridge was chairman, submitted a report recommending so great an extension of the system that it was said to provide social security "from the cradle to the grave." Some of the members of the house of commons desired to put the plan into effect immediately, but the prime minister pointed out that before it could be made effective a reorganization of economic life would be necessary in order to provide the financial resources needed to meet the proposed claims on social insurance. Later the cabinet proposed an alternative plan which followed the general principles of the Beveridge report but reduced some of the suggested benefits in order to make the project more feasible financially. Extensive improvements in the educational system are also under consideration. Evidently the British during this war, as they did during the last war, are dreaming of a better social order when peace comes again, but this time the government is giving more attention to practical plans for the purpose of making the dream come true.

Ireland: Sinn Fein

After 1918, Ireland presented a problem of great difficulty. The outbreak of the war stilled the Irish controversy only for a brief interval. In 1914 the Ulsterites and the Irish Nationalists put aside their enmity and began to enlist for the common cause. At that very time a new movement, initiated a few years before, was working secretly to promote rebellion. The new factor was Sinn Fein (we ourselves). It seems to have grown from a nationalistic revival of Celtic literature and traditions which had been taking place for some years. In 1905, when the phrase first became common, it apparently meant no more than idle talk about Irish independence. Before long it became the name of a secret society which was not content with home rule but sought Irish independence. It appears to have had the support of only a small minority. In 1916, however, it staged a rebellion in connivance with Germany. The Sinn Feiners seized several of the public buildings in Dublin and held them against attack. Since German aid failed to materialize, the revolt was easily quelled.

Attempted settlements, 1917–1918

Though the rebellion had little support, it convinced the cabinet that it would be well to proceed with home rule at once. In 1917 Lloyd George announced the intention of the government to give home rule immediately, excepting the six Protestant counties of Ulster.

The Unionists of Ulster promptly protested against home rule for the rest of Ireland, and the Irish Nationalists objected to the omission of the six counties from its scope. Lloyd George then hit upon the plan of a convention representing different sections of Irish opinion. The convention struggled for a long time. Finally in 1918 it proposed a scheme of government much like that provided by the act of 1914. The principal difference was the stronger guarantee given to the Irish Unionists for the protection of their minority rights. The report was adopted by a majority, but it was opposed by the solid Unionist vote. Since the Irish could not agree among themselves, the British government was no further ahead. If it carried the report into legislation, it would force upon the part of Ireland which had been loyal and had furnished more than its proportional share of volunteers a separation from Great Britain which it did not want, in order to satisfy a part of Ireland which had begun to oppose volunteer service and had indulged in open rebellion in conjunction with Britain's enemies.

Before this dilemma had been met, the government extended conscription to Ireland. Outside of Ulster opposition was nearly universal. Though the act was suspended before it actually went into operation, the harm was done. Sinn Fein, which previously had possessed the adherence of only a minority, gained supporters rapidly. The results appeared in the parliamentary election of 1918. The Unionists obtained 25 seats, the Irish Nationalists retained only 7, and Sinn Fein had 73. The Sinn Fein members refused to attend the British parliament. Early in 1919 they met in Dublin, declared themselves a constituent assembly, and proclaimed an Irish republic. It was a declaration of civil war. Great Britain had to decide whether parts of the country could at will break away from the whole and make themselves independent. After the declaration of a republic, killings and destruction of property began. The government declared martial law in the most disturbed districts, and in 1920 sent over an army of occupation. *Irish revolt, 1918-1920*

With the other hand the government held out the olive branch of a new home rule measure. It proceeded on the principle that the claim of the six Protestant counties of Ulster to self-determination within the empire was no less valid than the claim of the rest of Ireland. The country was therefore divided into northern Ireland, containing the six Protestant counties of Ulster, and southern Ireland, containing the rest. Each was given a single-chambered parliament with a responsible ministry. Each could legislate for its own section in all fields except a few, such as the army, the navy, coinage and customs and excise taxes, which were left under the control of the British parliament. The *Fourth Home Rule Bill* two Irish parliaments were to elect a council of forty to administer the services which the two parliaments should agree to have administered uniformly throughout the whole island. The two parliaments could at any time by identical acts supersede themselves and the council by a single parliament for all Ireland. Ulster accepted, and is working under the plan at present. Southern Ireland would have nothing to do with it.

Irish Free State

Late in 1921 Lloyd George offered southern Ireland the status of a dominion. The offer was accepted. In 1922 the Irish Free State was established, with a position within the empire similar to that occupied by Canada. A considerable minority in southern Ireland, which opposed any settlement short of complete independence, kept up a civil war against the new government. The British left the Irish to fight it out among themselves. Finally in 1923 de Valera, the leader of the rebels, announced that they would cease armed resistance, and the new state settled down to several years of comparative quiet. The calm was ruffled after de Valera became president in 1932. He held that the treaty of 1921 was not morally binding, and he sought to make the whole of Ireland an independent republic, but with retention of external association in the British Commonwealth of Nations. In pursuit of this objective he had the oath prescribed by the treaty, which contained an expression of faithfulness to the king, abolished. When he finally refused to continue the payments due from the Free State to England under the Land Purchase Acts and other agreements, the British government retaliated by imposing tariffs on Irish agricultural products imported into Great Britain. De Valera responded with duties upon British goods brought into the Free State. The accession of George VI in 1936 provided opportunity for another step toward independence. The Irish parliament passed two acts which removed the king from parliament and deprived the governor-general of certain functions performed in the king's name, but retained the king for the purpose of external relations in such matters as making treaties or appointing consuls. Within these limits the Irish Free State acknowledged the succession of George VI. The limitations of the powers of the king in the internal affairs of the Free State were largely matters of form. Parliament is no longer summoned in the king's name and bills are not signed in his name by the governor-general. In the next year a new constitution was adopted which incorporated all of these constitutional changes. It claims application to the whole of Ireland, but concedes that the legislation enacted by the parliament of the Irish Free State will not extend to northern Ireland until a union of the two parts has been accomplished.

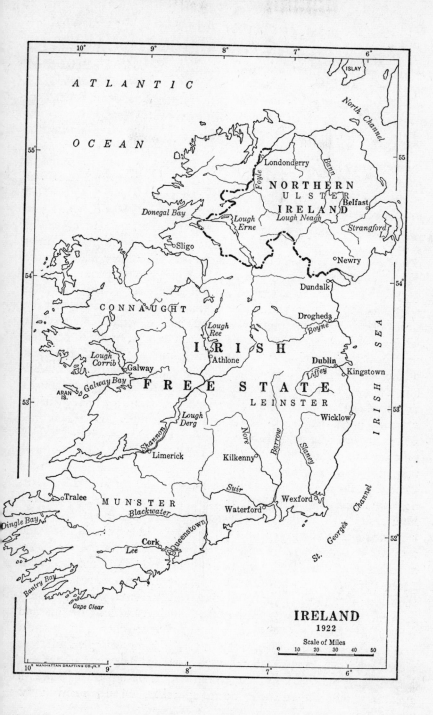

ATLANTIC

OCEAN

ISLAY

North Channel

Londonderry

Foyle

NORTHERN
U L S T E R
IRELAND

Bann

Belfast

Donegal Bay

*Lough
Erne*

Lough Neagh

*Strangford
L.*

Sligo

Newry

Dundalk

C O N N A U G H T

Drogheda

Boyne

*Lough
Ree*

I R I S H

*Lough
Corrib*

Athlone

Galway

Dublin

Liffey

Kingstown

F R E E   S T A T E

ARAN
IS.

Galway Bay

L E I N S T E R

*Lough
Derg*

Wicklow

Shannon

I R I S H   S E A

Nore

Barrow

Slaney

Limerick

Kilkenny

Tralee

M U N S T E R

Suir

Wexford

Blackwater

Waterford

St. George's Channel

Dingle Bay

Cork

Lee

Queenstown

Bantry Bay

Cape Clear

IRELAND
1922

Scale of Miles

0   10   20   30   40   50

MANHATTAN DRAFTING CO., N.Y.

The tariff war naturally imposed greater hardships upon the Free State than it did upon Great Britain. It was finally brought to an end in 1938 as part of a comprehensive agreement by which Great Britain hoped to render Ireland more friendly. This arranged for the end of the special duties established by each country against the other, for a large reduction of the debt owed by the Irish Free State, for prompt payment of the reduced amount, and for the withdrawal of the British from the harbor defenses of certain Irish ports which they occupied in accordance with the treaty of 1921. In return for the last concession the government of the Irish Free State promised that the defenses of the ports would be maintained and that its territory would not be allowed to become a base for an attack upon Great Britain by any foreign power. At the outbreak of war in Europe in 1939 Eire, as the Irish Free State was officially named in the constitution, declared its neutrality. When the British government proposed to apply conscription to northern Ireland, Eire protested so vigorously that the policy was abandoned, but similar protests against the stationing of American troops in northern Ireland went unheeded. The loss of Irish ports handicapped the British navy and the presence of German and Japanese diplomatic representatives was awkward for Great Britain at times, but Eire has kept its neutrality and its territory has not become a base for an attack on Great Britain.

The cabinet of Lloyd George which established the Irish Free State also brought about an important constitutional reorganization in India. New government for India, 1919 Pronounced political unrest developed in India during the closing years of the war. The educated native leaders began to agitate for dominion status and home rule, and secured a large popular following. In 1917 Montagu, secretary of state for India, announced in parliament that the policy of the government was to increase gradually the share of the Indians in their own government with a view to the ultimate realization of self-government. He then went to India to study the situation. In 1918, in conjunction with the viceroy, Lord Chelmsford, he submitted a report which became the basis of an act passed the next year. In the new organization the electorate was enlarged to include about 5,000,000. In the central and the provincial councils the elected element was given a larger majority. The provincial councils were given more of a legislative and parliamentary character by the establishment of the principle of dyarchy. The ministers responsible to a legislative council administered only certain fields, called the transferred services, such as education and public health. Other fields, such as justice and police, were designated as reserved services. They were administered by the governor and his agents, who were responsible only to the British parliament. The legislative council granted taxation and legislated in all fields, but "in the last resort where a 'reserved' subject was concerned, the governor had power to make financial provision against the will of the chamber, and to secure essential legislation; whereas in the case of a 'transferred' subject the chamber could impose its will on a 'minister.'"[2] The principle of dyarchy was not extended to the council of the central executive. No responsible ministers and no transferred services existed in the central government. The council could refuse legislation and supplies, but the viceroy could impose taxation or enact legislation which the assembly had refused to pass. The council could make it difficult for the machinery of government to run, but it could not stop the wheels entirely.

The natives generally regarded the amount of self-government as inadequate. An influential group of Indian political leaders decided at first to have nothing to do with the new constitution. Later they changed their attitude to participation and obstruction in the councils. Another group of the dissatisfied decided to cooperate for the purpose of obtaining its ultimate modification. By 1927, however, the dyarchy was working so well that Baldwin's government advanced by two years the appointment of a commission, authorized by the act of 1919, to study the working of the dyarchy and report what further steps toward self-government might be taken. The report was published in 1930. It recommended the abolition of the dyarchy in the provinces and the substitution of ministers responsible to their elected legislatures for all departments of government. The central government was to be a federation of provinces including not only British India but also the native states. The central executive, however, was to remain a British official who was not responsible to the federal assembly representing the provinces. This report was subsequently debated at round-table conferences in which the different parties and opinions of India were represented, and it was studied also by a select committee of parliament. Finally, in 1935, an India Act was passed. The provinces were given the type of government contemplated in the original report. Each was to have a legislature with a ministry completely responsible for the government, except that the British governor of the province could intervene to prevent any grave threat to peace or to safeguard the interests of minorities. In the federation the natives received more powers than had been intended at first. The assembly, in which both the

More autonomy, 1935

---

[2] Paraphrased from *These Eventful Years*, ii, 317.

British provinces and the native states were to be represented, was to have a responsible ministry by whom the governor-general was to be guided; but defense, foreign relations and religion were to remain under the control of the governor-general, who was also to have power to maintain the peace and to protect the interests of minorities. In 1937 the autonomous governments granted to the provinces became operative, but the projected changes in the central government have not yet been effected. Negotiations for the inclusion of the native states were proceeding with their princes when the war caused their suspension in 1939.

The war produced a critical situation in India. As early as 1936 the All India National Congress, which represents the largest and most influential group of natives, had announced its opposition to Indian assistance in any war in which Great Britain might become engaged. In 1939, when the British declaration of war against Germany automatically brought India into the war, the Congress renewed its stand and has maintained it ever since. The action caused the responsible ministries in seven of the British provinces to resign, necessitating their rule by the British governors. The leaders of the Congress refused to cooperate with the central government. Opposition has also been expressed by some civil disobedience, but this policy has been supported only half-heartedly by the Congress and it has not been applied on a large scale. On the other hand, native princes have helped the British with troops and money, loyalists in the British provinces have volunteered for military service and made voluntary gifts of money, and Indian war industries have expanded greatly. Indian troops have fought valiantly on many fronts and a large native army is organized for the defense of India.

An offer of self-government

The conquest of Burma by the Japanese in 1942 opened the door for the invasion of India and made the problem of obtaining united support for the British war effort acute. The British government therefore sent Sir Stafford Cripps, a member of the British war cabinet, to negotiate with the Indian leaders. He brought an offer of self-government at the close of the war. At that time a body elected by the Indians would be given power to frame a new constitution which would give India dominion status or complete independence. If any part of India preferred not to accept the new constitution, it could retain its present constitutional position, with freedom to join the union later if it should so desire. Meanwhile the Indian parties were asked to work together in support of the war. The All India National Congress rejected the offer because self-government was not to be established immediately and because some states might be left outside the union. The Moslem League, representing a large minority, declined to accept the proposal because its purpose was to create a united Indian state and the Mohammedans wanted separate Hindu and Moslem states. There the question of Indian self-government hangs fire, but the British offer still remains open.

Egypt

Another thorny imperial problem was presented by Egypt. The constitutional position of Great Britain in Egypt had always been anomalous. Nominally Egypt was dependent on Turkey before 1914. Actually it was practically independent before 1882 and was controlled by British representatives thereafter. British rule, which conferred great benefits upon the natives, for long aroused no pronounced opposition. During the twentieth century a new generation, which realized little of what Great Britain had done for Egypt, began to demand a larger degree of self-government. The movement was moderate in character, and it had not gone far when the war came. When Turkey entered the war, Great Britain declared a formal protectorate over Egypt in order to safeguard its position in Egypt against Turkey. During the course of the war the shibboleth of the independence of Egypt spread among the natives. In 1919 the Egyptians demanded independence, resorting to riots, assassinations, and violence of many sorts to express the strength of their desire. After an investigation, Lloyd George's government in 1922 abolished the protectorate and granted Egypt independence subject to four reservations which were subsequently to be settled by treaty. They were security for the communication of the empire, the defense of Egypt against foreign attack, the protection of foreign interests in Egypt, and British control of the Sudan.

For a long time the settlement worked indifferently. The Egyptian government established in 1923 at the election of the first parliament under the new Egyptian constitution was not willing to accept the reservations as a basis of negotiations. It demanded the complete withdrawal of British control from Egypt. In 1924 the British commander of an Egyptian army, who was governor of the Sudan, was murdered by Egyptian fanatics. The Egyptians continued nominally to govern themselves, but the presence of a British high commissioner and British troops rendered the self-government shadowy. This unsatisfactory state of affairs was finally concluded in 1936 by a treaty between Great Britain and Egypt. Great Britain agreed to withdraw her troops except those in the canal zone, and they were to be recalled whenever Egypt should be prepared to take over its defense. An alliance was established for twenty years, by which each state agreed to support the other in case of war. Egypt was expected not to give military aid but to allow the British free use of Egyptian territory, harbors and transportation facilities. In the Egyptian Sudan rights and privileges which had been taken away from Egypt after the assassination of the governor in 1924 were restored. Thus Egypt finally became independent.

The treaty of 1936 was put to the test when Great Britain declared war on Germany in 1939. The Egyptian government at once informed the British government that it would fulfill its obligations under the treaty and obtained assurance that the British would send reinforcements sufficient for the defense of Egypt. The Egyptian government severed diplomatic relations with Germany and sent home or took into custody German nationals, but did not declare war. It followed the same policy when Italy entered the war in 1940. After Italy attacked Egypt and the Sudan, some sentiment developed in favor of active participation in the war, but the government held back and kept their country out of war. Egypt has, however, carried out the treaty loyally and the relations with Britain have been cordial in the main.

The most striking and significant effect of the first world war upon the constitutional organization of the empire was the creation of the British Commonwealth of Nations. The participation of the self-governing dominions in the war served not only to strengthen their loyalty to the empire but also to sharpen their consciousness of nationhood. An imperial conference held during the war recommended a constitutional readjustment which should recognize "the Dominions as autonomous nations of an Imperial Commonwealth" and give to them "an adequate voice in foreign policy and in foreign relations."[3] At the close of the war they asked and received representation at the Peace Conference, and they obtained separate representation in the League of Nations. At the imperial conference held in 1921 they were consulted with regard to the foreign and imperial problems of the empire, but no attempt was made to define the constitutional relations of the dominions to Great Britain. Later Canada and the Irish Free State established their own diplomatic representatives at Washington, setting a precedent which has since been followed elsewhere by other dominions. It was also settled that one member of the Commonwealth might negotiate a treaty not binding on the other members, and Canada refused to ratify a treaty negotiated by Great Britain alone. Such incidents as these caused the imperial conference of 1926 to formulate a statement concerning the constitutional status of "the group of self-

The British Common-wealth of Nations

---

[3] Cited by Zimmern, *The Third British Empire*, p. 29.

governing communities composed of Great Britain and the Dominions."
It reads: "They are equal in status, in no way subordinate one to
another in any aspect of their domestic or external affairs, though
united by a common allegiance to the Crown, and freely associated as
members of the British Commonwealth of Nations." [4] In order to give
more definite legal validity to some of the implications of this definition, the British parliament in 1931 enacted the Statute of Westminster.
This acknowledged that the crown could no longer disallow a law
enacted by a dominion parliament, declared that no legislation of the
British parliament was applicable to any dominion except at the request
of a dominion, and defined in broad terms the power of the parliaments of the dominions to legislate with regard to their own affairs.
It also stated that any change in the law concerning the succession
to the crown would require the consent of the parliaments of the
dominions as well as that of the British parliament. The law leaves
the dominions practically independent and establishes no constitutional
or legal obstacle to the withdrawal of a dominion from the Commonwealth. The position became dramatically clear when the necessity for
the ratification of the abdication of Edward VIII by the parliaments
of the dominions made it apparent that a dominion accepted the king
established by the British parliament only at its own option. Yet the
bond of empire has not been broken. The self-governing members of
the Commonwealth are united by a common allegiance to the crown [5]
and by recognition of the value to them of association and cooperation
in the British Commonwealth of Nations.

Recently the value of this association appears to have been somewhat
enhanced by the material bond of trade fostered by preferential tariffs.
The suggestion of a preferential tariff was made by the dominions in
some of the early imperial conferences which took place late in the
nineteenth century, and Canada, followed by some of the other dominions, gave Great Britain some preferences in her markets. Great
Britain had nothing to offer in return as long as it maintained free
trade, and Joseph Chamberlain's advocacy of a British preferential tariff
was slow to bear fruit. The tariffs imposed by Great Britain during the
war and intermittently thereafter allowed for some preference to the
dominions, but they extended to comparatively few commodities. It
was not until the general protective tariff was established in 1932 that
British statesmen had anything with which to bargain. They took

---

[4] Cited by Somervell, *Reign of King George*, p. 378; Marriott, *Modern England*,
p. 466.

[5] This seems now to have been reduced to small limits by the Irish Free State.

prompt advantage of it, and in the same year an imperial conference was held at Ottawa to arrange preferential agreements. They found the statesmen from the dominions to be hard bargainers, but they succeeded in making some agreements. These agreements appear to have done more to promote the trade of the dominions than that of Great Britain, but they may have helped to strengthen the bond of interest within the Commonwealth. At an imperial conference held in 1937 in London after the coronation of George VI the representatives of the dominions expressed their willingness to cooperate in the task of imperial defense, and in 1939 the dominions promptly followed Great Britain into the war.

In some of the crown colonies there developed among the native populations during and after the first world war a desire for a larger amount of self-government. Between 1921 and 1937 the British government responded by granting more liberal constitutions to several colonies. The degree of self-government varied greatly, because complete self-government given to a people not sufficiently well educated and too backward socially and economically would be likely to result in chaos. In Malta, where the population, though in large majority non-British, seemed capable of exercising political power with a proper sense of responsibility, a bicameral legislature with a responsible ministry received complete control of local affairs as distinguished from imperial interests and policies. The latter were left in the hands of the governor appointed by the British government and aided by an appointed executive council. British Guiana, on the other hand, where the native population was less advanced, was given only a legislative council in which the official members and the members nominated by the governor outnumbered the members elected by the people. This slow advance toward self-government in the crown colonies was greatly accelerated by the present war. Since this war was being fought for freedom, the British began to give more attention to the limited degree of political liberty which existed in some of their colonies. The movement toward the extension of self-government received a sharp stimulus when the conquest of Malaya and Burma by the Japanese in 1942 made it apparent that large groups of the natives were hostile to British rule. In 1940, in the midst of war, parliament authorized the expenditure for ten years of as much as five million pounds annually to promote the social and economic advancement of backward colonies. The primary purpose was to help prepare the native peoples for larger participation in their own government. In the same year Ceylon was granted a legislative council in which the elected members had a large majority.

The crown colonies

In 1942 the island became so important strategically that this government was suspended, but the action was accompanied with the promise that Ceylon would be given full responsible government in all fields of internal civil administration after the war. This type of government, which had been extended to Malta in 1921, was revoked there in 1936 on account of local troubles caused by Italian machinations, but its restoration has been promised after the war. Cyprus and Burma have been assured more self-government when the war is concluded. In British Guiana the elected members of the legislative council were placed in a majority in 1943, and in the same year a more liberal constitution was offered to Jamaica. Thus Britain has begun to travel much more rapidly toward self-government in the crown colonies, with the ultimate goal of such complete independence as the dominions now enjoy when the native peoples have been adequately educated to its use.

In answer to the suggestions of critics outside the empire that British colonies should be placed under international control, Churchill in 1943 gave a vigorous denial, but said that Britain was prepared to cooperate with neighboring friendly nations in planning for the development of the British colonies. What the British government envisaged was the establishment of regional commissions on which all the friendly states with colonial possessions in an area would be represented. The commission would plan for the promotion of the welfare of the colonies in the region, but would have power only to recommend policies. Each state would retain full responsibility for the government of its own colonies. One such arrangement has already been made. In 1942 Great Britain and the United States established a Caribbean commission to provide for social and economic cooperation of the two powers with regard to their possessions in that area. So far the commission has been concerned chiefly with problems raised by the war, such as the supply of food and shipping, but within that limited field it has accomplished useful results.

Projects for international cooperation in the colonial sphere

FROM ONE WORLD WAR TO ANOTHER

Foreign
affairs:
Britain at
the Peace
Confer-
ence

AFTER the conclusion of the war in 1918, the terms of peace were established at Paris by a conference of the twenty-seven allied and associated powers which had been at war with one or more of the central powers. In the serious effort made to arrive at a just peace, Great Britain took a leading part. Lloyd George, the chief British spokesman, seemed to be actuated less than President Wilson by principles of abstract justice, and less than Clemenceau by materialistic considerations. His purpose appeared to be to secure treaties which would meet with British popular approval, and his objectives varied somewhat with the vagaries of British popular opinion, to which he was particularly sensitive. Lloyd George, however, was influenced by his colleagues and by the numerous experts who were attached to the British delegation. Many sections of the treaties were written by commissions composed of experts representing the great powers, and ratified with small change by the responsible delegates. On many of those problems which the heads of the delegations settled among themselves Lloyd George relied on the information and advice supplied by his advisers. That advice did not all tend in the same direction, but it was liberal in the main. The whole British delegation was sometimes hampered in its desire to support what appeared to be the ideal solution of a specific problem by the secret treaties, such as that of London.[1] Negotiated under the strain of the war largely to secure new alliances or to cement old ones, they proposed to pare and cut territories without regard for the desires of the inhabitants in a way worthy of the diplomacy of Habsburg and Valois. Some of the British representatives were disposed at times to advise the other signatory powers to forego this or that claim arising under one secret treaty or another, but, true to the British tradition, they honored their signatures when called upon to do so.

The terms of peace were embodied in a number of treaties signed during 1919 and 1920, though the treaty with Turkey had to be rewritten in 1923. The result of chief importance was the creation of the League of Nations, which seemed to offer the only avenue of escape

---

[1] Above, p. 791.

from the ultimate return of international anarchy such as produced the events of July, 1914. Its principal purpose was to maintain international peace and security, although it undertook several other useful functions, such as the improvement of the conditions under which laborers worked and the suppression of the trade in opium. Its main organs of government were an assembly, in which all of the many countries having membership in the League were represented, a council, in which certain great powers had permanent seats and a few lesser powers were represented in rotation, the permanent court of international justice and a permanent secretariat. The assembly was a deliberative body which established general policies and exerted an influence on the actions of the council. The council was more in the nature of an executive authority. It attempted to settle political disputes between countries which were referred to it, and either it or the assembly could take cognizance of any international relations which threatened to disturb the peace. If an act of aggression against a member of the League occurred, the council was to advise what the other members should do to help the attacked member. If a member resorted to war contrary to its obligation under the covenant of the League to keep the peace, the other members were bound to sever commercial and financial relations with the offender, and the council was to recommend what military or naval contingents each of the other members should contribute to the armed forces to be used against the breaker of the covenant. The court could determine any disputed international question submitted to it by the parties concerned and render advisory opinions on questions referred to it by the council of the League.

Reparations

The other European settlement which affected Great Britain most directly was that of the reparations exacted from Germany. Though it had been agreed at the time of the armistice that reparations should be demanded only for damages inflicted upon civilians, the cost of war pensions was included. One billion pounds was demanded as an immediate payment, and a reparations commission was established to settle upon the total sum within two years. The attempt to obtain excessive reparations, for which Lloyd George was largely responsible, worked to the disadvantage of Great Britain. It delayed the restoration of normal economic conditions in Europe and thus retarded the development of British industry and commerce, on which the prosperity of the people depended more largely than in any other country in Europe.

War guilt

The initial clause of the section of the treaty dealing with reparations, which came to be known as the war guilt clause, had an unfortunate effect. It required Germany to accept responsibility for all loss and damage inflicted upon the allied and associated governments and their nationals because the war was due to the aggression of Germany and her allies. It recognized that the sum, which would have included the costs of the war, was beyond the capacity of Germany to pay, and it exacted compensation only for damage done to the civilian population and their property. The clause was introduced at the peace conference as a compromise in order to break a deadlock between the representatives of the United States, who opposed the inclusion of the costs of war, and the representatives of France and Great Britain, who wanted the costs included. The real purpose of the clause was to exclude the costs of the war and thus to reduce the amount of reparations. To Germans this acknowledgment of responsibility for having begun the war was the most galling aspect of the treaty. They thought of themselves as having fought a war of defense against encirclement by the triple entente, just as the peoples of the allied countries thought that they had fought a defensive war against German aggression. Because Germans regarded the charge as false, they considered reparations a penalty imposed upon them unjustly. In the course of time they began to view other clauses in the same light, until they felt that all the requirements placed upon them by the treaty were penalties for an offense which they had not committed. This view was grossly exaggerated; but because Germans believed it, the execution and maintenance of the treaty became a constant source of trouble after 1919.

The territorial settlements in Europe concerned Great Britain primarily because she had to underwrite them as a member of the League of Nations. Germany returned Alsace-Lorraine to France, ceded to France the coal mines of the Saar basin, and placed the district under control of the League of Nations for fifteen years. Both banks of the Rhine were demilitarized, and allied armies, chiefly French, were placed in occupation of the left bank for fifteen years, with power to extend the period of occupation if Germany failed to pay reparations. Germany was also disarmed, and the allies agreed to reduce their own armaments in due course. Belgium had her neutrality abrogated and received small bits of territory on her eastern frontier. Northern Schleswig was restored to Denmark as the result of a plebiscite. On the east most of Posen, West Prussia, and a part of Silesia went to Poland, which appeared on the map as an independent nation for the first time since 1795. In order to give Poland access to the sea, Danzig, in which the Germans constituted an overwhelming majority, had the facilities of its port placed largely under Polish control, though the city in other respects was given self-government under supervision of the League of

Territorial adjustments: Europe

Nations. In southeastern Europe Austria-Hungary had already fallen apart. The treaties had only to confirm the results and settle the frontiers. Austria, Hungary, Bulgaria and Turkey were all reduced in size. Roumania and Greece were enlarged. Servia was expanded into the large Jugoslavia, and Czechoslovakia appeared as a new state. Poland received Galicia. Italy secured large portions of Austria located on her northern and northeastern frontiers.

Some of these territorial settlements contained extensive possibilities of friction. The German territory which Poland received split Germany into two parts, making it necessary for a German traveling by land between East Prussia and any other part of his country to cross Poland; it brought under Polish rule well over a million Germans and gave Poland the larger part of the second richest industrial district in Germany. Poland also acquired, largely by the use of armed force, considerable minorities of Ukrainian and other Russian-speaking peoples. These minorities were protected by a special treaty, but it failed miserably to obtain fair treatment for them. Between the German government of Danzig and the Polish government perennial quarrels developed. Czechoslovakia in proportion to its total population received even larger minorities. There were three and one-half million Germans, who, though they had previously been under Austrian and not German rule, were strongly antagonistic to the Czechs, and substantial minorities of Magyars and Ukrainians. The minorities in Czechoslovakia were not oppressed as severely as those in Poland, but they were nevertheless dissatisfied with the treatment accorded to them. Roumania and Jugoslavia were also awarded large minorities. Their mistreatment, however, was less dangerous to international peace, since they had no powerful country such as Germany to advocate their cause. The problem of the Turkish minority obtained by Greece was largely eliminated when the Turks, by defeating the Greeks in 1922, recovered much of the former Turkish territory which had been assigned to Greece by the treaty of 1920. The remaining Turks were sent to Turkey in exchange for the dispatch to Greece of the Greeks resident in Turkey. A source of international friction was thus removed at the cost of great suffering to the million and more people who were uprooted from their homes. In the Austrian territories which went to Italy there were significant minorities of Germans and Jugoslavs whose fate was far from happy under Italian rule.

In the distribution of colonial possessions Great Britain obtained the lion's share. The German colonial empire was surrendered entire, to be divided among the victors. Japan took the German rights in the

Colonies

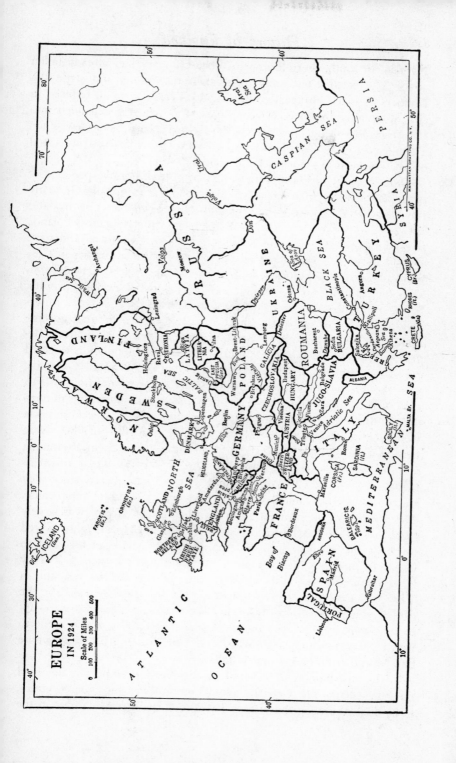

EUROPE
IN 1924

Scale of Miles
100 200 300 400 500

Chinese territory of Shantung and the islands in the northern Pacific. Great Britain received the islands in the southern Pacific, giving them with one exception to Australia and New Zealand. In Africa Great Britain added to her holdings small portions of the former German colonies on the Guinea coast and German East Africa. The Union of South Africa received German Southwest Africa. From Turkey Great Britain obtained Palestine and Mesopotamia. These vast territories were not ceded to the British Empire in outright ownership, but were held as mandates from the League of Nations. The mandatory power reported to the League of Nations annually and was responsible to the League in some measure for the exercise of its power. The extent of the power granted under the mandate varied with the nature of the community governed thereby. German Southwest Africa was governed as an integral part of the South African Union, while Mesopotamia, at the other extreme, was administered with a view to its ultimate independence, which it received in 1932 under the name of Iraq. In the mandated territories the nationals of all powers had equal economic rights.

After the Peace Conference, the exceedingly difficult problem of restoring normal conditions in the world, and particularly in Europe, long exercised British statesmen. Many international conferences were held in which Lloyd George took a prominent and influential part. In the course of these conferences Great Britain and France gradually drifted apart, until, in 1922, serious rifts appeared. In a conference of all the powers, including Russia and Germany, which met at Genoa under the aegis of Lloyd George to plan the economic and financial rehabilitation of Europe, France limited her participation, opposed many of the important suggestions of Great Britain, and contributed materially to the failure of the conference. They also differed in their attitude toward Turkey,[2] but their most serious disagreement was over reparations. On this question British opinion changed after the treaty when it became evident that Germany had only goods with which to pay reparations. These goods came into competition with British goods and they provided the Germans with no money for the purchase of British goods. Lloyd George therefore urged that reparations be made moderate in amount and easy in terms of payment, in order that Germany might recover economically. France desired to exact the last mark, but could not be persuaded that a demand for more than Germany could pay would defeat her own end.

Reparations

[2] Above, p. 801.

The amount of reparations was set early in 1921 at thirty-three billion dollars, which was probably three or four times what Germany
could pay. Meanwhile the Germans had been dilatory in their payments. Lacking hope of paying all, they soon began to display a lack
of will to pay any. By 1922, however, economic conditions were so bad
in Germany that payment was not possible, and Great Britain urged
that payments be suspended for a time. To this France would not listen,
and early in 1923 French troops occupied the Ruhr, a rich industrial
district in Germany, for the purpose of seizing the products of the
mines and factories in payment of reparations. The occupation was
followed by an inflation in Germany which soon rendered German
money practically worthless. Members of the middle class lost the
savings which placed them economically and socially above the
average wage earner. They became an embittered middle-class proletariat. Though Germany's financing of the war too much by loans
and too little by taxes and the government's financial policies after the
war had prepared the way for the depreciation of the mark, reparations
were an important cause of it. The despairing middle class regarded
reparations and the attempt of the French to collect them by force as
the sole cause of their losses, and they were filled with hatred for France.

The occupation also further strained French relations with Great
Britain. The Conservative cabinet protested vainly that it was a violation of the Treaty of Versailles. MacDonald, while he was prime
minister in 1924, succeeded in improving relations with France by
the application of his pacific principles to international affairs. France
by that time had learned the futility of the occupation of the Ruhr as
satisfaction for anything more than pride, and was beginning to recognize that reparations constituted an economic rather than a political
problem. Already it had agreed to the study of the problem by a committee of experts, such as had been suggested by Secretary Hughes of
the United States. The committee was headed by Charles Dawes, who
later became vice-president of the United States. It provided a plan for
balancing the budget and stabilizing the currency of Germany, and a
plan for the payment of reparations. The French government had not
intended originally to go the full length of the Dawes plan, but it was
persuaded to accept the project largely through the efforts of the
British prime minister. The French troops were ultimately withdrawn from the Ruhr, Germany returned to a gold basis and a balanced
budget and made the first payments of reparations as scheduled.

Though the Dawes plan worked well in some respects, it was found
unsatisfactory in others. In 1928 the interested powers appointed an-

other commission to work out a final settlement of the problem of reparations. Again the chairman was an American, Owen D. Young. This commission established the amounts of payments to be made annually and made various other alterations. Payments would cease in 1966, provided the debts owed by the allied powers to the United States had then been paid. Otherwise they would continue at a reduced rate until 1988. At the latter date the total sum of reparations which Germany would have paid would be in the neighborhood of thirty-one billion dollars. Included in this agreement was the evacuation of the Rhineland. When the proposals of the commission were finally ratified in 1930, the last of the foreign troops marched out of Germany five years before the date established by the Treaty of Versailles for the end of the occupation.

The Young plan

The Young plan had hardly begun to operate before the economic depression became pronounced. In 1931 President Hoover issued a proposal for the suspension during one year of payments on all inter-governmental debts which was accepted by all of the countries concerned. It soon became evident, however, that Germany could not continue to maintain reparations, and in 1932 representatives of the creditor nations met at Lausanne. They agreed to set aside the German reparations debt and to substitute for it a down payment of bonds, not to be put on the market for three years, amounting to seven hundred and fifty million dollars. At the same time they agreed among themselves not to ratify the arrangement until a satisfactory settlement had been made between themselves and their creditors. Since the United States was not prepared to reduce the debts which the creditors of Germany owed it, the Lausanne agreement never went into effect. Neither were any further payments of reparations made. The Nazi party which came to power in Germany in 1933 substituted for "Germany cannot pay" the slogan, "Germany will not pay."

The end of reparations

Another problem which caused international difficulties was the French desire for security. It was based upon the fear of another attack by Germany. France had been invaded twice by Germany within fifty years, and the French feared that the Germans might again cause them agony like that through which they had just passed. It was a very real fear which persisted for many years. The need for security consequently became a fixed idea with the French, just as resentment of the war guilt clause and of the alleged penal nature of the Treaty of Versailles became an unalterable point of view with the Germans. It affected profoundly the policies which the French government followed in international affairs after 1918.

French security

France obtained from the Treaty of Versailles much less security than the French wanted, and it soon lost one protection which the treaty provided. In the course of the negotiations Clemenceau, at the insistence of Lloyd George and Wilson, gave up a demand that the Rhine should become the western frontier of Germany in return for proposed treaties by which Great Britain and the United States would undertake to support France with all their forces if Germany should make an unprovoked attack upon France. When the United States senate refused in 1920 to ratify the Treaty of Versailles, both of the proposed alliances fell through, because they were mutually interdependent. The French government attempted to repair the damage by negotiating bilateral alliances with neighbors of Germany. The first alliance was formed with Belgium in 1920. In the next year a treaty with Poland provided that each would aid the other if it were attacked without provocation, and in 1924 Czechoslovakia was brought into the system by an agreement that the two powers would consult together with regard to the help to be given if either should become subject to unprovoked aggression.

The strongest alliance which France sought was not obtained. Negotiations begun with Great Britain late in 1921 for a similar treaty were dropped by the French government after the occupation of the Ruhr in 1923. The terms offered by the British were not very satisfactory to the French. The British were not willing to supplement the alliance with a military convention which would make British military help automatic and immediate in case of a German invasion of France, and they wanted to limit their help to the actual invasion of France, with no promise of military aid if Germany occupied the demilitarized zone on the Rhine. The French government therefore ceased negotiations lest the British government use them to exert pressure for the withdrawal of French troops from the Ruhr. After the French failure in the Ruhr, the entente between the two powers was reestablished. Both countries felt the need of it, but the friendship was somewhat strained at times when the French government, in order to retain it, had to make more concessions and be more conciliatory to Germany than some of its members desired, or when some British statesmen thought that the concessions were too few or too dilatory.

Although French foreign policy was perhaps more strongly influenced by the desire for security than that of any other country, many other countries were anxious to have security from aggression. As soon as the League of Nations began to discuss general disarmament, which the treaty required it to initiate, it discovered that a guarantee of safety

(margin notes)
French alliances

Relations with Great Britain

General security

would have to go hand in hand with reduction of armaments. The assembly, therefore, proposed a treaty of mutual assistance, which was formulated in 1923. It provided for all the signers to come to the military aid of any one of their number subjected to a war of aggression. The British were not prepared to undertake military commitments on so large a scale, and the treaty appears to have found little favor elsewhere. MacDonald, though he would not accept the treaty, wanted to satisfy the French desire for security. He suggested modifications of the treaty to which the prime minister of France agreed. The new document was drawn up in 1924 and was called the Geneva protocol. It met some of the criticisms of the treaty of mutual assistance by providing for the arbitration of disputes and by attempting to define aggression, but any signatory power might still be called upon to wage war in any part of the world. When the British considered the new plan, the Labor cabinet had been succeeded by a Conservative cabinet which was unwilling to cooperate because the definition of aggression was unsatisfactory and the military commitments were again too extensive geographically.

Before this plan was dropped, Stresemann, the German foreign minister, who had initiated a conciliatory policy toward France as a better means of obtaining a revision of the Treaty of Versailles, had suggested a German guarantee of the frontiers of some of the countries bordering on Germany. The British government became convinced of the value of the proposal and the French government proved willing to substitute it for the earlier more general plan. The pacts of security were finally embodied in a number of documents at a conference held in Locarno in 1925. The pact of chief importance was the guarantee by France, Germany, Belgium, Italy and Great Britain of the frontier between France and Germany and of the demilitarization of the zones on the Rhine established by the Treaty of Versailles. If disputes arose, they were to be settled by diplomacy, conciliation or arbitration; but if the frontier was violated by unprovoked aggression, the other powers would give military help to the invaded country. Pacts with regard to Germany's eastern boundary were established with Poland and Czechoslovakia, but they arranged only for arbitration and gave no such guarantee as did the western Locarno pacts. This was partly because Germany was not satisfied with her eastern boundary and partly because Italy and Great Britain did not sign the eastern pacts. British statesmen did not want to assume liability for upholding settlements which they thought might deserve revision in a portion of Europe where Great Britain appeared to have no direct interests. Nevertheless,

Locarno pacts

the Locarno pacts completed the process of the substitution of good will in international relations for the rivalry, suspicion and ill will which had been growing steadily from 1919 to 1924.

General
disarma-
ment

Unfortunately the era of good feeling did not endure, largely because the Germans did not obtain from participation in the pacts all that they desired. In 1926 Germany was given a permanent seat in the council of the League and four years later the last foreign troops were withdrawn from German soil, but the Germans regarded the pacts as a step toward general disarmament which would bring other nations down to an equality with Germany. Previously the French had refused to consider this promise contained in the Treaty of Versailles until they had security, and the Locarno pacts were designed to fulfill this condition. The first step toward disarmament was taken in 1926 when the council of the League appointed a commission to prepare a program for a disarmament conference. It took several years to accomplish the task, and during that period public opinion in both Germany and France began to deteriorate. In Germany the Nationalists and the Nazis opposed Stresemann's policy from the first, and by 1930 the Nazis had become a strong opposition party. After Stresemann's death in 1929, his successor found it increasingly difficult to maintain the policy of conciliatory accomplishment of Germany's rehabilitation in the world. In France a current of public opinion, which regarded the Locarno pacts as an insufficient addition to French security to counterbalance the surrender of any military advantages, gained strength. After 1930 it caused any further concessions to Germany to cease. Against this background of unfavorable public opinion the disarmament conference met in 1932, thirteen years after the signing of the Treaty of Versailles. At the conference the French representatives said that France would not disarm until it had greater security and they proposed that an international armed force should be placed at the disposal of the League of Nations. To the Germans this did not appear to be disarmament; it seemed to be merely putting the arms in another place. Their representatives demanded equality with other nations and ultimately they threatened to rearm if the other powers would not disarm to Germany's level. The representatives of Great Britain offered no general plan and their attitude in favor of disarmament seemed to be less decisive than that of the British public. Their moderate position, however, left them more free to seek for common ground between French security and German equality. When a deadlock was reached, this was what they tried to do. The attempt failed because the two policies as interpreted by their respective proponents were irreconcilable. In 1933, after the Nazis came to power under Hitler's leadership, the German representatives were recalled and notice was given that Germany would withdraw from the League. The failure of the disarmament conference was one of the first turning points in the direction of war.

The foreign policy which the Nazis had advocated in their election campaign was the substitution of aggressive for conciliatory diplomacy as a means of righting what the Germans called the wrongs of Versailles. Withdrawal from the conference and from the League represented the first application of the new policy; the second was rearmament. Though no particular secret was made of it, Hitler did not announce it until 1935. He claimed that rearmament was being undertaken because the allies had nullified the disarmament clauses of the Treaty of Versailles by failing to disarm. Great Britain, France and Italy protested and obtained from the League a reproof of Germany for a unilateral breach of that treaty. The three powers also called a conference at Stresa to arrange for united opposition to any further unilateral breach of the treaty which Germany might attempt, but they failed to attain a strong united front, and before long, events caused Italy to break away from Great Britain and France and to veer toward Germany. Thus no active attempt was made to prevent German rearmament.

German rearmament

One result of the failure of the disarmament conference and of Germany's subsequent rearmament was that Great Britain began to increase its armaments. In 1934 Baldwin put forward the view that the frontier of Great Britain for the purpose of defense had come to be the Rhine and he asked for an increased appropriation for the air force. The sum was modest, but the principle was important. At a time when strict economy was still the policy of the government, the prime minister announced that if disarmament finally failed, Great Britain would build to rival the strongest air force of any of its neighbors. This marked the abandonment of economy on armament which had been followed for many years. By 1936 a plan had been formulated for a large increase in the army and navy as well as the air force, and from then until 1939 the expenditures for increased armaments mounted steadily. Great Britain protected itself further by negotiating a naval agreement with Germany in 1935. Germany was to confine the tonnage of its surface navy to thirty-five per cent of Great Britain's and to have equality in submarines. Since Germany had already begun to

British armaments

build naval ships, it seemed to British statesmen advantageous to limit the amount, but to the French Great Britain appeared to be approving German rearmament.

France also began to look to its armaments, and as further protection it sought an alliance with Russia. Before beginning negotiations the French government consulted the British government. British statesmen had never looked favorably upon the French alliances with Poland and Czechoslovakia, for they saw a dangerous source of friction in the settlements of Germany's eastern frontier that had been made in 1919. If they caused war between Germany and its eastern neighbors, France was committed; and if France should enter a war against Germany, Great Britain probably could not stand aside in isolation. The projected treaty did not have the same element of danger because Russia did not border on Germany, but it was likely to revive among Germans the fear of their country's encirclement. The British government suggested that in order to avoid giving offense to Germany a multilateral pact should be formed that would include Germany and all the small eastern states as well as Russia. Recognizing that the proposed pact was really directed against Germany, Hitler declined. France therefore concluded a bilateral pact with Russia in 1935. If either state were threatened with aggression by a European state, the two would consult together. If either should become subject to unprovoked aggression, the other would come to the immediate assistance of its attacked partner. Meanwhile Hitler broke the "iron ring" around Germany by arranging a non-aggression pact with Poland in 1934. Since there had previously been much friction between Germany and Poland, this treaty removed the most serious threat from the east and left Hitler free to deal with the western powers.

These alliances were followed by the Italian conquest of Ethiopia which provided Germany with a new friend and divided the powers of western and central Europe into democratic and totalitarian camps. In 1922 the Fascists, whose doctrines were later copied to a large extent by the German Nazis, seized the government of Italy and set up Mussolini as a dictator. To him war was a desirable state of society, and the main purpose of Italian warriors should be to make the Mediterranean again an Italian sea, as it had been in the days of the Roman empire. In 1935 it became apparent that Mussolini was preparing to put these ideals into practice by conquering the native state of Ethiopia in northeastern Africa. Ethiopia, being a member of the League, asked that body for protection against the threatened aggression. The British public wanted to make the question a test of the League's power to

Margin notes:
New alliances

The Ethiopian crisis

maintain peace, and British statesmen feared that Ethiopia if united to the other Italian possessions in northeastern Africa might become a menace to British interests in that neighborhood. Great Britain, as a consequence, took the leadership in the League's effort to keep the peace, but all the attempts to conciliate Italy failed. They included a proposal, made at a conference of representatives of Great Britain, France and Italy which was held at the suggestion of the council of the League, to grant Italy, with the consent of the emperor of Ethiopia, an extensive economic concession in that country. Mussolini refused the offer, and in the autumn his troops invaded Ethiopia.

Faced with war, the League declared Italy to be the aggressor and applied economic sanctions. These sanctions had the fatal weakness of failing to include oil, and Italy could obtain that commodity from the United States, which was not a member of the League. When the League began to discuss the inclusion of oil, Mussolini threatened war against any country that tried to enforce this sanction. The power which would probably have to enforce it, if it were applied, was Great Britain. Actuated perhaps by a desire to keep his country out of war, Hoare, the British foreign minister, united with Laval, the French prime minister, who had wavered in his opposition to Italy, in offering Italy a large portion of Ethiopia. This was generally regarded as a betrayal of the League; in Great Britain it caused such widespread criticism that Hoare resigned. The League, however, gave up the attempt to extend sanctions to oil. Mussolini, who had rejected the offer, continued the war until Ethiopia was conquered completely in 1936. The effect of this opposition upon Italy was to change decisively the orientation of its foreign policy. Before the Ethiopian affair Italy had usually, though not without exception, worked with Great Britain and France. In 1936 the Italian and German governments made agreements for cooperation which became a virtual alliance known as the Rome–Berlin Axis. Thereafter Great Britain and France were generally faced with the opposition of Germany and Italy.

The Ethiopian crisis also had a profound effect upon the League. That body had previously settled some disputes which might have led to war, but its power to protect weak states against the aggression of powerful nations was already distrusted before 1935. In addition to its failure to prevent the rearmament of Germany, the League had failed to prevent the Japanese conquest of Manchuria. When the Japanese invasion began in 1931, the League with the cooperation of the United States tried to persuade Japan to halt the invasion and to settle the dispute with China over Manchuria by negotiation. When this policy

Twilight
of the
League

had no result, the council of the League appointed a commission, headed by Lord Lytton and including an American member, to investigate on the spot. This commission reported that Japan had violated its obligation under the covenant of the League. The assembly adopted the report, but did nothing to force Japan to abide by its obligation. The smaller states in the League desired to have economic sanctions applied to Japan, but their enforcement would have fallen upon the greater powers, and mainly upon Great Britain with its navy. Enforcement was likely to mean war, and if the British government had been willing to take the risk, it could not have counted upon the support of public opinion for a war undertaken to uphold the integrity of a country so remote. The faith of the smaller countries in the protection of the League had been shaken, and with the Ethiopian crisis it was lost completely. The Hoare-Laval incident caused such countries to fear even that they might be sacrificed to keep the greater powers out of war. Hence many of them began to seek other means of protection. Belgium deserted its alliance with France for neutrality, Poland substituted cooperation with Germany for cooperation with France and the League, and other states made similar attempts to find security.

German occupation of the Rhineland

Hitler took advantage of the preoccupation of the western powers with the Ethiopian crisis in 1936 to send troops into the demilitarized sections of the Rhineland and to proclaim the resumption of full German sovereignty over the area. In justification he asserted that the Franco-Russian mutual assistance pact violated the Locarno pacts. The truth or falsity of this claim was beside the issue. If Germany thought the Locarno pacts had been violated, its means of redress were prescribed by the pacts.[3] It had no right unilaterally to declare a multilateral treaty void. The French government appears to have been somewhat undecided on what should be done to meet this serious threat to French security, but it realized that any opposition involving the use of force must have the support of Great Britain. Members of the French cabinet forthwith went to London to consult with the British cabinet. Apparently British statesmen did not think that the Locarno pacts committed Britain to give military aid to France unless France was actually invaded. The question was finally submitted to the League. The council declared that Germany had broken the Locarno pacts and the Treaty of Versailles, but it made no recommendation of military sanctions.

This event resulted in the establishment of a definite alliance between

---

[3] Above, p. 831.

Great Britain and France later in the same year. The government of each country made a unilateral statement to the effect that its country would give military assistance to the other if it should be attacked without provocation. The statements were followed by military conversations and agreements.

The conflict of interests between the two alliances was demonstrated during the course of the Spanish civil war. This war began in 1936 when a party commonly called the nationalists, but which was predominantly fascist, revolted against the party in control of the government, which was called republican but had a strong communist tinge. Russia sent supplies and some technicians to help the republicans, and Germany and Italy sent supplies and troops to aid the nationalists. In both Great Britain and France public sympathy was divided between the two parties; neither country was yet prepared militarily or psychologically for war. At the instance of France a non-intervention committee was formed which included many European states. It tried to prevent foreign states from providing the belligerents with supplies or soldiers and to secure the withdrawal of troops which had been sent. Great Britain, supported by France, took the leadership in proposing means of accomplishing these ends and its proposals were met by counter-proposals, delays of acceptance and evasions from Italy, supported by Germany. The work of the committee made evident a steady decline of respect for international obligations on the part of the fascist powers. Early in 1938 the situation became so serious that it caused Eden, the British foreign secretary, to resign. Chamberlain wanted to accept a request of the Italian government to hold conversations on the questions at issue between the two governments. Eden felt that so little reliance could be placed upon the word of the Italian government that it was useless to negotiate further until that government had withdrawn its troops from Spain as evidence of its good faith. Despite its many failures, the committee did help to prevent the civil war, which ended in 1939 with victory for the fascist nationalists, from expanding into a general European war.

The conversations with Italy were important chiefly as an illustration of Chamberlain's policy of appeasement. His thought was that the division of Europe between dictator and democratic powers threatened the peace of the continent unless the four powers could settle their differences and reach a friendly understanding by means of discussion. The negotiations resulted in several agreements. Each power ratified an informal understanding, which had been reached the year before, whereby the existing status in the western Mediterranean would be maintained. Italy promised to reduce the size of its army in Libya, Great Britain undertook to recommend to the League the recognition of Ethiopia as an Italian possession, and several other causes of friction were to be removed. The agreements were not to become effective until a settlement had been reached with regard to Spain, and it was not until near the close of 1938 that the British government brought them into force.

Before these negotiations were concluded, Germany, by the annexation of Austria in 1938, threatened the peace of Europe much more seriously than Italy had done. The peace of 1919 left Austria so small and so barren of economic resources that it seemed doubtful whether its people would be able to make a living. The Austrians desired union with Germany, but that was forbidden by the treaties. The sentiment in behalf of union appears, nevertheless, to have survived for a long time. As late as 1931 a partial economic union was attempted as a means of alleviating the economic depression, but it was declared by the permanent court to run counter to the prohibition in the treaties of 1919. After the Nazis came to power in Germany, public opinion in Austria apparently began to regard the union with less favor, and an abortive attempt of Austrian Nazis in 1934 to seize control of the Austrian government, which it was suspected had the support of the German Nazis, helped to strengthen this trend in Austrian opinion. Two years later Austria secured from Germany a treaty by which each government agreed not to interfere in the internal political affairs of the other country. This protection of Austrian independence proved to be worthless because Hitler disregarded his word. Early in 1938 he ordered the chancellor of Austria to admit Austrian Nazi leaders to important posts in the government. Though this was obviously the first step toward annexation, the chancellor was compelled to obey. He could not oppose Germany's might with the Austrian army and he could turn to no other power for help. He did attempt to ascertain Austrian public opinion by holding a plebiscite on the question of union or independence, but Hitler, fearful that the vote might be for independence, did not allow the plebiscite to take place. On March 11 a German army marched into Austria without opposition, and Austria was annexed to Germany by means of force.

In Great Britain the method by which the union was brought about caused some indignation. The British government expressed its condemnation but it could do nothing to prevent the union. The agreement made at Stresa in 1935 called for consultation of Italy, France and Great Britain if Austrian independence were threatened. In 1938,

German annexation of Austria

British attitude

however, Italy was a member of the Axis with Germany; hence
Mussolini expressed his approval of the annexation. France, which had
been strongly opposed to the union ever since 1919, was in the midst
of a cabinet crisis and was not prepared to take any effective action.
Great Britain never had been opposed to a revision of the treaty which
would make the union possible, and in 1938 it was by no means certain
that the union was not desired by the majority of Austrians.

The incident left Europe apprehensive of further German aggression.
It soon became apparent that the next blow was likely to be directed
against Czechoslovakia. A large German minority, commonly called
the Sudeten Germans, was located in the Czechoslovak province of
Bohemia, mainly in the regions adjacent to Germany and Austria.
This minority had lived in Bohemia for centuries, subject first to
Bohemian and later to Austrian rule. In the early years of the twentieth
century, when the German element in the population was kept politically dominant by the Austrian government, there was strong antagonism between the Germans and the Czechs, a Slavic-speaking people,
who were in the majority. With the creation of Czechoslovakia in 1919,
the Czechs became politically dominant. The Germans were protected
by a minorities treaty, but they were not happy about their position. A
small group of irreconcilables wanted union with Germany, but the
large majority wanted autonomy within Czechoslovakia. By 1938 the
majority of the Sudeten Germans were organized in a single party
under the leadership of Henlein. Nominally it was not a Nazi party,
but after the annexation of Austria it became so. Many moderates
were stirred by that event to a strong nationalistic fervor and others
feared a concentration camp if they did not support union with Germany. Henlein, however, demanded of the Czechoslovak government
only a large degree of autonomy for the Sudeten Germans within
Czechoslovakia.

When this demand was made, Chamberlain foresaw that its refusal
might cause Germany to attack Czechoslovakia. In that event France
was bound by treaty to aid Czechoslovakia, and if France became
involved in war with Germany, Great Britain would probably have to
support France. Chamberlain therefore decided to try to avoid war by
appeasing Germany. He persuaded the French government to join in
notifying the Czechoslovak government that the two powers wanted the
Sudeten problem worked out peacefully within Czechoslovakia. The
British government then sent an adviser who attempted to persuade
the Czechoslovak government to grant what Henlein demanded.
The Czechoslovak government was loath to concede all the demands,

The
Sudeten
Germans

British
interven-
tion

since some of them threatened that state's sovereignty over the Sudeten Germans; but after several proposed compromises were rejected by Henlein, it finally offered a large part of the original demands. Henlein also refused this proposal. On September 12 Hitler announced that he would help the Sudeten Germans, and shortly afterward Henlein stated that they would be satisfied only with annexation to Germany.

The attempted appeasement had failed and a European war seemed nearly inevitable. Yet, if the majority of the Sudeten Germans really wanted to be placed under German rule, a war to keep them in Czechoslovakia hardly seemed justified. Chamberlain, in a last effort to avert war, determined to seek a personal interview with Hitler; this took place in Germany on September 15. Apparently Chamberlain learned that Hitler would accept nothing short of the annexation of the Sudeten lands, but he received a promise that the German leader would claim no more territory in Europe. Chamberlain thereupon returned to London and persuaded the French government to join in putting pressure on the Czechoslovak government to make the cession. Areas whose populations were more than fifty per cent German were to be ceded without plebiscites, but plebiscites were to be held where the majorities were doubtful. Deprived of the support of Great Britain and France, Czechoslovakia could only give way. With the cession assured, Chamberlain returned to Germany to arrange with Hitler the details of the transfer of territory. He found that instead of an international commission to take charge of the cession and to hold plebiscites in doubtful areas, Hitler proposed to occupy the territory which he desired with an army and not to bother with plebiscites. Chamberlain forwarded Hitler's plan to the Czechoslovak government, but this time neither Britain nor France advised acceptance, and both countries began to prepare for war.

War seemed unavoidable, when Mussolini secured a conference of Great Britain, France, Germany and Italy at Munich on September 29. The resulting treaty was a compromise. The occupation was to be made by the German army one zone at a time, but the frontier was to be established by an international commission which could designate districts in which plebiscites were to be held. The four powers guaranteed the new boundaries of Czechoslovakia. The treaty, however, proved to be a compromise in name only. The international commission accepted the boundary which Hitler desired and no plebiscites were ever held. When Chamberlain returned from Munich, he was hailed with acclaim for keeping Britain out of war when it was unprepared, but the relief was accompanied with an uneasy feeling that

Margin notes: Chamberlain and Hitler

Munich

an immoral settlement had been condoned in the face of threatened force.

It soon became evident that the British had accepted humiliation in vain. In March, 1939, Hitler occupied the remainder of Czechoslovakia except a small portion which he allowed to go to Hungary. This not only broke the promise which he had given, but it also meant that the purpose of German aggression had undergone a decisive change. Up to that time Hitler had claimed that German territorial expansion was for the purpose of bringing German-speaking peoples under German rule. For the present venture no such claim could be made. It was conquest of a people merely to add to German territory and to contribute to the economic welfare of Germans.

The rest of Czecho-slovakia

The effect on British public opinion was to render prevalent the view that Hitler must be stopped. Chamberlain responded with a public speech in which he said that Great Britain was ready to oppose Germany's further expansion by such forceful methods. The French prime minister spoke for France in similar terms. When Hitler a few days later demanded the return of Danzig to Germany and a sovereign right of way across the Polish Corridor, the British and French governments each gave a unilateral undertaking to give Poland all the support in its power if Polish independence were threatened. This was soon followed by the announcement that Great Britain was ready to co-operate with all nations resisting aggressors, and after the seizure of Albania by Italy on April 7, Britain and France pledged help specifically to Greece and Roumania. The crux of this new policy was the guarantee given to Poland, and in that there was one weakness. The settlements in Danzig and the Corridor had worked badly, and Germany may have had a reasonable claim for the revision of the treaty with regard to them. Chamberlain met this by stating in several speeches that Great Britain was willing to have these questions settled by negotiation between Germany and Poland, provided it was done in an atmosphere of peace and with no threat to Polish independence.

British alliance with Poland

With the issue thus defined, both Germany and Great Britain sought alliances. Hitler had no difficulty in obtaining a military alliance from Mussolini. Great Britain turned to Russia but had no success. Such an alliance was likely to mean Russian participation in the war, and Hitler had a better proposal to make. All he asked was that Russia remain out of the war. Russia agreed and the non-aggression pact was made public on August 21. It meant that Hitler was free to deal with France and Great Britain as soon as he had conquered Poland, without fear of attack from the rear. There followed a hectic week of

The com-ing of war

negotiation, chiefly between Great Britain and Germany, to avert war. At the end Hitler proposed the most moderate settlement with Poland he had yet suggested, but it was offered under such circumstances that it does not appear to have been honestly intended as a basis of negotiation. On September 1 German troops invaded Poland.

Conquest of Poland

The conquest of Poland took less than a month. By the coordination of planes, tanks and infantry and the use of larger armies, the German invaders overwhelmed the Poles. Shortly before the victory was completed, a Russian army occupied eastern Poland, and by agreement with Germany Russia kept that portion of Poland, leaving the rest to Germany.

British and French strategy

Great Britain and France entered the war against Germany on September 3. They could not send troops to Poland and the destruction of the Polish airfields by German planes at the beginning of the invasion prevented the possibility of aid from the air. The French invaded the western part of Germany, but the diversion was not on a sufficient scale to have any effect upon Poland's fate. After the fall of this nation, the French armies and the British army which had been sent to France remained on the defensive behind the Maginot line, a system of forts and defenses which protected the eastern frontier of France as far north as Belgium. The Germans had a similar line of defenses on their western boundary, known as the Westwall or the Siegfried line. For the rest of the winter the war consisted of artillery duels and occasional clashes of patrols in the area between the two lines. The war of defense was chosen deliberately on the part of the French and the British, because they hoped by control of the sea to deprive Germany of food and other supplies and eventually to force a surrender with as little expenditure of life as possible. The system of blockade which had been put into effect so successfully in the preceding war was renewed, and this time it was extended to the seizure of exports from Germany. Some German surface raiders were destroyed, but German submarines sank a significant amount of allied shipping. On the whole, however, the blockade had made an effective beginning by the spring of 1940.

The fall of France

The Germans had no intention of battering themselves against the Maginot line while they awaited starvation. On April 9 German armies invaded Denmark and Norway. The British contested the occupation of the latter country without success. Germany thus added to its supplies of food and other materials, and acquired bases for submarines and planes for use against Great Britain. On May 10 the Germans invaded Holland, Belgium and Luxemburg. In five days the Dutch

army, after suffering great losses, surrendered, and Belgium followed
on May 28. This left the British and French troops which had come
to the help of the Belgians surrounded, because the Germans had broken
into France and had occupied the northeastern part of the country clear
to the coast. The surrounded troops retreated to Dunkirk, where the
greater part of them were evacuated by means of the navy and a large
number of boats of all types manned for the most part by volunteers.
It was a bad defeat for the British, but they could find some comfort in
the escape of their forces from a position in which surrender or annihilation seemed certain. The French could find no alleviative circumstances.
The Germans pressed steadily south and the French retired before them.
On June 10 Mussolini, convinced that Germany would win, declared
war on France and sent an Italian army to invade southeastern France.
On June 16 the French sought an armistice and a few days later the war
ended. France accepted German occupation of northern France and of
the entire Atlantic coast line, and Italian occupation of a section of
southeastern France. The government of the portion which was not
occupied thereafter collaborated with Germany.

When the French government was preparing to surrender, Churchill
released it from its undertaking not to make a separate peace, provided
the French navy was turned over to Great Britain or interned in ports
not under German or Italian control. In the armistice with Germany
the French government disregarded this undertaking, whereupon the
British determined to prevent French ships from coming under German and Italian control as far as possible. French naval vessels in ports
under British control were forcibly interned unless they would voluntarily cooperate with the British navy. The commander of the French
ships in the Algerian port of Oran refused either to cooperate with the
British navy or to intern his ships in British or neutral ports. A British
fleet therefore attacked the French fleet and sank or damaged several
ships, though some escaped and reached the French port of Toulon.
The *Richelieu,* a French battleship stationed at Dakar, was also attacked and seriously damaged.

The fall of France left Great Britain in a desperate situation. The
internal defenses against a possible German invasion by sea were inadequate, there were not enough trained soldiers under arms and the
supply of weapons was not sufficient. The superiority of the British
navy, on the other hand, made a sea-borne invasion a difficult problem
for the Germans. Before it could be attempted, moreover, control of
the air was necessary. The battle of Britain began in the air and the
British defense was so successful that the battle never advanced be-

The
French
navy

The battle
of Britain

yond that stage. The Germans had more planes, but the British had better fighter planes and better pilots. The early raids were made daily with comparatively small numbers of planes and were directed mainly against military objectives and port facilities. In August the nature of the raids changed. The bombers came in large groups, and their targets were the crowded cities, particularly London. They wrought great destruction of civilian life and property, but the British spirit, instead of breaking, rose to the occasion. British fighter planes had been taking steady toll of the German bombers, but on the mass raids they inflicted losses so much greater than those which they sustained that the Germans gave up such raids by day and confined their attacks mainly to raids on a smaller scale at night. Any danger of immediate invasion was thus removed. "Never," said Churchill, "in the field of human conflict was so much owed by so many to so few."

North Africa, 1940–41

The entry of Italy into the war threatened the British position in the Mediterranean and North Africa. In the summer of 1940 an Italian army conquered British Somaliland and another one invaded western Egypt from Libya. Before the end of the year a strongly reinforced British army drove the Italian army out of Egypt and pursued it until, in the spring of 1941, the eastern part of Libya was in the possession of the British. At the same time other British forces recovered British Somaliland and conquered all of Italian East Africa, including Ethiopia. The series of victories over the Italians was rounded out by a decisive defeat of the Italian fleet off Cape Matapan in the Mediterranean in March, 1941.

The eastern Mediterranean

Meanwhile a serious threat to the British had been developing in the eastern Mediterranean. Late in October, 1940, the Italians attacked Greece from Albania. The Greeks withstood the invasion and soon forced the Italians back into Albania, where they continued to retreat until the Germans came to their rescue. Late in 1940 and early in 1941 Germany obtained the cooperation of Roumania, Hungary and Bulgaria and sent armies through these countries to the borders of Greece and Jugoslavia. On April 6 they invaded both countries. The British sent troops to help the Greeks in accordance with their undertaking of 1939, but the Greeks were forced to surrender in three weeks. The Germans then conquered and occupied by an air-borne invasion the island of Crete to which the British forces had withdrawn from Greece. Jugoslavia capitulated before Greece did, but many of the Jugoslavs were soon able to institute guerrilla warfare against the Germans.

While these campaigns were taking place, the Germans were sending troops to Libya to assist the Italians. In the spring of 1941 the joint armies cleared the province of British troops, except for a garrison which remained in the port of Tobruk. The British were able to recover the lost territory in the autumn, but early in 1942 the Germans and Italians pushed them back into Egypt, where the British finally held them at El Alamein.

The victories of the Axis in Greece and Libya in 1941 raised the threat that the Germans might come down through the countries to the east of the Mediterranean and attack Egypt and the Suez from two sides at once. German influence in those countries was already strong. To eliminate this danger Great Britain occupied Iraq and French Syria. In the latter invasion British soldiers were assisted by Free French troops.

Throughout this period Great Britain continued its blockade, but the extensive conquests of the Germans so increased the resources available to them that it became a less effective weapon. The German attacks on British shipping, on the other hand, proved a serious menace to British supplies. The acquisition of air bases in Norway, along the Atlantic coast and in the Mediterranean area made it possible for Germany to increase the attacks upon shipping from the air. The surface ships of the German navy were used mainly for raids upon commercial shipping, and though the British watched them closely and kept them confined to harbors a large part of the time, they occasionally slipped out and did much damage. The British sank some of them in 1941 and thereafter the danger from this source declined somewhat. The greatest losses were inflicted by German submarines, and by the end of 1941 they had assumed alarming proportions. The difficulties were increased because the Mediterranean was unsafe for shipping, and longer voyages around Africa were therefore necessary. In 1940 the German occupation of Norway caused about sixty Norwegian warships and a large number of merchant ships to be placed at the disposal of the British, but by the summer of 1941 British ships were being sunk faster than they could be replaced.

In this crisis Great Britain began to receive some help from the United States. At the beginning of the war in 1939, the United States revised its neutrality legislation to permit the export of arms, but required that they should be paid for in cash before they left the country and should not be carried on American ships. The law also prevented American ships from entering ports in the war zone to carry any other goods. Popular sympathy was with the democratic powers, but it was not strong enough to justify the risk of becoming entangled in the war. With the fall of France in 1940, the American people began to realize that they might not be safe from Nazi aggression, which obviously could be limited only by superior might. With so large a part of the Atlantic coast of Europe in Nazi possession, with the possible expansion of Nazi control to the Atlantic coast of the French colonies in Africa and with the independence of Britain endangered, the world suddenly seemed smaller and the necessity of preparing for defense became a dominant consideration. This was soon followed by the thought that one of the best modes of defense was to help Great Britain defend itself. In September the United States gave that nation fifty destroyers and in return received land for building air and naval bases in British possessions from Newfoundland through the British West Indies to British Guiana. A little later President Roosevelt announced that the United States would increase greatly its production of planes, guns and ships for Great Britain and other powers opposed to the Axis. Early in 1941 congress passed the lease-lend act which enabled the government to furnish billions of dollars' worth of material aid to countries whose defense was vital to that of the United States, and Great Britain received the largest share. In the course of the year the United States took over control of Greenland and Iceland, which had been Danish possessions, for sea and air bases. Along with them it assumed the patrol by planes and ships of the longer part of the route across the Atlantic. After a German submarine attacked an American destroyer, President Roosevelt ordered ships and planes to shoot first if German submarines or raiders were discovered in waters vital for the defense of this country. Finally congress removed the restrictions on American ships entering the war zone, and the American merchant marine began to carry goods to Great Britain.

The entry of Russia

On June 22, 1941, the Nazis provided Great Britain with a powerful ally by invading Russia without warning. On a front hundreds of miles long the Germans pushed the Russian armies back to a line extending from below Leningrad to Rostov. They did not succeed, however, in their main objective, which was to annihilate the Russian armies. The Russian spaces were so great that the Germans could not occupy with safety a part of the Soviet Union unless the Soviet armies were rendered ineffective. The advance was made, moreover, at considerable cost. The Russians often succeeded in wiping out the German spearheads which penetrated their lines; and if the Germans broke through effectively, they always found reserve Russian divisions a few miles farther on. The Germans did not attain superiority in the air, and their supply lines were long and were subject to attack by Russian guerrillas. The Russians still had many great industrial plants east of the Urals and they were receiving supplies from Great Britain and the United States. The military help which Germany received from Finland, Bulgaria, Roumania, Hungary and Italy did not offset these advantages. At the close of 1941 the Germans had not succeeded in taking either Leningrad or Moscow, though they were only a few miles from both cities.

On December 7, 1941, Japan supplied Great Britain with another powerful ally and with another powerful enemy by attacking the United States navy at Pearl Harbor without warning. The attack was caused by the diplomatic opposition of the United States to Japan's ambition to build in eastern Asia and the southern Pacific a vast dominion under its control. After the conquest of Manchuria and its organization as the puppet kingdom of Manchukuo, Japan in 1937 invaded China. In 1940 the Japanese obtained from France an extensive degree of control in French Indo-China, began to extend their influence in Siam, which was becoming known as Thailand, and were making threats against the Dutch East Indies. It was obvious that the British and American possessions in the Far East stood in the way of the Japanese ambitions and that Japan was closely associated with the enemies of Great Britain in Europe. In 1937 Japan had entered the Axis, and in 1940 it had made with Germany and Italy a military alliance directed particularly against the United States. From the beginning of the invasion of China the United States and Great Britain opposed Japanese aggression diplomatically, and after Great Britain became occupied with the war in Europe the United States tended to take the leadership in this policy. During 1941 relations between the United States and Japan grew steadily more strained. Japan protected its back door by a treaty of neutrality with the Soviet Union, and the government of the United States received assurance from Churchill that it would have the support of Great Britain if its policy led to war with Japan. Thus the attack on Pearl Harbor brought the United States into the war against Germany and Italy as well as against Japan, and Great Britain declared war on Japan.

The entry of the United States

With remarkable speed the Japanese conquered an immense amount of territory. The British possessions of Hong Kong, Malaya and Burma fell within a few months. This brought Japan to the gates of India and gave it control of the Burma Road, the only route by which the western powers could get supplies to China. The Dutch East Indies and the Philippines soon followed the British possessions, and by June, 1942, the Japanese were in New Guinea threatening Australia with attack. On the sea the Americans defeated Japanese fleets in the

Japanese conquests

battles of Midway, the Coral Sea and the Solomon Islands. These victories not only saved the United States from attack but also kept open the sea lanes to Australia and prevented a possible invasion of that country. The British contributed by occupying the French island of Madagascar in order to protect the route to the east around the Cape of Good Hope. The British sent reinforcements to India, and the United States sent troops to New Zealand, Australia and some neighboring islands to the east of that continent which the Japanese had not occupied. Before the end of 1942 American forces had landed on Guadalcanal and were contesting its possession with the Japanese, and American and Australian troops were fighting the Japanese in New Guinea. These expeditions constituted as yet hardly more than an offensive defense to protect Australia and the sea route to it, but they later became the initial steps in the reconquest of the islands held by Japan.

Until late in 1942 Great Britain and the United States stood on the defensive and were forced to accept disastrous defeats, but the way was being prepared to wrest the initiative from the Axis powers. On January 1, 1942, twenty-six countries, designated as the United Nations, signed a treaty providing for cooperation against the common enemy. They included the exiled governments of countries occupied by the Axis powers, the British dominions, some Latin American countries and the four major powers—Great Britain, the United States, the Soviet Union and China. Plans were formulated for coordinated action and committees were appointed to carry them out. The arrangements most important for their immediate consequences were those made by Churchill and Roosevelt in two series of conversations. It was decided to make the principal military effort in the European theater, to place British and American forces working together under unified commands and to attack Germany and Italy in North Africa.

These plans were brought to fruition in the autumn of 1942. On October 24 the British at El Alamein, reinforced and supplied with adequate weapons, inflicted upon the Germans and Italians a severe defeat and forced them to retreat. The British then pursued them across Libya. On November 7, in one of the largest amphibious operations yet attempted during the war, American and British troops were landed in Morocco and Algeria. The French put up a short token resistance, but French officers who desired a free France soon brought the opposition to an end. The Germans at once occupied southern France, whereupon the French fleet at Toulon was sunk by the French. The Germans also began to send reinforcements to Tunisia in such numbers that

Marginal notes:

Prepara-
tions for
an offense

North
Africa,
1942–43

its conquest became a difficult task. In the spring, however, the British drove the Germans and Italians fleeing across Libya into Tunisia and pushed them to the north. The Americans and British on the west forced the Germans facing them to retreat into the same area. Penned between the allied armies and the sea, with no chance of escape, the German and Italian armies surrendered in May, leaving North Africa in the undisputed possession of the allies.

By that time the tide of war was turning against the Axis powers in other quarters. In Russia, as well as in North Africa and the Pacific, the turn came late in 1942. During the winter of 1941–42 the Russians pushed the Germans back in a number of places, but they were able to capture few of the strong points in the German line. In the summer the Germans began to advance again, occupying the Crimea and pushing south toward the oil wells of the Caucasus and east toward the Volga. At Stalingrad on that river both armies fought a conquer-or-die battle; the Russians won in January, 1943. Thereafter they took the offensive and maintained it until the last of the Germans were driven out of Russia in 1944. The Russian armies pursued the retreating Germans into the Baltic states, Poland and the Balkans. At the end of 1944 the Germans had not been ousted entirely from the Baltic states, though some Russian troops were at the frontier of East Prussia. The Russian advance in Poland had been halted at Warsaw. In the southeast Bulgaria and Roumania had been forced to make peace with the allies, Russian armies were driving German and Hungarian armies before them in Hungary and Czechoslovakia, and other Russian forces had entered Jugoslavia to cooperate with the native guerrillas who had been fighting the Germans throughout the war. In the north, Finland had been overwhelmed and required to abandon its alliance with Germany and to make terms with Russia.

The war in Russia, 1941–44

The battle of the Atlantic followed a similar course. An enormous increase of production in the United States during 1942 provided vast quantities of supplies. Some went across the Pacific and some of those for Russia went around Africa to the Persian gulf and thence overland through Iran. In the previous year the British and Russians had forced the ruler of Iran, who was favorable to the Nazis, to permit this transit, and allied soldiers were kept there to maintain it. But a large part of the supplies for Russia, for Great Britain and for American armies had to go across the northern Atlantic subject to intensive attack by hostile submarines and planes. In 1942 the allied losses in all parts of the world amounted to over four million gross tons of ships and of the supplies which they carried. By that time the United States and Great

The Atlantic, 1942–44

Britain were building ships faster than they were being sunk, but a decrease of the sinkings was imperative. This was accomplished during the next two years. In 1943 the sinkings declined substantially and during 1944 they were reduced still further.

The attainment of superiority in the air was also a slow process. As soon as the Germans began to bomb Britain, the British air force began to retaliate. The number of raids and the number of planes on each raid mounted steadily. In 1941 Germany and the territories it held appear to have received more bombs than Britain did. In the next year American planes and crews based in Britain helped to increase the havoc being wrought. In the north African campaign of that year allied planes had superiority. Throughout the next two years the bombing of industrial plants, oil supplies and communications in Germany and the lands occupied by the Germans increased steadily in frequency and amount, and the opposition of German planes as steadily declined. German planes were being destroyed so much faster than they were being built that in 1944 Germany began to hoard them for use when the need was exceptionally great. German raids on England declined to such an extent that in 1944 some of the blackout restrictions were lifted for the first time since 1939. On the battle-fields of 1944 German soldiers often shouted vainly for the help of planes as the French and British had done four years before.

In 1943, two months after the campaign ended in Tunisia, allied troops were transported from North Africa to the beaches of Sicily, and in a swift campaign the island was conquered. On September 3 the allied armies crossed the Strait of Messina to the mainland. On the same day the surrender of Italy took place, Mussolini having been previously overthrown. This left only the Germans to fight, but they, aided by the mountainous terrain, gave the allies strong opposition. When an amphibious landing was made at Salerno on September 9, the Germans nearly drove the invaders back into the sea. After this initial difficulty was overcome, a junction of the allied armies was soon accomplished. They captured Naples, but to the north on the Garigliano, where several armies had been defeated in the past, the allied progress stopped for the winter. More troops were landed in January, 1944, at Anzio well to the north of the Garigliano, but the Germans contained them. Finally, on May 11, the allies began an offensive which forced the Germans to retreat. Rome was liberated, the Germans continuing to flee until they were in the Apennines north of Florence; here they established a line of defense rendered strong by the nature of the terrain. For the remainder of 1944 the allies hammered at this line, making painfully slow progress.

Air power in Europe

Invasion of Sicily and Italy

The most spectacular campaign in 1944 was the invasion of France. On June 6 British, Canadian and American troops, which had been transported from Britain by the largest armada of ships employed during the war, landed on the eastern side of the Cotentin peninsula. The Germans, who had been fortifying the coast of France for a long time in anticipation of an invasion, made the landing costly but could not prevent the establishment of beachheads. They then massed their troops in an attempt to confine the invaders to the Cotentin. They held the British and Canadians around Caen, but the Americans, after capturing the port of Cherbourg, went down the western side of the peninsula and broke through into Brittany. After the Germans failed to close the gap at Avranches, they were forced to retreat. The allies swept through northern and central France at an astounding rate of speed. Paris was freed on August 25, and most of eastern France, Belgium and part of the Netherlands were soon cleared of Germans. On August 15, in one of the best-executed amphibious operations of the war, American and French armies were landed on the Riviera. They soon took Toulon and Marseilles, and then chased the fleeing Germans up the Rhone valley and through the Belfort gap. By September the allied armies had outrun their supplies, making it necessary to slow up and reorganize before invading Germany. This gave the Germans an opportunity to strengthen their defenses in front of the Siegfried line. The advance into Germany was consequently very slow, and in December it was stopped entirely by a German break through the allied lines for several miles into Belgium. The counter-offensive reached no important objectives before it was stopped. It made clear what had been becoming apparent for some time, that the war of movement had changed to a war of attrition.

Invasion of France

Late in 1944 British troops entered Greece and helped the Greek guerrillas to drive the Germans out. They restored the exiled conservative government, and this led to civil war. The radical Greeks, who had arms, tried to secure control of the government by force. The British, insisting that a change in government must be accomplished by peaceful, democratic procedure, attempted to suppress the rebellion. The incident had unfortunate political repercussions in Great Britain. The liberal elements suspected that the British government was waging war on Greeks who had fought to liberate their country, in order to maintain a Greek government which was favorable to Great Britain but unpopular in Greece. Churchill denied the allegation in the house of commons and obtained a vote of confidence. Eventually a regency was established, a new cabinet designed to be representative of all parties was appointed, and a truce ended the civil war.

The British in Greece

War in
the
Pacific

In the Pacific, as elsewhere, the allies were able to take the offensive in 1943. During the course of the year Guadalcanal and other islands in the Solomon group were captured, landings were made on others, and the Japanese on New Guinea were steadily pressed back. Air and naval superiority became so great that the Japanese convoys carrying troops and supplies to these outlying sections of the new empire were sunk with regularity. It was estimated that only one of ten of their ships got through the allied blockade. By the spring of 1944 these islands in the southwest Pacific no longer offered any strategic obstacle to offensives farther afield. In the northeastern Pacific the Japanese, who had occupied Attu and Kiska in the Aleutian Islands, were conquered on the former and withdrew from the latter in 1943. Thereafter American bombers utilized these islands as bases for frequent raids upon the Kuriles in northern Japan. Late in 1943 the American navy began to assault Japanese islands in the central Pacific. The general pattern called for bombing by planes for a period, shelling from ships, and then amphibious landings on some of the islands in the group. In 1943 and 1944 several islands were conquered in the Gilberts, the Marshalls, the Carolines and the Marianas. The conquered islands included Guam, which the Japanese had seized from the United States early in the war. These islands provided new airfields for land-based planes and made it possible to neutralize many of the unconquered Japanese islands in the central Pacific and to extend the air raids to additional parts of the Japanese holdings. In June, 1944, Superfortress planes began to raid the main Japanese islands from bases in China and later from Saipan. At the same time heavy raids on the Philippines were initiated. The latter were followed on October 20 by the landing of American troops on Leyte in the central Philippines. Before the end of the year all organized resistance had ceased on Leyte, and the island of Mindoro to the north was in the process of being conquered. The invasion of the Philippines tempted the Japanese fleet, which had kept its principal strength withdrawn from the area where the constantly growing American fleet was operating, to combat. Its attempt to surprise the American fleet at Leyte failed, and American planes and ships inflicted upon it an overwhelming defeat.

After the Japanese conquests closed the Burma Road, the allies could get supplies to China only in small quantities by plane. The Americans established an air force in China, but in 1944 the Japanese conquered a large part of southwestern China and forced the Americans to abandon some of their best fields. Campaigns were made in Burma in order to open a road to China and to push the Japanese back from the Indian

China and
Burma

frontier. One begun in the autumn of 1942 was unsuccessful, but one undertaken a year later, in which British, Indians, Americans and Chinese participated, cleared part of northern Burma of the Japanese, and by the close of 1944 a road to China was nearing completion. The Japanese retaliated by invading the state of Manipur in India, but they were driven out late in 1944.

CHRONOLOGICAL TABLES

Kent

Ethelbert, 560–616

Northumbria

Ethelfrith, 593–617
Edwin, 617–633
Oswald, 635–642
Oswy, 642–670
Ecgfrith, 670–685

Mercia

Penda, 626–655
Ethelbald, 716–757
Offa II, 757–796
Cenulf, 796–821

Wessex

Ine, 688–726
Egbert, 802–839
Ethelwulf, 839–858
Ethelbald, 858–860
Ethelbert, 860–866
Ethelred, 866–871

England

Alfred, 871–899
Edward, 899–924
Ethelstan, 924–939
Edmund, 939–946
Edred, 946–955
Edwig, 955–959
Edgar, 959–975
Edward, 975–978
Ethelred, 978–1016
Edmund, 1016
Canute, 1017–1035
Harold, 1035–1040
Harthacanute, 1040–1042

Edward, 1042–1066
Harold, 1066
William I, 1066–1087
William II, 1087–1100
Henry I, 1100–1135
Stephen, 1135–1154
Henry II, 1154–1189
Richard I, 1189–1199
John, 1199–1216
Henry III, 1216–1272
Edward I, 1272–1307
Edward II, 1307–1327
Edward III, 1327–1377
Richard II, 1377–1399
Henry IV, 1399–1413
Henry V, 1413–1422
Henry VI, 1422–1461
Edward IV, 1461–1483
Edward V, 1483
Richard III, 1483–1485
Henry VII, 1485–1509
Henry VIII, 1509–1547
Edward VI, 1547–1553
Mary, 1553–1558
Elizabeth, 1558–1603
James I, 1603–1625
Charles I, 1625–1649
Interregnum, 1649–1660
Charles II, 1660–1685
James II, 1685–1688
William III and Mary, 1689–1702
Anne, 1702–1714
George I, 1714–1727
George II, 1727–1760
George III, 1760–1820
George IV, 1820–1830
William IV, 1830–1837
Victoria, 1837–1001

Edward VII, 1901–1910 Edward VIII, 1936
George V, 1910–1936 George VI, 1936–

HEADS OF CABINETS

Sir Robert Walpole, 1721–1742
John Carteret, 1742–1744
Henry Pelham, 1744–1754
Duke of Newcastle, 1754–1756
William Pitt, 1756–1757
William Pitt and the Duke of Newcastle, 1757–1761
Duke of Newcastle and Lord Bute, 1761–1762
Lord Bute, 1762–1763
George Grenville, 1763–1765
Lord Rockingham, 1765–1766
William Pitt, Lord Chatham, 1766–1768
Duke of Grafton, 1768–1770
Lord North, 1770–1782
Lord Rockingham, 1782
Lord Shelburne, 1782–1783
Charles James Fox and Lord North, 1783
William Pitt, the Younger, 1783–1801
Henry Addington, 1801–1804
William Pitt, the Younger, 1804–1806
Charles James Fox, 1806–1807
Duke of Portland, 1807–1809
Spencer Perceval, 1809–1812
Lord Liverpool, 1812–1827
George Canning, 1827
Lord Goderich, 1827
Duke of Wellington, 1828-1830
Earl Grey, 1830–1834
Lord Melbourne, 1834
Sir Robert Peel, 1834–1835
Lord Melbourne, 1835–1841
Sir Robert Peel, 1841–1846
Lord John Russell, 1846–1852
Lord Derby and Benjamin Disraeli, 1852
Lord Aberdeen, 1852–1855
Lord Palmerston, 1855–1858
Lord Derby and Disraeli, 1858–1859
Lord Palmerston, 1859–1865
Lord Russell, 1865–1866
Lord Derby and Disraeli, 1866–1868
William E. Gladstone, 1868-1874

Benjamin Disraeli, 1874–1880
Gladstone, 1880–1885
Lord Salisbury, 1885–1886
Gladstone, 1886
Lord Salisbury, 1886–1892
Gladstone, 1892–1894
Lord Rosebery, 1894–1895
Lord Salisbury, 1895–1902
Sir Arthur Balfour (later Lord Balfour), 1902–1905
Sir Henry Campbell-Bannerman, 1905–1908
Herbert H. Asquith (later Lord Oxford and Asquith), 1908–1916
David Lloyd George, 1916–1922
Andrew Bonar Law, 1922–1923
Stanley Baldwin, 1923–1924
J. Ramsay MacDonald, 1924
Stanley Baldwin, 1924–1929
Ramsay MacDonald, 1929–1931 (Labor); 1931–1935 (National)
Stanley Baldwin, 1935–1937
Neville Chamberlain, 1937–1940
Winston Churchill, 1940–

SUGGESTIONS FOR FURTHER READING

BIBLIOGRAPHIES

The Sources and Literature of English History (second ed., London, 1915) by Charles Gross provides a thorough, critical bibliography of works on the period before 1485 published before 1915. Similar bibliographies for the Tudor and Stuart periods have been edited respectively by Conyers Read (Oxford, 1933) and Godfrey Davies (Oxford, 1928). One of the best selective critical bibliographies of the whole period is that contained in the appendices of the twelve volumes of *The Political History of England,* edited by W. Hunt and R. L. Poole (London, 1906–11). The *Oxford History of England,* which is in the course of publication, will provide similar bibliographies brought up to date. H. L. Cannon in his *Reading References for English History* (Boston, 1910) groups the materials in chronological sections and gives references to the specific chapters or pages of the books cited. There are several bibliographies of particular aspects of English history such as H. Hall's *Select Bibliography for the Study, Sources and Literature of English Mediæval Economic History* (London, 1914) and C. Gross' *Bibliography of British Municipal History* (New York, 1897). Many of the special studies cited below contain valuable bibliographies.

CHAPTER I.—THE LAND AND ITS EARLY INHABITANTS

Two stimulating books on the relations between history and geography are E. C. Semple's *Influences of Geographic Environment on the Basis of Ratzel's System of Anthropo-Geography* (New York, 1911), Ratzel having been practically the founder of the modern study of human geography, and J. Brunhes' *Human Geography,* translated by Le Compte and edited by Bowman and Dodge (Chicago, 1920). H. B. George's *Relations of Geography and History* (Oxford, 1901) is a good, brief manual. *The Principles of Human Geography* (New York, 1921) by E. Huntington and S. W. Cushing is an elementary discussion of the principal geographic factors which influence human activities.

The best work on the physical geography of the British Isles for the purposes of the historical reader is H. J. Mackinder's *Britain and the British Seas* (New York, 1914). *An Historical Geography of England before A.D. 1800,* ed. by H. C. Darby (Cambridge, 1936) explains the salient geographical factors in relation to history, period by period. A good example of elementary geographies is *The Clarendon Geography:* part ii, *The British Isles* (Oxford, 1919), by F. D. Herbertson, revised by O. J. R. Howarth. J. R. and A. S. Green's *Short Geography of the British Isles* (London, 1879) is still useful. The last chapter of H. J. Fleure's *Human Geography in Western Europe* (second ed., London, 1919) presents suggestive views.

The following books deal with the prehistory of Europe, treating Britain only incidentally. H. F. Osborn's *Men of the Old Stone Age* (New York, 1915) and W. J. Sollas' *Ancient Hunters* (third ed., New York, 1924) are comprehensive treatments of the paleolithic stage. The former is exceptionally clear. M. C. Burkitt's *Prehistory* (Cambridge, 1921) gives the reader a real appreciation of the value of the evidence for the same period. G. G. MacCurdy's *Human Origins* (2 vols., New York, 1924) is a good manual of the whole period. C. E. Vulliamy's *Our Prehistoric Forerunners* (New York, 1925) is a briefer manual devoted mainly to the stage of stone. M. C. Burkitt's *Old Stone Age* (Cambridge, 1933) and *Our Early Ancestors* (Cambridge, 1926) provide an excellent survey of the stone age based upon a conservative interpretation of the evidence available at the times of publication. From them may be gleaned a brief account of British prehistory during the period. V. G. Childe's *Bronze Age* (Cambridge, 1930) performs a like service for the period to which it relates. His *Prehistory of Scotland* (London, 1935) also casts much light upon English prehistory, beginning with the mesolithic stage. His critical summary of various views on Celtic origins is convenient.

N. Ault's *Life in Ancient Britain* (London, 1920) is a delightful, brief survey of the whole prehistoric period. Robert Munro, who has long studied the subject, summarizes his findings in a volume in the *Home University Library* called *Prehistoric Britain* (London, about 1914). J. R. Moir, who is mainly responsible for establishing belief in eolithic man, presents his discoveries in *The Antiquity of Man in East Anglia* (Cambridge, 1927). Archaeologists who accept his fundamental conclusions suspend judgment on others, pending further discoveries. H. F. Osborn presents his views upon these questions and the Piltdown man in *Man Rises to Parnassus* (Princeton, 1927). D. A. E. Garrod's *Upper Paleolithic Age in Britain* (Oxford, 1926) presents an important record and summary of the upper paleolithic finds in Britain, J. G. D. Clark's *Mesolithic Age in Britain* (Cambridge, 1932) does the same for this later period, and R. E. M. Wheeler's *Prehistoric and Roman Wales* (Oxford, 1925) is of a similar nature. *Ancient Britain and the Invasions of Julius Caesar* (Oxford, 1907) by T. Rice Holmes is useful on the later phases of prehistory. *Archaeology in England and Wales, 1914-1931* (London, 1932) by T. D. Kendrick and C. F. C. Hawkes is an indispensable summary of the discoveries during these years and estimate of their significance. The record is kept current by an annual review of new finds by C. and J. Hawkes in the *Archaeological Journal* beginning with volume xc (1933). S. Casson gives a brief estimate of the significance of the British discoveries of the preceding twenty-five years in his *Progress of Archaeology* (London, 1934). *Celtic Britain* (London, 1904) by J. Rhys is based largely upon philological evidence. H. Peake formulates a brilliant hypothesis with regard to the arrival of the Celts in Britain in his *Bronze Age and the Celtic World*

(London, 1922), and H. Hubert gives attention to the origin of the British Celts in his *Rise of the Celts* (London, 1934). The paper by G. C. Dunning and C. Hawkes on "The Belgae of Gaul and Britain" in *Archaeological Journal,* lxxxvii, 150–353 (1931), is valuable.

On general questions of race W. Z. Ripley's *Races of Europe* (New York, 1910) should be consulted, though some parts of it are antiquated. C. S. Coon's *Races of Europe* (New York, 1939) incorporates more recent evidence. R. B. Dixon's *Racial History of Man* (New York, 1923) adopts a new classification of races, but with results which are suggestive and illuminating. An excellent brief description of the European races in the light of recent information is chapter iv of H. J. Peake's *English Villages* (London, 1922). On the racial history of Britain *British Barrows* (Oxford, 1877) by W. Greenwell and G. Rolleston is fundamental. J. Beddoe's *Races of Britain* (London, 1885) is a standard work. H. J. Fleure's *Races of England and Wales* (London, 1923) and his "Racial History of the British People" in *Geographical Review,* v. 216–231 (1918) are good brief surveys of the results of recent research.

CHAPTER II.—ROMAN BRITAIN AND THE ANGLO-SAXON CONQUEST

F. J. Haverfield is the scholar who has done most to make the history of Roman Britain known to us. His articles are widely scattered, but three, which present summaries of his views, may be cited. *Roman Britain* is chapter xiii of the second volume of the *Cambridge Medieval History* (New York, 1911), the *Romanization of Roman Britain* is printed by the Oxford Press as a separate pamphlet (second ed., 1912), and the fullest but not the latest statement is given in his *Roman Occupation of Britain* (Oxford, 1924) published posthumously. R. G. Collingwood's *Roman Britain* (London, 1934) is a revision of his earlier work of the same title which incorporates the results of the discoveries made in the intervening period. Since the author is one of the foremost English scholars engaged in research on the Roman period, this brief survey constitutes a reliable and convenient guide. He provides a fuller and more recent account of the period which adds much to what was known in Haverfield's time in *Roman Britain and the English Settlements* (Oxford, 1936) by him and J. N. L. Myres. His *Archaeology of Roman Britain* (London, 1930) describes all types of Roman remains and throws much light upon the civilization of the period. G. Macdonald's *Roman Britain, 1914–1928* (London, n. d.) explains the significance of the research accomplished during the period indicated, and Kendrick and Hawkes bring the story down to 1931 in their *Archaeology in England and Wales, 1914-1931*. This aspect of the subject is kept up to date by the annual survey of archaeological finds published by R. G. Collingwood and M. V. Taylor in the *Journal of Roman Studies*. C. Oman's account of the period in chapters iii to x of his *England before the Norman Conquest* (London, 1910) is still useful, but it has to be corrected in places by the light of recent research. Chapter ii in book i of P. Vinogradoff's *The Growth of the Manor* (London, 1905) deals primarily with legal and economic aspects of the rural organization, but it provides a convenient recent summary of the point of view of the historians who tend to minimize the extent of the Roman influence during the period of the occupation.

Accounts of the Anglo-Saxon conquest are contained in volume i of R. H. Hodgkin's *History of the Anglo-Saxons* (Oxford, 1935), and in *Roman Britain and the English Settlements* by Collingwood and Myres. They correlate the most recent archaeological discoveries with the other evidence, and carry further the work begun by H. M. Chadwick in his *Origin of the English Nation* (Cambridge, 1907). These researches modify fundamentally some of the views expressed by earlier writers with regard to the course of the conquest and the nature of the institutions of the early Anglo-Saxons, but the new hypotheses do not appear in every instance to be as sound as the old ones. The view that the Anglo-Saxon conquest was one of extermination is upheld by the following: E. A. Freeman, *Four Oxford Lectures* (London, 1888), pp. 61–112; J. R. Green, *The Making of England* (New York, 1882), chapter iv; P. Vinogradoff, *The Growth of the Manor,* book ii, chapter i. The contrary view is expounded by F. Seebohm, whose hypotheses are conveniently summarized in the last chapter of his *English Village Community* (second ed., London, 1883), and by W. J. Ashley in his introductory chapter to *The Origin of Property in Land* (London, 1904) by Fustel de Coulanges. C. Oman estimates critically the early accounts of the conquest and describes Anglo-Saxon institutions as they are portrayed in the laws and other documents of the seventh and eighth centuries in chapters xi, xii, xiii, xvii, and xviii of his *England before the Norman Conquest.* F. G. M. Beck in his section on the "Teutonic Conquest of Britain" in the first volume of the *Cambridge Medieval History* provides a brief treatment which takes into account the researches of Chadwick and the archaeological finds which had been made at the time. Much of the archaeological evidence is discussed synthetically by E. T. Leeds in his *Archaeology of the Anglo-Saxon Settlements* (Oxford, 1913), and publication by the same author of a new synthesis which incorporates the results of subsequent research is announced (1936) under the title *Anglo-Saxon Art and Archaeology.* G. B. Brown is interested primarily in the artistic side of Anglo-Saxon archaeological remains, but his *Arts in Early England,* which is still in course of publication, contains much of historical value. The Germanic character as it appears in the early literature is well portrayed in the first chapter of E. Dale's *National Life and Character in the Mirror of Early English Literature* (Cambridge, 1907). The institutions of the early Germans are described by F. B. Gummere in his *Germanic Origins* (New York, 1892) which has been edited with notes on the later literature by F. P. Magoun, Jr., under the title *Founders of England* (New York, 1930). It is scholarly and interesting.

CHAPTER III.—THE DEVELOPMENT OF ANGLO-SAXON ENGLAND

Hodgkin's narrative, which becomes even more interesting for this period, carries the story to the close of the reign of Alfred. Oman's work continues to be useful. J. R. Green's two books, *The Making of England* and *The Conquest of England* (New York, 1882–84), set forth a brilliant narrative of the whole period. The author sometimes states hypotheses as facts, and since he wrote much new information has been brought to light. F. M. Stenton's *Anglo-Saxon England* (Oxford, 1943) presents the mature conclusions of a scholar who is thoroughly familiar with the sources and literature of the period. The first three volumes of E. A. Freeman's *History of the Norman Conquest* (second ed., Oxford, 1870) constitute a classic narrative of the later part of the period, though it requires correction on some points. A convenient manual on the history of Christianity in the Anglo-Saxon period is W. Hunt's *The English Church from Its Foundation to the Norman Conquest* (London, 1907).

The brief description of the expansion of the Northmen and of the culture which they carried abroad given by C. H. Haskins in his *Normans in European History* (Boston, 1915) catches the spirit of the movement. The same work tells the story of Normandy and the Normans. A. Mawer's *The Vikings* (Cambridge, 1913) is a good summary of the viking movement, and T. D. Kendrick provides a more extensive account in *A History of the Vikings* (New York, 1930). *Social Scandinavia in the Viking Age* (New York, 1920) by M. W. Williams is the most extensive description in English of the Scandinavian civilization at the time of the expansion.

Good biographies of Alfred are C. Plummer's *Life and Times of Alfred the Great* (Oxford, 1902) and B. A. Lees' *Alfred the Great* (New York, 1915). L. M. Larson's *Canute the Great* (New York, 1912) puts the career of Canute in its proper Scandinavian setting, and provides a trustworthy and readable account of his reign. A brief, instructive life of Dunstan is given by W. Stubbs in the introduction to *Memorials of Saint Dunstan,* which may be found conveniently in his *Historical Introductions to the Rolls Series* (London, 1902). J. Armitage Robinson tells the story of the religious movement of the tenth century and corrects earlier views in many particulars in his *Times of St. Dunstan* (Oxford, 1923).

CHAPTER IV.—ANGLO-SAXON INSTITUTIONS

The best brief manuals for an introduction to the constitutional history of this and later periods are A. B. White's *Making of the English Constitution* (second ed., New York, 1925), W. A. Morris's *Constitutional History of England to 1216* (New York, 1930), and G. B. Adams' *Constitutional History of England* (revised ed., by R. L. Schuyler New York, 1934). W. Stubbs gives a comprehensive survey in his *Constitutional History of England* (volume i, sixth ed., Oxford, 1897). Facts are rarely misstated, but many of the inferences drawn from the obscure evidence have been superseded by the intensive researches of later scholars. The changed views are made apparent by comparison with Morris. F. W. Maitland's *Domesday Book and Beyond* (Cambridge, 1897) contains brilliant essays. P. Vinogradoff's *Growth of the Manor* (London, 1905) and *English Society in the Eleventh Century* (Oxford, 1908) are weighty pronouncements, but they are rather difficult of assimilation except by the more advanced student. These authors hold the point of view that the Anglo-Saxons began life in England with the freeman as the basic social unit. The contrary thesis is advanced by F. Seebohm in his *English Village Community* (London, 1883), whose descriptions of agrarian organization are valuable. His hypotheses, however, should be compared with those of the authors previously mentioned. H. M. Chadwick's *Studies on Anglo-Saxon Institutions* (Cambridge, 1905) is a work of fundamental importance, written primarily for the advanced student. Of the Anglo-Saxon laws Pollock and Maitland provide a useful summary in chapter ii of the first volume of their *History of English Law* (second ed., Cambridge, 1898). H. C. Lea's *Superstition and Force* (second ed., Philadelphia, 1870) is a stimulating work on German legal procedure. Articles of exceptional value on special topics are those by W. A. Morris on "The Office of Sheriff in the Anglo-Saxon Period," *English Historical Review,* xxxi, 20–40 (1916), and F. Liebermann, *The National Assembly in the Anglo-Saxon Period* (Halle, 1913).

The economic development of the Anglo-Saxons is surveyed in book i of W. Cunningham's *Growth of English Industry and Commerce during the Early and Middle Ages* (fifth ed., Cambridge 1915). The last three sections of chapter ii in volume i of H. D. Traill's *Social England* (second ed., New York, 1894) deal with trade, industry, and material civilization. C. M. Andrews describes rural life in his *Old English Manor* (Baltimore, 1892). C. Stephenson's *Borough and Town* (Cambridge, 1932) is a brilliant study of Anglo-Saxon boroughs. J. Tait suggests some modifications of his conclusions in a review in *English Historical Review,* xlviii, 642-48 (1933). Tait has written much else of value on the boroughs, mainly in scattered studies. A list of them will be found in *Historical Essays in Honour of James Tait* (Manchester, 1933). Many of his studies are now collected in his *Medieval English Borough* (Manchester, 1936).

Hunt's work mentioned previously remains the standard manual on the ecclesiastical history of the period. The story of the conversion is told by W. Bright in *Chapters of Early English Church History* (Oxford, 1878). J. L. G. Meissner's *Celtic Church in England after the Synod of Whitby* (London, 1929) and T. Allison's *English Religious Life in the Eighth Century* (London, 1929) are useful and interesting.

An excellent comprehensive survey of the intellectual development of the Anglo-Saxons may be obtained from M. R. James' chapters in volume iii of the *Cambridge Medieval History* (New York, 1922) which deal with

Europe in general, and M. L. W. Laistner has a good chapter on the topic in his *Thought and Letters in Western Europe A.D. 500 to 900* (New York, 1931). Chapters ii and iii of E. Dale's *National Life and Character in the Mirror of Early English Literature* relate largely to this subject. The education provided by the European schools of the period is described summarily by D. C. Munro in his *Middle Ages* (New York, 1921, pp. 82-85). The body of information received by the European scholars of this period from the classical past is the subject of H. O. Taylor's delightful essay on *The Classical Heritage of the Middle Ages* (New York, 1901). A. F. Leach in his *Schools of Medieval England* (London, 1915, chapters i-vi) gives a history of Anglo-Saxon schools. The best account of Bede and his works is given by C. Plummer in the introduction to his edition of Bede's *Ecclesiastical History* (Oxford 1896). A. F. West's *Alcuin and the Rise of the Christian Schools* (New York, 1892) is interesting and in-structive. J. J. Jusserand gives a charming survey of Anglo-Saxon literature in the first volume of his *Literary History of the English People* (New York, 1906), and *The Cambridge History of English Literature* provides a more extensive account (volume i, New York, 1907). C. G. Osgood's *Voice of England* (New York, 1935) is a stimulating survey of the history of English literature, but it is not very full on the medieval period.

CHAPTER V.—NORMAN ENGLAND

G. B. Adams in his *History of England from the Norman Conquest to the Death of John* (London, 1905) and H. W. C. Davis in his *England under the Normans and Angevins* (New York, 1905) give good general accounts of the Norman period. Both are scholars who have made special studies of the period. The last two volumes of Freeman's *History of the Norman Conquest* give the most comprehensive survey of the period. Free-man belittles the extent of the Norman influence upon English institutions, and some of his views have been superseded; but he holds the interest of the reader, and his work is still of fundamental importance. Freeman's *William the Conqueror* (London, 1903) summarizes much of his larger work, while F. M. Stenton's *William the Conqueror* (New York, 1908) is a careful independent study presented in popular form.

On constitutional history the first four books mentioned in the preceding section continue to serve the same purposes for this period. C. Petit-Dutail-lis's *The Feudal Monarchy in France and England from the Tenth to the Thirteenth Century* (London, 1936) is a suggestive survey by a scholar thoroughly familiar with the subject. The constitutional changes resulting from the Norman conquest receive a stimulating discussion from G. B. Adams in the first two chapters of *The Origin of the English Constitution* (New Haven, 1912). His *Councils and Courts in Anglo-Norman England* (New Haven, 1926) is an important piece of research. The first volume of Pollock and Maitland's *History of English Law* (second ed., Cambridge, 1898) contains a survey of the institutions of Normandy before the conquest (chapter iii) and of the institutions of England under Norman rule (chapter iv) and a full discussion of the legal aspects of English feudalism (book ii). The studies of C. H. Haskins on Norman institutions are essential for an understanding of English institutions in the Norman period. Some of his conclusions are summarized in his *Normans in European History,* and the results of his extensive researches are presented fully in *Norman Institutions* (Cambridge, 1918). J. H. Round in his *Feudal England* (London, 1895) establishes the fact that feudalism was introduced into England in the time of William the Conqueror and treats many other problems of the Norman period in a keenly critical spirit.

Good, brief, general views of feudalism are given by G. B. Adams in chapter ix of his *Civilization during the Middle Ages* (revised ed., New York, 1914) and by E. Emerton in chapter xiv of his *Mediaeval Europe* (Boston, 1903). The only rounded survey of English feudalism during the reigns of the Norman kings is given by F. M. Stenton in *The First Century of English Feudalism, 1066-1166* (Oxford, 1932). It presents with clarity the conclusions of a thorough scholar.

The general development of the church is presented in convenient form by W. R. W. Stephens in his *English Church from the Norman Conquest to the Accession of Edward I* (London, 1901). On the relations between church and state H. Böhmer's *Kirche und Staat in England und in der Normandie im XI und XII Jahrhundert* (Leipzig, 1899) is of cardinal importance, but some of his conclusions have been corrected by Z. N. Brooke in his *English Church and the Papacy from the Conquest to the Reign of John* (Cambridge, 1933), which is by far the best account of the development of papal authority in England during the period.

C. W. David's *Robert Curthose* (Cambridge, 1920) is important for the relations between England and Normandy. J. H. Round in his *Geoffrey de Mandeville* (London, 1892) presents a series of critical studies which constitute a more or less connected narrative of most of Stephen's reign. Freeman's *The Reign of William Rufus* (2 vol., Oxford, 1882) has the same merits and defects as his *Norman Conquest.* A. J. Macdonald's *Lanfranc* (Oxford, 1926) and R. W. Church's *Saint Anselm* (London, 1888) are good biographies.

CHAPTER VI.—HENRY II AND THE ENGLISH CONSTITUTION

Brilliant, brief surveys of Henry's constitutional reforms are given by Stubbs in his introduction to the second volume of Benedict of Peterborough's Chronicle, which is reprinted in *Historical Introductions to the Rolls Series;* by Pollock and Maitland in book i, chapter vi, of *The History of English Law* (second ed.); and by Haskins in chapter iv of *The Normans in European History.* More extensive treatments are provided by Stubbs and Morris in their constitutional histories. Morris incorporates the results of recent research. Pollock and Maitland deal with the legal and judicial reforms authoritatively in other parts of their work, and

Haskins says the last word on the Norman side of the story in his *Norman institutions*. Mrs. J. R. Green's *Henry II* (London, 1888) is a fascinating story of the reign, and L. F. Salzman's *Henry II* (Boston, 1914) is a good account. R. L. Poole's *Exchequer in the Twelfth Century* (Oxford, 1912) is a thorough, scholarly exposition of the subject. The works by Adams and by Davis previously mentioned and K. Norgate's *England under the Angevins* (2 vols., London, 1887) give good general accounts of the reign. The volume by Stephens on the history of the church continues to be useful. Brooke brings out the effect of the controversy with Becket upon the relations with the papacy. Good lives of Becket are those by Morris (second ed., London, 1885) and W. H. Hutton (second ed., Cambridge, 1926).

CHAPTER VII.—THE ANGEVIN EMPIRE

The works by Adams, Davis, and Norgate, mentioned at the close of the last chapter, deal with the subject of the present chapter. The closing years of the Angevin empire are treated briefly by Haskins in chapter v of *The Normans in European History,* and in greater detail by Norgate in *Richard the Lion Heart* (London, 1924) and *John Lackland* (London, 1902). The most thorough study of this aspect of the subject is F. M. Powicke's *Loss of Normandy, 1189-1204* (Manchester, 1913). The relations between the kings of France and the kings of England in this period are surveyed from the French point of view in the third volume of *Histoire de France* (Paris, 1901) edited by E. Lavisse, and treated in great detail from the same point of view by A. Cartellieri in his *Philipp II August* (4 vols., Leipzig, 1899-1921). A good manual to which to turn for a brief view of continental developments in this and other periods of the Middle Ages is C. Stephenson's *Mediaeval History* (New York, 1935). S. Painter's *William Marshal* (Baltimore, 1933) is an interesting biography of a knight who took a leading part in the affairs of the period.

The best guide to the early history of Wales is J. E. Lloyd's *History of Wales* (2 vols., second ed., London, 1912). The single volume by J. Rhys and D. Brynmor-Jones on the *Welsh People* (New York, 1900) is also good. Volume i of P. Hume Brown's *History of Scotland* (Cambridge, 1902) is a trustworthy guide on that subject. A brief account of Ireland's early history is P. W. Joyce's *Short History of Ireland* (London, 1911). R. Dunlop's *Ireland from the Earliest Times to the Present Day* (Oxford, 1922) is excellent but exceedingly brief. G. H. Orpen's *Ireland under the Normans* (4 vols., Oxford, 1911-20) is a scholarly work on the period from 1169 to 1333. On early Irish culture H. Zimmer's *The Irish Element in Medieval Culture* (New York, 1891) is the work of an enthusiastic scholar. The few pages devoted to the subject by M. R. James in chapters xix and xx of the third volume of *The Cambridge Medieval History* (Cambridge, 1922) are suggestive.

On the crusades D. C. Munro has two illuminating chapters in his *Mid-*

dle Ages (New York, 1921), and his *Kingdom of the Crusaders* (New York, 1935) presents in brief and simple form the results of a lifetime of research. Other good single volumes in English are by T. A. Archer and C. L. Kingsford on *The Crusades* (New York, 1895) and by W. B. Stevenson on *The Crusaders in the East* (Cambridge, 1907). B. Kugler's *Geschichte der Kreuzzüge* (second ed., Berlin, 1891) is a standard work. R. Röhricht's *Geschichte des Königreichs Jerusalem* (Innsbruck, 1898) is the best authority on that aspect of the subject. The story of Richard's crusade is told by Stubbs in the preface to *Itinerarium Regis Ricardi*, which may be found in *Historical Introduction to the Rolls Series,* and by S. Lane-Poole in *Saladin and the Fall of the Kingdom of Jerusalem* (New York, 1903).

Chapter VIII.—The King and the Barons

The works of Adams, Davis, and Norgate continue to be of value. A. Luchaire's *Innocent III, les Royautés vassales du Saint-Siège* (Paris, 1908) contains an excellent brief account of the relations between John and the pope. F. M. Powicke's *Stephen Langton* (Oxford, 1928) is a study of the career of a leader of thought and action during the reign of John and the early years of Henry III. Its author possesses the happy faculty of presenting the results of research in a form which is interesting to the general reader. W. S. McKechnie's *Magna Carta* (second ed., Glasgow, 1914) is the standard commentary on the Great Charter. The view that it is a feudal document is set forth by G. B. Adams in chapter v of his *Origin of the English Constitution* (New Haven, 1912). Its subsequent history is traced by F. Thompson in *The First Century of Magna Carta* (Minneapolis, 1925).

General surveys of the reign of Henry III are given by Davis in the work previously mentioned and by T. F. Tout in his scholarly *History of England from the Accession of Henry III to the Death of Edward III* (London, 1905). More detailed works on the period of the minority are K. Norgate's *The Minority of Henry the Third* (London, 1912) and G. J. Turner's "The Minority of Henry III" in *Transactions of the Royal Historical Society,* new series, xviii, 245-295; third series, i, 205-262 (London, 1904, 1907). R. F. Treharne presents a thorough and scholarly study in his *Baronial Plan of Reform, 1258-1263* (Manchester, 1932). A. Gasquet's *Henry the Third and the Church* (London, 1905) is a delightful essay. The material is taken from the sources, but they are sometimes handled uncritically. A. L. Smith's *Church and State in the Middle Ages* (Oxford, 1913) treats the relations between England and the papacy during the middle years of Henry's reign. It is based upon a critical study of Matthew Paris, and it is a suggestive and stimulating book. The best biography of Simon de Montfort is by C. Bémont (revised ed., translated by E. F. Jacob, Oxford, 1930).

CHAPTER IX.—INTELLECTUAL AND RELIGIOUS DEVELOPMENT

The best general work on the development of thought in the Middle Ages is H. O. Taylor's *Mediæval Mind* (third ed., 2 vols., New York, 1919). R. L. Poole gives an insight into the thought and an estimate of the influence of the leading scholars of the epoch in his *Illustrations of the History of Medieval Thought and Learning* (second ed., London, 1920). C. H. Haskins' *Renaissance of the Twelfth Century* (Cambridge, 1927) is a series of brilliant studies. Good brief chapters on the subject may be found in L. Thorndike's *History of Medieval Europe* (chapter xx), and E. Emerton's *Mediæval Europe* (chapter xiii). An excellent guide to the principal authors and their works is J. E. Sandy's *History of Classical Scholarship* (vol. i, Cambridge, 1903). C. H. Haskins' *Studies in the History of Mediæval Science* (Cambridge, 1924) is stimulating and profound. L. Thorndike's *A History of Magic and Experimental Science during the First Thirteen Centuries of Our Era* (4 vols., New York, 1923-34) is a mine of information on the aspect of the subject which it treats. A good elementary *History of Philosophy* is F. Thilly's (New York, 1914), and more extensive general treatments are M. de Wulf's *History of Mediæval Philosophy* (translated by E. C. Messenger, 2 vols., London, 1926) and F. Ueberweg's *Grundriss der Geschichte der Philosophie* (edited by B. Geyer, vol. ii, Berlin, 1928). An earlier edition of the latter has been translated.

The standard history of the universities is H. Rashdall's *Universities of Europe in the Middle Ages,* edited by F. M. Powicke and A. B. Emden (3 vols., Oxford, 1936). D. C. Munro gives a good brief chapter (xxxi) to the subject in his *Middle Ages.* R. S. Rait's *Life in the Medieval University* (Cambridge, 1912) is based largely on Rashdall's work. Articles by Haskins in the *American Historical Review* (volumes iii, x) provide instructive and amusing sidelights on student life, and his *Rise of the Universities* (New York, 1923) is a delightfully humorous summary of profound studies. A. Mansbridge gives a suggestive sketch of the early history of English universities in his *Older Universities of England: Oxford and Cambridge* (Boston, 1923). C. E. Mallet's *History of the University of Oxford* (New York, 1924); H. C. Maxwell Lyte's *History of the University of Oxford* (London, 1886); and J. B. Mullinger's *University of Cambridge from the Earliest Times* (Cambridge, 1873) are standard histories of the English universities.

The development of learning in England receives attention in all the general works cited. R. L. Poole's papers on *Learning and Science* in the third and fourth chapters of the first volume of Traill's *Social England* (New York, 1894) provide an able summary of the English development, and R. Graham's "Intellectual Influence of English Monasticism between the Tenth and the Twelfth Centuries" in *Transactions of the Royal Historical Society* (new series, xvii, 23-65) throws much light on the subject. The sixth and seventh chapters of W. Stubbs' *Seventeen Lectures on the*

Study of Medieval and Modern History (Oxford, 1886) treat learning and literature in the time of Henry II. Miss Norgate in *England under the Angevin Kings* (ii, 438-468) deals with the same subject. Of the leading English scholars of the period there are many good biographies. The best estimate of the work of Roger Bacon is given in *Roger Bacon Essays,* edited by A. G. Little (Oxford, 1914). Of the numerous general works on the vernacular literature of the period three of the most interesting and instructive are W. H. Schofield's *English Literature from the Norman Conquest to Chaucer* (New York, 1906); *The Cambridge History of English Literature,* volume i (New York, 1907); and J. J. Jusserand's *Literary History of the English People,* volume i. The first two have bibliographies.

A brief historical sketch of English architecture may be found in K. Baedeker's *Great Britain* (pp. xxxv-lxiii of the sixth ed., Leipzig, 1906). More extensive works are C. H. Moore's *Mediæval Church Architecture of England* (New York, 1912), T. G. Jackson's *Gothic Architecture in France, England, and Italy* (Cambridge, 1915), F. Bond's *An Introduction to English Church Architecture* (2 vols., London, 1913), A. W. Clapham's *English Romanesque Architecture before the Conquest* and *After the Conquest* (Oxford, 1930, 1934).

David Knowles' *The Monastic Order in England* (Cambridge, 1940) provides a comprehensive history of the subject to 1216. Abbot Gasquet's *English Monastic Life* (fourth ed., London, 1910) deals sympathetically and understandingly with the life of the monastery but gives no history of the movement. A. H. Thompson's *English Monasteries* (Cambridge, 1913) is concerned primarily with the same subject, but has a brief historic sketch. D. H. S. Cranage in his *Home of the Monk* (3rd ed., Cambridge, 1934) describes the monastic buildings and gives sidelights on the nature of the life in them. E. Margaret Thompson's *The Carthusian Order in England* is an excellent history of one order of monks, but E. L. Taunton's *The English Black Monks of St. Benedict* (2 vols., London, 1898) is a series of sketches rather than a systematic history as far as it relates to the medieval period. E. Power's *Medieval English Nunneries* (Cambridge, 1922) is a thorough study. R. H. Snape's *English Monastic Finances in the Later Middle Ages* (Cambridge, 1926) breaks new ground, but does not penetrate far below the surface. Briefer but stimulating studies, taking somewhat different points of view, may be found in chapters iii, ix and xv of M. Bateson's *Mediæval England* (New York, 1904) and in chapter iii of A. Jessopp's *Coming of the Friars* (London, 1905).

The last work also has a delightful essay on the friars, which may be supplemented by chapter vi, of equal charm, in the first volume of H. C. Lea's *History of the Inquisition of the Middle Ages* (New York, 1888). A. G. Little's *Studies in English Franciscan History* (Manchester, 1917) is a series of interesting essays based largely on unpublished documents, and E. Hutton's *Franciscans in England* (London, 1926) is a popular work.

B. E. R. Formoy's *The Dominican Order in England before the Reformation* (London, 1925) and B. Jarrett's *The English Dominicans* (London, 1921) provide information concerning that order.

CHAPTER X.—LIFE IN COUNTRY AND TOWN

Good general surveys of the subject are provided by E. Lipson's *Economic History of England,* volume i, *The Middle Ages* (7th ed., London, 1937); E. P. Cheyney's *Introduction to the Industrial and Social History of England* (chapters ii-iv, second ed., New York, 1921); W. J. Ashley's *Introduction to English Economic History and Theory* (volume i, London, 1888); W. Cunningham's *Growth of English Industry and Commerce during the Early and Middle Ages* (fifth ed., Cambridge, 1915); and A. P. Usher's *Introduction to the Industrial History of England* (chapters iv-vii, Boston, 1920).

On the manor N. J. Hone's *The Manor and Manorial Records* (London, 1906) is a good general survey. N. Neilson, whose knowledge of the subject is profound, portrays the life of the peasants in *Mediæval Agrarian Economy* (New York, 1936), and H. S. Bennett provides a more extensive treatment in his *Life on the English Manor: A Study of Peasant Conditions, 1150-1400* (Cambridge, 1938). G. G. Coulton brings together much valuable evidence about the life of the villagers in his *Medieval Village* (Cambridge, 1926). Chapter ii of A. Jessopp's *The Coming of the Friars* is a graphic pen picture of the life of the villagers. Good studies on the history and organization of single manors are N. Neilson's *Economic Conditions on the Manors of Ramsey Abbey* (Bryn Mawr Dissertation, 1898); F. G. Davenport's *The Economic Development of a Norfolk Manor* (Cambridge, 1906); N. S. B. and E. C. Gras, *The Economic and Social History of an English Village (Crawley Hampshire) A.D. 909-1928* (Cambridge, 1930). P. Vinogradoff in *Villainage in England* (Oxford, 1892) and in book iii of *The Growth of the Manor* (London, 1905) gives special attention to the legal side of the story. N. S. B. Gras in *The Evolution of the English Corn Market* (Cambridge, 1915) presents new views on the development of manorial as well as of urban economy. On baronial life see S. Painter's *Studies in the History of the English Feudal Barony* (Baltimore, 1943) and N. Denholm-Young's *Seignorial Administration in England* (Oxford, 1937).

There is no good comprehensive work on the English towns of this period, although there are some good studies of special aspects of the subject and a few good histories of individual boroughs. Stephenson brings the story of origins down to the beginning of the thirteenth century, and Tait's studies on the boroughs of this period are important. Other studies of various aspects are F. W. Maitland's *Township and Borough* (Cambridge, 1898); A. Ballard's *Domesday Boroughs* (Oxford, 1904) and *The English Borough in the Twelfth Century* (Cambridge, 1914); M. Bateson's "Laws of Breteuil" in *English Historical Review,* volumes xv, xvi, dealing with baronial boroughs; and her introduction to volume ii of *Borough Customs* (Selden Society, London, 1906), dealing with the local customs of the towns. On the government of medieval towns C. W. Colby's "Growth of Oligarchy in English Towns" in *English Historical Review* (v, 633-653) is important. J. Tait's *Mediæval Manchester and the Beginnings of Lancashire* (Manchester, 1904); M. Bateson's introduction to volume i of *Records of the Borough of Leicester* (Cambridge, 1899); and M. D. Harris's *Life in an Old English Town: a History of Coventry* (London, 1898) are good studies of individual boroughs.

The Gild Merchant (volume i, Oxford, 1890) by C. Gross is an exhaustive and authoritative study of that subject, but there is no work of similar scope on the craft gilds. S. Kramer's *English Craft Gilds and the Government* (New York, 1905) deals mainly with a later period. J. M. Lambert's *Two Thousand Years of Gild Life* (Hull, 1891), F. A. Hibbert's *Influence and Development of English Gilds, as Illustrated by the History of the Craft Gilds of Shrewsbury* (Cambridge, 1891) and G. Unwin's *Gilds and Companies of London* (London, 1908) are among the best of the studies of the craft gilds of particular boroughs for the purposes of the general reader.

The development and organization of English commerce and industry in this period also have to be followed mainly in special studies or in sections of works devoted to other subjects, such as those dealing with the Hanseatic League or with Italian commerce. L. F. Salzman's *English Industries of the Middle Ages* (new ed., London, 1923) is of value for the industrial side of the subject, and chapter iii of the introduction to *The Early English Customs System* (Cambridge, 1918) by N. S. B. Gras contains many stimulating suggestions on various aspects of the subject. On the fairs and the courts of pie powder the introduction of C. Gross to *Select Cases concerning the Law Merchant* (Selden Society, London, 1908) is a brief but suggestive study, while the law merchant is treated by W. Mitchell in his *Early History of the Law Merchant* (Cambridge, 1904), and by F. R. Sanborn in *Origins of the Early English Maritime and Commercial Law* (New York, 1930). The best account of the origin of the staple is given by T. F. Tout in his *Place of the Reign of Edward II* (Manchester, 1914). Further information on the staple in this period may be found in A. L. Jenckes' *Origin, Organization, and the Location of the Staples of England* (Philadelphia, 1908) and G. F. Ward's "Early History of the Merchants Staplers" in *English Historical Review* (xxxiii, 297-319). On foreign financiers and traders in England the following give a small selection: W. Cunningham, *Alien Immigrants to England* (London, 1897); R. J. Whitwell, "Italian Bankers and the English Crown," *Transactions of the Royal Historical Society* (new series, xvii, 175-233); C. Walford, "Outline History of the Hanseatic League, more particularly in its Bearings upon English Commerce," *ibid.* (ix, 82-136); W. E. Rhodes, "Italian Bankers in England and their Loans to Edward I and Edward II" in *Historical*

Essays by Members of the Owens College, Manchester (London, 1902); A. Schaube, *Handelsgeschichte der romanischen Völker des Mittelmeergebiets bis zum Ende der Kreuzzüge* (England, pp. 392-417; Munich, 1906); A. Schaube, "Die Wollausfuhr Englands vom Jahre 1273," in *Vierteljahrschrift für Social- und Wirtschaftsgeschichte* (vi, 39-72, 159-185); A. M. Hyamson, *A History of the Jews in England* (London, 1908).

Chapter vi of L. H. Haney's *History of Economic Thought* (New York, 1911) gives a brief exposition of the economic theories of the Middle Ages, and G. O'Brien's *Essay on Mediæval Economic Teaching* (London, 1920) provides a more extensive discussion.

CHAPTER XI.—THE CONSTITUTION UNDER EDWARD I

The best brief account of the reign is given by T. F. Tout in his *History of England from the Accession of Henry III to the Death of Edward III* (New York, 1905). The best biographies are Tout's *Edward the First* (London, 1893) and E. Jenks' *Edward Plantagenet* (New York, 1902).

The constitutional developments of the period are surveyed summarily by G. B. Adams in the fifth and sixth chapters of *Constitutional History of England* (New York, 1921). The same author dwells at greater length on certain aspects of them in the last two chapters of his *Origin of the English Constitution*. T. F. Tout's *Chapters in the Administrative History of Mediæval England* (6 vols., Manchester, 1920-30) throws much light on the central administrative machine, which previous historians had neglected. The standard authority on the council is J. F. Baldwin's *The King's Council in England during the Middle Ages* (Oxford, 1913).

Local administration and the inquests of 1274-75 receive elucidation in H. M. Cam's *Studies in the Hundred Rolls: Some Aspects of Thirteenth Century Administration,* published in volume vi of *Oxford Studies in Social and Legal History* (Oxford, 1921). W. A. Morris's *Early English County Court* (Berkeley, 1926) and his *Medieval English Sheriff* (London, 1927) are thorough and scholarly studies.

The story of parliament as told by many writers carries back into this period views of the legislative functions and of the organization of parliament which belong only to a later period. Stubbs' chapters on the subject in his *Constitutional History* have this fault, although they contain the most detailed narrative we have. F. W. Maitland, in the introduction to the volume in the series of *Chronicles and Memorials* published under direction of the Master of the Rolls cited as *Memoranda de Parliamento,* or as *Records of the Parliament holden at Westminster* (London, 1893), was the first to emphasize the essentially judicial character of parliament in Edward's time. C. H. McIlwain followed with a brilliant essay on the *High Court of Parliament* (New Haven, 1910) and A. F. Pollard develops the view still further in his *Evolution of Parliament* (2nd ed., London, 1926). A brief clear exposition of the development of representation in central assemblies is given in White's section on the subject in his *Making of the*

English Constitution. This is supplemented by his "Some early Instances of Concentration of Representatives in England," *American Historical Review,* xix (1914), 735-750. D. Pasquet's *Essay on the Origins of the House of Commons* (Cambridge, 1925) is an excellent study. M. V. Clarke's *Medieval Representation and Consent* (London, 1936) presents fresh views and materials which are most suggestive. The earlier training of the people for participation in the government is described by White in his *Self-Government at the King's Command* (Minneapolis, 1933). Important new evidence about the origin of parliament is presented by H. G. Richardson in "The Origins of Parliament," *Transactions of the Royal Historical Society,* fourth series, xi (1928), 137-183, and by H. G. Richardson and G. O. Sayles in "Early Records of the English Parliament," *Bulletin of the Institute of Historical Research,* v (1928), 129-154; vi (1929), 71-88, 129-155. For what the new research has added to the old see C. H. McIlwain in *Cambridge Medieval History,* vii (New York, 1932), 664-715, and H. M. Cam in *Bulletin of the International Committee of Historical Sciences,* ix (1937), 413-418. On parliament and taxation J. F. Willard's *Parliamentary Taxes on Personal Property, 1290 to 1334* (Cambridge, 1934) is authoritative.

Edward's relations with the clergy and the pope have not received proper attention. The salient aspects are generally mentioned in the narrative histories of the reign. The first two chapters of W. W. Capes's *The English Church in the Fourteenth and Fifteenth Centuries* (London, 1909) deal cursorily with the subject.

CHAPTER XII.—EXTERNAL AFFAIRS, 1272-1399

By far the best brief survey of the subjects treated in this chapter may be found in the appropriate sections of Tout's *History of England from the Accession of Henry III to the Death of Edward III,* which may be supplemented by the next volume in the series, C. Oman's *History of England from the Accession of Richard II to the Death of Richard III* (London, 1906), for the Hundred Years' War during Richard's reign. The chapters which relate to the subject in K. H. Vickers' *England in the Later Middle Ages* (London, 1914) provide a convenient but not a particularly well-balanced narrative. External affairs during the reign of Edward I are treated briefly in the lives of that monarch mentioned at the beginning of the last chapter.

The affairs of Wales during the reign of Henry III are best treated in the second volume of J. E. Lloyd's *History of Wales* (third ed., London, 1939). T. F. Tout's "Wales and the March during the Baron's Wars" in *Historical Essays by Members of the Owens College, Manchester* (London, 1902) is an excellent study of a limited but important period. *The Welsh People* (New York, 1900) by J. Rhys and D. Brynmor-Jones is less satisfactory, but it covers also the reign of Edward I. *The Welsh Wars of Edward I* (Oxford, 1901) by J. E. Morris is a thorough study.

On relations with Scotland the first volume of P. Hume Brown's *History of Scotland* (Cambridge, 1912) continues to be the best manual. A valuable treatment of the relations of Edward I to Scotland is given by Sir J. H. Ramsay in his *Dawn of the Constitution* (London, 1908).

The narrative of the Hundred Years' War given by W. Longman in his *History of the Life and Times of Edward the Third* (2 vols., London, 1869) relies too much upon Froissart and is in part antiquated; but H. Mackinnon's *History of Edward the Third* (London), published thirty-one years later, represents much less of an improvement than might reasonably be expected. The relations between England and France during the whole period are excellently treated from the French point of view in E. Lavisse's *Histoire de France* (volume iii, part 2 and volume iv, part 1, Paris, 1911). *Les Préliminaires de la Guerre de Cent Ans* (Paris, 1902) by E. Déprez is a thorough discussion of the causes, and H. Denifle's *La Désolation des Églises, Monastères et Hôpitaux en France, pendant la Guerre de Cent Ans* (2 vols., Paris, 1897-99) is a scholarly study which treats other aspects of the war besides those designated in the title. E. C. Lodge's *Gascony under English Rule* (London, 1926) may be consulted on relations between England and Gascony. H. Pirenne's *Histoire de Belgique* (second ed., volumes i, ii, Bruxelles, 1902, 1908) contains an excellent account of the relations between England and Flanders, and *The Low Countries and the Hundred Years' War, 1326-1347* (Ann Arbor, 1929) by H. S. Lucas is a thorough study of the Netherlandish phase of the war. Many aspects of the war after 1369 are treated in S. Armitage-Smith's *John of Gaunt* (Westminster, 1904).

CHAPTER XIII.—POLITICAL AND CONSTITUTIONAL DEVELOPMENTS OF THE FOURTEENTH CENTURY

Many of the works cited in the two preceding chapters deal also with the subject of the present chapter. T. F. Tout gives a well-rounded view of the reign of Edward II and presents a new estimate of its constitutional significance in his *Place of the Reign of Edward II in English History* (Manchester, 1914). *The Baronial Opposition to Edward II* (Cambridge, 1918) by J. C. Davies is an important detailed study based on materials in manuscript. There are as yet no thorough studies of the reign of Edward III. A. Steel's *Richard II* (Cambridge, 1941) is a critical study. J. H. Ramsay's *Genesis of Lancaster* (2 vols., Oxford, 1913) is a useful chronological guide.

The following works on constitutional development should be noted in addition to those cited above. H. L. Gray's *The Influence of the Commons on Early Legislation* (Cambridge, 1932) is an essential work on parliamentary development in the fourteenth and fifteenth centuries. Some other aspects are treated by H. C. Richardson and G. O. Sayles in "Parliaments of Edward III," *Bulletin of the Institute of Historical Research,* viii (1931), 65-82; ix (1932), 1-18. L. O. Pike's *Constitutional History of the House of Lords* (London, 1894) has to be checked by the later researches on council and parliament. On administrative development Tout's *Chapters* remains the standard comprehensive work. *The English Government at Work, 1327-1336,* vol. i, *Central and Prerogative Administration,* edited by J. F. Willard and W. A. Morris (Cambridge, 1940), is an intensive study. See also B. Wilkinson's *The Chancery under Edward III* and *Studies in the Constitutional History of the Thirteenth and Fourteenth Centuries* (Manchester, 1929, 1937). The courts and other aspects of constitutional development are treated in W. S. Holdsworth's *History of English Law,* volume i (London, 1903) and sketched in A. T. Carter's *History of English Legal Institutions* (fourth ed., London, 1910). The best study of the justices of the peace is B. H. Putnam's introduction to *Proceedings before the Justices of the Peace in the Fourteenth and Fifteenth Centuries* (London, 1938). See also her *Enforcement of the Statutes of Labourers* (Columbia University, 1908).

CHAPTER XIV.—SOCIAL, ECONOMIC, AND RELIGIOUS DEVELOPMENTS OF THE FOURTEENTH CENTURY

Many of the works cited under chapters ix and x deal with the fourteenth century as well as the thirteenth. General works on the more purely social aspects of the subject are A. Abram's *English Life and Manners in the Later Middle Ages* (London, 1913), which is a suggestive but not a thorough treatment; D. Chadwick's *Social Life in the Days of Piers Plowman* (Cambridge, 1922), which presents the evidence concerning social life to be found in the poem; J. J. Jusserand's *Piers Plowman* (New York, 1894) and his delightful *English Wayfaring Life in the Middle Ages* (London, 1889); E. Dale's *National Life and Character in the Mirror of Early English Literature,* chapter v (Cambridge, 1907); and G. G. Coulton's *Chaucer and his England* (New York, 1908).

The black death and the detailed effects are treated excellently by C. Creighton in volume i of his *History of Epidemics in Britain* (Cambridge, 1891) and by F. A. Gasquet in his *Black Death of 1348 and 1349* (second ed., London, 1908); but their estimate of the mortality should be viewed in the light of the conclusions of A. P. Usher in his *Introduction to the Industrial History of England* (Boston, 1920), pp. 92-97, and of A. E. Levett and A. Ballard in their "Black Death" in *Oxford Studies in Social and Legal History,* volume v (Oxford, 1916). A. Jessopp devotes two of the interesting essays in his *Coming of the Friars and Other Essays* (London, 1905) to the plague in East Anglia.

The changes in the rural life of the fourteenth century were set in a new light by the studies of T. W. Page presented in *The End of Villainage in England* (American Economic Association, New York, 1900). These have been supplemented and in some part corrected by E. P. Cheyney in *Eng. Hist. Rev.,* xv, 20-37 (1900); H. L. Gray in the same, xxix, 625-651 (1914); K. G. Feiling in the same, xxvi, 333-338 (1911); N. S. B. Gras in chapter i of his *Evolution of the English Corn Market* (Cambridge, 1915); and by Levett and Ballard in their work cited above. A critical summary of the conclusions of recent writers on the subject is given by E. Power in "The Effects of the Black Death on Rural Organization in England," *History*, new series, iii (1919), 109-116. B. H. Putnam's *Enforcement of the Statutes of Labourers* (Columbia University, 1908) is a thorough treatment of the topic. Two books which deal primarily with a later period, but contain some additional information on this subject, are W. Denton's *England in the Fifteenth Century* (London, 1888) and G. Schanz's *Englishe Handelspolitik gegen Ende des Mittelalters* (Leipzig, 1881).

Excellent accounts of the Peasants' Revolt are given in G. M. Trevelyan's *England in the Age of Wycliffe,* chapter vi (new ed., London, 1909); C. Oman's *History of England (1377-1485)*, chapter ii (London, 1906) and *The Great Revolt of 1381* (Oxford, 1906); and in the more extensive study of A. Réville, *Le Soulèvement des Travailleurs d'Angleterre en 1381,* edited by C. Petit-Dutaillis (Paris, 1898). E. Powell's *The Rising in East Anglia in 1381* (Cambridge, 1896) gives the detailed story of the revolt in that section. The causes and general characteristics of the rising are reviewed in the light of the recent literature by C. Petit-Dutaillis in *Studies and Notes supplementary to Stubbs' Constitutional History*, ii, 252-304 (Manchester, 1914).

Finance and Trade under Edward III, edited by G. Unwin (Manchester, 1918), is a study of phases of commercial development. H. L. Gray treats "Production and Exportation of English Woollens in the Fourteenth Century" in the light of previously unexplored material in *Eng. Hist. Rev.,* xxxix, 13-35. Much of interest on the tin industry is contained in G. R. Lewis' *The Stannaries* (Boston, 1908). On the merchants, see A. Law, "The English Nouveaux Riches in the Fourteenth Century," *Transactions of the Royal Historical Society,* new series, ix, 49-73; and A. Beardwood, *Alien Merchants in England, 1350-1377* (Cambridge, 1931).

Religious conditions in the fourteenth century are set forth generally by G. M. Trevelyan in chapters iv and v of *England in the Age of Wycliffe,* and something may be gleaned from W. W. Capes in his *The English Church in the Fourteenth and Fifteenth Centuries* (London, 1909). A more thorough study on one aspect of the subject is given by H. G. Richardson in "The Parish Clergy of the Thirteenth and Fourteenth Centuries," *Transactions of the Royal Historical Society,* third series, vi, 89-128 (London, 1912). The subject still lacks adequate investigation. The latest and best biography of Wycliffe is H. B. Workman's (2 vols., Oxford, 1926); an excellent brief one is R. L. Poole's (New York, 1890). G. Mollat surveys very briefly the history of papal provisions in England during the fourteenth century in his *La Collation des Bénéfices ecclésiastiques sous les Papes d'Avignon* (Paris, 1921), and J. F. Baldwin on pages lvi-lxv of his introduction to *Select Cases before the King's Council* (Selden Society, Cambridge, 1918) traces summarily the opposition to provisions before the statute of 1351. A. Deeley's "Papal Provision and Royal Patronage in the Early Fourteenth Century," *English Historical Review,* xliii (1928), 497-527, is an excellent study of certain aspects of the subject. E. Perroy's *L'Angleterre et le grand Schisme d'Occident* (Paris, 1933) is a scholarly treatment of the relations with the papacy in the later portion of the period. E. B. Graves in his "Legal Significance of the Statute of Praemunire of 1353," *Anniversary Essays in Mediæval History* by students of Charles Homer Haskins (Boston, 1929), pp. 57-80, brings out the real meaning of this statute; and W. T. Waugh does the like for the third statute in his "Great Statute of Praemunire," *English Historical Review,* xxxvii (1922), 173-205.

On the history of the Lollards Trevelyan gives a suggestive outline in chapters viii and ix of his *England in the Age of Wycliffe,* and W. H. Summers presents a useful study of a corner of the subject in his *Lollards of the Chiltern Hills* (London, 1906). The most elaborate work is Gairdner's *Lollardy and the Reformation,* volume i (London, 1908), but it is discursive, prejudiced, and far from thorough.

The volume of comment on the literature of this period is very large. C. S. Baldwin's *Three Mediæval Centuries of Literature in England, 1100-1400* (Boston, 1932) and W. H. Schofield's *English Literature from the Norman Conquest to Chaucer* (New York, 1906), in addition to the general works mentioned above, serve as an introduction to the subject. Good accounts of Chaucer and his work are J. L. Lowes' *Geoffrey Chaucer and the Development of his Genius* (Boston, 1934); G. L. Kittredge's *Chaucer and his Poetry* (Cambridge, 1915); and R. K. Root's *Poetry of Chaucer* (revised ed., Boston, 1922).

Universities and the thought of the period are treated in the books cited in chapter ix.

CHAPTER XV.—LANCASTER AND YORK

A brief account which reflects new views resulting from recent research is provided by K. B. McFarlane and C. H. Williams in chapters xi and xii of volume viii of *The Cambridge Medieval History* (Cambridge, 1936). The works of Oman and Vickers supply fuller guides to the political narrative. The third volume of Stubbs' *Constitutional History* is useful for political history as well as constitutional. J. H. Ramsay's *Lancaster and York* (2 vol., Oxford, 1892), though uncritical, can be consulted with profit on a period of which our knowledge still suffers for lack of sufficient research. R. B. Mowat's *Wars of the Roses* (London, 1914) is a convenient summary.

J. H. Wylie's *History of England under Henry the Fourth* (4 vols., London, 1884-98) is based on wide research and treats the subject in great detail, but it is poorly organized. His three volumes on *The Reign of Henry the Fifth* (Cambridge, 1914-29), the third of which was completed by W. T. Waugh, are in better perspective. C. L. Kingsford's *Henry V* (New York, 1901) is a scholarly biography. R. B. Mowat's *Henry V* (Boston, 1919) is somewhat briefer. M. E. Christie's *Henry VI* (London, 1922) is a popular biography. A. G. Bradley's *Owen Glyndwr* (New York, 1901) is useful for Welsh history. K. H. Vickers' *Humphrey, Duke of Gloucester* (London, 1907) is an excellent study of this interesting figure. C. Oman's *Warwick the Kingmaker* (London, 1891) is a brief popular biography. C. L. Scofield's *Life and Reign of Edward the Fourth* (2 vols., London, 1923) is a thorough and a readable study based on extensive researches in the archives. It is particularly full on foreign affairs, but devotes comparatively little attention to constitutional, economic, and social developments. On the reign of Richard III J. Gairdner's *History of the Life and Reign of Richard the Third* (second ed., London, 1879) is the standard authority.

The Hundred Years' War is treated at disproportionate length to its comparative importance in relation to other events in many of the works previously cited. R. A. Newhall's *English Conquest of Normandy, 1416-1424* (New Haven, 1924) is a thorough study of the military history. L. V. D. Owen's *The Connection between England and Burgundy during the First Half of the Fifteenth Century* (Oxford, 1909) is a convenient outline of the subject. The French point of view of the later years of the war receives a thorough exposition in G. du Fresne de Beaucourt's *Histoire de Charles VII* (6 vols., Paris, 1881-91), and the whole period receives an excellent briefer treatment in the fourth volume of E. Lavisse's *Histoire de France* (Paris, 1911). Relations between Edward IV and Louis XI are studied by G. Périnelle and J. Calmette in *Louis XI et l'Angleterre (1461-1483)* (Paris, 1930). A scholarly and interesting life of Joan of Arc is that of F. C. Lowell (Boston, 1896).

On constitutional development the best general treatises are White's and Adams's and F. W. Maitland's *Constitutional History of England* (Cambridge, 1911). The third volume of Stubbs' great work is still the best authority on the constitutional history of the period, and his views of parliamentary development in this period require less revision in the light of the studies of Baldwin, McIlwain, and Pollard than is the case in earlier periods. Gray's *Influence of the Commons* is essential for parliamentary history, and M. McKisack corrects older views concerning the composition of the house of commons in her *Representation of English Boroughs in the Middle Ages* (London, 1932). Baldwin's work on the council may be supplemented in some particulars by T. F. Plucknett's "Place of the Council in the Fifteenth Century" in *Transactions of the Royal Historical Society* (1918), pp. 157-189. S. B. Chrimes's *English Constitutional Ideas in the Fifteenth Century* (Cambridge, 1936) rests largely on legal sources.

CHAPTER XVI.—THE BEGINNINGS OF THE MODERN ERA

A good general work on the period of the Tudors is A. D. Innes' *England under the Tudors* (London, 1905), and still better is H. A. L. Fisher's *History of England from the Accession of Henry VII to the Death of Henry VIII* (London, 1906). Against the background of a profound knowledge of the period C. Read sketches for us in *The Tudors* (New York, 1936) the personalities of the rulers of the house of Tudor and makes shrewd estimates of their accomplishments. The first volume of W. Busch's *England under the Tudors* (London, 1895) is the most thorough account of the reign of Henry VII. J. Gairdner's *Henry the Seventh* (London, 1889), though briefer, is the work of an authority on the subject, and G. Temperley's *Henry VII* (Boston, 1914) is also good. Lectures xv and xvi in W. Stubb's *Seventeen Lectures on the Study of Medieval and Modern History* (Oxford, 1886) present a masterly summary of the reign. A good summary is given in *Cambridge Modern History,* i, chapter xiv (New York, 1902). An ancient work, which should still be read for the keenness of its insight and its literary qualities, is Lord Bacon's *History of the Reign of King Henry the Seventh.*

On the continental side of foreign relations useful summaries may be found in C. J. H. Hayes' *Political and Cultural History of Modern Europe,* i, part i, chapter i (New York, 1933; with excellent bibliographies), R. Lodge's *Close of the Middle Ages,* chapter xvi (London, 1904), and A. H. Johnson's *Europe in the Sixteenth Century,* chapter i (London, 1903). The French side of the story is set forth in E. Lavisse's *Histoire de France,* iv, part ii, pp. 420-435; v, part i, pp. 1-87 (Paris, 1911); the Spanish, in R. B. Merriman's *Rise of the Spanish Empire,* ii, chapter xiv (New York, 1918); the German, in J. Janssen's *History of the German People,* volume ii, book iv, chapter iii (St. Louis, n.d.), and R. W. Seton Watson's *Maximilian I* (Westminster, 1902); and the Flemish in H. Pirenne's *Histoire de Belgique,* iii (Bruxelles, 1923).

Brief accounts of the Irish situation may be found in R. Dunlop's *Ireland* (Oxford, 1922), E. Curtis's *History of Medieval Ireland* (New York, 1923), and W. O. Morris's *Ireland, 1494-1905* (Cambridge, 1909). R. Bagwell's *Ireland under the Tudors* (volume i, London, 1885) is the most thorough work.

Economic developments of the fifteenth century and of the reign of Henry VII may be followed in the general works of Cheyney, Cunningham, Ashley, and Lipson already cited.

A good brief summary of the commercial expansion in Europe generally is given by C. Hayes in his *Political and Cultural History of Modern Europe,* i, part i, chapter ii. G. Schanz's *Englische Handelspolitik* (2 vols., Leipzig, 1881) is the standard authority on the commercial history of the early Tudors. Mrs. J. R. Green's *Town Life in the Fifteenth Century* (2 vols., New York, 1894) deals with commerce and industry as well as town life. It has the Green dramatic touch, but it utilizes only a small part of the available evidence. *Studies in English Trade in the Fifteenth Century,* ed. by E. Power and M. M. Postan (London, 1933), are scholarly researches on important aspects of commercial development before 1485. Giuseppi gives an excellent summary of the conditions under which foreign merchants did business in England in his "Alien Merchants in England in the Fifteenth Century," *Transactions of the Royal Historical Society,* new series, ix, 75-98. Good brief accounts of the Merchant Adventurers are given on pp. xv to xxxix of W. E. Lingelbach's *Merchant Adventurers of England* (Philadelphia, 1902), and in C. P. Lucas's *Beginnings of English Overseas Enterprise* (Oxford, 1917). The story of the Hanseatic League is entertainingly told in the sixth chapter of R. Pauli's *Pictures of Old England* (London, 1861). On the crafts and industrial organization A. P. Usher's *Introduction to the Industrial History of England,* G. Unwin's *Industrial Organization in the Sixteenth and Seventeenth Centuries* (Oxford, 1904), and S. Kramer's *English Craft Gilds and the Government* (New York, 1905) may be consulted.

Good brief accounts of enclosures and their effects are given in E. Lipson's *Economic History of England,* volume i, chapter iv; R. E. Prothero's *English Farming Past and Present* (fifth ed., London, 1936); E. P. Cheyney's *Social Changes in England in the Sixteenth Century as reflected in Contemporary Literature* (Philadelphia, 1895); and W. H. R. Curtler's *Enclosure and Redistribution of Our Land* (Oxford, 1920). W. Hasbach briefly places the enclosure movement in relation to previous agrarian development in the first chapter of his *History of the English Agricultural Labourer* (London, 1908). More thorough studies are E. F. Gay's "Inclosures in England in the Sixteenth Century," *Quarterly Journal of Economics,* xvii, 576-597; E. C. K. Gonner's *Common Land and Enclosure* (London, 1912); H. Bradley's *The Enclosures in England* (New York, 1918); R. H. Tawney's *The Agrarian Problem in the Sixteenth Century* (London, 1912); the introduction to I. L. Leadam's *Domesday of Enclosures, 1517-18* (London, 1897); and the article by Gay and Leadam on "The Inquisitions of Depopulation in 1517 and the 'Domesday of Enclosures,'" in *Transactions of the Royal Historical Society,* new series, xiv, 231-303.

How the political conditions of the fifteenth century reacted on social life is set forth in the introduction to the *Paston Letters* (London, 1908) edited by J. Gairdner, and a more rounded view of social life, based largely on the same evidence, is presented in H. S. Bennett's *The Pastons and Their England* (Cambridge, 1922). C. L. Kingsford's interesting and scholarly studies in this field are set forth in *Prejudice and Promise in XVth Century England* (Oxford, 1925). W. Denton's *England in the Fifteenth Century* (London, 1888) supplies much valuable information about rural life, but some of the conclusions based on statistics and prices should be accepted with reserve. A. Abram's *English Life and Manners in the Later Middle*

Ages (London, 1913) relates mainly to the fifteenth century. C. Plummer's introduction to Fortescue's *Governance of England* (Oxford, 1885) gives a good brief survey of the effects of the internal disorder.

With the reign of Henry VII Stubbs deserts us as a guide to constitutional developments, and there is no similar comprehensive work to take its place for the modern period; but K. Pickthorn provides a thorough study of the constitution under Henry VII in his *Early Tudor Government: Henry VII* (Cambridge, 1934), and A. F. Pollard gives a suggestive summary in the introduction to his *Reign of Henry VII*, i, pp. xxviii-xliv (London, 1913). The constitutional histories of Adams and Maitland contain brief sketches of the constitution under the Tudors, and D. J. Keir's *Constitutional History of Modern Britain, 1485-1937* (New York, 1938) treats the modern period on a more extensive scale in the light of more recent research. McIlwain, Pollard, Pike, and Baldwin continue the stories of parliament and the council. On the court of star chamber C. L. Scofield's *Study of the Court of Star Chamber* (Chicago, 1900) is fundamental, and it can be supplemented by the introduction to I. S. Leadam's *Select Cases before the King's Council in the Star Chamber* (2 vols., Selden Society, 1903, 1911). Suggestive new views are presented by A. F. Pollard in "Council, Star Chamber, and Privy Council under the Tudors," *English Historical Review*, xxxvii, 337-360, 519-539; xxxviii, 42-60.

On the literature of the fifteenth century the general guides which have been cited earlier may still be followed. C. L. Kingsford's *English Historical Literature in the Fifteenth Century* (Oxford, 1913) is authoritative.

C. E. Mallet provides the best account of Oxford in this period in volume i of his *History of the University of Oxford* (London, 1924). On the development of schools and the spread of elementary education A. F. Leach gives a comprehensive view in chapter xii of his *Schools of Medieval England* (London, 1915).

J. Burckhardt's *Civilization of the Period of the Renaissance in Italy* (2 vols., London, 1878) is still one of the best general works to consult for an understanding of the spirit of the Renaissance. G. Voight's *Die Wiederbelebung des classischen Alterthums* (third ed., Berlin, 1893) is a standard work. J. A. Symonds' *Short History of the Renaissance in Italy* (New York, 1894) is less thorough but has a lighter touch. Some aspects of the subject are admirably treated in brief form in E. M. Hulme's *Renaissance and Reformation* (revised ed., New York, 1915), chapters v-vii, xix, xxix, xxx.

Two good brief treatments of the literary revival in England may be found in chapter ii of F. A. Gasquet's *Eve of the Reformation* (London, 1913) and in chapter i of L. Einstein's *Italian Renaissance in England* (New York, 1902). The latter also treats other aspects of the subject, and the same author presents stimulating views of the spirit and significance of the English Renaissance in his *Tudor Ideals* (New York, 1921). F. Seebohm's *Oxford Reformers* (second ed., London, 1869) is a graphic but somewhat overdrawn account of the intellectual revival. P. S. Allen's *Age of Erasmus* (Oxford, 1914) contains much of significance upon the English renaissance. Vickers has two good chapters on the duke of Gloucester's part in the movement in his *Humphrey, Duke of Gloucester* (London, 1907). Sidney Lee deals charmingly with some of the literary aspects in his *Great Englishmen of the Sixteenth Century* (New York, 1904). H. O. Taylor's *Thought and Expression in the Sixteenth Century* (volume ii, New York, 1920) is the product of ripe scholarship.

Biographies of some of the leaders of the movement in England are R. W. Chambers' *Thomas More* (New York, n.d.), J. H. Lupton's *Life of John Colet* (London, 1887), and E. Emerton's *Desiderius Erasmus* (New York, 1899). The last is excellent.

Of the geographical discoveries of the period and their general significance, good brief accounts are given in chapter ii of J. A. Williamson's *Short History of British Expansion* (London, 1922), and in chapters i and ii of *Cambridge Modern History*, volume i. The medieval background is given by C. R. Beazley in his *Dawn of Modern Geography* (volume ii, London, 1901). They are placed in their European setting by W. C. Abbott in his *Expansion of Europe* (volume i, New York, 1918).

On English explorations see C. R. Beazley's *John and Sebastian Cabot* (London, 1898), H. Harrisse's *John Cabot* (London, 1896), and J. A. Williamson's *Maritime Enterprise, 1485-1558* (Oxford, 1913).

Chapter XVII.—Henry VIII

A. F. Pollard's *Henry VIII* (London, 1905) is the best account of the reign. It is both scholarly and interesting. J. S. Brewer's *Reign of Henry VIII* (2 vols., London, 1884) carries the story in great detail to the death of Wolsey, and is particularly valuable for foreign affairs. The author tends to judge the ethical standards of the sixteenth century by the conventions of the mid-Victorian era. J. A. Froude takes up the story at 1529 and carries it to 1588 in his *History of England* (12 vols., New York, 1865-70). Despite mistakes of detail and prejudice in favor of Henry VIII, the work is based on such wide research and tells the story so graphically that it remains the standard comprehensive history of the period. K. Pickthorn's *Early Tudor Government: Henry VIII* (Cambridge, 1934) is a narrative of internal political affairs with emphasis on the constitutional side. R. B. Merriman's *Life and Letters of Thomas Cromwell* (2 vols., Oxford, 1902) is a masterly product of thorough scholarship. P. Friedman's *Anne Boleyn* (2 vols., London, 1884) is excellent. Good biographies of Wolsey are M. Creighton's (London, 1888) and A. F. Pollard's (London, 1929).

On the European side of foreign affairs most of the books mentioned in the previous chapter continue to be of use. To them may be added L. Ranke's *History of the Reformation in Germany* (3 vols., London, 1845-47), E. Armstrong's *The Emperor Charles V* (2 vols., London, 1910), M. Creighton's *History of the Papacy* (vols. iv, v, 1887, 1894), and L. Pastor's *History of the Popes* (vols. vii-xii, St. Louis, 1912-14).

Of the Reformation in Europe P. Smith's *Age of the Reformation* (New York, 1920) is an excellently rounded survey and E. M. Hulme's *Renaissance and Reformation* provides a stimulating summary in briefer scope. Both books contain selected biographies.

The ecclesiastical changes in England receive brief, scholarly treatment in J. Gairdner's *English Church in the Sixteenth Century* (London, 1904). On the background of the movement it should be compared with F. A. Gasquet's *Eve of the Reformation* (London, 1913). The former is coldly Protestant in tone and the latter is warmly Catholic. R. S. Arrowsmith's *Prelude to the Reformation* (London, 1923) is the best study of the background. P. Janelle brings forward some new views and new evidence on the separation in his *L'Angleterre catholique à la Veille du Schisme* (Paris, 1935). R. W. Dixon's *History of the Church of England* (third ed., 6 vols., London, 1895-1902) is a more extensive treatment of the Reformation from the Anglican point of view. A. F. Pollard's *Thomas Cranmer* (New York, 1904) is a delightful biography.

F. A. Gasquet sets forth with his usual charm the fruits of extensive studies in his *Henry VIII and the English Monasteries* (2 vols., sixth ed., London, 1902). It is somewhat too sympathetic with the monasteries. A. Savine's "English Monasteries on the Eve of the Dissolution" in the first volume of Vinogradoff's *Oxford Studies in Social and Legal History* (Oxford, 1909) is a thorough, complicated analysis of important evidence on the economic and social aspects of monastic organization. M. H. and R. Dodds make a careful study in their *Pilgrimage of Grace, 1536-1537, and the Exeter Conspiracy, 1538* (2 vols., London, 1915). B. F. Westcott's *General View of the History of the English Bible* (third ed., New York, 1916) and H. E. Jacobs' *Lutheran Movement in England* (Philadelphia, 1894) are valuable for the aspects which they treat.

CHAPTER XVIII.—PROTESTANT AND CATHOLIC

A. F. Pollard's *History of England from the Accession of Edward VI to the Death of Elizabeth* (London, 1910) is a brilliant treatment of the period and his *England under Protector Somerset* (London, 1900) is also excellent. R. Davey's *The Nine Days' Queen, Lady Jane Grey* (London, 1909) is interesting. J. M. Stone's *History of Mary I, Queen of England* (London, 1901) is of value, but it is prejudiced in favor of Mary. The early chapters of M. A. S. Hume's *Two English Queens and Philip* (London, 1908) deal with Mary's reign. The biography of Mary's influential adviser is provided by J. A. Muller in his *Stephen Gardiner and the Tudor Reaction* (New York, 1926).

On foreign affairs additional works of interest are H. Forneron's *Histoire de Philippe II* (4 vols., Paris, 1882-87) and his *Les Ducs de Guise et leur Époque* (2 vols., Paris, 1877).

On the religious changes J. Lingard's *History of England* (volume vii, second ed., London, 1823) should be consulted in addition to the works earlier mentioned. It is antiquated, but still of some value for its Catholic point of view. C. H. Smyth's *Cranmer and the Reformation under Edward VI* (Cambridge, 1926) contains much valuable information. F. A. Gasquet and E. Bishop's *Edward VI and the Book of Common Prayer* (third ed., London, 1891) and F. Proctor and W. H. Frere's *New History of the Book of Common Prayer* (London, 1910) explain the innovations of the reign of Edward VI.

On the Elizabethan settlement Dixon continues to be one of the best guides. W. H. Frere gives a reliable summary in his *English Church in the Reigns of Elizabeth and James I* (London, 1904). Fuller treatments are given by H. Gee, who is an Anglican, in his *Elizabethan Clergy and the Settlement of Religion, 1558-1564* (Oxford, 1898) and by the Catholic scholar, H. N. Birt, in his *Elizabethan Religious Settlement* (London, 1907).

On the economic and social conditions of the period W. Cunningham's *Growth of English Industry and Commerce during the Early and Middle Ages* (fifth ed., Cambridge, 1915) contains a good brief survey. E. P. Cheyney's *Social Changes in England in the Sixteenth Century as reflected in Contemporary Literature* (1895) is an interesting description of the changes in rural life. C. Oman's "The Tudors and the Currency" in *Trans. Royal Hist. Soc.*, new series, xiv, 231-303 is useful on that subject. On the increase of the precious metals A. Soetbeer's *Edelmetall-Produktion und Werthverhältniss zwischen Gold und Silber seit der Entdeckung Amerikas bis zur Gegenwart* (Gotha, 1879) should be compared with C. H. Haring's "American Gold and Silver Production in the First Half of the Sixteenth Century" in *Quarterly Journal of Economics*, xxix, 433-474. Literature on enclosures is listed under chapter xvi.

CHAPTER XIX.—EXTERNAL RELATIONS UNDER ELIZABETH

All of the works which treat generally of Elizabeth's reign necessarily deal extensively with foreign affairs. Those by Innes, Pollard, and Froude have been mentioned previously. J. E. Neale's *Elizabeth* (London, 1934) is the best short life of the queen, and J. B. Black's *Reign of Elizabeth* (New York, 1936) is well reviewed. E. S. Beesley's *Queen Elizabeth* (London, 1892) is a brief biography. M. Creighton's *Queen Elizabeth* (New York, 1900) is a suggestive and stimulating appreciation of the reign. E. P. Cheyney's *History of England from the Defeat of the Armada to the Death of Elizabeth* (2 vols., New York, 1914-26) fills the gap between the works of Froude and of Gardiner, the historian of the Stuarts. It is the mature, seasoned work of a thorough scholar, and as interesting as it is authoritative. M. A. S. Hume, who was familiar with the Spanish sources, deals largely with foreign relations in an entertaining manner, but not always accurately, in his *Two English Queens and Philip* (London, 1908), *The Courtships of*

Queen Elizabeth (New York, 1898), *The Year After the Armada* (New York, 1896), and *Treason and Plot* (New York, 1901). J. R. Seeley's *Growth of British Policy* (volume i, Cambridge, 1895) contains a well-ordered survey of the significance of England's external policies in this period, but it is sometimes unreliable. C. Read's *Mr. Secretary Walsingham and the Policy of Queen Elizabeth* (3 vols., Oxford, 1925) contains a detailed, thorough, interesting, and scholarly exposition of England's foreign policy in the critical period from 1570 to 1590. It is based primarily on manuscripts, many of which have not before been utilized. The best brief survey for a quick grasp of the European situation generally is M. Creighton's *Age of Elizabeth* (Boston, 1876), though A. H. Johnson's *Europe in the Sixteenth Century* (London, 1903) is better, if one can read but a single volume. Many chapters in the *Cambridge Modern History* are valuable, but its cooperative character deprives it of interest as a continuous narrative. M. Philippson's *West-Europa im Zeitalter von Philipp II, Elisabeth und Heinrich IV* (Berlin, 1882) is a standard survey of the period.

Of France's part in European affairs L. Batiffol's *Century of the Renaissance* (New York, 1916) supplies a good short story, and the sixth volume of Lavisse's *Histoire de France* maintains the general excellence of that work. H. M. Baird's *History of the Rise of the Huguenots of France* (2 vols., New York, 1879); E. Armstrong's *French Wars of Religion* (London, 1892); A. W. Whitehead's *Gaspard de Coligny* (London, 1904); and J. W. Thompson's more recent *Wars of Religion in France, 1559-1576* (Chicago, 1909) are of interest and importance on a phase of French history of great significance in relation to England. Kervyn de Lettenhove's *Les Huguenots et les Gueux* (6 vols., Bruges, 1883-85) is important for the relations with the Dutch as well as with the French.

M. A. S. Hume's *Philip II* (London, 1897) is a brief biography. H. Forneron's *Histoire de Philippe II* is more interesting and on a larger scale. R. Altamira's *Historia de España* (volume iii, third ed., Barcelona, 1913) is a standard Spanish history. C. E. Chapman's *History of Spain* (New York, 1918) is based largely upon it.

On the revolt of the Netherlands P. J. Blok's *History of the People of the Netherlands* (volume iii, New York, 1900) and H. Pirenne's *Histoire de Belgique* (volumes iii, iv, Bruxelles, 1919-23) are standard and excellent works. R. Putman's *William the Silent* (2 vols., New York, 1895) and F. Harrison's (London, 1897) are good biographies of the leader of the movement. M. Philippson's *La Contre-Révolution religieuse au xvi⁰ Siècle* (Bruxelles, 1884) is an interesting exposition of the subject. A. W. Ward supplies a brief work on the *Counter-Reformation* (London, 1889) in English.

On the early relations of Elizabeth with Scotland F. W. Maitland's chapter on "The Anglican Settlement and the Scottish Reformation" in the second volume of the *Cambridge Modern History* is the delightful product of deep research. The history of Scotland is told reliably but dryly by P. Hume Brown in his *History of Scotland* (volume ii, Cambridge, 1902). Mary Stuart's dramatic career has attracted many writers. The following are interesting accounts of her life or of important parts of it: A. Lang, *Mystery of Mary Stuart* (third ed., New York, 1902); J. Hosack, *Mary Queen of Scots and Her Accusers* (2 vols., Edinburgh, 1870-74); T. F. Henderson, *Mary, Queen of Scots* (2 vols., London, 1905); S. Cowan, *Mary, Queen of Scots* (2 vols., London, 1901); M. Philippson, *Marie Stuart et la Ligue catholique universelle* (Brussells, 1886).

Of the work of the Tudor seamen W. Raleigh's *English Voyages of the Sixteenth Century* (Glasgow, 1910) is a charming appreciation. J. A. Williamson's *Maritime Enterprise, 1485-1558* (Oxford, 1913) is a scholarly and interesting treatment of the subject, and in his *Short History of British Expansion* (London, 1922) he carries the story through Elizabeth's reign in more compressed and less interesting form. J. A. Froude's *English Seamen in the Sixteenth Century* (New York, 1917) relates mainly to Elizabeth's reign. Cheyney's *History* contains several interesting chapters on the subject. J. S. Corbett's *Sir Francis Drake* (London, 1894), an excellent brief biography, and *Drake and the Tudor Navy* (2 vols., new ed., London, 1899), a larger, more specialized and more interesting work, are written by an authority on naval history.

The story of the Armada is best told by Corbett in his *Drake and the Tudor Navy*, much new evidence on that subject having come to light in the last generation. His *Successors of Drake* (new ed., London, 1919) also deals with the later naval warfare with Spain, and Cheyney's *History* has an important chapter on that subject.

The most thorough treatment of Ireland in the sixteenth century is given in R. Bagwell's *Ireland under the Tudors* (3 vols., London, 1885-90). W. O. Morris gives a brief summary in his *Ireland, 1494-1905* (Cambridge, 1909), and P. Wilson's *The Beginnings of Modern Ireland* (London, 1912) is a history of the English in Ireland under Henry VIII and his two successors. In the introduction to his first volume of *Ireland under the Commonwealth* (Manchester, 1913) R. Dunlop gives a clear, succinct survey of Elizabeth's policy in Ireland.

Chapter XX.—Elizabethan England

Two cooperative works which cover many of the topics treated in this chapter are H. D. Traill's *Social England* (volume iii, New York, 1895) and *Shakespeare's England* (2 vols., Clarendon Press, Oxford, 1916).

The general histories of the church in the previous chapter deal with the relations of the government to the Catholics and the Puritans. A. J. Klein's *Intolerance in the Reign of Elizabeth* (Boston, 1917) is a good brief survey of the subject. J. H. Pollen's *English Catholics in the Reign of Elizabeth* (London, 1920) is a scholarly study by a Catholic, and A. O. Meyer's *England and the Catholic Church under Queen Elizabeth* (London, 1916) is also an important study. R. B. Merriman's "Some Notes on the Treatment of the English Catholics in the Reign of Elizabeth," in *American Historical Review*, xiii, 480-500, is a significant discussion of some aspects of the subject, and in chapter xi of C. Read's *Mr. Secretary Walsingham* the subject is surveyed impartially in the light of much new evidence. H. W. Clark's *History of English Nonconformity* (volume i, London, 1911) is a comparatively brief survey of that part of the story, and C. Burrage's *Early English Dissenters* (volume i, Cambridge, 1912) presents much new evidence. A. F. S. Pearson's *Thomas Cartwright and Elizabethan Puritanism, 1535-1603* (Cambridge, 1925) is a good study. E. L. Taunton's *History of the Jesuits in England* (London, 1901) and A. Jessopp's *One Generation of a Norfolk House* (third ed., New York, 1914) deal with the activities of secular priests and Jesuits in England.

The best general survey of economic development is E. Lipson's *Economic History of England* (volumes ii, iii, London, 1931), and it is usefully supplemented by W. Cunningham's *Growth of English Industry and Commerce in Modern Times* (fifth ed., part i, Cambridge, 1912). On industry G. Unwin's *Industrial Organization in the Sixteenth and Seventeenth Centuries* (Oxford, 1904) is a standard work, but it has to be supplemented by studies based upon the extensive research which has taken place in recent years. J. U. Nef provides an excellent brief explanation of the rise of large-scale industries in his "Progress of Technology and the Growth of Large Scale Industry in Great Britain, 1540-1640," *The Economic History Review*, v, 3-24 (London, 1934). It is, however, necessary to turn to the histories of single industries. Among the best of these are T. S. Ashton's *Iron and Steel in the Industrial Revolution* (Manchester, 1924); H. Heaton, *The Yorkshire Woollen and Worsted Industries* (London, 1921); A. K. H. Jenkins, *The Cornish Miner* (London, 1927); G. R. Lewis, *The Stannaries* (Cambridge, 1908); E. Lipson, *The History of the Woollen and Worsted Industries* (London, 1921); J. U. Nef, *The Rise of the British Coal Industry* (2 vols., London, 1932); H. Hamilton, *The English Brass and Copper Industries to 1800* (London, 1926); and *The Cotton Trade and Industrial Lancashire* (Manchester, 1931) by A. P. Wadsworth and J. de L. Mann. Agriculture is covered in the works cited in chapter xvi. Commercial expansion is surveyed generally in J. A. Williamson's *Short History of British Expansion* (London, 1922) and in part iii of the first volume of Cheyney's *History of England from the Defeat of the Armada*. The latter is the more interesting, but the former is conveniently organized. A convenient, somewhat superficial outline of the history of the trading companies is given by G. Cawston and A. H. Keane in *Early Chartered Companies* (London, 1896). W. R. Scott's *Joint Stock Companies* (3 vols., Cambridge, 1910-12) is a thorough study of the aspect it treats. Gerson, Vaughn and Deardorff's *Studies in the History of English Commerce in the Tudor Period* (Philadelphia, 1912), A. L. Rowland and G. B. Manhart's *Studies in English Commerce and Exploration in the Reign of Elizabeth* (Philadelphia, 1924), A. C. Wood's *History of the Levant Company* (Oxford, 1935), and M. Epstein's *Early*

History of the Levant Company (London, 1908) are special studies of value. The standard account of the relations of the Hanse to England in Elizabeth's reign is R. Ehrenberg's *Hamburg und England im Zeitalter der Königin Elizabeth* (Jena, 1896). E. M. Leonard's *Early History of English Poor Relief* (Cambridge, 1900) and W. H. Price's *English Patents of Monopoly* (Cambridge, 1913) are thorough and reliable studies of the subjects which they treat.

G. Schmoller's *Mercantile System* (New York, 1896) puts the system in its historical setting. L. H. Haney's *History of Economic Thought* (chapter vii, New York, 1911) provides a very brief summary of its principles. E. F. Heckscher's *Mercantilism* (2 vols., New York, 1935) is a comprehensive treatment. The classic exposition of its faults is found in book iv of Adam Smith's *Wealth of Nations*.

Society is described by H. Hall in *Society in the Elizabethan Age* (third ed., London, 1888); H. T. Stephenson in *Elizabethan People* (New York, 1910); M. S. Byrne in *Elizabethan Life in Town and Country* (London, 1926); and L. F. Salzman in *England in Tudor Times: Its Social Life and Industries* (London, 1926). Wallace Notestein's *History of Witchcraft in England* (Washington, 1911) is an interesting and scholarly treatment of a typical phase of the life of the times.

On the thought and the education of the times L. Einstein's *Tudor Ideals* (New York, 1921) is a stimulating book. Chapter xv of the second volume of J. E. Sandys's *History of Classical Scholarship* (Cambridge, 1908) provides a convenient "Who's Who" of the field. J. B. Mullinger's *History of the University of Cambridge* (volume ii, 1884) and C. E. Mallet's *History of the University of Oxford* (volume ii, New York, 1924) are the best guides to the situation in the universities, though A. Mansbridge has a few suggestive pages in his *Older Universities* (Boston, 1923).

The literature on Elizabethan literature is extensive. The second volume of J. J. Jusserand's *Literary History of the English People* (in two parts, New York, 1906-09) and volumes iii-v of the *Cambridge History of English Literature* (New York, 1909-10) supply a good introduction to the subject, and the latter has bibliographies. F. E. Schelling's *English Literature during the Lifetime of Shakespeare* (New York, 1910) is a standard brief manual. F. E. Schelling's *Elizabethan Drama* (2 vols., Boston, 1908) and E. K. Chambers' fuller *Elizabethan Stage* (4 vols., Oxford, 1923) are standard works. S. Lee in his *Great Englishmen of the Sixteenth Century* (New York, 1904) catches the spirit of literature and learning in the sixteenth century in a series of charming biographical sketches. Of the many biographies of Shakespeare those by J. Q. Adams (Boston, 1923) and E. K. Chambers (2 vols., Oxford, 1930) may be mentioned.

Chapter XXI.—The Government of the Tudors

K. Pickthorn's *Early Tudor Government* carries the story to 1547. The introduction to G. W. Prothero's *Select Statutes and other Constitutional*

Documents Illustrative of the Reigns of Elizabeth and James I (fourth ed., Oxford, 1913) is a remarkably clear and concise exposition of the constitution as it existed at the close of the Tudor period. E. P. Cheyney in his *History of England from the Defeat of the Armada* gives a fuller and a very scholarly and interesting description of the organization and working of the government in the last years of Elizabeth. Chapter x of G. B. Adams' *Constitutional History* is a suggestive consideration of the significance of the changes, giving comparatively little attention to the institutions themselves. The introductory sections of J. R. Tanner's *Tudor Constitutional Documents* (Cambridge, 1922) provide a concise summary. Period iii of F. W. Maitland's *Constitutional History* presents many facts not found conveniently elsewhere in brief compass and has the usual illuminating touch of the author. What he says about parliament should be compared with McIlwain's *High Court of Parliament* and Pollard's *Evolution of Parliament*. These works are essential for the understanding of the parliamentary development. Professor A. F. Pollard has a wide and deep knowledge of the Tudor constitution, but he has never set it forth in convenient form. Scattered pages of his *Evolution, Henry VIII, England under Protector Somerset, History of England from the Accession of Edward VI*, and various articles, of which the most important are those on "Council, Star Chamber, and Privy Council under the Tudors" in *English Historical Review* (volumes xxxvii and xxxviii), provide a treatment than which none is more stimulating and suggestive for the portion of the field it covers. F. Dietz's *English Government Finance, 1485-1558* (University of Illinois Studies in the Social Sciences, volume ix, No. 3, Urbana, 1920) and his *English Public Finance, 1558-1641* (New York, 1932) are significant studies. E. Porritt's *Unreformed House of Commons* (2 vols., Cambridge, 1903); C. G. Bayne's "First House of Commons of Queen Elizabeth" in *English Historical Review* (volume xxiii); and E. J. Neale's "Peter Wentworth" in the same, volume xxxix, pp. 36-54, 175-205, may be consulted profitably on certain aspects of parliamentary history.

E. Percy's *Privy Council under the Tudors* (Oxford, 1907) is a convenient survey of the whole period, but it needs to be supplemented by the works already mentioned and by Baldwin's *King's Council* which carries the subject to the close of the reign of Henry VIII. The local councils are treated in C. A. J. Skeel's *The Council in the Marches of Wales* (London, 1904) and R. R. Reid's *King's Council in the North* (London, 1921).

On the courts and the law C. L. Scofield's *Study of the Court of Star Chamber* (Chicago, 1900), R. G. Usher's *Rise and Fall of the High Commission* (Oxford, 1913), and I. S. Leadam's introductions to his *Select Cases before the King's Council in the Star Chamber* and *Select Cases in the Court of Requests* (Selden Society, 1898, 1903) are special studies of importance. F. W. Maitland's *English Law and the Renaissance* (Cambridge, 1901) is a delightful essay on the influence of the Roman law.

Of local government as a whole E. P Cheyney's *European Background of American History* (chapters xiv-xvi, New York, 1904) and the chapters devoted to the subject in the second volume of his *History of England from the Defeat of the Armada* provide by far the best accounts. On the parish S. L. Ware's "The Elizabethan Parish in its Ecclesiastical and Financial Aspects" in *Johns Hopkins University Studies in Historical and Political Science* (volume xxvi, Baltimore, 1908) and T. Smith's *The Parish* (second ed., London, 1857) may be consulted. E. Trotter's excellent *Seventeenth Century Life in the Country Parish* (Cambridge, 1919) relates to a little later period. R. Gneist's *History of the English Constitution* offers a suggestive point of view of the justices of the peace in chapters xxx and xxxvi of the second volume (New York, 1886), and C. A. Beard's *Office of Justice of the Peace* (New York, 1904) contains a useful description of their organization and functions. Special aspects are thoroughly treated in E. M. Leonard's *Early History of English Poor Relief* (Cambridge, 1900), S. and B. Webb's *English Local Government*; *The Story of the King's Highway* (chapters i, ii, London, 1913), and G. S. Thomson's *Lords Lieutenants in the Sixteenth Century* (London, 1923).

CHAPTERS XXII, XXIII.—KING VERSUS PARLIAMENT; THE ROYAL AUTHORITY VERSUS THE LIBERTIES OF THE SUBJECT

S. R. Gardiner's *History of England, 1603-1642* (10 vols., London, 1883-84) is the authoritative work on which most briefer recent narratives are mainly based. G. M. Trevelyan's *England under the Stuarts* (sixth ed., New York, 1914) is a well-rounded, readable, and suggestive narrative. F. C. Montague's *History of England, 1603-1660* (London, 1907) is fuller on the political narrative. G. Davies incorporates in his *Early Stuarts, 1603-1660* (Oxford, 1937) the results of recent research.

The introduction to Prothero's *Select Statutes* and the works of G. B. Adams and F. W. Maitland supply good brief surveys of the constitutional development. There is no adequate treatment of the subject. J. R. Tanner gives a very satisfactory survey of the relations between king and parliament in his *English Constitutional Conflicts of the Seventeenth Century* (Cambridge, 1928). The views of Gardiner on that subject should be checked by Wallace Notestein's *Winning of the Initiative by the House of Commons* (London, 1925), which is of fundamental importance, and by chapter v of McIlwain's *High Court of Parliament*. F. H. Relf's *Petition of Right* (Minneapolis, 1917) explains the constitutional significance of the petition by a detailed study of the circumstances of its production. Several others of the books mentioned in the previous section continue to be useful for the constitutional history of the present period.

On the political theories of the times G. P. Gooch's *History of English Democratic Ideas in the Seventeenth Century* (second ed., by H. J. Laski, Cambridge, 1927), J. F. Figgis' *Divine Right of Kings* (second ed., Cambridge, 1914), and the introduction to C. H. McIlwain's *Political Works of James I* (Cambridge, 1918) are excellent.

On religious questions Frere continues to offer guidance on the history of the church to the close of the reign of James. W. H. Hutton, who takes up the story in the next volume of the series, presents the Anglican point of view. The latter's *William Laud* (Boston, 1895) is also useful. The early chapters of H. H. Henson's *Puritanism in England* (London, 1912) and his *Studies in English Religion in the Seventeenth Century* (London, 1903) are penetrating and suggestive essays. The works of Burrage and Clark continue to be of service on the Puritans and the Separatists. R. G. Usher's *Reconstruction of the English Church* (2 vols., New York, 1910) is a scholarly work. A comparison of Father J. Gerard's *What Was the Gunpowder Plot?* (London, 1897) with S. R. Gardiner's *What Gunpowder Plot Was* (London, 1897) provides not only information about the Catholics but also an amusing and instructive illustration of right and wrong ways to interpret historical evidence.

England's foreign policy Gardiner treats at length, and L. von Ranke's *History of England Principally in the Seventeenth Century* (vol. i, Oxford, 1875) is valuable on this aspect of the subject. J. R. Seeley's *Growth of British Policy* (2 vols., Cambridge, 1895) is suggestive, though its generalizations cannot always be accepted without question.

Hayes provides a brief, convenient survey of European political development. His work may be supplemented by S. R. Gardiner's *Thirty Years' War* (London, 1891) and H. O. Wakeman's *Europe, 1598-1715* (New York, 1894). For France J. B. Perkins' *Richelieu* (New York, 1900) and the early chapters of his *France under Mazarin* (volume i, second ed., New York, 1886) may be added to Lavisse; for Spain, Altamira's work; and for the Netherlands, Blok's *History*.

E. Edwards' *Life of Sir Walter Raleigh* (volume i, London, 1868) is a standard treatment of one of the most many-sided men of the time; and J. Spedding's *Account of the Life and Times of Francis Bacon* (2 vols., Boston, 1878) is a reliable life of the statesman. H. D. Traill's *Lord Strafford* (London, 1889) is a useful, brief biography. H. Haynes' *Henrietta Maria* (New York, 1912) gives an organized account of the queen's activities.

On the continental American colonies numerous histories of the American colonial period supply bibliographies. Interesting and authoritative general narratives of moderate length are E. Channing's *History of the United States* (volume i, New York, 1907) and L. G. Tyler's *England in America, 1580-1652* (New York, 1904). A. P. Newton's *Colonising Activities of the English Puritans* (New Haven, 1914) deals particularly with the English background, and J. T. Adams in his *Founding of New England* (Boston, 1921) reaches significant conclusions about the Puritan migration. The early history of the Pilgrims is treated in R. G. Usher's *The Pilgrims and Their History* (New York, 1918). On the West Indies volume ii of C. P. Lucas' *Historical Geography of the British Colonies* (Oxford, 1890) is a convenient manual. Good brief accounts of the establishment of the East

India Company in India are given in W. W. Hunter's *Brief History of the Indian Peoples* (24th ed., Oxford, 1907) and A. Lyall's *Rise and Expansion of the British Dominion in India* (fifth ed., London, 1910). W. W. Hunter's *History of British India* (2 vols., London, 1900) is a more extensive treatment.

CHAPTER XXIV.—THE CIVIL WAR AND THE INTERREGNUM

S. R. Gardiner carries his monumental work to 1656. C. H. Firth continues Gardiner's work to 1658 in his *Last Years of the Protectorate* (2 vols., London, 1909). The best life of Cromwell is C. H. Firth's *Oliver Cromwell* (New York, 1906). Good brief sketches are H. Johnstone's *Oliver Cromwell and His Times* (London, 1912) and F. Harrison's *Oliver Cromwell* (London, 1912). On Military history C. H. Firth's *Cromwell's Army* (London, 1912) is the standard authority. Various aspects of the Commonwealth and Protectorate receive scholarly treatment in F. A. Inderwick's *The Interregnum* (London, 1891), L. Jenks' *Constitutional Experiments, 1649-1660* (Cambridge, 1890), and L. F. Brown's *Political Activities of the Baptists and Fifth Monarchy Men in England during the Interregnum* (Washington, 1912). They place emphasis chiefly on the constitutional side.

Additional works of interest on the political theories of the period are W. A. Dunning's *History of Political Theories from Luther to Montesquieu*, chapters vii, viii (New York, 1905); C. Borgeaud's *Rise of Modern Democracy* (London, 1894); the introduction to volume i of the *Clarke Papers*, edited by C. H. Firth (Camden Society, 1891); and T. C. Pease's *The Leveller Movement* (Washington, 1916).

Further works on the religious question are W. A. Shaw's *English Church during the Civil Wars and under the Commonwealth* (2 vols., London, 1900), R. Barclay's *Inner Life of the Religious Societies of the Commonwealth* (London, 1876), and G. B. Tatham's *The Puritans in Power* (Cambridge, 1913). W. C. Braithwaite's *Beginnings of Quakerism* (London, 1912) is the standard work on the Quakers in this period. Interesting biographies are R. M. Jones's *Story of George Fox* (New York, 1919) and F. J. Powicke's *Life of the Reverend Richard Baxter* (London, 1924).

On Ireland R. Bagwell's *Ireland under the Stuarts* (3 vols., London, 1909-16) is the most thorough scholarly work on the whole period. The introduction to the first volume of R. Dunlop's *Ireland under the Commonwealth* (Manchester, 1913) provides a reliable and an admirable brief exposition. P. H. Brown's *History of Scotland* is still a safe guide on that aspect of the subject.

The best account of the imperial policy of the period is G. L. Beer's *Origins of the British Colonial System, 1578-1660* (New York, 1908). The same author writes on "Cromwell's Policy in Its Economic Aspects" in *Political Science Quarterly*, xvi, 582-611; xvii, 46-70. J. R. Seeley's *Growth of British Policy* and his *Expansion of England* (Boston, 1883) explain, sometimes too simply, the commercial and colonial rivalries during the period, and J. S. Corbett's *England in the Mediterranean* (volume i, London, 1904) is of fundamental importance on the growth and significance of naval power. Seeley and Corbett also treat the Anglo-Dutch war. P. J. Blok in his *History of the Netherlands* (volume iv, New York, 1907) approaches the subject from the Dutch side.

CHAPTER XXV.—THE RESTORATION AND THE REVOLUTION

On the reign of Charles II there is no work comparable in scope to Gardiner's for the earlier period, but T. B. Macaulay's *History of England* (best ed. by Firth, 6 vols., London, 1913-15) treats the period from 1685 to 1702 on a similar scale. Though the product of extensive research, it is not free from errors, and it betrays a Whig bias. It is noted for its vivid style. G. N. Clark's *Later Stuarts, 1660-1714* (Oxford, 1934), D. Ogg's *England in the Reign of Charles II* (Oxford, 1934), and K. Feiling's *British Foreign Policy, 1660-1672* (London, 1930) throw much new light upon the period. R. Lodge's *History of England from the Restoration to the Death of William III* (London, 1910) is a good account of the political development. Trevelyan's *England under the Stuarts* and L. von Ranke's *History of England* continue to be of service for this period.

Important studies on the politics of the period of Charles II are W. C. Abbot's "The Long Parliament of Charles II," *Eng. Hist. Rev.,* xxi, 21-56, 254-285; his "Origin of English Political Parties," *Am. Hist. Rev.,* xxiv, 578-602; C. B. R. Kent's *Early History of the Tories* (London, 1908), and K. Feiling's *History of the Tory Party, 1640-1714* (Oxford, 1924).

The constitutional significance of the period is sketched admirably in chapter xiv of G. B. Adam's *Constitutional History of England*, and somewhat more fully by Tanner in *English Constitutional Conflicts*.

Hutton's *English Church* is the best brief guide on the religious development of the period. J. H. Overton's *Life in the English Church, 1660-1714* (London, 1885) and J. Stoughton's *History of Religion in England*, volumes iii-v (new ed., London, 1881) contain much good material on the subject, though the latter is rather dull. C. J. Abbey's *The English Church and Its Bishops, 1700-1800* (2 vols., London, 1887) is a standard work on the eighteenth century. A. A. Seaton's *Theory of Toleration under the Later Stuarts* (Cambridge, 1911) and H. F. R. Smith's *Theory of Religious Liberty in the Reigns of Charles II and James II* (Cambridge, 1911) are interesting essays. F. Bate's *Declaration of Indulgence* (London, 1908) is a special study of interest.

Good biographies are J. Corbett's *Monk* (London, 1889); W. D. Christie's *Life of Anthony Ashley Cooper, First Earl of Shaftesbury* (London, 1871); H. D. Traill's briefer *Shaftesbury* (London, 1888); V. Barbour's *Henry Bennet, Earl of Arlington* (Washington, 1914); and H. C. Foxcroft's *Life and Letters of Halifax* (2 vols., London, 1898).

With this period begins the abundance of contemporary narratives and memoirs which continues to the present day. Some of those which are likely to interest the casual reader and are at the same time valuable historical evidence are G. Burnet's *History of His Own Time* (6 vols., second ed., Oxford, 1833); S. Pepys' *Diary* and J. Evelyn's *Diary* (both in several editions).

On foreign affairs the works of Hayes and Wakeman continue to be good guides. O. Airy's *The English Restoration and Louis XIV* (London, 1888) is a convenient outline. Several of the works previously cited on France and the Netherlands continue to be of value. To them may be added A. Hassall's convenient *Louis XIV* (New York, 1895), the early chapters of J. B. Perkin's *France under the Regency* (Boston, 1892), A. T. Mahan's suggestive *Influence of Sea Power upon History* (second ed., Boston, 1891), and the general survey in M. Philippson's *Das Zeitalter Ludwigs des Vierzehnten* (Berlin, 1889).

P. H. Brown's *History of Scotland* is still the best general guide to the history of Scotland. His *Legislative Union of England and Scotland* (Oxford, 1914) and W. L. Mathieson's *Scotland and the Union* (Glasgow, 1905) are excellent studies.

The second volume of W. E. H. Lecky's *History of England in the Eighteenth Century* (New York, 1887) contains a good account of the relations with Ireland in this period. *Revolutionary Ireland and Its Settlement* (London, 1911) by R. H. Murray is an important study. A. E. Murray's *Commercial and Financial Relations between England and Ireland* (London, 1903) is a valuable study of the economic policy.

CHAPTER XXVI.—THE LAST OF THE STUARTS

Most of the general works mentioned in the previous section cover the period of the present chapter. W. H. Lecky's *History of England in the Eighteenth Century* (8 vols., New York, 1882-90) is the standard work. It is the work of an impartial scholar who interprets history broadly, relegates the political narrative to its proper place, emphasizes social, economic, and intellectual developments, and makes of it a narrative less stylistic but fully as interesting as Macaulay's. I. S. Leadam's *History of England from the Accession of Anne to the Death of George II* (London, 1909) is a clear, detailed narrative of political events. G. M. Trevelyan's *England under Queen Anne* (3 vols., London, 1930-34) is the best comprehensive account of the reign. The other general histories of Anne's reign are for the most part superficial or antiquated, but Earl Stanhope's *Reign of Queen Anne* (third ed., London, 1871) is a product of research which can still be used to advantage to supplement Lecky, since it emphasizes political and military affairs and tells the story in an interesting fashion. W. M. Morgan's *English Political Parties and Leaders in the Reign of Queen Anne* (New Haven, 1920) is an excellent piece of research which takes a new view of Anne's character and throws much light on parties and politics. M. E. Grew's *William Bentinck and William III* (London, 1924) is a valuable biography based largely on the papers of Bentinck, who was William's friend and trusted adviser. W. S. Churchill's *Marlborough, His Life and Times* (6 vols., New York, 1933-38) is an interesting biography of one of the foremost leaders of the period.

F. W. Head's *The Fallen Stuarts* (Cambridge, 1901) is a suggestive and illuminating brief treatment of the foreign policy of the period built around the central theme of the exiled Stuarts. A. T. Mahan's *Influence of Sea Power upon History* (Boston, 1891) brings out the significance of the naval warfare in relation to the whole war and to the national development in an interesting and authoritative manner. J. S. Corbett does the like for the warfare in the Mediterranean in his *England in the Mediterranean* (2 vols., London, 1904). J. W. Fortescue's *History of the British Army* (volume i, London, 1899) deals thoroughly with the campaigns and their significance. G. N. Clark's *Dutch Alliance and the War against French Trade* (Manchester, 1923) is an interesting study of a significant aspect of the war begun in 1689. Detailed treatments of international affairs from continental points of view are given by C. von Noorden in his *Europäische Geschichte im achtzehnten Jahrhundert* (3 vols., 1870-82) and by A. Legrelle in his *Notes et Documents sur la Paix de Ryswick* (Paris, 1894) and his *La Diplomatie française et la Succession d'Espagne* (second ed., 6 vols., Paris, 1895-1900).

M. T. Blauvelt's *Development of Cabinet Government in England* (New York, 1902) is a useful history of that institution, but since it appeared further studies have added much to our knowledge of its early history. These studies are E. R. Turner's in *Am. Hist. Rev.*, xviii, 751-768, xix, 27-43, 772-793; H. W. V. Temperley's in *Eng. Hist. Rev.*, xxvii, 682-699, xxviii, 127-131; E. I. Carlyle's in *Eng. Hist. Rev.*, xxvii, 251-273; W. R. Anson's in *Eng. Hist. Rev.*, xxix, 56-78, 325-327. E. R. Turner's *The Privy Council of England in the Seventeenth and Eighteenth Centuries* (2 vols., Baltimore, 1927-28) and *The Cabinet Council of England in the Seventeenth and Eighteenth Centuries* (2 vols., Baltimore, 1930-32) are the products of extensive researches which have not always been well digested.

CHAPTER XXVII.—ECONOMIC, SOCIAL, AND INTELLECTUAL ASPECTS OF STUART ENGLAND

Most of the subjects discussed in this chapter are treated in the fourth volume of Traill's *Social England*, and several of them find place in Davies' *Early Stuarts*, Clark's *Later Stuarts*, and Ogg's *England in the Reign of Charles II*.

On the economic development the greater part of the works cited above in chapter xx continue to be of service. W. A. S. Hewin's *English Trade and Finance chiefly in the Seventeenth Century* (London, 1892) is a survey of several aspects of economic history. R. E. Prothero's *English Farming Past and Present* (London, 1912) is an excellent brief survey of the agricultural situation. On enclosures see Gonner's "Progress of Inclosure during the Seventeenth Century," *Eng. Hist. Rev.*, xxiii, 477-501; and Leonard's "Inclosure of Common Fields in the Seventeenth Century," *Trans. Royal*

Hist. Soc., new series, xix, 101-146. The standard *History of the Bank of England* is by A. Andréadès (second ed., London, 1924).

G. L. Beer's *Old Colonial System* (2 vols., New York, 1912) is by far the best work on imperial commercial policy. It is a scholarly and interesting narrative, based largely on sources in manuscript previously unutilized. The following are brief, suggestive treatments which present several different points of view: W. J. Ashley, *Surveys Historic and Economic* (London, 1900), pp. 309-335; G. B. Hertz, *Old Colonial System* (Manchester, 1905), chapter iii; H. E. Egerton, *Causes and Character of the American Revolution* (Oxford, 1923), chapter iii; W. H. Lecky, *History of England in the Eighteenth Century,* volume ii, chapter v, section on *The Colonies;* E. Channing, *History of the United States* (volumes i, ii, New York, 1907-20); *The Cambridge History of the British Empire,* volume i (New York, 1929). It should be borne in mind that the great increase in our knowledge of this subject, resulting from the researches of the present generation, has altered profoundly the point of view generally presented by American historians of the previous generation.

The simplest and most instructive way to grasp the part played by the mercantile system in the seventeenth century is to read some of the contemporary pamphlets upon it. Two of the best, which are readily available, are Thomas Mun's *England's Treasure by Foreign Trade* (New York, 1895) and Josiah Child's *A New Discourse of Trade* (London, 1694). A good, brief, modern interpretation of it is presented in volume iii, chapter iv, of Lipson's *Economic History.*

The first two chapters of Trevelyan's *England under the Stuarts* provide a delightful survey of English life under the first two Stuarts. M. James's *Social Problems and Policy during the Puritan Revolution, 1640-1660* (London, 1930) is a thorough and interesting study. The third chapter of the first volume of Macaulay's *History of England* is a famous picture of society in the England of the restoration. Despite some sweeping statements that lack sufficient evidential foundation, it is a masterly description. It should be supplemented by the pertinent portions of the works by Davies, Ogg and Clark, and by other studies cited in this paragraph. W. C. Sydney's *Social Life in England from the Restoration to the Revolution* (New York, 1892) contains much of interest, but it is poorly organized and uncritical. M. Coate's *Social Life in Stuart England* (New York, 1925) gives an excellent brief description of the daily life of the various social classes. E. Trotter's *Seventeenth Century Life in the Country Parish* (Cambridge, 1919) and M. Campbell's *The English Yeoman under Elizabeth and the Early Stuarts* (New Haven, 1942) are excellent studies. J. E. Gillespie's *Influence of Overseas Expansion on England to 1700* (New York, 1920) has much of interest on society. Pepys' *Diary* is a good road to an understanding of the social life of the restoration. Evelyn's *Diary* is also valuable for this purpose. J. J. Jusserand's *French Ambassador at the Court of Charles the Second* (New York, 1892) gives interesting sidelights on the court of Charles II. G. B.

Hertz (or Hurst) is of interest on many social aspects of the period in his *English Public Opinion after the Restoration* (1902). *The Memoirs of the Verney Family* edited by F. P. and M. M. Verney (4 vols., London, 1892-99) contain much information on social customs. J. Ashton's *Social Life in the Reign of Queen Anne* (2 vols., London, 1882) is informative and dull.

B. Wendell's *Temper of the Seventeenth Century in English Literature* (New York, 1904) is an illuminating and enjoyable series of essays which constitute a remarkably fine interpretation of the spirit of the literature of the period. L. Stephen carries the story into the next century with equal brilliance and charm in his *English Literature and Society in the Eighteenth Century* (New York, 1904). *The Cambridge History of English Literature* (volumes vii-ix, New York, 1911-13) is a standard survey.

Very brief summaries of the developments in science, philosophy, and political theory which point the way to further reading, if it is desired, may be found in *Cambridge Modern History*, v, chapter xxiii; F. Thilly, *History of Philosophy*, sections 43, 44, 48-52; and W. A. Dunning's *History of Political Theories from Luther to Montesquieu* (New York, 1919). See also the critical bibliography in Clark's *Later Stuarts*.

Chapter XXVIII.—Walpole and Pitt

To the general works on the period by Lecky and Leadam the following may be added. G. C. Robertson's *England under the Hanoverians* (London, 1911) is useful. B. Williams's *The Whig Supremacy, 1714-1760* (Oxford, 1939) is valuable for its utilization of more recent research. Lord Mahon's *History of England from the Peace of Utrecht to the Peace of Versailles* (third ed., 7 vols., Boston, 1853), despite its author's point of view that politics and wars made history, is interesting and valuable, though it has to be supplemented by more recent works. H. M. Ibert-Terry's *A Constitutional King, George the First* (London, 1927) contains much of interest on the personalities of the time. J. Morley's *Walpole* (London, 1890) is a readable brief biography. W. M. Coxe's *Memoirs of Sir Robert Walpole* (new ed., 3 vols., London, 1800) is much fuller. Though antiquated in parts, it is still the best biography we have on some aspects of the statesman's career. N. A. Brisco's *The Economic Policy of Robert Walpole* (New York, 1907) and S. H. Nulle's *Thomas Pelham-Holles, Duke of Newcastle, his early Political Career, 1693-1724* (Philadelphia, 1931) are useful studies.

The most extensive biographies of William Pitt are A. von Ruville's (3 vols., London, 1907) and B. Williams's (2 vols., London, 1913). The former is more thorough, but it is somewhat cold and tedious; the latter is more sympathetic and a bit more readable; both are essential for a thorough knowledge. W. D. Green's briefer *William Pitt* (New York, 1911) is based on original research and is well worth reading. F. Harrison's *Chatham* (New York, 1905) is in the nature of a brief appraisement of Pitt. Lord Rosebery's *Chatham: his Early Life and Connections* (London, 1910) is a pleasant narrative of a limited portion of his life. T. W. Riker's *Henry Fox, First Lord Holland* (2 vols., Oxford, 1911) is a scholarly work.

On the development of the cabinet and parties the following may be read in addition to the works mentioned in a previous list: chapter vii of Morley's *Walpole*; E. Jenks's *Parliamentary England* (chapters v, vi, New York, 1903); C. B. Realey's *The Early Opposition to Sir Robert Walpole, 1720-1727* (Philadelphia, 1931); and W. T. Laprade's *Public Opinion and Politics in Eighteenth Century England to the Fall of Walpole* (New York, 1936).

Of the many contemporary narratives, memoirs, and collections of letters, the following have been selected as particularly interesting and valuable for the light they shed on political history: H. Walpole's *Letters* (16 vols., Oxford, 1903-05) and his *Memoirs of the Reign of King George II* (second ed., 3 vols., London, 1846-47); Lord Hervey's *Memoirs of the Reign of George the Second* (3 vols., London, 1884); Earl Waldegrave's *Memoirs* (London, 1821); G. B. Doddington's *Diary* (London, 1785); *The Grenville Papers*, edited by W. J. Smith (volumes i, ii, London, 1852).

H. Hassall's *Balance of Power* (New York, 1896) provides a convenient brief narrative of continental history during the period. A. T. Mahan's *Influence of Sea Power on History* (Boston, 1891) summarizes excellently the diplomatic and martial relations of the European powers. E. Bourgeois's *Manuel historique de Politique étrangère* (2 vols., Paris, 1919-20) and his *La Diplomatie secrète au xviiie Siècle* (3 vols., Paris) are excellent works on diplomatic history. Lavisse's *Histoire de France* and Perkins's *France under Louis XV* (2 vols., Boston, 1897) are good general works on France. E. Armstrong's *Elizabeth Farnese* (London, 1892) and Altamira's *Historia de España* provide the Spanish background; and H. Tuttle's *History of Prussia under Frederick the Great* (3 vols., Boston, 1888-96), W. F. Reddaway's *Frederick the Great* (New York, 1904), and R. Koser's *König Friedrich der Grosse* (2 vols., Stuttgart, 1893-1905) tell the Prussian side of the story well.

Head's *Fallen Stuarts*; A. W. Ward's *Great Britain and Hanover* (Oxford, 1899); F. L. Edwards' *James first Earl Stanhope (1673-1721) and British Foreign Policy* (London, 1925); B. Williams's *Stanhope* (Oxford, 1932); and J. F. Chance's *George I and the Northern War* (London, 1909) deal with important aspects of British foreign policy. L. Wiesener's *Le Régent, l'Abbé Dubois et les Anglais* (3 vols., Paris, 1891-99) and P. Vaucher's *Robert Walpole et la Politique de Fleury* (Paris, 1924) are important for the relations between Great Britain and France.

On the causes of the war with Spain both chapter ii of G. B. Hertz's *British Imperialism in the Eighteenth Century* (London, 1908) and H. W. V. Temperley's "Causes of the War of Jenkins' Ear" in *Trans. Royal Hist. Soc.* (third series, iii, 197-236) should be read. J. W. Fortescue's *History of the British Army* (volume ii, London, 1899) and A. Arvers's *Guerre de la Succession d'Autriche* (Paris, 1893) deal particularly with the War of the Austrian Succession. On the Indian background of the Seven Years' War A. Lyall's *Rise and Expansion of British Dominion in India;* G. B. Malleson's brief *Lord Clive* (Oxford, 1907); his *Dupleix* (Oxford, 1895); C. W. Wilson's *Lord Clive* (London, 1890); G. Forrest's *Life of Lord Clive* (2 vols., London, 1918); P. Cultru's *Dupleix* (Paris, 1901); H. Weber's *La Compagnie française des Indes* (Paris, 1904) and the *Cambridge History of the British Empire* (volume iv, New York, 1929) are good works; on the American rivalry of the British and French the *Cambridge History of the British Empire,* volume i; R. G. Thwaite's *France in America* (New York, 1905); E. Channing's *History of the United States* (volume ii, New York, 1908); W. M. Sloane's *The French War and the Revolution* (New York, 1893); A. G. Bradley's *The Fight with France for North America* (New York, n.d.); and F. Parkman's *A Half-Century of Conflict* (2 vols., Boston, 1905) and his *Montcalm and Wolfe* (2 vols., Boston, 1899) may be used to advantage; while the European diplomatic background is treated in several of the general works mentioned, and also in R. Lodge's *Great Britain and Prussia in the Eighteenth Century* (Oxford, 1923), and R. Waddington's *Louis XV et le Renversement des Alliances* (Paris, 1896). Most of these works and many of the others previously mentioned deal with the Seven Years' War. R. Waddington's *La Guerre de Sept Ans* (5 vols., Paris, 1899-1914) and A. D. Schäfer's *Geschichte des siebenjährigen Kriegs* (3 vols., Berlin, 1867-74) give continental views of the struggle. J. Corbett's *England in the Seven Years' War* (2 vols., London, 1907) is chiefly naval. K. Hotblack's "Peace of Paris" in *Trans. Royal Hist. Soc.* (third series, volume ii) is important on the peace.

CHAPTER XXIX.—SOCIETY AND RELIGION IN THE EIGHTEENTH CENTURY

Social aspects of the period are treated excellently in A. S. Turberville's *English Men and Manners in the Eighteenth Century* (Oxford, 1926); J. B. Botsford's *English Society in the Eighteenth Century* (New York, 1924); M. D. George's *England in Transition* (London, 1931); A. E. Richardson's *Georgian England* (New York, 1931); *Johnson's England, an Account of the Life and Manners of his Age,* edited by A. S. Turberville (2 vols., Oxford, 1933); scattered sections of Lecky's *History;* and Miss Bateson's brief sections in Traill's *Social England,* volume v. W. M. Thackeray's *Four Georges* (many editions) gives a humorous touch to many of the social aspects. L. Stephen's *English Literature and Society in the Eighteenth Century* (London, 1904) is the delightful work of a master of the subject. W. C. Sydney's *England and the English in the Eighteenth Century* (2 vols., New York, 1891) and T. Wright's *Caricature History of the Georges* (London, 1876) present much curious and interesting information. Chapter iii of G. O. Trevelyan's *Early History of Charles James Fox* (New York, 1880) is a brilliant description of certain aspects of social life. A. E. Dobb's *Education and Social Movements, 1700-1850* (London, 1919) is important for the interrelations of two aspects of the subject. D. A. Winstanley surveys the conditions of life at the universities in his *University of Cambridge in the Eighteenth Century* (Cambridge, 1922).

Social life is best portrayed in the literature of the time, and almost any sort will bring one into contact with some aspects of it. Two of the best for the purpose are H. Walpole's *Letters,* edited by Mrs. P. Toynbee (16 vols., Oxford, 1903-05); and Lady Mary Wortley Montagu's *Letters and Works,* edited by Lord Wharncliffe (2 vols., London, 1887). D. Defoe's *Compleat English Gentleman,* edited by K. D. Bülbring (London, 1890), is a treasure, and the works of Defoe, Swift, and Addison generally contain much of interest and value. There are several descriptions by foreign observers, of which the best is C. de Saussure's *A Foreign View of England in the Reigns of George I and George II,* edited by van Muyden (New York, 1902).

The English Church in the Eighteenth Century (London, 1887) by C. J. Abbey and J. H. Overton is a standard and an excellent work. J. H. Overton also has an interesting volume on *The Evangelical Revival in the Eighteenth Century* (London, 1900). N. Sykes's *Church and State in England in the XVIIIth Century* (Cambridge, 1934) is a valuable study. Richard Green's *John Wesley* (London, 1905) is an appreciative biography. John Wesley's *Journal* (several editions) is a human document of great interest. On rationalism, deism, and the thought of the time generally L. Stephen's *History of English Thought in the Eighteenth Century* (third ed., 2 vols., New York, 1902) is a profound and interesting study.

CHAPTER XXX.—THE KING, THE CABINET, AND THE EMPIRE

Lecky's continues to be by far the best comprehensive narrative. The works of Lord Mahon and Robertson also cover this period. W. Hunt's *History of England from the Accession of George III to the Close of Pitt's First Administration* (New York, 1905) is a useful but not particularly interesting narrative.

On English politics in this period the best studies are D. A. Winstanley's *Personal and Party Government* (Cambridge, 1910), his *Lord Chatham and the Whig Opposition* (Cambridge, 1912); L. B. Namier's *The Structure of Politics at the Accession of George III* (2 vols., London, 1929), and his *England in the Age of the American Revolution* (London, 1930), and D. G. Barnes's *George III and William Pitt, 1783-1806* (Stanford University, 1939). The last two authors present new conclusions on the relations of George III to the cabinet different from those expressed above. C. W. Alvord's *The Mississippi Valley in British Politics* (2 vols., Cleveland, 1917) contains much of value on the subject. E. Jenks's *Parliamentary England* is a good brief narrative devoted mainly to this aspect. The first chapter of G. C. Lewis's *Essays on the Administration of Great Britain* (London, 1864) gives an excellent account of the ministerial changes which took place between 1782 and 1784.

The constitutional significance of politics in relation to the cabinet is well summarized in G. B. Adams's *Constitutional History of England* (chapter xvi) and in Blauvelt's *Development of Cabinet Government in England*. T. E. May's *Constitutional History of England* (fourth ed., 3 vols., London, 1873) and H. Jephson's *The Platform: its Rise and Progress* (volume i, New York, 1892) contain much of interest and importance.

The biographies of William Pitt mentioned in the preceding section cover part of this period. To them may be added E. Fitzmaurice's important *Life of William, Earl of Shelburne* (2 vols., London, 1912) and G. O. Trevelyan's *Early History of Charles James Fox* (New York, 1886), which is fascinating, though biased in favor of the Whigs. J. Drinkwater's *Charles James Fox* (New York, 1928) is an appreciation. R. Lucas's *Lord North* (2 vols., London, 1913) is the principal biography of that statesman.

Contemporary writings which bear on the political situation abound. The following are selected for their outstanding importance or for their interest: H. Walpole's *Letters, Memoirs of the Reign of King George III* (4 vols., New York, 1894) and *Last Journals* (2 vols., London, 1910); *The Grenville Papers*, edited by W. J. Smith (4 vols., London, 1852-53); *Autobiography and Political Correspondence of Augustus Henry, third Duke of Grafton,* edited by W. R. Anson (London, 1898); *Correspondence of George the Third with North*, edited by W. B. Donne (2 vols., London, 1867); *Correspondence of King George the Third*, edited by J. Fortescue (6 vols., London, 1927-28); E. Burke, "Thoughts on the Cause of the Present Discontents," *Works* (eighth ed., volume i, Boston, 1884).

The whole story of the relations between Great Britain and the colonies is told by Lecky with sympathy for the colonies. A more recent and impartial treatment is provided by *The Cambridge History of the British Empire* (volume i, Cambridge, 1929). G. O. Trevelyan's *The American Revolution* (4 vols., London, 1903-07) and his *George III and Charles Fox* (2 vols., London, 1912-14) are biased in favor of the colonies by a strong Whig partisanship. Of the many histories of the subject written by Americans, the following are suggested as presenting the results of recent research in an interesting and authoritative manner: E. Channing's *History of the United States* (volume iii, New York, 1920), and C. H. Van Tyne's *American Revolution* (New York, 1905). Of the older histories J. Fiske's *The American Revolution* (2 vols., Boston, 1891) is one of the most interesting. S. G. Fisher's *Struggle for American Independence* (2 vols., Philadelphia, 1908) presents some original points of view. The part taken by France in the war is told by J. B. Perkins in his *France in the American Revolution* (Boston, 1911). E. S. Corwin's *French Policy and the American Alliance of 1778* (Princeton, 1916) is a brilliant study devoted particularly to the causes of French intervention.

Recently two Americans and one Englishman, all of whom have long studied the subject, have treated the causes of the Revolution in the light of the latest evidence. Their works are C. H. Van Tyne's *Causes of the*

War of Independence (Boston, 1922), C. M. Andrews's *Colonial Background of the American Revolution* (New Haven, 1924), and H. E. Egerton's *Causes and Character of the American Revolution* (Oxford, 1923). They are interesting and scholarly. W. T. Laprade presents new evidence and points of view in his "Stamp Act in British Politics," *American Historical Review*, xxxv, 735-757 (New York, 1930). On the constitutional claims of the colonists W. T. Root's *Relations of Pennsylvania with the British Government* (New York, 1912) contains much of value. C. H. McIlwain's *American Revolution* (New York, 1923) is a learned monograph which supports the colonial view. It should be compared with the first essay in R. M. Schuyler's *Parliament and the British Empire* (New York, 1929), and with A. B. Keith's *Constitutional History of the first British Empire* (Oxford, 1930). R. G. Adams's *Political Ideas of the American Revolution* (Durham, 1922) is particularly good on the contemporary points of view of the colonists. D. M. Clark's *British Opinion and the American Revolution* (New Haven, 1930) is an excellent study of that aspect of the subject.

H. E. Egerton's *Short History of British Colonial Policy* (ninth ed., London, 1932) is a convenient manual on the subject. O. M. Dickerson's *American Colonial Government, 1696-1765* (Cleveland, 1912) gives the best account of the imperial administrative system, and W. T. Root's *Relations of Pennsylvania with the British Government* is of great value on this aspect. For excellent brief descriptions, see *Cambridge History of the British Empire*, volume i, and J. T. Adams, *Revolutionary New England* (Boston, 1923). A. H. Bayse's *The Lords Commissioners of Trade and Plantations, 1748-1782* (New Haven, 1925) and L. M. Penson's *Colonial Agents of the British West Indies* (London, 1924) are good studies. On the imperial policy followed from 1754 to 1765 G. L. Beer's *British Colonial Policy, 1754-1765* (New York, 1907) is scholarly and illuminating. It deals particularly with the economic side. The imperial policy from 1763 to 1774 is treated in the works dealing with the causes of the Revolution and with the Revolution itself. To them may be added G. E. Howard's *Preliminaries of the Revolution* (New York, 1905). G. B. Hurst has an interesting chapter on English opinion of colonial questions in his *Old Colonial System* (Manchester, 1905).

CHAPTER XXXI.—THE INDUSTRIAL REVOLUTION

The change in the view of the significance of the industrial revolution produced by recent researches is summarized admirably by H. L. Beales in *History*, xiv, 125-129 (London, 1930), and by H. Heaton in *Encyclopaedia of the Social Sciences*, viii, 3-12 (New York, 1932). Good brief surveys of the movement are provided by H. L. Beales, *The Industrial Revolution* (London, 1928); A. Redford, *The Economic History of England, 1760-1860* (London, 1931); F. C. Dietz, *The Industrial Revolution* (New York, 1927); L. C. A. Knowles, *Industrial and Commercial Revolu-*

tions in Great Britain during the Nineteenth Century, part 2 (fourth ed., London, 1926); and A. P. Usher, *Introduction to the Industrial History of England*, chapters ix-xiv (Boston, 1920). The last writer is particularly good on the mechanical changes, and he has carried this aspect of the subject further in his *History of Mechanical Inventions* (New York, 1929). The two best treatments of larger scope are *The Rise of Modern Industry* by J. L. and B. Hammond (New York, 1926) and *The Industrial Revolution in the Eighteenth Century* by P. Mantoux (New York, 1928). A. Toynbee, who was the first to indicate the importance of the movement, presented his studies in *Lectures on the Industrial Revolution* (third ed., London, 1890). He confined the development to too brief a period, made the transitions at both ends appear more abrupt than they were, and portrayed the effects upon labor as worse in some respects than later research indicates that they were, but much of his treatment is still of value. H. T. Wood's *Industrial England in the Middle of the Eighteenth Century* (London, 1910) and L. W. Moffit's *England on the Eve of the Industrial Revolution* (London, 1925) are useful on the conditions preceding the revolution and its beginnings. The phases of the revolution which developed between 1820 and 1850 are treated in J. H. Clapman's *Economic History of Modern Britain: The Early Railway Age* (Cambridge, 1926). W. Bowden's *Industrial Society in England towards the End of the Eighteenth Century* (New York, 1925) is a good discussion of the early effects upon capitalists and laborers. Mr. and Mrs. Hammond have made the most extensive studies of the fortunes of the laborers during the period in *The Village Labourer, 1760-1832, The Town Labourer, 1760-1832*, and *The Skilled Labourer, 1760-1832* (London, 1911-20). P. Gaskell's *Manufacturing Population of England* (London, 1833) is worth reading because it portrays the conditions of labor so graphically, but it should be compared with recent studies. E. W. Gilboy's *Wages in Eighteenth-Century England* (Cambridge, 1934) is an important contribution to the subject. The relation of changes of population to the revolution has received recent discussion by M. C. Buer in *Health, Wealth and Population in the Early Days of the Industrial Revolution* (London, 1926) and by T. H. Marshall in his "Population Problem during the Industrial Revolution," *Economic History*, i, 429-456 (London, 1929). The latter is a keen analysis of the principal arguments and evidence in this controverted subject. Several histories of individual industries are cited under chapter xx. To them may be added S. J. Chapman, *Lancashire Cotton Industry* (Manchester, 1904); G. W. Daniels *Early English Cotton Industry* (Manchester, 1920); T. S. Ashton and J. Sykes, *The Coal Industry of the Eighteenth Century* (Manchester, 1929); and V. W. Bladen, "The Potteries in the Industrial Revolution," *Economic History*, i, 117-130 (London, 1929). The biographies of the inventors and early entrepreneurs are often highly interesting. Among the most interesting and often the most valuable are those by S. Smiles in *Industrial Biography: Iron Workers and Tool-Makers* (Boston, 1864),

Lives of Boulton and Watt (London, 1865), and *Lives of the Engineers* (4 vols., London, 1862-68). T. H. Marshall's *James Watt* (London, 1925) is a brief, non-technical biography. Another recent biographical work is *Samuel Oldknow and the Arkwrights* by G. Unwin, A. Hulme and G. Taylor (Manchester, 1924). T. S. Ashton supplies an excellent critical bibliography of the secondary works on the subject in *Economic History Review*, v, 104-119 (London, 1934).

Of the agricultural changes R. E. Prothero's *English Farming Past and Present* provides an excellent survey. On the enclosures of this period R. Curtler's *Enclosure and Redistribution of Our Land* (Oxford, 1920) provides a convenient, summary view. W. Hasbach's *History of the English Agricultural Labourer* (London, 1908); G. Slater's *The English Peasantry and the Enclosure of the Common Fields* (London, 1907); and E. C. K. Gonner's *Common Land and Enclosure* (London, 1912) are studies of a more specialized type. T. H. Marshall presents new views and evidence in "Jethro Tull and the 'New Husbandry' of the Eighteenth Century," *Economic History Review*, ii, 41-60 (London, 1930).

CHAPTER XXXII.—WILLIAM PITT THE YOUNGER

The works of Lecky, Hunt, and Robertson cover this period. Lord Rosebery's *Pitt* (London, 1891) is a brief, interesting biography, based on no extensive research. Earl Stanhope's *Life of William Pitt* (4 vols., London, 1861-62) is more comprehensive, but needs to be supplemented by modern research. J. H. Rose's *Life of William Pitt* in two volumes, called *William Pitt and the National Revival* and *William Pitt and the Great War* (New York, 1924) is probably the best biography. All of these biographies are favorable to Pitt. A more impartial study of his career is still a desideratum. F. Salomon began a life, *William Pitt der Jüngere* (volume i, Leipzig, 1906), and published other studies, but they do not constitute a complete biography.

G. C. Lewis's *Administrations of Great Britain* (London, 1864) is a series of valuable essays on the politics of the period. J. W. Fortescue's *British Statesmen of the Great War* (Oxford, 1911) provides some brilliant Tory judgments of statesmen and politics. Biographies of Henry Dundas, Pitt's friend and colleague, are supplied by H. Furber (Oxford, 1931) and C. Matheson (London, 1933). The effects of the French Revolution on the internal affairs of England are excellently treated from somewhat different points of view by W. T. Laprade in his *England and the French Revolution* (Baltimore 1909); by W. P. Hall in his *British Radicalism, 1791-1797* (New York, 1912); P. A. Brown in *The French Revolution in English History* (London, 1918); R. Birley, *The English Jacobins* (Oxford, 1924); and G. S. Veitch in his *Genesis of Parliamentary Reform* (London, 1913). H. Jephson's *The Platform* (volume i, New York, 1892) and May's *Constitutional History* are useful on liberty of opinion during the period.

W. L. Mathieson's *England in Transition, 1789-1832* (London, 1920) is an interesting study of social, economic, and intellectual developments.

Interesting contemporary glimpses of internal affairs may be found in Lord Holland's *Memoirs of the Whig Party* (2 vols., London, 1852-54); Elizabeth Lady Holland's *Journal* (i, London, 1909); and *The Windham Papers,* ed. Rosebery (2 vols., London, 1913).

The latest survey of Pitt's foreign policy is presented in the first volume of *The Cambridge History of British Foreign Policy* (New York, 1922). E. D. Adams's *Influence of Grenville on Pitt's Foreign Policy* (Washington, 1904) deals with significant aspects. J. H. Rose's two volumes are important.

Of the bountiful literature on revolutionary and Napoleonic Europe the following are selected as good introductory works: S. Mathews's *French Revolution* (New York, 1909) is brief and interesting; L. Madelin's *French Revolution* (New York, 1916) is brilliant and enjoyable, though prejudiced; and H. E. Bourne's *Revolutionary Period in Europe* (New York, 1914) is a broader and better balanced survey. The following more recent works are excellent: L. R. Gottschalk, *The Era of the French Revolution* (Boston, 1929); C. D. Hazen, *The French Revolution* (2 vols., New York, 1932); L. Gershoy, *The French Revolution and Napoleon* (New York, 1933); C. Brinton, *A Decade of Revolution, 1789-1799* (New York, 1934). A. Fournier's *Napoleon I* (second ed., 2 vols., London, 1912) and J. H. Rose's *Life of Napoleon I* (2 vols., New York, 1901) are standard biographies.

On the course of the war between England and France many of the works already cited are useful. In addition, J. W. Fortescue's *History of the British Army* (volumes iv-x, London, 1899-1910); A. T. Mahan's *Influence of Sea Power upon the French Revolution and Empire* (2 vols., Boston, 1892); and his *Life of Nelson* (second ed., Boston, 1899) are important and interesting.

Good works to consult for the French side of the story are E. Lavisse's *Histoire de France contemporaine* (volumes i-iii, Paris, 1920-21) and A. Sorel's *L'Europe et la Révolution française* (8 vols., Paris, 1889-1904).

On British control of India A. Lyall's *Rise and Expansion of British Dominion in India* (London, 1894) is still a serviceable brief guide. The results of more recent research are presented in volume iv of *Cambridge History of the British Empire* (Cambridge, 1929), which is the same as volume v of *Cambridge History of India.* C. Ilbert's *Government of India* (Oxford, 1898) contains a good brief summary of the governmental development. L. J. Trotter's *Warren Hastings* (Oxford, 1890) is a brief biography of the chief figure in Indian affairs.

J. A. Froude's *The English in Ireland* (3 vols., New York, 1873-75) and W. H. Lecky's *History of Ireland in the Eighteenth Century* (5 vols., New York, 1893) still give the best secondary accounts of the relations with Ireland in this period. J. R. Fisher's *End of the Irish Parliament*

(London, n. d.) is a convenient summary based on these two more extensive works. W. O. Morris's *Ireland* (revised ed., Cambridge, 1909) presents a briefer summary. W. H. Lecky's interesting study of the *Leaders of Public Opinion in Ireland* (New York, 1872) is devoted largely to this period. H. M. Hyde's *Rise of Castlereagh* (London, 1933) is important on the union.

CHAPTER XXXIII.—THE NAPOLEONIC ERA, 1801-1815

On the war the majority of the works cited in the previous section continue to be of service. C. Oman's *History of the Peninsular War* (5 vols., Oxford, 1902-14) is a thorough study. L. Madelin provides a good general account of the French side of affairs in this period in *Le Consulat et l'Empire* (Paris, 1932). J. Fortescue's *Wellington* (London, 1925) and P. Guedalla's *Wellington* (New York, 1931) are interesting biographies. C. K. Webster's *Congress of Vienna, 1814-1815* (Oxford, 1919) is a brief survey by a scholar thoroughly familiar with the subject. A. W. Ward's *Period of Congresses* (3 pts., London, 1919) is also an excellent brief survey. F. E. Melvin's *Napoleon's Navigation System* (University of Pennsylvania, 1909) and E. F. Heckscher's *Continental System* (Oxford, 1922) are excellent detailed studies of the continental system. Of the causes and results of the war with the United States a convenient summary with references is given by R. G. Adams in *History of the Foreign Policy of the United States* (New York, 1925).

The general history of England receives a comprehensive, well-balanced treatment in A. F. Fremantle's *England in the Nineteenth Century* (2 vols., 1801-10, New York, 1929-30). *The History of England from Addington's Administration to the Close of William IV's Reign* by G. C. Brodrick and J. K. Fotheringham (London, 1906) provides a clear narrative of political events. G. M. Trevelyan's *British History in the Nineteenth Century* (London, 1922) is a suggestive survey. C. Oman's *England in the Nineteenth Century* (London, 1917) is a convenient summary of political events.

The story of cabinets and party politics is excellently told in the works of G. C. Lewis and J. W. Fortescue already mentioned. W. Harris provides a history of *The Radical Party in Parliament* (London, 1885), but C. B. R. Kent's *English Radicals* (London, 1899) is a better treatment. E. I. Carlyle's *William Cobbett* (London, 1904) is a good biography of this radical leader. W. Reitzel's *Progress of a Plough-Boy to a Seat in Parliament as Exemplified in the History of the Life of William Cobbett* (London, 1933) is a series of extracts from Cobbett's writings which provide a connected story of his life. Other interesting contemporary glimpses of personalities and parties are given in *Windham Papers*, ed. Rosebery (2 vols., Boston, 1913); *The Creevey Papers,* edited by H. Maxwell (New York, 1904); Lord Holland's *Further Memoirs of the Whig Party* (New York, 1905). John Gore's *Creevey's Life and Times* (London, 1934) supplements *The Creevey Papers.*

On the economic and social conditions of the period W. Smart's *Economi̇ Annals of the Nineteenth Century, 1801-1820* (London, 1910) is the most thorough and the most interesting. W. Cunningham's *Growth of English Industry and Commerce in Modern Times* (Cambridge, 1917) is a good survey of the economic side. A. W. Acworth's *Financial Reconstruction in England, 1815-1822* (London, 1925) and W. F. Galpin's *Grain Supply of England during the Napoleonic Period* (New York, 1925) are excellent studies. G. Slater's *Making of Modern England* (Boston, 1914) is concerned primarily with social history. It is a suggestive treatment from a liberal point of view.

CHAPTER XXXIV.—THE END OF THE TORY RÉGIME, 1815-1830

Several narrative histories begin with 1815. J. A. R. Marriott's *England since Waterloo* (New York, 1913) is an excellent, readable narrative in a single volume. S. Walpole's *History of England from the Conclusion of the Great War in 1815* (5 vols., London, 1878-86) is the most thorough and extensive work, and it is also a delightful narrative. His judgments of men should be compared with J. W. Fortescue's *British Statesmen* and C. Alington's charming *Twenty Year's* (Oxford, 1921). É. Halévy's *History of the English People* (3 vols., New York, 1924—n.d.) covers the period from 1815 to 1841. It compares in scale and interest with Walpole's work, which it supplements but does not supersede. It is based primarily on printed sources. H. Martineau's *History of England during the Thirty Years' Peace: 1816-1846* (2 vols., London, 1849-50) is an interesting narrative written nearly contemporaneously from the liberal point of view. E. L. Woodward's *Age of Reform, 1815-1870* (Oxford, 1938) incorporates the results of recent research.

H. Jephson's *The Platform* should be consulted on the radical agitation and its repression. S. Bamford's *Passages in the Life of a Radical* (2 vols., London, 1893) and G. Wallas's *Life of Francis Place* (fourth ed., London, 1925) supply interesting contemporary views of the movement and its fundamental ideas.

Economic and social conditions are treated by the books mentioned in the preceding section. To them should be added W. Smart's *Economic Annals, 1821-1830* (London, 1917) and S. and B. Webb's *History of Trade Unionism* (second ed., London, 1920), which is authoritative and interesting. Brief surveys are provided by J. F. Rees in *Social and Industrial History of England, 1815-1918* (London, 1920) and G. H. Perris in *Industrial History of Modern England* (London, 1914). E. P. Cheyney's *Modern English Reform* (Philadelphia, 1931) is a suggestive survey of the reform movement in this and later periods.

The following treat special aspects of the Tory reforms: *legal:* T. H. Ward, *Reign of Queen Victoria,* i, pp. 281-329 (London, 1887); *fiscal:* L. Levi, *History of British Commerce,* part iii (second ed., London, 1880) and W. Huskisson's *Speeches,* volumes ii, iii (London, 1831); *repeal of the combination acts:* G. Wallas, *Life of Francis Place,* chapter viii; S. and B. Webb, *History of Trade Unionism,* chapter ii (second ed., London, 1920); G. Howell, *Labour Legislation, Labour Movements and Labour Leaders,* chapters i-vii (London, 1902); M. D. George, "The Combination Laws reconsidered," *Economic History,* i, 214-228 (London, 1929); *Catholic emancipation:* W. H. Lecky, *Leaders of Public Opinion in Ireland,* pp. 222-581; R. Dunlop, *Daniel O'Connell,* chapters i-x (New York, 1900); C. S. Parker, *Sir Robert Peel,* chapters iii, iv; Robert Peel, *Memoirs,* volume i.

On the currents of public opinion which produced the reforms A. V. Dicey's *Lectures on the Relations between Law and Public Opinion* (London, 1905) is a stimulating book. Chapter xxiv in volume x of the *Cambridge Modern History* (New York, 1907) is a good summary. W. L. Davidson's *Political Thought in England, the Utilitarians from Bentham to J. S. Mill* (London, 1915) is a brief treatise. E. Albee's *History of English Utilitarianism* (London, 1902); L. Stephen's *English Utilitarians* (3 vols., London, 1900); and É. Halévy's *Formation du Radicalisme philosophique* (3 vols., Paris, 1901-04) are all excellent on that aspect of the subject. The essence of J. S. Mill's influential views may be derived from his *Principles of Political Economy* (book iv, chapters vi, vii) and W. Cunningham's *Growth of English Industry and Commerce in Modern Times,* section 266. C. M. Atkinson has written a life of *Jeremy Bentham* (London, 1905).

S. Walpole's *Life of Spencer Perceval* (second ed., 2 vols., London, 1889) is an excellent biography. H. W. V. Temperley's *Life of Canning* (London, 1905) is the best biography of that statesman. A. Hassall's *Viscount Castlereagh* (New York, 1904) is convenient.

Interesting contemporary views are expressed in J. Bagot's *George Canning and his Friends* (2 vols., London, 1909); S. Romilly's *Memoirs* (3 vols., London, 1840); and G. C. F. Greville's *Journal of the Reigns of King George IV, King William IV and Queen Victoria* (new ed., 8 vols., London, 1888).

General works on foreign policy are R. W. Seton-Watson's *Britain in Europe, 1789-1914* (New York, 1937) and *Cambridge History of British Foreign Policy.* C. K. Webster's *Foreign Policy of Castlereagh* (London, 1925) and H. Temperley's *Foreign Policy of Canning, 1822-1827* (London, 1925) are thorough studies of importance. W. A. Phillips's *Confederation of Europe* (New York, 1914) is also an excellent study of this period.

CHAPTER XXXV.—AN EPOCH OF REFORM, 1830-1846

The general histories mentioned in the last section continue to treat the present period. Brodrick and Fotheringham's volume ends at 1837, whence the narrative is carried on to 1901 by S. Low and L. C. Sanders in their *History of England during the Reign of Victoria* (London, 1907). H. Paul's *History of Modern England* (5 vols., New York, 1904-06), which begins with 1845, is useful and entertaining. W. M. Molesworth's *History of England from the Year 1830-1874* (new ed., 3 vols., London, 1874) is an interesting contemporary narrative. G. K. Clark's *Peel and the Conservative Party* (London, 1929) is a good study of the politics of the period from 1832 to 1841. H. W. C. Davis's *Age of Grey and Peel* (Oxford, 1929) deals with men and issues rather than with events. S. Macoby's *English Radicalism, 1832-1852* (London, 1935) traces the politics of the period from the point of view of the radicals. J. L. and B. Hammond's *Age of the Chartists, 1832-1854* (London, 1930) sets the story in its social background.

From the abundant biographical literature the following are selected either for the importance of their subjects or for the significance of their contributions. Most of them are thoroughly interesting. G. M. Trevelyan, *Lord Grey of the Reform Bill* (London, 1920); A. Aspinall, *Lord Brougham and the Whig Party* (Manchester, 1927); S. J. Reid, *Life and Letters of the First Earl of Durham* (2 vols., London, 1906); C. W. New, *Lord Durham* (Oxford, 1929); S. Walpole, *Life of Lord John Russell* (2 vols., London, 1889); J. Morley, *Life of Richard Cobden* (Boston, 1881); J. A. Hobson, *Richard Cobden, the International Man* (New York, 1919); G. M. Trevelyan, *Life of John Bright* (Boston, 1913); J. R. Thursfield, *Peel* (London, 1891); A. A. W. Ramsay, *Sir Robert Peel* (London, 1928); C. S. Parker, *Sir Robert Peel* (3 vols., London, 1891-99); S. Lee, *Queen Victoria* (New York, 1903); L. Strachey, *Queen Victoria* (New York, 1921). Two standard biographies on the grand scale which begin to be useful in this period are J. Morley's *Life of Gladstone* (3 vols., London, 1903), and W. F. Monypenny's *Life of Benjamin Disraeli,* continued by G. E. Buckle (6 vols., New York, 1910-20).

Contemporary memoirs of interest and broad significance are Lord Melbourne's *Papers* (London, 1889); Robert Peel's *Memoirs* (2 vols., London, 1856); John Earl Russell's *Recollections and Suggestions* (Boston, 1875); *Early Correspondence of Lord John Russell,* edited by R. Russell (2 vols., London, 1913); *Later Correspondence of Lord John Russell* (2 vols., London, 1925); and *The Croker Papers,* edited by L. J. Jennings (2 vols., New York, 1884).

Of parliament before the reform E. Porritt's *Unreformed House of Commons* (2 vols., Cambridge, 1903) presents a thorough and an interesting study; May's *Constitutional History* (edition by Holland, i, 220-289) gives an excellent brief view; and J. Grego's *History of Parliamentary Elections* (new ed., London, 1892) contains many interesting anecdotes. W. M. Molesworth in his *History of the Reform Bill* (London, 1865) and J. A. Roebuck in his *History of the Whig Ministry of 1830* (2 vols., London, 1852) supply contemporary accounts of its passage more or less biased. J. R. M. Butler's *Passing of the Great Reform Bill* (London, 1914) is a modern impartial study. C. Seymour's *Electoral Reform in England and Wales* (New Haven, 1915) is the most thorough study of its effects.

A History of Factory Legislation (Westminster, 1903) by B. L. Hutchins and A. Harrison is an excellent study. E. Hodder's *Life and Work of the Seventh Earl of Shaftesbury* (London, 1893) deserves to be better known than it is. P. Gaskell's *Artisans and Machinery* (London, 1836) is a graphic picture of unreformed conditions by a contemporary. Mrs. S. Webb's *The Case for the Factory Acts* (New York, 1901) contains some historical information. Nothing portrays more strikingly the conditions in the factories than the evidence in the volume of *Parliamentary Papers* for 1816 entitled *Report of the Select Committee on the State of Children Employed in the Manufactures of the United Kingdom* (see, for example, pp. 20-28). *Robert Owen* is the subject of biographies by F. Podmore (London, 1924) and G. D. H. Cole (London, 1925).

G. Nicholls's *History of the English Poor Law* (3 vols., 1854-99) is the standard work. Briefer treatments are given in W. B. Odgers's *Local Government* (chapter v, second ed., London, 1907) and T. W. Fowle's *The Poor Law* (London, 1881).

Of municipal reform W. B. Munro in his *Government of European Cities* (pp. 209-229, New York, 1909) gives a good brief account. Other good treatments may be found in J. Redlich's *Local Government in England*, edited by Hirst (i, 111-133, London, 1903) and S. and B. Webb's *English Local Government* (iii, chapter xi, London, 1908). A terse summary of the conditions existing before 1835 is presented in the "First Report of Commissioners appointed to inquire into the Municipal Corporations in England and Wales," *Parliamentary Papers, 1835*, pp. 16-49.

The story of Peel's introduction of free trade is told in his biographies and memoirs already mentioned and in Morley's *Cobden*. D. G. Barnes provides the background in his *History of the English Corn Laws* (London, 1930). S. Buxton's *Finance and Politics* (i, chapters iii, iv, London, 1888) gives an excellent brief statement of the significance of Peel's budgets. C. Shaw Lefevre's *Peel and O'Connell* (London, 1887), W. H. Lecky's *Leaders of Public Opinion in Ireland* and R. Dunlop's *Daniel O'Connell* are good and interesting guides to Irish affairs after 1830.

The *Cambridge History of British Foreign Policy* sets forth the results of recent research in convenient form. H. Bulwer's *Life of Palmerston* (2 vols., Philadelphia, 1871) continued by E. Ashley (2 vols., London, 1876) is inadequate but provides many documents. H. C. F. Bell's *Lord Palmerston* (2 vols., London, 1936) is now the standard biography. It is both scholarly and entertaining. John Hall's *England and the Orleans Monarchy* (New York, 1912) is important on relations with France.

J. F. Driault's *La Question d'Orient* (third ed., Paris, 1905) is a capital survey of the eastern question. J. A. R. Marriott's *Eastern Question* (Oxford, 1918); F. Schevill's *History of the Balkan Peninsula* (New York, 1922); W. S. Davis's *Short History of the Near East* (New York, 1922); and W. Miller's *Ottoman Empire, 1801-1913* (Cambridge, 1913) also present good résumés of the subject. H. L. Hoskins explains some aspects of

Britain's interest in the problem in *British Routes to India* (New York, 1928).

H. E. Egerton's *Short History of British Colonial Policy* and the second volume of the *Cambridge History of the British Empire* survey the policies of the period discussed above. H. Merivale's *Lectures on Colonization* (London, 1861) is still valuable, and W. P. Morrell's *British Colonial Policy in the Age of Peel and Russell* (Oxford, 1930) is a good recent study. E. Porritt's *Fiscal and Diplomatic Freedom of the British Oversea Dominions* (Oxford, 1922) contains much of value on colonial policies. For the government see H. T. Manning, *The British Colonial Government after the American Revolution, 1782-1820* (New Haven, 1933). Contemporary views with regard to the empire are explained by R. Coupland, *American Revolution and the British Empire* (London, 1930), P. Knaplund, *Gladstone and Britain's Imperial Policy* (New York, 1927) and C. A. Bodelson, *Studies in Mid-Victorian Imperialism* (New York, 1924). Lord Durham's *Report* (London, 1902) is of fundamental importance on the establishment of responsible government, and W. P. M. Kennedy's *Constitution of Canada* (Oxford, 1922) contains a brief account of its establishment in Canada.

The comprehensive work on the history of the empire is the *Cambridge History of the British Empire* (8 vols., 7 published, New York, 1929-40). P. Knaplund's *The British Empire, 1815-1939* (New York, 1941) is the most comprehensive brief history of the modern period and A. P. Newton's *A Hundred Years of the British Empire* (New York, 1940) is also excellent. Brief accounts of the expansion of the empire are H. E. Egerton's *Origin and Growth of Greater Britain* (Oxford, n. d.) and W. H. Woodward's *Short History of the Expansion of the British Empire* (sixth ed., Cambridge, 1931). C. Wittke's *History of Canada* (revised ed., New York, 1933) and E. Jenks's *History of the Australasian Colonies* (third ed., Cambridge, 1912) are good short histories.

On Chartism R. S. Gammage's *History of the Chartist Movement* (London, 1894); M. Hovell's *The Chartist Movement* (Manchester, 1918); E. Dolléans, *Le Chartisme* (Paris, 1912); J. West, *History of the Chartist Movement* (London, 1920); P. W. Slosson, *Decline of the Chartist Movement* (New York, 1916); and B. F. Rosenblatt, *Social and Economic Aspects of the Chartist Movement* (New York, 1916) may be consulted.

W. L. Mathieson's *English Church Reform* (New York, 1923) is an excellent study of that movement. R. W. Church's *Oxford Movement* (London, 1891) is an account of the movement by a participant, and S. L. Ollard's *Short History of the Oxford Movement* (London, 1915) is the work of a sympathetic student of a later generation.

CHAPTER XXXVI.—AFFAIRS CHIEFLY FOREIGN AND IMPERIAL, 1846-1865

Many of the works cited in the previous chapter cover the period of the present chapter also. S. Walpole's *History of England* is continued in his

History of Twenty-five Years (4 vols., London, 1904-08). J. F. Bright's *History of England, Period IV, 1837-1880* (New York, 1888) is a convenient annalistic compilation. H. Cox's *Whig and Tory Administrations, 1855-1868* (London, 1868) is still useful.

In addition to the biographies and memoirs noted in the last chapter the following are particularly good for one reason or another: Earl of Malmesbury, *Memoirs of an Ex-Minister* (3 vols., Leipzig, 1885); E. Fitzmaurice, *Life of Earl Granville* (2 vols., London, 1905-06); Lord Stanmore, *A Memoir of Sidney Herbert* (2 vols., 1906); C. S. Parker, *Life and Letters of Sir James Graham* (2 vols., London, 1907); *Letters of Queen Victoria, 1837-1861,* second series, *1862-1878,* ed. by A. C. Benson and Viscount Esher (5 vols., London, 1907-26); *The Diaries of John Bright,* ed. by P. Bright (London, 1930); and *Gladstone and Palmerston, being the Correspondence of Lord Palmerston with Mr. Gladstone, 1851-1865,* ed. by P. Guedalla (New York, 1928).

A. W. Kinglake's *Invasion of the Crimea* (6 vols., New York, 1868-99) is the most extensive history of the Crimean War, but it is partisan and makes many errors. S. Lane-Poole's *Life of Stratford Canning* (2 vols., 1868) explains some of the most important diplomatic transactions that preceded the war. A good explanation of the immediate causes is B. Schmitt's "Diplomatic Preliminaries of the Crimean War," *Am. Hist. Rev.* (xxv, 36-57); new views are presented by V. J. Puryear in *England, Russia and the Straits Question, 1844-1856* (Berkeley, 1931); and the most thorough study of the background is H. Temperley's *England and the Near East: the Crimea* (New York, 1936). B. K. Martin's *Triumph of Lord Palmerston* (New York, 1924) is an interesting study of the influence of British public opinion upon the entry of Great Britain into the war. Good brief accounts of the Near-Eastern question are cited in the previous section. A French view of the immediate diplomatic background is presented by A. Debidour in his *Histoire diplomatique de l'Europe* (volume ii, Paris, 1891).

J. F. Rhodes in his *History of the United States,* iv, chapter xxii (New York, 1899) and W. A. Dunning in his *British Empire and the United States* (New York, 1919) set forth the seasoned views of American scholars with regard to the relations between Great Britain and the United States. E. D. Adams's *Great Britain and the American Civil War* (2 vols., New York, 1925) is a more thorough study.

On the history of British India the *Cambridge History of India* (volumes v, vi, same as volumes iv, v of *Cambridge History of the British Empire*) is a standard manual. A. Lyall's *Rise of British Dominion in India* is a good brief survey, and V. A. Smith's *Oxford History of India* (Oxford, 1919) is of similar scope. They may be supplemented by L. J. Trotter's *History of India under Queen Victoria from 1836 to 1880* (2 vols., London, 1886). W. H. Hutton's *Marquess of Wellesley* (Oxford, 1893) and W. W. Hunter's *Marquess of Dalhousie* (Oxford, 1895) are good brief biographies.

A standard history of the mutiny is T. R. Holmes's *History of the Indian Mutiny* (fifth ed., London, 1913). G. W. Forrest's *History of the Indian Mutiny* (3 vols., Edinburgh, 1904-12) is more detailed. On the changes in government C. Ilbert's *Government of India* (second ed., Oxford, 1907) is an authoritative manual.

CHAPTER XXXVII.—GLADSTONE AND DISRAELI, 1865-1885

Most of the narratives and some of the biographies mentioned in the last three sections continue to be useful. Particularly important are Morley's *Gladstone* and Monypenny and Buckle's *Disraeli*. Morley's work is supplemented by Viscount Gladstone's *After Thirty Years* (London, 1928) and P. Guedalla's *The Queen and Mr. Gladstone* (New York, 1934). R. C. K. Ensor's *England, 1870-1914* (Oxford, 1936) is now the best general treatment of the period. The fifth volume of Bright's *History of England* is a well-balanced narrative of the principal events from 1880 to 1901. R. H. Gretton's *History of England, 1880-1910* (2 vols., Boston, 1913) is useful but discursive. H. E. Gorst's *The Fourth Party* (London, 1906) throws much light on party politics. Additional biographies and memoirs which contain much valuable material are *Letters of Queen Victoria, Second Series,* edited by G. E. Buckle (2 vols., London, 1926); G. Cecil's *Life of Robert, Marquis of Salisbury* [to 1892] (4 vols., London, 1921-32); A. Lang's *Life, Letters, and Diaries of Sir Stafford Northcote* (2 vols., Edinburgh, 1890); W. Churchill's *Lord Randolph Churchill* (2 vols., London, 1906); Syed Sirdar Ali Khan's *Life of Lord Morley* (London, 1923); B. Holland's *Life of Spencer Compton, eighth Duke of Devonshire* (2 vols., London, 1911); Viscount Morley's *Recollections* (2 vols., New York, 1917); A. G. Gardiner's *Life of Sir William Harcourt* (2 vols., London, 1923); J. L. Garvin's *Life of Joseph Chamberlain* (to 1900, 3 vols., London, 1932-34); B. E. C. Dugdale's *Arthur James Balfour* (2 vols., New York, 1937); and S. Lee's *King Edward VII* (volume i, New York, 1925). Recent estimates of Gladstone and Disraeli are O. Burdett's *Gladstone* (London, 1927), E. Clarke's *Benjamin Disraeli* (New York, 1926), M. Maurois's *Disraeli* translated by Miles (London, 1927), and W. P. Hall's *Mr. Gladstone* (New York, 1931).

On parliamentary reform G. L. Dickinson's *Development of Parliament during the Nineteenth Century* (London, 1895) is a brilliant essay. F. E. Gillespie's *Labor and Politics in England, 1850-1867* (Durham, 1927) traces the political activities of labor, particularly in relation to parliamentary reform. H. Cox's *History of the Reform Bills of 1866 and 1867* (London, 1868) is a useful contemporary account, and J. H. Park's *English Reform Bill of 1867* (New York, 1920) is a recent study. Seymour's study (above) is important, Holland's continuation of May's *Constitutional History* is good, and S. Walpole's *The Electorate and the Legislature* (London, 1892) is a convenient brief survey.

On the constitution and the government A. L. Lowell's *Government of England* (2 vols., New York, 1910) is a brilliant and comprehensive treatise.

W. Bagehot's *English Constitution* (revised ed., New York, 1908) is a stimulating study of cabinet government as a working machine, and A. V. Dicey's *Introduction to the Study of the Law of the Constitution* (third ed., London, 1889) is equally interesting on the legal aspects. On the relations of the cabinet to the queen they should be supplemented by F. Hardie's *Political Influence of Queen Victoria, 1861-1901* (Oxford, 1935). The development of parties is best told in M. Ostrogorski's *Democracy and the Organization of Political Parties* (volume i, New York, 1902).

On Ireland L. Paul-Dubois's *Contemporary Ireland* (London, 1908) is readable and impartial. E. R. Turner's *Ireland and England* (New York, 1919) is a convenient summary. On the land problem see J. E. Pomfret's *The Struggle for Land in Ireland, 1800-1923* (Princeton, 1930).

The development of labor and trade unions is traced by G. D. H. Cole in his *Short History of the British Working Class Movement* (3 vols., New York, 1927) and S. and B. Webb in *The History of Trade Unionism* (new ed., New York, 1920).

The Cambridge History of British Foreign Policy is a brief guide. P. Knaplund's *Gladstone's Foreign Policy* (New York, 1935) is an excellent study based in part upon unprinted documents. G. P. Gooch's *History of Europe, 1878-1919* (New York, 1923) and J. A. Spender's *Fifty Years of Europe* (second ed., London, 1936) are good, general guides on international relations. They are supplemented by W. L. Langer's more intensive and thorough *European Alliances and Alignments, 1871-1890* (New York, 1931). In this period the documents of the German foreign office published in *Die grosse Politik* become of fundamental importance. Many of them have been translated by E. T. S. Dugdale in *German Diplomatic Documents, 1871-1914* (4 vols., New York, 1928-31). A Commission de Publication des Documents relatifs aux Origines de la Guerre de 1914 of the Ministère des Affaires étrangères is now publishing *Documents diplomatiques français, 1871-1914* (Paris, 1929-). R. W. Seton-Watson's *Disraeli, Gladstone and the Eastern Question* (London, 1935) is a thorough study. Other studies useful on the eastern question are M. W. Tyler's *The European Powers and the Near East, 1875-1908* (Minneapolis, 1925) and D. E. Lee's *Great Britain and the Cyprus Convention Policy of 1878* (Cambridge, 1934). On relations with Germany see W. O. Aydelotte, *Bismarck and British Colonial Policy: The Problem of South West Africa, 1883-1885* (Philadelphia, 1937) and R. S. Sontag, *Germany and England: Background of Conflict* (New York, 1938).

The best introductory survey of the part played by imperialism in the international relations of Europe is P. T. Moon's *Imperialism and World Politics* (New York, 1927). M. E. Townsend's *Rise and Fall of Germany's Colonial Empire, 1884-1918* (New York, 1930) is excellent, and J. Darcy's *France et Angleterre: Cent Années de Rivalité coloniale* (Paris, 1904) is still useful. General surveys of Great Britain's part in the partition of Africa are given in E. Sanderson's *Great Britain in Modern Africa* (London, 1907);

J. S. Keltie's *Partition of Africa* (second ed., London, 1895); H. H. Johnston's *History of the Colonization of Africa* (Cambridge, 1913); and C. P. Lucas's *Partition and Colonization of Africa* (Oxford, 1922). L. Woolf deals with the conflicting interests of the powers in his *Empire and Commerce in Africa* (New York, 1920), and N. D. Harris summarizes the development of European control of Africa in his *Europe and Africa* (Boston, 1927). Lord Cromer's *Modern Egypt* (2 vols., New York, 1916) and Viscount Milner's *England in Egypt* (London, 1892) are authoritative and interesting works. On other parts of Africa the following may be recommended: P. L. McDermott, *British East Africa* (second ed., London, 1895); C. Eliot, *The East African Protectorate* (London, 1905); M. Kingsley, *The Story of West Africa* (London, 1899); E. D. Morel, *Nigeria* (London, 1911); A. C. Burns, *History of Nigeria* (London, 1929); R. I. Lovell, *The Struggle for South Africa, 1875-1899* (New York, 1934); and E. A. Walker, *A History of South Africa* (2nd ed., New York, 1939). B. Williams provides an impartial biography of *Cecil Rhodes* (London, 1921).

On the federation of Canada C. Wittke's *History of Canada* (revised ed., New York, 1933) and W. P. M. Kennedy's *Constitution of Canada* (Oxford, 1922) may be consulted.

CHAPTER XXXVIII.—THE GROWTH OF IMPERIALISM, 1885-1905

With this period the recent works of J. A. R. Marriott, *Modern England (1885-1932), a History of my Own Times* (London, 1934) and J. A. Spender, *Great Britain, Empire and Commonwealth, 1886-1935* (London, n. d.) become important guides. The two volumes of the epilogue of É. Halévy's *Histoire du Peuple anglais au XIXe Siècle* (Paris, 1926-32) begin with 1895. The first volume has been translated. Significant biographies and memoirs which have not been mentioned previously are J. A. Spender and C. Asquith, *Life of Asquith* (2 vols., London, 1932); Marquess of Crewe, *Lord Rosebery* (New York, 1931); Lord Newton, *Lord Lansdowne* (London, 1929); and *The Letters of Queen Victoria, third series, 1886-1901* (3 vols., New York, 1930-32).

On Irish home rule the following may be mentioned in addition to the works on Ireland cited in the previous section. A. V. Dicey's *England's Case Against Home Rule* (London, 1887) is a moderate presentation of the arguments of the opposition. M. MacDonagh's *Home Rule Movement* (Dublin, 1920) is a brief historical treatment by an Irishman, and E. Barker's *Ireland in the Last Fifty Years* (second ed., Oxford, 1919) is a briefer survey of a broader scope by an Englishman.

Some of the works on foreign and imperial policies cited in the preceding section cover this period as well. The *British Documents on the Origins of the War, 1898-1914*, edited by G. P. Gooch and H. Temperley (11 vols., London, 1926-   ) are of primary importance. A. F. Pribram's *England and the International Policy of the European Powers, 1871-1914* (Oxford, 1931) is a brief interpretative sketch. Good general treatments of

European diplomatic relations of the period are E. Brandenburg's *From Bismarck to the World War* (London, 1927); J. A. Spender's *Fifty Years of Europe* (London, 1933); and W. I. Langer's *The Diplomacy of Imperialism* (2 vols., New York, 1935). Various aspects of British relations with Germany are treated by J. V. Fuller, *Bismarck's Diplomacy at its Zenith* (Cambridge, 1922); O. Hammann, *The World Policy of Germany* (New York, 1927); R. J. S. Hoffman, *Great Britain and the German Trade Rivalry, 1875-1914* (Philadelphia, 1933); G. P. Gooch on Holstein in his *Studies in Modern History* (London, 1931); and E. M. Earle, *Turkey, the Great Powers and the Bagdad Railway* (New York, 1924). The following are good German treatments of the negotiations of 1898-1901: W. Becker, *Fürst Bülow und England, 1897-1909* (Bamberg, 1929); G. Ritter, *Die Legende von der verschmähten englischen Freundschaft, 1898-1901* (Freiburg, 1929); W. Löding, *Die deutsch-englischen Bündnisverhandlungen, 1898 bis 1901* (Hamburg, 1929); and H. von Hoyningen genannt Huene, *Untersuchungen zur Geschichte des deutsch-englischen Bündnisproblems, 1898-1901* (Breslau, 1934). Baron von Eckardstein's *Ten Years at the Court of St. James'* (London, 1921) should be used with caution. On the Sudan M. B. Giffen's *Fashoda* (Chicago, 1930) is a thorough study. For French views see C. de Freycinet, *La Question d'Égypte* (Paris, 1905) and J. Cocheris, *La Situation internationale de l'Egypte et du Soudan* (Paris, 1903). British policy in the Far East may be gleaned from the following: R. S. McCordock, *British Far Eastern Policy, 1894-1900* (New York, 1931); P. Joseph, *Foreign Diplomacy in China, 1894-1900* (London, 1928); H. B. Morse and H. F. MacNair, *Far Eastern International Relations* (Boston, 1931); and H. M. Vinacke, *History of the Far East in Modern Times* (fourth ed., New York, 1942).

Good short accounts of imperial development may be found in J. A. Williamson, *Short History of British Expansion* (London, 1922) and H. Robinson, *Development of the British Empire* (Boston, 1922). More comprehensive surveys are given by the *Cambridge History of the British Empire* and C. P. Lucas in his *Historical Geography of the British Colonies* (7 vols., Oxford, 1906-25). *The Economic Development of the British Overseas Empire* (London, 1924) by L. C. A. Knowles relates mainly to the last century. W. P. Hall's *Empire to Commonwealth* (New York, 1928) is an excellent survey which begins in this period. H. Jenkyns's *British Rule and Jurisdiction beyond the Seas* (Oxford, 1902) is a standard constitutional manual for the period and A. B. Keith's *Responsible Government in the Dominions* (2nd ed., 2 vols., Oxford, 1912) is a more comprehensive treatise. In addition to the works on British colonies in Africa cited above, the following are useful for this period: H. M. Hole, *The Making of Rhodesia* (London, 1926); H. Johnston, *Uganda Protectorate* (2 vols., New York, 1902); L. Wolf, *Life of the First Marquess of Ripon* (2 vols., London, 1927); W. B. Worsfold, *Reconstruction of the New Colonies under Lord Milner* (2 vols., London, 1913). On Australia the following may be consulted: E. Scott, *Short History of Australia* (fourth ed., London, 1926); G. W. Rusden, *History of Australia* (3 vols., 1908); and R. B. Wise, *Making of the Australian Commonwealth, 1889-1900* (London, 1913).

On the development of imperial ideas in Great Britain in the closing years of the nineteenth century R. Jebb's *Britannic Question* (New York, 1913) is a stimulating little book. Other good works are G. R. Parkin's *Imperial Federation* (1913); L. S. Amery's *Union and Strength* (New York, n. d.); J. A. Hobson's *Imperialism* (London, 1905); A. B. Silburn's *Colonies and Imperial Defense* (London, 1909); J. D. Rees's *Current Political Problems* (New York, n. d.), and C. E. T. Stuart-Linton's *Problem of Empire Governance* (London, 1912). A. B. Keith treats the constitutional issues involved in his *Imperial Unity and the Dominions* (Oxford, 1916).

The reforms in local government are treated by Redlich and Hirst, *Local Government in England;* W. B. Odgers, *Local Government;* and A. Shaw, *Municipal Government in Great Britain* (New York, 1895).

CHAPTER XXXIX.—OTHER PHASES OF ENGLISH LIFE AND THOUGHT IN THE NINETEENTH CENTURY

A good brief survey of the economic development is provided by F. C. Dietz in his *Industrial Revolution*, a satisfactory fuller treatment is L. C. A. Knowles' *Industrial and Commercial Revolutions in Great Britain during the Nineteenth Century*, and the most thorough study is J. H. Clapham's *Economic History of Modern Britain* which extends to 1886. Other convenient volumes on the subject are A. P. Usher, *Introduction to the Industrial History of England;* C. R. Fay, *Great Britain from Adam Smith to the Present Day* (London, 1928); C. M. Waters, *Economic History of England, 1066-1874* (Oxford, 1925); and G. H. Perris, *Industrial History of Modern England* (second impression, London, 1920). To the works on special topics cited previously may be added E. A. Pratt, *History of Inland Transport and Communication in England* (London, 1912); W. T. Jackman, *Development of Transportation in Modern England* (2 vols., Cambridge, 1916); E. C. Stevens, *English Railways: their Development and their Relations to the State* (London, 1915); R. J. Cornewall Jones, *The British Merchant Service* (London, 1898); J. Kennedy, *The History of Steam Navigation* (1903); H. W. Macrosty, *The Trust Movement in British Industry* (London, 1907).

To the several works on social development which have been mentioned in earlier sections should be added *Early Victorian England, 1830-1865*, edited by G. M. Young (2 vols., Oxford, 1934); O. F. Christie's *Transition from Aristocracy, 1832-1867* (New York, 1928); and Ensor's illuminating chapters on the subject. The last volume of Traill's *Social England* is less useful than some of its predecessors.

The following deal with aspects of religious development and thought: C. S. Carpenter, *Church and People, 1789-1889* (London, 1933); H. C. G.

Moule, *The Evangelical School in the Church of England* (London, 1901); A. W. Harrison, B. A. Barber, G. C. Hornby and E. T. Davis, *The Methodist Church, Its Origin, Divisions and Re-union* (London, 1932); A. Peel, *These Hundred Years: A Centenary History of the Congregational Union of England and Wales, 1831-1931* (London, 1931); J. M. Robertson, *A History of Free Thought in the Nineteenth Century* (2 vols., London, 1929); and V. F. Starr, *Development of English Theology in the Nineteenth Century* (1913). On the Oxford Movement see above, p. 880.

Osgood's *Voice of England* is an interesting brief survey of the literature, and the *Cambridge History of English Literature* provides a fuller treatment. Both have bibliographies. The following are a few of the more recent critical treatments of the literature of the nineteenth century: E. Bernbaum, *Guide through the Romantic Movement* (New York, 1930); F. E. Pierce, *Currents and Eddies in the English Romantic Movement* (New Haven, 1918); H. Walker, *The Literature of the Victorian Era* (New York, 1921); O. Elton, *A Survey of English Literature, 1780-1880* (4 vols., London, 1924); A. H. Thorndike, *Literature in a Changing Age* (New York, 1920); S. T. Williams, *Studies in Victorian Literature* (New York, 1923); J. W. Cunliffe, *English Literature during the Last Half Century* (New York, 1919); C. Weygandt, *A Century of the English Novel* (New York, 1925); D. Cecil, *Early Victorian Novelists* (New York, 1935); E. A. Baker, *The History of the English Novel* (volumes vi-viii, London, 1935-37); B. I. Evans, *English Poetry in the Later Nineteenth Century* (London, 1933).

D. C. Somervell deals briefly with the thought of some of the writers in his *English Thought in the Nineteenth Century* (New York, 1929), and R. H. Murray at greater length in his *Studies in the English Social and Political Thinkers of the Nineteenth Century* (2 vols., Cambridge, 1929). C. Brinton makes a thorough study of the *Political Ideas of the English Romanticists* (Oxford, 1926), and carries the history of political thought through the whole period in his *English Political Thought in the Nineteenth Century* (London, 1933). J. Holbrook's *Eighteen Nineties* deals with the last decade of the century.

Of the general histories of science W. D. D. Dampier-Whetham's *History of Science and Its Relations with Philosophy and Religion* (New York, 1929) is one of the most suggestive. The treatment of the nineteenth century in *A Short History of Science* by W. T. Sedgwick and H. W. Tyler (New York, 1917) is briefer, but it makes the salient aspects stand out. Its bibliographies include histories of individual sciences and scientists. R. J. Harvey-Gibson's *Two Thousand Years of Science* (second ed., London, 1931) is less comprehensive than Dampier-Whetham's survey, but it clarifies what it treats. J. T. Merz's *History of European Thought in the Nineteenth Century* (4 vols., Edinburgh, 1914-23) is a good synthesis. Traill's *Social England* is useful for the part taken by British scientists to 1885.

CHAPTER XL.—THE ROADS TO UTOPIA AND ARMAGEDDON

Many works cited in chapters xxxvii and xxxviii continue to be of value for this period. J. A. Farrer's *England under Edward VII* (London, 1922) is a good survey of the reign. D. C. Somervell's *Reign of King George the Fifth* (London, n. d.) not only deals with the events but also explains the contemporary views of them.

C. Hayes's *British Social Politics* (Boston, 1913), which consists of extensive extracts from parliamentary speeches and other documents, provides interesting information about the liberal reforms. P. Alden's *Democratic England* (New York, 1912) discusses the principal reforms from the point of view of a liberal. F. A. Ogg's *Economic Development of Modern Europe* (New York, 1917) and his *Social Progress in Contemporary Europe* (New York, 1912) contain good summaries of British social reforms. A. P. Usher's *Introduction to the Industrial History of England* (Boston, 1920) treats some of them briefly and excellently. H. Beer's *History of British Socialism* (2 vols., London, 1919) is a standard work on the subject.

On special aspects of the social reforms the following may be suggested: V. S. Clark's "Woman and Child Wage-Earners in Great Britain" in *United States Bureau of Labor, Bulletin* (no. 80, 1909, pp. 1-87), which is a valuable exposition of the laws regulating the hours and conditions of labor; C. Black's *Sweated Industry* (London, 1907); Porritt's "British National Insurance Act" in *Political Science Quarterly* (June, 1912, pp. 260-280); and E. Dewsnup's *Housing Problem in England* (Manchester, 1907). The rural problem is treated by F. E. Green in his *History of the English Agricultural Labourer, 1870-1920* (London, 1920).

On the reform of the house of lords the third volume of May's *Constitutional History,* edited by Holland, and A. L. P. Dennis's "Impressions of British Party Politics, 1909-1911" and "The Parliament Act of 1911" in *Am. Pol. Sci. Rev.* (volumes v, vi, 1911-12) may be consulted.

The following biographical or autobiographical material is important and interesting: S. Lee, *King Edward VII* (volume ii, New York, 1927); J. A. Spender, *Life of Sir Henry Campbell-Bannerman* (2 vols., London, 1923); G. M. Trevelyan, *Grey of Fallodon* (Boston, 1937); H. Nicolson, *Sir Arthur Nicolson, Bart., first Lord Carnock* (London, 1930); Earl of Oxford and Asquith, *Fifty Years of British Parliament* (2 vols., Boston, 1926) and *Memories and Reflections, 1852-1927* (2 vols., Boston, 1928); Viscount Haldane, *An Autobiography* (New York, 1929); Viscount Snowden, *Autobiography* (2 vols., London, 1934-35); *Journals and Letters of Viscount Esher,* edited by M. V. Brett (2 vols., London, 1934); W. S. Blunt, *My Diaries* (2 vols., New York, 1922); *Diary of Lord Bertie of Thame, 1914-1918,* edited by H. G. Lennox (2 vols., New York, 1925); G. Buchanan, *My Mission to Russia* (2 vols., Boston, 1923).

S. B. Fay's *Origins of the World War* (2 vols., New York, 1928) is an impartial and scholarly guide to the international relations of the period.

G. L. Dickinson's *International Anarchy, 1904-1914* (New York, 1926) presents keen judgments. B. E. Schmitt's "Triple Alliance and Triple Entente, 1902-1914" in *American Historical Review,* xxix, 449-473 (New York, 1924) is a useful brief survey, and his *Coming of the War, 1914* (2 vols., New York, 1930) is a thorough study of the diplomacy immediately preceding the war. Writings by English statesmen who had a part in the events are H. H. Asquith's *Genesis of the War* (London, 1923); W. S. Churchill's *The World Crisis, 1911-1918* (4 vols., New York, 1923-27); Viscount Haldane's *Before the War* (London, 1920); and Grey of Fallodon, *Twenty-five Years* (2 vols., New York, 1925). A German criticism of the last is presented by H. Lutz in *Lord Grey and the World War* (New York, 1928). Earl Loreburn's *How the War Came* (London, 1918) is an early English criticism of Grey's policies. To the documentary publications previously noted should be added *Un Livre noir, 1910-1916* (Russian documents, 3 vols., Paris, n. d.); B. von Siebert and C. A. Schreiner, *Entente Diplomacy and the World War* (Russian, New York, 1921); *Oesterreich-Ungarns Aussenpolitik von der bosnischen Krise 1908 bis zum Kriegsausbruch 1914* (9 vols., 1930). Some significant memoirs of foreign statesmen are Fürst von Bülow, *Memoirs* (2 vols., Boston, 1931); T. von Bethmann-Holwegg, *Betrachtung zum Weltkriege* (2 vols., Berlin, 1919-22), translated in part as *Reflections on the World War;* Admiral von Tirpitz, *My Memoirs* (2 vols., New York, 1919); Wilhelm II, *The Kaiser's Memoirs* (New York, 1922); S. D. Sazonoff, *Fateful Years, 1909-1916* (London, 1928); K. M. Lichnowsky, *My Mission to London, 1912-1914* (New York, 1918); R. Poincaré, *The Origins of the War* (London, 1922) and *Au Service de la France* (10 vols., Paris, 1926-33). Two French treatments of the background of the war are E. Bourgeois and G. Pagès, *Les Origines et les Responsabilités de la grande Guerre* (second ed., Paris, 1922) and E. Renouvin, *The Immediate Origins of the War* (New Haven, 1928); two German are M. Montgelas, *The Case for the Central Powers* (New York, 1925) and T. Wolff, *The Eve of 1914* (New York, 1936). Studies of special subjects are E. N. Anderson, *The First Moroccan Crisis, 1904-1906* (Chicago, 1930); J. Caillaux, *Agadir* (Paris, 1919); E. L. Woodward, *Great Britain and the German Navy* (Oxford, 1935); B. E. Schmitt, *The Annexation of Bosnia* (Cambridge, 1937); and E. C. Helmreich, *The Diplomacy of the Balkan Wars, 1912-1913* (Cambridge, 1938).

A good history of the war in a single volume is C. R. M. F. Cruttwell's *A History of the Great War, 1914-1918* (Oxford, 1934). An official *History of the Great War Based on Official Documents* is still in course of publication. It is divided into the following sections: *Official Military History of the War* by J. E. Edmonds; *Naval Operations* by J. S. Corbett and H. Newbolt; *Seaborne Trade* by C. E. Fayle; *The Merchant Navy* by A. Hurd; and *The War in the Air* by W. Raleigh and H. A. Jones. The Carnegie Endowment is publishing an extensive *Economic and Social History*

History of England

of the World War by many scholars in many volumes. The following biographical or autobiographical materials are important for the English part in the war: D. Lloyd George, *War Memoirs* (5 vols., Boston, 1933-37); H. Wilson, *Life and Diaries,* edited by C. E. Callwell (2 vols., New York, 1927); E. G. F. French, *Life of Field-Marshal Sir John French, First Earl of Ypres* (London, 1931); D. Cooper, *Haig* (2 vols., London, 1935). Among the memoirs of foreign commanders are J. J. C. Joffre, *Personal Memoirs* (2 vols., New York, 1932); Foch, *Mémoires pour servir à l'Histoire de la Guerre de 1914-1918* (2 vols., Paris, 1931); E. von Ludendorff, *Ludendorff's Own Story* (2 vols., New York, 1919); P. von Hindenburg, *Out of My Life* (new ed., London, 1933); C. von Hötzendorf, *Aus meiner Dienstzeit, 1906-1918* (5 vols., Wien, 1922-25). An excellent survey of Great Britain's internal organization for the purpose of war is given by H. L. Gray in his *War Time Control of Industry: The Experience of England* (New York, 1918).

Current bibliographies on international affairs in this period and the next may be found in *Foreign Affairs.*

CHAPTER XLI.—INTERNAL AND IMPERIAL DEVELOPMENTS, 1918-1944

Narrative histories, biographies and works on special topics cited in previous chapters cover a large part of the present period. The narrative of recent years can be followed in *The Annual Register.* A. Hutt's *The Post-War History of the British Working Class* (New York, 1938) is a good account of that aspect of the subject.

The chapters added by R. L. Schuyler to the revised edition of G. B. Adams's *Constitutional History* (New York, 1934) constitute a thoughtful survey of recent constitutional developments. Descriptions of the government are given by R. Muir, *How Britain Is Governed* (New York, 1930); F. A. Ogg, *English Government and Politics* (New York, 1929); R. K. Gooch, *The Government of England* (New York, 1937); W. I. Jennings, *Cabinet Government* (Cambridge, 1936) and *The British Constitution* (Cambridge, 1941); and A. B. Keith, *The British Cabinet, 1830-1938* (London, 1939). On special aspects see C. K. Allen, *Bureaucracy Triumphant* (Oxford, 1931); Lord Hewart, *The New Despotism* (New York, 1929); H. Finer, *The British Civil Service* (London, 1927) and *English Local Government* (New York, 1934).

Aspects of economic developments are treated by C. Day, *Economic Development in Modern Europe* (New York, 1933); J. P. Day, *An Introduction to World Economic History since the Great War* (London, 1940), and J. H. Richardson, *British Economic Foreign Policy* (New York, 1936). The following deal with the economic and social topics indicated by their titles: F. Morley, *Unemployment Relief in Great Britain* (London, 1924); R. C. Davison, *The Unemployed* (London, 1929) and *British Unemployment Policy: The Modern Phase since 1930* (New York, 1938); H. F.

Hohman, *The Development of Social Insurance and Minimum Wage Legislation in Great Britain* (Boston, 1933); R. Graves and A. Hodge, *The Long Week End: A British Social History, 1918-1939* (New York, 1941); W. Beveridge, *Social Insurance and Allied Services* (London, 1942).

W. A. Phillips's *The Revolution in Ireland, 1906-1923* (London, 1923) is a good treatment of the subject. Other works on Ireland are D. Figgis, *The Irish Constitution* (Dublin, 1922); L. Kohn, *The Constitution of the Irish Free State* (London, 1932); D. R. Gwynn, *The Irish Free State, 1922-1927* (London, 1928). A. W. Bromage explains the treaty of 1938 in "Anglo-Irish Accord," *Political Science Quarterly,* liii (1938), 516-32.

The following deal with various phases of the recent history of India: E. A. Horne, *Political System of British India* (Oxford, 1922); C. Ilbert, *Government of India* (Oxford, 1922); V. Chirol, *India Old and New* (London, 1921) and *India* (New York, 1926); E. J. Thompson, *Reconstructing India* (New York, 1930); E. J. Thompson and G. T. Garratt, *Rise and Fulfillment of British Rule in India* (New York, 1934); V. Anstey, *The Economic Development of India* (third ed., London, 1936); G. N. Joshi, *The New Constitution of India* (London, 1937); W. R. Smith, *Nationalism and Reform in India* (New Haven, 1938).

On recent events in Egypt see Lord Lloyd, *Egypt since Cromer* (2 vols., London, 1933-34); V. Chirol, *The Egyptian Problem* (London, 1920); M. Harris, *Egypt under the Egyptians* (London, 1925); E. W. Newman, *Great Britain in Egypt* (London, 1928); H. A. MacMillan, *The Anglo-Egyptian Sudan* (London, 1934).

Good guides on the British Commonwealth of Nations are A. Zimmern's *Third British Empire* (London, 1926); W. P. Hall, *Empire to Commonwealth* (New York, 1928); W. Y. Elliott, *The New British Empire* (New York, 1932); R. M. Dawson, *The Development of Dominion Status, 1900-1936* (London, 1937); W. K. Hancock, *Survey of British Commonwealth Affairs* (2 vols., Oxford, 1937-42).

The present organization of the empire is described by Royal Institute of International Affairs, *The British Empire* (second ed., London, 1938) and A. B. Keith, *The Government of the British Empire* (New York, 1935). The present trend of colonial policy is estimated by R. S. Kain in "Britain's New Colonial Policy," *Yale Review,* xxxiii (1944), 498-515. The recent situation in various colonies is treated by L. A. Mills, *British Rule in Eastern Asia* (Minneapolis, 1942) and *Ceylon under British Rule, 1795-1932* (London, 1933); J. L. Christian, *Modern Burma* (Berkeley, 1942); M. R. Dilley, *British Policy in the Kenya Colony* (New York, 1937); C. R. Niven, *A Short History of Nigeria* (London, 1937).

CHAPTER XLII.—FROM ONE WORLD WAR TO ANOTHER

Two good general histories of the period are *The World since 1914* by W. C. Langsam (fifth ed., New York, 1943) and *This Age of Conflict* by

F. P. Chambers, C. P. Grant and C. C. Bayley (New York, 1943). Good general accounts of international relations are presented by E. H. Carr, *International Relations since the Peace Treaties* (London, 1938), G. M. A. Gathorne-Hardy, *Short History of International Affairs, 1920-1938* (New York, 1939), and C. G. Haines and R. J. S. Hoffman, *The Origins and Background of the Second World War* (London, 1943). A. B. Keith's *The Causes of the War* (London, 1940) is a logical analysis of the subject. On British foreign policy C. Sipple's *British Foreign Policy since the World War* (Iowa City, 1932) is useful. E. H. Carr's *Britain; a Study of Foreign Policy from the Versailles Treaty to the Outbreak of the War* (London, 1939) is a good brief guide. W. N. Medlicott's *British Foreign Policy since Versailles* (London, 1940) is excellent. R. W. Seton-Watson's *Britain and the Dictators* (New York, 1938) is continued in his *From Munich to Danzig* (London, 1939). They constitute a valuable discussion of British foreign policy, though the author's sympathies sometimes appear. A. Wolfers' *Britain and France between Two Wars* (New York, 1940) is a thorough and illuminating study of the relations of Great Britain and France to each other and to the other countries of Europe. An annual survey of international developments since 1919 is provided by A. Toynbee's *Survey of International Affairs* (London, 1920-).

H. W. V. Temperley's *History of the Peace Conference of Paris* (6 vols., London, 1920-24) is the most comprehensive work on the subject. *What Really Happened at Paris,* edited by E. M. House and C. Seymour (New York, 1921), is an excellent survey of the conference and its results by American delegates and advisers; C. H. Haskins and R. H. Lord, two of the American advisers, explain the European territorial settlements in *Some Problems of the Peace Conference* (Cambridge, 1920); A. Tardieu's *Truth about the Treaty* (Indianapolis, 1921) presents the French view of proceedings and contains many valuable documents; R. S. Baker's *Woodrow Wilson and World Settlement* (3 vols., New York, 1922) is particularly valuable for its documents. P. Birdsall's *Versailles Twenty Years After* (New York, 1941) has the advantage of perspective and contains much that is new. Documentary records of negotiations are *The Treaty of St. Germain,* edited by N. Almond and R. H. Lutz (Stanford University, 1935); *Reparations at the Paris Peace Conference,* edited by P. M. Burnett (2 vols., New York, 1940); *The German Delegation at the Paris Peace Conference,* edited by A. Luckau (New York, 1941). D. Lloyd George's *Memoirs of the Peace Conference* (2 vols., New Haven, 1939) is valuable but should be used with caution.

The following provide information concerning the organization and activities of the League of Nations: C. Howard-Ellis, *The Origin, Structure and Working of the League of Nations* (Boston, 1928); F. Morley, *The Society of Nations: Its Organization and Constitutional Development* (Washington, 1932); J. I. Knudson, *A History of the League of Nations*

(Atlanta, 1938); M. E. Burton, *The Assembly of the League of Nations* (Chicago, 1941); M. O. Hudson, *The Permanent Court of International Justice* (New York, 1934).

Impartial estimates of conditions on the eastern frontier of Germany are given by I. F. D. Morrow, *The Peace Settlement in the German-Polish Borderlands: A Study of Conditions Today in the Pre-War Prussian Provinces of East and West Prussia* (London, 1936), E. Wiskemann, *Czechs and Germans: A Study of the Struggles in the Historic Provinces of Bohemia and Moravia* (London, 1938), and H. M. Ball, *Post-War German-Austrian Relations: The Anschluss Movement, 1918-1936* (Stanford University, 1937).

On recent international relations in the Far East H. S. Quigley and G. H. Blakeslee's *The Far East* (Boston, 1938) and Vinacke's work noted above may be consulted.

On the immediate background of the war in Europe O. E. Benson's *Through the Diplomatic Looking Glass* (Norman, 1939) is useful. N. Henderson, who was British ambassador to Germany from 1937 to 1939, gives an account of his work in *Failure of a Mission* (New York, 1940). The British government presents some of the pertinent documents in *Documents concerning German-Polish Relations and the Outbreak of Hostilities between Great Britain and Germany on September 3, 1939* (London, 1939), and the German government, in *Documents on the Events preceding the Outbreak of War* (New York, 1940).

The course of the war is followed by E. McInnis in his *The War: First Year* (Oxford, 1940 and annually thereafter).

INDEX

Abbots, 50, 79, 90-92, 99, 164, 185, 196, 230, 314, 315, 380
Abélard, 156
Aberdeen, Lord, 668, 669, 676-679
Aboukir Bay, 607
Abyssinia, *see* Ethiopia
Act, 264; artisans' dwelling, 705; Ashbourne, 720, 723; ballot, 699; British North America, 695, 696; Canada, 658; conventicle, 450; county councils, 723; declaratory, 555; defense of the realm, 807; disestablishment, 696, 697, 720; education, 698, 741, 798; emergency powers, 806, 808; encumbered estates, 672; factory, 648-650, 705; factory and workshop, 705, 729; five mile, 450; house and town planning, 770, 771; in conditional restraint of annates, 312, 382; India, 596, 597, 685, 816; Indian councils, 777; industrial courts, 808; judicature, 699, 700; land purchase, 720, 721, 814; licensing, 742; molasses, 495, 496, 551-553; municipal corporations, 449, 457, 642; mutiny, 464; navigation, 250, 288, 439, 440, 471, 637; occasional conformity, 481; parish councils, 727; property qualification, 480, 481; public health, 704, 705, 748; Quebec, 658; regulating, 596, 597; riot, 507; schism, 481; seditious meetings, 612; septennial, 508; settlement, 464, 484, 485, 539; six articles, 316, 321, 322, 332; stamp, 553, 554; succession, 313; sugar, 553; supremacy, 336; test, 453, 464, 481, 642; toleration, 464; trade boards, 770; trade disputes and trade unions, 810; trades disputes, 767; treason, 313, 321, 464; treasonable practices, 612, 613; triennial, 423, 464; uniformity, 321, 328, 336, 450; union, 465, 466; workmen's compensation, 729, 769
   See also Statute
Acts, combination, 613, 638, 639; enclosure, 569, 570; liberticide, 631; of trade, 494-497, 551, 555; Poyning's, 286, 437, 610; six, 631, 632
Addington, Henry, 612, 622
Addison, Joseph, 500, 501, 505, 752
Adela, 99, 102

Administration, 109, 114, 117, 143, 192-196, 198, 209, 223, 227, 234, 235, 237, 478, 482, 493, 508, 698, 699, 794, 795
Adrianople, 24
Aelfric, 79
Afghanistan, 677, 682, 702, 708, 710, 779
Africa, 2, 301, 347, 439, 452, 472, 525, 526, 528, 561, 564, 656, 708-710, 712-714, 724, 725, 732, 747, 827, 834, 835, 844, 846, 848, 849
Agadir, 781 ·
Agassiz, Louis, 760
Agincourt, 264
Agreement of the people, 434, 435, 437
Agricola, 23, 25
Agriculture, 5, 8, 13-15, 17, 28, 30, 36, 63, 64, 67, 76, 139, 170, 174-179, 189, 290, 291, 295, 324-328, 360, 404, 487, 488, 566-571, 626-630, 641, 745-747, 757, 803, 805, 806, 810, 811; board of, 571
Aidan, 30, 127
Aids, 102, 139; feudal, 82, 139, 193
Air fields, 842, 853
Air force, 833
Air power, 843-845, 850, 852, 853
Air raids, 844, 850
Airplanes, 842, 844, 846, 849, 850
Aix-la-Chapelle, peace of, 518, 520
Alabama, 688, 689, 702, 731
Albania, 841, 844
Albert, prince consort, 674, 675, 687, 688
Alcuin, 78
Aldhelm, 78, 79
Aleutian Islands, 852
Alfred, 43-47, 51, 52, 57, 58, 78, 79
Algeciras, 777, 778
Algeria, 848
All India National Congress, 817
Alliance, 735, 736; against France, 471; Austrian, 508, 509; Burgundian, 275; dual, 735, 739; Dutch, 454; Franco-Belgian, 830, 834; Franco-Czechoslovakian, 830, 834, 839; Franco-Polish, 830, 834; Franco-Russian, 834, 836; French, 305, 306, 308, 318, 344, 442, 451, 453, 454, 508, 509, 830, 836, 837; German-Polish, 834; grand, 475; Italo-German, 835, 839, 841; Japanese, 739,